Cool Radio.

Grundig, together with the F.A. Porsche Design Group, has developed a revolutionary new product in every sense. With an aluminum paint finish, leather cover, and stylish details, Grundig scores again with this amazingly compact and impressive digital direct-frequency-entry radio!

GRUNDIG

1998 passport
to world band radio

COMPLEAT IDIOT'S GUIDE TO GETTING STARTED

WHAT TO LISTEN WITH
1998 PASSPORT REPORTS

Gahan Wilson

FEBC

J. Macmillan, USN&WR/LA Times Syndicate

1998 passport
to world band radio

ISSN 0897-0157

International Broadcasting Services, Ltd.

Our reader is the most important person in the world!

Editorial

Editor-in-Chief	Lawrence Magne
Editor	Tony Jones
Contributing Editors	Jock Elliott (U.S.), Craig Tyson (Australia)
Consulting Editors	John Campbell (England), Don Jensen (U.S.)
WorldScan® Contributors	Gabriel Iván Barrera (Argentina), James Conrad (U.S.), Alok Dasgupta (India), Graeme Dixon (New Zealand), Manosij Guha (India), Anatoly Klepov (Russia), Marie Lamb (U.S.), *Número Uno*/Jerry Berg (U.S.), Toshimichi Ohtake (Japan), *Radio Nuevo Mundo* (Japan), Henrik Klemetz (Colombia), Takayuki Inoue Nozaki (Japan), Nikolai Rudnev (Russia), Don Swampo (Uruguay), David Walcutt (U.S.)
WorldScan® Software	Richard Mayell
Laboratory	Sherwood Engineering Inc.
Artwork	Gahan Wilson, cover; Leigh Ann Smith, text
Graphic Arts	Bad Cat Design; Mike Wright, layout
Printing	World Color Press

Administration

Publisher	Lawrence Magne
Associate Publisher	Jane Brinker
Advertising & Distribution	Mary Kroszner, MWK
Offices	IBS North America, Box 300, Penn's Park PA 18943, USA; World Wide Web: http://www.passport.com *Advertising & Distribution:* Phone +1 (215) 794-3410; Fax +1 (215) 794 3396; E-mail mwk@passport.com *Editorial:* Fax +1 (215) 598 3794 *Orders (24 hours):* Phone +1 (215) 794-8252; Fax +1 (215) 794 3396; E-mail mwk@passport.com; World Wide Web (secure) https://www.comcat.com/~mwk/orderform.htm
Media Communications	Jock Elliott, Pickering Lane, Troy NY 12180, USA; Fax +1 (518) 271 6131; E-mail media@passport.com

Bureaus

IBS Latin America	Tony Jones, Casilla 1844, Asunción, Paraguay; Fax +595 (21) 390 675; E-mail schedules@passport.com
IBS Australia	Craig Tyson, Box 2145, Malaga WA 6062; Fax +61 (9) 342 9158; E-mail addresses@passport.com
IBS Japan	Toshimichi Ohtake, 5-31-6 Tamanawa, Kamakura 247; Fax +81 (467) 43 2167; E-mail ibsjapan@passport.com

Library of Congress Cataloging-in-Publication Data
Passport to World Band Radio.
1. Radio Stations, Shortwave—Directories. I. Magne, Lawrence
    TK9956.P27   1997   384.54′5   97-22739
    ISBN 0-914941-45-3

PASSPORT, PASSPORT TO WORLD BAND RADIO, *WorldScan, Radio Database International, RDI White Papers* and *White Papers* are registered trademarks of International Broadcasting Services, Ltd., in the United States, Canada, United Kingdom and various other parts of the world.

THE WORLD
OF WORLD BAND RADIO

WORLD TIME EXAMPLE: 1300 World Time is 7AM (−6 hours) in Chicago. For more, see ADRESSES PLUS section.

+11 +12 −11 −10 −9 −8 −7 −6 −5 −4 −3 −2

Palana, Russia

Anchor Point, Alaska, USA

Petropavlovsk-Kamchatskiy, Russia

Calgary AB, Canada

Vancouver BC, Canada

Toronto ON, Canada
Montréal PQ, Canada
Greenbush ME, USA
Sackville NB, Canada
St. John's NF, Canada
Halifax NS, Canada
Noblesville IN, USA
Bethel PA, USA
Red Lion PA, USA
Upton KY, USA
Nashville TN, USA
McCaysville GA, USA
Greenville NC, USA
Cypress Creek SC, USA
Macon GA, USA
Birmingham AL, USA
New Orleans LA, USA
Okeechobee FL, USA
Miami FL, USA
Havana, Cuba

Salt Lake City UT, USA
Boulder CO, USA
Delano CA, USA
Rancho Simi CA, USA
Dallas TX, USA
Mesquite NM, USA

Hermosillo, Mexico

Kekaha, Kauai Island, Hawai'i, USA

Naalehu, "Big Island," Hawai'i, USA

Linares, Mexico
Mérida, Mexico
México City, Mexico
Veracruz, Mexico
Puerto Cabezas, Nicaragua
Guatemala City, Guatemala
Tegucigalpa, Honduras
San José, Costa Rica
Santa Fé de Bogotá, Colombia
Villavicencio, Colombia
Florencia, Colombia
Quito, Ecuador
Tena, Ecuador
Loja, Ecuador
Iquitos, Perú
Cajamarca, Perú
Pucallpa, Perú
Guayaramerín, Bolivia
Cobija, Bolivia
Lima, Perú
Cusco, Perú
Arequipa, Perú
La Paz, Bolivia
Santa Cruz, Bolivia
Sucre, Bolivia
Asunción, Paraguay
Villarrica, Paraguay
Encarnación, Paraguay

Santo Domingo, Dominican Republic
Anguilla
Antigua
Bonaire, Netherlands Antilles
Caracas, Venezuela
Puerto Ayacucho, Venezuela
Georgetown, Guyana
Paramaribo, Surinam
Montsinéry, French Guiana
Cayenne, French Guiana

Belem, Brazil
Manaus, Brazil

Porto Velho, Brazil
Salvador, Brazil
Cuiabá, Brazil
Brasília, Brazil
Goiânia, Brazil

Belo Horizonte, Brazil
Rio de Janeiro, Brazil
São Paulo, Brazil
Curitiba, Brazil
Foz do Iguaçu, Brazil
Florianópolis, Brazil
Porto Alegre, Brazil
Artigas, Uruguay
Montevideo, Uruguay
Buenos Aires, Argentina

Tarawa, Kiribati

Honiara, Solomon Islands

Port-Vila, Vanuatu

Tahiti, French Polynesia

Mendoza, Argentina
Santiago, Chile
Malargüe, Argentina

Temuco, Chile

Rangitaiki, New Zealand

Levin, New Zealand

Coyhaique, Chile

Base Esperanza, Antarctica (−3)

+11 +12 −11 −10 −9 −8 −7 −6 −5 −4 −3 −2

Maldives, the Absolute Dream

Where even the sharks are friendly . . .
by Manosij Guha

Mahuraba! Or Welcome . . . to the Absolute Dream. Tiny dots of islands scattered around the Equator, and dipped in the ultramarine blue of the Indian Ocean. Palm fringed, sparkling chalk-white beaches, see-through turquoise lagoons—so transparent one can see right to the bottom. This is the paradise called MALDIVES.

Paradise Gained

The Maldives. A place many people have heard of, but few know much about. This is probably because Maldives is one of Nature's untouched treasures. As far back as the 14th century, the famous Moroccan traveler, Ibn Battuta, described the Maldives as "one of the wonders of the world." And "Flower of the Indies," wrote Marco Polo in his chronicles. Truly a natural wonder, the islands rarely reach six feet or two meters above sea level. The Maldivian atolls are a classic discovery in their own right—the word

"atoll" itself being derived from the national language, Dhivehi.

The islands are surrounded by shallow crystal-clear lagoons enclosed by coral reefs, providing visitors with a breathtaking view of life in the underwater world. Formed above peaks emerging from the depths of the ocean, upon layers of both living and dead coral, and remnants of other marine life, the islands are generally covered with dense tropical vegetation. The tropical climate varies little, making it a yearlong tourist destination.

> Maldives' land mass is only about twice the size of Washington, DC.

The 1,190 tiny specks of islands in 26 atoll formations have a total area of only 115 square miles or 298 square kilometers, about twice the size of Washington, DC. These islands are scattered over a wide area of endless sea, about 35,000 square miles or 90,000 square kilometers,

---

Voice of Maldives staffers leave for afternoon prayers at a nearby mosque.   M. Guha

9

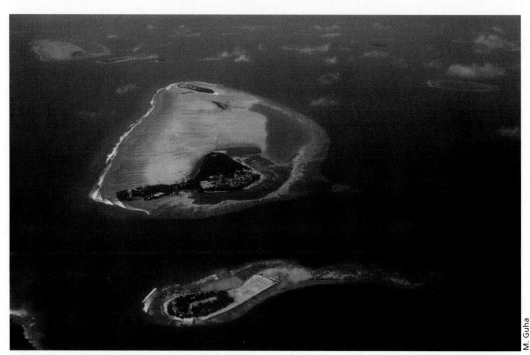

The Maldives atoll lies only slightly above sea level. Maldivians fear that icecap melting resulting from global warming may cause their islands to disappear.

with a spread of up to 500 miles or 820 kilometers. The closest neighbors are India, 260 miles or 420 kilometers to the north, and Sri Lanka, 445 miles or 720 kilometers to the east. With a population of about 250,000, only 199 islands are inhabited out of which 74 have been set aside exclusively as resort islands for tourists.

Paradise Found

The origins of the Maldivians are lost in ancient history. There are historical and archaeological records which suggest that the islands have been inhabited for over 5,000 years. There are also indications that the Maldive islands, being on an important trade route, were settled by people from all over the world.

This leaves the exact origins of the people cloaked in the pages of history.

However, the main stock of Maldivian people, as seen from physical features and supported by historical evidence of migration, is predominantly Aryan or Dravidian.

The language spoken is Dhivehi, a tongue related to Sinhala from the Indo-Iranian group, with a strong Arabic influence. Like Arabic it is also penned from right to left and is the official language of the country, while English comes a close second, being widely used and understood.

Until 30 years ago, the Maldives had been an independent country under the dynastic rule of Sultans, except for a brief period of 15 and a half years of tyrannical Portuguese rule in the middle of the 16th century. Between 1887 and 1965, the Maldives was a British protectorate (mainly for a military base), and Her Majesty's government did not interfere

M. Guha

Water bungalows perch peacefully along the beachfront.

with the internal affairs of the country. Maldives regained full sovereignty in 1965 and it changed from a Sultanate to a republic on November 11th, 1968 with a single-party presidential form of government—a rather tight-fisted one at that.

After twenty years, the islands' idyllic calm was shattered when the capital city of Male' was taken hostage for a day in 1988 when some dissidents staged an uprising with the help of Tamil mercenaries imported from nearby Sri Lanka. The coup was quelled by 1,600 Indian paratroopers hurriedly flown in. Although the coup was unsuccessful, it revealed a certain amount of discontent among the populace, especially the younger generation. Since then, considerable efforts have been made to democratize the political process and liberalize the economy while still catering to the more conservative, traditional elites and clergy who oppose democratic reforms—a hangover from the Sultanate era. A considerable part of the republic's revenues have been spent in securing wider educational opportunities for the Maldivian people through the construction of new schools and the provision of government funded scholarships abroad.

> The stillness of the atolls is occasionally broken by the frenetic thumping of the *bodu beru* log drum.

But not all measures were populist. As external threat became a reality in this peace-loving nation, and to take care of national defense, a military draft was introduced and the National Security Service was started. It maintains a constant vigil with a gunboat at the entrance to the harbor, while another crisscrosses the atoll . . . a measure aimed more for confidence building than to thwart an external threat, given the rudimentary weapons they have. Or perhaps to scare away the high-speed boats of the new pirates—underworld dons of Bombay and Dubai, who find the Maldives' 1,190 islands provide them with the ultimate in hideouts.

The Maldivians are a warm, gentle, friendly people whose graceful lives are almost untouched by the hurly-burly pace most of us have come to accept as everyday living. Their easy laid back life is hard not to envy. With an almost zero crime rate, the highest punishment is banishment to a remote isle—what is capital punishment to some is paradise to others!

The stillness is loud in the atolls, but is occasionally broken by muezzin calling the faithful to prayer, or the frenetic thumping of the big *bodu beru* log drum. Foreigners are segregated from the local population so that they do not get tainted by western mores or political dissidence. But top dollars from tourism overrule questions of faith. Even though the Maldivian government follows a strict no-outsiders policy, sometimes a "native" island can be seen through a chink in the coral curtain. But they are mostly souvenir islands like Himafushi, where a brisk T-shirt trade has replaced the fishing pole and line.

> Other than fish and coconuts, almost everything is imported—even the soil on which majestic palms grow.

While Maldivian authorities are reluctant to discuss openly the social impact of tourism on their youthful population, 65 percent being under 25 years of age, the conservative way of life is clearly under pressure. "We are not allowed to visit the resorts, drink alcohol or party," complained one youth. "Are they trying to isolate us from the happenings around us?"

As the islands are far flung, efficient communications and water-transport are bare essentials—traditional *dhonis* or

A village elder takes his afternoon siesta on one of the island's communal hammocks.

ICOM Leads the Way with New PC Ready Scanners and Receivers

The whole world in a little black box! ICOM's newest receiver is a PC-external peripheral (no internal PC installation required). It's true plug and play world band convenience.

- 100% PC Controlled
- Wide Band 100 kHz – 1.3 GHz**
- All Mode AM, FM, WFM, SSB, CW
- 3 Selectable User Screens
- Unlimited Number of Memory Channels
- Runs on Windows® 3.1 or 95

NEW!

Plug and Play. Software, 6-pin RS-232C cable, antenna and AC adapter are **included**.

IC-PCR1000*

External, PC-controlled Wide Band Receiver
coming fall 1997*

IC-R8500

The Expert's Choice is Also Easy to Use

Plug and Play. Standard third party serial cable required for PC connection.

ICOM's latest base station is a handsome rig that will look as good in the home living room as in the listening shack. Built ready for easy PC control, the IC-R8500 is only a cable away from software customized operation. ☞

- Wide Band 100 kHz – 2 GHz**
- All Mode AM, FM, WFM, SSB, CW
- Commercial Grade
- Built-in CI-V Command Control
- Built-In RS-232C Port

- 1000 Memory Channels
- IF Shift & Noise Blanker
- Audio Peak Filter (APF)
- Auto Frequency Control
- 7 Different Scan Types

Uses "AA" Alkalines or Ni-Cds

☜ One of the IC-R10's great features is the **SIG NAVI scan**. While you listen to a paused frequency, the SIG NAVI scan looks for the next busy frequency within 100 kHz.

Select ICOM options required, depending on PC control or cloning task desired

IC-R10

Catch More Listening Excitement on the Go!

Whether you're new to scanning or a longtime listener, this rugged little handheld delivers!

- Wide Band 100 kHz – 1.3 GHz**
- All Mode, Including SSB
- PC Cloneable
- 1000 Memory Channels

- "Real-Time" Band Scope
- 7 Different Scan Types
- **EASY MODE** for Beginners
- Uses "AA" Ni-Cds (included) or Alkalines – your choice

Visit your ICOM dealer or call 425-450-6088 for free brochures

ICOM®
RECEIVERS

*This device has not been approved by the Federal Communications Commission. This device may not be offered for sale or lease, or be sold or leased until the approval of the FCC has been obtained.
**Cellular blocked: unblocked versions available only to FCC approved users.

©1997 ICOM America, Inc. 2380 116th Ave NE, Bellevue WA 98004 • 425-454-8155. All specifications are subject to change without notice or obligation. The ICOM logo is a registered trademark of ICOM, Inc. Microsoft, Windows and Windows 95 are registered trademarks of Microsoft Corporation. PASS98

http://www.icomamerica.com

The traditional *dhoni* boat is constructed in time-honored fashion. Dhonis are increasingly losing favor to motorboats with modern electronics.

country boats are being replaced by launches and speedboats, which are a sign of upward mobility. Gone are the days when *dhonis* could sail by the stars for days without modern navigational tools. Now each has its own diesel and radio, with fishing sonar and navigational radar thrown in at times.

Fish, coconuts and other produce from an overabundant Nature are the only domestic items that dominate the Maldivian economy. The stores are well stocked with imported goods. Almost every item is imported—fresh fruit and vegetables from Pakistan, oil from the Gulf, cars and electronics from Japan. This island nation probably has more foreign exchange reserves than any other South Asian country. One can walk into any Male' store and buy the latest in Levis or Sonys, pay in dollars, and get small change in the same currency.

Paradise Rediscovered

Ancient turboprops chartered from Sri Lanka in the 1970s brought the first tourists to the Maldives, which was at best a risky adventure.

"There was no visa. Hotel owners made their own visa stamps as tourists demanded something to show on their passports," reminisces Dr Ibrahim Maniku, Chairman of Universal Resorts, the largest resort-chain owner in the Maldives. "The small planes landed on the semi-prepared strips of the erstwhile British airbase in Gan, with a lone coconut tree and nothing else.

"We ourselves lifted their bags to our office in Male', Maniku continues. "Italian tourists came with shotguns to shoot fish, something that is unthinkable now. What started as a one or two day detour for sun 'n' sand frolic became a booming tourist trade."

RCSS™ REMOTE

RCSS™ Remote
pictured with optional
wideband receiver
internally installed.

Simultaneous High Speed Data and Full Duplex Audio Over a Single Phone Line.

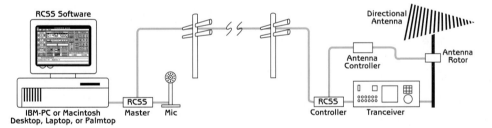

R CSS™ Remote provides a unique solution to remote systems control. It enables high speed data and full duplex wideband audio over any standard or cellular phone line. Audio and data are transferred simultaneously, not time sliced, providing true real time control.

Remote operation can be fully automated with RCSS™ software. A simple point and click graphical user interface via Microsoft Win-

dows™ provides quick learning and easy operation. RCSS™ software is also available separately to provide automated control of AOR and ICOM receivers, among others.

The RCSS™ master unit can be used with any serial terminal including desktops, laptops, and the new palmtops. RCSS™ Remote is housed in a rugged aluminum case for military style dependability. It is constructed using several processors and the latest DSP technology

available. All RCSS™ components are fully shielded from RF leakage. Power is supplied from either AC or DC sources for portability.

The RCSS™ modular design allows the configuration to be modified as user needs expand. Special user developed programs can be uploaded for custom applications.

For more information call, write, fax, or e-mail today. Or, via computer, visit our web page at http://www.sasiltd.com/sasi

SYSTEMS & SOFTWARE
INTERNATIONAL • LTD

Systems & Software International is in its 10th year, and manufactures all equipment in the USA. Please contact us at:
4639 Timber Ridge Drive, Dumfries, Virginia, 22026-1059, USA; **(703) 680-3559;** Fax (703) 878-1460; E-mail 74065.1140@compuserve.com

A Maldivian Air Taxi seaplane glides alongside the quay. Maldives' many islands make it impractical to use conventional runways for inter-island hopping.

Tourism is central to the prosperity of the archipelago's small population of a quarter-million Sunni Muslims. It accounts for 20 percent of the GDP and 70 percent of the foreign exchange earnings. Visitors arrive by the chartered planeload all year round to this oversold paradise, but it comes at a cost—that of the fragile eco-system. Seventy-four islands with their coconut palms, white sandy beaches and fish-filled lagoons have been developed as resorts, each run by a single company and offering such water sports as scuba diving, snorkeling, sailing and canoeing. One Dutch entrepreneur has gone to the extent of recreating a complete Spanish galleon and turning it into a trendy hotel afloat.

With names such as Full Moon and Kurumba replacing the original Furana-fushi and Vihamanafushi, the resort islands are miles apart not so much in physical distance from the local popula-tion as in terms of culture. These islands are virtual oases, taking freewheeling Western ways to the other extreme.

> Italians used to come with shotguns to shoot fish, something that is unthinkable now.

Alcohol is prohibited in the native islands but flows freely in the resort islands, where U.S. greenbacks are the de facto currency and the local Rufiya is frowned upon. Here, everything is created synthetically, and importation en masse is the name of the game. The majestic water bungalows owe their origins to Malaysia, with an occasional Hawaiian thatch firing up a resort designer's imagi-nation. Even the soil on which majestic palms grow is imported from Sri Lanka, as are the gardeners who landscape the

M. Guha

Maldivian fisherwoman prepares *spuntino alfresco* from the day's catch.

Sharks lurk in the warm waters, but visitors have little to fear. For local divers, hand-feeding the sharks is fun. "It's not just the people of the Maldives, even the sharks are friendly here," jests Tom Gerreau, a diving instructor and avid nature conservationist, originally from Jamaica, who has adopted these islands as his home away from home. "The sharks are quite well fed and are not dangerous," he declares. "In fact, there have never been any incidents with sharks." And these well-mannered toothy creatures are becoming something of a tourist attraction. But why are the sharks so friendly? "Spearfishing and fishing nets are prohibited in the Maldives, so the fish are friendly and totally unafraid of divers," he explains.

Paradise Retained

Islands come and go in this Indian Ocean archipelago, and no one is keeping a precise tally. "How do you define an island," asks Abdul Hussain Rashid, the Maldivian minister for environment? "We cannot precisely say how many there are. It is an ongoing process and it's hard to keep track." The government has more or less settled on the figure of 1,190.

Scientists across the world studying global warming are worried that the seas swollen by the melting of the polar icecaps could deluge the Maldives. "There is a consensus, but how much, when, how soon it will come—over that there is still debate," observes minister Hussain.

With the highest point only eight feet or 2.4 meters above the enveloping sea, the Maldives is one of the world's lowest-lying nations—even a small rise in the world's ocean could spell the end. "We are environmentally a very delicate place," elaborates minister Hussain. "The average land height in the Maldives is 1.3 meters [four feet above sea level],

serene Japanese gardens. Drinking water is very much in short supply and is collected from rainwater, which is adequate during the monsoons. At other times the precious liquid is created from desalinated seawater, which makes it costlier than gasoline. Ironically, one of the resorts has its own Coca-Cola bottling plant, so a Coke bottle costs a buck less than a bottle of water!

As in any *nouveau riche* country, the Maldives faces an acute human resource crunch, which compels resort owners to allow foreigners to join the workforce. Thirty-eight percent of workers in the tourist industry are expats from Sri Lanka, India, Bangladesh, the Philippines and some European countries. They form the "invisible hands" who maintain the five-star resorts in tip-top condition while they themselves live a deplorable existence—cramped living quarters, long working hours and completely cut-off from their families whom they can visit only once every two years.

and 80 percent is below 1 meter [three feet]. It is a question of survival now, the survival of the islands themselves. We don't know what is going to happen to them."

For millennia, since the 26 atolls rose up from the ocean floor, coral reefs have been nature's defense for the 513-mile or 828-kilometer archipelago. An eccentric German marine biologist gives nature a helping hand. Professor Rheinhart Hilbertz, almost indistinguishable in his scuba gear opines, "by passing a mild electric charge between pieces of coral, they seem to grow faster. Furthermore, they can be formed in a wide variety of shapes and sizes as required."

In the Maldives land is by far the costliest commodity, as much of it is reclaimed by dumping custom-made concrete boulders into the sea. To bolster defenses around Male', hundreds of three-ton, four-legged blocks called Tetrapods have been piled, creating a giant concrete seawall that dissipates the wrath of the waves, but allows water to flow through the gaps between them. But pressure from the increasing population and a new affluence have led to an increased demand for new land and houses. For years, coral has been mined from shallow reefs for use as building material. Realizing the folly of removing what protects the islands from pounding surf, the Maldivian government has set aside certain reefs for mining.

Further exacerbating the global warming issue is large-scale deforestation in the inhabited islands, as the trappings of modern life and encroaching industrialization loom large. In order to reduce dependence on imports and to promote industry, prime forest land is being

M. Guha

A local girl bicycles past the Voice of Maldives' guarded entrance.

cleared. As a result, the environmentally conscious government now finds itself in something of a quandary.

Voice of Maldives, the Sound of Paradise

Our destination is a short and bumpy taxi ride away, through the coral-cobbled streets of Male' and on to the far side of the island. (All rides are short here, as the entire length of the capital island can be covered in 15 minutes.) There, on a seaside alley called *Moonlight Higun*— Moonlight Way—stands an old colonial villa, which contains the island-nation's only radio station, the Voice of Maldives.

This dowager villa is enclosed in a high-walled compound, its entrance

M. Guha

Antennas for the Voice of Maldives lie alongside a favorite surfers' beach.

guarded by an armed soldier who at times takes a break from the tedium by playing with children bicycling in the street. The reclaimed beach in front doubles as an antenna farm, besides being a surfer hangout for a few wannabe kahunas.

> A dowager villa is home to the only radio station, the Voice of Maldives. Wannabe kahunas surf near its antennas.

The station building, overlooking the international airport, houses three recording studios, one continuity studio, a newsroom, the transmitter hall, an administration office, a training center for budding radio professionals, and a technical facility. However, next door are new facilities with administrative offices and 12 more studios that are scheduled to open shortly. Downtown, there is also a theater complex with three studios for recording orchestras, talks and features.

World Band Starts in 1962

The Voice of Maldives has roughly 150 employees and, except for advertising income, it is entirely funded and run by the government. The station came into being in 1962 with a tiny studio and a reconditioned British-made RACAL shortwave communications transmitter imported from Sri Lanka. This modest transmitter used to pump out a maximum of one kilowatt in the 90 meter band.

The station was expanded in 1969 with the induction of a three kilowatt locally made shortwave transmitter which broadcast on 9335 kHz and 7400 kHz, split into day and evening shifts. But as the vast majority of the population had AM radios, a mediumwave AM operation was hastily started, which put out a weak signal around 1500 kHz via a two kilowatt locally made transmitter. This frequency drifted widely, so frequent retuning of the transmitter was necessary. This state of affairs continued until 1982.

> The station's first studios and transmitters were handmade from discarded communications equipment.

"In those days, we did everything by hand, and we actually made all studio equipment ourselves, besides our first few transmitters," reminisces Maizan Ahmed Maniku, the station's first engineer and now its Director General of Engineering. "The raw material came from discarded communications equipment."

Things looked up in 1982 when the Australian government, as part of extensive aid to the Maldivian government, thoughtfully donated a five kilowatt mediumwave AM TBC transmitter. About this time the frequency was shifted to 1449 kHz, in keeping with ITU regulations.

Old Transmitter, Off in 1995, Still Functions

The shortwave operation was put to its first real test in 1989, when the capital of Male' was briefly seized by dissidents. One of the first installations to be captured was the island's radio station, but not until after an SOS went out to the world. But as shortwave operations on the antediluvian transmitter became unreliable and costly to maintain, the transmitter was permanently switched off in 1995.

Well . . . not quite. Confides maintenance engineer-cum-technician Rasheed, "It was very troublesome to get replacements for the burnt-out tubes, as the manufacturers themselves had stopped manufacturing them. So there would be long breaks in transmissions, sometimes for weeks, until the spares arrived."

The local news in Divehi in progress at a Voice of Maldives studio. Lace curtains make an attractive substitute for sound tiles.

He goes on, "But the transmitter is in running condition, and can be switched on in an emergency. In fact, we switch it on every now and then on 5998.5 kHz for training newscasters, using a few watts."

At present, this is the extent of world band radio from the Maldives—DX as pristine as Maldives' waters. However, Voice of Maldives engineers are also trying to refurbish a German Techimatic transmitter. This point-to-point shortwave sender of indeterminate power runs on 110 Volts and can operate from 2 through 30 MHz. Alas, it needs a refit and a number of spares in order to be able to take to the airwaves.

Given the unreliability of the old signal, along with inadequate transmitting facilities and the wide area the station had to cover—roughly 55,000 square miles, or 90,000 square kilometers—the shortwave operation was gradually scaled down. Shortwave was discontinued entirely when a 10 kW Harris DX-10 mediumwave AM transmitter was installed in 1995. This

Barefoot technician catches up on local news while keeping an eye on the station's transmitters.

carries the primary service on 1449 kHz and continues to this day. The old 5 kW transmitter serves as standby and is tuned to 1458 kHz, where it is likely to be revived to air a second channel in the future.

Daily Service Includes English

The primary service starts at 0025 World Time with its distinctive birdcall sign-on, followed by prayers from the Koran in Arabic. Programs are in the local language, Dhivehi, and continue until about 1015, when there is a technical break. The evening service resumes at 1200, and continues through to 1800, when the station signs off with a choir singing the Maldivian national anthem.

However, during the Muslim holy month of Ramadan, the station operates continuously from 0200 until 2100, when the overworked transmitter gets a well-deserved break.

Programs in English are heard daily for two hours between 1700 and 1900, with news in English at 1800 to 1810. Ten-minute newscasts in Dhivehi punctuate the schedule at 0200, 0900, 1100, 1400 and 1700. Even though the station is almost totally funded by the government, advertisements form an important source of revenue. And judging by their frequency, the revenue seems to be significant.

The Voice of Maldives enjoys an estimated listenership of 130,000. Its medium-wave AM signal reaches not only the outlying islands, but also further afield to Sri Lanka and southern India, as indicated by listener's letters in the popular mailbag program.

Government and Pirate FM Expanding

In the evenings, there is also a four-hour FM service between 1500 and 1900 nominally on 103.8 MHz, but which drifts widely. This music-only channel continuously plays lilting melodies in Dhivehi, which are often punctuated by raucous songs from Hindi films, underlining the Subcontinental influence. The only identification comes during the relay of the nightly news from the mediumwave AM service.

Power? Pure DX, a feeble ten Watts from a suitcase transmitter fed by an audio cassette deck, all provided by a not-so-generous grant from UNESCO. This service can be heard only in Male' and the islands in its immediate vicinity, but it has already had a major impact. The Maldivian government has been quick to notice that FM is popular, owing to its superior reception and audio quality, and has already sanctioned the purchase of a pair of one kilowatt FM transmitters to run on 99.0 and 89.0 MHz in order to setup an island-wide FM network.

Network coordination has already been done with TV Maldives, which is on a similar expansion binge. It proposes to network outlying transmitters via a hired Intelsat satellite transponder, with one audio sub-carrier earmarked for the fledgling FM radio station. Given the efficient island-wide mobile phone network provided by a British transnational company and the extensive use of maritime radio, linking the broadcast transmitters should not be a problem.

But that is not the only FM activity emanating from the Maldives. Pirate broadcasting on FM is surprisingly common, and the ill-equipped telecom authorities cannot trace them easily because of their microwatt power and nimble mobility. "These are voices of the real youth who think it is time for some real freedom," declares a teenager on the condition of anonymity.

AM Locked into Low Power

The islands' radio mainstay thus is still the venerable mediumwave AM channel. But reception, especially at night, is marred by interference. "We cannot increase power [on 1449 kHz] because of complaints from the international airport," laments engineer Maniku. Hardly surprising, as the airport island is so close to the station that you can swim to it.

New World Band Facility Recommended

So, there is once again a need for a viable world band radio service. As the Australian government traditionally has been a significant donor to the Maldives, it has been approached to provide financial and technological assistance to establish a shortwave service.

Everything Ready . . .

The Australian government has reacted swiftly by including a 10 kW shortwave transmitter in its aid package—ironic, perhaps, given Radio Australia's recent controversial cutbacks. To get this off the ground, a team of Australian experts has concluded a survey of the islands. The result was that they selected Maafushi, an inhabited island in the South Male' atoll, for erecting the proposed new shortwave station. Since then, the Maldivian government has acquired the land required to set up the facility.

. . . but Approval Awaited

Yet, even though the survey report was submitted some time ago, the station is still awaiting the final nod. Local cognoscenti whisper that the deal will not be clinched until President Gayoom pays a much-awaited state visit "Down Under."

Until then, world band radio from the Maldives remains nothing more than a dog-eared file on the station engineer´s table . . . unless, of course, a wayward engineer decides to give a trainee newscaster a taste of the real thing!

Manosij Guha is news producer for the ARD German television network's India bureau in New Delhi. The official Maldives Website is www.visitmaldives.com.

Ten of the Best:
1998's Top Shows

World band radio is the nerve center for the world's news—real news from everywhere, not the parochial "lifestyle reports" and safety-scares-of-the-week that have dominated TV since the end of the Cold War.

But world band also knows how to have a good time. There's entertainment aplenty, including sports and music from near and far—and no soaps! First-class drama and comedy, too, just like in radio's pre-television heyday. And because world band radio is largely public radio, ads rarely intrude.

PASSPORT's comprehensive guide to hundreds of world band shows is "What's On Tonight" farther back in this book. That *TV Guide*-type section takes you, hour-by-hour, through the full gamut of choices of what's being aired in English. What follows is a sampling of the best of these shows for 1998.

As always, times given are World Time. "Winter" and "summer" refer to seasons in the Northern Hemisphere.

"Newshour"
BBC World Service

When it comes to news, Britannia rules the airwaves and the BBC World Service is king. No other broadcaster offers the same depth and breadth of coverage of what is happening in the world. And amidst this wealth of riches, the jewel in the crown is "Newshour," sixty minutes of news and reports from around the globe.

The choice of subjects is wide-ranging, and includes national, regional and international stories. Fast-breaking news is regularly updated throughout the program, with in-depth analysis of major topics being a regular feature.

But not all is politics and crises—lighter stories are also offered, and there are business updates and news of major sports events. There are two separate daily editions, at 1300 and 2000.

"Newshour" is the Mother of All Newscasts. If you need a daily fix of news, this is definitely it.

Ten Best

The Voice of Russia's "Folk Box" is enjoyed by a wide variety of listeners worldwide. H. Karashoff

Nic Newman and Robin Lustig present the incomparable "Newshour," heard twice daily over the BBC World Service.

Officially, listeners in *North America* have just the one opportunity, at 1300 on 5965 (winter), 6195, 9515, 9590 (or 11865), 9740 and 15220 kHz. However, those in eastern North America can also try the frequencies for Europe at 2000.

Timings for *Europe* are 1300 on 9410, 12095, 15575 and 17640 kHz; and 2000 on 3955 (winter), 6180, 6195, 7325, 9410 and (summer) 12095 and 15575 kHz.

In the *Middle East*, the 1300 broadcast is available year-round on 11760, 15565, 15575 and (winter) 17640 kHz. The first half hour of the 2000 transmission is also available in winter on 9410 kHz.

Southern Africa has easy access to both editions: 1300 on 6190, 11940 and 21660 kHz; and 2000 on 3255, 6190 and 11835 (or 15400) kHz.

In *East Asia*, there's just the one slot, 1300 on 5990 and 9740 kHz. Listeners in *Southeast Asia* can hear the same broadcast on 6195, 9740 and (summer) 15310 kHz. In winter, the 2000 transmission is also available, on 9740 and 11955 kHz.

For *Australasia*, it's 1300 on 9740 kHz, and 2000 on 5975 (or 11955) and 9740 kHz.

"Folk Box"
Voice of Russia

The Voice of Russia's admirable "Folk Box" is a treasure-chest of music from all over the former Soviet Union. It is folk music in the original meaning of the term, music of the people.

From Karelian wedding dances to the throat singing of Central Asia, the variety of musical styles is endless. Balalaikas

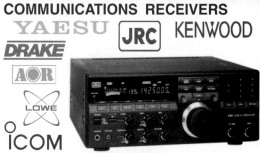

R. Crane

Near the studios of the Voice of Russia is the world's largest bell.

frequencies at 2131 Thursday. In summer, same days but one hour earlier, tune in at 2331 on 7125, 7250 and 9665 kHz; and 0131 and 0431 on 12010, 12050, 13645 (0431 only), 13665, 15180 and 15595 kHz.

There are two winter airings for *Europe*: 2131 Thursday on 5940, 6110, 7170, 7180, 7320, 7440 and 9890 kHz; and 1831 Friday on 6130, 7180, 7440 and 9890 kHz. In summer, tune in at 2031 Thursday on 7250, 7350, 7370, 7440, 9665, 9710, 9740. 9765, 9775, 9880 and 11840 kHz; and 1731 Friday on 9765, 9775 and 9880 kHz.

Winters, best bet for the *Middle East* is 1531 Monday on 4940, 4975, 5925, 7130, 7165, 9470, 9585, 9635, 9840 and 15205 kHz; in summer, try one hour earlier on 4740, 4940, 4975, 9595, 11665, 11835 and 11985 kHz.

In *Southern Africa*, winters, try 1831 Friday on 7325 and 9505 kHz; in summer, one hour earlier, go for 9440, 9975 and 11775 kHz.

There's nothing for *East Asia*, so best is to try the channels for *Southeast Asia*. Winters, tune in at 0931 Wednesday and Saturday on 7220 and 17860 kHz; and 1231 Tuesday and Wednesday on 9820, 9875, 11655, 13785, 17755 and 17860 kHz. Summers, one hour earlier, it's 0831 on 15470, 15490, 17610 and 17795 kHz; and 1131 on 11655, 15460, 15490, 15510, 17560, 17610, 17755, 17775 and 17795 kHz.

In *Australasia*, tune in at 0931 Wednesday and Saturday on 9675, 9835, 9875 and 17860 kHz; midyear, it's one hour earlier on 9810, 9835, 11800, 15490 and 17610 kHz.

and accordions share the stage with rubabs, changs and shepherds' flutes, and even the ubiquitous Jew's harp puts in an occasional appearance.

The music is as exotic as it is enjoyable, and you can also hear about local customs associated with songs and dances featured in the show. "Folk Box" is one of the best, if not *the* best, of its kind.

Winters in *North America*, the best chance for easterners is 0031 Monday and Saturday (Sunday and Friday evenings local American date) on 5940 and 7125 kHz. For western parts, choose from 0231 Tuesday on 5920, 5930, 7345 and 9580 kHz; and 0531 Thursday on 5920, 5930 and 7330 kHz. Listeners in eastern North America can also try the European

"Science in Action"
BBC World Service

The title says it all. This is a show which spotlights the practical applications of scientific discoveries, from the near-sublime to the slightly ridiculous, and is not without its moments of humor. The list of topics is as varied and comprehensive as science itself, and covers the whole gamut of technical advances on the scientific front.

Among the most interesting items are those dealing with medical issues, such as organ transplants and artificial limbs, but terrestrial and space exploration also provide fascinating insights into the inter-relation between man and machine. On a more esoteric level, you can hear about all sorts of strange phenomena, like how the power of music can increase the body's resistance to colds.

There's something for everyone, especially those with inquisitive minds, and it is in plain English—no scientific gobbledygook here!

First slot for *North America* is 1530 Friday on 9515, 9590 (or 11865), 15220 and 17840 kHz; with a repeat at 0530 Saturday on 5975 and 6175 kHz. Listeners in western North America can also listen at 1430 Friday on 9740 kHz.

Europe has three opportunities: 1530 Friday on 6195, 9410, 12095 and 15575 kHz; 0530 Saturday on 3955, 6195, 7120 (or 7150), 9410 and 12095 kHz; and 1830 Saturday on 3955 (winter), 6180, 6195, 9410 and (summer) 12095 and 15575 kHz. These slots are also available for the *Middle East:* 1530 on 9410 (or 15575) and 12095 kHz; 0530 on 11760 and 15575 kHz (9410 and 12095 also available in winter); and 1830 on 9410 and (summer) 12095 and 15575 kHz.

For *Southern Africa*, it's 1930 Friday on 3255, 6190 and 11835 (or 15400) kHz; or 0730 Saturday on 6190, 9600, 11940 and 15400 kHz.

Timings for *East Asia* are: 1430 Friday on 5990 and 9740 kHz; and 2330 Saturday (Sunday local date) on 5965, 7180 (winter), 9580, 11945, 11955 and (summer) 15380 kHz. These same broadcasts are heard in *Southeast Asia* at 1430 on 6195 and 9740 kHz; and 2330 on 3915 (winter), 6195, 7110 and 11955 kHz. Winter night owls

can also try 1830 Saturday (early Sunday morning local date) on 9740 kHz.

The first airing for *Australasia* is at 1430 Friday on 9740 kHz, with a repeat four hours later (at 1830) on the same frequency. The third and final slot is at 2330 Saturday (Sunday morning local date) on 11955 kHz.

"Saturday Concert" Radio Prague

One of the rare pluses of communism was that government-run stations in Eastern Europe usually aired lots of music for overseas listeners.

Few did this better than Radio Prague. Its concerts of Czech and Slovak folk music were among the best on the air, and there were also regular programs of jazz and classical music.

But in recent years, traditional Czech music all but disappeared from Radio Prague's lineup. Now, though, part of the Czech Republic's large musical heritage has made a small but welcome comeback.

Each Saturday (Sunday in some areas), you can hear 23 minutes of music from Central Europe, with folk and classical music alternating with jazz and pop. This is fine for those with broad musical tastes, but it is a bit rough if you only like one particular kind of music—you have a month's wait before the next show!

But it is worth the wait. Czech classical music has long been held in high esteem, and today's musicians continue the tradition of their predecessors. Little need be said about the country's folk music—it has always been a favorite with world band audiences. The jazz output is less well known, but Czechs have been playing great jazz for many a decade. Indeed, Czech old-time jazz from the thirties is a treat for the ears. As for pop music, long gone is the monolithic output of communist times; today's musicians can be as innovative as their counterparts in other European countries.

Timings for *North America* are 1404 Saturday (winter only) on 13580 kHz; 2234 Saturday on 5930 (winter), 7345 and (summer) 11600 kHz; 0004 Sunday (Saturday evening in the Americas) on 5930 and 7345 kHz; 0104 Sunday on 6200 and 7345 kHz; and 0304 Sunday on 5930 and 7345 kHz. Most of these frequencies are intended for eastern North America; listeners farther west should try the 0304 slot.

The show is available Saturdays for *Europe* at 0804 and 1134 on 7345 and 9505 kHz; 1704 on 5930 kHz; 1804 on 5835 (or 5930) kHz; and 2104 on 5930 kHz. All times are one hour earlier in summer.

Listeners in the *Middle East* have two opportunities: 1004 Saturday (one hour earlier in summer) on 17485 kHz; and 0334 Sunday, winters on 7350 kHz, and summers on 9480 kHz.

Best bet for *Southern Africa* is Saturday at 1004 winter on 21705 kHz; and 1704 summer on 15640 kHz.

For *Australasia*, try Saturday (Sunday, Down Under) at 1804 winter on 9430 kHz; 2004 summer on 11600 kHz; and 2134 summer on 9495 or 11600 kHz.

"Christian Message from Moscow" Voice of Russia

No, this is not an Eastern European version of hard-sell American evangelism. In fact, it is about as far removed as you can get. What you do get is a fair share of history, a little philosophy and scholarship, some magnificent music, and spirituality in the broadest sense of the word.

It has sometimes been said that to understand the Russian soul you must first know something about Russian Orthodoxy. This program goes a long way to underlining that argument. The format varies, depending on whether the subject matter is current or historical. It might be

a young Orthodox priest philosophizing about why he is not an atheist ("when one enters a church one should take off one's cap, and not one's head"). On the other hand, if the subject matter is historical, you may get a yarn in the finest Russian tradition, with a backdrop of balalaikas or ancient choral music. Whatever the topic, this is a program steeped in atmosphere.

"Christian Message from Moscow" can be enjoyed by listeners of all faiths, even non-believers. It goes a considerable way to explaining why Russian Orthodoxy is a powerful and growing force in that vast country.

Winters in *North America*, best bet for easterners is 2331 Sunday on 5940, 7125 and 7170 kHz. Farther west, tune in at 0431 Sunday (Saturday evening local American date) on 5920, 5930, 7345 and 9580 kHz. This slot is also available for eastern North America on 7125 kHz, but reception can be iffy. Better is to try the 1931 and 2031 frequencies for Europe. In summer, one hour earlier, listen at 2231 Sunday on 7125, 7250 and 9665 kHz. The 0331 Sunday slot is heard on 7125 kHz (East Coast), and in western parts on 12010, 12050, 13645, 13665, 15180 and 15595 kHz.

There are two winter airings for *Europe*: 2031 Saturday and 1931 Sunday on 4920, 5940, 6110, 6130, 7440 and 9890 kHz. In summer, tune in at 1831 on 7290, 7350, 9765, 9775 and 9880 kHz; and 1931 on 7290, 7350, 7440, 9775 and 9880 kHz.

Best timing for the *Middle East* is 1431 winter Saturdays on 7130, 7165, 9470, 9840 and 15205 kHz. There's no specific summer slot for the region, but try dialing around one hour earlier in the 11650-12050 and 15100-15600 kHz segments.

In *Southern Africa*, your best winter chance is at 1931 Sunday on 7325 and 9505 kHz; in summer, one hour earlier, try 9975, 11765 and 11775 kHz.

There's nothing much targeted to *East*

Asia, so best is to try the channels for *Southeast Asia*. Winters, tune in at 0831 Saturday on 7220, 12035 and 15460 kHz; and 1131 Sunday on 11655, 13785, 15460, 15490, 15560, 17755 and 17860 kHz. Summers, it's 0731 Saturday on 15470, 15580, 17580, 17610 and 17795 kHz; and 1031 Sunday on 7330, 11655, 15490, 15510, 17560, 17610, 17775 and 17795 kHz.

Australasia has just a single slot for winter: 0831 Saturday on 9875 and 12025 kHz. Also worth a try are the channels for Southeast Asia at 1131 Sunday. Midyear, choose from 0731 Saturday on 15560, 15570 and 17610 kHz; and 1031 Sunday on 9810, 9835, 11800, 15490 and 17610 kHz.

"Andy Kershaw's World of Music" BBC World Service

In a typical program, the first item off the block is a recording of Mongolian nose music, followed by West African rhythms from Guinea and a "rural rocker" from Neil Young. Next, a song from John Fogerty, formerly of Creedence Clearwater Revival, some Scottish airs, then sounds from the Asian underground. The show closes with a touch of the South Seas—choral music from Tahiti.

For most of us this is a rare combination of sounds, but for followers of "Andy Kershaw's World of Music" it is regular fare. Some of the recordings are discovered on his travels to out-of-the-way places—Timbuktu was one of his ports of call—and others are sent to him by listeners, friends and contacts scattered around the world.

Despite regularly leaping from one musical extreme to another, the show is not disjointed. Skillful presentation and a careful selection of records ensure a smooth passage from beginning to end. Not least of the attractions is the element of surprise—you never know what's coming up next.

BBC Photograph Library

"Andy Kershaw's World of Music" has the juice! To the delight of listeners, it covers everything from Guinean rhythms to Tahitian choral music.

Other world band stations have tried similar shows, but with relatively little success. Andy Kershaw has the juice, and his world of music is a tough act to imitate.

In *North America*, you can hear Kershaw at 2330 Saturday on 5975, 6175 and 9590 kHz. Unfortunately, there is no second chance to tune in.

Europe, like North America, gets just a single slot: 0830 Saturday on 6195 (winter), 7325, 9410, 12095, 15575 and 17640 kHz. Same timing for the *Middle East*, but on 11760, 15565, 15575 and (winter) 17640 kHz.

In *Southern Africa*, the first airing is at 1830 Saturday on 3255, 6190 and 15400 kHz; with a repeat at 1130 the following Friday on 6190, 11940 and 21660 kHz.

Deutsche Welle's "NewsLink" team provides the *ne plus ultra* in coverage of European affairs. It is heard weekdays in much of the world.

Broadcasts for *East Asia* are at 1030 Thursday on 9740 and 21660 kHz; and 0730 Friday on 9740, 11955 (or 17760), 15360 and 21660 kHz. Audible in *Southeast Asia* at the same times: 1430 on 6195 and 9740 kHz; and 0730 on 9740, 11955 and 15360 kHz. For those who can stay awake, there is an additional winter slot at 1830 Monday on 9740 kHz.

The first airing for *Australasia* is at 1830 Monday on 9740 kHz, with repeats at 1030 Thursday (April to October only) on 11765 kHz, and 0730 Friday on 7145, 11955 and 15360 kHz.

"NewsLink"
Deutsche Welle

When it comes to news programs, world band is a mixed bag. Some smaller stations report only on international stories,

usually covered far more knowledgeably and in greater detail by broadcasting giants like the BBC or VOA. Yet others, like Radio Finland, restrict themselves to news from within their own countries. Strangely enough, good regional or continental coverage—that mid-ground between national and international reporting—is relatively rare, especially as concerns Europe.

The BBC World Service has an excellent regional report, "Europe Today," but for some inexplicable reason it is mainly beamed to European audiences. Most of the world, it seems, has little interest in what is happening in Europe—or so the BBC would have us believe.

Deutsche Welle, on the other hand, has always leaned heavily towards coverage of European affairs, and its pioneering "European Journal" has been a valuable source of continental news and analysis.

Playing to this success, in 1997 the station decided to merge its two main news programs—"European Journal" and "Newsline Cologne"—into the new and more streamlined "NewsLink."

The result is a fast-moving 25-minute show with the accent squarely on Europe. Granted, important international stories are not ignored, but it is European news and reports which hold center stage. "NewsLink" is simply invaluable as a source of information for followers of the European scene.

For *North America*, the show is available Tuesday through Saturday (local weekday evenings in the Americas) at 0106, winters on 5960, 6040, 6085 and 6145 kHz; and summers on 6040, 6085, 6145, 9640 and 11810 kHz. The next broadcast is two hours later, at 0306, winters on 6045, 6085, 9535 and 9650 kHz; and summers on 6085, 6185, 9535, 9615 and 9640 kHz. The third and final airing (best for western North America) is at 0506, winters on 6120, 6145, 6185 and 9650 kHz; and summers on 5960, 6045, 6185 and 9515 kHz.

Europe has just the one slot: 2006 Monday through Friday, winters on 7285 kHz, and summers on 7170 and 9615 kHz.

Best bet for the *Middle East* is 0606 Monday through Friday, winters on 21705 kHz, and summers on 21680 kHz.

In *Southern Africa*, you can choose from three transmissions each weekday. The first is at 0406, winters on 6015, 6065, 7225, 7265 and 9565 kHz; and summers on 5990, 6015, 7225, 9565 and 11765 kHz. A second broadcast can be heard at 0906 on 9565, 15145 (winter), 15205 (summer), 15410, 17800 and 21600 kHz; and the final edition goes out at 1606, winter on 7195, 9735, 11810, 13610 and 15145 kHz; and summer on 7130, 9735, 11810 and 17800 kHz.

There is nothing beamed to East Asia, but listeners in *Southeast Asia* can listen at 2306 Monday through Friday (Tuesday through Saturday in the target area),

winters on 6000, 6160 and 7235 kHz; and summers on 5980, 7235 and 9690 kHz.

Australasia gets two bites. The first is at 0906, winters on 6160, 7380, 11715 and 17820 kHz; and summers on 6160, 12055, 17715 and 21680 kHz. The second edition goes out at 2106 on 7115 (summer), 9670, 9765 and 11785 kHz. Note that the 2106 broadcast is heard Tuesday through Saturday, local dates in the target area.

"Music and Musicians" Voice of Russia

World band radio is hardly the ideal-fidelity medium for music, particularly classical, although some of the newer receivers with synchronous selectable sideband sound pretty good. Yet, some of the finest classical-music programs are aired on world band.

One of these is "Music and Musicians," the only show from the Voice of Russia to be allocated more than 30 minutes. That unassuming title gives little indication of the wealth of exceptional music that is contained within this gem of a program.

Russian composers and artists predominate, but not to the exclusion of others from farther afield. The show has no fixed format, and you are just as likely to hear live performances from Moscow's Musical Assembly Festival as recordings of symphonies from Rachmaninoff or Shostakovich. Variety is plentiful, and performances range from sublime interpretations of centuries-old choral works to classical compositions written for, and played on, panpipes.

There are short, informative notes about the music, composers and festivals featured in the program, but it is the music itself which is given pride of place. Add to this a relaxed presentation, and you have good reason to pull up an armchair for 45 minutes of pure entertainment.

There are two slots scheduled for *North*

Get It Firsthand
With Drake World Band
The Finest Line of Products For The Shortwave Enthusiast.

R8B Communications Receiver

SW8 Worldband Receiver

SW2 Shortwave Receiver

SW1 Shortwave Receiver

Drake's current line of world band communication receivers continues its history of excellence. Drake has something for everyone - regardless of skill or interest level.

For the avid enthusiast, the top of the line R8B offers serious performance with Selectable Sideband Synchronous Detection and five built-in filters. For the listener on the go, the SW8 provides all the advanced features of a tabletop unit, but is completely portable. Expensive taste with a small budget? The SW2 fits the bill. The SW2 boasts expensive features like Selectable Sideband Synchronous Detection, 100 programmable memories and an optional infrared remote control - all at a moderate price. Just getting started? The SW1 is perfect for the beginning hobbyist. User friendly operation lets you pull in AM broadcasts from the far corners of the world.

Whatever your level of interest, you'll appreciate the craftsmanship, quality and performance that is built into every Drake communications receiver.

R.L. Drake Company
phone 513-746-4556

230 Industrial Dr.
fax 513-743-4510

Franklin, OH 45005 U.S.A.
on-line www.rldrake.com

RNW

The pride of Radio Netherlands' "Documentary" staff is Syrian-born Eric Beauchemin, who has won several international awards. The show's topics range from gypsies to Trappist monks, with lots of sound bites.

Winters in the *Middle East*, try 1711 Saturday on 7130, 7210, 7255, 7275, 7305 and 9585 kHz; summers, one hour earlier, on 9615, 9675, 11725, 11775, 11850 and 11945 kHz. This slot is also available for *Southern Africa*, winters on 7115, 7255, 7275, 7325 and 9505 kHz; and summers on 9440, 9615, 9675, 9975 and 11775 kHz.

There's nothing for *East Asia*, so best is to try the channels for *Southeast Asia*. Winter timings are 0811 Sunday and Monday on 7220, 12035 and 15460 kHz; and 1311 Sunday on 4740, 4975, 15460 and 17860 kHz. In summer, tune in one hour earlier: 0711 on 15470, 15580, 17580, 17610 and 17795 kHz; and 1211 on 4740, 4975, 11655, 11785, 15110, 15435, 15490, 15510, 17610, 17755, 17775 and 17795 kHz.

In *Australasia*, "Music and Musicians" can be heard winters at 0811 Sunday and Monday on 9875 and 12025 kHz; midyear, it's one hour earlier on 11800, 15560 and 17610 kHz.

"Documentary" Radio Netherlands

Radio Netherlands is the only international broadcaster which can give the BBC World Service a run for its money in the production of documentaries. Winner of several prestigious international awards, the Radio Netherlands English team is as prolific as it is excellent.

The range of topics is seemingly limitless. Jazz, gypsies, secret police, tigers, violent women, racism, Brahms, the brews of Trappist monks, international poverty, childbirth and the Titanic are just some of the subjects to come under the scrutiny of the documentary team.

The programs are well researched, and put together with admirable professionalism. Good use of sound bites helps create a propitious atmosphere, and there is very much a "local" feel to each of the programs. They are broadcast on Wednesday and Friday of each week.

America, and both are for the western half of the continent. Winters, tune in at 0211 Sunday and Monday (Saturday and Sunday evenings in North America) on 5920, 5930, 7345, 9580, 12030 and 13665 kHz; and in summer, one hour earlier, on 12010, 12050, 13665, 15180 and 15195 kHz. Listeners in the East can try the channels for Europe at 2211 (2111 in summer).

Europe has two opportunities, both on Saturday. Winters, choose from 1711 on 4920, 5940, 6110, 6130, 7180, 7440 and 9890 kHz; and 2211 on 5940, 6110, 7125, 7205, 7320, 7360, 7400, 7440 and 9890 kHz. Summer timings are 1611 on 7290, 7350, 9730, 9765, 9775, 9880 and 15430 kHz; and 2111 on 7250, 7370, 7440, 9665, 9710, 9740, 9765, 9775, 9880 and 11840 kHz.

First slot for eastern *North America* is at 0054 Thursday (Wednesday evening in the Americas) on 6020, 6165 and (summer) 9845 kHz; with a repeat at 2354 Friday on the same frequencies. Farther west, tune in at 0454 Thursday on 5995 (9590 in summer) and 6165 kHz.

The timings for *Europe* are a little more complicated: winters, it's 1254 Wednesday and 1154 Friday on 6045 and 7190 kHz; and summers, one hour earlier on 6045 and 9650 kHz. Listeners in the *Middle East* get only half a loaf—1354 Wednesday and 1454 Friday on 13700 kHz, but only in winter. Strangely, there's nothing beamed their way during the summer months.

In *Southern Africa*, look for good all-year reception at 1754 Wednesday and 1854 Friday on 6020 kHz.

For *East* and *Southeast Asia*, try 0954 Wednesday and 1054 Friday, winters on 7260 and 9810 kHz; and summers on 12065 and 13710 kHz. In *Australasia*, the first airing is at 0754 Wednesday, winters (summer Down Under) on 9830 and 11895 kHz, and summers on 9720 and 9820 kHz. A repeat broadcast can be heard at 0854 Friday, winters on 5965, 9830 and 13700 kHz; and summers on 9720 and 9820 kHz. Too, the transmissions for East and Southeast Asia often provide good reception in much of Australasia.

"Focus on Faith"
BBC World Service

If you are looking for spiritual guidance or inspiration, you've come to the wrong place—"Focus on Faith" offers you neither. Instead, it takes a hard secular look at what is happening in the world of religion. Here, nothing is sacred.

The program is evenhanded and all-embracing. Financial shenanigans in the Vatican are given the same coverage as a Jewish shemozzle in Gaza or the debate about homosexual priests in the Anglican church. A story on Islamic fundamentalists gets the same impartial treatment as a report on Zoroastrianism.

"Focus on Faith" is an eye-opener, spotlighting many of the conflicts and incongruities of the world's religions. For those who believe that religion is only for the religious, here is a show that proves otherwise.

The first airing for *North America* is at 0230 Friday (Thursday evening local American date) on 5975, 6175, 9515 (winter) and 9590 (or 9895) kHz; and is repeated nine hours later (at 1130) on 5965, 6195 and 15220 kHz.

Europe has two Friday slots: 1130 on 9410, 12095, 15575 and 17640 kHz; and 1830 on 3955 (winter), 6180, 6195, 9410 and (summer) 12095 and 15575 kHz. These same two slots are also available for the *Middle East*: at 1130 on 11760, 15565, 15575 and (winter) 17640 kHz; and at 1830 on 9410 and (summer) 12095 and 15575 kHz.

In *Southern Africa*, choose from 0915 Friday on 6190, 11940 and 15400 kHz; and 0330 Saturday on 3255, 6005, 6190 and 9600 kHz.

The first opportunity for *East Asia* is at 0530 Friday on 9740, 11955 (or 17760), 15360 and 21660 kHz; with a repeat five hours later, at 1030, on 9740 and (summer) 21660 kHz. These same two slots are also available for *Southeast Asia*: 0530 on 9740, 11955, 15310 (summer) and 15360 kHz; and 1030 on 6195, 9740 and (summer) 11765 and 15310 kHz. For night owls, there is an additional winter slot at 1930 Friday on 9740 kHz.

First shot for *Australasia* is at 0530 Friday on 11955 and 15360 kHz, with repeats at 1030 (April to October only) on 11765 kHz, and 1930 on 9740 kHz.

Prepared by the staff of PASSPORT TO WORLD BAND RADIO.

Compleat Idiot's Guide to Getting Started

Four "Must" Tips to Catch the World

World band radio is information and entertainment, on the spot—your unfiltered connection to what's going on all over. But it's not as easy to receive as conventional radio, so here are four "must" tips to get started.

"Must" #1: Set Clock for World Time

World band schedules use a single worldwide time, *World Time*. After all, world band radio is global, with nations broadcasting around-the-clock from virtually every time zone.

Imagine the chaos if each broadcaster used its own local time for scheduling. In England, 9 PM is different from nine in the evening in Japan or Canada. How would anybody know when to tune in?

World Time, or Coordinated Universal Time (UTC), was formerly and in some circles still is known as Greenwich Mean Time (GMT). It is keyed to the Greenwich meridian in England and is announced in 24-hour format, like military time. So 2 PM, say, is 1400 ("fourteen hundred") hours.

There are four easy ways to know World Time. First, you can tune to one of the standard time stations, such as WWV in Colorado and WWVH in Hawaii in the United States, or CHU in Ottawa, Canada. WWV and WWVH are on 5000, 10000 and 15000 kHz around-the-clock, with WWV also on 2500 and 20000 kHz; CHU is on 3330, 7335 and 14670 kHz. There, you will hear time "pips" every second, followed just before the beginning of each minute by an announcement of the exact World Time. Boring, yes, but very handy when you need it.

> World band uses a single worldwide time, *World Time*.

Second, you can tune to one of the major international broadcasters, such as London's BBC World Service or Washington's Voice of America. Most announce World Time at the top of the hour.

Third, you can access the Internet Web site http://www.greenwich2000.com/time.htm, but you'll need to have your slow-loading graphics switched on

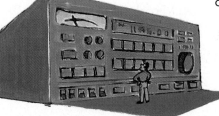

John Pivarnik tunes in the world while outdoors in rural Bucks County, Pennsylvania. Howard Karashoff

to see the clock display. This site also provides gobs of information about all aspects of UTC.

Fourth, here are some quick calculations.

If you live on the East Coast of the United States, *add* five hours winter (four hours summer) to your local time to get World Time. So, if it is 8 PM EST (the 20th hour of the day) in New York, it is 0100 hours World Time.

On the U.S. West Coast, add eight hours winter (seven hours summer).

In Britain, it's easy—World Time (oops, Greenwich Mean Time) is the same as local winter time. However, you'll have to subtract one hour from local summer time to get World Time.

Elsewhere in Western Europe, subtract one hour winter (two hours summer) from local time.

Live elsewhere? Flip through the next few pages until you come to "How to Set Your World Time Clock."

Once you know the correct World Time, set your radio's clock so you'll have it handy whenever you want to listen. No 24-hour clock? Pick up the phone and order one (world band specialty firms sell them for as little as $10, see box). Unless you enjoy doing weird computations in your head (it's 6:00 PM here, so add five hours to make it 11:00 PM, which on a 24-hour clock converts to 23:00 World Time—but, whoops, I forgot that it's summer and I should have added four hours instead of five . . .), it'll be the best ten bucks you ever spent.

Bargains in World Time Clocks

For the relatively unfamiliar 24-hour World Time, digital clocks are much easier to read than timepieces with hands. Here are four value-priced choices that work well and are easy to find.

MFJ-24-107B, $9.95. Despite its paucity of features, this battery-powered "Volksclock" does the trick.

NI8F LCD, $14.95. Same as the MFJ, above, but with a handsome walnut frame instead of aluminum. It is less likely than MFJ models to scratch surfaces. From Universal Radio.

MFJ's "Volksclock" costs less than ten dollars, but does the trick.

MFJ 114, $39.95. If you want your World Time *VISIBLE*, here's a bold alternative. MFJ's 114 uses tall (2¼ inches or 60 mm) bright-red LEDs instead of the small, low-contrast LCD screens used by most other digital timepieces. Unlike LCD clocks, which are battery powered, the 114 plugs into the wall, using a battery only for backup.

MFJ-108B, $19.95. For those who also want local time. Two battery-powered LCD clocks—24-hour format for World Time, separate 12-hour display for local time—side-by-side.

ECW-40, $2,345. Don't like cheap? Try this GPS-fed multiple-format satellite chronometer, intended mainly for radio stations, with World Time and World Day accurate to the nearest microsecond. From Eventide Inc., Little Ferry, NJ 07643 USA (www.eventide.com/broadcst/ecw40bro.htm).

Simply the Best

With Grundig you can search to the ends of the earth, and no one unlocks the

mysteries of radio better than Grundig. Technology, value, service...

GRUNDIG IS SIMPLY THE BEST.

GRUNDIG

"Must" #2: Wind Your Calendar

What happens at midnight, World Time? A new *World Day* arrives as well. This can trip up even experienced listeners—sometimes radio stations, too.

Remember: Midnight World Time means a new day. So if it is 9 PM EST Wednesday in New York, it is 0200 hours World Time *Thursday*. Don't forget to "wind your calendar"!

"Must" #3: Know How to Find Stations

Passport provides station schedules three ways: by country, by time of day and by frequency. By-country is best to hear a given station. "What's On To-night," the time-of-day section, is like *TV Guide* and includes program details. The by-frequency Blue Pages are for when you're dialing around the bands.

> There are several "neighborhoods" where stations are clustered, and each has different characteristics.

Frequencies may be given either in kilohertz (kHz) or Megahertz (MHz). The only difference is three decimal places, so 6175 kHz is the same as 6.175 MHz.

But forget all the technobabble. All you need to know is that 6175, with or without decimals, refers to a certain spot on your radio's dial.

Here are the main "neighborhoods" where you'll find world band stations and when they're most active. Except for the 4750-5075 kHz segment, which has mainly low-powered Latin American and African stations, you'll discover a huge variety of stations.

Frequency	Activity
4750-5075 kHz	Night and twilight, mainly during winter
5730-6205 kHz	Night and twilight; sometimes day, too
7100-7595 kHz	Night, early morning and late afternoon
9350-10000 kHz	Night (except winter), early morning and late afternoon
11550-12160 kHz	Night (except winter) and day, especially dusk
13570-13870 kHz	Day and, to a limited degree, night
15000-15710 kHz	Day and, to a limited degree, night
17500-17900 kHz	Day and, rarely, night
21450-21850 kHz	Day only

Burning Rubber: Passport's Five-Minute Start

In a hurry? Here's how to get to get going with the most fire and least smoke:

1. Wait until evening, when signals are strongest. If you live in a concrete-and-steel building, put your radio by a window or sit on the balcony.

2. Make sure the radio is plugged in or has fresh batteries. Extend the telescopic antenna fully and vertically. Set the DX/local switch (if there is one) to "DX," but otherwise leave the controls the way they came from the factory.

3. Turn on your radio. Set it to 5900 kHz and begin tuning slowly toward 6200 kHz. You will now begin to encounter a number of stations from around the world. Adjust the volume to a level that is comfortable for you. *Voilà!* You are now an initiate of world band radio.

Other times? Read this chapter, especially the "Best Times and Frequencies for 1998" sidebar.

You're already used to hearing mediumwave AM and FM stations at the same place on the dial, day and night. But things are a lot different when you roam the international airwaves.

Daytime, you'll find most stations above 11500 kHz; night, below 10000 kHz.

World band radio is like a global bazaar where a variety of merchants come and go at different times. Similarly, stations enter and leave a given spot on the dial throughout the day and night. Where you once tuned in, say, a French station, hours later you might find a Russian or Chinese broadcaster roosting on that same spot.

Or on a nearby perch. If you suddenly hear interference from a station on an adjacent channel, it doesn't mean something is wrong with your radio; it probably means another station has begun broadcasting on a nearby frequency. There are more stations on the air than there is space for them, so sometimes they try to outshout each other.

To cope with this, purchase a radio with superior adjacent-channel rejection, also known as selectivity. The lab measurements and listening tests in PASSPORT REPORTS, a major section of this book, tell you how successfully the various radios leap this hurdle.

One of the most pleasant things about world band radio is cruising up and down the airwaves. Daytime, you'll find most stations above 11500 kHz; night, below 10000 kHz.

Teacher Neil Carleton has headed the Shortwave Listening Clubs at the Glen Tay and G.L. Comba public schools in Ontario. Classrooms around the world now use world band radio to educate youngsters.

The tradition of Marcel Marceau lives on in Helsinki, where this young mime entertains passersby.

Tune slowly, savor the sound of foreign tongues sprinkled alongside English shows. Enjoy the music, weigh the opinions of other peoples and the events that shape their lives.

If a station fades out, there is probably nothing wrong with your radio. The atmosphere's *ionosphere* bounces world band signals earthward, like a dribbled basketball, and it changes constantly. The result is that broadcasters operate in different parts of the world band spectrum, depending upon the time of day and season of the year.

That same changeability can also work in your favor, especially if you like to eavesdrop on signals not intended for your part of the world. Sometimes stations from exotic locales—places you would not ordinarily hear—become surprise arrivals at your radio, thanks to the shifting characteristics of the ionosphere.

"Must" #4: Get A Radio That Really Works

Choose carefully, but you shouldn't need a costly set. Cheap radios should be avoided—they suffer from one or more major defects. But with one of the better-rated portables, usually less than the price of a VCR, you'll be able to hear much of what world band has to offer.

You won't need an outside antenna, either, unless you're using a tabletop model. All portables, and to some extent portatops, are designed to work off the built-in telescopic antenna. But try to purchase a radio with digital frequency

Setting Your World Time Clock

PASSPORT's "Addresses PLUS" lets you arrive at the local time in another country by adding or subtracting from World Time. Use that section to determine the time within a country you are listening to.

   This box, however, gives it from the other direction—that is, what to add or subtract from your local time to determine World Time where you're at. Use this to set your World Time clock.

Where You Are	To Determine World Time

North America

Newfoundland St. John's NF, St. Anthony NF	Add 3½ hours winter, 2½ hours summer
Atlantic St. John NB, Battle Harbour NF	Add 4 hours winter, 3 hours summer
Eastern New York, Atlanta, Toronto	Add 5 hours winter, 4 hours summer
Central Chicago, Nashville, Winnipeg	Add 6 hours winter, 5 hours summer
Mountain Denver, Salt Lake City, Calgary	Add 7 hours winter, 6 hours summer
Pacific San Francisco, Vancouver	Add 8 hours winter, 7 hours summer
Alaska Anchorage, Fairbanks	Add 9 hours winter, 8 hours summer
Hawaii Honolulu, Hilo	Add 10 hours year round

Europe

United Kingdom, Ireland and Portugal London, Dublin, Lisbon	Same time as World Time winter, subtract 1 hour summer
Continental Western Europe; parts of Central and Eastern Continental Europe Paris, Berlin, Stockholm, Prague, Rome, Madrid	Subtract 1 hour winter, 2 hours summer
Elsewhere in Continental Europe Belarus, Bulgaria, Cyprus, Estonia, Finland, Greece, Latvia, Lithuania, Moldova, Romania, Russia (Kaliningradskaya Oblast), Turkey and Ukraine	Subtract 2 hours winter, 3 hours summer

display. Its accuracy will make tuning far easier than with outmoded slide-rule tuning.

Does that mean you should avoid a tabletop or portatop model? Hardly, especially if you listen during the day, when signals are weaker, or to hard-to-hear stations. The best-rated tabletop, and even portatop, models can bring faint and difficult signals to life—especially when they're connected to a good external antenna. But if you just want to hear the big stations, you'll do fine with a moderately priced portable. PASSPORT REPORTS rates virtually all available models.

Universal Radio's Fred Osterman troubleshoots a world band receiver.

> Portables don't need an outside antenna, as they are designed to work off the built-in antenna.

Radio in hand, read or at least glance over your owner's manual—yes, it *is* worth it. You'll find that, despite a few unfamiliar controls, your new world band receiver isn't all that much different from radios you have used all your life. Experiment with those controls so you'll become comfortable with them. After all, you can't harm your radio by twiddling switches and knobs.

———————————

Prepared by Jock Elliott, Tony Jones and Lawrence Magne.

Mideast & Southern Africa

Egypt, Israel, Lebanon and Syria	Subtract 2 hours winter, 3 hours summer
South Africa, Zambia and Zimbabwe	Subtract 2 hours year round

East Asia & Australasia

China, including Taiwan	Subtract 8 hours year round
Japan	Subtract 9 hours year round
Australia: *Victoria, New South Wales, Tasmania*	Subtract 11 hours local summer, 10 local winter (midyear)
Australia: *South Australia*	Subtract 10½ hours local summer, 9½ hours local winter (midyear)
Australia: *Queensland*	Subtract 10 hours year round
Australia: *Northern Territory*	Subtract 9½ hours year round
Australia: *Western Australia*	Subtract 8 hours year round
New Zealand	Subtract 13 hours local summer, 12 hours local winter (midyear)

Best Times and Frequencies for 1998

With world band, if you dial around randomly, you're almost as likely to get dead air as you are a favorite program. For one thing, a number of world band segments are alive and kicking by day, while others are nocturnal. Too, some fare better at specific times of the year.

"Neighborhoods" Where to Tune

Official "neighborhoods," or segments, of the shortwave spectrum are set aside for world band radio by the International Telecommunication Union. However, the ITU countenances some broadcasting outside these parameters, so the "real world" situation is actually more generous. This is what's shown below.

This guide is most accurate if you're listening from north of Africa or South America. Even then, what you'll actually hear will vary—depending upon such variables as your precise location, where the station transmits from, the time of year and your radio (e.g., see Propagation in the glossary). Although world band is active 24 hours a day, signals are usually best from around just before sunset until sometime after midnight. Too, try a couple of hours on either side of dawn.

Here, then, are the most attractive times and frequencies for world band listening, based on reception conditions forecast for the coming year. Unless otherwise indicated, frequency ranges are occupied mainly by international broadcasters, but also include some domestic stations or overseas relays of domestic stations. In the Americas, 3900-4000 kHz and 7100-7300 kHz are reserved for use by amateur radio ("hams"), even though world band transmissions from other parts of the world manage to be heard there. **Nights** refers to your local hours of darkness, plus dawn and dusk.

Rare Reception Winter Nights

2 MHz (120 meters) **2300-2500 kHz** (overwhelmingly domestic stations)

Limited Reception Winter Nights

3 MHz (90 meters) **3200-3400 kHz** (mostly domestic stations)
Good-to-Fair during Winter Nights in Europe and Asia
Limited Reception during Winter Nights Elsewhere
4 MHz (75 meters) **3900-4080 kHz** (international and domestic stations, primarily not in or beamed to the Americas—3900-3950 mainly Asian and Pacific transmitters; 3950-4000 also includes European and African transmitters)

Some Reception during Nights
Regional Reception Daytime

5 MHz (60 meters) **4700-5100 kHz** (mostly domestic stations)

Excellent during Nights
Regional Reception Daytime

6 MHz (49 meters) **5730-6250 kHz**

An Indonesian peasant boy listens to the FEBC on his compact world band portable.

Good during Nights except Mid-Winter
Variable during Mid-Winter Nights
Regional Reception Daytime

7 MHz (41 meters) **7100-7600 kHz (also 6890-6995 kHz)** (7100-7300 kHz, no American-based transmitters and few transmissions targeted to the Americas)

Good during Summer Nights
Some Reception Daytime and Winter Nights
Good Asian and Pacific Reception Mornings in America

9 MHz (31 meters) **9250-10000 kHz (also 9020-9080 kHz)**
11 MHz (25 meters) **11500-12160 kHz**

Good during Daytime
Generally Good during Summer Nights

13 MHz (22 meters) **13570-13870 kHz**
15 MHz (19 meters) **15000-15800 kHz**

Good during Daytime
Variable, Limited Reception Summer Nights

17 MHz (16 meters) **17480-17900 kHz**

Limited Reception during Daytime

19 MHz (15 meters) **18900-19020 kHz**
21 MHz (13 meters) **21450-21850 kHz**

Inactive at Present

25 MHz (11 meters) **25670-26100 kHz**

First Tries:
Ten Easy Catches

Here are ten English-language stations you can enjoy wherever you are. All times are World Time, explained elsewhere in PASSPORT.

EUROPE
France

After years of being lavishly funded, **Radio France Internationale** has finally begun to feel the financial axe. Nevertheless, RFI's overall financial situation continues to be enviable compared to that of many of its fellow broadcasters, such as Radio Australia. Although broadcasting predominantly in French, the station's output in English continues to be heard over various parts of the globe. The timing of its English broadcasts are not the most convenient, but quality programs and slick presentation justify the extra effort to listen to the station.

North America: 1200-1255, year-round, on 13625 kHz. For a second (seasonal) channel, try 11615, 15530 or 17575 kHz. Reception still poor? Try 15540 kHz via their relay in Gabon. Though targeted at West Africa, the Gabon signal is nonetheless audible in parts of eastern North America and the Caribbean. The 1600 broadcast to Africa (see below) is also sometimes audible in eastern North America.

Europe: 1200-1255 on 9805, 15155 and 15195 kHz.

Middle East: 1400-1455 on 17560 kHz; 1600-1655 on 9485 or 11615 kHz, and 1700-1730 (targeted at East Africa) on 9485, 11615 or 15460 kHz.

Asia: 1200-1255 on 11600 kHz, and 1400-1455 on 7110 (or 11910) and 12030 (or 15405) kHz.

Africa: RFI's broadcasts for Africa are among the best sources of news about that continent, and can often be heard well in other parts of the world. Audible at 1600-1655 on 11615, 11700, 12015 and 15530 kHz; and at 1600-1730 on one or more channels from 11615, 15210 and 15460 kHz. The 1200 transmission for Europe and North America also goes out to West Africa on 15540 kHz.

American juggles for donations in Germany. Pocket portables make world band reception a popular pastime among international travelers. S. Crane

The Boukan Ginen group appears over Radio France Internationale.

Europe: 2000-2050, winters on 7285 kHz; and summers on 7170 and 9615 kHz.

Middle East: 0600-0650, winters on 21705 kHz; and summers on 21680 kHz.

Southern Africa: 0400-0450 winters (summer in the Southern Hemisphere) on 6015, 6065, 7225, 7265 and 9565 kHz; summers on 5990, 6015, 7225, 9565 and 11765 kHz. The second slot is at 0900-0950 on 9565, 15145 (winter), 15205 (summer), 15410, 17800 and 21600 kHz; and the third and final broadcast goes out at 1600-1650, winter on 7195, 9735, 11810, 13610 and 15145 kHz; and summer on 7130, 9735, 11810 and 17800 kHz.

Asia and the Pacific: 0900-0950 winters on 6160, 7380, 11715 and 17820 kHz; summers on 6160, 12055, 17715 and 21680 kHz. A second broadcast goes out at 2100-2150 on 7115 (summer), 9670, 9765 and 11785 kHz. There's also an additional transmission for South and Southeast Asia at 2300-2350, winters on 6000, 6160 and 7235 kHz; summers on 5980, 7235 and 9690 kHz.

Germany

Germany's ubiquitous **Deutsche Welle** has also undergone some belt tightening, but fortunately their English broadcasts remain intact. DW's well-established format of news and features is being further streamlined, with emphasis on regional coverage of world events. The station's strength is in-depth European news, plus there's coverage of events in Africa and the Asia-Pacific region. Professionalism and technical excellence generally continue to be hallmarks of this news-oriented station.

North and Central America: 0100-0150 winters on 5960, 6040, 6085 and 6145 kHz; summers on 6040, 6085, 6145, 9640 and 11810 kHz. The next edition is at 0300-0350: winters on 6045, 6085, 9535 and 9650 kHz; summers on 6085, 6185, 9535, 9615 and 9640 kHz. The third and final broadcast goes out at 0500-0550, winters on 6120, 6145, 6185 and 9650 kHz; and summers on 5960, 6045, 6185 and 9515 kHz. This last slot is best for western North America.

Holland

Radio Nederland, also known as **Radio Netherlands** and more formally as **Radio Nederland Wereldomroep**, continues to ride high in the popularity charts thanks to a pleasing blend of news, information and cultural programs. Innovative and sometimes controversial, it has a dynamism rarely equaled by other international broadcasters. A worldwide network of relay transmitters ensures you can hear this station just about anywhere in the world.

North America: Easily heard throughout much of North America at 2330-0125 on 6020, 6165 and (summer) 9845 kHz. For western parts, try 0430-0525 on 5995 (summers on 9590) and 6165 kHz. Too, the broadcasts for Africa at 1830-2025 on 15315 and 17605 kHz are often well heard in many parts of North America.

YACHT BOY 400

THE ULTIMATE IN DIGITAL TECHNOLOGY

Noted for its exacting controls, including fine tuning, volume and high/low tone controls.

Multi-Function Liquid Crystal Display: The LCD shows simultaneous displays of time, frequency, band, alarm function and sleep timer.

The Digital Key Pad: The key pad itself is a marvel of performance with 40 pre-set stations. It's intelligently designed and easy to use.

GRUNDIG
made for you

Grundig's Yacht Boy 400 has received rave reviews from the shortwave press for combining a wealth of sophisticated features in one compact, portable package that doesn't cost a fortune. It incorporates features found on stationary shortwave systems that cost thousands, such as outstanding audio quality, precise 0.1 kHz increment tuning, up/down slewing, frequency scanning, signal strength indication, and single-sideband signal demodulation.

But the Yacht Boy advantage mentioned most often in reviews was its ease of use for the novice listener. Following the included shortwave guide, in moments you can be listening to foreign broadcasts beamed to North America.

Soon, you will be scanning the airwaves to tune in exotic music programs and sports events from faraway locales. Yacht Boy even picks up shortwave amateur (ham radio) broadcasts and shortwave aviation/military frequencies (cockpit-to-tower communications). The possibilities for family fun, education, and enjoyment are boundless.

For travel or home use, Grundig adds in a dual-time travel clock with snooze and sleep timer. FM band is stereophonic with your headphones. The lighted LCD panel is easy to read in the dark. Comes with a form-fitting pouch, integral telescoping antenna and advanced external antenna on a compact reel, carry-strap, batteries, and complete instructions.

RNW

Anne Blair Gould, Science Editor of Radio Netherlands' English Service.

Europe: 1130-1325 winters on 6045 and 7190 kHz; 1030-1225 summers on 6045 and 9650 kHz.

Middle East: There is nothing specifically targeted to this area, but try the winter frequency of 13700 kHz at 1330-1525.

Southern Africa: 1730-1925 on 6020 kHz.

East Asia: 0930-1125 winters on 7260

RNW

Nick Meanwell now heads Radio Netherlands' English Service.

and 9810 kHz, and summers on 12065 and 13710 kHz.

Australia and the Pacific: 0730-0825 winters (summer in Australasia) on 9830 and 11895 kHz, and summers on 9720 and 9820 kHz; 0830-0925 winters on 5965, 9830 and 13700 kHz; summers on 9720 and 9820 kHz; 0930-1025 winters on 5965 kHz. Too, the 0930-1125 broadcasts for East Asia are often well received in parts of Australasia.

Russia

Many world band stations are having to cope with reduced budgets, but here is one whose funds have virtually dried up. Yet, a few faithful staffers continue to make the **Voice of Russia** a popular choice for millions of listeners. Although there are interesting newscasts, many programs are cultural, and the musical output is legendary. No longer the dominant transmitting power of Cold War lore, the Voice of Russia has nevertheless succeeded in making its signal widely available by stepping up the power of the remaining transmitters at its disposal.

Eastern North America: Reception quality varies, but best is usually late afternoon and early evening. Winter, try the following frequencies: 5940 (2230-0100 and 0300-0400), 7125 (2300-0200 and 0400-0600), 7170 (2300-2400) and 7400 (2000-2300). Best summer channels are 7125 (2230-0100 and 0300-0500), 7250 (2200-0100) and 9665 (2030-2400). In addition, try frequencies beamed to Europe—a number of them often make it to eastern North America. If you don't find anything on these channels, dial around nearby. The Voice of Russia is not renowned for sticking to its frequencies, but it often stays within the same segments of the world band spectrum.

Western North America: 0200-0800 (one hour earlier in summer). Reception in western parts is more reliable than farther

Voice of Russia's popular English-language team includes Olga Troshina, Joe Adamov, Lyubov Tsaronskaya and Mzina Koroloua. Ms. Troshina answers listeners' letters, while "Jolly Joe" has been an announcer at the station since the Germans were at the gates of Moscow.

east, and channel usage is more predictable. Not all frequencies are in use for the entire period, but several of them are. In winter, choose from 5920, 5930, 7175, 7330, 7345, 9580 and 12030 kHz; for summer reception, try 12000, 12010, 12050, 13645, 13665, 15180 and 15595 kHz.

Europe: Nominally 1700-2300, but opens earlier on some channels. Is one hour earlier in summer. Best winter choices are in the 6, 7 and 9 MHz segments. Try 4920, 5940, 6110, 6130, 7180, 7320 (2130-2300), 7400 and 9890 kHz. For summer, dial around the 7, 9, 11 and 15 MHz ranges. Worth a look are 7370 (2030-2200), 7440, 9665, 9775, 9810, 9880, 11840 (2100-2200) and 15400 kHz. Times vary for each channel.

Middle East: 1400-1900 (one hour earlier in summer). Winter, try the likes of 4740, 4940, 4975, 5925, 7130, 7165, 7275, 9470, 9585 and 9635 kHz. Best summer bets

can be found amongst 9595, 9675, 9830, 11775, 11835, 11945, 11985, 15350 and 15540 kHz. Times vary for each channel, and some frequencies carry languages other than English for part of the time.

Southern Africa: 1500-2100, although start time may be earlier in some cases. One hour earlier in summer. Channels can vary, but for winter try 7255, 7325, 9470 and 9505 kHz; in summer, go for 9975, 11765 and 11775 KHz. If these are unsatisfactory, dial around nearby. Too, some frequencies targeted at the Middle East are also audible in southern Africa.

East Asia: Currently very little on offer, due to limited availability of transmitters in the Russian Far East. Try at 1000-1200 winter in the 5940-6060 kHz range, and 2000-2200 summer on 7300 kHz.

Southeast Asia: 0600-1400, winter on 11655, 12035, 12055, 13785, 15460, 15490, 15560, 17755 and 17860 kHz; summer on

Mikhail Sergeyev (with tie), director of the GPR-2 world band transmission facilities in St. Petersburg, Russia. On left are American visitors Art Bell, Jr. and Bob Crane of the C. Crane Company, which distributes world band products.

7330, 11655, 15110, 15230, 15460, 15490, 15510, 15560, 17560, 17610, 17755, 17775 and 17795 kHz. Times vary for each channel, and some frequencies carry languages other than English for part of the time.

Australasia: 0600-1200, winter (summer Down Under) on 9835, 9875, 12025, 15470, 17570, 17860 and 21790 kHz; summer on 9810, 9835, 11800, 15490, 15560, 17570 and 17610 kHz. Not all frequencies are available for the full period.

Switzerland

Swiss Radio International stresses hard news during the week, with lighter fare on weekends. Close proximity to important international agencies like the Red Cross enables SRI to cover humani-

tarian and Third World issues often absent from conventional news media. But not all SRI fare is international—some programs have a strong local flavor.

North America: 0100-0130 on 6135, 9885 and 9905 kHz; 0400-0430 on 6135 and 9885 kHz; and 0400-0500 on 9905 kHz.

Europe: (everything one hour earlier in summer) 0615-0630 and 0715-0730 on 5840 (winter), 6165 and (summer) 9535 kHz, 1100-1130 and 1300-1400 on 6165 and 9535 kHz; 1800-1830 on 7410 (replaced summers by 9905) kHz, and 2000-2030 on 6165 kHz.

Middle East: 2000-2030 winters on 9905 kHz, and summers on 12075 kHz.

Southern Africa: 0600-0630 on 9885, 11860 and 13635 kHz.

East and Southeast Asia: 1100-1130 winters on 9885, 11995 and 13635 kHz;

Radio drama is alive and well at the BBC World Service. Esmeralda Bhil and Athol Fugard are actors in Fugard's own play, "Valley Song."

North America: Winter mornings, easterners can listen at 1100-1200 on 5965 kHz; 1200-1300 on 5965 and 15220 kHz; 1300-1400 on 5965, 9515, 9590 and 15220 kHz; 1400-1615 on 9515, 9590 (till 1600) and 17840 kHz; and 1615-1700 on 17840 kHz (also available Saturdays on 9515 kHz). The summer schedule is 1000-1200 on 5965 kHz; 1200-1400 on 9515 and 15220 kHz; 1400-1630 on 9515 (to 1700 Saturday), 15220 (till 1600) and 17840 kHz; and 1630 to 1800 on 17840 kHz. Listeners in or near the Caribbean area can tune in at 1000-1100 on 6195 kHz; 1100-1400 on 6195 and 15220 kHz; and 1400-1700 on 17840 kHz.

For winter reception in western North America, try 1200-1300 on 9740 and 15220 kHz; 1300-1400 on 9515, 9590, 9740 and 15220 kHz; 1400-1600 on 9515, 9590, 9740, 15220 and 17840 kHz; and 1600-1900 on 17840 kHz. In summer, it's 1200-1300 on 9740 and 15220 kHz; 1300-1400 on 9515, 9740, 11865 and 15220 kHz; 1400-1600 on 9515, 9740, 11865, 15220 and 17840 kHz; and 1600-1800 on 17840 kHz. Note that 9740 kHz carries programs for Asia and the Pacific, which are often different from those targeted at North America.

Early evenings in eastern North America, go for 5975 kHz at 2100-2200. This slot contains the informative "Caribbean Report," aired at 2115-2130 Monday through Friday, and which is also carried on 15390 and 17715 kHz.

Throughout the evening, most North Americans can listen in at 2200-0700 (0800 in winter) on a number of frequencies. Times vary, but workhorse channels are 5975, 6175 and 9590 kHz.

Europe: A powerhouse 0300-2330 (one hour earlier in summer) on 3955, 6180, 6195, 7325, 9410, 12095, 15485, 15575 and 17640 kHz (times vary for each channel).

Middle East: 0300-2000 year-round. Key frequencies (times vary according to whether it is winter or summer) are 9410, 11760, 12095, 15565, 15575 and 17640 kHz.

and summers on 13635, 15415 and 17515 kHz. The broadcast is repeated at 1300-1330 on 7230, 7480, 12075 (15120 in summer) and 13635 kHz.

Australasia: 0900-0930 on 9885, 12075 (17515 in summer) and 13685 kHz.

United Kingdom

The **BBC World Service** is still the world's leading international broadcaster, despite major restructuring and the privatization of some of its services. Gone are several audience favorites, replaced by others of doubtful entertainment value. Too, many programs are now produced independently of the BBC, so the quality is uneven. On the positive side, the programming lineup still contains a number of jewels, and the "Beeb" continues to remain ahead of other organizations when it comes to news and news analysis.

Southern Africa: 0300-2200 on (among others) 3255, 6005, 6190, 9600, 11940, 15400, 21470 and 21660 kHz (times vary for each channel).

East and Southeast Asia: 0000-0300 on 6195 (till 0200), 15280 (except 0030-0100) and 15360 kHz; 0300-0330 on 15360 and 21660 kHz; 0330-0500 on 11955, 15280 and 21660 kHz; 0500-0945 on 6195 (from 0900), 9740, 11955 (till 0900), 15280 (0500-0530 and 0900-0945), 15360 and 21660 kHz; 0945-1100 on 6195, 9740, 15360 (till 1030) and 21660 kHz; 1100-1300 on 6195, 9580, 9740 and 11955 kHz; 1300-1615 on 5990, 6195 and 9740 kHz; and 1615-1745 (to Southeast Asia) on 3915 and 7135 (or 7160) kHz. For morning reception, try 2100-2200 on 3915, 5965, 6120 (11945 in summer) and 6195 kHz; 2200-2300 on 5905 (9890 in summer), 5965, 6195, 7110 and 11955 kHz; and 2300-0030 on 6195, 7110, 9580, 11945 and 11955 kHz. In winter, 9740 kHz (1830-2200) and 11955 kHz (2000-2200) are also available for Southeast Asia.

Australasia: 0500-0600 on 11955 and 15360 kHz; 0600-0815 on 7145, 11955 and 15360 kHz; 0815-0900 on 11955 and 15360 kHz; 0900-1030 on 15360 kHz (replaced April to October by 11765 kHz, 0900-1130); 1100-1130 on 6100 or 9700 kHz; 1130-1615 on 9740 kHz; 1830-2000 on 9740 kHz; 2000-2200 on 9740 and 11955 kHz; and 2200-2400 on 11955 kHz. At 2200-2300, 12080 kHz is also available for some parts of the region. From April to October, 5975 kHz is also in use at 2000-2200.

ASIA
Japan

Radio Japan is now easily heard just about anywhere in the world, either direct from Tokyo or via one or more of its overseas relays. Until relatively recently, technical advances were not accompanied by corresponding improvements in the

Much of China's population is not of majority Han origin. Shown, a midwife of the minority Miao tribe.

station's programming, but this is now changing. Livelier presentation and more upbeat programs have gone some way to redressing past criticism of staid and stuffy programming. All broadcasts have a strong Japanese flavor and usually last an hour.

Eastern North America: 1100 on 6120 kHz, and again at 0300 (0100 summer) on 5960 kHz. Also try 0100 on 11790 and 13630 kHz.

Western North America: 0100 on 11790 and 13630 kHz; 0300 on 11790 (winter) and 13630 kHz; 0500 on 6110 kHz; 0600 (summer) on 9835 and 12030 kHz; 1400 (winter) on 9535 and 11705 kHz; 1500, 1700 and (winter) 1900 on 9535 kHz; and 2100 (summer) on 13630 kHz. There is also a 30-minute broadcast to Hawaii, western North America and Central America at 0500-0530 winters on 9835, 11895 and 12000 kHz; and summers on 11895, 13630 and 15230 kHz.

R. Crane

Guards keep watch at Taiwan's Chang Kai Shek Memorial.

Middle East: 0700 on 15165 (or 15230) kHz, and 1700 on 11880 kHz.

Southern Africa: 1500 on 15355 kHz.

Asia: 0100 on 11840 (winter), 11860, 11890, 13650 (winter), 15475 (winter), 15500 (summer), 15590 (summer) and 17810 kHz; 0300 (winter) on 11840 and 17810 kHz; 0500 (winter) on 11740 and 17810 kHz, and (summer) on 11840 kHz; 0600 on 11740 (summer), 11840 (summer), 11910, 15550 (summer) and 17810 kHz; 0700 on 11740, 11840 (summer), 15590 (winter) and 17810 kHz; 0900 (winter) on 7125 and 11815 kHz; 1100 on 7125 and 11815 kHz; 1200 (summer) on 7125 and 11815 kHz; 1400 on 7200 and (winter) 11880 and 12045 kHz; 1500 on 7200, 7225 (winter), 7240 (summer), 9750 (summer), 11730 (summer) and (for winter) 11880 kHz; 1700 on 6035, 7200, 7225 and 11880 (replaced summer by 11730) kHz; 1900 (winter) on 6035 and 7200 kHz; 2100 (winter) on 6035, 9560 and 9825 kHz; and (summer) on 6035 and (till 2130) 6090 kHz; and 2300 (winter) on 9560 and 9825 kHz. Transmissions to Asia are often heard in other parts of the world, as well.

Australasia: 0100 (summer) on 21610 kHz; 0300 (summer) on 17685 kHz; 0500 on 11920 kHz; 0600 on 11850 (or 11920) kHz; 0700 on 11850 and 11920 kHz; 0900 (winter) on 11850 kHz; 1900 (winter) on 6035 and 7140 kHz; and 2100 and 2300 (both winter only) on 11850 kHz.

Europe: 0500 on 7230 kHz; 0600 on 5975 kHz (summers also on 7230 kHz); 0700 on 7230 kHz; 1700 (summer) on 7110 kHz; and 2300 (winter) on 6180 kHz.

CRI

The China Agricultural University's soccer team takes on a team from Taiwan.

China

China Radio International, a modern reincarnation of the old Radio Peking (later Radio Beijing), bears little resemblance to its predecessor of the Mao era. Business reviews now replace the former tirades against capitalist running dogs, and criticism of Western countries is more subtle and subdued. Political propaganda has been superseded by informative features about China, its people and culture,

R. Crane

Taiwan's Chang Kai Shek monument at night.

and Chinese popular music now shares the stage with the more traditional variety.

Like its neighbor, Radio Japan, CRI is now an easy catch. New transmitters on Chinese soil and relay facilities in four continents ensure ample coverage.

Eastern North America: 0000-0100 on 9710 and 11695 kHz; 0300-0400 on 9690, 9710 and 11695 kHz; 0400-0500 on 9730 kHz; and 0500-0600 (0400-0500 in summer) on 9560 kHz.

Western North America: As for eastern parts except for 9690 at 0300. Also at 1400-1600 (one hour earlier in summer) on 7405 kHz.

Europe: 2000-2200 on 6950 and 9920 kHz; 2200-2230 (2100-2130 in summer) on 3985 kHz; 2100-2200 (summer) on 9880 kHz; and 2200-2300 (winter) on 7170 kHz.

Middle East: There are no specific broadcasts for this area, but try the transmission to Europe at 2000-2200; also

1900-2000 on 6955 (11515 in summer) and 9440 kHz.

Southern Africa: 1600-1700 on 15110 and 15130 kHz; 1700-1800 on 7150, 7405 and 9570 kHz; and 2000-2130 on 11715 and 15110 kHz.

Asia: 1200-1400 on 9715 and 11660 kHz; and 1400-1600 on 7495, 9535 and 9785 kHz.

Australasia: 0900-1100 on 9785 (or 15440) and 11755 kHz; 1200-1300 on 7385 and 11795 kHz; and 1300-1400 on 7385 kHz.

NORTH AMERICA
Canada

Despite surviving the latest in a seemingly endless series of fiscal crises, **Radio Canada International** continues to face an uncertain future. It is woefully underfunded, and relies heavily for program

Bob McDonald, host of the award-winning science program "Quirks and Quarks" over Radio Canada International.

material on the domestic service of its parent organization, the Canadian Broadcasting Corporation—itself on a tight budget. Although mainly of interest to Canadians abroad, much of the output still appeals to a general audience.

North America: Reception is better in eastern North America than farther west, although evening broadcasts reach a wider area. Winters, the first daytime slot is at 1300-1400 (weekdays till 1500) on 9640 and 11855 kHz. There is also a three-hour Sunday broadcast at 1400-1700 on the same frequencies. In summer the same broadcasts go out one hour earlier on 9640 (except for 1300-1600 Sunday), 11855 and 13650 kHz. During winter, evening broadcasts air at 2300-0100 on 5960 and 9755 kHz (6010 and 6040 kHz are also available part of the time); 0200-0300 on 6155, 9535, 9755 and 11725 kHz; and 0300-0400 on 6155 and 9755 kHz. The summer schedule is 2200-2400 on 5960, 9755 and 13670 kHz; 0100-0200 on 9535, 9755, 11715 and 13670 kHz (only 9755 kHz is available 0130-0200 weekday evenings); and 0200-0300 on 6120, 9535, 9755, 11715 and 13670 kHz (6120, 9535

and 11715 kHz not available 0230-0300 Tuesday through Saturday).

The evening transmission for Africa is also audible in parts of North America; winters at 2100-2230 on 11945, 13690, 15150 and 17820 kHz; and summers one hour earlier on 13670, 15150 and 17820 kHz.

Europe: Winters at 1430-1500 on 9555, 11915, 11935 and 15325 kHz; 2100-2200 on 5925, 5995, 7235, 9805 and 13650 kHz; and 2200-2230 on 5995, 7235 and 9805 kHz. Summer broadcasts are one hour earlier: 1330-1400 Monday through Saturday on 17820 kHz, and daily on 11935 and 15325 kHz; and 2000-2130 on 5995, 7235, 11690, 13650, 15325 and (till 2100) 17870 kHz.

Europe, Middle East and Africa: 0600-0630 winter weekdays on 6050, 6150, 9740, 9760 and 11905 kHz. Summers, it goes out one hour earlier on 6050, 7295, 11835 and 15430 kHz.

Middle East: Winters, at 0400-0430 on 6150, 9505 and 9645 kHz; 1430-1500 on 9555, 11935 and 15325 kHz; and 2000-2100 on 5995 kHz. In summer, try 0400-0430 on 9715, 11835 and 11975 kHz; 1330-1400 on 15325 kHz; and 2000-2130 on 5995 kHz.

Southern Africa: 2100-2230 winter (summer in Southern Hemisphere) on 13690, 15150 and (to 2200) 17820 kHz; and 2000-2130 summer on 13670, 15150 and 17820 kHz.

Asia: To East Asia at 1200-1230, winter on 6150 and 11730 kHz, and summer on 9660 and 15195 kHz; 1330-1400 on 6150 (summers on 11795) and 9535 kHz; to South Asia at 1630-1700 on 7150 and 9550 kHz; and to Southeast Asia at 2200-2230 on 11705 kHz.

United States

Something of the Rodney Dangerfield of international broadcasting, the **Voice of America** now faces a threat from an

unexpected quarter—competitors within its own stable. When the Cold War ended, it was assumed that American surrogate broadcasting, such as Radio Free Europe and Radio Liberty, would cease. However, that was before American politicians decided there was a need for a "Radio Free Asia" for Asia and a "Radio-TV Martí" for Cuba—even a "Radio Free Africa" and a "Radio Free Iran" have been proposed to further balkanize official American international broadcasting. The VOA thus has to scratch with others for a declining pool of funds, as well as for transmitter time. The VOA's English for Europe has already disappeared from the world bands, and the evening service for the Americas is now switched off on weekends.

If this weren't enough, the VOA's relatively autonomous parent organization, the USIA, is scheduled to be incorporated into the State Department—the result of pressure from Senator Jesse Helms. Whether the VOA's hard-won journalistic credibility will survive unscathed remains to be seen.

Yet, the "Voice" still has a variety of interesting programs in its repertory. Aside from mainstream programming, there are popular regional variations which are heard well outside their intended target areas, including within the United States.

North America: The two best times to listen are at 0000-0200 Tuesday through Saturday (local weekday evenings in the Americas) on 5995, 6130, 7405, 9455, 9775 and 13740 kHz (with 11695 kHz also available at 0000-0100); and 1000-1100 daily on 6165, 7405 and 9590 kHz. This is when the VOA broadcasts to South America and the Caribbean. The African

VOA's popular Kim Andrew Elliott, presenter of "Communications' World," enjoys a dip with his wife Jinling and son Ian.

André Piston

Paris, toujours Paris! Among international broadcasters, Radio France Internationale is one of the largest, carrying francophone culture to the corners of the earth.

Service can also be heard in much of North America—try part of the morning broadcast on 6035 (0500-0700); 1600-1800 on 13710, 15445 and 17895 kHz; and 1800-2200 (Saturday to 2130) on 15410, 15580 and (from 2000) 17725 kHz.

Europe lost its VOA channels to the financial axe in September 1995, and was left to rely on broadcasts beamed to other areas. Try 0400-0700 on 7170 kHz, 1500-1800 on 15205 kHz, and 1700-2200 on 9760 kHz.

Middle East: 0400-0500 summer on 15205 kHz; 0500-0700 on 11825 (winter) and 15205 kHz (11965 kHz is also available summers at 0400-0600); 1400-1500 (winter) on 15205 kHz; 1500-1800 on 9700 and 15205 kHz; 1700-1900 (winter) on 6040 kHz; and 1800-2200 on 9760 kHz.

Southern Africa: 0300-0500 on 6080, 7280 (summer), 7340 (to 0430), and 9575

kHz; 0400-0600 (winter) on 9775 kHz; 0500-0700 on 6035 kHz; 1600-2200 (to 2130 Saturday) on 7415, 11920 (winter), 12040 (winter), 13710, 15410, 15445, 15580 and 17895 kHz (not all available for the full broadcast).

Australasia: 1000-1200 on 5985, 9645 (from 1100), 11720 and 15425 kHz; 1200-1330 on 11715 and 15425 kHz, 1330-1500 on 9645 (till 1400) and 15425 kHz; 1900-2000 on 9525, 11870 and 15180 kHz; 2100-2200 on 11870, 15185 and 17735 kHz; 2200-2400 on 15185, 15305 and 17735 kHz; and 0000-0100 on 15185 and 17735 kHz.

East and Southeast Asia: 1100-1200 on 9760, 11720 and 15160 kHz; 1200-1330 on 9760, 11715 and 15160 kHz; 1330-1500 on 9760 and 15160 kHz; 2200-2400 on 15290, 15305, 17735 and 17820 kHz; and 0000-0100 on 15290, 17735 and 17820 kHz.

Real Radios Glow in the Dark

by Fred Osterman

Shortwave listening was different back then.

Thirty-five years ago, today's baby boomers were only teenagers. Radio electronics was a popular outlet for technically inclined youngsters, and in those simpler days they often became interested simply for the magic and excitement.

Freebies from radio stations also attracted young listeners. A listener in the early sixties might receive Bulgarian recipe books, cultural magazines, folk-music recordings, pennants—even Iraqi cigarettes!

But there was also a serious side. In the 1960's, shortwave radio was the best way to obtain breaking news directly from overseas. In those days prior to satellite TV feeds, shortwave radio afforded the most diverse and immediate source for information on the state of the world. Shortwave—today better known as world band radio—still fulfills this function, but it now shares the scene with other media, such as the World Wide Web and CNN.

Running Dogs and Moscow Mufflers

Shortwave listening had a sharper edge back then, a greater sense of urgency. Today, a news broadcast from the Voice of Russia may not sound much different from a bulletin on the Voice of America.

> World band radio did more than anything else to end communism behind the Iron Curtain.

Not so during the Cold War. The struggle between East and West was on, and it was hardball. *Democracy vs. communism* was slugged out on the airwaves, where it was pure excitement.

Shortwave radio was the principal vehicle of persuasion employed by the superpowers and their client states. Radio Moscow, Radio Peking, Radio Prague and bizarre little Radio Tirana were running full transmitter schedules.

In the other corner, the BBC, the Voice of America, Radio Free

---

Marie Mudd's granddaughter relives the past by enjoying her grandparents' 1942 Philco 42-380 console, recently restored to perfection inside and out. Howard Karashoff

Shortwave radio was the principal method to spread the competing doctrines of communism and democracy. Even small communist countries such as Bulgaria, Cuba and Albania had big voices on world band.

Europe and Radio Liberty were on the air, but faced a barrage of intentional jamming. Despite this, throughout the Cold War shortwave radio was always the best way to pierce the Iron Curtain. Indeed, after the Cold War ended it was widely acknowledged that world band radio had done more than anything else to end communism in Russia and Eastern Europe.

Jamming was not the only unpleasant manifestation of the Cold War to be heard on shortwave. The Soviets experimented with a type of over-the-horizon radar that emitted a wideband tapping signal reminiscent of a woodpecker at work. This intrusion became so pervasive that one electronics manufacturer produced an audio filter called the *Moscow Muffler* specifically to combat this blight of the airwaves.

Sometimes Cold War programming wasn't much better than the interference.

If you were listening to Albania thirty years ago, you might hear an announcer, sounding like Dracula's wife, exulting how the "great genius, Stalin, showed his political enemies no mercy"—Marxist terminology for having them shot.

Tempus fugit. Albania, once a bastion of godless communism, now leases a former propaganda transmitter to Trans World Radio, a Christian broadcaster. Thirty years ago, a TWR relay on Mars would have seemed more likely.

> Sounding like Dracula's wife, the announcer praised "the great genius, Stalin" for having his political enemies shot.

During the so-called Great Proletarian Cultural Revolution, Radio Peking would let loose with such soporific Maoist diatribes as, "People of the world unite, and defeat the U.S. aggressors and all their running dogs!"—repeated over and again for a full hour to ensure you got the point. Now, Radio Peking has been reinvented as the thoroughly bourgeois China Radio International, which airs such fire-breathing fare as "Business Review."

Today, the only broadcaster with that "good old Stalinist flavor" is Radio Pyongyang in famine-plagued North Korea. Their daily diatribes will keep you depressingly up to speed on the latest Marxist dogma in this worker's paradise. Catch it while you can—it is the dying voice of a bygone era.

Mrs. Mao's Music for Blacklisted Kids

Listeners in the sixties who requested a verification card—QSL—from a communist bloc country sometimes got more than they bargained for. Propaganda budgets were almost unlimited for potential converts anywhere, and few profited more than the world's postal services.

A few days after your Radio Peking QSL arrived, a *Peking Review* magazine would appear, followed by colorful calendars, pennants, more magazines, pamphlets, Mao posters, Mao buttons and, of course, Mao's famous Little Red Book. If you were so inclined you could request and receive free leather-bound volumes of Mao's complete "thoughts," as well as LP recordings of revolutionary operas composed by—who else?—Mrs. Mao. These monthly mailings often continued for years.

For a time in the United States, mail like this arrived marked, "Opened and inspected by the U.S. Post Office." In the mid-sixties, some listeners even received official postcards stating ominously that certain mail for them had been confiscated by the authorities because it had been deemed to be "communist propaganda." If you wanted it, you had to sign

Communist broadcasters were quick to verify reception reports with "QSL" postcards. An unsolicited barrage of propaganda usually followed, as well.

CBS

Jackie Gleason had a lifelong love affair with world band radio. Although he had two modern Sony ICF-2010 portables—he always had two of each model, in case one acted up—his favorite radios were tube-type heavyweights. *"Real* sets," he called them.

congenial program included barrel-organ music, quizzes, short features on daily life in Holland and calls to listeners. Startz also featured a make-believe teatime, complete with whinnying horses and quacking ducks—sadly, fare too innocent for today's broadcasting environment.

The Rule of Big Iron

World politics have changed beyond anyone's expectations, and shortwave equipment has changed just as dramatically. Shortwave and amateur radios in the fifties and sixties were dominated by such venerable American manufacturers as Hammarlund, Hallicrafters and National. Their prevailing philosophy was simple—the bigger and heavier, the better.

Big Iron radios coming out of Chicago were not unlike Big Iron cars coming out of Detroit. In the 1988 PASSPORT TO WORLD BAND RADIO, world band enthusiast Jackie Gleason called these "real sets"—gear which, like The Great One himself, had the necessary girth and poundage to command respect.

> Big Iron radios coming out of Chicago were like Big Iron cars coming out of Detroit—the bigger and heavier, the better. Tipping the scales at 70 pounds or 32 kg, the Hallicrafters SX-101 receiver was a chiropractor's dream.

and return the card. Fearing blacklisting, few did.

Nevertheless, government files were started on a number of world band listeners of the era. Federal gumshoes must have been sorely disappointed to find that among their potential Red sympathizers was an apolitical 11-year-old who received similar material from South Africa's Radio RSA, Vatican Radio and the BBC World Service.

Dutch Horses at Teatime

The Cold War generated an avalanche of shortwave propaganda, but there was delightful programming, too. If Radio Tirana was the coldest place on the dial, Radio Nederland was one of the warmest. Among other things, it was home to the long-running "Happy Station," where host Eddie Startz made friends worldwide. His

Until the late sixties, when smaller radios produced by the R.L. Drake Company drove Big Iron rigs into extinction, the emphasis continued to be on size and weight. While car makers were focusing on broader wheelbases and bigger fins, radio manufacturers equally duked it out on weight and acreage. In 1959, a Hallicrafters ad even boasted how they had produced, like an electronic Joe Louis, *"The new heavyweight champion— employs heaviest chassis in the industry."* Tipping the scales at 70 pounds, or 32 kg,

Five hundred dollars was a vast sum in the mid 1960's, but that is what it took to own the venerable Hammarlund HQ-180AC.

this SX-101 receiver was a chiropractor's dream.

These metal monsters are now fondly and accurately referred to as boat anchors. Perhaps the most coveted was the huge Hammarlund HQ-180/A. At 19 by 10.5 by 13 inches, or 482 by 266 by 330 mm, this behemoth was the dream receiver of the sixties. One had to mow many a lawn to pay the onerous tariff of $500 for this classic.

Hit-and-Miss Tuning a Challenge

Not only were radios bigger and harder to lift, they were more difficult to use. Poor dial accuracy was the principal challenge to operating a general coverage shortwave receiver in the fifties and sixties—affordable digital displays were years away.

The analog "needle" dials of many sets featured less than one inch per Megacycle, or Mc/s. (The politically correct, yet less-descriptive term Megahertz had not yet found favor.) Until you "got to know" your receiver, it was impossible to determine whether you were tuning 11.8 or 11.9 Mc/s.

Better radios had calibrated "bandspreads," which were electronically stretched-out dials. However, except for

the dual dials on the National NC-140 and NC-190, these bandspreads were rarely calibrated for world band frequencies. All that was offered was a simple 0-100 scale.

The industrious listener would carefully construct charts or graphs to interpolate world band frequencies based on known stations. Without such effort, getting back to the same frequency the following night was almost impossible. It was not uncommon to spend more time *finding* the signal on a radio dial than actually listening to it.

> It used to be common to spend more time *finding* the signal on a radio dial than actually listening to it.

Eventually, if you were skilled and a little lucky, you could accurately return to a 5 kHz channel. Compare that with today, when most tabletop models are precise to a tenth or even a hundredth of a kilohertz!

Vintage world band radios are growing in popularity. Last July, Mitch Cohen, host of "Nickel Serenade" over New Jersey's WWJZ-AM, gave away a Zenith Trans-Oceanic portable as first prize in a listeners' contest.

L. Magne/Davis Publications

Radio magazines in the 1960s and 1970s featured photographs of shortwave enthusiasts at their listening posts. Shown, PASSPORT's Larry Magne, featured as a young man in the Spring-Summer 1972 *Communications World.*

Finding a signal was only the first challenge—staying on the frequency was also a chore. Until the advent of solid state circuits, shortwave radios used drifty vacuum tubes. Experienced listeners would switch on their radios half an hour before they were actually going to listen, just so the circuit could settle down. Some perfectionists never even turned their radios off.

> Tube sets were abandoned in droves. Technology marched on, and those companies which hesitated to change, failed.

Tubes are the ultimate non-binary devices, and are prone to aging. Typically, they don't die abruptly but, like old soldiers, progressively fade away. Getting around the resulting drop in weak-signal sensitivity requires periodic circuit realignment and tube replacement.

Selectivity was, and is, an important attribute of any radio. Some receivers of the fifties and sixties used an inboard Q-multiplier circuit, and Heath even offered a popular outboard Q-multiplier kit. These allowed for variable selectivity and tunable notch filtering—two huge virtues—but their skirt selectivity was abysmal and operation was tricky. Improved crystal, mechanical and ceramic bandwidth filters, as well as built-in IF and AF notch filters, rendered the Q-multiplier obsolete.

Few Schedule References

Many information sources we enjoy today were not available three decades ago. For the world band listener the only annual reference was the *World Radio TV Handbook*, whose 300 or so pages were shared among shortwave, mediumwave AM, longwave, FM and TV worldwide.

So I Opened the Valve and It All Went Down the Tubes

by John Wilson

Winston Churchill said that the U.S. and Britain are two nations separated by a common language. This was never better illustrated than by the words "valve" and "tube" to describe the same thermionic device on which the whole science and art of radio was built.

My engineering background and the fact that I am British lead me to understand that a valve is a device for regulating the flow of something, such as water, oil, air—or even electrons—so a device for regulating electron flow is surely a valve?

On the other hand, a device for regulating water flow may be a faucet, which over here we call a tap, but surely a tap is a knock on the windowpane,

857B tubes from a 1944 RCA shortwave transmitter look more like vacuum flasks or Christmas tree ornaments than "tubes" or "valves."

and Taps may be the tune played by the bugler at West Point, except that over here we call that the Last Post, which in New York may be the final edition of today's newspaper.

As for a tube; well, a tube is a pipe down which something flows in an unregulated fashion, which is just as well for the Australians to whom a tube means a can of beer, and it certainly flows unregulated down there. Ask an Australian what he thinks of a hot tube, and he will visualise a beer that hasn't been in the icebox rather than a glowing 6L6 or 807, neither of which are tubular in any case, and how could you call a 417A valve a tube when the Americans themselves call it a "doorknob"? (And dare I mention the 9001 valve, christened the "acorn"?)

So maybe my next receiver will start off with a doorknob feeding push-pull acorns, with later stages using tubes which are non-tubular, but don't think that the Americans have all the strange names because we Brits developed a series of valves in the 1930s which were sold as "Catkins". Sounds more like a canned pet food than a valve/tube.

And the Lord said unto Moses, "Tell thy people that real radios glow in the dark."

John Wilson, formerly of Lowe Electronics, now delves into analog electronics at the radio research and measurement laboratory, Exeter University. He is also a regular contributor to Short Wave Magazine. *His pastimes include bicycling in the Devon countryside and diminishing his cellar's enviable inventory of vintage wines.*

R.L. Drake Company

In 1969, the innovative R.L. Drake Company produced a revolutionary new tabletop model for the shortwave listener. The SPR-4 broadcast receiver was solid state (no tubes), stable, selective, and provided an astounding dial accuracy of better than ±1 kHz.

Yaesu

Yaesu earned high-marks for its general coverage FRG-7 "Volksreceiver." This reliable model is still a great find on the used market at under $300.

There was virtually nothing for the program-oriented listener, much less the utility or non-broadcast enthusiast, although there were excellent weekly printed DX bulletins—free to participants—from Radio Sweden's "Sweden Calling DXers."

This soon changed. The first edition of the *Confidential Frequency List* hit the shelves in 1968. Priced at $1.95, this 35-page guide to utility stations was considered to be "it"! By contrast, the current *Confidential Frequency List* runs 450 pages and shares the market scene with the *Guide to Utility Stations* at 586 pages.

Popular Electronics, Communications World and other radio magazines of the day did include shortwave frequency schedules. They also regularly featured photos of noted radio aficionados. For example, the 1972 Spring-Summer issue of *Communications World* featured Richard Wood, Ed Shaw and Larry Magne (shown)—names still recognized by some of today's shortwave cognoscenti.

Receivers Begin Changing in Late Sixties

Shortwave listening and DXing 35 years ago had the frustration of incredibly poor dial accuracy, marginal selectivity, lack of stability and spotty reference material. Yet, the evolution of electronics would soon liberate listeners from these unwelcome challenges.

Radio Shack

The Realistic DX-300 and DX-302 were among the earliest models to boast digital frequency display, but both were mediocre performers.

JRC

In 1979, the Japan Radio Company introduced the professional-quality NRD-515 communications receiver to the consumer market. To this day, this tank-tough receiver, shown here with speaker and 96-channel memory option, is used by Passport in jungle conditions to gather data on stations.

In 1966, the R.L. Drake Company, in cooperation with Radio New York Worldwide, introduced the tube-powered SW-4A tabletop world band receiver. It was stable, an excellent performer, and its linear analog dial was accurate to the nearest two kilohertz. At the same time, the SW-4A ushered in a new era where tabletop receivers would be bereft of the sort of full, mellow audio that had until then been the norm.

Three years later Drake introduced a solid-state communications receiver, the SPR-4. It had a linear analog dial that was accurate to plus or minus 1 kHz—closer than 0.5 kHz if you were careful and had good eyes. Like the SW-4A, it used a number of plug-in crystals, each of which covered a 500 kHz range, so the entire shortwave spectrum wasn't covered.

Thereafter, responding to Drake's success and advances in solid-state circuitry, radios became smaller, more accurate, easier to use and more affordable. Pioneering these, from South Africa of all places, was the DX-quality Barlow-Wadley XCR-30, introduced in 1972. This was a large, tough analog portable with linear tuning accurate to five kilohertz, using a Wadley-loop frequency circuit to cover the entire shortwave spectrum.

In 1976, Yaesu inaugurated the linear-tuned analog FRG-7, a refined tabletop version of the XCR-30. Affectionately referred to as the "Frog Seven," this tireless volksreceiver combined performance, affordability and excellent dial accuracy. Many are still in regular use today.

But a few years later these analog wonders would fade away as the digital revolution came to world band radio, and there would be no turning back. By 1977, digital tabletop and portable receivers were available outside military-intelligence circles from only three firms: Japan's Panasonic, (West) Germany's Schaub-Lorenz and America's McKay Dymek. But two years later, the roster had expanded

This vintage Sony CRF-320 "portable," heavier than most tabletop models, is still in regular use at China Radio International's new offices in Beijing.

to include Drake, Kenwood, Japan Radio Company, Radio Shack, Sony and Hitachi. Among these, the outstanding Drake R-7, Japan Radio NRD-505 and Sony ICF-6800W are even today prized as benchmark models.

With these sorts of advanced receivers, shortwave listening and DXing became much easier. Selectivity improved, instability vanished and radios became reliable and virtually maintenance-free.

Tube sets were abandoned in droves for modern solid-state, digital receivers. Technology marched on, and those companies which hesitated to change, failed. Most Hallicrafters, Hammarlund and National radios were slowly and cheaply sold off at hamfests and yard sales. Values plummeted.

Today's Radios, Yesterday's Dream . . .

In 1972, the editors of *Communications World* magazine designed a theoretical "ultimate receiver" (see illustration), which featured digital readout and broad coverage of the radio spectrum. Keypads and presets, or memories, had not even

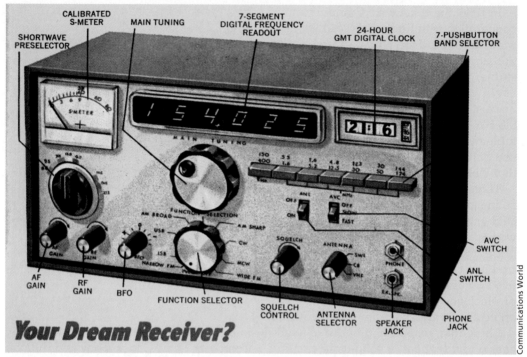

Labels on the receiver image:

SHORTWAVE PRESELECTOR · CALIBRATED S-METER · MAIN TUNING · 7-SEGMENT DIGITAL FREQUENCY READOUT · 24-HOUR GMT DIGITAL CLOCK · 7-PUSHBUTTON BAND SELECTOR · AVC SWITCH · ANL SWITCH · PHONE JACK · SPEAKER JACK · ANTENNA SELECTOR · SQUELCH CONTROL · FUNCTION SELECTOR · BFO · RF GAIN · AF GAIN

Your Dream Receiver?

Communications World

Most of the features of this 1972 imaginary "dream receiver" have found their way into today's models. But some features common today—programmable channel memories, keypad entry, computer interfaces and alphanumeric displays—were beyond even the dream stage back then.

been dreamed of then, and the idea of connecting a shortwave receiver to a computer would have been considered absurd—computers took up entire rooms back then.

. . . Yesterday's Radios, Today's Dream

In the mid-nineties, prices for classic used receivers finally started going back up. Demand and interest in vintage shortwave radios was fueled by two factors. To begin with, many current radio enthusiasts were purchasing their first receiver *again!* They say there is no love like your first love, and in radio . . . you can go back again.

Additionally, the time has finally arrived when that unreachable dream receiver of one's youth can be purchased for a few days' pay. The venerable

HQ-180 and SX-122 now seem eminently affordable.

> To many veteran listeners, tube radios seem more *real* than their contemporaries. Today's receivers won't take the chill off the room, provide a warm surface for the cat to nap on, or provide the robust audio of yesterday's sets.

But the allure of older receivers may have more to do with ambiance than affordability. There is a very different feeling and challenge to operating tube sets. To many veteran listeners, tube radios seem more *real* than their contemporaries. Today's receivers won't take the chill off the room, provide a warm surface for the cat to nap on, or provide the robust audio of yesterday's sets.

Simply put, the rich fidelity of the better

tube receivers cannot be duplicated by modern radios at any price. With these, the interval signal of the BBC's Big Ben and the kookaburra bird call over Radio Australia had a realistic, three-dimensional sound.

Today, there is less music on shortwave than thirty or forty years ago; perhaps this is because music used to sound better on those veteran receivers. Sadly, music on today's technically advanced radios doesn't begin to compare to that which emanated from an ordinary Philco console in the parlor (see photo at beginning of chapter).

Power-Sucking Fire Bottles *vs.* Silicon Valley

Years back, adolescents routinely tore into the innards of their Ford flathead V-8 engines. Now, it takes a factory service station with networked computers and Silicon Valley parts to repair even the simplest of modern automobiles.

> Today's surface-mounted components require hands steady enough to circumcise a gnat.

So it is with shortwave radios. Servicing and modifying tube radios is utterly unlike working with modern sets. Today's surface-mounted components require microscopic vision and hands steady enough to circumcise a gnat. Because of this, some listeners have hung onto their tube sets; but for most, the call back to these power-sucking fire bottles is a relatively recent phenomenon.

For a number of enthusiasts the allure is history, for others nostalgia. Freudians may even claim that these restorations are an attempt to defer mortality. Whatever,

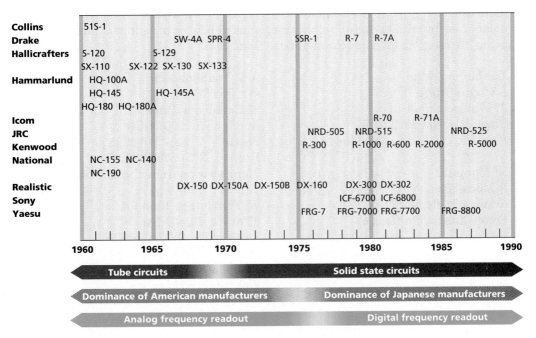

The 1970s was a decade of dramatic change in shortwave radio equipment. Tube circuits gave way to solid state design, digital displays were introduced, and the center of receiver production shifted from America to Japan.

Finding Your Vintage Receiver

For many the thrill of the chase is half the pleasure. As with antique hunting, large doses of imagination, luck and persistence are required.

To get started on the right track, here are the places to go and the people to know.

- Amateur radio hamfests, called "rallies" in the U.K.
- Estate sales
- Pawn shops
- Auctions, especially at military bases
- Military bases
- Monthly radio periodicals
- Goodwill shops
- Yard sales
- Amateur ("ham") radio dealers
- Surplus dealers, such as Fair Radio
- Newspaper classified ads
- Chat groups and Websites on the Internet

Owner's and Service Manuals

There are a number of specialty firms that can sell you manuals for older communications receivers. In most cases they offer quality photocopies of original manuals, but originals are sometimes available . . . for a price. Contact these companies by mail or online with your specific needs, or order their catalog—some are free, others a couple of dollars or so.

The Manual Man
P.A. Markavage
27 Walling Street
Sayreville, NJ 08872 USA
Phone/fax: +1 (732) 238-8964

HI-Manuals
P.O. Box 802
Council Bluffs, IA 51502 USA
Email: himan@radiks.net

A.G. Tannenbaum
P.O. Box 386
22 Schiavone Drive
Ambler, PA 19002 USA
Phone: +1 (215) 540-8055
Fax: +1 (215) 540 8327
Web: www.agtannenbaum.com

W7FG Vintage Manuals
3300 Wayside Drive
Bartlesville, OK 74006 USA
Phone: +1 (918) 333-3754
Email: w7fg@w7fg.com
Web: www.w7fg.com

Do You Need Professional Help?

The following craftsmen offer restoration and service of vintage radios, but it is important to contact them by mail or phone *before* sending your radio.

When shipping something as beefy and delicate as a vintage receiver, remember to use a tough, extra-large container. Surround the radio generously on all sides with plastic "peanuts" or other packing material, then double-box and wrap the entire business liberally with shipping tape. Don't forget to insure it, but remember that all you'll get back on a claim is what you paid for the receiver—not the sweat equity you put into it. So pack it as though your life depends on every tube and dial arriving unscathed.

Barbara Eslinger

Since 1990 former executive Bob Eslinger has been restoring and repairing vintage tube-type radio receivers, including for world band aficionado Dave Letterman. In 1997 Eslinger, whose reputation has led to a one-year backlog of work, expanded into new facilities. His firm, Antique Radio Restoration & Repair, now includes a staff of expert technicians and an inventory of over 50,000 tubes.

Bob Eslinger
Antique Radio Restoration & Repair
20 Gary School Road
Pomfret Center, CT 06259 USA
Phone: +1 (860) 928-2628
Email: radiodoc@neca.com
Web: www.neca.com/~radiodoc
Specialty: Tube-type radios only.

Tom Miller Electronics
22516 S. Normandie SP41B
Torrance, CA 90502 USA
Phone: +1 (310) 320-8980

RTO Electronics
5585 Hochberger
Eau Claire, MI 49111 USA
Phone: +1 (616) 461-3057
Specialty: Heathkits

Great Northern
Alan Jesperson
P.O. Box 17338
Minneapolis, MN 55417 USA
Phone: +1 (612) 727-2489
Email: mte612@aol.com

Tubes, Variable Capacitors and Buggy Whips

Thirty years ago you could walk into any radio store and simply ask for a "35Z5/GT." The salesman (*not* salesperson) would reach around without taking a step, then hand you the tube. Don't try this nowadays at your local TV-VCR shop—you'll just get a blank stare.

The leading source for such vintage "musts," as well as the AM Wireless Transmitter Kit #K-488, is this friendly firm:

Antique Electronic Supply
6221 S. Maple Avenue
Tempe, AZ 85283 USA
Phone: +1 (602) 820-5411
Fax: (800) 706 6789 or (602) 820 4643

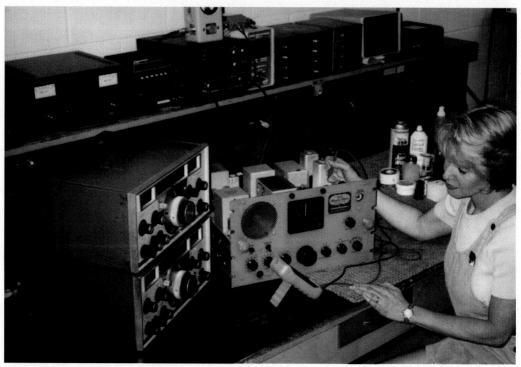

Expert firms specialize in the repair and restoration of vintage communications receivers. Here, Barbara Rogers brings alignment into original factory specs.

these vintage leviathans from the Great Tube Era are once again being collected, cared for, restored . . . and enjoyed.

Unearthing Big Beauties

Finding vintage hardware can be a challenge (see sidebar). Most local amateur radio clubs hold a "hamfest" once a year; these outdoor sale, swap and trading sessions can be a rich source for vintage receivers.

Expect to find radios in every state of preservation from pristine to pathetic. Don't overlook those carcasses, though—many avid collectors seek a well-preserved primary specimen, and afterward buy a second, nonworking, "junker" as a parts source.

Hamfests occurring around the Washington, DC beltway, such as the Gaithersburg Hamfest, can be a rich source for exotic "spook" radios from military and intelligence sources. These spy rigs could tell many a story if they could talk as well as they listen. Brands seldom seen in other areas of the country, such as Racal and Watkins-Johnson, can be found at Gaithersburg. When federal agencies upgrade models, or nearby contractors close out inventory, these orphaned receivers often find their way there. As the military adopts satellite circuits, even more commercial-grade shortwave receivers are likely to make their way to the surplus market.

Many vintage radios are sold without either an owner's manual or a service manual. An owner's manual not only helps you understand and operate a radio, but is helpful if service is required. It typically includes instructions on the operation of the receiver and, usually, a basic schematic. A service or technical manual always includes a schematic, plus additional diagnostic and technical information, instructions for alignment and restringing dials, a parts list, circuit photographs and so on. Fortunately, there are companies that specialize in providing out-of-print owner's and service manuals (see sidebar).

Shocking News

After you have found your "new" old radio, the temptation is to take it home, plug it in and start turning knobs with both hands. Bad idea.

Today's solid-state receivers are incredibly safe—getting a shock is unlikely unless you remove the cover and start poking about. But it is much easier to get

a serious jolt from a tube-type receiver with high-voltage circuitry, especially when it is old. An aged capacitor can short to ground, sending lethal voltages to the chassis. Or a transformer winding may fail. So remember, your vintage radio has the potential (pun intended) to give you the biggest shock of your life . . . or even the *last* shock of your life!

If you do not have the equipment and experience to diagnose vintage circuits, then seek out an expert specialist. Fortunately, there are companies (see sidebar) that specialize in servicing and restoring older receivers. It is important to realize and appreciate that these special skills do command a price. But a professional restoration will preserve history and create an heirloom which can be appreciated for generations to come.

Universal Radio

Many people, and *all* felines, prefer tube radios over solid-state receivers.

Restoration Guidelines

Restoring a vintage radio, just like renovating a vintage car or old house, raises philosophical questions. How far should the restoration go? Should only original parts be used? Is an equivalent contemporary part acceptable? How closely should the original appearance and color be preserved?

Some are self-answering. For example, power-supply "can" capacitors vary in size, shape and performance specifications. Today, new ones that look and perform identically are virtually unavailable, yet rarely do the original "caps" work properly. So restorers tend to leave the old can capacitors in place as "dummies," bypassing them with small, modern replacements secreted within the bowels of the chassis.

Old Programs for Old Radios

Fortunately, the BBC World Service, Voice of Russia and other world band stations still offer radio drama and comedy, just as domestic networks did "back in the glory days." These shows are new or recent productions, not recordings from yesteryear. Yet, there is a way to bring the past back to life.

Virtually all vintage shortwave receivers also cover the mediumwave AM band. Among beady-eyed nostalgia buffs there is nothing quite like tuning in the Lone Ranger, the Whisperer, Fibber McGee and Molly, or a "live" Benny Goodman concert on their veteran radios. Problem is, few locations have this sort of fare available on AM; yet, it is sometimes to be found on FM, CDs or even Web radio over the Internet (see the book, PASSPORT TO WEB RADIO).

Solution? The K-488 AM-band Wireless Transmitter Kit, $22.95 plus shipping in kit form from Antique Electronic Supply, or $139 assembled from Antique Radio Restoration & Repair. Connect this microtransmitter to the audio output of your PC, FM receiver or CD player, and—presto!—a feeble signal goes out to any nearby AM radio. Pure to the core, this tube-type flea-powered device is patterned after the phonograph-to-radio link used for a 1939 Zenith "wireless record player."

Shortwave listening was different a generation ago, but in some ways it remains unchanged: listening to exotic lands, hearing news from fresh perspectives. Also unchanged is the excitement of un-boxing a new radio, not reading the instructions and attaching an antenna.

Some collectors possess a missionary zeal for collecting and resuscitating radios on the verge of extinction. Rescuing an unappreciated, sick radio from the obscurity of a yard sale and restoring it to its original health, look and vitality can be exceptionally satisfying. History is preserved, and the golden age of radio—at least in one real sense—is brought back to life for all to hear.

Fred Osterman is president of Universal Radio Inc. and editor of Shortwave Receivers Past and Present.

further Reading

Shortwave Receivers Past & Present—Second Edition
by Fred Osterman; Universal Radio Research, 6830 Americana Parkway, Reynoldsburg, OH 43068 USA; phone (800) 431-3939 or +1 (614) 866-4267; fax +1 (614) 866 2339; email dx@universal-radio.com; Web www.universal-radio.com.

This 351-page publication features over 500 tabletop communications receivers produced by 70 American and international manufacturers from 1945 to 1996. Entry information includes type, dates sold, photograph, features, factory specifications and market valuation.

Radios By Hallicrafters
by C. Dachis; Schiffer Publishing, 77 Lower Valley Road, Atglen, PA 19310 USA; phone +1 (610) 593-1777; fax +1 (610) 593 2002.

A marvelous book with over 1,000 photos of radio receivers, transmitters, speakers, early TV sets and accessories carrying the famous Hallicrafters label.

Communications Receivers—The Vacuum Tube Era
by R.S. Moore, R.S.M., P.O. Box 27, LaBelle, FL 33975 USA; phone +1 (305) 853-0184.

The golden age of vacuum tube receivers is revisited in this comprehensive book covering the period 1932 to 1981.

Heathkit—A Guide to the Amateur Radio Products
by Chuck Penson WA7ZZE; Electric Radio Press, Inc., 14643 County Road G, Cortez, CO 81321 USA; phone/fax +1 (970) 564-9185.

The definitive guide to all amateur, shortwave and related accessories offered by the Heath Company.

The Pocket Guide to Collins Amateur Radio Equipment 1946-1980
by Jay H. Miller, KK5IM; Trinity Graphics Systems, 5402½ Morningside Avenue, Dallas, TX 75206 USA; phone +1 (214) 826-0448.

A compact, well-organized guide to the venerable Collins line of amateur radio equipment.

Zenith Trans-Oceanic, the Royalty of Radios
by John Bryant, AIA and Harold Cones, Ph.D.; Schiffer Publishing, 77 Lower Valley Road, Atglen PA 19310 USA; phone +1 (610) 593-1777; fax +1 (610) 593 2002.

Here is the engrossing forty year history of the world's most romantic, celebrated and expensive series of portable shortwave radios.

Monthly magazines for the radio collector:

Antique Radio Classified
P.O. Box 2
1 River Road
Carlisle, MA 01741 USA
Phone: +1 (508) 371-0512

Electric Radio
14643 County Road G
Cortez, CO 81321 USA

Radio Bygones
9 Wetherby Close
Broadstone
Dorset BH18 8JB, England

1998 PASSPORT REPORTS

How to Choose a World Band Radio

Some electronic goodies, like VCRs, have evolved into commodity products. With a little common sense you can pretty much get what you want without fuss or bother.

Not so world band receivers, which vary greatly from model to model. As usual, money talks—but even that's a fickle barometer. Some models use old technology, or misapply new technology, so they're unhandy or function poorly. But others can perform nicely, indeed.

Crammed with Stations

World band radio is a jungle: *1,100 channels*, with stations scrunched cheek-by-jowl. This crowding is much greater than on FM or mediumwave AM. To make matters worse, the international voyage often causes signals to be weak and quivery. To cope, a radio has to perform some exceptional electronic gymnastics. Some succeed, others don't.

This is why PASSPORT REPORTS was created. Since 1977 we've tested hundreds of world band

products—the good, the bad and the ugly. These evaluations include rigorous hands-on use by veteran listeners and newcomers alike, plus specialized lab tests we've developed over the years.

> World band radios need to perform exceptional electronic gymnastics. Some succeed, others don't.

These form the basis of this PASSPORT REPORTS, and for premium models are detailed to the nth degree in our acclaimed series of Radio Database International White Papers®.

Five Things to Check for

Before you pore over which radio does what, here's a basic checklist to get oriented.

What to spend? Don't be fooled by the word "radio"—able world band radios are sophisticated devices. Yet, for all they do, they cost only about as much as a VCR.

If you're just starting out,

New for 1998 are (left, counterclockwise) the Drake SW2, JRC NRD-345, Grundig Traveller III, Sharper Image VA100 and Sangean ATS 303. Right, Sony ICF-2010; top, a restored 1937 Truetone.   Howard Karashoff

Konrad Kroszner

For the most part, new radios are the best performers. Yet, some vintage models can also provide excellent results. Shown, the Drake R-7 and, to its right, the Drake R-4B with an outboard digital frequency display.

figure the equivalent of what sells in the United States for $100-200, or which sells for £60-130 in the United Kingdom, in a model with two- and-a-half stars or more. If you're looking for top performance, shoot for a portable with three-and-a-half stars—at least $350 or £360—or look into one of the sophisticated portatop or tabletop models that cost somewhat more.

> Don't be fooled by the word "radio"–
> able world band radios are sophisticated devices.

If price isn't a reliable guide, why not go for the cheapest? Research shows that once the novelty wears thin, most people quit using cheap radios, especially those under $80 or £60. It's like driving a lawn tractor instead of a car on a highway—it's cheaper, all right, but not up to the

task. On most stations low-cost radios sound terrible, and they're clumsy to tune.

What do you want to hear? Just the big stations? Or do you also hanker for soft voices from exotic lands? Decide, then choose a model that surpasses your expected needs by a good notch or so—this helps ensure against disappointment without wasting money. After all, you don't need a Ferrari to go to the mall, but you also don't want a golf cart for the autobahn.

Keep in mind that, except to some extent for the Sony ICF-2010, portables don't do brilliantly with tough signals—those that are weak, or hemmed in by interference from other stations. If it's important to you to ferret out as much as possible, think four stars—perhaps five—in a portatop or tabletop. The rub is that these cost much more, usually several hundred dollars or a few hundred pounds, or more.

Where are you located? Signals are strongest in and around Europe, second-best in eastern North America. If you live in either place, you might get by with any of a number of reasonably rated models.

Elsewhere in the Americas, or in Hawaii or Australasia, choose with more care. You'll need a receiver that's unusually sensitive to weak signals—some sort of extra antenna will help, too.

Where you live partially determines which radio you should pick.

If you're an urban listener in a high-rise building, you may find an ordinary portable radio to be insufficient—try to hedge your bet by buying one on a money-back basis. Sometimes the best choice is a tabletop or portatop model fed by a simple outboard antenna mounted at or just outside a window or balcony. For more on this, see the introduction to the tabletop section of this PASSPORT REPORTS.

What features make sense? Separate features into those which affect performance and those that don't (see sidebars). Don't rely on performance features alone, though. As PASSPORT REPORTS demonstrates, much more besides features goes into performance.

Where to buy? Unlike TVs and ordinary radios, world band sets don't test well in stores other than the few specialty showrooms that have proper outdoor antennas. Even there, given the fluctuations over time in world band reception,

PASSPORT Standards: Our 20th Year

Our reviewers, and no one else, have written everything in PASSPORT REPORTS. These include our laboratory findings, all of which are done independently for us by a specialized contract laboratory that is recognized as the world's leader in this field. (For more on this, please see the Radio Database International White Paper, *How to Interpret Receiver Lab Tests and Measurements*.)

Our review process is completely separate from any advertising, and our team members may not accept review fees from manufacturers or "permanently borrow" radios. Neither International Broadcasting Services nor any of its editors owns any stake in, or is employed by, firms which manufacture, sell or distribute world band radios, antennas or related hardware.

PASSPORT recognizes superior products regardless of when they first happen to appear on the market. So we don't bestow annual awards, which recognize only models released during a given year. Some years, many worthy models are introduced, whereas in other years virtually none appear. Thus, a "best" receiver for one year may be markedly inferior to a "non-best" receiver from another year.

Instead, we designate each exceptional model, regardless of its year of introduction, as *Passport's Choice*.

This edition marks the 20th year our organization has been adhering to these standards. We hope to be doing more of the same for years to come.

Features for Superior Performance

The bottom line is that a signal should not just come in, but also sound pleasant. There are several features that help bring this about—some are concerned with keeping out unwanted sounds, others with enhancing the audio quality of the station you're trying to hear.

For example, *multiple conversion* (also called *double conversion*, *up conversion*, *dual conversion* or *two IFs*) is important to rejecting spurious "image" signals—unwanted growls, whistles, dih-dah sounds and the like. Few models under $100 or £70 have it; nearly all over $150 or £100 do. This borders on a "must" for all but casual listening.

Also look for two or more *bandwidths* for superior rejection of stations on adjacent channels. Bandwidths are measured at -6 dB, and in a radio with multiple bandwidths one should measure between 4 kHz and 7 kHz, another between 2 kHz and 3 kHz. Most portables come with only one bandwidth, which should measure between 4 kHz and 6 kHz.

Look for properly functioning *synchronous selectable sideband* (synchronous detection with selectable sideband), a superb high-tech feature for enhanced adjacent-channel rejection and reduced fading. Large speakers are another aural plus, as are *tone controls*—preferably continuously tunable with separate bass and treble adjustments.

For world band reception, *single-sideband* (SSB) reception capability is irrelevant, but it's essential if you want to eavesdrop on utility or "ham" signals. On costlier models you'll get it whether you want it or not.

Heavy-hitting tabletop models and their portatop cousins are designed to flush out virtually the most stubborn signal. Look for a tunable *notch filter* to zap howls; *passband offset*, also known as *passband tuning* and *IF shift*, for superior adjacent- channel rejection and audio contouring, especially in conjunction with synchronous selectable sideband; and multiple *AGC* decay rates (e.g., *AGC slow*, *AGC fast*), ideally with selectable *AGC off*.

A *noise blanker* sounds like a better idea than it really is, given the received-frequency technology in use. But at some electrically noisy locations it is essential.

Digital signal processing (DSP) is the latest high-tech attempt to enhance mediocre signal quality. Thus far it has been much smoke, little fire.

With portables, an *AC adaptor* not only reduces operating costs, it may also improve weak-signal performance. However, with tabletop models an *inboard AC power supply* is marginally handier than an outboard AC adaptor, and supposedly is less likely to cause a fire.

Looking ahead, the exciting possibility exists that *digital shortwave transmissions* may be feasible. If compatible with analog receivers (in-band, on-channel), it could supplement and gradually replace the current analog-only mode in years to come. This should result in much-improved reception quality for the listener, with reduced transmission costs for the broadcaster. But don't look anytime soon for radios that can receive these transmissions—they don't exist yet.

long-term satisfaction is hard to gauge from a spot test.

However, to some extent you can evaluate audio quality and ergonomics in a store. Even if a radio can't pick up much world band in the building, you can get a thumbnail idea of fidelity by listening to some mediumwave AM stations. By playing with the radio, you can also get a feel for handiness of operation.

If you're not familiar with a store you're trying, a good way to judge it is to use the old *Guide Michelin* trick. Visibly bring along or mention your PASSPORT. Reputable dealers—reader feedback suggests most are—welcome it as a sign you are serious and knowledgeable. The rest react accordingly.

Otherwise, whether you buy in a mall or through the mail makes little difference. Use the same street smarts you employ when buying anything sophisticated.

> Quality of repairs tends to correlate with price.

Are repairs important? Judging from our experience and reports from readers, the quality and availability of repairs tends to correlate with price. At one extreme, some off-brand portables from China are essentially unserviceable, although most outlets will exchange a defective unit within warranty. On the other hand, superb service is available for most tabletop and portatop models.

Features for Handy Operation

The single most desirable operating feature for a world band radio is *digital frequency readout*—this is a virtual "must" to find stations quickly. A *24-hour clock* for World Time is another "must," and it's best if you can see it whether the radio is on or off. However, standalone 24-hour clocks and watches are available if the radio you want doesn't come with a World Time clock.

Other important features to look for are direct-access tuning via *keypad* and *presets* ("memories"); and any combination of a *tuning knob*, up/down *slewing controls* or *"signal-seek" scanning* to hunt around for stations.

Sets with digital frequency readout virtually always have presets, and *vice versa*. These two features are especially important. First, there are so many channels that if you can't see the frequencies displayed digitally, you have to resort to hit-and-miss tuning by ear. Second, world band stations, unlike local stations, don't stay on the same frequency all the time. Being able to store the frequencies of favorite broadcasters into presets makes it much handier to tune them in regularly.

Useful, but less important, is an *on/off timer*, especially if it can control a separate tape recorder—better, some timer-controlled models come with built-in cassette recorders. Also look for an *illuminated display*; *single-keystroke callup* (a separate button for each preset, rather than having to use the 1-0 keypad); *numerically displayed seconds* on the 24-hour clock; and a good *signal-strength indicator*. Travelers should stick to portables with locks that keep the power from being switched on accidentally.

Better portables are almost always serviced or replaced within warranty. If you can possibly swing it, insist upon a replacement. Repairs to portables, even from the most respected of manufacturers, can be a nightmare.

After warranty expiration, nearly all factory-authorized service for portables tends to fall woefully short, sometimes making radios worse instead of better. Grundig worldwide—and, in the United States, Radio Shack and Sangean— spring to mind as exceptions to some extent. However, note that Sangean offices service only Sangean-brand products, not those made by Sangean for other firms and sold under other names.

On the other hand, for tabletop and

Outdoor Antennas: Who Needs Them?

If you're wondering what accessory antenna you'll need for your new radio, the answer for portables and portatops is usually simple: none, or almost none, as all come with built-in telescopic antennas. Indeed, for evening use in Europe or eastern North America nearly all portables perform *less* well with sophisticated outboard antennas than with their built-in ones.

"Volksantenna" Best for Portables

But if you listen during the day, or live in such places as the North American Midwest or West, your portable may need more oomph. The best solution in the United States is also the cheapest: ten bucks or so for Radio Shack's 75-foot (23-meter) "SW Antenna Kit," which comes with insulators and other goodies, plus $2 for a claw clip. This sort of "inverted-L" antenna itself may be a bit too long for your circumstances, but you can always trim it.

Alternatively, many electronics and world band specialty firms sell the necessary parts and wire for you to make your own inverted-L antenna. An appendix in the Radio Database International White Paper® *Evaluation of Popular Outdoor Antennas* gives minutely detailed step-by-step instructions for making and erecting such an antenna.

Basically, you attach the antenna to your radio using a claw clip, which is clamped onto your radio's rod antenna—this is usually better than the set's external antenna input socket, which may have a desensitizing circuit. Then run the antenna out a window, as high as is safe and practical, to some tall point, like a tree. Unless you want to become Crispy the Cadaver, *keep your antenna clear of any hazardous wiring—the electrical service to your house, in particular—and respect heights.* If you live in an apartment, run it to your balcony or window—as close to the fresh outdoor air as possible.

This "volksantenna"—best disconnected when you're not listening, and especially when thunder, snow or sand storms are nearby—will probably help with most signals. But if it occasionally makes a station sound worse, just disconnect the claw clip and use your radio's telescopic antenna.

portatop models factory-authorized service is usually available to keep them purring for many years to come. Drake, Watkins-Johnson, AOR and Lowe are legendary in this regard. Drake and Watkins-Johnson are especially valued because they have a decades-long track record of maintaining a healthy parts inventory, even for older models.

Of course, nothing quite equals service at the factory itself. So if repair is especially important to you, bend a little toward the home team: Drake and Watkins-Johnson in the United States, Grundig in Germany, Lowe and AOR in the United Kingdom, Japan Radio and AOR in Japan, and so on.

Specialized Antennas for Tabletop Models

It's a different story with tabletop receivers. They require an external antenna, either passive or electrically amplified ("active"). Although portatop models don't require an outboard antenna, they invariably work better with one.

Amplified antennas use short wire or rod elements, but beef up incoming signals with high-gain electronic circuitry. For apartment dwellers and some others, they can be a godsend—provided they work right. Choosing a suitable amplified antenna for your tabletop or portatop receiver takes some care, as some are pretty awful. Yet, certain models—notably, Britain's Datong AD 370—work relatively well.

If you have space outdoors, a passive outdoor wire antenna is much better, especially when it's designed for world band frequencies. Besides not needing problematic electronic circuits, a good passive antenna also tends to reduce interference from the likes of fluorescent lights and electric shavers—noises which amplified antennas boost, right along with the signal. As the cognoscenti put it, the "signal-to-noise ratio" tends to be better with passive antennas.

Eavesdropper antennas usually come with built-in lightning protectors. For other makes of antennas, you can purchase a modestly priced lightning protector, such as is made by Alpha Delta. Or, if you have deep pockets, there's the $295 Ten-Tec Model 100 protector, which automatically shuts out your antenna and power cord when lightning appears nearby. Still, with any outdoor antenna, especially if it is high out in the open, it's best to disconnect it and affix it to something like an outdoor ground rod if there is lightning nearby. Otherwise, sooner or later, you may be facing a costly repair bill.

A surge protector on the radio's power cord is good insurance, too. These are available at any computer store, and cheap MOV-based units are usually good enough. But you can also go for the whole hog, as we do, with the innovative $150 Zero Surge ZS 900 (U.S. phone 800/996-6696; elsewhere +1 908/996-7700).

Many firms—some large, some tiny—manufacture world band antennas. Among the best passive models—all under $100 or £60—are those made by Antenna Supermarket ("Eavesdropper") and Alpha Delta Communications, available from world band stores. A detailed report on these is in the same Radio Database International White Paper® mentioned above, *Evaluation of Popular Outdoor Antennas*.

Portables for 1998

Interested in hearing major world band stations? If so, a good portable provides real value. Unless you live in a high-rise, the best digitally tuned portables will almost certainly meet your needs—especially evenings, when signals are strongest.

That's singularly true in Europe and the Near East, or even along the east coast of North America. Signals tend to come in well in these places, where virtually any well-rated portable should be all you need.

Weak Signals?

But signals are weaker in places like central and western North America, Australasia, and the Caribbean or Pacific islands. There, focus on models PASSPORT has found to be unusually sensitive to weak signals (see box).

Yet, even in Europe and eastern North America daytime signals tend to be weaker than at night. If you listen then—some programs are heard in North America only during the day—weak-signal performance should be a priority.

Longwave Useful for Some

The longwave band is still used for some domestic broadcasts in Europe, North Africa and Russia. If you live in or travel to these parts of the world, longwave coverage is a slight plus for daytime listening to regional radio stations, especially in the hinterland. Otherwise, forget it.

Keep in mind, though, that when a low-cost analog model is available with longwave, that band may be included at the expense of some world band coverage.

Coping with Quality Control Variations

In general, you can depend on Panasonic to produce a consistently reliable, and reliably consistent, product. Sangean models made in Taiwan—under their name or as OEM under other names—fall close behind. At the other end are off-brand products made in China. The rest fall somewhere between, although thus far even name-brand models made in China have tended to be less robust than those made

---

Grundig's new G2000A compact portable has been cleverly designed by F.A. Porsche.   Grundig

Pulling In Weak Stations

Many portables are designed to work well in Europe, where mighty signals can overwhelm radio innards. To get around this, engineers limit signal sensitivity to make a radio "hear" all stations as though they weaker than they really are. Problem is, if you are listening from western or central North America, New Zealand or other region where signals tend to be weak, something else is needed. Something sensitive to weak signals.

Best Weak-Signal Radios

Best is to purchase a radio designed to work well where signals are weak. Here are PASSPORT's choices, listed in order of their ability to flush out anemic signals. While this ability centers around sensitivity to weak signals, there are other factors taken into account, such as the ability to produce intelligible audio at low signal levels. Keep in mind that sample-to-sample variations can affect weak-signal sensitivity and that, as our detailed ratings show, several other models are close runners-up to the following:

- Sony ICF-2010 (where available)
- Grundig Yacht Boy 305 (as available)

Not good enough? If mobility isn't crucial and your pockets are deep, go for one of the better portatop or tabletop models with a worthy external antenna designed for non-portable receivers, such as those made under the "Eavesdropper" and "Alpha Delta" labels.

Make Your Radio "Hear" Better

Regardless of which portable you own, you can give it at least some additional sensitivity on the cheap.

Sony's new AN-LP1 amplified antenna can be used with a wide variety of world band portables.

How cheap? Nothing, for starters.

Find Your Room's "Sweet Spots"

Just wander around the room looking for "sweet spots." Stations may improve if the radio is placed in one of these endowed locations than if you simply plop it down. Try near windows, appliances, telephones and the like; although at times these locations make things worse by introducing electrical noise. Just keep experimenting.

If your portable has an AC adaptor, try that, then batteries; usually the AC adaptor does a better job. Best is the adaptor designed for your radio by the manufacturer and certified by the appropriate safety authorities, such as Underwriters Laboratories. If you travel abroad, look for a multivoltage version—standard on a few models.

Outdoor Antenna Best

An outdoor antenna can help. With portable antennas, simplest is best. Use an alligator or claw clip to connect several meters or yards of insulated wire, elevated outdoors above the ground, to your set's telescopic antenna. It's fast and cheap, yet effective.

Fine Print: Under the right conditions, outdoor wire antennas can feed static electricity, along with signals you want, right into your radio. You'd expect this with thunderstorms and lightning pounding away. But what you might not anticipate is that you can also get this snap, crackle and pop during breezy snowstorms or sand storms.

Static electricity fries semiconductors faster than you can say "Colonel Sanders," so use outdoor antennas only when needed, disconnecting them during stormy conditions and when the radio is off. And try to avoid touching the antenna during dry weather, as you may discharge static electricity from your body right into the radio.

More Fine Print: Outboard antennas can sometimes cause "overloading," usually at certain times of the day on one or more frequency segments with lots of strong signals. You'll know this when you tune around and most of what you hear sounds like murmuring in a TV courtroom scene. Remedy: Disconnect the wire antenna and use to the telescopic rod.

Fancy outdoor wire antennas? These are designed for tabletop and portatop models. For portables, a length of ordinary insulated wire works better and costs less.

If you are in a weak-signal part of the world, such as the North American Midwest or West, and want something with more oomph, best is to erect an inverted-L (so-called "longwire") antenna. This is available as a kit through Radio Shack (278-758, $9.99) and some other radio specialty outlets, or may be easily constructed from detailed instructions found in the recently revised RDI White Paper, *Popular Outdoor Antennas*.

Indoor Solutions, Too

Antennas, like football players, almost always do best outdoors. But if your supplementary antenna simply must be indoors, it can work to best advantage if you place it along the middle of a window with Velcro or tape. Another solution, if you're listening in a reinforced-concrete building which absorbs radio signals, is to use the longest telescopic car antenna you can find. Affix it outdoors, almost horizontally, onto a windowsill or balcony rail.

Amplified, or "active," antennas often do more harm than good with portables. Yet, those made by Sony have consistently tested out to be relatively problem-free, even if they do little to actually boost signal strength. Their high card is that they have long cords which allow you to place the antenna near the outdoors, where reception tends to be best, but to leave the radio sitting where you listen.

Inexpensive electronic signal-booster devices usually fare much more poorly than Sony's offerings, although anecdotal evidence suggests that some can help in given listening situations. Purchase these on a money-back basis so you can experiment with little risk.

elsewhere. Although some Sony models once had an above-average defect rate, in recent years we've noticed a marked improvement.

If you purchase a genuinely defective world band portable, insist upon an exchange. Many vendors and virtually all world band specialty outlets will be cooperative if a just-sold radio turns out to be defective or "DOA"; others even have 30-day or similar return policies.

That's because manufacturers' repair facilities have an atrocious record when it comes to fixing world band portables. (Grundig is a commendable exception during the warranty; after-warranty service is performed by designated independent agents, which reportedly are of high quality but slow). In North America, Sangean-*branded* models, not those manufactured for other companies by Sangean, also tend to be treated better for service; so long as their North American office remains in operation, this should continue to be the case. Of course, the longer you own a radio, the less likely it is you'll be able to have it exchanged, so check it out carefully after you purchase it.

Shelling Out

Only observed approximate selling, or "street," prices (including VAT, where applicable) are cited in PASSPORT. Of course, street prices vary plus or minus, so take them as the general guide they are meant to be.

Duty-free shopping? For the time being, in some parts of the European Union it may save you ten percent or more, *provided* you don't have to declare the radio at your destination. Check on warranty coverage, though. In the United States, where prices are already among the world's lowest, you're better off buying from shortwave specialty outlets and other stores or catalog houses. Canada,

as well—and, to an increasing extent, the United Kingdom and Germany.

Some countries, such as Singapore, offer genuine bargain, at least on some models. However, don't look for anything comparable in Beijing, where even Chinese-made radios are overpriced.

In Japan the go-go days of bargain hunting in Tokyo's famous Akihabara are over, at least for the time being. World band radios are no longer widely available, with only a few outlets, such as X-One and T-Zone, having much selection. Even Japanese-made radios are now usually cheaper in the United States.

Naturally, all prices are as we go to press and may fluctuate. Recently, though, prices have been remarkably stable—even dropping slightly—so the prices in PASSPORT should be fairly accurate throughout 1998

We try to stick to plain English, but some specialized terms have to be used. If you come across something that's not clear, check it out in the glossary farther back in this edition.

Virtually All Available Models Included

We've scoured the earth to evaluate nearly every digital portable currently produced that at least meets minimum standards of performance. Here, then, are the results of our hands-on and laboratory tests.

What Passport's Ratings Mean

Star ratings: ★ ★ ★ ★ ★ is best, ★ is a dog. We award stars solely for overall performance and meaningful features, plus to some extent ergonomics and build quality. Price, appearance, country of manufacture and the like are not taken into account. To facilitate comparison, the same rating system is used for portable and portatop models, reviewed elsewhere in this PASSPORT. Whether a radio is portable, a portatop or a tabletop model, a given rating—three stars, say—means largely the same thing.

A rating of three or more stars should please most who listen to major stations regularly during the evening. However, for a throwaway on trips, a small portable with as little as one-and-a-half stars may suffice.

If you are listening from a weak-signal part of the world, such as central and western North America or Australasia, lean strongly towards models that have weak-signal sensitivity among the listed advantages. Too, check out the portatop and tabletop sections of this PASSPORT REPORTS.

Passport's Choice. La crème de la crème. Our test team's personal picks of the litter—digital portables we would buy or have bought for our personal use.

¢: denotes a price-for-performance value. A designated model may or may not be truly inexpensive, but it *will* provide exceptional performance for the relatively reasonable amount of money spent.

How Models Are Listed

Models are listed by size; and, within size, in order of world band listening suitability. Street, or typical selling, prices are given. Unless otherwise indicated, each digital model includes:

• Tuning by keypad, up/down slewing, presets and scanning.
• Digital frequency readout.
• Coverage of the world band shortwave spectrum from at least 3200-26100 kHz.
• Coverage of the usual 87.5-108 MHz FM band.
• Coverage of the AM (mediumwave) band in selectable 9 and 10 kHz channel increments from 513-1705 kHz.

POCKET PORTABLES
Handy for Travel, Poor for Home

Pocket portables weigh under a pound, or half-kilogram, and are somewhere between the size of an audio cassette box and one of the larger hand-held calculators. They operate off two to four ordinary small "AA" (UM-3 penlite) batteries. These diminutive models do one job well: provide news and entertainment when you're traveling, especially abroad. Their great virtue is that they can be stashed on your person, where corrupt or naive security and customs personnel seldom look.

Don't expect much more, once the novelty has worn off. Listening to tiny speakers can be tiring, so most pocket portables aren't suitable for hour-after-hour listening except through good headphones. This isn't an attractive option, given that none has the full array of Walkman-type features, such as a hidden antenna.

Too, none of the available digitally tuned pocket portables are as sensitive to weak signals as they could be, although some come close. Outboard antennas, sometimes supplied, help—but they defeat the point of having a pocket model: hassle-free portability.

Best bet? If price and sound quality through the speaker are paramount, try Sangean's relatively affordable ATS 606A or ATS 606p, also available as the Roberts R617 and Siemens RK 659. Or look at the inexpensive Grundig Traveller II Digital—also sold as the Grundig TR II Digital and Grundig Yacht Boy 320. Otherwise, check out Sony's innovative but pricey ICF-SW100S and ICF-SW100E.

Don't forget to look over the large selection of compact models, just after the pocket portables reviewed in this section. They're not much larger, so they also travel well. But, unlike their smaller cousins, compacts usually sound better because they have larger speakers and stronger audio amplification.

Sony's innovative ICF-SW100S/E pocket portable is a traveler's dream. It also appears to be more robust than when it was first introduced.

★ ★ ★

Sony ICF-SW100S

Price: $359.95 in the United States. CAN$499.00-599.00 in Canada. £239.95 in the United Kingdom.
Pro: Extremely small. Superior overall world band performance for size. Excellent synchronous detection with selectable

sideband. Good audio when earpieces (supplied) are used. FM stereo through earpieces. Exceptional number of helpful tuning features, including "page" storage with presets. Tunes in precise 100 Hz increments. Worthy ergonomics for size and features. Illuminated display. Clock for many world cities, which can be made to work as a *de facto* World Time clock. Timer/snooze features. Travel power lock. Receives longwave and Japanese FM bands. Amplified outboard antenna (supplied), in addition to usual built-in antenna, enhances weak-signal reception. High-quality travel case for radio. *Except for North America:* Self-regulating AC adaptor, with American and European plugs, adjusts automatically to all local voltages worldwide.
Con: Tiny speaker, although an innovative design, has mediocre sound and limited loudness. Weak-signal sensitivity could be better, although outboard active antenna (supplied) helps. Expensive. No tuning knob. Clock not readable when station frequency displayed. As "London Time" is used by the clock for World Time, the summertime clock adjustment cannot be used if World Time is to be displayed accurately. Rejection of certain spurious signals ("images"), and 10 kHz "repeats"

Passport's Choice

For 1998, *Passport's Choice* portables are limited to those very few which combine either outstanding performance or a combination of superior performance and value pricing.

The legendary **Sony ICF-2010** is the undisputed King of the Hill. With performance that's unmatched by any other model, plus one-touch presets, this is the only portable that approaches the quality of a portatop or tabletop receiver.

There are no cheap or pocket models that qualify, but two exceptional values among compacts are the advanced-technology **Sony ICF-SW7600G** and quality-audio **Grundig Yacht Boy 400**. Neither equals the '2010, but at just over half the price they make attractive alternatives.

when synchronous selectable sideband off, could be better. In some urban locations, FM signals (from 87.5 to 108 MHz) can break through into world band segments with distorted sound, e.g. between 3200 and 3300 kHz. Synchronous selectable sideband tends to lose lock if batteries not fresh, or if NiCd cells are used. Batteries run down faster than usual when radio off. "Signal-seek" scanner sometimes stops 5 kHz before a strong "real" signal. No meaningful signal-strength indicator. Mediumwave AM reception only fair. Mediumwave AM channel spacing adjusts peculiarly. Flimsy battery cover. In early production samples, the cable connecting the two halves of the "clamshell" case tended to lose continuity with extended or rough use; this appears to have been resolved in production starting around early 1996, but only time will tell for certain. *North America:* AC adaptor 120 Volts only.

Note: Although Sony's factory alignment procedures now seem to be commendably precise, with any compact or pocket Sony portable having synchronous selectable sideband it doesn't hurt to check in the store, or immediately after purchase, to ensure it was aligned properly at the factory: 1) put fresh batteries into the radio, 2) tune in a local mediumwave AM station, and 3) adjust the "sync" function back and forth between LSB and USB. If all is well, the audio will sound similar in both cases—*similar*, not identical, as there will always be at least some difference. However, if one choice sounds significantly muddier and bassier than the other, the unit is probably out of alignment and you should select another sample.

Verdict: An engineering *tour de force.* Speaker and, to a lesser extent, weak-signal sensitivity keep it from being all it could have been. Yet, it still is the handiest pocket portable around, and one of the niftiest gift ideas in years.

★ ★ ★

Sony ICF-SW100E

Price: £149.95 in the United Kingdom. AUS$649.00 in Australia. Not distributed by Sony within North America.
Verdict: This version, available in Europe but not North America, nominally includes a case, tape-reel-type passive antenna and earbuds. Otherwise, it is identical to the Sony ICF-SW100S, above.

Enhanced for 1998
★ ★ ★

Roberts R617
Sangean ATS 606A
Sangean ATS 606p
Siemens RK 659

Price: *R617:* £124.95 in the United Kingdom. *ATS 606p:* $179.95 in the United States. CAN$279.00 in Canada. Around $250 within European Community. *ATS 606A:* $149.95 in the United States. CAN$239.00 in Canada. Around $230 within European Community. AUS$249.00 in Australia.
Pro: Exceptional simplicity of operation for technology class. Speaker audio

Sangean's small ATS 606, already a superior value, has been improved for 1998.

quality superior for size class, improves with (usually supplied) earpieces. Various helpful tuning features. Keypad has exceptional feel and tactile response. Longwave. World Time clock, displayed separately from frequency, and local clock. Alarm/snooze features. Travel power lock. Clear warning when batteries weak. Stereo FM via earpieces. Superior FM reception. Superior quality of construction. *ATS 606p:* Reel-in passive wire antenna. Self-regulating AC adaptor, with American and European plugs, adjusts automatically to most local voltages worldwide.

Con: No tuning knob. World Time clock readable only when radio is switched off. Display not illuminated. Keypad not in telephone format. No meaningful signal-strength indicator. No carrying strap or handle. *ATS 606A:* AC adaptor extra.

Verdict: Now with more precise tuning—1 kHz instead of 5 kHz increments—and more presets, the revised version is a sensible choice, thanks to superior sound through the speaker. If the regular "A" Sangean version seems Spartan, there's the "p" version, complete with handy goodies.

The Grundig Traveller II Digital performs reasonably for the price.

Grundig Traveller II Digital
Grundig TR II Digital
Grundig Yacht Boy 320

Price: *Traveller II Digital and TR II Digital:* $99.95 in the United States. CAN$129.95 in Canada. *Yacht Boy 320:* £59.95 in the United Kingdom.

Pro: Price. Superior audio quality for pocket size. 24-hour clock with alarm feature and clock-radio capability. Up/down slew tuning with "signal-seek" scanning. Illuminated LCD. Travel power lock (*see* Con). FM in stereo through earpieces, not included.

Con: Poor rejection of certain spurious signals ("images"). Doesn't cover 7400-9400 kHz world band range, although like other single-conversion sets it can be tricked into receiving the lower part of this range at reduced strength by tuning the 6505-6700 kHz "image" frequencies. Lacks keypad and tuning knob. Few presets (e.g., only five for 2300-7400 kHz range). Tunes world band only in coarse 5 kHz steps. Even-numbered frequencies displayed with final zero omitted; e.g., 5.73 rather than conventional 5.730 or 5730. Poor spurious-signal ("image") rejection. So-so adjacent-channel rejection (selectivity). Unhandy "SW1/SW2" switch to go between 2300-7400 kHz and 9400-26100 kHz ranges. World Time clock not displayed independent of frequency. Nigh-useless signal-strength indicator. LCD illumination not disabled when travel power lock activated. No carrying strap or handle. AC adaptor extra. No longwave.

Verdict: Warts and all, a decent offering at an attractive price, with audio quality superior to that of most pocket models. Grundig's slightly larger, but better, Yacht Boy 305, as available, is worth considering as a comparably priced alternative.

COMPACT PORTABLES

Good for Travel, Fair for Home

Compacts tip in at one to two pounds, under a kilogram, and are typically sized 8 × 5 × 1.5 inches, or 20 × 13 × 4 cm. Like pocket models, they feed off "AA" (UM-3 penlite) batteries—but, usually, more of them. They travel almost as well as smaller models, but sound better and usually receive better, too. For some travelers, they also suffice as home sets—something pocket units can't really do. However, if you don't travel abroad often, you may find better value and performance in a lap portable.

Which stand out? Three, in particular, provide an unusually favorable intersection of price and performance. Grundig's Yacht Boy 400 has superior audio quality and two bandwidths, and it's straightforward to operate. For hearing signals hemmed in by interference, the Sony ICF-SW7600G brings real affordability to synchronous selectable sideband, and its build quality now appears to be superior. Both are outstanding buys, especially if you don't live where signals are relatively weak.

If you live in a weak-signal area, consider the Grundig Yacht Boy 305 which, to the extent it is available, is a relative bargain. Otherwise, step up to the larger and better Sony ICF-2010, or even a portatop or tabletop model. But between the similarly priced YB 400 and ICF-SW7600G, the latter has a slight edge in such weak-signal parts of the world as central and western North America.

"Bells and whistles"? Among three-star models, the Sony ICF-SW55 and the Sangean ATS 909 are laden with snazzy operating features and accessories that come standard. However, neither has the one feature that really counts: synchronous selectable sideband.

For superior quality of construction, look to Panasonic or those Sangean products made at its Taiwan factory (not its factories in China). For simplicity of operation, there are the various Grundig Yacht Boy compacts, especially the 305, as well as the Sony ICF-SW40, among others.

★ ★ ★¼   *Passport's Choice*

Grundig Yacht Boy 400

Price: $199.95 in the United States. CAN$249.95 in Canada. £119.95 in the United Kingdom. £119.95 in the United Kingdom. AUS$399.00 in Australia.

Pro: Unusually good value. Audio quality clearly tops in size category. Two bandwidths, both well-chosen. Easy to operate and ergonomically superior for advanced-technology radio. A number of helpful tuning features, including keypad, up/down slewing, 40 station presets, "signal seek" frequency scanning and scanning of station presets. Signal-strength indicator. World Time clock with second time zone, any one of which is shown at all times; however, clock displays seconds only when radio is off. Illuminated display.

Grundig's Yacht Boy 400 is one of the best values in world band radios.

Alarm/snooze features. Demodulates single-sideband signals, used by hams and utility stations, with unusual precision for a portable. Fishing-reel-type outboard passive antenna to supplement telescopic antenna. Generally superior FM performance. FM in stereo through headphones. Longwave.

Con: Circuit noise ("hiss") can be slightly intrusive with weak signals. AC adaptor not standard or offered; in North America, Grundig recommends the Radio Shack adaptor #273-1455. No tuning knob. At some locations, there can be breakthrough of powerful AM or FM stations. Keypad not in telephone format. No LSB/USB switch.

Verdict: An excellent choice. The Grundig Yacht Boy 400's audio quality is what sets this model apart, even though circuit noise with weak signals could be lower. (It helps if you clip on several yards or meters of strung-out doorbell wire to the built-in antenna).

Tips for Globetrotting

Airport security and customs personnel at major gateways are accustomed to world band portables, which have become a staple among world travelers. Yet, a few simple practices will help in avoiding hassles:

- Take along a pocket or compact model, nothing larger. Portable radios are a favorite of terrorists for stashing explosives, but for their misdeeds to succeed they need a radio of reasonable proportions.
- Models with built-in recorders (see next chapter), especially if they're not small, may attract unfavorable attention. With these, give yourself a few extra minutes to clear security.
- Stow your radio in a carry-on bag, not in checked luggage or on your person.
- Take along fresh batteries so you can demonstrate that the radio actually works, as gutted radios can be used to carry illegal material. To ensure batteries haven't run down by accident in your carry-on, be sure to activate your radio's power lock, if it has one; if it doesn't, remove at least one power battery from the radio.
- If asked what the radio is for, state that it is for your personal use.
- If traveling in zones of war or civil unrest, or off the beaten path in much of Africa or parts of South America, take along a radio you can afford to lose, and which fits inconspicuously on your person in a pocket.
- If traveling to Bahrain, avoid taking a radio which has the word "receiver" on its case, as security personnel have been known to mistakenly believe that "receiver" connotes a device used for espionage. If this is impractical, use creative, but not amateurish or obvious, means to disguise or eliminate the offending term.

Theft? Remember that radios, cameras, binoculars, laptop computers and the like are almost always stolen to be resold. The more worn the item looks—affixing scuffed stickers helps—the less likely it is to be confiscated by corrupt inspectors or stolen by thieves.

★ ★ ★¼ *Passport's Choice*

The Sony ICF-SW7600G is the least costly radio with synchronous selectable sideband, an advanced-technology feature which makes listening more pleasant.

Sony ICF-SW7600G
Sony ICF-SW7600GS

Price: *ICF-SW7600G:* $199.95 in the United States. CAN$299.00 in Canada. £129.95 in the United Kingdom. AUS$499.00 in Australia. ¥2,700 (about $325) in China. *ICF-SW7600GS:* $269.95 in the United States.

Pro: Unusually good value. Far and away the least-costly model available with high-tech synchronous detection coupled to selectable sideband; this generally performs very well, reducing adjacent-channel interference and fading distortion on world band, longwave and mediumwave AM signals (*see* Con). Single bandwidth, especially when the synchronous-detection feature is used, exceptionally effective at adjacent-channel rejection. Numerous helpful tuning features, including keypad, two-speed up/down slewing, 20 presets (ten for world band) and "signal-seek, then resume" scanning. Demodulates single-sideband signals, used by hams and utility stations, with unusual precision for a portable. World Time clock, easy to set. Tape-reel-type outboard passive antenna accessory comes standard. Snooze/timer features. Illuminated display. Travel power lock. FM stereo through earpieces or headphones. Receives longwave and Japanese FM bands. Dead-battery indicator. Comes standard with vinyl carrying case. *ICF-SW7600GS:* Comes with AN-LP1 active antenna system.

Con: Certain controls, notably for synchronous selectable sideband, located unhandily at the side of the cabinet. No tuning knob. Clock not readable when radio is switched on. No meaningful signal-strength indicator. No AC adaptor comes standard, and polarity difference disallows use of customary Sony adaptors. No earphones/earpieces come standard.

Note: Although Sony's factory alignment procedures now appear to be commendably precise, with any compact or pocket Sony portable having synchronous selectable sideband it doesn't hurt to check in the store, or immediately after purchase, to ensure it was aligned properly at the factory: 1) put fresh batteries into the radio, 2) tune in a local mediumwave AM station, and 3) adjust the "sync" function back and forth between LSB and USB. If all is well, the audio will sound similar in both cases—*similar*, not identical, as there will always be at least some difference. However, if one choice sounds significantly muddier and bassier than the other, the unit is probably out of alignment and you should select another sample.

Verdict: An excellent choice. The best compact model available for rejecting adjacent-channel interference and selective fading distortion—a major plus—but audio quality otherwise is *ordinaire*. A worthy value, mainly because it comes with synchronous selectable sideband that's normally found only on costly receivers. Quality control, after hiccups in early production, now appears to be *better* than most.

Important Things to Look For

- **Helpful tuning features.** Digitally tuned models are by now so superior and cost-effective that they are virtual "musts." Most such models come with such useful tuning aids as direct-frequency access via keypad, presets (programmable channel memories), up-down tuning via tuning knob and/or slew keys, band/segment selection, and signal-seek or other scanning. In general, the more such features a radio has, the easier it is to tune—no small point, given that a hundred or more channels may be audible at any one time. However, there is the occasional model, identified in PASSPORT REPORTS under "Con," with tuning features that are so sophisticated that they can make tuning excessively complicated for some users.

- **Worthy audio quality.** Few models, especially among portables, have rich, full audio—for mellow sound, you're better off with a reconditioned vintage receiver (see article elsewhere in this edition). But some are distinctly better than others. If you listen regularly and have either exacting ears or difficulty in hearing, focus on those models with superior audio quality—and try to buy on a money-back or exchange basis.

- **Effective adjacent-channel rejection ("selectivity").** World band stations are packed together about twice as closely as ordinary mediumwave AM stations, so they tend to interfere with each other. Radios with superior selectivity are better at rejecting this. However, better selectivity also means less high-end ("treble") audio response, so having more than one "bandwidth" allows you to choose between superior selectivity ("narrow bandwidth") when it is warranted, and more realistic audio ("wide bandwidth") when it is not.

- **Synchronous selectable sideband.** When it is designed and manufactured correctly, this advanced feature further improves audio quality and selectivity. First, it virtually eliminates distortion resulting from fading. Second, because each world band signal consists of two identical "halves," in a number of situations it can simultaneously reduce adjacent-channel interference by selecting the "better half." *Tip:* On some portables with this feature that have only one bandwidth, you can usually increase high-end ("treble") audio response by detuning the radio one or two kilohertz with the synchronous selectable sideband feature activated. (Of course, you can detune *any* radio, but if it doesn't have this feature distortion will tend to increase the more you detune.)

- **Sensitivity to weak signals.** How a radio sounds doesn't mean much if the radio can't cough up the station in the first place. Most models have adequate sensitivity for listening to major stations if you're in such parts of the world as Europe, North Africa or the Near East. However, in places like North America west of the east coast, or Australasia, received signals tend to be weak, and thus sensitivity becomes a crucial factor.

- **Superior ergonomics or ease of use.** Certain radios are easier to use than others. In some cases, that's because they don't have features which complicate operation. For example, a radio without single-sideband reception (for hearing hams and other non-world-band signals) is inherently more foolproof to use for world band than one with this feature. However, even models with complex features can be designed to operate relatively intuitively.

★ ★ ★

Sony ICF-SW55
Sony ICF-SW55E

Price: $349.95 in the United States.
CAN$499.00-599.00 in Canada. £239.95
in the United Kingdom. AUS$819.00 in
Australia.

Pro: Although sound emerges through a
small port, rather than the usual speaker
grille, audio quality is better than most in
its size class. Dual bandwidths. Tunes in
precise 0.1 kHz increments (displays only
in 1 kHz increments). Controls neatly and
logically laid out. Innovative tuning system, including factory pre-stored station
presets and displayed alphabetic identi-
fiers for groups ("pages") of stations.
Weak-signal sensitivity a bit better than
most. Good single-sideband reception,
although reader reports continue to complain of some BFO "pulling" or "wobbling"
(not found in our unit). Comes complete
with carrying case containing reel-in wire
antenna, AC adaptor, DC power cord and
in-the-ear earpieces. Signal/battery
strength indicator. Local and World Time
clocks, either (but not both) of which is
displayed separately from frequency.
Summer time adjustment for local time

The Sony ICF-SW55 has good audio and handy
features, but lacks synchronous selectable sideband,
found in the similarly priced Sony ICF-2010.

clock. Snooze/alarm features. Five-event
(daily only) timer nominally can automatically turn on/off certain cassette
recorders—a plus for VCR-type multiple-
event recording. Illuminated display.
Receives longwave and Japanese FM
bands.

Con: "Page" tuning system difficult for
some to grasp. Operation sometimes

• **World Time clock.** Unless you listen to nothing more than the same one or
two stations, a World Time clock (24-hour format) borders on a "must." You can
buy these separately for as little as $10, but many radios come with them built in.
Best among the built-ins is one that always displays World Time; worst is a radio
that has to be switched off for the clock to display, or which has a 12-hour-format
clock. As a compromise, some models have a button that allows you to display
the time briefly while the radio is on.

• **AC adaptor.** Back when portables were larger, they sometimes had built-in
AC power supplies and could be plugged right into the wall, as well as run off
batteries. Now, an outboard AC adaptor ("wall wart") is needed. An AC adaptor
that comes standard with the radio is best, as it is designed to work with that
particular radio, and a multivoltage adaptor is ideal if you spend a lot of time
traveling abroad. It's a sad commentary that $60 telephone answering machines
and the like come standard with an AC adaptor, but not most world band portables costing far more.

unnecessarily complicated by any yardstick, but especially for listeners in the Americas. Spurious-signal rejection, notably in higher world band segments, not fully commensurate with price class. Wide bandwidth somewhat broad for world band reception. Display illumination dim and uneven. Costly to operate from batteries. Cabinet keeps antenna from tilting fully, a slight disadvantage for reception of some FM signals.

Verdict: If the ICF-SW55's operating scheme meets with your approval—for example, if you are comfortable utilizing the more sophisticated features of a typical VCR or computer—and you're looking for a small portable with good audio, this radio is a superior performer in its size class. It can also tape like a VCR, provided you have a suitable recorder to connect to it.

★ ★ ★

Radio Shack DX-398
Roberts R861
Sangean ATS 909
Siemens RK 777

Price: *Radio Shack:* $249.99 in the United States. *Roberts:* £199.95 in United Kingdom. *Sangean:* $299.95 in the United States. CAN$429.00 in Canada.

The Sangean ATS 909, sold under various names, is similar to the Sony ICF-SW55.

Pro: Exceptionally wide range of tuning facilities and hundreds of presets, including one which works with a single touch. Alphanumeric station descriptors. Two voice bandwidths, well-chosen. Tunes single sideband in unusually precise 0.04 kHz increments. Sensitivity to weak signals slightly above average. Superb multi-voltage AC adaptor with North American and European plugs. Travel power lock. 24-hour clock shows at all times, and can display local time in various cities of the world. 1-10 digital signal-strength indicator. Clock radio function offers three "on" times for three discrete frequencies. Snooze feature. FM performs well overall, has RDS feature, and is in stereo through earpieces, included. Superior quality of construction.

Con: Tuning knob tends to mute stations during bandscanning; remediable by modification via at least one American dealer (C. Crane). Large for a compact. Signal-seek scanner tends to stop on few active shortwave signals. Although scanner can operate out-of-band, reverts to default (in-band) parameters after one pass. Two-second wait between when preset is keyed and station becomes audible. Under certain conditions, alphanumeric station descriptor stays on full time, regardless of when designated station is active, and can even repeat the same single station ID throughout all channels in the world band spectrum; solution, commanding the set to revert to page 29 every time this happens, adds to tuning complexity. "Page" tuning system difficult for some to grasp, preceding aside. No carrying handle or strap. 24-hour clock set up to display home time, not World Time, although this is easily overcome by not using world-cities-time feature. Clock does not compensate for daylight (summer) time in each displayed city. RDS, which can automatically display FM-station IDs and update clock, requires strong signal to activate. AC adaptor lacks UL approval.

Verdict: Not tops in its class, but the best offering from Sangean in years, though software is not the best. Especially appropriate for those seeking a wide range of operating features or superior tuning of single-sideband signals.

★ ★ ★

Grundig Yacht Boy 500

Price: £139.95 in the United Kingdom. AUS$599.00 in Australia. Also available in the Middle East and Africa, but not the Americas.

Pro: Attractive layout. Audio-boost circuitry for superior volume. 40 presets. Displays operator-assigned alphanumeric names for stations in presets. RDS circuitry for FM. ROM with 90 factory-preassigned world band channels for nine international broadcasters. Two 24-hour clocks, either one of which displays full time. Battery-low indicator. FM in stereo via headphones. Travel power lock. Three-increment signal-strength indicator. Elevation panel. Single-sideband reception via LSB/USB key. Illuminated display. Timer/snooze features. Comes with worldwide dual-voltage AC adaptor and two types of plugs. Audio quality pretty good. Longwave.

Con: Circuit noise relatively high. Lacks tuning knob. Telescopic antenna tends to get in the way of right-handed users. Volume slider fussy to adjust. Keypad not in telephone format. Key design and layout increase likelihood of wrong key being pushed. Owner's manual, although thorough, poor for quick answers. Twenty-four hour clocks display without leading zeroes. Elevation panel flimsy. Socket for AC adaptor appears to be flimsy. Factory-preassigned channels, of use mainly to beginners, relatively complex for beginners to select. AC adaptor lacks UL seal of approval. Relatively high number of spurious "birdie" signals.

Grundig's world band radios are all made in Asia except the Yacht Boy 500, shown, and the similar Yacht Boy 360. Both are made in Portugal and are available outside North America.

Verdict: Attractive design, good performance, with powerful audio and a number of interesting features. Withal, for most users, slightly better performance can be had in other models for the same price or less.

★ ★ ★

Grundig Yacht Boy 360

Not tested. According to the manufacturer, similar to the Yacht Boy 500, preceding, but with fewer features and in a horizontal, rather than vertical, layout. £89.95 in the United Kingdom; not sold in North America.

Panasonic is not a major presence in world band, but its RF-B45 is a nice performer and well built.

Panasonic RF-B45
Panasonic RF-B45DL
National B45

Price: *RF-B45:* $169.95 in the United States. CAN$239.00 in Canada. AUS$399.00 in Australia. *RF-B45DL:* £139.95 in the United Kingdom. The equivalent of US$220-320 in the European Union. RP-38 120/220 VAC adaptor or RP-65 120 VAC adaptor extra.
Pro: Worthy performance for price category. Easy to operate for advanced-technology radio. A number of helpful

The Sangean ATS-808A is sold under various names. It is a bargain, given its level of performance.

tuning features. Signal-strength indicator. World Time clock. Alarm/snooze features. Demodulates single-sideband signals, used by hams and utility stations. Long-wave. Superior quality of construction.
Con: No tuning knob. Weak-signal sensitivity a bit lacking. Adjacent-channel rejection (selectivity) a bit broad. Clock not displayed separately from frequency. No display illumination. AC adaptor extra.
Verdict: A nice little radio, fairly priced, with Panasonic's superior build quality. Problem is, try to find one!

Enhanced for 1998

Aiwa WR-D1000
Roberts R809
Sangean ATS-808A
Siemens RK 661

Price: *Aiwa:* $199.95 in the United States. *Roberts:* £99.99 in the United Kingdom. *Sangean:* $139.95 in the United States. CAN$249.95 in Canada. AUS$299.00 in Australia. *Siemens:* 399.00 DM in Germany.
Pro: A solid value. Relatively simple to operate for technology class. Dual band-widths, unusual in this size radio (see Con). Various helpful tuning features. Weak-signal sensitivity a bit better than most. Keypad has exceptional feel and tactile response. Longwave. World Time clock, displayed separately from frequency, and local clock. Alarm/snooze features. Signal strength indicator. Travel power lock. Stereo FM via earpieces, included. Superior FM reception. Superior quality of construction.
Con: Fast tuning mutes receiver when tuning knob is turned quickly. Narrow bandwidth performance only fair. Spurious-signal ("image") rejection very slightly substandard for class. Pedestrian audio. Display not illuminated. Keypad not in telephone format. No carrying strap or handle. AC adaptor extra.

Note: Aiwa cabinet styled differently.

Verdict: With more presets, the revised version of this classic Sangean offering continues to be a good value, with relative simplicity of operation and good overall performance. However, mediocre for bandscanning.

★ ★½   ¢

Grundig Yacht Boy 305

Price: $129.95 in the United States. CAN$149.95 in Canada. £85 in the United Kingdom.

Pro: Unusually good value. Commendably sensitive to weak world band and mediumwave AM signals for a portable. Above-average selectivity and audio quality. Various helpful tuning features. Travel power lock. Stereo FM via earpieces, not supplied.

Con: Spurious-signal ("image") rejection below norm for rating group, especially annoying for listening within Europe and

The Grundig Yacht Boy 305 is an exceptional value for weak-signal locations like western North America and Australasia. Catch it while you can, as its future is uncertain.

other strong-signal parts of the world. Tends to overload in the presence of powerful signals, a shortcoming for listening with Europe and other strong-signal parts of the world. No AC adaptor. No tuning knob. Build quality appears to be slightly below average.

World Band Wound Up

If you want a radio that doesn't depend upon batteries or house current to do its job, the BayGen Freeplay radio may be your answer. It is powered by a spring which takes 20 seconds to wind up for over half an hour of listening pleasure.

Various dealers offer it throughout the world, usually for around $100-120 (under CAN$150 in Canada, around £70 in the United Kingdom), and Coca-Cola even offers a razzleberry-red version. That's a bit steep for what it is, but the profits from sales in developed countries are used to help subsidize sales within poorer parts of Africa.

For your money, you get a three-band receiver with FM, mediumwave AM and world band: Model "A" tunes 3.2-12.1 MHz, whereas Model "B" covers 5.8-18 MHz. The Freeplay is analog-tuned and has limited fidelity, but is adequate for hearing major stations.

J. Macmillan, USN&WR/LA Times Syndicate

The BayGen radio is given away and sold in Africa by various organizations, including Coca-Cola.

Note: As of presstime, this model's future is up in the air, but at the very least it should be available for a number of months.

Verdict: A great choice, or a lesser choice, depending upon where you're located. On the one hand, it's priced reasonably, is exceptionally sensitive to weak signals, and has worthy selectivity and audio quality—but only for those in weak-signal parts of the world, such as the Americas (especially central and western North America), Australasia, the Caribbean and the Pacific islands. Equally, the '305's tendency to overload and generate various types of spurious signals makes it a lesser choice for use within Europe, North Africa and the Near East. If weak-signal sensitivity is not paramount, but the price is attractive, consider *inter alia* the similarly priced Sangean ATS-808A, which has better spurious-signal rejection.

★ ★½   ¢

Sony ICF-SW30

Price: $99.95 in the United States. CAN$179.95 in Canada. £89.95 in the United Kingdom. AUS$299.00 in Australia.
Pro: Excellent value for locations where Grundig Yacht Boy 305 not suitable. Superior reception quality, with excellent adjacent-channel rejection (selectivity) and spurious-signal rejection. Weak-

signal sensitivity a bit better than most. Easy to operate for advanced-technology radio. World Time and local time clock. Audio, although lacking in bass, unusually intelligible. Alarm/snooze features. Travel power lock. FM stereo through headphones, not supplied. Battery-life indicator. Receives Japanese FM band.

Con: No keypad or tuning knob. Synthesizer chugging and poky slewing degrade bandscanning. Only seven world band station presets. Does not cover two minor world band segments (2 and 3 MHz), the new 19 MHz segment and a scattering of other world band channels. Clock not displayed independent of frequency. Radio suddenly goes dead when batteries get weak. No longwave. AC adaptor, much-needed, is extra.

Verdict: Among the best-performing radios in the "value" category, and simple to operate, but tuning convenience is pedestrian. An excellent buy if you listen to only a limited number of stations.

★ ★½

Sony ICF-SW40

Price: $129.95 in the United States. £89.95 in the United Kingdom.
Pro: Relatively affordable. Technologically unintimidating, using advanced digital

Sony's ICF-SW30 offers much performance for the money, but is unhandy to operate.

The Sony ICF-SW40 is great for technophobes, but not much else.

circuitry in a radio disguised as slide-rule, or analog, tuned. 24-hour clock. Double-conversion circuitry, unusual in price class, reduces likelihood of reception of spurious "image" signals. Two "on" timers and snooze facility. Travel power lock. Illuminated LCD. Covers Japanese FM band.

Con: Single bandwidth is relatively wide, reducing adjacent-channel rejection. No keypad. Lacks coverage of 1625-1705 kHz portion of North American mediumwave AM band. No single-sideband or synchronous selectable sideband.

Verdict: If you're turned off by things digital and complex, Sony's ICF-SW40 will feel like an old friend in your hands. Otherwise, look elsewhere.

Radio Shack's DX-375 is an outstanding value when on sale at reduced price.

★ ★½   ¢

Radio Shack/Realistic DX-375

Price: Usually $99.99, but as low as $69.99 during special sales in the United States. Not available in Australia.

Pro: Excellent value at $100, rises to an outstanding value when on sale. Several handy tuning features. Weak-signal sensitivity a bit above average. Relatively easy to use for digital portable in its price class. Stereo FM through headphones, not supplied. Travel power lock. Timer. 30-day money-back trial period in the United States.

Con: Mediocre spurious-signal ("image") rejection. Unusually long pause of silence when tuning from channel to channel. Antenna swivel sometimes needs tightening. AC adaptor plug easy to insert accidentally into headphone socket. Build quality, although adequate, appears to be slightly below average. Static discharges sometimes disable microprocessor (usually remediable if batteries are removed for a time, then replaced). No World Time clock. AC adaptor extra. No longwave.

Verdict: No Volvo, but if you absolutely, positively don't want to spend more than $100, this is an excellent choice. When on sale at around $70, it is easily the best buy among low-cost offerings.

New for 1998
★ ★

Grundig G2000A "Porsche Design"

Price: $149.95 in the United States, CAN$199.95 in Canada.

Pro: Arguably the most functionally attractive world band radio on the market, with generally superior ergonomics that include an effective and handy lambskin protective case. Superior adjacent-channel rejection—selectivity—for price and size class. Keypad (in proper telephone format), handy meter-band carousel control, "signal-seek" scanning and up/down slew tuning. Twenty station presets, of which ten are for world band and the rest for FM and mediumwave AM stations. World Time clock. Timer/snooze/alarm. Illuminated display. Travel power lock. Microprocessor reset control.

Con: Sensitivity mediocre between 9400-26100 kHz, improving slightly between 2300-7400 kHz. Poor spurious-signal

Winner of the 1998 World Band Beauty Pageant is the new Grundig G2000A, designed by Porsche. The radio's layout is as practical as it is attractive, but performance is pedestrian.

("image") rejection. Does not tune such important world band ranges as 7405-7550 and 9350-9395 kHz. Tunes world band only in coarse 5 kHz steps and displays in nonstandard XX.XX MHz/XX.XX₅ MHz format characteristic of low-cost Chinese radios. No tuning knob. Annoying one-second pause when tuning from one channel to the next. Old-technology SW1/SW2 switch complicates tuning. Protruding power button can get in the way of nearby slew-tuning and meter-carousel keys. Leather case makes it difficult to retrieve folded telescopic antenna. Magnetic catches weak on leather case. No carrying strap. No longwave. Signal-strength indicator nigh useless. Clock not displayed separately from frequency. AC adaptor extra.

Comment: Strong signals within the 7405-7595 kHz range can be tuned, at reduced strength, via the "image" signal 900 kHz down; e.g., 7425 kHz may be heard on 6525 kHz.

Verdict: Five stars for design, two for performance, but who ever complained that Marilyn Monroe couldn't sing? The Grundig G2000A redefines how a world band radio should look and feel. Hopefully Grundig puts this talent to use with future models that operate as spectacularly as they look.

Evaluation of New Model: Conceived in California, designed in Germany and manufactured in China, the new Grundig G2000A is the most interesting-looking radio that's come along since the introduction of Sony's "clamshell" ICF-SW100. For starters, there's a hard lambskin case instead of the traditional separate travel pouch. To use the radio, simply lift the front part of the case, like a handbag, so it clings magnetically to the back. This exposes the radio's controls, while the case serves as an elevation panel to place the faux-aluminum radio at a handy angle (see photo). It's ingenious . . . and thoroughly effective.

The Porsche design philosophy, whether with cars or other products, has always been that form follows function. So it is with the G2000A. Aside from the antenna's being clumsy to retrieve, the case's magnetic catches being weaker than they should be, and the protruding power button sometimes getting in the way of other controls, the ergonomics are sensible.

Tuning is by keypad in the customary telephone format, plus there are 20 presets (ten for world band), up/down slew buttons which tune world band in 5 kHz increments, "signal-seek" scanning and a meter-band carousel button. There is no tuning knob, and an SW1/SW2 switch unnecessarily complicates operation. World band coverage is from 2300-26100 kHz except, alas, for a "hole" between 7405-9393 kHz where a number of stations operate.

The illuminated LCD includes a digital frequency readout in XX.XX MHz format for even channels, XX.XX₅ MHz format for odd channels—an offbeat arrangement found only in low-cost Chinese-made radios. Sharing that display is a World Time clock with alarm/snooze functions. The clock readout replaces the frequency display when the radio is off, or with the radio on by pressing a button. The LCD also has a marginally useful signal-strength indicator. Other features include a travel power lock and a microprocessor reset in case the microprocessor crashes.

When tuning from one channel to the next with the slew control, you have to wait one second before there is any sound. Sensitivity to weak signals is also not all it could be, especially above 9400 kHz, making it a suboptimal choice for listeners in Australasia or near the west coast of North America.

Adjacent-channel rejection, or selectivity, is superior, but rejection of spurious "image" signals is poor. World band audio quality is at least as good as you would expect from a receiver of this size, although FM audio lacks low-frequency response.

Grundig's new G2000A is reminiscent of the Porsche made years ago that had a Volkswagen engine: a visual knockout and fine features, but it just putts along when it comes to weak-signal performance.

The Grundig Traveller III is virtually the same radio as the Grundig G2000A, but cheaper and with less visual panache. But for that same money you can also get a Grundig Yacht Boy 305, which is better yet.

New for 1998
★ ★

Grundig Traveller III

Price: $129.95 in the United States, CAN$149.95 in Canada.
Pro: Superior adjacent-channel rejection—selectivity—for price and size class. Keypad (in proper telephone format), handy meter-band carousel control, "signal-seek" scanning and up/down slew tuning. Twenty station presets, of which ten are for world band and the rest for FM and mediumwave AM stations. World Time clock. Timer/snooze/alarm. Travel power lock. Microprocessor reset control.
Con: Sensitivity mediocre between 9400-26100 kHz, improving slightly between 2300-7400 kHz. Poor spurious-signal ("image") rejection. Does not tune such important world band ranges as 7405-7550 and 9350-9395 kHz. Tunes world band only in coarse 5 kHz steps and displays in nonstandard XX.XX MHz/XX.XX5 MHz

format characteristic of cheap Chinese radios. No tuning knob. Annoying one-second pause when tuning from one channel to the next. Old-technology SW1/SW2 switch complicates tuning. No carrying strap. No longwave. Signal-strength indicator nigh useless. Clock not displayed separately from frequency. Display not illuminated. AC adaptor extra.
Comment: Strong signals within the 7405-7595 kHz range can be tuned, at reduced strength, via the "image" signal 900 kHz down; e.g., 7425 kHz may be heard on 6525 kHz.
Verdict: Virtually identical to the Grundig G2000A, preceding, but cheaper and without the Porsche pizzazz and illuminated dial. Not the most appropriate choice for use in western North America and Australasia.

★ ★   ¢

Electro Brand Digital Tesonic R-3000

Price: *Electro:* $49.99 in the United States. *R-3000:* ¥620 (about US$71) in China.
Pro: Relatively inexpensive for a model with digital frequency display, keypad and station presets (18 for world band, 18 for

The Electro Brand Digital is sold under various names. Its construction quality isn't the best, but it offers many features at a rock-bottom price.

FM and mediumwave AM). Up/down slew tuning with "signal-seek" scanning. Slightly better adjacent-channel rejection (selectivity) than usual for price category. World Time and local clocks (see Con). Alarm/snooze timer. Illuminated display. FM stereo via optional headphones. *Some versions:* AC adaptor included.

Con: Mediocre build quality, with one sample having poor sensitivity, another having skewed bandwidth filtering. Inferior dynamic range and spurious-signal rejection. Does not tune 5800-5815, 9300-9495, 11500-11575, 13570-13870, 15000-15095, 18900-19020 kHz and some other useful portions of the world band spectrum. No tuning knob. Tunes world band only in coarse 5 kHz steps. No longwave. No signal-strength indicator. No travel power lock (lock provided serves another function), but power switch not easy to turn on accidentally. Clocks do not display independent of frequency. Static discharges occasionally disable microprocessor in high-static environments (usually remediable if batteries are removed for a time, then replaced). *Some versions:* No AC adaptor.

Verdict: Made by the Disheng Electronic Cooperative, Ltd., in Guangzhou, China, this bargain-priced model has excellent features, with much-improved performance over our original test unit in 1992. However, lacks complete frequency coverage and appears to have unusually high sample-to-sample variations in performance.

Duracell Batteries Leaking

We've used Duracell alkaline batteries by the hundreds. They used to perform just fine, but over the past couple of years we've been encountering swelling and leaking, especially with "D" cells. Battery leakage is no small matter—it can seriously corrode costly electronic equipment.

This hasn't happened just once or twice, but on several occasions from different production batches purchased at various outlets. All have been used years before their stamped expiration dates. However, compared to "D" cells, and to some extent "C" cells, "AA" Duracells appear to be holding up relatively well.

Whether this is endemic with all makes of alkaline batteries, perhaps as a result of environmentally friendly reformulations, remains to be seen. However, we have been testing a variety of sizes of Eveready "Energizer" alkaline cells. While it's too early to issue a definitive verdict, thus far we haven't encountered any swelling or leakage.

Until this is resolved, carefully inspect new batteries—especially "D" cells—for signs of swelling, and check them every couple of months if you leave them inside your radio.

Sangean ATS 303

Price: $89.95 in the United States.

Pro: LCD has large digits and excellent contrast at all viewing angles. Weak-signal sensitivity better than most. Five station preset buttons retrieve up to ten world band and ten AM/FM stations. Easy-to-set World Time clock. Timer/snooze/alarm. Travel power lock. Stereo FM via earpieces.

Con: Intolerably slow tuning by single-speed up/down slew buttons—no tuning knob or other remedy beyond presets and scanning. Mediocre spurious-signal ("image") rejection and adjacent-channel rejection (selectivity), plus some distorted spurious FM broadcast signals may intrude within the world band spectrum. Does not tune such important world band ranges as 7305-7600 and 9300-9495 kHz. Tunes world band only in coarse 5 kHz steps. Old-technology SW1/SW2 switch complicates tuning. No longwave. Signal-strength indicator nigh useless. No display illumination. Clock not displayed separately from frequency. No carrying strap or handle. AC adaptor extra.

Comment: Strong signals within the 7305-7595 kHz range can be tuned, at reduced strength, via the "image" signal 900 kHz down; e.g., 7425 kHz may be heard on 6525 kHz.

Caution: Made in China, according to an informed industry source. However, our unit and a number of others inspected at an American dealership had no indication of the country of manufacture on the radio, packaging or accompanying literature. As a result, some dealers and consumers have unwittingly presumed the ATS 303 is made in Taiwan, where Sangean's build quality is superior to anything that has come out of China thus far. Hopefully by the time you read this the country of origin will be properly indicated.

The new Sangean ATS 303 is handicapped by tortoise-slow tuning and misses many world band frequencies. A number of similarly priced alternatives are better.

Verdict: Somewhat superior sensitivity to weak signals and excellent LCD notwithstanding, tortoise-slow tuning, missed frequencies and mediocre performance make this a model to avoid.

Evaluation of New Model: The new Sangean ATS 303, which comes with no outboard AC adaptor, has ten presets for shortwave—five for below 7.3 MHz, five for above 9.5 MHz; ten more are for FM and mediumwave AM. There's also signal-seek scanning and up/down slew buttons which tune in 5 kHz increments. Absent altogether are a keypad and tuning knob.

Alas, slewing is painfully slow. Coupled with the lack of a keypad or tuning knob, this makes the '303 one of the most tiresome receivers we have ever tested for dialing up and down the bands—it's like trying to surf the Internet with a 4800 or 9600 kb/s modem. The '303's SW1/SW2 switch, a technological relic, also complicates tuning.

The LCD, with large digits, has excellent contrast no matter which angle you view it from. Although it lacks illumination, this display can be a real boon if your eyes are weak. The 24-hour World Time clock, which is easy to set, is shared with the frequency display, although a button can be pressed to see the time while you're listening. There is also a power-lock switch to keep the radio from being turned on accidentally.

Selectivity (adjacent-channel rejection) and spurious-signal rejection are mediocre, so you tend to hear more interference from other signals than you would on a better radio. Audio quality is passable. The lone performance plus is that sensitivity to weak signals is a cut above average—important if you live where world band signals tend to be weak.

Incredibly for a new model, the '303 does not even tune the 7305-9495 kHz range. A check of PASSPORT's Blue Pages shows just how many stations are missed, notably within the 7305-7550 and 9350-9495 kHz segments.

No matter how well a radio performs, it isn't of much use if it can't tune where stations operate.

★ ★

Bolong HS-490

Price: ¥360 (about US$41) in China.
Pro: Inexpensive for a model with digital frequency display, ten world band station presets, and ten station presets for mediumwave AM and FM. World Time clock (see Con). Tape-reel-type outboard passive antenna accessory comes standard. AC adaptor. Illuminated display. Alarm/snooze features. FM stereo (see Con) via earbuds, included.
Con: Requires patience to get a station, as it tunes world band only via 10 station presets and multi-speed up/down slewing/scanning. Tunes world band only in coarse 5 kHz steps. Even-numbered frequencies displayed with final zero omitted; e.g., 5.75 rather than conventional 5.750 or 5750. Poor spurious-signal ("image") rejection. So-so adjacent-channel rejection (selectivity). World Time clock not displayed independent of frequency. Does not receive relatively unimportant 6200-7100 kHz portion of world band spectrum. Does not receive 1615-1705 kHz portion of expanded AM band in the Americas. No signal-strength indicator. No travel power lock. Mediumwave AM tuning increments not switchable, which may make for inexact tuning in some parts of the world other than where the radio was purchased. FM selectivity and capture ratio mediocre. FM stereo did not trigger on our unit.
Verdict: Made by a joint venture between Xin Hui Electronics and Shanghai Huaxin Electronic Instruments. No prize, but as good you'll find among the truly cheap, which probably accounts for its being the #1 seller among digital world band radios in China.

Cheap but no bargain is the Bolong HS-490, a best-seller within China.

★ ★

Lowe SRX-50
Amsonic AS-908
Galaxis G 1380/4
Morphy Richards R191
Yorx AS-908

Price: *Lowe:* £39.95 in the United Kingdom. *Galaxis:* About the equivalent of

US$33 in the European Union. *Morphy Richards:* £37.00 in the United Kingdom. *Yorx:* CAN$56 in Canada.

Pro: Inexpensive for a model with digital frequency display, five world band station presets (ten on the Yorx), plus ten station presets for mediumwave AM and FM. Relatively simple to operate for technology class. Illuminated display. Alarm/snooze features. FM stereo via headphones. *Except Yorx:* World Time clock. Longwave. *Yorx:* Ten, rather than five, world band station presets. AC adaptor and stereo earpieces come standard. *Galaxis and Lowe:* Headphones included.

Con: Substandard build quality. No tuning knob; tunes only via station presets and multi-speed up/down slewing/scanning. Tunes world band only in coarse 5 kHz steps. Even-numbered frequencies displayed with final zero omitted; e.g., 5.75 rather than conventional 5.750 or 5750. Poor spurious-signal ("image") rejection. Mediocre selectivity. Does not receive 1605-1705 kHz portion of expanded AM band in the Americas. No signal-strength indicator. No travel power lock. Clock not displayed independent of frequency display. Mediumwave AM tuning increments not switchable, which may make for inexact tuning in some parts of the world other than where the radio was purchased. Power switch has no position labeled "off," although "auto radio" power-switch position performs a comparable role. *Except Yorx:* Does not tune important 5800-5895, 17500-17900 and 21750-21850 kHz segments; 15505-15695 kHz tunable only to limited extent (see Comment). No AC adaptor. *Yorx:* Does not receive 7300-9499 and 21750-21850 kHz portions of the world band spectrum. Clock in 12-hour format.

Comment: Strong signals within the 15505-15800 kHz range can be tuned via the "image" signal 900 kHz down; e.g., 15685 kHz may be heard on 14785 kHz.

Verdict: Outclassed by newer models.

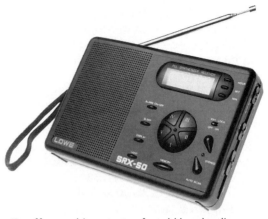

To offer newbies a taste of world band radio, England's Lowe Electronics offers the low-cost SRX-50, made in China. It is sold under various other brand names, as well.

★ ★

Elektro AC 101

Price: $49.95 plus $4 shipping by mail order in the United States. About the equivalent of US$50 in China.

Pro: One of the least costly portables with digital frequency display and presets (ten for world band, ten for AM/FM) and "signal-seek" scan tuning. Slightly more selective than usual for price category. Relatively simple to operate for technology class. World Time clock. Alarm/snooze features. Illuminated display. FM stereo via optional headphones.

Con: Mediocre build quality. Relatively lacking in weak-signal sensitivity. No tuning knob; tunes only via presets and multi-speed up/down slewing. Tunes world band only in coarse 5 kHz steps. Mediumwave AM tuning steps do not conform to channel spacing in much of the world outside the Americas. Frequency display in confusing XX.XX/XX.XX5 MHz format. Poor spurious-signal ("image") rejection. Mediocre dynamic range. Does not tune relatively unimportant 6200-7100 and 25600-26100 kHz world band segments. Does not receive longwave band or 1615-1705 kHz portion of expanded AM band in the Americas. No signal-strength indicator. No travel power lock switch. No AC adaptor. Antenna swivels, but does not rotate; swivel breaks relatively easily. Limited dealer network.

Verdict: Audi cockpit, moped engine.

★ ★

**Rodelsonic Digital World Band
Rodelvox Digital World Band
Amsonic AS-138
Dick Smith Digitor A-4336
Sootoade 65B 119 UCY Digital
Shimasu PLL Digital
World Wide 4 Band Digital Receiver**

Price: *Rodelvox and Rodelsonic:* $99.95 plus $6.95 shipping in United States.

Amsonic: ¥265 (about US$31) in China. *Dick Smith Digitor:* AUS$79.95. *Scotcade:* £29.99 plus shipping in the United Kingdom.

Pro: Relatively inexpensive for a model with digital frequency display and 20 station presets (ten for world band, ten for mediumwave AM and FM). Relatively simple to operate for technology class. Alarm/snooze features with World Time clock. Illuminated display. FM stereo via optional headphones.

Con: Poor build quality. Modest weak-signal sensitivity. No tuning knob; tuned only by station presets and multi-speed up/down slewing/scanning. Tunes world band only in coarse 5 kHz steps. Even-numbered frequencies displayed with

World Band in Your Car

Becker, the German firm which provides gilt-edged radios for Mercedes-Benz, offers the Mexico 2340 world band car radio, $549.95 in the United States. It is available throughout much of Europe and North America, and comes with the usual stereo features, including an inboard cassette drive and optional outboard CD changer.

Unlike most world band radios, those in cars have to overcome electrical noise from ignitions, microprocessor chips, wiper motors and the like. Diesels generate no ignition noise, but even they are a poor substitute for the relative quiet of a home environment.

There's not much you can do about electrical noise, but it's generally not serious enough to dampen listening to major world band stations. The Becker is sensitive enough for this and more, and you can improve weak-signal sensitivity by replacing your car's telescopic antenna with one that's longer, or the one offered by some Becker dealers.

Michael Pilla Photography

The Becker Mexico 2340, made in Germany, provides high-fidelity listening inside automobiles.

Ergonomics for Safe Driving

When you're driving along crowded roads, you can't devote much attention to the nuances of tuning stations. Ergonomics thus are not a luxury, but an important safety issue, just as with cellular car phones.

Fortunately, the Becker has reasonable ergonomics, albeit with a learning curve, weird keypad and no tuning knob. There are ten one-push buttons to call up presets—ten presets for world band, 30 for FM—as well as for direct-frequency entry. An even bigger plus is that its "signal-seek" scan circuit works well. Tuning is precise, too—1 kHz increments throughout the longwave, mediumwave AM and world band ranges.

There's only one bandwidth, an ergonomic virtue even if normally two band-widths would be better. It is well chosen, being narrow enough to keep most interference at bay, yet wide enough to let through surprisingly pleasant audio.

Indeed, the Becker sounds magnificent for listening to world band programs, better than virtually any regular tabletop or portable model. If your ears crave rich, full audio, then the 2340 may have you looking forward to driving just to hear how pleasant world band can really sound. And not just world band—FM and mediumwave AM also perform commendably, and the FM comes with an RDS system for automatic identification of stations.

Limited Frequency Coverage

However, frequency coverage is only between 5900 and 15700 kHz. Daytime, that means you miss the 17, 19, 21 and 26 MHz segments, although of these only the first and third really count. Evenings, you can't tune in the growing roster of stations between 5730-5895 kHz, much less the Latin American and other stations found between 4750-5100 kHz.

Ditto the mediumwave AM band, which covers only 531-1600 kHz. That's a hundred kilohertz—ten channels—lower than the upper limit of AM in North America, and one silly kilohertz higher than the 530 kHz occupied by a couple of Canadian stations.

Birdies, Images, Chugging and Pauses

There are spurious "images" from signals 900 kHz higher, as well as a few silent-carrier "birdies," including one covering time stations on 10000 kHz. These cause no more of a problem than they do on some worthy small portables, such as the Grundig Yacht Boy 305. But they are there, and on a radio in this price class they shouldn't be.

Tuning can annoy, too. There's chugging during bandscanning, and the radio has to stop to "think" in silence for a second or two when coming onto a new station.

"World on Wheels" Works Well

Fortunately—after all, outside of Singapore and some other Asian locales it's the only serious act in town—the great-sounding Becker Mexico 2340 generally checks out well. And, unlike most other car radios that seem to be made like Dixie cups, it is manufactured to perform dependably over the passage of time.

final zero omitted; e.g., 5.75 rather than conventional 5.750. Poor spurious-signal ("image") rejection. Mediocre dynamic range. Does not receive 1635-1705 kHz portion of expanded AM band in the Americas. No signal-strength indicator. Clock in 12-hour format, not displayed independent of frequency. No travel power lock. No AC adaptor. Quality of construction appears to be below average. Mediumwave AM tuning increments not switchable, which may make for inexact tuning in some parts of the world other than where the radio was purchased. *Except Scotcade:* Does not tune important 7305-9495 and 21755-21850 kHz segments. No longwave.

Note: The Amsonic is available in at least five versions: AS-138 for China, AS-138-0 for Europe, AS-138-3 for USA/Canada, AS-138-4 for Japan, and AS-138-6 for other countries and Europe. Each version has FM and mediumwave AM ranges and channel spacing appropriate to the market region, plus the Japanese version replaces coverage of the 21 MHz band with TV audio.

Comment: Strong signals within the 7305-7595 kHz range can be tuned via the "image" signal 900 kHz down; e.g., 7435 kHz may be heard on 6535 kHz.

Verdict: Poorly made, no bargain.

The Jäger PL-440 is overpriced for what it offers.

★★

Jäger PL-440
Omega

Price: *Jäger:* $79.95 plus $6.00 shipping in the United States. *Omega:* 1,500 francs in Belgium.

Pro: Relatively inexpensive for a model with digital frequency display. Tuning aids include up/down slewing buttons with "signal-seek" scanning, and 20 station presets (five each for world band, FM, longwave and mediumwave AM). Relatively simple to operate for technology class. World Time clock. Snooze/timer features. Longwave. Antenna rotates and tilts, unusual in price class. Travel power lock.

Con: Mediocre build quality. Limited coverage of world band spectrum omits important 5800-5945, 15605-15695, 17500-17900 and 21450-21850 kHz ranges, among others. No tuning knob; tunes only via station presets and multi-speed up/down slewing/scanning. Tunes world band only in coarse 5 kHz steps. Tortoise-slow band-to-band tuning, remediable by using station presets as band selectors. Slow one-channel-at-a-time slewing is the only means for bandscanning between world band segments. Slightly insensitive to weak signals. Poor adjacent-channel rejection (selectivity). Even-numbered frequencies displayed with final zero omitted; e.g., 5.75 rather than conventional 5.750 or 5750. No signal-strength indicator. Clock not displayed independent of frequency display. Display not illuminated. Not offered with AC adaptor. Does not receive 1605-1705 kHz portion of expanded AM band in the Americas. Lacks selector for 9/10 kHz mediumwave AM steps.

Verdict: An Omega not to watch out for.

★½ **Aroma SEG SED-ECL88C** and **Giros R918**. Avoid.

LAP PORTABLES
Good for Home, Fair for Travel

If you're looking for a home set, yet one that also can be taken out in the backyard and on the occasional trip, a lap portable is probably your best bet. These are large enough to perform well and can sound pretty good, yet are compact enough to tote in your suitcase now and then. Most take 3-4 "D" (UM-1) or "C" (UM-2) cells, plus they may also use a couple of "AA" (UM-3) cells for their fancy computer circuits.

How large? Typically just under a foot wide—that's 30 cm—and weighing in around 3-4 pounds, or 1.3-1.8 kg. For air travel, that's okay if you are a dedicated listener, but a bit much otherwise. Too, larger sets with snazzy controls occasionally attract unwanted attention from suspicious customs and airport-security personnel in some parts of the world.

One model stands out for most listeners: the high-tech Sony ICF-2010, formerly also sold as the ICF-2001D. The revised Sony ICF-SW77, like opera, is not for everybody. With this high-tech wonder, it's either love or hate—little between.

Grundig's long-awaited Satellit 900 remains in the wings. According to the manufacturer, the original chip for it ceased to be manufactured, so the radio is being redesigned and improved to incorporate a newer chip. The official word from Grundig as we go to press is, "The Satellit radios (including the Satellit 900) will be coming out in 1998."

The best world band portable on the market is the Sony ICF-2010, a brisk seller that is available throughout North America. Elsewhere, it has to be ordered by post from American world band specialty firms.

★ ★ ★½   *Passport's Choice*

Sony ICF-2010

Price: $349.95 in the United States. CAN$599.00 in Canada. ¥4,500 (about $540) in China. Not distributed at retail in several parts of the world, but is available worldwide by mail order from U.S. and Canadian world band specialty firms.

Pro: High-tech synchronous detection with selectable sideband, thanks to a Sony proprietary chip with sideband phase canceling; on the '2010, this feature performs very well, indeed, reducing adjacent-channel interference and fading distortion on world band, longwave and mediumwave AM signals. This is further aided by two bandwidths which offer superior tradeoff between audio fidelity and adjacent-channel rejection (selectivity). Use of 32 separate station preset buttons in rows and columns is ergonomically the best to be found on any model, portable or tabletop, at any price—simply pushing one button one time brings in your station, a major convenience. Numerous other helpful tuning features. Weak-signal sensitivity better than most. Tunes and displays in precise 0.1 kHz increments. Separately displayed World Time clock. Alarm/snooze features, with four-event timer. Illuminated LCD. Travel power lock. Signal-strength indicator. Covers longwave and the Japanese FM band. FM unusually sensitive to weak signals, making it appropriate for fringe reception in some areas (see Con). Superior overall reception of fringe and distant

(DX) mediumwave AM signals. Some passable reception of air band signals (most versions). AC adaptor.

Con: Audio quality only average, with mediocre tone control. Because there are so many controls and high-tech features, they may initially intimidate or confuse, although thereafter this model tends to be straightforward to use. Station presets and clock/timer features immediately erase whenever computer batteries are replaced, and also sometimes when set is jostled (changing to a different brand of battery sometimes helps); this erasing also sometimes happens irregularly with no apparent cause on aging units. Wide bandwidth tends to be broad for world band reception, but narrower aftermarket (non-Sony) replacement filters reportedly cause sound to be muffled. "Signal-seek" scanning works poorly. Telescopic antenna swivel gets slack with use, requiring periodic adjustment of tension screw. Synchronous selectable sideband alignment can drift slightly with temperature and battery voltage, causing synchronous selectable sideband reception to be more muffled in one sideband than the other,

Sony ICF-2010: Engineering Triumph

In the early 1980s, I received a call from a group of Sony world band engineers who were visiting the United States. They wanted to meet with me, and as I was on the road I stopped by their motel in Cherry Hill, New Jersey.

The youngest of the group kept quiet throughout much of the conversation, but towards the end he indicated he was designing a new world band portable. The design strategy was refreshingly simple: He would look over the comments and suggestions from reviewers and customers, and try to design something that would address what they wanted, and a bit more. He also appeared to have a solid understanding of shortwave listening, which back then was something of a fad among young men in Japan.

The result, introduced in 1984—yes, *1984*, that's not a typo!—was the Sony ICF-2010, and the rest is history. Also offered for several years as the ICF-2001D, it is festooned not only with features, but also with banks of dedicated buttons to operate the radio without having to remember arcane numbers or wade through software trees. Not incidentally, it includes an all-time first: synchronous select-able sideband, which emanates from a proprietary chip developed by Sony for stereo AM.

Because the '2010 was so thoughtfully designed and technologically advanced, it was not only the best portable then, it still is now, some *14 years later*. Nothing in the history of world band radio—or much else in consumer electronics—comes close to equaling this record. Sony of America tells us not only that the '2010 continues to sell briskly, but that they have no plans whatsoever to discontinue it.

Compare this design *tour de force* with some of the models thrown on the market lately from Chinese, Taiwanese and other manufacturers—including the occasional stubbed toe from Sony. Even now, we see brand-new models that don't even cover world band segments that have been in use for over 15 years, or which have such broad selectivity as to border on the useless.

particularly with the narrow bandwidth. Synchronous selectable sideband does not switch off automatically during tuning. Lacks up/down slewing. Keypad not in telephone format. LCD clearly readable only when radio viewed from below. Chugs slightly when tuned. 100 Hz tuning resolution means that non-synchronous single-sideband reception can be mistuned by up to 50 Hz. In urban areas, FM band can overload badly, causing false "repeat" signals to appear (see Pro). Air band insensitive to weak signals. Recently, some Sony of America repair facilities appear to have assumed that any model introduced more than a few years ago must have been discontinued, and have refused to provide service for the '2010; this problem has been addressed by Sony, but should you encounter it, anyway, contact Sony headquarters in Park Ridge, New Jersey and press the matter with vigor. **Verdict:** Our panelists, like opinionated Supreme Court justices, usually issue split decisions, but not with this model. Since its introduction, it has always been, and very much still is, our unanimous favorite among portables. It is among the

Yet, such is the standard set by the '2010 that when Sony tried to discontinue it a few years back and replace it with a "new, improved" model, the ICF-SW77, the newbie had to be recalled. It was tweaked and returned to the market, but the '2010 continues to be sold, anyway, at least in some parts of the world.

Why hasn't the '2010 simply been upgraded slightly, to have improved audio quality, better FM dynamic range, more reliable memory retention and perhaps tighter bandwidth filters?

Truth is, the '2010 couldn't pass muster today at any firm, as with all those buttons and snappy features it simply costs too much to produce. However, the '2010 has been saved from museum status because its development costs were completely written off years ago. This has allowed it to remain profitable even with its relatively high production cost.

In the real world of large corporate engineering, trying to tweak the '2010 would rock the boat with a Pandora's box of procedures and approvals. Ergo, the Little Radio That Could quietly continues to lead the pack "as is."

Over the years, I've lost track of the name of that Sony engineer—perhaps appropriately, given the Japanese preference for group identity. But now, almost a decade and a half later, we should take a moment to tip our hats to this quiet, anonymous gentleman and his colleagues. Imagine what it would be like if men and women like him were designing PCs, for example—computers that could last five or six years instead of three or four simply by regarding the customer as someone to be pleased, rather than forced to the trough as often as possible.

Alas, there is no equivalent of the '2010 among PCs or much else these days. But somewhere in Japan there is an engineer long on common sense—someone who understood that engineering comes only *after* a full understanding of what can be done to cater to customers.

—Lawrence Magne

best for rejection of one of world band's major bugaboos, adjacent-channel interference, and yet it is able to retain a relatively wide audio bandwidth for listening pleasure. Alone among sophisticated receivers, it allows dozens of stations to be brought up literally at the single touch of a button. Except for everyday audio quality and urban FM, Sony's high-tech offering is the best performing portable—regardless of where you live—and is the only portable to approach portatop and tabletop performance.

An *RDI WHITE PAPER* is available for this model.

★ ★ ★½

Sony ICF-SW77
Sony ICF-SW77E

Price: $469.95 in the United States. CAN$699.00 in Canada. £339.95 in the United Kingdom. AUS$1,249.00 in Australia. ¥8,000 (about $960) in China.
Pro: A rich variety of tuning features, including innovative computer-type graphical interface not found on other world band models. Synchronous selectable sideband, which in most samples performs as it should, is exceptionally handy to operate; it significantly reduces fading distortion and adjacent-channel

Sony's ICF-SW77 is a solid performer, with an operating system that some love but others disdain.

interference on world band, longwave and mediumwave AM signals. Two well-chosen bandwidths provide superior adjacent-channel rejection. Tunes in exacting 50 Hz increments; displays in precise 100 Hz increments. Two illuminated multi-function liquid crystal displays. Pre-set world band segments. Keypad tuning. Tuning "knob" with two speeds. 162 station presets, including 96 frequencies stored by country or station name. "Signal-seek" scanning. Separately displayed World Time and local time clocks. Station name appears on LCD when station presets used. Signal-strength indicator. Flip-up chart for calculating time differences. VCR-type five-event timer controls radio and optional outboard recorder alike. Continuous bass and treble tone controls. Superior FM audio quality. Stereo FM through headphones. Receives longwave and Japanese FM. AC adaptor.
Con: Excruciatingly complex for many, but by no means all, to operate. Station presets can't be accessed simply, as they can on most models. Synthesizer chugging, as bad as we've encountered in our tests, degrades the quality of tuning by knob. Dynamic range only fair. Synchronous selectable sideband subject to imperfect alignment, both from factory and from seeming drift after purchase, causing synchronous selectable sideband reception to be more muffled in one sideband than the other, particularly with the narrow bandwidth. Flimsy telescopic antenna. Display illumination does not stay on with AC power. On mediumwave AM band, relatively insensitive, sometimes with spurious sounds during single-sideband reception; this doesn't apply to world band reception, however. Mundane reception of difficult FM signals. Signal-strength indicator over-reads.
Verdict: The '77, a generally superior performer since it was improved a few years back, uses innovative high technology in an attempt to make listening easier. Results, however, are a mixed

bag: What is gained in convenience in some areas is lost in others. The upshot is that whether using the '77 is enjoyable or a hair-pulling exercise comes down to personal taste. In our survey some relish it, most don't. Best bet: If you're interested, try it out first.

★ ★½

Radio Shack/Realistic DX-390
Roberts R827
Sangean ATS-818

The ATS-818 is one of Sangean's best performers. It is also available in North America as the Radio Shack DX-390 and in the United Kingdom as the Roberts R827.

Price: *Radio Shack/Realistic:* Usually $219.99, but as low as $169.99 during special sales, plus optional #273-1655 AC adaptor at Radio Shack stores in the United States. CAN$299.95 plus #273-1454 AC adaptor in Canada. No longer available in Australia. *Roberts:* £149.95 in the United Kingdom. *Sangean:* $174.95 in the United States. CAN$289.00 in Canada. £149.95 in the United Kingdom. AUS$349.00 in Australia.

Pro: Superior overall world band performance. Numerous tuning features, including 18 world band station presets. Two bandwidths for good fidelity/interference tradeoff. Superior spurious-signal ("image") rejection. Illuminated display. Signal-strength indicator. Two 24-hour clocks, one for World Time, with either displayed separately from frequency. Alarm/snooze/timer features. Travel power lock. FM stereo through headphones. Longwave. Superior quality of construction. *Sangean:* AC adaptor. *Radio Shack/Realistic:* 30-day money-back trial period in United States.

Con: Mutes when tuning knob turned quickly, making bandscanning difficult (*see* Note, below). Wide bandwidth a bit broad for world band reception. Keypad not in telephone format. For single-sideband reception, relies on a touchy variable control instead of separate LSB/USB switch positions. Does not come with tape-recorder jack. *Radio Shack/Realistic:* AC adaptor, which some readers complain causes hum and buzz, is extra.

Note: Tuning-knob muting reportedly can be eliminated, albeit with some side effects, by disabling or removing diode D29, according to reader Steven Johnson. We can't vouch for this or any other homebrew modification, but if you are comfortable working with electronic circuitry and wish to take the plunge, you can get further information by writing him at P.O. Box 80042, Fort Wayne IN 46898 USA. He tells us he will be glad to reply, but please enclose a self-addressed stamped envelope, or outside the United States a self-addressed envelope with 3 IRCs or $1, to cover return postage.

Verdict: A decent, predictable radio— performance and features, alike—but mediocre for bandscanning.

_____

The PASSPORT *portable-radio review team includes Lawrence Magne, Jock Elliott and Tony Jones, with laboratory measurements performed independently by Sherwood Engineering. Additional research by John Campbell, George Zeller and Craig Tyson.*

World Band Cassette Recorders

What happens if your favorite show comes on at an inconvenient time? Why, tape it, of course, with a world band cassette recorder—just like on your VCR.

Two models are offered, and there's no question which is better: the Sony. It's lots smaller, too, so it is less likely to raise eyebrows among airport security personnel. But its price difference over the Sangean—a nice, serviceable model—is considerable. Wrestle with your conscience, then decide.

Keep in mind that a few ordinary portables can be programmed to switch not only themselves on and off, but also a cassette recorder. Less handy, but it can be cheaper.

Enhanced for 1998

★ ★ ★¼

Sony ICF-SW1000T
Sony ICF-SW1000TS

Passport's Choice

Price: *ICF-SW1000T:* $499.95 in the United States. CAN$779.00 in Canada. £399.95 in the United Kingdom. *ICF-SW1000TS:* $549.95 in the United States.

Pro: Built-in recorder has two user-programmable on/off events. Relatively small, important for airport security. Synchronous selectable sideband reduces adjacent-channel interference and fading distortion on world band, longwave and mediumwave AM signals (*see Con*). Single bandwidth, especially when the sync feature is used, exceptionally effective at adjacent-channel rejection. Numerous helpful tuning features, including keypad, two-speed up/down slewing, 32 presets and "signal-seek" scanning. Effectively demodulates single-sideband signals, used by hams and utility stations. World Time clock, easy to set. Snooze/timer features. Illuminated display. Travel power lock. Easy on batteries. FM stereo through earpieces (supplied). Receives longwave and Japanese FM bands. Tape-reel-type outboard passive antenna accessory included. Dead-battery indicator. Comes standard with lapel mic and vinyl carrying case. *ICF-SW1000TS:* Comes with AN-LP1 active antenna system.

Con: Costly. Incredibly at this price, only one bandwidth, and no AC adaptor comes standard. Synchronous selectable sideband tends to lose lock if batteries not fresh, or if NiCd cells are used. No tuning knob. Clock not readable when radio switched on except for ten-seconds when button is pushed. No meaningful signal-strength indicator. No recording-level indicator. Lacks built-in mic and stereo mic facility. Lacks flip-out elevation panel; uses less-handy plug-in elevation tab, instead. FM sometimes overloads. Telescopic antenna exits from the side, which limits tilting choices for FM.

Note: With any compact or pocket Sony portable having synchronous selectable sideband, it's a good idea to check in the store, or immediately after purchase, to ensure it was aligned properly at the factory: 1) put fresh batteries into the radio, 2) tune in a local mediumwave AM station, and 3) adjust the "sync" function back and forth between LSB and USB. If all is well, the audio will sound similar in both cases—*similar*, not identical, as there will always be at least some difference. However, if one choice sounds significantly muddier and bassier than the other, the unit is probably out of alignment and you should select another sample.

Verdict: An innovative, neat little package—but it doesn't come cheap.

Radio Shack/Realistic DX-392
Roberts RC828
Sangean ATS-818CS
Siemens RK 670

★ ★½   ¢

Price: *Radio Shack:* Usually $259.99 in the United States, but as low as $199.99 during special sales. *Roberts:* £199.95 in the United Kingdom. *Sangean:* $249.95 in the United States; CAN$359.00 in Canada; AUS$399.95 in Australia.

Pro: Built-in cassette recorder. Price low relative to competition. Superior overall world band performance. Numerous tuning features, including 18 world band station presets. Two bandwidths for good fidelity/interference tradeoff. Superior spurious-signal ("image") rejection. Illuminated display. Signal-strength indicator. Two 24-hour clocks, one for World Time, with either displayed separately from frequency. Alarm/snooze/timer features. Travel power lock. FM stereo through headphones. Longwave. Built-in condenser mic. Superior quality of construction, including tape deck. *Sangean:* Supplied with AC adaptor. *Radio Shack/Realistic:* 30-day money-back trial period (in United States).

Con: Recorder has no multiple recording events, just one "on" time only (quits when tape runs out). Mutes when tuning knob turned quickly, making band-scanning difficult (see Note under review of regular Sangean ATS-818 portable). Wide bandwidth a bit broad for world band reception. Keypad not in telephone format. For single-sideband reception, relies on a touchy variable control instead of separate LSB/USB switch positions. Recorder has no level indicator, no stereo and no counter. Fast-forward and rewind controls installed facing backwards. *Radio Shack/Realistic:* AC adaptor, which some readers complain causes hum and buzz, is extra.

Verdict: Good value, but only single-event.

Best bet in world band cassette recorders is the Sony ICF-SW1000T, now also available with an outboard amplified antenna as the ICF-SW100TS.

Sangean's ATS-818CS, also available in North America from Radio Shack, in the U.K. from Roberts and in Europe from Siemens. Only single-event recording, but reasonably priced.

Oldies, Some Goodies

The following digital models reportedly have been discontinued, yet may still be available new at a limited number of retail outlets. Cited are typical recent sale prices in the United States ($) and United Kingdom (£). Prices elsewhere may differ.

★ ★ ★½   **Grundig Satellit 700**

An excellent offering, the favorite model of a broad swathe of regular world band program listeners. Withal, notably for bandscanning, not quite all it should be. Occasionally still available for under $500 in the United States, under CAN$650 in Canada and around £370 in the United Kingdom.

Panasonic RF-B65
Panasonic RF-B65D
Panasonic RF-B65L
★ ★ ★   **National B65**

A slightly fancier version of the current Panasonic RF-B45, this model is well constructed and easy to use. A good choice for Europe or eastern North America, where world band signals are relatively strong. Under $270 or £170.

★ ★ ★   **Sony ICF-SW7600**

Worthy and proven all-around performer. Similar to the current Sony ICF-SW7600G (see), but without synchronous selectable sideband. Under $200 or £180.

★ ★ ★   **Sangean ATS-808**   ¢

Very similar to the current ATS-808A, but a better value if you can find one. Under $120 in the United States.

★ ★ ★   **Sangean ATS 606**

Very similar to the current Sangean ATS 606A, but cheaper. Under $130 or CAN$220.

★ ★ ★½   **Sony ICF-SW33**

A good performer, but inconvenient to tune—something of a fancier version of the current Sony ICF-SW30. Still widely available at under $180, CAN$200 or £135.

Roberts R801
Sangean ATS 800A
★ ★   **Siemens RP 647G4**

Not competitive within its price class. Under $90 or CAN$130.

★ ★   **Sangean ATS-202**

Pocket model with lackluster performance and limited frequency coverage. Under $100 or CAN$120.

Analog Portables

With digitally tuned portables now commonplace and affordable, there's little reason to purchase an analog, or slide-rule-tuned, model. They lack every tuning aid except a knob, and their coarse indicators make it almost impossible to tell the frequency.

Among new models for 1998 is the Sony ICF-SW600, which is a bargain, considering its superior quality of sound and inboard power supply. It is being discontinued in the United States, where units should still be available throughout much of 1998, but will continue to be sold in various other parts of the world. The new "clamshell" Sony ICF-SW12 is noteworthy only for its sophisticated digital clock/alarm.

Pocket Analog Portables

★ ★ **Sony ICF-SW22.** Tiny, with superior spurious signal ("image") rejection, but tinny sound and limited frequency coverage.

★½ **Aiwa WR-A100, Grundig Yacht Boy 207, Grundig Yacht Boy 217, InterNational WR-689, Panasonic RF-B11, Radio Shack/Realistic DX-351, Roberts R101, Sangean MS-101, Sangean MS-103, Sangean MS-103L, Sangean SG-789A, Sangean SG-789L, Sharper Image VA100, Sony ICF-SW12.**

★ **International R-110**

Compact Analog Portables

★½ **Amsonic AS-912, Cougar H-116, Elektro AC 100, International AC 100, Kchibo KK-168, Kchibo KK-210B, MCE-7760, National B20, Pace, Panasonic RF-B20, Panasonic RF-B20L, Radio Shack/Realistic DX-350, Roberts R621, Sangean SG 621, Sangean SG 631, Sangean SG-700L, SEG Precision World SED 110, Siemens RK 710, Sony ICF-SW10, SoundTronic Multiband Receiver, TEC 235TR.**

★ **Apex 2138, Cougar H-88, Cougar RC210, Garrard Shortwave Radio 217, Grundig Traveller II (analog version), International MT-718, Opal OP-35, Panashiba FX-928, Precision World SED 901, Shiba Electronics FX-928, Siemens RK 702, Silver International MT-798, Windsor 2138.**

Analog Lap Portables

★ ★ ¢ **Sony ICF-SW600.** Superior audio and built-in AC power supply.

★ **Alconic Series 2959, Dick Smith D-2832, Electro Brand 2971, Electro Brand SW-2000, Rhapsody Multiband, Shimasu Multiband, Steepletone MBR-7, Steepletone MBR-8, Venturer Multiband.**

Analog Oldies

★ ★ **Sony ICF-4900II, Sony ICF-4920, Sony ICF-5100, Sony ICF-7601, Sony ICF-SW15, Sony ICF-SW20.**

★½ **Grundig Yacht Boy 230, Magnavox AE 3205 GY, Magnavox D1835, Magnavox OD1875BK, Philips AE 3205 GY, Philips D1835, Philips OD1875BK.**

★ **National B10, Panasonic RF-B10.**

Portatop Receivers for 1998

Superior Performance at Home or Outdoors

Most of us buy a world band radio not for just one room, but to be used throughout the house—maybe outdoors, too. That's why portables sell so well. Yet, even the very best portables don't sound as good as some tabletop models. Nor can they cut the mustard with really tough signals, although the Sony ICF-2010 comes close.

Solution: Combine the most desirable characteristics of portables and tabletops into one single receiver, a portatop. For years, now, manufacturers have been nibbling at the edges of this idea. Finally, they're getting it right.

What Passport's Ratings Mean
(Good Fine Print)

Star ratings: ★ ★ ★ ★ ★ is best. PASSPORT awards stars solely for overall performance and meaningful features, plus to some extent ergonomics and build quality. Price, appearance, country of manufacture and the like are not taken into account. With portatop models there is roughly equal emphasis on the ability to flush out tough, hard-to-hear signals, and program-listening quality with stronger broadcasts.

Passport's Choice. La crème de la crème. Our test team's personal picks of the litter—models we would buy or have bought for our personal use.

¢: A bargain.

Prices: Approximate selling, or "street," prices (including VAT, where applicable). Prices vary plus or minus, so take them as the general guide they are meant to be.

★ ★ ★ ★ ½ *Passport's Choice*

Drake SW8

Price: $779.95 in the United States. CAN$1,129.95 in Canada. £699.00 in the United Kingdom. AUS$1,599.00 in Australia.

Drake's SW8 carries the winning combination of full-sized portability and near-superset performance.

Since 1994, Drake has been improving its innovative SW8 receiver—as well as raising the price. Now, it is a solid performer for fastidious listeners and DXers who don't wish to compromise performance when portability is required.

Pro: Portatop design approaches tabletop performance with many of the conveniences of a portable; portability made easier by optional carrying case. Above-average audio quality with internal speaker or headphones. High-tech synchronous selectable sideband feature reduces adjacent-channel interference and fading distortion on world band, longwave and mediumwave AM signals. Three bandwidths provide worthy adjacent-channel rejection. Continuous tone control. Numerous helpful tuning aids, including 70 presets. Helpful signal-strength indicator, digital. Single-sideband reception well above the portable norm. Weak-signal sensitivity excellent with external antenna. Superior blocking performance aids usable sensitivity. Two timers and 24-hour clocks (see Con). Display illuminated. FM, in mono through speaker but stereo through headphones, performs well. Covers longwave down to 100 kHz and VHF aeronautical band. Superior factory service. Fifteen-day money-back trial period if ordered from the factory or certain dealers.

Con: Sounds "hissy" when used with built-in antenna; clipping on a length of wire to the built-in antenna helps greatly. Bereft of certain features—among them notch filter, adjustable noise blanker and passband tuning—found on premium-priced tabletop models. Ergonomics mediocre, including pushbuttons that rock on their centers. Key pushes must each be done within three seconds, lest receiver wind up being mistuned or placed into an unwanted operating mode. Wide bandwidth—nominally 6 kHz, actually 7.8 kHz—a bit broader than it should be. Drake's 120 VAC power supply, via a separate outboard adaptor. Telescopic antenna doesn't swivel fully for best FM reception. Clocks don't display when frequency is shown. Carrying/elevation handle clunky to adjust, with adjustment stops that can break if handle forced. Optional MS8 outboard speaker not equal to receiver's fidelity potential.

Verdict: The current version of the Drake SW8 is very nearly everything a top-notch portatop should be: performance only a skootch below that of the fanciest tabletop supersets, yet at a price that's lower, with portability and FM thrown in. A superior all-around receiver for use both indoors and out, but hiss with built-in antenna continues to be a drawback.

An *RDI WHITE PAPER* is available for this model.

Enhanced Version Planned for 1998
★ ★ ★ ★

Lowe HF-150
Lowe HF-150E

Price, without keypad or other options:
HF-150: $499.95 in the United States (add about $130 for HF-150M marine version,

not tested). CAN$899.00 in Canada. £389.95 in the United Kingdom (add about £20 for HF-150M marine version, not tested). AUS$1,150.00 in Australia. *HF-150E:* £499.00. *Keypad:* $89.95 in the United States. £39.95 in the United Kingdom.

Pro: *HF-150:* Attractive price for level of performance. Top-notch world band and mediumwave AM audio quality—a treat for the ears—provided a good external speaker or simple headphones are used. High-tech synchronous detection reduces fading distortion on world band, longwave and mediumwave AM signals. Synchronous detection circuit, which holds lock unusually well, also allows for either selectable-sideband or double-sideband reception. Synchronous detector switches out automatically during tuning, which aids in bandscanning. Exceptionally rugged cast-aluminum housing of a class normally associated with professional-grade equipment. Mouse keypad, virtually foolproof and a *de rigeur* option, performs superbly for tuning and presets. Sixty presets store frequency and mode. Tunes, but does not display, in exacting 8 Hz

Entertainer David Letterman, who can afford any radio, uses the Lowe HF-150 to hear the BBC World Service, his favorite station.

increments, the most precise found in any model with portable characteristics. Single-sideband reception well above the portable norm. Small footprint saves space and adds to portability. Optional accessory kit, necessary for real portability, provides telescopic antenna, rechargeable nickel-cadmium batteries (four hours per charge) and shoulder strap with built-in antenna. High weak-signal sensitivity with accessory antenna helps make for exceptional portable performance and obviates the need for a large outdoor antenna. Excellent operating manual. Available with IF-150 optional computer interface. Superior factory service.

Con: *HF-150:* Grossly inferior front-end selectivity can result in creation of spurious signals if the radio is connected to a significant external antenna or used near mediumwave AM transmitters; depending upon several variables, this may be a couple of kilometers or miles, or it may be several. (Lowe's excellent optional PR-150 preselector eliminates this disadvantage, albeit at a hefty cost in treasure, bulk and simplicity of operation. Also, Kiwa Electronics's BCB Rejection Filter accomplishes much the same thing more simply and at lower cost. However, neither solution is practical during portable operation.) Requires AK-150 option to be a true portatop. Lacks FM broadcast reception, normally found on portables. Built-in speaker produces only okay audio quality as compared to simple earphones or a good external speaker. No tone control. Frequency displays no finer than 1 kHz resolution. Lacks lock indicator or similar aid (e.g., finer frequency-display resolution) for proper use of synchronous detector, which can result in less-than-optimum detector performance. Keypad overpriced. Bereft of certain features—among them notch filter, adjustable noise blanker and passband tuning—found on premium-priced tabletop models. Lacks signal-strength indicator. Operation of some front-panel button functions tends to be confusing until you get the hang of it. Light weight allows radio to slide on table during operation more than do heavier models. Lacks much-needed elevation feet. Erratic contact on outboard-speaker socket. Display not illuminated. AC power supply via a separate outboard adaptor, rather than inboard. *Portable operation:* Telescopic antenna tilts properly, but is clumsy to rotate. Comes with no convenient way to attach keypad to cabinet (remediable by affixing sticky-backed Velcro). This—plus the use of an outboard AC adaptor, the need for an external speaker or headphones for proper fidelity, and no dial illumination—all conspire to make this model less handy to tote around than a conventional portable.

Enhancement Planned for 1998: According to the manufacturer, the HF-150E "Europa" version, due out shortly, will have improved bandwidth filters, much-needed front-end bandpass filters, screened RF coils and high-quality diodes as used in other "Europa" models.

Verdict: The shortcomings of the pioneering HF-150 portatop are by now beginning to loom large, although the upcoming "Europa" version, not yet available to be tested, should help resolve certain of these, such as front-end selectivity. The regular HF-150 sorely needs to be upgraded with some sort of workable front end, a better speaker, dial illumination, FM broadcast reception and true portability, among other improvements. Yet, at under $600 with keypad in the United States it remains a tough and affordable little radio. Its outstanding synchronous selectable sideband provides superb fidelity on world band, longwave and mediumwave AM—*if* you don't live near any longwave or mediumwave AM transmitters. If audio quality is your overriding passion, with other factors being secondary, this is the portatop model to get—indeed, for audiophiles this is arguably the *tabletop* model to get, provided you use a high-quality outboard passive or amplified speaker or headphones. But beware the possible need at your location for an outboard preselector or high-pass filter, as front end selectivity on this radio is as bad as we've ever encountered.

An *RDI WHITE PAPER* is available for this model.

Choosing a Premium Receiver?

Get premium advice before you buy!

If you could, you'd spend weeks with each receiver, learning its charms and foibles. Seeing for yourself how it handles—*before* you spend.

Now, you can do the next best thing—better, some folks insist. Radio Database International White Papers®, from the PASSPORT® TO WORLD BAND RADIO library of in-depth test reports, put the facts right into your hands.

We test run each receiver for you. Put it through comprehensive laboratory and bench tests to find out where it shines. And where it doesn't.

Then our panel takes over: DXers, professional monitors, program listeners—experts all. They're mean, grumpy, hypercritical . . . and take lots of notes. They spend weeks with each receiver, checking ergonomics and long-run listening quality with all kinds of stations. Living with it day and night.

With PASSPORT's RDI White Papers®, these findings—the good, the bad and the ugly—are yours, along with valuable tips on how to operate your radio to best advantage. Each receiver report covers one model in depth, and is $6.95 postpaid in the United States; US$6.95 or CAN$9.95 in Canada; US$9.95 airmail in the European Union, Scandinavia, Australia, New Zealand and Japan; US$14.95 registered air elsewhere. Separate reports are

available for each of the following premium radios:

AOR AR3030
AOR AR7030*
Drake R8B*
Drake SW8
Icom IC-R71A/D/E (while supplies last)
Icom IC-R9000
Japan Radio NRD-535/NRD-535D
Kenwood R-5000
Lowe HF-150
Sony ICF-2010/ICF-2001D
Yaesu FRG-100
***Available from early 1998**

Reports for other models will be added throughout 1998. Request our latest info sheet, or visit our Web site at http://www.passport.com.

Other PASSPORT RDI White Papers available:

How to Interpret Receiver Specifications and Lab Tests
Popular Outdoor Antennas

Available from world band radio dealers or direct. For VISA/MasterCard orders, call our 24-hour automated order line: +1 (215) 794-8252, or fax +1 (215) 794 3396 or Website www.passport.com. Or send your check or money order (Pennsylvania add 42¢ per report), specifying which report or reports you want, to:

U.S.: EEB, Grove, Universal
Canada: Sheldon Harvey (Radio Books)
Japan: IBS Japan
Latin America: IBS Latin America

Passport RDI White Papers
Box 300
Penn's Park, PA 18943 USA

"We strongly recommend the PASSPORT RDI White Papers before purchasing any receiver over $100. The *Consumer Reports* of shortwave radio." —What's New, *Monitoring Times*

Tabletop Receivers for 1998

Banner Year for New Models

Tabletop receivers exist to flush out tough game—faint stations, often swamped by competing signals. That's why they are prized by serious radio aficionados known as "DXers," a term derived from telegraph code meaning long distance.

But these tabletop models aren't for everybody. If all you want to hear are non-DX stations and a portable can't quite hack it, you can also get excellent results with a portatop model.

Outstanding Models for 1998

1998 is a banner year for new and revised tabletop models—two from Drake, two from Lowe, and one each from AOR, Japan Radio and Icom. American prices range from $280 to $1,850, with European prices being anywhere from about the same to half-again more and Australian prices being higher yet.

Of these, the Drake R8B is a knockout, once again underscoring that Drake has

become to non-portable world band receivers what Hewlett-Packard is to laser printers—offering top-flight performance and worthy ergonomics at lowball prices, resulting in dominant market share.

Well, in North America, anyway, as Drake products are decidedly more costly in Europe. There, the good news is that the superb British-made AOR AR7030, also available in America, is now offered in an enhanced "Plus" version.

Additionally, Japan Radio, whose construction standards are among the industry's finest, has entered the value segment with the NRD-345. And the new Target HF3, sold in North America as the Lowe SRX100, sets a new standard for low-cost tabletop receivers.

Still, for most applications there is still not a tabletop model under $500 that is really attractive. In that price class, the portable Sony ICF-2010 continues to make more sense for most.

For scanner buffs who also want worthy world band reception, the new Icom IC-R8500 should do

The new Drake SW2, left, and Japan Radio NRD-345 compare favorably with the Sony ICF-2010 portable. Atop radio at left is a Sherwood SE-3 accessory and speaker.   Howard Karashoff

the trick. It's not tops for world band, but among "dc-to-daylight" receivers on the sunny side of $2,000 it is the best choice.

Finally, the gilt-edged Watkins-Johnson HF-1000 "ultimate superset" has undergone a number of enhancements since its introduction in 1994, and sometime in 1998 Japan Radio plans to introduce the NRD-545 with digital signal processing and filtering.

More "Wall Warts" Appear

An unwelcome footnote is that more new models are showing up with outboard "wall wart" AC adaptors in lieu of traditional inboard power supplies. These allow manufacturers to forego UL and certain other safety approvals, so long as the adaptor is properly certified. However, these adaptors are believed to be somewhat more prone to catch fire, even when they are properly fused and the radio is off. A few also radiate spurious AC fields, causing hum via the antenna lead-in. Best bets are either to avoid receivers with outboard AC adaptors, or to switch your receiver on at the adaptor using a switched plug strip.

Big Guns for American West—Aussies, too

Tabletop supersets, like portatops, are the heavy artillery needed where signals are weak, but folks are strong. Places like the North American Midwest and West, or Australia and New Zealand. Even elsewhere there can be a problem when world band signals have to follow paths over or near the geomagnetic North Pole. To check, place a string on a globe—a map won't do—between you and where signals come from. If the string passes near or above latitude 60% N, beware.

Hear More Daytime Signals

With the end of the Cold War, some stations have compressed their hours of transmission. The result is that some excellent English-language programs are heard only during the day.

Daytime signals are weaker, especially when they're not beamed to your part of the world. However, thanks to the scattering properties of shortwave, you can still eavesdrop on many of these "off-beam" signals. But it's harder, and that's where a well-rated tabletop's longer reach comes in.

Good High-Rise Listening, but No FM

In high-rise buildings—especially in urban areas—portables can disappoint. Reinforced buildings soak up signals from afar, and local broadcast and cellular transmitters can interfere.

Here, your best bet for bringing in tough stations is to connect a good tabletop or portatop model to an insulated-wire antenna that runs along, or protrudes just outside, a window or balcony. Also try an ordinary telescopic car antenna sticking out from a window or balcony ledge, flagpole-style. If your radio has a built-in preamplifier, all the better. With portatop models, the built-in preamplifier can be accessed by connecting your antenna to the receiver's whip-antenna input.

You can also try amplified ("active") antennas that have reception elements and amplifiers in separate modules, not together as part of the same cabinet. Properly made active antennas are found only at world band specialty outlets, but even these sometimes produce false signals—although Datong models have traditionally been superior in this regard. The quality of performance of active antennas is very location-specific, so try to purchase these on a returnable basis.

Most tabletop receivers are pricier than portables. For that extra money you tend to get not only better performance, but also a better-made device. However, what you rarely find in a tabletop is reception of the everyday 87.5-108 MHz FM band. It's an omission based on the evolution of shortwave receivers along a non-consumer-electronics path—specifically, most tabletop receiver manufacturers have roots in, or also still manufacture, equipment for the "ham" radio community.

External Antenna a "Must"

Nearly all tabletop models require an outboard world band antenna. Even those that have a built-in antenna should have a first-rate outboard antenna to perform to full advantage.

Tabletop performance is greatly determined by antenna quality and placement. A first-rate world band outdoor wire antenna, such as those made by Antenna Supermarket and Alpha Delta, usually sells for under $100—a bargain, given all they do. If you don't live in an apartment, this is the way to go. Check with the PASSPORT Radio Database International White Paper, *Popular Outdoor Antennas*, for the full scoop.

Virtually Every Model Tested

Every tabletop receiver evaluated, regardless of its introduction year, has been put through stringent testing hurdles we have honed since 1977, when we first started reviewing world band equipment.

First, receivers are thoroughly tested in the laboratory, using techniques we developed specially for the strenuous requirements of world band reception. Each receiver then undergoes extensive hands-on evaluation, usually for months, before we begin preparing our detailed internal report. That report, in turn, forms the basis for this PASSPORT REPORTS.

Unabridged Reports Available
These unabridged laboratory and hands-on test results are too exhaustive to reproduce here. However, for many serious tabletop models they are available as PASSPORT's Radio Database International White Papers—details on availability are elsewhere in this book.

Tips for Using this Section

Receivers are listed in order of suitability for listening to difficult-to-hear world band stations. Important secondary consideration is given to audio fidelity and ergonomics. We cite street prices, which are as of when we go to press. Of course,

Passport's Choice

For 1998, *Passport's Choice* tabletop models are limited to that handful which has been found to have superlative performance.

Only four models have earned this distinction—the **Watkins-Johnson HF-1000, Drake R8B, AOR AR7030** and the **Japan Radio NRD-535D**. Of these, the Drake will almost certainly have the widest appeal because of price and operating convenience. Yet, the current version of the Watkins-Johnson is the ultimate in world band DX machines, albeit by only a slight amount, and for less money the unusual AOR comes quite close. The Japan Radio offering stands out for its superior ergonomics and quality of construction, along with competitive DX performance.

these prices vary plus or minus, so take them as the general guide they are meant to be.

Unless otherwise stated, all tabletop models have:

- Digital frequency synthesis and display.
- Full coverage of at least the 155-29999 kHz longwave, mediumwave AM and shortwave spectra—including all world band frequencies—but no coverage of the FM broadcast band (87.5-108 MHz).
- A wide variety of helpful tuning features.
- Synchronous selectable sideband, which reduces interference and fading distortion.
- Proper demodulation of non-world-band shortwave signals. These include single-sideband and CW (Morse code); also, with suitable ancillary devices, radioteletype and radio fax.
- Meaningful signal-strength indication.
- Illuminated display.

What Passport's Rating Symbols Mean

Star ratings: ★ ★ ★ ★ ★ is best. We award stars mainly for overall performance and meaningful features, plus to some extent ergonomics and build quality. Price, appearance, country of manufacture and the like are not taken into account. With tabletop models there is a slightly greater emphasis than with portables or portatops on the ability to flush out tough, hard-to-hear signals, as this is one of the main reasons these sets are chosen.

Passport's Choice. La crème de la crème. Our test team's personal picks of the litter—models we would buy or have bought for our personal use.

¢: No, this doesn't mean cheap. *None* of these models is cheap! Rather, it denotes a model that costs appreciably less than usual for the level of performance provided.

PROFESSIONAL-GRADE MONITOR RECEIVERS

Get what you pay for? Not necessarily.

Costly professional-grade monitor receivers are designed and made for military, commercial and surveillance applications. These activities have only some things in common with the needs of world band listeners, unless you're bouncing around mountain trails in a Hummer. Result: They usually provide little or no improvement in performance over regular tabletop models costing a fraction as much.

There is one exception, the Watkins-Johnson HF-1000, especially when equipped with the fidelity-enhancing Sherwood SE-3 accessory. But be prepared not only for sticker shock, but also to be exacting in selecting and erecting a suitable antenna if you want it to soar to its full potential.

Retested for 1998

★ ★ ★ ★ ★   *Passport's Choice*

Watkins-Johnson HF-1000

Price: *HF-1000:* $3,799.00 in the United States. CAN$5,400 in Canada. £4,495.00 in the United Kingdom. AUS$7,900 in Australia. *Sherwood SE-3 MK III accessory:* $495.00 plus shipping worldwide.

Pro: Unsurpassed reception of weak world band DX signals. Exceptional reception of "utility" stations. Generally superior audio quality (*see* Con), especially when used with the Sherwood SE-3 fidelity-enhancing accessory and a worthy external speaker (*see* below). Unparalleled bandwidth flexibility, with no less than 58 outstandingly high-quality bandwidths. Digital signal processing (DSP). Tunes and displays in extremely precise .001 kHz increments. Extraordinary operational flexibility—virtually every receiver parameter is adjustable. One hundred station presets. Synchronous detection reduces distortion with world band, mediumwave AM and longwave signals (*see* Con). Built-in preamplifier. Tunable notch filter. Highly adjustable scanning of both frequency ranges and channel presets. Easy-to-read displays. Large tuning knob. Can be fully and effectively computer and remotely controlled. Passband tuning (*see* Con). Built-in test equipment (BITE) diagnostics. Built-in 455 kHz IF output makes for instant installation of Sherwood SE-3 accessory (*see* below). Superior factory service.

Con: Very expensive. Static and modulation splash sound harsher than with most other models, although this has been improved somewhat in the latest version of the receiver's operating software. Complex to operate to full advantage. Synchronous detection not sideband-selectable, so it does not aid in reduction of adjacent-channel interference. Requires coaxial antenna feed line to avoid receiver-generated digital noise emanating from audio output connector; however, thanks to a connector design change this problem is now less serious than it was with early production units (indeed, early production units also emanated digital noise from the headphone socket, but this was quickly resolved with a new, no-noise socket). Passband tuning operates only in CW mode. Jekyll-and-Hyde ergonomics: sometimes wonderful, sometimes awful. No traditional cabinet, and front-panel rack "ears" protrude. In principle, mediocre front-end selectivity; however, problems were not apparent during listening tests; and, if needed (say, if you live very close to a mediumwave AM station), a sub-octave preselector option can be added or installed at factory. Cumbersome operating manual.

Note: Within the Americas and many other parts of the world, the $599.95 op-

The "ultimate superset" for DXing is the Watkins-Johnson HF-1000, originally designed for the U.S. government's most sensitive intelligence-gathering operations. Fully equipped, this "James Bond Special" comes to $4,893.95 . . . not including speaker!

tional sub-octave preselector offered by Watkins-Johnson is rarely necessary. However, within Europe and other strong-signal parts of the world, the preselector may improve spurious-signal rejection.

Improved Performance with Accessory: George Zeller, one of our panelists, has been using his personal HF-1000 in combination with a Sherwood SE-3 outboard accessory for some time, now, to enhance performance at home and on DX-peditions. George reports emphatically that, yes, even this top-rated $3,800 receiver is noticeably better with the SE-3, and installation takes about one minute and no tools. For starters, the receiver has only double-sideband synchronous detection, whereas the SE-3 allows it to have synchronous selectable sideband, a major improvement. The receiver's passband tuning operates only in the CW mode, but the SE-3 allows for passband tuning in all modes. Too, with the SE-3 in use no receiver-generated digital noise is present, as the receiver's audio output no longer needs to be used. Finally, with the SE-3 the receiver's audio quality improves noticeably.

Verdict: In its latest incarnation, the HF-1000 is, by a hair, the ultimate machine for down-and-dirty DXing where money is no object. With a final solution to the digital hash problem—and the addition of a tone control, passband tuning and synchronous selectable sideband—the '1000 would have been even better, especially for program listening. Fortunately, the Sherwood SE-3 accessory remedies all these problems, and improves audio fidelity, to boot. For those who don't wish to go the SE-3 route, the Alpha-Delta "DX-Ultra" antenna eliminates nearly all the hash problem. Thus, the HF-1000 now is exceptionally well-suited to demanding aficionados with suitable financial wherewithal—provided they want a high degree of manual receiver control.

★ ★ ★ ★

Icom IC-R9000

Price: $6,199.00 to authorized purchasers in the United States. CAN$9,399.00 in Canada. £4,080.00 in the United Kingdom. No longer available in Australia.

Pro: Exceptional tough-signal performance (*see* Note, below). Flexible, above-average audio for a tabletop model when used with suitable outboard speaker. Three AM-mode bandwidths (*see* Note, below). Tunes and displays frequency in precise 0.01 kHz increments. Video display of radio spectrum occupancy, a rarely found feature. Sophisticated scanner/timer. Extraordinarily broad coverage of radio spectrum, including portions forbidden to be listened to by the general public in the United States. Exceptional assortment of flexible operating controls and sockets. Good ergonomics. Superb reception of utility and ham signals. Two 24-hour clocks.

Icom's IC-R9000 includes a video display.

Con: In the United States, certain members of Congress have been overheard saying rude things over their non-digital cellular phones, so the Federal government now bans sales to the public of receivers, such as the '9000, which can hear cellular frequencies—notwithstanding that cellular is going digital and thus will no longer be amenable to eavesdropping. Dreadfully expensive. No synchronous selectable sideband. Power supply runs hot, although over the years this does not appear to have caused premature component failure. Both AM-mode bandwidths too broad for most world band applications. Both single-sideband bandwidths almost identical. Dynamic range merely adequate. Reliability, especially when roughly handled, may be wanting. Front-panel controls of only average construction quality.

Note: The above star rating can be viewed as conservative if, at a minimum, the barn-wide 11.3 kHz AM-mode bandwidth filter is changed to something in the vicinity of 4.5-5.5 kHz. Too, when suitably enhanced by Sherwood Engineering, the R9000 reportedly is an outstanding receiver; however, we have not tested this upgraded version, and for it to work Sherwood has to modify the 10.7 MHz IF output to 455 kHz.

Verdict: The Icom IC-R9000, with at least one changed AM-mode bandwidth filter—available from some world band specialty firms—is pretty much right up there with the best-performing models for DX reception of faint, tough signals. That is, of course, if you're allowed to buy one in the first place; best bet for Americans is to order one by mail from Canada. This is especially true if you have the fingers of a safecracker and don't mind using the set's SSB circuitry to manually tune AM-mode signals (so-called manual ECSS reception). Where it shines is if you want a visual indication of spectrum occupancy and certain other characteristics of stations within a designated segment of the radio spectrum. Nevertheless, this model has been around for several years, and other models now offer virtually the same level, or even better, construction quality and performance, plus synchronous selectable sideband—sadly lacking on the 'R9000—for far less money.

 An *RDI WHITE PAPER* is available for this model.

The Drake R8B, new for 1998, gets everything right and costs less than most other PASSPORT's CHOICE tabletop models. A winner!

TABLETOP RECEIVERS

If you want a top performer to unearth tough signals, read on. Five-star tabletop models should satisfy even the fussiest, and four-star models are no slouches, either.

The best tabletop models are the Ferraris and Mercedes of the radio world. As with their automotive counterparts, like-ranked receivers may come out of the curve at the same speed, though how they do it can differ greatly from model to model. So if you're thinking of choosing from the top end, study each contender in detail.

New for 1998

★ ★ ★ ★ ★ *Passport's Choice*

Drake R8B

Price: $1,199.00 for factory-direct orders in the United States. CAN$1,689.00 in Canada. Prices elsewhere to be determined after production commences.
Pro: Superior all-round performance for listening to world band programs and hunting faint signals. Superior audio quality, especially with suitable outboard speaker or headphones. Highly improved selectable-sideband synchronous detector excels at reducing distortion caused by fading, and at diminishing or eliminating adjacent-channel interference. Five bandwidths, four suitable for world band, among the best configurations of any model tested. Highly flexible operating controls, including a powerful tunable AF notch filter and an excellent passband tuning control. Superior reception of mediumwave AM, amateur and utility signals. Tunes and displays in precise 0.01 MHz increments. Superior blocking performance. Slow/fast/off AGC with superior performance characteristics. Superior noise blanker. Sophisticated scanning functions. All station presets can be quickly accessed via tuning knob and slew buttons. Built-in preamplifier. Accepts two antennas which are selectable via front panel. Two 24-hour clocks, with seconds displayed numerically and timer features. Superior factory service. Fifteen-day money-back trial period if ordered from the factory or certain dealers. *Tentative:* Superior dynamic range, which will be cross-checked when production units become available.
Con: Notch filter extremely fussy to adjust, to the point where many listeners report that they don't bother using it. Virtually requires a good outboard speaker for non-headphone listening, but the optional Drake MS8 outboard speaker is not equal to the receiver's audio potential; try a good amplified computer speaker or high-efficiency passive speaker instead. Lightweight tuning knob lacks flywheel effect.
Note about Unit Tested: A late-development pre-production unit was tested, as this was all which was available as we went to press. Although our tests suggest

that this prototype probably performs very close to what we would expect from a production unit, some differences are inevitable. Thus, we will retest the R8B in depth when it becomes available as a production receiver, then issue the results as a new RDI White Paper.

Verdict: Yes, the Watkins-Johnson HF-1000 is a skootch better as a DX receiver. And yes, the AOR AR7030 has slightly superior dynamic range, audio fidelity and synchronous detection. And yes, the Japan Radio NRD-535 has the best ergonomics. But the Drake R8B is the only receiver we have ever tested—portable, portatop or tabletop—that gets *everything* right, where there isn't something important missing or sputtering, or ergonomics are wanting.

Evaluation of New Model: The R8B tabletop communications receiver is electrically identical to its predecessor, the R8A, but with much-improved selectable-sideband synchronous detection, 1000 memory presets and faster scanning. This new receiver covers from 0.1 MHz (0.15 MHz in the European version) through 30 MHz, and an optional VHF converter adds coverage of 35-55 and 108-174 MHz. Reception modes are AM, LSB, USB, CW, RTTY and narrow-band FM. The R8B, which uses a first-rate inboard power supply, can be operated from 90-110, 108-132, 180-220 or 216-264 VAC, 50-60 Hz, or from 11-16 VDC through a DC connector on the rear panel.

The R8B incorporates features highly desired by program listeners and tough-signal hunters, including no less than five usable bandwidths (four for voice), passband tuning control (for all modes except NBFM), selectable-sideband synchronous detection, two VFOs, 1000 memory presets that store just about every receiver operating parameter, two selectable antenna inputs, keypad and multi-speed knob tuning, up/down slewing in 100 kHz increments, all-mode squelch, a variety of sophisticated scanning options, a tunable audio notch filter, two-level noise blanking that works extremely well, two 24-hour clocks, a timer, an attenuator, a switchable shortwave preamplifier, an analog signal-strength meter, a front-panel-display dimmer, plus RF gain and tone controls. A large LCD serves as "information central" for the R8B, displaying the status of just about every receiver control.

You can tag each memory preset with a seven-digit alphanumeric name, as well as its numeric frequency. A nice touch is that a function key allows you to decide whether or not the name of the preset should be displayed when poking through the memory channels.

The R8B can display the frequency as 9.750 MHz, 9.750.0 MHz, 9.750.00 MHz, 9750 kHz, 9750.0 kHz or 9750.00 kHz, depending upon which display and tuning-step options you select. To tilt the receiver at comfortable angle for tabletop operation, the R8B comes equipped with a sturdy flip-down metal rod.

There is a single button for selecting each of the five bandwidths, plus an AUTO button that automatically selects the bandwidth for you—an option few are likely to utilize. There is also a button for each of the operating modes, so in all this receiver is ergonomically acceptable.

In our earlier lab tests, the R8A earned high ratings in virtually every measurement of receiver performance. The only notable exceptions were dynamic range and the related third-order intercept point, which were only fair. Since both affect a receiver's ability to handle powerful nearby signals, an improvement here would be welcome.

So we were pleasantly surprised to find a substantial improvement in the R8B's third-order intercept point. In most measurements of receiver performance, we had expected the R8B to be virtually identical to the R8A, and most of our laboratory measurements bore this out. Those differences we did find—such as the improved third-order intercept point—could be the result of our having tested a pre-production unit, or it could even reflect the normal variation from sample-to-sample. We will know better once we fully test a production unit.

The biggest change in the R8B results from what is essentially a "transplant." Drake's "doctors" removed the old R8A synchronous detection circuit and replaced it with the newer and better "sync" circuit used in the latest version of the Drake SW8 portatop. The result is a greatly improved synchronous detector that offers the options of double-sideband or select-able-sideband synchronous detection.

To activate the synchronous detector, you press the AM button. Press it a second time, and the receiver is in double-sideband synchronous detection. You can then use the R8B's outstanding passband tuning control, like on the R8A, to "roll" to either sideband. Or you can use the R8B's new facility to switch to either the lower or upper sideband.

The new synchronous circuit works very well, indeed, holding lock solidly—although not as resolutely as, say, the Sherwood SE-3. This improvement alone is easily worth the extra hundred dollars the "B" version costs, as the R8A's sync-lock performance was mediocre even with strong signals. With this improvement, Drake's R8-series receivers go from "almost, but not quite" to "they really got it right this time!"

Our lab tests show there is even more good news concerning the new synchronous circuits. Audio distortion, which was already quite good in the R8A, has been improved in the R8B to less than 1% at every point of measurement—a superb showing. Nevertheless, high-frequency audio response is not quite equal to that of a few competing models, such as the AOR AR7030.

With the addition of worthy selectable-sideband synchronous detection, the

Drake R8B has established itself as a "crackin' good" tabletop superset that should provide years of satisfying performance for both program listeners and DXers alike.

An *RDI WHITE PAPER* will be available for this model in early 1998.

Enhanced for 1998

★ ★ ★ ★ ★ *Passport's Choice*

AOR AR7030

Price: $1,149.95 in the United States. CAN$1,899.00 in Canada. £749.00 in the United Kingdom. AUS$1,995.00 in Australia. New "AR7030 Plus" upgrade option adds £150 in the United Kingdom, $299.95 in the United States.

Pro: In terms of sheer performance for program listening, as good a radio as we've ever tested. Except for sensitivity to weak signals (see Con), easily overcome, the same comment applies to DX reception. Exceptionally quiet circuitry. Superior audio quality. Synchronous selectable sideband performs quite well for reduced fading and easier rejection of interference. Synchronous detection circuit allows for either selectable-sideband or double-sideband reception. Best dynamic range of any consumer-grade radio we've ever

Don't let appearances deceive. The five-star AOR AR7030 "Plus" looks stylishly simple, but is a superlative performer.

tested. Nearly all other lab measurements are top-drawer. Four voice bandwidths (2.3, 7.0, 8.2 and 10.3 kHz), with cascaded ceramic filters, come standard; up to six, either ceramic or mechanical, upon request (see Con). Superior audio quality, so it's well suited to listening to programs hour after hour. Advanced tuning and operating features aplenty, including passband tuning. Tunable AF notch and noise blanker now available, but as an option. Notch filter extremely effective, with little loss of audio fidelity. Built-in preamplifier (see Con). Automatically self-aligns all bandwidths for optimum performance, then displays the measured bandwidth of each. Remote keypad (see Con). Accepts two antennas. IF output. Optional improved processor unit now has 400 memories, including 14-character alphanumeric readout for station names. World Time clock, which displays seconds, calendar and newly expanded timer/snooze features. Superior mediumwave AM performance. Superior factory service.

Con: Most unusual and complex ergonomics of any radio we've ever tested, with operation via a maze of software trees and branches. Some panelists feel they are completely unacceptable, whereas others feel that operation is fine once you get used to it after studying the helpful owner's manual. Already-complicated operation made even slightly more so in "Plus" version. Remote control unit, which has to be aimed carefully at the receiver, is required if you want to use certain features, such as direct frequency entry; not all panelists were enthusiastic about this arrangement, wishing that a mouse-type umbilical cable had been used instead. Although remote keypad can operate from across a room, the LCD characters are too small and lack sufficient intensity to be seen from such a distance. LCD omits certain important information, such as signal strength, when radio in various status modes.

Sensitivity to weak signals good, as are related noise-floor measurements, but could be a bit better; a first-rate antenna overcomes this. Because of peculiar built-in preamplifier/attenuator design in which the two are linked, receiver noise rises slightly when preamplifier used in +10 dB position, or attenuator used in –10 dB setting; however, "Plus" option remedies this. When six bandwidths used (four standard ceramics, two optional mechanicals), ultimate rejection, although superb with widest three bandwidths, cannot be measured beyond –80/–85 dB on narrowest three bandwidths because of phase noise; still, ultimate rejection is excellent even with these three narrow bandwidths. Lacks, and would profit from, a bandwidth of around 4 or 5 kHz; a Collins mechanical bandwidth filter of 3.5 kHz (nominal at –3db, measures 4.17 kHz at –6 dB) is an option. Such Collins filters, in the two optional bandwidth slots, measure as having poorer shape factors (1:1.8 to 1:2) than the standard-slot MuRata ceramic filters (1:1.5 to 1:1.6). LCD emits some digital electrical noise, potentially a problem if an amplified (active) antenna is used with its pickup element (e.g. telescopic rod) placed near the receiver. Minor microphonics (audio feedback), typically when internal speaker is used, noted in laboratory; in actual listening, however, this is not noticeable. Uses outboard AC adapter instead of built-in power supply.

Note: The features of the "Plus" version can be incorporated into existing regular models by skilled electronic technicians. Contact the manufacturer or its agents for specifics.

Verdict: AOR's sterling performer is now even better in the new "AR7030 Plus" incarnation, albeit at an additional cost of around $300. But operation, already peculiar and cumbersome in the "barefoot" version, is even more complex in the "Plus" version.

Give the radio, "Plus" or otherwise, five stars for performance, with a big question mark for ergonomics. Were it not for these ergonomics and slightly limited sensitivity to weak signals, the '7030 would be the best DX choice available on the sweet side of a Watkins-Johnson HF-1000. This is a radio you'll really need to get your hands on for a few days before you'll know whether it's love or hate—or something in between.

Evaluation of "Plus" Enhancements:
The standard '7030 model is still available, but the new "AR7030 Plus" option package contains several important features, notably a tunable audio notch filter to reduce heterodyne "whistles" and a noise blanker to help overcome local electrical noises. The notch filter is extremely effective, both in manual tuning operation and in a "smart" mode where the receiver searches for and eliminates heterodyne noises. Our lab measurements show the notch depth to be a monster 55 dB using a 700 Hz beat note. The notch is tight, too, with a 50 Hz width at –10 dB and 12 Hz at –30 dB. This notch filter is a real Terminator, killing annoying heterodyne whistles as dead as a Perdue chicken.

The optional noise blanker works vigorously, and can attenuate local noise under some circumstances. But, as is unfortunately the case with today's crop of noise blankers, signals from stations must exceed the level of noise before the blanker clicks in to do its stuff.

AOR has upgraded the microprocessor to handle the optional features. In the "Plus" version, the receiver now has 400 memories, including 14-character alphanumeric labels that let you put, say, "R. Australia" on 9580. Memory editing and searching have also been improved. No less than ten timers are incorporated that can turn the radio on at specific hours and days, much like the operation of a VCR.

The "Plus" option has significantly improved the '7030, which was already

an outstanding radio. However, it also adds around $300 to the receiver's already-high cost, which is a bit like paying extra for a high-performance suspension on a Ferrari. World band receivers in this price class normally provide a notch and noise blanker as standard equipment—AOR should do the same with the '7030.

 An *RDI WHITE PAPER* will be available for both versions of this model in early 1998.

★ ★ ★ ★ ★   *Passport's Choice*

Japan Radio NRD-535D

Price: $1,699.00 in the United States. CAN$2,949.00 in Canada. £2,499.00 in the United Kingdom. AUS$4,099.95 in Australia.
Evaluation: See below.

★ ★ ★ ★ ★½

Japan Radio NRD-535

Price: $1,199.00 in the United States. CAN$1,749.00 in Canada. £1,525.00 in the United Kingdom. AUS$3,299.95 in Australia.
Pro: One of the best and quietest DX receivers ever tested. Top-notch ergonomics, including non-fatiguing display. Construction quality slightly above average. Computer-type modular plug-in circuit boards ease repair. Highly flexible oper-

Among supersets, the Japan Radio NRD-535 series has the best ergonomics. Superior build quality, too.

ating controls, including 200 superb station presets, tunable notch filter and passband tuning. Superior reception of utility and ham signals. One of the few receivers tested that tunes frequency in exacting 0.001 kHz increments. Displays frequency in precise 0.01 kHz increments. Slow/fast/off AGC. Superior front-end selectivity. Sophisticated scan functions. World Time clock with timer features; displays seconds, albeit only if a wire inside the receiver is cut. Excellent optional NVA-319 outboard speaker. *NRD-535D:* Synchronous selectable sideband for reduced fading and easier rejection of interference. Continuously variable bandwidth in single-sideband (narrow bandwidth) and AM (wide bandwidth) modes.

Con: Audio quality, although improved over some earlier Japan Radio offerings, still somewhat muddy. Dynamic range and blocking performance adequate, but not fully equal to price class. Excessive beats, birdies and radiated digital noise. AGC sometimes causes "pop" sounds. Clock shares readout with frequency display. Clock not visible when receiver off. Front feet do not tilt receiver upwards. *NRD-535:* No synchronous selectable sideband. *NRD-535D:* Synchronous detection circuit locking performance suboptimal, notably with passband tuning in use. Variable bandwidth comes at the expense of deep-skirt selectivity.

Note: Also available in a specially upgraded "NRD-535SE" version for $1,995 from Sherwood Engineering in the United States. More complicated to operate than the regular NRD-535D, but performance, especially fidelity, is exemplary. Informally rated ★ ★ ★ ★ for ergonomics, ★ ★ ★ ★ ★ for performance, in 1994 PASSPORT.

Verdict: An exceptional receiver for snaring tough DX signals, notably in the "D" version, with the best ergonomics we've come across in a tabletop model. However, its lack of full-fidelity audio makes it far from the ideal receiver for listening to the more easily-heard world band programs over periods of time. Superior quality of construction.

An *RDI WHITE PAPER* is available that covers both factory versions of this model.

New for 1998
★ ★ ★ ★½

Japan Radio "NRD-345SE"

Price: $1,195.00 plus shipping worldwide.
Evaluation of Enhanced Model: Sherwood Engineering is introducing the Japan Radio "NRD-345SE," the unofficial moniker for its version of the '345 when sold by Sherwood equipped with the Sherwood SE-3 fidelity-enhancing accessory and requisite IF output. The outboard SE-3 allows for first-rate synchronous selectable sideband and superior audio quality.

We tested a pre-production sample of this version, and it sounded very good, indeed—a major improvement in audio quality and interference rejection over the barefoot '345. The downside is that this version costs $400 more and complicates operation.

The "SE" version resolves most of the '345's shortcomings with aplomb, notably if you're listening within North America. However, Europeans should note that it does nothing to improve the '345's pedestrian dynamic range.

For other details, *see* Japan Radio NRD-345, below.

New for 1998
★ ★ ★ ★

Japan Radio NRD-345
Japan Radio NRD-345G

Price: *NRD-345:* $799.95 in the United States. £795.00 in the United Kingdom. AUS$1,790.00 in Australia. *NRD-345G:* £899.00 in the United Kingdom.

Pro: Superior build quality by any yardstick, but especially for price. Excellent ergonomics, including superb tuning knob. Tunes in very precise 0.005 kHz increments with four manually selectable tuning speeds; displays to nearest 0.01 kHz. Superior weak-signal sensitivity and spurious-signal rejection. Two switchable antenna inputs, one low-impedance and the other high-impedance. Clock/timer functions. Tone control helps shape audio which, although lacking in treble, is already reasonably good and has minimal distortion. Slow/fast/off AGC (see Con). Memory scanning. Signal-strength indicator is analog. Double-fused for safety and protection. Worthy owner's manual.

Con: No tunable notch filter. Lacks passband tuning. Synchronous detector not sideband-selectable and provides little improvement even in double-sideband. Mediocre dynamic range limits strong-signal handling. Uses AC adaptor instead of built-in power supply. World Time clock does not display independent of frequency. AGC "off" virtually useless because of no RF gain control. Mediumwave AM performance suffers from reduced sensitivity and limited dynamic range.

Verdict: First rate ergonomics and build quality, along with good performance, make this new offering an attractive value.

Evaluation of New Model: The NRD-345 covers, in precise 5 Hz increments, 100 kHz to 30 MHz in the AM, synchronous-AM, lower-sideband, upper-sideband and fax modes. It is equipped with two worthy bandwidths, nominally 4 kHz and 2 kHz, plus a slot for an optional third bandwidth for which a number of quality JRC filters are available; two VFOs; 100 memories that store frequency, mode, AGC time constant, attenuator status, VFO, bandwidth and noise-blanker status; clock/timer; noise blanker; meter-band entry capability; switchable high-and low-impedance antenna inputs; an RS-232C port for computer control of the receiver;

The new Japan Radio NRD-345 offers JRC's legendary fit and finish for less money. First-rate ergonomics, also.

a keypad in standard telephone format (three-over-three over centered "1"); an excellent analog signal-strength meter, not some antsy digital indicator (signal-strength indicators, like automobile speedometers, are better when they are analog); an illuminated yellow liquid-crystal display (LCD); adjustable slow/fast/off AGC; and memory scanning. In short, the '345 has most of the features that world band listeners want and need.

Missing, however, are two goodies that dedicated DXers find helpful for coaxing faint signals out of a recalcitrant ether: a tunable notch filter and passband tuning. Too, the '345 operates off an outboard AC adaptor, although to JRC's credit there is secondary fusing on the receiver itself.

Measuring a compact $9\frac{3}{4} \times 4 \times 9\frac{1}{2}$ inches, or 250 mm × 100 mm × 238 mm, the '345 is a handsomely built receiver with the high level of fit and finish that listeners have come to expect from all JRC products.

Ergonomics are on an equally high plane. At the upper left of the front panel is a power switch, with settings for on, off and timer. To the right is the signal-strength meter, then farther right is the backlit LCD which serves as information central for the receiver. It displays bandwidth, frequency in the appropriate XX,XXX.XX kHz format, mode, AGC status, attenuator status, VFO and memory channel. At the upper right of the front panel is the keypad, which is made of hard-plastic buttons that are well-spaced, along with a quartet of buttons for clear, MHz, kHz and enter.

A graceful sculpted line divides the top and bottom halves of the front panel of the '345. At the lower left are clock and timer buttons, as well as a large headphone jack. Just to the right are a knob for adjusting the level of the noise blanker, and buttons for activating scanner and noise-blanker functions. There is also a "PASS" button that, curiously, is not for passband tuning. Instead, it is a "passover" button for selecting memory channels to pass over while in scanning mode. (However, there is no sabbath button to allow the radio to rest on the seventh day.)

At the center of the radio is a large, free-spinning tuning knob, complete with knurled rubber perimeter and a deep speed dimple—it's a delight to operate. On either side of the tuning knob are up and down buttons that can be used for slewing frequency or changing mode. In addition, surrounding the tuning knob are buttons for setting memory channel operations, writing to memory, selecting bandwidth, changing VFOs, activating the mode selection functions and locking the receiver. At the lower-right corner of the front panel are buttons for the attenuator and AGC functions, and knobs for volume and tone control.

Atop cabinet is a small upward-firing speaker. Below is metal bail equipped with soft rubber pads—flip it down, and the receiver sits at a minimum proper angle for comfortable operation.

Tuning speeds—5 Hz, 100 Hz, 1 kHz and 10 kHz—are manually selected by pressing the kHz or MHz buttons, which many prefer over the VRIT approach in which software automatically changes the tuning rate as the knob is spun faster or slower.

In most measurements of receiver performance, the '345 clearly shows its high-performance heritage. Sensitivity is excellent-to-superb at world band and longwave frequencies, although medium-wave AM-band sensitivity, internally attenuated, is only fair. Image rejection is excellent, and first IF rejection is superb. AGC performance is decent and stability is excellent.

The 4 kHz bandwidth (nominal) actually measures narrower than the factory specification, and also has a good shape factor. The 2 kHz bandwidth (nominal) measures 2.3 kHz, with an excellent shape factor. Audio quality is reasonably good, with distortion in the AM mode being good-to-excellent. In the AM-synchronous mode, distortion is even less—excellent-to-superb—and in the single-sideband mode distortion is superb throughout. There's also a treble tone control to help shape the audio.

But there are problems. For starters, dynamic range and third-order intercept points are poor at 5 kHz spacing and, unfortunately, synthesizer noise prevents making a measurement at 20 kHz spacing. This is clearly not the ultimate in receivers for strong-signal handling, especially in powerhouse-signal locations like Europe, North Africa and the Near East. However, in North America this is much less of a consideration, especially as you go west.

Too, the synchronous detector that Japan Radio has engineered for the '345 is clearly substandard. First, it is double-sideband only, which means you can't select one sideband over another to escape or reduce adjacent-channel interference. A double-sideband synchronous detector that works well is better than no synchronous detector, as the owners of the now-discontinued Lowe HF-225 and 225 Europa will attest, but synchronous selectable sideband is far preferable.

Absent synchronous selectable sideband, it is relatively unimportant that the '345's synchronous detector, such as it is, barely works. When faced with a fading signal that produces distortion, laboratory tests show that the synch circuit reduces distortion, but the surging of audio through the speaker or headphones is still unacceptably high. To solve the problem, Sherwood Engineers is to offer an improved version, the "NRD-345SE" (see above for evaluation).

The bottom line is that the Japan Radio NRD-345 is an interesting world band tabletop receiver that delivers a lot for the money. With improved dynamic range, an additional bandwidth and an improved synchronous detector, it could be—but isn't, yet—a real bargain. The costlier "SE" version resolves most of these shortcomings with aplomb, especially if you're listening within North America.

New for 1998
★ ★ ★ ★

Icom IC-R8500

Price: $1,849.00 in the United States. CAN$2,999.00 in Canada. £1,549.00 in the United Kingdom. AUS$3,300.00 in Australia.

Pro: Wide-spectrum multimode coverage from 0.1-2000 MHz includes longwave, mediumwave AM, shortwave and scanner frequencies all in one receiver. Physically very rugged, with professional-grade cast-aluminum chassis and impressive computer-type innards. Generally superior ergonomics, with generous-sized front panel having large and well-spaced controls, plus outstanding tuning knob with numerous tuning steps. 1,000 presets and 100 auto-write presets have handy naming function. Superb weak-signal sensitivity. Pleasant, low-distortion audio aided by audio peak filter. Passband tuning ("IF shift"). Unusually readable LCD. Tunes and displays in precise 0.01 kHz increments. Three antenna connections. Clock-timer, combined with record output and recorder-activation jack, make for

If you want a receiver that is both a superior world band radio and a solid scanner, the new Icom IC-R8500 is the best choice. It covers from 0.1-2000 MHz with a wide variety of reception modes.

superior hands-off recording of favorite programs.

Con: No synchronous selectable sideband. Bandwidth choices for world band and other AM-mode signals leap from a very narrow 2.7 kHz to a broad 7.1 kHz with nothing between, where something is most needed; third bandwidth is 13.7 kHz, too wide for world band, and no provision is made for a fourth bandwidth filter. Only one single-sideband bandwidth. Unhandy carousel-style bandwidth selection with no permanent indication of which bandwidth is in use. Poor dynamic range, surprising at this price point. Passband tuning ("IF shift") does not work in the AM mode, used by world band and mediumwave AM-band stations. No tunable notch filter. Built-in speaker mediocre. Uses outboard AC adaptor instead of customary inboard power supply.

Versions Available: The Icom IC-R8500 is available in two identically priced versions, "02" and "03." The "02" incarnation, sold to the public in the United States, is the same as the "03" version, but does not receive the *verboten* 824-849 and 869-894 MHz cellular bands. In the U.S., the "03" version is available legally only to government-approved organizations, although others reportedly have been bootlegging the "03" version by mail order from Canada. Outside the United States, the "03" version is usually the only one sold.

Sherwood SE-3: Also tested with Sherwood SE-3 non-factory accessory, which was outstanding at adding selectable synchronous sideband and provides passband tuning in the AM mode used, among other things, by world band stations. This and replacing the widest bandwidth with a 4 to 5 kHz bandwidth dramatically improve performance on shortwave, mediumwave AM and longwave.

Verdict: The large new Icom IC-R8500 is really a scanner that happens to cover world band, rather than *vice versa*. As a standalone world band receiver, it makes little sense, but it is well worth considering if you want worthy scanner and shortwave performance all in one rig.

Evaluation of New Model: For world band listeners, the IC-R8500 is among the most interesting of the "DC-to-daylight" receivers. As wideband as it is physically large, it covers 0.1-1999.99 MHz (except in the United States, where it omits the 824-849 and 869-894 MHz cellular gaps) in the AM, single-sideband, CW, narrow-FM and wide-FM modes. So it tunes not only world band, but also scanner frequencies for fire, police and the like.

This physically rugged receiver comes with a professional-grade cast-aluminum chassis having a computer-type board layout using ribbon cables and zero-insertion-force connectors. Also helping assure long-term reliability is that the '8500, unlike its older and better '9000 cousin, runs cool. This is the upside of what is basically a downside, that the '8500 uses an outboard AC adaptor instead of an inboard power supply.

The '8500's features include three AM-mode voice bandwidths for *inter alia* world band reception, one bandwidth for single-sideband reception, plus another for CW; passband tuning ("IF shift"); an audio peak filter; an adjustable BFO; ten tuning steps that are manually adjustable from 10 Hz to 1 MHz, plus a programmable tuning step; 1000 presets (memories); 100 skip channels; 100 auto-write presets (memories); a naming function for memory banks and memory channels; a noise blanker; three antenna connectors; a robust tilt bail for elevating the front panel; a three-step attenuator; an RS-232 port for computer control; various scanning capabilities; a clock-timer; a record jack; and a recorder-activation jack.

There are two (fast and slow) AGC decay choices, and in practice they appear to be adequate, although the AGC cannot be switched off and there's no IF output.

For this kind of money, you expect these things. What you don't expect in 1998 is to find no notch filter and no synchronous selectable sideband—not even double-sideband synchronous detection. And the passband tuning does not work in the AM mode. As we found in separate tests, these last two shortcomings are remedied to a fare-thee-well by the excellent and proven Sherwood SE-3 accessory, although this adds to cost and complication.

The '8500 is quite large, so the dedicated controls can be and are well-spaced and large enough even for a farmer's fingers. It also has an outstanding tuning knob with a separately rotating and friction-free speed dimple. The LCD is unusually readable, with no ghosting. All these ergonomic pluses combine to make the '8500 exceptionally pleasurable to operate hour-after-hour. The '8500 provides the sort of solid "feel" formerly associated only with the greatest of tube-type communication receivers of yore.

Still, ergonomics could have been better. Bandwidths are selected carousel-style, which is unhandy, and there is no indication whatsoever of which bandwidth is in use except for a few seconds after the bandwidth is changed. Frequency entry, in classic Icom fashion, is also a tad more complicated than on some other models.

Nevertheless, the '8500 shines in many measurements of receiver performance.

Sensitivity to weak world band signals is almost without equal. Spurious signals are few and weak, and the noise blanker works nicely. Distortion is low, helping make for pleasant audio quality when a suitable outboard speaker or headphones is used. However, the built-in speaker disappoints.

There are other problems. The '8500's dynamic range is poor at 5 kHz spacing, making this receiver potentially inappropriate for flushing out faint world band stations in frequency proximity to powerhouse signals. North Americans and Aussies probably won't notice, but *caveat emptor* in places like Europe and the Near East, where field strengths are relatively high.

The wide bandwidth for world band and other AM-mode signals is a barn-wide 13.7 kHz, too broad for virtually anything other than listening to local mediumwave AM-band signals. The medium bandwidth for world band listening, nominally 5.5 kHz, actually measures 7.1 kHz—adequate as "wide," but not as intermediate. The narrow bandwidth, which measures 2.7 kHz, is excellent for reception of congested signals, but at the cost of muffled audio.

This receiver desperately needs a fourth AM-mode bandwidth to fill in the "hole" between 2.7 kHz and 7.1 kHz. Something in the vicinity of 4 to 5 kHz would be ideal, but there appears to be no way to add one short of replacing one of the existing bandwidth filters. Too, a second, narrower, single-sideband bandwidth would have been helpful, but the receiver doesn't come with one, nor does there appear to be any provision for an aftermarket upgrade.

With its robust construction and other admirable qualities, Icom's IC-R8500 should be a top-choice superset. But it lacks synchronous selectable sideband, a proper complement of bandwidths and worthy dynamic range, among other shortcomings. Nevertheless, with the Sherwood SE-3 and improved filtering,

the '8500 is about as good as there is in a dc-to-daylight receiver that performs well for world band listening and DXing.

★ ★ ★ ★

Kenwood R-5000

Price: $999.95 in the United States. CAN$1,339.00 in Canada. £924.95 in the United Kingdom. AUS$2,040.00 in Australia.

Pro: Good audio, provided a suitable outboard speaker is used. Exceptionally flexible operating controls, including tunable notch filter and passband tuning. Tunes and displays frequency in precise 0.01 kHz increments. Excellent reception of utility and ham signals. Superior frequency-of-repair record. In some parts of the world, easier to find than other tabletop models.

Con: No synchronous selectable sideband. Ergonomics only fair—especially keypad, which uses an offbeat horizontal format. Mediocre wide bandwidth filter supplied with set; replacement with high-quality YK-88A-1 substitute adds around $95 to cost. Audio significantly distorted at tape-recording output.

Note: Some R-5000 units have been found to develop significant hum after long-term use. The manufacturer advises that this is caused by deterioration of the IF board's ground connection to the chassis. The remedy is to clean the IF board foil under the mounting screws, then re-affix those screws snugly.

There have been almost as many rumors about a "new Kenwood receiver" as Elvis sightings. Nevertheless, all that's offered is the R-5000, introduced a decade back.

Verdict: The Kenwood R-5000's combination of superior tough-signal performance and good audio quality once made it a top choice for tough-signal DXing, as well as listening to world band programs. Now, to the extent it's still available it is fast becoming a technological also-ran.

 An *RDI WHITE PAPER* is available for this model.

New for 1998
★ ★ ★ ★

Lowe HF-250E

Price (including remote control):
$1,299.95 in the United States.
CAN$1,999.00 in Canada. £795.00 in the United Kingdom. AUS$2,500.00 in Australia. £676.00 plus shipping elsewhere.
Pro: Top-notch world band and mediumwave AM audio quality, aided by effective tone control, so it's well suited to listening to world band programs hour after hour. Clean, simple panel keeps operating controls to a minimum. Synchronous detection circuit allows for either selectable-sideband for reduced fading and easier rejection of interference, or double-sideband reception for reduced fading (*see* Con). Four worthy voice bandwidths. Exceptionally rugged cast-aluminum housing of a class normally associated with professional-grade

Lowe's new HF-250E is a worthy and durable receiver, but not competitively priced for what it does.

equipment. Relatively small footprint. Digital display unusually easy to read. World Time clock shows seconds numerically (*see* Con). Superior factory service.
Con: Synchronous detector only okay in holding lock with signals suffering from flutter fading. Operation of some front-panel button functions tends to be confusing until you get the hang of it. Nonstandard keypad layout. Bereft of certain features—among them notch filter, adjustable AGC and passband tuning—found on some premium-priced models. Occasional minor hum from AC adaptor unless antenna uses coaxial-cable feedline. Signal-strength indicator has small numbers, hard to read. Clock not displayed when frequency is showing. Minor "braap" chugging within some frequency ranges.
Verdict: Think of the Lowe HF-250E as a cleaned-up HF-150 that while generally moving forward, also took a couple of steps backward with the offbeat keypad and "on-during-bandscanning" synchronous detector that could be better at holding lock. It's a hardy, advanced-fidelity receiver for the dedicated listener to world band programs.
Evaluation of New Model: The Lowe HF-250E is touted as an enhanced-performance replacement for the recently discontinued HF-250. Among the improvements, according to Lowe, are that "magnetically shielded coils and higher spec switching diodes and capacitors are used in the bandpass filter stages. This gives a much lower receiver noise floor, better suited to topical band DXing for example." In addition, the 10, 7 and 4 kHz AM nominal bandwidths of the '250 have been replaced by 7, 4.5 and 3.5 kHz nominal bandwidths.

The receiver covers from 30 kHz to 30 MHz, with AM, LSB, USB, CW, narrowband FM, and both double-sideband and selectable-sideband synchronous detection—a six-LED display indicates which mode has been selected. There's an analog signal strength meter, indicators for synchronous lock and memory mode, along with an X.XXX.X MHz frequency display. The HF-250E tunes in commendably precise 8 Hz steps, but displays the frequency only to the nearest 100 Hz. There are 255 memory channels that store frequency, mode and filter settings. There are also three AM-mode bandwidths, a bandwidth for single-sideband reception and an audio filter for CW.

There's a substantial metal tuning knob with a speed dimple and, for those old enough to recall the practice, the knob is "spinnable." The knob spins freely and, aided by variable-rate incremental tuning (when the knob rotates rapidly, the tuning rate kicks into a higher gear), the digits blindingly whiz by on the frequency display. Missing, however, are certain sophisticated controls that faint-signal hunters use to coax the last vestiges of intelligibility out of whispers on the airwaves: a notch filter and passband tuning.

In most measurements of receiver performance, the 250E earns excellent ratings. All four bandwidths have excellent shape factors and ultimate rejection, an improvement over the previous model. The 7 kHz nominal bandwidth measures 5.8 kHz, and the 4.5 kHz nominal bandwidth actually comes in at 4.9 kHz. Because these two bandwidths are so similar, their flexibility and utility are reduced.

Dynamic range is only fair-to-good when measured at 20 kHz separation, but rises to fair-to-excellent at the more demanding separation of 5 kHz. This is a step down in performance from the previous model, but is still worthy. In addition, mediumwave AM sensitivity, measured at 1 MHz and 2 MHz, is only good, whereas it had been good-to-excellent in the "plain-old" HF-250.

Our laboratory measurements of overall audio distortion shows a slight "disimprovement" from the '250 to the '250E.

AM distortion which had been excellent-to-superb, is now good-to-excellent. Distortion in the single-sideband mode is superb when the volume is low, but decreases to only good when the volume is cranked up. And AM-synchronous distortion, which formerly received ratings of good, excellent and superb at various audio frequencies, has declined to fair, good and superb. In all, the Lowe HF-250E is still a fine-sounding radio, but a skootch less than it used to be.

Finally, unimproved in the HF-250E is the ergonomically tortuous infrared remote control. It can turn the receiver on or off, mute, change modes, switch filters, control the attenuator and memories and even slew frequencies—albeit at a crawl. However, its key layout is bizarre and it has *no* volume control.

The HF-250E represents a limited step forward and a partial step back. Overall, it is an excellent receiver with museum-class cabinetry and worthy overall performance.

★ ★ ★ ★   ¢

AOR AR3030

Price: $699.95 in the United States. CAN$1,499.00 or less in Canada. £499.00 in the United Kingdom. AUS$1,599.00 in Australia.
Pro: Good-to-excellent in most laboratory measurements of receiver performance.

AOR's AR3030, never terribly distinctive, looks increasingly undistinguished alongside new models.

Relatively low price. Two well-chosen bandwidths. Tunes in very precise 0.005 kHz increments, displays in precise 0.01 Hz increments. Various scanning schemes. Easy-to-use, well-laid-out controls are largely intuitive and easy to operate. Very low audio distortion in single-sideband mode. Synchronous detector reduces distortion with world band, mediumwave AM and longwave signals (see Con). Superior weak-signal sensitivity within certain world band segments, such as 9 MHz (see Con). Small. Light. Can be run off batteries for short periods. Easy-to-read display. Can be computer controlled.

Con: Dynamic range, only fair at 5 kHz spacing, can cause overloading in and around 9 MHz segment. Weak-signal sensitivity only fair within tropical segments. Synchronous detector is not sideband-selectable, so it doesn't aid in reduction of adjacent-channel interference. Synchronous detector must be exactly center-tuned; otherwise, it may distort with a powerful station. Lacks some of the exotic controls that DXers can use, such as a notch filter and passband tuning. Needs an external speaker or headphones to take full advantage of its otherwise-good audio. Tilt bail does not latch properly. Small tuning knob. Non-standard layout for numeric keypad. Runs off external AC adaptor, rather than internal power supply—albeit one that is approved by Underwriters Laboratories. Increasingly hard to find.

A good, unpretentious choice, but Yaesu's FRG-100 now has to share its price bracket with competitors.

Verdict: A decent little receiver at an attractive price that offers generally pleasant results for program listening.

An *RDI WHITE PAPER* is available for this model.

★ ★ ★ ★   ¢

Yaesu FRG-100

Price: $599.95 in the United States. CAN$899.00 in Canada. £459.00 in the United Kingdom. AUS$999.00 in Australia.

Pro: Excellent performance in many respects. Relatively low price. Covers 50 Hz to 30 MHz in the LSB, USB, AM and CW modes. Includes three bandwidths, a noise blanker, selectable AGC, two attenuators, the ability to select 16 preprogrammed world band segments, two clocks, on-off timers, 52 tunable station presets that store frequency and mode data, a variety of scanning schemes and an all-mode squelch. A communications-FM module, 500 Hz CW bandwidth and high-stability crystal are optional.

Con: No keypad for direct frequency entry (remediable, see Note, below). No synchronous selectable sideband. Lacks features found in "top-gun" receivers: passband tuning, notch filter, adjustable RF gain. Simple controls and display, combined with complex functions, can make certain operations confusing. Dynamic range only fair. Uses AC adaptor instead of built-in power supply.

Note: An outboard accessory keypad is virtually a "must" for the FRG-100, and is a no-brainer to attach. Brodier E.E.I. (3 Place de la Fontaine, F-57420 Curvy, France) makes the best keypad, sold direct and through Universal Radio in the United States, Martin Lynch in England and Charly Hardt in Remscheid, Germany. Reasonably similar is the costlier QSYer—SWL Version, available from Stone Mountain Engineering Company in Stone

Mountain GA 30086 USA. These we've tested, but another, the KPAD100, has since appeared from Lowe Electronics in the United Kingdom.

Verdict: While sparse on features, in many respects the Yaesu FRG-100 succeeds in delivering worthy performance within its price class. Its lack of a keypad for direct frequency entry is now easily remediable (*see Note, above*).

 An *RDI WHITE PAPER* is available for this model.

New for 1998
★ ★ ★½

Drake SW2

Price: *Receiver:* $499.00 in the United States. CAN$699.00 in Canada. £499.00 in the United Kingdom. AUS$1,050.00 in Australia. *Infrared remote control:* $49.00 in the United States. CAN$75.00 in Canada. £49.95 in the United Kingdom.

Pro: Synchronous selectable sideband performs unusually well for reduced fading and easier rejection of interference; also, synchronous detector works in double-sideband mode. Several useful tuning features, including keypad, slewing and 100 presets. Superb dynamic range

puts most other receivers to shame, regardless of price. This, combined with generally superior weak-signal sensitivity, make for generally good mediumwave DX performance. Pleasant audio with minimal distortion. Worthy ergonomics, including outstandingly easy-to-read frequency display with dimmer. Superior factory service. Fifteen-day money-back trial period if ordered from the factory or certain dealers.

Con: Only one (7 kHz) of two voice bandwidths usable in AM mode, used for world band reception. Tunes in relatively coarse 50 Hz steps with some minor chugging. No notch filter, passband tuning, manually selectable AGC or noise blanker. No clock or timer. "Wall wart" AC adaptor instead of internal power supply. Optional remote control, which doesn't control volume, not worth the money for most, although its utility is aided by the receiver's bright LEDs, which can be read easily across a room.

Verdict: Tantalizingly close, but no Havana. Imagine a V-8 engine with a double-barrel carburetor where the manufacturer has plugged up one of the barrels, then think of radio. The Drake SW2 is a fine all-round performer, but even though it has two voice bandwidths—one narrow, one wide—only the wide, alas, is accessible for world band.

Drake's new SW2 would be a much better choice if it had more than one bandwidth for listening to world band stations.

Evaluation of New Model: The SW2 is a relatively small receiver, only $10^{7}/_{8} \times 4^{3}/_{8} \times 7^{5}/_{8}$ inches, or $276 \times 111 \times 193$ mm. The speaker is aimed forward, as it should be, and there is a yellow, green and red LED display that includes a passable digital signal-strength indicator and a delightful XXXXX.X kHz frequency readout bright and large enough for all but the feeblest of eyes. Frequency displays are as important to bandscanners as monitors are to PC users, so kudos to Drake for this "bright idea."

To the lower-right of that display is a large plastic tuning knob with knurled edges and a handy "speed" dimple. Also on the front are up/down slewing buttons, a straightforward-to-operate keypad in proper telephone layout, and a mini-jack for headphones. An optional infrared remote control is offered, but is of little practical use. Power, alas, is supplied by an external "wall wart" AC adaptor.

In all, no gripes about ergonomics. The layout is intuitive and easy to use, and the display is a delight to the eyes.

The SW2 covers 100 kHz to 30 MHz in the AM, synchronous selectable sideband, synchronous double sideband, and conventional upper-and lower-sideband modes. There are 100 presets (memories) which store frequency, mode and detector mode.

Although the SW2 offers synchronous selectable sideband to increase long-term program listening pleasure, as well as single-sideband for receiving ham and utility signals, there are none of the advanced controls, such as passband tuning and a notch filter, that serious DXers have come to cherish for squeezing the last erg out of difficult signals.

The SW2 has pleasant audio quality, and our laboratory measurements confirm that most measurements of distortion are excellent-to-superb. However, the relatively coarse 50 Hz tuning increments sometimes degrade single-sideband audio quality, making "ECSS" tuning of limited value.

Weak-signal sensitivity is good, excellent or superb across the radio spectrum covered. Image rejection is good, and dynamic range measured at 20 kHz spacing is superb—commendable for any receiver, but astonishing at this price point. However, the receiver's synthesizer was noisy enough to keep us from making dynamic range measurements at the more-stringent spacing of 5 kHz. There are some weak "birdies," but none are strong enough to cause listening problems.

But there's a catch. The SW2 is hobbled by substandard selectivity, or adjacent-channel rejection. The problem is that bandwidth is not selectable independent of mode, so only the wider of the two voice bandwidths can be used for world band listening. Also, that bandwidth is nominally 6 kHz at –6 dB, but actually measures 7 kHz at –6 dB and 15 kHz at –60 dB. This not only is a bit wide, but its shape factor is not the best by today's standards. The result is that stations one channel (5 kHz) away can more readily interfere with the broadcast you're trying to hear.

The receiver's synchronous selectable sideband performs unusually well and helps resolve these combined shortcomings. However, this relief works only if the other sideband is free from adjacent-channel interference.

Similarly, the SW2's AGC is not manually switchable, being like bandwidth selected automatically by mode. Switchable "fast," "slow" and "off" would have been preferable—especially considering the SW2 comes with an RF gain control, needed when an AGC is switched off—and would have cost next to nothing to include.

Drake has come close very close to creating a simple but superior performer in the under-$500 class. But at least so long as it continues to be handicapped by its inflexible bandwidth setup, the SW2 will be something of a disappointment.

New for 1998

★ ★ ★   ¢

Lowe SRX100
Target HF3

Price: *Lowe:* $279.95 in the United States. CAN$399.00 in Canada. *Target:* £159.95 in the United Kingdom. AUS$439.00 in Australia.

Pro: Low price. Superior rejection of spurious "image" signals. Third-order intercept point indicates superior strong-signal handling capability. Bandwidths have superb ultimate rejection.

Con: Unusually frustrating to operate, with only one preset, no keypad and variable-rate tuning knob is exceptionally difficult to control. When switched on, goes not to the last-tuned frequency and mode, but rather to the frequency and mode in the lone preset. Volume control fussy to adjust. Bandwidths not selectable independent of mode. The only AM-mode bandwidth, used for world band reception, is somewhat wide because of broad skirt selectivity. Single-sideband bandwidth too great. Synthesizer tunes in relatively coarse 1 kHz increments, supplemented by an analog fine-tuning "clarifier" control. Single sideband requires both tuning controls to be adjusted, and also has "warbly" audio apparently resulting from synthesizer instability. No synchronous selectable sideband, notch filter or passband tuning. Frequency readout off by 2 kHz in single-sideband mode. Uses AC adaptor instead of built-in power supply. No clock, timer or snooze feature. No elevation feet or tilt bail. LCD not illuminated.

Verdict: Surprisingly good world band performance for the price, but devilishly frustrating to operate.

Evaluation of New Model: Ensconced in a plastic case with a top-firing speaker, the diminutive Target HF3, sold in North America as the Lowe SRX100, is about the size of a large paperback. There are

The Lowe SRX100, also sold as the Target HF3, performs surprisingly well at a bargain-basement price. However, it is devilishly frustrating to operate.

only three knobs, four buttons and a highly readable digital display on the face of the receiver. That display, which is not illuminated, shows mode, frequency to the nearest kilohertz, and signal strength via digital bars.

The SRX100/HF3 covers longwave, mediumwave AM and shortwave in the AM, upper-sideband and lower-sideband modes. There are two bandwidths, nominally 3.8 kHz for single-sideband and 6 kHz for AM. There is one—count 'em, *one!*—memory preset. There is no keypad for entering frequencies and no provision for connecting one, and there are no flip-down feet or an elevation rod to prop the receiver at a comfortable operating angle.

When the receiver is switched on, it automatically goes to the frequency and mode that were last stored in the single memory preset—*not* the frequency and mode in use when you last switched the receiver off. The tuning knob has four tuning rates—10 kHz per revolution, 100 kHz, 1 MHz and 10 MHz—which are automatically selected depending upon how fast the tuning knob is turned. This is known as variable-rate incremental tuning, or VRIT.

Assisting high-speed tuning is a knob that spins freely and has been weighted to produce flywheel inertia. Give it a hefty flick, and display digits begin whirling like a slot machine gone mad. Overshooting is even possible if you inadvertently give the knob an energetic twitch while making a "final approach" from a couple hundred kilohertz away. Boink!—suddenly you're two Megahertz from where you wanted to be.

There are other peculiarities. For example, when the receiver is turned on, if you want to change the mode, you must use the up button in some cases, the down button in others. A single carousel control would have been handier.

Unlike virtually every other world band tabletop receiver, the SRX100/HF3 does not automatically compensate for the BFO offset that results when you switch from the AM mode to either upper or lower sideband. As a result, the frequency readout is two kilohertz off. Additionally, because of cost-cutting in the frequency synthesizer's design, even with precision tuning the SRX100/HF3 "warbles" like a twin-propeller airplane with engines out of sync.

The SRX100/HF3's eccentricities aside, how does it perform? The answer depends very much on what performance measurement you're looking at. Ultimate rejection of the two bandwidths is superb, a pleasant surprise at this price. But while the 6 kHz nominal bandwidth actually measures a bit under the factory specification of 5.6 kHz, the shape factor is a whopping 1:3. That means the bandwidth filter is over 17 kHz wide at –60 dB, so you can sometimes hear stations 10 kHz away.

The SSB bandwidth, which is supposed to be 3.8 kHz, actually measures 4.8 kHz, which means there is very little difference between the two bandwidths, although the shape factor of the single-sideband bandwidth is good. Had it met factory specification it would have been a good alternative bandwidth for world band listening. Unfortunately, on the SRX100/HF3 there is no way to select bandwidth independent of mode.

Image rejection is important, and here it is excellent—a major plus at this price. First IF rejection is poor, although should be a problem only under certain unusual circumstances.

Dynamic range is fair-to-good, but the more revealing signal-handling measurement of third-order intercept point is excellent-to-superb. This is a better showing that we've found with supersets costing *beaucoup* times more. However, weak-signal sensitivity throughout the receiver's tuning range is only fair, so a good antenna is called for.

When listening to a station "in the clear," the SRX100/HF3 sounds quite pleasant, although overall audio distortion is 10-15% at lower frequencies, a poor showing. Distortion improves markedly to excellent-to-superb at higher frequencies in both modes. This means there will be a certain amount of subconscious "audio fatigue" during long listening sessions, although few receivers in this price class do better.

The bottom line is that the bargain-priced Lowe SRX100/Target HF3 is a welcome surprise—maddeningly frustrating to operate, but a decent little performer.

★ ★½   ¢

Radio Shack/Realistic DX-394

Price: $249.99 in the United States. CAN$399.99 in Canada. £229.95 in the United Kingdom. AUS$599.95 in Australia.
Pro: Low price, dropped even further for 1998. Advanced tuning features include 160 tunable presets (*see* Con). Tunes and displays in precise 0.01 kHz. Modest size, light weight and built-in telescopic antenna provide some portable capability. Bandwidths have superior shape factors and ultimate rejection. Two 24-hour clocks, one of which shows independent of frequency display. Five programmable timers. 30/60 minute snooze feature. Noise blanker. 30-day money-back trial period in the United States.

Radio Shack offers what in many countries is the lowest-priced tabletop model, the DX-394. No prize, but it's fairly priced for what it does.

Con: What appear to be four bandwidths turn out to be virtually one bandwidth, and it is too wide for optimum reception of many signals. Bandwidths, such as they are, not selectable independent of mode. No synchronous selectable sideband. Presets cumbersome to use. Poor dynamic range for a tabletop, a potential problem in Europe and other strong-signal parts of the world if an external antenna is used. Overall distortion, although acceptable, higher than desirable.

Verdict: This is Radio Shack's first foray into the tabletop market in years. The result is a radio of modest dimensions and equally modest performance, but in North America it is sensibly priced for what it does.

★ ★½   ¢

Drake SW1

Price: $299.95 in the United States. CAN$399.00 in Canada. AUS$620.00 in Australia.
Pro: Low price, especially for high level of construction quality. Dynamic range,

sensitivity to weak signals and certain other performance variables above average for price class. Pleasant audio. Large, bright digital display using LEDs much easier to read indoors than most. Easiest and simplest to use of any tabletop tested, with quality ergonomics. Superior factory service. 15-day money-back trial period if ordered from the factory or certain dealers.
Con: Mediocre adjacent-channel rejection (selectivity) from the single bandwidth. No features—*nada*, not even a signal-strength indicator—except for tuning. No single sideband. No synchronous selectable sideband. Increments for tuning and frequency display are relatively coarse. Annoying chugging during bandscanning. Uses AC adaptor instead of built-in power supply.
Verdict: Okay as far as it goes, but where's the radio? And why such mediocre selectivity and loud chugging? Still, in many respects, such as quality of construction and service, Drake's SW1 offers real value at an exceptionally low price. Because of build quality and service, no other model of world band radio of any type under $400 comes as close to being a "friend for life."

The PASSPORT *tabletop-model review team consists of Jock Elliott, Lawrence Magne and George Zeller, with Tony Jones; also, George Heidelman and Craig Tyson. Laboratory measurements by J. Robert Sherwood.*

Drake's low-cost SW1 tabletop is priced like a portable. Yet, it will almost certainly outlast them by a wide margin.

Where to Find It: Index to Digital Radios for 1998

PASSPORT TO WORLD BAND RADIO tests nearly every model on the market. This index lists all digital models tested, with those that are new or enhanced for 1998 being in **bold**. Additionally, 75 analog portables are rated on page 131 and another on page 111, whereas several recently discontinued digital portables are rated on page 130.

For premium receivers and antennas, there are also comprehensive PASSPORT® Radio Database International White Papers®. Each RDI White Paper®—$6.95 in North America, $9.95 airmail to Europe and Australasia—contains virtually all our panel's findings and comments during hands-on testing, as well as laboratory measurements and what these mean to you. They are available from key world band dealers, or you can contact our 24-hour automated VISA/MC order channels (voice +1 215/794-8252, fax +1 215/794 3396 or Website http://www.passport.com), or write us at PASSPORT RDI White Papers, Box 300, Penn's Park, PA 18943 USA.

[1]*Radio Database International White Paper*® available.
[2]*Radio Database International White Paper*® available after early 1998.

Don Moore

The little mountain village of Nahualá in Guatemala is home to one of the best-heard of Latin America's tiny stations, La Voz de Nahualá, 3360 kHz. The broadcaster is part of a community education and development program that has been headed by a Roman Catholic nun from Spokane, Washington, since the 1960s.

WorldScan®

What's On Tonight?

PASSPORT's Hour-by-Hour Guide to English World Band Shows

World band radio is the preferred choice of millions, and no wonder. It's affordable, easy to use and offers a vast range of programs at the touch of a button.

And what programs! Solid news, along with the greatest variety of music and entertainment—shows you don't find on ordinary radio or TV. There's almost too much to choose from, so here is our pick of the better shows from all over—and where and when to hear them. To help you separate the gold from the bronze, here are some handy symbols:

- ■ Station with programs that are almost always superior
- ● First-class program

To be as helpful as possible throughout the year, PASSPORT's Blue Pages include not just observed activity and factual schedules, but also those which we have creatively opined will take place. This predictive information is original from us, and although it's of real value when tuning the airwaves, it is inherently not so exact as factual data.

Key frequencies are given for North America, Europe, East Asia and Australasia, plus general coverage of the Mideast, Southern Africa and Southeast Asia. Information on secondary and seasonal channels, as well as channels for other parts of the world, are in Worldwide Broadcasts in English and the Blue Pages.

Times are given in World Time, days as World Day, both explained in the glossary and "Compleat Idiot's Guide to Getting Started." Many stations announce World Time on the hour. "Summer" and "winter"? These refer to seasons in the Northern Hemisphere. Many stations supplement their programs with newsletters, tourist brochures, magazines, books and other goodies—often free. See Addresses PLUS for how you can get them.

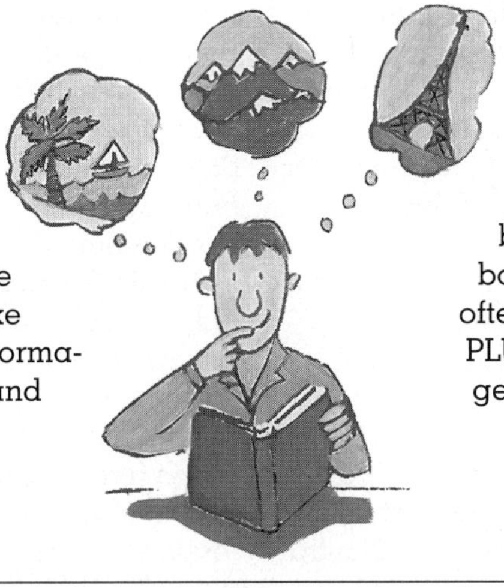

HCJB's antenna farm, 20 miles east of Quito, Ecuador. Much of the station's hardware is made by station engineers and evangelical colleagues. HCJB

0000-0559
North America–Evening Prime Time
Europe & Mideast–Early Morning
Australasia & East Asia–Midday and Afternoon

00:00

■BBC World Service for the Americas. The 1997 decision to reduce the number of program "streams" from five to three resulted in the rescheduling of much of the BBC World Service's broadcasting output. With the program lineup still in a state of flux, it is difficult to predict what further changes will occur in 1998. In the meantime, though, this is what you get. The first half-hour consists of the comprehensive ●*Newsdesk*, which is then followed by a 15-minute feature and ●*Britain Today*. Pick of the litter are Thursday's ●*From Our Own Correspondent* (Wednesday evening, local American date) and Sunday's ●*Letter from America*. On other days you can hear the likes of *Good Books* (Monday), *The Farming World* (Wednesday) and Saturday's *From the Weeklies*. Audible on 5975, 6175, 9515 (winter) and 9590 kHz.

■BBC World Service for Asia. Similar to the service for the Americas, except for some of the features at 0030. Audible in East and Southeast Asia till 0030 on 7110, 9580, 11945 and 15280 kHz; and for a full hour on 6195 and 15360 kHz.

Radio Bulgaria. Winters only at this time. *News*, then Tuesday through Friday there's 15 minutes of current events in *Today*, replaced Saturday by *Weekly Spotlight*. The remainder of the broadcast is given over to features dealing with Bulgarian life and culture, and includes some lively Balkan folk music. Sixty minutes to eastern North America and Central

America on 7480 and 9700 kHz. One hour earlier in summer.

Radio Exterior de España ("Spanish National Radio"). *News*, then Tuesday through Saturday (local weekday evenings in the Americas) it's *Panorama*, which features a recording of popular Spanish music, a commentary or a report, a review of the Spanish press, and weather. The remainder of the program is a mixture of literature, science, music and general programming. Tuesday (Monday evening in North America), there's *Sports Spotlight* and *Cultural Encounters*; Wednesday features *People of Today* and *Entertainment in Spain*; Thursday brings *As Others See Us* and, biweekly, *The Natural World* or *Science Desk*; Friday has *Economic Report* and *Cultural Clippings*; and Saturday offers *Window on Spain* and *Review of the Arts*. The final slot is give over to a language course, *Spanish by Radio*. On the remaining days, you can listen to Sunday's *Hall of Fame*, *Distance Unknown* (for radio enthusiasts) and *Gallery of Spanish Voices*; and Monday's *Visitors' Book*, *Great Figures in Flamenco* and *Radio Club*. Sixty minutes to eastern North America on 6055 kHz.

Radio Canada International. Winters only at this time. Tuesday through Saturday (weekday evenings in North America), it's the final hour of the CBC domestic service news program ●*As It Happens*, which features international stories, Canadian news and general human interest features. Sundays feature ●*Quirks and*

> Millions of North Koreans may be starving, but about all you'll hear on Radio Pyongyang are reverences to the "Beloved Comrade and Great Leader," the late Kim II Sung.

Quarks (science), replaced Monday by the cultural *Tapestry*, both from the CBC's domestic output. To North America on 5960 and 9755 kHz. One hour earlier in summer.

Voice of Russia World Service. Beamed to eastern North America at this hour. Winters, *news* and opinion take up the first 30 minutes, followed by some excellent musical fare during the second half-hour. Monday and Saturday (Sunday and Friday evenings local American days), there's the incomparable ●*Folk Box*; Thursday brings ●*Music at Your Request*; and Friday features Russian jazz. Summers, it's *News*, followed Tuesday through Saturday by *Focus on Asia and the Pacific*, with *Mailbag* on the remaining days. These are followed on the half-hour by ●*Audio Book Club* (Sunday), *This is Russia* (Tuesday, Thursday and Saturday), ●*Moscow Yesterday and Today* (Wednesday and Friday) or *Russian by Radio* (Monday). Not the easy catch it used to be, so you have to dial around a bit. Winters, the pickings are slim, indeed; try 5940 and 7125 kHz. Failing these, try other frequencies in the 7 MHz segment, or the bottom end of the 6 MHz range (5900-5940 kHz). Best summer options are 7125 and 7250 kHz.

Radio Yugoslavia. Monday through Saturday (Sunday through Friday, local American evenings) and summers only at this time. *News* and information with a strong local flavor, and worth a listen if you are interested in the region. Thirty minutes to eastern and central North America on 9580 and 11870 kHz. One hour later in winter.

Radio Pyongyang, North Korea. Millions may be starving in the country, but it is unlikely you'll hear much about it on Radio Pyongyang. Much of the programming is still dedicated to lauding the "Great Leader" and "Beloved Comrade," the late Kim Il Sung. The last of the old-style communist stations, and unlikely to change, at least for the time being. Sixty

boring minutes to Southeast Asia and Central America (also audible in parts of western North America) on 11845, 13650 and 15230 kHz.

Radio Ukraine International. Summers only at this time. An hour's ample coverage of just about everything Ukrainian, including news, sports, politics and culture. Well worth a listen is ●*Music from Ukraine*, which fills most of the Monday (Sunday evening in the Americas) broadcast. Sixty minutes to eastern North America on 7150, 9550 and 12040 kHz; and for European night owls on 5905, 6010, 6020, 6090, 7180, 7240 and 9560 kHz. One hour later in winter.

Radio Australia. Part of a 24-hour service to East Asia and the Pacific, but which can also be heard at this time in western North America. Begins with world *news*, then features. Best of the weekday programs is Tuesday's *Science Show*; weekends, try Saturday's *Feedback* (a listener-response program) and *Indian Pacific*, replaced Sunday by *Oz Sounds* and *Correspondents' Report*. In East Asia, try 13605, 13755, 15415 and 17750 kHz; for the Pacific, choose from 12080, 13755, 15510 and 17795 kHz.

Radio Prague, Czech Republic. *News*, then Tuesday through Saturday (weekday evenings in the Americas), there's *Current Affairs*. These are followed by one or more features. Tuesday has *Magazine '96*; Wednesday, it's *Talking Point* and *Media Czech*; Thursday's slots are *The Arts* and *From the Archives*; Friday brings *Economic Report* and *I'd Like You to Meet . . .*; and Saturday it's *Between You and Us*. Sunday's offering is a thoroughly enjoyable musical feature which offers a different style of music each week, alternating between classical, folk, contemporary and jazz. This is replaced Monday by *The Week in Politics*, *From the Weeklies* and *Media Czech*. Thirty minutes to eastern North America on 5930 and 7345 kHz.

Voice of America. The first half of a

Robert Crane

Buddhist monk collects rocks for a temple in Taiwan's marble mountains.

HCJB—Voice of the Andes, Ecuador. The first of four hours of continuous programming to eastern North America on 9745 kHz. Tuesday through Saturday (weekday evenings in North America), it's a combination of *Insight for Living* and *Focus on the Family*. Weekend fare includes *Musical Mailbag* (0030 Sunday) and *Mountain Meditations* (same time Monday).

Radio Thailand. *Newshour*. Not the exotic fare you'd expect from a country like Thailand. Thirty minutes for East African insomniacs, winters on 9680 kHz and summers on 9690 kHz. An extra half hour is available for listeners in Asia on 9655 and 11905 kHz.

China Radio International. *News* and commentary, followed Wednesday through Saturday (Tuesday through Friday evenings in the Americas) by *Current Affairs*. These are followed by various feature programs, such as *Cultural Spectrum* (Friday); *Listeners' Letterbox* (Monday and Wednesday); *China Scrapbook*, *Cooking Show*, *Chinese Folk Tales* and ●*Music from China* (Sunday); *Sports Beat* and *Song of the Week* (Monday); *Learn to Speak Chinese* (Tuesday and Thursday); and Saturday's *In the Third World*. Mondays, there is also a biweekly *Business Show* which alternates with *China's Open Windows*. One hour to eastern North America on 9710 and 11695 kHz.

All India Radio. The final 45 minutes of a much larger block of programming targeted at Southeast Asia, and heard well beyond. On 7150, 9705, 9950 and 11620 kHz.

Radio Cairo, Egypt. The final half-hour of a 90-minute broadcast to eastern North America on 9900 kHz. See 2300 for specifics.

Radio New Zealand International. A friendly package of *news* and features sometimes replaced by live sports commentary. Part of a much longer broadcast for the South Pacific, but also heard in

two-hour weekday evening broadcast to the Caribbean and Latin America (nothing at weekends). *News*, followed by split programming. Listeners in the Caribbean get ●*Report to the Caribbean* and *Music USA*. For Latin America there's ●*VOA Business Report* (replaced Friday evening by *Newsline*) and news and features in Special (slow-speed) English. These include a science or environment report during the first four days, replaced Friday evening by ●*American Stories*. The service to the Caribbean is on 6130, 9455 and 11695 kHz; and listeners in Latin America can choose from 5995, 7405, 9775 and 13740 kHz. The final hour of a separate service to East and Southeast Asia and Australasia (see 2200) can be heard on 7215, 9770, 9890 (winter), 11760, 15185, 15290, 17735 and 17820 kHz.

parts of North America (especially during summer) on 15115 kHz.

WWCR, Nashville, Tennessee. Carries a variety of disestablishmentarian programs at this hour, depending on the day of the week. Winters on 5065 kHz, there's "The Voice of Liberty" and "The Hour of Courage"; in summer it's "Protecting your Wealth", "World of Prophecy" and "Full Disclosure Live." On 7435 kHz, look for yet more of the same.

WJCR, Upton, Kentucky. Twenty-four hours of gospel music targeted at North America on 7490 kHz. Also heard elsewhere, mainly during darkness hours. For more religious broadcasting at this hour, try **WGTG** on 5085 kHz, **WYFR-Family Radio** on 6085 kHz, and **KTBN** on (winters) 7510 or (summers) 15590 kHz. For something a little more controversial, tune to Dr. Gene Scott's University Network, via **WWCR** on 13845 kHz or **KAIJ** on 13815 kHz. Traditional Catholic programming can be heard via **WEWN** on 7425 kHz.

00:30

Radio Netherlands. *News*, then Tuesday through Sunday (Monday through Saturday evenings in North America) there's ●*Newsline*, a current affairs program. These are followed by a different feature each day, including the well-produced ●*Research File* (science, Tuesday); *Mirror Images* (arts in Holland, Wednesday); the excellent ●*Documentary* (Thursday); *Media Network* (Friday); ●*A Good Life* (Saturday); and Sunday's ●*Weekend*. Monday's features are a listener-response program and *Sounds Interesting*. Fifty-five minutes to North America on 6020, 6165 and (summers) 9845 kHz; and a full hour to South Asia (also widely heard in other parts of the continent, as well as Australasia), winters on 5905 and 7305 kHz, and summers on 9855 and 11655 kHz.

Radio Austria International. ●*Report from Austria*, which includes a brief bulletin of *news*, followed by a series of current events and human interest stories. Ample coverage of national and regional issues, and an excellent source for news of Central and eastern Europe. Thirty minutes to North America on 7325 or 9655 kHz.

Radio Vlaanderen Internationaal, Belgium. Winters only at this time; Tuesday through Saturday (weekday evenings in North America), there's *News*, *Press Review* and *Belgium Today*, followed by features like *Focus on Europe* (Tuesday), *Living in Belgium* and *Green Society* (Wednesday), *The Arts* and *Around Town* (Thursday), *Economics* and *International Report* (Friday), and *The Arts* and *Tourism* (Saturday). Weekend features include *Music from Flanders* (Sunday) and Monday's *P.O. Box 26* and *Radio World*. Thirty minutes to eastern North America on 5900 (or 6030) kHz; also audible on 9925 kHz, though beamed elsewhere. One hour earlier in summer.

Radio Sweden. Tuesday through Saturday (weekday evenings in the Americas), it's *news* and features in *Sixty Degrees North*, concentrating heavily on Scandinavian topics. Tuesday's accent is on sports; Wednesday has electronic media news; Thursday brings *Money Matters*; Friday features ecology or science and technology; and Saturday offers a review of the week's news. Sunday, there's *Spectrum* (arts) or *Sweden Today* (current events), while Monday's offering is *In Touch with Stockholm* (a listener-response program) or the musical *Sounds Nordic*. Thirty minutes to South America, also audible in eastern North America on 6065 and (winter) 9850 kHz.

Radio Vilnius, Lithuania. A half hour that's heavily geared to *news* and background reports about events in Lithuania. Of broader appeal is *Mailbag*, aired every other Sunday (Saturday evenings local American date). For a little Lithuanian music, try the next evening, following the

MFJ's high performance *tuned* active antenna rivals long wires hundreds of feet long!

MFJ-1020B

$69⁹⁵

Receive strong clear signals from all over the world with this indoor tuned active antenna that rivals the reception of long wires hundreds of feet long!

"World Radio TV Handbook" says MFJ-1020B is a "fine value . . . fair price . . . performs very well indeed!" Set it on your desktop and listen to the world!

No need to go through the hassle of putting up an outside antenna you have to disconnect when it storms.

Covers 300 kHz to 30 MHz so you can pick up all of your favorite stations. And discover new ones you couldn't get before. Tuned circuitry minimizes intermodulation, improves selectivity and reduces noise from phantom signals, images and out-of-band signals.

Adjustable telescoping whip gives you maximum signal with minimum noise. Full set of controls for tuning, band selection, gain and On-Off/Bypass. 5x2x6 in.

Also, doubles as preselector with external antenna . Use 9 volt battery or 110 VAC with MFJ-1312, $12.95.

MFJ tunable DSP filter

MFJ-784B
$249⁹⁵

Super filter uses state-of-the-art *Digital Signal Processing* technology!

It *automatically* searches for and eliminates *multiple* heterodynes.

Tunable, pre-set and programmable "brick wall" filters with 60 dB *attenuation just 75 Hz away from cutoff frequency* literally knocks out interference signals.

Adaptive noise reduction reduces random background noise up to 20 dB.

Works with all signals including all voice, CW and data signals. Plugs between radio and speaker or phones.

Dual Tunable Audio Filter

MFJ-752C
$99⁹⁵

Two separately tunable filters let you peak desired signals and notch out interference at the same time. You can peak, notch, low or high pass signals to eliminate heterodynes and interference. Plugs between radio and speaker or phones. 10x2x6 in.

Super Active Antenna

"World Radio TV Handbook" says MFJ-1024 is a "first rate easy-to-operate active antenna . . . quiet . . . excellent dynamic range . . . good gain . . . low noise . . . broad frequency coverage."

Mount it outdoors away from electrical noise for maximum signal, minimum noise. Covers 50 KHz to 30 MHz.

Receives strong, clear signals from all over the world. 20dB attenuator, gain control, ON LED. Switch two receivers and aux. or active antenna. 6x3x5 in. remote has 54 inch whip, 50 ft. coax. 3x2x4 in. 12 VDC or 110 VAC with MFJ-1312, $12.95.

MFJ-1024 **$129⁹⁵**

Eliminate noise and interference

MFJ-1026
$139⁹⁵

NEW! **Completely** cancel interfering signals, power line noise and lightning crashes *before they get into your receiver*. Dramatic results! Works on all modes -- SSB, AM, CW, FM -- and on all shortwave bands. Plugs between your external antenna and receiver. Use built-in active antenna or external antenna to pick up noise and interference for cancellation. Use 12 VDC or 110 VAC with MFJ-1312B, $12.95.

MFJ Antenna Matcher

MFJ-959B
$99⁹⁵

Matches your antenna to your receiver so you get maximum signal and minimum loss.

Preamp with gain control boosts weak stations 10 times. 20 dB attenuator prevents overload. Pushbuttons let you select 2 antennas and 2 receivers. Covers 1.6-30 MHz. 9x2x6 inches.

SWL's Guide for Apartments

World renowned MFJ-36 SWL expert Ed **$9⁹⁵** Noll's book tells you what shortwave bands to listen to, the best times to tune in, how to DX and QSL, how to send for schedules and construct indoor antennas plus more!

Easy-Up Antennas Book

How to build and put up inexpensive, fully tested wire antennas using readily available parts that'll bring signals in like you've never heard before. Antennas

MFJ-38
$16⁹⁵ from 100 KHz to 1000 MHz.

High-Q Passive Preselector

High-Q passive LC preselector that lets you boost your favorite stations while rejecting images, intermod and other phantom signals. 1.5-30 MHz.

MFJ-956
$39⁹⁵

MFJ Lightning Surge Protector for 50 ohm coax

NEW!

MFJ-270 **MFJ** *Lightning*
$29⁹⁵ *Surge Protector* safeguards your expensive shortwave receiving equipment from damaging static electricity and lightning induced surges. Ultra-fast gas discharge tube safely shunts up to 5,000 amps of peak impulse current harmlessly to independent ground. Plugs between antenna and receiver. Does not protect against a direct lightning hit.

High-Gain Preselector

MFJ-1045C
$69⁹⁵

High-gain, high-Q receiver preselector covers 1.8-54 MHz. Boost weak signals 10 times with low noise dual gate MOSFET. Reject out-of-band signals and images with high-Q tuned circuits. Pushbuttons let you select 2 antennas and 2 receivers. Dual coax and phono connectors. Use 9-18 VDC or 110 VAC with MFJ-1312, $129.95.

MFJ Communications Speaker

NEW! **Top** grade Mylar speaker in speech-enhancing baffle. AM, SSB, FM, CW never sounded so crystal-clear! Swivel mount. Handles 8 watts. 8 ohms. 6 foot cord, 3.5 mm mono plug.

MFJ-281
$9⁹⁵

Multimode *Digital* Decoder

MFJ-1278B
$299⁹⁵

Discover digital communications on shortwave with MFJ-1278B, your receiver and computer.

Listen to worldwide packet networks, watch hams exchange *color SSTV* pictures. Marvel at *full color* FAX news photos. See weather changes on highly detailed weather maps. Eavesdrop on late breaking news on RTTY. Copy CW.

Requires MFJ *Multi-Com™* software. $59.95. Specify DOS or WINDOWS. Includes RS-232 cable.

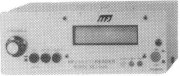

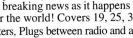

news. To eastern North America winters on 5890 kHz, and summers on 9855 kHz.

Voice of the Islamic Republic of Iran. One hour of *news*, commentary and features with a strong Islamic slant. Targeted at North and Central America. Try 6015, 6150, 6175, 7180, 9022 and 9670 kHz. Apart from 9022 kHz, channel usage tends to be variable.

Radio Thailand. *Newshour*. Thirty minutes to North America winters on 11905 kHz, and summers on 15395 kHz.

00:50

Radio Roma-RAI International, Italy. *News* and some uninspiring Italian music make up this 20-minute broadcast to North America. Better than what it used to be, but there's still room for improvement. On 6010, 9675 and 11800 kHz.

01:00

■**BBC World Service for the Americas.** Thirty minutes of ●*Newsdesk* followed by one or more features. Pick of the pack are Wednesday's ●*Discovery* (Tuesday evening, local American date) and Thursday's ●*Omnibus*. Audible in North America on 5975, 6175, 9515 (winter) and 9590 kHz.

■**BBC World Service for Asia.** Ten minutes of *World News*, followed by five minutes of the religious *Pause for Thought* and a quarter-hour feature. Tuesday through Saturday, it's analysis of current events in ●*The World Today*, replaced Sunday by ●*Health Matters*, and Monday by *The Farming World*. The second half-hour is equally split between *World News* and ●*Sports Roundup*. Audible in East and Southeast Asia on 6195, 15280 and 15360 kHz.

Radio Canada International. Summers only. *News*, followed Tuesday through Saturday (weeknights local American date) by *Spectrum* (topics in

the news), which in turn is replaced Sunday by *Innovation Canada* (science) and ●*Earth Watch*. On Monday (Sunday evening in North America) there's *Arts in Canada* and a listener-response program. Sixty minutes to North America on 6120 and 9755 kHz. You can also try 9535, 11715 and 13670 kHz, but they are only available for the first 30 minutes, except for weekends. One hour later in winter.

■**Deutsche Welle,** Germany. *News*, followed Tuesday through Saturday (weekday evenings in the Americas) by the comprehensive ●*NewsLink*—commentary, interviews and background reports on European events. This is followed by ●*Man and Environment* (Tuesday), ●*Insight* (Wednesday), *Living in Germany* (Thursday) or *Economic Notebook* on Saturday. Sunday fare consists of *Sports Report*, *Inside Europe* and *Mailbag*; and is replaced Monday by *Commentary*, *Arts on the Air* and *German by Radio*. Fifty minutes of very good reception in North America and the Caribbean, winters on 5960, 6040, 6085, 6145 and 9640 kHz; and summers on 6040, 6085, 6145, 9640 and 11810 kHz.

Radio Slovakia International. *Slovakia Today*, a 30-minute window on Slovak life and culture. Tuesday (Monday evening in the Americas), there's a potpourri of short features; Wednesday puts the accent on tourism and Slovak personalities; Thursday's slot is devoted to business and economy; and Friday brings a mix of politics, education and science. Saturday offerings include cultural features, *Slovak Kitchen* and the off-beat *Back Page News*; while Sunday brings the "*Best of*" series. Monday's fare is very much a mixed bag, and includes *Listeners' Tribune* and some enjoyable Slovak music. A friendly half hour to eastern North America and Central America on 5930 and 7300 kHz, and to South America on 9440 kHz.

Radio Norway International. Mondays (Sunday evenings, local American date) only. *Norway Now*. Thirty minutes of *news* and chat from and about Norway. To North and Central America winters on 7465 kHz, and summers on 9560 kHz.

Radio Budapest, Hungary. Summers only at this time. *News* and features, some of which are broadcast on a regular basis. These include Monday's *Bookshelf* (local Sunday evening in North America), a press review (Tuesday, Wednesday, Friday and Saturday), *Profiles* (Wednesday), and *Focus on Business* (Thursday). Thirty minutes to North America on 6120 and 9580 kHz. One hour later in winter.

Radio Prague, Czech Republic. Repeat of the 0000 broadcast. Thirty minutes to North America on 6200 and 7345 kHz.

Swiss Radio International. *Newsnet.* A workmanlike compilation of news and background reports on world and Swiss events. Somewhat lighter fare on Sunday (Saturday evening in North America), when the biweekly *Capital Letters* (a listener-response program) alternates with *Name Game* and *Sounds Good*. A half hour to North America and the Caribbean on 6135, 9885 and 9905 kHz.

Radio Japan. *News*, then Tuesday through Saturday (weekday evenings local American date) there's 10 minutes of *Asian Top News* followed by a half-hour feature. Take your pick from *Profile* (Tuesday), *Enjoy Japanese* (Wednesday and Friday), *Town and Around* (Thursday) and Saturday's *Music and Book Beat*. On the remaining days, look for *Asia Weekly* (Sunday) or Monday's *Let's Learn Japanese* and *Viewpoint*. The broadcasts end with the daily *Tokyo Pop-in*. One hour to eastern North America summers only on 5960 kHz via the powerful relay facilities of Radio Canada International in Sackville, New Brunswick. Also year-round to western North America on 11885, 9605 (winter)

and (summer) 11790 kHz. Also available to Asia on 11840, 11860, 11890/11900, 11910, 17810 and 17845 kHz.

Radio Exterior de España ("Spanish National Radio"). Repeat of the 0000 transmission. To eastern North America on 6055 kHz.

Radio For Peace International, Costa Rica. One of the few remaining places where you can still find the peace and "peoplehood" ideals of the Sixties. This hour is the start of English programming—the initial hour being in Spanish. *FIRE* (Feminist International Radio Endeavour) is one of the better offerings from the mélange of programs that make up RFPI's eight-hour cyclical blocks of predominantly counterculture programming. Sixty minutes of variable reception in Europe and the Americas on 7385, 7585 and (summer) 15050 kHz. Some transmissions are in the single-sideband mode, which can be properly processed only on certain radios.

The VOA's excellent *Report to the Americas* is the best bet for following events in the Western Hemisphere.

Voice of Vietnam. A relay via the facilities of the Voice of Russia. Begins with *news*, then there's *Commentary* or *Weekly Review*, followed by short features and some pleasant Vietnamese music (especially at weekends). Repeated at 0230 on the same channel. Thirty minutes to eastern North America; winters on 5940 kHz, and summers on 7250 kHz.

Voice of Russia World Service. Continuous programming to North America at this hour. *News*, features and music. Tuesday through Saturday, winters, it's *Focus on Asia and the Pacific*, replaced summers by ●*Commonwealth Update*. The second half-hour contains some interesting fare. In summer, look for Tuesday's ●*Folk Box* (Monday evening local American date), ●*Music at Your Request* (Wednesday and Friday), Russian jazz (Thursday and Saturday), and ●*Music and Musicians* (from 0111, Sunday

PASSPORT editor Craig Tyson feeds backyard visitors at his home near Perth, Western Australia.

and Monday). Pick of the winter fare is ●*Moscow Yesterday and Today* (Wednesday and Friday) and Sunday's ●*Audio Book Club*. Most of the remaining days feature *This is Russia*, except for Monday, when you can hear *Russian by Radio*. Where to tune? In eastern North America winters, shoot for 7125 kHz—there's not much else. The former summer slots have now given way to Russian broadcasts, so there's little you can do except to try the channels targeted at western parts. For western North America, it's summers only. Try 12000, 12010, 12050, 13665, 15180 and 15595 kHz.

Radio Habana Cuba. The start of four hours of continuous programming to eastern North America, and made up of *news* and features such as *Latin America Newsline*, *DXers Unlimited*, *The Mailbag Show* and ●*The Jazz Place*, interspersed with some good Cuban music. To eastern North America on 6000 and 9820 kHz. Also available on 9830 kHz upper sideband, though not all radios, unfortunately, can process such signals.

Radio Australia. *News*, then Monday through Friday it's *Dateline*, followed on the half-hour by a feature: *Innovations* (Monday), *Arts Australia* (Tuesday), *Science File* (Wednesday), *Book Talk* (Thursday) and *Earthbeat* on Friday. Weekends, there's *Oz Sounds* and *Arts Australia* (Saturday), and *The Europeans* (Sunday). Continuous programming to East Asia and the Pacific, and also audible in western North America. On 12080, 13605, 13755, 15415, 15510, 17750 and 17795 kHz. Some channels may carry a separate sports service on winter Saturdays.

Radio Yugoslavia. Monday through Saturday (Sunday through Friday, local

American evenings) and winters only at this time. *News* and short reports, dealing almost exclusively with local and regional topics. Worth a listen. Thirty minutes to eastern and central North America on 6195 and 7115 kHz. One hour earlier in summer.

HCJB—Voice of the Andes, Ecuador. Tuesday through Saturday (weekday evenings in North America) it's *Studio 9*, featuring nine minutes of world and Latin American *news*, followed by 20 minutes of in-depth reporting on Latin America. The final portion of *Studio 9* is given over to one of a variety of 30-minute features— including *You Should Know* (issues and ethics, Tuesday), *El Mundo Futuro* (science, Wednesday), *Ham Radio Today* (Thursday), *Woman to Woman* (Friday), and the unique and enjoyable ●*Música del Ecuador* (Saturday). On Sunday (Saturday evening in the Americas), the news is followed by *DX Partyline*, which in turn is replaced Monday by *Saludos Amigos*— HCJB's international friendship program. Continuous programming to eastern North America on 9745 kHz.

Voice of America. The second and final hour of a weekday evening broadcast to the Caribbean and Latin America (nothing at weekends). Starts with 10 minutes of *news*, which is then followed by the outstanding ●*Report to the Americas*, a series of news features about the United States and other countries in the hemisphere. Far and away the best show of its kind. The hour is rounded off with a five-minute editorial. To the Americas on 5995, 6130, 7405, 9455, 9775 and 13740 kHz.

Radio Ukraine International. Winters only at this time; see 0000 for program details. Sixty minutes of informative programming targeted at eastern North America and European night owls. For North America, try 5915 and 7150 kHz; in Europe, choose from 5905, 5940, 6010, 6020, 7205 and 7290 kHz. One hour earlier in summer.

Radio New Zealand International. A package of *news* and features sometimes replaced by live sports commentary. Part of a much longer broadcast for the South Pacific, but also heard in parts of North America (especially during summer) on 15115 kHz.

Radio Tashkent, Uzbekistan. *News* and features with a strong Uzbek flavor; some exotic music, too. A half hour to West and South Asia and the Mideast, occasionally heard in North America; winters on 5955, 5975, 7105 and 7285 kHz; summers on 7190, 9375, 9530 and 9715 kHz.

FEBC Radio International, Philippines. *Good Morning from Manila*, a potpourri of secular and religious programming targeted at South and Southeast Asia, but heard well beyond. The first 60 minutes of a two-hour broadcast on 15450 kHz.

"American Dissident Voices", **WRNO.** This time summers only. Neo-Nazi anti-Israel program, hosted by Kevin Alfred Strom. Only of interest to those with similar beliefs. Thirty minutes Sunday (Saturday evening local American date) on 7355 kHz; try four hours later on 7395 kHz if preempted by live sports. Targeted at North America, but reaches beyond. Is followed by "Herald of Truth", another disestablishmentarian program of a similar vein.

WWCR, Nashville, Tennessee. Carries a variety of disestablishmentarian programs at this hour, depending on the day of the week. Winters, there's "Protecting your Wealth", "World of Prophecy" and "Full Disclosure Live" on 5065 kHz; while 7435 kHz carries a similar bunch of programs.

WJCR, Upton, Kentucky. Continues with country gospel music for North American listeners on 7490 kHz. Also with religious programs to North America at this hour are **WGTG** on 5085 kHz, **WYFR-Family Radio** on 6065 and 9505 kHz,

WWCR on 13845 kHz and **KTBN** on 7510 kHz. For traditional Catholic programming, tune to **WEWN** on 7425 kHz.

01:30

Radio Sweden. *News* and features of mainly Scandinavian content; see 0030 for specifics. Thirty minutes to Asia and Australasia on one or more frequencies. Try 7120 and 7290 kHz.

Radio Netherlands. *News*, followed Tuesday through Saturday by ●*Newsline*, a current affairs program. Then there's a different feature each day, including ●*A Good Life* (Tuesday); *Sounds Interesting* (Thursday); ●*Research File* (science, Friday) and ●*Documentary* (Saturday). Making up the week are Sunday's award-winning ●*Roughly Speaking* and Monday's *Wide Angle* and *Siren Song*. One hour to South Asia (also widely heard in other parts of the continent, as well as Australasia); winters on 5905, 7305, 9860 and 11655 kHz; and summers on 9855 and 11655 kHz.

Voice of Greece. Preceded and followed by programming in Greek. Approximately 10 minutes of English *news*, then Greek music, a short feature about the country, and more music. Resumes programming in Greek at 0200. To North America on any three frequencies from 6260, 7448, 9420, 9935 and 11645 kHz.

01:45

Radio Tirana, Albania. Approximately 10 minutes of *news* and commentary from one of Europe's least known countries. To North America on 6115 and 7160 kHz.

02:00

■BBC World Service for the Americas. Opens with 30 minutes of ●*Newsday*, then there's a half-hour feature. Monday through Thursday (Sunday through Wednesday evenings in the Americas), the spotlight is on the arts, in *Meridian*. This is replaced Friday by ●*Focus on Faith*, a secular look at the world of religion; Saturday by ●*People and Politics*; and Sunday by classical music. Audible in North America on 5975, 6175, 9515 (winter) and 9590 kHz.

■BBC World Service for Asia. ●*Newsday*, followed on the half-hour by one or more features. Pick of the litter is Tuesday's ●*Discovery*, one of world band's top science shows. Other interesting offerings include ●*One Planet* (Wednesday), ●*Assignment* (Friday) and Saturday's ●*People and Politics*. Continuous to East and Southeast Asia on 15280 and 15360 kHz.

Radio Cairo, Egypt. Repeat of the 2300 broadcast, and the first hour of a 90-minute potpourri of *news* and features about Egypt and the Arab world. Fair reception and mediocre audio quality to North America on 9475 kHz.

Radio Argentina al Exterior—R.A.E. Tuesday through Saturday only. *News* and short features dealing with aspects of life in Argentina, interspersed with samples of the country's various musical styles, from tango to zamba. Fifty-five minutes to North America on 11710 kHz.

Radio Budapest, Hungary. This time winters only; see 0100 for specifics. Thirty minutes to North America on 5905 and 9840 kHz. One hour earlier in summer.

Radio Canada International. Starts off with *News*, then Tuesday through Saturday winter (week-nights local American date) it's *Spectrum*. Sunday, there's *Innovation Canada* and the environmental ●*Earth Watch*, replaced Monday by *The Arts in Canada* and *Mailbag*. Summers, *News* is followed by features taken from the Canadian Broadcasting Corporation's domestic output. Tuesday through Saturday, there's *The Best of Morningside*; Sunday features *Double Exposure* and *Canadian Air Farce*; and Monday has

The Inside Track (sports) and *Now the Details*, a current affairs feature. One hour winters to North America and the Caribbean on 6155, 9535, 9755, 9780 and 11725 kHz; and summers on 6120 (except 0230-0300, Tuesday through Saturday), 9755 and 13670.

Radio Yugoslavia. Winters only at this time. *News* and information with a strong regional slant. Thirty minutes to western North America on 6195 and 7130 kHz. Worth a listen.

■**Deutsche Welle,** Germany. *News,* then Tuesday through Saturday there's the fast-moving ●*NewsLink*—commentary, interviews, background reports and analysis of European events. A feature follows just after the half-hour. Choose from ●*Man and Environment* (Tuesday), ●*Insight* (Wednesday), *Living in Germany* (Thursday), *Spotlight on Sport* (Friday) and *Economic Notebook* on Saturday. These are replaced Sunday by *Sports Report*, *Development Forum* (alternates with *Women on the Move*) and *Mailbag*; and the Sunday lineup features *Commentary*, *Inside Europe* and a series of features which rotate on a weekly basis. Fifty minutes nominally targeted at South Asia, but widely heard elsewhere. Winters on 6035, 7265, 7285, 7355, 9515 and 9615 kHz; and summers on 7285, 9615, 9690, 11945, 11965 and 12045 kHz.

HCJB—Voice of the Andes, Ecuador. A mixed bag of religious and secular programming, depending on the day of the week. Tuesday (Monday evening in North America) is given over to *The Least of These* and *Let My People Think*; Wednesday airs *Simply Worship* and *Unshackled*; and Thursday brings *The Book and the Spade*, *Inside HCJB* and *Rock Solid!* On Friday, you can hear *Radio Reading Room* and *Inspirational Classics*; Saturday has the Europe-oriented *On-Line*

followed by *On Track* (contemporary Christian music); Sunday features *Rock Solid!* and *Solstice* (a youth program); and Monday is devoted to *Radio Reading Room* and the *L'Abri Lectures* (or their substitute). Continuous to eastern North America on 9745 kHz.

Voice of Free China, Taiwan. *News,* followed by features. The last is *Let's Learn Chinese*, which has a series of segments for beginning, intermediate and advanced learners. Other features include *Jade Bells and Bamboo Pipes* (Monday), *Kaleidoscope* and *Main Roads and Byways* (Tuesday), *Music Box* (Wednesday), *Perspectives* and *Journey into Chinese Culture* (Thursday), *Confrontation* and *New Record Time* (Friday), *Reflections* (Saturday) and *Adventures of Mahlon and Jeanie* and *Mailbag Time* (Sunday). One hour to North and Central America on 5950, 9680 and 11740 kHz; to East Asia on 7130 and 15345 kHz; and to Southeast Asia on 11825 kHz.

Voice of Russia World Service. Continuous to North America at this hour. *News*, features and music to suit all tastes. Winter fare includes ●*Commonwealth Update* (0211 Tuesday through Saturday), ●*Music and Musicians* (same time Sunday and Monday), and after 0230, ●*Folk Box* (Tuesday), ●*Music at Your Request* (Wednesday and Friday) and Russian jazz on Thursday and Saturday. Best in summer is ●*Audio Book Club* at 0231 Thursday and Saturday; though some listeners may prefer *Science and Engineering* (0211 Wednesday), the business-oriented *Newmarket* (0211 Tuesday) or the many-faceted *Kaleidoscope* (0231 Tuesday). A listener-response program is aired at 0211 Thursday through Monday. Note that these days are World Time; locally in North America it will be the previous evening. There's nothing for

> Tired of alternative rock? Tap your feet to the tango, still alive and well over Radio Argentina al Exterior.

02:00

eastern North America at this hour, but listeners farther west have a good choice of channels. Winters, choose from 5920, 5930, 7345, 9580 and 12030 kHz; summers, from 12000, 12010, 12050, 13645, 13665, 15180 and 15595 kHz.

Radio Habana Cuba. See 0100 for program details. Continues to eastern North America on 6000 and 9820 kHz. Also available on 9830 kHz upper sideband.

Radio Australia. Continuous programming to East Asia and the Pacific, and well heard in western North America. Begins with *World News*, then Monday through Friday there's *Australia Talks Back*. Weekend fare includes Saturday's ●*Ockham's Razor* (science) and *Health Report*, replaced Sunday by *Fine Music Australia* and *Religion Report*. On 12080, 13605, 15240, 15415, 15510, 17750 and 17795 kHz. Some of these channels may carry a separate sports service on summer weekends and winter Saturdays.

Radio For Peace International, Costa Rica. Part of an eight-hour cyclical block of social-conscience and counterculture programming audible in Europe and the Americas on 7385, 7585 and (summer) 15050 kHz. One of international broadcasting's more unusual features, *The Far Right Radio Review*, can be heard at 0200 Wednesday (Tuesday evening in the Americas). As we go to press, there's a communications feature, *World of Radio*, at the same time Sunday, but the timing of this program tends to change. Some transmissions are in the single-sideband mode, which can be properly processed only on some radios.

Radio Korea International, South Korea. Opens with *news* and commentary, followed Tuesday through Thursday (Monday through Wednesday evenings in the Americas) by *Seoul Calling*. Weekly features include *Echoes of Korean Music* and *Shortwave Feedback* (Monday), *Tales from Korea's Past* (Tuesday), *Korean Cultural Trails* (Wednesday), *Pulse of Korea* (Thursday), *From Us to You* (a listener-response program) and *Let's Learn Korean* (Friday), *Let's Sing Together* and *Korea Through Foreigners' Eyes* (Saturday), and Sunday's *Discovering Korea*, *Korean Literary Corner* and *Weekly News*. Sixty minutes to the Americas on 11725, 11810 and 15575 kHz; and to East Asia on 7275 kHz.

FEBC Radio International, Philippines. The final 30 minutes of *Good Morning from Manila* (see 0000 for specifics), followed by a half hour of religious fare. Targeted at South and Southeast Asia on 15450 kHz, but heard well beyond.

Radio Romania International. *News*, commentary, press review and features on Romania. Regular spots include Wednesday's *Youth Club* (Tuesday evening, local American date), Thursday's *Romanian Musicians*, and Friday's *Listeners' Letterbox* and ●*Skylark* (Romanian folk music). Fifty-five minutes to North America on 5990, 6155, 9510, 9570 and 11940 kHz.

"American Dissident Voices",
WRNO. Winter Sundays only (Saturday evenings, local American date) at this time. See 0100 for program details. Thirty minutes to North America and beyond on 7355 kHz; try four hours later on 7395 kHz if preempted by live sports.

WWCR, Nashville, Tennessee. Carries a variety of disestablishmentarian programs at this hour, depending on the day of the week, and whether it is summer or winter. These include "Protecting Your Wealth", "World of Prophecy" and "Radio Free America"; choose between 5065 and 2390 (or 7435) kHz.

WJCR, Upton, Kentucky. Continues with country gospel music for North American listeners on 7490 kHz. Also with religious broadcasts to North America at this hour are **WYFR-Family Radio** on 6065 and 9505 kHz, **WWCR** on 5935 kHz, **KAIJ** on 5810 kHz, and **KTBN** on 7510 kHz. Traditional Catholic programming can be heard via **WEWN** on 7425 kHz.

02:30

Radio Austria International. Repeat of the 0030 broadcast. A half hour to the Americas on 9655 (or 7325), 9870 and 13730 (or 9495) kHz.

Radio Sweden. *News* and features concentrating heavily on Scandinavia. See 0030 for program details. Thirty minutes to North America on one or more channels from 6090, 7115, 7120 and 7290 kHz.

Radyo Pilipinas, Philippines. Monday through Saturday, the broadcast opens with *Voice of Democracy* and closes with *World News.* These are separated by a daily feature: *Save the Earth* (Monday), *The Philippines Today* (Tuesday), *Changing World* (Wednesday), *Business Updates* (Thursday), *Brotherhood of Men* (Friday), and Saturday's *Listeners and Friends.* Sunday fare consists of *Asean Connection, Sports Focus* and *News Roundup.* Approximately one hour to South and East Asia on 17760, 17865 and 21580 kHz.

Radio Budapest, Hungary. Summers only at this time. *News* and features, some of which are broadcast on a regular basis. These include Tuesday's *Musica Hungarica* (local Monday evening in North America), *Focus on Business* and *The Weeklies* (Thursday), *Letter Home* (Friday) and *Profiles* (Sunday). Thirty minutes to North America on 9840 and 11910 kHz. One hour later in winter.

Voice of Vietnam. Repeat of the 0100 broadcast; see there for specifics. A relay to eastern North America via the facilities of the Voice of Russia, winters on 5940 kHz, and summers on 7250 kHz.

Radio Netherlands. Repeat of the 0030 transmission. Fifty-five minutes to South Asia, but heard well beyond, on 9855 (or 9860) and 11655 kHz.

> Central Europe has always been a bountiful source of musical entertainment, and Radio Prague's Saturday night concert continues that tradition.

Radio Tirana, Albania. Still being run on a shoestring budget. Programs consist mainly of *news* about the country plus some lively Albanian music. Twenty-five minutes to North America on 6140 and 7160 kHz.

02:50

Vatican Radio. Concentrates heavily, but not exclusively, on issues affecting Catholics around the world. Twenty minutes to eastern North America, winters on 6095 and 7305 kHz, and summers on 7305 and 9605 kHz.

03:00

■**BBC World Service for the Americas.** Five minutes of world *news,* followed by 10 minutes of the best business and financial reporting to be found on the international airwaves. The next quarter-hour is devoted to the popular and highly informative ●*Sports Roundup.* These are followed Tuesday through Saturday (weekday evenings in the Americas) by ●*The World Today* (analysis of current events) and ●*Off the Shelf* (book readings). Best of the remaining offerings at this hour is ●*From Our Own Correspondent* at 0330 Sunday. Audible in North America on 5975, 6175, 9515 (till 0330, winters only) and 9590/9895 kHz.

■**BBC World Service for Europe (and the Mideast).** Identical to the service for the Americas, except for 0330-0400 Monday through Saturday, summers, when Europeans can hear the latest news, analysis and comment in ●*Europe Today.* To eastern Europe on 6195 and (summers) 6180 and 9410 kHz; and to the Mideast on 9410 and 11760 kHz. In summer, the first frequency carries *Europe Today,* while 11760 kHz carries mainstream programming.

■BBC World Service for Africa. As for Europe and the Americas until 0330, then Monday through Friday it's *Network Africa*, a fast-moving breakfast show. On Saturday it's ●*Focus on Faith*, replaced Sunday by *African Quiz* or *Postmark Africa*. If you are interested in what's happening in the continent, tune to 3255, 6005, 6190 and 9600 kHz.

■BBC World Service for Asia. *World News* and ●*Sports Roundup*, followed on the half-hour by the weekday ●*Off the Shelf* (readings from world literature). The final 15 minutes are taken up by a feature, the best of which is Friday's ●*Learning World* (when not substituted by another program). The Saturday slot is given over to *The Vintage Chart Show*, and Sunday's offering is *Global Business*. Continuous to East and Southeast Asia till 0330 on 15360 and 21660 kHz, and thereafter only to East Asia on 11955, 15280 and 21660 kHz.

Radio Canada International. Winters only at this time. Starts off with *News*, then Tuesday through Saturday (weeknights local American date) there's *Report to Peacekeepers*. Weekends, there's a full hour of programs from the domestic service of RCI's parent organization, the Canadian Broadcasting Corporation: *Double Exposure* and *Royal Canadian Air Farce* (Sunday), replaced Monday by *The Inside Track* and *Now the Details*. To eastern North America and the Caribbean on 6155, 9755 and 9780 kHz. One hour earlier in summer.

Voice of Free China, Taiwan. Similar to the 0200 transmission, but with the same programs broadcast one day later. To North and Central America on 5950 and 9680 kHz; to East Asia on 11745 and 15345 kHz; and to Southeast Asia on 11825 kHz.

China Radio International. Repeat of the 0000 transmission. One hour to North America on 9690, 9710 and 11695 kHz.

■Deutsche Welle, Germany. *News*, then Tuesday through Saturday (weekday evenings in North America) it's ●*NewsLink*—a comprehensive package of interviews, background reports and analysis of European events. The remainder of the broadcast is taken up by a repeat of the feature from the 0100 broadcast (see there for specifics). Sunday and Monday, there's a repeat of the 0100 transmission, except that *Religion and Society* replaces Sunday's *Mailbag*. Fifty minutes to North America and the Caribbean, winters on 6045, 6085, 9535 and 9650 kHz; and summers on 6085, 6185, 9535, 9615 and 9640 kHz.

Voice of America. Three and a half hours (four at weekends) of continuous programming aimed at an African audience. Monday through Friday, there's the informative and entertaining ●*Daybreak Africa*, followed by 30 minutes of *Studio 38*. Weekend programming consists of *News* and *VOA Saturday/VOA Sunday*, a mixed bag of sports, science, business and other features. Although beamed to Africa, this service is widely heard elsewhere, including parts of the United States. Try 6035 (winter), 6080, 6115 (summer), 7105, 7280 (summer), 7290, 7340 (till 0330), 7415 (winter), 9575 and 9885 kHz.

Voice of Russia World Service. Continues to North America. *News*, then winters it's a listener-response program (Thursday through Monday), the business-oriented *Newmarket* (Tuesday), or *Science and Engineering* (Wednesday). At 0331, there's ●*Audio Book Club* (Thursday and Saturday), *Kaleidoscope* (Tuesday), *Russian by Radio* (Friday), and mostly music on the remaining days. Note that these days are World Time, so locally in North America it will be the previous evening. In summer, look for the daily *News and Views* at 0311. Apart from ●*Christian Message from Moscow* (Sunday) and ●*Audio Book Club* (Monday), the 0330 summer slot is allocated to "alternative programs." These can be quality shows from the station's archives, mind-numbing religious paid programming, or anything in-between. For eastern North America there's little on offer, but try 5940 kHz in winter and 7125 kHz in summer. Western North America gets a better deal— good winter bets are 5920, 5930, 7345 and 9580 kHz; in summer, go for 12000, 12010, 12050, 13645, 13665, 15180 and 15595 kHz.

Radio Australia. *News*, followed Monday through Friday by *The World Today* (includes sports news on the half-hour). These are replaced weekends by Saturday's *Book Reading* and *Science File*, and Sunday's *Feedback* and *Correspondents' Reports*. Continuous to East Asia and the Pacific, and also audible in western North America. On 12080, 13605, 15240, 15415, 15510, 17750 and 17795 kHz. Some of these channels may carry a separate sports service at weekends. A popular choice with many listeners.

Radio Habana Cuba. Continuous programming to eastern North America, and a repeat of the 0100 programs at this hour. On 6000 and 9820 kHz, and also available on 9830 kHz upper sideband.

Radio Norway International. Winter Mondays (Sunday evenings, local American date) only. *Norway Now*. News and features from one of the friendliest stations on the international airwaves. Thirty minutes to western North America on 7465 kHz.

Radio Thailand. *Newshour*. Thirty minutes to western North America winters on 11890 kHz, and summers on 15395 kHz. Also available to Asia on 9655 and 11905 kHz.

Radio Ukraine International. Summers only at this time. See 0400 for program specifics. Sixty minutes to eastern North America on 7150, 9550 and 12040 kHz; and for European night owls on 6010, 6020 and 6090 kHz. One hour later in winter.

HCJB, from Quito, Ecuador, is one of the oldest world band stations on the air. Although it is partly staffed by non-Latinos, its sensitivity to and promotion of Ecuadorian culture have helped make it a favorite among listeners.

HCJB—Voice of the Andes, Ecuador. Predominantly religious programming at this hour. Try *Joy International*, a selection of Christian music favorites, at 0330 Monday (local Sunday in North America). Continuous programming to the eastern United States and Canada on 9745 kHz.

Radio Prague, Czech Republic. *News*, then Tuesday through Saturday (weekday evenings in the Americas), there's *Current Affairs*. These are followed by one or more features. Take your pick from *Magazine '96* (Tuesday), *Talking Point* and *Media Czech* (Wednesday), *The Arts* and *From the Archives* (Thursday), *Economic Report* and *I'd Like You to Meet . . .* (Friday) and Saturday's *Between You and Us*. Sunday's showpiece is a thoroughly enjoyable musical feature which offers a different style of music each week, alternating between classical, folk, contemporary and jazz. This is replaced Monday by *The Week in Politics*, *From the Weeklies* and *Media Czech*. A half hour to North America on 5930 and 7345 kHz.

Radio Cairo, Egypt. The final half-hour of a 90-minute broadcast to North America on 9475 kHz.

Radio Japan. *News*, followed by the weekday *Radio Japan Magazine Hour*. This consists of *News Commentary*, *Japan*

Diary, *Close Up*, a feature (two on Tuesday) and a final news bulletin. Monday (Sunday evening in North America), you can hear *Sports Column*, Tuesday features *Japanese Culture* and *Today*, Wednesday has *Asian Report*, Thursday brings *Crosscurrents*, and Friday's offering is *Business Focus*. Weekend fare is made up of Saturday's *This Week* and Sunday's *Hello from Tokyo*. Sixty minutes to western North America winters on 9605 and 11960 kHz, and summers on 11790 and 15230 kHz. Available to East and Southeast Asia on 11840 and 17810 kHz. Winters only, can also be heard in eastern North America on 5960 kHz.

Croatian Radio. Summers only at this time. *News* from Croatian Radio's Zagreb studio (length of bulletin varies). Best received in Europe and eastern North America, but also heard elsewhere. On 5895 kHz, with 9495 additionally available for eastern North America. One hour later in winter.

Radio New Zealand International. A friendly broadcasting package targeted at a regional audience. Part of a much longer transmission for the South Pacific, but also heard in parts of North America (especially during summer) on 15115 kHz. Often carries commentaries of local sporting events.

Voice of Turkey. Summers only at this time. *News*, followed by *Review of the Turkish Press* and features (some of them arcane) with a strong local flavor. Selections of Turkish popular and classical music complete the program. Fifty minutes to eastern North America on 7300 or 9655 kHz, to the Mideast on 9685 kHz, and to Southeast Asia and Australasia on 17705 kHz. One hour later during winter.

WJCR, Upton, Kentucky. Continues with country gospel music for North American listeners on 7490 kHz. Also with religious programs to North America at this hour are **WGTG** on 5085 kHz, **WYFR-Family Radio** on 6065 and 9505 kHz,

WWCR on 5935 kHz, **KAIJ** on 5810 kHz and **KTBN** on 7510 kHz. For traditional Catholic fare, try **WEWN** on 7425 kHz.

"For the People," WHRI, Noblesville, Indiana. A two-hour edited repeat of the 1900 (1800 in summer) broadcast. Promotes classic populism—an American political tradition going back to 1891. Suspicious of concentrated wealth and power, *For the People* promotes economic nationalism ("buying foreign amounts to treason"), little-reported health concepts and a sharply progressive income tax, while opposing the "New World Order" and international banking. This two-hour talk show, hosted by former deejay Chuck Harder, can be heard Tuesday-Saturday (Monday through Friday local days) on 5745 kHz. Targeted at North America, but heard beyond.

Radio For Peace International, Costa Rica. Continues with a variety of counterculture and social-conscience features. There is also a listener-response program at 0330 Wednesday (Tuesday evening in the Americas). Audible in Europe and the Americas on 7385, 7585 and (summer) 15050 kHz. Some transmissions are in the single-sideband mode, which can be properly processed only on some radios.

WWCR, Nashville, Tennessee. "Radio Free America", a populist show hosted by Tom Valentine for two hours Tuesday through Saturday (Monday through Friday evenings, local American date). Winters, starts at this time; summers, it is already at its halfway point. Well heard in North America on 5065 kHz.

03:30

United Arab Emirates Radio, Dubai. *News*, then a feature devoted to Arab and Islamic history or culture. Twenty-five minutes to North America on 11945, 13675, 15400 and 21485 kHz; heard best during the warm-weather months.

Find Your Place in the World with Grundig

Grundig's Yacht Boy 400 –

Powerful enough to hear the world, yet small enough to fit in your hand. This award-winning radio features 40 presets for quick recall plus selectable wide/narrow bandwidth filter, and built-in clock with dual alarms and sleep timer. Cover AM/FM/LW and continuous short wave bands from 1.6 to 30 MHZ. Complete with travel case and carrying strap.

Grundig's Yacht Boy 305 –

This new world band radio features circuitry superior to comparable analog (dial tune) radios. Its digital technology allows you to precisely "fine tune" distant signals for crystal clear reception and rock-solid frequency stability. To catch the news, weather or even music from around the world, simply autoscan through AM, FM or the shortwave spectrum.

Grundig's Compact World Traveller II Digital –

The Grundig digital, portable AM/FM/SW radio is big on features, yet small enough to fit into a pocket or handbag. Keep track of time and events at home or away with…
- Dual quartz controlled alarm clocks • sleep timer
- 20 station memory • auto search and manual tuning
- protective travel pouch, *Grundig Shortwave Listening Guide.*

Radio Sweden. Repeat of the 0230 transmission. See 0030 for program details. Thirty minutes to North America on 7115 or 7120 kHz.

Radio Prague, Czech Republic. Repeat of the 0300 broadcast (see there for specifics). A half hour to the Mideast and beyond. Winters on 7350 kHz, and summers on 9480 and 11600 kHz.

Radio Budapest, Hungary. This time winters only; see 0230 for specifics. Thirty minutes to North America on 6195 and 9840 kHz. One hour earlier in summer.

RDP International—Radio Portugal. Tuesday through Saturday (weekday evenings in North America) and summers only at this time. See 0430 for specifics. Thirty minutes of *news* and features about Portugal. Only fair reception in eastern North America—worse to the west—on 6150 and 9570 kHz. One hour later in winter.

Voice of Greece. Actual start time subject to slight variation. Ten to fifteen minutes of English *news*, preceded by long periods of Greek music and programming. To North America on any three frequencies from 6260, 7448, 9420, 9935 and 11645 kHz.

04:00

■BBC World Service for the Americas. Starts with the half-hour ●*Newsdesk*, followed Tuesday through Saturday (local weekday evenings in the Americas) by the eclectic and entertaining ●*Outlook*. The hour is rounded off by a five minute feature. These are replaced Sunday by ●*From Our Own Correspondent*. A full hour of top-notch programming to North America on 5975 and 6175 kHz.

■BBC World Service for Europe (and the Mideast). As for the Americas, except for 0430-0500 Monday through Saturday (Monday through Friday in summer), when Europeans can hear the latest news, analysis and comment in

●*Europe Today*. Continuous to Europe on 3955, 6180, 6195 and (summer) 9410 and 12095 kHz; and to the Mideast on 9410 (winter), 11760 and 15575 kHz. The 9410 kHz channel has the European program, while the other frequencies carry mainstream programming.

■BBC World Service for Africa. ●*Newsdesk*, followed at 0430 Monday through Friday by *Network Africa*, Saturday by *African Quiz* or *Postmark Africa*, and Sunday by *The Arts House*. Targeted at African listeners, but also heard elsewhere, on 3255, 6005, 6190, 7160 and 9600 kHz.

■BBC World Service for Asia. First it's ●*Newsdesk*, then Monday through Saturday the accent's on youth or popular music. Pick of the pack are Wednesday's ●*Megamix* and Friday's inimitable ●*John Peel*. The Sunday offering is ●*From Our Own Correspondent*. Continuous to East Asia on 11955, 15280 and 21660 kHz.

Radio Habana Cuba. Continuous programming to eastern North America. Consists of Cuban and Latin American *news*, features about Cuba, and some lively and enjoyable music from the island. On 6000 and 9820 kHz. Also available on 9830 kHz upper sideband.

Swiss Radio International. Repeat of the 0100 broadcast to North America on 6135, 9885 and 9905 kHz. Look for an additional 30-minute feature on 9905 kHz which is a simulcast of SRI's satellite programming.

HCJB—Voice of the Andes, Ecuador. The first of three hours of continuous programming to western North America on 9745 kHz. Tuesday through Saturday (weekday evenings in North America) it's *Studio 9*, featuring nine minutes of world and Latin American *news*, followed by 20 minutes of in-depth reporting on Latin America. The final portion of *Studio 9* is given over to one of a variety of 30-minute features—including *You Should Know* (issues and ethics, Tuesday), *El Mundo*

C. Tyson

Sydney, Australia's, multimodal urban transportation system integrates trains, ferries, buses and automobiles.

Futuro (science, Wednesday), *Ham Radio Today* (Thursday), *Woman to Woman* (Friday), and the unique and enjoyable ●*Música del Ecuador* (Saturday). On Sunday (Saturday evening in the Americas), the news is followed by *DX Partyline*, which in turn is replaced Monday by *Saludos Amigos*—HCJB's international friendship program.

Radio Australia. *News*, then Monday through Friday it's *Pacific Beat*, divided into two parts by 10 minutes of sports news on the half-hour. These are replaced weekends by *Pacific Focus* followed by Saturday's *Indian Pacific* or Sunday's *Australia Today*. Continuous to East Asia and the Pacific, and also heard in western North America. On 12080, 13605, 15240, 15510, 17750 and 17795 kHz. Some channels may carry separate sports programming at weekends.

■**Deutsche Welle, Germany.** *News*, then Tuesday through Saturday there's the highly informative ●*NewsLink* (interviews, background reports and analysis of European events), replaced Monday by *Commentary* and *Inside Europe*. Monday through Friday, the last part of the broadcast is given over to ●*Good Morning Africa*, with *Economic Notebook* in the Saturday slot. The Sunday lineup features *Sports Report*, *Focus on Development* (alternates with *Women on the Move*), *Religion and Society* and *Hits in Germany*. A 50-minute broadcast aimed primarily at eastern and southern Africa, but also heard in parts of the Mideast and eastern North America. Winters on 6015, 6065, 7225, 7265 and 9565 kHz; and summers on 5990, 6015, 7225, 9565 and 11765 kHz.

Radio Canada International. *News*, then Tuesday through Saturday it's the topical *Spectrum*. This is replaced Sunday by the science feature *Innovation Canada*, and Monday by a listener-response program. Thirty minutes to the Mideast, winters on 6150, 9505 and 9645 kHz; summers on 9715, 11835 and 11975 kHz.

China Radio International. Repeat of the 0000 transmission. One hour to North America on 9730 and (summer) 9560 kHz.

Radio Norway International. Summer Mondays (Sunday evenings in the target area) only. *Norway Now*. A half hour of *news* and human-interest stories targeted at western North America on 7465 (or 7520) kHz.

Radio Bulgaria. Summers only at this time. Starts with 15 minutes of *news*, followed Tuesday through Friday by *Today* (current events), and Saturday by *Weekly Spotlight*, a summary of the major political events of the week. At other times, there are features dealing with multiple aspects of Bulgarian life and culture, including some lively Balkan folk music. To eastern North America and Central America on 9485 and 11720 kHz. One hour later in winter.

Voice of America. Directed to Africa and the Mideast, but widely heard elsewhere. *News*, followed Monday through Friday by ●*VOA Business Report*. On the half-hour, the African service continues with ●*Daybreak Africa*, replaced to other areas by *Studio 38*—a look at American lifestyles. Weekends, the *news* is followed by 50 minutes of *VOA Saturday/VOA Sunday*. To North Africa and the Mideast on 7170 (North Africa only), and (summer) 11965 and 15205 kHz. The mainstream African service is available on 6035 (winter), 6080, 7180 (winter), 7265 and 7280 (summer), 7290, 7415 (winter), 9575, 9775 (winter) and (till 0430) 9885 kHz. Reception of some of these channels is also possible in parts of North America.

Channel Africa, South Africa. Thirty

minutes of mostly news-related fare. To southern Africa on 5955 kHz.

Radio Romania International. Similar to the 0200 transmission (see there for specifics). Fifty-five minutes to North America on 5990, 6155, 9510, 9570 and 11940 kHz.

Radio Ukraine International. Winters only at this time. An hour's ample coverage of just about everything Ukrainian, including news, sports, politics and culture. Well worth a listen is ●*Music from Ukraine*, which fills most of the Monday (Sunday evening in the Americas) broadcast. Sixty minutes to North America on 5915 and 7150 kHz. One hour earlier in summer.

Voice of Turkey. Winters only at this time. See 0300 for specifics. Fifty minutes to eastern North America on 9655 kHz, to the Mideast on 9685 kHz, and to Southeast Asia and Australasia on 9560 kHz. One hour earlier in summer.

Radio Ukraine International provides a panoramic view of things Ukrainian—rousing music, too.

WJCR, Upton, Kentucky. Continues with country gospel music for North American listeners on 7490 kHz. Also with religious programs to North America at this hour are **WGTG** on 5085 kHz, **WYFR-Family Radio** on 6065 and 9505 kHz, **WWCR** on 5935 kHz, **KAIJ** on 5810 kHz and **KTBN** on 7510 kHz. Traditional Catholic programming is available via **WEWN** on 7425 kHz

Kol Israel. Summers only at this time. *News* for 15 minutes from Israel Radio's domestic network. To Europe and eastern North America on 7465 and 9435 kHz, and to Australasia on 17545 kHz. One hour later in winter.

Radio New Zealand International. Continues with regional programming for the South Pacific. Part of a much longer broadcast, which is also heard in parts of North America (especially during summer) on 15115 kHz. Sometimes carries commentaries of local sporting events.

Norham Radio Inc.

Friendly & Qualified Staff + Experienced Advice + Competitive Pricing = Customer Satisfaction

Canada's Leader in Shortwave Radio & Scanners

 ICOM

IC-R10E Compact Handheld Receiver

- .5 to 1300 MHz coverage (with 800 MHz)
- All mode reception (AM, NFM, WFM, SSB, CW)
- Built in Band Scope
- 15 different tuning steps .1 to 1MHz
- 7 Scan methods
- 1000 memory channels
- Computer controllable (optional CT-17)
- Powered by 4 AA nicads (included),
  Regular AA alkaline cells or 12v DC

IC-R8500E Communications Receiver

- .1 to 2000 MHz coverage (with 800 MHz)
- All mode reception AM, NFM, WFM, SSB, CW
- TV reception with optional TV-R7000 & monitor
- 13 different tuning steps .1 to 1 MHz
- Versitile scanning functions
- 1000 memory channels
- Built in RS232 computer interface
- Powered by 12v DC (adaptor included)

ALINCO

DJ-X10 Wide Range Receiver

- .1 to 2000 MHz coverage (with 800 MHz)
- All mode reception AM, NFM, WFM, SSB, CW
- Signal strength meter and Channel Scope
- Alphanumeric display
- 1200 memory channels
- Dual VFO's simultaneously displayed
- Clock and Priority watch
- Powered by rechargable nicad (included)

AOR

AOR-8000 Handheld Scanner

- .5 to 1900 MHz coverage (with 800 MHz)
- All mode reception AM, NFM, WFM, SSB, CW
- Signal strength meter and Band Scope
- Internal ferrite antenna improves low bands
- Alphanumeric display
- 1000 memory channels
- Dual VFO's simultaneously displayed
- Computer controllable (Software optional)
- Powered by rechargable AA nicads (included)

YUPITERU
MVT-7100 Handheld Scanner

- .5 to 1600 MHz coverage (with 800 MHz)
- All mode reception AM, NFM, WFM, SSB, CW
- Rotary tuning knob
- Signal strength meter
- High speed search and scan
- 1000 memory channels
- Illuminated keypad
- Built in RF attinuator
- Powered by rechargable AA nicads (included)

YUPITERU
MVT-9000 Handheld Scanner

- .5 to 2000 MHz coverage (with 800 MHz)
- All mode reception AM, NFM, WFM, SSB, CW
- Rotary tuning knob
- Signal strength meter and Band Scope
- High speed search and scan
- 1000 memory channels
- Illuminated keypad
- Built in AM antenna
- Powered by rechargable AA nicads (included)

Please call for exact pricing and shipping. All USA orders shipped Express

Visit Our Retail Store :
4373 Steeles Ave. W., North York, On M3N 1V7
Store Hours :
Monday-Friday : 10am - 6pm
Saturday : 10am - 2pm, Closed Sunday

Phone or Mail Order :
(416) 667-1000
VISA   MasterCard

FAX :(416) 667-9995   www.norham.com
E-Mail: norham@fox.nstn.ca

RFPI

Radio for Peace International, although in Costa Rica, was created by a United Nations resolution and is staffed in large part by Americans. Its programs focus on the rights and conditions of minorities, women and the poor, among others.

Radio For Peace International, Costa Rica. Part of an eight-hour cyclical block of predominantly social-conscience and counterculture programming. Some of the offerings at this hour include a women's news-gathering service, *WINGS*, (0430 Friday); a listener-response program (same time Saturday); and *The Far Right Radio Review* (0400 Sunday). Audible in Europe and the Americas on 7385, 7585 and (summer) 15050 kHz. Some transmissions are in the single-sideband mode, which can be properly processed only on some radios.

Voice of Russia World Service. Continuous to North America at this hour. Winters, it's *News and Views*, replaced Tuesday through Saturday summers by the timely ●*Commonwealth Update*. The final half-hour contains some interesting fare. Summer pickings include *Jazz Show* (Monday), ●*Music at Your Request* (Wednesday), ●*Folk Box* (Thursday), *Kaleidoscope* (Friday) and Sunday's retrospective ●*Moscow Yesterday and Today*. Winters, the Sunday slot is filled by ●*Christian Message from Moscow*, replaced Monday by ●*Audio Book Club*. The remaining days feature "alternative programs"—religious paid programming or a show from the Voice of Russia's archives or transcription department. In eastern North America, try 7125 kHz. Reception is iffy, but you may be lucky. Farther west, best winter bets are 5920, 5930, 7345 and 9580 kHz; in summer, try 12000, 12010, 12050, 13645, 13665, 15180 and 15595 kHz.

"For the People," WHRI, Noblesville, Indiana. See 0300 for specifics. The second half of a two-hour broadcast targeted week-nights to North America on 5745 kHz.

Croatian Radio. Several minutes of *news* (length varies) from Croatian

Radio's Zagreb studio. Best heard in Europe and eastern North America, but also heard elsewhere. On 5895 kHz, with 9495 kHz also available summers for eastern North America.

WWCR, Nashville, Tennessee. Carries a variety of disestablishmentarian programs at this hour, depending on the day of the week, and whether it is summer or winter. These include "America First Radio," "Hour of the Time," "Duncan Long Show" and "Radio Free America"; choose between 5065 and 2390 (or 7435) kHz.

Corner (Saturday). There are no broadcasts on Sunday or Monday (Saturday and Sunday evenings local North American days). Only fair reception in eastern North America—worse to the west—on 6150 and 9570 kHz. One hour earlier in summer.

Radio Yugoslavia. Summers only at this time. *News* and short background reports heavily geared to local issues. Worth a listen if you are interested in the region. Thirty minutes to western North America on 9580 and 11870 kHz.

04:30

Radio Netherlands. *News*, then Tuesday through Sunday (Monday through Saturday evenings in North America) there's ●*Newsline*, a current affairs program. These are followed by a different feature each day, including the well-produced ●*Research File* (science, Tuesday); *Mirror Images* (arts in Holland, Wednesday); the excellent ●*Documentary* (Thursday); *Media Network* (Friday); ●*A Good Life* (Saturday); and Sunday's ●*Weekend*. Monday's features are a listener-response program and *Sounds Interesting*. Fifty-five minutes to western North America on 5995 (winter), 6165 and (summer) 9590 kHz.

Radio Austria International. Summers only at this time. ●*Report from Austria*, which includes a brief bulletin of *news*, followed by a series of current events and human interest stories. An excellent source for news of central and eastern Europe. Thirty minutes to Europe on 6155 and 13730 kHz. One hour later in winter.

RDP International—Radio Portugal. Winters only at this time. *News*, which usually takes up at least half the broadcast, followed by features: *Visitor's Notebook* (Tuesday), *Musical Kaleidoscope* (Wednesday), *Challenge of the 90's* (Thursday), *Spotlight on Portugal* (Friday), and *Listeners' Mailbag* and *Collector's*

05:00

■**BBC World Service for the Americas.** Thirty minutes of ●*Newsday*, then some of the BBC's best output, most of which starts on the half-hour. Take your choice from *The Works* (technology, Monday), ●*Discovery* (science, Tuesday), ●*One Planet* (development, Wednesday), ●*The Learning World* (education, 0545 Thursday), ●*Assignment* (Friday), ●*Science in Action* (Saturday) and world theater at its best in Sunday's ●*Play of the Week*. Audible in North America (better to the west) on 5975 and 6175 kHz.

■**BBC World Service for Europe (and the Mideast).** Identical to the service for the Americas, except for 0530-0600 weekdays, when some frequencies carry ●*Europe Today*. In winter, listeners in Europe can choose from 3955, 6180, 6195 and 9410 kHz; summers, the program is only available on 3955 and 6195 kHz. Summer mainstream programming can be heard on 6180, 7120, 9410 and 12095 kHz. *Europe Today* can be heard in the Mideast only in winter, on 9410 kHz, while mainstream output is on 11760, 12095 (winter) and 15575 kHz.

■**BBC World Service for Africa.** Thirty minutes of ●*Newsday*, then weekdays it's a continuation of *Network Africa*. This is replaced Saturday by *Talk About Africa* and Sunday by *Postmark Africa*.

Continuous programming on 3255, 6005, 6190, 7160, 9600, 15420 and 17885 kHz.

■BBC World Service for Asia and the Pacific. ●*Newsday* and a variety of features and entertainment. Quality offerings include ●*Omnibus* (0530 Tuesday) and ●*Focus on Faith* (same time Friday). Sports fans should not miss Wednesday's comprehensive package of news, interviews and features in *Sports International*. Continuous to East and Southeast Asia on 9740, 11955, 15280 and 15360 kHz; and to Australasia on 11955 and 15360 kHz.

■Deutsche Welle, Germany. Repeat of the 50-minute 0100 transmission to North America, winters on 6120, 6145, 6185 and 9650 kHz; and summers on 5960, 6045, 6185 and 9515 kHz. This slot is by far the best for western North America.

Radio Exterior de España ("Spanish National Radio"). *News*, then Tuesday through Saturday (local week-nights in North America) it's *Panorama*, which features a recording of popular Spanish music, a commentary or a report, a review of the Spanish press, and weather. The remainder of the program is a mixture of literature, science, music and general programming. Tuesday (Monday evening in North America), there's *Sports Spotlight* and *Cultural Encounters*; Wednesday features *People of Today* and *Entertainment in Spain*; Thursday brings *As Others See Us* and, biweekly, *The Natural World* or *Science Desk*; Friday has *Economic Report* and *Cultural Clippings*; and Saturday offers *Window on Spain* and *Review of the Arts*. The final slot is give over to a language course, *Spanish by Radio*. On the remaining days, you can listen to Sunday's *Hall of Fame, Distance Unknown* (for radio enthusiasts) and *Gallery of Spanish Voices*; and Monday's *Visitors' Book, Great Fig-*

Great Figures in Flamenco is Spanish National Radio's tribute to one of the country's major assets.

ures in Flamenco and *Radio Club*. Sixty minutes to North America on 6055 kHz.

Radio Canada International. Summer weekdays only. See 0600 for program details. To Europe, Africa and the Mideast on 6050, 7295, 11835 and 15430 kHz. One hour later during winter.

Vatican Radio. Summers only at this time. Twenty minutes of programming oriented to Catholics. To Europe on 5880 and 7250 kHz. Frequencies may vary slightly. One hour later in winter.

China Radio International. This time winters only. Repeat of the 0000 broadcast; one hour to North America on 9560 kHz.

HCJB—Voice of the Andes, Ecuador. A mixed bag of religious and secular programming, depending on the day of the week. Tuesday (Monday night in North America) is given over to *The Least of These* and *Let My People Think*; Wednesday airs *Simply Worship* and *Unshackled*; and Thursday brings *The Book and the Spade, Inside HCJB* and *Rock Solid!* On Friday, you can hear *Radio Reading Room* and *Inspirational Classics*; Saturday has the Europe-oriented *On-Line* followed by *On Track* (contemporary Christian music); Sunday features *Musical Mailbag* and *Afterglow*; and Monday is devoted to *Radio Reading Room* and *The Sower*. Continuous programming to western North America on 9745 kHz.

Voice of America. Continues with the morning broadcast to Africa and the Mideast. Starts with *News*, followed weekdays by *VOA Today*—a conglomeration of business, sports, science, entertainment and virtually anything else that may be newsworthy. On weekends, the news is followed by an extended edition of *VOA Saturday/VOA Sunday*. To the Mideast and North Africa on 7170, 9700 and 11825

(winter), 11965 (summer) and 15205 kHz; and to the rest of Africa on 5970, 6035, 6080, 7195 (summer), 7295 (winter), 9630 (summer), 9775 (winter) and 12080 kHz. Some of these channels provide reasonable reception in parts of North America.

Radio Bulgaria. Winters only at this time; see 0400 for specifics. A distinctly Bulgarian potpourri of news, commentary, interviews and features, plus a fair amount of music. Sixty minutes to eastern North America and Central America on 7480 and 9700 kHz. One hour earlier in summer.

Radio Habana Cuba. Repeat of the 0100 transmission. To western North America winter on 6000 kHz, and summer on 9820 kHz. Also available to Europe on 9830 kHz upper sideband.

Channel Africa, South Africa. Thirty minutes of mostly news-related fare. To West Africa on 9675 or 11900 kHz, and sometimes heard in Europe and eastern North America.

Voice of Nigeria. The first hour of a daily broadcast intended for listeners in West Africa, but also heard in parts of Europe and North America (especially during winter). Features vary from day to day, but are predominantly concerned with Nigerian and West African affairs. On 7255 kHz.

Radio New Zealand International. Continues with regional programming for the South Pacific. Part of a much longer broadcast, which is also heard in parts of North America (especially during summer) on 9570 or 11900 kHz.

Radio Australia. *News*, then Monday through Friday there's *Dateline*, *Australia Today* and the retrospective *On This Day*. Weekends, look for *Oz Sounds* and Saturday's *The Sports Factor*, replaced Sunday by *The Media Report*. Continuous to East Asia and the Pacific, and also heard in western North America. On 12080, 13605, 15240, 15510 and 17795 kHz. Some channels may carry alternative sports programming at weekends.

Voice of Russia World Service. Continues winters to eastern North America, and year-round to western North America. Tuesday through Saturday, winters, the first half-hour features *News* and ●*Commonwealth Update*, the latter replaced summers by *Focus on Asia and the Pacific*. At 0531 winters, look for some interesting musical shows, including ●*Music at Your Request* (Wednesday), ●*Folk Box* (Thursday), and Monday's jazz feature. Other interesting offerings include Friday's *Kaleidoscope* and Sunday's ●*Moscow Yesterday and Today*. Summers, this slot is given over to either ●*Moscow Yesterday and Today* (Tuesday, Thursday and Saturday) or, on the remaining days, *This is Russia*. For the technically minded, try *Science and Engineering* at 0511 Sunday. Winters to eastern North America on 7125 kHz, and to western parts on 5920, 5930 and (from 0530) 7330 kHz. Summers in western North America, choose from 12000, 12010, 12050, 12070 (from 0530), 13645, 13665, 15180 and 15595 kHz. Also available summers for East and Southeast Asia and Australasia on 15470 and 17570 kHz.

Radio For Peace International, Costa Rica. Continues at this hour with a potpourri of United Nations, counterculture and other programs. These include *WINGS* (news for and of women, 0530 Wednesday) and *Vietnam Veterans Radio Network* (0530 Thursday). Audible in Europe and the Americas on 7385 and 7585 kHz. Some transmissions are in the single-sideband mode, which can be properly processed only on some radios.

Kol Israel. Winters only at this time. *News* for 15 minutes from Israel Radio's domestic network. To Europe and eastern North America on 7465 and 13755 kHz, and to Australasia on 17545 kHz. One hour earlier in summer.

Radio Japan. Repeat of the 0300 broadcast, except that Sunday's *Hello from Tokyo* is replaced by *Let's Learn*

Japanese and *Viewpoint*; and the daily end-of-broadcast news gives way to *Tokyo Pop-in*. Sixty minutes to Europe winters on 5975 and 6150 kHz, and summers on 7230 kHz; to East and Southeast Asia on 11725, 11740 and 17810 kHz; to Australasia on 11920 kHz; and to western North America on 6110 kHz. There is also a 30-minute broadcast to West North America and Central America on 11885, 11895, 11960 (winter) and (summer) 15230 kHz.

Croatian Radio. Winters only at this time. Several minutes of *news* (length varies) from Croatian Radio's Zagreb studio. Best heard in Europe and eastern North America, but also heard elsewhere. On 5895 kHz. One hour earlier in summer.

Radio Pyongyang, North Korea. A soporific hour of old-fashioned communist propaganda. To Europe on 11740 and 13790 kHz.

WWCR, Nashville, Tennessee. Carries a variety of disestablishmentarian programs at this hour, depending on the day of the week, and whether it is summer or winter. These include winter's "America First Radio", "Hour of the Time" and "Duncan Long Show"; and summer's "Herald of Truth", "The Hour of Courage" and "Seventieth Week Magazine." On 5065 and 2390 (or 7435) kHz.

WJCR, Upton, Kentucky. Continues with country gospel music for North American listeners on 7490 kHz. Also with religious programs to North America at this hour are **WGTG** on 5085 kHz, **WYFR-Family Radio** on 5985 kHz, **WWCR** on 5935 kHz, **KAIJ** on 5810 kHz and **KTBN** on 7510 kHz. For traditional Catholic programming (some of which may be in Spanish), tune to **WEWN** on 7425 kHz.

Oberengadin, Graubünden, in the Swiss Alps. Swiss Radio International brings Alpine music to the four corners of the world.

Foto Schweiz Tourismus

05:15

Swiss Radio International. Summers only at this time. Fifteen minutes of *news* to Europe on 6165 and 9535 kHz. One hour later in winter.

05:30

Radio Austria International. ●*Report from Austria*; see 0430 for more details. Thirty minutes year-round to North America on 6015 kHz, and winters only to Europe and the Mideast on 6155, 13730, 15410 and 17870 kHz.

United Arab Emirates Radio, Dubai. See 0330 for program details. To East Asia and Australasia on 15435, 17830 and 21700 kHz.

Radio Thailand. Thirty minutes of *news* and short features. To Europe on 15115 kHz. Also available to Asia on 9655 and 11905 kHz.

Radio Romania International. *News*, commentary, a press review, and one or more short features. Thirty minutes to southern Africa (and heard elsewhere) on 11810 (or 11740), 11940, 15250 (or 15270), 15340 (or 15365), 17745 (winter) and 17790 kHz.

06:00

■BBC World Service for the Americas.
Except Sunday (Saturday evening in western North America), the hour starts with 15 minutes of *World News*. This is followed Tuesday through Saturday by a quarter-hour of analysis of current events in ●*The World Today*, replaced Monday by a feature. Sunday, it's a continuation of ●*Play of the Week*, which can run to either 0630 or 0700. The second half-hour is given over to one or more features. These include ●*Omnibus* (Monday), *Sports International* (Wednesday) and an arts program, *Meridian* on Thursday and Saturday. If Sunday's radio theater ends early, look for *A Jolly Good Show* during the final 30 minutes. Continuous to North America (better to the west) on 5975 and 6175 kHz.

■BBC World Service for Europe (and the Mideast). Identical to the service for the Americas, except for 0630-0700 winter weekdays on 3255 and 6195 kHz, when listeners in western Europe can hear ●*Europe Today*. Continuous to Europe on 3955 (winter), 6180, 6195, 7325, 9410, 11780, 12095 and 15575 kHz; and to the Mideast on 9410 (winter), 11760, 12095 (winter) and 15575 kHz.

■BBC World Service for Africa.
Opens with 15 minutes of *World News*, then Monday through Friday it's ●*Sports Roundup* and the breakfast show *Network Africa*. Saturday fare consists of Alistair Cooke's ●*Letter from America* followed by a repeat of the 0430 show, and Sunday airs a quarter-hour feature and *African Perspective*. Continuous to most parts of the continent on 6005, 6190, 7160, 9600, 11835 (midyear), 11940 and 15420 kHz.

■BBC World Service for Asia and the Pacific. *World News*, followed Tuesday through Saturday by ●*The World Today*, and replaced Sunday by ●*Letter from America* and Monday by *Seven Days* (current events). Offerings on the half-hour include the arts show *Meridian* (Sunday, Wednesday, Thursday and Saturday), *Composer of the Month* (Tuesday) and *Music Review* (Friday). Continuous to East and Southeast Asia on 9740, 11955, 15360 and 21660 kHz; and to Australasia on 7145, 11955 and 15360 kHz.

■Deutsche Welle, Germany. Repeat of the 50-minute 0400 transmission to Africa, and beamed to West Africa at this hour. Also well heard in parts of Europe, especially during summer. Winters on 7225, 9565, 11765, 13790, 17820 and 21705 kHz; and summers on 11915, 13790, 15185, 17820, 17860 and 21680 kHz. Good reception in the Mideast on 21705/21680 kHz.

Radio Habana Cuba. Repeat of the 0200 transmission. To western North America winter on 6000 kHz, and summer on 9820 kHz. Also available to Europe on 9830 kHz upper sideband.

Croatian Radio. Monday through Friday, summers only at this time; actually starts a little late, and is preceded by a few minutes of Croatian. Several minutes of on-the-spot *news* (length varies) from one of Europe's most troubled areas. Intended mainly for Europe and Australasia at this hour, but also heard elsewhere. On 5920, 7165, 9830 and (irregularly) 13830 kHz. One hour later during winter.

Radio Norway International. Summer Sundays only. *Norway Now*. Thirty minutes of *news* and human-interest stories. To Europe on 7180 kHz, and to Australasia on 7295 and 9590 kHz.

Swiss Radio International. *Newsnet.* A workmanlike compilation of news and background reports on world and Swiss events. Look for some lighter fare on Saturdays, when the biweekly *Capital Letters* (a listener-response program) alternates with *Name Game* and *Sounds Good.* A half hour to Africa on 9885, 11860 and 13635 kHz. The last frequency is best for southern Africa.

Radio Canada International. Winter weekdays only. Thirty minutes targeted at Canadian peacekeepers overseas. To Europe, Africa and the Mideast on 6050, 6150, 9740, 9760 and 11905 kHz. One hour earlier in summer.

Voice of America. Final segment of the transmission to Africa and the Mideast. Monday through Friday, the mainstream African service carries just 30 minutes of ●*Daybreak Africa*, with other channels carrying a full hour of *news* and *VOA Today*—a mixed bag of popular music, interviews, human interest stories, science digest and sports news. Weekend programming is the same to all areas—a bulletin of *news* followed by 50 minutes of *VOA Saturday/VOA Sunday.* To North Africa and the Mideast on 5995 (winter), 7170, 9680 (summer), 11805, 11825 (winter), 11965 (summer) and 15205 kHz; and to mainstream Africa on 5970, 6035, 6080, 7195 (summer), 7285 and 7295 (winter), 9630 (summer), 11950, 12080 and (winter) 15600 kHz. Several of these channels give fair reception in parts of North America.

Radio Australia. *News*, then Monday through Friday it's *Pacific Beat*, with a break for the latest sports news on the half-hour. Weekend fare consists of *Feedback* and *Arts Australia* (Saturday), replaced Sunday by ●*Ockham's Razor* and

Correspondents' Report. Continuous to East Asia and the Pacific, and also audible in western North America. On 12080, 13605, 15240, 15415, 15510, 17750 and 21725 kHz. Some channels may carry an alternative sports program until 0630 at weekends (0730 midyear).

Voice of Nigeria. The second (and final) hour of a daily broadcast intended for listeners in West Africa, but also heard in parts of Europe and North America (especially during winter). Features vary from day to day, but are predominantly concerned with Nigerian and West African affairs. On 7255 kHz.

Radio New Zealand International. Continues with regional programming for the South Pacific. Part of a much longer broadcast, which is also heard in parts of North America (especially during summer) on 9570 or 11900 kHz.

Voice of Russia World Service. *News*, then winters it's *Focus on Asia and the Pacific* (Tuesday through Saturday), *Science and Engineering* (Sunday), and *Mailbag* (Monday). In summer, the news is followed by *Science and Engineering* (Monday, Friday and Saturday), the business-oriented *Newmarket* (Tuesday and Thursday), and a listener-response program on Tuesday and Sunday. The second half-hour is given over to ●*Moscow Yesterday and Today* (Tuesday, Thursday and Saturday in winter; Wednesday and Friday for summer); *Russian by Radio* (Sunday and Monday, summer); and *This is Russia* on the remaining days. Continuous to western North America winters on 5920, 5930, 7175 and 7330 kHz; and summers on 12000, 12010, 12050, 12070, 13645, 13665, 15180 and 15595 kHz. Also heard in Southeast Asia and Australasia at this time. For winter (local summer in Australia), try 12025, 12035, 12055, 15460, 15470, 17570, 17580 and 21790 kHz; in

> Radio Australia provides sharp comment about the scientific world in *Ockham's Razor.*

summer, go for 15460, 15490, 15560, 17570, 17580, 17610 and 17795 kHz.

Radio For Peace International, Costa Rica. Continues with counterculture and social-conscience programs—try Monday's *The Far Right Radio Review.* Audible in Europe and the Americas on 7385 and 7585 kHz. Some transmissions are in the single-sideband mode, which can be properly processed only on some radios.

Channel Africa, South Africa. Thirty minutes of mostly news-related fare. To West Africa on 11900 kHz, and sometimes heard in Europe and eastern North America.

Vatican Radio. Winters only at this time. Twenty minutes with a heavy Catholic slant. To Europe on 4005 and 5882 kHz. One hour earlier in summer. Frequencies may vary slightly.

WJCR, Upton, Kentucky. Continues with country gospel music to North America on 7490 kHz. Also with religious programs for North American listeners at this hour are **WYFR-Family Radio** on 5985 kHz, **WWCR** on 5935 kHz, **KAIJ** on 5810 kHz, **KTBN** on 7510 kHz, and **WHRI-World Harvest Radio** on 5760 and 7315 kHz. Traditional Catholic fare (some of it may be in Spanish) is available on 7425 kHz.

Voice of Malaysia. Actually starts at 0555 with opening announcements and program summary, followed by *News.* Then comes *This is the Voice of Malaysia,* a potpourri of news, interviews, reports and music. The hour is rounded off with *Personality Column.* Part of a 150-minute broadcast to Southeast Asia and Australia on 6175, 9750 and 15295 kHz.

Radio Japan. Repeat of the 0300 transmission, except that the end-of-broadcast news is replaced by *Tokyo Pop-in.* Sixty minutes to East and Southeast Asia on 11725, 11860 and 17810 kHz; and to Australasia on 11850 kHz.

HCJB—Voice of the Andes, Ecuador. Tuesday through Saturday (week-nights

in North America), it's strictly religious fare: *Psychology for Living, Stories of Great Christians* and *Nightsounds.* Weekends, Sunday features *Rock Solid!* and *Solstice* (a youth program), and Monday brings *Mountain Meditations* and the throughly enjoyable ●*Música del Ecuador.* The last of three hours of continuous programming to western North America on 9745 kHz.

06:15

Swiss Radio International. Fifteen minutes of *news* to Europe on 5840 (winter), 6165 and (summer) 9535 kHz.

06:30

Radio Austria International. Winters only at this time. ●*Report from Austria* (see 0030). A half hour via the Canadian relay, aimed primarily at western North America on 6015 kHz.

Radio Vlaanderen Internationaal, Belgium. Summers only at this time. *News,* then *Press Review* (except Sunday), followed Monday through Friday by *Belgium Today* (various topics) and features like *The Arts* (Monday and Thursday, *Tourism* (Monday), *Focus on Europe* (Tuesday), *Living in Belgium* and *Green Society* (Wednesday), *Around Town* (Thursday), and *Economics* and *International Report*(Friday). Weekend features consist of Saturday's *Music from Flanders* and Sunday's *P.O. Box 26* (a listener-response program) and *Radio World.* Thirty minutes to Europe on 5985 and 9925 kHz; and to Australasia on 9925 kHz. One hour later in winter.

Radio Romania International. Actually starts at 0631. A nine-minute news broadcast to Europe winters on 7105, 9510, 9570, 9665 and 11745 kHz; and summers on 9550, 9665 and 11810 kHz.

Catch the World with
GRUNDIG

A world of adventure with the Grundig Yacht Boy 400 shortwave radio. Hear news (in English) direct from the world's capitals... as it happens. The compact, easy to use portable covers all short-wave frequencies plus AM & FM. With keypad entry and digital readout, you won't miss any of the international action!

With the Grundig Traveller III, there is no dialing—ever. To search any broadcast band use Auto Scan and the Traveller III stops at the next station. Twenty memories store your favorite stations for instant retrieval at the push of a button. Plus the digital-display clock is quartz-accurate.

A Grundig worldband radio is great for an armchair explorer of any age. Great for international travellers too.

Visit Universal Radio to see the complete line of Grundig Worldband radios priced from $50.

Quality shortwave and amateur radio equipment since 1942.

Universal Radio, Inc.
6830 Americana Pkwy.
Reynoldsburg, Ohio 43068
☎ 800 431-3939
☎ 614 866-4267

Studio 11 of Radio Romania International, recording a session of "Youth Club." From left, Georgiana Zachia, Lisaura Ungureanu, Ioana Masariu, Dan Balamar and Frederica Dochinoiu.

06:45

Radio Romania International. *News*, commentary, a press review and short features, with interludes of lively Romanian folk music. Fifty-five minutes to East Asia and Australasia on 11740, 11840, 15250, 15270, 15405, 17720 and 17805 kHz, some of which are seasonal.

07:00

■**BBC World Service for Europe, the Mideast and the Americas.** Fifteen minutes of *World News*, followed Monday through Friday by ●*Off the Shelf* (readings from world literature). Weekends at this hour, it's either Saturday's *From the Weeklies* or Sunday's ●*Letter from America*. The final 30 minutes consist of a mixed bag of features and entertainment. Especially worth a listen are *The Vintage*

Chart Show (Monday), *Composer of the Month* (classical music, Thursday) and Saturday's ●*Brain of Britain* (or its substitute). Winters only to North America on 5975 and 6175 kHz; and year-round to Europe on 6180, 6195, 7325, 9410, 12095 and 15575 kHz. Some of these frequencies may only be available till 0730. Also audible in the Mideast on 11760, 15565, 15575 and (winters) 17640 kHz.

■**BBC World Service for Africa.** During the first half-hour, similar to the service for Europe and the Americas, except for 0715-0730 Sunday, when *Good Books* replaces *Letter from America*. Pick of the 0730 offerings are ●*The Learning World* (Wednesday), ●*Health Matters* (Thursday), ●*Science in Action* (Saturday) and Sunday's ●*From Our Own Correspondent*. Continuous on 6190, 9600, 11940, 15400 (from 0730) and 17830 kHz.

■**BBC World Service for Asia and**

the Pacific. Until 0730, the same as for Europe and the Americas, except for an alternative feature at 0715 Sunday. On the half-hour, look for some of the best of the BBC's output, though not necessarily for all tastes. The Sunday slot is filled by the popular *A Jolly Good Show;* Tuesday brings the inimitable ●*John Peel;* Wednesday, it's ●*One Planet;* Thursday, there's ●*The Learning World* and *Record News;* Friday's presentation is the eclectic ●*Andy Kershaw's World of Music;* and Saturday features ●*People and Politics.* Continuous to East and Southeast Asia on 9740, 11955, 15280 and 15360 kHz; and to Australasia on 7145, 11955, 15360 and 21660 kHz.

Voice of Malaysia. First, there is a daily feature with a Malaysian theme (except for Thursday, when *Talk on Islam* is aired), then comes a half hour of *This is the Voice of Malaysia* (see 0600), followed by 15 minutes of *Beautiful Malaysia.* Not much doubt about where the broadcast originates! Continuous to Southeast Asia and Australia on 6175, 9750 and 15295 kHz.

Radio Prague, Czech Republic. Summers only at this time. See 0800 for specifics. Thirty minutes to Europe on 7345 and 9505 kHz. One hour later in winter.

Radio Australia. *News,* then Monday through Friday it's *Dateline,* followed on the half-hour by a feature: *The Sports Factor* (Monday), *Health Report* (Tuesday), *Law Report* (Wednesday), *Religion Report* (Thursday) and *Media Report* on Friday. Weekends, look for *Pacific Focus* followed by Saturday's *Australia Today* or Sunday's *Science File.* Continuous programming to East Asia and the Pacific, also audible in western North America. On 12080, 13605, 15240, 15415, 15510, 17750 and 21725 kHz.

Radio For Peace International, Costa Rica. The final 60 minutes of an eight-hour cyclical block of United Nations, counterculture and social-conscience programming. Audible in Europe and the

Americas on 7385 and 7585 kHz. Some transmissions are in the single-sideband mode, which can be properly processed only on some radios.

Voice of Russia World Service. *News,* followed Tuesday through Saturday summers by the informative ●*Commonwealth Update.* The second half-hour includes two of the Voice of Russia's best—●*Audio Book Club* (Wednesday and Friday) and ●*Christian Message from Moscow* (Saturday). At 0711 Sunday and Monday, it's time to sit back and enjoy the excellent ●*Music and Musicians.* Winter's offerings are a mixed bag, with *Science and Engineering* (0711 Monday, Friday and Saturday) alternating with *Mailbag* (Sunday and Wednesday) and the business-oriented *Newmarket.* The final 25 minutes or so is divided between *This is Russia* (Tuesday, Thursday and Saturday), ●*Moscow Yesterday and Today* (Wednesday and Friday), and *Russian by Radio* on the remaining days. To western North America (winters only) on 5920, 5930, 7175 and 7330 kHz. Also year-round to Southeast Asia and Australasia, winters on 12025, 12035, 12055, 15460, 15470, 17560, 17570 and 21790 kHz; and summers on 15470, 15560, 17570, 17580, 17610 and 17795 kHz.

WJCR, Upton, Kentucky. Continues with country gospel music for North American listeners on 7490 kHz. Also with religious programs to North America at this hour are **WWCR** on 5935 kHz, **KAIJ** on 5810 kHz, **KTBN** on 7510 kHz, and **WHRI-World Harvest Radio** on 5745 and 9495 kHz. For traditional Catholic programming, tune **WEWN** on 7425 kHz.

Radio Norway International. Winter Sundays only. *Norway Now.* A half hour of *news* and human-interest stories targeted at Australasia on 7180 kHz.

Croatian Radio. Monday through Friday winters, and summer weekends at this time. Actually starts a little late, and is preceded by a few minutes of Croatian.

Several minutes of English *news* (length varies) from one of Croatian Radio's domestic networks. In times of crisis, one of the few sources of up-to-date news on what is actually happening in the region. To Europe and Australasia on 5920, 7165, 9830 and (irregularly) 13830 kHz.

Radio New Zealand International. Continues with regional programming for the South Pacific. Part of a much longer broadcast, which is also heard in parts of North America (especially during summer) on 6100, 9570 or 9700 kHz.

Voice of Free China, Taiwan. Repeat of the 0200 transmission. Best heard in southern and western parts of the United States on 5950 kHz.

Radio Japan. Monday through Friday, it's *Radio Japan News Round* followed by *Radio Japan Magazine Hour*, which consists of *Close Up* and a feature (two on Tuesday). On Monday you can hear *Sports Column*, Tuesday has *Japanese Culture* and *Today*, Wednesday features *Asian Report*, Thursday brings *Crosscurrents*, and Friday's offering is *Business Focus*. Weekend fare is made up of a bulletin of *news*, followed by Saturday's *This Week* or Sunday's *Let's Learn Japanese* and *Viewpoint*. The broadcast ends with a daily *news* summary. Sixty minutes to Europe on 5975 (winter), 7230 and 15165 kHz; to the Mideast on 15165 kHz; to Africa on 15165 and 17815 kHz; to East and Southeast Asia on 11725, 11740, 17810 and 21610 kHz; and to Australasia on 11850 and 11920 kHz.

HCJB—Voice of the Andes, Ecuador. Sixty minutes of religious programming— the first part of a much longer broadcast to Australasia on 9445 or 9645 kHz.

Swiss Radio International. Winters only at this time. Fifteen minutes of *news* to Europe on 5840 and 6165 kHz. One hour earlier in summer.

Radio Netherlands. *News*, then Monday through Saturday it's ●*Newsline* followed by a feature. Pick of the pack are ●*Research File* (science, Monday); ●*A Good Life* (Friday); ●*Weekend* (Saturday) and Wednesday's award-winning ●*Documentary*. On the remaining days, you can hear *Mirror Images* (arts in Holland, Tuesday) and *Media Network* (communications, Thursday). Sunday fare consists of *Sincerely Yours* (a listener-response program) and *Sounds Interesting*. To Australasia winters on 9720 and 9820 kHz; and midyear on 9830 and 11895 kHz. Well worth a listen.

Radio Austria International. Summers only at this time. ●*Report from Austria*, which includes a short bulletin of *news* followed by a series of current events and human interest stories. Good coverage of national and regional issues. Thirty minutes to Europe on 6155 and 13730 kHz, and to the Mideast on 15410 and 17870 kHz. One hour later in winter.

Radio Vlaanderen Internationaal, Belgium. Winters only at this time. See 0630 for program details. Thirty minutes to Europe on 5985 (or 5910) and 9920 (or 9925) kHz, with the latter channel also available for Australasia. One hour earlier in summer.

HCJB—Voice of the Andes, Ecuador. The first 30 minutes of a two-hour broadcast to Europe, and mostly religious fare at this time. On 5865 or 9765 kHz.

Voice of Greece. Actual start time varies slightly. Ten minutes of English news from and about Greece. Part of a longer broadcast of predominantly Greek programming. To Europe and Australasia on two or more channels from 7450, 9425 and 11645 kHz.

KTWR-Trans World Radio, Guam. Actually starts at 0740. The first part of a

BBC

John Peel has been a weekly fixture on the BBC World Service for over 20 years. His sardonic presentation of offbeat rock, which emanates from a spare room in his house, has earned him a cult following worldwide.

95-minute transmission of evangelical programming targeted at East Asia on 15200 kHz.

08:00

■**BBC World Service for Europe (and the Mideast).** *News*, then the religious *Pause for Thought*, followed by a wide variety of programming, depending on the day of the week. At 0830, try ●*The Greenfield Collection* (classical music, Sunday), ●*Everywoman* (for and about women, Tuesday), the unique and inimitable ●*John Peel* ("action for all the family," Friday) or the eclectic and unpredictable ●*Andy Kershaw's World of Music* (Saturday). Continuous to Europe on 6195 (winter), 7325, 9410, 12095, 15575 and 17640 kHz; and to the Mideast on 11760, 15565 (weekends only), 15575 and (winter) 17640 kHz.

■**BBC World Service for Asia and the Pacific.** As for Europe and the Mideast, but with different features on some days. Look for classical music on Sunday, Tuesday and Saturday (start times vary); ●*The Vintage Chart Show* (0830 Wednesday), ●*From Our Own Correspondent* and ●*Brain of Britain* or its substitute (Thursday), and ●*Everywoman* (0830 Friday). Continuous to East and Southeast Asia on 9740, 11955, 15360 and 21660 kHz; and to Australasia on 11955 and 15360 kHz.

HCJB—Voice of the Andes, Ecuador. Continuous programming to Europe and Australasia. For Europe there's *Studio 9* (or weekend variations); see 0900 for specifics. Australasia gets a full hour's serving of predominantly religious fare. To Europe on 5865 or 9765 kHz; and to Australasia on 9445 or 9645 kHz.

Voice of Malaysia. *News* and commentary, followed Monday through Friday by *Instrumentalia*, which is replaced weekends by *This is the Voice of Malaysia* (see 0600). The final 25 minutes of a much longer transmission targeted at Southeast Asia and Australia on 6175, 9750 and 15295 kHz.

Croatian Radio. Summer weekdays and winter weekends at this hour. Actually starts a little late, and is preceded by a few minutes of Croatian. Several minutes of English *news* from one of the domestic networks. A good way to keep abreast of events in one of Europe's most volatile regions. To Europe and Australasia on 5920, 7165, 9830 and (irregularly) on 13830 kHz.

Radio Norway International. Summer Sundays only. *Norway Now*. A pleasant half hour of *news* and human-interest stories from and about Norway. To Australasia on 17860 kHz.

Radio Prague, Czech Republic. Winters only at this time. *News*, then Monday through Friday there's *Current Affairs*.

These are followed by one or more features. Monday has *Magazine '96*; Tuesday, it's *Talking Point* and *Media Czech*; Wednesday has *From the Archives* and *The Arts*; Thursday brings *Economic Report* and *I'd Like You to Meet . . .*; and Friday there's *Between You and Us*. Saturday's offerings include a musical feature, replaced Sunday by *The Week in Politics*, *From the Weeklies* and *Media Czech* Thirty minutes to Europe on 7345 and 9505 kHz. One hour earlier in summer.

Radio Australia. Part of a 24-hour service to Asia and the Pacific, but which can also be heard at this time throughout much of North America. Begins with *News*, then Monday through Friday there's a relay from the Radio National domestic service. Weekends, it's *Grandstand Sports Wrap* followed on the half-hour by Saturday's *Indian Pacific* or Sunday's *Innovations*. To East Asia and the Pacific on 5995, 9580, 9710, 12080, 15510 and (until 0830) 15415, 17750 and 21725 kHz. Best heard in North America on 9580 kHz.

YLE Radio Finland. Summers only at this time. *News*, followed by short features from and about Finland. Mainstay of the broadcast is the daily *Compass North*, 12 minutes (nine on Saturday) of general interest stories about life in Finland. Saturdays at 0823, look for a world band curiosity, *Nuntii Latini* (news in Latin), which has something of a cult following. Thirty minutes to Southeast Asia and Australasia on 13645 and 15185 kHz.

WJCR, Upton, Kentucky. Continues with country gospel music to North America on 7490 kHz. Other U.S. religious broadcasters operating at this hour include **WWCR** on 5935 kHz, **KAIJ** on 5810 kHz, **KTBN** on 7510 kHz, and **WHRI-World Harvest Radio** on 5745 and 9495 kHz. Traditional Catholic programming can be heard via **WEWN** on 7425 kHz.

Voice of Russia World Service. *News*, then Tuesday through Saturday winters, it's ●*Commonwealth Update*. Choice pickings from the second half-hour include ●*Audio Book Club* (Wednesday and Friday) and ●*Christian Message from Moscow* (Saturday). From 0811 on Sunday and Monday you can listen to the sublime sounds of the Voice of Russia's showpiece of classical music—the highly enjoyable ●*Music and Musicians*. In summer, the *news* is followed Tuesday through Saturday by *Focus on Asia and the Pacific*. This in turn gives way, on the half-hour, to some entertaining musical fare—●*Folk Box* (Wednesday and Saturday), *Yours for the Asking* (Monday), ●*Music at Your Request* (Tuesday), and Friday's *Jazz Show*. The only exception is Thursday's eclectic *Kaleidoscope*. Continuous to East and Southeast Asia and Australasia, winters on 9875, 12025, 12035, 12055 and 15460 kHz; and summers on 15490, 15560, 17610 and 17795 kHz.

The Voice of Russia's *Christian Message from Moscow* gives a fascinating insight into Russian Orthodoxy.

KTWR-Trans World Radio, Guam. Part of a longer transmission of evangelical programming targeted at East Asia on 15200 kHz.

Radio New Zealand International. *News* and features, music or special programs for the South Sea Islands, all with a distinctly Pacific flavor. Sometimes includes relays from the domestic National Radio. Part of a much longer broadcast for the South Pacific, but well heard in North America winters on 9700, and summers on 6100 kHz.

Radio Korea International, South Korea. Opens with *news* and commentary, followed Monday through Wednesday by *Seoul Calling*. Weekly features include *Echoes of Korean Music* and *Shortwave Feedback* (Sunday), *Tales from Korea's Past* (Monday), *Korean Cultural Trails* (Tuesday), *Pulse of Korea* (Wednesday),

08:00

From Us to You (a listener-response program) and *Let's Learn Korean* (Thursday), *Let's Sing Together* and *Korea Through Foreigners' Eyes* (Friday), and Saturday's *Discovering Korea, Korean Literary Corner* and *Weekly News Focus*. Sixty minutes to Europe on 13670 kHz.

specifics. Thirty minutes to Europe on 9710 kHz. One hour later in winter.

Voice of Armenia. Summer Sundays only. Mainly of interest to Armenians abroad. Thirty minutes of Armenian *news* and culture. To Europe on 15270 (or 15170) kHz. One hour later in winter.

08:30

Radio Austria International. Winters only at this time. The comprehensive ●*Report from Austria*; see 0430 for more details. A half hour to Europe on 6155 and 13730 kHz; to East Asia on 15240 (or 15455) kHz; and to Australia and the Pacific on 17870 kHz.

Radio Slovakia International. *Slovakia Today*—30 minutes of *news*, reports and features, all with a distinct Slovak flavor. Tuesday, there's a potpourri of short features; Wednesday puts the accent on tourism and Slovak personalities; Wednesday has a historical feature; Thursday's slot is devoted to business and economy; and Friday brings a mix of politics, education and science. Saturday has a strong cultural content; Sunday features the *"Best of"* series; and Monday brings *Listeners' Tribune* and some enjoyable Slovak music. To Australasia on 11990, 15460 (or 17485) and 17570 (or 21705) kHz.

Radio Netherlands. The second of three hours aimed at Australasia. *News*, followed Monday through Saturday by ●*Newsline*, then a feature program. Choice pickings include ●*A Good Life* (Monday), ●*Research File* (Thursday), ●*Roughly Speaking* (Saturday) and Friday's ●*Documentary*. Other offerings include *Music 52-15* (Tuesday), *Sounds Interesting* (Wednesday) and Sunday's *Siren Song*. Winters on 5965, 9830 and 13700 kHz; and midyear on 9720 and 9820 kHz.

Radio Vilnius, Lithuania. Summers only at this time; see 0930 for program

09:00

■**BBC World Service for Europe (and the Mideast).** Starts with *News* and ●*World Business Report/Review*, and ends with ●*Sports Roundup*. The remaining time is taken up by one or more features, the pick of which are ●*From Our Own Correspondent* (0915 Sunday), ●*The Learning World* (same time Friday) and *The Works* (technology, 0915 Saturday). Continuous to Europe on 9410, 12095, 15575 and 17640 kHz; and to the Mideast on 11760 (till 0915), 15565, 15575 and (winter) 17640 kHz.

■**BBC World Service for Asia and the Pacific.** Starts and ends like the service for Europe, but the features are different. Monday through Friday, the programs are mainly of an educational nature. Weekends, look for ●*Omnibus* (0915 Saturday) and *Good Books* (same time Sunday). Continuous to East and Southeast Asia on 6195, 9740, 15280 (till 0945), 15360 and 21660 kHz; and to Australasia on 11765 or 15360 kHz.

■**Deutsche Welle,** Germany. *News*, then Monday through Friday there's the fast-moving ●*NewsLink*—commentary, interviews, background reports and analysis of European events. A feature follows just after the half-hour. Monday's offering is *Headcrash* (computers), *Science and Technology, Media Mag* or *Made in Germany*, depending on the week of the month. On other days, choose from ●*Man and Environment* (Tuesday), ●*Insight* (Wednesday), *Living in Germany* (Thursday) and *Spotlight on Sport* (Friday). The Saturday lineup consists of *Commentary,*

Germany This Week, Mailbag Africa and *Saturday Special.* Sunday, there's *Commentary, Arts on the Air* and *German by Radio.* Fifty minutes to southern Africa on 9565, 15145 (winter), 15205 (summer), 15410, 17800 and 21600 kHz.

■**Deutsche Welle,** Germany. *News,* followed Monday through Friday by some excellent backup reports and analysis in ●*NewsLink* and ●*Asia-Pacific Report.* Weekends, the news is followed by *Commentary* and features. Saturday offerings are *Germany This Week, Talking Point* and *Religion and Society;* replaced Sunday by *Arts on the Air* and *German by Radio.* Fifty minutes to Asia and Australasia winters on 6160, 7380, 11715 and 17820 kHz; and summers on 6160, 12055, 17715 and 21680 kHz.

Radio New Zealand International. Continuous programming for the islands of the South Pacific, where the broadcasts are targeted. Summers on 6100 kHz, and winters on 9700 kHz. Audible in much of North America.

Radio Vlaanderen Internationaal, Belgium. Monday through Saturday, summers only at this time. *News* and *Press Review,* followed Monday through Friday by *Belgium Today* (various topics) and features like *Tourism* (Monday), *Focus on Europe* (Tuesday), *Living in Belgium* and *Green Society* (Wednesday), *The Arts* (Monday and Thursday), *Around Town* (Thursday), and *Economics* and *International Report*(Friday). Saturday features *Music from Flanders.* Thirty minutes to Europe on 6035 kHz, and to Africa on 15545 and 17595 kHz. One hour later in winter.

Croatian Radio. Monday through Friday, winters only at this time. Actually

starts a little late, and is preceded by news in Croatian. Several minutes of on-the-spot *news* from the Balkan cauldron. To Europe and Australasia on 5920, 7165, 9830 and (irregularly) 13830 kHz. One hour earlier during summer.

HCJB—Voice of the Andes, Ecuador. Monday through Friday it's *Studio 9*, featuring nine minutes of world and Latin American *news*, followed by 20 minutes of in-depth reporting on Latin America. The final portion of *Studio 9* is given over to one of a variety of 30-minute features—including *You Should Know* (issues and ethics, Monday), *El Mundo Futuro* (science, Tuesday), *Ham Radio Today* (Wednesday), *Woman to Woman* (Thursday) and Friday's thoroughly entertaining ●*Música del Ecuador*. On Saturday, the news is followed by *DX Partyline*, which in turn is replaced Sunday by *Saludos Amigos*—HCJB's international friendship program. Continuous to Australasia on 9445 or 9645 kHz. A separate half-hour of religious programming for Europe can be heard on 5985 or 9765 kHz.

China Radio International. *News* and commentary, followed Tuesday through Friday by *Current Affairs*. These are followed by various feature programs, such as *Cultural Spectrum* (Thursday); *Listeners' Letterbox* (Sunday and Tuesday); *China Scrapbook*, *Cooking Show*, *Chinese Folk Tales* and ●*Music from China* (Saturday); *Sports Beat* and *Song of the Week* (Sunday); *Learn to Speak Chinese* (Monday and Wednesday); and Friday's *In the Third World*. Sundays, there is also a biweekly *Business Show* which alternates with *China's Open Windows*. One hour to Australasia on 9785 (or 15440) and 11755 kHz.

Voice of Mongolia. Most days, it's *news*, reports and short features, all with a Mongolian flavor. Here's a chance to

learn about one of the most remote countries on the planet. The entire Sunday broadcast is given over to exotic Mongolian music. Thirty minutes to East Asia (and audible in parts of Australasia) on 15170 (or 12085) kHz. Frequencies may vary a little.

Voice of Russia World Service. Tuesday through Saturday, winters, *News* is followed by *Focus on Asia and the Pacific*. This is replaced summers by a variety of features—Wednesday and Sunday offer the business-oriented *Newmarket*, Thursday features *Science and Engineering*, and there's a listener-response program on Monday, Tuesday and Friday. In winter, the second half-hour concentrates mainly on music, with the main attractions being ●*Folk Box* (Wednesday and Saturday), ●*Music at Your Request* (Tuesday), and Friday's *Jazz Show*. For summer, there's *This is Russia* (Wednesday and Friday), *Timelines* (Saturday and Sunday), ●*Audio Book Club* (Monday), and ●*Moscow Yesterday and Today* on the remaining days. Sixty minutes of continuous programming beamed to East and Southeast Asia and the Pacific. Winters, try 7220, 9835, 9875 and 17860 kHz; and summers on 7390, 9810, 11800, 17595, 17610 and 17795 kHz.

Swiss Radio International. Thirty minutes of *news* and background reports on world and Swiss events. Look for some lighter fare on Saturdays, when *Capital Letters* (a biweekly listener-response program) alternates with *Name Game* and *Sounds Good*. To Australasia on 9885, 12075 (winter), 13685 and (summer) 17515 kHz.

Radio Prague, Czech Republic. This time summers only. Repeat of the 0700 broadcast (see 0800 for program specifics). Thirty minutes to the Mideast and beyond on 17485 kHz; and to West Africa on 15640 kHz.

> If you enjoy Chinese food, try some of the recipes in Saturday's *Cooking Show* from China Radio International.

Radio Australia. *News*, followed Monday through Friday by *Dateline*, a summary of the latest sports news, and *Australia Today*. These are replaced weekends by Saturday's 50-minute *Science Show* and Sunday's *Hindsight* and *On This Day*. Continuous to East Asia and the Pacific on 9580 and 11640 kHz, and heard in North America on 9580 kHz.

Radio For Peace International, Costa Rica. *FIRE* (Feminist International Radio Endeavour). Repeat of the 0100 broadcast. To the Americas on 7385 and 7585 kHz.

KTWR-Trans World Radio, Guam. The final quarter-hour of a 95-minute transmission of evangelical programming targeted at East Asia on 15200 kHz, and the final hour of a similar 65-minute broadcast to Australasia on 11835 kHz. A secular media show, *Pacific DX Report*, can be heard at 0900 Tuesday on 15200 kHz, and at 0940 Saturday on 11835 kHz.

WJCR, Upton, Kentucky. Continues with country gospel music to North America on 7490 kHz. Other U.S. religious broadcasters operating at this hour include **WWCR** on 5935, **KAIJ** on 5810, **KTBN** on 7510 kHz, and **WHRI-World Harvest Radio** on 5745 and 9495 kHz. Traditional Catholic programming is aired via **WEWN** on 7425 kHz.

Radio Japan. Repeat of the 0300 broadcast; see there for specifics. Up-to-the-minute news from and about the Far East. Sixty minutes to East and Southeast Asia on 6090 (winter), 9610 (summer) and 15190 kHz; and to Australasia on 11850 kHz.

09:30

Radio Austria International. Monday through Saturday, summers only at this time. ●*Report from Austria*, which includes a short bulletin of *news* followed by a series of current events and human interest stories. Ample coverage of national and regional issues. To East Asia on 15455 kHz; and to Australasia on 17870 kHz.

Radio Netherlands. *News*, then Monday through Saturday it's ●*Newsline* followed by a feature. Pick of the pack are ●*Research File* (science, Monday); ●*A Good Life* (Friday); ●*Weekend* (Saturday) and Wednesday's award-winning ●*Documentary*. On the remaining days, you can hear *Mirror Images* (arts in Holland, Tuesday) and *Media Network* (communications, Thursday). Sunday fare consists of *Sincerely Yours* (a listener-response program) and *Sounds Interesting*. One hour to East and Southeast Asia, winters on 7260 and 9810 kHz; and summers on 12065 and 13705 kHz. Also available winters to Australasia on 5965 and 9830 kHz. Recommended listening.

Radio Vilnius, Lithuania. Winters only at this time. A half hour that's mostly *news* and background reports about events in Lithuania. Of broader appeal is *Mailbag*, aired every other Sunday. For a little Lithuanian music, try the second half of Monday's broadcast. To Europe on 9710 kHz. One hour earlier in summer.

FEBC Radio International, Philippines. Opens with *World News Update*, then it's mostly religious features. For something with a more general appeal, try Thursday's *Mailbag* or Sunday's *DX Dial* (a show for radio enthusiasts). The first half-hour of a 90-minute predominantly religious broadcast targeted at East and Southeast Asia on 11635 kHz.

Voice of Armenia. Winter Sundays only. Mainly of interest to Armenians abroad. Thirty minutes of Armenian *news* and culture. To Europe on 15270 kHz. One hour earlier in summer.

10:00

■**BBC World Service for Europe, the Mideast and the Americas.**
●*Newsdesk*, followed on the half-hour by a mixed bag of features. These include

BBC

Although the BBC World Service has undergone a major reorganization, it continues to be the finest station in the English language.

●*Omnibus* (Monday), ●*One Planet* (Wednesday), ●*Discovery* (science, Thursday), ●*Assignment* (Friday) and *Global Business* (Sunday). Continuous to Europe on 9410, 12095, 15575 and 17640 kHz; and to the Mideast on 11760, 15565, 15575 and (winter) 17640 kHz. To eastern North America, summers only, on 5965 kHz. Listeners in the Caribbean area can tune to 6195 kHz.

■BBC World Service for Asia and the Pacific. Thirty minutes of ●*Newsdesk*, then features. Worth a listen are *The Works* (technology, Monday), ●*One Planet* (the environment, Wednesday), ●*Andy Kershaw's World of Music* (Thursday), the secular ●*Focus on Faith* (Friday) and the eclectic ●*Anything Goes* on Saturday. Continuous to East and Southeast Asia on 6195, 9740, 15360 (till 1030) and 21660 kHz; and to Australasia on 11765 or 15360 kHz (varies on a seasonal basis).

Radio Australia. *News*, followed by two features. Choose from *Australian Music Show* and *Innovations* (Monday), *At Your Request* and *Arts Australia* (Tuesday), *Blacktracker* and *Science File* (Wednesday), *Oz Country Style* and *Book Talk* (Thursday), *Music Deli* and *Earthbeat* (Friday), *Jazz Notes* and *Indian Pacific* (Saturday) and *Oz Sounds* and *Correspondents' Report* on Sunday. Continuous

to Asia and the Pacific on 9580 kHz, and also easily audible in much of North America.

Swiss Radio International. Summers only at this time. *Newsnet*—news and background reports on world and Swiss events. Look for some lighter fare on Saturdays, when the bi-weekly *Capital Letters* (a listener-response program) alternates with *Name Game* and *Sounds Good*. Thirty minutes to Europe on 6165 and 9535 kHz. One hour later in winter.

Radio Prague, Czech Republic. This time winters only. Repeat of the 0800 broadcast (see there for specifics). Thirty minutes to the Mideast and beyond on 17485 kHz, and to Africa on 21705 kHz.

Radio New Zealand International. A mixed bag of Pacific regional *news*, features, and relays of the domestic National Radio network. Continuous to the Pacific; summers on 6100 kHz, and winters on 9700 kHz. Easily audible in much of North America.

Voice of Vietnam. Begins with *news*, then there's *Commentary* or *Weekly Review*, followed by short features and some pleasant Vietnamese music (especially at weekends). Heard extensively on 9840 and (winters) 12020 or (summers) 15010 kHz. Targeted to Asia at this hour.

Radio Vlaanderen Internationaal, Belgium. Monday through Saturday, winters only at this time. See 0900 for program details. Thirty minutes to Europe on 6035 kHz, and to Africa on 15510 and 17595 kHz. One hour earlier in summer.

KTWR-Trans World Radio, Guam. A 60-minute block of religious programming targeted at East Asia on 9865 kHz.

Voice of America. The start of VOA's daily broadcasts to the Caribbean. *News*, followed Monday through Friday by *VOA Today*—a compendium of news, sports, science, business and other features. Replaced weekends by *VOA Saturday/ VOA Sunday*, which have less accent on news, and more on features. On 6165,

7405 and 9590 kHz. For a separate service to Australasia, see the next item.

Radio Jordan. Summers only at this time. A partial relay of the station's domestic broadcasts, beamed to Europe on 11690 kHz. One hour later in winter.

Voice of America. *News*, followed Monday through Friday by *Stateside*, a look at issues and personalities in different walks of American life. This is replaced Saturday by ●*Encounter* and *Communications World*, and Sunday by *Critic's Choice* and a feature in slow-speed English. To Australasia on 5985, 11720, and 15425 kHz.

Radio For Peace International, Costa Rica. Another hour of counterculture and social-conscience programs. Offerings at this hour include *The Far Right Radio Review* (1000 Wednesday)

and *My Green Earth* (a nature program for children, 1030 Monday). Continuous to North and Central America on 7385 and 7585 kHz. Some transmissions are in the single-sideband mode, which can be properly processed only on some radios.

China Radio International. Repeat of the 0900 broadcast. One hour to Australasia on 9785 (or 15440) and 11755 kHz.

FEBC Radio International, Philippines. The final hour of a 90-minute mix of religious and secular programming for East and Southeast Asia. Monday through Friday, it's *Focus on the Family*, then a 15-minute religious feature, *Asian News Update* (on the half-hour) and *In Touch*. All weekend offerings are religious in nature. On 11635 kHz.

All India Radio. *News*, then a composite program of commentary, press

review and features, interspersed with ample servings of enjoyable Indian music. To East Asia on 11585 and 17840 kHz; and to Australasia on 13700, 15050 and 17387 kHz.

WJCR, Upton, Kentucky. Continues with country gospel music to North America on 7490 kHz. Other U.S. religious broadcasters operating at this hour include **WWCR** on 5935 kHz, **KTBN** on 7510 kHz, **WYFR-Family Radio** on 5950 kHz, and **WHRI-World Harvest Radio** on 6040 and 9495 kHz. For traditional Catholic programming, try **WEWN** on 7425 kHz.

Voice of Russia World Service. *News*, followed winters by a variety of features. Sunday and Wednesday it's business in *Newmarket*, Thursday features *Science and Engineering*, and there's a listener-response program on Monday, Tuesday and Friday. The second half-hour brings ●*Audio Book Club* (Monday), ●*Moscow Yesterday and Today* (Tuesday and Thursday), *Timelines* (Saturday and Sunday) and *This is Russia* on the remaining days. In summer, the news is followed Tuesday through Saturday by the timely ●*Commonwealth Update*, replaced Sunday by *Mailbag* and Monday by *Science and Engineering*. At 1030, the Sunday slot is filled by ●*Christian Message from Moscow*, replaced Monday by the aptly named *Kaleidoscope*. The remaining days feature "alternative programs"—religious paid programming or a show from the Voice of Russia's archives or transcription department. Continuous to Asia and the Pacific. For East and Southeast Asia and Australasia, try the winter channels of 7220, 9835, 9875, 13785, 15490, 15560, 17755 and 17860 kHz; and summer, choose from 7330, 7390, 9800, 9810, 9835, 11800, 15435, 15490, 15510, 17560, 17610, 17775 and 17795 kHz.

HCJB—Voice of the Andes, Ecuador. The final 60 minutes of a four-hour package of religious and secular programming to Australasia on 9445 or 9645 kHz.

Radio Korea International, South Korea. Summers only at this time. Starts off with *News*, followed Monday through Wednesday by *Economic News Briefs*. The remainder of the 30-minute broadcast is taken up by a feature: *Shortwave Feedback* (Sunday), *Seoul Calling* (Monday and Tuesday), *Pulse of Korea* (Wednesday), *From Us to You* (Thursday), *Let's Sing Together* (Friday) and *Weekly News Focus* (Saturday). On 11715 kHz via their Canadian relay, so this is the best chance for North Americans to hear the station. One hour later in winter.

Radio Prague, Czech Republic. This time summers only. Repeat of the 0700 broadcast (see 0800 for program specifics). A half hour to Europe on 7345 and 9505 kHz. One hour later during winter.

Radio Netherlands. *News*, followed Monday through Saturday by ●*Newsline*, then a feature program. Top choices include ●*A Good Life* (Monday), ●*Research File* (Thursday), ●*Roughly Speaking* (Saturday) and Friday's ●*Documentary*. Other offerings include *Music 52-15* (Tuesday), *Sounds Interesting* (Wednesday) and Sunday's *Siren Song*. Fifty-five minutes to East and Southeast Asia winters on 7260 and 9810 kHz, and summers on 12065 and 13710 kHz (also audible in Australasia). Summers, also available to Europe on 6045 and 9860 kHz.

Radio Austria International. ●*Report from Austria* (see 0930). A half hour to Europe Monday through Saturday winters on 6155 and 13730 kHz; to East Asia on 15240 kHz; and to Australasia on 17870 kHz. In summer, Sundays only to East Asia on 15455 kHz, and to Australia and the Pacific on 17870 kHz.

United Arab Emirates Radio, Dubai. *News*, then a feature dealing with one or more aspects of Arab life and culture. Weekends, there are replies to listeners' letters. To Europe on 13675, 15395, 17630 and 21605 kHz.

■BBC World Service for Europe, the Mideast and the Americas.
●*Newsdesk*, followed on the half-hour by a variety of features, depending on the day of the week. Try *Sports International* (Wednesday), ●*The Learning World* and ●*From Our Own Correspondent* (Thursday), ●*Focus on Faith* (Friday), ●*People and Politics* (Saturday) and the aptly named ●*Anything Goes* on Sunday. Continuous to eastern North America and the Caribbean on 5965, 6195 and 15220 kHz (weekdays, for the first half-hour, 6195 and 15220 kHz carry alternative programs for the Caribbean). Also to Europe on 9410, 12095, 15575 and 17640 kHz; and to the Mideast on 11760, 15565, 15575 and (winter) 17640 kHz.

■BBC World Service for Asia and the Pacific. Thirty minutes of ●*Newsdesk*, then a feature. Weekdays (except Thursday), *Meridian* spotlights the arts; Saturday's slot is devoted to classical music in *Music Review*; and Sunday brings the first half-hour of ●*Play of the Week* (world theater). Continuous to East and Southeast Asia on 6195, 9580, 9740 and 11955 kHz. The first half-hour is available to Australasia via Radio New Zealand International on 9700 (or 6100) kHz, and the service is then resumed via the BBC's own facilities on 9740 kHz.

Voice of Asia, Taiwan. One of the few stations to open with a feature: *Asian Culture* (Monday), *Touring Asia* (Tuesday), *World of Science* (Wednesday), *World Economy* (Thursday), and music on the remaining days. There is also a listener-response program on Saturday. After the feature there's a bulletin of news, and no matter what comes next, the broadcast always ends with *Let's Learn Chinese.* One hour to Southeast Asia on 7445 kHz.

Radio Australia. *News*, then Monday through Friday it's *Dateline*, followed on the half-hour by a summary of the latest sports news, and *Countrywide*. Weekend fare consists of *Fine Music Australia* (Saturday) or *Jazz Notes* (Sunday), followed by *Australia Today*. Continuous to Asia and the Pacific (also well heard in much of North America) on 9580 kHz.

HCJB—Voice of the Andes, Ecuador. First 60 minutes of a four-hour block of religious programming to the Americas on 12005 and 15115 kHz. Try *Morning in the Mountains*, a mix of secular and religious items at 1130 weekdays.

Voice of America. *News*, then Saturday it's *Agriculture Today* and ●*Press Conference USA*; Sunday there's ●*New Horizons* and ●*Issues in the News*; and weekdays have *Music USA*. To East Asia on 6110 (winter), 6160 (summer), 9760, 11705 (winter), 11720 and (summer) 15160 kHz; and to Australasia on 5985, 9645, 11720 and 15425 kHz. Some of these channels provide good reception in Southeast Asia.

Radio Jordan. A partial relay of the station's domestic broadcasts. Targeted at Europe, but also heard winters in eastern North America. On 11690 kHz.

Voice of Russia World Service. Continuous programming to Asia and the Pacific. Starts with *News*, then Tuesday through Saturday winters, it's the informative ●*Commonwealth Update*, replaced Sunday by *Mailbag* and Monday by *Science and Engineering*. Summers at this time, there's *News and Views*, with the second half-hour mostly given over to a variety of musical styles, including the top-rated ●*Folk Box* (Tuesday and Wednesday), the classical ●*Music at Your Request* (Monday and Saturday), and Thursday's *Jazz Show*. Odd man out is Sunday's *This is Russia*. Winters at 1130, the Sunday slot is given over to ●*Christian Message from Moscow*, replaced Monday by the eclectic *Kaleidoscope*. The remain-

Radio Singapore International's English language staff. Front, from left, Belinda Yeo, Josephine Huang, Haslinda Amin, Merrilyn Fong, Anushia Sabai and Jane Ong. Rear, Sakuntala Gupta and William Teo.

ing days feature "alternative programs"—quality shows from the station's archives, mind-numbing religious paid programming, or anything in-between. Winters to Southeast Asia on 13785, 15460, 15490, 15560, 17755 and 17860 kHz; summers on 9800, 9835, 15430, 15435, 15460, 15490, 15510, 15560, 17560, 17610, 17755 and 17795 kHz. Several of these channels are also audible in parts of Australasia.

Voice of Vietnam. Repeat of the 1000 broadcast. A half hour to Asia on 7285 and 9730 kHz. Both frequencies vary somewhat.

Voice of the Islamic Republic of Iran. Ninety minutes of *news*, commentary and features, much of it reflecting the Islamic point of view. Targeted at the Mideast and South and Southeast Asia on 11745, 11790, 11875 (summer), 11930 and 15260 kHz.

Radio Singapore International. A three-hour package for Southeast Asia, and widely heard elsewhere. Starts with a summary of *news* and weather conditions in Asia and the Pacific, followed by a wide variety of short features, depending on the day of the week. These include Monday's eclectic *Frontiers*, Tuesday's *Kaleidoscope*, the literary *Bookmark* (Friday), and *Dateline RSI* (a listener-participation program, Sunday). At 1120 Monday through Friday, it's the *Business and Market Report*. There's *news* on the half-hour, then weekdays there's a brief press review, music, and either *Newsline* (1145 Monday, Wednesday and Friday) or *Business World* (same time, Tuesday and Thursday). Weekends, it's *The Week Ahead* (1133 Saturday and Sunday), *Regional Press Review* and *Newsline* (Saturday) or *The Sunday Interview*. On 6015 and 6155 kHz.

CBC North-Québec, Canada. Summers only at this time; see 1200 for specifics. Intended for a domestic audience, but also heard in the northeastern United States on 9625 kHz.

Swiss Radio International. Thirty minutes of *news* and background reports on world and Swiss events. Look for some lighter fare on Saturdays, when *Capital Letters* (a biweekly listener-response program) alternates with *Name Game* and *Sounds Good.* To Europe winters on 6165 and 9535 kHz, and year-round to East Asia and Australasia on 9885 and 11995 (winter), 13635 (all-year) and (summer) 15415 and 17515 kHz.

Radio Japan. On weekdays, opens with *Radio Japan News Round*, with news oriented to Japanese and Asian affairs. This is followed by *Radio Japan Magazine Hour*, which includes features like *Sports Column* (Monday), *Japanese Culture* and *Today* (Tuesday), *Asian Report* (Wednesday), *Crosscurrents* (Thursday) and *Business Focus* (Friday). *Commentary* and *News* round off the hour. These are replaced Saturday by *This Week*, and Sunday by *Hello from Tokyo.* One hour to North America on 6120 kHz, and to East and Southeast Asia on 6090 (winter), 9610 (summer) and 15350 kHz.

Radio For Peace International, Costa Rica. Continues with a variety of counterculture and social-conscience features. There is also a listener-response program at 1130 Wednesday. To North and Central America on 7385 and 7585 kHz. Some transmissions are in the single-sideband mode, which can be properly processed only on some radios.

Radio Pyongyang, North Korea. The last of the old-time communist stations, with quaint terms like "Great Leader" and "Unrivaled Great Man" being the order of the day. Starts with "news", with much of the remainder of the broadcast given over to revering the late Kim Il Sung. Abominably bad programs, but worth the occasional listen just to hear how awful they are. A soporific hour to Southeast Asia and Central America (also audible in parts of western North America) on 9975, 11335 and 13650 kHz; and to the Mideast and beyond on 9640 kHz.

WJCR, Upton, Kentucky. Continues with country gospel music to North America on 7490 kHz. Other U.S. religious broadcasters operating at this hour include **WWCR** on 5935 (or 15685) kHz, **KTBN** on 7510 kHz, **WYFR-Family Radio** on 5950 and 7355 (or 11830) kHz, and **WHRI-World Harvest Radio** on 6040 and 9495 kHz. Traditional Catholic programming (some of which may be in Spanish) can be found on **WEWN** on 7425 kHz.

11:30

Radio Korea International, South Korea. Winters only at this time. See 1030 for program details. A half hour on 9650 kHz via their Canadian relay, so a good chance for North Americans to hear the station. One hour earlier in summer.

Radio Netherlands. *News*, followed Monday through Saturday by ●*Newsline*, then a feature program. Choice winter pickings include ●*A Good Life* (Monday), ●*Research File* (Thursday), ●*Roughly Speaking* (Saturday) and Friday's ●*Documentary.* Other offerings include *Music 52-15* (Tuesday), *Sounds Interesting* (Wednesday) and Sunday's *Siren Song.* Pick of the summer pack are ●*Research File* (science, Monday); ●*A Good Life* (Friday); ●*Weekend* (Saturday) and Wednesday's award-winning ●*Documentary.* On the remaining days, you can hear *Mirror Images* (arts in Holland, Tuesday) and *Media Network* (communications, Thursday). Sunday fare consists of *Sincerely Yours* (a listener-response program) and *Sounds Interesting.* One hour to western Europe on 6045 and (winter) 7190 or (summer) 9860 kHz.

Radio Prague, Czech Republic. Winters only at this time. Repeat of the 0700 transmission (see 0800 for specifics). A half hour to Europe on 7345 and 9505 kHz. One hour earlier in summer.

Radio Sweden. Summers only at this time; see 1230 for program details. To North America on 11650 and 15240 kHz.

1200-1759
Western Australia & East Asia—Evening Prime Time
North America—Morning
Europe & Mideast—Afternoon and Early Evening

12:00

■**BBC World Service for Europe, the Mideast and the Americas.** *World News*, then Monday through Saturday there's 10 minutes of specialized business and financial reporting. Weekdays, these are followed by ●*Britain Today* and a quarter-hour feature. Choose from *Seven Days* (current events, Monday), ●*Health Matters* (Tuesday), *Science Update* (Wednesday), *Record News* (classical music, Thursday) and a science feature on Friday. At 1215 Saturday, off-the-wall humor and popular music make up *A Jolly Good Show*, replaced Sunday by the religious *Songs of Praise*. ●*Sports Roundup* follows at 45 minutes past the hour, except for Saturday, when it is replaced by *Good Books*. Continuous to North America and the Caribbean on 5965 (winter), 6195, 9515 (summer) and 15220 kHz. Weekdays, for the first 15 minutes, 6195 and 15220 kHz carry alternative programming for the Caribbean. Also to Europe on 9410, 12095, 15575 and 17640 kHz; and to the Mideast on 11760, 15565, 15575 and (winter) 17640 kHz.

■**BBC World Service for Asia and the Pacific.** Monday through Saturday, opens with *World News* and ●*World Business Report/Review*. Weekdays, these are followed by ●*Britain Today* ●*Off the Shelf* (readings of world literature) and ●*Sports Roundup*, replaced Saturday by ●*Science in Action* and Alistair Cooke's ●*Letter from America*. Sunday is given over to the second half of ●*Play of the Week* (followed by ●*Andy Kershaw's World of Music* if it ends by 1230). Continuous to East and Southeast Asia on

6195, 9740, 11955 and 15280 kHz; and to Australasia on 9740 kHz.

Radio Canada International. Summer weekdays only. Tuesday through Saturday, it's a shortened version of the Canadian Broadcasting Corporation's domestic news program ●*As It Happens*, which is replaced Sunday by ●*Quirks and Quarks*, and Monday by *Double Exposure* and *Royal Canadian Air Farce*. Sixty minutes to North America and the Caribbean on 9640, 11855 and 13650 kHz. One hour later in winter. For a separate service to Asia, see the next item.

Radio Canada International. *News*, followed Monday through Friday by *Spectrum* (topical events). Saturday features the environmental *Earth Watch*, and *The Mailbag* occupies the Sunday slot. Thirty minutes to East and Southeast Asia, winters on 6150 and 11730 kHz, and summers on 9660 and 15195 kHz.

Radio Tashkent, Uzbekistan. *News* and commentary, followed by features such as *Life in the Village* (Wednesday), a listeners' request program (Monday), and local music (Thursday). Heard better in Asia, Australasia and Europe than in North America. Thirty minutes winters on 5060, 5975, 6025 and 9715 kHz; and summers on 7285, 9715 and 15295 kHz.

■**Radio France Internationale.** The first 30 minutes consist of *news* and correspondents' reports, with a review of the French press rounding off the half-hour. The next 25 minutes are given over to a series of short features, including Sunday's *Paris Promenade* and *Club 9516* (a listener-response program); the weekday *RFI Europe*; sports (Monday and Thursday); *Arts in France*, *Books* and

Science Probe (Tuesday); *Bottom Line* (business and finance) and *Land of France* (Wednesday); the biweekly *North/South* (or *Planet Earth*) and *The Americas* (Thursday); *Film Reel* and *Made in France* (Friday); and Saturday's *Focus on France*, *Spotlight on Africa* and *Counterpoint* (human rights) or *Echoes from Africa*. A fast-moving information-packed 55 minutes to Europe on 9805, 15155 and 15195 kHz; and to North America on 13625 and 11615, 15530 or 17575 kHz (depending on the season). In eastern North America, you can also try 15540 kHz, targeted at West Africa.

Polish Radio Warsaw, Poland. This time summers only. Fifty-five minutes of news, commentary, features and music—all with a Polish accent. Monday through Friday, it's *News from Poland*—a potpourri of news, reports and interviews. This is followed by *Jazz, Folk, Rock and Pop from Poland* (Monday), *Request Concert* and *A Day in the Life of . . .* (Tuesday), the historical *Flashback* and a regular feature (Wednesday), a communications feature and *Letter from Poland* (Thursday), and *Business Week* followed by classical music (Friday). The Saturday broadcast begins with a bulletin of *news*, then there's *Weekend Press* (a review of the week's papers), *Europe East* (correspondents' reports from all over eastern Europe) and an arts magazine, *Focus*. Sundays, you can hear *Weekend Commentary*, *Panorama* (a window on day-to-day life in Poland) and *Postbag*, a listener-response program. To Europe on 6095, 7145, 7270, 9525 and 11815 kHz. This last frequency can sometimes be heard in the northeastern United States and southeastern Canada, interference permitting. One hour later in winter.

Radio Australia. *News*, then a relay of the Radio National domestic network.

> Polish Radio Warsaw's *Europe East* covers events in lesser-known parts of the Continent.

Continuous to Asia and the Pacific (and well heard in much of North America) on 5870 (or 9580), 5995, 6080 and 11800 kHz.

Radio Jordan. A partial relay of the station's domestic broadcasts. Targeted at Europe, but also heard winters in eastern North America. On 11690 kHz.

Radio Bulgaria. Summers only at this time. *News*, then Monday through Thursday there's 15 minutes of current events in *Today*. This is replaced Friday by *Weekly Spotlight*, a summary of the week's major political events. The remainder of the broadcast is given over to features dealing with Bulgaria and its people, plus some lively folk music. Sixty minutes to East Asia on 13790 kHz. One hour later during winter.

Radio Ukraine International. Summers only at this time. An hour's ample coverage of just about everything Ukrainian, including news, sports, politics and culture. To northern Europe on 7150 kHz, and to North America on 12050 kHz. One hour later in winter.

Croatian Radio. Summers only at this time; actually starts a little late, and is preceded by a bulletin in Croatian. Several minutes of English *news* (length varies) from one of the domestic networks. A valuable source of up-to-the-minute information from the region. Heard best in Europe at this hour, but also audible in eastern North America. On 5920, 7165 and 13830 kHz. One hour later in winter.

Swiss Radio International. Summers only at this time. Sixty minutes of *news*, background reports and features, and a simulcast of SRI's satellite programming. To Europe on 6165 and 9535 kHz. One hour later in winter.

Radio Korea International, South Korea. Opens with *news* and commentary, followed Monday through Wednesday by *Seoul Calling*. Weekly features include *Echoes of Korean Music* and *Shortwave Feedback* (Sunday), *Tales from Korea's Past* (Monday), *Korean Cultural Trails* (Tuesday), *Pulse of Korea* (Wednesday), *From Us to You* (a listener-response program) and *Let's Learn Korean* (Thursday), *Let's Sing Together* and *Korea Through Foreigners' Eyes* (Friday), and Saturday's *Discovering Korea*, *Korean Literary Corner* and *Weekly News Focus*. Sixty minutes to East Asia on 7285 kHz.

CBC North-Québec, Canada. Part of an 18-hour multilingual broadcast for a domestic audience, but which is also heard in the northeastern United States. Weekend programming at this hour is in English, and features *news* followed by the enjoyably eclectic ●*Good Morning Québec* (Saturday) or *Fresh Air* (Sunday). Starts at this time winters, but summers it is already into the second hour. On 9625 kHz.

HCJB—Voice of the Andes, Ecuador. Continuous religious programming to North America on 12005 and 15115 kHz. Monday through Friday, there's the live—and lively—*Morning in the Mountains*.

Radio Norway International. Summer Sundays only. *Norway Now,* a friendly 30-minute package of *news* and features aimed at Europe on 9590 kHz, and East Asia on 13800 and 15305 kHz.

Radio Singapore International. Continuous programming to Southeast Asia and beyond. Starts with a brief summary of *news,* then the musical *E-Z Beat*. This is followed weekdays by the *Business and Market Report, news* on the half-hour, and then a feature. Monday, it's *Bookmark,* replaced Tuesday by *Reflections,* and Wednesday by *Frontiers*. Thursday brings *Snapshots,* and Friday has a listener-participation program, *Dateline RSI*. These are replaced Saturday by *Snapshots, Asean Notes* and *Arts Arena,* and Sunday by *Frontiers* and *Kaleidoscope*. On 6015 and 6155 kHz.

Voice of Free China, Taiwan. *News,*

followed by features. The last is *Let's Learn Chinese,* which has a series of segments for beginning, intermediate and advanced learners. Other features include *Jade Bells and Bamboo Pipes* (Monday), *Kaleidoscope* and *Main Roads and Byways* (Tuesday), *Music Box* (Wednesday), *Perspectives* and *Journey into Chinese Culture* (Thursday), *Confrontation* and *New Record Time* (Friday), *Reflections* (Saturday) and *Adventures of Mahlon and Jeanie* and *Mailbag Time* (Sunday). One hour to East Asia on 7130 kHz, and to Australasia on 9610 kHz.

Voice of America. *News,* followed Monday through Friday by *Stateside.* End-of-week programming consists of Saturday's *On the Line* and *Communications World,* and Sunday's ●*Encounter* and *Studio 38*. To East Asia on 6110 (or 6160), 9760, 11705 (winter), 11715 and (summer) 15160 kHz; and to Australasia on 9645, 11715 and 15425 kHz. Some of these channels are also well heard in Southeast Asia.

China Radio International. *News* and a variety of features—see 0900 for specifics. One hour to Southeast Asia on 9565, 9715 and 11660 kHz; and to Australasia on 7385 and 11795 kHz.

Radio Nacional do Brasil (Radiobras), Brazil. Monday through Saturday, you can hear *Life in Brazil* or *Brazilian Panorama,* a potpourri of news, facts and figures about this huge and fascinating land, garnished with samplings of the country's various styles of music. The *Sunday Special,* on the other hand, is devoted to one particular theme, and often contains lots of exotic Brazilian music. Eighty minutes to North America on 15445 kHz.

Voice of Russia World Service. Continuous programming to Asia at this hour. Winters, it's *News and Views,* then twenty-five minutes of entertainment. ●*Music at Your Request* (Monday and Saturday) and ●*Folk Box* (Tuesday and Wednesday) are undoubtedly the choice offerings. On the remaining days, look for *This is Russia* (Sunday), *Yours for the Asking* (Friday) and Thursday's *Jazz Show.* Tuesday through Saturday, summers, there's *Focus on Asia and the Pacific*, then ●*Moscow Yesterday and Today* (Wednesday and Friday), *This is Russia* (Tuesday and Thursday), *Russian by Radio* (Monday) or music. Pick of the pack is ●*Music and Musicians* at 1311 Sunday. Winters in Southeast Asia, try 9875 (from 1230), 13785, 17755 and 17860 kHz; best in summer are 15435, 15490, 15510, 17610, 17755, 17775 and 17795 kHz.

WJCR, Upton, Kentucky. Continues with country gospel music to North America on 7490 kHz. Other U.S. religious broadcasters operating at this hour include **WGTG**

on 9400 kHz, **WWCR** on 5935 (or 13845) and 15685 kHz, **KTBN** on 7510 kHz, **WYFR-Family Radio** on 5950, 6015 (or 7355), 11830 and 11970 (or 17750) kHz, and **WHRI-World Harvest Radio** on 6040 and 9495 kHz. For traditional Catholic programming, tune **WEWN** on 7425 kHz.

12:15

Radio Cairo, Egypt. The start of a 75-minute package of news, religion, culture and entertainment, much of it devoted to Arab and Islamic themes. The initial quarter-hour consists of virtually anything, from quizzes to Islamic religious talks, then there's *news* and commentary, which in turn give way to political and cultural items. To Asia on 17595 kHz.

R.S. Makedonias

Greece's Radiophonikos Stathmos Makedonias, already widely heard, may soon be using powerful 250 kW transmitters. Shown, program staffers Mrs. Gianakidou (left), Mrs. Hadjidimitriou, Mr. Karamaounas, Mr. Tsoukalos, Mrs. Pakalidou and Mrs. Vouzi.

12:30

Radio Austria International. Summers only at this time. Thirty minutes of ●*Report from Austria.* An excellent source for news of central and eastern Europe. To Europe and eastern North America on 6155 and 13730 kHz. One hour later in winter.

Radio Bangladesh. *News,* followed by Islamic and general interest features and pleasant Bengali music. Thirty minutes to Southeast Asia, also heard in Europe, on 7185 and 9550 kHz. Frequencies may vary slightly.

Radio Netherlands. Winters only at this time. *News,* then Monday through Saturday it's ●*Newsline* followed by a feature. Select offerings include ●*Research File* (science, Monday); ●*A Good Life* (Friday); ●*Weekend* (Saturday) and Wednesday's award-winning ●*Documentary.* On the remaining days, you can hear *Mirror Images* (arts in Holland, Tuesday) and *Media Network* (communications, Thursday). Sunday fare consists of *Sincerely Yours* (a listener-response program) and *Sounds Interesting.* Fifty-five minutes to Europe on 6045 and 7190 kHz. One hour earlier in summer.

YLE Radio Finland. Summers only at this time; see 1330 for program specifics. To North America on 11900 and 15400 kHz. One hour later in winter.

Voice of Vietnam. Repeat of the 1000 transmission. A half hour to Asia on 9840 and 12020 (or 15010) kHz. Frequencies may vary slightly.

Radio Thailand. Thirty minutes of *news* and short features. To Southeast Asia and Australasia, winters on 9810 kHz, and summers on 9885 kHz.

Voice of Mongolia. Repeat of the 0900 broadcast (see there for specifics). Thirty minutes to Australasia on 12085 kHz. Frequencies may vary slightly. Occasionally heard in eastern North America.

Voice of Turkey. This time summers only. Fifty minutes of *news*, features and Turkish music beamed to Europe on 9445 kHz, and to the Mideast and Southwest Asia on 9630 kHz. One hour later in winter.

Radio Sweden. Monday through Friday, it's *news* and features in *Sixty Degrees North*, concentrating heavily on Scandinavian topics. Monday's accent is on sports; Tuesday has electronic media news; Wednesday brings *Money Matters*; Thursday features ecology or science and technology; and Friday offers a review of the week's news. Saturday's slot is filled by *Spectrum* (arts) or *Sweden Today*, and Sunday fare consists of *In Touch with Stockholm* (a listener-response program) or the musical *Sounds Nordic*. A half hour to Asia and Australasia on 9835 (winter), 13740 and 15240 kHz.

Radio Vlaanderen Internationaal, Belgium. Summer Sundays only at this time. *News*, *P.O. Box 26* (a listener-response program) and *Radio World*. Thirty minutes to eastern North America on 13610 kHz, and to Southeast Asia on 15540 kHz. One hour earlier in summer.

Radio Korea International, South Korea. Starts off with *news*, followed Monday through Wednesday by *Economic News Briefs*. The remainder of the broadcast is taken up by a feature: *Shortwave Feedback* (Sunday), *Seoul Calling* (Monday and Tuesday), *Pulse of Korea* (Wednesday), *From Us to You* (Thursday), *Let's Sing Together* (Friday) and *Weekly*

Radio Canada International's *Quirks and Quarks* is the most irreverent science show on world band.

News Focus (Saturday). Thirty minutes to East and Southeast Asia on 9570, 9640 and 13670 kHz.

Voice of Greece. Summers only at this time, and actually starts around 1235. Several minutes of English news surrounded by a lengthy period of Greek music and programming. To North America on 15175 and 15650 kHz. One hour later during winter.

■**BBC World Service.** ●*Newshour*—the crème de la crème of all news shows. Sixty minutes of quality reporting, broadcast worldwide at this hour. Available to North America and the Caribbean on 5965 (winter), 6195, 9515, 9590 (winter), 9740, 11865 (summer) and 15220 kHz. Audible in Europe on 9410, 12095, 15575 and 17640 kHz; in the Mideast on 11760, 15565, 15575 and (winter) 17640 kHz; and in southern Africa on 6190, 11940 and 21660 kHz. Heard in East and Southeast Asia on 5990, 6195 and 9740 kHz; and in Australasia on 9740 kHz.

Radio Canada International. Tuesday through Friday winters, it's a shortened version of the Canadian Broadcasting Corporation's domestic news program ●*As It Happens*. This is replaced Sunday by ●*Quirks and Quarks*, and Monday by *Double Exposure* and *Royal Canadian Air Farce*. For summer, it's the weekdays-only *Best of Morningside*. Sixty minutes to North America and the Caribbean on 9640, 11855 and (summer) 13650 kHz. For an additional service, see the next item.

Radio Canada International. Summers only at this time; see 1400 for program details. Sunday only to North America and the Caribbean on 11855 and 13650 kHz.

Swiss Radio International. Repeat of

the 1100 broadcast. *Newsnet*—a workmanlike compilation of news and background reports on world and Swiss events. Somewhat lighter fare on Saturday, when the biweekly *Capital Letters* (a listener-response program) alternates with *Name Game* and *Sounds Good*. Look for an additional 30-minute feature to Europe, which is a simulcast of SRI's satellite programming. A full hour winters to Europe on 6165 and 9535 kHz, and 30 minutes year-round to East and Southeast Asia on 7230, 7480, 12075 (winter), 13635 and (summer) 15120 kHz.

Radio Norway International. Sundays only. *Norway Now*. A friendly half hour of *news* and human-interest stories, winters to Europe on 9590 kHz, to East Asia on 7315 (or 11850) kHz, and to Southeast Asia and Western Australia on 15605 kHz; in summer, the broadcast is aimed at eastern North America on 15340 kHz, and at Southeast Asia and Western Australia on 13800 kHz.

Radio Nacional do Brasil (Radiobras), Brazil. The final 20 minutes of the broadcast beamed to North America on 15445 kHz.

Radio Vlaanderen Internationaal, Belgium. Monday through Saturday, summers only at this time. Repeat of the 0900 broadcast; see there for program details. Thirty minutes to eastern North America on 13610 kHz, and to Southeast Asia on 15540 kHz. One hour later in winter.

China Radio International. See 0900 for specifics. One hour to western North America summers on 7405 kHz; and year-round to Southeast Asia on 9565, 9715 and 11660 kHz; and to Australasia on 7385 kHz.

Polish Radio Warsaw, Poland. This time winters only. *News*, commentary, music and a variety of features. See 1200 for specifics. Fifty-five minutes to Europe on 6095, 7145, 7270, 9525 and 11815 kHz. The last frequency can also be heard in southeastern Canada and the northeast-

ern United States, interference permitting. One hour earlier in summer.

Radio Prague, Czech Republic. Summers only at this time. *News*, then Monday through Friday there's *Current Affairs*. These are followed by one or more features. Monday has *Magazine '96*; Tuesday, it's *Talking Point* and *Media Czech*; Wednesday has *The Arts* and *From the Archives*; Thursday brings *Economic Report* and *I'd Like You to Meet . . .*; and Friday there's *Between You and Us*. Saturday's showpiece is a thoroughly enjoyable musical feature which offers a different style of music each week, alternating between classical, folk, contemporary and jazz. This is replaced Sunday by *The Week in Politics*, *From the Weeklies* and *Media Czech*. Thirty minutes to South and Southeast Asia on 13580 kHz, and to East Africa and beyond on 17485 kHz. Can also be heard in the Mideast.

Radio Cairo, Egypt. The final half-hour of the 1215 broadcast, consisting of listener participation programs, Arabic language lessons and a summary of the latest news. To Asia on 17595 kHz.

CBC North-Québec, Canada. Continues with multilingual programming for a domestic audience. *News*, then winter Saturdays it's the second hour of ●*Good Morning Québec*, replaced Sunday by *Fresh Air*. In summer, the news is followed by *The House* (Canadian politics, Saturday) or the highly professional ●*Sunday Morning*. Weekday programs are mainly in languages other than English. Audible in the northeastern United States on 9625 kHz.

Radio Ukraine International. Winters only at this time. A 60-minute potpourri of all things Ukrainian. Inaugurated in summer 1997. Try the 5915-6080 and 7105-7250 kHz ranges for northern Europe, and the 9800-9990 and 12030-12060 kHz segments for North America and Australasia. One hour earlier in summer.

Radio Romania International. First

afternoon broadcast for European listeners. *News*, commentary, press review, and features about Romanian life and culture, interspersed with some lively Romanian folk music. Fifty-five minutes winters on 11940, 15390 and 17745 kHz; summers on 9690, 11940, 15365 and 17720 kHz.

Croatian Radio. Winters only at this time; actually starts a little late, and is preceded by news in Croatian. Several minutes of on-the-spot *news* from Croatian Radio's Zagreb studio. Best heard in Europe at this hour, but also audible in eastern North America. On 5920, 7165, and 13830 kHz. One hour earlier during summer.

Radio Australia. *News*, then a relay of the Radio National domestic network. Continuous to Asia and the Pacific (and well heard in much of North America) on 5870 (or 9580), 5995, 6080 and 11800 kHz.

Radio Singapore International. The third and final hour of a daily broadcasting package to Southeast Asia and beyond. Starts with a summary of the latest *news*, then it's pop music. On the half-hour, there's a 10-minute *news* bulletin (replaced by a short summary at weekends), followed by *Newsline* (Monday, Wednesday and Friday), *Business World* (Tuesday and Thursday), *Regional Press Review* (Saturday), or *The Sunday Interview*. On 6015 and 6155 kHz.

WJCR, Upton, Kentucky. Continues with country gospel music to North America on 7490 kHz. Other U.S. religious broadcasters operating at this hour include **WGTG** on 9400 kHz, **WWCR** on 5935 (or 13845) and 15685 kHz, **KTBN** 7510 kHz, **WYFR-Family Radio** on 5950, 6015 (or 9705), 11830 and 11970 (or 17750) kHz, and **WHRI-World Harvest Radio** on 6040 and 15105 kHz. Traditional Catholic programming is available via **WEWN** on 7425 kHz.

Voice of Russia World Service. Continues to much of southern Asia. *News*, then very much a mixed bag depending on the day and season. Winter programming includes *Focus on Asia and the Pacific* (Tuesday through Saturday) and Sunday's ●*Music and Musicians*, both of which start at 1311. During the second half-hour, look for the retrospective ●*Moscow Yesterday and Today* (Wednesday and Friday), *This is Russia* (Tuesday and Thursday), and *Russian by Radio* on Monday. At 1311 in summer, there's the business-oriented *Newmarket* (Tuesday), *Science and Engineering* (Sunday), and a listener-response program on most of the other days. ●*Audio Book Club* (Monday) and ●*Christian Message from Moscow* (Saturday) are the obvious choices from 1330 onwards, and alternate with *Kaleidoscope* (Tuesday and Thursday), *Russian by Radio* (Wednesday and Friday) or a music program. Winters in Southeast Asia, try 15460 and 17860 kHz; best for summer are 15460, 15560, 17610 and 17795 kHz.

13:00

HCJB—Voice of the Andes, Ecuador. Sixty minutes of religious broadcasting. Continuous to the Americas on 12005 and 15115 kHz.

FEBC Radio International, Philippines. The first 60 minutes of a three-hour (mostly religious) package to South and Southeast Asia. Weekdays, starts with *Good Evening Asia*, which includes *News Insight* and a number of five-minute features (world band enthusiasts should look for Wednesday's *DX Dial*). Other offerings include *World News Update* (1330 Monday through Saturday) and *News from the Philippines* (1335 weekdays). Most of the remaining features are religious in nature. On 11995 kHz.

Voice of America. *News*, followed most days by features for students of English. One notable exception is *Critic's Choice* at 1310 Sunday. To East Asia on 6110 (winter), 6160 (summer), 9760, 11705 (winter) and (summer) 15160 kHz; and to Australasia on 9645 and 15425 kHz. Also on 11715 kHz to both areas until 1330. Some of these channels are easily audible in Southeast Asia.

13:30

United Arab Emirates Radio, Dubai. *News*, then a feature devoted to Arab and Islamic history and culture. Twenty-five minutes to Europe (also audible in eastern North America) on 13675, 15395, 17630 and 21605 kHz.

Radio Austria International. Winters only at this time. ●*Report from Austria* (see 1230 for more details). Thirty minutes to Europe and eastern North America on 6155 and 13730 kHz. One hour earlier in summer.

Radio Vlaanderen Internationaal, Belgium. Winter Sundays only at this time. *News*, *P.O. Box 26* (a listener-response program) and *Radio World*. Thirty minutes to eastern North America on 13670 kHz. One hour later in winter. May also be available to Southeast Asia—try 15540 kHz or nearby.

Radio Yugoslavia. Summers only at this time. *News* and short reports with a strong regional flavor. Thirty minutes to Australasia on 11835 kHz. Worth a listen, especially if you are interested in the region.

Voice of Turkey. This time winters only. *News*, followed by *Review of the Turkish Press* and features (some of them arcane) with a strong local flavor. Selections of Turkish popular and classical music complete the program. Fifty minutes to Europe on 9445 kHz, and to the Mideast and Southwest Asia on 9630 kHz. One hour earlier in summer.

YLE Radio Finland. Winters only at this time. *News*, followed by short features from and about Finland. Mainstay of the broadcast is the daily *Compass North*, 12 minutes (nine on Saturday) of general interest stories about life in Finland. Saturdays at 1353, look for a world band curiosity, *Nuntii Latini* (news in Latin). A half hour to North America on 11735 and 15400 kHz. One hour earlier in summer.

Radio Canada International. *News*, followed Monday through Friday by *Spectrum* (topical events), Saturday by *Innovation Canada*, and Sunday by a listener-response program. To East Asia on 6150 (winter), 11795 (summer) and 9535 kHz. Also to Europe, the Mideast and Africa, summers only, on 11935, 15325 and (Monday through Saturday) 17820 kHz.

RDP International—Radio Portugal. Monday through Friday, summers only, at this time. See 1430 for program details. Thirty minutes to the Mideast and South Asia on 21515 kHz. One hour later during winter.

Radio Netherlands. Repeat of the 0730 broadcast. Beamed to South Asia on 9890/9895, 13700 and 15585 kHz, and widely heard winters in the Mideast on 13700 kHz.

Tipografia Vaticana

Ing. Dr. Venuti shows Pope John Paul II a prototype of the new operations control system of Vatican Radio.

Radio Sweden. See 1230 for program details. Thirty minutes to North America on 11650 and 15240 kHz.

Voice of Vietnam. Begins with *news*, then there's *Commentary* or *Weekly Review*, followed by short features and some pleasant Vietnamese music (especially at weekends). A half hour to East Asia on 9840 and 12020 (or 15010) kHz. Also audible in parts of North America, especially during summer.

Voice of Greece. Winters only at this time, and actually starts around 1335. Several minutes of English news, surrounded by lots of Greek music and programming. To North America on 9420 and 15650 kHz. One hour earlier during summer.

All India Radio. The first half-hour of a 90-minute package of exotic Indian music, regional and international *news*, commentary, and a variety of talks and features of general interest. To Southeast Asia and beyond on 9545, 11620 and 13710 kHz.

Radio Tashkent, Uzbekistan. *News* and commentary, then features. Look for an information and music program on Tuesdays, with more music on Sundays. Apart from Wednesday's *Business Club*, most other features are broadcast on a non-weekly basis. Heard in Asia, Australasia, Europe and occasionally in North America; winters on 5060, 5975, 6025 and 9715 kHz; and summers on 7285, 9715 and 15295 kHz.

13:45

Vatican Radio. Twenty minutes of religious and secular programming to Southeast Asia and Australasia on 9500, 11625 and 13765 (or 15585) kHz.

14:00

■ **BBC World Service for Europe, the Mideast and the Americas.** *World News*, then Monday through Friday it's the long-running and eclectic ●*Outlook*, followed by programs aimed at a younger audience. These include ●*Megamix* (Wednesday) and *Multitrack* (Tuesday, Thursday and Friday). Weekend programming consists of Saturday's *Sportsworld* and a Sunday feature followed by Alistair Cooke's ●*Letter from America*. Continuous to North America and the Caribbean on 9515, 9590 (winter), 11865 (summer), 15220 and 17840 kHz. Audible in Europe on 9410, 12095, 15575 and 17640 kHz; and in the Mideast on 12095 (winter), 15565, 15575 and (winter) 17640 kHz.

■ **BBC World Service for Asia and the Pacific.** Monday through Friday, it's 30 minutes of *East Asia Today*, followed by some of the best of the BBC's output: ●*Discovery* (Tuesday), *Sports International* (Wednesday), ●*Assignment* (Thursday) and ●*Science in Action* (Friday). Saturday goes live in *Sportsworld*, and pick of the Sunday fare is ●*Health Matters*, heard in the final 15-minute slot. Continuous to East and Southeast Asia on 5990, 6195 and 9740 kHz; and to Australasia on 9740 kHz. Also audible in western North America on 9740 kHz.

Radio Japan. Repeat of the 0600 broadcast; see there for specifics. One hour to western North America on 9535 and 11705 kHz, and to Asia on 6090 (winter), 9610 (summer), 9695 (winter), 11895 and (summer) 11915 kHz.

■**Radio France Internationale.** *News*, press reviews and correspondents' reports, with emphasis on events in Asia and the Mideast. These are followed, on the half-hour, by two or more short features (see the 1200 broadcast for specifics, although there may be one or two minor alterations). Fifty-five minutes of interesting and well-produced programming to the Mideast and beyond on 17560 kHz.

Voice of Russia World Service. Winters, it's *News* and a variety of features—*Newmarket* (business, Tuesday), *Science and Engineering* (Sunday), a preview of the coming week's programs (Saturday), and *Mailbag* (a listener-response show) on the remaining days. These are followed on the half-hour by ●*Audio Book Club* (Monday), *Kaleidoscope* (Tuesday and Thursday), *Russian by Radio* (Wednesday and Friday), ●*Christian Message from Moscow* (Saturday) or music. Summer offerings include the daily *News and Views* followed by some of the station's better entertainment features. Try Monday's ●*Folk Box* and Friday's ●*Music at Your Request*, both of which should please. For different tastes, there's also *Jazz Show* (Wednesday), *Timelines* (Saturday), *Kaleidoscope* (Sunday) and *Yours for the Asking* (Tuesday and Thursday).

Mainly to the Mideast, West Asia and eastern and southern parts of Africa at this hour. For the Mideast, best winter channels are 7130, 7165, 9470 and 9840 kHz; in summer, check out 4740, 4940, 4975, 9595, 11835, 11945, 11985, 15350 and 15540 kHz. For southern Africa winters, try 9470 kHz; midyear, the channels tend to be variable—best bet is to dial around the 11 and 15 MHz segments.

Radio Australia. *News*, then a relay of the Radio National domestic network. Continuous to Asia and the Pacific (and well heard in much of North America) on 5870, 5995, 9415 and 11800 kHz.

Radio Prague, Czech Republic. Winters only at this time. *News*, then Monday through Friday there's *Current Affairs*. These are followed by one or more features. Choose from *Magazine '96* (Monday), *Talking Point* and *Media Czech* (Tuesday), *The Arts* and *From the Archives* (Wednesday), *Economic Report* and *I'd Like You to Meet . . .* (Thursday) and *Between You and Us* on Friday. Saturday brings a thoroughly enjoyable musical feature which offers a different style of music each week, alternating between classical, folk, contemporary and jazz. This is replaced Sunday by *The Week in Politics, From the Weeklies* and *Media Czech*. Thirty minutes to eastern North America on 13580 kHz, and to East Africa and beyond on 17485 kHz.

Voice of America. The first of several hours of continuous programming to the Mideast. *News*, then Monday through Friday it's *Asia Report*. Weekends, look for Saturday's ●*Music USA-Jazz* (music from the Conover archives) and Sunday's *The Concert Hall*—both should please. At 1455, there's a daily editorial. Winters on 15205 kHz, and summers on 15255 kHz. Also available to East Asia winters on 6110, 9760 and 11705 kHz; and summers on 6160, 9760 and 15160 kHz. To Australasia on 15425 kHz.

Kol Israel. Summers only at this time.

A 30-minute relay from Israel Radio's domestic network. To Europe and eastern North America on 12077 and 15615 kHz. One hour later in winter.

China Radio International. *News* and commentary, followed Tuesday through Friday by *Current Affairs*. These are followed by various feature programs, such as *Cultural Spectrum* (Thursday); *Listeners' Letterbox* (Sunday and Tuesday); *China Scrapbook, Cooking Show, Chinese Folk Tales* and ●*Music from China* (Saturday); *Sports Beat* and *Song of the Week* (Sunday); *Learn to Speak Chinese* (Monday and Wednesday); and Friday's *In the Third World*. Sundays, there is also a biweekly *Business Show* which alternates with *China's Open Windows*. One hour to western North America on 7405 kHz.

Radio Vlaanderen Internationaal, Belgium. Monday through Saturday, winters only at this time. Repeat of the 1000 broadcast; see 0900 for program details. Thirty minutes to eastern North America on 13670 kHz. May also be available to Southeast Asia—try 15540 kHz or nearby.

All India Radio. The final hour of a 90-minute package of regional and international *news*, commentary, features and exotic Subcontinental music. To Southeast Asia and beyond on 9545, 11620 and 13710 kHz.

Radio Algiers International, Algeria. Winters only at this time. *News*, then local French and Arab popular music, with an occasional brief feature also thrown in. One hour of so-so reception in Europe, and occasionally heard in eastern North America. On 11715 and 15160 kHz (may also appear on 15205, 15215 or 17745 kHz).

Radio Canada International. *World Report* and the Canadian Broadcasting Corporation's popular ●*Sunday Morning*. A three-hour broadcast starting at 1400 winters, and 1300 summers. Sunday only to North America and the Caribbean on 9640 (winter), 11855 and (summer) 13650 kHz.

HCJB—Voice of the Andes, Ecuador.

14:00

Another hour of religious fare to the Americas on 12005 and 15115 kHz.

CBC North-Québec, Canada. Continues with multilingual programming for a domestic audience. *News*, followed winter Saturdays by *The House* (Canadian politics). In summer, it's *The Great Eastern*, a magazine for Newfoundlanders. Sundays, there's the excellent ●*Sunday Morning*. Weekday programs are in languages other than English. Audible in the northeastern United States on 9625 kHz.

Radio Jordan. A partial relay of the station's domestic broadcasts. Targeted at Europe, but also heard winters in eastern North America. On 11690 kHz.

FEBC Radio International, Philippines. Continues with mostly religious programming for South and Southeast Asia. For some secular fare, try *World News Update* (1430 Monday through Saturday) and *DX Dial* (for radio enthusiasts, 1440 Saturday). On 11995 kHz, and widely heard beyond the target areas.

Radio Thailand. Thirty minutes of *news* and short features for Southeast Asia and Australasia; winters on 9530 kHz, and summers on 9830 kHz.

WJCR, Upton, Kentucky. Continues with country gospel music to North America on 7490 kHz. Other U.S. religious broadcasters operating at this hour include **WGTG** on 9400 kHz, **WWCR** on 13845 and 15685 kHz, **KTBN** on 7510 kHz, **WYFR-Family Radio** on 5950, 9705 (winter), 11830 and 17750 kHz, and **WHRI-World Harvest Radio** on 6040 and 15105 kHz. For traditional Catholic fare, try **WEWN** on 7425 kHz.

CFRX-CFRB, Toronto, Canada. Audible throughout much of the northeastern United States and southeastern Canada during the hours of daylight with a modest, but clear, signal on 6070 kHz. This pleasant, friendly station carries news, sports, weather and traffic reports—most of it intended for a local audience. Call in if you'd like at +1 (514) 790-0600—comments from outside Ontario are welcomed.

14:30

Radio Netherlands. Repeat of the 0830 transmission; see there for program specifics. Beamed to South Asia, and heard well beyond; winters on 9895, 13700 and 15585 kHz; summers on 9890, 12090 and 15585 kHz. Good reception winters in the Mideast on 13700 kHz.

Radio Canada International. This time winters only. *News*, followed Monday through Friday by *Spectrum* (current events), Saturday by *Innovation Canada* (science), and Sunday by *The Mailbag* (a listener-response program). Thirty minutes to Europe, the Mideast and Africa on 9555, 11915, 11935 and 15325 kHz. One hour earlier in summer.

Radio Romania International. Fifty-five minutes of *news*, commentary, features and some enjoyable Romanian folk music. Targeted at the Mideast and South Asia winters on 11740, 11810 and 15335 kHz; an summers on 11775 and 15335 kHz.

Radio Sweden. Winters only at this time. Repeat of the 1330 broadcast; see 1230 for program specifics. *News* and features (sometimes on controversial subjects not often discussed on radio), with the accent strongly on Scandinavia. Thirty minutes to North America on 11650 and 15240 kHz.

RDP International—Radio Portugal. Monday through Friday, winters only, at this time. *News*, then features: *Visitor's Notebook* (Monday), *Musical Kaleidoscope* (Tuesday), *Challenge of the 90's* (Wednesday), *Spotlight on Portugal* (Thursday), and *Listeners' Mailbag* and *Collector's Corner* (Friday). Thirty minutes to the Mideast and South Asia on 21515 kHz. One hour earlier in summer.

15:00

■ **BBC World Service for Europe, the Mideast and the Americas.** *News*, then Monday through Thursday there's 10 minutes of ●*Sports Roundup*. The remainder is a thoroughly mixed bag of programs, depending on the day of the week. On the half-hour, try ●*The Greenfield Collection* (classical music, Tuesday), ●*Everywoman* (for and about women, Wednesday), ●*John Peel* (defies description, Thursday) and ●*Science in Action* (Friday). Weekends, there's live action in Saturday's *Sportsworld*, and Sunday features classical music. Continuous to North America on 9515, 9590 (winter), 11865 (summer), 15220 and 17840 kHz. Audible in Europe on 6195 (winter), 9410, 12095 and 15575 kHz; and in the Mideast on 9410 (winter), 12095 and (summer) 15575 kHz.

■ **BBC World Service for Asia and the Pacific.** Monday through Friday, it's 30 minutes of *East Asia Today*, followed by ●*Outlook*. A five-minute feature rounds off the hour. Weekends, the action's in Saturday's *Sportsworld*, which is replaced Sunday by features or music. Continuous to East and Southeast Asia on 5990, 6195 and 9740 kHz; and to Australasia on 9740 kHz.

China Radio International. See 0900 for program details. One hour to western North America winters on 7405 kHz. One hour earlier during summer.

Radio Australia. *News*, then a relay of the Radio National domestic network. Continuous to Asia and the Pacific (and well heard in western North America) on 5870, 5995, 9415, 9615, 11660 and 11800 kHz.

Radio Pyongyang, North Korea. Repeat of the 1100 broadcast (see there for details). One hour to Southeast Asia and Central America (also heard in parts of western North America) on 11335, 11735 and 13650 kHz; and to the Mideast and Africa on 9640 and 9975 kHz.

Voice of America. Continues with programming to the Mideast and beyond. *News*, then Monday through Friday there's *All About English*. Weekend fare consists of *On the Line* (politics, Saturday) and ●*New Horizons* (science, Sunday). The second half-hour consists of news and features in slow-speed English. Winters on 9575 and 15205 kHz, and summers on 9700, 15205 and 15255 kHz. Also heard in parts of Europe. The same programs with one exception—*Agriculture Today* replaces *On the Line* at 1510 Saturday—is available to South and Southeast Asia on 6110, 6160 (summer), 7125, 7215, 9645, 9760 and 15395 kHz.

Kol Israel. Winters only at this time. A 30-minute relay from Israel Radio's domestic network. To Europe and eastern North America on 9390 and 11685 kHz. One hour earlier in summer.

Radio Norway International. Winter Sundays only. *Norway Now*. News and features from and about Norway. A pleasant thirty minutes to the Mideast on 9520 and 11730 kHz.

Radio Canada International. Continuation of the CBC domestic program ●*Sunday Morning*. Sunday only to North America and the Caribbean on 9640 (winter), 11855 and (summer) 13650 kHz.

Radio Jordan. A partial relay of the station's domestic broadcasts. Targeted at Europe, but also heard winters in eastern North America. On 11690 kHz.

Radio Japan. *News*, then weekdays there's 10 minutes of *Asian Top News* followed by a half-hour feature. Take your pick from *Profile* (Monday), *Enjoy Japanese* (Tuesday, repeated Thursday), *Town and Around* (Wednesday) and Friday's *Music and Book Beat*. Weekends, look for *Asia Weekly* (Saturday) or Sunday's *Hello from Tokyo*. The broadcasts end with the daily *Pop-in* (Sunday excepted) and a summary of *news*. To western North America on 9535 kHz; to Southern Africa on 15355 kHz; and to South and Southeast Asia winters on 7240 and 9695 kHz, and summers on 11880/11930 and 11915 kHz.

Voice of Russia World Service. Predominantly news-related fare for the first half-hour, then a mixed bag, depending on the day and season. At 1531 winter, look for ●*Folk Box* (Monday), *Jazz Show* (Wednesday),*Timelines* (Saturday), *Yours for the Asking* (Tuesday and Thursday), ●*Music at Your Request* (Friday) and the eclectic *Kaleidoscope* (Sunday). Summers at this time, the Saturday and Sunday slots are given over to ●*Moscow Yesterday and Today*. At the same time weekdays you can hear "alternative programs"—religious paid programming or a show from the Voice of Russia's archives or transcription department. Continuous to the Mideast winters on 4940, 4975, 5925, 7130, 7165, 9470, 9585 and 9840 kHz; and summers on 4740, 4940, 4975, 9675, 11775, 11835, 11945 and 15540 kHz. In southern Africa, good winter channels are 7115, 9470 and 9585 kHz; best for midyear are 9440, 9975, 11765 and 11775 kHz.

Voice of Mongolia. *News*, reports and short features, with Sunday featuring lots of exotic local music. Thirty minutes to South and Southeast Asia on 9720 and 12085 kHz. Frequencies may vary slightly.

FEBC Radio International, Philippines. The final 60 minutes of a three-hour (mostly religious) broadcast to South and Southeast Asia. For secular programming, try the five-minute *World News Update* at 1530 Monday through Saturday, and a listener-response feature at 1540 Saturday. On 11995 kHz, and often heard outside the target area.

WJCR, Upton, Kentucky. Continues with country gospel music to North America on 7490 kHz. Other U.S. religious broadcasters operating at this hour include **WGTG** on 9400 kHz, **WWCR** on 13845 and 15685 kHz, **KTBN** on 7510 (or 15590) kHz, and **WYFR-Family Radio** on 11830 and (winter) 15215 kHz. Traditional Catholic pro-

Report from Austria offers a well-presented package of news and stories from Central Europe.

gramming is available from **WEWN** on 7425 kHz.

CFRX-CFRB, Toronto, Canada. See 1400.

Radio Netherlands. A repeat of the 1330 broadcast; see 0730 for program specifics. Fifty-five minutes winters to South Asia and beyond on 9890/9895 and 12090 kHz.

Radio Austria International. Winters only at this time. ●*Report from Austria*, a half hour of news and human interest stories. Ample coverage of national and regional issues, and a valuable source of news about central and eastern Europe. To Europe on 6155 and 13730 kHz; to the Mideast on 9870 kHz; and to South and Southeast Asia on 11780 kHz.

Voice of the Islamic Republic of Iran. Sixty minutes of *news*, commentary and features, most of it reflecting the Islamic point of view. To South and Southeast Asia (and also heard elsewhere) on 9575 (winter), 11790 (winter), 11875 (summer), 15260 and 17750 kHz.

■ **BBC World Service for Europe, the Mideast and the Americas.** Summer weekdays, it's a daily diet of quality news reporting. The first half hour consists of ●*Europe Today*, an up-to-the minute look at European events. Then, on the half-hour, there's the incomparable ●*World Business Report*, followed 15 minutes later by ●*Britain Today*. Much of the weekend programming is live sports, with *World News* (1600 Saturday) and ●*Europe Today* (same time Sunday) being the only exceptions. Monday through Friday winters, there's 15 minutes of *World News* followed by ●*The World Today* (analysis of current events) and a quarter-hour feature. The final 15 minutes are the same, year round. Winter Sundays, *Europe Today* airs one hour later, and is replaced by a news summary and feature. Continuous to North America and the Caribbean on 9515 and 17840 kHz, though the first channel is available for the full hour only on Saturday. Audible in Europe on 6195 (winter), 9410, 12095 and 15575 kHz; and in the Mideast on 9410 (winter), 12095 and (summer) 15575 kHz.

■ **BBC World Service for Asia and the Pacific.** *World News*, then weekdays it's a series of shows (mainly rock or popular music) geared to a youthful audience. *Multitrack* airs on Monday, Wednesday and Friday, with ●*Megamix* the Tuesday replacement. Weekend fare is heavily sports-oriented. To East and Southeast Asia till 1615 on 5990, 6195 and 9740 kHz; and then to Southeast Asia on 3915 and 7135 (or 7160) kHz. Audible in Australasia (till 1615) on 9740 kHz.

■**Radio France Internationale.** *News*, press reviews and correspondents' reports, with particular attention paid to events in Africa. These are followed by two or more short features (basically a repeat of the 1200 broadcast, except for weekends when there is more emphasis on African themes). A fast-moving fifty-five minutes to Africa on 11615, 11700, 12015, 15460 and 15530 kHz. Also heard on 9485 and 15210 kHz on a seasonal basis. Available to parts of the Mideast on 11615 and 15460 kHz (9485 kHz may replace either or both of these channels in winter). Some of these frequencies are also audible, to a varying degree, in eastern North America. Best bet is 11700 kHz.

United Arab Emirates Radio, Dubai. Starts with a feature on Arab history or culture, then music, and a bulletin of *news* at 1630. Answers listeners' letters at weekends. Forty minutes to Europe (also heard in eastern North America) on 13675, 15395, 17630 and 21605 kHz.

FEBC's Burmese-language transmissions, aired on world band from the Philippines, are prepared by Saw Set Tone (left), Za Win Tun and their spouses.

■**Deutsche Welle,** Germany. *News*, then Monday through Friday there's ●*NewsLink* (interviews, backup reports and analysis of European events) and *Africa Report*. Weekends, the news is followed by *Commentary* and features. Saturday's lineup includes *Talking Point*, *Africa in the German Press* and *People and Places*; Sunday brings *Arts on the Air* and *Africa Highlight*. Fifty minutes aimed primarily at eastern, central and southern Africa, but also audible in the Mideast. Winters on 7195, 9735, 11810, 13610 and 15145 kHz; and summers on 7130, 9735, 11810 and 17800 kHz.

Radio Korea International, South Korea. Opens with *news* and commentary, followed Monday through Wednesday by *Seoul Calling*. Weekly features include *Echoes of Korean Music* and *Shortwave Feedback* (Sunday), *Tales from Korea's Past* (Monday), *Korean Cultural Trails* (Tuesday), *Pulse of Korea* (Wednesday), *From Us to You* (a listener-response program) and *Let's Learn Korean* (Thursday), *Let's Sing Together* and *Korea Through Foreigners' Eyes* (Friday), and Saturday's

Discovering Korea, Korean Literary Corner and *Weekly News Focus.* One hour to East Asia on 5975 kHz, and to the Mideast and much of Africa on 9515 and 9870 kHz.

Radio Norway International. Summer Sundays only. *Norway Now.* A half hour of *news* and human-interest stories targeted at western North America on 11840 kHz, East Africa on 13805 kHz, and South Asia and beyond on 11860 kHz.

Radio Pakistan. Fifteen minutes of *news* from the Pakistan Broadcasting Corporation's domestic service, followed by a similar period at dictation speed. Intended for the Mideast and Africa, but heard well beyond on several channels. Choose from 9485, 9515, 9785, 11570, 11745, 11935, 13590 and 15555 kHz.

Radio Prague, Czech Republic. Summers only at this time. *News*, reports and features with a distinctly Czech slant, including *The Week in Politics* and *From the Weeklies* (Sunday), *Magazine '96* (Monday), *Talking Point* and *Media Czech* (Tuesday), *The Arts* and *From the Archives* (Wednesday), *Economic Report* and *I'd Like You to Meet . . .* (Thursday), *Between You and Us* (Friday) and a Saturday musical feature that's well worth a listen. A half hour to Europe on 5930 kHz, and to East Africa and the Mideast on 17485 kHz. One hour later in winter.

Radio Algiers International, Algeria. Winters only at this time. *News*, then local French and Arab popular music, with an occasional brief feature also thrown in. One hour of so-so reception in Europe, and occasionally heard in eastern North America. On 11715 and 15160 kHz (may also appear on 15205, 15215 or 17745 kHz).

Channel Africa, South Africa. Thirty minutes of mostly news-related fare. To southern Africa on 6120 (or 7155) and 9685 kHz.

Voice of Vietnam. *News*, followed by *Commentary* or *Weekly Review*, then some short features and pleasant Vietnamese music (especially at weekends). A half

hour to Africa (and heard well beyond) on 9840 and 12020 (or 15010) kHz.

Radio Australia. *News*, then a relay of the Radio National domestic network. Continuous to Asia and the Pacific (and well heard in western North America) on 5870, 5995, 6080, 9415, 9615 and 11660 kHz.

Radio Ethiopia. An hour-long broadcast divided into two parts by the 1630 *news* bulletin. Regular weekday features include *Kaleidoscope* and *Women's Forum* (Monday), *Press Review* and *Africa in Focus* (Tuesday), *Guest of the Week* and *Ethiopia Today* (Wednesday), *Ethiopian Music* and *Spotlight* (Thursday) and *Press Review* and *Introducing Ethiopia* on Friday. For weekend listening, try *Contact* and *Ethiopia This Week* (Saturday), or Sunday's *Listeners' Choice* and *Commentary.* Best heard in parts of Africa and the Mideast, but sometimes audible in Europe. On 7165, 9560 and 11800 kHz.

Radio Jordan. A partial relay of the station's domestic broadcasts. Summers, the final half hour; but a full 60 minutes in winter. Targeted at Europe, but also heard winters in eastern North America. On 11690 kHz.

Voice of Russia World Service. *News*, then very much a mixed bag, depending on the day and season. Winters, there's *Focus on Asia and the Pacific* (Tuesday through Friday) and *Mailbag* (Monday and Saturday), with Sunday's program preview making up the week. On the half-hour, the Saturday and Sunday slots are given over to ●*Moscow Yesterday and Today.* At the same time weekdays you can hear "alternative programs"—religious paid programming or a show from the Voice of Russia's archives or transcription department. Pick of the summer programming is ●*Music and Musicians* (1611 Saturday). Other options (all at 1611) include *Science and Engineering* (Tuesday and Wednesday), *Mailbag* (Thursday and Sunday) and the business-oriented *Newmarket* (Monday and Friday). At 1631, choose from ●*Moscow Yesterday and Today* (Tuesday and Thursday), *Timelines* (Sunday) and *This is Russia* (Monday and Wednesday). Continuous to the Mideast winters on 4940, 4975, 6175, 7210, 7275, 9470, 9585 and 9635 kHz; and summers on 9675, 11775, 11835 and 11945 kHz. For southern Africa, try 7255, 7325, 9470 and 9505 kHz in winter; and 9440, 9675, 9975 and 11775 kHz midyear. Also available summers to Europe on 7440, 9775, 9880 and (irregularly) 15400 kHz.

Radio Canada International. Winters only. Final hour of CBC's ●*Sunday Morning.* Sunday only to North America and the Caribbean on 9640 and 11855 kHz.

"Rush Limbaugh Show," WRNO, New Orleans, Louisiana. Summer weekdays only at this time. The first sixty minutes of a three-hour live package. Arguably of little interest to most listeners outside North America, but popular and controversial within the United States. To North America and Caribbean on 7355 (or 15420) kHz.

China Radio International. *News* and commentary, followed Tuesday through Friday by *Current Affairs.* These are followed by various feature programs, such as *Cultural Spectrum* (Thursday); *Listeners' Letterbox* (Sunday and Tuesday); *China Scrapbook, Cooking Show, Chinese Folk Tales* and ●*Music from China* (Saturday); *Sports Beat* and *Song of the Week* (Sunday); *Learn to Speak Chinese* (Monday and Wednesday); and Friday's *In the Third World.* Sundays, there is also a biweekly *Business Show* which alternates with *China's Open Windows.* One hour to Southern Africa on 15110 and 15130 kHz.

Voice of America. Several hours of continuous programming aimed at an African audience. Monday through Friday, starts with *news* and features for listeners who use English as a second language. Followed on the half-hour by *Africa World Tonight.* Weekends, it's a full hour of *Nightline Africa*—special news and features on African affairs. Heard well beyond the target area—including North America—on a number of frequencies. Try 6035, 11920, 12040, 13600, 13710, 15225, 15410, 15445 and 17895 kHz, some of which are seasonal. In North America, try 13710, 15410, 15445 and 17895 kHz. For a separate service to the Mideast and beyond, see the next item.

Voice of America. *News*, then weekdays it's news and reports in *Mideast Edition.* This is followed on the half-hour by *Music USA.* Saturday's fare is *On the Line* and *Press Conference USA*, replaced Sunday by ●*Encounter* (current events) and *Studio 38* (American lifestyles). To the Mideast (also heard in parts of Europe), winters on 9575 and 15205 kHz, and summers on 9700, 15205 and 15255 kHz. Available to South and Southeast Asia on 6110, 6160 (summer), 7125, 7215, 9645, 9760 and 15395 kHz.

WJCR, Upton, Kentucky. Continues with country gospel music to North America on 7490 kHz. Other U.S. religious broadcasters operating at this hour include **WGTG** on 9400 kHz, **WWCR** on 13845 and 15685 kHz, **KTBN** on 15590 kHz, and **WYFR-Family Radio** on 11705 (or 15215) and 11830 kHz. Traditional Catholic programming can be heard via **WEWN** on 7425 kHz.

CFRX-CFRB, Toronto, Canada. See 1400.

16:30

Radio Slovakia International. Summers only at this time; see 1730 for specifics. Thirty minutes of friendly programming to western Europe on 5915, 6055 and 7345 kHz. One hour later in winter.

Radio Canada International. *News*, then Monday through Friday it's *Spectrum* (current events). *Innovation Canada* airs on Saturday, and a listener-response program occupies Sunday's slot. A half hour to Asia on 7150 and 9550 kHz.

16:30

Radio Austria International. See 1530 for more details. An informative half-hour of ●*Report from Austria*. Available summers to Europe on 6155 and 13730 kHz, and to the Mideast on 11855 kHz; also year-round to South and Southeast Asia, winters on 11780 kHz, and summers on 13710 kHz.

Radio Cairo, Egypt. The first 30 minutes of a two-hour package of Arab music and features reflecting Egyptian life and culture, with *news* and commentary about events in Egypt and the Arab world. There are also quizzes, mailbag shows, and answers to listeners' questions. To southern Africa on 15255 kHz.

17:00

■ **BBC World Service for Europe, the Mideast and the Americas.** Winter weekdays, the first half hour consists of ●*Europe Today* (reports and analysis), and then there's business and financial news in ●*World Business Report*. In summer, look for 15 minutes of *World News* followed by ●*The World Today* and a quarter-hour feature. The final slot is the year-round ●*Sports Roundup*. Weekends, look for some interesting fare that rotates on a seasonal basis. Continuous to North America on 17840 kHz; to Europe on 3955 (winters), 6180, 6195, 9410, 12095 and 15575 kHz; and to the Mideast on 9410 and 12095 kHz. Some of the European channels are also heard in eastern North America.

■ **BBC World Service for Africa.** *World News*, *Focus on Africa*, *African News* and ●*Sports Roundup*. Part of a 21-hour daily service to the African continent on a variety of channels, including 3255, 6190, 15400 and 17830 kHz. The last two channels are widely heard outside Africa, including parts of North America.

■ **BBC World Service for Asia.** Weekdays, the lineup is five minutes of *World News*, followed by ●*World Business*

Report (financial news), ●*The World Today* (analysis of current events) and ●*Off the Shelf* (readings from world literature). Weekend fare consists of Saturday's ●*World Business Review* and *A Jolly Good Show*, and Sunday's *Write On* (a listener-response program) and ●*Omnibus*. Continuous to Southeast Asia (till 1745) on 3915 and 7135 (or 7160) kHz.

Radio Prague, Czech Republic. See 1600 for specifics. A half hour of *news* and features year-round to Europe on 5930 kHz; also winters to East Africa (and audible in parts of the Mideast) on 9430 kHz, and summers to central and southern Africa on 15640 kHz.

Radio Australia. *News*, then a relay of the Radio National domestic network. Continuous to Asia and the Pacific (and well heard in western North America) on 5870, 5995, 6080, 9415, 9615 and 11660 kHz.

Swiss Radio International. World and Swiss *news* and background reports. Information at the expense of entertainment, though Saturday's programming has a lighter touch to it. Thirty minutes to northern Europe, winters on 7410 kHz, and summers on 9905 kHz.

Polish Radio Warsaw, Poland. This time summers only. Fifty-five minutes of news, commentary, features and music—all with a Polish flavor. Monday through Friday, it's *News from Poland*—a compendium of news, reports and interviews. This is followed by *A Day in the Life . . .* and *Request Concert* (Monday), a regular feature which alternates on a weekly basis (Tuesday), *Letter from Poland* and a communications show (Wednesday), classical music and the historical *Flashback* (Thursday), and Friday's *Business Week* followed by *Focus* (the arts in Poland). The Saturday broadcast begins with a bulletin of *news*, then there's *Weekend Commentary*, *Panorama* (a window on day-to-day life in Poland) and a listener-response program, *Postbag*. Sundays, you can hear *Europe East* (correspondents' reports from all over eastern Europe) and *Jazz, Folk, Rock and Pop from Poland*. Fifty-five minutes to Europe on 6000, 6095, 7270 and 7285 kHz. One hour later during winter.

Radio Jordan. Winters only at this time. The final 30 minutes of a partial relay of the station's domestic broadcasts. Targeted at Europe, but also heard in eastern North America. On 11690 kHz.

Voice of Russia World Service. *News*, then it's a mixed bag, depending on the day of the week. Pick of the litter is undoubtedly ●*Music and Musicians* (1711 Saturday). Other shows at the same time include *Science and Engineering* (Tuesday and Wednesday), *Mailbag* (Thursday and Sunday) and the business-oriented *Newmarket* (Monday and Friday). On the half-hour, choose from ●*Moscow Yesterday and Today* (Tuesday and Thursday), *Timelines* (Sunday) and *This is Russia* (Monday and Wednesday). Summers, there's the daily *News and Views* followed by a variety of features. Best of these are ●*Music at Your Request* (Thursday), ●*Folk Box* (Friday), *Kaleidoscope* (Sunday) and Tuesday's *Jazz Show*. Other options include Sunday's *This is Russia* and Wednesday's *Yours for the Asking*. Continuous to Europe winters on 4920, 5940, 6110, 6130, 7180, 7440 and 9890 kHz; and summers on 7440, 9775, 9880 and (irregularly) 15400 kHz. Also to the Mideast winters on 7130, 7210, 7255, 7275, 7305 and 9585 kHz; and summers on 9595, 9675 and 11775 kHz. In southern Africa, try 7255, 7325, 9470 and 9505 kHz in winter; and 9975 and 11775 kHz midyear.

Radio For Peace International, Costa Rica. The first daily edition of *FIRE* (Feminist International Radio Endeavour), and the start of the English portion of an eight-hour cyclical block of predominantly social-conscience and counterculture

Take a journey into history with *Moscow Yesterday and Today,* aired over the Voice of Russia.

programming. Audible in North America and elsewhere on 15050 kHz.

Radio Japan. Repeat of the 1500 broadcast, except that Sunday's *Hello from Tokyo* is replaced by *Let's Learn Japanese* and *Viewpoint*. One hour to the Mideast on 11930 kHz; to western North America on 9535 kHz; and to Asia on 6035/6150 (East), 7280/11880 (South) and (Southeast) 9580 kHz.

Channel Africa, South Africa. Thirty minutes of mostly news-related fare. To West Africa on 11900 kHz, and sometimes heard in Europe.

China Radio International. Repeat of the 1600 transmission. One hour to East and Southern Africa on 7150 (or 7160), 7405, 9570 and (midyear) 11910 kHz.

Voice of America. Continuous programming to the Mideast and North Africa. *News*, then Monday through Friday it's the interactive *Talk to America*. Weekends, there's Saturday's *American Agenda* and *Communications World*, and Sunday's *Critic's Choice* and ●*Issues in the News*. Winters on 6040, 9760 and 15205 kHz; and summers on 9700, 9760 and 15255 kHz. Also available to Europe, winters on 15120 kHz, ands summers on 15135 kHz. For a separate service to Africa, see the next item.

Voice of America. Programs for Africa. Monday through Saturday, identical to the service for Europe and the Mideast (see previous item). On Sunday, opens with *News*, then it's *Voices of Africa* and ●*Music Time in Africa*. Audible well beyond where it is targeted. On 11920 (winter), 12040 (winter), 15410, 15445 and 17895 kHz. For yet another service (to Asia and the Pacific), see the next item.

Voice of America. Monday through Friday only. *News*, followed by the interactive *Talk to America*. Sixty minutes to Asia on 5990, 6045, 6110, 6160, 7125, 7150, 7170, 7215, 9525, 9550, 9645, 9670,

17:00

9770, 9795, 11945, 12005 and 15255 kHz, some of which are seasonal. For Australasia, try 9525, 11945 and 15255 kHz in winter; and 7150 and 7170 kHz midyear. Some of these channels also carry weekend programming to South and Southeast Asia (same shows as for Europe and the Mideast, above).

■**Radio France Internationale.** An additional half-hour (see 1600) of predominantly African fare. To East Africa on any two frequencies from 9485, 11615, 15210 and 15460 kHz. Also audible in parts of the Mideast, and occasionally heard in eastern North America.

Radio Cairo, Egypt. See 1630 for specifics. Continues with a broadcast to southern Africa on 15255 kHz.

"Rush Limbaugh Show," **WRNO,** New Orleans, Louisiana. Monday through Friday only; see 1600 for specifics. Starts at this time winters; summers, it's already into the second hour. Continuous to North America and the Caribbean on 7355 (or 15420) kHz.

WJCR, Upton, Kentucky. Continues with country gospel music to North America on 7490 kHz. Other U.S. religious broadcasters operating at this hour include **WGTG** on 9400 kHz, **WWCR** on 13845 and 15685 kHz, **KTBN** on 15590 kHz, and **WHRI-World Harvest Radio** on 13760 and 15105 kHz.

CFRX-CFRB, Toronto, Canada. See 1400.

17:30

Radio Netherlands. Targeted at Africa, but heard well beyond. *News*, followed Monday through Saturday by *Newsline* and a feature. Top choices include ●*Research File* (Monday), ●*A Good Life* (Friday), and Saturday's ●*Weekend*. For other interesting offerings, try *Mirror Images* (Tuesday) or Wednesday's documentaries, many of which are excellent. Other programs include Thursday's *Media*

Network and Sunday's *Sounds Interesting*. Monday through Friday there is also a *Press Review*. One hour on 6020, 7120 (summer), 9605 (winter) and 11655 kHz.

Radio Slovakia International. Winters only at this time. *Slovakia Today*, a 30-minute look at Slovak life and culture. Tuesday, there's a mixed bag of short features; Wednesday puts the accent on tourism and Slovak personalities; Thursday's slot is devoted to business and economy; and Friday brings a mix of politics, education and science. Saturday offerings include cultural items, *Slovak Kitchen* and the off-beat *Back Page News*; and Sunday brings the *"Best of"* series. Monday's show is more relaxed, and includes *Listeners' Tribune* and some enjoyable Slovak music. A friendly half hour to western Europe on 5915, 6055 and 7345 kHz. One hour earlier in summer.

Radio Romania International. *News*, commentary, a press review, and one or more short features. Thirty minutes to eastern and southern Africa (also audible in parts of the Mideast). Winters on 9750, 11740 and 11940 kHz; and summers on 9550, 9750, 11830 and 11940 kHz.

17:45

All India Radio. The first 15 minutes of a two-hour broadcast to Europe and Africa, consisting of regional and international *news*, commentary, a variety of talks and features, press review and exotic Indian music. Continuous till 1945. To Europe on 7410, 9950 and 11620 kHz; and to Africa on 11935, 13780 and 15075 kHz. Easily audible in the Mideast, but dial around to find the best frequency for your location.

Voice of Armenia. Monday through Friday, summers only at this time. Mainly of interest to Armenians abroad. Fifteen minutes of *news* from and about Armenia. To eastern Europe and the Mideast on 4810, 4990 and 7480 kHz. One hour later in winter.

1800-2359
Europe & Mideast—Evening Prime Time
East Asia—Early Morning
Australasia—Morning
eastern North America—Afternoon
western North America—Midday

18:00

■ **BBC World Service for Europe, the Mideast and the Americas.** Thirty minutes of ●*Newsdesk*, with the next half-hour containing some varied and interesting fare. Sunday, there's the first part of ●*Play of the Week* (world theater), replaced Monday by ●*Brain of Britain* (or its substitute), and Tuesday by ●*One Planet* (the environment). Then it's ●*The Works* (technology, Wednesday). ●*Assignment* (Thursday), ●*Focus on Faith* (a secular look at religion, Friday) and ●*Science in Action* on Saturday. Continuous five-star programming to Europe on 3955 (winter), 6180, 6195, 9410 and (summer) 12095 and 15575 kHz; and to the Mideast on 9410 and (summer) 12095 and 15575 kHz. Some of these channels provide fair to good reception in eastern North America. Also available winters to much of North America on 17840 kHz.

■ **BBC World Service for Africa.** ●*Newsdesk*, then Monday through Friday it's *Focus on Africa*. Weekends, Saturday gives us ●*Andy Kershaw's World of Music*, and Sunday it's time for *A Jolly Good Show*. Continuous programming to the African continent (and heard well beyond) on 3255, 6005 (from 1830), 6190, 9630 (from 1830), 15400 and 17830 kHz. The last two channels are audible in parts of North America.

Radio Kuwait. The start of a three-hour package of *news*, Islamic-oriented features and western popular music. Some interesting features, even if you don't particularly like the music. There is a full program summary at the beginning of each transmission, to enable you to pick and choose. To Europe and eastern North America on 11990 kHz.

Voice of Vietnam. Begins with *news*, then there's *Commentary* or *Weekly Review*, followed by short features and some pleasant Vietnamese music (especially at weekends). A half hour to Europe on 9840 and 12020 (or 15010) kHz.

Radio For Peace International, Costa Rica. Part of a continuous eight-hour cyclical block of predominantly social-conscience and counterculture programming. One of international broadcasting's more unusual features, *The Far Right Radio Review*, can be

From Antarctica to the Himalayas, David Lee Travis has been playing requests for listeners in every part of the globe for over 18 years.

heard at 1800 Tuesday. To North America and beyond on 15050 kHz.

Radio Vlaanderen Internationaal, Belgium. Summers only at this time. See 1900 for program details. Thirty minutes to Europe on 5910 kHz, and to Africa on 13645 kHz. One hour later in winter.

All India Radio. Continuation of the transmission to Europe, Africa and the Mideast (see 1745). *News* and commentary, followed by programming of a more general nature. To Europe on 7410, 9950 and 11620 kHz; and to Africa on 11935, 13780 and 15075 kHz. In the Mideast, choose the channel best suited to your location.

Radio Prague, Czech Republic. Winters only at this time. *News*, then Monday through Friday there's *Current Affairs*. These are followed by one or more features. Choose from *Magazine '96* (Monday), *Talking Point* and *Media Czech* (Tuesday), *The Arts* and *From the Archives* (Wednesday), *Economic Report* and *I'd Like You to Meet . . .* (Thursday) and *Between You and Us* on Friday. Saturday's showpiece is a thoroughly enjoyable musical feature which offers a different style of music each week, alternating between classical, folk, contemporary and jazz. This is replaced Sunday by *The Week in Politics, From the Weeklies* and *Media Czech.* A half hour to Europe on 5835 kHz, and to Australasia on 9430 kHz.

Radio Norway International. Summer Sundays only. *Norway Now.* Repeat of the 1200 transmission. Thirty minutes of friendly programming from and about Norway. To Europe on 7485 kHz, to the Mideast on 9590 kHz, and to Africa on 13805 and 15220 kHz.

Croatian Radio. Summers only at this time; actually starts a little late, and is preceded by a bulletin in Croatian. A short English newscast from one of the domestic networks. Heard best in Europe on 5895 and 7165 kHz, but also audible in eastern North America on 13830 kHz. Sometimes preempted by live sports commentary in Croatian. One hour later in winter.

Radio Australia. *News,* then Sunday through Thursday it's *Pacific Beat.* On the remaining two days, look for a relay of the Radio National domestic network. Continuous to Asia and the Pacific (and well heard in western North America) on 5995, 6080, 7240, 9415, 9615 and 11880 kHz.

Radio Nacional do Brasil (Radiobras), Brazil. Monday through Saturday, you can hear *Life in Brazil* or *Brazilian Panorama,* a potpourri of news, facts and figures about this fascinating land, interspersed with examples of the country's various unique musical styles. The *Sunday Special,* on the other hand, is devoted to one particular theme,

> Radio Nacional do Brasil's *Sunday Special* often contains exotic Brazilian music.

and often contains lots of exotic Brazilian music. Eighty minutes to Europe on 15265 kHz.

Polish Radio Warsaw, Poland. This time winters only. See 1700 for program specifics. *News,* music and features, covering multiple aspects of Polish life and culture. Fifty-five minutes to Europe on 6000, 6095, 7270 and 7285 kHz. One hour earlier in summer.

Voice of Russia World Service. Predominantly news-related fare during the initial half-hour, with *News and Views* the daily winter offering. In summer, it's ●*Commonwealth Update* Monday through Friday, and the business-oriented *Newmarket* on Saturday. Sunday has a program preview. At 1830, winter features include Tuesday's *Jazz Show,* Wednesday's *Yours for the Asking,* Thursday's ●*Music at Your Request* and Friday's exotic ●*Folk Box.* Other options include *This is Russia* (Sunday) and *Kaleidoscope* (Monday). Apart from *This is Russia* (Saturday) and ●*Christian Message from*

Moscow (Sunday), the 1830 summer slot is allocated to "alternative programs." These can be regular shows, Voice of Russia transcription programs or mind-numbing religious paid programming. Continuous to Europe winters on 6130, 7180, 7440 and 9890 kHz; and summers on 9765, 9775, 9810, 9880 and (irregularly) 15400 kHz. Some of these channels can be heard in parts of eastern North America. Also to the Mideast winters on 7305 kHz. For southern Africa, try 7175, 7305, 7325 and 9505 kHz in winter, and 9440, 9675, 9975 and 11775 kHz midyear.

Voice of America. Continuous pro-gramming to the Mideast and North Africa. Repeat of the 1600 broadcast except at 1810 weekends, when you can hear ●*Encounter* (Saturday) and *Agriculture Today* (Sunday). On 6040 (winter) and 9760 kHz. Also audible in parts of Europe. For a separate service to Africa, see the next item.

Voice of America. Monday through Friday, it's 60 minutes of *Africa World Tonight*. Weekends, there's Saturday's *Agriculture Today* or Sunday's ●*Encounter*, followed on the half-hour by *news* and features in "Special" (slow-speed) English. To Africa, but heard well beyond, on 6035, 7415, 11920, 11975, 12025, 13710, 15410, 15580 and 17895 kHz, some of which are seasonal.

Radio Pyongyang, North Korea. The last of the old-time communist stations, with quaint terms like "Great Leader" and "Beloved Comrade" still in regular use. Much of the broadcast is given over to revering the late Kim Il Sung, both in words and music. Awful programs, but worth the occasional listen just to hear how bad they are. One hour to Europe on 6575 and 9345 kHz; and to North America (better to the west) on 11700 and 13760 kHz.

Radio Cairo, Egypt. See 1630 for spe-cifics. The final 30 minutes of a two-hour broadcast to southern Africa on 15255 kHz.

Radio Omdurman, Sudan. A one-hour package of *news* and features (often from a pro-government viewpoint), plus a little ethnic Sudanese music. Better heard in Europe than in North America, but occa-sionally audible in the eastern United States. On 9200 kHz.

"Rush Limbaugh Show," WRNO, New Orleans, Louisiana. Monday through Friday only; see 1600 for specifics. Con-tinuous to North America and the Carib-bean on 7355 (or 15420) kHz.

"For the People," WHRI, Noblesville, Indiana. Summers only at this time; see 0300 for specifics. Three hours of live populist programming targeted at North America on 9495 kHz. One hour later in winter.

WJCR, Upton, Kentucky. Continues with country gospel music to North America on 7490 kHz. Other U.S. religious broadcast-ers operating at this time include **WGTG** on 9400 kHz, **WWCR** on 13845 and 15685 kHz, **KTBN** on 15590 kHz, and **WHRI-World Harvest Radio** on 13760 and 15105 kHz. For traditional Catholic pro-gramming, tune **WEWN** on 7425 kHz.

CFRX-CFRB, Toronto, Canada. See 1400.

18:15

Radio Bangladesh. *News*, followed by Islamic and general interest features; some nice Bengali music, too. Thirty min-utes to Europe on 7185 and 9550 kHz, and irregularly to the Mideast on 15520 kHz. Frequencies may be slightly variable.

Radio Tirana, Albania. Summers only at this time. Approximately 10 minutes of *news* and commentary from and about Albania. To Europe on 7270 and 9570 kHz. One hour later during winter.

18:30

■ **BBC World Service for Asia and the Pacific.** The first 30 minutes of a much longer transmission of continuous pro-

Radio Slovakia International airs programs worldwide in English, Slovak, French, German and Russian.

Slovenský Rozhlas

gramming, and which is dedicated to features at this hour. Pick of the pack are ●*Andy Kershaw's World of Music* (an eclectic delight, Monday), ●*Everywoman* (for and about women, Tuesday), and ●*Science in Action* (self-explanatory, Friday). Winters to Southeast Asia, year-round to Australasia, on 9740 kHz.

Radio Netherlands. Well heard in parts of North America, despite being targeted at Africa. *News*, followed Monday through Saturday by *Newsline* and a feature, several of which are excellent. Take your pick from ●*A Good Life* (Monday), *Music 52/15* (Tuesday) *Sounds Interesting* (Wednesday), ●*Research File* (Thursday), the award-winning ●*Documentary* (Friday) and Saturday's ●*Roughly Speaking.* These are replaced Sunday by *Wide Angle* and *Siren Song.* Sixty minutes on 6020, 7120 (summer), 9605 (winter), 9895 (summer), 11655, 15315 and 17605 kHz. The last two frequencies, via the relay in the Netherlands Antilles, are best for North American listeners.

Radio Slovakia International. Summers only at this time; see 1930 for specifics. Thirty minutes of *news* and features with a strong Slovak flavor. To western Europe on 5915, 6055 and 7345 kHz. One hour later in winter.

Voice of Turkey. This time summers only. *News*, followed by *Review of the Turkish Press*, then features on Turkish history, culture and international relations, interspersed with enjoyable selections of the country's popular and classical music. Fifty minutes to western Europe on 9445 and 9535 kHz. One hour later in winter.

Radio Sweden. Monday through Friday, it's *news* and features in *Sixty Degrees North*, concentrating heavily on Scandinavian topics. Monday's accent is on sports; Tuesday has electronic media news; Wednesday brings *Money Matters*; Thursday features ecology or science and technology; and Friday offers a review of the week's news. Saturday's slot is filled by *Spectrum* (arts) or *Sweden Today*, and Sunday fare consists of *In Touch with Stockholm* (a listener-response program) or the musical *Sounds Nordic*. Thirty minutes to Europe, the Mideast and Africa on 6065, 7240 (or 11615) and 9655 kHz.

Radio Korea International, South Korea. Starts off with *news*, followed Monday through Wednesday by *Economic News Briefs*. The remainder of the broadcast is taken up by a feature: *Shortwave Feedback* (Sunday), *Seoul Calling* (Monday and Tuesday), *Pulse of Korea* (Wednesday), *From Us to You* (Thursday), *Let's Sing Together* (Friday) and *Weekly News Focus* (Saturday). Thirty minutes to Europe summers on 3955 kHz. This station reorganized its schedule for summer 1996, so the former winter timing of 2000 is almost certainly subject to change. Try 1830 or 1930 on 3970 kHz.

Radio Tirana, Albania. Summers only at this time. *News*, with much of the remainder of the broadcast being devoted to lively Albanian music. Thirty minutes to Europe on 7270 and 9740 kHz. One hour later during winter.

Radio Yugoslavia. Summers only at this time. *News* and background reports with a strong regional slant. Thirty minutes to Europe on 6100 kHz, and to Southern Africa on 9720 kHz. One hour later during winter.

Voice of Armenia. Monday through Friday, winters only at this time. Mainly of interest to Armenians abroad. Fifteen minutes of *news* from and about Armenia. To eastern Europe and the Mideast on 4810, 4990 and 7480 kHz. One hour earlier in summer.

■ **BBC World Service for Europe, the Mideast and the Americas.** Monday through Saturday, starts with a brief summary of the latest *news*. This is followed weekdays by the popular and long-running ●*Outlook* and five minutes of the religious *Pause for Thought*. On the half-hour, the programs are geared to younger listeners: *Multitrack* (Monday, Wednesday and Friday), ●*Megamix* (Tuesday) and ●*John Peel* (Thursday). Pick of the weekend fare is Sunday's continuation of ●*Play of the Week* and, if the play ends by 1930, the aptly-named ●*Anything Goes*. Continuous to Europe on 3955 (winter), 6180, 6195, 9410 and (summer) 12095 and 15575 kHz; and to the Mideast on 9410 and (summer) 15575 kHz. Some of the European channels are also audible in eastern North America.

■ **BBC World Service for Africa.** A series of features aimed at the African continent, but worth a listen even if you live farther afield. The list includes *Fast Track* and *Meridian On Screen* (Monday), *Money Focus* (Tuesday), *Talkabout Africa* and ●*One Planet* (Wednesday), ●*Assignment* and ●*The Works* (Thursday), *African Perspective* and ●*Science in Action* (Friday), ●*Omnibus* and *Meridian* (Saturday) and *Postmark Africa* and *The Art House* on Sunday. Continuous programming to the African continent (and

heard well beyond) on 3255, 6005, 6190, 9630, 11835 (summer), 15400 and 17830 kHz. The last two channels are audible in parts of North America.

■ **BBC World Service for Asia and the Pacific.** Monday through Friday (Tuesday through Saturday local Asian days), five minutes of *World News* are followed by human-interest stories in ●*Outlook*. The second half-hour has something for every taste, depending on the day of the week. Take your pick from *Composer of the Month* (classical music, Monday), ●*Brain of Britain* or a substitute quiz (Tuesday), *Sports International* (Wednesday), *Meridian On Screen* (cinema, Thursday) and ●*Focus on Faith* (a secular look at religion, Friday). Saturday fare is split between ●*From Our Own Correspondent* and the religious *In Praise of God*, replaced Sunday by classical music and a 15-minute feature. Continuous to Australasia on 9740 kHz, and available winters to Southeast Asia on the same frequency.

Radio Nacional do Brasil (Radiobras), Brazil. Final 20 minutes of the 1800 broadcast to Europe on 15265 kHz.

Radio Vlaanderen Internationaal, Belgium. Winters only at this time. Weekdays, there's *News*, *Press Review* and *Belgium Today*, followed by features like *Focus on Europe* (Monday), *Living in Belgium* and *Green Society* (Tuesday), *The Arts* (Wednesday and Friday), *Around Town* (Wednesday), *Economics* and *International Report* (Thursday), and *Tourism* (Friday). Weekend features include *Music from Flanders* (Saturday) and Sunday's *P.O. Box 26* (a listener-response program) and *Radio World*. Twenty-five minutes to Europe on 5910 kHz; also to Africa (and heard elsewhere) on 9925 kHz. One hour earlier in summer.

Radio Australia. Begins with *News*, then there's *Pacific Beat* and/or *Pacific Focus*. Continuous programming to Asia and the Pacific on 5995, 6080, 7240, 9415 and 11880 kHz

Croatian Radio. Winters only at this time; actually starts a little late, and is preceded by a bulletin in Croatian. A short English newscast from one of the domestic networks. Heard best in Europe on 5895 and 7165 kHz, and also audible in eastern North America on 11635 kHz. Sometimes preempted by live sports commentary in Croatian. One hour earlier in summer.

Radio Norway International. Winter Sundays only. *Norway Now. News* and features from and about Norway. Thirty minutes to Europe on 5960 kHz, to Australasia on 7115 kHz; and to Africa on 7485 and 9590 kHz.

Radio Kuwait. See 1800; continuous to Europe and eastern North America on 11990 kHz.

Kol Israel. Summers only at this time. ●*Israel News Magazine.* Thirty minutes of even-handed and comprehensive news reporting from and about Israel. To Europe and North America on 7465, 11605 and 15615 kHz; to Central and South America on 9435 kHz, and to Africa and South America on 15640 kHz. One hour later in winter.

All India Radio. The final 45 minutes of a two-hour broadcast to Europe, Africa and the Mideast (see 1745). Starts off with *news*, then continues with a mixed bag of features and Indian music. To Europe on 7410, 9950 and 11620 kHz; and to Africa on 11935, 13780 and 15075 kHz. In the Mideast, choose the channel best suited to your location.

Radio Bulgaria. Summers only at this time. *News*, then Monday through Thursday there's 15 minutes of current events in *Today*, replaced Friday by *Weekly Spotlight*, a summary of the week's major political stories. The remainder of the broadcast is given over to features dealing with Bulgaria and Bulgarians, and includes some lively ethnic music. To

Europe, also audible in eastern North America, on 9700 and 11720 kHz. One hour later during winter.

Radio Pyongyang, North Korea. Repeat of the 1800 transmission (see there for details). One hour to the Mideast and Africa on 6575, 9600 and 9975 kHz.

HCJB—Voice of the Andes, Ecuador. The first of three hours of religious and secular programming targeted at Europe. Monday through Friday it's *Studio 9*, featuring nine minutes of world and Latin American *news*, followed by 20 minutes of in-depth reporting on Latin America. The final portion is given over to one of a variety of 30-minute features—including *You Should Know* (issues and ethics, Monday), *El Mundo Futuro* (science, Tuesday), *Ham Radio Today* (Wednesday), *Woman to Woman* (Thursday) and Friday's exotic and enjoyable ●*Música del Ecuador*. On Saturday, the news is followed by *DX Partyline*, which in turn is replaced Sunday by *Saludos Amigos*—HCJB's international friendship program. Winter on 11960 kHz, and summer on 15540 kHz.

Radio Budapest, Hungary. Summers only at this time. *News* and features, some of which are broadcast on a regular basis. These include Sunday's *Bookshelf* a press review (Monday, Tuesday, Thursday and Friday), *Profiles* (Tuesday), and *Focus on Business* (Wednesday). Thirty minutes to Europe on 3975, 7155 and 9755 kHz. One hour later in winter.

■**Deutsche Welle,** Germany. A repeat of the 1600 broadcast. Fifty minutes nominally aimed at West Africa, but heard well beyond, including eastern North America. Winters, try 9640, 9765, 11785, 11810, 13690, 15135 and 15425 kHz; in summer, go for 7250, 9640, 9670, 9735, 11785, 11810, and 13790 kHz.

Radio Romania International. *News*, commentary, press review and features. Regular spots include *Youth Club* (Tuesday), *Romanian Musicians* (Wednesday),

Chief Engineer René Usquiawo and his assistant prepare to air a taped program at Bolivia's official station, Radio Illimani on 4945 and 6025 kHz from La Paz.

and Thursday's *Listeners' Letterbox* and ●*Skylark* (Romanian folk music). Fifty-five minutes to Europe; winters on 6105, 7105, 7195 and 9510 kHz; and summers on 9550, 9690, 11810 and 11940 kHz. Also audible in eastern North America.

Radio Japan. Repeat of the 1500 transmission; see there for specifics. One hour to East and Southeast Asia on 6035/6150 and 9580 kHz; to Australasia on 6035, 7140 and 11850 kHz; and to western North America on 9535 kHz.

Voice of Russia World Service. *News*, followed winter weekdays by ●*Commonwealth Update*, and Saturday by *Newmarket*. Summers, choose from *Science and Engineering* (Thursday), *Newmarket* (Wednesday and Sunday) and *Mailbag* most other days. Winters at 1930, the Saturday slot is filled by *This is Russia*, replaced Sunday by ●*Christian Message from Moscow*. The remaining days feature "alternative programs"—religious paid programming or a show from the Voice of Russia's archives or transcription department. In summer it's a choice between *This is Russia* (Tuesday and Thursday), ●*Christian Message from*

Moscow (Saturday) and ●*Moscow Yesterday and Today* on the remaining dates. To Europe winters on 5940, 6110, 6130, 7180, 7400 and 9890 kHz; and summers on 7440, 9665, 9775, 9880 and (irregularly) 15400 kHz. Some of these channels are audible in parts of eastern North America. Also available to southern Africa, winters on 7255, 7325, 9470 and 9505 kHz; and midyear on 9440 and 11765 kHz.

Voice of Greece. Winters only at this time, and actually starts about three minutes into the broadcast, following some Greek announcements. Approximately ten minutes of *news* from and about Greece. To Europe on 9375 or 9380 kHz.

Radio Thailand. A 60-minute package of *news*, features and (if you're lucky) enjoyable Thai music. To Northern Europe winters on 7295 kHz, and summers on 7210 kHz. Also available to Asia on 9655 and 11905 kHz.

Radio Yugoslavia. Sunday through Friday, and summers only at this time. *News* and information with a strong regional flavor. Thirty minutes to Australasia on 7230 kHz.

Radio For Peace International,

Costa Rica. Continues with a variety of counterculture and social-conscience features. There is also a listener-response program at 1930 Tuesday. Audible in Europe and North America on 15050 kHz.

Swiss Radio International. This time summers only. World and Swiss *news* and background reports, with some lighter and more general features on Saturdays. Thirty minutes to Europe on 6165 kHz. One hour later during winter.

Voice of Vietnam. Repeat of the 1800 transmission (see there for specifics). A half hour to Europe on 9840 and 12020 (or 15010) kHz.

Voice of America. Continuous programming to the Mideast and North Africa. *News*, then Monday through Friday it's *Europe Edition* and *Dateline*. Weekends, the news is followed by *Newsline* and *Press Conference USA* (Saturday) or ●*Music USA-Standards* (Sunday). On 9760 and (summer) 9770 kHz. Also heard in parts of Europe. For a separate service to Africa, see the next item.

Voice of America. *News*, then Monday through Friday there's *Europe Edition*, an editorial and *World of Music*. Weekends, choose from Saturday's *Voices of Africa* and *Press Conference USA*, and Sunday's *Newsline* and ●*Music Time in Africa*. Continuous to most of Africa on 6035, 7375, 7415, 11920, 11975, 12025, 13710, 15410, 15445 and 15580 kHz, some of which are seasonal.For yet another service, to Australasia, see the following item.

Voice of America. Weekday programs are the same as for the Mideast (see above). On weekends, look for *Newsline* followed by *Press Conference USA* (Saturday) or ●*Music USA-Standards* (Sunday). One hour to Australasia on 9525, 11870 and 15180 kHz.

"Rush Limbaugh Show," WRNO, New Orleans, Louisiana. See 1600 for specifics. Winters only at this time. The final sixty minutes of a three-hour presentation. Popular and controversial within the United States, but of little interest to most other listeners. To North America and the Caribbean on 7355 (or 15420) kHz.

Radio Korea International, South Korea. Repeat of the 1600 broadcast. Sixty minutes to East Asia on 5975 and 7275 kHz.

Radio Argentina al Exterior—R.A.E. Monday through Friday only. *News* and short features dealing with Argentinian life and culture, interspersed with fine examples of the country's various musical styles, from chamamé to zamba. Fifty-five minutes to Europe on 15345 kHz.

"For the People," WHRI, Noblesville, Indiana. See 0300 for specifics. Monday through Friday only. A three-hour populist package broadcast live to North America on 9495 kHz.

WJCR, Upton, Kentucky. Continues with country gospel music to North America on 7490 kHz. Other U.S. religious broadcasters operating at this time include **WGTG** on 9400 kHz, **WWCR** on 13845 and 15685 kHz, **KTBN** on 15590 kHz, and **WHRI-World Harvest Radio** on 13760 kHz. For traditional Catholic programming, try **WEWN** on 7425 kHz.

CFRX-CFRB, Toronto, Canada. See 1400.

19:15

Radio Tirana, Albania. Winters only at this time. Approximately 10 minutes of *news* and commentary from and about Albania. To Europe on 6270 and 7270 kHz. One hour earlier during summer.

19:30

Polish Radio Warsaw, Poland. Summers only at this time. Weekdays, it's *News from Poland*— news, reports and interviews on the latest events in the country. What follows is very much a mixed bag, depending on the day of the week. Monday has a regular feature which alternates on a weekly basis; Tuesday, there's *Letter from Poland* and *DX Club* (a media show); Wednesday's slots are given over to the retrospective *Flashback* and classical music; Thursday features *A Day in the Life . . .* and *Focus* (the arts in Poland); and Fiday's offerings are *Business Week* and *Postbag* (a listener-response program). The Saturday transmission begins with a bulletin of *news*, then there's *Weekend Press* (a review of Poland's newspapers), *Europe East* (correspondents' reports), and later in the broadcast, *Jazz, Folk, Rock and Pop from Poland*. Sundays, you can hear *Panorama* (a window on day-to-day life in Poland) and *Request Concert*. Fifty-five minutes to Europe on 6035, 6095 and 7285 kHz. One hour later during winter.

Radio Slovakia International. Winters only at this time. *Slovakia Today*, a 30-minute review of Slovak life and culture. Monday, there's a potpourri of short features; Tuesday spotlights tourism and Slovak personalities; Wednesday is devoted to business and economy; and Thursday brings a mix of politics, education and science. Friday offerings include cultural items, cooking recipes and the off-beat *Back Page News*; and Saturday has the *"Best of"* series. Sunday's show is a melange of this and that, and includes *Listeners' Tribune* and some enjoyable Slovak music. A friendly half hour to western Europe on 5915, 6055 and 7345 kHz. One hour earlier in summer.

Voice of Turkey. Winters only at this time. See 1830 for program details. Some rather unusual programming and friendly presentation make this station worth a listen. Fifty minutes to Europe on 9445 kHz. One hour earlier in summer.

Voice of the Islamic Republic of Iran. Sixty minutes of *news*, commentary and features with a strong Islamic slant. Not the lightest of programming fare, but reflects a point of view not often heard in western countries. To Europe on 7260 and 9022 kHz.

Radio Yugoslavia. Winters only at this time. *News* and short reports with a strong local flavor. Thirty minutes to Europe on 6100 kHz, and to Southern Africa on 9720 kHz. One hour earlier in summer.

Radio Austria International. Winters only at this time. News and human-interest stories in ●*Report from Austria*. A half hour to Europe on 5945 and 6155 kHz; and to southern Africa on 9495 (or 13730) kHz.

Radio Netherlands. *News*, followed Monday through Saturday by *Newsline* and a feature. Take your choice from ●*Research File* (Monday), ●*A Good Life* (Friday), and Saturday's ●*Weekend*. For other interesting offerings, try *Mirror Images* (Tuesday) or Wednesday's documentaries, many of which are excellent. Other programs include Thursday's *Media Network* and Sunday's *Sounds Interesting*. Fifty-five minutes to Africa on 6020, 7120 (summer), 9605 (winter), 9895 (summer), 11655, 15315 and 17605 kHz. The last two frequencies are heard well in many parts of North America.

Voice of Mongolia. *News*, reports and short features, with Sunday featuring lots of exotic local music. Thirty minutes to Europe on 9720 and 12015 kHz. Frequencies may vary slightly.

Radio Roma-RAI International, Italy. Actually starts at 1935. Approximately 12 minutes of *news*, then music. Twenty lackluster minutes to western Europe winters on 6030 and 7235 kHz, and summers on 6015, 7130 and 9670 kHz.

19:50

Vatican Radio. Summers only at this time. Twenty minutes of programming oriented to Catholics. To Europe on 4005, 5880 and 7250 kHz. One hour later in winter.

20:00

■ **BBC World Service.** ●*Newshour*. The best. Sixty minutes of quality reporting, and the standard for all in-depth news shows from international broadcasters. Good reception in Europe on 3955 (winters), 6180, 6195, 9410 and (summers) 12095 and 15575 kHz. Some of these channels are also easily heard in parts of eastern North America. Audible in Africa on 3255, 6005, 6190, 9630, 11835 (summer), 15400 and 17830 kHz. Available winters to the Mideast (till 2030) on 9410 kHz. Winters to Southeast Asia and year-round to Australasia on 9740 and 11955 kHz. An additional frequency, 5975 kHz, is available for Australasia from April to October.

■**Deutsche Welle,** Germany. *News,* then Monday through Friday it's 25 minutes of the comprehensive ●*NewsLink* (interviews, background reports and analysis of European events). The remainder of the broadcast is given over to a feature, the best of which are Tuesday's ●*Man and Environment* and Wednesday's ●*Insight.* The other offerings are *Economic Notebook* (Monday), *Living in Germany* (Thursday) and *Spotlight on Sport* (Friday). The Saturday lineup is *Sports Report,* *Germany This Week* and ●*Weekend;* and is replaced Sunday by *Commentary, Arts on the Air* and *German by Radio.* Fifty minutes to Europe winters on 7285 kHz, and summers on 7170 and 9615 kHz.

Radio Canada International. Summers only at this time. The first hour of a 90-minute broadcast to Europe and beyond. *News,* followed Monday through Friday by *Spectrum* (current events), which is replaced Saturday by *Innovation Canada* and ●*Earth Watch,* and Sunday by *Arts in Canada* and *The Mailbag.* To Europe and Africa on 5995 (also available in the Mideast), 7235, 11690, 13650, 13670, 15150, 15325, 17820 and 17870 kHz. Some of these are audible in parts of North America. One hour later during winter.

Radio Damascus, Syria. Actually starts at 2005. *News,* a daily press review, and different features for each day of the week. These can be heard at approximately 2030

and 2045, and include *Arab Profile* and *Palestine Talk* (Monday), *Syria and the World* and *Listeners Overseas* (Tuesday), *Around the World* and *Selected Readings* (Wednesday), *From the World Press* and *Reflections* (Thursday), *Arab Newsweek* and *Cultural Magazine* (Friday), *Welcome to Syria* and *Arab Civilization* (Saturday), and *From Our Literature* and *Music from the Orient* (Sunday). Most of the transmission, however, is given over to Syrian and some western popular music. One hour to Europe, often audible in eastern North America, on 12085 and 13610 (or 15095) kHz.

Radio Norway International. Summer Sundays only. *Norway Now.* Thirty friendly minutes to Australasia on 9590 kHz.

Swiss Radio International. Thirty minutes of *Newsnet*—news and background reports on world and Swiss events. Somewhat lighter fare on Saturday, when the biweekly *Capital Letters* (a listener-response program) alternates with *Name Game* and *Sounds Good.* To Europe winters on 6165 kHz (one hour earlier in summer), and year-round to North and West Africa and the Mideast (also audible in eastern North America) on 5850 (winter), 9885, 9905 (winter), and (summer) 12075 and 13635 kHz.

Radio Australia. Starts with *News,* then Sunday through Thursday it's *Dateline* followed by *Pacific Beat.* These are replaced Friday by *Oz Sounds* and *Health Report,* and Saturday by *Australia All Over.* Continuous to Asia and the Pacific on 5995, 9415, 9615 and 11880 kHz.

Voice of Russia World Service. *News,* then summers it's more of the same in *News and Views,* replaced winters by a series of features. These include *Science and Engineering* (Thursday), the business-oriented *Newmarket* (Wednesday and Sunday) and *Mailbag* most other days. Winters on the half-hour, it's a choice between *This is Russia* (Tuesday and Thursday), ●*Christian Message from*

Moscow (Saturday) and ●*Moscow Yesterday and Today* on the remaining dates. Summer offerings at this time are ●*Music at Your Request* (Wednesday), *Jazz Show* (Friday), *Yours for the Asking* (Tuesday), ●*Folk Box* (Thursday), *Kaleidoscope* (Saturday) and Sunday's *Timelines*. Continuous to Europe winters on 4920, 5940, 6110, 6130, 7180, 7400 and 9890 kHz; and summers on 7370 (from 2030), 9665, 9795, 9810 and 9880 kHz. Some of these channels are audible in eastern North America. Also available winters to southern Africa on 7325 kHz.

Radio Kuwait. The final sixty minutes of a three-hour broadcast to Europe and eastern North America (see 1800). Regular features at this time include *Theater in Kuwait* (2000), *Saheeh Muslim* (2030) and *News in Brief* at 2057. On 11990 kHz.

Radio Bulgaria. This time winters only; see 1900 for specifics. Sixty minutes of *news* and entertainment, including lively Bulgarian folk rhythms. To Europe, also heard in eastern North America, on 7335 and 9700 kHz. One hour earlier during summer.

Voice of Greece. Summers only at this time and actually starts about three minutes into the broadcast, after a little bit of Greek. Approximately ten minutes of *news* from and about Greece. To Europe on 7430 or 9420 kHz.

Radio Prague, Czech Republic. Summers only at this time. *News*, then Monday through Friday there's *Current Affairs*. These are followed by one or more features. Monday has *Magazine '96*; Tuesday, it's *Talking Point* and *Media Czech*; Wednesday brings *The Arts* and *From the Archives*; Thursday features *Economic Report* and *I'd Like You to Meet . . .*; and Friday it's *Between You and Us*. The Saturday offering is a thoroughly enjoyable musical feature which offers a different style of music each week, alternating between classical, folk, contemporary and jazz. Sunday, it is replaced by *The Week in Politics, From the Weeklies* and *Media Czech*. Thirty minutes to Europe on 5930 kHz, and to South Asia and Australasia on 11600 kHz.

Radio Algiers International, Algeria. Summers only at this time. *News*, then local French and Arab popular music, with an occasional brief feature also thrown in. One hour of so-so reception in Europe, and occasionally heard in eastern North America. On 11715 and 15160 kHz.

Radio Budapest, Hungary. Winters only at this time. *News* and features, some of which are broadcast on a regular basis. These include Monday's *Musica Hungarica, Focus on Business* and *The Weeklies* (Wednesday), *Letter Home* (Thursday) and *Profiles* (Saturday). Thirty minutes to Europe on 3975, 5970 and 9840 kHz. One hour earlier in summer.

China Radio International. *News* and commentary, followed Tuesday through Friday by *Current Affairs*. These are followed by various feature programs, such as *Cultural Spectrum* (Thursday); *Listeners' Letterbox* (Sunday and Tuesday); *China Scrapbook, Cooking Show, Chinese Folk Tales* and ●*Music from China* (Saturday); *Sports Beat* and *Song of the Week* (Sunday); *Learn to Speak Chinese* (Monday and Wednesday); and Friday's *In the Third World*. Sundays, there is also a biweekly *Business Show* which alternates with *China's Open Windows*. One hour to Europe on 6950 and 9920 kHz, and to East and Southern Africa on 9440, 11715 and 15110 kHz.

Radio Nacional de Angola ("Angolan National Radio"). The first 30 minutes or so consist of a mix of music and short features, then there's *news* near the half-hour. The remainder of the broadcast is given over to some thoroughly enjoyable Angolan music. Sixty minutes to Southern Africa on 3354 and 9535 kHz, with the second frequency also audible in parts of Europe and eastern North America, especially during winter.

RDP International—Radio Portugal.
Monday through Friday, summers only, at
this time. *News*, then features: *Visitor's
Notebook* (Monday), *Musical Kaleidoscope*
(Tuesday), *Challenge of the 90's* (Wednesday), *Spotlight on Portugal* (Thursday),
and *Listeners' Mailbag* and *Collector's
Corner* (Friday). Thirty minutes to Europe
on 6130, 9780 and 9815 kHz. Sometimes
preempted by live soccer commentary in
Portuguese. One hour later in winter.

"For the People," WHRI, Noblesville,
Indiana. Monday through Friday only;
see 0300 for specifics. Part of a three-hour
populist package broadcast live to North
America on 9495 kHz.

**Radio Exterior de España ("Spanish
National Radio").** Monday through Friday only at this time. *News*, followed by
Panorama (Spanish popular music, commentary, press review and weather), then
a couple of features: *Sports Spotlight* and
Cultural Encounters
(Monday); *People of
Today* and *Entertainment in Spain* (Tuesday);
As Others See Us and,
biweekly, *The Natural
World* or *Science Desk* (Wednesday);
Economic Report and *Cultural Clippings*
(Thursday); and *Window on Spain* and
Review of the Arts (Friday). The broadcast ends with a language course, *Spanish by Radio*. Sixty minutes to Europe on
6125 kHz, and to Africa on 11775 kHz.
One hour later on weekends.

Kol Israel. Winters only at this time.
Thirty minutes of *news* and in-depth reporting from and about Israel. To Europe
and North America on 7418, 7465 and
9435 kHz; to Central and South America
on 9845 kHz; and to Africa and South
America on 13750 kHz. One hour earlier
in summer.

YLE Radio Finland. Summers only at
this time; see 2100 for specifics. A half hour
to western Europe and beyond on 6120
and 9855 kHz. One hour later in winter.

HCJB—Voice of the Andes, Ecuador.
Continues with a three-hour block of
religious and secular programming to
Europe. Monday is given over to *The
Least of These* and *Let My People Think*;
Tuesday airs *Simply Worship* and
Unshackled; and Wednesday brings *The
Book and the Spade*, *Inside HCJB* and
Rock Solid! On Thursday, you can hear
Radio Reading Room and *Inspirational
Classics*; Friday has the Europe-oriented
On-Line followed by *On Track* (contemporary Christian music); Saturday features
Musical Mailbag and *Solstice* (a youth
program); and Sunday is devoted to *Radio
Reading Room* and *Joy International*.
Winters on 11960 kHz, and summers on
15540 kHz.

Voice of America. *News*, then listeners
in the Mideast can hear the weekday
Border Crossings (a musical call-in show),
Saturday's ●*Music U.S.A. (Jazz)* (the
Conover archives) or
Sunday's *Concert Hall*.
On 9760, (summer) 9770
and (winter) 15205 kHz.
For African listeners
there's the weekday
Africa World Tonight, replaced weekends
by *Nightline Africa*. Choose from 6035,
7375, 7415, 11975, 13710, 15410, 15445,
15580, 17725 and 17755 kHz, some of
which are seasonal. Both transmissions
are heard well beyond their target areas,
including parts of North America.

Radio For Peace International,
Costa Rica. Part of an eight-hour cyclical
block of predominantly social-conscience
and counterculture programming. Some
of the offerings at this hour include a
women's news-gathering service, *WINGS*,
(2030 Thursday) and a listener-response
program (same time Friday). Audible in
Europe and North America on 15050 kHz.

WJCR, Upton, Kentucky. Continues with
country gospel music to North America on
7490 kHz. Other U.S. religious broadcasters which operate at this time include

> A must for jazz aficionados is the VOA's
> *Music USA (Jazz)*. Here, you can listen to
> the best of the great Conover archives.

WGTG on 9400 kHz, **WWCR** on 13845 and 15685 kHz, **KTBN** on 15590 kHz, and **WHRI-World Harvest Radio** on 13760 kHz. For traditional Catholic programming, tune **WEWN** on 7425 kHz.

CFRX-CFRB, Toronto, Canada. See 1400.

20:30

Radio Sweden. Summer weekends only at this time. Saturday, there's *Spectrum* (arts) or *Sweden Today* (current events). Sunday fare consists of *In Touch with Stockholm* (a listener response program) or the musical *Sounds Nordic.* Thirty minutes to Europe, Africa and the Mideast on 6065, 9430 and 9655 kHz.

Voice of Vietnam. *News,* followed by *Commentary* or *Weekly Review,* then some short features and pleasant Vietnamese music (especially at weekends). A half hour to Europe on 9840 and 12020 (or 15010) kHz.

Radio Thailand. Fifteen minutes of *news* targeted at Europe. Winters on 9535 (or 11805) kHz, and summers on 9680 kHz. Also available to Asia on 9655 and 11905 kHz.

Polish Radio Warsaw, Poland. Winters only at this time. See 1930 for program specifics. Fifty-five minutes of *news,* music and features spotlighting Poland past and present. To Europe on 6035, 6095 and 7285 kHz. One hour earlier during summer.

Radio Habana Cuba. A 60-minute package of *news* (predominantly about Cuba and Latin America), features about the island and its people, and some lively and enjoyable Cuban music. To Europe winters on 9585 (upper sideband) and 9620 kHz, and summers on 13715 and (upper sideband) 13725 kHz. Also well heard in parts of eastern North America.

Radio Tashkent, Uzbekistan. *News* and commentary, then features; some exotic music, too. Most features are broadcast on a non-weekly basis. To

Europe and West Asia on 7105 (winter), 9540 and (summer) 9545 kHz.

Voice of Armenia. Summers only at this time. Mainly of interest to Armenians abroad. Thirty minutes of Armenian *news* and culture. To Europe on 7480 (or 11615) and 9965 kHz. Sometimes audible in eastern North America. One hour later in winter.

Radio Roma-RAI International, Italy. Actually starts at 2025. Twenty minutes of *news* and music targeted at the Mideast, winters on 7105, 9685 and 11840 kHz; and summers on 7120, 9710 and 11840 KHz. Better than what it used to be, but still has a long way to go.

20:45

All India Radio. The first 15 minutes of a much longer broadcast, consisting of a press review, Indian music, regional and international *news,* commentary, and a variety of talks and features of general interest. Continuous till 2230. To western Europe on 7410, 9950 and 11620 kHz; and to Australasia on 7150, 9910, 11620 and 11715 kHz. Early risers in Southeast Asia can try the Australasian channels.

Vatican Radio. Winters only at this time, and actually starts at 2050. Twenty minutes of predominantly Catholic fare. To Europe on 4015 and 5882 kHz. Frequencies may vary slightly. One hour earlier in summer.

21:00

■ **BBC World Service for Europe and the Americas.** *World News,* then ten minutes of specialized business and financial reports (except Sunday, when there's a listener-response program). These are followed by ●*Britain Today* or ●*Caribbean Report* (see 2115 for specifics). Features on the half-hour include *Music Review* (Sunday), ●*People and Politics* (Friday) and an arts program, *Meridian* (Tuesday,

Wednesday, Thursday and Saturday). Continuous to Europe on 3955 (winters), 6180, 6195, 7325, 9410 and (summers) 12095 kHz; and to eastern North America and the Caribbean on 5975 kHz.

■ **BBC World Service for Africa.** Part of a 21-hour daily service to the African continent, and the final hour for southern Africa. Starts with a brief summary of the latest news, followed Monday through Saturday by ●*World Business Report/Review*. Best of the remaining shows are ●*Discovery* (science, Wednesday), ●*From Our Own Correspondence* (2115 Thursday and 2130 Saturday), ●*People and Politics* (2130 Friday) and ●*Health Matters* (2115 Saturday). On 3255, 6005 and 6190 kHz.

■ **BBC World Service for Asia and the Pacific.** *World News*, a business report and a wide variety of features. Pick of the litter are ●*Discovery* (science, 2130 Tuesday), ●*One Planet* (the environment, same time Wednesday), ●*The Learning World* and ●*Assignment* (Thursday), ●*The Works* (technology, 2130 Friday) and ●*The Greenfield Collection* (same time Saturday). Continuous to East and Southeast Asia on 3915, 5965, 5990, 6120 (winter), 6195, 9740 (winter), 11945 (summer) and (winter) 11955 kHz; and to Australasia on 5975 (midyear), 9740 and 11955 kHz.

Radio Exterior de España ("Spanish National Radio"). Weekends only at this time. *News*, then Saturday there's *Hall of Fame*, *Distance Unknown* (for radio enthusiasts) and *Gallery of Spanish Voices*; replaced Sunday by *Visitors' Book*, *Great Figures in Flamenco* and *Radio Club*. Sixty minutes to Europe on 6125 kHz, and to Africa on 11775 kHz. One hour earlier, Monday through Friday.

Radio Ukraine International. Summers only at this time. *News*, commentary, reports and interviews, covering multiple aspects of Ukrainian life. Saturdays feature a listener-response program, and most of Sunday's broadcast is a show-

piece for Ukrainian music. Sixty minutes to Europe and beyond on 5905, 6010, 6020, 6090, 7180, 7240, 9560, 9640 and 13590 kHz; and to Australasia on 7380 kHz. Also audible in parts of eastern North America. One hour later in winter.

Radio Canada International. Winters, the first hour of a 90-minute broadcast; summers, the last half-hour of the same. Winters, there's *News*, followed Monday through Friday by *Spectrum* (current events), which is replaced Saturday by *Innovation Canada* and ●*Earth Watch*, and Sunday by *Arts in Canada* and a listener-response program. Summer weekdays, it's the CBC domestic service's ●*The World at Six*, with weekend fare consisting of *Royal Canadian Air Farce* (Saturday) and Sunday's *The Inside Track*. To Europe and Africa winters on 5995, 7235, 9735, 9805, 11945, 13650, 13670, 13690, 15150 and 17820 kHz; and summers on 5995 (also for the Mideast), 7235, 11690, 13650, 13670, 15150, 15325 and 17820 kHz. Some of these are also audible in parts of North America.

Radio Vlaanderen Internationaal, Belgium. Summers only at this time. Repeat of the 1800 transmission (see 1900 for program details). Thirty minutes daily to Europe on 5910 kHz. One hour later in winter.

Radio Prague, Czech Republic. Winters only at this time; see 2000 for program details. *News* and features dealing with Czech life and culture. A half hour to eastern North America on 5930 kHz, and to West Africa on 7345 kHz.

Radio Bulgaria. This time summers only. *News*, then Monday through Thursday there's 15 minutes of current events in *Today*, replaced Friday by *Weekly Spotlight*, a summary of the week's major political stories. The remainder of the broadcast is given over to features dealing with multiple aspects of Bulgarian life and culture, and includes some lively and entertaining folk music. One of the first things you'll discover is that bagpipes aren't confined to Scotland! To Europe and eastern North America on 9700 and 11720 kHz. One hour later during winter.

China Radio International. Repeat of the 2000 transmission. One hour to Europe on 6950 and 9920 kHz. A 30-minute shortened version is also available summers (2100-2130) on 6165 kHz.

RDP International—Radio Portugal. Winter weekdays only at this time. *News*, followed by a feature about Portugal; see 2000 for more details. Thirty minutes to Europe on 6130, 9780 and 9815 kHz. Sometimes preempted by live soccer commentary in Portuguese. One hour earlier in summer.

Voice of Russia World Service. The first 30 minutes have the accent heavily on *news*, the only exceptions being summer weekends—●*Music and Musicians* (2111 Saturday) and *Science and Engineering* (same time Sunday). Winters on the half-hour, look for a choice of features: *Yours for the Asking* (Tuesday), *Jazz Show* (Friday), ●*Music at Your Request* (Wednesday), ●*Folk Box* (Thursday), *Kaleidoscope* (Saturday) and *Timelines* (Sunday). Summers, these are replaced by *Science and Engineering* (Monday and Friday), the business-oriented *Newmarket* (Tuesday), *This is Russia* (Sunday) and a listener-response program on other days. Continuous to Europe winters on 5940, 6110, 7170 (from 2130), 7180, 7320 (from 2130), 7400 and 9890 kHz; and summers on 7370 (from 2030), 9665, 9765, 9775 9880 and 11840 kHz. Several of these channels are also audible in eastern North America.

Radio Budapest, Hungary. Summers only at this time. *News* and features, some of which are broadcast on a regular basis. These include Monday's *Musica Hungarica*, *Focus on Business* and *The Weeklies* (Wednesday), *Letter Home* (Thursday) and *Profiles* (Saturday). Thirty minutes to Europe on 3975, 7250 and 9835 kHz. One hour later in winter.

Samoeun Intal, director of FEBC's Cambodian service, lost virtually her entire family in the Khmer Rouge killing fields of Cambodia.

Radio Australia. *News*, then Sunday through Thursday there's a 20-minute relay of the Radio National domestic service, replaced Friday by *Feedback* (a listener-response show). On the half-hour, look for a feature: *Earthbeat* (Sunday), *Innovations* (Monday and Friday), *Arts Australia* (Tuesday), *Science File* (Wednesday) and *Book Talk* on Thursday. Saturday's offering is *Australia All Over*. Continuous to Asia and the Pacific (and also audible in parts of North America) on 5995, 7240, 9415, 9615, 11695, 11880, 12080 and 13755 kHz, some of which are only available for the first or second half-hour.

■**Deutsche Welle,** Germany. *News*, then Monday through Friday (Tuesday through Saturday local Asian days) it's 25 minutes of ●*NewsLink* (interviews, background reports and analysis of European events). The remainder of the broadcast is taken up by a feature: *Economic Notebook* (Monday), ●*Man and Environment* (ecology, Tuesday), ●*Insight* (Wednesday), *Living in Germany* (Thursday) and *Spotlight on Sport* (Friday). The Saturday lineup is *Sports Report*, *Development Forum* (alternates with *Women on the Move*) and *Mailbag*; and is replaced Sunday by *Commentary*, *Inside Europe* and *Hits from Germany*. Fifty minutes to East Asia and Australasia on 7115 (summer), 9670, 9765 and 11785 kHz. A separate service, which differs only in that the weekend features are repeats of the 1600 transmission to Africa, is also broadcast at this time. To West Africa and beyond (also heard in eastern North America), winters on 9615, 9690, 11865 and 15285 kHz; and summers on 9735, 11865 and 15135 kHz.

Radio Japan. Repeat of the 1700 transmission; see there for specifics. One hour to East and Southeast Asia winters on 6035, 7125 and 7140 kHz; and summers on 6035, 9535 and 9560 kHz. Also to Australasia on 11850 kHz. There is also a separate 10-minute *news* broadcast to Southeast Asia on 7190 or 11685 kHz.

Radio Yugoslavia. *News* and short background reports, mostly about local issues. An informative half-hour summers to Europe on 6100 and 6185 kHz.

Radio Pyongyang, North Korea. An hour of old-style communist propaganda, and boring, to boot. Catch it while you can—the country is in such dire straits, anything could happen. To Europe on 6575 and 9345 kHz; and to North America (better to the west) on 11700 and 13760 kHz.

Radio Romania International. *News*, commentary and features (see 1900), interspersed with some thoroughly enjoyable Romanian folk music. One hour to Europe winters on 5955, 5990, 7105 and 7195 kHz; summers on 5990, 7105, 7195 and 9690 kHz. Also audible in eastern North America.

Radio Korea International, South Korea. Repeat of the 1900 broadcast; see 1600 for program details. Sixty minutes to Europe on 6480 and 15575 kHz.

Radio For Peace International, Costa Rica. Continues at this hour with a potpourri of United Nations, counterculture and other programs. These include *WINGS* (news for and of women, 2130 Tuesday) and *Vietnam Veterans Radio Network* (same time Wednesday). Audible in Europe and North America on 15050 kHz.

YLE Radio Finland. Winters only at this time. *News*, followed by short features from and about Finland. Mainstay of the broadcast is the daily *Compass North*, 12 minutes (nine on Saturday) of general interest stories about life in Finland. Saturdays at 2123, look for a world band curiosity, *Nuntii Latini* (news in Latin), which has something of a cult following. Thirty minutes to Europe on 6120 kHz. One hour earlier in summer.

HCJB—Voice of the Andes, Ecuador. The final sixty minutes of a three-hour block of predominantly religious programming to Europe. Pick of the first half-hour is undoubtedly ●*Música del Ecuador*, at 2100 Monday. Weekdays at 2130, you can listen to *Nightsounds;* and the weekend fare consists of Saturday's *Sports Spectrum* and *Afterglow*, replaced Sunday by *Mountain Meditations* and *Songs in the Night*. Winters on 11960 kHz, and summers on 15540 kHz.

Radio Tirana, Albania. Summers only at this time. Still being run on a virtually non-existent budget, so broadcasts are mainly limited to *news* and pleasant Albanian music. Thirty minutes to Europe on 7110 and 9515 kHz. One hour later during winter.

Voice of America. Monday through Friday, it's a full hour of *World Report*. Weekends, there's *News* and a variety of features, depending on the area served. Pick of the litter is the science program ●*New Horizons* (2110 Sunday). Other offerings include ●*Issues in the News* (Africa, 2130 Sunday; Australasia, same time Saturday), *Studio 38* (Mideast and Australasia, 2130 Sun), *On the Line* (all areas, 2110 Saturday) and *Communications World* (Mideast, 2130 Saturday). To the Mideast and North Africa winters on 6070, 9595, 9760 and 15205 kHz; and summers on 6040, 9535 and 9760 kHz; to Africa on 6035, 7375, 7415, 11975, 13710, 15410, 15445, 15580 and 17725 kHz (some of which are seasonal); and to Southeast Asia and the Pacific on 11870, 15185 and 17735 kHz.

All India Radio. Continues to western Europe on 7410, 9950 and 11620 kHz; and to Australasia on 7150, 9910, 11620 and 11715 kHz. Look for some authentic Indian music from 2115 onwards. The European frequencies are audible in parts of eastern North America, while those for Australasia are also heard in Southeast Asia.

"For the People," WHRI, Noblesville, Indiana. winters only at this time. Monday through Friday only; see 0300 for specifics. The final hour of a three-hour populist package broadcast live to North America on 9495 kHz. One hour earlier in summer.

CFRX-CFRB, Toronto, Canada. See 1400. Summers at this time, you can hear ●*The World Today*, 90 minutes of news, interviews, sports and commentary. On 6070 kHz.

21:15

Radio Damascus, Syria. Actually starts at 2110. *News*, a daily press review, and a variety of features (depending on the day of the week) at approximately 2130 and 2145. These include *Arab Profile* and *Economic Affairs* (Sunday), *Camera and Masks* and *Selected Readings* (Monday), *Reflections* and *Back on the Stage* (Tuesday), *Listeners Overseas* and *Palestine Talking* (Wednesday), *From the World Press* and *Arab Women in Focus* (Thurs-

day), *Arab Newsweek* and *From Our Literature* (Friday), and *Human Rights* and *Syria and the World* (Saturday). The transmission also contains Syrian and some western popular music. Sixty minutes to North America and Australasia on 12085 and 13610 (or 15095) kHz.

■**BBC World Service for the Caribbean.** ●*Caribbean Report*, although intended for listeners in the area, can also be clearly heard throughout much of eastern North America. This brief, 15-minute program provides comprehensive coverage of Caribbean economic and political affairs, both within and outside the region. Monday through Friday only, on 6110, 15390 and 17715 kHz.

Radio Cairo, Egypt. The start of a 90-minute broadcast devoted to Arab and Egyptian life and culture. The initial quarter-hour of general programming is followed by *news*, commentary and political items. This in turn is followed by a cultural program until 2215, when the station again reverts to more general fare. A Middle Eastern melange, including exotic Arab music, beamed to Europe on 9900 kHz.

WJCR, Upton, Kentucky. Continuous gospel music to North America on 7490 kHz. Other U.S. religious broadcasters operating at this hour include **WGTG** on 9400 kHz, **WWCR** on 13845 and 15685 and kHz, **KTBN** on 15590 kHz, and **WHRI-World Harvest Radio** on 13760 kHz. Traditional Catholic programming is available from **WEWN** on 7425 kHz.

21:30

BBC World Service for the Falkland Islands. *Calling the Falklands* is one of the curiosities of international broadcasting, and consists of news and features for this small community in the South Atlantic. Often includes unusual topics, with such diverse themes as remote ocean islands and Argentinian politics. Fifteen minutes

Tuesdays and Fridays on 11680 kHz—easily heard in eastern North America.

Radio Austria International. Summers only at this time. Thirty minutes of news and human-interest stories in ●*Report from Austria.* A worthy source of national and regional news. To Europe on 5945 and 6155 kHz; and to southern Africa on 13730 kHz. One hour later during winter.

Radio Prague, Czech Republic. Summers only at this time. See 2230 for program details. A half hour to Australasia on 9495 or 11600 kHz, and to West Africa on 9440 or 11600 kHz.

Voice of the Islamic Republic of Iran. Sixty minutes of *news*, commentary and features with a strong Islamic slant. To Australasia on 6175 and 9670 kHz, but may be subject to change.

Voice of Armenia. Winters only at this time. Mainly of interest to Armenians abroad. Thirty minutes of Armenian *news* and culture. To Europe on 7480 and 9965 kHz, and sometimes audible in eastern North America. One hour earlier in summer.

Radio Tashkent, Uzbekistan. Repeat of the 2030 broadcast (see there for specifics). To Europe and West Asia on 7105 (winter), 9540 and (summer) 9545 kHz.

Radio Sweden. Thirty minutes of predominantly Scandinavian fare (see 1830 for specifics). Year-round to Europe on 6065 kHz, and summer to Africa and the Mideast on 6065, 9430 and 9655 kHz. May be weekends only during winter.

22:00

■ **BBC World Service for Europe and the Americas.** Thirty minutes of the comprehensive ●*Newsdesk*, then weekdays there's 15 minutes of analysis in ●*The World Today.* This is replaced Sunday by the informative ●*Health Matters.* Monday through Saturday, the final quarter-hour is devoted to ●*Sports Roundup.* At 2230 Saturday, there's the first part of ●*Play of the Week,* a *tour de force* of world theater. Sixty minutes of quality programming to North America and the Caribbean on 5975, 6175 and 9590 kHz. Also available to Europe, winters for the full hour, summers for the first 30 minutes, on 3955 (winter), 6195, and (till 2230) 7325 and 9410 kHz.

■ **BBC World Service for Asia and the Pacific.** Starts with 30 minutes of ●*Newsdesk*, and ends with a quarter-hour of ●*Sports Roundup.* In-between, it's the weekday ●*World Business Report* (Tuesday through Saturday local Asian days), Saturday's *From the Weeklies,* or Sunday's ●*Letter from America.* Continuous to East and Southeast Asia on 5905 (winter), 5965, 6195, 7110, 9890 (summer) and 11955 kHz; and to Australasia on 11955 and 12080 kHz.

Remote ocean islands and Argentinean politics are just some of the unusual topics you can hear on the BBC World Service for the Falkland Islands.

Radio Bulgaria. Winters only at this time; see 2100 for specifics. Sixty minutes of *news* and features from and about Bulgaria, interspersed with lively Bulgarian folk music. To Europe and eastern North America on 7105 and 9700 kHz. One hour earlier in summer.

Radio Cairo, Egypt. The second half of a 90-minute broadcast to Europe on 9900 kHz; see 2115 for program details.

Voice of America. The beginning of a three-hour block of programs to East and Southeast Asia and the Pacific. *News,* followed Sunday through Thursday (Monday through Friday in the target areas) by *VOA Today.* On the remaining days, it's *VOA Saturday* or *VOA Sunday.* Fortunately, the shows are better than their titles. To East and Southeast Asia on 7215, 9705 (summer), 9770, 9890 (winter), 11760, 15185, 15290, 15305, 17735 and 17820 kHz; and to Australasia on 15185, 15305,

AWR-Asia

Lolita Collegado is the listener mail secretary for Adventist World Radio-Asia. Each flag on the map represents a country from which listeners have written.

17735 and 17820 kHz. There is a separate 30-minute week-night service to Africa which features *Music USA* on 6035, 7340 (summer), 7375 (summer), 7415, 11975 and (winter) 12080 and 13710 kHz.

Radio Australia. *News*, then a selection of some of the station's most popular programs: *Music Deli* and *Australia Today* (Sunday), *Australian Music Show* (Monday), *At Your Request* (Tuesday), *Blacktracker* (Wednesday), *Australian Country Style* (Thursday), *Hindsight* (Friday) and Saturday's call-in extravaganza, *Australia All Over.* Continuous to Asia and the Pacific (and audible in parts of North America) on 11695, 13755, 15510 and 17795 kHz.

Voice of Russia World Service. *News*, then Monday through Friday winters, it's *Focus on Asia and the Pacific.* This is followed at 2230 by *Science and Engineering* (Monday and Friday), the business-oriented *Newmarket* (Tuesday) and a

listener-response program on Wednesday and Thursday. Pick of the weekend programs is the inimitable ●*Music and Musicians* (2211 Saturday), replaced Sunday by *Science and Engineering* and *This is Russia.* Summers, there's the weekday ●*Commonwealth Update*, substituted weekends by a preview of upcoming shows. The second half-hour is a mixed bag, with two obvious choices being Tuesday's ●*Audio Book Club* and Sunday's ●*Christian Message from Moscow.* Other offerings include *Russian by Radio* (Monday and Wednesday) and *Timelines* (Friday and Saturday). Winters to Europe on 5940, 6110, 7205, 7320, 7360, 7400 and 9890 kHz (some of which are audible in eastern North America); and summers to eastern North America on 7125 (from 2230), 7250 and 9665 kHz.

Voice of Free China, Taiwan. *News*, then features. The last is *Let's Learn Chinese*, which has a series of segments for beginning, intermediate and advanced learners. Other features include *Jade Bells and Bamboo Pipes* (Monday), *Kaleidoscope* and *Main Roads and Byways* (Tuesday), *Music Box* (Wednesday), *Perspectives* and *Journey into Chinese Culture* (Thursday), *Confrontation* and *New Record Time* (Friday), *Reflections* (Saturday) and *Adventures of Mahlon and Jeanie* and *Mailbag Time* (Sunday). Sixty minutes to western Europe, winters on 5810 and 9985 kHz, and summers on 15600 and 17750 kHz.

Croatian Radio. Summers only at this time. Starts a little late, and is preceded by news in Croatian. Several minutes of English *news* from what is still one of Europe's most volatile regions. Best in Europe and eastern North America at this hour, but also heard elsewhere. On 5895 and 11635 kHz. One hour later during winter.

Radio Budapest, Hungary. Winters only at this time; see 2100 for specifics. Thirty minutes to Europe on 3975, 5970 and 9835 kHz. One hour earlier in summer.

Voice of Turkey. Summers only at this time. *News*, followed by *Review of the Turkish Press* and features with a strong local flavor. Selections of Turkish popular and classical music complete the program. Fifty minutes to Europe on 7280 and 9655 kHz, to eastern North America on 9655 kHz, and to much of Asia and Australasia on 9560 kHz. One hour later during winter.

Radio Yugoslavia. Winters only at this time. Repeat of the 1930 broadcast. Thirty minutes to Europe on 6100 and 6185 kHz. One hour earlier in summer.

China Radio International. Repeat of the 2000 broadcast. One hour to Europe winters on 7170 kHz, summers on 9880 kHz. A shortened version is also available winters at 2200-2230 on 3985 kHz.

Radio Vlaanderen Internationaal, Belgium. Winters only at this time. Repeat of the 1900 broadcast; see there for program details. Thirty minutes to Europe on 5910 kHz, also audible in parts of eastern North America. One hour earlier in summer.

Radio Canada International. This time winters only. The final half-hour of a 90-minute broadcast. Monday through Friday, it's the CBC domestic service's ●*The World at Six*, with weekend fare consisting of Saturday's *Royal Canadian Air Farce* and Sunday's *The Inside Track*. To Europe and Africa on 5995, 7235, 9735, 9805, 11945, 13690 and 15150 kHz. For a separate summer service, see the following item.

Radio Canada International. Summers only; a relay of CBC domestic programming, except for the final 30 minutes weekends. Monday through Friday, there's ●*The World at Six*; Saturday and Sunday, *The World This Weekend*. On the half-hour, the weekday ●*As It Happens* is replaced Saturday by *The Mystery Project* and Sunday by *Now the Details*. Sixty minutes to North America on 5960, 9755 and 13670 kHz. One hour later in winter. For a separate year-round service to Asia, see the next item.

Radio Canada International. Monday through Friday, it's ●*The World At Six*; Saturday and Sunday summer, *The World This Weekend*. Winter weekends, look for Saturday's *Royal Canadian Air Farce* and Sunday's *The Inside Track*. Thirty minutes to Southeast Asia on 11705 kHz.

Radio Norway International. Sundays only. *Norway Now*. Thirty minutes of *news* and human-interest stories from and about Norway. Winters to East Asia on 7115 kHz, and to eastern North America on 6200 kHz; in summer, to Australasia on 9485 kHz.

Radio Tirana, Albania. Winters only at this time. Still being run on a shoestring budget, so broadcasts are often limited to *news* and pleasant Albanian music. Thirty minutes to Europe on 5985 and 7170 kHz. One hour earlier during summer.

Radio Roma, Italy. Approximately ten minutes of *news* followed by a quarter-hour feature (usually music). An uninspiring 25 minutes to East Asia on 6150, 9565 and 11815 kHz.

Radio Ukraine International. Winters only at this time. A potpourri of all things Ukrainian, with the Sunday broadcast often featuring some excellent music. Sixty minutes to Europe, Africa, the Mideast and beyond on 5905, 5940, 6010, 6020, 7115 and 7205 kHz; and to Australasia on 7380 kHz. Also audible in parts of eastern North America. One hour earlier in summer.

Radio For Peace International, Costa Rica. Continues with counterculture and social-conscience programs—try *The Far Right Radio Review* at 2200 Sunday. Audible in Europe and North America on 7385 and 15050 kHz.

All India Radio. The final half-hour of a transmission to western Europe and Australasia, consisting mainly of news-related fare. To Europe on 7410, 9950 and 11620 kHz; and to Australasia on 7150, 9910, 11620 and 11715 kHz. Frequencies for Europe are audible in parts of eastern North America, while those for Australasia are also heard in Southeast Asia.

WJCR, Upton, Kentucky. Continues with country gospel music to North America on 7490 kHz. Other U.S. religious broadcasters heard at this hour include **WGTG** on 5085 or 9400 kHz, **WWCR** on 13845 kHz, **KAIJ** on 13815 kHz, **KTBN** on 15590 kHz, and **WHRI-World Harvest Radio** on 5745 (or 13760) kHz. For traditional Catholic programming, try **WEWN** on 7425 kHz.

CFRX-CFRB, Toronto, Canada. If you live in the northeastern United States or southeastern Canada, try this pleasant little local station, usually audible for hundreds of miles/kilometers during daylight hours on 6070 kHz. At this time, you can hear ●*The World Today* (summers, starts at 2100)—90 minutes of news, sport and interviews.

22:30

Radio Sweden. Winters only at this time. Repeat of the 2130 broadcast (see 1830 for program details). Thirty minutes of *news* and features, with the accent heavily on Scandinavian topics. To Europe on 6065 kHz.

Radio Austria International. Winters only at this time. The informative and well-presented ●*Report from Austria.* Ample coverage of national and regional issues. Thirty minutes to Europe on 5945 and 6155 kHz; and to southern Africa on 9495 (or 13730) kHz. One hour earlier in summer.

Radio Prague, Czech Republic. *News,* reports and features with a strong local flavor. These include *Magazine '96* (Monday), *Talking Point* and *Czech Media* (Tuesday), *The Arts* and *From the Archives* (Wednesday), *Economic Report* and *I'd Like You to Meet . . .* (Thursday), *Between You and Us* (Friday) and some of the best of Czech music on Saturday. The Sunday lineup consists of *The Week in Politics, From the Weeklies* and *Media Czech.* A half hour to eastern North America on 5930 (winter), 7345 and (summers) 11600 kHz.

Voice of Greece. Actually starts around 2235. Fifteen minutes of English news from and about Greece. Part of a much longer, predominantly Greek, broadcast. To Australasia on 9425 kHz.

Radio Habana Cuba. Sixty minutes of *news* (mainly about Cuba and Latin America), features about the country and its inhabitants, and some enjoyable Cuban music. To the Caribbean and southern United States on 6180 kHz.

22:45

All India Radio. The first 15 minutes of a much longer broadcast, consisting of Indian music, regional and international *news,* commentary, and a variety of talks and features of general interest. Continuous till 0045. To Southeast Asia (and beyond) on 7150, 9705, 9950 and 11620 kHz.

Vatican Radio. Twenty minutes of religious and secular programming to

22:45

East and Southeast Asia and Australasia on 6065, 7305, 9600 and 11830 kHz, some of them seasonal.

23:00

■ **BBC World Service for Europe and the Americas.** Sunday through Friday, opens with five minutes of *World News*, followed weekdays by the popular and long-running ●*Outlook*. Except for the weekend, the second half-hour is targeted at a younger audience, with *Multitrack* occupying the Monday, Wednesday and Friday slots. This is replaced Tuesday by ●*Megamix*, and Thursday by *The Vintage Chart Show*. Saturday, it's a continuation of ●*Play of the Week* (world theater), which runs to either 2330 or 2400. If it's the earlier time, look for the many-splendored ●*Andy Kershaw's World of Music* at 2330. Sunday fare consists of three short features and the religious *In Praise of God*. Continuous to North America and the Caribbean on 5975, 6175 and 9590 kHz. In winter, also available to Europe till 2315 (2330 Saturday) on 3955 and 6195 kHz.

■ **BBC World Service for Asia and the Pacific.** *World News*, then Sunday through Friday (Monday through Saturday local Asian dates) there's *East Asia Today*. This, in turn, is followed Monday through Friday by ●*The World Today* (analysis of current events). Some interesting content despite the lackluster titles. The hour is rounded off with a 15-minute feature, the best of which is Friday's informative ●*Health Matters*. Pick of the remaining programs are ●*From Our Own Correspondent* and ●*Science in Action* (Saturday) and ●*Anything Goes* (2330 Sunday). Continuous to East and Southeast Asia on 6195, 7110, 9580, 11945 and 11955 kHz; and to Australasia on 11955 kHz.

Voice of Turkey. Winters only at this hour. See 2200 for program details. Fifty minutes to Europe on 7280 and 9445 kHz, to eastern North America on 9655 kHz,

and to much of Asia and Australasia on 9560 kHz. One hour earlier in summer.

■ **Deutsche Welle,** Germany. Repeat of the 2100 broadcast. Fifty minutes to Southeast Asia, winter on 6000, 6160, and 7235 kHz; and summer on 5980, 7235 and 9690 kHz.

Radio Japan. Very similar to the 1500 transmission (see there for specifics), except that Monday through Friday the news is extended at the expense of *Tokyo Pop-in*. Sixty minutes to Europe on one or more channels from 5965, 6055 and 6155 kHz; to East and Southeast Asia winter on 7125 and 7140 kHz, and summer on 9535 and 9560 kHz; and to Australasia on 11850 kHz.

Radio Australia. *News*, then Sunday through Thursday it's *Dateline*, replaced Friday by *Book Reading*. The second half-hour consists of a feature: *Media Report* (Sunday), *The Sports Factor* (Monday), *Health Report* (Tuesday), *Law Report* (Wednesday), *Religion Report* (Thursday) and *Australia Today* on Friday. Saturday brings a continuation of *Australia All Over*. Continuous to Asia and the Pacific (and audible in western North America) on 11695, 12080, 13755, 15510, 17750 and 17795 kHz.

Radio Canada International. Summer weekdays, the final hour of ●*As It Happens*; winters, the first 30 minutes of the same, preceded by the up-to-the-minute news program ●*World at Six*. Summer weekends, look for ●*Quirks and Quarks* (Saturday, science) and *Tapestry* (Sunday, culture). These are replaced winter by *The World This Weekend* (both days), *Mystery Project* (Saturday) and *Now the Details* (Sunday). To eastern North America on 5960 and 9755 kHz, with 13670 kHz also available in summer.

Croatian Radio. Winters only at this time. Actually starts a little late, and is preceded by news in Croatian. Several minutes of English *news* from Croatian Radio's Zagreb studio. Best in Europe and eastern North America, but also heard elsewhere. On 5895 kHz. One hour earlier in summer.

Radio Pyongyang, North Korea. Repeat of the 2100 transmission. One hour of old-time communist propaganda to North America (better to the west) on 11335, 11700, 13760 and 15130 kHz.

Radio For Peace International, Costa Rica. The final 60 minutes of a continuous eight-hour cyclical block of United Nations, counterculture and social-conscience programming. Audible in Europe and the Americas on 7385 and 15050 kHz.

Radio Cairo, Egypt. The first hour of a 90-minute potpourri of exotic Arab music and features reflecting Egyptian life and culture, with *news* and commentary about events in Egypt and the Arab world. There are also quizzes, mailbag shows, and answers to listeners' questions. Fair reception and mediocre audio quality to North America on 9900 kHz.

Radio Romania International. *News,* commentary and features, interspersed with some thoroughly enjoyable Romanian folk music. Fifty-five minutes to Northern Europe and eastern North America. Try 7135, 9570, 9625 and 11940 kHz.

Radio Bulgaria. Summers only at this time. A potpourri of news and features with a strong Bulgarian flavor. Starts with *News,* then Monday through Thursday there's 15 minutes of current events in *Today,* replaced Friday by *Weekly Spotlight,* a summary of the week's major political stories. The remainder of the broadcast is given over to features dealing with Bulgaria and Bulgarians, and includes some lively ethnic music. Sixty minutes to eastern North America on 7480 and 9435 kHz. One hour later during winter.

Voice of Russia World Service. *News,* then winter weekdays, try the informative ●*Commonwealth Update*, with the pick of the second half-hour being Tuesday's ●*Audio Book Club* and Sunday's ●*Christian Message from Moscow*. Other

features include *Russian by Radio* (Monday and Wednesday) and *Timelines* (Friday and Saturday). Summers, there's the daily *News and Views,* followed by *Yours for the Asking* (Monday), ●*Music at Your Request* (Wednesday), *Jazz Show* (Thursday), ●*Folk Box* (Friday and Sunday) and *This is Russia* (Saturday). To eastern North America winters on 5940, 7125 and 7170; and summers on 7125, 7250 and 9665 kHz.

Voice of America. *News,* then it's a continuation of the programs from the 2200 broadcast. Continuous programming to East and Southeast Asia on 7215, 9705 (summer), 9770, 9890 (winter), 11760, 15185, 15290, 15305, 17735 and 17820 kHz; and to Australasia on 15185, 15305, 17735 and 17820 kHz.

WWCR, Nashville, Tennessee. Carries a variety of disestablishmentarian programs at this hour, depending on the day of the week, and whether it is summer or winter. These include winter's "Norman Resnick Show" and summer's "The Hour of Courage" and "The Voice of Liberty." On 5065 kHz.

WJCR, Upton, Kentucky. Continuous country gospel music to North America on 7490 kHz. Other U.S. religious broadcasters heard at this time include **WGTG** on 5085 kHz, **WWCR** on 13845 kHz, **KAIJ** on 13815 kHz, **KTBN** on 15590 kHz, and **WHRI-World Harvest Radio** on 5745 kHz. For traditional Catholic programming, tune **WEWN** on 7425 kHz.

CFRX-CFRB, Toronto, Canada. See 2200.

23:30

Radio Vlaanderen Internationaal, Belgium. Summers only at this time. Weekdays, there's *News, Press Review* and *Belgium Today,* followed by features like *Focus on Europe* (Monday), *Living in Belgium* and *Green Society* (Tuesday), *The Arts* (Wednesday and Friday), *Around Town* (Wednesday), *Economics* and *Inter-*

Don Moore

Radio Bahá'í's family-oriented religious programs mesh well with the traditional society of the local Quichua-speaking Indians in Otavalo, northern Ecuador.

national Report (Thursday), and Tourism (Friday). Weekend features include Music from Flanders (Saturday) and Sunday's P.O. Box 26 (a listener-response program) and Radio World. Twenty-five minutes to eastern North America on 9925 kHz; also audible on 11690 (or 13800) kHz, targeted at South America.

Radio Netherlands. News, followed Monday through Saturday by ●Newsline, then a feature program. Quality offerings include ●A Good Life (Monday), ●Research File (science, Thursday), the award-winning ●Documentary (Friday) and Saturday's ●Roughly Speaking. The rest of the week's lineup consists of Music 52/15 (Tuesday), Sounds Interesting (Friday) and Sunday's double-bill, Wide Angle and Siren Song. One hour to North America on 6020, 6165 and (summers) 9845 kHz.

All India Radio. Continuous programming to Southeast Asia. A potpourri of news, commentary, features and exotic Indian music. On 7150, 9705, 9950 and 11620 kHz.

Voice of Vietnam. News, then it's Commentary or Weekly Review. These are followed by short features and some pleasant Vietnamese music (especially at weekends). A half hour to Asia (also heard in Europe) on 9840 and 12020 (or 15010) kHz.

Voice of Greece. Actually starts around 2335. Ten minutes of English news from and about Greece. Part of a much longer multilingual broadcast. To Central America (and well heard in eastern North America) on any two (sometimes three) frequencies from 9395, 9425. 9935, 11595 and 11640 kHz.

Prepared by Don Swampo and the staff of PASSPORT TO WORLD BAND RADIO.

Worldwide Broadcasts in English—1998

Country-by-Country Guide to Best-Heard Stations

Dozens of countries reach out to us in English, and this section covers the times and frequencies where you're likely to hear them. If you want to know which shows are on hour-by-hour, check out the "What's On Tonight" section.

Some tips so you don't waste your time:

• **Best times and frequencies:** "Best Times and Frequencies," earlier in this book, tells where each world band segment is found. It also gives helpful specifics as to when and where to tune.

In general, it is best to listen during the late afternoon and evening, when most programs are beamed your way; in your local winter, tune the world band segments within the 5730-7600 kHz range (5730-15800 kHz local summer). Around breakfast, you can also explore segments within the 5730-15800 kHz range for a smaller, but interesting, number of selections.

• **Strongest (and weakest) frequencies:** Frequencies shown in italics—say, *6175* kHz—tend to be the best, as they are from transmitters that may be located near you. Frequencies with

no target zones are typically from transmitters designed for domestic coverage, so these are the least likely to be heard well by you unless you're in or near that country.

Programs Change Times Midyear

Some stations shift broadcast times by one hour midyear, typically April through October. These are indicated by ◄ (one hour earlier) and ►▶ (one hour later). Stations may also extend their hours of transmission, or air special programs, during national holidays or sports events.

Eavesdropping on World Music

Broadcasts in other than English? Turn to the next section, "Voices from Home," or the Blue Pages. Keep in mind that stations for kinsfolk abroad sometimes carry delightful chunks of indigenous music. They make for exceptional listening, regardless of language.

Schedules Prepared for Entire Year

To be as helpful as possible throughout the year, PASSPORT's schedules consist of not just observed activity, but also schedules which we have creatively opined will be in use during the forthcoming year. This latter material is original from us, and therefore will not be so exact as factual information.

Most frequencies are aired year round. Those that are only used seasonally are labeled **S** for summer (midyear, typically April through October), and **W** for winter.

Times and days of the week are in World Time, explained in "Setting Your World Time Clock" earlier in the book, as well as in the glossary.

ALBANIA
RADIO TIRANA

0145-0200	6115 (E North Am), 7160 (N America)
0230-0300	6140 (E North Am), 7160 (N America)
1845-1900	**S** 9570 (W Europe)
1945-2000 ▣	**W** 6270, 7270 (W Europe)
2100-2130	**S** 7110, **S** 9515
2200-2230	**W** 5985, **W** 7170

ALGERIA
RTV ALGERIENNE—(Europe)

1400-1500	**W** 11715, **W** 15160
2000-2100	**S** 11715, **S** 15160

ANGOLA
A VOZ DO GALO NEGRO—(S Africa)

1830-1845	5985/6095

RADIO NACIONAL—(S Africa)

2000-2100	3354 & 9535

ARGENTINA
RADIO ARGENTINA AL EXTERIOR-RAE

0200-0300	Tu-Sa 11710 (Americas)
1900-2000	M-F 15345 (Europe & N Africa)

ARMENIA
VOICE OF ARMENIA

0930-1000 ▣	Su 15270 (Europe)
1845-1900 ▣	M-F 4810 (E Europe, Mideast & W Asia), M-F 4990 & M-F 7480 (Mideast & N Africa)
2130-2200 ▣	9965 (Europe & C America)
2130-2200	**W** 7480 (Europe)

AUSTRALIA
ABC/CAAMA RADIO—(Australasia)

0000-0830	4835 & 4910
0830-2130	2310 & 2325
2130-2400	4835 & 4910

ABC/RADIO RUM JUNGLE—(Australasia)

0830-2130	2485
2130-0830	5025

DEFENCE FORCES RADIO—(Mideast)

0430-0630	13525 USB

RADIO AUSTRALIA

0000-0200	13755 (Pacific & W North Am)
0000-0400	17750 (E Asia & SE Asia)
0000-0600	17795 (Pacific & W North Am)
0000-0800	9660 (Pacific), 13605 (E Asia)
0000-0900	12080 (S Pacific), 15510 (Pacific & C America)
0100-0400	15415 (E Asia & SE Asia)
0200-0800	15240 (Pacific & N America)
0600-0830	11880 (Pacific & N America)
0600-0900	15415 (E Asia & SE Asia)
0800-0900	5995 & 9710 (Pacific)
0800-1300	9580 (Pacific & N America)
0830-1200	6080 (Pacific & E Asia)
1200-1800	5870 (Pacific & W North Am)
1300-2130	5995 (Pacific & W North Am)
1330-1700	11660 (E Asia & SE Asia)
1700-2130	11880 (Pacific)
1800-2000	6080 (Pacific)
2100-2200	9660 (Pacific), 12080 (S Pacific)
2100-2400	17795 (Pacific & W North Am)
2130-2300	11695 (E Asia & SE Asia)
2130-2400	13755 (Pacific & W North Am)
2200-2400	15510 (Pacific & C America)
2300-2400	9660 (Pacific), 12080 (S Pacific)

AUSTRIA
RADIO AUSTRIA INTERNATIONAL

0030-0100	9655/7325 (E North Am)
0230-0300	**W** 9495 (S America), 9655/7325 (E North Am), 9870 (C America), **S** 13730 (S America)
0430-0500	**S** 13730 (E Europe)
0530-0600	*6015* (N America), **W** 6155 (Europe), **W** 13730 (E Europe), **W** 15410 & **W** 17870 (Mideast)
0630-0700	**W** *6015* (N America)
0730-0800	**S** 6155 (Europe), **S** 13730 (E Europe), **S** 15410 & **S** 17870 (Mideast)
0830-0900	**W** 6155 (Europe), **W** 13730 (N Europe), **W** 15240 (E Asia), **W** 17870 (Australasia)
0930-1000	**S** M-Sa 15455 (E Asia), **S** M-Sa 17870 (Australasia)
1030-1100	**W** M-Sa 6155 (Europe), **W** M-Sa 13730 (N Europe), **W** M-Sa 15240 & **S** Su 15455 (E Asia), **S** Su 17870 & **W** M-Sa 17870 (Australasia)

1230-1300	**S** 6155 (Europe), **S** 13730 (W Europe & E North Am)
1330-1400	**W** 6155 (Europe), **W** 13730 (W Europe & E North Am)
1530-1600	**W** 6155 (Europe), **W** 9655 (Mideast), **W** 11780 (S Asia & SE Asia), **W** 13730 (S Europe & W Africa)
1630-1700	**S** 6155 (Europe), **W** 11780 & **S** 13710 (S Asia & SE Asia), **S** 13730 (S Europe & W Africa)
1930-2000	**W** 5945 & **W** 6155 (Europe), **W** 9495 (S Africa)
2130-2200	**S** 5945 & **S** 6155 (Europe), **S** 13730 (S Africa)
2230-2300	**W** 5945 & **W** 6155 (Europe), **W** 9495 (S Africa)

BANGLADESH
BANGLADESH BETAR
| 1230-1300 | 7185 & 9550 (SE Asia) |
| 1815-1900 | 7185 & 9550 (Europe), 15520 (Irr) (Mideast) |

BELGIUM
RADIO VLAANDEREN INTERNATIONAL
0030-0100	**W** 5900 (E North Am), **W** 9925 (S America)
0730-0800 ◪	5985 (Europe), 9925/9920 (S Europe & Australasia)
0900-0930	**S** M-Sa 15545 (Africa)
1000-1030 ◪	M-Sa 6035 (Europe), M-Sa 17610/ 17595 (Africa)
1000-1030	**W** M-Sa 15510 (Africa)
1230-1300	**S** Su 13610 (E North Am), **S** Su 15540 (SE Asia)
1300-1330	**S** M-Sa 13610 (E North Am), **S** M-Sa 15540 (SE Asia)
1330-1400	**W** Su 13670 (E North Am)
1400-1430	**W** M-Sa 13670 (E North Am)
1800-1830	**S** 13645 (Africa)
1900-1930 ◪	5910 (Europe)
1900-1930	**W** 9925 (Africa)
2200-2230 ◪	5910 (Europe)
2200-2230	**W** 9925 (Europe)
2330-2400	**S** 9925 (E North Am), **S** 11690 (S America)

BRAZIL
RADIO NACIONAL DO BRASIL-RADIOBRAS
| 1200-1320 | 15445 (N America & C America) |
| 1800-1920 | 15265 (Europe & Mideast) |

BULGARIA
RADIO BULGARIA
0000-0100 ◪	7480 (E North Am), 9700 (E North Am & C America)
0400-0500	**S** 11720 (E North Am)
0500-0600 ◪	9700 (E North Am & C America)
0500-0600	**W** 7480 (E North Am)
1130-1230	**S** 13790 (E Asia)

Dr. Esteban Sywulka, Director, and Pastor José Castañeda officiate at ceremonies celebrating the 34th anniversary of Guatemala's Radio Maya. With the right listening equipment, the station is sometimes faintly audible evenings throughout the Americas on 3324.8 kHz.

1230-1330	**W** 9445/9810 (E Asia), **W** 11605 & **S** 15620 (S Asia & E Asia)
1900-2000	**S** 11720 (Europe)
2000-2100 ◪	9700 (Europe)
2000-2100	**W** 7335 (Europe)
2100-2200	**S** 11720 (Europe)
2200-2300 ◪	9700 (Europe)
2200-2300	**W** 7105 (Europe)

CAMBODIA
NATIONAL VOICE OF CAMBODIA—(SE Asia)
| 0000-0015 & 1200-1215 | 11940 |

CANADA
CANADIAN BROADCASTING CORP—(E North Am)
| 0000-0300 ◪ | Su 9625 |
| 0200-0300 ◪ | Tu-Sa 9625 |
| 0300-0310 & |
| 0330-0609 ◪ | M 9625 |
| 0400-0609 ◪ | Su 9625 |

0500-0609 ◪	Tu-Sa 9625
1200-1255 ◪	M-F 9625
1200-1505 ◪	Sa 9625
1200-1700 ◪	Su 9625
1600-1615 &	
1700-1805 ◪	Sa 9625
1800-2400 ◪	Su 9625
1945-2015,	
2200-2225 &	
2240-2330 ◪	M-F 9625

CFCX, Montreal—(E North Am)
24 Hr   6005 (Irr)

CFRX-CFRB, Toronto—(E North Am)
1045-0300 ◪   6070

CFVP-CKMX, Calgary—(W North Am)
24 Hr   6030

CHNX-CHNS—(E North Am)
24 Hr   6130

CKZN-CBN, St. John's NF—(E North Am)
0930-0500 ◪   6160

CKZU-CBU, Vancouver—(W North Am)
24 Hr   6160

RADIO CANADA INTERNATIONAL

0000-0030	**W** Tu-Sa 6040 (C America), **W** Tu-Sa 11940 (C America & S America)
0000-0100 ◪	9755 (E North Am)
0000-0100	**W** 5960 (E North Am)
0100-0130	**S** 9535 & **S** 11715 (C America & S America), **S** 13670 (S America)
0130-0200	**S** Su/M 9535 & **S** Su/M 11715 (C America & S America), **S** Su/M 13670 (S America)
0200-0230	**S** 6120 (E North Am & C America), 9535 & **S** 11715 (C America & S America)
0200-0300 ◪	9755 (E North Am & C America)
0200-0300	**W** 6155 & **S** 9755 (E North Am & C America), **W** 11725 (C America & S America), **S** 13670 (S America)
0200-0330	**W** 9780 (C America & S America)
0230-0300	**S** Su/M 6120 (E North Am & C America), **S** Su/M 9535, **W** 9535 & **S** Su/M 11715 (C America & S America)
0300-0330	**W** 6155 (E North Am & C America), **W** 9755 (C America)
0330-0400	**W** Su/M 6155 (E North Am & C America), **W** Su/M 9755 (C America)
0400-0430	**W** 6150, **W** 9505, **W** 9645, **S** 9715, **S** 11835 & **S** 11975 (Mideast)
0500-0530	**S** M-F 7295 (W Europe & N Africa), **S** M-F 15430 (Africa)
0600-0630 ◪	M-F 6050 (Europe)
0600-0630	**W** M-F 6150 (Europe), **W** M-F 9740 (Africa), **W** M-F 9760 (Europe & N Africa), **W** M-F 11905 (Mideast)
1200-1230	**S** 9660 (E Asia), **W** 11730 & **S** 15195 (SE Asia)
1200-1300	**S** 13650 (E North Am & C America)
1230-1300	**W** 6150 (E Asia)
1300-1400 ◪	9640 (E North Am), 11855 (E North Am & C America)
1300-1400	**S** Su-F 13650 (E North Am & C America)
1330-1357	9535 (E Asia)
1330-1400	**W** 6150 & **S** 11795 (E Asia), **S** 15325 & **S** M-Sa 17820 (Europe)
1400-1500 ◪	M-F 9640 (E North Am), Su-F 11855 (E North Am & C America)
1400-1600	**S** Su 13650 (E North Am & C America)
1400-1700	**W** Su 9640 (E North Am)
1430-1500 ◪	11935 (Europe & Mideast)
1430-1500	**W** 9555 (Europe & Mideast), **W** 11915 & **W** 15325 (Europe)
1500-1700 ◪	Su 11855 (E North Am & C America)
1630-1657	7150 & 9550 (S Asia)
1630-1700	6550 (E Asia)
2000-2100	**S** 13650 (Europe & N Africa), **S** 17820 (Africa), **S** 17870 (Europe & N Africa)
2000-2130	**S** 11690 (Europe), **S** 13670 (Africa), **S** 15325 (Europe)
2100-2130	13650 (Europe & N Africa), 17820 (Africa)
2100-2230 ◪	5995 (Europe), 7235 (S Europe & N Africa), 15150 (Africa)
2100-2230	**W** 9735 (Africa), **W** 9805 (W Europe & N Africa), **W** 11945 (W Africa), **W** 13690 (Africa)
2130-2200	**W** 13650 (Europe & N Africa), **W** 17820 (Africa)
2200-2230	11705 (SE Asia), **S** 15305 (C America & S America)
2200-2300	**S** 5960 (E North Am), **S** 13740 (C America)
2200-2400	**S** 13670 (C America & S America)
2300-2330	**W** 6040 (C America), **W** 9535, 11940 & **S** 15305 (C America & S America)
2300-2400 ◪	9755 (E North Am)
2300-2400	5960 (E North Am)
2330-2400	**W** Sa/Su 6040 (C America), **W** Sa/Su 9535, Sa/Su 11940 & **S** Sa/Su 15305 (C America & S America)

CHINA

CHINA RADIO INTERNATIONAL

0000-0100	9710 & 11695 (N America)
0300-0400	9690 (N America & C America), 9710 & 11695 (N America)
0400-0500	9730 (W North Am)
0500-0600 ◪	9560 (N America)
0900-1100	9785/15440 & 11755 (Australasia)
1140-1155	**W** 6995, **S** 8660 (SE Asia)
1200-1300	9715 (SE Asia), 11795 (Australasia)
1200-1400	11660 (SE Asia)
1210-1225	**W** 6995, **S** 8660 & 12110 (SE Asia)
1300-1400	**S** 11980 (SE Asia)
1400-1500	9535 & 11825 (S Asia)

1400-1600	7405 (W North Am)
1400-1600	7160 & 9785 (S Asia)
1440-1455	W 6995, S 8660 (SE Asia)
1600-1700	*15110* (C Africa & S Africa), *15130* (S Africa)
1700-1800	5220 (E Asia), 7160/7150 (E Africa & S Africa), 7405 (Africa), 9570 (E Africa & S Africa), S 11910 (E Africa)
1900-2000	W 6955 (N Africa & W Africa), S 11515 (Mideast & N Africa)
1900-2100	9440 (N Africa & W Africa)
2000-2100	S 7160
2000-2130	*11715* (S Africa), *15110* (C Africa & S Africa)
2000-2200	5220 (E Asia), 6950 & 9920 (Europe)
2200-2230	*3985* (Europe)
2200-2300	W *7170* & S *9880* (Europe)

CHINA (TAIWAN)
VOICE OF FREE CHINA
0200-0300	*5950* (E North Am), 7130 (E Asia), *11740* (C America)
0200-0400	*9680* (W North Am), 11825 (SE Asia), 15345 (E Asia)
0300-0400	*5950* (E North Am & C America), 11745 (E Asia)
0700-0800	*5950* (C America)
1200-1300	7130 (E Asia), 9610 (Australasia)
2200-2300	W *5810*, W *9985*, S *15600* & S *17750* (Europe)

VOICE OF ASIA—(SE Asia)
1100-1200	7445

COSTA RICA
ADVENTIST WORLD RADIO
0500-0600	5030 & 6150 (C America), 7375 (C America & S America), 9725 (C America)
1100-1300	5030 & 6150 (C America), 7375 (C America & S America), 9725 & 13750 (C America)
1600-1700	Sa/Su 9725 & Sa/Su 13750 (C America)
2300-2400	5030, 6150, 9725 & 13750 (C America)

RADIO FOR PEACE INTERNATIONAL
0100-1200	7585 USB (C America)
0100-1600	7385 (C America & N America)
1700-2400	15050 (N America)
2200-2400	7385 (C America & N America)

CROATIA
CROATIAN RADIO
0400-0410 &	
0500-0510	5895 (Eu & N America)
1300-1310	W 13830 (E North Am)
1900-1910	5895 (Europe)
1900-1910	W 11635 (N America)
2300-2310	5895 (Europe)

Faro del Caribe, "Lighthouse of the Caribbean," has broadcast religious programs from the outskirts of San Jose, Costa Rica, for decades. As the surrounding neighborhood has become increasingly urbanized, they have been forced to move their antennas out to the countryside.

Don Moore

CUBA
RADIO HABANA CUBA
0100-0500	6000 (E North Am), 9820 (N America)
0100-0700	9830 USB (E North Am & Europe)
0500-0700	W 6000 & S 9820 (W North Am)
2030-2130	W 9585 USB, W 9620, S 13715 & S 13725 USB (Europe & E North Am)
2230-2330	6180 (C America)

CZECH REPUBLIC
RADIO PRAGUE
0000-0030	5930 & 7345 (E North Am)
0100-0130	6200 & 7345 (E North Am)
0300-0330	5930 (N America), 7345 (E North Am)
0330-0400	W 7350 (Mideast & S Asia), S 9480 (Mideast)
0800-0830	7345 (W Europe)
0900-0930	S 15640 (W Africa), S 17485 (Mideast & S Asia)

Located in an old warehouse, Ecuador's La Voz de los Caras, 4795 kHz, broadcasts to the world from Bahía de Caráquez. Once Ecuador's most important port, it has been forgotten since the harbor silted over several decades ago.

1000-1030	☒ 17485 (Mideast & E Africa)
1130-1200 ⇐	7345 (N Europe), 9505 (W Europe)
1300-1330	☒ 13580 (S Asia & SE Asia)
1400-1430 ⇐	17485 (E Africa)
1400-1430	☒ 13580 (E North Am)
1600-1630	☒ 17485 (E Africa)
1700-1730	5930 (W Europe), ☒ 9430 (E Africa), ☒ 15640 (C Africa)
1800-1830	☒ 5835 (W Europe), ☒ 9430 (Australasia)
2000-2030	☒ 5930 (W Europe), ☒ 11600 (S Asia & Australasia)
2100-2130	☒ 5930 (E North Am), ☒ 7345 (W Africa)
2230-2300	☒ 5930, 7345 & ☒ 11600 (E North Am)

ECUADOR
HCJB-VOICE OF THE ANDES
0000-0400	9745 (E North Am)
0000-1600	21455 USB (Europe & Australasia)
0400-0700	9745 (W North Am)

0700-1100	9445/9645 (Australasia)
0730-0930	9765 (Europe)
1100-1600	12005 (C America), 15115 (N America & S America)
1900-2200	☒ 11960 & ☒ 15540 (Europe), 21455 USB (Europe & Australasia)

EGYPT
RADIO CAIRO
0000-0030	9900 (E North Am)
0200-0330	9475 (N America)
1215-1330	17595 (S Asia)
1630-1830	15255 (C Africa & S Africa)
2030-2200	15375 (W Africa)
2115-2245	9900 (Europe)
2300-2400	9900 (E North Am)

ETHIOPIA
RADIO ETHIOPIA
1600-1700	7165, 9560 & 11880 (E Africa)

FINLAND
YLE RADIO FINLAND
1030-1100	☒ 13645 & ☒ 15235 (SE Asia & Australasia)
1130-1200	☒ 15240 (E Asia & SE Asia), ☒ 17825 (SE Asia & Australasia)
1230-1300	☒ 11900 (N America)
1330-1400 ⇐	15400 (N America)
1330-1400	☒ 11735 (N America)
2030-2100	☒ 9855 & ☒ 15440 (Europe & W Africa)
2130-2200	☒ 6120 (Europe & W Africa)

FRANCE
RADIO FRANCE INTERNATIONALE
1200-1300	9805 (E Europe), *11600* (SE Asia), ☒ 11615 (E North Am & C America), *13625* (C America & N America), 15155 & 15195 (E Europe), ☒ 15530 (C America), *15540* (W Africa), ☒ *17575* (Irr) (C America & N America)
1400-1455	*5220* (Asia)
1400-1500	*7110* (S Asia), ☒ 12030 & ☒ 15405 (S Asia & SE Asia), *17560* (Mideast)
1600-1700	☒ 9485 (N Africa, Mideast & E Africa), 11615 (N Africa), ☒ 11615 (Mideast), *11700* (W Africa), *12015* & 15530 (S Africa)
1600-1730	☒ 15210 & ☒ 15460 (E Africa)

GERMANY
DEUTSCHE WELLE
0100-0150	*6040* & *6085* (N America), 6145, ☒ 9640 & ☒ *11810* (N America & C America)
0200-0250	☒ 6035, ☒ *7265*, 7285, ☒ *7355*, ☒ 9515, *9615*, ☒ 9690, ☒ *11965* & ☒ *12045* (S Asia)
0300-0350	☒ 6045, *6085* & *6185* (N America),

	9535 & **S** 9615 (N America & C America), **S** 9640 & **W** 9650 (N America)
0400-0450	**S** 5990 & 6015 (S Africa), **W** 6065, 7225, **W** 7265, 9565 & **S** 11765 (Africa)
0500-0550	5960 (N America), **S** 6045 (N America & C America), **W** 6120 & **W** 6145 (N America), 6185 (W North Am), **S** 9615 (N America)
0600-0650	**W** 7225, **W** 9565, **W** 11765, **S** 11915, **S** 13790 & **S** 15185 (W Africa), 17820 (E Asia), **S** 17860 (W Africa), **S** 21680 & **W** 21705 (Mideast)
0900-0950	6160 (Australasia), **W** 7380 (E Asia), 9565 (Africa), **W** 11715 (SE Asia & Australasia), **W** 15145 (E Africa), 15410 (S Africa), **S** 17715, **W** 17780 (Africa), 17800 (W Africa), 21600 (Africa) & **S** 21680 (SE Asia & Australasia)
1100-1150	**S** 15370 (C Africa & W Africa), **W** 15410 (W Africa), **S** 17765 & 17800 (W Africa)
1600-1650	6170 (S Asia), **W** 7120 (S Africa), **S** 7130 (S Africa), 7225 & **W** 7305 (S Asia), 9735 (Africa), **S** 9875 & **S** 13690 (S Asia), 11810 (S Africa), **W** 13610 (C Africa & S Africa), **W** 15145 (E Africa & S Africa), **S** 17800 (Africa)
1900-1950	**S** 7250, 9640 & **S** 9670 (Africa), **S** 9735, **W** 9765 & **S** 11785 (W Africa), **W** 11785 (Africa), 11810 (W Africa), **W** 13690 (E Africa), **S** 13790, 15135 & **W** 15425 (W Africa)
2000-2050	**S** 7170 (W Europe), **W** 7285 & **S** 9615 (Europe)
2100-2150	**S** 7115 & 9670 (SE Asia & Australasia), **W** 9690 (Africa), **S** 9735 (W Africa), 9765 & 11785 (SE Asia & Australasia), 11865 (W Africa), **W** 15275 (W Africa & Americas)
2300-2350	**S** 5980 (S Asia & SE Asia), **W** 6000 (SE Asia), **W** 6130, 7235, **S** 9690 & **S** 12045 (S Asia & SE Asia)

GHANA
GHANA BROADCASTING CORPORATION
0000-0100	4915
0530-0915	3366, 4915
0915-1115	M-F 4915 (Irr)
0915-1200	Sa/Su//Holidays 4915
1200-1700	M-F 6130
1200-2400	4915
1700-2400	3366

GREECE
FONI TIS HELLADAS
0130-0200	**W** 7448, **W** 9420 & 9935/6260 (N America)

0330-0345	**W** 7448 & **W** 9420 (N America)
0745-0755	7450, **S** 9425 & 11645 (Europe & Australasia)
1235-1245	**S** 15175 (Europe & N America)
1335-1345 ⬅	15650 (Europe & N America)
1335-1345	**W** 9420 (Europe & N America)
1840-1855	11645 & 15150 (Africa)
1900-1910	**W** 9375/9380 (Europe)
2000-2010	**S** 7430/9420 (Europe)
2235-2245	9425 (Australasia)
2335-2350	**S** 9395 (C America & S America), **S** 9425 (C America & Australasia), **W** 9425 (C America), 11595 & **W** 11640 (S America)

GUAM
KSDA-ADVENTIST WORLD RADIO
1030-1100	9530 (E Asia)
1330-1400	9650 (E Asia)
1600-1700	**S** 7395 & **W** 7400 (S Asia)
2130-2200	**W** 9495 & **S** 15310 (E Asia)
2300-2400	**S** 11775 & 11895 (SE Asia)

KTWR-TRANS WORLD RADIO
0740-0915	15200 (SE Asia)
0855-1000	11830 (Australasia)
1000-1100	9865 (E Asia)
1500-1630	11580 (S Asia)

GUYANA
VOICE OF GUYANA
0800-2400	5950/3290

HOLLAND
RADIO NETHERLANDS
0000-0125	6020 (E North Am), 6165 (N America), **S** 9845 (E North Am)
0030-0225	**W** 5905, **W** 7305, **S** 9855 & **S** 11655 (S Asia)
0130-0325	**W** 9860 (S Asia)
0230-0325	11655 (S Asia)
0430-0525	**W** 5995, 6165 & **S** 9590 (W North Am)
0730-0825	**W** 11895 (Australasia)
0730-1025	**W** 9830 (Australasia)
0830-0925	**W** 13700 (Australasia)
0930-1125	**W** 7260 (E Asia), **W** 9810 (SE Asia), **S** 12065 & **S** 13710 (E Asia & Australasia)
1030-1225	**S** 9860 (W Europe)
1130-1325 ⬅	6045 (W Europe)
1130-1325	**W** 7190 (W Europe)
1330-1525	**W** 13700 (Mideast & S Asia)
1330-1625	**S** 9890 & **W** 9895 (S Asia)
1730-2025	6020 (S Africa), **S** 7120 & **W** 9605 (E Africa), **S** 11655 (W Africa)
1830-2025	15315 & 17605 (W Africa)
1830-2125	**S** 9895 (W Africa)
2330-2400	6020 (E North Am), 6165 (N America), **S** 9845 (E North Am)

HUNGARY
RADIO BUDAPEST
0100-0130	⑤ 9840 (N America)
0200-0230 ▣	11870 (N America)
0200-0230	Ⓦ 6190 & Ⓦ 9850 (N America)
0230-0300	⑤ 9840 (N America)
0330-0400 ▣	11870 (N America)
0330-0400	Ⓦ 5965 & Ⓦ 9850 (N America)
1900-1930	⑤ 6140 (N Europe), ⑤ 7130 (W Europe)
2000-2030 ▣	3975 (Europe), 9835 (W Europe)
2000-2030	Ⓦ 5970 (N Europe), Ⓦ 7250 (W Europe)
2200-2230 ▣	3975 (Europe), 5935 (N Europe), 7250 & 9835 (W Europe)

INDIA
ALL INDIA RADIO
1000-1100	11585 (E Asia), 13700, 15050 & 17387 (Australasia), 17840 (E Asia)
1330-1500	9545, 11620 & 13710 (SE Asia)
1745-1945	7410 (N Europe), 9950 & 11620 (W Europe), 11935, 13780 & 15075 (E Africa)
2045-2230	7150 (Australasia), 7410 (W Europe), 9910 (Australasia), 9950 (W Europe), 11620 (W Europe & Australasia), 11715 (Australasia)
2245-0045	7150 & 9705 (SE Asia), 9950 (E Asia), 11620 (E Asia & SE Asia)

INDONESIA
VOICE OF INDONESIA
0100-0200 &	
0800-0900	9525 (Asia & Pacific)
2000-2100	9525 (Europe)

IRAN
VOICE OF THE ISLAMIC REPUBLIC
0030-0130	Ⓦ 6150/6015 (Europe & C America), ⑤ 6175 (C America), Ⓦ 7100 (N America), ⑤ 7180 (C America), ⑤ 7260 (E North Am), 9022 (N America), Ⓦ 9670 (E North Am)
1100-1230	11745 (Mideast), ⑤ 11790 (W Asia), Ⓦ 11790 (S Asia & SE Asia), ⑤ 11875 (S Asia), 11930 (Mideast), 15260 & 17750 (S Asia & SE Asia)
1530-1630	Ⓦ 9575 (S Asia), Ⓦ 11790 (S Asia & SE Asia), ⑤ 11875 (S Asia), 15260 & 17750 (S Asia & SE Asia)
1930-2030	7260 & 9022 (Europe)
2130-2230	⑤ 6175 & ⑤ 9670 (Australasia)

IRELAND
UCB EUROPE—(W Europe)
24 Hr	6200

WEST COAST RADIO IRELAND
0100-0200	Ⓦ Th 5910 & ⑤ Th 9875 (E North Am)

1500-1600	Ⓦ Sa 5970/6015 & ⑤ Sa 6175 (Europe)
1800-1900	Ⓦ Th 11665 (Africa & Australasia)
1900-2000	⑤ Th 15625 (Africa & Australasia)

ISRAEL
KOL ISRAEL
0400-0415	⑤ 9435 (Europe)
0500-0515 ▣	7465 (W Europe & E North Am), 17545 (Australasia)
0500-0515	Ⓦ 5885 (Europe)
1400-1430	⑤ 12077 & ⑤ 15615 (W Europe & E North Am)
1500-1530	Ⓦ 9390 & Ⓦ 11685 (W Europe & E North Am)
1900-1930	⑤ 11605 (W Europe & E North Am), ⑤ 15615 (W Africa & S America), ⑤ 15640 (C America & S America)
2000-2030 ▣	9435 (W Europe & E North Am)
2000-2030	Ⓦ 7418 (Europe), Ⓦ 7465 (W Europe & E North Am), Ⓦ 9845 & Ⓦ 13750 (S America)

ITALY
IRRS-SHORTWAVE—(Europe)
0630-0830 ▣	3985
0830-1430 ▣	7125
1430-1700 ▣	F-Su 3985

RADIO ROMA-RAI INTERNATIONAL
0050-0110	6010 (E North Am), 9675 (E North Am & C America), 11800 (N America & C America)
0425-0440	5975 & 7275 (S Europe & N Africa)
1935-1955	Ⓦ 6030, 7235, ⑤ 9670 & ⑤ 11905 (N Europe)
2025-2045	Ⓦ 5990, 7110, 9710 & ⑤ 11840 (Mideast)
2200-2225	6150, 9565 & 11815 (E Asia)

JAPAN
RADIO JAPAN/NHK
0000-0100	⑤ 6155 & ⑤ 6180 (Europe)
0100-0200	⑤ 5960 (E North Am), Ⓦ 9605 (W North Am), 11860 (SE Asia), 11890 (S Asia), 13630 (W North Am), 15500/15475 (E Asia), 17810 (SE Asia), 17845 (S Asia)
0300-0400	Ⓦ 5960 (E North Am), Ⓦ 9605 (W North Am)
0500-0530	11895 (C America), ⑤ 15230 (W North Am)
0500-0600	6110 (W North Am & C America), Ⓦ 6150 (Europe)
0500-0800	11725 (E Asia), 11920 (Australasia)
0600-0700	5975 (Europe), 15550 (S Asia)
0600-0800	7230 (Europe), 11740 & 17810 (SE Asia)
0700-0800	11850 (Australasia), 15230/15165 (Mideast), 17815 (C Africa), 21610 (SE Asia)

0900-1000	**S** 9610 (E Asia), 15190 (SE Asia)
1100-1200	*6120* (E North Am), **S** 9610 (E Asia)
1400-1500	**S** 9610 (E Asia), **W** *11705* (W North Am)
1400-1600	7200 & **W** 9695 (SE Asia)
1500-1600	**W** 7240 (S Asia), **S** 9750 (E Asia), **S** 11730 (S Asia), *15355* (S Africa)
1700-1800	6035 (E Asia), **W** *7280* (S Asia), 9535 (W North Am), 9580 (SE Asia), *11880* (Mideast & N Africa), **S** *11880* (S Asia)
1900-2000	*6035* & 7140 (Australasia), 9580 (SE Asia), 11850 (Australasia)
2100-2110	**W** 7190, **S** 9570 & 11685 (SE Asia)
2100-2200	*6035* & **W** 7125 (SE Asia), **W** 9560 (E Asia), 11850 (Australasia), 13630 (W North Am)
2300-2400	**W** 7125 & **S** 9535 (SE Asia), **W** 9560 (E Asia), 11850 (Australasia)

KOREA (DPR)
RADIO PYONGYANG

0000-0100	11845, 13650 & 15230 (SE Asia & C America)
1100-1200	9975 & 11335 (SE Asia & C America)
1500-1600	9640 (Mideast & Africa), 9975 (Africa), 13650 (SE Asia & C America)
1800-1900	6575 & 9345 (Europe), 11700 & 13760 (N America)
1900-2000	6520 & 9600 (Mideast & N Africa), 9975 (Africa)
2100-2200	6575 & 9345 (Europe)
2300-2400	11335, 11700, 13760 & 15130 (N America)

KOREA (REPUBLIC)
RADIO KOREA INTERNATIONAL

0200-0300	7275 (E Asia), 11725 & 11810 (S America), 15575 (N America)
0800-0900	13670 (Europe)
1030-1100	**S** *11715* (E North Am)
1130-1200	**W** *9650* (E North Am)
1200-1300	7285 (E Asia)
1230-1300	9570 (SE Asia), 9640 (E Asia), 13670 (SE Asia)
1600-1700	5975 (E Asia), 9515 & 9870 (Mideast & Africa)
1900-2000	5975 & 7275 (E Asia)
2100-2130	**S** *3970* (Europe)
2100-2200	6480 & 15575 (Europe)
2200-2230	**W** *3970* (Europe)

KUWAIT
RADIO KUWAIT—(Europe & E North Am)

1800-2100	11990

LEBANON
VOICE OF LEBANON

0900-0915,
1315-1330 &
1800-1815 **▭**	6550

LIBERIA
LIBERIAN COMMUNICATIONS NETWORK

0800-1800	6100
1800-0200	5100

LITHUANIA
RADIO VILNIUS

0030-0100	**W** *5890*, **S** *9855* (E North Am)
0930-1000 **▭**	9710 (Europe)

MALAWI
MALAWI BROADCASTING CORPORATION

0250-0815	3380, 5993
1510-2210	3380

MALAYSIA
VOICE OF MALAYSIA

0500-0830	6175 (SE Asia), 9750 (SE Asia & Australasia), 15295 (Australasia)

MOLDOVA
RADIO MOLDOVA INTERNATIONAL

0330-0355 &
0430-0455	**W** *7500* & **S** *7520* (E North Am)
2200-2225 &
2230-2255	**W** *7500* & **S** *7520* (Europe)

MONACO
TRANS WORLD RADIO—(W Europe)

0755-0905 **▭**	7115
0905-0920 **▭**	Su-F 7115
1230-1300 **▭**	Sa/Su 7115

MONGOLIA
VOICE OF MONGOLIA

0900-0930	12085/15170 (E Asia)
1230-1300	12085 (Australasia)
1500-1530	9720, 12085 (Asia)
1930-2000	9720, 12015 (Europe)

NAMIBIA
NAMIBIAN BROADCASTING CORPORATION

0000-0600 **➡**	3290
0400-0600 **➡**	3270
0600-1600 **➡**	4930, 4965
1600-1910 **➡**	3270
1600-2400 **➡**	3290

NEW ZEALAND
RADIO NEW ZEALAND INTERNATIONAL—
(Pacific)

0000-0458	15115
0459-0758	**S** 9795
0500-0758	**W** 11905
0758-0816	**W** Sa/Su 9700 & **S** M-F 9795
0758-0817	**S** Sa/Su 6100
0816-1206	**W** 9700
0817-1206	**S** 6100
1206-1650	**W** 6070 (Irr) & **S** 6100 (Irr)
1650-1752	**W** M-F 6070

1650-1951   **S** M-F 6145
1753-1850   **W** M-F 9810
1952-2306 **➡** 11735
2307-2400   15115

NIGERIA
VOICE OF NIGERIA—(Africa)
0500-0700 & 1000-1100   7255
1500-1700 & 1900-2100   7255

NORWAY
RADIO NORWAY INTERNATIONAL
0100-0130   **W** M 7465 (E North Am &
           C America), **S** M 9560 (N America)
0300-0330   **W** M 7465 (W North Am)
0400-0430   **S** M 7520 (W North Am)
0600-0630   **S** Su 7295 (Australasia), **S** Su
           9590 (W Africa & Australasia)
0700-0730   **W** Su 7180 (W Europe & Australasia)
0800-0830   **S** Su 17855 (Australasia)
1200-1230   **S** Su 9590 (Europe), **S** Su 13800 &
           S Su 15305 (E Asia)
1300-1330   **W** Su 9590 (Europe), **W** Su 9795
           (E Asia), **S** Su 13800 (SE Asia &
           Australasia), **S** Su 15340
           (N America), **W** Su 15605 (SE Asia
           & Australasia)
1400-1430   **W** Su 11840 (N America)
1500-1530   **W** Su 9520 & **W** Su 11730 (Mideast)
1600-1630   **S** Su 11860 (S Asia), **S** Su 13805
           (E Africa)
1800-1830   **S** Su 7485 (Europe), **S** Su 9590
           (Mideast), **S** Su 13805 (W Africa),
           S Su 15220 (C Africa)
1900-1930   **W** Su 5930 (Australasia), **W** Su
           5960 (Europe), **W** Su 7485
           (W Africa), **W** Su 9590 (C Africa)
2000-2030   **S** Su 9590 (Australasia)
2200-2230   **W** Su 6200 (E North Am), **W** Su
           7115 (E Asia), **S** Su 9485
           (Australasia)

PAPUA NEW GUINEA
NBC
0730-0900   9675/4890
1200-1930   M-Sa 4890
2200-0730   9675

PHILIPPINES
FEBC RADIO INTERNATIONAL
0100-0300   15450 (S Asia & SE Asia)
0930-1100   11635 (E Asia & Australasia)
1300-1600   11995 (S Asia & SE Asia)
RADYO PILIPINAS
0230-0330   **W** 11805, **S** 11885 & 15120 (Mideast)

POLAND
POLISH RADIO WARSAW
1300-1355 **▣** 6095, 7145, 7270 & 9525 (W Europe),
           11815 (W Europe & E North Am)

1800-1855 **▣** 6000, 6095, 7270 & 7285 (W Europe)
2030-2125 **▣** 6035, 6095 & 7285 (W Europe)

PORTUGAL
RDP INTERNATIONAL-RADIO PORTUGAL
0430-0500 **▣** Tu-Sa 6150 & Tu-Sa 9570 (E North
           Am)
1430-1500 **▣** M-F 21515 (Mideast & S Asia)
2100-2130 **▣** M-F 6130, M-F 9780 & M-F 9815
           (Europe)

ROMANIA
RADIO ROMANIA INTERNATIONAL
0200-0300 &
0400-0500   5990, 6155, 9510, 9570 & 11940
           (E North Am)
0530-0600   11940 (C Africa), **W** 15250 (C Africa
           & S Africa), **S** 15270 (E Asia),
           S 15340, **W** 15365, **W** 17720 &
           W 17745 (C Africa & S Africa),
           17790 (S Africa)
0632-0641   **W** 7105, **S** 9550, 9665, **W** 11775 &
           S 11810 (Europe)
0645-0745   **S** 11740 (E Asia), **S** 11840 & 15250
           (Australasia), **S** 15270 & **W** 15405
           (E Asia), 17720 & **W** 17805
           (Australasia)
1300-1400   **S** 9690 & 11940 (Europe), **S** 15365,
           W 15390 & **S** 17720 (W Europe)
1430-1530   **W** 11740 & **S** 11775 (S Asia), **W**
           11810 (Mideast & S Asia), 15335
           (S Asia)
1730-1800   **S** 9550, 9750 & **W** 11740 (S Africa),
           S 11830 & 11940 (C Africa &
           S Africa)
1900-2000   **W** 6105, **W** 7105, **W** 7195, **W** 9510,
           S 9550, **S** 9690, **S** 11810 & **S**
           11940 (Europe)
2100-2200   5990, 7105, 7195, **W** 9510 & **S** 9690
           (Europe)
2300-2400   7135 (Europe), 9570 (E North Am),
           9625 (Europe), 11940 (E North Am)

RUSSIA
VOICE OF RUSSIA
0000-0100   **W** *7180* (N Europe, E North Am &
           C America), **S** *7250* (E North Am),
           S *9665* (E North Am & C America),
           S *9820* & **S** *9830* (S America)
0000-0200 **▣** *7125* (E North Am)
0000-0500   **S** 9620 (E North Am & C America)
0000-0600   **W** *7105* (Europe & E North Am)
0100-0200   **W** *7440* (S America)
0100-0500   **S** 15180 (W North Am)
0100-0700   **S** 12010, **S** 12050, **S** 13665 &
           S 15580 (W North Am)
0200-0300   **W** 12030 & **W** 13640 (W North Am)
0200-0400   **W** 7345 (W North Am)
0200-0700   **S** 13645 (W North Am)
0200-0800   **W** 5920 & **W** 7270 (W North Am)

Radio Cajamarca, 4279 kHz, is one of the many tiny Peruvian stations which uses low-powered transmitters to reach the far corners of their country and beyond. Tradition holds that the building behind the station contains the room where Spanish conquistadores held the last great Inca leader, Atahualpa, for ransom. If Atahualpa's vassals could fill the room with gold to a point as high as he could touch on the wall, then the emperor would go free. They did, but Spanish leader Pizarro reneged on his promise, and Atahualpa was strangled and burned across the street a few days later.

0300-0400	**W** 5940 (E North Am)
0300-0500	**S** 7230 (C America)
0400-0600 ⬅	7125 (E North Am)
0400-0600	**W** 7180 (N Europe, E North Am & C America)
0400-0800	**W** 7175 (W North Am)
0430-0800	**W** 7330 (W North Am)
0500-0800	**W** 5930 (W North Am), **S** 17580 (SE Asia)
0500-0900	**S** 15470 (E Asia & Australasia)
0530-0700	**S** 12040 (W North Am)
0530-0800	**W** 5905 (W North Am)
0600-0700	**S** 15490 (SE Asia & Australasia)
0600-0800	**W** 15470, 17570 & **W** 21790 (Australasia)
0600-0900	**S** 15560 (SE Asia & Australasia), **W** 17560 (SE Asia)
0600-1100	**W** 12025 (Australasia)
0800-1000	**S** 15580 (E Asia & SE Asia)
0800-1100	**W** 9685 (SE Asia)
0800-1300	**W** 17860 (S Asia, SE Asia & Australasia), **W** 17880 (Australasia)
0830-1100	**S** 11800 (S Pacific)
0830-1200	**W** 12005 (Australasia)
0930-1100	**W** 7305 (SE Asia)
0930-1200	**W** 9450 (Australasia)
1000-1100	**S** 15430 (W Europe & E North Am), **W** 17755 (S Asia & SE Asia)
1000-1200	**S** 7150 (E Asia), **S** 9800 & **S** 9835 (Australasia), **W** 15490 (S Asia & SE Asia), **W** 15560 (S Asia), **S** 17560 (Australasia)
1000-1300	**S** 11880 (S Asia), **W** 13785 & *15170* (S Asia & SE Asia), **S** 15490 (S Asia), **S** *17775* (S Asia & SE Asia)
1000-1400	**S** 17610 (S Asia & SE Asia)
1030-1300	**S** 11655 (S Asia)
1100-1200	**W** 12055, **S** 15460, **S** 15560 & **W** 17890 (SE Asia)
1100-1300	**S** 9920 (Australasia), **W** *15120* (S Asia), *15430* (W Europe & E North Am), *17755* (S Asia & SE Asia)
1200-1300	**W** 9725 (W Asia & S Asia), **S** 11785 & **S** 15110 (S Asia), **S** 15230 (W Asia & S Asia), **S** 15510 (S Asia & SE Asia)
1200-1400 ⬅	4740 (W Asia & S Asia)

1230-1300	**W** 9875 (S Asia & SE Asia), **S** 15435 (S Asia)
1300-1400 ◀	*4975* (W Asia & S Asia)
1300-1400	**W** 12055, **S** 15460, **W** 15470 & **S** 15560 (SE Asia), **S** *17755* (S Asia & SE Asia)
1300-1500	**S** *15340* (W Africa & S America), **S** *15430* (W Europe & E North Am)
1400-1500	**S** 9800 & **S** 9835 (Australasia), **S** 11985 (Mideast & W Asia)
1400-1600	**W** 7130 & **W** 7165 (Mideast & W Asia), **S** *11835* & **W** 12065 (Mideast), **S** *15320* (Mideast & W Asia), **S** 15540 (Mideast), **S** 15560 (Mideast & E Africa)
1400-1700	**S** *11945* & **S** 15350 (Mideast & E Africa), **S** 17525
1400-1800	**W** 9470 (C Africa & S Africa)
1430-1600	**S** *9595* (W Asia & S Asia)
1500-1600	**W** *11765* (Mideast & W Asia), **S** 12035 (Mideast & E Africa), *15430* (W Europe & E North Am), **S** *17750* (Mideast)
1500-1700 ◀	*4740, 4940 & 4975* (W Asia & S Asia)
1500-1700	**W** 9635 (Mideast), **W** *9905* (W Asia & S Asia), **W** *11945* (Mideast & C Africa)
1500-1800	**W** 7115 (N Europe), **W** 7325 (C Africa & S Africa)
1500-1900	**S** *9365* (Mideast & E Africa), **S** 9675 (Mideast & S Africa), **S** *9975* (S Africa), **S** 11775 (N Africa & E Africa)
1500-2000	**S** *15400* (N Europe & E North Am)
1500-2200	**S** 9880 (Europe)
1530-1600	**W** 6005 (Mideast & W Asia)
1600-1700	**W** 5925 (N Africa), **W** Su-F 6005 (Mideast & W Asia), **W** 6175 (Mideast & N Africa), **S** 7240 (N Europe), **S** 7245 & **W** 7275 (Mideast & E Africa), **S** 7290 (N Europe), **W** 7330 (Europe), **S** 7350 (N Europe), **S** 9615 (C Africa & S Africa), **W** 9865 (W Africa), **S** *11675* (N Europe), **S** 11725 (E Africa), **W** *11865* (C Africa), **S** *15430* (W Europe & E North Am)
1600-2000	**W** 7210 (Mideast & E Africa), **W** 9505 (S Africa)
1600-2100	**W** 9490 (W Africa)
1600-2200	**S** 9480 (N Europe)
1600-2400	**W** *7180* (N Europe, E North Am & C America)
1630-1800	**S** 7440 (Europe & W Africa)
1630-1900	**W** 7175 & **W** *13670* (W Africa)
1700-1800	**W** *4740* (W Asia & S Asia), **W** 5995 & **W** 6055 (N Europe), *6590* (E Asia), **W** 9560 (Mideast), **S** *17875* (W Africa)
1700-2000	**W** 7255 (E Africa & S Africa)

1700-2200	**W** 5940 (N Europe)
1700-2300	**W** 7205 (N Europe & W Europe), **W** 9890 (N Europe)
1730-1800	**W** 7130 (Mideast & W Asia), **W** *9585* (Mideast & N Africa), **S** 12065 (Mideast & W Asia)
1800-2000	**S** 7240 & **S** 7290 (N Europe), **S** *11945* (Mideast & E Africa)
1800-2100	**S** *11675* (N Europe)
1800-2200	**S** 7350 (N Europe)
1830-2000	**S** 11765 (Mideast & E Africa)
1900-2000	**S** Su/M/W/F 7300 (E Asia & SE Asia), **S** 7440 (Europe & W Africa), **S** *17875* (W Africa)
1900-2100	**W** 7325 & **W** 9470 (C Africa & S Africa), **W** *9585* (Mideast & N Africa)
1900-2300	**W** 5995 & **W** 6055 (N Europe)
1930-2000	**W** 7200 (E Africa & S Africa)
2000-2100	**W** 7175 (W Africa), **W** 9795 (S Europe), **W** *13670* (W Africa)
2000-2200	**S** 7300 (E Asia & SE Asia)
2030-2400	**S** 9665 (E North Am & C America)
2100-2200	**S** 9580 (Europe), **S** 9710 (Europe & W Africa), **S** *11840* (W Europe & E North Am)
2100-2400	**S** *11750* (E North Am)
2120-2300	**W** 7400 (W Europe & C America)
2130-2200	**W** 7170 (Europe)
2130-2300	**S** 7250 (E North Am)
2200-2300	**W** 7140 & **W** 7360 (Europe)
2220-2400	**W** 5940 (E North Am)
2230-2400	**S** *11840* (C America)
2300-2400	**W** *7105* (Europe & E North Am), **W** 7170 (Europe), **W** 7205 & **W** *9550* (C America), **W** 9795 (S America)
2330-2400 ◀	*7125* (E North Am)

FEBA RADIO—(W Asia & S Asia)

1500-1558	M-Sa 9810

SIERRA LEONE
SIERRA LEONE BROADCASTING SERVICE

0600-0830 & 1700-2330	3316

SINGAPORE
RADIO SINGAPORE INTERNATIONAL—(SE Asia)

1100-1400	6015 & 6155

RADIO CORPORATION OF SINGAPORE

1400-1700 & 2300-1100	6155

SLOVAKIA
ADVENTIST WORLD RADIO

0400-0430	**W** 9450 (S Asia), **S** 9455 (E Africa)
2100-2200	**S** 6055 (W Europe)
2200-2300	**S** 11610 (N Africa & W Africa)

RADIO SLOVAKIA INTERNATIONAL

0100-0130	5930 & 7300 (E North Am & C America), 9440 (S America)
0830-0900	11990, **S** 15460, **W** 17485, **S** 17570 & **W** 21705 (Australasia)
1730-1800 &	
1930-2000 ◼	5915, 6055 & 7345 (Eu)

SOLOMON ISLANDS
SOLOMON ISLANDS BROADCASTING CORP

0000-0030	M-F 5020, M-F 9545
0000-0230	Sa 5020, Sa 9545
0030-0230	Su 5020, Su 9545
0100-0800	M-F 5020, M-F 9545
0500-0800	Sa 5020, Su 5020, Sa 9545, Su 9545
0815-1130	Su 5020, Su 9545
0830-0900	M-F 5020, M-F 9545
0845-1100	Sa 9545
0845-1130	Sa 5020
0915-0930 &	
0945-1130	M-F 5020, M-F 9545
1900-1930	Sa 5020
1900-2030	M-F 5020
1945-2400	Sa 5020
2000-2015 &	
2030-2330	Su 5020
2045-2400	M-F 5020
2100-2330	Su 9545
2100-2400	M-F 9545, Sa 9545

SOUTH AFRICA
CHANNEL AFRICA

0300-0330	5955 (E Africa & C Africa)
0400-0430	5955 (S Africa)
0500-0530	**S** 9675 & **W** 11900 (W Africa)
1600-1630	**S** 6120/**W** 7155 (S Africa), 9685 (Af)
1700-1730	11900 (W Africa)

TRANS WORLD RADIO—(W Africa)

0600-0630	11730
0630-0645	Sa/Su 11730

SPAIN
RADIO EXTERIOR DE ESPANA

0000-0200 &	
0500-0600	6055 (N & C America)
2000-2100	M-F 6125 (Europe) & 11775 (Africa)
2100-2200	Sa/Su 6125 (Europe), Sa/Su 11775 (Africa)

SRI LANKA
SRI LANKA BROADCASTING CORPORATION

0030-0430	9730 & 15425 (S Asia)
1030-1130	11835 (SE Asia & Australasia), 17850 (E Asia)
1230-1600	9730 & 15425 (S Asia)

SUDAN
RADIO OMDURMAN—(Europe, Mideast & Africa)

1800-1900	9200

SWAZILAND
TRANS WORLD RADIO

0430-0500	3200 (S Africa)
0430-0530	6100/6070 (S Africa)
0430-0700	4775 (S Africa)
0505-0735	9500 (C Africa)
0605-0735	9650 (S Africa)
0735-0805	**W** Sa/Su 6100 (S Africa), Sa/Su 9500 (C Africa), Sa/Su 9650 (S Africa)
1600-1830	9500 (C Africa)
1745-1800	M-F 3200 (S Africa)
1800-2015	3200 (S Africa)

SWEDEN
RADIO SWEDEN

0030-0100	6065 & **W** 9850 (S America)
0230-0300 ◼	6090 (N America)
0330-0400 ◼	7115 (N America)
1230-1300 ◼	11650 (N America), 15240 (E North Am)
1430-1500 ◼	15240 (E North Am)
1430-1500	**W** 11650 (N America)
1930-2000 ◼	6065 (Europe), 9655 (Mideast)
2030-2100 ◼	6065 (Europe)
2130-2200 ◼	Sa/Su 6065 (Europe & Mideast)
2230-2300 ◼	6065 (Europe)

SWITZERLAND
SWISS RADIO INTERNATIONAL

0100-0130	6135 & 9885 (E North Am), *9905* (N America & C America)
0400-0430	6135 (W North Am), 9885 (N America)
0400-0500	*9905* (N America & C America)
0515-0530	**S** 9535 (E Europe)
0600-0630	9885 & 11860 (W Africa), 13635 (S Africa)
0615-0630 ◼	6165 (Europe & N Africa)
0615-0630	**W** 5840 & **S** 9535 (E Europe)
0715-0730 ◼	6165 (Europe & N Africa)
0715-0730	**W** 5840 (E Europe)
0900-0930	*9885*, **W** 12075, 13685 & **S** 17515 (Australasia)
1100-1130 ◼	6165 (Europe & N Africa), 9535 (S Europe & W Europe)
1100-1130	**W** 9885, **W** 11995, 13635, **S** 15415 & **S** 17515 (E Asia)
1300-1330	*7230* (SE Asia), *7480* (E Asia), **W** 12075, 13635 & **S** 15120 (SE Asia)
1300-1400 ◼	6165 (Europe & N Africa), 9535 (S Europe & W Europe)
1600-1630	**W** 9885 & 12075 (C Asia & S Asia), 13635 & **S** 15530 (W Asia & S Asia)
1700-1730	**W** 7410 & **S** 9905 (N Europe)
2000-2030 ◼	6165 (Europe & N Africa)
2000-2030	**S** 9885 (N Africa)

SYRIA
RADIO DAMASCUS

2005-2105	12085 & 13610/15095 (Europe)

2110-2210	12085 (N America), 13610/15095 (Australasia)

TANZANIA
RADIO TANZANIA—(E Africa)
0330-0430 &	
0900-1030	5050
1030-1530	Sa/Su 5050
1530-1915	5050

THAILAND
RADIO THAILAND
0000-0030	W 9680 & S 9690 (S Asia & E Africa)
0000-0100	9655 & 11905 (Asia)
0030-0100	W 11905 & S 15395 (N America)
0300-0330	9655 (Asia), W 11890 (W North Am), 11905 (Asia), S 15395 (W North Am)
0530-0600	11905 (Asia), 15115 (Europe)
1230-1300	W 9810 & S 9885 (SE Asia & Australasia), 11905 (Asia)
1400-1430	W 9530 & S 9830 (SE Asia & Australasia)
1900-2000	S 7210 & W 9535 (N Europe), 9655 & 11905 (Asia)
2030-2045	W 9535 (Europe), 9655 (Asia), S 9680 (Europe), 11905 (Asia)

TURKEY
VOICE OF TURKEY
0300-0350	S 17705 (S Asia, SE Asia & Australasia)
0400-0450 ▣	9655 (Europe & E North Am), 9685 (Mideast & W Asia)
0400-0450	W 9560 (W Asia, S Asia & Australasia)
1330-1420 ▣	9445 (Europe), 9630 (W Asia & S Asia)
1830-1850	S 9535 (Europe)
1930-2020 ▣	9445 (Europe)
2300-2350 ▣	7280 (Europe), 9560 (W Asia, S Asia & Australasia), 9655 (Europe & E North Am)

UGANDA
RADIO UGANDA
0300-0600	4976/3340, 5026
1245-1300	Sa/Su 7110, Sa/Su 7195
1300-2100	4976/3340, 5026

UKRAINE
RADIO UKRAINE INTERNATIONAL
0000-0100	S 7150 & S 9550 (E North Am)
0100-0200	W 6010 (W Europe & C America), W 6055 (Arctic & W North Am), W 9620 (W Africa & S America)
0130-0200	W 5915 (W Europe & E North Am)
0300-0400	S 7150 & S 9550 (E North Am)
0400-0500	W 5915 (W Europe & E North Am), W 6010 (W Europe & C America),

	W 7205 (W Europe, W Africa & S America)
2100-2200	S 6010 (S Europe & N Africa), S 6020 (E Europe), S 7375 (Australasia), S 9560 (S Europe & N Africa), S 9875 (S Africa)
2200-2300 ▣	5905 (S Europe & N Africa), 6080 (W Asia)
2200-2300	W 4795 & W 4820 (Europe), W 5940 (S Europe & N Africa), W 6010 (N Europe, W Europe & C America), W 6020 (N Europe & E North Am), W 6055 (Mideast, E Africa & Arctic), W 6130 (W Europe, N Africa & E North Am), W 7135 (W Asia), W 7205 (W Europe, W Africa & S America), W 7240 (W Europe), W 9620 (W Africa & S America)

UNITED ARAB EMIRATES
UAE RADIO IN DUBAI
0330-0400	11945, 13675, 15400 & 21485 (E North Am & C America)
0530-0600	15435 (Australasia), 17830 (E Asia), 21700 (Australasia)
1030-1110, 1330-1400 & 1600-1640	13675 & 15395 (Europe), 17630 (N Africa), 21605 (Europe)

UNITED KINGDOM
BBC WORLD SERVICE
0000-0030	*11945 (E Asia)*
0000-0100	*5965 (S Asia)*, W *9580 (E Asia)*
0000-0200	*6195 (SE Asia), 9410 (W Asia & S Asia), 11750 (S America)*
0000-0230	*9590 (C America & S America), 9915 (S America)*
0000-0300	*11955 (S Asia)*
0000-0330	*5970 (S America & C America), 6175 (N America), 15360 (SE Asia)*
0000-0530	*15280 (E Asia)*
0000-0700	*5975 (N America & C America)*
0000-2230	W *Sa 6195 (Europe)*
0100-0200	W *5965* & S *9605 (S Asia)*
0200-0300	S *6195 (E Europe)*, S *9410 (Europe)*, W *9410 (W Asia & S Asia), 9605 (S Asia)*
0200-0330	*6135 (E Africa)*, S *9760 (W Asia & S Asia)*
0230-0330	*7325 (S America)*, S *9895 (C America & S America)*
0230-0430	W *9590 (C America & S America)*
0300-0330	*11850 & 15340 (E Asia), 15380 (SE Asia)*
0300-0400	*6005 (W Africa & S Africa)*, S *6180 (Europe)*
0300-0430	W *9605 (W Asia & S Asia)*
0300-0500	*11955 (E Asia)*, W *12095 (E Africa)*
0300-0530	W *17790 & 21660 (E Asia)*

0300-0600   *3255* (S Africa)
0300-0730   6195 (Europe)
0300-0800   *9600* (S Africa)
0300-0815   **W** 3955 (Europe)
0300-0915   *11760* (Mideast), *15310* (W Asia & S Asia)
0300-2200   *6190* (S Africa)
0300-2230   9410 (Europe)
0330-0430   **W** *6175* (N America), *9610 & 11730* (E Africa)
0400-0500   **S** 12095 (Europe)
0400-0600   *15575* (W Asia)
0400-0715   *7160* (W Africa & C Africa)
0400-0730   *6005* (W Africa), *6180* (Europe)
0430-0600   **W** 7150 (Europe)
0430-0615   15420 (E Africa)
0430-0800 ⬅   *6175* (C America)
0500-0700   **W** *17640* (E Africa)
0500-0800   *15360* (SE Asia & Australasia)
0500-0900   *11955* (SE Asia & Australasia)
0500-1130   *9740* (SE Asia)
0500-1500   17885 (E Africa)
0500-2100   12095 (Europe)
0530-0900   **S** *15280* (E Asia)
0530-1030   *21660* (SE Asia)
0600-0730   **W** *11780* (Europe & N Africa), *15565* (W Asia)
0600-0800   **W** *11940* (S Africa), *17790* (S Asia)
0600-0810   **W** 7145 (Australasia)
0600-0915   7325 (Europe)
0600-1615   **W** 15575 (Europe)
0615-0700   15420 (E Africa)
0700-0730   *17830* (Africa)
0700-0800   **W** *5975* (N America & C America), **W** 17640 (Europe)
0700-2000   15485 (W Europe & N Africa)
0715-1000   *15400* (W Africa)
0730-0900   Sa/Su *15565* (W Asia)
0730-1000   *17830* (W Africa & C Africa)
0800-1400   **W** *11750* (S Asia)
0800-1500   17640 (E Europe & Mideast)
0800-1600   *11940* (S Africa)
0900-0930   *15575* (W Asia)
0900-1000   **W** *6065, 9580,* **S** *11765 & 11955* (E Asia), *15190* (S America), *15280* (E Asia & SE Asia)
0900-1030   *15360* (E Asia, SE Asia & Australasia)
0900-1500   *15565* (W Asia)
0900-1615   *6195* (SE Asia)
0900-1630   17705 (N Africa)
0900-1800   *11750* (S Asia)
0915-0930 ⬅   11680, 13745, 15325 & 17695 (E Europe)
0915-1000   **W** 9750 (E Europe), *17760* (E Asia & SE Asia)
0930-1500   *15575* (Mideast & W Asia)
1000-1100   **S** *5965* (E North Am), Sa/Su *15400* (W Africa), Sa/Su *17830* (W Africa & C Africa)
1000-1130   Sa/Su *15190* (S America), *17790* (S Asia)
1000-1400   *6195* (C America & N America), *11760* (Mideast), *15310* (W Asia & S Asia)
1100-1130   *11955* (E Asia), *15400* (W Africa), *17790* (S America)
1100-1200   *5965* (E North Am)
1100-1300   *9580* (E Asia), *11955* (SE Asia)
1100-1400   *15220* (Americas)
1100-1700   *21660* (S Africa)
1100-2100   *17830* (W Africa & C Africa)
1130-1615   9740 (SE Asia & Australasia)
1200-1230   *15105* (W Africa)
1200-1300   **S** *9515* (E North Am)
1200-1400   **W** *5965* (E North Am)
1300-1415   *15420* (E Africa)
1300-1600   **W** *9590 &* **S** *11865* (W North Am)
1300-1615   **W** *5990* (E Asia), *9515* (E North Am)
1300-1700   *21470* (E Africa)
1400-1415   *11860 & 21490* (E Africa)
1400-1500   **S** *15310* (S Asia)
1400-1600   *15220* (N America)
1400-1700   *17840* (Americas)
1415-1430   Sa/Su *11860,* Sa/Su *15420 &* Sa/Su *21490* (E Africa)
1430-1500   M-F *15400* (W Africa)
1500-1530   *11860 & 15420* (E Africa), *17880* (C Africa), 21490 (E Africa)
1500-1700   **S** 6195 (Europe), *15400* (W Africa)
1500-1745   **S** *7180* (E Asia)
1500-1830   5975 (S Asia)
1600-1745   *3915 &* **W** *7135* (SE Asia)
1600-1800   **S** *3255 &* **W** *11940* (S Africa)
1615-1700   Sa *9515* (E North Am), *15420* (E Africa)
1615-1830   *9510 & 9740* (S Asia)
1630-1745   *11860* (E Africa)
1700-1745   **S** *6005 & 9630* (E Africa)
1700-1800   **S** *17840* (W North Am & C America)
1700-1830   7160 (Mideast & W Asia)
1700-1900   *15420* (E Africa), **W** *17840* (W North Am)
1700-1930   *15400* (W Africa & S Africa)
1700-2200   6180 (Europe)
1700-2230   6195 (Europe)
1700-2330   **W** 3955 (Europe)
1730-1800   **W** 7210 (W Europe), **W** 9685 (E Europe)
1800-2200   *3255* (S Africa)
1830-2130   *9630* (E Africa)
1830-2200   *6005* (E Africa), *9740* (Australasia)
1900-2000   *5975* (Mideast & W Asia)
1930-2100   **S** *11835 &* **W** *15400* (S Africa)
1930-2300   *11835* (W Africa)
1930-2315   **S** 15400 (W Africa)
2000-2200   *11955* (Australasia)
2000-2230   7325 (Europe)
2000-2400   *11750* (S America)
2100-2200   *3915* (SE Asia), *5965 &* **W** *6120* (E Asia)

2100-2230	**S** 12095 (Europe)
2100-2400	5975 (N America & C America), 6195 (SE Asia)
2115-2130	M-F 15390 & M-F 17715 (C America)
2130-2145	Tu/F 11680 (Atlantic & S America)
2200-2230	**S** 9915 (S America)
2200-2300	**W** 5905 (E Asia), 9660 (Pacific), **S** 9890 (E Asia), 12080 (S Pacific)
2200-2400	6175 (N America), **W** 7110 (SE Asia), 9590 (N America), 11955 (SE Asia & Australasia)
2230-2315	**W** 6195 (Europe)
2230-2400	9915 (S America)
2300-2315	**W** 11835 (W Africa)
2300-2400	5965, 7180, **W** 9580 & 11945 (E Asia)
2315-2330	**W** Sa 11835 (W Africa)
2315-2400	**W** Sa 6195 (Europe)
2330-2345	6140 (SE Asia)

USA

FAMILY RADIO—(S Asia)

0100-0200 &	
1610-1810	11550

HERALD BROADCASTING SYNDICATE

0000-0057	W/F-M 7535 (E North Am), M/W/F 9430 (C America & S America), 15665 (E Asia)
0100-0157	7535 (N America), M 9430 (C America & S America)
0200-0257	Su/M 5850 (W North Am), M/Th 7535 (W North Am & C America)
0300-0357	5850 (W North Am), M/W 7535 (E Africa)
0400-0457	M/W 9840 (C Africa & S Africa)
0500-0557	W 7535 (Europe)
0600-0657	Tu/F 7535 (W Europe)
0800-0857	Sa/Su 7535 (Europe), Sa-Th 9845 (Australasia), Su 15665 (E Europe)
0900-0957	Tu/Th 7535 (Europe), **S** 9385 (Australasia), **W** Su/M/W/F 9430 (E Asia), **W** 13840 (Australasia), **S** Su/M/W/F 15665 (E Asia)
1000-1057	M/W/Th 6095 (E North Am), Su 7395 (S America), **W** Th/Sa-Tu 9355 & **S** Th/Sa-Tu 15665 (E Asia), Th/Sa-Tu 15725 (SE Asia)
1100-1157	Tu/F-Su 6095 (E North Am), W/F 7395 (C America & S America), Tu/Th/Sa 9355 (E Asia)
1200-1257	M/W/Th 6095 (E North Am), M/W/F 9355 (SE Asia), Su 9430/9385 (Australasia), Sa 9455 (C America & S America)
1300-1357	Sa-Th 6095 (N America), 9355 (S Asia), Tu/F 9455 (W North Am & C America)
1400-1457	9355 (E Asia)
1600-1657	Sa 18930 (E Africa)
1700-1800	Tu/Th/Sa 18930 (C Africa)
1800-1857	**W** Su/M/W/F 9355 (Europe & Mideast), Th-Tu 9385 (S Africa), **W** Su 11550 (E Europe), **S** Su/M/W/F 13770 (Europe & Mideast), **S** Su 15665 (E Europe), Su/W 18930 (S Africa)
1900-1957	**W** Su/Tu/Th/Sa 9355 (Europe & Mideast), F-M 9385 (S Africa), **W** Su/Tu/Th 11550 (E Europe), **S** Su/Tu/Th/Sa 13770 (Europe & Mideast), **S** Su/Tu/Th 15665 (E Europe)
2000-2057	**W** W/Su 5850 (Europe), **S** F-Tu 9355 (Australasia), **S** Su/W 13770 (Europe), **W** F-Tu 13840 (Australasia)
2100-2157	**W** Su 5850 (E North Am & Europe), **W** W/Sa-M 7510 & **S** Su 13770 (Europe), **S** W/Sa-M 15665 (W Europe)
2200-2257	Su/Th 7510 (Europe), **S** Su/Th 13770 (W Europe), **S** Su/W 13770 (S Europe & W Africa), **W** Su/W 13770 & **S** W/Su 15280 (S America)
2300-2357	Su/W 7510 (S Europe & W Africa), **W** Su/M 13770 & **S** Su/M 15280 (S America)

KAIJ—(N America)

0000-1400	5810
1400-2400	13815
1500-2230	15725

KJES

0100-0200	7555 (W North Am)
0200-0230	7555 (E North Am)
1300-1400	11715 (E North Am)
1400-1500	11715 (W North Am)
1800-1900	15385 (Australasia)

KNLS-NEW LIFE STATION—(E Asia)

0800-0900	**W** 6150 & **S** 9615
1300-1400	7365

KTBN—(E North Am)

0000-0100	**W** 7510 & **S** 15590
0100-1500	7510
1500-1600	**W** 7510 & **S** 15590
1600-2400	15590

KVOH-VOICE OF HOPE—(C America)

0100-0500	9975

KWHR

0000-0100	Tu-Su 17510 (E Asia)
0000-0700	17555 (Australasia)
0100-0400	17510 (E Asia)
0400-0500	**W** 17510 (E Asia)
0400-0800	**S** 17880 (E Asia)
0500-0800	**W** 9930 (E Asia)
0700-1300	11565 (Australasia)
0800-0900	9930 (E Asia)
0900-1000	Su-F 9930 (E Asia)
1000-1100	9930 (E Asia)
1100-1200	Su-F 9930 (E Asia)
1300-1400	Sa 9930 (E Asia)
1300-1900	6020 (Australasia)
1430-1500	Sa/Su 9930 (E Asia)

1500-1600	9930 (E Asia)
1600-1800	6120 (Australasia)
1800-2000	13625 (Australasia)
1900-2400	17555 (Australasia)
2000-2100	[W] M-F 11980 & [S] M-F 15405 (E Asia)
2300-2330	M-F 17510 (E Asia)
2330-2400	Su-F 17510 (E Asia)

UNIVERSITY NETWORK—(S Asia)

0300-0700	[S] 17655
0700-1600	[S] 15500
0800-1100	[W] 17600
1330-1700	[W] 9835

VOA-VOICE OF AMERICA

0000-0100	7215 & [S] 9770 (SE Asia), [W] 9770 (SE Asia & Australasia), [W] 9890 (SE Asia), Tu-Sa 11695 (C America & S America), 11760 (SE Asia), 15185 (SE Asia & S Pacific), 15290 (E Asia), 17735 (E Asia & Australasia), 17820 (E Asia)
0000-0200	Tu-Sa 5995, Tu-Sa 6130, Tu-Sa 7405, Tu-Sa 9455, Tu-Sa 9775 & Tu-Sa 13740 (C America & S America)
0100-0300	7115, 7205, [S] 9635, [W] 9740, [W] 9850, 11705, [S] 11725, [S] 11820, 15250, [W] 15300, 17740 & 17820 (S Asia)
0300-0330	Su-Th 4960 (W Africa & C Africa), 7340 (C Africa & E Africa)
0300-0400	[W] 6035 & [S] 6115 (E Africa & S Africa), 7105 (S Africa)
0300-0430	9885 (Africa)
0300-0500	6080 (S Africa), [S] 7280 (Africa), 7290 (C Africa & E Africa), [W] 7415 (Africa), 9575 (W Africa & S Africa)
0400-0500	[W] 6035 (W Africa & S Africa), [S] 7265 (S Africa & E Africa), [S] 15205 (Mideast & S Asia)
0400-0600	[W] 9775 (C Africa & E Africa)
0400-0700	7170 (N Africa), [S] 11965 (Mideast)
0500-0600	[W] 7295 (W Africa), [W] 9700 (N Africa & W Africa)
0500-0630	5970 (W Africa & C Africa), 6035 (W Africa & S Africa), 6080 & [S] 7195 (W Africa), [S] 9630 & 12080 (Africa)
0500-0700	[W] 11825 (Mideast), 15205 (Mideast & S Asia)
0600-0630	[W] 7285 (W Africa), 11950 (N Africa & E Africa), [W] 15600 (C Africa & E Africa)
0600-0700	[W] 5995 & [S] 9680 (N Africa), 11805 (N Africa & W Africa)
0630-0700	Sa/Su 5970 (W Africa & C Africa), Sa/Su 6035 (W Africa & S Africa), Sa/Su 6080, [S] Sa/Su 7195 & [W] Sa/Su 7285 (W Africa), [S] Sa/Su 9630 (Africa), Sa/Su 11950 (N Africa & E Africa), Sa/Su 12080 (Africa), [W] Sa/Su 15600 (C Africa & E Africa)
1000-1100	6165, 7405 & 9590 (C America)
1000-1200	5985 (Pacific & Australasia), 11720 (E Asia & Australasia)
1000-1500	15425 (SE Asia & Pacific)
1100-1300	[W] 6110 & [S] 6160 (SE Asia)
1100-1400	9645 (SE Asia & Australasia)
1100-1500	9760 (E Asia, S Asia & SE Asia), [W] 11705 & [S] 15160 (E Asia)
1200-1330	11715 (E Asia & Australasia)
1230-1300	Sa 7769 USB (E North Am)
1300-1800	[W] 6110 & [S] 6160 (S Asia & SE Asia)
1400-1800	7125, 7215 & 9645 (S Asia), [W] 15205 (Mideast & S Asia), [S] 15255 (Mideast), 15395 (S Asia)
1500-1700	[W] 9575 (Mideast & S Asia), 9760 (S Asia & SE Asia), [S] 15205 (Europe, N Africa & Mideast)
1500-1800	[S] 6110 (SE Asia), [S] 9700 (Mideast)
1600-1700	6035 (W Africa), 13600 (C Africa & E Africa), 13710 (Africa), 15225 (S Africa)
1600-1800	[W] 12040 & 15445 (E Africa), 17895 (Africa)
1600-2000	[W] 11920 (E Africa)
1600-2130	15410 (Africa)
1700-1800	M-F 5990 & M-F 6045 (E Asia), [S] M-F 7150 (SE Asia & S Pacific), [S] M-F 7170 (E Asia & Australasia), [W] M-F 9525 (E Asia, SE Asia & S Pacific), [S] M-F 9550 & [W] M-F 9670 (E Asia & SE Asia), [S] M-F 9770 (S Asia & SE Asia), M-F 9770 (E Asia), [W] M-F 9795 (S Asia & SE Asia), [W] M-F 11945 (E Asia & Australasia), [W] 15120 & [S] 15135 (Europe), [W] M-F 15255 (E Asia & Australasia)
1700-1900	[W] 6040 (N Africa & Mideast)
1700-2100	[S] 9760 (N Africa & Mideast), [W] 9760 (Mideast & S Asia)
1800-1900	[S] 7415 & [S] 17895 (Africa)
1800-2000	[W] 12025 (E Africa)
1800-2130	6035 (W Africa), [W] 13710 (Africa), 15580 (W Africa)
1830-1900	[W] Sa/Su 7150, [S] Sa/Su 7170, [S] Sa/Su 7330, [W] Sa/Su 9845, [S] Sa/Su 9860 & [W] Sa/Su 15445 (E Africa)
1900-1930	Sa 4950 (W Africa & C Africa)
1900-2000	9525 & 11870 (Australasia), 15180 (Pacific)
1900-2100	[S] 9770 (N Africa & Mideast)
1900-2130	[S] 7375, 7415 & [S] 15445 (Africa)
1930-2030	4950 (W Africa & C Africa)
2000-2030	11855 (W Africa)
2000-2100	17755 (W Africa & C Africa)
2000-2130	17725 (W Africa)
2000-2200	[W] 15205 (Mideast & S Asia)
2030-2100	Sa/Su 4950 (W Africa & C Africa)
2100-2200	[S] 6040 & [W] 6070 (Mideast), [S] 9535 (N Africa & Mideast), [W] 9595 (Mideast), 9760 (E Europe & Mideast), 11870 (Australasia)

American radio's "Northern Exposure" is KNLS—New Life Station, operating from the frosty hinterland of Anchor Point, Alaska.

2100-2400	*15185* (SE Asia & S Pacific), *17735* (E Asia & Australasia)	
2130-2200	Su-F *6035* (W Africa), **S** Su-F 7375 & Su-F *7415* (Africa), Su-F *11975* (C Africa), **W** Su-F *13710*, Su-F *15410* & **S** Su-F *15445* (Africa), Su-F 15580 (W Africa), Su-F 17725 (W Africa)	
2200-2230	M-F *6035* (W Africa), **S** M-F *7340*, **S** M-F 7375, M-F 7415, **W** M-F *12080* & **W** M-F *13710* (Africa)	
2200-2400	7215 (SE Asia), **S** 9705 (SE Asia & Australasia), **S** 9770 (SE Asia), **W** 9770 (SE Asia & Australasia), **W** 9890 & *11760* (SE Asia), *15290* (E Asia), *15305* (E Asia & Australasia), *17820* (E Asia)	

VOICE OF HOPE

1400-1600	*12120* (S Asia)
1800-2100 ▭	*9310* (Europe)

WEWN

0000-0400	5825 (Europe & E North Am), 7425 (W North Am & C America)
0400-0500	**S** Tu-Su 5825 & **W** 5825 (Europe & E North Am), **S** Tu-Su 7425 & **W** 7425 (W North Am & C America)
0500-0600	**W** Tu-Su 5825 (Europe & E North Am), **W** Tu-Su 7425 (W North Am & C America)
0600-0700	**S** 5825 (Europe & E North Am), **S** 7425 (W North Am & C America)
0700-0800	7425 (W North Am & C America)
0700-1000	5825 (Europe & E North Am)
0800-1300	7425 (N America & C America)
1000-1200	**W** 7465 (Europe)
1200-1600	15665 (Europe)
1300-1400	7425 (E North Am)
1300-1600	11875 (W North Am & C America)
1600-1700	**S** M-Sa 11875 & **W** 11875 (E North Am), **S** M-Sa 13615, **S** Su 13615 & **W** 13615 (W North Am & C America), **S** M-Sa 15665 & **W** 15665 (Europe)
1700-1800	**W** M-Sa 11875 (E North Am), **W** M-Sa 13615 (W North Am & C America), **W** M-Sa 15665 (Europe)
1800-1900	**S** 11875 (E North Am), **S** 13615 (W North Am & C America)
1800-2000	**S** 15745 (Europe)
1900-2200	11875 (E North Am), **W** 17695 (Europe)
1900-2400	13615 (W North Am & C America)
2000-2200	7425 (E North Am), **S** 13695 (Europe)

2000-2400	5825 (Europe & E North Am)
2200-2400	**S** 11820 (Europe)

WGTG—(W North Am & C America)

0000-0600	5085
1000-2155	9400
2155-2255	**S** 9400
2200-2300	**W** 5085
2300-2400	5085

WINB-WORLD INTERNATIONAL BROADCASTING

1700-1900	15715 (Europe)
1900-2200	11740 (Europe)
2200-0300	11950 (C America)

WJCR

24 Hr	7490 (E North Am)
1500-0300 ◁	13595 (W North Am & E Asia)

WMLK—(Europe, Mideast & N America)

0400-0900 &	
1700-2200	Su-F 9465

WORLD HARVEST RADIO

0000-0300	5745 (E North Am)
0145-0200	M 7315 (C America)
0200-0230	Tu-Su 7315 (C America)
0230-0400	7315 (C America)
0300-1000	5760/5745 (E North Am)
0400-0600	Tu-Su 7315 (C America)
0600-0800	7315 (C America)
0800-0900	Sa/Su 7315 (C America)
0900-1000	7315 (C America)
1000-1300	6040 (E North Am & C America)
1300-1500	6040 (E North Am)
1300-1800	15105 (C America)
1500-2200	13760 (E North Am & W Europe)
1800-2400	9495 (N America & C America)
2200-2400	5745 (E North Am)

WRMI-R MIAMI INTERNATIONAL—(N America & C America)

0000-0100 ◁	Tu-Su 9955
0100-0115 ◁	Su-F 9955
0115-0145 ◁	M 9955
0145-0300 ◁	M-Sa 9955
0300-0400 ◁	Su 9955
0400-0430 ◁	Su/Tu/Sa 9955
0430-0445 ◁	Tu-Sa 9955
0445-0500 ◁	M-Su 9955
0500-1100 ◁	M-Sa 9955
1300-1400 ◁	Su 9955
1400-1445 ◁	Sa/Su 9955
1445-1500 ◁	9955
1500-1700 ◁	M-Sa 9955
1700-1715 ◁	M-F 9955
1715-1730 &	
1730-1900 ◁	Su-F 9955
1900-2000 ◁	9955
2000-2115 ◁	Su-F 9955
2115-2200 ◁	9955
2200-2230 &	
2230-2400 ◁	M-Sa 9955

WRNO WORLDWIDE—(E North Am)

0000-0300	**S** 7355

0400-0700 ◁	7395
1400-1500	**S** 7395
1500-1600	7395
1600-2300	7355/15420
2300-2400	**S** 7355

WWBS (Projected)

0100-1300 ◁	11910

WWCR

0000-0100	7435 (E North Am), 13845 (W North Am)
0000-0300	5065/5070 (E North Am & Europe)
0000-0400	3215 (E North Am)
0100-1000	2390 (E North Am)
0100-1200	5935 (E North Am & Europe)
0200-0300	**W** M 5065/5070 (E North Am & Europe)
0200-0400	Tu-Su 5065/5070 (E North Am & Europe)
0300-0400	**S** M 5065/5070 (E North Am & Europe)
0400-0900	3210 (E North Am)
0400-1100	5065/5070 (E North Am & Europe)
0900-1000	**S** 3210 (E North Am)
0900-1100	**W** 7435 (E North Am)
1000-1100	**S** 15685 (E North Am & Europe)
1000-2200	9475 (E North Am)
1100-1200	**W** 5065/5070 (E North Am & Europe)
1100-1300	7435 (E North Am)
1100-2100	15685 (E North Am & Europe)
1200-1400	**W** 5935 (E North Am & Europe), **S** 13845 (W North Am)
1200-1500	**S** 12160 (E North Am & Europe)
1300-1500	**W** 7435 (E North Am)
1400-2400	13845 (W North Am)
1500-2300	12160 (E North Am & Europe)
2100-2200	**S** 15685 (E North Am & Europe)
2200-2300	**S** 9475 & **W** 9475 (E North Am)
2200-2400	7435 (E North Am)
2215-2245 ◁	F-Tu 15685 (E North Am & Europe)
2245-2400 ◁	Sa/Su 15685 (E North Am & Europe)
2300-2400	5065/5070 (E North Am & Europe), 9475 (E North Am)

WYFR-FAMILY RADIO

0000-0100	6085 (E North Am)
0004-0100	**S** 9505 (W North Am)
0100-0445	6065 (E North Am), 9505 (W North Am)
0400-0745	9985 (Europe)
0500-0600	**S** 11580 & **W** 11695 (Europe)
0500-0700	5985 (W North Am)
0600-0745	7355 (Europe)
0700-0800	**W** 9455 & **S** 13695 (W Africa)
1000-1500	5950 (E North Am)
1100-1200	**S** 11830 (W North Am)
1100-1245	**W** 7355 (W North Am)
1200-1245	**S** 6015 (W North Am)
1200-1345	**W** 11970 (C America)
1200-1700	11830 (W North Am), **S** 17750 (C America)
1300-1400	13695 (E North Am)

1400-1700	W 17760 (C America)
1600-1700	21525 (C Africa & S Africa)
1600-1745	S 21745 (Europe)
1600-1800	W 17555 (Europe)
1600-1845	15695 (Europe)
1604-1700	S 11705 & W 15215 (W North Am)
1800-1900	W 9825 & W 9835 (N Africa)
1800-1945	17555 (Europe)
1845-1900	S 15695 (Europe)
1945-2145	S 17555 (Europe)
2000-2045	21525 (C Africa & S Africa)
2000-2100	S 5810 (Europe)
2000-2200	W 7355 (Europe)
2000-2245	W 15565 & S 17845 (W Africa)
2045-2245	S 21525 (C Africa & S Africa)
2100-2245	W 11580 (C Africa & S Africa)

VATICAN STATE
VATICAN RADIO
0140-0200	5980, W 7335, S 9650 & S 11935 (S Asia)
0250-0310	W 6095 & 7305 (E North Am), S 9605 (E North Am & C America)
0320-0350	7360 & 9660/5865 (E Africa)
0500-0530	W 7360 (E Africa), 9660 (Africa), 11625 & S 13765 (E Africa)
0600-0620 ◄	4010/4005 (Europe), 6245/5860 (W Europe)
0630-0700	W 7360 (W Africa), W 9660 (Africa), S 11625 (W Africa), W 11625 (Africa), S 13765 (W Africa), S 15570 (Africa)
0730-0745 ◄	M-Sa 4010/4005 (Europe), M-Sa 6245/5860 (W Europe), M-Sa 7250 & M-Sa 9645 (Europe), M-Sa 11740 (W Europe & N Africa), M-Sa 15210/15215 (Mideast)
1020-1030	M-Sa 17550 (Africa)
1120-1130 ◄	M-Sa 6245 & M-Sa 7250 (Europe), M-Sa 11740 (W Europe), M-Sa 15210 (Mideast)
1120-1130	W 17585 (Africa)
1345-1405	W 9500, 11625 & S 13765 (Australasia), 15585 (SE Asia)
1545-1600	W 9500, 11640 & S 15585 (S Asia)
1600-1630	W Sa 9500, Sa 11640 & Sa 15585 (S Asia)
1600-1635	W Sa 9660 (E Africa)
1615-1630	S 7250 (N Europe), S 11810 (Mideast)
1715-1730 ◄	6245 (Europe), 9645 (W Europe)
1715-1730	W 7250 (Mideast)
1730-1800	W 7305 & W 9660 (E Africa), 11625 (E Africa & S Africa), S 13765 (E Africa), S 15570 (Africa)
2000-2030	W 7355 & 9645 (Africa), 11625 & S 13765 (W Africa)
2050-2110 ◄	3945/4005 (Europe), 5882/5885 (W Europe)

VIETNAM
VOICE OF VIETNAM
0100-0130 &	
0230-0300	W 5940 & S 7250 (E North Am)
0330-0400	S 7260 (C America)
1000-1030	9840, W 12020 & S 15010 (SE Asia)
1100-1130	7285 & 9730 (SE Asia)
1230-1300	9840, W 12020 & S 15010 (E Asia & Americas)
1330-1400	9840, W 12020 & S 15010 (SE Asia)
1600-1630	9840, W 12020 & S 15010 (Africa)
1800-1830,	
1900-1930 &	
2030-2100	9840, W 12020 & S 15010 (Europe)
2330-2400	9840, W 12020 & S 15010 (E Asia & Americas)

YEMEN
REPUBLIC OF YEMEN RADIO—(Mideast & E Africa)
0600-0700 &	
1800-1900	9780

YUGOSLAVIA
RADIO YUGOSLAVIA
0000-0030	S M-Sa 9580 & S M-Sa 11870 (E North Am)
0100-0130	W M-Sa 6195 & W M-Sa 7115 (E North Am)
0200-0230	W 6195 & W 7130 (W North Am)
0430-0500	S 9580 & S 11800 (W North Am)
1330-1400	W 11835 (Australasia)
1900-1930	S Su-F 7230 (Australasia)
1930-2000 ◄	6100 (W Europe), 9720 (S Africa)
2200-2230 ◄	6100 (Europe), 6185 (W Europe)

ZAMBIA
CHRISTIAN VOICE—(S Africa)
0355-0700	3330/6065
0700-1600	6065
1600-2200	3330/4965

RADIO ZAMBIA-ZNBC
0250-0530	4910/6265
0250-0600	6165
0530-1500	7220
0600-1430	6165/7235
1430-2200	6165
1500-2205	4910/6265

ZIMBABWE
ZIMBABWE BROADCASTING CORPORATION
0300-0530	3396
0800-1630	5975, 6045/7285
1700-2200	4828/3396

2245-2305	W 6065 (SE Asia), W 7305 (E Asia), 9600 & 11830 (Australasia)	

Voices from Home—1998

Country-by-Country Guide to Native Broadcasts

For some listeners, English offerings are merely icing on the cake. Their real interest is in eavesdropping on broadcasts for *nativos*—the home folks. These can be enjoyable regardless of language, especially when they offer traditional music from other cultures.

Some you'll hear, many you won't—depending on your location and receiving equipment. Keep in mind that native-language broadcasts tend to be weaker than those in English, so you may need more patience and better hardware. PASSPORT REPORTS tests for which radios are best.

Times and days of the week are in World Time, explained in "Setting Your World Time Clock" earlier in the book, as well as in the glossary; for local times, see "Addresses PLUS." Midyear, some stations are an hour earlier (◀▭) or later (l) for summer savings time, typically April through October. Stations may also extend their hours during holidays or for sports events.

Frequencies in *italics* may be best, as they come from relay transmitters that might be near you. Frequencies with no target zones are typically from transmitters designed for domestic coverage, so these are the least likely to be heard well by you unless you're in or near that country.

When to Tune

Some broadcasts come in best during the day within world band segments from 9300 to 17900 kHz. However, signals from Latin America and Africa peak near or during darkness, especially from 4700 to 5100 kHz. See "Best Times and Frequencies" earlier in this book for solid guidance.

Schedules Prepared for Entire Year

To be as helpful as possible throughout the year, PASSPORT's schedules consist of not just observed activity and other factual data, but also of schedules which we have creatively opined will be in use. This latter material is original from us, and therefore will not be so exact as factual information.

Most frequencies are aired year round. Those used only seasonally are labeled **S** for summer (midyear), and **W** for winter.

ARGENTINA—Spanish
RADIO ARGENTINA AL EXTERIOR-RAE
0000-0200	Tu-Sa 15345 (Americas)
1200-1400	M-F 11710 (S America)
2200-2300	M-F 15345 (Europe & N Africa)
2300-2400	M-F 15345 (Americas)

RADIO NACIONAL
0000-0200	Su/M 15345 (Americas)
0900-1200	M-F 15345
0900-1500	6060 (S America)
1500-1600	M-F 15345 (S America)
1800-2300	Sa/Su 15345 (Europe & N Africa)
2300-2400	Su/M 15345 (Americas)

ARMENIA—Armenian
VOICE OF ARMENIA
0100-0130 ▭	9965 (S America)
1730-1830 ▭	4810 (E Europe, Mideast & W Asia), 4990 & 7480 (Mideast & N Africa)
1900-2000	**S** 7480 (Europe)
2000-2100	7480 (Europe)
2000-2200 ▭	4810 (E Europe, Mideast & W Asia), 4990 (Mideast & N Africa)
2100-2130 & 2215-2245 ▭	9965 (Europe & C America)

AUSTRIA—German
RADIO AUSTRIA INTERNATIONAL
0000-0030	**W** 9495 (S America), 9655/7325 (E North Am), 9870 & **S** 13730 (S America)
0100-0200	9870 (S America)
0100-0230	**W** 9495 (S America), 9655/7325 (E North Am), **S** 13730 (S America)
0200-0230	9870 (C America)
0300-0330	**W** 9495 (S America), 9870 (C America), **S** 13730 (S America)
0400-0430	M-Sa 6155 (Europe), M-Sa 13730 (E Europe)
0430-0500	**W** 6155 (Europe), **W** 13730 (E Europe)
0500-0510	17870 (Mideast)
0500-0530	*6015* (N America), 6155 (Europe), 13730 (E Europe), 15410 (Mideast)
0510-0530	M-Sa 17870 (Mideast)
0530-0600	**S** 6155 (Europe), **S** 13730 (E Europe), **S** 15410 & **S** 17870 (Mideast)

0600-0610	15410 (Mideast)
0600-0630	*6015* (N America), 6155 (Europe), 13730 (E Europe), 17870 (Mideast)
0610-0630	M-Sa 15410 (Mideast)
0630-0700	**W** 6155 (Europe), **W** 13730 (E Europe), **W** 15410 & **W** 17870 (Mideast)
0700-0730	6155 (Europe), 13730 (E Europe), 15410 & 17870 (Mideast)
0800-0830	6155 (Europe), 13730 (N Europe), **W** 15240 (E Asia), 17870 (Australasia)
0830-0900	**S** 6155 (Europe), **S** 13730 (N Europe), **S** 17870 (Australasia)
0900-0930	**S** 15455 (E Asia), 17870 (Australasia)
0900-1030	6155 (Europe), 13730 (N Europe), **W** 15240 (E Asia)
0930-1000	**S** Su 15455 (E Asia), **S** Su 17870 & **W** 17870 (Australasia)
1000-1030	**S** 15455 (E Asia), 17870 (Australasia)
1030-1100	**W** Su 6155 (Europe), **S** 13730 & **W** Su 13730 (N Europe), **W** Su 15240 & **S** M-Sa 15455 (E Asia), **S** M-Sa 17870 & **W** Su 17870 (Australasia)
1100-1130	6155 (Europe), 13730 (W Europe & E North Am), **S** 15455 (E Asia)
1200-1230	6155 (Europe), 13730 (W Europe & E North Am)
1230-1300	**W** 6155 (Europe), **W** 13730 (W Europe & E North Am)
1300-1330	6155 (Europe), 13730 (W Europe & E North Am)
1400-1430	M-Sa 6155 (Europe), M-Sa 13730 (S Europe & W Africa)
1430-1500	**S** 6155 (Europe), **S** 13730 (S Europe & W Africa)
1500-1530	6155 (Europe), **W** 9655 (Mideast), **W** 11780 (S Asia & SE Asia), 13730 (S Europe & W Africa)
1500-1630	**S** 11855 (Mideast), **S** 13710 (S Asia & SE Asia)
1530-1600	**S** 6155 (Europe), **S** 13730 (S Europe & W Africa)
1600-1630	6155 (Europe), **W** 11780 (S Asia & SE Asia), 13730 (S Europe & W Africa)
1600-1730	**W** 9655 (Mideast)
1630-1700	**W** 6155 (Europe), **W** 13730 (S Europe & W Africa)
1700-1730	6155 (Europe), **W** 11780 & **S** 13710 (S Asia & SE Asia), 13730 (S Europe & W Africa)
1800-1810	**S** 11855 & **S** 13730 (Mideast)
1800-1930	5945 & 6155 (Europe)
1810-1830	**S** M-Sa 13730 (Mideast)
1830-1900	**S** 13730 (Mideast)
1900-1930	**W** 9495 (S Africa)
1900-2030	**S** 13730 (S Africa)
1930-2000	**S** 5945 & **S** 6155 (Europe)

2000-2030	5945 & 6155 (Europe), ▦ 9495 (S Africa)
2100-2130 &	
2200-2230	5945 & 6155 (Europe), ▦ 9495 & ▪ 13730 (S Africa)
2300-2330	M-Sa 9870 (S America)

BELGIUM
RADIO VLAANDEREN INTERNATIONAL
Dutch

0500-0600	▪ 7240 (S Europe), ▪ 11640 (Africa)
0600-0700	▦ 5985 (Europe), ▦ 9925 (Africa)
0700-0730 ◄	5985 (Europe), 9925/9920 (S Europe & Australasia)
0730-0830	▪ M-Sa 7190 (Europe)
0830-0900 ◄	M-Sa 6035 & M-Sa 9925 (Europe)
0830-0930	▦ M-Sa 9905 (Europe)
0900-0930 ◄	6035 & 9925 (Europe)
0900-1100 ◄	Su 17610/17595 (Africa)
0930-1100 ◄	Su 6035 & Su 9925 (Europe)
1000-1100	▪ 15545 (Africa)
1100-1130	▪ 11640 (Europe), ▪ 17595/17690 (Africa)
1100-1200 ◄	M-Sa 6035 (Europe), 17610/17595 (Africa)
1100-1200	▦ 15510 (Africa)
1200-1230 ◄	6035 (Europe)
1200-1230	▦ 9925 (Europe), ▪ 13610 (E North Am), ▪ 15540 (SE Asia), ▦ 17610/17595 (Africa)
1230-1300	▪ M-Sa 13610 (E North Am), ▪ M-Sa 15540 (SE Asia)
1300-1330	▦ 13670 (E North Am)
1300-1700	▪ Su 11640 (Europe)
1330-1400	▦ M-Sa 13670 (E North Am)
1400-1530	▦ Su 5915 (Europe)
1400-1700 ◄	Su 9925 (Europe), Su 17690 (Africa)
1430-1600	▪ Sa 9925 (Europe)
1530-1700	▦ Sa/Su 5915 (Europe)
1600-1630	▪ 9925 (S Europe & N Africa), ▪ 13795 (Mideast), ▪ 17640 (Africa)
1700-1730	▦ 9925 (Mideast), ▦ 11765 (Africa)
1800-1830 ◄	5910 & 9925 (Europe)
1800-1830	▦ 9925 (Europe)
1800-2010	▪ W/Sa 13685 (Africa)
1900-2000	▪ 9925 (Europe), ▪ 13645 (Africa)
1900-2110	▦ W/Sa 9940 (Africa)
2000-2030	▪ 9925 (Europe)
2000-2100	▦ 5910 (Europe), ▦ 9925 (Africa)
2100-2130 ◄	5910 (Europe)
2100-2130	▦ 9925 (Europe), ▦ Su 9925 (Africa)
2200-2300	▪ 9925 (E North Am), ▪ 11690 (S America)
2300-2400	▦ 5900 (E North Am), ▦ 9925 (S America)

French

0800-0830 ◄	6035 & 9925 (Europe), 15545 (Africa)
0930-1000	▪ M-Sa 15545 (Africa)
1030-1100 ◄	M-Sa 6035 (Europe), M-Sa 17610/

	17595 (Africa)
1030-1100	▦ M-Sa 15510 (Africa)
1330-1400	▪ M-Sa 13610 (E North Am), ▪ M-Sa 15540 (SE Asia)
1430-1500	▦ M-Sa 13670 (E North Am)
1830-1900	▪ 13645 (Africa)
1930-2000 ◄	5910 (Europe)
1930-2000	▦ 9925 (Africa)
2130-2200	▪ 9925 (E North Am), ▪ 13800 (S America)
2230-2300	▦ 5900 (E North Am), ▦ 9925 (S America)

BRAZIL—Portuguese
RADIO NACIONAL DA AMAZONIA

0700-0800 ➡	M-F 6180, M-F 11780
0800-2400 ➡	6180, 11780

RADIO BANDEIRANTES

24 Hr	6090, 9645, 11925

RADIO NACIONAL DO BRASIL-RADIOBRAS

0115-0215	Tu-Sa 11780 (N America)
0415-0515	Tu-Sa 11765 (N America)
1630-1750	15265 (Europe & Mideast)

CANADA—French
CANADIAN BROADCASTING CORPORATION—(E North Am)

0100-0300 ◄	M 9625
0300-0400 ◄	Su 9625 & Tu-Sa 9625
1300-1310 &	
1500-1555 ◄	M-F 9625
1700-1715 ◄	Su 9625
1900-1945 ◄	M-F 9625
1900-2310 ◄	Sa 9625

RADIO CANADA INTERNATIONAL

0000-0030	▪ Tu-Sa 9535 & ▪ Tu-Sa 11940 (C America & S America), ▪ Tu-Sa 13670 (S America)
0000-0100	▪ 5960 (E North Am)
0100-0130	▦ 9535 & ▦ 11725 (C America & S America)
0100-0200 ◄	9755 (E North Am & C America)
0130-0200	▦ Su/M 9535 & ▦ Su/M 11725 (C America & S America)
0230-0300	▪ Tu-Sa 6120 (E North Am & C America), ▪ Tu-Sa 9535 & ▪ Tu-Sa 11715 (C America & S America)
0300-0330	▦ 6025, ▦ 9505, ▪ 9760 & ▪ 11835 (Mideast)
0330-0400	▦ Tu-Sa 6155 (E North Am & C America), ▦ Tu-Sa 9755 (C America)
0530-0600	▪ M-F 7295 (W Europe & N Africa), ▪ M-F 15430 (Africa)
0630-0700 ◄	M-F 6050 (Europe)
0630-0700	▦ M-F 6150 (Europe), ▦ M-F 9740 (Africa), ▦ M-F 9760 (Europe & N Africa), ▦ M-F 11905 (Mideast)
1200-1230	▦ 6150 (E Asia)
1200-1300	▪ 15305 (E North Am & C America)

1230-1300	**S** *9660* (E Asia), **W** *11730* & **S** *15195* (SE Asia)
1300-1400 ◩	9650 (E North Am & C America)
1300-1400	**W** 15425 (C America)
1300-1600	**S** Su 15305 (E North Am & C America)
1400-1500	**S** M-Sa 15305, **S** *15325* & **S** M-Sa 17820 (Europe), **S** M-Sa 17895 (W Europe & Africa)
1400-1700	**W** Su 15325 (C America)
1500-1600 ◩	*11935* (Europe & Mideast)
1500-1600	**W** *9555* (Europe & Mideast), **W** *11915* & **W** M-Sa 15325 (Europe), **W** 17820 (W Europe & Africa)
1900-2000	**S** 11700 (Europe), **S** 13670 (Africa), **S** 15325 (Europe), **S** 17820 (Africa), **S** 17870 (Europe & N Africa)
2000-2100 ◩	*5995* (Europe), 7235 (S Europe & N Africa), 15150 (Africa)
2000-2100	**W** *9735* (Africa), **W** 9805 (W Europe & N Africa), **W** 11945 (W Africa), **W** 13650 (Europe & N Africa), **W** 13690 & **W** 17820 (Africa)
2130-2200	**S** 11690 (Europe), **S** 13650 (Europe & N Africa), **S** 13670 (Africa), **S** 13740 (C America), **S** 15305 (C America & S America), **S** 17820 (Africa)
2230-2300 ◩	*5995* (Europe), 7235 (S Europe & N Africa), 9755 (E North Am & C America)
2230-2300	**W** 5960 (E North Am), **W** *9735* (Africa), *11705* (SE Asia), **W** 11945 (W Africa), **W** 13690 (Africa), **S** 15305 (C America & S America)

CHINA
CENTRAL PEOPLE'S BROADCASTING STATION

Chinese

0000-0030	**W** 5320, 10260, **S** 15550
0000-0100	5880, 5915, 5955, 6125, 6750, **W** 6790, **W** 7770, **W** 7935, 9080, 9170, **S** 11000, 11740, **S** 15390, **S** 15500
0000-0200	4800, 9755, 9775
0000-0300	**W** 6890, 9610/9530, **S** 11040
0000-0600	6840, 7504, 9064, 9290, 11610, 11800, 12120
0030-0200	11630
0030-0600	15550
0055-0612	11100, 11935, 15710
0100-0200	**W** 9080, **S** 17605
0100-0210	**W** 11740
0100-0211	**S** 17700
0100-0600	15390, 15500
0200-0600	7315, 17605
0211-0600	17700
0300-0600	11040

0355-0604	11000, 15880
0600-0855	W-M 6840, W-M 7315, W-M 9290, W-M 11800, W-M 12120, W-M 15390, W-M 15550, W-M 17605
0600-0900	Th/Sa-M 7504, Th/Sa-Tu 11040, Th/Sa-Tu 15500
0600-0955	Th/Sa-Tu 9064, Th/Sa-Tu 11610
0600-1000	Th/Sa-Tu 17700
0604-0930	W-M 15880
0604-0955	W-M 11000
0855-0930	17605
0855-0945	15550
0855-1000	7315, 12120
0855-1023	15390
0855-1100	11800
0855-1731	6840, 9290
0900-0955	**W** Th/Sa-Tu 6890, **W** Th/Sa-Tu 7770, **S** Th/Sa-Tu 11040, **S** Th/Sa-Tu 15500
0900-1731	7504
0930-0955	**W** W-M 5090, **S** W-M 15880
0930-1100	**W** 9080, **S** 17605
0945-1130	**W** 5320, **S** 15550
0955-1100	**W** 6890, 11000, **S** 11040, **S** 15880
0955-1200	**W** 7770, **S** 15500
0955-1230	4800
0955-1400	**W** 7620, **S** 11935
0955-1600	9064
0955-1700	**W** 6015, **S** 11100
0955-1804	**W** 5090
0955-2400	**W** 5125, **S** 9380
1000-1100	**W** 11740, **S** 17700
1000-1330	**W** 4460, **S** 12120
1000-1600	**W** 5163, **S** 9755, 11610
1023-1200	**S** 15390
1024-1200	**W** 7935
1030-1200	9775
1045-1500	**S** 13610
1100-1300	11630
1100-1345	**W** 7345, **S** 11675/11825
1100-1600	6890, 7440, 7516, 11740
1100-1731	**W** 3220, 5880, 6125, 6750, 9080, 9800, **S** 11800
1100-1804	**W** 6790, **S** 9170, **S** 11000
1130-1731	5320
1200-1330	10260
1200-1731	7935
1230-1600	7770
1300-1600	4800, 9775
1330-1600	11630
1330-1731	4460
1400-2300	7620
1700-2230	6015
2000-2230	4460
2000-2300	5320
2000-2330	**W** 3220, **S** 11800
2000-2400	5880, 5915, 5955, 5995, 6125, 6750, 6840, 7504, 7935, 9080, 9290, 9610/9530
2055-2200	**S** 11000/6790

2055-2300	**W** 5090, **S** 9170
2055-2400	**W** 6790
2100-2330	4905, 5163, 6890, 7516, 7770, 11630
2100-2400	9064, 10260, 11610, 11740
2200-2400	**S** 11000
2230-2400	**W** 4460, 4800, **W** 6015, 9775, **S** 11100, **S** 12120
2300-2400	**W** 5320, **W** 7620, 9170, **S** 11935, **S** 15550
2330-2400	**W** 6890, **W** 7770, 9755, **S** 11040, 11800, **S** 15500

CHINA RADIO INTERNATIONAL
Chinese
0200-0300	*9690* (N America & C America), *9710 & 11695* (N America), 15435 (S America)
0300-0400	*9730* (W North Am)
0400-0500	*9710 & 11695* (N America)
0900-1000	9480 (E Asia), 9945 & 11500 (Australasia), 15180 (E Asia)
0900-1100	6590 (E Asia), 11840, 11945 & 12015 (SE Asia)
1200-1400	11945 & 15260 (SE Asia)
1300-1400	9440 (SE Asia)
1500-1600	**S** 7110, 9457 (S Asia), **S** 11980 (S Asia & E Africa)
1730-1830	**W** 4020 & 5250 (E Asia), 7110, 7335 & 7800 (Europe & N Africa), 9820 (N Africa & W Africa)
2000-2100	**W** 6955 (N Africa & W Africa), 7185, **W** 7435 & 7660 (E Europe), **W** 7780 (W Africa), **W** 9710 (E Africa), **S** 11650 (E Europe)
2100-2130 ⬅	*6165* (Europe)
2230-2300	9535 (E Asia), *9770* (C Africa & S Africa), *11790* (C Africa & E Africa)
2230-2330	6140 (SE Asia), **W** 7110 (Australasia), 7190, **W** 7230 (SE Asia), 7335, **S** 8260 (E Asia), 9440, 9870, **S** 11685 & 12015 (SE Asia), 12065, 15400 (SE Asia)

Cantonese
0100-0200	*9710 & 11695* (N America)
1000-1100	11915 (Australasia)
1100-1200	7335, 11945 (SE Asia)
1700-1800	**W** 6920, 9900 & **S** 11575 (S Asia & E Africa)
1900-2000	**W** 7780 (W Africa)

CHINA (TAIWAN)
BROADCASTING CORPORATION OF CHINA
Chinese
0000-0100	**S** 15125, 15270
0000-0400	7295
0000-0700	9280 (E Asia)
0000-0900	9610
0000-1700	11725, 11885
0100-1700	15125
1100-1200 &	
1300-1500	9610

2055-2400	11885, **S** 15125
2100-2400	11725
2200-2400	*5950* (E North Am), 9610, *11740* (C America), *11855* (W North Am), 15270, *15440* (C America)

VOICE OF FREE CHINA
Chinese
0000-0100	**W** *9690*, **W** *11720*, **S** *15130* & **S** *17805* (S America)
0100-0200	**W** *11825, 15215* & **S** *17845* (S America)
0400-0500	*5950* (E North Am & C America), 7130 (SE Asia), *9680* (W North Am), 11825, 15270 & 15345 (SE Asia)
0700-0800	7130 (SE Asia)
0900-1000	7445 (SE Asia), 9610 (Australasia), 11745 (E Asia), 11915, 15270 & 15345 (SE Asia)
1200-1300	11745 (E Asia), 15270 (SE Asia)
1900-2000	9955 (Mideast & N Africa), **W** *9985*, **S** *15600*, **S** *17750* & **W** *17760* (Europe)

Cantonese
0100-0200	*5950* (E North Am), *15440* (C America)
0300-0400	*11740* (C America)
0500-0600	*5950* (E North Am & C America), *9680* (W North Am), 11825, 11915, 15270 & 15345 (SE Asia)
1000-1100	7285, 7445 & 11915 (SE Asia)
1100-1200	15270 (SE Asia)
1300-1400	11550/11915 & 15345 (SE Asia)

VOICE OF ASIA
Chinese
0500-0700	7285 (E Asia)
0700-1100	9280 (E Asia)
0800-0900	7285 (E Asia)
1300-1445 &	
1450-1500	7445 (SE Asia)

Cantonese
0800-0900	7445 (E Asia)

CARACOL COLOMBIA
24 Hr	5077

ECOS DEL ATRATO
1000-0500	5019

RADIO NACIONAL
1100-0445	4955

CROATIAN RADIO
0000-0100 ⬅	5895 (Europe)
0208-0300 &	
0308-0400 ⬅	5895 (Europe & E North Am)
0410-0500 &	
0510-0600 ⬅	5895 (Europe & N America)
0600-0700 ⬅	5895 & 9830 (Europe)
0600-0700	**W** 13830 (Australasia)
0700-0710 ⬅	Sa/Su 5920 (Europe)

1230-1300	13830 (N America)
1310-1800	13830 (E North Am)
1600-1900 ▣	5895 (Europe)
1900-1910	S 11635 (N America)
1910-2200	11635 (N America)
1910-2300 &	
2310-2400 ▣	5895 (Europe)

CUBA—Spanish
RADIO HABANA CUBA

0000-0100	6000 (E North Am)
0000-0300	9550 & 11970 (S America)
0000-0500	5965 (C America), 6070 (C America & W North Am), 9505 (S America), 11760 (Americas), 13715/11875 (S America)
0200-0500	6180 (E North Am)
1100-1400	9550 (C America & S America)
1100-1500	6180 & 11760 (C America)
1200-1400	15340 (S America)
1200-1500	6070 (C America & W North Am)
2100-2300	W 9820 (Europe & N Africa), 9830 USB (E North Am & Europe), 11760 & S 13680 (Europe & N Africa)

RADIO REBELDE
24 Hr	5025

CYPRUS
CYPRUS BROADCASTING CORP—(Europe)
Greek
2215-2245	F-Su 6180, W F-Su 7105, S F-Su 7205, W F-Su 9675 & F-Su 9760

RADIO MONTE CARLO—(N America)
Arabic
0400-0420 ▣	5960 & 9755

DOMINICAN REPUBLIC—Spanish
RADIO CRISTAL INTERNACIONAL
2100-0300	5012

ECUADOR—Spanish
HCJB-VOICE OF THE ANDES
1030-1400	9765 (N America), 11960 (S America)
	1030-0504 6050 (S America)
1400-0504	15140 (N America & S America)
2130-2230	W 12025 & 15550 (Europe)

RADIO QUITO
24 Hr	4919

EGYPT—Arabic
EGYPTIAN RADIO
0000-0030 ▣	9700 (N Africa), 11665 (C Africa & E Africa), 15285 (Mideast)
0150-0700 ▣	12050 (Europe & E North Am)
0200-2200 ▣	9755 (N Africa & Mideast)
0300-0600 ▣	9850 (N Africa & Mideast)
0300-2400 ▣	15285 (Mideast)
0350-0700 ▣	9620 & 9770 (N Africa)
0350-1800 ▣	11665 (Mideast)
0350-2400 ▣	9800 (Mideast)

0600-1400 ▣	11980 (N Africa & Mideast)
0600-1410 ▣	15480
0700-1100 ▣	15115 (W Africa)
0700-1500 ▣	11785 (N Africa)
0700-1530 ▣	12050 (Europe, E North Am & E Africa)
1100-2400 ▣	9850 (N Africa)
1245-1900 ▣	17670 (N Africa)
1530-2400 ▣	12050 (Europe & N America)
1800-2400 ▣	9700 (N Africa)
1900-2400 ▣	11665 (C Africa & E Africa)

RADIO CAIRO
0000-0045	15220 (C America & S America), 17770 (S America)
0030-0330	9900 (E North Am)
0330-0430	9900 (W North Am)
1015-1215	17745 (Mideast & S Asia)
1100-1130	17800 (C Africa & S Africa)
1245-1600	15220 (C Africa)
2000-2200	11990 (Australasia)
2345-2400	15220 (C America & S America), 17770 (S America)

FRANCE—French
RADIO FRANCE INTERNATIONALE
0000-0030	S 15440 (SE Asia)
0000-0100	W 5920 (C America), W 7120 (S Asia & SE Asia), 9800 (S America), S 9805 (S Asia & SE Asia), S 11670 (C America), 12025 (SE Asia)
0000-0200	9715 (S America), 9790 (C America)
0100-0200	W 11600 & S 15440 (S Asia)
0200-0300	5920 (C America & N America), 9715 (S America)
0200-0500	9800 (C America)
0300-0400	7315 (Mideast)
0300-0445	5990 (E Europe)
0300-0500	S 7280 (E Europe), S 9550 (Mideast), S 11700 (E Africa)
0300-0600	6045 (E Europe), W 7280 & S 11685 (Mideast)
0300-0700	9790 (Africa)
0300-0800	7135 (Africa)
0400-0500	5920 (C America & N America), 5925 (N America), S 6175 (S Africa), 9805 (Mideast)
0400-0600 ▣	9805 (E Africa)
0400-0600	4890 (C Africa), W 5945 (E Africa & Mideast), W 7315 (Mideast), S 9745 (E Europe)
0445-0545	W 5990 (E Europe)
0500-0600	S 9805 (E Europe), 11700 & S 15155 (E Africa)
0500-0700 ▣	11995 (E Africa)
0500-0700	W 5925 & S 7305 (N Africa), W 9550 & S 15605 (Mideast)
0500-0800	7280 (E Europe)
0600-0700	W 5990 & W 6045 (E Europe), 9845 (W Africa), 15155 & S 17800 (E Africa)

Don Moore

In Guatemalan villages, everyone knows where the radio station is, so La Voz de Atitlán, 2390 kHz, needs no fancy sign. Until peace accords were signed in 1996, Guatemala was the site of a long and deadly guerilla war, and Santiago Atitlán was the focal point of military death squads. La Voz de Atitlán has always been a voice for peasant rights, so in 1980 the station manager, Gaspar Culán, and several staffers were kidnaped and murdered, as was, later, an Oklahoma priest. The station was closed for several years, but reopened in response to pressure from the Roman Catholic church.

0600-0800	**W** 9745 (E Europe), **W** 11685 (Mideast), 11700 (Africa), **S** 17620 (E Africa)
0600-0900 ⬅	9790 (N Africa)
0600-1200	9805 (E Europe)
0700-0800	**W** 7305 & **S** 9845 (N Africa), 15605 (Mideast), 17800 (E Africa), **S** 17850 (Africa)
0700-0900	**W** 11790 (E Europe), **W** 21620 (E Africa)
0700-1300	11670 (E Europe)
0700-1600	15315 (N Africa & W Africa)
0700-1700	15300 (Africa)
0800-0900	**W** 15135 & **S** 17800 (E Africa)
0800-1100	15605 (Mideast & S Asia)
0800-1200	15155 & 15195 (E Europe)
0800-1400	17650 (Mideast)
0800-1600	11845 (N Africa), 17850 (Africa)
0800-1700	17620 (Africa)
0900-1100	**S** 17795 (E Africa), **W** 21580 (C Africa & S Africa)
0900-1500	21620 (E Africa)

1000-1600	21685 (Irr) (W Africa)
1030-1125	5220 (E Asia)
1030-1130	**W** 9790 (C America), 11670 (S America), 11700 (Australasia), **W** 13625 & 15435 (Irr) (S America)
1030-1200	**W** 7140 (E Asia), **W** 9830 & **S** 11710 (SE Asia), **S** 17575 (Irr) (C America & N America)
1100-1200	6175 (W Europe), **W** 11700 (E North Am), 11890 (SE Asia), **S** 13625 & **S** 15365 (E North Am), 17795 (S Africa)
1100-1500	21580 (C Africa & S Africa)
1130-1200	**W** 15530 (C America)
1200-1300	**W** 11670 & 13640 (C America), 15435 & **S** 17560 (S America)
1200-1400	9790 (C Africa)
1300-1400	9805, **S** 11615 & **W** 11670 (E Europe), 13625 (C America & N America), **W** 15155 & 15195 (E Europe)
1330-1400	**S** M-Sa 13640 (C America), 15435 (S America), M-Sa 15515 (C America

& N America), *17560* (S America),
W M-Sa *17860* (C America)

1400-1500	11615 (E Europe), **S** *15525* (C America & N America), 15605 (Mideast), **W** *17575* (C America)
1400-1600	**S** 15155 & **S** 15195 (E Europe), **W** 15460 & 17795 (E Africa)
1430-1600	**S** *15515* (C America & N America), *17860* & **W** *21645* (C America)
1500-1600	**W** 9605 (E Europe), **S** 11615 (Mideast), **W** 11670 (E Europe), **S** 15405 (S Asia & SE Asia), **S** 21580 (C Africa & S Africa), **S** 21620 (E Africa)
1500-1700	**W** 9790 (N Africa, S Asia & SE Asia)
1500-1800	**W** 11995 (E Africa)
1600-1700	**W** 12030 (S Asia & SE Asia)
1600-1800	**S** *15525* & **W** *17630* (S America)
1600-1900	**W** 7160 (N Africa), **W** 11965 (W Africa)
1700-1800	**W** 9790 (Africa), **S** 9805 & **S** 11670 (E Europe)
1700-2200	15300 (Africa)
1730-1800	**S** 15210 (E Africa)
1730-1900	**W** 9485 & **S** 15460 (E Africa)
1800-1900	**W** 5900 & **W** 7135 (E Europe), 11705 (Africa)
1800-2000	**W** 7315 (E Africa)
1800-2100	**W** 6175 (N Africa), **S** 9495 (E Europe), **S** 11995 (E Africa)
1800-2200	*7160* (C Africa), 9790 (Africa)
1900-2100	**W** 7135 & **S** 9605 (E Europe), **S** 11705 (Africa), **S** 11965 (W Africa)
1900-2200	7160 (N Africa & W Africa), 9485 (E Africa), **S** *17630* & **W** *21765* (S America)
2000-2100	5915 (E Europe)
2000-2200	7315 (E Africa)
2100-2200	**S** 5900 & **W** 5915 (E Europe), **W** 5945 (E Africa & Mideast), 6175 (N Africa), **S** 9805 (E Europe)
2200-2300	**W** 5920 (C America), 9715 (S America), **S** 11670 (C America)
2200-2400	9790 (C America)
2300-2400	**W** 7120 (S Asia & SE Asia), **W** *9570* (SE Asia), *9715* (S America), **S** 9805 (S Asia & SE Asia), *12025* & **S** *15440* (SE Asia)

GABON—French
AFRIQUE NUMERO UN

0500-2300	9580 (C Africa)
0700-1600	17630 (W Africa)
1600-1900	15475 (W Africa & E North Am)

GERMANY—German
BAYERISCHER RUNDFUNK

24 Hr	6085

DEUTSCHE WELLE

0000-0150	**S** 9730 (C America), **W** *11795* & **S** *15410* (S America)
0000-0155	**S** 9545 (N America & C America), **S** *9680* (S Asia & SE Asia), *9765* (C America), *13780* (S America)
0000-0200	6075 (Europe), 9545 (S America), **W** *9690* (S Asia & SE Asia)
0000-0300	**W** 7225 & **S** *9795* (S Asia)
0000-0355	**W** *11785* (W Africa & Americas)
0000-0400	**W** 7130 (S Europe & S America)
0000-0600	3995 (Europe), 6100 (N America & C America)
0200-0400	**W** 6145 (C America), **S** 7130 (N Africa & S America)
0200-0555	**S** 9735 (N America)
0200-0600	6075 (Europe & N America), 9545 (E Africa & S Africa)
0400-0555	**S** 11795 (Africa)
0400-0600	6085 (N America), **W** *7195* (S Africa), **W** *7235* (W Africa), **S** *9535* (N America & C America), **S** *9700* (S Africa), **W** 9735 (Mideast & Africa)
0500-0600	**S** 9735 (Australasia)
0600-0800	*6185* (Australasia)
0600-0955	**W** 9670 (E Europe & W Asia), *9690*, 9735 & 11795 (Australasia), **S** 11865 (E Europe & W Asia), **S** *21640* (SE Asia & Australasia)
0600-1000	15275 (Africa), 17845 (SE Asia & Australasia)
0600-1800	13780 (S Europe)
0600-2000	6075 (Europe), 9545 (S Europe)
0800-0955	**W** 11865 (E Asia)
0900-1355	*15135* (Africa)
1000-1355	**W** 11865 (E Asia), **W** 12080 (E Europe & W Asia), **S** 13780 (C Asia & E Asia), **S** 15275 (Mideast), **S** 15640 (E Asia), 17845 (S Asia & SE Asia), **S** *17845* (E Asia)
1000-1400	**W** 7340 (E Asia), **W** *9480* (S Asia & SE Asia), **S** *12000* (E Asia), **S** *15490* (SE Asia & Australasia), **S** 17560 (W Africa)
1000-1600	**W** 15275 (S Europe)
1100-1300	**S** *11765* (Europe)
1200-1350	**S** *15285* (S America)
1200-1355	*15285* (N America & C America)
1200-1400	**W** *11805* (Europe), **W** *17765* (S America)
1300-1900	6140 (N Europe)
1400-1600	**W** 9595 & **S** *9655* (S Asia)
1400-1700	**W** *13790* (N America & C America), *17715* (N America), *17765* (S America)
1400-1755	**W** 9620 (S Asia), **W** *15135* (Mideast & Africa), **S** *21560* (Mideast)
1400-1800	**W** 7315 (S Asia), **S** 11795 (Mideast), **S** *12055* & **S** 15275 (S Asia)
1600-1755	**S** 9655 (S Asia)
1600-2000	**W** 7445 (Mideast & E Africa), **S** 9835 (Mideast)

1800-2000	W 11795 (W Africa & S America)
1800-2155	W 7125 (SE Asia & Australasia), W 7215 (Africa), S 9655 (SE Asia & Australasia), W 9735 (S Africa)
1800-2200	S 7185 (Africa), S 15275 (W Africa & S America), 17860 (W Africa & Americas)
2000-2200	6075 (Europe & Africa), 9545 & 11795 (W Africa & S America), 17810 (N America & S America)
2000-2400	3995 (Europe)
2200-2355	9715 (E Asia), S 17860 (C America)
2200-2400	W 5925 & W 6010 (E Asia), 6075 (Europe), 6100 (N America & C America), S 7315 (S Asia & SE Asia), 9545 (S America), S 9545 (N America & C America), W 9690 (S Asia & SE Asia), S 9730 & 9765 (C America), W 11785 (W Africa & Americas), S 11795 (E Asia), W 11795 & 13780 (S America), W 15275 (C America), S 15410 (S America)

DEUTSCHLANDRADIO—(Europe)

| 24 Hr | 6005 |

SUDDEUTSCHER R'FUNK—(Europe)

| 0455-2305 | 6030 |

SUDWESTFUNK—(Europe)

| 24 Hr | 7265 |

GREECE—Greek

FONI TIS HELLADAS

0000-0130 &	
0200-0330	W 7448, W 9420 & 9935/6260 (N America)
0330-0345	9935/6260 (N America)
0400-0525	W 7450, 9425/9420, W 11645 & 15650 (Mideast)
0600-0745	7450, S 9425 & 11645 (Europe & Australasia)
0900-0950	15415/15630 (E Asia), 15650 (Australasia)
1000-1135	9425 & 9915 (Mideast)
1200-1230	W 9420 (Mideast), W 11645 & W 15650 (Africa)
1200-1235 &	
1245-1350	S 15175 (Europe & N America)
1300-1335	15650 (Europe & N America)
1300-1335	W 9420 (Europe & N America), 11645 (C Asia)
1345-1450	15650 (Europe & N America)
1345-1450	W 9420 (Europe & N America)
1400-1430	S 9420, 11645 & S 15630 (Mideast)
1500-1600	W 7450 (Europe), S 9375, 9420 & 11645 (E Europe)
1710-1725	W 7450, S 9375, 9425/9420 & S 11645 (E Europe)
1800-1840	11645 & 15150 (Africa)

1800-1900	W 7450, W 9395, W 9425 & W 11595 (Europe)
1900-2100	W 9420 (Europe)
1900-2150	7450 (Europe), S 9420/7430 (Europe, N America & Australasia)
2100-2235	9425 (Australasia)
2100-2250	W 6260 (Europe)
2200-2300	W 6260 (N America)
2200-2305	S 9395 (C America & S America), 11595 (S America)
2300-2335	S 9425 (C America & Australasia)

RADIOFONIKOS STATHMOS MAKEDONIAS

0500-1700	S 9935 (Europe)
0500-1730	S 11595 (Mideast)
0600-0800	7430/6245 (Europe)
0600-1730	W 9935 (Mideast)
0600-1900	W 11595 (Europe)
1400-2200	7430 (Europe)
1500-2200	S 6260 (Europe)
1730-2200	9935 (Mideast)
1900-2300	W 6245 (Europe)
2200-2300	W 7430 (Europe), W 9935 (Mideast)

HOLLAND—Dutch
RADIO NEDERLAND WERELDOMROEP

0000-0025	7285, 9590, **W** 12065 & **S** 13695 (SE Asia)
0130-0225	6020 (C America), 6165 (N America), **S** 9895 (E North Am), 15315 (S America)
0330-0425	**S** 9855 & **W** 9860 (E Africa), 11655 (Mideast)
0500-0600	**S** 6145 (W Europe), **S** 7130 (Europe)
0530-0625	**W** 5995, 6165 & **S** 9715 (W North Am)
0600-0800	**S** 11935 (S Europe)
0630-0725	**W** 7130 & **W** 7240 (Europe), **S** 9615, 9720 & **W** 11660 (Australasia)
0630-0855	**W** 6020 (S Europe)
0630-1700	5955 (Europe), 9895 (S Europe)
0800-1700	**S** 13700 (S Europe)
0900-1255	**W** 11895 (S Europe)
0930-1025	6020 (C America)
1030-1125	9720 & 9820 (Australasia), 17580 (SE Asia), 21480 (E Asia)
1330-1425	**S** 5930 & **W** 5930 (E Asia), **W** 7375 (E Asia & SE Asia), **S** 12065 & **S** 13755 (SE Asia), **W** 13770 (Australasia)
1430-1525	**W** 7365 & **W** 13770 (S Asia)
1530-1625	**S** 12090 (S Asia & E Asia)
1600-1700	**S** 7310 (W Europe)
1600-1825	**W** 6015 (S Europe & W Africa)
1630-1725	6020 (S Africa), 11655 (E Africa)
1730-1825	**S** 9895 (Mideast), **W** 9895 (E Africa), **S** 13700 (Mideast), 17605 & 21590 (W Africa)
1830-1925	**S** Su 13700 (W Africa)
2030-2125	6015 (S Africa), **S** 7120 (C Africa & S Africa), **W** 11655 & 15315 (W Africa), **S** Su 15525 (N America & S America), **S** 17605 (W Africa)
2030-2225	6020 (N Africa & W Africa)
2130-2225	6030 & **S** 9895 (C America), **W** 11730 (E North Am), **S** 13700 (S America), **S** 15155 (E North Am), 15315 (S America)
2330-2400	7285, 9590, **W** 12065 & **S** 13695 (SE Asia)

HUNGARY—Hungarian
RADIO BUDAPEST

0000-0100 ◄	M 9835 (S America)
0000-0100	**W** M 6165 (S America), **S** 9840 (N America), **W** M 11955 (S America)
0100-0200 ◄	11870 (N America)
0100-0200	**W** 6190 & **W** 9850 (N America)
0130-0230	**S** 9840 (N America)
0230-0330 ◄	11870 (N America)
0230-0330	**W** 5965 & **W** 9850 (N America)
0900-1000	**S** 15160 (Australasia)
1000-1100 ◄	15395 & 17750 (Australasia)

1000-1100	**S** Su 15160 & **W** 15220/21685 (Australasia)
1100-1200 ◄	Su 15395 & Su 17750 (Australasia)
1100-1200	**S** Su 5970 (W Europe), **S** Su 11905 (N Europe), **W** Su 15220/21685 (Australasia)
1200-1300 ◄	Su 9835/9825 (Europe)
1200-1300	**W** Su 5945 (W Europe), **W** Su 7220 (N Europe), **W** Su 11910 (N Europe & E Europe)
1300-1400	**S** Su 11905 (N Europe)
1400-1500 ◄	Su 5970 (W Europe), Su 9835 (Europe)
1400-1500	**W** Su 7220 (N Europe), **W** Su 11950 (N Europe & E Europe)
1800-1900	**S** 5975 (N Europe), **S** 7130 (W Europe)
1900-2000 ◄	3975 (Europe), 9835 (W Europe)
1900-2000	**W** 5975 (N Europe), **W** 7250 (W Europe)
2000-2100	**S** 6140 (N Europe), **S** 7130 (W Europe)
2100-2200 ◄	3975 (Europe), 9835 (W Europe)
2100-2200	**W** 5970 (N Europe), **W** 7185 (W Europe)
2200-2300	**S** 6085 & **S** 11910 (S America)
2300-2400 ◄	9835 (S America)
2300-2400	**S** Su 6085, **W** 6165, **S** Su 11910 & **W** 11955 (S America)

INDIA—Hindi
ALL INDIA RADIO

0315-0415	11855 (Mideast & W Asia), 15075 (W Asia, Mideast & E Africa), 15180 & 17387 (E Africa)
1615-1730	7410 (Mideast & W Asia), 9950 & 13770 (E Africa)
1945-2045	7410, 9950 & 11620 (W Europe)
2300-2400	9910, 11740 & 13795 (SE Asia)

IRAN—Persian
VOICE OF THE ISLAMIC REPUBLIC

0000-0030	**W** 7100 & **S** 7130 (Mideast & Europe)
0000-1230	15084
0130-1330	15365 (W Asia & S Asia)
1300-2400	15084
1630-1730	7230 (Europe)
1630-1930	6175/6005 & **W** 7180 (W Asia)
1630-2400	**W** 7100 & **S** 7130 (Mideast & Europe)

ITALY—Italian
RADIO ROMA-RAI INTERNATIONAL

0000-0050	6010 (E North Am), 9575 (S America), 9675 (E North Am & C America), 11800 (N America & C America), 11880 (S America)
0130-0230	6110 & 11765 (S America)
0130-0305	6010 (E North Am), 9575 (S America),

	9675 (N America & C America), 11800 (E North Am & C America), 11880 (S America)
0415-0425	5975 & 7275 (S Europe & N Africa)
0435-0510	▣ 9670, ▣ 11800, ◪ 11880 & ◪ 15400 (E Africa)
1000-1100	*11925* (Australasia)
1320-1650	Su 21535 (S America), Su 21710 (C Africa & S Africa)
1400-1430	15245/15250 & 17780 (E North Am)
1500-1525	5990, 7290 & ◪ 9670 (S Europe & N Africa)
1555-1625	5990, 7290 & 9755 (Europe)
1700-1800	7235, ◪ 9535 & ▣ 9710 (N Africa), 11840 & 15230 (Africa), *15320* (S Africa), 17870 (E Africa)
1830-1905	15245/15250 & 17780 (E North Am)
2230-2400	6010 (E North Am), 9575 (S America), 9675 (E North Am & C America), 11800 (N America & C America), 11880 (S America)

JAPAN—Japanese
RADIO JAPAN/NHK

0000-0100	*6155 & 6180* (Europe)
0200-0300	*5960* (E North Am), *11860* (SE Asia), 13630 (W North Am), 15500/15475 (E Asia)
0200-0500	11840 (E Asia)
0300-0330	13700 (E Africa)
0300-0400	*9515* (Mideast), *11895* (C America), 13630 (W North Am)
0300-0430	◪ 15230 (W North Am)
0300-0500	17810 (SE Asia)
0400-0500	*5960* & ▣ *6095* (Europe), *6110* (W North Am & C America), ◪ *7230* (Europe), *17820* (Mideast & N Africa)
0600-0700	◪ 15230 (W North Am)
0800-0900	*11920* (Australasia), *15220* (W Africa), *17815* (C Africa)
0800-0930	6070 & 9685 (S America)
0800-1000	*11740* (SE Asia), 11850 (Australasia)
0800-1100	7125 & ▣ 7125 (E Asia), 11815 (SE Asia)
0900-1500	9855 (SE Asia)
1000-1100	◪ *6120* (E North Am), *17780* (S Africa)
1200-1300	▣ *6120* (E North Am)
1300-1400	*11705* (W North Am), *15400* (W Africa), *21490* (C Africa)
1300-1500	*12045* (S Asia)
1600-1700	6035 (E Asia), 9535 (W North Am)
1700-1800	7225 (S Asia)
1800-1900	7140 (Australasia), *11880* (Mideast)
1800-2000	6035 (E Asia), 9535 (W North Am)
1800-2100	7110 (Europe)
1900-2100	*6035* (Australasia)
2000-2100	6090 (E Asia), *7210* (Europe), 13630 (W North Am)
2000-2400	◪ 9560 (E Asia), 11665 (SE Asia)

2200-2300	*6055 & 6115* (Europe), *9685* (S America), 11850 (Australasia)

RADIO TAMPA

0000-0800	3925, 9760
0000-1000	6115
0000-1300	3945
0000-1730	6055, 9595
0800-1730 &	
2020-2300	3925
2030-2400	6055, 9595
2300-2400	3925, 3945, 6115, 9760

JORDAN—Arabic
RADIO JORDAN

0400-0600 ◄═	9630 (N Africa & E Africa)
0400-0810	11810 (Mideast, SE Asia & Australasia)
0400-0815 ◄═	15435 (W Europe)
0600-0900 ◄═	11835 (E Europe)
0830-1515	11810 (Mideast, SE Asia & Australasia)
1100-1300 ◄═	15355 (N Africa & C America)
1633-2155 ◄═	13630/7155 (N Africa & E Africa)
1800-2155 ◄═	9830 (W Europe)
2200-0208 ◄═	11935 (W Europe & E North Am), 15435 (S America)

AWR-Asia broadcasts from Guam in 22 languages, using powerful 100 kW transmitters and far-reaching curtain antennas.

KOREA (REPUBLIC)—Korean
RADIO KOREA INTERNATIONAL

0000-0100	5975 (E Asia), 15575 (N America)
0100-0200	7275 (E Asia)
0300-0400	7275 (E Asia), 11725 & 11810 (S America), 15575 (N America)
0700-0800	7550 (Europe)
0900-1000	7550 (S America)
0900-1100	5975 & 7275 (E Asia), 9570 (Australasia), 13670 (Europe)
1000-1100	6135 (E Asia)
1100-1130	*6145* (E North Am), 9640 (E Asia), *9650* (E North Am), 11725 (S America)
1300-1400	9640 (E Asia), 13670 (SE Asia)
1700-1900	5975 (E Asia), 7550 & 15575 (Europe)
2100-2200	5975 & 7275 (E Asia), 9640 (SE Asia)
2300-2400	5975 (E Asia), 15575 (N America)

KUWAIT—Arabic
RADIO KUWAIT

0000-0530	11675 (W North Am)
0200-1305	6055 & 15495 (Mideast)
0400-0805	15505 (E Europe)
0445-0930	15110 (S Asia & SE Asia)
0815-1740	15505 (W Africa & C Africa)
0900-1505	17885 (E Asia)
0930-1605	13620 (Europe & E North Am)
1315-1730	15110 (S Asia & SE Asia)
1315-2130	9880 (Mideast)
1615-1800	11990 (Europe & E North Am)
1745-2300	15505 (Europe & E North Am)
1800-2400	9855 (Europe & E North Am), 15495 (W Africa & C Africa)

LEBANON
VOICE OF LEBANON
Arabic & French

0355-2225 ⬅	6550

LIBYA—Arabic
RADIO JAMAHIRIYA

0000-0445 ⬅	11850/15435 (N Africa & Mideast), 15235/9700 (W Africa & S America), 15415 (Europe)
1115-1730 ⬅	11850/15435 (N Africa & Mideast)
1115-1800 ⬅	15415 (Europe)
1115-2400 ⬅	15235/9700 (W Africa & S America)
1800-2400 ⬅	11850/15435 (N Africa & Mideast)
1915-2400 ⬅	15415 (Europe)

LITHUANIA—Lithuanian
RADIO VILNIUS

0000-0030	**W** 5890 (E North Am), **S** *9855* (E North Am)
0900-0930 ⬅	9710 (Europe)

MEXICO—Spanish
RADIO EDUCACION

0000-1200 ⬅	6185

RADIO MEXICO INTERNATIONAL—(W North Am & C America)

0000-0400 ⬅	9705
0400-0500 ⬅	Mon 9705
1300-1500 ⬅	5985 & 9705
1900-2000 ⬅	5985 & 9705
2200-2400 ⬅	5985 & 9705

RADIO MIL

24 Hr	6010

MOROCCO
RADIO MEDI UN—(Europe & N Africa)
French & Arabic

0500-0100	9575

RTV MAROCAINE
Arabic

0000-0500	11920 (N Africa & Mideast)
1000-2100	15345 (N Africa)
1100-1500 & 2200-2400	15335 (Europe)

PARAGUAY—Spanish
RADIO ENCARNACION

0700-0300 ➡	11939

RADIO NACIONAL

0700-1700 ➡	9735 (S America & E North Am)
1700-2000 ➡	9735 (Irr) (S America)
2000-0300 ➡	9735 (S America & E North Am)

PHILIPPINES—Tagalog
RADYO PILIPINAS—(Mideast)

1730-1930	**S** 11720, **W** 11730, 11890 & 15190

POLAND—Polish
POLISH RADIO WARSAW

1130-1200 ⬅	5995 & 7285 (Europe)
1200-1225 ⬅	7270 (W Europe), 7285 (E Europe)
1530-1625	**S** 9690 (W Europe)
1630-1725 ⬅	6000 & 7145 (W Europe), 7285 (E Europe)

1630-1725	W 9670 (W Europe)
2200-2255 ◨	6035 (E Europe), 6095 (W Europe)

PORTUGAL—Portuguese
RDP INTERNATIONAL-RADIO PORTUGAL

0000-0430 ◨	6150 & 9570 (E North Am), 9600 (S America), 9635 (C America & S America), 11840 (S America)
0430-0500 ◨	Su/M 6150 & Su/M 9570 (E North Am), Su/M 9600 (S America), Su/M 9635 (C America & S America), Su/M 11840 (S America)
0600-0800 ◨	M-F 6130/6155 (Europe)
0700-0800 ◨	M-F 9780 (Europe)
0745-0900 ◨	M-F 9630 (Europe)
0800-1000 ◨	Sa/Su 17595 (SE Asia), Sa/Su 17680/15515 (E Africa & S Africa), Sa/Su 21655 (W Africa & S America)
0800-1400 ◨	6130 & 9780 (Europe)
0900-1030 ◨	Sa/Su 9615 (Europe)
1000-1200 ◨	17680/15515 (E Africa & S Africa), 21655 (W Africa & S America), M-F 21720 (E Africa & S Africa)
1200-1300 ◨	M-F 17595 (SE Asia)
1200-1800 ◨	Sa/Su 17680/15515 (E Africa & S Africa), Sa/Su 21655 (W Africa & S America)
1300-1430 ◨	M-F 21515 (Mideast & S Asia)
1300-2100 ◨	Sa/Su//Holidays 15200 (E North Am), Sa/Su//Holidays 17745 (C America)
1400-1800 ◨	Sa/Su 6130 & Sa/Su 9780 (Europe)
1500-1900 ◨	Sa/Su 21515 (Mideast & S Asia)
1800-2100 ◨	6130, 9780 & M-F 9815 (Europe), 21655 (W Africa & S America)
1800-2200 ◨	15515 (E Africa & S Africa)
1900-2000 ◨	Sa/Su 21515 (Irr) (Mideast & S Asia)
2100-2300 ◨	21655 (Irr) (W Africa & S America)
2100-2345 ◨	9780 (Irr) (Europe)
2100-2400 ◨	9570 (Irr) (E North Am), 11840 (Irr) (S America)
2200-2300 ◨	15515 (Irr) (E Africa & S Africa)

ROMANIA—Romanian
RADIO ROMANIA

0000-0300	S 6105 (W Europe)
0300-0700	9570 (W Europe)
0500-0800	W 11970 (Europe)
0600-0800	W 15105 (Europe, N Africa & Mideast)
0700-1200	S 11940 (Europe)
0800-1430	15105 (Europe, N Africa & Mideast)
0800-1500	W 17720 (Europe)
1200-2100	S 11790 (Europe)
1430-2100	S 15105 (Europe, N Africa & Mideast)
2100-2400	S 6105 (W Europe)

RADIO ROMANIA INTERNATIONAL

0000-0100	9510 & 11940 (E North Am)
0100-0200	9570 (S America)

0600-0614	W 7105, S 9550, 9665, W 11775 & S 11810 (Europe)
0715-0815	S Su 11740 & Su 15335 (W Asia), Su 15370 & Su 17790 (SE Asia)
0815-0915	S Su 11810 (C Africa), Su 15335 (S Africa), Su 15380 (C Africa), S Su 17745 (S Africa), W Su 17790 (W Africa)
0915-1015	Su 9570 (Europe), W Su 9590 (W Europe), Su 9665, Su 11775 & Su 11810 (N Africa), S Su 11970 (Europe & Atlantic)
1130-1200	S 11790 (Europe)
1300-1330	S 11775 (Europe), W 15365 & W 17790 (Australasia)
1630-1700	W 7105, S 9510, W 9665 & S 11775 (Mideast)
1730-1800	W 5990, W 6105, W 7195 & S 9510 (Europe)
2000-2030	W 7175 (Europe), S 9625 (W Europe), W 9690 (Europe), S 11790 (W Europe)
2230-2300	W 9530 (W Europe), 9570 & S 11830 (E North Am), W 11830 (S America)
2300-2400	W 5990 (C America), 7105 & W 9550 (Australasia), W 11940 (S America)

SAUDI ARABIA—Arabic
BROADCASTING SERVICE OF THE KINGDOM

0300-0600	7150, 9555 (Mideast), 9620/9885 (N Africa), 9720 (W Asia), 11740/11935 (C Asia), W 11785, S 11870, S 17745/17780 & W 17745/17720 (C Asia)

Most world band radios are pedestrian in places like Africa. Still, world band is the main link with the outside for millions too poor to afford televisions or telephones. Here, an East African listens to FEBA, which operates from facilities in the Seychelles.

Mullah Faiz Mohammad Goth of the Karachi Adventist Hospital, part of the international operation which includes Adventist World Radio.

0300-1700	9580 (Mideast & E Africa)
0300-2100	10990 (Irr) ISL & 10990 (Irr) ISU (Mideast)
0600-0700	7150
0600-0900	11710 (N Africa), 11950 (W Asia)
0600-1200	11820 (Mideast)
0900-1200	17880/17895 (SE Asia), 21495/21530 (E Asia & SE Asia)
0900-1500	15060 (N Africa)
1200-1500	15230/15175 (W Europe), 15380 (W Asia)
1200-1600	15165 (N Africa), 15280 (Mideast)
1500-1800	11780 (N Africa), 11910/11965 (W Europe), 11950 (W Asia)
1600-1800	9730 (C Africa), 11710 (N Africa), 11835 (Mideast)
1700-2100	6020 (Mideast & E Africa)
1800-2100	9705/9775 (W Asia)
1800-2300	9555 (N Africa), 9870 (W Europe), 11935 (N Africa)
2100-2300	3868 (Irr) USB (Mideast)

SINGAPORE—Chinese
RADIO SINGAPORE INTERNATIONAL—(SE Asia)

1100-1400	6000 & 6120

RADIO CORPORATION OF SINGAPORE

1400-1700 &	
2300-1100	6000

SLOVAKIA—Slovak
RADIO SLOVAKIA INTERNATIONAL

0130-0200	5930 & 7300 (E North Am & C America), 9440 (S America)
0900-0930	11990, **S** 15460, **W** 17485, **S** 17570 & **W** 21705 (Australasia)
1500-1600	**S** 5915 (W Europe)
1600-1700 **◄**	6055 (W Europe), 7345 (S Europe)
1600-1700	**W** 5940 (W Europe)
1800-1830 **◄**	5915 & 6055 (W Europe), 7345 (S Europe)
2000-2030 **◄**	5915, 6055 & 7345 (W Europe)

SPAIN—Spanish
RADIO EXTERIOR DE ESPANA

0000-0100	Su/M 5970 (C America), Su/M 11815 (N America), Su/M 17870 (S America)
0000-0200	11945 (S America)
0000-0500	6125 (S America), 9540 (N America & C America), 9620 (S America)
0100-0400	Tu-Sa 3210 (C America), Tu-Sa 5970 (N America), Tu-Sa 5990 (S America)

0200-0500	6055 (N America & C America)
0500-0700	9650 (Australasia), 9685 (Europe), 9760 (Australasia), **W** 11890 (Mideast), 11920 (Europe), **S** 15125 (Mideast)
0600-0910	12035 (Europe)
0900-0910	17715 (S America)
0900-1200	Su 9620 (W Europe)
0900-1700	**W** 15110 & **S** 17890 (Mideast)
0900-1900	17755 (W Africa & S Africa)
0910-0940	Su-F 12035 (Europe), Su-F 17715 (S America)
0940-1515	12035 (Europe)
0940-1900	17715 (S America)
1000-1200	*9620 (E Asia)*
1100-1400	M-F *3210* (C America), M-F *9630* (N America), M-F *11815* (S America)
1200-1400	*5220 (E Asia)*, *11910 (SE Asia)*
1200-1515	9620 (W Europe)
1200-1800	17845/21570 (C America & S America)
1300-1800	Sa/Su *11815* (N America)
1400-1800	Sa/Su *5970* (C America), Sa/Su *17870/11880* (S America)
1515-1600	Sa/Su 9620 (W Europe), Sa/Su 12035 (Europe)
1600-1700	Su 9620 (W Europe), 12035 (Europe), M-Sa 15210 (W Africa & C Africa)
1700-2000	Sa/Su 6125 (W Europe)
1700-2235	7275 (Europe)
1800-1900	**S** Sa/Su 17845/21570 (C America & S America)
1800-2235	*5970* (C America), *11815* (N America), *17870* (S America)
1900-2000	**S** Sa/Su 17845/15125 (C America & S America)
1900-2200	**W** 11880 & **S** 17870 (E North Am & C America)
2000-2100	Sa 6125 (W Europe), **S** Sa 17845/15125 (C America & S America)
2200-2235	11880 (E North Am & C America)
2200-2300	6130 (N Africa), **W** 9580 & **S** 15110 (Mideast)
2235-2255	Su *5970* (C America), Su *11815* (N America), Su 11880 (E North Am & C America), Su *17870* (S America)
2235-2300	Su 7275 (Europe)
2255-2400	*5970* (C America), *11815* (N America), 11880 (E North Am & C America), *17870* (S America)
2300-2400	6125 (S America), 9540 (N America & C America), 9620 & 11945 (S America)

RADIO SWEDEN

0000-0030	6065 & **W** 9850 (S America)
0100-0130	**W** 7120 (E Asia & Australasia)
0200-0230 ◧	6090 (N America)
0300-0330	7115 (N America)

0500-0710 ◧	M-F 6065 (Europe), M-F 13625 (Europe & N Africa)
0700-0900 ◧	Sa 6065 (Europe), Sa 13625 (Europe & N Africa)
0800-1000 ◧	Su 6065 (Europe), Su 13625 (Europe & N Africa)
1000-1030	**S** Sa/Su 15120 (E Asia & Australasia)
1100-1130 ◧	Sa/Su 6065 (Europe)
1100-1130	**S** 15120 (C America & S America)
1100-1200	**S** 13740 (Asia & Australasia)
1130-1200 ◧	6065 (Europe), 11650 (E North Am)
1130-1200	**W** 13625 (Europe & N Africa)
1300-1330	**W** 9835/9830 (S Asia)
1500-1530 ◧	15240 (E North Am)
1500-1530	**W** 11650 (N America)
1545-1600 ◧	6000 (E Europe), 11650 (N America)
1545-1600	**S** 11650 (Europe & Africa), **S** 13765 (Mideast)
1545-1700 ◧	6065 (Europe)
1600-1615	**S** M-F 11650 (Europe & Africa), **S** M-F 13765 (Mideast)
1700-1715 ◧	M-F 6065 (Europe)
1900-1930 ◧	6065 (Europe & Mideast), 9655 (Mideast)
2030-2100	**S** M-F 9655 (Europe & Africa)
2100-2130 ◧	6065 (Europe & Mideast)
2200-2230 ◧	6065 (Europe)

SWISS RADIO INTERNATIONAL
French

0200-0230	6135 & 9885 (E North Am), *9905* (N America & C America)
0400-0445	**S** 9535 (E Europe)
0430-0500	6135 (W North Am), 9885 (N America)
0500-0545 ◧	6165 (Europe & N Africa)
0500-0545	**W** 5840 (E Europe)
0530-0600	**S** 9535 (E Europe)
0630-0700 ◧	6165 (Europe & N Africa)
0630-0700	**W** 5840 & **S** 9535 (E Europe), 9885 & 11860 (W Africa), 13635 (S Africa)
0730-0800	**W** 5840 (E Europe)
0730-1100 ◧	6165 (Europe & N Africa)
0930-1000	*9885*, **W** 12075, 13685 & **S** 17515 (Australasia)
1130-1200	**W** 9885, **W** 11995, 13635, **S** 15415 & **S** 17515 (E Asia)
1200-1230 ◧	6165 (Europe & N Africa), 9535 (S Europe & W Europe)
1330-1400	*7230 (SE Asia)*, *7480 (E Asia)*, **W** 12075, 13635 & **S** 15120 (SE Asia)
1500-1530	**W** 9885 & 12075 (C Asia & S Asia), 13635 & **S** 15530 (W Asia & S Asia)
1800-1815	**W** 5850, 9885/9745 & **S** 12075 (Mideast)
1830-1845	**W** 7410 (N Europe)
1930-2000 ◧	6165 (Europe & N Africa)
2100-2130	**S** 9840/9870 (S Africa), **W** 9885 (E Africa), 9905 (S Africa), 11640

(W Africa & S Africa), **W** *13635* (S Africa)

2215-2230   9885 (S America), 9905 (C America), *11650* (S America)

German

0030-0100   6135 & 9885 (E North Am), *9905* (N America & C America)

0330-0400   6135 (W North Am), 9885 (N America), *9905* (N America & C America)

0500-0515   **S** 9535 (E Europe)

0600-0615 ◨   6165 (Europe & N Africa)

0600-0615   **W** 5840 (E Europe)

0730-0800   9885 & 11860 (W Africa), 13635 (S Africa)

1000-1030   *9885*, **W** 12075, 13685 & **S** 17515 (Australasia)

1130-1200 ◨   6165 (Europe & N Africa), 9535 (S Europe & W Europe)

1200-1230   **W** 9885, **W** 11995, 13635, **S** 15415 & **S** 17515 (E Asia)

1430-1445   *7230* (SE Asia), *7480* (E Asia), **W** 12075, 13635 & **S** 15120 (SE Asia)

1530-1600   **W** 9885 & 12075 (C Asia & S Asia), 13635 & **S** 15530 (W Asia & S Asia)

1600-1900 ◨   6165 (Europe & N Africa)

1730-1800   **W** 7410 & **S** 9905 (N Europe)

1815-1830   **W** 5850, 9885/9745 & **S** 12075 (Mideast)

2130-2200   **S** 9840/9870 (S Africa), **W** 9885 (E Africa), 9905 (S Africa), 11640 (W Africa & S Africa)

2230-2300   9885 (S America), 9905 (C America), *11650* (S America)

Italian

0300-0315   6135 & 9885 (E North Am), *9905* (N America & C America)

0445-0500   **S** 9535 (E Europe)

0500-0530   6135 (W North Am), 9885 (N America), *9905* (N America & C America)

0545-0600 ◨   6165 (Europe & N Africa)

0545-0600   **W** 5840 (E Europe)

0600-0615   **S** 9535 (E Europe)

0700-0715 ◨   6165 (Europe & N Africa)

0700-0715   **W** 5840 (E Europe)

0700-0730   9885 & 11860 (W Africa), 13635 (S Africa)

0830-0900   *9885*, **W** 12075, 13685 & **S** 17515 (Australasia)

1230-1245   **W** 9885, **W** 11995, 13635, **S** 15415 & **S** 17515 (E Asia)

1230-1300 ◨   6165 (Europe & N Africa), 9535 (S Europe & W Europe)

1400-1430   *7230* (SE Asia), *7480* (E Asia), **W** 12075, 13635 & **S** 15120 (SE Asia)

1400-1600 ◨   6165 (Europe & N Africa)

1645-1700   **W** 5850, 9885/9745 & **S** 12075 (Mideast)

1800-1830   **W** 7410 & **S** 9905 (N Europe)

1845-1900   **S** 12075 (Mideast)

1900-1930 ◨   6165 (Europe & N Africa)

2045-2100   **S** 9840/9870 (S Africa), **W** 9885 (E Africa), 9905 (S Africa), 11640 (W Africa & S Africa), **W** *13635* (S Africa)

2300-2330   9885 (S America), 9905 (C America), *11650* (S America)

SYRIA—Arabic
RADIO DAMASCUS

2215-2315   12085 & 13610/15095 (S America)

SYRIAN BROADCASTING SERVICE

0600-1600 ◨   15095/13610

0600-1700 ◨   12085

THAILAND—Thai
RADIO THAILAND

0000-1700   6070, 7115

0100-0200   9655 & 11905 (Asia), **W** 11905 & **S** 15395 (N America)

0330-0430   9655 (Asia), **W** 11890 (W North Am), 11905 (Asia), **S** 15395 (W North Am)

1330-1400   **W** 7145 (E Asia), 9655 & 11905 (Asia), **S** 11955 (E Asia)

1800-1900   9655 (Asia), **S** 9690 & **W** 11855 (Mideast), 11905 (Asia)

2045-2115   **W** 9535 (Europe), 9655 (Asia), **S** 9680 (Europe), 11905 (Asia)

2200-2400   6070, 7115

TURKEY—Turkish
VOICE OF TURKEY

0000-0400   **S** 11725 (Europe & N America)

0000-0800 ◨   9445 (Europe & E North Am), 9460 (Europe)

0000-0800   **W** 11710 (Europe & E North Am)

0000-1000 ◨   15385 (Europe)

24 Hr   11955 (Mideast)

0400-0700   **S** 9505 (Europe, N America & C America)

0400-0900   **S** 21715 (W Asia, S Asia & Australasia)

0500-1000 ◨   11925 & 15145 (W Asia)

0500-1000   **W** 9560 (W Asia, S Asia & Australasia)

0700-0900   **S** 13670 (Europe)

0800-2200 ◨   9460 (Europe & E North Am)

1000-1500   **S** F 15625 (N Africa & E Africa)

1000-1700   15350 (Europe)

1000-2300 ◨   9560 (W Asia, S Asia & Australasia)

1100-1600   **W** F 7150 (N Africa)

1300-1500   **S** 13670 (Europe)

1600-2200   **S** 7115 (N Africa & Mideast)

1600-2300 ◨   5980 (Europe)

1700-2300   **W** 7255 (Mideast & Africa)

1700-2400 ◨   15385 (Europe)

2100-2400   **S** 11725 (Europe & N America)

2200-2400 ◨   9445 (Europe & E North Am), 9460 (Europe)

| 2200-2400 | W 11710 (Europe & E North Am) |
| 2300-2350 | S 11810 (Europe & E North Am) |

UNITED ARAB EMIRATES—Arabic
UAE RADIO FROM ABU DHABI
0000-0200	9605 (Irr) (Mideast)
0200-0400	6180 (Mideast), W 15315 (E Asia)
0200-0500	S 17855 (Australasia)
0200-0700	W 9605 (Mideast)
0200-0900	W 11970 (Mideast)
0500-0700	S 21735 (Australasia)
0600-0800	S 15265 (Europe)
0600-0900	W 13605 (Europe)
0700-1100	S 17760 (N Africa)
0700-1400	W 17760 (Australasia)
0900-1100	S 17825 & S 21735 (E Asia)
0900-1400	W 15280 & W 15380 (Mideast) W 17885 (Australasia)
1100-1300	S 15315 & W 21735 (E Asia)
1300-1600	W 9605 (Australasia)
1400-1800	W 9695 (N Africa)
1400-2200	9770 (Europe)
1500-1700	S 13605 (Mideast)
1500-1800	S 15265 (N Africa)
1500-2200	S 9605 (Mideast)
1600-2200	6180 (Irr) (N Africa & Mideast), 11710 (Europe)

UAE RADIO IN DUBAI
0000-0200	11795 (Irr) (Europe, E North Am & C America), 13675 (Irr) (E North Am & C America)
0230-0330	11945, 13675, 15400 & 21485 (E North Am & C America)
0400-0530	15435 (Australasia), 17830 (E Asia), 21700 (Australasia)
0600-1030, 1110-1330 & 1400-1600	13675 & 15395 (Europe), 17630 (N Africa), 21605 (Europe)
1640-2055	11795, 13675 & 15395 (Europe), 17630 (N Africa)
2055-2400	11795 (Irr) (Europe, E North Am & C America), 13675 (Irr) (E North Am & C America)

VENEZUELA—Spanish
ECOS DEL TORBES
0900-1300	4980
1300-1900	9640
2000-0400	4980

RADIO TACHIRA
0130-0400	4830 (Irr)
1000-1300 & 2000-0130	4830

VIETNAM—Vietnamese
VOICE OF VIETNAM
0000-0100	9840, W 12020 & S 15010 (E Asia & Americas)
0000-1000	12035

0000-1600	10059
0130-0230	W 5940 & S 7250 (E North Am)
0300-0900	W 12020
1700-1800	9840, W 12020 & S 15010 (Europe)
2200-2400	10059, 12035

YUGOSLAVIA—Serbian
RADIO YUGOSLAVIA
0000-0030	S Su 9580 & S Su 11870 (E North Am)
0030-0100	W 6195, W 7115 & S 9580 (E North Am), S 11870 (E North Am)
0100-0130	W Su 6195 & W Su 7115 (E North Am)
0130-0200	W 6195 & W 7115 (E North Am)
1400-1430	W 11835 (Australasia)
2000-2030	Sa 6100 (W Europe), Sa 7230 (Australasia)
2030-2100	6100 (W Europe), 7230 (Australasia)
2100-2130	Sa 6100 (W Europe), Sa 7230 (Australasia)
2330-2400	S 9580 (E North Am), S 11870 (E North Am)

Addresses PLUS—1998

E-Mail and Postal Addresses . . . PLUS World Wide Web Sites, Phones and Faxes, Contact Personnel, Bureaus, Future Plans, Items for Sale, Free Gifts . . . PLUS Summer and Winter Times in Each Country!

The rest of this book tells how stations reach you, but this section is different. It spins the bottle the other way by showing how you can reach the stations. It also reveals other ways that stations can inform and entertain you.

"Applause" Replies

When radio was new, listeners sent in "applause" cards not only to let stations know about reception quality, but also how much their shows were—or were not—being appreciated. By way of saying "thanks," stations would reply with a letter or attractive card verifying ("QSLing" in radio lingo) that the station the listener reported hearing was, in fact, theirs. While they were at it, some would also throw in a free souvenir of their station—a calendar, perhaps, or a pennant or sticker.

This is still being done today. You can see how by looking under Verification in the glossary farther back in this book, then making use of Addresses PLUS for contact specifics.

Electronic Bazaar

Stations sell offbeat items, too. Besides the obvious, such as world band radios, some stations peddle native recordings, books, magazines, station T-shirts, ties, tote bags, aprons, caps, watches, clocks, pens, knives, letter openers, lighters, refrigerator magnets, keyrings and other collectables. One Miami-based station will even sell you airtime for a dollar a minute!

Paying Postfolk

Most stations prefer to reply to listener correspondence—even e-mail—via the postal system. That way, they can send out printed schedules, verification cards and other "hands-on" souvenirs. Big stations usually do so for free, but smaller ones often want to be reimbursed for postage costs.

Hong Kong is China's economic gateway to the world, while China Radio International is their global voice.   Robert Crane

Pastor Ed Lapiz, in short-sleeved shirt, and Jonathan Mortiz host FEBC's "Kumusta Po Kabayan?" for Filipino overseas contract workers in Saudi Arabia and the Gulf states.

Most effective, especially for Latin American and Indonesian stations, is to enclose some unused (mint) stamps from the station's country. These are available from Plum's Airmail Postage, 12 Glenn Road, Flemington NJ 08822 USA, phone +1 (908) 788-1020, fax +1 (908) 782 2612. Too, you can try DX Stamp Service, 6137 Patriot Drive, Apt. 13, Ontario NY 14519-8606 USA, phone +1 (315) 524-8806; or DX-QSL Associates, 434 Blair Road NW, Vienna VA 22180 USA.

One way to help ensure your return-postage stamps will be used as you intended is to stick them onto a pre-addressed return airmail envelope (self-addressed stamped envelope, or SASE).

You can also prompt reluctant stations by donating one or more U.S. dollars, preferably hidden from prying eyes by a piece of foil-covered carbon paper or the like. Registration helps, too, as cash tends to get stolen. Additionally, International Reply Coupons (IRCs), which recipients may exchange locally for air or surface stamps, are available at many post offices worldwide. Thing is, they're relatively costly, are not fully effective, and aren't accepted by postal authorities in all countries.

Stamp Out Crime

Yes, even in 1998 mail theft is a problem in several countries. We identify these, and for each one offer proven ways to avoid theft.

Remember that some postal employees are stamp collectors, and in certain countries they freely steal mail with unusual stamps. When in doubt, use everyday stamps or, even better, a postal meter. Another option is to use an aerogram.

¿Que Hora Es?

World Time, explained elsewhere in this book, is essential if you want to find out when your favorite station is on. But if you want to know what time it is in any given country, World Time and Addresses PLUS work together to give you the most accurate local times within each country.

How accurate? The United States' official expert on international local times tells us that her organization finds PASSPORT's local times to be the most accurate available from any source, anywhere.

So that you don't have to wrestle with seasonal changes in your own local time, we give local times for each country in terms of hours' difference from World Time, which stays the same year-round. For example, if you look below under "Algeria," you'll see that country is World Time +1; that is, one hour ahead of World Time. So, if World Time is 1200, the local time in Algeria is 1300 (1:00 PM). On the other hand, México City is World Time –6; that is, six hours behind World Time. If World Time is 1200, in México City it's 6:00 AM. And so it goes for each country in this section. Times shown in parentheses are for the middle of the year—roughly April-October; specific dates of seasonal-time changeovers for individual countries can be obtained (U.S. callers only) by dialing toll-free 1-800-342-5624.

Spotted Something New?

Has something changed since we went to press? A missing detail? Please let us know! Your update information, especially photocopies of material received from stations, is highly valued. Contact the IBS Editorial Office, Box 300, Penn's Park, PA 18943 USA, fax +1 (215) 598 3794, e-mail addresses@passport.com.

Many thanks to the kindly folks and helpful organizations mentioned at the end of this chapter for their cooperation in the preparation of this section. Without you, none of this would have been possible.

Using PASSPORT's Addresses PLUS Section

- **Stations included:** All stations known to reply, however erratically, or new stations which possibly may reply, to correspondence from listeners.
- **Leased-time programs:** Private non-political organizations that lease air time, but which possess no world band transmitters of their own, are not necessarily listed. However, they may be reached via the stations over which they are heard.
- **Postal addresses.** Communications addresses are given. These sometimes differ from the physical locations given in the Blue Pages.
- **E-mail addresses and URLs.** Given in Internet format. Periods, commas and semicolons at the end of an address are normal sentence punctuation, *not* part of that address. Individuals can often be reached by e-mail by using their last name before the "@".
- **Fax numbers.** To help avoid confusion, fax numbers are given without hyphens, telephone numbers with hyphens, and are configured for international dialing once you add your country's international access code (011 in the United States and Canada, 010 in the United Kingdom, and so on). For domestic dialing within countries outside the United States, Canada and the Caribbean, replace the country code (1-3 digits preceded by a "+") by a zero.
- **Giveaways.** If you want freebies, say so politely in your correspondence. These are usually available until supplies run out.

R. Walton

Oregonian Richard Walton's collection of world band portables includes two prized oldies, the beefy Grundig Satellit 650 (being tuned) and to its right the large Sony ICF-6800W. Both have superb audio quality.

- **Web radio.** World band stations which also have RealAudio, StreamWorks or comparable Web audio programming are indicated by 📧.
- **Unless otherwise indicated, stations:**
  — Reply regularly within six months to most listeners' correspondence in English.
  — Provide, upon request, free station schedules and verification ("QSL") postcards or letters (see "Verification" in the glossary for further information). We specify when other items are available for free or for purchase.
  — Do not require compensation for postage costs incurred in replying to you. Where compensation is required, details are provided.
- **Local times.** These are given in difference from World Time. For example, "World Time –5" means that if you subtract five hours from World Time, you'll get the local time in that country; so if it were 1100 World Time, it would be 0600 local time in that country. Times in (parentheses) are for the middle of the year—roughly April-October.

AFGHANISTAN World Time +4:30
NOTE: Postal service to this country is occasionally suspended.
Radio Afghanistan, P.O. Box 544, Kabul, Afghanistan. Rarely replies.

ALBANIA World Time +1 (+2 midyear)
Radio Tirana, External Service, Rruga Ismail Qemali, Tirana, Albania. Phone: +355 (42) 23-239. Fax: (External Service) +355 (42) 23 650; (General Directorate) +355 (42) 26 203. Contact: Bardhyl Pollo, Director of External Services; Adriana Bislea, English Department; or Diana Koci; (Technical Directorate) Itfan Mandija, Chief of Radio Broadcasting, Technical Directorate; or Rifat Kryeziu, Director of Technical Directorate. Budget cutbacks have caused the once-vigorous Correspondence Section to be completely eliminated, so getting any sort of reply is not easy. Reception reports are sometimes verified with QSL cards printed in Munich and donated by the "Radio Tirana Listener Club" in Germany. Try enclosing $1 with your letter, it might help.
Trans World Radio—*see* Monaco.

ALGERIA World Time +1 (+2 midyear)
Radio Algiers International—same details as "Radio Algérienne," below.
Radio Algérienne (ENRS)
NONTECHNICAL AND GENERAL TECHNICAL: 21 Boulevard des Martyrs, Algiers 16000, Algeria. Phone: (general) +213 (2) 590-700; (head of international relations) +213 (2) 594-266; (head of technical direction) +213 (2) 692-867. Fax: +213 (2) 605 814. Contact: (nontechnical) L. Zaghlami; Chaabane Lounakil, Head of International Arabic Section; Mrs. Zehira Yahi, Head of International Relations; or Relations Extérieures; (technical) M. Lakhdar Mahdi, Head of Technical Direction. Replies irregularly. French or Arabic preferred, but English accepted.
FREQUENCY MANAGEMENT OFFICE: Télédiffusion d'Algérie, route de Bainem, B.P. 50, Bouzareah, Algeria. Fax: +213 (2) 797 390 or +213 (2) 941 390. Contact: Mouloud Lahlou, Director General.

ANGOLA World Time +1
NOTE: Because of the unsettled conditions prevalent in Angola, except for the first three stations given below, few of the former stations have been active in recent years. Whether most will eventually be reactivated is unknown at this time.
A Voz da Resistência do Galo Negro(VORGAN) (Voice of the Resistance of the Black Cockerel), Free Angola Information Service, 1629 K Street NW, Suite 503, Washington DC 20006 USA. Phone: +1 (202) 775-0958. Fax: +1 (202) 785 8063. URL: (UNITA) www.sfiedi.fr/kup/index.html#anglais. Contact: Kalik Chaka, Director of Information; or Jardo Muekalia, Chief Representative to the United States. Pro-UNITA, led by Joseph Savimbi—once a rebel organization, but which is now considered to be part of the legitimate Angolan political structure. This station will eventually be privatized as soon as all political issues have been settled. The new station will be called Radio Despertar (Wake Up Radio). Transmits from Jamba in the central highlands of Angola.
Emissora Provincial de Benguela (when operating), C.P. 19, Benguela, Angola. Contact: Simão Martíns Cuto, Responsável Administrativo; Carlos A.A. Gregório, Diretor; or José Cabral Sande. $1 or return postage required. Replies irregularly.
Emissora Provincial de Bié (if reactivated), C.P. 33, Kuito, Bié, Angola. Contact: José Cordeiro Chimo, O Diretor. Replies occasionally to correspondence in Portuguese.
Emissora Provincial de Moxico (if reactivated), C.P. 74, Luena, Angola. Contact: Paulo Cahilo, Diretor. $1 or return postage required. Replies to correspondence in Portuguese.
Other **Emissora Provincial** stations (if reactivated)—same address, etc., as Rádio Nacional, below.

Rádio Nacional de Angola, C.P. 1329, Luanda, Angola. Fax: +244 (2) 391 234. Contact: Bernardino Costa, Public Opinion Office; Sra. Luiza Fancony, Diretora de Programas; Lourdes de Almeida, Chefe de Seção; or Cesar A.B. da Silva, Diretor Geral. Formerly replied occasionally to correspondence, preferably in Portuguese, but replies have been more difficult recently. $1, return postage or 2 IRCs most helpful.

ANTARCTICA World Time –2 (–3 midyear) Base Antárctica Esperanza

Radio Nacional Arcángel San Gabriel—LRA36, Base Esperanza, Tierra del Fuego, Antártida e Islas del Atlántico Sur, 9411 Argentina. Contact: Luis Dupuis; Victor Hugo Figueroa, Jefe base; or Sra. Adriana Figueroa. Return postage required. Replies to correspondence in Spanish, and sometimes to correspondence in English and French, depending upon who is at the station. If no reply, try sending your correspondence (but don't write the station's name on your envelope) and 2 IRCs via the helpful Gabriel Iván Barrera, Casilla 2868, 1000 Buenos Aires, Argentina; fax +54 (1) 322 3351.

ANGUILLA World Time –4

Caribbean Beacon, Box 690, Anguilla, British West Indies. Phone: +1 (809) 497-4340. Fax: +1 (809) 497 4311. Contact: Monsell Hazell, Chief Engineer. $2 or return postage helpful. Relays Dr. Gene Scott's University Network—see USA.

ANTIGUA World Time –4

BBC World Service—Caribbean Relay Station, P.O. Box 1203, St. John's, Antigua. Phone: +1 (809) 462-0994. Fax: +1 (809) 462 0436. Contact: (technical) G. Hoef, Manager; Roy Fleet; or R. Pratt, Company Engineer. Nontechnical correspondence should be sent to the BBC World Service in London (see).

Deutsche Welle—Relay Station Antigua—same address and contact as BBC World Service, above. Nontechnical correspondence should be sent to the Deutsche Welle in Germany (see).

ARGENTINA World Time –3

"De Coleccion," Casilla 96, 1900 La Plata, Argentina. Phone: +54 (21) 270-507; or +54 (21) 216-607. Contact: Jorge Bourdet, Editor. Program aired on shortwave from a local medium wave station from La Plata city. Beamed to Antarctica on Sundays only in the SSB mode. Include 2 IRCs when writing.

Radiodifusión Argentina al Exterior—RAE, C.C. 555 Correo Central, 1000 Buenos Aires, Argentina. Phone: +54 (1) 325-6368. Fax: +54 (1) 325 9433. URL: (experimental website) www.primenet.com/~miglia/rae.htm. Contact: (general) Paul F. Allen, Announcer, English Team; John Anthony Middleton, Head of the English Team; María Dolores López; Rodrigo Calderón, English Department; or Sandro Cenci, Chief, Italian Section; (administration) Señorita Perla Damuri, Directora; (technical) Gabriel Iván Barrera, DX Editor; or Patricia Menéndez. Free paper pennant and tourist literature. Return postage or $1 appreciated.

Radio La Colifata—LT22, Casilla 17, 1640 - Martínez (B.A.), Argentina. E-mail: colifata@interactive.com.ar. Contact: Alfredo Olivera, Director General; or Norberto Pugliese, Producción onda corta. Verifies reception reports and replies to correspondence in Spanish. Return postage (2 IRCs) required. Normally transmits only on FM, from its location in the Dr. J. T. Borda Municipal Neuropsychiatric Hospital, but occasionally has special programs broadcast via stations like WRMI, USA. Programs are produced by residents of the hospital.

Radio Malargüe (when active), Esq. Aldao 350, 5613 Malargüe, Argentina. Contact: Eduardo Vicente Lucero, Jefe Técnico; Nolasco H. Barrera, Interventor; or José Pandolfo, Departamento Administración. Free pennants. Return postage necessary. Prefers correspondence in Spanish.

Radio Nacional Buenos Aires, Maipú 555, 1006 Buenos Aires, Argentina. Phone: +54 (1) 325-9100. Fax: (general)

+54 (1) 325 9433; (technical) +54 (1) 325 5742. Contact: Patricia Ivone Barral, Directora Nacional; Patricia Claudia Dinale de Jantus, Directora Administrativa; or María Eugenia Baya Casal, Directora Operativa. $1 helpful. Prefers correspondence in Spanish, and usually replies via RAE (see above). If no reply, try sending your correspondence (but don't write the station's name on your envelope) and 1 IRC via the helpful Gabriel Iván Barrera, Casilla 2868, 1000 Buenos Aires, Argentina; fax +54 (1) 322 3351.

Radio Nacional Mendoza (when active), Av. Emilio Civit 460, 5500 Mendoza, Argentina. Phone: (administrative) +54 (61) 38-15-27. Phone/fax: (general) +54 (61) 25-79-31. Fax: +54 (61) 38 05 96. Contact: (general/administrative) Lic. Jorge Horacio Parvanoff, Director; (technical) Juan Carlos Fernández, Jefe del Departamento Técnico. Free pamphlets and stickers. Replies to correspondence, preferably in Spanish, but English also accepted. Plans to replace transmitter.

Radio Rivadavia (when operating to Antarctica), Arenales 2467, 1124 Buenos Aires, Argentina. Fax: +54 (1) 824 6927.

ARMENIA World Time +3 (+4 midyear)

Armenian Radio—see Voice of Armenia for details.

Lutherische Stunde (religious program aired over Radio Intercontinental), Postfach 1162, D-27363 Sottrum, Germany.

Mitternachtsruf (religious program aired via Radio Intercontinental), Postfach 62, D-79807 Lottstetten, Germany; Postfach 290, Eicholzstrasse 38, CH-8330 Pfaffikon, Switzerland; or P.O. Box 4389, W. Columbia, SC 29171 USA. Contact: Jonathan Malgo or Paul Richter. Free stickers and promotional material.

Radio Intercontinental

MAIN ADDRESS: Vardanants 28, No. 34, Yerevan 70 Armenia.
GERMAN ADDRESS: D-51702 Bergneustad, Germany.
SWITZERLAND ADDRESS: (Mitternachtsruf) Postfach 8051, Zurich, Switzerland.

Voice of Armenia, Radio Agency, Alek Manoukyan Street 5, 375025 Yerevan, Armenia. Phone: +374 (2) 558-010. Fax: +374 (2) 551 513. Contact: V. Voskanian, Deputy Editor-in-Chief; R. Abalian, Editor-in-Chief; Armenag Sansaryan, International Relations Bureau; or Levon Ananikian. Free postcards and stamps. Replies slowly. At present telephone, fax and mail services in and out of Armenia are very erratic. Until mid-October 1997 station will be conducting their 50th anniversary public relations campaign from Canada. The contact address until mid-October 1997 is: Mr. Armenag Sansaryan, Voice of Armenia, International Relations Bureau, 6055 Balmoral, Brossard PQ J4Z 2H5 Canada. Phone/fax: +1 (514) 445 6592. Mr Sansaryan will be moving back to Armenia around mid-October 1997.

ASCENSION World Time exactly

BBC World Service—Atlantic Relay Station, English Bay, Ascension (South Atlantic Ocean). Fax: +247 6117. Contact: (technical) Jeff Cant, Staff Manager; M.R. Watkins, A/Assistant Resident Engineer; or Mrs. Nicola Nicholls, Transmitter Engineer. Nontechnical correspondence should be sent to the BBC World Service in London (see).

Radio Japan, Radio Roma and Voice of America/IBB— via BBC Ascension Relay Station—All correspondence should be directed to the regular addresses in Japan, Italy and USA (see).

AUSTRALIA World Time +11 (+10 midyear) Victoria (VIC), New South Wales (NSW), Australian Capital Territory (ACT) and Tasmania (TAS); +10:30 (+9:30 midyear) South Australia (SA); +10 Queensland (QLD); +9:30 Northern Territory (NT); +8 Western Australia (WA)

Australian Broadcasting Corporation Northern Territory HF Service—ABC Darwin, Administrative Center for the Northern Territory Shortwave Service, ABC Box 9994, GPO Darwin NT 0820, Australia. Phone: +61 (8) 8943-3222, +61 (8) 8943-3229, or +61 (8) 8943-3231; (engineering) +61 (8) 8943-3210. Fax: +61 (8) 8943 3235 or +61 (8) 8943 3208.

Contact: (general) Sue Camilleri, Broadcaster and Community Liaison Officer; Yvonne Corby; Christine Kakakios; or Fred McCue, Producer, "Mornings with Michael Mackenzie"; (technical) Peter Camilleri, Production Manager. Free stickers. Free "Traveller's Guide to ABC Radio." T-shirts US$20. Three IRCs or return postage helpful.

Australian Defence Forces Radio, Department of Defence, EMU (Electronic Media Unit) ANZAC Park West, APW 1-B-07, Reid, Canberra, ACT 2601, Australia. Phone: +61 (2) 6266-6669. Fax: +61 (2) 6266 6565. Contact: (general) Adam Iffland, Presenter; (technical) Hugh Mackenzie, Managing Presenter; or Brian Langshaw. SAE and 2 IRCs needed for a reply. Station replies to verification inquiries only. At last check, transmissions were emanating from a 40 kW single-sideband transmitter in Canberra at HMAS Harman.

BBC World Service via Radio Australia—For verification direct from the Australian transmitters, contact Arie Schellars, Assistant Transmission Manager, Master Control, at Radio Australia (see). Nontechnical correspondence should be sent to the BBC World Service in London (see).

CAAMA Radio—ABC, Central Australian Aboriginal Media Association, Bush Radio Service, P.O. Box 2924, Alice Springs NT 0871, Australia. Phone: +61 (8) 8952-9204. Fax: +61 (8) 8952 9214. Contact: Merridie Satoar, Department Manager; Mark Lillyman, News Director; Nova Mack, Receptionist; or Owen Cole, CAAMA General Manager; (administration) Graham Archer, Station Manager; (technical) Warren Huck, Technician. Free stickers. Two IRCs or return postage helpful.

📻**Radio Australia—ABC**
STUDIOS AND MAIN OFFICES: GPO Box 428G, Melbourne VIC 3001, Australia. Phone: ("Openline" voice mail for listeners' messages and requests) +61 (3) 9626-1825; (general) +61 (3) 9626-1800; (management) +61 (3) 9626-1901; (technical) +61 (3) 9626 1912/3/4; (ABC programs) +61 (3) 9626-1916. Fax & Faxpoll: (general) +61 (3) 9626 1899; (management) +61 (3) 9626 1903; (technical) +61 (3) 9626 1917. E-mail: (English Service) raelp@radioaus.abc.net.au; (Pacific Services) rapac@radioaus.abc.net.au; (Radio and Television Transmissions) ratx@radioaus.abc.net.au; (Internet and World Wide Web Coordinator) naughton.russell@a2.abc.net.au; (others) roz@radioaus.org.au or raust3@ozemail.com.au. URLs: (general) www.abc.net.au/ra/default.htm; (RealAudio in English) www.wrn.org/stations/abc.html; (overview) www.dca.gov.au/pubs/creative_nation/filmtv.htm; (latest program schedule) www.abc.net.au/ra/stopress.htm. Contact: (general) Susan Jenkins, Correspondence Officer; Roger Broadbent, Head, English Language Programming; Judi Cooper, Business Development Manager; Jean-Gabriel Manguy, Chief Executive; Ms. Lisa T. Breeze, Publicist; Denis Gibbons, Producer, "Feedback"; Catherine McCafferty, Audience Liaison; or Dan Gordon; (technical) Nigel Holmes, Transmission Manager, Transmission Management Unit; Arie Schellaars, Assistant Transmission Manager, Master Control; or Neil Deer, Controller, Resources & Distribution. T-shirts available. As from the 1st of July 1997, Radio Australia has been operating at a greatly reduced capacity. Budget cuts of more than 50% in 1997 and continuing over the next 3 years, will reduce this station's ability to broadcast successfully on shortwave. Despite this situation, Radio Australia will attempt to answer listener's letters and reports, even though this will largely depend on the availability of resources and a reply may no longer be possible in all cases. Radio Australia deeply regrets the impact which the funding cuts will have on listener's reception of its broadcasts, but are hopeful that the situation will improve in the future.
NEW YORK BUREAU, NONTECHNICAL: Room 2260, 630 Fifth Avenue, New York NY 10020 USA. Phone: (representative) +1 (212) 332-2540; or (correspondent) +1 (212) 332-2545. Fax: +1 (212) 332 2546. Contact: Maggie Jones, North American Representative.

LONDON BUREAU, NONTECHNICAL: 54 Portland Place, London W1N 4DY, United Kingdom. Phone: +44 (171) 631-4456. Fax: (administration) +44 (171) 323 0059, (news) +44 (171) 323 1125. Contact: Robert Bolton, Manager.
BANGKOK BUREAU, NONTECHNICAL: 209 Soi Hutayana off Soi Suanplu, South Sathorn Road, Bangkok 10120, Thailand. Fax: +66 (2) 287 2040. Contact: Nicholas Stuart.
SAN FRANCISCO OFFICE, SCHEDULES: 2654 17th Avenue, San Francisco CA 94116 USA. Phone: +1 (415) 564-9968. Contact: George Poppin. This address, a volunteer office, only provides Radio Australia schedules to listeners. All other correspondence should be sent directly to the main office in Melbourne.

Radio Rum Jungle—ABC (program studios), Top Aboriginal Bush Association, Corner Speed Street & Gap Road, Batchelor NT 0870, Australia. Phone: +61 (8) 8952-3433. Fax: +61 (8) 8952 2093. Contact: Mae-Mae Morrison, Announcer; Andrew Joshua, Chairman; or George Butler. Three IRCs or return postage helpful. May send free posters.

Radio VNG (official time station)
PRIMARY ADDRESS: National Standards Commission, P.O. Box 282, North Ryde, NSW 2113, Australia. Toll-free telephone number (Australia only) (008) 251-942. Phone: +61 (2) 9888-3922. Fax: +61 (2) 9888 3033. E-mail: richardb@ozemail.com.au. Contact: Dr. Richard Brittain, Secretary, National Time Committee. Station offers a free 16-page booklet about VNG and free promotional material. Free stickers and postcards. Three IRCs helpful. May be forced to close down if sufficient funding is not found.
ALTERNATIVE ADDRESS: VNG Users Consortium, GPO Box 1090, Canberra ACT 2601, Australia. Fax: +61 (2) 6249 9969. Contact: Dr. Marion Leiba, Honorary Secretary. Three IRCs appreciated.

AUSTRIA World Time +1 (+2 midyear)
📻**Radio Austria International**
MAIN OFFICE: Würzburggasse 30, A-1136 Vienna, Austria. Phone: (general) +43 (1) 87878-2130; (voice mail) +43 (1) 87878-3636; (technical) +43 (1) 87878-2629. Fax: (general) +43 (1) 87878 4404; (technical) +43 (1) 87878 2773. E-mail: (general) info@rai.ping.at; ("Kurzwellen Panorama") kwp@rai.ping.at; (technical) hfbc@orf.at. URLs: (general) www.ping.at/rai/; (RealAudio in English and German) www.wrn.org/stations/orf.html. Contact: (general) Vera Bock, Listener's Service; "Postbox"/"Hörerbriefkasten" listeners' letters shows; ("Kurzwellen Panorama") Wolf Harranth, Editor; or Christine Soucek, Listener'Service; (administration) Prof. Paul Lendvai, Director; Dr. Edgar Sterbenz, Deputy Director; (English Department) David Ward; (German Department) Helmut Blechner; (French Department) Robert Denis; (Spanish Department Jacobo Naar-Carbonell; (Internet Service) Marianne Veit or Oswald Klotz; (technical) Ing. Ernst Vranka, Frequency Manager; or Ing. Klaus Hollndonner, Technical Director. Free stickers and program schedule twice a year, as well as quiz prizes. Mr. Harranth seeks collections of old verification cards and letters for the highly organized historical archives he is maintaining.
WASHINGTON NEWS BUREAU: 1206 Eaton Ct. NW, Washington DC 20007 USA. Phone: +1 (202) 822-9570. Contact: Franz R. Kössler.

AZERBAIJAN World Time +3 (+4 midyear)
Azerbaijani Radio—see Radio Dada Gorgud for details.
Radio Dada Gorgud (Voice of Azerbaijan), Medhi Hüseyin küçəsi 1, 370011 Baku, Azerbaijan. Phone: +7 (8922) 398-585. Fax: +7 (8922) 395 452. Contact: Mrs. Tamam Bayatli-Öner, Director. Free postcards. $1 or return postage helpful. Replies occasionally to correspondence in English.

BAHRAIN World Time +3
Radio Bahrain (if reactivated), Broadcasting & Television, Ministry of Information, P.O. Box 702, Al Manāmah, Bahrain. Phone: (Arabic Service) +973 781-888; (English Service)

+973 629-085. Fax: (Arabic Service) +973 681 544; (English Service) +973 780 911. Contact: A. Suliman (for Director of Broadcasting). $1 or IRC required. Replies irregularly.

BANGLADESH World Time +6
Bangladesh Betar
NONTECHNICAL CORRESPONDENCE: External Services, Shahbagh Post Box No. 2204, Dhaka 1000, Bangladesh. Phone: +880 (2) 865-294. Fax: +880 (2) 862 021. Contact: Quazi Mahmudur Rahman, Director, Liaison; Fakhrul Islam, Deputy Director; Syed Zaman; A.K. Jahidul Huq, Assistant Director; or Ashraf ul-Alam, Assistant for Director.
TECHNICAL CORRESPONDENCE: National Broadcasting Authority, NBA House, 121 Kazi Nazrul Islam Avenue, Dhaka 1000, Bangladesh. Phone: +880 (2) 818-734 or +880 (2) 865-294. Fax: +880 (2) 817 850. Contact: Nurul Islam, Station Engineer, Research; Mohammed Romizuddin Bhuiya, Senior Engineer (Research Wing). Verifications not common from this office.

BELARUS World Time +2 (+3 midyear)
Belarussian Radio—see Radio Belarus for details.
Grodno Radio—see Radio Belarus for details.
Mogilev Radio—see Radio Belarus for details.
Radio Belarus, ul. Krasnaija 4, 220807 Minsk, Belarus. Phone: +7 (172) 395-875, +7 (172) 334-039 or +7 (172) 333-922. Fax: +7 (172) 366 643 or +7 (172) 648 182. URLs: (official site of German department) www.nestor.minsk.by/radiorod/; (unofficial site in English, set up by a friendly enthusiast) http://ourworld.compuserve.com/homepages/castner/radio_gb.htm. Contact: Michail Tondel, Chief Editor Overseas Service; or Jürgen Eberhardt, Editor German Service. Free Belarus stamps.
Radio Minsk—see Radio Belarus for details.
Voice of Orthodoxy (program)
MINSK OFFICE: V. Pristavko, P.O. Box 17, 220012 Minsk, Belarus. Aired via transmission facilities of Radio Trans Europe, Portugal, and the Voice of Hope, Lebanon. Correspondence and reception reports welcomed.
PARIS OFFICE: B.P. 416-08, F-75366 Paris Cedex 08, France. Contact: Valentin Korelsky, General Secretary.

BELGIUM World Time +1 (+2 midyear)
☞Radio Vlaanderen Internationaal
NONTECHNICAL AND GENERAL TECHNICAL: P.O. Box 26, B-1000 Brussels, Belgium. Phone: +32 (2) 741-5611, +32 (2) 741-3807 or +32 (2) 741-3802. Fax: (administration and Dutch Service) +32 (2) 732 6295; (other language services) +32 (2) 732 8336. BBS: +32 (3) 825-3613. E-mail: rvi@brtn.be. URLs: (general) www.brtn.be/rvi/; (RealAudio in English and Dutch) www.wrn.org/stations/rvi.html. Contact (general) Deanne Lehman, Producer, "P.O. Box 26" letterbox program; Liz Sanderson, Head, English Service; Maryse Jacob, Head, French Service; Martina Luxen, Head, German Service; Ximena Prieto, Head, Spanish Service; (administration) Monique Delvaux, Directeur; (general technical) Frans Vossen, Producer, "Radio World." Sells RVI T-shirts (large/extra large) for 400 Belgian francs. Remarks and reception reports can also be sent c/o the following diplomatic addresses:
NIGERIA EMBASSY: 1A, Bak Road, Ikoyi-Island, Lagos, Nigeria.
ARGENTINA EMBASSY: Defensa 113, 8% Piso, 1065 Buenos Aires, Argentina.
INDIA EMBASSY: 50 N Shanti Path Chanakyapuri, New Delhi 110021, India.
Radio Vlaanderen International is to undergo drastic restructuring reforms to cut costs by restricting broadcasts and reducing the number of employees. These reforms will be implemented at the end of October 1997. Spanish, German and Arabic broadcasts will end. The Dutch, French and English language services will continue but in a different format. Overall shortwave broadcasts will be reduced from the present level of 300 hours per week to only 140 hours.

FREQUENCY MANAGEMENT OFFICE: BRTN, Ave. Reyerslaan 52, B-1043 Brussels, Belgium. Phone: +32 (2) 741-5571. Fax: +32 (2) 741 5567. E-mail: hugo.gauderis@brtn.be. Contact: Hugo Gauderis or Willy Devos, Frequency Manager.

BENIN World Time +1
Office de Radiodiffusion et Télévision du Benin, La Voix de la Révolution, B.P. 366, Cotonou, Bénin; this address is for Cotonou and Parakou stations, alike. Contact: (Cotonou) Damien Zinsou Ala Hassa; Emile Desire Ologoudou, Directeur Generale; or Leonce Goohouede; (technical) Anastase Adjoko, Chef de Service Technique (Radio Parakou, general) J. de Matha, Le Chef de la Station, or (Radio Parakou, technical) Léon Donou, Le Chef des Services Techniques. Return postage, $1 or IRC required. Replies irregularly and slowly to correspondence in French.

BHUTAN World Time +7 (+6 midyear)
Bhutan Broadcasting Service
STATION: Department of Information and Broadcasting, Ministry of Communications, P.O. Box 101, Thimphu, Bhutan. Phone: +975 223-070. Fax: +975 223 073. Contact: (general) Ashi Renchen Chhoden, News and Current Affairs; Narda Gautam; or Sonam Tshong, Executive Director; (technical) C. Proden, Station Engineer; or Technical Head. Two IRCs, return postage or $1 required. Replies extremely irregularly; correspondence to the U.N. Mission (see following) may be more fruitful.
UNITED NATIONS MISSION: Permanent Mission of the Kingdom of Bhutan to the United Nations, Two United Nations Plaza, 27th Floor, New York NY 10017 USA. Fax: +1 (212) 826 2998. Contact: Mrs. Kunzang C. Namgyel, Third Secretary; Mrs. Sonam Yangchen, Attaché; Ms. Leki Wangmo, Second Secretary; Thinley Dorrji, Second Secretary; or Hari K. Chhetri, Second Secretary. Free newspapers and booklet on the history of Bhutan.

World Time −4
NOTE ON STATION IDENTIFICATIONS: Many Bolivian stations listed as "Radio . . ." may also announce as "Radio Emisora . . ." or "Radiodifusora . . ."
Galaxia Radiodifusión—see Radio Galaxia, below.
Hitachi Radiodifusión—see Radio Hitachi, below.
Paititi Radiodifusión—see Radio Paititi, below.
Radio Abaroa, Calle Nicanor Gonzalo Salvatierra 249, Riberalta, Beni, Bolivia. Contact: René Arias Pacheco, Director. Return postage or $1 required. Replies rarely to correspondence in Spanish.
Radio A.N.D.E.S., Casilla No. 16, Uyuni, Provincia Antonio Quijarro, Departamento de Potosí, Bolivia. Phone: +591 (69) 32-145. Owners: La Federación Unica de Trabajadores Campesinos del Altiplano Sud. Contact: Francisco Quisbert Salinas, Secretario Permanente del Consejo de Administración; Audo Ramos Colque; Rita Salvatierra Bautista; or César Gerónimo Alí Flores, Reporteros. Spanish preferred. Return postage in the form of two U.S. dollars appreciated, as the station depends on donations for its existence.
Radio Animas, Chocaya, Animas, Potosí, Bolivia. Return postage or $1 required. Replies irregularly to correspondence in Spanish.
Radio Camargo—see Radio Emisoras Camargo, below.
Radio Carlos Palenque, Casilla de Correo 8704, La Paz, Bolivia. Phone: +591 (2) 354-418, +591 (2) 375-953, +595 (2) 324-394 or +595 (2) 361-176. Fax: +591 (2) 356 785. Contact: Rodolfo Beltrán Rosales, Jefe de Prensa de "El Metropolicial." Free postcards and pennants. $1 or return postage necessary.
Radio Centenario "La Nueva"
MAIN OFFICE: Casilla 818, Santa Cruz de la Sierra, Bolivia. Phone: +591 (3) 529-265. Fax: +591 (3) 524 747. Contact: Napoleón Ardaya Borja, Director. May send a calendar. Free stickers. Return postage or $1 required. Audio cassettes of contemporary Christian music and Bolivian folk music $10,

including postage; CDs of Christian folk music $15, including postage. Replies to correspondence in English and Spanish. *U.S. BRANCH OFFICE:* LATCOM, 1218 Croton Avenue, New Castle PA 16101 USA. Phone: +1 (412) 652-0101. Fax: +1 (412) 652 4654. Contact: Hope Cummins.

Radio Colonia—*see* Radio Televisión Colonia.

Radio Cosmos (if reactivated), Casilla 1092, Cochabamba, Bolivia. Phone: +591 (42) 50-423. Fax: +591 (42) 51 173. Contact: Laureano Rojas, Jr. $1 or return postage required. Replies to correspondence in Spanish.

Radiodifusoras Integración—*see* Radio Integración, below.

Radiodifusoras Minería, Casilla de Correo 247, Oruro, Bolivia. Phone: +591 (52) 52-736. Contact: Dr. José Carlos Gómez Espinoza, Gerente y Director General; or Srta. Costa Colque Flores, Responsable del programa "Minería Cultural." Free pennants. Replies to correspondence in Spanish.

Radiodifusoras Trópico, Casilla 60, Trinidad, Beni, Bolivia. Contact: Eduardo Avila Alberdi, Director. Replies slowly to correspondence in Spanish. Return postage required for reply.

Radio Eco
MAIN ADDRESS: Correo Central, Reyes, Ballivián, Beni, Bolivia. Contact: Gonzalo Espinoza Cortés, Director. Free station literature. $1 or return postage required. Replies to correspondence in Spanish.
ALTERNATIVE ADDRESS: Rolmán Medina Méndez, Correo Central, Reyes, Ballivián, Bolivia.

Radio Eco San Borja (San Borja la Radio), Correo Central, San Borja, Ballivián, Beni, Bolivia. Contact: Gonzalo Espinoza Cortés, Director. Free station poster promised to correspondents. Return postage appreciated. Replies slowly to correspondence in Spanish.

Radio El Mundo, Casilla 1984, Santa Cruz de la Sierra, Bolivia. Phone: +591 (3) 464-646. Fax: +591 (3) 465 057. Contact: Freddy Banegas Carrasco, Gerente; Lic. José Luis Vélez Ocampo C., Director; or Lic. Juan Pablo Sainz, Gerente General. Free stickers and pennants. $1 or return postage required. Replies irregularly to correspondence in Spanish.

Radio Emisora Dos de Febrero, Vaca Diez 400, Rurrenabaque, Beni, Bolivia. Contact: John Arze von Boeck. Free pennant, which is especially attractive. Replies occasionally to correspondence in Spanish.

Radio Emisora Galaxia—*see* Radio Galaxia, below.

Radio Emisora Padilla—*see* Radio Padilla, below.

Radio Emisora San Ignacio, Calle Ballivián s/n, San Ignacio de Moxos, Beni, Bolivia. Contact: Carlos Salvatierra Rivero, Gerente y Director. $1 or return postage necessary.

Radio Emisora Villamontes—*see* Radio Villamontes, below.

Radio Emisoras Camargo, Casilla 09, Camargo, Provincia Nor-Cinti, Bolivia. Contact: Pablo García B., Gerente Propietario. Return postage or $1 required. Replies slowly to correspondence in Spanish.

Radio Emisoras Minería—*see* Radiodifusoras Minería.

Radio Estación Frontera—*see* Radio Frontera, below.

Radio Fides, Casilla 9143, La Paz, Bolivia. Fax: +591 (2) 379 030. Contact: Pedro Eduardo Pérez Iribarne, Director; Felicia de Rojas, Secretaria; or Roxana Beltrán C. Replies occasionally to correspondence in Spanish.

Radio Frontera, Casilla 179, Cobija, Pando, Bolivia. Contact: Lino Miahuchi von Ancken, CP9AR. Free pennants. $1 or return postage necessary. Replies to correspondence in Spanish.

Radio Galaxia (if reactivated), Calle Beni s/n casi esquina Udarico Rosales, Guayaramerín, Beni, Bolivia. Contact: Dorián Arias, Gerente; Héber Hitachi Banegas, Director; or Carlos Arteaga Tacaná, Director-Dueño. Return postage or $1 required. Replies to correspondence in Spanish.

Radio Grigotá (if reactivated), Casilla 203, Santa Cruz de la Sierra, Bolivia. Phone/fax: +591 (3) 326-443. Fax: +591 (3) 362 795. Contact: (general) Victor Hugo Arteaga B., Director General; (technical) Tania Martins de Arteaga, Gerente Administrativo. Free stickers, pins, pennants, key rings and posters. $1 or return postage required. Replies occasionally to correspondence in English, French, Portuguese and Spanish. May replace old Philips transmitter.

Radio Hitachi (Hitachi Radiodifusión), Calle Sucre 20, Guayaramerín, Beni, Bolivia. Contact: Héber Hitachi Banegas, Director. Return postage of $1 required.

Radio Illimani, Casilla 1042, La Paz, Bolivia. Phone: +591 (2) 376-364. Fax: +591 (2) 359 275. Contact: Rubén D. Choque, Director; or Lic. Manuel Liendo Rázuri, Gerente General. $1 required, and your letter should be registered and include a tourist brochure or postcard from where you live. Replies irregularly to friendly correspondence in Spanish.

Radio Integración, Casilla 7902, La Paz, Bolivia. Contact: Lic. Manuel Liendo Rázuri, Gerente General; Benjamín Juan Carlos Blanco Q., Director Ejecutivo; or Carmelo de la Cruz Huanca, Comunicador Social. Free pennants. Return postage required.

Radio Juan XXIII (Veintitrés), Avenida Santa Cruz al frente de la plaza principal, San Ignacio de Velasco, Santa Cruz, Bolivia. Phone: +591 (962) 2188. Contact: Fernando Manuel Picazo Torres, Director; or Pbro. Elías Cortezon, Director. Return postage or $1 required. Replies occasionally to correspondence in Spanish.

Radio La Cruz del Sur, Casilla 1408, La Paz, Bolivia. Contact: Hazen Parent, General Director; or Pastor Rodolfo Moya Jiménez, Director. Pennant $1 or return postage. Replies slowly to correspondence in Spanish.

Radio La Palabra, Parroquia de Santa Ana de Yacuma, Beni, Bolivia. Phone: +591 (848) 2117. Contact: Padre Yosu Arketa, Director. Return postage necessary. Replies to correspondence in Spanish.

Radio La Plata, Casilla 276, Sucre, Bolivia. Phone: +591 (64) 31-616. Fax: +591 (64) 41 400. Contact: Freddy Donoso Bleichner.

Radio Libertad (if reactivated), Casilla 5324, La Paz, Bolivia. Phone: +591 (2) 365-154. Fax: +591 (2) 363 069. Contact: (general) Oscar Violetta Barrios; (technical) Lic. Teresa Sanjinés Lora, Gerente General. Depending upon what's on hand, pamphlets, stickers, pins, pennants, purses, pencil sharpeners, key rings and calendars. If blank cassette and $2 is sent, they will be happy to dub recording of local music. Sells T-shirts for $10. Return postage or $1 required for reply. Upon request, they will record for listeners any type of Bolivian music they have on hand, and send it to that listener for the cost of the cassette and postage; or, if the listener sends a cassette, for the cost of postage. Replies fairly regularly to correspondence in English and Spanish.

Radio Loyola, Casilla 40, Sucre, Bolivia. Phone: +591 (64) 30-222. Fax: +591 (64) 42 555. URL: (experimental RealAudio) www.nch.bolnet.bo/loyola.ram. Contact: (general) Lic. José Weimar León G., Director; (technical) Tec. Norberto Rosales. Free stickers and pennants. Replies occasionally to correspondence in English, Italian and Spanish. Considering replacing 18-year old transmitter.

Radio Mauro Núñez (if reactivated), Centro de Estudios para el Desarrollo de Chuquisaca (CEDEC), Casilla 196, Sucre, Bolivia. Phone: +591 (64) 25-008. Fax: +591 (64) 32 628. Contact: Jorge A. Peñaranda Llanos; Ing. Raúl Ledezma, Director Residente "CEDEC"; José Peneranda; or Jesús Urioste. Replies to correspondence in Spanish.

Radio Minería—*see* Radiodifusoras Minería.

Radio Movima, Calle Baptista No. 24, Santa Ana de Yacuma, Beni, Bolivia. Contact: Rubén Serrano López, Director; Javier Roca Díaz, Director Gerente; or Mavis Serrano, Directora. Return postage or $1 required. Replies irregularly to correspondence in Spanish.

Radio Nacional de Huanuni, Casilla 681, Oruro, Bolivia. Contact: Rafael Linneo Morales, Director General; or Alfredo Murillo, Director. Return postage or $1 required. Replies irregularly to correspondence in Spanish.

Radio Norte, Calle Warnes 195, 2do piso del Cine Escorpio, Montero, Santa Cruz, Bolivia. Phone: +591 (92) 20-970. Contact: Leonardo Arteaga Ríos, Director.

Radio Padilla (when active), Padilla, Chuquisaca, Bolivia. Contact: Moisés Palma Salazar, Director. Return postage or $1 required. Replies to correspondence in Spanish.

Radio Paitití, Casilla 172, Guayaramerín, Beni, Bolivia. Contact: Armando Mollinedo Bacarreza, Director; Luis Carlos Santa Cruz Cuéllar, Director Gerente; or Ancir Vaca Cuéllar, Gerente-Propietario. Free pennants. Return postage or $3 required. Replies irregularly to correspondence in Spanish.

Radio Panamericana, Casilla 5263, La Paz, Bolivia. Contact: Daniel Sánchez Rocha, Director. Replies irregularly, with correspondence in Spanish preferred. $1 or 2 IRCs helpful.

Radio Perla del Acre, Casilla 7, Cobija, Departamento de Pando, Bolivia. Return postage or $1 required. Replies irregularly to correspondence in Spanish.

Radio Pío XII (Doce), Casilla 434, Oruro, Bolivia. Phone: +591 (52) 53-168. Contact: Pbro. Roberto Durette, OMI, Director General. Return postage necessary. Replies occasionally to correspondence in Spanish.

Radio San Gabriel, Casilla 4792, La Paz, Bolivia. Phone: +591 (2) 355-371. Phone/fax: +591 (2) 321 174. Contact: Hno. José Canut Saurat, Director General; or Sra. Martha Portugal, Dpto. de Publicidad. $1 or return postage helpful. Free book on station, Aymara calendars and *La Voz del Pueblo Aymara* magazine. Replies fairly regularly to correspondence in Spanish. Station of the Hermanos de la Salle Catholic religious order.

Radio San Miguel, Casilla 102, Riberalta, Beni, Bolivia. Phone: +591 (852) 8268. Contact: Félix Alberto Rada Q., Director; or Gerin Pardo Molina, Director. Free stickers and

Tips for Effective Correspondence

Write to be read. Winning correspondence, on paper or by e-mail, is interesting and helpful from the recipient's point of view, yet friendly without being chummy. Comments on specific programs are almost always appreciated.

They don't know English? No problem. A basic form of translation service, performed by computer, is available for free via Globalink over the World Wide Web at www.globalink.com/xlate.html. That same organization—and many more, including some university language departments—will do translations by human beings, usually for a modest fee.

Incorporate language courtesies. Writing in the broadcaster's tongue is always a plus—this section of PASSPORT indicates when it is a requirement—but English is usually the next-best bet. In addition, when writing in any language to Spanish-speaking countries, remember that what gringos think of as the "last name" is actually written as the penultimate name. Thus, Juan Antonio Vargas García, which can also be written as Juan Antonio Vargas G., refers to Sr. Vargas; so your salutation should read, *Estimado Sr. Vargas.*

What's that "García" doing there, then? That's *mamita's* father's family name. Latinos more or less solved the problem of gender fairness in names long before the Anglos.

But, wait—what about Portuguese, used by all those lovely stations in Brazil? Same concept, but in reverse. *Mamá's* father's family name is penultimate, and the "real" last name is where English-speakers are used to it, at the end.

In Chinese, the "last" name comes first. However, when writing in English, Chinese names are sometimes reversed for the benefit of *weiguoren*—foreigners. Use your judgement. For example, "Li" is a common Chinese last name, so if you see "Li Dan," it's "Mr. Li." But if it's "Dan Li," and certainly if it's been anglicized into "Dan Lee," he's already one step ahead of you, and it's still "Mr. Li" (or Lee). Less widely known is that the same can also occur in Hungarian. For example, "Bartók Béla" for Béla Bartók.

If in doubt, fall back on the ever-safe "Dear Sir" or "Dear Madam," or use e-mail, where salutations are not expected. And be patient—replies by post usually take weeks, sometimes months. Slow responders, those that tend to take six months or more to reply, are cited in this section, as are erratic repliers.

pennants; has a different pennant each year. Return postage or $1 required. Replies irregularly to correspondence in Spanish. Feedback on program "Bolivia al Mundo" (aired 0200-0300 World Time) especially appreciated.

Radio Santa Ana, Calle Sucre No. 250, Santa Ana de Yacuma, Beni, Bolivia. Contact: Mario Roberto Suárez, Director; or Mariano Verdugo. Return postage or $1 required. Replies irregularly to correspondence in Spanish.

Radio Santa Cruz, Emisora del Instituto Radiofónico Fé y Alegría (IRFA), Casilla 672 (or 3213), Santa Cruz, Bolivia. Phone: +591 (3) 531-817. Fax: +591 (3) 532 257. Contact: Padre Francisco Flores, S.J., Director General; Srta. María Yolanda Marco E., Secretaria; Señora Mirian Suárez, Productor, "Protagonista Ud.", Director General; or Lic. Silvia Nava S. Free pamphlets, stickers and pennants. Return postage required. Replies to correspondence in English, French and Spanish.

Radio Sararenda, Casilla 7, Camiri, Santa Cruz, Bolivia. Phone: +591 (952) 2121. Contact: Freddy Lara Aguilar, Director; or Kathy Arenas, Administradora. Free stickers and photos of Camiri. Replies to correspondence in Spanish.

Radio Televisión Colonia (when active), Correo Central, Yapacani, Santa Cruz de la Sierra, Bolivia. Phone/fax: +591 (933) 61-64. Fax: +591 (933) 60 00. Contact: (general) Yrey Fausto Montaño Ustárez, Gerente Propietario; (technical) Ing. Rene Zambrana. Replies to correspondence in English, French, Italian, Japanese, Portuguese and Spanish. Free pamphlets, stickers, pins, pennants and small handicrafts made by local artisans. Return postage required for reply.

Radio Villamontes, Avenida Méndez Arcos No. 156, Villamontes, Departamento de Tarija, Bolivia. Contact: Gerardo Rocabado Galarza, Director. $1 or return postage required.

BOSNIA-HERCEGOVINA World Time +1 (+2 midyear)
Radio & Television of Bosnia-Hercegovina, Bulevar Mese Selimovica 4, BH-71000 Sarajevo, Bosnia-Hercegovina. Phone: +387 (71) 646-014 or +387 (71) 455-124. Fax: +387 (71) 645 142 or +387 (71) 455 104. Contact: Milenko Vockic, Director; Mr. N. Dizdarevic; or Rodzic Nerin.

BOTSWANA World Time +2
Radio Botswana, Private Bag 0060, Gaborone, Botswana. Phone: +267 352-541. Fax: +267 357 138. Contact: (general) Ted Makgekgenene, Director; or Monica Mphusu, Producer, "Maokaneng/Pleasure Mix"; (technical) Kingsley Reebang. Free stickers, pennants and pins. Return postage, $1 or 2 IRCs required. Replies slowly and irregularly.

Voice of America/VOA-IBB—Botswana Relay Station
TRANSMITTER SITE: Voice of America/IBB, Botswana Relay Station, Moepeng Hill, Selebi-Phikwe, Botswana. Phone: +267 810-932. Fax: +267 810 252. Contact: Dennis G. Brewer, Station Manager. This address for specialized technical correspondence only. All other correspondence should be directed to the regular VOA address (see USA).

BRAZIL World Time –1 (–2 midyear) Atlantic Islands; –2 (–3 midyear) Eastern, including Brasília and Rio de Janeiro, plus the town of Barra do Garças; –3 (–4 midyear) Western; –4 (–5 midyear) Acre. Some northern states keep midyear time year round.
NOTE: Postal authorities recommend that, because of the level of theft in the Brazilian postal system, correspondence to Brazil be sent only via registered mail.

Emissora Rural A Voz do São Francisco (when operating), C.P. 8, 56300-000 Petrolina PE, Brazil. Contact: Maria Letecia de Andrade Nunes. Return postage necessary. Replies to correspondence in Portuguese.

Rádio Alvorada (Londrina), Rua Senador Souza Naves 9, 9 Andar, 86010-921 Londrina PR, Brazil. Contact: Padre José Guidoreni, Diretor. Pennants $1 or return postage. Replies to correspondence in Portuguese.

Rádio Alvorada (Parintins), Travessa Leopoldo Neves 503, 69150-000 Parintins AM, Brazil. Contact: Raimunda Ribeira da Motta, Diretora. Return postage required. Replies occasionally to correspondence in Portuguese.

Rádio Alvorada (Rio Branco), Avenida Ceará 2150—Altos de Gráfica Globo, 69900-470 Rio Branco AC, Brazil. Occasionally replies to correspondence in Portuguese.

Rádio Anhanguera, C.P. 13, 74823-000 Goiânia GO, Brazil. Contact: Rossana F. da Silva; or Eng. Domingos Vicente Tinoco. Return postage required. Replies to correspondence in Portuguese.

Rádio Aparecida, Avenida Getulio Vargas 185, 12570-000 Aparecida SP, Brazil; or C.P. 14547, 03698-970 Aparecida SP, Brazil. Phone: +55 (12) 565-1133. Fax: +55 (12) 565 1138. Contact: Padre C. Cabral; Savio Trevisan, Departamento Técnico; Cassiano Macedo, Producer, "Encontro DX"; or João Climaco, Diretor Geral. Return postage or $1 required. Replies occasionally to correspondence in Portuguese.

Rádio Bandeirantes, C.P. 372, Rua Radiantes 13, Morumbí, 01059-970 São Paulo SP, Brazil. Fax: +55 (11) 843 5391. E-mail: rbradio@netalpha.com.br. URL: www.netalpha.com.br/bandeirantes/. Contact: Samir Razuk, Diretor Geral; Carlos Newton; or Salomão Esper, Superintendente. Free stickers, pennants and canceled Brazilian stamps. $1 or return postage required.

Rádio Baré, Avenida Santa Cruz Machado 170 A, 69010-070 Manaus AM, Brazil. Contact: Fernando A.B. Andrade, Diretor Programação e Produção. The Diretor is looking for radio catalogs.

Radiobrás—see Rádio Nacional da Amazônia and Rádio Nacional do Brasil.

Rádio Brasil, C.P. 625, 13000-000 Campinas, São Paulo SP, Brazil. Contact: Wilson Roberto Correa Viana, Gerente. Return postage required. Replies to correspondence in Portuguese.

Rádio Brasil Central, C.P. 330, 74001-970 Goiânia GO, Brazil. Contact: Ney Raymundo Fernández, Coordinador Executivo; Sergio Rubens da Silva; or Arizio Pedro Soarez, Diretor Gerente. Free stickers. $1 or return postage required. Replies to correspondence in Portuguese.

Rádio Brasil Tropical, C.P. 405, 78005-970 Cuiabá MT, Brazil. Physical address: Rua Joaquim Murtinho 1456, 78020-830 Cuiabá MT, Brazil. Phone: +55 (65) 321-6882 or +55 (65) 321-6226. Fax: +55 (65) 624 3455. E-mail: rcultura@nutecnet.com.br. URL: www.solunet.com.br/rcultura/radio6.htm. Contact: Klécius Antonio dos Santos, Diretor Comercial. Free stickers. $1 required. Replies to correspondence in Portuguese.

Rádio Caiari, C.P. 104, 78900-000 Porto Velho RO, Brazil. Contact: Carlos Alberto Diniz Martins, Diretor Geral. Free stickers. Return postage helpful. Replies irregularly to correspondence in Portuguese.

Rádio Canção Nova, C.P. 15, 12630-000 Cachoeira Paulista SP, Brazil. Contact: Benedita Luiza Rodrigues; Ana Claudia de Santana; or Valera Guimarães Massafera, Secretária. Free stickers, pennants and station brochure sometimes given upon request. $1 helpful.

Rádio Capixaba, C.P. 509, 29000-000 Vitória ES, Brazil. Contact: Jairo Gouvea Maia, Diretor; or Sofrage do Benil. Replies occasionally to correspondence in Portuguese.

Rádio Carajá (when active), C.P. 520, 75001-970 Anápolis GO, Brazil. Contact: Nilson Silva Rosa, Diretor Geral. Return postage helpful. Replies to correspondence in Portuguese.

Rádio Clube do Pará, C.P. 533, 66000-000 Belém PA, Brazil. Contact: Edyr Paiva Proença, Diretor Geral; or José Almeida Lima de Sousa. Return postage required. Replies irregularly to correspondence in Portuguese.

Rádio Clube de Rondonópolis, C.P. 190, 78700-000 Rondonópolis MT, Brazil. Contact: Canário Silva, Departamento Comercial; or Saúl Feliz, Gerente-Geral. Return postage helpful. Replies to correspondence in Portuguese.

Rádio Clube Varginha, C.P. 102, 37000-000 Varginha MG,

Brazil. Contact: Juraci Viana. Return postage necessary. Replies slowly to correspondence in Portuguese.

Rádio Coari—*see* Rádio Educação Rural-Coari.

Rádio Cultura Araraquara, Avenida Feijó 583 (Centro), 14801-140 Araraquara SP, Brazil. Phone: +55 (16) 232-3790. Fax: +55 (16) 232 3475. E-mail: cultura@techs.com.br. URLs: http://200.246.30.1/cultura/; www.techs.com.br. Contact: Antonio Carlos Rodrigues dos Santos. Return postage required. Replies slowly to correspondence in Portuguese.

Rádio Cultura de Campos, C.P. 79, 28100-970 Campos RJ, Brazil. $1 or return postage necessary. Replies to correspondence in Portuguese.

Rádio Cultura do Pará, Avenida Almirante Barroso 735, 66090-000 Belém PA, Brazil. Contact: Ronald Pastor; or Augusto Proença, Diretor. Return postage required. Replies irregularly to correspondence in Portuguese.

Rádio Cultura de Foz do Iguaçu (Onda Corta), C.P. 84, 85852-520 Foz do Iguaçu PR, Brazil. Phone: +55 (45) 574-3010. Contact: Francisco Pires dos Santos, Gerente-Geral. Return postage necessary. Replies to correspondence in Portuguese. Carries Rede Transamérica programming at night, but all correspondence should be sent to Rádio Cultura.

Rádio Cultura Ondas Tropicais, Rua Barcelos s/n Praça 14, 69020-060 Manaus AM, Brazil. Phone: +55 (92) 633-3857/2030. Fax: +55 (92) 633 3332. Contact: Luíz Fernando de Souza Ferreira; or Maria Jerusalem dos Santos, Chefe da Divisão de Rádio. Replies to correspondence in Portuguese. Return postage appreciated. Station is part of the FUNTEC, Fundação Televisão e Rádio Cultura do Amazonas network.

Rádio Cultura São Paulo, Rua Cenno Sbrighi 378, 05036-900 São Paulo SP, Brazil. Contact: Thais de Almeida Dias, Chefe de Produção e Programação; Sra. Maria Luíza Amaral Kfouri, Chefe de Produção; Valvenio Martins de Almeida; or José Munhoz, Coordenador. $1 or return postage required. Replies slowly to correspondence in Portuguese.

Rádio Difusora Cáceres, C.P. 297, 78200-000 Cáceres MT, Brazil. Contact: Sra. Maridalva Amaral Vignardi. $1 or return postage required. Replies occasionally to correspondence in Portuguese.

Rádio Difusora de Aquidauana, C.P. 18, 79200-000 Aquidauana MS, Brazil. Phone: +55 (67) 241-3956 or +55 (67) 241-3957. Contact: Primaz Aldo Bertoni, Diretor. Free tourist literature and used Brazilian stamps. $1 or return postage required. This station sometimes identifies during the program day as "Nova Difusora," but its sign-off announcement gives the official name as "Rádio Difusora, Aquidauana."

Rádio Difusora de Londrina, C.P. 1870, 86000-000 Londrina PR, Brazil. Contact: Walter Roberto Manganoti, Gerente. Free tourist brochure, which sometimes seconds as a verification. $1 or return postage helpful. Replies irregularly to correspondence in Portuguese.

Rádio Difusora do Amazonas, C.P. 311, 69000-000 Manaus AM, Brazil. Contact: J. Joaquim Marinho, Diretor. Joaquim Marinho is a keen stamp collector and especially interested in Duck Hunting Permit Stamps. Will reply to correspondence in Portuguese or English. $1 or return postage helpful.

Rádio Difusora do Maranhão (when active), C.P. 152, 65000-000 São Luís MA, Brazil. Contact: Alonso Augusto Duque, BA, Presidente; José de Arimatéa Araújo, Diretor; or Fernando Souza, Gerente. Free tourist literature. Return postage required. Replies occasionally to correspondence in Portuguese.

Rádio Difusora Jataí, C.P. 33 (or Rua de José Carvalhos Bastos 542), 75800-000 Jataí GO, Brazil. Contact: Zacarías Faleiros, Diretor Gerente.

Rádio Difusora Macapá (when active), C.P. 2929, 68900-000 Macapá AP, Brazil. Contact: Francisco de Paulo Silva Santos or Rui Lobato. $1 or return postage required. Replies irregularly to correspondence in Portuguese.

Rádio Difusora Poços de Caldas, C.P. 937, 37701-970 Poços de Caldas MG, Brazil. URL: www.pocos-net.com.br/

Rio's Carnival, a time of celebration and music when virtually all of Brazil shuts down. Tiju

difusora/am.htm. Contact: Marco Aurelio C. Mendoça, Diretor. $1 or return postage required. Replies to correspondence in Portuguese.

Rádio Difusora Roraima, Avenida Capitão Ene Garcez 830, 69304-000 Boa Vista RR, Brazil. Contact: Francisco G. França, Diretor Gerente; Marcia Seixas, Diretora Geral; Benjamin Monteiro, Locutor; or Francisco Alves Vieira. Return postage required. Replies occasionally to correspondence in Portuguese.

Rádio Difusora "6 de Agosto," Rua Pio Nazário 31, 69930-000 Xapuri AC, Brazil. Contact: Francisco Evangelista de Abreu. Replies to correspondence in Portuguese.

Rádio Difusora Taubaté, Rua Dr. Sousa Alves 960, 12020-030 Taubaté SP, Brazil. No contact details available at press time but station plans to increase its power from 500 watts to 1 kW.

Rádio Educação Rural—Campo Grande, C.P. 261, 79002-233 Campo Grande MS, Brazil. Phone: +55 (67) 384-3164, +55 (67) 382-2238 or +55 (67) 384-3345. Contact: Ailton Guerra, Gerente-Geral; Angelo Venturelli, Diretor; or Diácono Tomás Schwamborn. $1 or return postage required. Replies to correspondence in Portuguese.

Rádio Educação Rural—Coari, Praça São Sebastião 228, 69460-000 Coari AM, Brazil. Contact: Lino Rodrigues Pessoa, Diretor Comercial; Joaquim Florencio Coelho, Diretor Administrador da Comunidade Salgueiro; or Elijane Martins Correa. $1 or return postage helpful. Replies irregularly to correspondence in Portuguese.

Rádio Educadora Cariri, C.P. 57, 63100-000 Crato CE, Brazil. Contact: Padre Gonçalo Farias Filho, Diretor Gerente. Return postage or $1 helpful. Replies irregularly to correspondence in Portuguese.

Rádio Educadora da Bahia, Centro de Rádio, Rua Pedro Gama 413/E, Alto Sobradinho Federação, 40236-900 Salvador BA, Brazil. Contact: Elza Correa Ramos; or Walter Sequieros R. Tanure. $1 or return postage required. May send local music CD. Replies to correspondence in Portuguese.

Rádio Educadora de Bragança (when active), Rua Barão do Rio Branco 1151, 68600-000 Bragança PA, Brazil. Contact: José Rosendo de S. Neto or Zelina Cardoso Gonçalves. $1 or return postage required. Replies to correspondence in Portuguese.

Rádio Educadora de Guajará Mirim, Praça Mario Correa No.90, 78957-000 Guajará Mirim RO, Brazil. Contact: Padre Isidoro José Moro. Return postage helpful. Replies to correspondence in Portuguese.

Rádio Gaúcha, Avenida Ipiranga 1075 2do andar, Azenha, 90169-900 Porto Alegre RS, Brazil. Phone: +55 (51) 223-6600. E-mail: gaucha@rdgaucha.com.br. URL: www.rdgaucha.com.br/. Contact: Marco Antônio Baggio, Gerente de Jornalismo/Programação; Armindo Antônio Ranzolin, Diretor Gerente; or Geraldo Canali. Replies occasionally to correspondence, preferably in Portuguese.

Rádio Gazeta, Avenida Paulista 900, 01310-940 São Paulo SP, Brazil. Fax: +55 (11) 285 4895. Contact: Shakespeare Ettinger, Superv. Geral de Operação; Bernardo Leite da Costa; José Roberto Mignone Cheibub, Gerente Geral; or Ing. Aníbal Horta Figueiredo. Free stickers. $1 or return postage necessary. Replies to correspondence in Portuguese.

Rádio Globo, Rua do Russel 434-Glória, 22213-900 Rio de Janeiro RJ, Brazil. Contact: Marcos Libretti, Diretor Geral. Replies irregularly to correspondence in Portuguese. Return postage helpful.

Rádio Globo, Rua das Palmeiras 315, 01288-900 São Paulo SP, Brazil. Contact: Ademar Dutra, Locutor, "Programa Ademar Dutra"; or José Marques. Replies to correspondence, preferably in Portuguese.

Rádio Guaíba, Rua Caldas Junior 219, 90019-900 Porto Alegre RS, Brazil. Return postage may be helpful.

Rádio Guaraní, Avenida Assis Chateaubriand 499, Floresta, 30150-101 Belo Horizonte MG, Brazil. Contact: Junara Belo, Setor de Comunicações. Replies slowly to correspondence in Portuguese. Return postage helpful.

Rádio Guarujá
STATION: C.P. 45, 88000-000 Florianópolis SC, Brazil. Contact: Acy Cabral Tieve, Diretor; Joana Sempre Bom Braz, Assessora de Marketing e Comunicação; or Rosa Michels de Souza. Return postage required. Replies irregularly to correspondence in Portuguese.
NEW YORK OFFICE: 45 West 46 Street, 5th Floor, Manhattan, NY 10036 USA.

☞**Rádio Inconfidência**, C.P. 1027, 30650-540 Belo Horizonte MG, Brazil. Fax: +55 (31) 296 3070. E-mail: inconfidencia@plugway.com.br. URL: (includes RealAudio) www.plugway.com.br/inconfidencia/. Contact: Isaias Lansky, Diretor; Manuel Emilio de Lima Torres, Diretor Superintendente; Jairo Antolio Lima, Diretor Artístico; or Eugenio Silva. Free stickers and postcards. $1 or return postage helpful.

Rádio Integração, Rua Alagoas 270, 69980-000 Cruzeiro do Sul AC, Brazil. Contact: Oscar Alves Bandeira, Gerente. Free 1997 anniversary pennant. Return postage helpful.

Rádio IPB AM, Rua Itajaí 473, Bairro Antonio Vendas, 79041-270 Campo Grande MS, Brazil. Contact: Iván Páez Barboza, Diretor Geral (hence, the station's name, "IPB"); Pastor Laercio Paula das Neves, Dirigente Estadual; Agenor Patrocinio S., Locutor; Pastor José Adão Hames; or Kelly Cristina Rodrigues da Silva, Secretária. Return postage required. Replies to correspondence in Portuguese.

☞**Rádio Itatiaia**, Rua Itatiaia 117, 31210-170 Belo Horizonte MG, Brazil. Fax: +55 (31) 446 2900. E-mail: itatiaia@itatiaia.com.br. URL: (includes RealAudio) www.itatiaia.com.br/. Contact: Lúcia Araújo Bessa, Assistente da Diretória.

Rádio Jornal "A Crítica," C.P. 2250, 69061-970 Manaus AM, Brazil.

Rádio Marajoara (when active), Travessa Campos Sales 370, Centro, 66019-904 Belém PA, Brazil. Contact: Elizete Maria dos Santos Pamplona, Diretora Geral; or Sra. Neide Carvalho, Secretária da Diretoria Executiva. Return postage required. Replies irregularly to correspondence in Portuguese.

Rádio Marumby, C.P. 62 (C.P. 296 is the alternative box), 88010-970 Florianópolis SC, Brazil; or (missionary parent organization) Gideões Missionários da Última Hora—GMUH, Ministéreo Evangélico Mundial, Rua Joaquim Nunes 244, C.P. 4, 88340-000 Camboriú SC, Brazil. Contact: Davi Campos, Diretor Artístico; Dr. Cesino Bernardino, Presidente,

GMUH; Pb. Claudiney Nunes, Diretor; Dr. Nildair Santos, Coordinador; or Jair Albano, Producer. $1 or return postage required. Free diploma and stickers. Replies to correspondence in Portuguese.

Rádio Marumby, Curitiba—see Rádio Novas de Paz, Curitiba, below.

Rádio Meteorologia Paulista, C.P. 91, 14940-970 Ibitinga, São Paulo SP, Brazil. Contact: Roque de Rosa, Diretora. Replies to correspondence in Portuguese. $1 or return postage required.

Rádio Mundial, Rua da Consolação 2608, 1° Andar, CJ. 11, 01416-000 Consolação, São Paulo SP, Brazil. Fax: +55 (11) 258 5838 or +55 (11) 258 0152.

Rádio Nacional da Amazônia, Radiobrás, SCRN 702/3 Bloco B Lote 16/18, Ed. Radiobrás, 70323-900 Brasília DF, Brazil. Fax: +55 (61) 321 7602. URL: http:www.radiobras.gov.br/radioamz.htm. Contact: (general) Luíz Otavio de Castro Souza, Diretor; Fernando Gómez da Camara, Gerente de Escritório; or Januario Procopio Toledo, Diretor. Free stickers, but no verifications.

Rádio Nacional do Brasil—Radiobrás, External Service, C.P. 08840, 70912-790, Brasília DF, Brazil. Fax: +55 (61) 321 7602. URL: www.radiobras.gov.br/. Contact: Renato Geraldo de Lima, Manager; Michael Brown, Announcer; or Gaby Hertha Einstoss, Correspondence Service. Free stickers. Correspondence welcomed in English and other languages. Unlike Radiobrás' domestic service (preceding entry), Radiobrás' External Service verifies regularly.

Rádio Nacional São Gabriel da Cachoeira, Avenida Alvaro Maia 850, 69750-000 São Gabriel da Cachoeira AM, Brazil. Contact: Luíz dos Santos França, Gerente; or Valdir de Souza Marques. Return postage necessary. Replies to correspondence in Portuguese.

Rádio Novas de Paz, C.P. 22, 80000-000 Curitiba PR, Brazil. Contact: João Falavinha Ienzen, Gerente. $1 or return postage required. Replies irregularly to correspondence in Portuguese.

Rádio Nova Visão
STUDIOS: Rua do Manifesto 1373, 04209-001 São Paulo SP, Brazil. Contact: José Eduardo Dias, Diretor Executivo; Rev. Iván Nunes; or Marlene P. Nunes, Secretária. Return postage required. Replies to correspondence in Portuguese. Free stickers. Relays Rádio Trans Mundial fulltime.
TRANSMITTER: C.P. 551, 97000-000 Santa Maria RS, Brazil; or C.P. 6084, 90000-000 Porto Alegre RS, Brazil. Reportedly issues full-data verifications for reports in Portuguese or German, upon request, from this location. If no luck, try contacting, in English or Dutch, Tom van Ewijck, via e-mail at egiaroll@mail.iss.lcca.usp.br.

Rádio Oito de Setembro, C.P. 8, 13690-000 Descalvado SP, Brazil. Contact: Adonias Gomes. Replies to corrrespondence in Portuguese.

Rádio Pioneira de Teresina, Rua 24 de Janeiro 150 sul/centro, 64001-230 Teresina PI, Brazil. Contact: Luíz Eduardo Bastos; or Padre Tony Batista, Diretor. $1 or return postage required. Replies slowly to correspondence in Portuguese.

Rádio Poti (if reactivated), C.P. 145, 59001-970 Natal RN, Brazil. Contact: Cid Lobo. Return postage helpful. Replies slowly to correspondence in Portuguese.

Rádio Progresso (when operating), Estrada do Belmont s/n, B% Nacional, 78903-400 Porto Velho RO, Brazil. Return postage required. Replies occasionally to correspondence in Portuguese.

Rádio Record
STATION: C.P. 7920, 04084-002 São Paulo SP, Brazil. Contact: Mário Luíz Catto, Diretor Geral. Free stickers. Return postage or $1 required. Replies occasionally to correspondence in Portuguese.
NEW YORK OFFICE: 630 Fifth Avenue, Room 2607, New York NY 10111 USA.

Rádio Ribeirão Preto (if reactivated), C.P 814, 14001-970 Ribeirão Preto SP, Brazil. Contact: Lucinda de Oliveira,

Secretária; Luis Schiavone Junior; or Paulo Henríque Rocha da Silva. Replies to correspondence in Portuguese.

Rádio Rio Mar, Rua José Clemente 500, 69010-070 Manaus AM, Brazil. Replies to correspondence in Portuguese. $1 or return postage necessary.

Rádio Rural Santarém, Rua Floriano Peixoto 632, 68005-060 Santarém PA, Brazil. Contact: João Elias B. Bentes, Gerente Geral; or Edsergio de Moraes Pinto. Replies slowly to correspondence in Portuguese. Free stickers. Return postage or $1 required.

Rádio Sentinela, Travessa Ruy Barbosa 142, 68250-000 Obidos PA, Brazil. Contact: Max Hamoy; or Maristela Hamoy. Return postage required. Replies occasionally to correspondence in Portuguese.

Rádio Timbira (when active), Rua do Correio s/n, Bairro de Fátima, 65030-340 São Luís MA, Brazil. Contact: Sandoval Pimentel Silva, Diretor Geral. Free picture postcards. $1 helpful. Replies occasionally to correspondence in Portuguese; persist.

Rádio Transamérica—see Rádio Cultura Foz do Iguaçu.

Rádio Trans Mundial, Caixa Postal 18300 (Aeroporto), 04699-970 São Paulo SP, Brazil. Program aired via Rádio Nova Visão—see above.

Rádio Tropical (if reactivated), C.P. 23, 78600-000 Barra do Garças MT, Brazil. Contact: Alacir Viera Cándido, Diretor e Presidente; or Walter Francisco Dorados, Diretor Artístico. $1 or return postage required. Replies slowly and rarely to correspondence in Portuguese.

Rádio Tupí (if reactivated), Avenida Nadir Dias Figueiredo 1329, 02110-901 São Paulo SP, Brazil. Contact: Alfredo Raymundo Filho, Diretor Geral; Celso Rodrigues de Oliveira, Asesor Internacional da Presidencia; Montival da Silva Santos; or Elia Soares. Free stickers. Return postage required. Replies occasionally to correspondence in Portuguese.

Rádio Universo, C.P. 7133, 80000-000 Curitiba PR, Brazil. Contact: Luíz Andreu Rúbio, Diretor. Replies occasionally to correspondence in Portuguese.

Rádio Verdes Florestas, C.P. 53, 69981-970 Cruzeiro do Sul AC, Brazil. Contact: Marlene Valente de Andrade. Return postage required. Replies occasionally to correspondence in Portuguese.

Rede Transamérica—see Rádio Cultura Foz do Iguaçu.

BULGARIA   World Time +2 (+3 midyear)
Radio Bulgaria
NONTECHNICAL AND TECHNICAL: P.O. Box 900, 1000, Sofia-Z, Bulgaria. Phone: +359 (2) 661-954 or +359 (2) 854-633. Fax: (general, usually weekdays only) +359 (2) 871 060, +359 (2) 871 061 or +359 (2) 650 560; (Managing Director) +359 (2) 662 215; (Frequency Manager) +359 (2) 963 4464. E-mail: (private employee e-mail, but will reach German language section) tgeorgi@mail.techno-link.com. Contact: (general) Mrs. Iva Delcheva, English Section; Kristina Mihailova, In Charge of Listeners' Letters, English Section; Christina Pechevska, Listeners' Letters, English Section; Svilen Stoicheff, Head of English Section; or Sta. Katia Tomor, Sección Española; (administration and technical) Anguel H. Nedyalkov, Managing Director; (technical) Atanas Tzenov, Director. Free tourist literature, postcards, stickers, T-shirts, bookmarks and pennants. Gold, silver and bronze diplomas for correspondents meeting certain requirements. Free sample copies of *Bulgaria* magazine. Replies regularly, but sometimes slowly. Return postage helpful, as the station is financially overstretched due to the economic situation in the country. For concerns about frequency usage, contact BTC, below, with copies to Messrs. Nedyalkov and Tzenov of Radio Bulgaria. FREQUENCY MANAGEMENT AND TRANSMISSION OPERATIONS: Bulgarian Telecommunications Company (BTC), Ltd., 8 Totleben Blvd., 1606 Sofia, Bulgaria. Phone: +359 (2) 88-00-75. Fax: +359 (2) 87 58 85 or +359 (2) 80 25 80. Contact: Roumen Petkov, Frequency Manager; or Mrs. Margarita Krasteva, Radio Regulatory Department.

Radio Horizont, Bulgarian Radio, 4 Dragan Tsankov Blvd., 1040 Sofia, Bulgaria. Phone: +359 (2) 652-871. Fax: (weekdays) +359 (2) 657 230. Contact: Borislav Djamdjiev, Director; Iassen Indjev, Executive Director; or Martin Minkov, Editor-in-Chief.

Radio Varna, 22 blv. Primorski, 9000 Varna, Bulgaria. Replies irregularly. Return postage required.

BURKINA FASO   World Time exactly
Radiodiffusion-Télévision Burkina, B.P. 7029, Ouagadougou, Burkina Faso. Phone: +226 310-441. Contact: (general) Raphael L. Onadia or M. Pierre Tassembedo; (technical) Marcel Teho, Head of Transmitting Centre. Replies irregularly to correspondence in French. IRC or return postage helpful.

BURMA—see MYANMAR.

BURUNDI   World Time +2
La Voix de la Révolution, B.P. 1900, Bujumbura, Burundi. Phone: +257 22-37-42. Fax: +257 22 65 47 or +257 22 66 13. Contact: (general) Grégoire Barampumba, Head of News Section; or Frederic Havugiyaremye, Journaliste; (administration) Gérard Mfuranzima, Le Directeur de la Radio; or Didace Baranderetse, Directeur Général de la Radio; (technical) Abraham Makuza, Le Directeur Technique. $1 required.

CAMBODIA   World Time +7
National Radio of Cambodia
STATION ADDRESS: Monivong Boulevard No. 106, Phnom Penh, Cambodia. Phone: +855 (23) 23-369 or +855 (23) 22-869. Fax: + 855 (23) 27 319. Contact: (general) Miss Hem Bory, English Announcer; Kem Yan, Chief of External Relations; or Touch Chhatha, Producer, Art Department; (administration) In Chhay, Chief of Overseas Service; Som Sarun, Chief of Home Service; Van Sunheng, Deputy Director General, Cambodian National Radio and Television; or Ieng Muli, Minister of Information; (technical) Oum Phin, Chief of Technical Department. Free program schedule. Replies irregularly and slowly. Do not include stamps, currency, IRCs or dutiable items in envelope. Registered letters stand a much better chance of getting through.

CAMEROON   World Time +1
NOTE: Any CRTV outlet is likely to be verified by contacting via registered mail, in English or French with $2 enclosed, James Achanyi-Fontem, Head of Programming, CRTV, B.P. 986, Douala, Cameroon.

Cameroon Radio Television Corporation (CRTV)—Bafoussam (when active), B.P. 970, Bafoussam (Ouest), Cameroon. Contact: (general) Boten Celestin; (technical) Ndam Seidou, Chef Service Technique. IRC or return postage required. Replies irregularly in French to correspondence in English or French.

Cameroon Radio Television Corporation (CRTV)—Bertoua (when active), B.P. 230, Bertoua (Eastern), Cameroon. Rarely replies to correspondence, preferably in French. $1 required.

Cameroon Radio Television Corporation (CRTV)—Buea (when active), P.M.B., Buea (Sud-Ouest), Cameroon. Contact: Ononino Oli Isidore, Chef Service Technique. Three IRCs, $1 or return postage required.

Cameroon Radio Television Corporation (CRTV)—Douala (when active), B.P. 986, Douala (Littoral), Cameroon. Contact: (technical) Emmanual Ekite, Technicien. Free pennants. Three IRCs or $1 required.

Cameroon Radio Television Corporation (CRTV)—Garoua, B.P. 103, Garoua (Nord/Adamawa), Cameroon. Contact: Kadeche Manguele. Free cloth pennants. Three IRCs or return postage required. Replies irregularly and slowly to correspondence in French.

Cameroon Radio Television Corporation (CRTV)—Yaoundé, B.P. 1634, Yaoundé (Centre-Sud), Cameroon. Phone: +237 214-077 or +237 214-088. Fax: +237 204 340. Contact: (technical or nontechnical) Gervais Mendo Ze,

Directeur-Général; (technical) Eyebe Tanga, Directeur Technique. $1 required. Replies slowly (sometimes extremely slowly) to correspondence in French.

World Time –3:30 (–2:30 midyear) Newfoundland; –4 (–3 midyear) Atlantic; –5 (–4 midyear) Eastern, including Quebec and Ontario; –6 (–5 midyear) Central; except Saskatchewan; –6 Saskatchewan; –7 (–6 midyear) Mountain; –8 (–7 midyear) Pacific, including Yukon

BBC World Service via RCI/CBC—For verification direct from RCI's CBC shortwave transmitters, contact Radio Canada International (see below). Nontechnical correspondence should be sent to the BBC World Service in London (see).

Canadian Forces Network Radio—see Radio Canada International, below. Free pennants and calendars.

📻**Canadian Broadcasting Corporation (CBC)—English Programs**, P.O. Box 500, Station A, Toronto, Ontario, M5W 1E6, Canada. Phone: +1 (416) 975-3311. URLs: (general, including RealAudio) www.cbc.ca/; (CBC Web sites and e-mail addresses) www.cbc.ca./aboutcbc/address/address.html. CBC prepares some of the programs heard over Radio Canada International (see).

📻**Canadian Broadcasting Corporation (CBC)—French Programs**—see Radio Canada International, below, for mailing address. E-mail (comments on programs): auditoire@montreal.src.ca. Welcomes correspondence sent to this address but cannot reply due to shortage of staff. URL: (includes RealAudio) www.radio-canada.com/index.htm. CBC prepares some of the programs heard over Radio Canada International (see).

CBC Northern Quebec Shortwave Service—see Radio Canada International, below.

CFCX-CIQC/CKOI (when operating)

TRANSMITTER (CFCX); ALSO, STUDIOS FOR CIQC ENGLISH-LANGUAGE PROGRAMS: CFCX-CIQC, Radio Montréal, Mount Royal Broadcasting, Inc., 1200 McGill College Avenue, Suite 300, Montréal, Quebec, H3B 4G7 Canada. Phone: +1 (514) 766-2311, then press keys for appropriate department. Fax: +1 (514) 393 4659. Contact: Ted Silver, Programme Director; (technical) Kim Bickerdike, Technical Director. Currently off shortwave due to transmitter problems. Station has recently been very difficult to contact by both phone and mail, so the above address and contact details may no longer be valid.

FRENCH-LANGUAGE PROGRAM STUDIOS: CKOI, Metromedia CMR, Inc., 211 Gordon Avenue, Verdun, Quebec, H4G 2R2 Canada. Fax: (CKOI—Programming Dept.) +1 (514) 766 2474; (sister station CKVL) +1 (514) 761 0136. URL: www.netmusik.com/Empire/empire_histo.html. Free stickers and possibly T-shirts. Correspondence in French preferred, but English and Spanish accepted.

📻**CFRX-CFRB**

MAIN ADDRESS: 2 St. Clair Avenue West, Toronto, Ontario, Canada, M4V 1L6. Phone:(main switchboard) +1 (416) 924-5711; (access line) +1 (416) 872-CFRB; (news centre) +1 (416) 924-6717; (talk shows) +1 (416) 872-1010. Fax: +1 (416) 323 6830. E-mail: (unofficial, belongs to an employee at the station) iain@trends.ca. URL: (includes RealAudio) www.trends.ca/~iain/CFRB/. Contact: (nontechnical) Bob Macowycz, Operations Manager; or Gary Slaight, President; (technical) Ian Sharp. Reception reports should be sent to verification address, below.

VERIFICATION ADDRESS: Ontario DX Association, P.O. Box 161, Station 'A', Willowdale, Ontario, Canada, M2N 5S8. Phone: +1 (416) 293-8919. Fax: +1 (416) 293 6603. E-mail: 70400.2660@compuserve.com. Contact: Steve Canney. Free CFRB/CFRX information sheet and ODXA brochure enclosed with verification. Reception reports are processed quickly if sent to this address, rather than to the station itself.

CFVP-CKMX, AM 1060, Standard Broadcasting, P.O. Box 2750, Stn. "M", Calgary AB, T2P 4P8 Canada. Phone: (general) +1 (403) 240-5800; (news) +1 (403) 240-5844; (technical) +1 (403) 240-5867. Fax: (general and technical) +1 (403) 240 5801; (news) +1 (403) 246 7099. Contact: (general) Gary Russell, General Manager; or Beverley Van Tighem, Exec. Ass't.; (technical) Ken Pasolli, Technical Director.

CHNX-CHNS, P.O. Box 400, Halifax NS, B3J 2R2 Canada. Phone: +1 (902) 422-1651. Fax: +1 (902) 422 5330. E-mail: chns@ns.sympatico.ca. Contact: Garry Barker, General Manager; (programs) Troy Michaels, Operations Manager; (technical) Wayne Harvey, Chief Engineer. Program schedules, stickers and small souvenirs sometimes available. Return postage or $1 helpful. Replies irregularly.

CHU (official time and frequency station), Time and Frequency Standards, Bldg. M-36, National Research Council, Ottawa ON, K1A 0R6 Canada. Phone: (general) +1 (613) 993-5186; (administration) +1 (613) 993-1003 or +1 (613) 993-2704. Fax: +1 (613) 993 1394. E-mail: radio.chu@nrc.ca. URL: www.ems.nrc.ca. Contact: Dr. R.J. Douglas, Programme Leader. Official standard frequency and World Time station for Canada on 3330, 7335 and 14670 kHz. Brochure available upon request. Those with a personal computer, Bell 103 standard modem and appropriate software can get the exact time, via CHU's cesium clock, off the air from their computer; details available upon request.

CKZN-CBN, CBC, P.O. Box 12010, Station "A", St. John's NF, A1B 3T8 Canada. Phone: +1 (709) 576-5155. Fax: +1 (709) 576 5099. Contact: (general) Heather Elliott, Communications Officer; (technical) Shawn R. Williams, Manager, Regional Engineering, Newfoundland Region. Free CBC sticker and verification card with the history of Newfoundland included. Don't enclose money, stamps or IRCs with correspondence, as they will only have to be returned.

CKZU-CBU, CBC, P.O. Box 4600, Vancouver BC, V6B 4A2 Canada. Toll-free telephone (U.S & Canada only) 1-800-961-6161. Phone: (general) +1 (604) 662-6000; (engineering) +1 (604) 662-6064. Fax: +1 (604) 662 6350; (engineering) +1 (604) 662 6350. URL: www.cbc.ca. Contact: (general) Public Relations; (technical) Dave Newbury, Transmission Engineer.

📻**Radio Canada International**

NOTE: (Canadian Forces Network Radio and CBC Northern Quebec Service): The following RCI address, fax and e-mail information for the Main Office and Transmission Office is also valid for the Canadian Forces Network Radio and CBC Northern Quebec Shortwave Service, provided you make your communication to the attention of the particular service you seek to contact.

MAIN OFFICE: P.O. Box 6000, Montréal, Quebec, H3C 3A8 Canada. Phone: (general) +1 (514) 597-7500; (Audience Relations) +1 (514) 597-7555; (English and French programming) +1 (514) 597-7551; (Russian programming) +1 (514) 597-6866; (CBC's "As It Happens' Talkback Machine") +1 (416) 205-3331. Fax: (RCI) +1 (514) 284 0891 or +1 (514) 284 9550; (English and French Programming) +1 (514) 597 7617; (Canadian Forces Network) +1 (514) 597 7893. E-mail: (general) rci@montreal.ca; (Audience Relations) rci@cam.org. URL: (includes RealAudio) www.rcinet.ca/en/index.htm. Contact: (general) Maggy Akerblom, Director of Audience Relations; Ousseynou Diop, Manager, English and French Programming; Allan Familiant, Program Director; or Mark Montgomery, Producer/Host, the "Mailbag"; (administration) Bob O'Reilly, Executive Director; (technical—verifications) Bill Westenhaver, CIDX. Free stickers and other small station souvenirs. 50th Anniversary T-shirts, sweatshirts, watches, lapel pins and tote bags available for sale; write to the above address for a free illustrated flyer giving prices and ordering information.

TRANMISSION OFFICE: P.O. Box 6000, Montréal PQ, H3C 3A8 Canada. Phone: +1 (514) 597-7616/17/18/19/20. Fax: +1 (514) 284 9550 or +1 (514) 284 2052. E-mail: (Théorêt) gtheoret@montreal.src.ca; (Bouliane) jbouliane@montreal.src.ca. Contact: (general) Gérald Théorêt, Frequency Manager; (administration) Jacques Bouliane, Director of Engineering. This office only for informing about transmitter-related problems (interference, modulation quality, etc.), especially by fax. Verifications not given out at this office; requests for verification should be sent to the main office, above.

TRANSMITTER SITE: CBC, P.O. Box 1200, Sackville NB, E0A 3CO Canada. Phone: +1 (506) 536-2690/1. Fax: +1 (506) 536 2342. Contact: Marc Leblanc, Plant Manager. All correspondence not concerned with transmitting equipment should be directed to the appropriate address in Montréal, above. Free tours given during normal working hours.

RCI MONITORING STATION: P.O. Box 322, Station C, Ottawa, ON K1Y 1E4, Canada. Phone: +1 (613) 831-2801. Fax: +1 (613) 831 0342. Contact: Derek Williams, Plant Manager.

LABOR REPRESENTATION AND RCI BOOSTERS' ORGANIZATION: Coalition to Restore Full RCI Funding, SCFP Local 675, 1250 de la Visitation, Montréal, Quebec, H2L 3B4 Canada. Phone: +1 (514) 844-2262. Fax: +1 (514) 521 3082. E-mail: rci@cam.org. Contact: Wojtek Gwiazda. Local 675 is active in maintaining RCI as an active force in international broadcasting, and welcomes correspondence from like-minded individuals and organizations.

WASHINGTON NEWS BUREAU: CBC, National Press Building, Suite 500, 529 14th Street NW, Washington DC 20045 USA. Phone: +1 (202) 638-3286. Fax: +1 (202) 783 9321. Contact: Jean-Louis Arcand, David Hall or Susan Murray.

LONDON NEWS BUREAU: CBC, 43-51 Great Titchfield Street, London W1P 8DD, England. Phone: +44 (171) 412-9200. Fax: +44 (171) 631 3095.

PARIS NEWS BUREAU: CBC, 17 avenue Matignon, F-75008 Paris, France. Phone: +33 (1) 43-59-11-85. Fax: +33 (1) 44 21 15 14.

Radio Monte-Carlo Middle East (via Radio Canada International)—*see* Cyprus.

Shortwave Classroom, Naismith Memorial Public School, P.O. Box 280, Almonte ON, K0A 1A0 Canada. Phone: (weekdays during school season) +1 (613) 256-3773; (other times) +1 (613) 256-2018. Fax: (during school season) +1 (613) 256 3825. E-mail: as167@freenet.carleton.ca. Contact: Neil Carleton, Organizer. *The Shortwave Classroom* newsletter, three times per year, for "$10 and an accompanying feature to share with teachers in the newsletter." Ongoing nonprofit volunteer project of teachers and others to use shortwave listening in the classroom to teach about global perspectives, media studies, world geography, languages, social studies and other subjects. Interested teachers and parents worldwide are invited to make contact.

CENTRAL AFRICAN REPUBLIC   World Time +1

Radio Centrafrique, Radiodiffusion-Télévision Centrafricaine, B.P. 940, Bangui, Central African Republic. Contact: (technical) Jacques Mbilo, Le Directeur des Services Techniques; or Michèl Bata, Services Techniques. Replies on rare occasions to correspondence in French; return postage required.

CHAD   World Time +1

Radiodiffusion Nationale Tchadienne—N'djamena, B.P. 892, N'Djamena, Chad. Contact: Djimadoum Ngoka Kilamian. Two IRCs or return postage required. Replies slowly to correspondence in French.

Radio Diffusion Nationale Tchadienne—Radio Abéché, B.P. 105, Abéché, Ouaddai, Chad. Return postage helpful. Replies rarely to correspondence in French.

Radiodiffusion Nationale Tchadienne—Radio Moundou, B.P. 122, Moundou, Logone, Chad. Contact: Dingantoudji N'Gana Esaie.

CHILE   World Time –3 (–4 midyear)

Radio Esperanza

OFFICE: Casilla 830, Temuco, Chile. Phone/fax: +56 (45) 240-161. Contact: (general) Juanita Cárcamo, Departemento de Programación; Eleazar Jara, Dpto. de Programación; Ramón P. Woerner K., Publicidad; or Alberto Higueras

Staffers from China Radio International's English Service stand under the station's old logo, when it was known as "Radio Beijing."

Martínez, Locutor; (verifications) Juanita Carmaco M., Dpto. de Programacíon; (technical) Juan Luis Puentes, Dpto. Técnico. Free pennants, stickers, bookmarks and tourist information. Two IRCs, $1 or 2 U.S. stamps appreciated. Replies, usually quite slowly, to correspondence in Spanish or English.

STUDIO: Calle Luis Durand 03057, Temuco, Chile. Phone/fax: +56 (45) 240-161.

Radio Santa María, Apartado 1, Coyhaique, Chile. Phone: +56 (67) 23-23-98, +56 (67) 23-20-25 or +56 (67) 23-18-17. Fax: +56 (67) 23 13 06. Contact: Pedro Andrade Vera, Coordinador. $1 or return postage required. May send free tourist cards. Replies to correspondence in Spanish and Italian.

Radio Triunfal Evangélica, Calle Las Araucarias 2757, Villa Monseñor Larrain, Talagante, Chile. Phone: +56 (1) 815-4765. Contact: Fernando González Segura, Obispo de la Misión Pentecostal Fundamentalista. Two IRCs required. Replies to correspondence in Spanish.

CHINA   World Time +8; still nominally +6 ("Urümqi Time") in the Xinjiang Uighur Autonomous Region, but in practice +8 is observed there, as well.

NOTE: China Radio International, the Central People's Broadcasting Station and certain regional outlets reply regularly to listeners' letters in a variety of languages. If a Chinese regional station does not respond to your correspondence within four months—and many will not, unless your letter is in Chinese or the regional dialect—try writing them c/o China Radio International.

Central People's Broadcasting Station (CPBS)—China National Radio, Zhongyang Renmin Guangbo Diantai, P.O. Box 4501, CN-100866 Beijing, China. Phone: +86 (10) 6851-2435 or +86 (10) 6851-5522. Fax: +86 (10) 6851 6630. Contact:

Wang Changquan, Audience Department, China National Radio. Tape recordings of music and news $5 plus postage. CPBS T-shirts $10 plus postage; also sells ties and other items with CPBS logo. No credit cards. Free stickers, pennants and other small souvenirs. Return postage helpful. Responds regularly to correspondence in English and Standard Chinese (Mandarin). Although in recent years this station has officially been called "China National Radio" in English-language documents, all on-air identifications in Standard Chinese continue to be "Zhongyang Renmin Guangbo Dientai" (Central People's Broadcasting Station). CPBS-1 also airs Chinese-language programs co-produced by CPBS and Radio Canada International.

China Huayi Broadcasting Company, P.O. Box 251, Fuzhou City, 35001 Fujian, China. Contact: Lin Hai Chun, Announcer. Replies to correspondence in English and Chinese.

China National Radio—see Central People's Broadcasting Station/CPBS, above.

China Radio International
MAIN OFFICE, NON-CHINESE LANGUAGES SERVICE: 16A Shijingshan Street, 100039 Beijing, China. Phone: (director's office) +86 (10) 6889-1676; (Audience Relations.) +86 (10) 6889-1617 or +86 (10) 6889-1652; (English Newsroom) +86 (10) 609-2266; (current affairs) +86 (10) 801-3134; (administration) +86 (10) 6851-3135. Fax: (English Department) +86 (10) 6889 1378 or +86 (10) 6889 1379; (Audience Relations) +86 (10) 6851 3175 or (administration) +86 (10) 6851 3174. E-mail: (English Department) crieng@public.bta.net.cn. Contact: (general) Yanling Zhang, Head of Audience Relations; Ms. Chen Lifang, Mrs. Fan Fuguang, Ms. Qi Guilin, Audience Relations, English Department; Richard D. Hutto, Advisor, English Department; Zhang Hong Quan, Reporter, General Editor's Office; Dai Mirong and Qui Mei, "Listeners' Letterbox"; Zang Guohua, or Deputy Director of English Service; (technical) Liu Yuzhou, Technical Director; or Ge Hongzhang, Frequency Manager; (research) Ms. Zhang Yanling; (administration) Zhang Zhenhua, Director General, China Radio International; Wang Guoqing, Assistant Director, China Radio International. Free bi-monthly *The Messenger* magazine, pennants, stickers, desk calendars, pins, hair ornaments and such small souvenirs as handmade papercuts. T-shirts $5 and CDs $15. Two-volume, 820-page set of *Day-to-Day Chinese* language-lesson books $15, including postage worldwide; contact Li Yi, English Department. Various other Chinese books (on arts, medicine, etc.) in English available from Chen Denong, CIBTC, P.O. Box 399, Beijing, China; fax +86 (10) 841 2023. To remain on *The Messenger* magazine mailing list, listeners should write to the station at least once a year. CRI is also relayed via shortwave transmitters in Brazil, Canada, France, French Guiana, Mali, Russia, Spain and Switzerland.
MAIN OFFICE, CHINESE LANGUAGES SERVICE: Box 565, Beijing, China. Prefers correspondence in Chinese (Mandarin), Cantonese, Hakka, Chaozhou or Amoy.
BONN NEWS BUREAU: Am Buchel 81, D-53173 Bonn, Germany. Contact: Ma Xuming.
CHINA (HONG KONG) NEWS BUREAU: 387 Queen's Road East, Hong Kong, China. Contact: Zang Daolin, Bureau Chief; Zhang Xiujuan; or Zhang Jiaping.
WASHINGTON NEWS BUREAU: 2401 Calvert Street NW, Suite 1012, Washington DC 20008 USA. Phone: +1 (202) 387-6860. Phone/fax: +1 (202) 387-0459, but first call +1 (202) 387-6860 so fax can be switched on.
NEW YORK NEWS BUREAU: 630 First Avenue #35K, New York NY 10016 USA. Fax: +1 (212) 889 2076. Contact: Liu Hui, Bureau Chief.
PARIS NEWS BUREAU: 7 rue Charles Lecocq, F-75015 Paris, France. Contact: Huang Liangde, Chef de Bureau; Jia Yanjing; or Xiong Wei.
SYDNEY NEWS BUREAU: 121/226 Sussex Street, Sydney NSW 2000, Australia. Contact: Xu Rongmao, Bureau Chief; or Shi Chungyong.

TOKYO NEWS BUREAU: Meith Fuyoku Nakameguro 2F3-10-3 Kamimeguro, Megoro-ku, Tokyo 153, Japan. Phone/fax: +81 (3) 3719-8414. Contact: Zhang Guo-qing, Bureau Chief.

Fujian People's Broadcasting Station, Fuzhou, Fujian, China. $1 helpful. Replies occasionally and usually slowly.

Gansu People's Broadcasting Station, Lanzhou, China. Contact: Li Mei. IRC helpful.

Guangxi People's Broadcasting Station, No. 12 Min Zu Avenue, Nanning, 530022 Guangxi, China. Contact: Song Yue, Staffer; or Li Hai Li, Staffer. Free stickers and handmade papercuts. IRC helpful. Replies irregularly.

Heilongjiang People's Broadcasting Station, No. 115 Zhongshan Road, Harbin City, Heilongjiang, China. $1 or return postage helpful.

Honghe People's Broadcasting Station, Jianshe Donglu 32, 661400 Geji City, Yunnan, China. Contact: Shen De-chun, Head of Station; or Mrs. Cheng Lin, Editor-in-Chief. Free travel brochures.

Hubei People's Broadcasting Station, No. 563 Jie Fang Avenue, Wuhan, Hubei, China.

Jiangxi People's Broadcasting Station, Nanchang, Jiangxi, China. Contact: Tang Ji Sheng, Editor, Chief Editor's Office. Free gold/red pins. Replies irregularly. Mr. Tang enjoys music, literature and stamps, so enclosing a small memento along these lines should help assure a speedy reply.

Nei Monggol (Inner Mongolia) People's Broadcasting Station, Hohhot, Nei Monggol Zizhiqu, China. Contact: Zhang Xiang-Quen, Secretary; or Liang Yan. Replies irregularly.

Qinghai People's Broadcasting Station, Xining, Qinghai, China. Contact: Liqing Fangfang. $1 helpful.

Sichuan People's Broadcasting Station, Chengdu, Sichuan, China. Replies occasionally.

Voice of Jinling, P.O. Box 268, Nanjing, 210002 Jiangsu, China. Fax: +86 (25) 413 235. Contact: Strong Lee, Producer/Host, "Window of Taiwan." Free stickers and calendars, plus Chinese-language color station brochure and information on the Nanjing Technology Import & Export Corporation. Replies to correspondence in Chinese and to simple correspondence in English. $1 or return postage helpful.

Voice of Pujiang, P.O. Box 3064, 200002 Shanghai, China. Contact: Jiang Bimiao, Editor & Reporter.

Voice of the Strait, People's Liberation Army Broadcasting Centre, P.O. Box 187, Fuzhou, 350012 Fujian, China. Replies very irregularly.

Wenzhou People's Broadcasting Station, Wenzhou, China.

Xilingol People's Broadcasting Station, Xilinhot, Xilingol, China.

Xinjiang People's Broadcasting Station, No. 84 Tuanjie Lu (United Road), Urümqi, 830044 Xinjiang, China. Contact: Zhao Ji-shu. Free tourist booklet, postcards and used Chinese stamps. Replies to correspondence in Chinese and to simple correspondence in English.

Xizang People's Broadcasting Station, Lhasa, Xizang (Tibet), China. Contact: Lobsang Chonphel, Announcer. Free stickers and brochures. Enclosing an English-language magazine may help with a reply.

Yunnan People's Broadcasting Station, No 73 Renmin Road (W), Central Building of Broadcasting & TV, Kunming, 650031 Yunnan, China. Contact: Sheng Hongpeng or F.K. Fan. Free Chinese-language brochure on Yunnan Province, but no QSL cards. $1 or return postage helpful. Replies occasionally.

CHINA (TAIWAN)   World Time +8
📻**Broadcasting Corporation of China (BCC)**, 53 Jen'ai Road, SEC. 3, Taipei 10628, Taiwan, Republic of China. Phone: +886 (2) 771-0151. Fax: +886 (2) 751 9277. URL: (includes RealAudio) www.bcc.com.tw/.

Central Broadcasting System (CBS), 55 Pei'an Road, Tachih, Taipei 104, Taiwan, Republic of China. Phone: +886 (2) 591-8161. Contact: Lee Ming, Deputy Director. Free stickers.

Voice of Asia, P.O. Box 24-777, Taipei, Taiwan, Republic of China. Phone: +886 (2) 771-0151, X-2431. Fax: +886 (2) 751

9277. URL: http://bcc.com.tw/global/voa/voa.htm. Contact: (general) Vivian Pu, Co-Producer, with Isaac Guo of "Letterbox"; or Ms. Chao Mei-Yi, Deputy Chief; (technical) Engineering Department. Free shopping bags, inflatable globes, coasters, calendars, stickers and booklets. T-shirts $5.
Voice of Free China, P.O. Box 24-38, Taipei 106, Taiwan, Republic of China; or (physical address) 53, SEC, 3 Jen Ai Road, Taipei, Taiwan, Republic of China. Phone: +886 (2) 752-2825 or +886 (2) 771-0151. Fax: +886 (2) 751 9277. E-mail: overseas@bcc.com.tw. URL: www.bcc.com.tw/global/vofc/vofc.htm. Contact: (general) Daniel Dong, Chief, Listeners' Service Section; Paula Chao, Producer, "Mailbag Time"; Yea-Wen Wang; or Phillip Wong, "Perspectives"; (administration) John C.T. Feng, Director; or Dong Yu-Ching, Deputy Director; (technical) Wen-Bin Tsai, Engineer, Engineering Department; Tai-Lau Ying, Engineering Department; Tien-Shen Kao; or Huang Shuh-shyun, Director, Engineering Department. Free stickers, caps, shopping bags, *Voice of Free China Journal*, annual diary, "Let's Learn Chinese" language-learning course materials, booklets and other publications, and Taiwan stamps. Station offers listeners a free Frisbee-type saucer if they return the "Request Card" sent to them by the station. T-shirts $5. VoFC programs are relayed to the Americas via WYFR's transmitters in Okeechobee, Florida, USA (see).
OSAKA NEWS BUREAU: C.P.O. Box 180, Osaka Central Post Office, Osaka 530-091, Japan.
TOKYO NEWS BUREAU: P.O. Box 21, Azubu Post Office, Tokyo 106, Japan.
SAN FRANCISCO NEWS BUREAU: P.O. Box 192793, San Francisco CA 94119-2793 USA.

CLANDESTINE—*see* DISESTABLISHMENTARIAN.

COLOMBIA   World Time –5
NOTE: Colombia, the country, is always spelled with two o's. It is never written as "Columbia."
Armonías del Caquetá, Apartado Aéreo 71, Florencia, Caquetá, Colombia. Phone: +57 (88) 352-080. Contact: Padre Alvaro Serna Alzate, Director. Replies rarely to correspondence in Spanish. Return postage required.
Caracol Arauca—*see* La Voz del Cinaruco.
Caracol Colombia
MAIN OFFICE: Apartado Aéreo 9291, Santafé de Bogotá, D.C., Colombia. Phone: +57 (1) 337-8866. Fax: +57 (1) 337 7126. URL: (RealAudio in Spanish; news in Spanish & correspondence) www.caracol.com.co. Contact: Hernán Peláez Restrepo, Jefe Cadena Básica. Free stickers. Replies to correspondence in Spanish and English.
MIAMI OFFICE: 2100 Coral Way, Miami FL 33145 USA. Phone: +1 (305) 285-2477 or +1 (305) 285-1260. Fax: +1 (305) 858 5907.
Caracol Florencia (when active), Apartado Aéreo 465, Florencia, Caquetá, Colombia. Phone: +57 (88) 352-199. Contact: Guillermo Rodríguez Herrara, Gerente; or Vicente Delgado, Operador. Replies occasionally to correspondence in Spanish.
Caracol Villavicencio—*see* La Voz de los Centauros.
Colmundo Bogotá, Diagonal 58 No. 26A-29, Santafé de Bogotá, Colombia. Contact: María Teresa Gutiérrez, Directora Gerente; Jorge Hernández, Gerente de Programación; or Néstor Chamorro, Presidente de la Red Colmundo. Actively seeks reception reports from abroad, preferably in Spanish. Free stickers and program schedule.
Ecos del Atrato, Apartado Aéreo 196, Quibdó, Chocó, Colombia. Phone: +57 (49) 711-450. Contact: Absalón Palacios Agualimpia, Administrador. Free pennants. Replies to correspondence in Spanish.
Ecos del Orinoco (when active), Gobernación del Vichada, Puerto Carreño, Vichada, Colombia.
La Voz de la Selva—*see* Caracol Florencia.
La Voz de los Centauros (Caracol Villavicencio), Cra. 31 No. 37-71 Of. 1001, Villavicencio, Meta, Colombia. Phone:

+57 (86) 214-995. Fax: +57 (86) 623 954. Contact: Carlos Torres Leyva, Gerencia; or Olga Arenas, Administradora. Replies to correspondence in Spanish.
La Voz del Cinaruco (when active), Calle 19 No. 19-62, Arauca, Colombia. Contact: Efrahim Valera, Director. Pennants for return postage. Replies rarely to correspondence in Spanish; return postage required.
La Voz del Guainía (when active), Calle 6 con Carrera 3, Puerto Inírida, Guainía, Colombia. Contact: Luis Fernando Román Robayo, Director. Replies occasionally to correspondence in Spanish.
La Voz del Guaviare, Carrera 22 con Calle 9, San José del Guaviare, Colombia. Phone: +57 (986) 840-153/4. Fax: +57 (986) 840 102. Contact: Luis Fernando Román Robayo, Director General. Replies slowly to correspondence in Spanish.
La Voz del Llano, Calle 38 No. 30A-106, Villavicencio, Meta, Colombia. Phone: +57 (86) 624-102. Fax: +57 (86) 625 045. Contact: Alcides Antonio Jáuregui B., Director. Replies occasionally to correspondence in Spanish. $1 or return postage necessary.
La Voz del Río Arauca
STATION: Carrera 20 No. 19-09, Arauca, Colombia. Phone: +57 (818) 52-910. Contact: Jorge Flórez Rojas, Gerente; Luis Alfonso Riaño, Locutor; or Mario Falla, Periodista. $1 or return postage required. Replies occasionally to correspondence in Spanish; persist.
BOGOTÁ OFFICE: Cra. 10 No. 14-56, Of. 309/310, Santafé de Bogotá, D.C., Colombia.
La Voz del Yopal (when active), Calle 9 No. 22-63, Yopal, Casanare, Colombia. Phone: +57 (87) 558-382. Fax: +57 (87)

557 054. Contact: Pedro Antonio Socha Pérez, Gerente; or Marta Cecilia Socha Pérez, Subgerente. Return postage necessary. Replies to correspondence in Spanish.

Ondas del Meta (when active), Calle 38 No. 30A-106, Villavicencio, Meta, Colombia. Phone: +57 (86) 626-783. Fax: +57 (86) 625 045. Contact: Yolanda Plazas Agredo, Administradora. Free tourist literature. Return postage required. Replies irregularly and slowly to correspondence in Spanish. Plans to reactivate from a new antenna site.

Ondas del Orteguaza, Calle 16, No. 12-48, piso 2, Florencia, Caquetá, Colombia. Phone: +57 (88) 352-558. Contact: Sandra Liliana Vásquez, Secretaria; Señora Elisa Viuda de Santos; or Henry Valencia Vásquez. Free stickers. IRC, return postage or $1 required. Replies occasionally to correspondence in Spanish.

☞RCN (Radio Cadena Nacional)
MAIN OFFICE: Apartado Aéreo 4984, Santafé de Bogotá, D.C., Colombia. URL: (RealAudio, news & correspondence) http://rcn.com.co. Contact: Antonio Pardo García, Gerente de Producción y Programación. Will verify all correct reports for stations in the RCN network. Spanish preferred and return postage necessary.

Radiodifusora Nacional de Colombia
MAIN ADDRESS: Edificio Inravisión, CAN, Av. Eldorado, Santafé de Bogotá, D.C., Colombia. Phone: +57 (1) 222-0415. Fax: +57 (1) 222 0409 or +57 (1) 222 8000. Contact: Rubén Dario Acero or Dra. Athala Morris. Tends to reply slowly.
CANAL INTERNACIONAL: Apartado Aéreo 93994, Santafé de Bogotá, D.C., Colombia. Contact: Jesús Valencia Sánchez.

Radio El Sol (when active), Villa Moreno (Nariño), Colombia. Contact: Pastor Guayguán.

Radio Macarena (when active), Calle 38 No. 32-41, piso 7, Edif. Santander, Villavicencio, Meta, Colombia. Phone: +57 (986) 626-780. Phone/fax: +57 (986) 624-507. Contact: (general) Pedro Rojas Velásquez; or Carlos Alberto Pimienta, Gerente; (technical) Sra. Alba Nelly González de Rojas, Administradora. Sells religious audio cassettes for 3,000 pesos. Return postage required. Replies slowly to correspondence in Spanish. Considering installing a more powerful transmitter and Audimax audio processor.

Radio Melodía (Cadena Melodía) (when active), Apartado Aéreo 58721, Santafé de Bogotá, D.C., Colombia; or Apartado Aéreo 19823, Santafé de Bogotá, D.C., Colombia. Phone: +57 (1) 217-0423, +57 (1) 217-0720, +57 (1) 217-1334 or +57 (1) 217-1452. Fax: +57 (1) 248 8772. Contact: Gerardo Páez Mejía, Vicepresidente; Elvira Mejía de Pérez, Gerente General; or Gracilla Rodríguez, Asistente Gerencia. Stickers and pennants. $1 or return postage.

Radio Mira, Apartado Aéreo 165, Tumaco, Nariño, Colombia. Phone: +57 (27) 272-452. Contact: Padre Jairo Arturo Ochoa Zea. Return postage required.

Radio Nueva Vida (when active), Apartado Aéreo 3068, Bucaramanga, Colombia. Phone: +57 (76) 443-195. Contact: Marco Antonio Caicedo, Director. Cassettes with biblical studies $3 each. Return postage. Replies to correspondence in Spanish.

Radio Super (Ibagué) (when active), Parque Murillo Toro 3-31, P. 3, Ibagué, Tolima, Colombia. Phone: +57 (82) 611-381. Fax: +57 (82) 611 471. Contact: Fidelina Caycedo Hernández; or Germán Acosta Ramos, Locutor Control. Free stickers. Return postage or $1 helpful. Replies irregularly to correspondence in Spanish.

COMOROS World Time +4
Radio Comoro (when operating), B.P. 250, Moroni, Grande Comore, Comoros. Phone: +269 732-531. Contact: Ali Hamdi Hissani; or Antufi Mohamed Bacar, Le Directeur de Programme. Return postage required. Replies very rarely to correspondence in French. Currently off air due to a technical problem with their shortwave transmitter but hope to be back on the air very soon.

CONGO (DEMOCRATIC REPUBLIC)
(formerly Zaïre) World Time +1 Western, including Kinshasa; +2 Eastern
La Voix du Peuple (formerly Radio CANDIP), B.P. 373, Bunia, Democratic Republic of Congo. Letters should preferably be sent via registered mail. $1 or return postage required. Correspondence in French preferred.

Radio Agatashya (if operating), Fondation Hirondelle, 3 Rue Traversiere, CH-1018 Lausanne, Switzerland. Phone: +41 (21) 647-2805. Fax:+41 (21) 647 4469. URL: www.hirondelle.org. A humanitarian station for the victims of Burundi, Rwanda and the Democratic Republic of the Congo. Sponsored by the Swiss government and the European Community.

Radio Bukavu (when active), B.P. 475, Bukavu, Democratic Republic of the Congo. Contact: Jacques Nyembo-Kibeya; Kalume Kavue Katumbi; or Baruti Lusongela, Directeur. $1 or return postage required. Replies slowly. Correspondence in French preferred.

Radio Kisangani (when active), B.P. 1745, Kisangani, Democratic Republic of the Congo. Contact: (general) Lumeto lue Lumeto, Directeur Regional; or Lumbutu Kalome, Directeur Inspecteur; (technical) Lukusa Kowumayi Branly, Technicien. $1 or 2 IRCs required. Correspondence in French preferred. Mail to this station may be interfered with by certain staff members. Try sending letters to Lumbutu Kalome at his private address: 10ᵉ Avenue 34, Zone de la Tshopo, Kisangani, Democratic Republic of the Congo. Registering letters may also help. Replies to North American listeners sometimes are mailed via the Oakland, California, post office.

Radio Lubumbashi (when active), B.P. 7296, Lubumbashi, Democratic Republic of the Congo. Contact: Senga Lokavu, Chef du Service de l'Audiovisuel; Bébé Beshelemu, Directeur; or Mulenga Kanso, Chef du Service Logistique. Letters should be sent via registered mail. $1 or 3 IRCs helpful. Correspondence in French preferred.

Radio-Télévision Nationale Congolaise, B.P. 3171, Kinshasa-Gombe, Democratic Republic of the Congo. Contact: Ayimpam Mwan-a-ngo, Directeur des Programmes, Radio; or Faustin Mbula, Ingenieur Technicien. Letters should be sent via registered mail. $1 or 3 IRCs helpful. Correspondence in French preferred

CONGO (REPUBLIC) World Time +1
NOTE: International mail to the Republic of Congo has been temporarily suspended because of civil unrest.
Radio Congo, Radiodiffusion-Télévision Congolaise, B.P. 2241, Brazzaville, Congo. Contact: (general) Antoine Ngongo, Rédacteur en chef; (administration) Albert Fayette Mikano, Directeur; or Zaou Mouanda. $1 required. Replies irregularly to letters in French sent via registered mail.

COSTA RICA World Time –6
Adventist World Radio, the Voice of Hope, AWR-PanAmerica, Apartado 1177, 4050 Alajuela, Costa Rica. Phone: +506 483-0550/551. Fax +506 483 0555. E-mail: rmadvent@racsa.sol.cr. URL: www.awr.org/awr-panamerica/. Contact: Victor Shepherd, General Manager; David Gregory, Program Director; Miss Miriam Pottinger; or Rosaura Barrantes B., Secretaria; (technical) Karl Thompson, Chief Engineer. Free stickers, calendars, Costa Rican stamps and religious printed matter. IRCs accepted but currency notes in a major world currency preferred, or return postage stamps appreciated. Also, *see* AWR listings under Guam, Guatemala, Italy, Kenya, Russia and USA.

Faro del Caribe Internacional y Misionera—TIFC
MAIN OFFICE: Apartado 2710, 1000 San José, Costa Rica. Phone: +506 (226) 2573 or +506 (226) 2618. Fax: +506 (227) 1725. E-mail: al@casa-pres.go.cr. Contact: Carlos A. Rozotto Piedrasanta, Director Administrativo; or Mauricio Ramires; (technical) Minor Enrique, Station Engineer. Free stickers, pennants, books and bibles. $1 or IRCs helpful.

U.S. OFFICE, NONTECHNICAL: Misión Latinoamericana, P.O. Box 620485, Orlando FL 32862 USA.

Radio Casino, Apartado 287, 7301 Puerto Limón, Costa Rica. Phone: +506 758-0029. Fax: +506 758 3029. Contact: Edwin Zamora, Departamento de Notícias; or Luis Grau Villalobos, Gerente; (technical) Ing. Jorge Pardo, Director Técnico; or Luis Muir, Técnico.

Radio Exterior de España—Cariari Relay Station, Cariari de Pococí, Costa Rica. Phone: +506 767-7308 or +506 767-7311. Fax: +506 225 2938.

Radio For Peace International (RFPI)
MAIN OFFICE: Apartado 88, Santa Ana, Costa Rica. Phone: +506 249-1821. Fax: +506 249 1095. E-mail: rfpicr@sol.racsa.co.cr. URLs: (general) www.clark.net/pub/cwilkins/rfpi/rfpi.html; (Far Right Radio Review) www.clark.net/pub/cwilkins/rfpi/frwr.html. Contact: (general) Debra Latham, General Manager of RFPI, Editor of *VISTA* and co-host of "RFPI Mailbag"; (programming) Joe Bernard, Program Coordinator; Willie Barrantes, Director, Spanish Department; María Suárez Toro and Katerina Anfossi Gómez, FIRE, Women's Programming; or James Latham, host, "Far Right Radio Review"; (nontechnical or technical) James L. Latham, Station Manager. Replies sometimes slow in coming because of the mail. Audio cassette presentations, in English or Spanish, from women's perspectives welcomed for replay over "FIRE" program. Quarterly *VISTA* newsletter, which includes schedules and program information, $35 annual membership ($50 family/organization) in "Friends of Radio for Peace International"; station commemorative T-shirts and rainforest T-shirts $20; thermo mugs $10 (VISA/MC). Actively solicits listener contributions—directly, as well as indirectly through well-wishers signing up with PeaceCOM's long distance telephone service (+1 541/345-3326), or making designated world band purchases from Grove Enterprises (1-800-438-8155). $1 or 3 IRCs appreciated. Limited number of places available for volunteer broadcasting and journalism interns; those interested should send resumé. If funding can be worked out, hopes to add a world band transmission facility in Salmon Arm, British Columbia, Canada. RFPI was created by United Nations Resolution 35/55 on December 5, 1980.
U.S. OFFICE, NONTECHNICAL: P.O. Box 20728, Portland OR 97294 USA. Phone: +1 (503) 252-3639. Fax: +1 (503) 255 5216. Contact: Dr. Richard Schneider, Chancellor CEO, University of Global Education (formerly World Peace University). Newsletter, T-shirts and so forth, as above. University of the Air courses (such as "Earth Mother Speaks" and "History of the U.N.") $25 each, or on audio cassette $75 each (VISA/MC).

Radio Reloj, Sistema Radiofónico H.B., Apartado 341, 1000 San José, Costa Rica. Contact: Roger Barahona, Gerente; or Francisco Barahona Gómez. Can be very slow in replying. $1 required.

Radio Universidad de Costa Rica, San Pedro de Montes de Oca, 1000 San José, Costa Rica. Phone: +506 225-3936. Contact: Marco González Muñoz; Henry Jones, Locutor de Planta; or Nora Garita B., Directora. Free postcards, station brochure and stickers. Replies slowly to correspondence in Spanish or English. $1 or return postage required.

Radiodiffusion Télévision Ivoirienne, B.P. 191, Abidjan 1, Côte d'Ivoire. Phone: +225 32-4800.

☞Croatian Radio
MAIN OFFICE: Hrvatska Radio-Televizija (HRT), Prisavlje 3, HR-41000 Zagreb, Croatia. Phone: (technical) +385 (1) 616-3355. Fax: (general) +385 (1) 616 3285; (technical) +385 (1) 616 3347. E-mail: (International Relations Department) ird@hrt.hr; (technical) zelimir.klasan@hrt.com.hr. URLs: (general) www.hrt.hr/; (program guide) www.hrt.hr/hr/program/; (RealAudio) www.hrt.hr/hr/audio/. Contact: (general) Vladimir Lusic, Head of International Relations; Darko

Kragovic; or Bozidar Tomanek; (technical) Zelimir Klasan. Free Croatian stamps. Subscriptions to *Croatian Voice*. $1 helpful. Replies irregularly and slowly.
WASHINGTON NEWS BUREAU: Croatian-American Association, 1912 Sunderland Place NW, Washington DC 20036 USA. Phone: +1 (202) 429-5543. Fax: +1 (202) 429 5545. URL: www.hrnet.org/CAA/. Contact: Bob Schneider, Director.

Radio Habana Cuba, P.O. Box 6240, Havana, Cuba. Phone: (general) +53 (7) 784-954 or +53 (7) 334-272; (English and Spanish Departments) +53 (7) 791-053; (French Department) +53 (7) 785-444. Fax: (general) +53 (7) 783 518; (English and Spanish Departments) +53 (7) 795 007; (French Department) +53 (7) 705 810. E-mail: (programming) radiohc@mail.infocom.etecsa.cu; (engineering, technical, "Dxers Unlimited" & reception reports) inforhc@mail.infocom.etecsa.cu; or acoro@tinored.cu. URL: www.radiohc.org/. Contact: (general) Lourdes López, Head of Correspondence Dept.; Jorge Miyares, English Service; or Mike La Guardia, Senior Editor; (administration) Ms. Milagro Hernández Cuba, General Director; (technical) Arnaldo Coro Antich, ("Arnie Coro"), Producer, "DXers Unlimited"; or Luis Pruna Amer, Director Técnico. Free wallet and wall calendars, pennants, stickers, keychains and pins. DX Listeners' Club. Free sample *Granma International* newspaper. Contests with various prizes, including trips to Cuba.

Radio Rebelde, Departamento de Relaciones Públicas, Apartado 6277, Havana 10600, Cuba. Contact: Noemí Cairo Marín, Secretaria, Relaciones Públicas; Iberlise González Padua, Relaciones Públicas; Marisel Ramos Soca, Relaciones Públicas; or Jorge Luis Más Zabala, Director, Relaciones Públicas. Replies very slowly, with correspondence in Spanish preferred.

☞Bayrak Radio—BRT International (when operating), Yeni Organize Sanayi Bolgesi, Lefkoşa, via Mersin 10, Turkey. Phone: +90 (392) 228-5555. E-mail: brt@emu.edu.tr. URL: (includes RealAudio) www.cc.emu.edu.tr/press/brt/brt.htm. Contact: Mustafa Tosun, Head of Transmission Department.

BBC World Service—East Mediterranean Relay Station, P.O. Box 4912, Limassol, Cyprus. Contact: Steve Welch. This address for technical matters only. Reception reports and nontechnical correspondence should be sent to the BBC World Service in London (*see*).

☞Cyprus Broadcasting Corporation, Broadcasting House, P.O. Box 4824, 1397 Nicosia, Cyprus; or (physical address) RIK Street, Athalassa, Nicosia, Cyprus. Phone: +357 (2) 422-231. Fax: +357 (2) 314 050. E-mail: rik@cybc.com.cy. URL: (includes RealAudio) www.cybc.com.cy/. Contact: (general) Pavlos Soteriades, Director General; (technical) Andreas Michaelides, Director of Technical Services. Free stickers. Replies occasionally, sometimes slowly. IRC or $1 helpful.

Radio Monte-Carlo Middle East, P.O. Box 2026, Nicosia, Cyprus. Contact: M. Pavlides, Chef de Station. This address for listeners to the RMC Arabic Service, which prepares its world band programs in Cyprus, but transmits them via facilities of Radio Canada International in Canada. For details of Radio Monte-Carlo's headquarters and other branch offices, *see* Monaco.

☞Radio Prague, Czech Radio, Vinohradská 12, 120 99 Prague, Czech Republic. Phone: (general) +420 (2) 2409-4608; (Czech Department) +420 (2) 2422-2236; (English Department) +420 (2) 2421-8349; (Internet) +420 (2) 2421 5456. Fax: (general) +420 (2) 2422 2236; (external programs, nontechnical and technical) +420 (2) 2421 8239; (domestic and external programs, technical) +420 (2) 232 1020. E-mail: (general) cr@radio.cz; (English Department) english@radio.cz; (reception reports, Nora Mikes) nora@werich.radio.cz; (free news texts) robot@radio.cz, writing "Subscribe English" (or other desired language) within the subject line; (technical, chief engineer) cip@radio.cz. URLs: (text and RealAudio in English, German, Spanish and French) www.radio.cz; (RealAudio in English and Czech) www.wrn.org/stations/prague.html; (text) http://town.hall.org/Archives/Mirrors/Prague; ftp://ftp.radio.cz; gopher://gopher.radio.cz. Contact: (general) Markéta Albrechtová; Lenka Adamová, "Mailbag"; Zdenek Dohnal; Nora Mikes, Listener Relations; L. Kubik; or Jan Valeška, Head of English Section; (administration) Dr. Richard Seeman, Director, Foreign Broadcasts; (technical, all programs) Oldrich Čip, Chief Engineer. Free stickers, key chains, and calendars; free Radio Prague Monitor Club "DX Diploma" for regular correspondents. History booklet called "Radio Prague, 1936-1996," now available. Free books available for Czech-language course called "Check out Czech." Samples of *Welcome to the Czech Republic* and *Czech Life* available upon request from Orbis, Vinohradská 46, 120 41 Prague, Czech Republic. Recent reports indicate that Radio Prague, due to budget cuts, will end its programs in German, French and Spanish by the end of 1997.

RFE-RL—see USA.

DENMARK World Time +1 (+2 midyear)

📻Radio Danmark

MAIN OFFICE: Rosenørns Allé 22, DK-1999 Frederiksberg C, Denmark. Phone: (Danish-language 24-hour telephone tape recording for schedule information) +45 3520-5796 for Europe/Africa, +45 3520-5797 for Eastern Hemisphere, +45 3520-5798 for Western Hemisphere; (office) +45 3520-5785 (0800-1500 UTC winter; 0700-1400 UTC summer); (voice mail) +45 3520-5791. Fax: + 45 3520 57 81. E-mail: (schedule and program matters) rdk@dr.dk; (technical matters and reception reports) rdk.ek@login.dknet.dk. URL: (includes RealAudio) www.dr.dk/rdk. Contact: (general) Lulu Vittrup, Audience Communications; or Bjorn Schionning; (technical) Erik Køie, Technical Adviser; or Dan Helto, Frequency Manager. Replies to correspondence in English or Danish. Will verify all correct reception reports; return postage ($1 or one IRC) appreciated. Uses transmitting facilities of Radio Norway International.

PRODUCTION OFFICE, ENGLISH PROGRAM: Box 666, DK-1506 Copenhagen, Denmark. E-mail: jui@dr.dk. Contact: Julian Isherwood, Producer, "Tune In" twice monthly (Saturday) letterbox program.

TRANSMISSION MANAGEMENT AUTHORITY: Telecom Denmark, Telegade 2, DK-2630 Taastrup, Denmark. Phone: +45 4252-9111, Ext. 5746. Fax: +45 4371 1143. Contact: Ib H. Lavrsen, Senior Engineer.

NORWEGIAN OFFICE, TECHNICAL: Details of reception quality may also be sent to the Engineering Department of Radio Norway International (see), which operates the transmitters currently used for Radio Danmark.

World Music Radio, P.O. Box 112, DK-8900, Randers, Denmark. Phone: +45 (70) 222-222. Fax: +45 (70) 222 888. E-mail: wmr@cybernet.dk. URL: www.wmr.dk. Contact: Stig Hartvig Nielsen. Return postage required. Transmits via Sentech facilities in South Africa (see).

DISESTABLISHMENTARIAN

NOTE ON STATIONS WITHIN THE UNITED STATES AND COSTA RICA: In the United States and Costa Rica, disestablishmentarian programs are aired within the provisions of national law, and thus usually welcome correspondence and requests for free or paid materials. Virtually all such programs in the United States are aired over a variety of private stations—WGTG in McCaysville, Georgia; WWCR in Nashville; WRNO near New Orleans; WHRI in Noblesville, Indiana; WRMI in Miami; and, arguably, KVOH in Los Angeles.

These programs usually refer to themselves as "patriotic," and include such traditional and relatively benign ideologies as populism and politically conservative evangelism. Among these categories, some go out of their way to disassociate themselves from bigotry. However, other pro-grams, with tiny but dedicated audiences, are survivalist, antisemitic, neo-fascist, ultra-nationalist or otherwise on the fringes of the political "right," including the much-publicized militia movement. Perhaps surprisingly, few are overtly racist, although racism is often implied.

These programs reflect the American climate of unfettered freedom of speech, as well as, in some cases, the more cynical American tradition of profiting from proselytization. ("Our society is about to be conquered by alien or internationalist forces. To cope with this, you'll need certain things, which we sell.") Thus, American disestablishmentarian programs often differ greatly from the sorts of broadcasting discourse allowed within the laws and traditions of most other countries.

Well removed from this genre is the relatively low-powered voice of Radio For Peace International (see), a largely American-staffed station in Costa Rica. RFPI airs disestablishmentarian-cum-social-conscience programs from the relatively internationalist perspective of the political "new left" that grew into prominence in North America and Europe during the late Sixties. It also regularly follows and reports on the aforementioned disestablishmentarian programs aired over stations within the United States.

NOTE ON STATIONS OUTSIDE THE UNITED STATES AND COSTA RICA: Outside the United States and Costa Rica, disestablishmentarian broadcasting activities, some of which are actually clandestine, are unusually subject to abrupt change or termination. Being operated by anti-establishment political and/or military organizations, these groups tend to be suspicious of outsiders' motives. Thus, they are most likely to reply to contacts from those who communicate in the station's native tongue, and who are perceived to be at least somewhat favorably disposed to their cause. Most will provide, upon request, printed matter in their native tongue on their cause

For more detailed information on clandestine (but not disestablishmentarian) stations, refer to the annual publication, Clandestine Stations List, about $10 or 10 IRCs postpaid by air, published by the Danish Shortwave Clubs International, Tavleager 31, DK-2670 Greve, Denmark; phone (Denmark) +45 4290-2900; fax (via Germany) +49 6371 71790; e-mail 100413.2375@compuserve.com; its expert editor, Finn Krone of Denmark, may be reached at e-mail Krone@dk-online.dk. For CIA media contact information, see USA. Also now available on the internet The Clandestine Radio Intel Webpage, specialising in background information on these stations and organised by region and target country. The page can be accessed via: www.qsl.net/yb0rmi/cland.htm.

"Agenda Cuba" (when operating), 7175 SW 8 Street, Suite 217, Miami FL 33144 USA. Contact: Pedro Solares. Program of the Agenda Cuba organization. Via WRMI, USA.

"Along the Color Line," Department of History, Columbia University, 611 Fayerweather Hall, New York NY 10027 USA. Phone: +1 (212) 854-7080. Fax: +1 (212) 854 7060. Contact: Dr. Manning Marable, Director of the Institute for Research in African-American Studies. Critiques a wide variety of domestic and international issues relevant to African-Americans. Via RFPI, Costa Rica.

"Alternative Radio," P.O. Box 551, Boulder CO 80306 USA. Phone: +1 (303) 444-8788. Contact: David Barsamian. Critiques such issues as multiculturalism, the environment, racism, American foreign policy, the media and the rights of indigenous peoples. Via RFPI, Costa Rica.

📻"American Dissident Voices," P.O. Box 90, Hillsboro WV 24946 USA (or P.O. Box 596, Boring OR 97009 USA). E-mail: (general) crusader@national.alliance; or triton@abszolute.org; (Strom) ka_strom@ix.netcom. URLs: (general) www.natall.com/SCHEDULE/sched.html; (TrueSpeech/WAV audio archives) www.natall.com/radio/radio.html; (usenet) alt.politics.nationalism.white. Contact: Kevin Alfred Strom, WB4AIO, Producer. $12 for audio cassette of any given program. $55 for latest book from Canadian neonazi

Ernst Zündel. *Free Speech* publication $40 per year. $2 for catalog of books and tapes. Free bumper stickers, "Who Rules *America*?" pamphlet and sample copies of *Patriot Review* newsletter. Program of the National Alliance, the most prominent neonazi organization in the United States. In its publicity, it claims to support "ordinary straight White America"; according to *The New York Times*, the National Alliance also states, "We must have a racially clean area of the earth." The show sometimes features William Pierce, chairman and founder of the American Nazi Party. Pierce, under the pen name "Andrew Macdonald," is the author of *The Turner Diaries*, which is felt may have given accused bomber Timothy McVeigh the idea and pyrotechnic knowledge for the Oklahoma City bombing. Via WRNO, and before that believed to be behind the U.S. clandestine station, "Voice of To-morrow," which became inactive not long before "American Dissident Voices" came on the air.

"A Voz da Resistencia do Galo Negro" ("Voice of the Resistence of the Black Cockerel")—see Angola.

📠**"Baker Report,"** 2083 Springwood Road #300, York PA 17403 USA. Phone: (show, toll-free in United States) 1-800-482-5560; (orders, toll-free in United States) 1-800-782-4843; (general number/voice mail) +1 (717) 244-1110. E-mail: baker@universalweb.com. URL: (includes RealAudio) www.universalweb.com/amerinet/baker/index.htm. Contact: Dr. Jeffrey "Jeff" Baker. Three months of *The Baker Report* periodical $24.95; also sells audio tapes of programs and other items. Anti-"New World Order," Freemasonry and the Illuminati, and distrustful of official versions of various events, including the Oklahoma City bombing. Via WGTG and WRMI, USA.

"Battle Cry Sounding"
HEADQUARTERS: Command Post, ACMTC, P.O. Box 90, Berino NM 88024 USA. Fax: +1 (505) 882 7325. E-mail: prophet@cibola.net. URL: www-user.cibola.net/~prophet/. Contact: General James M. Green. Voice of the Aggressive Christianity Missions Training Corps, which seeks to eliminate churches, synagogues, mosques and central governments, thence to replace them with fundamentalist "warrior tribes"; also, operates Women's International Mobilization Movement. Publishes *Wisdom's Cry*, *Words of the Spirit*, *Tribal Call* and *Battle Cry Sounding* periodicals, and offers various other publications, as well as video and audio tapes. Via facilities of WWCR and WRMI, USA.
AFRICA OFFICE: P.O. Box 2686, Jos North, Plateau State, Nigeria. Contact: Colonel Simon Agwale, Adjutant.

"British Israel World Federation (Canada)," 313 Sherbourne Street, Toronto ON, M5A 2S3 Canada. Phone: (office, weekdays) +1 (416) 921-5996; (Nesbitt) +1 (705) 435-5044; (McConkey) +1 (705) 485-3486. Fax: +1 (416) 921 9511. Contact: Douglas Nesbitt or John McConkey. Offers *The Prophetic* magazine and 90-minute audio cassettes of past programs. Although located in Canada, this is the only British Israel office in North America, and thus serves the United States, as well. According to Kenneth Stern in *A Force upon the Plain*, "Christian Identity [see "Herald of Truth" and "Scriptures for America"] began as British Israelism, which traced its roots to mid-nineteenth-century claims that white Christians were the 'true Israelites,' that Jews were offspring of Satan, and that blacks and other minorities were . . . subhuman." Via WWCR, USA.

"CounterSpin," Fairness and Accuracy in Reporting, 130 W. 25th Street, New York NY 10001 USA. Phone: +1 (212) 633-6700. E-mail: fair@igc.org. URL: www.fair.org/fair/. Media watchdog organization that reports on what it feels are propaganda, disinformation and other abuses of the media, as well as citing instances of "hard-hitting, independent reporting that cuts against the prevailing media grain." Via RFPI, Costa Rica.

📠**"Democratic Voice of Burma"** ("Democratic Myanmar a-Than")
STATION: DVB Radio, P.O. Box 6720, St. Olavs Plass, N-0130

Nobel Peace laureate and Burmese opposition leader Aung San Suu Kyi speaks over the Democratic Voice of Burma, which transmits from world band facilities in Norway.

Oslo, Norway. Phone: +47 (22) 20-0021. Phone/fax: +47 (22) 36-2525. E-mail: dvb@sn.no. URL: (includes RealAudio) www.communique.no/dvb/. Contact: (general) Dr. Anng Kin, Listener Liaison; Aye Chan Naing, Daily Editor; or Thida, host for "Songs Request Program"; (administration) Harn Yawnghwe, Director; or Daw Khin Pyone, Manager; (technical) Technical Dept. Free stickers and booklets to be offered in the near future. Norwegian kroner requested for a reply, but presumably Norwegian mint stamps would also suffice. Programs produced by Burmese democratic movements, as well as professional and independent radio journalists, to provide informational and educational services for the democracy movement inside and outside Burma. Opposes current Myanmar government. Transmits via the facilities of Radio Norway International and Deutsche Telekom, Germany.
AFFINITY GROUPS URLs:
BURMA NET. E-mail: (BurmaNet News editor, Free Burma Coalition, USA) strider@igc.apc.org; (Web coordinator, Free Burma Coalition, USA) freeburma@pobox.com. URL: (BurmaNet News, USA) http://sunsite.unc.edu/freeburma/listservers.html.
FREE BURMA COALITION. E-mail: justfree@ix.netcom.com. URL: http://danenet.wicip.org/fbc/.

"Democratic Voice of Iran" ("Seda-ye Azadi-khahan-e Iran"), BCM Box 5842, London, WC1N 3XX, United Kingdom; or Box 554, SE-114 79 Stockholm, Sweden. Fax: (France) +33 (1) 43 99 95 65; (Sweden) +46 (1) 831 4148; or (UK) +44 (541) 525 051. If corresponding with this station do not mention the name of the station or even the word "radio" on the envelope. Opposes current Iranian government. Believed to broadcast via a transmitter in Central Asia.

"Duncan Long Show" (when operating), American Freedom Network, P.O. Box 430, Johnstown CO 80534 USA. Phone: (talk show, toll-free within U.S.) 1-800-607-8255; (elsewhere) +1 (970) 587-5171; (order line, toll-free within U.S.) 1-800-205-6245. Fax: +1 (970) 587 5450. E-mail: duncan@kansas.net. URLs: www.kansas.net/~duncan; www.tfsksu.net/~duncan. Contact: Duncan Long, Host; or "Don W." Network Manager. Free sample of *USA Patriot News* monthly newspaper/catalog, otherwise $16/six months. Sells survival gear, night-vision goggles, Taiwanese shortwave radios, books and NTSC videos. VISA/MC/AX. Survivalist/militia how-to show, detailing such things as how and where to obtain, modify and use firearms and other military-type gear for various types of situations, including conventional, guerilla/special, biological and chemical combat, as well as "target shooting." Via WWCR, USA.

"Executive Intelligence Review Talks," EIR News Service, P.O. Box 17390, Washington DC 20041 USA. Phone: (Executive Intelligence Review) +1 (202) 544-7010; (Schiller Institute) +1 (202) 544-7018; (21st Century Institute, general information) +1 (202) 639-6821; (21st Century Institute, subscription information) +1 (703) 777-9451; (Ben Franklin Bookstore for LaRouche publications) toll-free daytimes only within United States 1-800-453-4108, elswhere +1 (703) 777-3661. Fax: +1 (202) 544 7105. E-mail: (technical) ralphgib@aol.com. URLs: (EIR Home Page) www.larouchepub.com/index.html; (LaRouche Associates) www.erols.com/larouche/. Contact: (general) Mel Kanovsky, Frank Bell; or, asking correspondence to be forwarded, Lyndon LaRouche; (technical) Ralph Gibbons. Publishes *Executive Intelligence Review* newsletter, $896/year, and a wide variety of other periodicals and books. Supports former U.S. presidential candidate Lyndon LaRouche's populist political organization worldwide, including the Schiller Institute and 21st Century Institute of Political Action. Via WWCR, USA.

"Far Right Radio Review"—see RFPI, Costa Rica, for contact information. Critiques populist and politically rightist programs emanating from various privately owned world band stations in the United States.

"FIRE" —RadioAward-winning multilingual (English and Spanish) feminist program produced by the Feminist International Radio Endeavour staff at Radio For Peace International in Costa Rica (see), led by María Suárez Toro. E-mail: fire@expreso.com. URL: www.igc.org/womensnet/beijing/news/fire.html. Financially supported by the Foundation for a Compassionate Society. See RFPI, Costa Rica, for more information.

"Food Not Bombs Radio Network"
PRODUCTION FACILITY: 350 7th Avenue #35, San Francisco CA 94118 USA. Phone: +1 (415) 330-5030. Contact: Richard Edmondson, Producer. Via RFPI, Costa Rica.
ORGANIZATIONAL ADDRESS: Food Not Bombs, 3145 Gary Blvd. #12, San Francisco CA 94118 USA; also, temporarily can be reached at 25 Taylor Avenue, San Francisco CA 94118 USA. Phone: (toll-free in the U.S.) 1-800-884-1136; (elsewhere) +1 (415) 351-1672. URL: www.webcom.com/~peace. $10 for starter kit and 128-page book for starting a food recovery program; NTSC video $15. Food Not Bombs is a political activist group concerned with American homeless people, with the radio program focusing on what it views as "oppressive local, state and federal policies." The producer is a former homeless person.

"For the People", P.O. Box 150, Tampa FL 33601-0150 USA. Phone: (general) +1 (904) 397-4390; (talk show, toll-free within the United States, 1400-1700 Eastern Time only) 1-888-822-8255. Fax: +1 (904) 397 4484 or +1 (904) 397 4491. E-mail: doug@forthepeople.org; cpa14782@gte.net; or hostmail@tstradio.com. URL: www.forthepeople.org. Contact: Chuck Harder, Host; or Brice Warnick, Producer. Free monthly *Station Listing & Program Guide* Flyer. Annual FTP membership $20 ($35 outside U.S.). Sells bi-weekly *News Reporter* newspaper, NTSC videos of past FTP broadcasts, T-

shirts and golf shirts; also a wide variety of books from its "For the People Bookstore"; free catalog upon request. VISA/MC. Publications and audio cassettes also available from "Eighth Day Books" (order line, toll-free within United States, 1-800-841-2541). Sells U.S.-made tabletop radio similar to Drake SW1 reviewed in PASSPORT REPORTS (see). The "For The People" talk show espouses American populism, a philosophy going back to 1891. FTP's governing non-profit organization supports trade restrictions, freedom of healthcare choice and progressive taxes on high incomes, while opposing racism and antisemitism. Have recently purchased a 50 kW shortwave transmitter which should be on the air soon. Live afternoons (local time) via WHRI, USA, and on tape evenings via WHRI and WWCR, USA; also in RealAudio (URL: www.whri.com/realaudio.htm; "Angel 1").

"Foro Militar Cubano," P.O. Box 140305, Coral Gables FL 33144-0305 USA. Contact: Frank Hernández Trujillo, Producer. Anti-Castro, anti-communist, privately supported by Cuban exiles and the Cuban American Veterans Association. Via WRMI, USA.

"Freedom's Call"—see WWCR, USA, for postal address. E-mail: bogritz@valint.net; or bo@talkamerica.com. URLs: www.bogritz.com/; www.talkamerica.com/bogritz.html; (StreamWorks audio) www.talkamerica.com/. Contact: James "Bo" Gritz. Opposes gun control, the Federal income tax, the "New World Order," Zionism, alleged Jewish "control" of such institutions as the Federal Reserve System, and the United Nations. Disputes official accounts of such events as the Oklahoma City bombing. Gritz, a retired U.S. Green Beret lieutenant colonel, America's most-decorated Vietnam veteran and former presidential candidate of the Populist Party (see "Radio Free America"), is the character upon whom the movie character "Rambo" is understood to have been based. Gritz is also credited, along with Jack McLamb (see "Officer Jack McLamb Show"), with being the key individual to persuade Randy Weaver to end the Ruby Ridge standoff. He leads two paramilitary/militia training organizations: Specially Prepared Individuals for Key Events (SPIKE), and the Idaho-based Constitutionalist Covenant Community. Via WWCR, USA.

"Full Disclosure Radio Show" (when operating), The Superior Broadcasting Company, P.O. Box 1533, Oil City PA 16301 USA. Phone: +1 (814) 676-2345. E-mail: glr@glr.com. URL: www.glr.com/net.html. Contact: Glen L. Roberts, Host. Sample newsletter $5. Offers a variety of electronics and related publications. Conservative talk show concerning such topics as political broadcasts and related communications, and eavesdropping. Via WGTG, USA.

"Herald of Truth," P.O. Box 1021, Harrison AK 72602 USA. Phone: +1 (501) 741-1119. Contact: Pastor Bob Hallstrom. Free packet of information and copies of broadcast transcripts, also available from Gospel Ministries, P.O. Box 9411, Boise ID 83707 USA; or via URL: www.melvig.org/gmo.html. Program of the Kingdom Identity Ministries, a Christian Identity organization believed to be associated with "Scriptures for America" (see), and reportedly descended from British Israelism (see "British Israel World Federation"). Vehemently opposes to what it calls "Jews, queers, aliens and minorities," and supports "white Christians," specifically those "Aryan Jacob Israel people" originating from Western Europe. Yet, also opposes a seemingly endless roster of conservative white Christian political leaders, including Rush Limbaugh and U.S. House Speaker Newt Gingrich, and claims the late U.S. President Franklin Roosevelt was a Jewish communist. Sells various books and audio cassettes, as well as the *Patriot Report* newsletter. Via WWCR and WRMI, USA; Christian Identity programs are also aired over other American world band stations, such as WRNO.

"Hightower Radio," Saddle Burr Productions, P.O. Box 13516, Austin TX 78711 USA. Phone: +1 (512) 477-5588. Fax: +1 (512) 478 8536. E-mail: hightower@essential.org. URL: www.essential.org/hightower/; (RealAudio) www-

2.realaudio.com/webactive/content/hightower.html. Contact: Jim Hightower. The term "maverick" comes from the contrarian way Texas pioneer Samuel Maverick and certain of his descendants handled cattle and other matters. Hightower Radio is considered to be heir to that spirit, featuring former Texas Agriculture Commissioner Jim Hightower, something of an establishment Texas disestablishmentarian and a gen-yew-wine Lone Star liberal. Via RFPI, Costa Rica.

"Holy Medina Radio" (when active)—*see* Radio Iraq International for contact information. Opposes the Saudi government.

"Hour of Courage," International Commerce Corporation, 135 S. Main Street, 7th Floor, Greenville SC 29601 USA. Phone: (toll-free within United States) 1-800-327-8606. Fax: +1 (803) 232 9309. Contact: Ron Wilson. *Creatures from Jeckyll Island* book $25. Forsees a conspiracy to take over the United States, opposes gun control, and is distrustful of official versions of various events, such as Waco. Also predicts the coming of a "greatest financial catastrophe in the world," and suggests that to protect against its consequences, listeners purchase precious metals from its sponsoring organization, Atlantic Bullion and Coin. Theme song: "Dixie." Via WWCR and WHRI, USA.

"Hour of the Time," The Harvest Trust, P.O. Box 1970, Eagar AZ 85925 USA. Phone/fax: +1 (520) 333-4578. E-mail: caji@pobox.com. URL: www.telepath.com/believer/page6.htm (broadcast transcripts downloadable as pkzip files from www.telepath.com/believer/page14.htm). Contact: William Cooper. Sells a variety of books, audio and video tapes. Newspaper *Veritas* available for prices ranging from $20 for six issues to $55 for 24 issues. Opposes "New World Order," the United Nations and the Federal Reserve; favors militias to resist potentially oppressive government. *Behold a Pale Horse* (Light Technology Publishing), a 1991 book by Cooper, covers his many claims, including about alien space invaders: "1 in 40 humans have been implanted with devices . . . aliens are building an army of implanted humans who can be activated and turned on us." Via WWCR, USA.

"Insight," The Progressive, 409 East Main Street, Madison WI 53703 USA. Phone: +1 (608) 257-4626. Fax: +1 (608) 257 3373. E-mail: editorial@progressive.org. URL: www.progressive.org/insight.htm. Contact: Matthew Rothschild, Editor. Radio outlet for *The Progressive* magazine, a disestablishmentarian publication founded in 1909. Via RFPI, Costa Rica.

"Intelligence Report," Wolverine Productions, P.O. Box 281, Augusta MI 49012 USA. Phone: +1 (616) 966-3002. Fax: +1 (616) 966 0742. Contact: (programs) John Stadtmiller. Sells various tapes and publications. Opposes the "New World Order" and supports the militia and survivalist movements. Aired via WWCR, USA.

"La Voz de Alpha 66," 1714 Flagler Street, Miami FL 33135 USA. Contact: Dr. Diego Medina, Producer. Anti-Castro, anti-communist; privately supported by the Alpha 66 organization. Via WHRI, USA.

"La Voz de la Fundación," 7300 NE 35th Terrace, Miami FL 33122 USA; or P.O. Box 440069, Miami FL 33122 USA. Phone: (general) +1 (305) 592-7768; (Pérez-Castellón) +1 (305) 599-3019. Fax: +1 (305) 592 7889. URLs: (Cuban American National Foundation parent organization) www.canfnet.org/; (La Voz de la Fundación) www.canfnet.org/english/prgvoz.htm. Contact: Ninoska Pérez-Castellón, Executive Producer; (technical) Mariela Ferretti. Free stickers. Anti-Castro, anti-communist; privately supported by the Cuban American National Foundation. Also, *see* Radio Martí, USA. Via WHRI and WRMI, USA.

"La Voz de la Junta Patriótica Cubana," 4600 NW 7 Street, Miami FL 33126 USA. Anti-Castro, anti-communist, privately supported by the Cuban Patriotic Council. E-mail: cabenedi@vais.net. URL: www.vais.net/~cabenedi/. Contact: Dr. Roberto Rodríguez de Aragón, Presidente de la Junta Patriótica Cubana; or Dr. Claudio F. Benedi-Beruff, Secretario de Relaciones Exteriores. Via WRMI, USA.

"La Voz del CID", 10021 SW 37th Terrace, Miami FL 33165 USA; if no result, try AFINSA Portugal, Ricardo Jorge 53, P-4000 Oporto, Portugal; Apartado de Correo 8130, 1000 San José, Costa Rica; or Apartado Postal 51403, Sabana Grande 1050, Caracas, Venezuela. Phone: (U.S.) +1 (305) 551-8484. Fax: (U.S.) +1 (305) 559 9365; (Portugal) +351 (2) 41 49 94. Contact: Alfredo Aspitia, Asistente de Prensa e Información; or Francisco Fernández. Anti-Castro, anti-communist; privately supported by Cuba Independiente y Democrática. Free political literature. Via their own clandestine transmitters in Central America, possibly Guatemala.

"La Voz del Puente de Jóvenes Profesionales Cubanos en el Exilio," P.O. Box 112452, Miami FL 33111-2453 USA. Contact: Rafael Sánchez-Aballi, Producer. Anti-Castro, supported by a group of Cuban professionals living in exile in Miami. Via WRMI, USA.

"Lightwave Mission Broadcasting"—*see* "Radio Newyork International listed under USA."

"Making Contact"
PRODUCTION OFFICE: David Barsamian, P.O. Box 551, Boulder CO 80306 USA. Phone: +1 (303) 444-8788. E-mail: contact@igc.org. URL: www.igc.org/MakingContact/. Via RFPI, Costa Rica.
ORGANIZATION OFFICE: National Radio Project, 830 Los Trancos Road, Portola Valley CA 94028 USA. Phone: +1 (415) 851-7256. Focuses on social and political problems and solutions within the United States and beyond.

"Mujer Cubana," 747 Ponce de Leon Blvd., Suite 409, Coral Gables FL 33134 USA. Program of a group of Cuban women exiles in Miami. Via WRMI, USA.

"National Radio of the Saharan Arab Democratic Republic," (when operating)—*see* "Voice of the Free Sahara," below, which is operated by the same group, the Frente Polisario.

"National Unity Radio" (when operating)—*see* Sudan National Broadcasting Corporation for contact information.

"New Dimensions Radio," P.O. Box 569, Ukiah CA 95482 USA. Program that looks at the independent media, how they affect political power and how they develop as alternatives to state controlled media. Via RFPI.

☞**"Norman Resnick Show,"** American Freedom Network, P.O. Box 430, Johnstown CO 80534 USA. Phone: (talk show, toll-free within U.S.) 1-800-607-8255; (elsewhere) +1 (970) 587-5171; (order line, toll-free within U.S.) 1-800-205-6245. Fax: +1 (970) 587 5450. URL: (RealAudio, via WHRI) www.whri.com/realaudio.htm ("Angel 2"); (StreamWorks, via American Freedom Network) www.amerifree.com/stream.htm. Contact: Norman "Dr. Norm" Resnick, Host. Free sample of *USA Patriot News* monthly newspaper/catalog. Sells survival gear, night-vision goggles, Taiwanese shortwave radios, books and NTSC videos. VISA/MC/AX. Former professor Resnick states that he is "an observant, kosher Jew." He describes his program as discussing "educational, social, political and economic issues from a Constitutional perspective," with emphasis on the activities on the U.S. Bureau of Alcohol, Tobacco and Firearms. Opposed *inter alia* to the "New World Order" and gun control. Via WWCR and WHRI, USA.

☞**"Officer Jack McLamb Show,"** P.O. Box 8712, Phoenix AZ 85066 USA. Phone: (McLamb) +1 (602) 237-2533. URLs: (general) www.police-against-nwo.com/; (RealAudio) www.whri.com/realaudio.htm ("Angel 1"). Program and sister organization, Police Against the New World Order, are headed by former Phoenix police officer Jack McLamb. Supports activities to convert American police officers and military personnel over to view and act favorably towards militias, as well as similar groups and armed individuals. Sells audio and video tapes, posters, *The Waco Whitewash*, *Vampire Killer 2000* and other publications. In *Vampire Killer 2000*, written by McLamb, he opposes, among many others, CBS News, financial interests of the Rothschild family, and gun control. McLamb is credited, along with "Bo" Gritz (*see*

"Freedom's Call"), with being a key individual in persuading Randy Weaver to end the Ruby Ridge standoff. Via WHRI, USA.

"Overcomer" ("Voice of the Last Day Prophet of God"), P.O. Box 691, Walterboro SC 29488 USA. Phone: (0900-1700 local time, Sunday through Friday) +1 (803) 538-3892. E-mail: rgstair@odys.com. URL: www.wwcr.com/stair.htm. Contact: Brother R.G. Stair. Sample "Overcomer" newsletter and various pamphlets free upon request. Sells a Sangean shortwave radio for $50, plus other items of equipment and various publications at appropriate prices. Primarily a fundamentalist Christian program from an exceptionally pleasant Southern town, but disestablishmentarian in such things as its characterizations of homosexuals in general, as well as the supposed homosexual and heterosexual activities of priests and nuns within the Roman Catholic Church. Also opposes Freemasonry, U.S. aid to Israel and reported abuses of powers of U.S. Federal authorities. Invites listeners to write in, giving the name of the station over which "The Overcomer" was heard and the quality of reception. Via WRNO and WWCR, USA.

"Preparedness Hour," American Freedom Network, P.O. Box 430, Johnstown CO 80534 USA. Phone: (talk show, toll-free within U.S.) 1-800-607-8255; (elsewhere) +1 (970) 587-5171; (order line, toll-free within U.S.) 1-800-205-6245. Fax: +1 (970) 587 5450. Contact: (general) Bob Speer, Host; or "Don W.", Network Manager; (sponsor) Jim Cedarstrom. Free sample of *USA Patriot News* monthly newspaper/catalog. Sells survival gear, night-vision goggles, Taiwanese shortwave radios, books and NTSC videos. VISA/MC/AX. Program concentrates on such survivalist skills as growing food, making soap and cheese, home childbirth and how to obtain and train mules or donkeys. Speer is described by his associates as a "SPIKE trainer" (Specially Prepared Individuals for Key Events) for retired U.S. Green Beret lieutenant colonel James "Bo" Gritz. Sponsored by Discount Gold, which urges listeners to invest in precious metals as an alternative to holding paper money or investments. Via WWCR, USA.

"Prophecy Club," P.O. Box 750234, Topeka KS 66675 USA. Phone/fax: (club) +1 (913) 478-1112; (sponsor, toll-free in U.S. only) 1-800-525-9556. Contact: Stan Johnson, Director. Club, which takes no cards or phone orders, offers free sample newsletter and catalog; also sells newsletter subscriptions, as well as videos in NTSC format for $28.75 within the United States and $30 elsewhere, including shipping. Also offers audio cassettes for $5.75 (U.S.) or $6 (elsewhere). Sponsor accepts cards and sells similar items. Organization states that it is devoted to study and research on Bible prophecy. Programs oppose, *i.a.*, the "New World Order" and Freemasonry. Via WWCR and WHRI, USA, as well as various AM, FM and television stations.

"Protecting Your Wealth," 9188 E. San Salvador Drive #203, Scottsdale AZ 85258 USA. Phone: (program, toll-free within United States) 1-800-598-1500; (sponsoring organization, toll-free within the United States) 1-800-451-4452; (elsewhere) +1 (602) 451-0575. Fax: +1 (602) 451 4394. Contact: Mike Callahan or Eric Ceadarstrom. Opposed to the "New World Order" and groups involved in paper-based financial markets. Supports rural-based survivalism, and claims that the purpose of anti-terrorism and related American legislation is to extend government control over people so as to strip them of their assets. Alleges that paper money, bonds and securities are controlled by an elite that is about to create a second Great Depression, rendering those assets worthless. As an alternative, urges people to invest in the precious metals sold by their sponsoring organization, Viking International Trading, as well as to move to the countryside with their shortwave radios and to purchase hoardable foods sold by a sister firm. Via WRMI and WWCR, USA.

"Radio Amahoro" ("Radio Voice of Peace for Rwanda")
STATION OFFICE: Inter-Africa Group, P.O. Box 1631, Addis Ababa, Ethiopia.
SPONSORING ORGANIZATION: Centre Amani/Europep, rue du Noyer 322, B-1040 Brussels, Belgium. Fax: +32 (2) 735 3916. Contact: Tatien Musabyimana, Director; or Guy Theunis, Administrateur. Free stickers. Christian humanitarian organization seeking peace and reconciliation among Rwandan tribes and refugees. Via Afrique Numéro Un (see Gabon) and Radio Ethiopia (see).

"Radio Free America"
NETWORK: Orbit 7 Radio Network. Phone: +1 (888) 467-2487; (Valentine) +1 (941) 353-9688. E-mail: orbit7@e-z.net. URLs: (general) http://orbit7.com/val.htm; (RealAudio) http://orbit7.com; or www.whri.com/realaudio.htm ("Angel 1"). Contact: Tom Valentine, Host. Via WHRI, USA.

"Radio Free Bougainville"
MAIN ADDRESS: 2 Griffith Avenue, Roseville NSW 2069, Australia. Phone/fax: +61 (2) 417-1066. E-mail: (Bougainville Freedom Movement) sashab@magna.com.au. URL: (Bougainville Freedom Movement) www.magna.com.au/~sashab/BFM.htm. Contact: Sam Voron, Australian Director. $5, AUS$5 or 5 IRCs required. Station's continued operation is totally dependent on the availability of local coconuts for power generation, currently the only form of power available for those living in the blockaded areas of the island of Bougainville. Station is opposed to the Papua New Guinea government, and supports armed struggle for complete independence and the "Bougainville Interim Government." With the recent signing of a peace agreement between Papua New Guinea authorities and the separatist movement of Bougainville, this station may soon stop broadcasting.
ALTERNATIVE ADDRESS: P.O. Box 1203, Honiara, Solomon Islands. Contact: Martin R. Miriori, Humanitarian Aid Coordinator. $1, AUS$2 or 3 IRCs required. No verification data issued from this address.

"Radio Free Somalia," 2 Griffith Avenue, Roseville NSW 2069, Australia. Phone/fax: +61 (2) 417-1066. Contact: Sam Voron, Australian Director. $5, AUS$5 or 5 IRCs required. Station is operated from Gaalkacyo in the Mudug region of northeastern Somalia by the Somali International Amateur Radio Club. Seeks volunteers and donations of radio equipment and airline tickets.

"Radio Kudirat," NALICON U.K, P.O. Box 9663, London SE1 3LZ, United Kingdom; or NALICON U.S.A, P.O. Box 175, Boston MA 02131 USA. Phone: (London) +1 (617) 364-4455. Fax: (London) +44 (171) 403 6985; (Boston) +1 (617) 364 7362. E-mail: (London) rkn@postlin.demon.co.uk; (Boston) nalicon@nalicon.com. Contact: Kayode Fayemi, Director of Communications, NALICON. Station set up to disseminate information concerning democracy, human rights and the environment in Nigeria. Anti-Nigerian government. Created by London-based Nigerian exile group, NALICON (National Liberation Council of Nigeria). Requests broadcast material and funds to maintain a regular broadcasting schedule. Welcomes scripts, and recordings from listeners and supporters. Transmits via the South African facilities of Sentech.

"Radio Message of Freedom" ("Radyo Pyam-e Azadi"), GPO Box 857, University Town, Peshawar, Pakistan. Contact: Qaribur Rehman Saeed, Director of Radio. Sponsored by the Islamic Party of Afghanistan rebel organization, headed by Golboddin Hekmatyar. Via its own transmitting facilities; once, and possibly still, located in Afghanistan.

"Radio Nadeco", 514 10th St NW, Suite 600, Washington DC 20004 USA. Phone: +1 (202) 347-1960. Fax: +1 (202) 347 0921. URL: www.panafrica.com/nadeco/nadeco.htm. Supports the National Democratic Coalition of Nigeria (Nadeco) and opposes the current Nigerian government. Transmits via WWCR, USA.

"Radio of the Provisional Government of National Union and National Salvation of Cambodia," Permanent Mission of Democratic Cambodia to the United Nations, 747 3rd Avenue, 8th Floor, New York NY 10017 USA. Contact: Phobel Cheng, First Secretary, Permanent Mission of Cambodia to the United Nations. Khmer Rouge station. Operates from a clandestine site within Cambodia.

"Radio of the Saudi Opposition from Najd and Hijaz" ("Idha'at al-Mu'aradah al-Sa'udiyah fi Najd wa al-Hijaz")— see Radio Iraq International for contact information. Opposes the Saudi government.

"Radio Revista Lux," P.O. Box 451132, Miami FL 33245-1132 USA; or (physical address) 75 NW 22 Avenue, Miami FL 33125 USA. Contact: René L. Díaz. Anti-Castro program of the Union of Electrical Plant and Gas Workers of Cuba in Exile (Sindicato de Trabajadores Eléctricos, Gas y Agua de Cuba en el Exilio). Via WRMI, USA.

"Radio Roquero," P.O. Box 18005 Fairfield OH 45018 USA. Contact: Víctor García Rivera, Producer. Anti-Castro program aired via WRMI, USA.

"Radio Voice of One Free Ethiopia" (Andit Netsa Ethiopia Dimts Radio Agelgilot"), P.O. Box 5801, Washington DC 20016 USA. Anti-Ethiopian and Eritrean governments. Encourages listener mail. Thought to transmit via a shortwave transmitter in Central Asia.

"Radio Voice of Peace for Rwanda"—see "Radio Amahoro," above.

"Radio Voice of the Mojahed"—see "Voice of the Mojahed," below.

"Republic of Iraq Radio, Voice of the Iraqi People" ("Idha'at al-Jamahiriya al-Iraqiya, Saut al-Sha'b al-Iraqi"), Broadcasting Service of the Kingdom of Saudi Arabia, P.O. Box 61718, Riyadh 11575, Saudi Arabia. Phone: +966 (1) 442-5170. Fax: +966 (1) 402 8177. Contact: Suliman A. Al-Samnan, Director of Frequency Management. Anti-Saddam Hussein "black" clandestine supported by CIA, British intelligence, the Gulf Cooperation Council and Saudi Arabia. The name of this station has changed periodically since its inception during the Gulf crisis. Via transmitters in Saudi Arabia.

"RFPI Reports"—see RFPI, Costa Rica, for contact information. News about human rights, social justice and the environment, mainly from Latin America and the Caribbean.

"Rush Limbaugh Show," EIB World Band, WABC, #2 Pennsylvania Avenue, New York NY 10121 USA; telephone (toll-free, USA only) 1-800-282-2882, (elsewhere) +1 (212) 613-3800; fax (during working hours) +1 (212) 563 9166. E-mail 70277.2502@compuserve.com. Via WRNO, USA. Reception reports concerning this program can also be sent with 2 IRCs or an SASE directly to WRNO.

"Scriptures for America," P.O. Box 766-c, Laporte CO 80535 USA. Phone: +1 (307) 745-5914. Fax: +1 (307) 745 5914. URLs: (general) www.logoplex.com/resources/sfa/; (FTP site) ftp://ftp.netcom.com/pub/SF/SFA/. Contact: Pastor Peter J. "Pete" Peters. A leader within the Christian Identity movement (also see "Herald of Truth" and "British Israel World Federation"). Peters vehemently opposes, inter alia, homosexuals, the Anti-Defamation League of the B'nai B'rith and other Jews and Jewish organizations, nonwhites, and international banking institutions. Also expresses suspicion of official and media responses to such events as the Oklahoma City bombing, and is supportive of militia activities. Like the relatively visible (e.g., advertising in U.S. World News & Report) Pastor Karl Schott of Christ's Gospel Fellowship/The Pathfinder in Spokane, Peters alleges that Christians whose ancestry is from selected parts of Europe are the true chosen people of Biblical prophecy. Free Scriptures for America Newsletter, brochures and catalog of publications and recordings. Via WWCR and WRNO, USA.

"Second Opinion"—see "Insight," above, for contact information. Various thinkers propose solutions to world problems. Via Radio for Peace International, Costa Rica.

"Seventieth Week Magazine," P.O. Box 771, Gladewater TX 75647 USA. Contact: Ben McKnight. Free "Flash Bulletins" booklets. Opposes "New World Order," believes United Nations and UFOs are plotting to take over the United States and commit genocide against Christians and patriots, and distrusts official versions of various events, such as the Oklahoma City bombing. Via WWCR, USA.

"Steppin' Out of Babylon," 2804 Piedmont Avenue, Berkeley CA 94705 USA. Phone: +1 (510) 540-8850. E-mail: sues@ricochet.net. Contact: Sue Supriano, Producer. Interviews with those protesting various conditions, including war, poverty and human-rights abuses. Via RFPI.

"The American Way" (when operating), P.O. Box 198, Hawthorne NJ 07507 USA. Phone: (sponsor, SDL Incorporated, toll-free in U.S.) 1-800-468-2646. Contact: Andrew M. Gause. Opposes inter alia the "New World Order" and the Federal Reserve System. Sponsored by a gold-and-silver coin dealer. Via WWCR.

"The CIA: Commentary and Critique," c/o RFPI, P.O. Box 88, Santa Ana, Costa Rica. Covers ongoing disclosures and current events involving the CIA and public efforts at initiating reforms of its activities. Presented by human rights activist Jennifer Harbury. Program hopes to contribute to world peace by gathering and disseminating much neede information about the covert work of the CIA. Via RFPI.

"The Neumaier Report," C/o RFPI, P.O. Box 88, Santa Ana, Costa Rica. Commentaries by Dr. John J. Neumaier professor emeritus of philosophy and social theory. Deals with how power elites and oligarchies function in relation to democracy and freedom. Via RFPI.

"This Way Out," Overnight Productions, P.O. Box 38327, Los Angeles CA 90038 USA. Phone: +1 (213) 874-0874. E-mail: tworadio@aol.com. URL: http://abacus.oxy.edu/QRD/www/media/radio/thiswayout/index.html or www.qrd.org/qrd/www/media/radio/thiswayout/. News, music, interviews and features from and about lesbians and gays, mainly but not exclusively within the United States. Via RFPI.

"Un Solo Pueblo" (when active)—see Radio Copán International, Honduras, for address; or write directly to the sponsoring organization at 8561 NW South River Drive, Suite 201, Medley FL 33166 USA; also, Organo del Centro de la Democracia Cubana, P.O. Box 161742, Miami FL 33116 USA. Anti-Castro, anti-communist; privately supported by the Coordinadora Social Demócrata Cubana.

"Vietnam Veterans Radio Network," 7807 N. Avalon, Kansas City MO 64152 USA. Contact: John ("Doc") Upton. This radio voice of the Vietnam Veterans Against the War mixes music, commentaries and sound bites concerning some of the more difficult aspects of the Vietnam War experience. Via RFPI.

"Voice of Arab Syria"—see Radio Iraq International for contact information.

"Voice of China" ("Zhongguo Zhi Yin Guangbo Diantai"), Democratization of China, P.O. Box 11663, Berkeley CA 94701 USA; Foundation for China in the 21st Century, P.O. Box 11696, Berkeley CA 94701 USA. Phone: +1 (510) 2843-5025. Fax: +1 (510) 2843 4370. Contact: Bang Tai Xu, Director. Mainly "overseas Chinese students" interested in the democratization of China. Financial support from the Foundation for China in the 21st Century. Have "picked up the mission" of the earlier Voice of June 4th, but have no organizational relationship with it. Transmits via facilities of the Central Broadcasting System, Taiwan (see).

"Voice of Eritrea"—see Radio Iraq International, Iraq, for contact information.

"Voice of Freedom" (if reactivated), 206 Carlton St., Toronto ON, Canada. Contact: Ernst Zündel. Neonazi, supporting Adolf Hitler, the Third Reich and the NSDAP, as well as denying established Holocaust history. Although Zündel's program, formerly broadcast over WWCR and WRNO, is currently not aired over world band, he is sometimes heard on "American Dissident Voices" (see). Zündel, whose conviction in Canada for defaming a distinctly identifiable group was eventually overturned, has authored a number of books, including The Hitler We Loved, and Why.

"Voice of Free Nigeria", P.O. Box 441395, Indianapolis IN 46244 USA. Phone: +1 (317) 216-4590. E-mail: fnm@ix.netcom.com. URL: http://pw2.netcom.com/~fnm. Contact: Tunde Okorodudu, President; or Mukhtar Dan' Iyan, Secretary General. Station operated by the Free Nigeria Movement (FNM). Anti-Nigerian government.

"Voice of Iranian Kurdistan", KDPI, c/o AFK, Boite Postale 102, F-75623 Paris Cedex, France. Anti-Iranian government.
"Voice of Iraqi Kurdistan" ("Aira dangi Kurdestana Iraqa") (when active), P.O. Box 2443, Merrifield VA 22116 USA; P.O. Box 1504, London W7 3LX, United Kingdom; KDP Press Office, P.O. Box 4912, London SE15 4EW, United Kingdom; Kurdiska Riksförbundet, Hornsgatan 80, SE-117 21 Stockholm, Sweden; or Kurdistan Press, Örnsvägen 6C, SE-172 Sundbyberg, Sweden. Phone: (KDP Press Office, London) +44 (171) 931-7764; (Stockholm) +46 (8) 668-6060 or +46 (8) 668-66088; (Sundbyberg) +46 (8) 298-332. E-mail: 101.564.3336@compuserve.com; (KDP Press Office, London) : 101701.153@compuserve.com. Fax: (KDP Press Office, London) +44 (171) 931 7765. URLs: (station) http://ourworld.compuserve.com/homepages/gara/; (Kurdistan Democratic Party-Iraq parent organization) www.kdp.pp.se/; or http://home1.swipnet.se/~w-11534/. Contact: (United States) Namat Sharif, Kurdistan Democratic Party. Sponsored by the Kurdistan Democratic Party, led by Masoud Barzani, and the National Democratic Iraqi Front. From its own transmitting facilities, reportedly located in the Kurdish section of Iraq.
"Voice of Kashmir Freedom" ("Sada-i Hurriyat-i Kashmir"), P.O. Box 102, Muzaffarabad, Azad Kashmir, via Pakistan. Favors Azad Kashmiri independence from India; pro-Moslem, sponsored by the Kashmiri Mojahedin organization. From transmission facilities believed to be in Pakistan.
"Voice of Liberty," Box 1776, Liberty KY 42539 USA; or Box 3987, Rex GA 32073 USA. Phone: (call-in) toll-free in United States 1-800-526-1776, or elsewhere +1 (404) 968-8865; (voice mail) +1 (404) 968-0330. Contact: Paul Parsons or Rick Tyler. Sells various audio cassettes, $50 starter kit and *News Front* newspaper. Supports the Voice of Liberty Patriots organization, and reportedly is affiliated with the Church of the Remnant and the "Intelligence Report" program (*see*). Opposed to certain practices of the Bureau of Alcohol, Tobacco and Firearms and various other law-enforcement organizations in the United States, abortion, and restrictions on firearms and Christian prayer. Via WWCR, USA.
"Voice of National Salvation" ("Gugugui Sori Pangsong"), Grenier Osawa 107, 40 Nando-cho, Shinjuku-ku, Tokyo, Japan. Phone: + 81 (3) 5261-0331. Fax: +81 (3) 5261 0332. Contact: Kuguk Chonson. Pro-North Korea, pro-Korean unification; supported by North Korean government. On the air since 1967, but not always under the same name. Via North Korean transmitters located in Pyongyang, Haeju and Wongsan.
"Voice of Oromo Liberation" ("Kun Segalee Bilisumaa Oromooti"), Postfach 510610, D-13366 Berlin, Germany; or SBO, P.O. Box 73247, Washington DC 20056 USA. Phone: (Germany) +49 (30) 494-1036. Fax: (Germany) +49 (30) 494 3372. Contact: Tayete Ferah, European Coordinator. Station of the Oromo Liberation Front of Ethiopia, an Oromo nationalist organization transmitting via facilities of Ukrainian Radio (*see*). Reply unlikely, but interesting correspondence with a suitable donation and SASE might trigger a favorable response.
"Voice of Palestine, Voice of the Palestinian Islamic Revolution" ("Saut al-Filistin, Saut al-Thowrah al-Islamiyah al-Filistiniyah")—*see* Voice of the Islamic Republic of Iran, over whose transmitters this program is clandestinely aired, for potential contact information. Supports the Islamic Resistance Movement, Hamas, which is anti-Arafat and anti-Israel.
"Voice of Peace," Inter-Africa Group, P.O. Box 1631, Addis Ababa, Ethiopia. Humanitarian organization, partially funded by UNICEF, seeking peace and reconciliation among warring factions in central and eastern Africa. Via Radio Ethiopia (*see*).
"Voice of Rebellious Iraq" ("Saut al-Iraq al-Tha'ir"), P.O. Box 11365/738, Tehran, Iran; P.O. Box 37155/146, Qom, Iran;

or P.O. Box 36802, Damascus, Syria. Anti-Iraqi regime, supported by the Shi'ite-oriented Supreme Assembly of the Islamic Revolution of Iraq, led by Mohammed Baqir al-Hakim. Supported by the Iranian government and transmitted from Iranian soil.
"Voice of Southern Azerbaijan" ("Bura Janubi Azerbaijan Sasi"), Vosa Ltd., Postfach 108, A-1193 Vienna, Austria. Phone: (Holland) +31 (70) 319-2189. This Azeri-language station is operated by the National and Independent Front of Southern Azerbaijan, which is opposed to Iranian and Armenian influence in Azerbaijan.
"Voice of the Communist Party of Iran" ("Seda-ye Hezb-e Komunist-e Iran"), B.M. Box 2123, London WC1N 3XX, United Kingdom; or O.I.S., Box 50040, SE-104 05 Stockholm, Sweden. E-mail: wpi@wpiran.org. URL: www.wpiran.org/. Sponsored by the Communist Party of Iran (KOMALA, formerly Tudeh).
"Voice of the Crusader"—*see* "Voice of the Mojahed," below.
"Voice of the Free Sahara" ("La Voz del Sahara Libre, La Voz del Pueblo Sahel") (when operating), Sahara Libre, Frente Polisario, B.P. 10, El-Mouradia, 16000 Algiers, Algeria; Sahara Libre, Ambassade de la République Arabe Saharaui Démocratique, 1 Av. Franklin Roosevelt, 16000 Algiers, Algeria; or B.P. 10, Al-Mouradia, Algiers, Algeria. Phone (Algeria): +213 (2) 747-907. Fax, when operating (Algeria): +213 (2) 747 984. Contact: Mohamed Lamin Abdesalem; Mahafud Zein; or Sneiba Lehbib. Free stickers, booklets, cards, maps, paper flags and calendars. Two IRCs helpful. Pro-Polisario Front; supported by Algerian government and aired via the facilities of Radiodiffusion-Télévision Algerienne.
"Voice of the Iranian Revolution" ("Aira Dangi Shurashi Irana")—*see* "Voice of the Communist Party of Iran," above, for details.
"Voice of the Iraqi People"—*see* "Radio of the Iraqi Republic from Baghdad, Voice of the Iraqi People," above.
"Voice of the Islamic Revolution in Iraq"—*see* "Voice of Rebellious Iraq," above, for contact information. Affiliated with the Shi'ite-oriented Supreme Assembly of the Islamic Revolution of Iraq, led by Mohammed Baqir al-Hakim.
"Voice of the Martyrs" ("Radioemission der Hilfsaktion Martyrerkirche"), Postfach 5540, D-78434 Konstanz, Germany. Possibly linked with Internationale Radioarbeits-Gemeinschaft fur die Martyrerkirche, which previously broadcast via Radio Trans-Europe, Portugal, as Radio Stephanusbotschaft. Sometimes uses facilities of Radio Intercontinental, Armenia.
"Voice of the Mojahed" ("Seda-ye Mojahed ast")
PARIS BUREAU: Mojahedines de Peuple d'Iran, 17 rue des Gords, F-95430 Auvers-sur-Oise, France. E-mail: (National Council of Resistence of Iran umbrella organization) mardom@iran-e-azad.org. URL: (People's Mojahedin Organization of Iran parent organization) www.iran-e-azad.org/english/pmoi.html. Contact: Majid Taleghani. Station replies very irregularly and slowly. Pre-prepared verification cards and SASE helpful, with correspondence in French or Persian almost certainly preferable. Sponsored by the People's Mojahedin Organization of Iran (OMPI) and the National Liberation Army of Iran.
OTHER BUREAUS: Voice of the Mojahed, c/o Heibatollahi, Postfach 502107, 50981 Köln, Germany; M.I.S.S., B.M. Box 9720, London WC1N 3XX, United Kingdom; P.O. Box 951, London NW11 9EL, United Kingdom; or P.O. Box 3133, Baghdad, Iraq. Contact: B. Moradi, Public Relations.
"Voice of the Tigray Revolution", P.O. Box 450, Mekelle, Tigray, Ethiopia. Contact: Fre Tesfamichael, Director. $1 helpful.
"Voice of the Worker"—same contact details as "Voice of the Communist Party of Iran" (*see* above).
"Voice of Tibet" Welhavensgate 1, N-0166 Oslo, Norway. Phone: +47 2211-4980. Fax: +47 2211 4988. E-mail: vot@sn.no. URL: www.twics.com/-tsgjp/tibrad.html. Contact: Svein

Wilhelmsen, Project Manager; Oystein Alme, Coordinator; or Kalsang Phuljung. Joint venture of the Norwegian Human Rights House, Norwegian Tibet Committee and World-View International. Programs, which are produced in Oslo, Norway, and elsewhere, focuses on Tibetan culture, education, human rights and news from Tibet. Anti-Chinese control of Tibet. Those seeking a verification for this program should enclose a prepared card or letter. Return postage helpful. Transmits via facilities of the Voice of Russia.

"Voz de la Ortodoxia," P.O. Box 35-1811, José Martí Station, Miami FL 33152 USA. Contact: Mario Jiménez. Program of the Partido Ortodoxo Cubano. Via WRMI, USA.

"WINGS," P.O. Box 33220, Austin TX 78764 USA. Phone/fax: +1 (512) 416-9000. E-mail: wings@igc.apc.org. URL: www.wings.org. Contact: Frieda Werden, Producer. News program of the Women's International News Gathering Service, covering such issues as women's rights, women activists and movements for sociopolitical change. Via RFPI, Costa Rica.

"World of Prophecy," 1708 Patterson Road, Austin TX 78733 USA. Contact: Texe Marrs. Conservative Christian program opposing various forms of government regulation and control, such as of the environment. Via WWCR and WHRI, USA.

DJIBOUTI World Time +3
Radiodiffusion-Télévision de Djibouti (if reactivated), B.P. 97, Djibouti. Return postage helpful. Correspondence in French preferred. This station is currently off the air due to transmitter failure. It is unlikely to come back on the air in the forseeable future, unless the French resuscitate the failed transmitter as part of the proposed, but as yet not approved, effort to install a Radio France Internationale relay in Djibouti.

DOMINICAN REPUBLIC World Time –4
Emisora Onda Musical (when active), Palo Hincado 204 Altos, Apartado Postal 860, Santo Domingo, Dominican Republic. Contact: Mario Báez Asunción, Director. Replies occasionally to correspondence in Spanish. $1 helpful.

La N-103/Radio Norte (when active), Apartado Postal 320, Santiago, Dominican Republic. Contact: José Darío Pérez Díaz, Director; or Héctor Castillo, Gerente.

Radio Amanecer Internacional, Apartado Postal 1500, Santo Domingo, Dominican Republic. Phone: +1 (809) 688-8067, +1 (809) 688-5609 or +1 (809) 688-5600. Fax: +1 (809) 227 1869. E-mail: amanecer@tricom.net. URL: http://jupiter.tricom.net/amanecer/. Contact: (general) Señora Ramona C. de Subervi, (technical) Ing. Sócrates Domínguez. $1 or return postage required. Replies slowly to correspondence in Spanish.

Radio Barahona (when active), Apartado 201, Barahona, Dominican Republic; or Gustavo Mejía Ricart No. 293, Apto. 2-B, Ens. Quisqueya, Santo Domingo, Dominican Republic. Contact: (general) Rodolfo Z. Lama Jaar, Administrador; (technical) Ing. Roberto Lama Sajour, Administrador General. Free stickers. Letters should be sent via registered mail. $1 or return postage helpful. Replies to correspondence in Spanish.

Radio Cima (when active), Apartado 804, Santo Domingo, Dominican Republic. Fax: +1 (809) 541 1088. Contact: Roberto Vargas, Director. Free pennants, postcards, coins and taped music. Roberto likes collecting stamps and coins.

Radio Cristal Internacional, Apartado Postal 894, Santo Domingo, Dominican Republic. Phone: +1 (809) 565-1460 or +1 (809) 566-5411. Fax: +1 (809) 567 9107. Contact: (general) Fernando Hermón Gross, Director de Programas; or Margarita Reyes; (administration) Darío Badía, Director General; or Héctor Badía, Director de Administración. Return postage appreciated.

Radio Quisqueya (when active), Apartado Postal 363, Puerto Plata, Dominican Republic; or Apartado Postal 135-2, Santo Domingo, Dominican Republic. Contact: Lic. Gregory Castellanos Ruano, Director. Replies occasionally to correspondence in Spanish and English.

Radio Santiago (when active), Apartado 282, Santiago, Dominican Republic.
Contact: Luis Felipe Moscos Finke, Gerente; Luis Felipe Moscos Cordero, Jefe Ingeniero; or Carlos Benoit, Announcer & Program Manager.

ECUADOR World Time –5 (–4 sometimes, in times of drought); –6 Galapagos
NOTE: According to HCJB's "DX Party Line," during periods of drought, such as caused by "El Niño," electricity rationing causes periods in which transmitters cannot operate because of inadequate hydroelectric power, as well as spikes which occasionally damage transmitters. Accordingly, many Ecuadorian stations tend to be irregular, or even entirely off the air, during drought conditions.
NOTE: According to veteran Dxer Harald Kuhl in Hard-Core-DX of Kotanet Communications Ltd., IRCs are exchangeable only in the cities of Quito and Guayaquil. Too, overseas airmail postage is very expensive now in Ecuador, so when in doubt enclosing $2 for return postage is appropriate.

Ecos del Oriente (when active), Sucre y 12 de Febrero, Lago Agrio, Sucumbíos, Ecuador. Phone: +593 (6) 830-141. Contact: Elsa Irene Velástegui, Secretaria. Sometimes includes free 20 sucre note (Ecuadorian currency) with reply. $2 or return postage required. Replies, often slowly, to correspondence in Spanish.

Emisora La Voz de Chinchipe—see Radio La Voz de Chinchipe.

Emisoras Gran Colombia (if reactivated), Casilla 17-01-2246, Quito, Ecuador (new physical address: Vasco de Contreras 689 y Pasaje "A", Quito, Ecuador). Phone: +593 (2) 443-147. Phone/fax: +593 (2) 442-951. Contact: Nancy Cevallos Castro, Gerente General. Return postage required. Replies to correspondence in Spanish. Their shortwave transmitter is out of order. While they would like to repair or replace it, for the time being they don't have the funds to do so, as they have just spent what extra money they had on new premises.

Emisoras Jesús del Gran Poder, Casilla 17-01-133, Quito, Ecuador. Phone: +593 (2) 513-077. Contact: Mariela Villarreal; Padre Angel Falconí, Gerente; or Hno. Segundo Cuenca OFM.

Emisoras Luz y Vida, Casilla 11-01-222, Loja, Ecuador. Phone: +593 (7) 570-426. Contact: Hermana (Sister) Ana Maza Reyes, Directora; or Lic. Guida Carrión H., Directora de Programas. Return postage required. Replies irregularly to correspondence in Spanish.

Escuelas Radiofónicas Populares del Ecuador (when active), Casilla 06-01-693, Riobamba, Ecuador. Fax: +593 (3) 961 625. Contact: Juan Pérez Sarmiento, Director Ejecutivo; or María Ercilia López, Secretaria. Free pennants and key rings. "Chimborazo" cassette of Ecuadorian music for 10,000 sucres plus postage; T-shirts for 12,000 sucres plus postage; and caps with station logo for 8,000 sucres plus postage. Return postage helpful. Replies to correspondence in Spanish.

Estéreo Carrizal (when active), Avenida Estudiantil, Quinta Velásquez, Calceta, Ecuador. Phone: +593 (5) 685-5470. Contact: Ovidio Velásquez Alcundia, Gerente General. Free book of Spanish-language poetry by owner. Replies to correspondence in Spanish.

HCJB World Radio, The Voice of the Andes
STATION: Casilla 17-17-691, Quito, Ecuador. Phone: +593 (2) 266-808 (X-4441 for the English Dept.). Fax: +593 (2) 447 263. E-mail: (English Dept.) english@hcjb.org.ec; (Spanish Dept.) spanish@hcjb.org.ec; (Japanese Dept.) japanese@hcjb.org.ec; (Frequency Management) irops@hcjb.org.ec or dlewis@hcjb.org.ec. URLs: www.hcjb.org/; www.hcjb.org.ec. Contact: (general) English [or other language] Department; "Saludos Amigos"—letterbox program; (administration) Glen Volkhardt, Director of Broadcasting; John Beck, Director of International Radio; or Curt Cole, Director, English Language Service; (technical) David Lewis, Frequency Man-

Indians coming to the Thursday market in Saquisilí, Ecuador, pass by the tiny offices of La Voz de Saquisilí, the town's only radio station. At present, the station is inactive because of the illness of the owner.

Don Moore

ager. Free religious brochures, calendars, stickers and pennants; free e-mail *The Andean Herald* newsletter. *Catch the Vision* book $8, postpaid. IRC or unused U.S. or Canadian stamps appreciated for airmail reply.

INTERNATIONAL HEADQUARTERS: HCJB World Radio, Inc., P.O. Box 39800, Colorado Springs CO 80949-9800 USA. Phone: +1 (719) 590-9800. Fax: +1 (719) 590 9801. E-mail: egiesbre@wrmf.org. Contact: Andrew Braio, Public Information; (administration) Richard D. Jacquin, Director, International Operations. Various items sold via U.S. address—catalog available. This address is not a mail drop, so listeners' correspondence, except those concerned with purchasing HCJB items, should be directed to the usual Quito address.

ENGINEERING CENTER: 2830 South 17th Street, Elkhart IN 46517-4008 USA. Phone: +1 (219) 294-8201. Fax: +1 (219) 294 8391. E-mail: webmaster@hcjbeng.org. URL: www.hcjbeng.org/. Contact: Dave Pasechnik, Project Manager; or Bob Moore, Engineering. This address only for those professionally concerned with the design and manufacture of transmitter and antenna equipment. Listeners' correspondence should be directed to the usual Quito address.

REGIONAL OFFICES: Although HCJB has over 20 regional offices throughout the world, the station wishes that all listener correspondence be directed to the station in Quito, as the regional offices do not serve as mail drops for the station.

La Voz de los Caras, Casilla 608, Calle Montúfar 1012, Bahía de Caráquez, Manabí, Ecuador. Fax: +593 (4) 690 305.

Contact: Ing. Marcelo A. Nevárez Faggioni, Director-General. Free 50th anniversary pennants, while they last. $2 or return postage required. Replies occasionally and slowly to correspondence in English and Spanish.

La Voz de Saquisilí—Radio Libertador (when active), Casilla 669, Saquisilí, Ecuador; or Calle 24 de Mayo, Saquisilí, Cotopaxi, Ecuador. Phone: +593 (3) 721-035. Contact: Eddy Roger Velástegui Mena, Director de Relaciones Públicas; Srta. Carmen Mena Corrales; or Arturo Mena Herrera, Gerente-Proprietario. $2 or mint Ecuadorian stamps for return postage; IRCs difficult to exchange. Eddy Velástegui M. is the only reliable responder at this station; but, as he is away at college most of the time, replies to correspondence tend to be slow and irregular. Spanish strongly preferred.

La Voz del Napo, Misión Josefina, Tena, Napo, Ecuador. Phone: +593 (6) 886-422. Contact: Ramiro Cabrera, Director. Free pennants and stickers. $2 or return postage required. Replies occasionally to correspondence in Spanish.

La Voz del Río Tarqui (when operating), Manuel Vega 653 y Presidente Córdova, Cuenca, Ecuador. Phone: +593 (7) 822-132. Contact: Sra. Alicia Pulla Célleri, Administración; or Sra. Rosa María Pulla. Replies irregularly to correspondence in Spanish. Has ties with station WKDM in New York.

La Voz del Upano
STATION: Vicariato Apostólico de Méndez, Misión Salesiana, 10 de Agosto s/n, Macas, Ecuador; or Casilla 602, Quito, Ecuador. Phone: +593 (7) 700-186. Contact: P. Domingo Barrueco C., Director. Free pennants and calendars. On one occasion, not necessarily to be repeated, sent tape of Ecua-

dorian folk music for $2. Otherwise, $2 required. Replies to correspondence in Spanish.

QUITO OFFICE: Procura Salesiana, Equinoccio 623 y Queseras del Medio, Quito, Ecuador. Phone: +593 (2) 551-012.

Radio Bahá'í, "La Emisora de la Familia," Casilla 10-02-1464, Otavalo, Imbabura, Ecuador. Phone: +593 (6) 920-245. Fax: +593 (6) 922 504. Contact: (general) William Rodríguez Barreiro, Coordinador; or Juan Antonio Reascos, Locutor; (technical) Ing. Tom Dopps. Free information about the Bahá'í faith, which teaches the unity of all the races, nations and religions, and that the Earth is one country and mankind its citizens. Free pennants. Return postage appreciated. Replies regularly to correspondence in English or Spanish. Enclosing a family photo may help getting a reply. Station is property of the Instituto Nacional de Enseñanza de la Fe Bahá'í (National Spiritual Assembly of the Bahá'ís of Ecuador). Although there are many Bahá'í radio stations around the world, Radio Bahá'í in Ecuador is the only one on shortwave.

Radio Buen Pastor—see Radio "El Buen Pastor."

Radio Católica Nacional del Ecuador (when active), Av. América 1830 y Mercadillo (Apartado 540A), Quito, Ecuador. Phone: +593 (2) 545-770. Contact: John Sigüenza, Director; or Sra. Yolanda de Suquitana, Secretaria; (technical) Sra. Gloria Cardozo, Technical Director. Free stickers. Return postage required. Replies to correspondence in Spanish.

Radio Católica Santo Domingo (if reactivated), Apartado Postal 17-24-0006, Santo Domingo de los Colorados, Pichincha, Ecuador. Contact: Nancy Moncada, Secretaria; Pedro Figueroa, Director de Programas; or Padre Gualberto Pérez Paredas, Director. Free pennants. Return postage or $2 helpful. Replies to correspondence in Spanish.

Radio Centro, Casilla 18-01-574, Ambato, Ecuador. Phone: +593 (3) 822-240 or +593 (3) 841-126. Fax: +593 (3) 829 824. Contact: Luis Alberto Gamboa Tello, Director Gerente; or Lic. María Elena de López. Free stickers. Return postage appreciated. Replies to correspondence in Spanish.

Radio Centinela del Sur (C.D.S. Internacional), Casilla 11-01-106, Loja, Ecuador. Fax: +593 (7) 562 270. Contact: (general) Marcos G. Coronel V., Director de Programas; or José A. Coronel V., Director del programa "Ovación"; (technical) José A. Coronel I., Director Propietario. Return postage required. Replies occasionally to correspondence in Spanish.

Radio Cumandá (if reactivated)

STATION: Principal y Espejo, Coca, Napo, Ecuador. Phone: +593 (6) 315-089. Contact: Angel Bonilla, Director.

OWNER: Luís Cordero 226, Machachi, Pichincha, Ecuador. Contact: José J. Quinga, Propietario.

Radiodifusora Cultural Católica La Voz del Upano—see La Voz del Upano, above.

Radiodifusora Cultural, La Voz del Napo—see La Voz del Napo, above.

Radio "El Buen Pastor," Asociación Cristiana de Indígenas Saraguros (ACIS), Reino de Quito y Azuay, Correo Central, Saraguro, Loja, Ecuador. Phone: +593 (2) 00-146. Contact: (general) Dean Pablo Davis, Sub-director; Segundo Poma, Director; Mark Vogan, OMS Missionary; Mike Schrode, OMS Ecuador Field Director; or Zoila Vacacela, Secretaria; (technical) Miguel Kelly. $2 or return postage in the form of mint Ecuadorian stamps required, as IRCs are difficult to exchange in Ecuador. Station is keen to receive reception reports; may respond to English, but correspondence in Spanish preferred. $10 required for QSL card and pennant.

Radio Federación Shuar (Shuara Tuntuiri), Casilla 17-01-1422, Quito, Ecuador. Phone/fax: +593 (2) 504-264. Contact: Manuel Jesús Vinza Chacucuy, Director; Yurank Tsapak Rubén Gerardo, Director; or Prof. Albino M. Utitiaj P., Director de Medios. Return postage or $2 required. Replies irregularly to correspondence in Spanish.

Radio Interoceánica (if reactivated), Santa Rosa de Quijos, Cantón El Chaco, Provincia de Napo, Ecuador. Contact: Byron Medina, Gerente; or Ing. Olaf Hegmuir. $2 or return postage required, and donations appreciated (station owned

by Swedish Covenant Church). Replies slowly to correspondence in Spanish or Swedish. Station's shortwave transmitter needs repair, but funds are not forthcoming, so it's anybody's guess if it will ever return to the air.

Radio Jesús del Gran Poder—see Emisoras Jesús del Gran Poder, above.

Radio La Voz del Río Tarqui—see La Voz del Río Tarqui.

Radio Luciérnaga del Cóndor, Yansatza, Zamora-Chinchipe, Ecuador.

Radio Luz y Vida—see Emisoras Luz y Vida, above.

Radio Municipal (if activated on world band), Alcaldía Municipal de Quito, García Moreno 887 y Espejo, Quito, Ecuador. Contact: Miguel Arízaga Q., Director. Currently not on shortwave, but hopes to activate a 2 kW shortwave transmitter—its old mediumwave AM transmitter modified for world band—on 4750 kHz once the legalities are completed. If this station ever materializes, which is looking increasingly doubtful, it is expected to welcome correspondence from abroad, especially in Spanish.

Radio Nacional Espejo, Casilla 17-01-352, Quito, Ecuador. Phone: +593 (2) 21-366. Contact: Marco Caceido, Gerente; or Mercedes B. de Caceido, Secretaria. Replies irregularly to correspondence in English and Spanish.

Radio Nacional Progreso, Casilla V, Loja, Ecuador. Contact: José A. Guamán Guajala, Director del programa "Círculo Dominical." Replies irregularly to correspondence in Spanish, particularly for feedback on "Círculo Dominical" program aired Sundays from 1100 to 1300. Return postage required.

Radio Oriental, Casilla 260, Tena, Napo, Ecuador. Phone: +593 (6) 886-033 or +593 (6) 886-388. Contact: Luis Enrique Espín Espinosa, Gerente General. $2 or return postage helpful. Reception reports welcome.

Radio Popular de Cuenca (when active), Av. Loja 2408, Cuenca, Ecuador. Phone: +593 (7) 810-131. Contact: Sra. Manena Escondón Vda. de Villavicencio, Directora y Propietaria. Return postage or $2 required. Replies rarely to correspondence in Spanish.

Radio Quito, Casilla 17-21-1971, Quito, Ecuador. Phone/fax: +593 (2) 508-301. Contact: Xavier Almeida, Gerente General; or José Almeida, Subgerente. Free stickers. Return postage required. Replies slowly, but regularly.

Sistema de Emisoras Progreso—see Radio Nacional Progreso, above.

EGYPT World Time +2 (+3 midyear)

WARNING: MAIL THEFT. Feedback from PASSPORT readership indicates that money is sometimes stolen from envelopes sent to Radio Cairo.

📧**Egyptian Radio**, P.O. Box 11511, 1186 Cairo, Egypt. URL: (RealAudio) www.sis.gov.eg/vidaudio/html/audiofm.htm. For additional details, see Radio Cairo, below.

Radio Cairo

NONTECHNICAL: P.O. Box 566, Cairo, Egypt. Contact: Mrs. Sahar Kalil, Director of English Service to North America & Producer, "Questions and Answers"; or Mrs. Magda Hamman, Secretary. Free stickers, postcards, stamps, maps, papyrus souvenirs, calendars and *External Services of Radio Cairo* book. Free booklet and individually tutored Arabic-language lessons with loaned textbooks from Kamila Abdullah, Director General, Arabic by Radio, Radio Cairo, P.O. Box 325, Cairo, Egypt. Arabic-language religious, cultural and language-learning audio and video tapes from the Egyptian Radio and Television Union sold via Sono Cairo Audio-Video, P.O. Box 2017, Cairo, Egypt; when ordering video tapes, inquire to ensure they function on the television standard (NTSC, PAL or SECAM) in your country. Once replied regularly, if slowly, but recently replies have been increasingly scarce. Comments welcomed about audio quality—see *TECHNICAL*, below. Avoid enclosing money (see *WARNING*, above). A new 500 kW shortwave transmitter is to be brought into service in the near future to improve reception.

NONTECHNICAL, HOLY KORAN RADIO: P.O. Box 1186, Cairo, Egypt. Contact: Abd al-Samad al Disuqi, Director. Operates only on 9755 kHz.

TECHNICAL: Broadcast Engineering Department, 24th Floor—TV Building (Maspiro), Egyptian Radio and Television Union, P.O. Box 1186/11151, Cairo, Egypt. Phone: +20 (2) 575-7155. Phone/fax: (propagation and monitoring office, set to automatically receive faxes outside normal working hours; otherwise, be prepared to request a switchover from voice to fax) +20 (2) 578-9491. Fax: +20 (2) 772 432; (ERTU projects) +20 (2) 766 909. E-mail: to be inaugurated shortly. Contact: Dr. Eng. Abdoh Fayoumi, Head of Propagation and Monitoring; or Nivene W. Laurence, Engineer. Comments and suggestions on audio quality and level especially welcomed.

ENGLAND—*see* UNITED KINGDOM.

EQUATORIAL GUINEA World Time +1
Radio Africa
TRANSMISSION OFFICE: Apartado 851, Malabo, Isla Bioko, Equatorial Guinea.
U.S. OFFICE FOR CORRESPONDENCE AND VERIFICATIONS: Pan American Broadcasting, 20410 Town Center Lane #200, Cupertino CA 95014 USA. Phone: +1 (408) 996-2033. Fax: +1 (408) 252 6855. E-mail: pabcomain@aol.com. Contact: (listener correspondence) Terry Kraemer; (general) Carmen Jung, Office & Sales Administrator; or James Manero. $1 in cash or unused U.S. stamps, or 2 IRCs, required for reply.
Radio East Africa—same details as "Radio Africa," above.
Radio Nacional de Guinea Ecuatorial—Bata (Radio Bata), Apartado 749, Bata, Río Muni, Equatorial Guinea. Phone: +240 08-382. Contact: José Mba Obama, Director. If no response try sending your letter c/o Spanish Embassy, Bata, enclosing $1 for return postage. Spanish preferred.
Radio Nacional de Guinea Ecuatorial—Malabo (Radio Malabo), Apartado 195, Malabo, Isla Bioko, Equatorial Guinea. Phone: +240 92-260. Fax: +240 92 097. Contact: (general) Román Manuel Mané-Abaga, Jefe de Programación; Ciprano Somon Suakin; or Manuel Chema Lobede; (technical) Hermenegildo Moliko Chele, Jefe Servicios Técnicos de Radio y Televisión. $1 or return postage required. Replies irregularly to correspondence in Spanish.

ERITREA World Time +3
Voice of the Broad Masses of Eritrea (Dimisi Hafash), EPLF National Guidance, Information Department, Radio Branch, P.O. Box 872, Asmara, Eritrea; Ministry of Information and Culture, Technical Branch, P.O. Box 243, Asmara, Eritrea; EPLF National Guidance, Information Department, Radio Branch, P.O. Box 2571, Addis Ababa, Ethiopia; EPLF National Guidance, Information Department, Radio Branch, Sahel Eritrea, P.O. Box 891, Port Sudan, Sudan. Phone: +291 (1) 119-100. Fax: +291 (1) 127 115. Contact: (Eritrea) Ghebreab Ghebremedhin; (Ethiopia and Sudan) Mehreteab Tesfa Giorgis. Return postage or $1 helpful. Free information on history of station, Ethiopian People's Liberation Front and Eritrea.

ESTONIA World Time +2 (+3 midyear)
Estonian Radio (Eesti Raadio)—same details as "Radio Estonia," below, except replace "Radio Estonia, External Service, The Estonian Broadcasting Company" with "Eesti Raadio." E-mail: webmaster@er.ee. URLs: (general) www.er.ee/er.html; (RealAudio) www.online.ee/raadio.htm.
Radio Estonia, External Service, The Estonian Broadcasting Company, 21 Gonsiori Street, EE-0100 Tallinn, Estonia. Phone: (general) +372 (2) 434-110 or +372 (2) 434 115; (English Service) +372 (2) 434-252. Fax: +372 (2) 434 457. E-mail: (specific individuals) format is lastname@er.ee, so the address for Tiina Sillam, say, would be sillam@er.ee; (general) webmaster@er.ee. URL: http://er.ee./tallinn/tallinn.html. Contact: (general) Silja Orusalu, Editor, I.C.A. Department; Harry Tiido; Mrs. Tiina Sillam, Head of English Service; Mrs. Kai Siidiratsep, Head of Service; Enno Turmen,

Head of Swedish Service; Juri Vilosius, Head of Finnish Service; Mrs. Mari Maasik, Finnish Service; or Elena Rogova; (administration) Kusta Reinsoo, Deputy Head of External Service. Free pennants. $1 helpful. Replies occasionally.

ETHIOPIA World Time +3
"Radio Amahoro"—*see* Disestablishmentarian listing earlier in this section.
Radio Ethiopia: (external service) P.O. Box 654; (domestic service) P.O. Box 1020—both in Addis Ababa, Ethiopia. Phone: (main office) +251 (1) 116-427; (engineering) +251 (1) 200-948. Fax: +251 (1) 552 263. Contact: (external service, general) Kahsai Tewoldemedhin, Program Director; Ms. Woinshet Woldeyes, Secretary, Audience Relations; Ms. Ellene Mocria, Head of Audience Relations; or Yohaness Ruphael, Producer, "Contact"; (administration) Kasa Miliko, Head of Station; (technical) Terefe Ghebre Medhin or Zegeye Solomon. Free stickers. Very poor replier.
Radio Fana (Radio Torch), P.O. Box 30702, Addis Ababa, Ethiopia. Contact: Mulugeta Gessese, General Manager; Mesfin Alemayehu, Head, External Relations; or Girma Lema, Head, Planning and Research Department. Station is autonomous and receives its income from non-governmental educational sponsorship. Seeks help with obtaining vehicles, recording equipment and training materials.
"Voice of Peace"—*see* Disestablishmentarian listing earlier in this section.

FINLAND World Time +2 (+3 midyear)
YLE Radio Finland
MAIN OFFICE: Box 78, FIN-00024 Helsinki, Finland. Phone: (general, 24-hour English speaking switchboard for both Radio Finland and Yleisradio Oy) +358 (9) 14801; (international information) +358 (9) 1480-3729; (administration) +358 (9) 1480-4320 or +358 (9) 1480-4316; (Technical Customer Service) +358 (9) 1480-3213. Fax: (general) +358 (9) 148 1169; (international information) +358 (9) 1480 3391; (Technical Affairs) +358 (9) 1480 3588. E-mail: rfinland@yle.fi; (Yleisradio Oy parent organization) fbc@yle.fi. URLs: (includes RealAudio in Finnish, Swedish, English, German, French, Russian and Classic Latin) www.yle.fi/fbc/radiofin.html; or (stored news audio in Finnish, Swedish, English, German, French and Russian) www.wrn.org/audio.html. Contact—Radio Finland: (English) Eddy Hawkins; (Finnish & Swedish) Pertti Seppä; (German & French) Dr. Stefan Tschirpke; (Russian) Timo Uotila and Mrs. Eija Laitinen; (administration) Juhani Niinistö, Head of External Broadcasting. Contact—Yleisradio Oy parent organization: (general) Marja Salusjärvi, Head of International PR; (administration) Arne Wessberg, Managing Director; or Tapio Siikala, Director for Domestic & International Radio. Sometimes provides free stickers and small souvenirs, as well as tourist and other magazines. Replies to correspondence, but does not verify reception reports (*see* Transmission Facility, below).
NUNTII LATINI (Program in Latin): P.O. Box 99, FIN-00024 Helsinki, Finland. Fax: +358 (9) 1480 3391. E-mail: nuntii.latini@yle.fi. URL: www.yle.fi/fbc/nuntii.html. Six years of Nuntii Latini now available in books I to III at US$30 each from: Bookstore Tiedekirja, Kirkkokatu 14, FIN-00170 Helsinki, Finland; fax: +358 (9) 635 017. VISA/MC/EURO.
FREQUENCY PLANNING: Bureau of Network Planning, Pl 20, FIN-00024 Helsinki, Finland. Phone: +358 (9) 1480-2787. Fax: +358 (9) 148 5260. E-mail: esko.huuhka@yle.yle.mailnet.fi. Contact: Esko Huuhka, Head of Network Planning.
MEASURING STATION: Yleisradio, FIN-05400 Jokela, Finland. Phone: +358 (9) 282-005/6. Fax: +358 (9) 417 2410. Contact: Kari Hautala, Monitoring Engineer.
TRANSMISSION FACILITY: Yleisradio Oy, Shortwave Centre, Preiviiki, Makholmantie 79, FIN-28660 Pori, Finland. Contact: Ms. Marjatta Jokinen. Issues full-data verification cards for good reception reports, and provides free illustrated booklets about the transmitting station.

NORTH AMERICAN OFFICE—LISTENER & MEDIA LIAISON: P.O. Box 462, Windsor CT 06095 USA. Phone: +1 (860) 688-5540 or +1 (860) 688-5098. Phone/fax: (24-hour toll-free within U.S. and Canada for recorded schedule and voice mail) 1-800-221-9539. Fax: +1 (860) 688 0113. E-mail: yleus@aol.com. Contact: John Berky, YLE Finland Transcriptions. Free *YLE North America* newsletter.

FRANCE World Time +1
Radio France Internationale (RFI)
MAIN OFFICE: B.P. 9516, F-75016 Paris Cedex 16, France. Phone: (general) +33 (1) 42-30-22-22; (International Affairs and Program Placement) +33 (1) 44-30-89-31 or +33 (1) 44-30-89-49; (Service de la communication) +33 (1) 42-30-29-51; (Audience Relations) +33 (1) 44-30-89-69/70/71; (Media Relations) +33 (1) 42-30-29-85; (Développement et de la communication) +33 (1) 44-30-89-21; (*Fréquence* **Monde**) +33 (1) 42-30-10-86; (English Department) +33 (1) 42-30-30-62; (Spanish Department) +33 (1) 42-30-30-48. Fax: (general) +33 (1) 42 30 30 71; (International Affairs and Program Placement) +33 (1) 44 30 89 20; (Audience Relations) +33 (1) 44 30 89 99; (other nontechnical) +33 (1) 42 30 44 81; (English Department) +33 (1) 42 30 26 74; (Spanish Department) +33 (1) 42 30 46 69. URLs: (general) www.rfi.fr/; (RealAudio and StreamWorks in French, English, Spanish & Portuguese) www.francelink.com/radio_stations/rfi/. Contact: Simson Najovits, Chief, English Department; J.P. Charbonnier, Producer, "Lettres des Auditeurs"; Joël Amar, International Affairs/Program Placement Department; Arnaud Littardi, Directeur du développement et de la communication; Nicolas Levkov, Rédactions en Langues Etrangères; Daniel Franco, Rédaction en français; Mme. Anne Toulouse, Rédacteur en chef du Service Mondiale en français; Christine Berbudeau, Rédacteur en chef, *Fréquence* **Monde**; or Marc Verney, Attaché de Presse; (administration) Jean-Paul Cluzel, Président-Directeur Général; (technical) M. Raymond Pincon, Producer, "Le Courrier Technique." Free *Fréquence* **Monde** bi-monthly magazine in French upon request. Free souvenir keychains, pins, lighters, pencils, T-shirts and stickers have been received by some—especially when visiting the headquarters at 116 avenue du Président Kennedy, in the chichi 16th Arrondissement. Can provide supplementary materials for "Dites-moi tout" French-language course; write to the attention of Mme. Chantal de Grandpre, "Dites-moi tout." "Le Club des Auditeurs" French-language listener's club ("Club 9516" for English-language listeners); applicants must provide name, address and two passport-type photos, whereupon they will receive a membership card and the club bulletin. RFI hopes to install a shortwave broadcasting center in Djibouti, which if approved could be operational in the not-too-distant future. Plans to stop shortwave broadcasting to Europe and North America. RFI exists primarily to defend and promote Francophone culture, but also provides meaningful information and cultural perspectives in non-French languages. The French government under both socialist and conservative leadership has given RFI consistent and substantial support, and with that support RFI has grown and continues to grow into a leading position in International broadcasting.
TRANSMISSION OFFICE, TECHNICAL: Direction de l'Equipement et de la Production, TDF—Groupe France Telecom, Ondes décamétriques, B.P. 518, F-92542 Montrouge Cedex, France. Phone: +33 (1) 46-57-77-83 or +33 (1) 49-65-11-61. Fax: +33 (1) 49 65 19 11 or +33 (1) 49 65 21 37. E-mail: (Bochent) 101317.2431@compuserve.com. URL: www.francetelecom.com/. Contact: Daniel Bochent, Chef du service ondes décamétriques; Alain Meunier, service ondes décamétriques; Mme. Annick Tusseau; Mme. Christiane Bouvet; or M. Michel Azibert, chef internationale. This office only for informing about transmitter-related problems (interference, modulation quality, etc.), especially by fax. Verifications not given out at this office; requests for verification should be sent to the main office, above.

UNITED STATES PROMOTIONAL, SCHOOL LIAISON, PROGRAM PLACEMENT AND CULTURAL EXCHANGE OFFICES: *NEW ORLEANS:* Services Culturels, Suite 2105, Ambassade de France, 300 Poydras Street, New Orleans LA 70130 USA. Phone: +1 (504) 523-5394. Phone/fax: +1 (504) 529-7502. E-mail: asteg@on101.com. Contact: Adam-Anthony Steg, Attaché Audiovisuel. This office promotes RFI, especially to language teachers and others in the educational community within the southern United States, and arranges for bi-national cultural exchanges. It also sets up RFI feeds to local radio stations within the southern United States.
NEW YORK: Audiovisual Bureau, Radio France Internationale, 972 Fifth Avenue, New York NY 10021 USA. Phone: +1 (212) 439-1452. Fax: +1 (212) 439 1455. Contact: Gérard Blondel or Julien Vin. This office promotes RFI, especially to language teachers and others within the educational community outside the southern United States, and arranges for bi-national cultural exchanges. It also sets up RFI feeds to local radio stations within much of the United States.
NEW YORK NEWS BUREAU: 1290 Avenue of the Americas, New York NY 10019 USA. Phone: +1 (212) 581-1771. Fax: +1 (212) 541 4309. Contact: Ms. Auberi Edler, Reporter; or Bruno Albin, Reporter.
WASHINGTON NEWS BUREAU: 529 14th Street NW, Suite 1126, Washington DC 20045 USA. Phone: +1 (202) 879-6706. Contact: Pierre J. Cayrol.
SAN FRANCISCO OFFICE, SCHEDULES: 2654 17th Avenue, San Francisco CA 94116 USA. Phone: +1 (415) 564-9968. Contact: George Poppin. This address, a volunteer office, only provides RFI schedules to listeners. All other correspondence should be sent directly to the main office in Paris.
Voice of Orthodoxy—see Belarus.

FRENCH GUIANA World Time –3
Radio France Internationale/Swiss Radio International—Guyane Relay Station, TDF, Montsinéry, French Guiana. Contact: (technical) Chef des Services Techniques, RFI Guyane. All correspondence concerning non-technical matters should be sent directly to the main addresses (see) for Radio France International in France and Swiss Radio International in Berne. Can consider replies only to technical correspondence in French.
RFO Guyane, Cayenne, French Guiana. Fax: +594 30 26 49. Free stickers. Replies occasionally and sometimes slowly; correspondence in French preferred, but English often okay.

FRENCH POLYNESIA World Time –10 Tahiti
RFO Polynésie Française (while still operating), B.P. 125, Papeete, Tahiti, 98 713 French Polynesia. Phone: +689 430-551. Fax: +689 413 155 or +689 425 041. E-mail: rfopolyfr@mail.pf. URL: www.tahiti-explorer.com/rfo.html. Contact: (general) Claude Ruben, Directeur; Patrick Durand Gaillard, Rédacteur en Chef; Jean-Raymond Bodin, Directeur des Programmes; (technical) Léon Siquin, Services Techniques. Free stickers, tourist brochures and broadcast-coverage map. Three IRCs, return postage, 5 francs or $1 helpful, but not mandatory. M. Siquin and his teenage sons Xavier and Philippe, all friendly and fluent in English, collect pins from radio/TV stations, memorabilia from the Chicago Bulls basketball team and other souvenirs of American pop culture; these make more appropriate enclosures than the usual postage-reimbursement items. This station, whose indigenous island programming of yore has become increasingly European and prosaic, once hoped to obtain new studios and transmitters. Alas, the effort came to naught. Now, only one of their three ancient world band transmitters continues to function regularly and, as a result, the station will abandon world band entirely sometime in the future when the final transmitter fails.

GABON World Time +1
Afrique Numéro Un, B.P. 1, Libreville, Gabon. Fax: +241 742 133. Contact: (general) Gaston Didace Singangoye; or A.

Letamba, Le Directeur des Programmes; (technical) Mme. Marguerite Bayimbi, Le Directeur [sic] Technique. Free calendars and bumper stickers. $1, 2 IRCs or return postage helpful. Replies very slowly.

RTV Gabonaise, B.P. 10150, Libreville, Gabon. Contact: André Ranaud-Renombo, Le Directeur Technique, Adjoint Radio. Free stickers. $1 required. Replies occasionally, but slowly, to correspondence in French.

GEORGIA World Time +4

Georgian Radio, TV-Radio Tbilisi, ul. M. Kostava 68, Tbilisi 380071, Republic of Georgia. Phone: (domestic service) +995 (8832) 368-362 or (external service) +995 (8832) 368-885 or +995 (8832) 360-063. Fax: +995 (8832) 368 665 or +995 (8832) 955 137. Contact: (external service) Helena Apkhadze, Foreign Editor; Tamar Shengelia; Mrs. Natia Datuaschwili, Secretary; or Maya Chihradze; (domestic service) Lia Uumlaelsa, Manager; or V. Khundadze, Acting Director of Television and Radio Department. Replies erratically and slowly, in part due to financial difficulties. Return postage or $1 helpful.

High Adventure Radio (Voice of Hope)—via Georgian Radio Relay—All correspondence should be directed to the office in the United Kingdom; see KVOH—High Adventure Radio, USA.

Republic of Abkhazia Radio, Abkhaz State Radio & TV Co., Aidgylara Street 34, Sukhum 384900, Republic of Abkhazia; however, as of press time, according to the station there is a total embargo on mail to the Republic of Abkhazia. Phone: +995 (8832) 24-867 or +995 (8832) 25-321. Fax: +995 (8832) 21 144. Contact: G. Amkuab, General Director; or Yury Kutarba, Deputy General Director. A 1992 uprising in northwestern Georgia drove the majority of ethnic Georgians from the region. This area remains virtually autonomous from Georgia.

GERMANY World Time +1 (+2 midyear)

Adventist World Radio, the Voice of Hope—see USA and Italy.

📻**Bayerischer Rundfunk**, Rundfunkplatz 1, D-80300 München, Germany. Phone: +49 (89) 5900-01. Fax: +49 (89) 5900 2375. E-mail: info@br-online.de. URLs: (general) www.br-online.de/; (RealAudio) www.br-online.de/. Contact: Dr. Gualtiero Guidi; or Jutta Paue, Engineering Adviser. Free stickers and 250-page program schedule book.

BBC World Service—see UNITED KINGDOM

Canadian Forces Network Radio—see CANADA.

Deutsche Telekom AG

JÜLICH ADDRESS: Rundfunksendstelle, Merscher Höhe D-52428 Jülich, Germany. Phone: +49 (2461) 697-372 or +49 (2461) 697-372. Fax: +49 (2461) 697 372. Contact: Gunter Hirte, Technical Advisor for High Frequency Broadcasting. *KÖLN ADDRESS:* Niederlassung 2 Köln, Service Centre Rundfunk, D-50482 Köln Germany. Phone: (Kraus) +49 (221) 575-4000; (Hufschlag) +49 (221) 575-4011. Fax: +49 (221) 575 4090. Contact: Egon Kraus, Head of Broadcasting Service Centre; or Josef Hufschlag, Customer Advisor for High Frequency Broadcasting.

This organization operates the transmitters used by Deutsche Welle, and also leased to various non-German world band stations.

📻**Deutsche Welle, Radio and TV International**

MAIN OFFICE: Raderbergguertel 50, D-50968 Cologne, Germany. Phone: (general) +49 (221) 389-2001/2; (listeners' mail) +49 (221) 389-2500; (Program Distribution) +49 (221) 389-2731; (technical) +49 (221) 389-3221 or +49 (221) 389-3208; (Public Relations) +49 (221) 2041. Fax: (general) +49 (221) 389 4155, +49 (221) 389 2080 or +49 (221) 389 3000; (listeners' mail) +49 (221) 389 2510; (English Service, general) +49 (221) 389 4599; (English Service, Current Affairs) +49 (221) 389 4554; (Public Relations) +49 (221) 389 2047; (Program Distribution) +49 (221) 389 2777; (technical) +49 (221) 389 3200 or +49 (221) 389 3240. E-mail: (general)

online@dwelle.de; (specific individuals or programs) format is firstname.lastname@dw.gmd.de, so to reach, say, Harald Schuetz, it would be harald.schuetz@dw.gmd.de (if this fails, try the format firstname@dwelle.de); (Program Distribution) 100302.2003@compuserve.com; (technical) (Pischalka) 100565.1010@compuserve.com; (Scholz) 100536.2173@compuserve.com. URLs: (general) www.dwelle.de/; (German program, including RealAudio) www.dwelle.de/dpradio/Welcome.html; (non-German languages, including RealAudio) www.dwelle.de/language.html. Contact: (general) Ursula Fleck-Jerwin, Audience Mail Department; Dr. Ralf Siepmann, Director of Public Relations; Michael Behrens, Head of English Service; or Dr. Burkhard Nowotny, Director of Media Department; Harald Schuetz; ("German by Radio" language course) Herrad Meese; (administration) Dieter Weirich, Director General; (technical—head of engineering) Peter Senger, Chief Engineer; (technical—Radio Frequency Department) Peter Pischalka; Frequency Manager; or Horst Scholz, Head of Transmission; (technical—Technical Advisory Service) Mrs. Silke Bröker. Free pennants, stickers, key chains, pens, *Deutsch—warum nicht?* language-course book, *Germany—A European Country and its People* book, and the excellent *DW-radio tune-in* magazine. Local Deutsche Welle Listeners' Clubs in selected countries. Operates via world band transmitters in Germany, Antigua, Canada, Madagascar, Portugal, Russia, Rwanda and Sri Lanka. Deutsche Welle is sheduled to move from Cologne to Bonn in the near future. *ELECTRONIC TRANSMISSION OFFICE FOR PROGRAM PREVIEWS:* Infomedia, 25 rue du Lac, L-8808 Arsdorf, Luxembourg. Phone: +352 649-270. Fax: +352 649 271. This office will electronically transmit Deutsche Welle program previews to you upon request; be sure to provide either a dedicated fax number or an e-mail address so they can reply to you.

BRUSSELS NEWS BUREAU: International Press Center, 1 Boulevard Charlemagne, B-1040 Brussels, Belgium. *U.S./CANADIAN LISTENER CONTACT OFFICE:* 2800 South Shirlington Road, Suite 901, Arlington VA 22206-3601 USA. Phone: +1 (703) 931-6644. *RUSSIAN LISTENER CONTACT OFFICE:* Nemezkaja Wolna, Abonentnyj jaschtschik 596, Glawpotschtamt, 190000 St. Petersburg, Russia. *TOKYO NEWS BUREAU:* C.P.O. Box 132, Tokyo 100-91, Japan. *WASHINGTON NEWS BUREAU:* P.O. Box 14163, Washington DC 20004 USA. Fax: +1 (202) 526 2255. Contact: Adnan Al-Katib, Correspondent.

DeutschlandRadio-Berlin, Hans-Rosenthal-Platz, D-10825 Berlin Schönberg, Germany. Phone: +49 (30) 8503-0. Fax: +49 (30) 8503 9009. E-mail: dlrb@dlf.de. URL (shared with Deutschlandfunk): www.d-radio.de/. Contact: Dr. Karl-Heinz Stamm.

Missionwerk Werner Heukelbach, D-51702 Bergneustadt 2, Germany. Contact: Manfred Paul. Transmits via the Voice of Russia. Replies to correspondence in English and German.

Radio Bremen, Betriebsdirektion, Postfach 330 320, D-28353 Bremen, Germany. Fax: +49 (421) 246 1010 or +49 (421) 246 2020. URL: www.radiobremen.de/. Contact: Jim Senberg. Free stickers and shortwave guidebook. Currently off shortwave due to cost saving measures which may, or may not, be permanent.

Radio Marabu, Box 1166, 49187 Belm, Germany. Phone: +49 (5406) 899 484. Fax: +49 (5406) 899 485. URL: www.mediaDD.de/radiomarabu/. Program heard via IRRS, Milano see Italy.

Süddeutscher Rundfunk, Neckarstrasse 230, D-70190 Stuttgart, Germany. Phone: +49 (711) 2881. Fax: +49 (711) 288 2600. E-mail: (general) pr@sdr.de; (technical) td@sdr.de. URL: www.sdr.de/radio/. Contact: Erich Fileru, Chief Engineer. Free stickers. This station will soon merge with Südwestfunk see next entry and be known as Südwestrundfunk.

Südwestfunk, Hans-Bredow-Strasse, D-76530 Baden-Baden,

D. Rosenau

Dietrich Rosenau of Berlin tunes in the world with top-flight receivers from AOR and Japan Radio.

Germany. Phone: +49 (7221) 920. Fax: +49 (7221) 922 010. E-mail: online@swf.de; (technical) technik@swf.de. URL: www.swf.de/. Contact: (technical) Prof. Dr. Hans Krankl, Chief Engineer. Sells a wide range of goods including books, videos, CDs, soft toys, T-shirts and caps, all of which are listed at www.tv-markt.de/swf/swf-home.shtml. This station is to merge with Süddeutscher Rundfunk and will then be known as Südwestrundfunk.

Südwestrundfunk—This new station will be the result of the merger between Süddeutscher Rundfunk and Südwestfunk. Based in Stuttgart, transmissions are scheduled to commence in October 1998.

Universelles Leben (Universal Life)

HEADQUARTERS: Postfach 5643, D-97006 Würzburg, Germany. Phone: +49 (931) 3903-0. Fax: (general) +49 (931) 3903 233; (engineering) +49 (931) 3903 299. E-mail: info@universelles-leben.org. URL: www.universelles-leben.org. Contact: Janet Wood, English Dept; "Living in the Spirit of God" listeners' letters program. Free stickers, publications and occasional small souvenirs. Transmits "The Word, The Cosmic Wave" (Das Wort, die kosmische Welle) via the Voice of Russia, WWCR (USA) and various other world band stations, as well as "Vida Universal" via Radio Miami Internacional and WHRI in the United States. Replies to correspondence in English, German or Spanish.

SALES OFFICE: Das WORT GmbH, Im Universelles Leben, Max-Braun-Str.2, D-97828 Marktheidenfeld/Altfeld, Germany. Phone: +49 (9391) 504-135. Fax: +49 (9391) 504 133. E-mail: info@das-wort.com. URL: www.das-wort.com/. Sells books, audio cassettes and videos related to broadcast material.

NORTH AMERICAN BUREAU: The Inner Religion, P.O. Box 3549, Woodbridge CT 06525 USA. Phone: +1 (203) 281-7771. Fax: +1 (203) 230 2703.

Voice of America/VOA-IBB Network Control Center (NCC), Senderstr. 32, D-85737 Ismaning, Germany. Phone: +49 (89) 9968-2208. Fax: +49 (89) 964 739. Contact: (administration) James Lambert, Manager; (technical) Ing. Innozenz Kastner; or Ing. Georg Pflaumbaum, Broadcast Operation Coordinator. This NCC location manages satellite interface in Germany for the IBB (*see*, USA).

GHANA   World Time exactly

WARNING—CONFIDENCE ARTISTS: Attempted correspondence with Radio Ghana may result in requests, perhaps resulting from mail theft, from skilled confidence artists for money, free electronic or other products, publications or immigration sponsorship. To help avoid this, correspondence to Radio Ghana should be sent via registered mail.

Ghana Broadcasting Corporation, Broadcasting House, P.O. Box 1633, Accra, Ghana. Phone: +233 (21) 221-161. Fax: +233 (21) 221 153 or +233 (21) 773 227. Contact: (general) Mrs. Maud Blankson-Mills, Acting Director of Corporate Affairs; (administration) B.A. Apenteng, Director of Radio; (technical) E. Heneath, Propagation Department. Mr. Markin states that he is interested in reception reports, as well as feedback on the program he produces, "Health Update," so directing your correspondence to him may be the best bet. Otherwise, replies are increasingly scarce, but whomever you send your correspondence to, you should register it, and enclose an IRC, return postage or $1.

GREECE   World Time +2 (+3 midyear)

Foni tis Helladas (Voice of Greece)

NONTECHNICAL: ERA-5, "The Voice of Greece", 432 Messogion Av., 153 42 Athens, Greece. Phone: +30 (1) 606-6308 or +30 (1) 606-6297. Fax: +30 (1) 606 6309. E-mail (program reports): fonel@hol.gr. URL: http://

Don Moore

Mayan Indians are the main target of Guatemala's many religious world band stations. This cultural weaving made by a listener celebrating the 37th anniversary of Radio Cultural, 3300 kHz, Guatemala's first evangelical radio broadcaster.

alpha.servicenet.ariadne-t.gr/Docs/Era5_12/html. Contact: Kosta Valetas, Director, Programs for Abroad. Free tourist literature.
TECHNICAL: Elliniki Radiophonia—ERA-5, General Directorate of Technical Services, 402 Messogion Av., 153 42 Athens, Greece. Phone: +30 (1) 639 7108 or +30 (1) 601-4700. Fax: +30 (1) 600 9608; or Elliniki Radiophonia Tileorasi S.A., Direction of Engineering and Development, P.O. Box 600 19, 153 10 Aghia Paraskevi Attikis, Athens, Greece. Phone: +30 (1) 601-4700 or +30 (1) 639-6762. Fax: +30 (1) 639 0652 or +30 (1) 600 9608. E-mail: skalai@leon.nrcps.ariadne-t.gr. Contact: (general) Demetri H. Vafeas, Chief Engineer; Ing. Dionysios Angelogiannis, Planning Engineer; Efstratios Kalaitzis, Technical Support; or Ing. Filotas Gianotas; (administration) Th. Kokossis, General Director; or Nicolas Yannakakis, Director. Technical reception reports may be sent via mail, fax or E-mail. Taped reports not accepted.
Radiophonikos Stathmos Makedonias—ERT-3, Angelaki 2, 546 21 Thessaloniki, Greece. Phone: +30 (31) 244-979. Fax: +30 (31) 236 370. E-mail: charter3@compulink.gr. Contact: (general) Mrs. Tatiana Tsioli, Program Director; or Lefty Kongalides, Head of International Relations; (technical) Dimitrios Keramidas, Engineer. Free booklets and other small souvenirs.
Voice of America/VOA-IBB—Kaválla Relay Station. Phone: +30 (5) 912-2855. Fax: +30 (5) 913 1310. Contact: Michael Nardi, Relay Station Manager. These numbers for urgent technical matters only. Otherwise, does not welcome direct correspondence; see USA for acceptable VOA Washington address and related information.
Voice of America/VOA-IBB—Rhodes Relay Station. Phone: +30 (241) 24-731. Fax: +30 (241) 27 522. Contact: Wesley

Robinson, Relay Station Manager. These numbers for urgent technical matters only. Otherwise, does not welcome direct correspondence; see USA for acceptable VOA Washington address and related information.

GUAM World Time +10
☞**Adventist World Radio, the Voice of Hope—KSDA**
AWR-Asia, P.O. Box 8990, Agat, Guam 96928 USA. Phone: +671 565-2000. Fax: +671 565 2983. E-mail: 70673.2552@compuserve.com; or (Benton) 74617.2361@ compuserve.com. URLs: (limited RealAudio, plus text) http:// ourworld.compuserve.com/homepages/awr_asia/; (general information) www.awr.org/awr-asia/index.html. Contact: (general) Lolita Colegado, Listener Mail Services; (technical) Elvin Vence, Chief Engineer; Gary Benton, Assistant Engineer. Free stickers, quarterly AWR Current, program schedule and religious printed matter. If enclosing return postage please use currency notes in a major world currency or return postage stamps. IRCs still accepted. Also, see AWR listings under Costa Rica, Guatemala, Italy, Kenya, Russia and USA.
Trans World Radio—KTWR
MAIN OFFICE, NONTECHNICAL: P.O. Box CC, Agana, Guam 96910 USA. Phone: +671 477-9701. Fax: +671 477 2838. E-mail: (general) wfrost@twr.hafa.net.gu; (technical) gzensen@twr.hafa.net.gu. URLs (transmission schedule): www.gospelcom.net/twr/t_guam.htm; www.guam.net/pub/ twr/; or www.gospelcom.net/twr/w_ap_guam.htm. Contact: (general) Karen Zeck, Listener Correspondence; James Elliott, Producer, "Friends in Focus" listeners' questions program; Wayne T. Frost, Program Director & Producer, "Pacific DX Report"; or Kathy Gregowski; (administration) Edward Stortro, Station Director; (technical) George Ross. Also, see USA. Free small publications.
FREQUENCY COORDINATION OFFICE: 1868 Halsey Drive, Asan, Guam 96922-1505 USA. Phone: +671 828-8637. Fax: +671 828 8636. E-mail: ktwrfreq@twr.hafa.net.gu. Contact: George Zensen, Chief Engineer.
AUSTRALIAN OFFICE: G.P.O. Box 602D, Melbourne 3001, Australia. Phone: +61 (3) 9872-4606. Fax: +61 (3) 9874 8890. Contact: John Reeder, Director.
CHINA (HONG KONG) OFFICE: Unit 1, Block A, Room 901, 9/F, Po Lung Centre, 11 Wang Chiu Road, Kowloon Bay, Kowloon, Hong Kong, China. Contact: Joyce Lok, Programme Manager.
INDIA OFFICE: P.O. Box 4310, New Delhi-110 019, India. Contact: N. Emil Jebasingh, Vishwa Vani; or S. Stanley.
"ARDXC REPORT" PROGRAM: ARDXC, Box 227, Box Hill 3128 VIC, Australia. URL: www.eagles.bbs.net.au/~andrewt/ ardxc/index/html. Return postage necessary.
SINGAPORE BUREAU, NONTECHNICAL: 273 Thomson Road, 03-03 Novena Gardens, Singapore 1130, Singapore.
TOKYO OFFICE: C.P.O. Box 1000, Tokyo Central Post Office, Tokyo 100-91, Japan. Fax: +81 (3) 3233 2650.

GUATEMALA World Time –6
Adventist World Radio, the Voice of Hope—Unión Radio, Apartado de Correo 51-C, Guatemala City, Guatemala. Phone: +502 365-2509, +502 365-9067 or +502 365-9072. Fax: +502 365 9076. E-mail: mundi@guate.net. Contact: D. Rolando García P., Gerente General. Free tourist and religious literature and Guatemalan stamps. Return postage, 3 IRCs or $1 appreciated. Correspondence in Spanish preferred. Also, see AWR listings under Costa Rica, Guam, Italy, Kenya, Russia and USA.
La Voz de Atitlán—TGDS, Santiago Atitlán, Guatemala. Contact: Juan Ajtzip Alvarado, Director; José Miguel Pop Tziná; or Esteban Ajtzip Tziná, Director Ejecutivo. Return postage required. Replies to correspondence in Spanish.
La Voz de Guatemala—TGW, 18 Calle 6-70 2do piso, Zona 1, Guatemala City, Guatemala.
La Voz de Nahualá, Nahualá, Sololá, Guatemala. Contact: (technical) Juan Fidel Lepe Juárez, Técnico Auxiliar; or F.

Manuel Esquipulas Carrillo Tzep. Return postage required. Correspondence in Spanish preferred.

Radio Buenas Nuevas, 13020 San Sebastián, Huehuetenango, Guatemala. Contact: Israel G. Rodas Mérida, Gerente. $1 or return postage helpful. Free religious and station information in Spanish. Sometimes includes a small pennant. Replies to correspondence in Spanish.

Radio Coatán, San Sebástian Coatán, Huehuetenango, Guatemala. Contact: Domingo Hernández, Director; or Virgilio José, Locutor.

Radio Chortís, Centro Social, 20004 Jocotán, Chiquimula, Guatemala. Contact: Padre Juan María Boxus, Director. $1 or return postage required. Replies irregularly to correspondence in Spanish.

Radio Cultural—TGNA, Apartado de Correo 601, Guatemala City, Guatemala. Phone: +502 (2) 427-45 or +502 (2) 443-78. Contact: Mariela Posadas, QSL Secretary; or Wayne Berger, Chief Engineer. Free religious printed matter. Return postage or $1 appreciated.

Radio K'ekchi—TGVC, 3ra Calle 7-15, Zona 1, 16015 Fray Bartolomé de las Casas, Alta Verapaz, Guatemala; (Media Consultant) David Daniell, Asesor de Comunicaciones, Apartado Postal 25, Bulevares MX, 53140 Mexico. Phone: (station) +502 950-0299; (Daniell, phone/fax) +52 (5) 572-9633. Fax: +502 950 0398. E-mail: (Daniell) DPDaniell@aol.com. Contact: (general) Gilberto Sun Xicol, Gerente; Anzelmo Cuc Chub, Director; or Mateo Botzoc, Director de Programas; (technical) Larry Baysinger, Ingeniero Jefe. Free paper pennant. $1 or return postage required. Replies to correspondence in Spanish.

Radio Mam, Acu'Mam, Cabricán, Quetzaltenango, Guatemala. Contact: Porfirio Pérez, Director. Free stickers and pennants. $1 or return postage required. Replies irregularly to correspondence in Spanish. Donations permitting (the station is religious), they would like to get a new transmitter to replace the current unit, which is failing.

Radio Maya de Barillas—TGBA, 13026 Villa de Barillas, Huehuetenango, Guatemala. Contact: José Castañeda, Pastor Evangélico y Gerente. Free pennants and pins. Station is very interested in receiving reception reports. $1 or return postage required. Replies occasionally to correspondence in Spanish and Indian languages.

Radio Tezulutlán—TGTZ, Apartado de Correo 19, 16901 Cobán, Guatemala. Contact: Sergio W. Godoy, Director; or Hno. Antonio Jacobs, Director Ejecutivo. Pennant for donation to specific bank account. $1 or return postage required. Replies to correspondence in Spanish.

GUINEA World Time exactly
Radiodiffusion-Télévision Guinéenne, B.P. 391, Conakry, Guinea. Contact: (general) Yaoussou Diaby, Journaliste Sportif; (administration) Momo Toure, Chef Services Administratifs; or Alpha Sylla, Directeur, Sofoniya I Centre de Transmission; (technical, studio) Mbaye Gagne, Chef de Studio; (technical, overall) Direction des Services Techniques. Return postage or $1 required. Replies very irregularly to correspondence in French.

GUYANA World Time –3
Voice of Guyana, Guyana Broadcasting Corporation, P.O. Box 10760, Georgetown, Guyana. Phone: +592 (2) 58734, +592 (2) 58083 or +592 (2) 62691. Fax: +592 (2) 58756, but persist as fax machine appears to be switched off much of the time. Contact: (general) Indira Anandjit, Personnel Assistant; (technical) Roy Marshall, Senior Technician; or Shiroxley Goodman, Chief Engineer. $1 or IRC helpful. Sending a spare sticker from another station helps assure a reply.

HOLLAND (THE NETHERLANDS) World Time +1 (+2 midyear)
Horizon 92.9 (when operating each northern summer), Horizon Worldwide, P.O. Box 80, NL-5595 ZH Leende, The Netherlands. E-mail: horizon.radio@club.tip.nl. Program re-

layed via IRRS Italy see. Provides local and regional news, holiday greetings, tourist information and music. Aimed at travellers and holiday makers in Europe. Aired from late June until the end of August on 3985 khz at 1930 UTC Saturdays and repeated Sundays at 0800 UTC on 7125 khz. Broadcasts are in Dutch with English announcements. Return postage appreciated.

Radio Nederland Wereldomroep (Radio Netherlands)
MAIN OFFICE: Postbus 222, 1200 JG Hilversum, The Netherlands. Phone: (general) +31 (35) 672-4211; (English Department) +31 (35) 672-4242; (Answerline) +31 (35) 672-4222; (Frequency Planning) +31 (35) 672-4425, +31 (35) 672-4825 or +31 (35) 672-4213; (Program Placement) +31 (35) 672-4258. Fax: (general) +31 (35) 672 4352, but indicate destination department on fax cover sheet; (Programme Directorate) +31 (35) 72 4252; (English Department) +31 (35) 672 4239; (Distribution & Frequency Planning Department) +31 (35) 672 4429 or +31 (35) 672 4207. E-mail: (general) letters@rnw.nl. ("Media Network") media@rnw.nl; (employee contact) firstname.lastname@rnw.nl, so to reach, say, Jonathan Marks, it would be jonathan.marks@rnw.nl. URLs: (general) www.rnw.nl/; (online publications and more) www.rnw.nl/en/pub/; (RealAudio) www.wrn.org/stations/rnw.html.
Contact: (general) Jonathan Marks, Director of Programs; Nick Meanwell, Head of English Language Service; Mike Shea, Network Manager English; Iris Walstra, English Correspondence; Diana Janssen, Producer, Media Network; Lee Martin, North American program placement; or Robert Chesal, Host, "Sounds Interesting" (include your telephone number); (administration) Lodewijk Bouwens, Director General; (technical, including for full-data verifications) Jan Willem Drexhage, Head of Distribution and Frequency Planning; or Ehard Goddijn. Full-data verification card if the report is correct and follows guidelines issued in the RNW flyer, "Writing Useful Reception Reports," available upon request. Semi-annual *On Target* newsletter also free upon request, as are stickers and booklets. RNW produces its own CDs, mainly of classical and world music. Visitors welcome, but it is helpful to call in advance.
WASHINGTON NEWS BUREAU: 1773 Lanier Place, Apt. 1, Washington DC 20009 USA. Phone: +1 (202) 265-9530. Contact: Arnoud Hekkens.
LATIN AMERICAN OFFICE: (local correspondence only) Apartado 880-1007, Ventro Colón, Costa Rica. This address solely for correspondence to RNW's Costa Rican employees, who speak only Spanish. All other correspondence should be sent directly to Holland.
NEW DELHI OFFICE: (local correspondence only) P.O. Box 5257, Chanakya Puri Post Office, New Delhi-110 021, India. All non-local correspondence should be sent directly to Holland.

American-born Robert Chesal has produced some 150 shows for Radio Netherlands.

HONDURAS World Time –6

La Voz de la Mosquitia (when operating)
STATION: Puerto Lempira, Dpto. Gracias a Dios, Honduras. Contact: Sammy Simpson, Director; or Larry Sexton. Free pennants.
U.S. OFFICE: Global Outreach, Box 1, Tupelo MS 38802 USA. Phone: +1 (601) 842-4615.

La Voz Evangélica—HRVC
MAIN OFFICE: Apartado Postal 3252, Tegucigalpa, M.D.C., Honduras. Phone: +504 34-3468/69/70. Fax: +504 33 3933. Contact: (general) Srta. Orfa Esther Durón Mendoza, Secretaria; Tereso Ramos, Director de Programación; Alan Maradiaga; or Modesto Palma, Jefe, Depto. Tráfico; (technical) Carlos Paguada, Director del Dpto. Técnico; (administration) Venancio Mejía, Gerente; or Nelson Perdomo, Director. Free calendars. Three IRCs or $1 required. Replies to correspondence in English, Spanish, Portuguese and German.
REGIONAL OFFICE, SAN PEDRO SULA: Apartado 2336, San Pedro Sula, Honduras. Phone: +504 57-5030. Contact: Hernán Miranda, Director.
REGIONAL OFFICE, LA CEIBA: Apartado 164, La Ceiba, Honduras. Phone: +504 43-2390. Contact: José Banegas, Director.

Radio Copán Internacional—HRJA (when operating)
STATION: Apartado 955, Tegucigalpa, M.D.C., Honduras.
MIAMI OFFICE: P.O. Box 526852, Miami FL 33152 USA. Phone: +1 (305) 267-1728. Fax: +1 (305) 267 9253. E-mail: 71163.1735@compuserve.com. Contact: Jeff White. Sells airtime for $1 per minute to anybody in any language to say pretty much whatever they want.

Radio HRET
STATION: Primera Iglesia Bautista, Domicilio Conocido, Puerto Lempira, Gracias a Dios 33101, Honduras. Fax: +504 980 018. Contact: Leonardo Alvarez López, Locutor y Operador; or Desiderio Williams, Locutor y Operador. Return postage necessary. Replies, sometimes slowly, to correspondence in Spanish.
NONTECHNICAL ENGLISH CORRESPONDENCE: David Daniell, Asesor de Comunicaciones, Apartado Postal 25, Bulevares, MX-53140, Mexico. Replies to correspondence in English and Spanish.
TECHNICAL ENGLISH CORRESPONDENCE: Ing. Larry Baysinger, 8000 Casualwood Ct., Louisville KY 40291 USA. Replies to correspondence in English and Spanish, but calls not accepted.

Radio HRMI, La Voz de Misiones Internacionales
STATION: Apartado Postal 20583, Comayaguela, M.D.C., Honduras. Phone: +504 339-029. Contact: Wayne Downs, Director. $1 or return postage helpful.
US OFFICE: IMF World Missions, P.O. Box 6321, San Bernardino CA 92412, USA. Phone +1 (909) 370-4515. Fax: +1 (909) 370 4862. E-mail: JKPIMF@msn.com. Contact: Dr. James K. Planck, President; or Gustavo Roa, Coordinator.

Radio Internacional, Apartado 1473, San Pedro Sula, Honduras. Phone: +504 528-181. Fax: +504 581 070. Contact: Víctor Antonio ("Tito") Handal, Gerente y Propietario; or Hugo Hernández y Claudia Susana Prieto, Locutores del "Desfile de Estrellas," aired Sunday at 0200-0500 World Time. Free stickers, stamps, postcards and one-lempira banknote. $1 helpful. Appears to reply regularly to correspondence in Spanish.

Radio Litoral (if reactivated), La Ceiba, Provincia Atlántida, Honduras. Contact: José A. Mejía, Gerente y Propietario. Free postcards. $1 or return postage necessary. Replies to correspondence in Spanish.

Radio Luz y Vida—HRPC, Apartado 303, San Pedro Sula, Honduras. Fax: +504 57 0394. Contact: C. Paul Easley, Director; Chris Fleck; or, to have your letter read over the air, "English Friendship Program." Return postage or $1 appreciated.

Sani Radio (if reactivated), Puerto Lempira, Dpto. Gracias a Dios, Honduras. Contact: Jacinto Molina G. or Mario S. Corzo. Return postage or $1 required.

HUNGARY World Time +1 (+2 midyear)

Radio Budapest
STATION OFFICES: Bródy Sándor utca 5-7, H-1800 Budapest, Hungary. Phone: (general) +36 (1) 138-7339, +36 (1) 138-8328, +36 (1) 138-7357 +36 (1) 138-8588, +36 (1) 138-7710 or +36 (1) 138-7723; (voice mail, English) +36 (1) 138-8320; (voice mail, German) +36 (1) 138-7325; (administration) +36 (1) 138-7503 or +36 (1) 138-8415; (technical) +36 (1) 138-7226 or +36 (1) 138-8923. Fax: (general) +36 (1) 138 8517; (administration) +36 (1) 138 8838; (technical) +36 (1) 138 7105. E-mail: (Radio Budapest, English) ango11@kaf.radio.hu; (Radio Budapest, German) nemetl@kaf.radio.hu; (Hungarian Information Resources) avadasz@bluemoon.sma.com; (technical) (Füszlás) Fuszfasla@muszak.radio.hu. URLs: (RealAudio in English and Hungarian) www.wrn.org/stations/hungary.html; (general) www.eunet.hu/radio; (shortwave program) www.glue.umd.edu/-gotthard/hir/entertainment/radio/; (North American Service via Hungarian Information Resources) http://mineral.umd.edu/hir/Entertainment/Radio/Shortwave. Contact: (English Language Service) Ágnes Kevi, Correspondence; Charles Taylor Coutts, Producer, "Gatepost" (listeners' letters' program) & Head of English Language Service; Louis Horváth, DX Editor; or Sándor Laczkó, Editor; (administration) Antal Réger, Director, Foreign Broadcasting; Dr. Zsuzsa Mészáros, Vice-Director, Foreign Broadcasting; János Szirányi, President, Magyar Rádió; or János Simkó, Vice President, Magyar Rádió; (technical) László Füszfás, Deputy Technical Director, Magyar Rádió; Külföldi Adások Főszerkesztösége; or Lajos Horváth, Műszaki Igazgatósá; (Hungarian Information Resources) Andrew Vadasz. Free *Budapest International* periodical, stickers, pennants, stamps and printed tourist and other material. Also, for those whose comments or program proposals are used over the air, T-shirts, baseball-style caps and ballpoint pens. *RBSWC DX News* bulletin free to all Radio Budapest Shortwave Club members. Advertisements considered. Plans to celebrate 40 years of the *DX Show* throughout 1997. Special QSL cards and verification letters will be issued. A series of Quiz programs and contests will be open to all listeners.
TRANSMISSION AUTHORITY: Ministry of Transport, Communications & Water Management, P.O. Box 87, H-1400 Budapest, Hungary. Phone/fax: +36 (1) 156-3493. Fax: +36 (1) 461 3392. E-mail: horvathf@cms.khvm.hu. Contact: Ferenc Horváth, Frequency Manager, Radio Communications Engineering Services.

ICELAND World Time exactly

Radio Alpha & Omega, Omega Television, P.O. Box 3340, IS-123 Reykjavík, Iceland. Phone: +354 567-6111. Fax: +354 568 3741. Contact: Eirikur Sigurbjoernson. This Christian station, which currently operates via leased-time transmission facilities in Jülich, Germany, sells tape recordings for $20.

Ríkisútvarpid, International Relations Department, Efstaleiti 1, IS-150 Reykjavík, Iceland. Phone: +354 515-3000. Fax: +354 515 3010. E-mail: isradio@ruv.is. URLs: www.ruv.is; (RealAudio) http://this.is/ruv. Contact: Dóra Ingvadóttir, Head of International Relations.

INDIA World Time +5:30

NOTE: The facility "New Broadcasting House" is being built to supplement the existing Broadcasting House on Parliament Street. It is to be used by the domestic and external services, alike, and is scheduled to be in full operation before 2001.

Ministry of Information & Broadcasting, Main Secretariat, A-Wing, Shastri Bhawan, New Delhi-110 001, India. Phone: (general) +91 (11) 338-4340, +91 (11) 338-4782 or +91 (11) 379-338; (Information & Broadcasting Secretary)

+91 (11) 338-2639. Fax: +91 (11) 338 3513, +91 (11) 338 7823, +91 (11) 338 4785, +91 (11) 338 7617 or +91 (11) 338 1043. Contact: (general) N.P. Nawani, Information & Broadcasting Secretary; (administration) C.M. Ibrahim, Minister for Information & Broadcasting.

Akashvani—Governing Body for All India Radio

ADMINISTRATION: Directorate General of All India Radio, Akashvani Bhawan, 1 Sansad Marg, New Delhi-110 001, India. Phone: (general) +91 (11) 371-0006; (Engineer-in-Chief) +91 (11) 371-0058; (Frequency Management) +91 (11) 371-0145 or +91 (11) 371-4062; (Director General) +91 (11) 371-0300 or +91 (11) 371-4061. Fax: +91 (11) 371 1956. E-mail: faair@giasdl01.vsnl.net.in. Contact: (general) Shashi Kant Kapoor, Director General; (technical) H.M. Joshi, Engineer-in-Chief; or A.K. Bhatnagar, Director -Frequency Assignments; (programming) +91 (11) 371 5411, (voice mail, English) +91 (11) 376-1166, (Hindi) +91 (11) 376-1144.

AUDIENCE RESEARCH: Audience Research Unit, All India Radio, Press Trust of India Building, 2nd floor, Sansad Marg, New Delhi-110 001, India. Phone: +91 (11) 371-0033. Contact: S.K. Khatri, Director.

CENTRAL MONITORING SERVICES: Central Monitoring Services, All India Radio, Ayanagar, New Delhi-100 047, India. Phone: (Director) +91 (11) 680-1763 or +91 (11) 680-2955; (Control Room) +91 (11) 680-2362. Fax: +91 (11) 680 2679, +91 (11) 680 2362 or +91 (11) 680 2955. Contact: V.K. Arora, Director.

INTERNATIONAL MONITORING STATION—MAIN OFFICE: International Monitoring Station, All India Radio, Dr. K.S. Krishnan Road, Todapur, New Delhi-110 012, India. Phone: (general) +91 (11) 581-461; (administration) +91 (11) 680-2306; (Frequency Planning) +91 (11) 573-5936 (Chhabra) or +91 (11) 573-5937 (Malviya). Contact: D.P. Chhabra or R.K. Malviya, Assistant Research Engineers—Frequency Planning.

NEWS SERVICES DIVISION: News Services Division, Broadcasting House, 1 Sansad Marg, New Delhi-110 001, India. Phone: +91 (11) 371-0084 or +91 (11) 373-1510. Contact: D.C. Bhaumik, Director General—News.

RESEARCH & DEVELOPMENT: Office of the Chief Engineer R&D, All India Radio, 14-B Ring Road, Indraprastha Estate, New Delhi-110 002, India. Phone: (general) +91 (11) 331-1711, +91 (11) 331-1762, +91 (11) 331-3532 or +91 (11) 331-3574; (Chief Engineer) +91 (11) 331 8329. Fax: +91 (11) 331 8329 or +91 (11) 331 6674. E-mail: rdair@giasdl01.vsnl.net.in. URL: www.air.kode.net. Contact: K.M. Paul, Chief Engineer.

TRANSCRIPTION & PROGRAM EXCHANGE SERVICES: Akashvani Bhawan, 1 Sansad Marg, New Delhi-110 001, India. Phone: +91 (11) 371-7927. Contact: D.P. Jatav, Director; or A.V. Bhavan, Chief Engineer.

All India Radio—Aizawl, Radio Tila, Tuikhuahtlang, Aizawl-796 001, Mizoram, India. Phone: +91 (3652) 2415. Contact: (technical) D.K. Sharma, Station Engineer.

All India Radio—Bangalore

HEADQUARTERS: see All India Radio—External Services Division.

AIR OFFICE NEAR TRANSMITTER: P.O. Box 5096, Bangalore-560 001, Karnataka, India. Phone: +91 (80) 261-243. Contact: (technical) C. Iyengar, Supervising Engineer.

All India Radio—Bhopal, Akashvani Bhawan, Shamla Hills, Bhopal-462 002, Madhya Pradesh, India. Phone: +91 (755) 540-041. Contact: (technical) C. Lal, Station Engineer.

All India Radio—Calcutta, G.P.O. Box 696, Calcutta—700 001, West Bengal, India. Phone: +91 (33) 281-705. Contact: (technical) R.N. Dam, Supervising Engineer.

All India Radio—Chennai

EXTERNAL SERVICES: see All India Radio—External Services Division.

DOMESTIC SERVICE: Kamrajar Salai, Mylapore, Chennai-600 004, Tamil Nadu, India. Phone: +91 (44) 845-975. Contact: (technical) S. Bhatia, Supervising Engineer.

All India Radio—Delhi—see All India Radio—New Delhi.

All India Radio—External Services Division

MAIN ADDRESS: Broadcasting House, 1 Sansad Marg, P.O. Box 500, New Delhi-110 001, India. Phone: (general) +91 (11) 371-5411; (Director) +91 (11) 371-0057. Contact: (general) P.P. Setia, Director of External Services; or S.C. Panda, Audience Relations Officer; (technical) S.A.S. Abidi, Assistant Director Engineering (F.A.). E-mail (Research Dept.): rdair@giasdl01.vsnl.net.in; (comments on programs) air@kode.net. URL: (includes RealAudio in English and other languages) www.allindiaradio.org. Free monthly *India Calling* magazine and stickers. Replies erratic. Except for stations listed below, correspondence to domestic stations is more likely to be responded to if it is sent via the External Services Division; request that your letter be forwarded to the appropriate domestic station.

VERIFICATION ADDRESS: Room 204, 1 Sansad Marg, P.O. Box 500, New Delhi-110 001, India. Contact: R.K. Bhatnagar, Director, Frequency Assignments.

All India Radio—Gangtok, Old MLA Hostel, Gangtok—737 101, Sikkim, India. Phone: +91 (359) 22636. Contact: (general) Y.P. Yolmo, Station Director; (technical) Deepak Kumar, Station Engineer.

All India Radio—Gorakhpur

NEPALESE EXTERNAL SERVICE: see All India Radio—External Services Division.

DOMESTIC SERVICE: Post Bag 26, Gorakhpur-273 001, Uttar Pradesh, India. Phone: +91 (551) 337-401. Contact: (technical) Dr. S.M. Pradhan, Supervising Engineer.

All India Radio—Guwahati, P.O. Box 28, Chandmari, Guwahati-781 003, Assam, India. Phone: +91 (361) 540-135. Contact: (technical) P.C. Sanghi, Superindent Engineer.

All India Radio—Hyderabad, Rocklands, Saifabad, Hyderabad-500 004, Andhra Pradesh, India. Phone: +91 (40) 234-904. Contact: (technical) N. Srinivasan, Supervising Engineer.

All India Radio—Imphal, Palau Road, Imphal-795 001, Manipur, India. Phone: +91 (385) 20-534. Contact: (technical) M. Jayaraman, Supervising Engineer.

All India Radio—Itanagar, Naharlagun, Itanagar-791 110, Arunachal Pradesh, India. Phone: +91 (3781) 4485. Contact: J.T. Jirdoh, Station Director; or Suresh Naik, Superintending Engineer. Verifications direct from station are difficult, as engineering is done by staff visiting from the Regional Engineering Headquarters at AIR—Guwahati (see); that address might be worth contacting if all else fails.

All India Radio—Jaipur, 5 Park House, Mirza Ismail Road, Jaipur-302 001, Rajasthan, India. Phone: +91 (141) 366-623. Contact: (technical) S.C. Sharma, Station Engineer.

All India Radio—Jammu—see Radio Kashmir—Jammu.

All India Radio—Kohima, Kohima-797 001, Nagaland, India. Phone: +91 (3866) 2121. Contact: (technical) K.G. Talwar, Superintending Engineer; K.K Jose, Assistant Engineer; or K. Morang, Assistant Station Engineer. Return postage, $1 or IRC helpful.

All India Radio—Kurseong, Mehta Club Building, Kurseong-734 203, Darjeeling District, West Bengal, India. Phone: +91 (3554) 350. Contact: (general) George Kuruvilla, Assistant Director; (technical) A.S. Guin, Chief Engineer; or R.K. Shina, Station Engineer.

All India Radio—Leh—see Radio Kashmir—Leh.

All India Radio—Lucknow, 18 Vidhan Sabha Marg, Lucknow-226 001, Uttar Pradesh, India. Phone: +91 (522) 244-130. Contact: R.K. Singh, Supervising Engineer. This station now appears to be replying via the External Services Division, New Delhi.

All India Radio—Mumbai

EXTERNAL SERVICES: see All India Radio—External Services Division.

COMMERCIAL SERVICE (VIVIDH BHARATI): All India Radio, P.O. Box 11497, 101 M K Road, Mumbai-400 0020, Maharashtra, India. Phone: (general) +91 (22) 203-1341 or +91 (22) 203-594; (director) +91 (22) 203-7702. Fax: +91 (22) 287 6040. Contact: Vijayalakshmi Sinha, Director.

DOMESTIC SERVICE: P.O. Box 13034, Mumbai-400 020, Maharashtra, India. Phone: +91 (22) 202-9853. Contact: S. Sundaram, Supervising Engineer; or Lak Bhatnagar, Supervisor, Frequency Assignments. Return postage helpful.

All India Radio—New Delhi, P.O. Box 70, New Delhi-110 011, India. Phone: (general) +91 (11) 371-0113. Contact: (technical) G.C. Tyagi, Supervising Engineer. $1 helpful.

All India Radio—Panaji

HEADQUARTERS: see All India Radio—External Services Division, above.

AIR OFFICE NEAR TRANSMITTER: P.O. Box 220, Altinho, Panaji-403 001, Goa, India. Phone: +91 (832) 5563. Contact: (technical) V.K. Singhla, Station Engineer; or G.N. Shetti, Assistant Engineer.

All India Radio—Port Blair, Dilanipur, Port Blair-744 102, South Andaman, Andaman & Nicobar Islands, Union Territory, India. Phone: +91 (3192) 20-682. Contact: (general) P.L. Thakur; (technical) Yuvraj Bajaj, Station Engineer. Registering letter appears to be useful. Don't send any cash with your correspondence as it appears to be a violation of their foreign currency regulations.

All India Radio—Ranchi, 6 Ratu Road, Ranchi-834 001, Bihar, India. Phone: +91 (651) 302-358. Contact: (technical) H.N. Agarwal, Supervising Engineer.

All India Radio—Shillong, P.O. Box 14, Shillong-793 001, Meghalaya, India. Phone: +91 (364) 224-443 or +91 (364) 222-781. Contact: (general) C. Lalsaronga, Director NEIS; (technical) H.K. Agarwal, Supervising Engineer. Free booklet on station's history.

All India Radio—Simla, Choura Maidan, Simla-171 004, Himachal Pradesh, India. Phone: +91 (177) 4809. Contact: (technical) B.K. Upadhayay, Supervising Engineer; or P.K. Sood, Assistant Station Engineer. Return postage helpful.

All India Radio—Srinagar—see Radio Kashmir—Srinagar.

All India Radio—Thiruvananthapuram, P.O. Box 403, Bhakti Vilas, Vazuthacaud, Thiruvananthapuram-695 014, Kerala, India. Phone: +91 (471) 65-009. Contact: (technical) K.M. Georgekutty, Station Engineer.

Radio Kashmir—Jammu, Begum Haveli, Old Palace Road, Jammu-180 001, Jammu & Kashmir, India. Phone: +91 (191) 544-411. Fax: +91 (191) 546 658. Contact: (technical) S.K. Sharma, Station Engineer.

Radio Kashmir—Leh, Leh-194 101, Ladakh District, Jammu & Kashmir, India. Phone: +91 (1982) 2263. Contact: (technical) L.K. Gandotar, Station Engineer.

Radio Kashmir—Srinagar, Sherwani Road, Srinagar—190 001, Jammu & Kashmir, India. Phone: +91 (194) 71-460. Contact: L. Rehman, Station Director.

Radio Tila—see All India Radio—Aizawl.

Trans World Radio

STUDIO: P.O. Box 4407, L-15, Green Park, New Delhi-110 016, India. Phone: +91 (11) 662-058. Fax: +91 (11) 686 8049. Contact: N. Emil Jebasingh, Director. This office is used for program production and answering listeners' correspondence, and does not have its own transmission facilities.

ON-AIR ADDRESS: P.O. Box 5, Andhra Pradesh, India.

INDONESIA World Time +7 Western: Waktu Indonesia Bagian Barat (Jawa, Sumatera); +8 Central: Waktu Indonesia Bagian Tengal (Bali, Kalimantan, Sulawesi, Nusa Tenggara); +9 Eastern: Waktu Indonesia Bagian Timur (Irian Jaya, Maluku)

NOTE: Except where otherwise indicated, Indonesian stations, especially those of the Radio Republik Indonesia (RRI) network, will reply to at least some correspondence in English. However, correspondence in Indonesian is more likely to ensure a reply.

Kang Guru II Radio English, Indonesia Australia Language Foundation, Kotak Pos 6756 JKSRB, Jakarta 12067, Indonesia. E-mail: kangguru@server.indo.net.id. URL: www.indo.net.id/commercial/waterfall/kangguru.html. Contact: Greg Clough, Kang Guru Project Manager. This program is aired over various RRI outlets, including Jakarta and Sorong. Continuation of this project, currently sponsored by Australia's AusAID, will depend upon whether adequate supplementary funding can be made available.

Radio Pemerintah Daerah TK II—RPD Poso, Jalan Jenderal Sudirman 7, Poso, Sulawesi Tengah, Indonesia. Contact: Joseph Tinagari, Kepala Stasiun. Return postage necessary. Replies occasionally to correspondence in Indonesian.

Radio Pemerintah Daerah Kabupaten TK II—RPDK Berau, Jalan SA Maulana, Tanjungredeb 77311, Kalimantan Timur, Indonesia. Contact: Kus Syariman or M. Auzi, Kepala Stasiun. Return postage necessary.

Radio Pemerintah Daerah Kabupaten—RPDK Bolaang Mongondow, Jalan S. Parman 192, Kotamobagu, Sulawesi Utara, Indonesia. Replies occasionally to correspondence in Indonesian.

Radio Pemerintah Daerah Kabupaten TK II—RPDK Buol-Tolitoli, Jalan Mohamed Ismail Bantilan No. 4, Tolitoli 94511, Sulawesi Tengah, Indonesia. Contact: Said Rasjid, Kepala Studio; Wiraswasta, Operator/Penyiar; or Muh. Yasin, SM. Return postage required. Replies extremely irregularly to correspondence in Indonesian.

Radio Pemerintah Daerah Kabupaten TK II—RPDK Ende, Jalan Panglima Sudirman, Ende, Flores, Nusa Tenggara Timor, Indonesia. Contact: (technical) Thomas Keropong, YC9LHD. Return postage required.

Radio Pemerintah Daerah Kabupaten TK II—RPDK Manggarai, Ruteng, Flores, Nusa Tenggara Timur, Indonesia. Contact: Simon Saleh, B.A. Return postage required.

Radio Pemerintah Daerah Kabupaten TK II—RPDK Tapanuli Selatan, Kotak Pos No. 9, Padang-Sidempuan, Sumatera Utara, Indonesia. Return postage required.

Radio Republik Indonesia—RRI Ambon, Jalan Jenderal Akhmad Yani 1, Ambon, Maluku, Indonesia. Contact: Drs. H. Ali Amran or Pirla C. Noija, Kepala Seksi Siaran. A very poor replier to correspondence in recent years. Correspondence in Indonesian and return postage essential.

Radio Republik Indonesia—RRI Banda Aceh, Kotak Pos No. 112, Banda Aceh, Aceh, Indonesia. Contact: S.H. Rosa Kim. Return postage helpful.

Radio Republik Indonesia—RRI Bandung, Stasiun Regional 1, Kotak Pos No. 1055, Bandung 40010, Jawa Barat, Indonesia. Contact: Drs. Idrus Alkaf, Kepala Stasiun; Mrs. Ati Kusmiati; or Eem Suhaemi, Kepala Seksi Siaran. Return postage or IRC helpful.

Radio Republik Indonesia—RRI Banjarmasin, Stasiun Nusantara 111, Kotak Pos No. 117, Banjarmasin 70234, Kalimantan Selatan, Indonesia. Contact: Jul Chaidir, Stasiun Kepala; or Harmyn Husein. Free stickers. Return postage or IRCs helpful.

Radio Republik Indonesia—RRI Bengkulu, Stasiun Regional 1, Kotak Pos No. 13 Kawat, Kotamadya Bengkulu, Indonesia. Contact: Drs. H. Harmyn Husein, Kepala Stasiun. Free picture postcards, decals and tourist literature. Return postage or 2 IRCs helpful.

Radio Republik Indonesia—RRI Biak (when operating), Kotak Pos No. 505, Biak, Irian Jaya, Indonesia. Contact: D. Latuperissa, Head of Station.

Radio Republik Indonesia—RRI Bukittinggi, Stasiun Regional 1 Bukittinggi, Jalan Prof. Muhammad Yamin No. 199, Aurkuning, Bukittinggi 26131, Propinsi Sumatera Barat, Indonesia. Fax: +62 (752) 367 132. Contact: Mr. Effendi, Sekretaris; Zul Arifin Mukhtar, SH; or Samirwan Sarjana Hukum, Producer, "Phone in Program." Replies to correspondence in Indonesian or English. Return postage helpful.

Radio Republik Indonesia—RRI Denpasar (when operating), P.O. Box 31, Denpasar, Bali, Indonesia. Replies slowly to correspondence in Indonesian. Return postage or IRCs helpful.

Radio Republik Indonesia—RRI Dili (when operating), Stasiun Regional 1 Dili, Jalan Kaikoli, Kotak Pos 103, Dili 88000, Timor-Timur, Indonesia. Contact: Harry A. Silalahi,

Kepala Stasiun; Arnoldus Klau; or Paul J. Amalo, BA. Return postage or $1 helpful. Replies occasionally to correspondence in Indonesian.

Radio Republik Indonesia—RRI Fak Fak, Jalan Kapten P. Tendean, Kotak Pos No. 54, Fak-Fak 98601, Irian Jaya, Indonesia. Contact: Bahrun Siregar, Kepala Stasiun; Aloys Ngotra, Kepala Seksi Siaran; or Richart Tan, Kepala Sub Seksi Siaran Kata. Station plans to upgrade its transmitting facilities with the help of the Japanese government. Return postage required. Replies occasionally.

Radio Republik Indonesia—RRI Gorontalo, Jalan Jenderal Sudirman, Gorontalo, Sulawesi Utara, Indonesia. Contact: Emod. Iskander, Kepala; or Saleh S. Thalib, Technical Manager. Return postage helpful. Replies occasionally, preferably to correspondence in Indonesian.

Radio Republik Indonesia—RRI Jakarta

STATION: Stasiun Nasional Jakarta, Kotak Pos No. 356, Jakarta, Jawa Barat, Indonesia. URL: (RealAudio via cyberstation Syahreza Radio) www.hway.net/syahreza/rri.htm. Contact: Drs.R. Baskara, Stasiun Kepala; or Drs. Syamsul Muin Harahap, Kepala Stasiun. Return postage helpful. Replies irregularly.

"DATELINE" ENGLISH PROGRAM: see Kang Guru II Radio English.

Radio Republik Indonesia—RRI Jambi

STATION: Jalan Jenderal A. Yani No. 5, Telanaipura, Jambi 36122, Propinsi Jambi, Indonesia. Contact: Marlis Ramali, Manager; M. Yazid, Kepala Siaran; or Buchari Mohammad, Kepala Stasiun. Return postage helpful.

Radio Republik Indonesia—RRI Jayapura, P.O. Box 1077, Jayapura 99222, Irian Jaya, Indonesia. Contact: Harry Liborang, Direktorat Radio; or Dr. David Alex Siahainenia, Kepala. Return postage helpful.

Radio Republik Indonesia—RRI Kendari, Kotak Pos No. 7, Kendari 93111, Sulawesi Tenggara, Indonesia. Contact: H. Sjahbuddin, BA; or Drs. Supandi. Return postage required. Replies slowly to correspondence in Indonesian.

Radio Republik Indonesia—RRI Kupang (Regional I), Jalan Tompello No. 8, Kupang, Timor, Indonesia. Contact: Alfonsus Soetarno, BBA, Kepala Stasiun; Qustigap Bagang, Kepala Seksi Siaran; or Said Rasyid, Kepala Studio. Return postage helpful. Correspondence in Indonesian preferred. Replies occasionally.

Radio Republik Indonesia—RRI Madiun (when operating), Jalan Mayor Jenderal Panjaitan No. 10, Madiun, Jawa Timur, Indonesia. Fax: +62 (351) 4964. Contact: Imam Soeprapto, Kepala Seksi Siaran. Replies to correspondence in English or Indonesian. Return postage helpful.

Radio Republik Indonesia—RRI Malang (when operating), Kotak Pos No. 78, Malang 65112, Jawa Timur, Indonesia; or Jalan Candi Panggung No. 58, Mojolangu, Malang 65142, Indonesia. Contact: Drs.Tjutju Tjuar Na Adikorya, Kepala Stasiun; Ml. Mawahib, Kepala Seksi Siaran; or Dra Hartati Soekemi, Mengetahui. Return postage required. Free history and other booklets. Replies irregularly to correspondence in Indonesian.

Radio Republik Indonesia—RRI Manado, Kotak Pos No. 1110, Manado 95124 Propinsi Sulawesi Utara, Indonesia. Fax: +62 (431) 63 492. Contact: Costher H. Gulton, Kepala Stasiun. Free stickers and postcards. Return postage or $1 required. Replies occasionally to correspondence in Indonesian.

Radio Republik Indonesia—RRI Manokwari, Regional II, Jalan Merdeka No. 68, Manokwari, Irian Jaya, Indonesia. Contact: P.M. Tisera, Kepala Stasiun; or Nurdin Mokogintu. Return postage helpful.

Radio Republik Indonesia—RRI Mataram, Stasiun Regional I Mataram, Jalan Langko No. 83 Ampenan, Mataram 83114, Nusa Tenggara Barat, Indonesia. Phone: +62 (364) 33-713 or +62 (364) 21-355. Contact: Drs. Hamid Djasman, Kepala; or Bochri Rachman, Ketua Dewan Pimpinan Harian. Free stickers. Return postage required. With sufficient return

postage or small token gift, sometimes sends tourist information and Batik print. Replies to correspondence in Indonesian.

Radio Republik Indonesia—RRI Medan, Jalan Letkol Martinus Lubis No. 5, Medan 20232, Sumatera, Indonesia. Phone: +62 (61) 324-222/441. Fax: +62 (61) 512 161. Contact: Kepala Stasiun, Ujamalul Abidin Ass; Drs. Syamsul Muin Harahap; Drs. S. Parlin Tobing, SH, Produsennya, "Kontak Pendengar"; Drs. H. Suryanta Saleh; or Suprato. Free stickers. Return postage required. Replies to correspondence in Indonesian.

Radio Republik Indonesia—RRI Merauke, Stasiun Regional 1, Kotak Pos No. 11, Merauke, Irian Jaya, Indonesia. Contact: (general) Drs. Buang Akhir, Direktor; Achmad Ruskaya B.A., Kepala Stasiun, Drs.Tuanakotta Semuel, Kepala Seksi Siaran; or John Manuputty, Kepala Subseksi Pemancar; (technical) Daf'an Kubangun, Kepala Seksi Tehnik. Return postage helpful.

Radio Republik Indonesia—RRI Nabire, Kotak Pos No. 110, Jalan Merdeka 74 Nabire 98801, Irian Jaya, Indonesia. Contact: Muchtar Yushaputra, Kepala Stasiun. Free stickers and occasional free picture postcards. Return postage or IRCs helpful.

Radio Republik Indonesia—RRI Padang, Kotak Pos No. 77, Padang 25121, Sumatera Barat, Indonesia. Phone: +61 (751) 28-363. Contact: Marlis Ramali; Syair Siak, Kepala Stasiun; or Amir Hasan, Kepala Seksi Siaran. Return postage helpful.

Radio Republik Indonesia—RRI Palangkaraya, Jalan M. Husni Thamrin No. 1, Palangkaraya 73111, Kalimantan Tengah, Indonesia. Phone: +62 (514) 21-779. Fax: +62 (514) 21778. Contact: Drs.Amiruddin; S. Polin; A.F. Herry Purwanto; Meyiwati SH; Supardal Djojosubrojo, Sarjana Hukum; Gumer Kamis; or Ricky D. Wader, Kepala Stasiun. Return postage helpful. Will respond to correspondence in Indonesian or English.

Radio Republik Indonesia—RRI Palembang, Jalan Radio No. 2, Km. 4, Palembang, Sumatera Selatan, Indonesia. Contact: Drs. H. Mursjid Noor, Kepala Stasiun; H.A. Syukri Ahkab, Kepala Seksi Siaran; or H.Iskandar Suradilaga. Return postage helpful. Replies slowly and occasionally.

Radio Republik Indonesia—RRI Palu, Jalan R.A. Kartini No. 39, 94112 Palu, Sulawesi Tengah, Indonesia. Phone: +62 (451) 21-621. Contact: Akson Boole; Untung Santoso; Nyonyah Netty Ch. Soriton, Kepala Seksi Siaran; or M. Hasjim, Head of Programming. Return postage required. Replies slowly to correspondence in Indonesian.

Radio Republik Indonesia—RRI Pekanbaru, Jalan Jenderal Sudirman No. 440, Kotak Pos 51, Pekanbaru, Riau, Indonesia. Phone: +62 (761) 22-081. Fax: +62 (761) 23 605. Contact: (general) Drs. Mukidi, Kepala Stasiun; Arisun Agus, Kepala Seksi Siaran; Drs. H. Syamsidi, Kepala Supag Tata Usaha; or Zainal Abbas. Return postage helpful.

Radio Republik Indonesia—RRI Pontianak, Kotak Pos No. 6, Pontianak 78111, Kalimantan Barat, Indonesia. Contact: Daud Hamzah, Kepala Seksi Siaran; Achmad Ruskaya, BA; Drs. Effendi Afati, Producer, "Dalam Acara Kantong Surat"; Subagio, Kepala Sub Bagian Tata Usaha; Suryadharma, Kepala Sub Seksi Programa; or Muchlis Marzuki B.A. Return postage or $1 helpful. Replies some of the time to correspondence in Indonesian (preferred) or English.

Radio Republik Indonesia—RRI Samarinda, Kotak Pos No. 45, Samarinda, Kalimantan Timur 75001, Indonesia. Phone: +62 (541) 43-495. Fax: +62 (541) 41 693. Contact: Siti Thomah, Kepala Seksi Siaran; Tyranus Lenjau, English Announcer; S. Yati; Marthin Tapparan; or Sunendra, Kepala Stasiun. May send tourist brochures and maps. Return postage helpful. Replies to correspondence in Indonesian.

Radio Republik Indonesia—RRI Semarang, Kotak Pos No. 1073, Semarang Jateng, Jawa Tengah, Indonesia. Phone: +62 (24) 316 501. Contact: Djarwanto, SH; Drs. Sabeni, Doktorandus; Drs. Purwadi, Program Director; Dra. Endang Widiastuti, Kepala Sub Seksi Periklanan Jasa dan Hak Cipta;

Bagus Giarto, Kepala Stasiun; or Mardanon, Kepala Teknik. Return postage helpful.

Radio Republik Indonesia—RRI Serui, Jalan Pattimura Kotak Pos 19, Serui 98211, Irian Jaya, Indonesia. Contact: Agus Raunsai, Kepala Stasiun; J. Lolouan, BA, Kepala Studio; Ketua Tim Pimpinan Harian, Kepala Seksi Siaran; or Drs. Jasran Abubakar. Replies occasionally to correspondence in Indonesian. IRC or return postage helpful.

Radio Republik Indonesia—RRI Sibolga (when operating), Jalan Ade Irma Suryani, Nasution No. 5, Sibolga, Sumatera Utara, Indonesia. Contact: Mrs. Laiya, Mrs. S. Sitoupul or B.A. Tanjung. Return postage required. Replies occasionally to correspondence in Indonesian.

Radio Republik Indonesia—RRI Sorong
STATION: Jalan Jenderal Achmad Yani No. 44, Klademak II, Kotak Pos 146, Sorong 98414, Irian Jaya, Indonesia. Phone: +62 (951) 21-003, +62 (951) 22-111, or +62 (951) 22-611. Contact: Drs. Sallomo Hamid; Tetty Rumbay S., Kasubsi Siaran Kata; Mrs. Tien Widarsanto, Resa Kasi Siaran; Ressa Molle; or Linda Rumbay. Return postage helpful.

"DATELINE" ENGLISH PROGRAM: See Kang Guru II Radio English.

Radio Republik Indonesia—RRI Sumenep, Jalan Urip Sumoharjo No. 26, Sumenep, Madura, Jawa Timur, Indonesia. Contact: Badarus Sjamsi, Kepala, Wseksi Siaran. Return postage helpful.

Radio Republik Indonesia—RRI Surabaya, Stasiun Regional 1, Kotak Pos No. 239, Surabaya 60271, Jawa Timur, Indonesia. Phone: +62 (31) 41-327. Fax: +62 (31) 42 351. Contact: Zainal Abbas, Kepala Stasiun; Drs.Agus Widjaja, Kepala Subseksi Programa Siaran; Usmany Johozua, Kepala Seksi Siaran; or Ny Koen Tarjadi. Return postage or IRCs helpful.

Radio Republik Indonesia—RRI Surakarta, Kotak Pos No. 40, Surakarta 57133, Jawa Tengah, Indonesia. Contact: H. Tomo, B.A., Head of Broadcasting. Return postage helpful.

Radio Republik Indonesia—RRI Tanjungkarang, Kotak Pos No. 24, Bandar Lampung 35213, Indonesia. Phone: +62 (721) 52-280. Fax: +62 (721) 62 767. Contact: M. Nasir Agun; Hi Hanafie Umar; Djarot Nursinggih, Tech. Transmission; Drs. Zulhaqqi Hafiz, Kepala Sub Seksi Periklanan; Asmara Haidar Manaf; or Sutakno, S.E., Kepala Stasiun. Return postage helpful. Replies in Indonesian to correspondence in English or Indonesian.

Radio Republik Indonesia—RRI Tanjungpinang, Stasiun RRI Regional II Tanjungpinang, Kotak Pos No. 8, Tanjungpinang 29123, Riau, Indonesia. Contact: M. Yazid, Kepala Stasiun; Wan Suhardi, Produsennya, "Siaran Bahasa Melayu"; or Rosakim, Sarjana Hukum. Return postage helpful. Replies occasionally to correspondence in Indonesian or English.

Radio Republik Indonesia—RRI Ternate, Jalan Kedaton, Ternate (Ternate), Maluku, Indonesia. Contact: (general) Abd. Latief Kamarudin, Kepala Stasiun; (technical) Rusdy Bachmid, Head of Engineering; or Abubakar Alhadar. Return postage helpful.

Radio Republik Indonesia Tual, Tual, Kepulauan Kai, Maluku, Indonesia.

Radio Republik Indonesia—RRI Ujung Pandang, RRI Nusantara IV, Kotak Pos No. 103, Ujung Pandang, Sulawesi Selatan, Indonesia. Contact: H. Kamaruddin Alkaf Yasin, Head of Broadcasting Department; Beni Koesbani, Kepala Stasiun; L.A. Rachim Ganie; Ashan Muhammad, Kepala Bidang Teknik; or Drs. Bambang Pudjono. Return postage, $1 or IRCs helpful. Replies irregularly and sometimes slowly.

Radio Republik Indonesia—RRI Wamena, RRI Regional II, Kotak Pos No. 10, Wamena, Irian Jaya 99501, Indonesia. Contact: Yoswa Kumurawak, Penjab Subseksi Pemancar. Return postage helpful.

Radio Republik Indonesia—RRI Yogyakarta, Jalan Amat Jazuli 4, Kotak Pos 18, Yogyakarta 55224, Jawa Tengah,

Indonesia. Fax: +62 (274) 2784. Contact: Phoenix Sudomo Sudaryo; Tris Mulyanti, Seksi Programa Siaran; Martono, ub. Kabid Penyelenggaraan Siaran; Mr. Kadis, Technical Department; or Drs. H. Hamdan Sjahbeni, Kepala Stasiun. IRC, return postage or $1 helpful. Replies occasionally to correspondence in Indonesian or English.

Radio Siaran Pemerintah Daerah TK II—RSPD Halmahera Tengah, Soasio, Jalan A. Malawat, Soasio, Maluku Tengah 97812, Indonesia. Contact: Drs. S. Chalid A. Latif, Kepala Badan Pengelola.

Radio Siaran Pemerintah Daerah TK II—RSPD Sumba Timur, Jalan Gajah Mada No. 10 Hambala, Waingapu, Nusa Tenggara Timur 87112, Indonesia. Contact: Simon Petrus, Penanggung Jawab Operasional. Replies slowly and rarely to correspondence in Indonesian.

Radio Siaran Pemerintah Daerah Kabupaten TK II—RSPDK Maluku Tengah, Jalan Pattimura, Masohi, Seram, Maluku Tengah, Indonesia. Contact: Toto Pramurahardja, BA, Kepala Stasiun; Pak Is. Rumalutur; or John Soumokil. Replies slowly to correspondence in Indonesian.

Radio Siaran Pemerintah Daerah Kabupaten Daerah TK II—RSPDKD Ngada, Jalan Soekarno-Hatta, Bjawa, Flores, Nusa Tenggara Tengah, Indonesia. Phone: +62 (384) 21-142. Contact: Drs. Petrus Tena, Kepala Studio.

Voice of Indonesia, Kotak Pos No. 1157, Jakarta 10001, Indonesia. Phone: +62 (21) 720-3467, +62 (21) 355-381 or +62 (21) 349-091. Fax: +62 (21) 345 7132. Contact: Anastasia Yasmine, Head of Foreign Affairs Section. Free stickers and calendars. Very slow in replying.

IRAN   World Time +3:30 (+4:30 midyear)
☞**Voice of the Islamic Republic of Iran**
MAIN OFFICE: IRIB External Services, P.O. Box 19395-6767, Tehran, Iran; or P.O. Box 19395-3333, Tehran, Iran. Phone: (IRIB Public Relations) +98 (21) 204-001/2/3 and +98 (21) 204-6894/5. Fax: (external services) +98 (21) 205 1635, +98 (21) 204 1097 or +98 (21) 291 095; (IRIB Public Relations) +98 (21) 205 3305/7; (IRIB Central Administration) +98 (21) 204 1051; (technical) +98 (21) 654 841. E-mail: (general) irib@dci.iran.com; (Research Centre) iribrec@dci.iran.com. URL: (RealAudio in Persian) http://netiran.com/PersianRadio.html; or http://194.126.32.20/irib/. Contact: (general) Hamid Yasamin, Public Affairs; Ali Larijani, Head; or Hameed Barimani, Producer, "Listeners Special"; (administration) J. Ghanbari, Director General; or J. Sarafraz, Deputy Managing Director; (technical) M. Ebrahim Vassigh, Frequency Manager. Free seven-volume set of books on Islam, magazines, calendars, book markers, tourist literature and postcards. Verifications require a minimum of two days' reception data, plus return postage. Station is currently asking their listeners to send in their telephone numbers so that they can call and talk to them directly. Upon request they will even broadcast your conversation on air. You can send your phone number to the postal address above or you can fax it to: + 98 (21) 205 1635. If English Service doesn't reply, then try writing the French Service in French.
ENGINEERING ACTIVITIES, TEHRAN: IRIB, P.O. Box 15875-4344, Tehran, Iran. Phone: +98 (21) 2196-6127. Fax: +98 (21) 204 1051, +98 (21) 2196 6268 or +98 (21) 172 924. Contact: Mrs. Niloufar Parviz.
ENGINEERING ACTIVITIES, HESSARAK/KARAJ: IRIB, P.O. Box 155, Hessarak/Karaj, Iran. Phone: +98 (21) 204-0008. Fax: +98 (21) 2196 6268. Contact: Mohsen Amiri.
BONN BUREAU, NONTECHNICAL: Puetzsir 34, 53129 Bonn, Postfach 150 140, D-53040 Bonn, Germany. Phone: +49 (228) 231-001. Fax: +49 (228) 231 002.
LONDON BUREAU, NONTECHNICAL: c/o WTN, IRIB, The Interchange Oval Road, Camden Lock, London NWI, United Kingdom. Phone: +44 (171) 284-3668. Fax: + 44 (171) 284 3669.
PARIS BUREAU, NONTECHNICAL: 27 rue de Liège, escalier

B, 1e étage, porte D, F-75008 Paris, France. Phone: + 33 (1) 42-93-12-73. Fax: +33 (1) 42 93 05 13.

Mashhad Regional Radio, P.O. Box 555, Mashhad Center, Jomhoriye Eslame, Iran. Contact: J. Ghanbari, General Director.

IRAQ World Time +3 (+4 midyear)

Holy Medina Radio—see Radio Iraq International, below, for contact information.

Radio Iraq International (Idha'at al-Iraq al-Duwaliyah) *MAIN OFFICE:* P.O. Box 8145, Baghdad, Iraq. Contact: Muzaffar 'Abd-al'-Al, Director; or Jamal Al-Samaraie, Head of Department. All broadcasting facilities in Iraq are currently suffering from severe operational difficulties. *INDIA ADDRESS:* P.O. Box 3044, New Delhi 110003, India.

Radio of Iraq, Call of the Kinfolk (Idha'at al-Iraq, Nida' al-Ahl)—same details as "Radio Iraq International," above.

Voice of Arab Syria—see Radio Iraq International, above, for contact information.

IRELAND World Time exactly (+1 midyear)

⏏Emerald Radio, P.O. Box 200, Dublin, Ireland. E-mail: global@emeraldradio.com. URL: (includes RealAudio) www.emeraldradio.com. Contact: Imelda Deegan; or Bernard Evans. Transmits via WWCR, USA.

Mid-West Radio
HEADQUARTERS: County Mayo Radio Limited, P.O. Box 1, Abbey Street, Ballyhaunis, Co. Mayo, Ireland. Phone: +353 (907) 30-553. Fax: +353 (907) 30 285. E-mail: soumayo@iol.ie. URL: www.mayo-ireland.ie/Mayo/Towns/BallyH/MWR/MWRsched.htm. Contact: P. Claffey, Managing Director; or J. O'Toole, Secretary. Broadcasts on world band occasionally, such as on St. Patrick's Day, to such places as North America, Europe, Africa and the Middle East, via facilities of the BBC World Service. Hopes to make service more regular, perhaps weekly, if funds permit. Correspondence welcomed.
WORLD BAND CORRESPONDENCE: Michael Commins, Murneen Post Office, Claremorris, Co. Mayo, Ireland. Phone/fax: +353 (94) 81-531. Verifies reception reports with a special QSL card.

⏏Radio Teleſís Eireann (Irish Overseas Broadcasting), P.O. Box 4950, Dublin 1, Ireland. Phone, offices: (general) +353 (1) 208-3111; (Broadcasting Development) +353 (1) 208-2350. Phone, concise news bulletins: (United States, special charges apply) +1 (900) 420-2411; (United Kingdom) +44 (891) 871-116; (Australia) +61 (3) 552-1140. Phone, concise sports bulletins: (United States, special charges apply) +1(900) 420-2412; (United Kingdom) +44 (891) 871-117; (Australia) +61 (3) 552-1141. Fax: (general) +353 (1) 208 3082; (Broadcasting Development) +353 (1) 208 3031. URLs: (general) www.rte.ie/; www.bess.tcd.ie/ireland/rte.html; (RealAudio in English and Gaelic) www.rte.ie/sounds.html; (RealAudio, some programs) www.wrn.org/stations/rte.html. Contact: Wesley Boyd, Director of Broadcast Development; Julie Hayde; or Bernie Pope, Reception. IRC appreciated. Offers a variety of video tapes (mostly PAL, but a few "American Standard"), CDs and audio casettes for sale from RTE Commercial Enterprises Ltd, Box 1947, Donnybrook, Dublin 4, Ireland; (phone) +353 (1) 208-3453; (fax) +353 (1) 208 2620. A full list of what's on offer can be viewed at www.rte.ie/lib/store.html#music. Via facilities of WWCR (USA) and Deutsche Telekom (Germany).

UCB Europe, P.O. Box 255, Stoke on Trent ST4 8YY, United Kingdom. E-mail: ucb@ucb.co.uk. URL: http://www.ucb.co.uk/. Contact: Graeme Wilson, Technical Manager.

West Coast Radio Ireland, Murneen Post Office, Claremorris, Co. Mayo, Ireland. Phone/fax: +353 (94) 81-531. E-mail: wcri@mayo-ireland.ie. URL: www.mayo-ireland.ie/shortwave.htm. Contact: Michael Commins; or Gerald Delany—see also *WORLD BAND CORRESPONDENCE,* above. Program originating in the studios of Mid-West Radio—see above, and transmitted via Deutsche Telecom at Jülich, Germany.

ISRAEL World Time +2 (+3 midyear)

Bezeq, The Israel Telecommunication Corp Ltd, Engineering & Planning Division, Radio & T.V. Broadcasting Section, P.O. Box 29555, Tel-Aviv 61294, Israel. Phone: +972 (3) 519-4490. Fax: +972 (3) 519 4614. URL: www.bezeq.co.il/. Contact: Rafael Shamir, Radio Frequency Manager; Johanan Rotem, Frequency Manager; or Marian Kaminski, Head of AM Radio Broadcasting. Bezeq is responsible for transmitting the programs of the Israel Broadcasting Authority (IBA), which *inter alia* parents Kol Israel. This address only for pointing out transmitter-related problems (interference, modulation quality, network mixups, etc.), especially by fax, of transmitters based in Israel. Verifications not given out at this office; requests for verification should be sent to English Department of Kol Israel (see below).

Galei Zahal, Zahal, Military Mail No. 01005, Israel. Phone: +972 (3) 512-6666. Fax: +972 (3) 512 6760. Contact: Yitshak Pasternak, Director. Israeli law allows the Galei Zahal, as well as the Israel Broadcasting Authority, to air broadcasts beamed to outside Israel.

⏏Kol Israel (Israel Radio, the Voice of Israel)
STUDIOS: Israel Broadcasting Authority, P.O. Box 1082, Jerusalem 91010, Israel. Phone: (general) +972 (2) 302-222; (Engineering Dept.) +972 (2) 535-051; (administration) +972 (2) 248-715. Fax: (English Service) +972 (2) 253 282; (Engineering Dept.) +972 (2) 388 821; (other) +972 (2) 248 392 or +972 (2) 302 327. E-mail: ask@israel-info.gov.il. URLs: (media and communications) gopher://israel-info.gov.il:70/00/cul/media/950900.med; (Foreign Ministry, general information on Israeli broadcasting) www.israel-mfa.gov.il; (RealAudio with English and Hebrew news, but only via download, then playback) www.artificia.com/html/news.cgi. Also available from Virtual Israel (RealAudio in Hebrew and English) at www.virtual.co.il/city_services/news/kol.html. Contact: (general) Sara Manobla, Head of English Service; Edmond Sehayeq, Head of Programming, Arabic, Persian & Yemenite broadcasts; Yishai Eldar, Senior Editor, English Service; (administration) Shmuel Ben-Zvi, Director; (technical, frequency management) Raphael Kochanowski, Director of Liaison & Coordination, Engineering Dept. Various political, religious, tourist, immigration and language publications. IRC required for reply.
SAN FRANCISCO OFFICE, SCHEDULES: 2654 17th Avenue, San Francisco CA 94116 USA. Phone: +1 (415) 564-9968. Contact: George Poppin. This address, a volunteer office, only provides Kol Israel schedules. All other correspondence should be sent directly to the main office in Jerusalem.

ITALY World Time +1 (+2 midyear)

Adventist World Radio, the Voice of Hope, AWR-Europe, Casella Postale 383, 47100 Forlì, Italy. Phone: +39 (543) 766-655. Fax: +39 (543) 768 198. E-mail: awritaly@mbox.queen.it. Contact: Erika Gysin, Listener Mail Services; or Sylva Kesheshian, Listener Mail Secretary. This office will verify reports for AWR broadcasts from Italy, Russia and Slovakia. Free religious printed matter, quarterly *AWR Current* newsletter, stickers, program schedules and other small souvenirs. Return postage, IRCs or $1 appreciated. The Italian government has awarded a shortwave license to AWR for its existing station at Forlì and for a new facility near Argenta scheduled for completion in 1999. AWR is currently considering proposals from manufacturers for this project. Also, see AWR listings under Costa Rica, Guam, Guatemala, Kenya, Russia and USA.
DX PROGRAM: "Radio Magazine," produced by Dario Villani.

European Christian Radio, Postfach 500, A-2345 Brunn, Austria. Fax: +39 (2) 29 51 74 63. Contact: John Adams, Director; or C.R. Coleman, Station Manager. $1 or 2 IRCs required.

Good Fun Radio, Treviso, c/o G.A.M.T., P.O. Box 3, Succ. 10, 31100 Treviso, Italy.

⏏Italian Radio Relay Service, IRRS-Shortwave, Nexus

NHK

Africa is a primary target for world band stations. Mohamed Juma of Tanzania is a regular listener to South Africa's Channel Africa and Radio Japan's Swahili service.

IBA, C.P. 10980, 20100 Milano, Italy; or alternatively to expedite cassette deliveries only, mail to: NEXUS-IBA, Attn. Anna Boschetti, Via F. D'Ovidio 6, 20131 Milano, Italy. Phone: +39 (2) 266-6971 or +39 (337) 297-778. Fax: +39 (2) 7063 8151. E-mail: (general) info@nexus.org; ("Hello There" program) ht@nexus.org; (reception reports of test transmissions) test@nexus.org; (other reception reports) reports@nexus.org; (International Public Access Radio, a joint venture of IRRS and WRMI, USA) IPAR@nexus.org; (Cotroneo) aec@nexus.org. URLs: (general) www.nexus.org; (RealAudio) www.nexus.org/IRN/index.html; (schedules) www.nexus.org/NEXUS-IBA/Schedules; (International Public Access Radio) www.nexus.org/IPAR. Contact: (general) Alfredo E. Cotroneo, President & Producer of "Hello There"; (technical) Ms. Anna S. Boschetti, Verification Manager. Free station literature. Two IRCs or $1 helpful.

Radio Europa International, via Gerardi 6, 25124 Brescia, Italy. Contact: Mariarosa Zahella. Replies irregularly, but return postage helpful.

Radio Europe, via Davanzati 8, 20158 Milan MI, Italy. Phone: +39 (2) 3931-0347. Fax: +39 (2) 8645 0149. E-mail: 100135.54@compuserve.com. Contact: Dario Monferini, Foreign Relations Director; or Alex Bertini, General Manager. Pennants $5 and T-shirts $25. $30 for a lifetime membership to Radio Europe's Listeners' Club. Membership includes T-shirt, poster, stickers, flags, gadgets, and so forth, with a monthly drawing for prizes. Application forms available from station. Sells airtime for $20 per hour. Two IRCs or $1 return postage appreciated.

Radio Internazionale Italia, Padova. E-mail: word@cdc.it. Contact: Paolo Tommasi; or this station now verifies via Dario Monferini—see next listing above.

Radio Maria Network Europe, relay Spoleto, Via Turati 7, 22036 Erba, Italy. Fax: +39 (31) 611 288. URL: www.cta.it/aziende/r_maria/info.htm.

Radio Mariquita/Alpen Adria, Treviso, c/o G.A.M.T., P.O. Box 3, Succ. 10, 31100 Treviso, Italy.

Radiorama Radio, C.P. 873, 34100 Trieste, Italy. Contact: Valerio G. Cavallo. Program over the Italian Radio Relay Service (see). Verifies directly.

📻 Radio Roma-RAI International (external services)
MAIN OFFICE: External/Foreign Service, Centro RAI, Saxa Rubra, 00188 Rome, Italy; or P.O. Box 320, Correspondence Sector, 00100 Rome, Italy. Phone: +39 (6) 33-17-2360. Fax: +39 (6) 33 17 18 95 or +39 (6) 322 6070. URLs: www.mix.it/rai; or www.mix.it/raiinternational/. Contact: (general) Rosaria

Vassallo, Correspondence Sector; or Augusto Milana, Editor-in-Chief, Shortwave Programs in Foreign Languages; Esther Casas, Servicio Español; (administration) Angela Buttiglione, Managing Director; or Gabriella Tambroni, Assistant Director. Free stickers, banners, calendars and *RAI Calling from Rome* magazine. Can provide supplementary materials, including on VHS and CD-ROM, for Italian-language video course, "Viva l' italiano," with an audio equivalent soon to be offered, as well. Is constructing "a new, more powerful and sophisticated shortwave transmitting center" in Tuscany; when this is activated, RAI International plans to expand news, cultural items and music in Italian and various other language services—including Spanish, Portuguese, Italian, plus new services in Chinese and Japanese. Responses can be very slow.
SHORTWAVE FREQUENCY MONITORING OFFICE: RAI Monitoring Station, Centro di Controllo, Via Mirabellino 1, 20052 Monza (MI), Italy. Phone: +39 (39) 388-389. Phone/fax (ask for fax): +39 (39) 386-222. E-mail: cqmonza@rai.it. Contact: Signora Giuseppina Moretti, Frequency Management.
ENGINEERING OFFICE, ROME: Via Teulada 66, 00195 Rome, Italy. Phone: +39 (6) 331-70721. Fax: +39 (6) 331 75142 or +39 (6) 372 3376. E-mail: isola@rai.it. Contact: Clara Isola.
ENGINEERING OFFICE, TURIN: Via Cernaia 33, 10121 Turin, Italy. Phone: +39 (11) 810-2293. Fax: +39 (11) 575 9610. E-mail: allamano@rai.it. Contact: Giuseppe Allamano.
NEW YORK OFFICE, NONTECHNICAL: 1350 Avenue of the Americas —21st floor, New York NY 10019 USA. Phone: +1 (212) 468-2500. Fax: +1 (212) 765 1956. Contact: Umberto Bonetti, Deputy Director of Radio Division. RAI caps, aprons and tote bags for sale at Boutique RAI, c/o the aforementioned New York address.
SAN FRANCISCO OFFICE, SCHEDULES: 2654 17th Avenue, San Francisco CA 94116 USA. Phone: +1 (415) 564-9968. Contact: George Poppin. This address, a volunteer office, only provides RAI schedules to listeners. All other correspondence should be sent directly to the main office in Rome.
Radio Speranza, Modena (when active), Largo San Giorgio 91, 41100 Modena, Italy. Phone/fax: +39 (59) 230-373. Contact: Padre Cordioli Luigi, Missionario Redentorista. Free Italian-language newsletter. Replies enthusiastically to correspondence in Italian. Return postage appreciated.
Radio Strike, Palermo, c/o R. Scaglione, P.O. Box 119, Succ. 34, 90144 Palermo, Italy.
RTV Italiana-RAI (domestic services)
CALTANISSETTA: Radio Uno, Via Cerda 19, 90139 Palermo, Sicily, Italy. Contact: Gestione Risorse, Transmission Quality Control. $1 required.
ROME: Centro RAI, Saxa Rubra, 00188 Rome, Italy. Fax: +39 (6) 322 6070. E-mail: grr@rai.it. URLs (experimental): (general) http:www.rai.it/; (RealAudio) www.rai.it/grr.
Tele Radio Stereo, Roma, Via Bitossi 18, 00136 Roma, Italy. Fax: + 39 (6) 353 48300.

IVORY COAST—*see* Côte d'Ivoire

JAPAN World Time +9
NHK Fukuoka, 1-1-10 Ropponmatsu, Chuo-ku, Fukuoka-shi, Fukuoka 810-77, Japan.
NHK Osaka, 3-43 Bamba-cho, Chuo-ku, Osaka 540-01, Japan. Fax: +81 (6) 941 0612. Contact: (technical) Technical Bureau. IRC or $1 helpful.
NHK Sapporo, 1-1-1 Ohdori Nishai, Chuo-ku, Sapporo 060, Japan. Fax: +81 (11) 232 5951.
NHK Tokyo/Shobu-Kuki, JOAK, 3047-1 Oaza-Sanga, Shoubu-cho, Minami Saitamagun, Saitama 346-01, Japan. Fax: +81 (3) 3481 4985 or +81 (480) 85 1508. IRC or $1 helpful. Replies occasionally. Letters should be sent via registered mail.
Radio Japan/NHK (external service)
MAIN OFFICE: 2-2-1 Jinnan, Shibuya-ku, Tokyo 150-01, Japan. Phone: +81 (3) 3465-1111. Fax: (general) +81 (3) 3481 1350; ("Hello from Tokyo" and Production Center) +81 (3)

3465 0966. E-mail: info@intl.nhk.or.jp. URLs: www.nhk.or.jp/rjnet. Contact: Chief Producer, "Hello from Tokyo"; Director of Public Relations; Director of Programming; Director of News Department; or Director of Production Center. Free *Radio Japan News* publication, sundry other small souvenirs and "Let's Learn/Practice Japanese" language-course materials.

Radio Tampa/NSB

MAIN OFFICE: Nihon Shortwave Broadcasting, 9-15 Akasaka 1-chome, Minato-ku, Tokyo 107, Japan. Fax: +81 (3) 3583 9062. E-mail: tampa@pub.softbank.co.jp. URL: www.softbank.co.jp/tampa/. Contact: H. Nagao, Public Relations; M. Teshima; Ms. Terumi Onoda; or H. Ono. Sending a reception report may help with a reply. Free stickers and Japanese stamps. $1 or 2 IRCs helpful.

NEW YORK NEWS BUREAU: 1325 Avenue of the Americas #2403, New York NY 10019 USA. Fax: +1 (212) 261 6449. Contact: Noboru Fukui, reporter.

JORDAN   World Time +2 (+3 midyear)

Radio Jordan, P.O. Box 909, Amman, Jordan. Phone: (general) +962 (6) 774-111; (International Relations) +962 (6) 778-578; (English Service) +962 (6) 757-410; (Arabic Service) +962 (6) 636-454; (Saleh) +962 (6) 748-048; (Al-Areeny) +962 (6) 757-404. Fax: +962 (6) 788 115. E-mail: (general) general@jrtv.gov.jo; (programs) rj@jrtv.gov.jo; (technical) eng@jrtv.gov.jo. URL: www.jrtv.com/radio.htm. Contact: (general) Jawad Zada, Director of English Service & Producer of "Mailbag"; Mrs. Firyal Zamakhshari, Director of Arabic Programs; or Qasral Mushatta; (administrative) Hashem Khresat, Director of Radio; Mrs. Fatima Massri, Director of International Relations; or Muwaffaq al-Rahayifah, Director of Shortwave Services; (technical) Fawzi Saleh, Director of Engineering; or Yousef Al-Areeny, Director of Radio Engineering. Free stickers. Replies irregularly and slowly. Enclosing $1 helps.

KAZAKHSTAN   World Time +6 (+7 midyear)

Kazakh Radio, Kazakh Broadcasting Company, 175A Zheltoksan Street, 480013 Almaty, Kazakhstan. Phone: +7 (3272) 630-763 or +7 (3272) 635-629. Fax: +7 (3272) 631 207. Contact: B. Shalakhmentov, Chairman; or S.D. Primbetov, Deputy Chairman.

Radio Almaty ("Radio Alma-Ata" and "Radio Almaty" in English Service, "Radio Kazakhstan" in Russian and some other services), 175A Zheltoksan Street, 480013 Almaty, Kazakhstan. Phone: +7 (3272) 637-694 or +7 (3272) 633-716. Fax: +7 (3272) 631 207. Contact: Mr. Gulnar. Correspondence welcomed in English, German, Russian, Korean and Kazakh. Station hopes to start up services in Chinese and Japanese, but not in the near future.

KENYA   World Time +3

Adventist World Radio, The Voice of Hope, AWR Africa, P.O. Box 10114, Nairobi, Kenya. Phone: +254 (2) 713-961. Fax: +254 (2) 713 907. E-mail: 74532.1575@compuserve.com. URL: www.awr.org/awr-africa/. Contact: Samuel Misiani, AWR Africa Region Director. Free home Bible study guides, program schedule and other small items. $1 preferred although IRCs still appreciated. Also, *see* AWR listings under Costa Rica, Guam, Guatemala, Italy, Russia and USA.

Kenya Broadcasting Corporation, P.O. Box 30456, Harry Thuku Road, Nairobi, Kenya. Phone: +254 (2) 334-567. Fax: +254 (2) 220 675. Contact: (general) Henry Makokha, Liaison Office; (administration) Philip Okundi, Managing Director; (technical) Augustine Kenyanjier Gochui; Lawrence Holnati, Engineering Division; or D. Githua, Assistant Manager Technical Services (Radio). IRC required. Replies irregularly.

KIRIBATI   World Time +12

Radio Kiribati, P.O. Box 78, Bairiki, Tarawa, Republic of Kiribati. Phone: +686 21187. Fax: +686 21096. Contact: (general) Atiota Bauro, Programme Organiser; Mrs. Otiri Laboia; or Moia Tetoa, Producer, "Kaoti Ami Iango," a program devoted to listeners views; (administration) Bill Reiher, Manager; (technical) Tooto Kabwebwenibeia, Broadcast Engineer; or T. Fakaofo, Technical Staff. Cassettes of local songs available for purchase. $1 or return postage required for a reply (IRCs not accepted).

KOREA (DPR)   World Time +9

Radio Pyongyang, External Service, Korean Central Broadcasting Station, Pyongyang, Democratic People's Republic of Korea (*not* "North Korea"). Phone: +850 (2) 812-301 or +850 (2) 36-344. Fax: +850 (2) 381 410. Phone and fax numbers valid only in those countries with direct telephone service to North Korea. Free book for German speakers to learn Korean, sundry other publications, pennants, calendars, newspapers, artistic prints and pins. Do not include dutiable items in your envelope. Replies are irregular, as mail from countries not having diplomatic relations with North Korea is sent via circuitous routes and apparently does not always arrive. Indeed, some PASSPORT readers continue to report that mail to Radio Pyongyang in North Korea results in their receiving anti-communist literature from *South* Korea, which indicates that mail interdiction has not ceased. One way around the problem is to add "VIA BEIJING, CHINA" to the address, but replies via this route tend to be slow in coming. Another gambit is to send your correspondence to an associate in a country—such as China, Ukraine or India—having reasonable relations with North Korea, and ask that it be forwarded. If you don't know anyone in these countries, try using the good offices of the following person: Willi Passman, Oberhausener Str. 100, D-45476, Mülheim, Germany. Include 3 IRCs to cover the cost of forwarding.

Regional Korean Central Broadcasting Stations—Not known to reply, but a long-shot possibility is to try corresponding in Korean to: Korean Central Broadcasting Station, Ministry of Posts and Telecommunications, Chongsung-dong (Moranbong), Pyongyang, Democratic People's Republic of Korea. Fax: +850 (2) 812 301 (valid only in those countries with direct telephone service to North Korea). Contact: Chong Ha-chol, Chairman, Radio and Television Broadcasting Committee.

KOREA (REPUBLIC)   World Time +9

Korean Broadcasting System (KBS), Yoido-dong 18, Youngdungpo-gu, Seoul, Republic of Korea 150-790. Phone: +82 (2) 781-2410. Fax: +82 (2) 761 2499. E-mail: webmaster@kbsnt.kbs.co.kr. URLs: www.kbs.co.kr/; (RealAudio) www.kbs.co.kr/radiofm/sound1.html.

Radio Korea International

MAIN OFFICE: Overseas Service, Korean Broadcasting System, Yoido-dong 18, Youngdungpo-gu, Seoul, Republic of Korea 150-790. Phone: (general) +82 (2) 781-3710 or +82 (2) 781-3721; (English Service) +82 (2) 781-3728/29/35; (Russian

FEBC

This famous arch in Vientiane, Laos continues to be lovingly maintained.

Service) +82 (2) 781-3714. Fax: +82 (2) 781 3799 or (toll-free fax lines now available for overseas listeners) (United States) 1-888-229-2312; (United Kingdom) 0800-89-5995; (Canada) 1-888-211-5865; (Australia) 1-800-142-644. URLs: www.kbs.co.kr/rki/rki.html; (RealAudio) www.kbs.co.kr/rki/rki.ram. Contact: (general) Chae Hong-Pyo, Director of English Service; Robert Gutnikov, English Service; Ms. Han Hee-joo, Producer/Host, "Shortwave Feedback"; Jong Kyong-Tae, Producer, Russian Service; H.A. Staiger, Deputy Head of German Service; Ms. Lee Hae-Ok, Japanese Service; or Ms. Kim Hae-Young, Producer, Japanese Service; (administration) Kim Sang-Soo, Executive Director; or Choi Jang-Hoon, Director. Free stickers, calendars, *Let's Learn Korean* book and a wide variety of other small souvenirs. *History of Korea* now available via Internet (see URL, above) and on CD-ROM (inquire).
WASHINGTON NEWS BUREAU: National Press Building, Suite 1076, 529 14th Street NW, Washington DC 20045 USA. Phone: +1 (202) 662-7345. Fax: +1 (202) 662 7347.

KUWAIT   World Time +3
Ministry of Information, P.O. Box 193, 13002 Safat, Kuwait. Phone: +965 241-5301. Fax: +965 243 4511. Contact: Sheik Nasir Al-Sabah, Minister of Information.
Radio Kuwait, P.O. Box 397, 13004 Safat, Kuwait. Phone: +965 241-0301 or +965 242-3774. URL: (RealAudio) www.radiokuwait.org/. E-mail: kwtfreq@ncc.moc.kw; or radiokuwait@radiokuwait.org. Fax: +965 241 5498, +965 245 6660 or +965 241 5946. Contact: (general) Manager, External Service; (technical) Nasser M. Al-Saffar, Controller, Frequency Management. Sometimes gives away stickers, calendars, pens or key chains.

KYRGYZSTAN   World Time +5 (+6 midyear)
Kyrgyz Radio, Kyrgyz TV and Radio Center, Prospekt Moloday Gvardil 63, 720 300 Bishkek, Kyrgyzstan. Fax: +7 (3312) 257 930. Contact: A.I. Vitshkov or E.M. Abdukarimov. Include your e-mail address (if you have one) when writing to the station; although the station is not online, at least one member of the staff, Natalya Moskvina, has access to an e-mail facility and has been known to reply via that route.

LAOS   World Time +7
Lao National Radio, Luang Prabang ("Sathani Withayu Kachaisiang Khueng Luang Prabang"), Luang Prabang, Laos; or B.P. 310, Vientiane, Laos. Return postage required (IRCs not accepted). Replies slowly and very rarely. Best bet is to write in Laotian or French directly to Luang Prabang, where the transmitter is located.
Lao National Radio, Vientiane, Laotian National Radio and Television, B.P. 310, Vientiane, Laos. Contact: Khoun Sounantha, Manager-in-Charge; Bounthan Inthasai, Deputy Managing Director; Miss Chanthery Vichitsavanh, Announcer, English Section who says, "It would be good if you send your letter unregistered, because I find it difficult to get all letters by myself at the post. Please use my name, and 'Lao Natl Radio, P.O. Box 310, Vientiane, Laos P.D.R.'It will go directly to me."; or Ms. Mativarn Simanithone, Deputy Head, English Section. The external service of this station tends to be erratic.

LATVIA   World Time +2 (+3 midyear)
Latvijas Radio, 8 Doma laukums, LV-1505 Riga, Latvia. Phone: (general) +371 720-6722; (Director General) +371 720-6747; (Program Director) +371 720-6750; (International Relations) +371 720-6757. Fax: (general) +371 720 6709; (International Relations) +371 782 0216; (Director General) +371 720 6709. E-mail: radio@radio.org.lv. URL: (includes RealAudio) www.radio.org.lv/. Contact: (general) Aivars Ginters, International Relations; or Mrs. Dârija Juðkevièa, Program Director; (administration) Dzintris Kolâts, Director General; (technical) Aigars Semevics, Technical Director. Replies to nontechnical correspondence in Latvian. Does not issue verification replies.
Radio Latvia, P.O. Box 266, LV-1098 Riga, Latvia. Contact: (general) Ms. Fogita Cimcus, Chief Editor, English.Free stickers and pennants. Unlike Latvijas Radio, preceding, Radio Latvia verifies regularly via the Chief Editor.

LEBANON   World Time +2 (+3 midyear)
Radio Lebanon, Radio Liban (when operation commences), Ministry of Information, Beirut, Lebanon. Hopes to inaugurate a major world band service.
The Voice of Charity, B.P. 850, Jounieh, Lebanon. E-mail: charity@cyberia.net.lb. Contact: Fr. Ellie Nakhoul, Managing Director. Program aired via Vatican Radio and founded by the Order of the Lebanese Missionaries. Basically, a Lebanese Christian educational radio program.
Voice of Hope, P.O. Box 77, Metulla 10292, Israel; or P.O. Box 3379, Limassol, Cyprus. Phone: (Israel) +972 (6) 959-174. Fax: (Israel) +972 (6) 997 827. E-mail: voh@zenon.logos.cy.net. URL: www.highadventure.org/voh_midd.html. Contact: Gary Hull, Station Manager; or Isaac Gronberg, Director. Free stickers. IRC requested.May send 214 page book *Voice of Hope* via USA headquarters *(see)*. Due to soaring electricity bills, station has reduced transmitter powers. Also, *see* KVOH—Voice of Hope/High Adventure Ministries, USA.
Voice of Lebanon, La Voix du Liban, B.P. 165271, Al-Ashrafiyah, Beirut, Lebanon. Phone/fax: +961 (1) 323-458. $1 required. Replies extremely irregularly to correspondence in French or Arabic, but usually willing to discuss significant matters by telephone. Operated by the Phalangist organization.
Voice of Orthodoxy—see Belarus.

LESOTHO   World Time +2
Radio Lesotho, P.O. Box 552, Maseru 100, Lesotho. Phone: +266 323-561. Fax: +266 310 003. Contact: (general) Mrs.

Florence Lesenya, Controller of Programmes; or Sekhonyana Motlohi, Producer, "What Do Listeners Say?"; (head of administration) Ms. Mpine Tente, Director; (technical) L. Monnapula, Acting Chief Engineer; or Peter L. Moepi, Studio Engineer. Return postage necessary.

LIBERIA World Time exactly
NOTE: Mail sent to Liberia may be returned as undeliverable.
ELBC, Liberian Broadcasting System, P.O. Box 10-594, 1000 Monrovia 10, Liberia. Phone: +231 22-4984 or +231 22-2758. Contact: Jesse B. Karnley, Director General, Broadcasting; or James Morlu, Deputy Director, Broadcasting. Operates on behalf of the Economic Community of West African States' peacekeeping force, ECOMOG.
Radio Liberia International, Liberian Communications Network/KISS, P.O. Box 1103, 1000 Monrovia 10, Liberia. Phone: +231 22-6963 or +231 22-7593. Fax: (during working hours) +231 22 6003. Contact: Issac P. Davis, Engineer-in-Charge/QSL Coordinator. $5 required for QSL card.

LIBYA World Time +1 (+2 midyear)
Radio Jamahiriya
MAIN OFFICE, EXTERNAL: P.O. Box 4677 (or P.O. Box 4396), Tripoli, Libya. Contact: R. Cachia. Arabic preferred.
MALTA OFFICE: European Branch Office, P.O. Box 17, Hamrun, Malta. This office, which may still be in operation, has historically replied more consistently than has the main office.
Libyan Jamahiriyah Broadcasting (domestic service), Box 9333, Soug al Jama, Tripoli, Libya. Phone: +218 (21) 603-191/5.

LITHUANIA World Time +2 (+3 midyear)
Lietuvos Radijo ir Televizijos Centras (LRTC), Sausio 13-osios 10, LT-2044 Vilnius, Lithuania. Phone: +370 (2) 459-397. Fax: +370 (2) 451 738.
This organization operates the transmitters used by Lithuanian Radio.
📻Lithuanian Radio
STATION: Lietuvos Radijas, Konarskio 49, LT-2674 Vilnius, Lithuania. Phone: (general) +370 (2) 633-182; (Grumadiene) +370 (2) 634-471; (Vilciauskas) +370 (2) 233-503. Fax: +370 (2) 263 282. E-mail: format is initial.lastname@rtv.lrtv.ot.lt, so to contact, say, Juozas Algirdas Vilciauskas, it would be jvilciauskas@rtv.lrtv.ot.lt. URLs: (RealAudio, including Radio Vilnius) www.lrtv.lt/lr.htm; www3.omnitel.net/virtual/lrtv.lt/lr.htm. Contact: (general) Mrs. Laima Grumadiene, Managing Director; or Mrs. Kazimiera Mazgeliene, Programme Director; (technical) Juozas Algirdas Vilciauskas, Technical Director.
ADMINISTRATION: Lietuvos Nacionalinis Radijas ir Televizija (LNRT), Konarskio 49, LT-2674 Vilnius, Lithuania. Phone: +370 (2) 263-383. Fax: +370 (2) 263 282. E-mail: (Ilginis) ailginis@rtv.lrtv.ot.lt. URLs: www.lrtv.lt/lrtv.htm; www3.omnitel.net/virtual/lrtv.lt.lrtv.htm. Contact: Arvydas Ilginis, Director General.
📻Radio Vilnius, Lietuvos Radijas, Konarskio 49, LT-2674 Vilnius, Lithuania. Phone: +370 (2) 633-182. Fax: +370 (2) 263 282. E-mail: ravil@rtv.lrtv.ot.lt. URL: see Lithuanian Radio, above. Contact: Ms. Rasa Lukaite, "Letterbox"; Audrius Braukyla, Editor-in-Chief; or Ilonia Rukiene, Head of English Department. Free stickers, pennants, Lithuanian stamps and other souvenirs. Transmissions to North America are via the facilities of Deutsche Telekom in Germany (see).

MADAGASCAR World Time +3
Radio Madagasikara, B.P. 1202, Antananarivo, Madagascar. Contact: Mlle. Rakotoniaina Soa Herimanitia, Secrétaire de Direction, a young lady who collects stamps; or Adolphe Andriakoto, Directeur. $1 required, and enclosing used stamps from various countries may help. Tape recordings accepted. Replies very rarely and slowly, preferably to friendly philatelist gentlemen who correspond in French.
Radio Nederland Wereldomroep—Madagascar Relay, B.P. 404, Antananarivo, Madagascar. Contact: (technical)

RTM director Tuan Haji Ahmed Shafiee Haji Yaman hosts a convention at the station's facilities in Kecil Kuching, Malaysia.

Rahamefy Eddy, Technische Dienst.; or J.A. Ratobimiarana, Chief Engineer. Nontechnical correspondence should be sent to Radio Nederland Wereldomroep in Holland (see).
Radio Television Tsioka Vao, P.O. Box 315, Tana, Madagascar. Phone: +261 (2) 21749. Contact: Detkou Dedonnais, Director.

MALAWI World Time +2
Malawi Broadcasting Corporation, P.O. Box 30133, Chichiri, Blantyre 3, Malawi. Phone: +265 671-222. Fax: +265 671 353 or +265 671 257. Contact: (general) Sam Gunde, Acting Director General; Joseph Mndeke, Director of Programmes; P. Chinseu; J.O. Mndeke; or T.J. Sineta; (technical) Joseph Chikagwa, Director of Engineering. Return postage or $1 helpful.

MALAYSIA World Time +8
Asia-Pacific Broadcasting Union, P.O. Box 1164, Pejabat Pos Jalan Pantai Bahru, 59700 Kuala Lumpur, Malaysia; or (street address) 2nd Floor, Bangunan IPTAR, Angkasapuri, 50614 Kuala Lumpur, Malaysia. Phone: +60 (3) 282-3590, +60 (3) 282-2480 or +60 (3) 282-3108. Fax: +60 (3) 282 5292. URL: www.rthk.org.hk/rthk/abu/. Contact: Dato' Jaafar Kamin, President; or Hugh Leonard, Secretary-General.
📻Radio Malaysia, Kuala Lumpur
MAIN OFFICE: RTM, Angkasapuri, Bukit Putra, 50614 Kuala Lumpur, Peninsular Malaysia, Malaysia. Phone: +60 (3) 282-5333 or +60 (3) 282-4976. Fax: +60 (3) 282 4735, +60 (3) 282 5103 or +60 (3) 282 5859. E-mail: sabariah@rtm.net.my. URL: (general) www.asiaconnect.com.my/rtm-net/; (RealAudio, live) www.asiaconnect.com.my/rtm-net/live/; (RealAudio, archives) www.asiaconnect.com.my/rtm-net/online/index.html. Contact (general) Madzhi Johari, Director of Radio; (technical) Ms. Aminah Din, Deputy Director Engineering; Abdullah Bin Shahadan, Engineer, Transmission & Monitoring; or Ong Poh, Chief Engineer. May sell T-shirts and key chains. Return postage required.
TRANSMISSION OFFICE: Controller of Engineering, Department of Broadcasting (RTM), 43009 Kajang, Selangor Darul Ehsan, Malaysia. Contact: Jeffrey Looi.

Radio Malaysia Kota Kinabalu, RTM, 88614 Kota Kinabalu, Sabah, Malaysia. Contact: Benedict Janil, Director of Broadcasting; or Hasbullah Latiff. Return postage required.

Radio Malaysia Sarawak (Kuching), RTM, Broadcasting House, Jalan P. Ramlee, 93614 Kuching, Sarawak, Malaysia. Phone: +60 (82) 248-422. Fax: +60 (82) 241 914. Contact: (general) Tuan Haji Ahmad Shafiee Haji Yaman, Director of Broadcasting; or Human Resources Development; (technical, but also nontechnical) Colin A. Minoi, Technical Correspondence; (technical) Kho Kwang Khoon, Deputy Director of Engineering. Return postage helpful.

Radio Malaysia Sarawak (Miri), RTM, Miri, Sarawak, Malaysia. Contact: Clement Stia. $1 or return postage helpful.

Radio Malaysia Sarawak (Sibu), RTM, Jabatan Penyiaran, Bangunan Penyiaran, 96009 Sibu, Sarawak, Malaysia. Contact: Clement Stia, Divisional Controller, Broadcasting Department. $1 or return postage required. Replies irregularly and slowly.

Voice of Islam—Program of the Voice of Malaysia (see), below.

Voice of Malaysia, Suara Malaysia, Wisma Radio, P.O. Box 11272-KL, 50740 Angkasapuri, Kuala Lumpur, Malaysia. Phone: +60 (3) 282-5333. Fax: +60 (3) 282 5859. Contact: (general) Mrs. Mahani bte Ujang, Supervisor, English Service; Hajjah Wan Chuk Othman, English Service; (administration) Santokh Singh Gill, Director; or Mrs. Adilan bte Omar, Assistant Director; (technical) Lin Chew, Director of Engineering. Free calendars and stickers. Two IRCs or return postage helpful. Replies slowly and irregularly.

MALDIVES   World Time +5
Voice of Maldives, Ministry of Information, Arts & Culture, Moonlight Higun, Malé 20-06, Republic of Maldives. Phone: (administration & secretaries) +960 321-642; (Director General) +960 322-577; (Director of Programs) +960 322-746; (Duty Officer) +960 322-841; (programme section) +960 322-842; (studio 1) +960 325-151; (studio 2) +960 323-416; (newsroom) +960 322-253, +960 324-506 or +960 324-507; (office assistant/budget secretary) +960 320-508; (FM Studio) +960 314-217; (technical, office) +960 322-444 or +960 320-941; (residence) +960 323-211. Fax: +960 328 357 or +960 325 371. E-mail: informat@dhivehinet.net.mv. Contact: Maizan Ahmed Manik, Director General-Engineering. Long inactive on the world bands, this station is expected to resume shortwave broadcasts in the near future with a newly installed 10 kilowatt transmitter on the island of Mafushi.

MALI   World Time exactly
Radiodiffusion Télévision Malienne, B.P. 171, Bamako, Mali. Phone: +223 22-47-27. Fax: +223 22 42 05. Contact: Karamoko Issiaka Daman, Directeur des Programmes; (administration) Abdoulaye Sidibe, Directeur General. $1 or IRC helpful. Replies slowly and irregularly to correspondence in French. English is accepted.

MALTA   World Time +1 (+2 midyear)
Voice of the Mediterranean (Radio Melita), P.O. Box 143, La Valletta, CMR 01, Malta. Phone: +356 240-421 or +356 248-080. Fax: +356 241 501. E-mail: vomradio@dream.vol.net.mt. URL: (unofficial site, set up by a friendly enthusiast) www.woden.com/~falcon/shedule.html. Contact: (administration) Richard Vella Laurenti, Managing Director; (German Service and listener contact) Ingrid Huettmann. Letters and reception reports welcomed in English, French, German or Arabic. Station is a joint venture of the Libyan and Maltese governments.

MAURITANIA   World Time exactly
Office de Radiodiffusion-Télévision de Mauritanie, B.P. 200, Nouakchott, Mauritania. Fax: +222 (2) 51264. Contact: Madame Amir Feu; Lemrabott Boukhary; Madame Fatimetou Fall Dite Ami, Secretaire de Direction; or Mr. Hane Abou. Return postage or $1 required. Rarely replies.

MAURITIUS   World Time +4
Mauritius Broadcasting Corporation, P.O. Box 48, Curepipe, Mauritius; (physical location) Louis Pasteur Street, Forest Side, Mauritius. Phone: +230 675-5001. Fax: +230 675 7332. URL: http://xensei.com/users/mbc/radio/. Contact: (general) Trilock Dwarka, Director General; or Mrs. Marie Michele Etienne, Officer in Charge of Programmes; (technical) Armoodalingum Pather, Chief Engineer; or Ashok Kariman, Deputy Chief Engineer. Currently inactive on world band, but hopes to reactivate transmissions eventually on 4855 and 9710 kHz.

MEXICO   World Time −6 (−5 midyear) Central, including D.F.; −7 (−6 midyear) Mountain; −8 (−7 midyear) Pacific
La Hora Exacta—XEQK, IMER, Margaritas 18, Col. Florida, 01030 México D.F., Mexico. Contact: Gerardo Romero.

La Voz de Veracruz—XEFT (when operating), Apartado Postal 21, 91700-4H. Veracruz, Ver., Mexico. Contact: C.P. Miguel Rodríguez Sáez, Sub-Director; or Lic. Juan de Dios Rodríguez Díaz, Director-Gerente. Free tourist guide to Veracruz. Return postage, IRC or $1 probably helpful. Likely to reply to correspondence in Spanish.

Radio Educación—XEPPM, SPE-333/92, Apartado Postal 21-940, 04021 México D.F., Mexico. Phone: (general) +52 (5) 559-8075 or +52 (5) 559-3102; (studio) +52 (5) 575-0919. Fax: +52 (5) 559 2301. Contact: (general) Lic. Susana E. Mejía Vázquez, Jefe del Dept. de Audiencia y Evaluación; or María Teresa Moya Malfavón, Directora de Producción y Planeación; (administration) Luis Ernesto Pi Orozco, Director General; (technical) Ing. Gustavo Carreño López, Subdirector, Dpto. Técnico. Free stickers, calendars, station photo and a copy of a local publication, *Audio Tinta Boletín Informativo*. Return postage or $1 required. Replies, sometimes slowly, to correspondence in English, Spanish, Italian or French.

Radio Huayacocotla—XEJN
STATION ADDRESS: "Radio Huaya," Dom. Gutierrez Najera s/n, Apartado Postal 13, 92600 Huayacocotla, Veracruz, Mexico. Phone: +52 (775) 8-0067. Fax: +52 (775) 8 0178. E-mail: framos@uibero.uia.mx. URL: http://mixcoac.uia.mx/~jsweeney/fce/huarad.html. Contact: Juan Antonio Vázquez; Alfredo Zepeda; Martha Silvia Ortiz López, Director de Programas; or Felipe de Jesús Martínez Sosa. Return postage or $1 helpful. Replies irregularly to correspondence in Spanish.
SPONSORING ORGANIZATION: Fomento Cultural y Educativo, A.C. Miguel Laurent 340, Col. Del Valle, 03100 México D.F., Mexico. Phone: +2 (5) 559-6000. Fax: +52 (5) 575 8357.

Radio México Internacional—XERMX, Grupo IMER, Instituto Méxicano de la Radio, Apartado Postal 21-300, 04021 México D.F., Mexico. Phone: +52 (5) 628-1700 or +52 (5) 534-5210. Fax: +52 (5) 604 8902 or +52 (5) 524 1758. E-mail: imer@mpsnet.com.mx. Contact: Lic. Juan Mort Martín del Campo, Gerente; or Julian Santiago, Host, "Mailbag." Free stickers, post cards and stamps. Welcomes correspondence, including inquiries about Mexico, in Spanish, English, French and Italian. Hopes to have an additional transmitter on the air by late 1997. $1 helpful.
SAN FRANCISCO OFFICE, SCHEDULES: 2654 17th Avenue, San Francisco CA 94116 USA. Phone: +1 (415) 564-9968. Contact: George Poppin. This address, a volunteer office, only provides Radio México International schedules to listeners. All other correspondence should be sent directly to the main office in México City.

Radio Mil—XEOI, NRM, Insurgentes Sur 1870, Col. Florida, 01030 México D.F., Mexico. Phone: (station) +52 (5) 662-1000 or +52 (5) 662-1100; (Núcleo Radio Mil network) +52 (5) 662-6060, +52 (5) 663-0739 or +52 (5) 663 0590. Fax: (station) +52 (5) 662 0974; (Núcleo Radio Mil network) +52 (5) 662 0979. Contact: Guillermo Salas Vargas, Presidente; Srta. Cristina Stivalet, Gerente; or Zoila Quintanar Flores. Free stickers. $1 or return postage required.

Radio Transcontinental de América—XERTA (when operating), Apartado Postal 653, 06002 México D.F., Mexico; or Torre Latinoamericana, piso 37, 06007, México D.F., Mexico. Phone: +52 (5) 510-9896. Fax: +52 (5) 510 3326. Plans to start an international service with as many as ten languages to promote Mexican tourism, products, etc.

Radio Universidad/UNAM—XEUDS, Apartado Postal No. 1817, 83000 Hermosillo, Sonora, Mexico. Contact: A. Merino M., Director; or Ing. Miguel Angel González Lopez, Subdirector de Ingenieria. Free tourist literature and stickers. $1 or return postage required. Replies irregularly to correspondence in Spanish.

Radio XEQQ, La Voz de la América Latina (on the rare occasions when operating), Sistema Radiópolis, Ayuntamiento 52, 06070 México D.F., Mexico; or Ejército Nacional No. 579 (6ᵗᵒ piso), 11520 México D.F., Mexico. Contact: (general) Sra. Martha Sandoval; (technical) Ing. Miguel Angel Barrientos, Director Técnico de Plantas Transmisoras. Free pennants. $1, IRC or return postage required. When operating, replies fairly regularly to correspondence in Spanish.

Radio XEUJ (when operating), Apartado Postal 62, 67700 Linares, Nuevo León, Mexico. Contact: (general) Marcelo Becerra González, Director General; or Joel Becerra Pecina; (technical) Ing. Gustavo Martínez de la Cruz. Free stickers, pennants and Mexican tourist cards. Replies irregularly to correspondence in Spanish, English or French. Considering replacing their transmitting equipment and extending hours of transmission.

Radio XEUW, Ocampo 119, 91700 Veracruz, Mexico. Contact: Ing. Baltazar Pazos de la Torre, Director General. Free pennants. Return postage required. Replies occasionally to correspondence in Spanish.

Tus Panteras—XEQM (when operating), Apartado Postal No. 217, 97000 Mérida, Yucatán, Mexico. Fax: +52 (99) 28 06 80. Contact: Arturo Iglesias Villalobos; L.C.C Roberto Domínguez Avila, Director General; or Ylmar Pacheco Gómez, Locutor. Replies irregularly to correspondence in Spanish.

"MOLDAVIAN REPUBLIC OF PRIDNESTROVYE" World Time +2 (+3 midyear)
NOTE: As direct mail service to this region is often nonexistent, the best way to contact the stations listed below is via Rumen Pankov, P.O. Box 199, 1000 Sofia-C, Bulgaria, enclosing 5 IRCs or $2, or 1 IRC and $1.
Radio Pridnestrovye, 10 Rosa Luxemburg Street, 278000 Tiraspol, Pridnestrovye, C.I.S.

MOLDOVA World Time +2 (+3 midyear)
Radio Moldova International
NOTE: As direct mail service to Moldova is often nonexistent, the best way to contact Radio Moldova International is via Rumen Pankov, P.O. Box 199, 1000 Sofia-C, Bulgaria, enclosing 5 IRCs or $2.
GENERAL CORRESPONDENCE: If direct mail service is available from your location, try Str. Miorița 1, 277028 Chișinău, Moldova. Phone: +373 (2) 721-792, +373 (2) 723-379 or +373 (2) 723-385. Fax: +373 (2) 723 329 or +373 (2) 723 307. Contact: Constantin Marin, International Editor-in-Chief; Alexandru Dorogan, General Director of Radio Broadcasting; Daniel Lacky, Editor, English Service; Veleriu Vasilica, Head of English Department; or Raisa Gonciar. Transmits via facilities of Radio România International. Free stickers and calendars.
RECEPTION REPORTS: Should direct mail service be available from your location, try RMI-Monitoring Action, P.O. Box 9972, 277070 Chișinău-70, Moldova.

MONACO World Time +1 (+2 midyear)
Radio Monte-Carlo
MAIN OFFICE: 16 Boulevard Princesse Charlotte, MC-98080 Monaco Cedex, Monaco. Phone: +377 (93) 15-16-17. Fax: +377 (93) 15 16 30 or +377 (93) 15 94 48. E-mail: via URL. URL: www.twr.org/monte.htm. Contact: Jacques Louret; Bernard

Poizat, Service Diffusion; or Caroline Wilson, Director of Communication. Free stickers. This station is on world band only with its Arabic Service.
MAIN PARIS OFFICE, NONTECHNICAL: 12 rue Magellan, F-75008 Paris, France. Phone: +33 (1) 40-69-88-00. Fax: +33 (1) 40 69 88 55 or +33 (1) 45 00 92 45.
PARIS OFFICE (ARABIC SERVICE): 78 Avenue Raymond Poincairé, F-75008 Paris, France. Phone: +33 (1) 45-01-53-30.
*CYPRUS OFFICE (ARABIC SERVICE)—see Cyprus.
Trans World Radio
STATION: B.P. 349, MC-98007 Monte-Carlo, Monaco-Cedex. Phone: +377 (92) 16-56-00. Fax: +377 (92) 16 56 01. URLs (transmission schedules): (Monte-Carlo) www.gospelcom.net/twr/t_monte_carlo.htm; (Albania) www.gospelcom.net/twr/t_albania.htm. Contact: (general) Mrs. Jeanne Olson; (administration) Richard Olson, Station Manager; (technical) Bernhard Schraut, Frequency Coordinator. Free paper pennant. IRC or $1 helpful. Also, see USA.
GERMAN OFFICE: Evangeliums-Rundfunk, Postfach 1444, D-35573 Wetzlar, Germany. Phone: +49 (6441) 957-0. Fax: +49 (6441) 957-120. E-mail: erf@erf.de; or siemens@arf.de. URL: www.erf.de. Contact: Jürgen Werth, Direktor.
HOLLAND OFFICE, NONTECHNICAL: Postbus 176, NL-3780 BD Voorthuizen, Holland. Phone: +31 (0) 34-29-27-27. Fax: +31 (0) 34 29 67 27. Contact: Beate Kiebel, Manager Broadcast Department; or Felix Widmer.
VIENNA OFFICE, TECHNICAL: Postfach 141, A-1235 Vienna, Austria. Phone: +43 (1) 863-1233 or +43 (1) 863-1247. Fax: +43 (1) 863 1220. E-mail: (Menzel) 100615.1511@compuserve.com; (Schraut) eurofreq@twr.org; bschraut@twr.org; or 101513.2330@compuserve.com; (Roswell) eurofreq@twr.org; or croswell@twr.org. Contact: Helmut Menzel, Director of Engineering; Bernhard Schraut, Frequency Coordinator; or Charles K. Roswell, Frequency Coordinator.
SWISS OFFICE: Evangelium in Radio und Fernsehen, Witzbergstrasse 23, CH-8330 Pfäffikon ZH, Switzerland. Phone: +41 (951) 0500. Fax: +41 (951) 0540. E-mail: erf@erf.ch. URL: www.erf.ch/.

MONGOLIA World Time +8
Mongol Radio (Mailing address same as Voice of Mongolia, see below). Phone: (administration) +976 (1) 23520 or +976 (1) 28978; (correspondence) +976 (1) 29766. E-mail: radiomongolia@magicnet.mn. URL: www.magicnet.mn/monradio/.
Radio Ulaanbaatar—see Voice of Mongolia, below.
Voice of Mongolia, C.P.O. Box 365, Ulaanbaatar 13, Mongolia. Phone: +976 (1) 321-624 or (English Section) +976 (1) 327-900. Fax: +976 (1) 323 096 or (English Section) +976 (1) 327 234. E-mail: (general) radiomongolia@magicnet.mn; or (International Relations Office) mrtv@magicnet.mn. Contact: (general) Mrs. Narantuya, Chief of Foreign Service; D. Batbayar, Mail Editor, English Department; N. Tuya, Head of English Department; Dr. Mark Ostrowski, Consultant, MRTV International Relations Department; or Ms. Tsegmid Burmaa, Japanese Department; (administration) Ch. Surenjav, Director; (technical) Ing. Ganhuu, Chief of Technical Department. Correpondence should be directed to the relevant language section and 2 IRCs or 1$ appreciated. Free pennants, postcards, newspapers and Mongolian stamps.

MOROCCO World Time exactly
Radio Medi Un
MAIN OFFICE: B.P. 2055, Tangier, Morocco. Contact: J. Dryk, Responsable Haute Fréquence. Two IRCs helpful. Free stickers. Correspondence in French preferred.
PARIS BUREAU, NONTECHNICAL: 78 Avenue Raymond Poincaré, F-75016 Paris, France. Phone: +33 (1) 45-01-53-30. Correspondence in French preferred.
RTV Marocaine, RTM, 1 rue al-Brihi, Rabat, Morocco. Phone: +212 (7) 70-17-40. Fax +212 (7) 70 32 08. Contact: (nontechnical and technical) Mrs. Naaman Khadija, Ingénieur d'Etat en Télécommunication; (technical) Tanone Mohammed

Yangon, Myanmar is home to Asia's most elaborate Buddhist temple that has not been vandalized or pilfered.

Jamaledine, Technical Director; Hammouda Mohamed, Engineer; or N. Read. Correspondence welcomed in English, French, Arabic or Berber—especially suggestions for times, languages and other relevant information concerning possible limited expansion of shortwave transmissions to new targets so Moroccan and North African affairs can be more widely disseminated and understood.

Voice of America/VOA-IBB—Morocco Relay Station, Briech. Phone: (office) +212 (9) 93-24-81; (transmitter) +212 (9) 93-22-00. Fax: +212 (9) 93 55 71. Contact: Wilfred Cooper, Manager. These numbers for urgent technical matters only. Otherwise, does not welcome direct correspondence; see USA for acceptable VOA Washington address and related information.

MOZAMBIQUE World Time +2

Rádio Maputo (when active)—see Radio Moçambique, below.

Rádio Moçambique (if operating), C.P. 2000, Maputo, Mozambique. Phone: +258 (1) 421-814, +258 (1) 429-826 or +258 (1) 429-836. Fax: +258 (1) 421 816. Contact: (general) João B. de Sousa, Administrador e Diretor Comercial; Daude Amade, Diretor de Programas; Iain Patrick Christie, Diretor; Orlanda Mendes, Produtor, "Linha Direta"; (technical) Eduardo Rufino de Matos, Diretor Técnico. Free medallions and pens. Cassettes featuring local music $15. Return postage, $1 or 2 IRCs required. Replies to correspondence in Portuguese or English. Means are being studied by which Rádio Moçambique, which the Mozambique prime minister says "is going through difficult times," may be properly financed and thus remain on the air. However, the station has recently reported a loss of its shortwave transmitting capabilities. Thieves have continually stolen copper wire at the transmitter station. It is quite unlikely the wire will be replaced due to the high cost involved. Another problem is that the shortwave transmitters are very old and finding spare parts for them is becoming increasingly difficult. Thus, this station appears to be planning a major transformation of its foreign broadcasting policy. It plans to target South Africa only, via medium wave and FM.

MYANMAR (BURMA) World Time +6:30

Radio Myanmar

STATION: GPO Box 1432, Yangon-11181, Myanmar; or Pyay Road, Yangon-11041, Myanmar. Phone: +95 (1) 31-355. Fax: +95 (1) 30 211. Contact: U. Ko Ko Htway, Director of Radio, Radio Division, M.R.T.D.

NAMIBIA World Time +2 (+1 midyear)

Radio Namibia/Namibian Broadcasting Corporation, P.O. Box 321, Windhoek 9000, Namibia. Phone: +264 (61) 291-3111. Fax: +264 (61) 217 760. URL: www.oneworld.org/cba/nbc.htm. Contact: P. Schachtschneider, Manager, Transmitter Maintenance. Free stickers.

NEPAL World Time +5:45

Radio Nepal, P.O. Box 634, Singha Durbar, Kathmandu, Nepal. Phone: (general) +977 (1) 223-910, +977 (1) 243-569 or +977 (1) 212-950; (engineering) +977 (1) 225-467. Fax: +977 (1) 221 952. URL: (includes RealAudio in English and Nepali) www.catmando.com/news/radio-nepal/. Contact: (general) S.R. Sharma, Executive Director; M.P. Adhikari, Deputy Executive Director; or S.K. Pant, Producer, "Listener's Mail"; (technical) Ram S. Kharki, Acting Director, Engineering. 3 IRCs necessary, but station urges that neither mint stamps nor cash be enclosed, as this invites theft by Nepalese postal employees.

NETHERLANDS ANTILLES World Time –4
Radio Nederland Wereldomroep—Bonaire Relay, P.O. Box 45, Kralendijk, Netherlands Antilles. Nontechnical correspondence should be sent to Radio Nederland Wereldomroep in Holland (see).

NEW ZEALAND World Time +13 (+12 midyear)
Kiwi Radio (unlicensed, but left alone by the government), P.O. Box 3103, Onekawa, Napier New Zealand. Phone: +64 (6) 835-9186. Fax: +64 (6) 835 4186. E-mail: kiwiradio@ writeme.com. URLs: www.geocities.com/CapeCanaveral/ 9885; or www-pp.hogia.net/jonny/fr/kiwi.html. Contact: Graham J. Barclay. Free stickers, schedule etc. New Zealand Tourist Information free upon request. Kiwi Radio T-shirts and history sets on cassette available for US $23 each airmail. Verification by QSL card. Return postage appreciated.
Radio New Zealand International (Te Reo Irirangi O Aotearoa, O Te Moana-nui-a-kiwa), P.O. Box 123, Wellington, New Zealand. Phone: +64 (4) 474-1437. Fax: +64 (4) 474 1433 or +64 (4) 474 1886. E-mail: rnzi@actrix.gen.nz. URLs: (general) www.actrix.gen.nz/biz/rnzi; (experimental Internet Audio Home Site) www.rnz.co.nz/. Contact: Florence de Ruiter, Listener Mail; Myra Oh, Producer, "Mailbox"; or Walter Zweifel, News Editor; (administration) Ms. Linden Clark, Manager; (technical) Adrian Sainsbury, Frequency Manager. Free stickers, schedule/flyer about station, map of New Zealand and tourist literature available. English/Maori T-shirts for US$20; Sweatshirts $40; interesting variety of CDs, as well as music cassettes and spoken programs, in Domestic "Replay Radio" catalog (VISA/MC). Three IRCs for verification, one IRC for schedule/catalog.
Radio Reading Service—ZLXA, P.O. Box 360, Levin 5500, New Zealand. Phone: +64 (6) 368-2229. Fax: +64 (6) 368 0151. E-mail: alittle@xtra.co.nz. Contact: (general) Ron Harper; Ash Bell; Brian Stokoe, Program Supervisor; (administration) Allen J. Little, Station Director. Free brochure, postcards and stickers. $1, return postage or 3 IRCs appreciated.
Radio RJK (unlicensed), P.O. Box 16-002, Tamatea, Napier, New Zealand. Transmits via the facilities of Kiwi Radio see above.
Radio Sue (unlicensed), c/o Kiwi Radio, P.O. Box 3103, Onekawa, Napier, New Zealand. Broadcasts via its own transmitter.

NICARAGUA World Time –6
Radio Miskut, Correo Central (Bragman's Bluff), Puerto Cabezas, R.A.A.N., Nicaragua. Phone: +505 (282) 2443. Fax: +505 (267) 3032. Contact: Evaristo Mercado Pérez, Director de Operación y de Programas. T-shirts $10, and *Resumen Mensual del Gobierno y Consejo Regional* and *Revista Informativa Detallada de las Gestiones y Logros* $10 per copy. Station has upgraded to a new shortwave transmitter and is currently improving its shortwave antenna. Replies slowly and irregularly to correspondence in English and Spanish. $2 helpful, as is registering your letter.

NIGER World Time +1
La Voix du Sahel, O.R.T.N., B.P. 361, Niamey, Niger. Fax: +227 72 35 48. Contact: (general) Adamou Oumarou; Zakari Saley; Souley Boubacou; or Mounkaïla Inazadan, Producer, "Inter-Jeunes Variétés"; (administration) Oumar Tiello, Directeur; (technical) Afo Sourou Victor. $1 helpful. Correspondence in French preferred. Correspondence by males with this station may result in requests for certain unusual types of magazines and photographs.

NIGERIA World Time +1
WARNING—MAIL THEFT: For the time being, correspondence from abroad to Nigerian addresses has a relatively high probability of being stolen.
WARNING—CONFIDENCE ARTISTS: For years, now, correspondence with Nigerian stations has sometimes resulted in letters from highly skilled "pen pal" confidence artists. These typically offer to send you large sums of money, if you will provide details of your bank account or similar information (after which they clean out your account). Other scams are disguised as tempting business proposals; or requests for money, free electronic or other products, publications or immigration sponsorship. Persons thus approached should contact their country's diplomatic offices. For example, Americans should contact the Diplomatic Security Section of the Department of State [phone +1 (202) 647-4000], or an American embassy or consulate.
Radio Nigeria—Enugu, P.M.B. 1051, Enugu (Anambra), Nigeria. Contact: Louis Nnamuchi, Assistant Director Technical Services. Two IRCs, return postage or $1 required. Replies slowly.
Radio Nigeria—Ibadan, P.M.B. 5003, Ibadan, Oyo State, Nigeria. Fax: +234 (22) 413 930. Contact: V.A. Kalejaiye, Technical Services Department; Rev. Olukunle Ajani, Executive Director; or Dare Folarin, Principal Public Affairs Officer. $1 or return postage required. Replies slowly.
Radio Nigeria—Kaduna, P.O. Box 250, Kaduna (Kaduna), Nigeria. Contact: Yusuf Garba, Ahmed Abdullahi, or Johnson D. Allen. $1 or return postage required. Replies slowly.
Radio Nigeria—Lagos, P.M.B. 12504, Ikoyi, Lagos, Nigeria. Contact: Babatunde Olalekan Raji, Monitoring Unit. Two IRCs or return postage helpful. Replies slowly and irregularly.
Voice of Nigeria, P.M.B. 40003 Falomo Post Office, Ikoyi, Lagos, Nigeria. Phone: +234 (1) 269-3078/3245/3075/. Fax: +234 (1) 269 1944. Contact: (general) Alhaji Lawal Yusuf Saulawa, Director Programmes; Mrs. Stella Bassey, Deputy Director Programmes; Alhaji Mohammed Okorejior, Acting Director News; or Livy Iwok, Editor; (administration) Alhaji Mallam Yaya Abubakar, Director General; Abubakar Jijiwa, Chairman; or Dr. Walter Ofonagoro, Minister of Information; (technical) J.O. Kurunmi, Deputy Director Engineering Services; O.I. Odumsi, Acting Director, Engineering; or G.C. Ugwa, Director Engineering. Replies from station tend to be erratic, but continue to generate unsolicited correspondence from supposed "pen pals" (see *WARNING—CONFIDENCE ARTISTS*, above); faxes, which are much less likely to be intercepted, may be more fruitful. Two IRCs or return postage helpful.

NORTHERN MARIANA ISLANDS World Time +10
Far East Broadcasting Company—KFBS Saipan
MAIN OFFICE: FEBC, P.O. Box 209, Saipan, Mariana Islands MP 96950 USA. Phone: +670 322-9088. Fax: +670 322 3060. E-mail: febc@itecnmi.com. URL: http://febc.org. Contact: Chris Slabaugh, Field Director; Mike Adams; or Robert Springer. Replies sometimes take months. Also, see FEBC Radio International, USA.
Herald Broadcasting Syndicate Northern Mariana Islands—KHBI Saipan, P.O. Box 1387, Saipan, Mariana Islands CM 96950-1387 USA; or write to Boston address (see USA). Phone: +670 234-6515. Fax: +670 234 5452. E-mail: (Station Manager) doming@khbi.com. URL: www.tfccs.com. Contact: (nontechnical) Alexander U. Igisaiar; or Doming F. Villar, Station Manager; (technical) Jess Emmanuel Domingo. Return postage is appreciated if writing to Saipan; no return postage necessary when writing to Boston. Visitors are welcome, preferably from 9 to 4 Monday through Friday, but contact transmitter site before arrival in Saipan to make arrangements.

NORWAY World Time +1 (+2 midyear)
☞Radio Norway International
MAIN OFFICE, NONTECHNICAL: Utenlandssendingen, NRK, N-0340 Oslo, Norway. Phone: (general) +47 (23) 048-441; (Norwegian-language 24-hour recording of schedule information +47 (23) 048-008 (Americas, Europe, Africa), +47 (23) 048-009 (elsewhere). Fax: (general) +47 (23) 047 134 or +47 (22) 605 719. E-mail: radionorway@nrk.no. URL: (includes RealAudio) www.nrk.no/radionyheter/radionorway/. Contact: (general) Kirsten Ruud Salomonsen, Head of External Broad-

casting; (technical) Gundel Krauss Dahl, Head of Radio Projects. Free stickers and flags.

FREQUENCY MANAGEMENT OFFICE: Statens Teleforvaltning, Dept. TF/OMG, Revierstredet 2, P.O. Box 447 Sentrum, N-0104 Oslo, Norway. Phone: +47 (22) 824-889. Fax: +47 (22) 824 891. E-mail: olavmo@online.no. Contact: Olav Mo Grimdalen, Frequency Manager.

WASHINGTON NEWS BUREAU: Norwegian Broadcasting, 2030 M Street NW, Suite 700, Washington DC 20036 USA. Phone: +1 (202) 785-1481 or +1 (202) 785-1460. Contact: Bjorn Hansen or Gunnar Myklebust.

SINGAPORE NEWS BUREAU: NRK, 325 River Valley Road #01-04, Singapore.

OMAN   World Time +4

BBC World Service—Eastern Relay Station, P.O. Box 6898 (or 3716), Ruwi Post Office, Muscat, Oman. Contact: Technical correspondence should be sent to "Senior Transmitter Engineer"; nontechnical goes to the BBC World Service in London (see United Kingdom).

☞**Radio Sultanate of Oman**, Ministry of Information, P.O. Box 600, Muscat, Post Code 113, Sultanate of Oman. URL: (RealAudio only) www.oman-tv.gov.om/. Fax: (general) +968 602 055 or +968 602 831; (technical) +968 604 629. Contact: (Directorate General of Technical Affairs) Abdallah Bin Saif Al Nabhani, Acting Chief Engineer; Rashid Haroon Al Jabry, Head of Radio Maintenance; or Ahmed Mohamed Al Balushi, Head of Studio's Engineering. Replies regularly, and responses are from one to two weeks. $1, return postage or 3 IRCs helpful.

PAKISTAN   World Time +5

Azad Kashmir Radio, Muzaffarabad, Azad Kashmir, Pakistan. Contact: (technical) M. Sajjad Ali Siddiqui, Director of Engineering; or Liaquatullah Khan, Engineering Manager. Registered mail helpful. Rarely replies to correspondence.

Pakistan Broadcasting Corporation—same address, fax and contact as "Radio Pakistan."

Radio Pakistan, P.O. Box 1393, Islamabad 44000, Pakistan. Phone: +92 (51) 813-802, +91 (51) 829-022 or +91 (51) 921-4947. Fax: +92 (51) 216 657 or +92 (51) 811 861. Contact: (technical) Anwer Inayet Khan, Senior Broadcast Engineer, Room No. 324, Frequency Management Cell; Syed Abrar Hussain, Controller of Frequency Management; Syed Asmat Ali Shah, Senior Broadcasting Engineer; or Nasirahmad Bajwa, Frequency Management. Free stickers, pennants and *Pakistan Calling* magazine. May also send pocket calendar. Very poor replier. Plans to replace two 50 kW transmitters with 500 kW units if and when funding is forthcoming.

PALAU   World Time +9

KHBN—Voice of Hope, P.O. Box 66, Koror, Palau 96940, Pacific Islands. Phone: +680 488-2162. Fax: +680 488 2163. E-mail: hampalau@belau.com. Contact: (general) Joseph Tan, Station Manager; (technical) Joe Fay, Chief Engineer. Free stickers and publications. IRC requested. Also, *see* KVOH—Voice of Hope/High Adventure Ministries, USA.

PAPUA NEW GUINEA   World Time +10

National Broadcasting Corporation of Papua New Guinea, P.O. Box 1359, Boroko, Papua New Guinea. Phone: + 675 325-5233 or +675 325-7175. Fax: +675 325 0796 or +675 325 6296. Contact: (general) Renagi R. Lohia, CBE, Managing Director and C.E.O.; or Francesca Maredei, Planning Officer; (technical) Bob Kabewa, Sr. Technical Officer; or F. Maredey, Chief Engineer. Two IRCs or return postage helpful. Replies irregularly.

Radio Bougainville, P.O. Box 35, Buka, North Solomons Province (NSP), Papua New Guinea. Fax: +675 939 912. Contact: Demas Kumaina, Provincial Programme Manager; Ms. Christine Talei, Assistant Provincial Manager; or Aloysius Laukai, Senior Programme Officer. Replies irregularly.

Radio Central, P.O. Box 1359, Boroko, NCD, Papua New Guinea. Contact: Steven Gamini, Station Manager; or Amos

Langit, Technician. $1, 2 IRCs or return postage helpful. Replies irregularly.

Radio Eastern Highlands (Karai Bilong Kumul), P.O. Box 311, Goroka, EHP, Papua New Guinea. Fax: +675 722 841. Contact: Ignas Yanam, Technical Officer; or Kiri Nige, Engineering Division. $1 or return postage required. Replies irregularly.

Radio East New Britain, P.O. Box 393, Rabaul, ENBP, Papua New Guinea. Fax: +675 923 254. Contact: Esekia Mael, Station Manager; or Otto Malatane, Provincial Program Manager. Return postage required. Replies slowly.

Radio East Sepik, P.O. Box 65, Wewak, E.S.P., Papua New Guinea. Fax: +675 862 405. Contact: Elias Albert, Assistant Provincial Program Manager; or Luke Umbo, Station Manager.

Radio Enga, P.O. Box 300, Wabag, Enga Province, Papua New Guinea. Phone: +675 571 213. Fax: +675 571 069. Contact: (general) John Lyein Kur, Station Manager; or Robert Papuvo, (technical) Felix Tumun K., Station Technician.

Radio Gulf, P.O. Box 36, Kerema, Gulf, Papua New Guinea. Contact: Robin Wainetta, Station Manager; or Timothy Akia, Provincial Program Manager.

Radio Madang, P.O. Box 2138, Madang, Papua New Guinea. Phone: +675 852-2415. Fax: +675 852 2360. Contact: (general) Damien Boaging, Senior Programme Officer; Geo Gedabing, Provincial Programme Manager; Peter Charlie Yannum, Assistant Provincial Programme Manager; or James Steve Valakvi, Senior Programme Officer; (technical) Lloyd Guvil, Technician.

Radio Manus, P.O. Box 505, Lorengau, Manus, Papua New Guinea. Phone: +675 470-9029. Fax: +675 470 9079. Contact: (technical and nontechnical) John P. Mandrakamu, Provincial Program Manager. Station is seeking the help of DXers and broadcasting professionals in obtaining a second hand, but still usable broadcasting quality CD player that could be donated to Radio Manus. Replies regularly. Return postage appreciated.

Radio Milne Bay, P.O. Box 111, Alotau, Milne Bay, Papua New Guinea. Contact: (general) Trevor Webumo, Assistant Manager; Simon Muraga, Station Manager; or Raka Petuely, Program Officer; (technical) Philip Maik, Technician. Return postage in the form of mint stamps helpful.

Radio Morobe, P.O. Box 1262, Lae, Morobe, Papua New Guinea. Fax: +675 472 6423. Contact: Ken L. Tropu, Assistant Program Manager; Peter W. Manua, Program Manager; Kekalem M. Meruk, Assistant Provincial Program Manager; or Aloysius R. Nase, Station Manager.

Radio New Ireland, P.O. Box 140, Kavieng, New Ireland, Papua New Guinea. Fax: +675 984 2489. Contact: Otto A. Malatana, Station Manager; or Ruben Bale, Provincial Program Manager. Return postage or $1 helpful.

Radio Northern, Voice of Oro, P.O. Box 137, Popondetta, Oro, Papua New Guinea. Contact: Roma Tererembo, Assistant Provincial Programme Manager; or Misael Pendaia, Station Manager. Return postage required.

Radio Sandaun, P.O. Box 37, Vanimo, Sandaun Province, Papua New Guinea. Phone: +675 857 1144/49/12. Fax: +675 857 1305. Contact: (nontechnical) Gabriel Deckwalen, Station Manager; Elias Rathley, Provincial Programme Manager; Mrs. Maria Nauot, Secretary; (technical) Paia Ottawa, Technician. $1 helpful.

Radio Simbu, P.O. Box 228, Kundiawa, Chimbu, Papua New Guinea. Phone: +675 735-1038 or +675 735-1082. Fax: +675 735 1012. Contact: (general) Tony Mill Waine, Provincial Programme Manager; Felix Tsiki; or Thomas Ghiyandiule, Producer, "Pasikam Long ol Pipel"; (technical) Gabriel Paiao, Station Technician. Cassette recordings $5. Free two-Kina banknotes.

Radio Southern Highlands, P.O. Box 104, Mendi, SHP, Papua New Guinea. Phone: +675 549-1020 or +675 549-1137. Fax: +675 549 1017. Contact: (general) Andrew Meles, Programme Manager; Miriam Piapo, Programme Officer; Benard Kagaro, Programme Officer; Lucy Aluy, Programme Officer; or Nicholas Sambu, Producer, "Questions & Answers"; (technical) Ronald Helori, Station Technician. $1 or return postage helpful; or donate a wall poster of a rock band, singer or American landscape.

Radio United Bougainville, Public Awareness Campaign Unit, P.O. Box 268, Buka, Papua New Guinea. Reportedly funded by the Bougainville Transitional Government, this essentially official station has been established to counter the rebel station, "Radio Free Bougainville" (see under Disestablishmentarian).

Radio Western, P.O. Box 23, Daru, Western Province, Papua New Guinea. Contact: (technical) Samson Tobel, Technician. $1 or return postage required. Replies irregularly.

Radio Western Highlands, P.O. Box 311, Mount Hagen, WHP, Papua New Guinea. Contact: (technical) Esau Okole, Technician. $1 or return postage helpful. Replies occasionally.

Radio West New Britain, P.O. Box 412, Kimbe, WNBP, Papua New Guinea. Fax: +675 983 5600. Contact: Valuka Lowa, Provincial Station Manager; Lemeck Kuam, Producer, "Questions and Answers"; or Esekial Mael. Return postage required.

PARAGUAY World Time −3 (−4 midyear)

La Voz del Chaco Paraguayo, Filadelfia, Dpto. de Boquerón, Chaco, Paraguay. This station, currently only on mediumwave AM, hopes to add a world band transmitter within the 60-meter (5 MHz) band. However, to date nothing concrete has come of this.

Radio Encarnación, Gral. Artigas casi Gral. B. Caballero, Encarnación, Paraguay. Phone: (general) +595 (71) 4376 or +595 (71) 3345; (press) +595 (71) 4120. Fax: +595 (71) 4099. $1 or return postage helpful.

Radio Guairá, Alejo García y Presidente Franco, Villarrica, Paraguay. Phone: +595 (541) 2385 or +595 (541) 3411. Fax: +595 (541) 2130. Contact: (general) Lídice Rodríguez Vda. de Traversi, Propietaria; (technical) Enrique Traversi. Welcomes correspondence in Spanish. $1 or return postage helpful.

Radio Nacional, Blas Garay 241 entre Yegros e Iturbe, Asunción, Paraguay. Phone: +595 (21) 449-213. Fax: +595 (21) 332 750. Contact: Fermín Espínola, Director General. Free tourist brochure. $1 or return postage required. Replies, sometimes slowly, to correspondence in Spanish.

PERU World Time −5 year-round in Loreto, Cusco and Puno. Other departments sometimes move to World Time −4 for a few weeks of the year.

NOTE: Obtaining replies from Peruvian stations calls for creativity, tact, patience—and the proper use of Spanish, not form letters and the like. There are nearly 150 world band stations operating from Perú on any given day. While virtually all of these may be reached simply by using as the address the station's city, as given in the Blue Pages, the following are the only stations known to be replying—even if only occasionally—to correspondence from abroad.

Estación C, Casilla de Correo 210, Moyobamba, San Martín, Peru.

Estación Tarapoto (if reactivated), Jirón Federico Sánchez 720, Tarapoto, Peru. Phone: +51 (94) 522-709. Contact: Luis Humberto Hidalgo Sánchez, Gerente General; or José Luna Paima, Announcer. Replies occasionally to correspondence in Spanish.

Estación Wari, Calle Nazareno 108, Ayacucho, Peru. Contact: Walter Muñoz Ynga I., Gerente.

Estación X (Equis) (when operating), Jirón Mariscal Castilla s/n, Yurimaguas, Alto Amazonas, Peru.

Estación Yurimaguas (if reactivated), Plaza de Armas No. 106, Yurimaguas, Loreto, Peru. Contact: Franklin Coral Zousa, Director Propietario, who may also be
contacted at his home address: Jirón Mariscal Castilla No. 104, Yurimaguas, Loreto, Peru.

Frecuencia Líder (Radio Bambamarca), Jirón Jorge Chávez 416, Bambamarca, Hualgayoc, Cajamarca, Peru. Phone: (office) +51 (74) 713-260; (studio) +51 (74) 713-249.

Contact: (general) Valentín Peralta Díaz, Gerente; Irma Peralta Rojas; or Carlos Antonio Peralta Rojas; (technical) Oscar Lino Peralta Rojas. Free station photos. *La Historia de Bambamarca* book for 5 Soles; cassettes of Peruvian and Latin American folk music for 4 Soles each; T-shirts for 10 Soles each (sending US$1 per Sol should suffice and cover foreign postage costs, as well). Replies occasionally to correspondence in Spanish. Considering replacing their transmitter to improve reception.

Frecuencia San Ignacio, Jirón Villanueva Pinillos 330, San Ignacio, Cajamarca, Peru. Contact: Franklin R. Hoyos Cóndor, Director Gerente; Oscar Vásquez Chacón, Locutor; or Ignacio Gómez Torres, Técnico de Sonido. Replies to correspondence in Spanish. $1 or return postage necessary.

La Super Radio San Ignacio (when operating), Avenida Víctor Larco 104, a un costado del campo deportivo, San Ignacio, Distrito de Sinsicap, Provincia de Otuzco, La Libertad, Peru.

La Voz de la Selva—see Radio La Voz de la Selva.

La Voz de Celendín—see Radio Frecuencia VH, below.

La Voz de Sayapullo, Distrito de Sayapullo, Provincia de Cajabamba, Región Nor Oriental del Marañón, Peru.

La Voz del Marañon—see Radio La Voz del Marañon.

Onda Azul—see Radio Onda Azul, below.

Ondas del Suroriente—see Radio Ondas del Suroriente, below.

Radio Adventista Mundial—La Voz de la Esperanza, Jirón Dos de Mayo No. 218, Celendín, Cajamarca, Peru. Contact: Francisco Goicochea Ortiz, Director; or Lucas Solano Oyarce, Director de Ventas.

Radio Altura (Cerro de Pasco), Casilla de Correo 140, Cerro de Pasco, Pasco, Peru. Contact: Oswaldo de la Cruz Vásquez, Gerente General. Replies to correspondence in Spanish.

Radio Altura (Huarmaca), Antonio Raymondi 3ra Cuadra, Distrito de Huarmaca, Provincia de Huancabamba, Piura, Peru.

Radio Amauta, Jirón Manuel Iglesias s/n, a pocos pasos de la Plazuela San Juan, San Pablo, Cajamarca, Nor Oriental del Marañón, Peru.

Radio América, Montero Rosas 1099 Santa Beatriz, Lima, Peru. Phone: +51 (14) 728-985. Fax: +51 (14) 719 909. Contact: Liliana Sugobono F., Directora.

Radio Ancash, Casilla de Correo 210, Huaraz, Peru. Phone: +51 (44) 721-381. Contact: Armando Moreno Romero, Gerente General. Replies to correspondence in Spanish.

Radio Andahuaylas, Jr. Ayacucho No. 248, Andahuaylas, Apurímac, Peru. Contact: Sr. Daniel Andréu C., Gerente. $1 required. Replies irregularly to correspondence in Spanish.

Radio Apurímac (when operating), Jirón Cusco 206 (or Ovalo El Olivo No. 23), Abancay, Apurímac, Peru. Contact: Antero Quispe Allca, Director General.

Radio Atahualpa (when active), Plaza Bolognesi s/n, Cajamarca, Peru; or Valle Riestra 1432, Urb. Colmenares Puerto Libre, Peru. Contact: José Suárez Suárez, Gerente.

Radio Atlántida

STATION: Jirón Arica 441, Iquitos, Loreto, Peru. Phone: +51 (94) 23-2276. Contact: Pablo Rojas Bardales.

LISTENER CORRESPONDENCE: Sra. Carmela López Paredes, Producer, "Trocha Turística," Jirón Arica 1083, Iquitos, Loreto, Peru. Free pennants and tourist information. $1 or return postage required. Replies to most correspondence in Spanish, the preferred language, and some correspondence in English. "Trocha Turística" is a bilingual (Spanish and English) tourist program aired weekdays 2300-2330.

Radio Ayabaca, Jirón Comercio 437, Ayabaca, Huancabamba, Peru.

Radio Ayaviri (La Voz de Melgar), Apartado 8, Ayaviri, Puno, Peru. Fax: +51 (54) 32 02 07, specify on fax "Anexo 127." Contact: (general) Sra. Corina Llaiqui Ochoa, Administradora; (technical) José Aristo Solórzano Mendoza, Director. Free pennants. Sells audio cassettes of local folk

Radio stations in the small towns of Andean Peru are generally homemade affairs. However, their signs usually proclaim a far greater status. Currently inactive, Radio Celendin claimed to be "a wave of love, peace and culture."

music for $5 plus postage; also exchanges music cassettes. Correspondence accepted in English, but Spanish preferred.

Radio Bahía, Jirón Alfonso Ugarte 309, Chimbote, Ancash, Peru. Contact: Margarita Rossel Soria, Administradora; or Miruna Cruz Rossel, Administradora.

Radio Bambamarca—see Frecuencia Líder, above.

Radio Cajamarca, Jirón La Mar 675, Cajamarca, Peru. Phone: +51 (44) 921-014. Contact: Porfirio Cruz Potosí.

Radio Chanchamayo, Jirón Tarma 551, La Merced, Junín, Peru.

Radio Chaski, Baptist Mid-Missions, Apartado 368, Cusco, Peru.

Radio Chincheros, Jirón Apurímac s/n, Chincheros, Departamento de Apurímac, Peru.

Radio Chota, Apartado 3, Jirón Fernando Vega 690, Chota, Cajamarca, Peru. Contact: Aladino Gavadía Huamán, Administrador. $1 or return postage required. Replies slowly to correspondence in Spanish.

Radio 5264 (Cinco Mil Doscientos Sesenta y Cuatro) (if reactivated), Jirón Ricardo Palma s/n, Chiriaco, Provincia Bagua, Dpto. Amazonas, Peru.

Radio Concordia, Av. La Paz 512-A, Arequipa, Peru. Contact: Pedro Pablo Acosta Fernández. Free stickers. Return postage required.

Radio Continental, Av. Independencia 56, Arequipa, Peru. Contact: J. Antonio Umbart D., Director General; or Leonor Núñez Melgar. Free stickers. Replies slowly to correspondence in Spanish.

Radio CORA, Compañía Radiofónica Lima, S.A., Paseo de la República 144, Centro Cívico, Oficina 5, Lima 1, Peru. Fax: +51 (14) 336 134. Contact: (general) Juan Ramírez Lazo, Director Gerente; Dra. Lylian Ramírez M., Directora de Prensa y Programación; Juan Ramírez Lazo, Director Gerente; or Ms. Angelina María Abie; (technical) Srta. Sylvia Ramírez

M., Directora Técnica. Free station sticky-label pads, bumper stickers and may send large certificate suitable for framing. Audio cassettes with extracts from their programs $20 plus $2 postage; women's hair bands $2 plus $1 postage. Two IRCs or $1 required. Replies slowly to correspondence in English, Spanish, French, Italian and Portuguese.

Radio Cosmos (when active), Jirón San Martín 484, Celendín, Provincia de Celendín, Departamento de Cajamarca, Peru. Return postage required. Correspondence in Spanish preferred.

Radio Cultural Amauta, Apartado 24, Huanta, Peru. Phone: +51 (64) 932-153. Contact: Vicente Saico Tinco.

Radio Cusco, Apartado 251, Cusco, Peru. Phone: +51 (84) 225-0851. Fax: +51 (84) 223 308. Contact: Sra. Juana Huamán Yépez, Administradora; or Raúl Siú Almonte, Gerente General; (technical) Benjamín Yábar Alvarez. Free pennants, postcards and key rings. Audio cassettes of Peruvian music $10 plus postage. $1 or return postage required. Replies irregularly to correspondence in English or Spanish. Station is looking for folk music recordings from around the world to use in their programs.

Radio del Pacífico, Casilla de Correo 4236, Lima 1, Peru. Contact: J. Petronio Allauca, Secretario, Departamento de Relaciones Públicas; or P.G. Ferreyra. $1 or return postage required. Replies occasionally to correspondence in Spanish.

Radiodifusoras Huancabamba, Calle Unión 409, Huancabamba, Piura, Peru.

Radio El Sol (if reactivated), Avenida Uruguay 355, 7%, Lima Peru.

Radio El Sol de los Andes, Jirón 2 de Mayo 257, Juliaca, Peru. Phone: +51 (54) 321-115. Phone/fax: +51 (54) 322-981. Contact: Armando Alarcón Velarde.

Radio Estación Uno, Barrio Altos, Distrito de Pucará, Provincia Jaén, Nor Oriental del Marañón, Peru.

Radio Frecuencia VH (La Voz de Celendín), Jirón José Gálvez 730, Celendín, Cajamarca, Peru. Contact: Fernando Vásquez Castro, Propietario.

Radio Frecuencia San Ignacio—see Frecuencia San Ignacio.

Radio Gotas de Oro, Primero de Mayo 278, Urbanización Urrunaga, Distrito José Leonardo Ortiz, Chiclayo, Peru. Phone: +51 (74) 256-090. Contact: Plutarco Chamba Febres, Director Propietario; Juan Vargas, Administrador; or Filomena Saldívar, Pauta Comercial. Return postage required.

Radio Horizonte (Chachapoyas), Apartado 69 (or Jirón Santo Domingo 639), Chachapoyas, Amazonas, Peru. Phone: +51 (74) 757-793. Fax: +51 (74) 757 004. Contact: Sra. Rocío García Rubio, Ing. Electrónico, Directora. Replies to correspondence in English, French, German and Spanish. $1 required.

Radio Horizonte (Chiclayo), Calle Incanato 387, Distrito José Leonardo Ortiz, Chiclayo, Peru. Phone: +51 (74) 222-486. Return postage required.

Radio Huamachuco, Jirón Bolívar 937, Huamachuco, La Libertad, Peru. Contact: Manuel D. Gil Gil, Director Propietario.

Radio Huancabamba (when operating), Calle Unión 610-Barrio Chalaco, Huancabamba, Piura, Peru. Fax: +51 (74) 320 229, specifying "Radio Huancabamba" on fax. Contact: (general) Fredy Alberca, General Manager; (administration) Edwin Arrieta. Free picture postcards. Replies occasionally to correspondence in English, French, Italian, Portuguese and Spanish. Hopes to replace transmitter. Off the air since 1996 when manager César Colunche Bustamante moved to San Ignacio where he operated Radio Melodia (now off the air) and Radio San Ignacio (see).

Radio Huanta 2000, Jirón Gervacio Santillana 455, Huanta, Peru. Phone: +51 (64) 932-105. Contact: Ronaldo Sapaico Maravi, Departmento Técnico; or Sra. Lucila Orellana de Paz, Administradora. Free photo of staff. Return postage or $1 appreciated. Replies to correspondence in Spanish.

Radio Huarmaca, Av. Grau 454 (detrás de Inversiones La Loretana), Distrito de Huarmaca, Provincia de Huancabamba, Región Grau, Peru. Contact: Simón Zavaleta Pérez. Return postage helpful.

Radio Ilucán, Jirón Lima 290, Cutervo, Región Nororiental del Marañón, Peru. Phone: +51 (74) 220-205, Anexo 10. Contact: José Gálvez Salazar, Gerente Administrativo. $1 required. Replies occasionally to correspondence in Spanish, and seems to be friendly with Mr. Takayuki Inoue Nozaki.

Radio Imagen, Casilla de Correo 42, Tarapoto, San Martín, Peru; or Apartado 254, Tarapoto, San Martín, Peru. Contact: Adith Chumbe Vásquez, Secretaria; or Jaime Ríos Tapullima, Gerente General. Replies irregularly to correspondence in Spanish. $1 or return postage helpful.

Radio Inca del Perú (when active), Av. Manco Cápac No. 263, Baños del Inca, Cajamarca, Peru. Contact: Josué Gonzalo Urteaga V., Director Gerente. Replies slowly to correspondence in Spanish.

Radio Integración, Av. Seoane 200, Apartado Postal 57, Abancay, Departamento de Apurímac, Peru. Contact: Zenón Hernán Farfán Cruzado, Propietario.

Radio Internacional del Perú (when operating), Jirón Bolognesi 532, San Pablo, Cajamarca, Peru.

Radio Interoceánica, Provincia de Azángaro, Departamento de Puno, Peru.

Radio Jaén (La Voz de la Frontera), Calle Mariscal Castilla 439, Jaén, Cajamarca, Peru.

Radio Juliaca (La Decana), Apartado Postal 67, Juliaca, San Román, Puno, Peru. Contact: Alberto Quintanilla Ch., Director.

Radio JVL, Jirón Túpac Amaru 105, Consuelo, Distrito de San Pablo, Provincia de Bellavista, Departamento de San Martín, Peru. Contact: John Wiley Villanueva Lara, a student of electronic engineering, who currently runs the station.

Radio La Hora, Av. Garcilazo 180, Cusco, Peru. Contact: Edmundo Montesinos Gallo, Gerente General. Free stickers, pins, pennants and postcards of Cusco. Return postage required. Replies occasionally to correspondence in Spanish. Hopes to increase transmitter power if and when the economic situation improves.

Radio La Inmaculada, Parroquia La Inmaculada Concepción, Frente de la Plaza de Armas, Santa Cruz, Provincia de Santa Cruz, Departamento de Cajamarca, Peru. This station may have changed its name to Radio Santa Fé, see below.

Radio Lajas, Jirón Rosendo Mendívil 589, Lajas, Chota, Cajamarca, Nor Oriental del Marañón, Peru. Contact: Alfonso Medina Burga, Gerente Propietario.

Radio La Merced, Calle Bolognesi s/n, Distrito de Tongod, Provincia de Santa Cruz, Cajamarca, Peru. Contact: Roberto Ramos Llatas, Director Gerente. $1 or return postage required. Formerly replied irregularly to correspondence in Spanish, but currently there is no postal delivery to the area.

Radio La Oroya, Apartado Postal No. 88, La Oroya, Provincia de Yauli, Departamento de Junín, Peru. Contact: Jacinto Manuel Figueroa Yauri, Gerente-Propietario. Free pennants. $1 or return postage necessary. Replies to correspondence in Spanish.

Radio Latina (when active), Av. Sáenz Peña 1558, Chiclayo, Lambayeque, Peru. Phone: +51 (74) 233-140. Contact: Carlos Tipara González, Director General. Currently off the air due to the transmitter being sold to Radio Gotas de Oro (see above).

Radio La Voz de Cutervo (if reactivated), Jirón María Elena Medina 644-650, Cutervo, Cajamarca, Peru.

Radio La Voz de Huamanga (if reactivated), Calle El Nazareno, 2do Pasaje No. 161, Ayacucho, Peru. Phone: +51 (64) 912-366. Contact: Sra. Aguida A. Valverde Gonzales. Free pennants and postcards.

Radio La Voz de La Selva, Casilla de Correo 207, Iquitos, Loreto, Peru. Phone: +51 (94) 241-515. Fax: +51 (94) 239 360. Contact: Julia Jauregui Rengifo, Directora; Marcelino Esteban Benito, Director; Pedro Sandoval Guzmán, Announcer; or Mery Blas Rojas. Replies to correspondence in Spanish.

Radio La Voz de Oxapampa, Av. Mullenbruck 469, Oxapampa, Pasco, Peru. Contact: Pascual Villafranca Guzmán, Director Propietario.

Radio La Voz de San Antonio, Jirón Alfonso Ugarte 732, Bambamarca, Cajamarca, Peru. Contact: Valentín Mejía Vásquez, Director General; Mauricio Rodríguez R.; Wilmer Vásquez Campos, Encargado Administración; Walter Hugo Silva Bautista. $1 or return postage required. Replies to correspondence in Spanish.

Radio La Voz de Santa Cruz (if reactivated), Av. Zarumilla 190, Santa Cruz, Cajamarca, Peru.

Radio La Voz del Campesino (if operating), San Miguel de El Faique, Provincia de Huancabamba, Peru. Contact: Alberto Soto Santos, Director Propietario.

Radio La Voz del Marañón, Jirón Bolognesi 130, Barrio La Alameda, Cajamarca, Nor Oriental del Marañón, Peru. Contact: Eduardo Díaz Coronado.

Radio Libertad de Junín, Apartado 2, Junín, Peru. Contact: Mauro Chaccha G., Director Gerente. Replies slowly to correspondence in Spanish. Return postage necessary.

Radio Líder, Portal Belén 115, 2do piso, Cuzco, Peru. Contact: Mauro Calvo Acurio, Propietario.

Radio Lircay, Barrio Maravillas, Lircay, Provincia de Angaraes, Huancavelica, Peru.

Radio Los Andes, Damián Nicolau 108-110, 2do piso, Huamachuco, La Libertad, Peru.

Radio Los Andes, Huarmaca, Huancabamba, Grau, Peru. Contact: William Cerro Calderón.

Radio LTC (Radio Comercial Collao), Jirón Unión 242, Juliaca, Puno, Peru. Phone: +51 (54) 322-452 or +51 (54) 322-560. Fax: +51 (54) 322 570. Contact: Mario Leónidas Torres, Gerente General.

Radio Luz y Sonido
STATION: Jirón Dos de Mayo 1286, Oficina 310, Apartado

280, Huánuco, Peru. Phone: +51 (64) 512-394. Fax: +51 (64) 511 985. E-mail: luz.sonido@hys.com.pe. Contact: (technical) Jorge Benavides Moreno; (nontechnical) Lic. Orlando Bravo Jesús. Return postage or $1 required. Replies to correspondence in Spanish, Italian and Portuguese. Sells video cassettes of local folk dances and religious and tourist themes.

Radio Madre de Dios, Apartado 37, Puerto Maldonado, Madre de Dios, Peru. Phone: +51 (84) 571-050. Contact: Alcides Arguedas Márquez, Director del programa "Un Festival de Música Internacional," heard Mondays 0100 to 0200 World Time. Sr. Arguedas is interested in feedback for this letterbox program. Replies to correspondence in Spanish. $1 or return postage appreciated.

Radio Majestad, Calle Real 1033, Oficina 302, Huancayo, Junín, Peru.

Radio Marañón (if reactivated), Apartado 50, Jaén (via Chiclayo), Peru. Phone/fax: +51 (74) 731-147. Contact: Padre Luis Távara Martín, S.J., Director. Return postage necessary. May send free pennant. Replies slowly to correspondence in Spanish.

Radio Máster, Jirón 20 de Abril 308, Moyobamba, Departamento de San Martín, Peru.

Radio Melodía, San Camilo 501, Arequipa, Peru.

Radio Melodía (if reactivated), Calle Comercio 140, San Ignacio, Región Nororiental del Marañón, Peru. Contact: César Colunche Bustamante at Radio San Ignacio address, see below.

Radio Mi Frontera, Calle San Ignacio 520, Distrito de Chirinos, Provincia de San Ignacio, Región Nor Oriental del Marañón, Peru.

Radio Mundial Adventista, Colegio Adventista de Titicaca, Casilla 4, Juliaca, Peru.

Radio Mundo, Calle Tecte 245, Cusco, Peru. Phone: + 51 (84) 232-076. Fax: +51 (84) 233 076. Contact: Valentín Olivera Puelles, Gerente. Free postcards and stickers. Return postage necessary. Replies slowly to correspondence in Spanish.

Radio Municipal de Cangallo (when active), Concejo Provincial de Cangallo, Plaza Principal No. 02, Cangallo, Ayacucho, Peru. Contact: Nivardo Barbarán Agüero, Encargado Relaciones Públicas.

Radio Nacional del Perú
ADMINISTRATIVE OFFICE: Avenida José Gálvez 1040 Santa Beatriz, Lima, Peru. Fax: +51 (14) 726 799. Contact: Henry Aragón Ybarra, Gerente; or Rafael Mego Carrascal, Jefatura de la Administración. Replies occasionally, by letter or listener-prepared verification card, to correspondence in Spanish. Return postage necessary.
STUDIO ADDRESS: Av. Petit Thouars 447, Lima, Peru.

Radio Naylamp, Avenida Huamachuco 1080, 2ᵈᵒ piso, Lambayeque, Peru. Phone: +51 (74) 283-353. Contact: Dr. Juan José Grández Vargas, Director Gerente; or Delicia Coronel Muñoz, who is interested in receiving postcards and the like. Feedback for Dr. J.J.'s weeknightly program "Buenas Tardes, Ecuador," from 0000 to 0100 World Time, appreciated. Free stickers, pennants and calendars. Return postage necessary.

Radio Nor Andina, Jirón José Gálvez 602, Celendín, Cajamarca, Peru. Contact: Misael Alcántara Guevara, Gerente; or Víctor B. Vargas C., Departamento de Prensa. Free calendar. $1 required. Donations (registered mail best) sought for the Committee for Good Health for Children, headed by Sr. Alcántara, which is active in saving the lives of hungry youngsters in poverty-stricken Cajamarca Province. Replies irregularly to casual or technical correspondence in Spanish, but regularly to Children's Committee donors and helpful correspondence in Spanish.

Radio Nor Peruana, Emisora Municipal (when active), Jirón Ortiz Arrieta 588, 2ᵈᵒ piso, Chachapoyas, Amazonas, Peru. Phone: +51 (44) 981-027. Contact: Fernando Serván Rocha, Director. Replies very slowly to correspondence in Spanish. Return postage necessary.

Radio Onda Azul (if reactivated), Apartado 210, Puno, Peru. Phone: +51 (54) 351-562. Fax: +51 (54) 352 233. Contact: (general) Mauricio Rodríguez R., Jefe de Producción y Programación; (technical) Marino Rojas Olazabal, Administrador. Free key rings, calendars and diaries. Return postage required. Replies to correspondence in Spanish.

Radio Onda Imperial, Calle Sacsayhuanan K-10, Urbanización Manuel Prado, Cusco, Peru.

Radio Ondas del Huallaga, Apartado 343, Jirón Leoncio Prado 723, Huánuco, Peru. Phone: +51 (84) 512-428. Contact: Flaviano Llanos Malpartida, Representante Legal. $1 or return postage required. Replies to correspondence in Spanish.

Radio Ondas del Río Marañón, Distrito de Aramango, Provincia de Bagua, Departamento de Amazonas, Región Nororiental del Marañón, Peru.

Radio Ondas del Río Mayo, Jirón Huallaga 348, Nueva Cajamarca, San Martín, Peru. Phone: +51 (94) 556-006. Contact: Edilberto Lucío Peralta Lozada, Gerente; or Víctor Huaras Rojas, Locutor. Free pennants. Return postage helpful. Replies slowly to correspondence in Spanish.

Radio Ondas del Suroriente, Jirón Ricardo Palma 510, Quillabamba, La Convención, Cusco, Peru.

Radio Oriente, Vicariato Apostólico, Calle Progreso 114, Yurimaguas, Loreto, Peru. Phone: +51 (94) 352-156. Phone/fax (ask to switch over to fax): +51 (94) 352-566. Contact: (general) Sra. Elisa Cancino Hidalgo; or Juan Antonio López-Manzanares M., Director; (technical) Pedro Capo Moragues, Gerente Técnico. $1 or return postage required. Replies occasionally to correspondence in English, French, Spanish and Catalan.

Radio Origen, Avenida Augusto B. Leguía 196, Huancavelica, Peru. Contact: Oscar Andrez Alvarado Yalico, Director General y Propietario. $1 or return postage required. Replies occasionally to correspondence in Spanish.

Radio Paccha (if reactivated), Calle Mariscal Castilla 52, Paccha, Provincia de Chota, Departamento de Cajamarca, Peru.

Radio Paucartambo, Jirón Conde de las Lagunas, 2ᵈᵒ piso, Frente al Hostal San José, Paucartambo, Pasco, Peru. Contact: Irwin Junio Berrios Pariona, Gerente General. Replies occasionally to correspondence in Spanish.

Radio Paucartambo, Emisora Municipal
STATION ADDRESS: Paucartambo, Cusco, Peru.
STAFFER ADDRESS: Manuel H. Loaiza Canal, Correo Central, Paucartambo, Cusco, Peru. Sr. Loaiza, who hosts the weeknightly music show, "El Bus Musical," heard from 2300-2400 World Time, seeks feedback on the program. Return postage or $1 required.

Radio Perú, Jirón Atahualpa 191, San Ignacio, Región Nororiental del Marañón, Peru. Contact: Oscar Vásquez Chacón, Director General; or Idelfo Vásquez Chacón, Director Propietario.

Radio Quillabamba, Apartado 76, Quillabamba, La Convención, Cusco, Peru. Contact: Padre Francisco Panera, Director. Replies very irregularly to correspondence in Spanish.

Radio Reina de la Selva, Jirón Ayacucho 944, Plaza de Armas, Chachapoyas, Región Nor Oriental del Marañón, Peru. Contact: José David Reina Noriega, Gerente General; or Jorge Oscar Reina Noriega, Director General. Replies irregularly to correspondence in Spanish. Return postage necessary.

Radio San Francisco Solano, Parroquia de Sóndor, Calle San Miguel No. 207, Distrito de Sóndor, Huancabamba, Piura, Peru. Contact: Padre Manuel J. Rosas C., Vicario Parroquial. Station operated by the Franciscan Fathers. Replies to correspondence in Spanish. $1 helpful.

Radio San Ignacio (La Voz de la Frontera), Jirón Mercado 218, San Ignacio, Cajamarca, Peru. Contact: Pedro Alfonso Morales y Sáenz, Director General; César Colunche Bustamante; or Dr. Daniel Carrillo Mendoza, Asesor legal y jurídico. This station was sold to Colunche Bustamante late 1996. Also, see next entry.

Radio San Ignacio (La Voz de la Peruanidad), Jirón Santa Rosa 751, San Ignacio, Región Nororiental del Marañon, Peru. Phone/fax (via Evaristo Campos): +51 (74) 716-238. Contact: César Colunche Bustamante, Director Propietario; or Fredy Colunche.

Radio San Juan (if reactivated), Pasaje San Martín 300, Urbanización Alto Mochica, Trujillo, Peru. Phone: +51 (44) 263-592. Contact: Santiago López Valderrama, Gerente.

Radio San Juan, Distrito de Aramango, Provincia de Bagua, Departamento de Amazonas, Región Nororiental del Marañón, Peru.

Radio San Juan, 28 de Julio 420, Lonya Grande, Provincia de Utcubamba, Región Nororiental del Marañón, Peru. Contact: Prof. Víctor Hugo Díaz Hidrovo; or Edilberto Ortiz Chávez, Locutor.

Radio San Martín (when active), Jirón Progreso 225, Tarapoto, San Martín, Peru. Contact: Fernando Tafur Arévalo, Gerente General. May send stickers and magazines. Return postage required. Replies occasionally to correspondence in Spanish.

Radio San Miguel de El Faique, Distrito de El Faique, Provincia de Huancabamba, Departamento de Piura, Peru.

Radio San Nicolás, Jirón Amazonas 114, Rodríguez de Mendoza, Peru. Contact: Juan José Grández Santillán, Gerente; or Violeta Grández Vargas, Administradora. Return postage necessary.

Radio San Miguel, Av. Huayna Cápac 146, Huánchac, Cusco, Peru. Contact: Sra. Catalina Pérez de Alencastre, Gerente General; or Margarita Mercado. Replies to correspondence in Spanish.

Radio San Miguel Arcángel, Jirón Grau 493, San Miguel de Pallaques, Cajamarca, Peru.

Radio Santa Fé, Parroquia La Inmaculada Concepción, Frente de la Plaza de Armas, Santa Cruz, Provincia de Santa Cruz, Departamento de Cajamarca, Peru.

Radio Santa Rosa, Casilla 4451, Lima 1, Peru. Phone: +51 (14) 277-488. Fax: +51 (14) 276 791. Contact: Padre Juan Sokolich Alvarado; or Lucy Palma Barreda. Free stickers and pennants. $1 or return postage necessary. 180-page book commemorating station's 35th anniversary $10. Replies to correspondence in Spanish.

Radio Satélite E.U.C., Jirón Cutervo No. 543, Cajamarca, Santa Cruz, Peru. Contact: Sabino Llamo Chávez, Gerente. Free tourist brochure. $1 or return postage required. Replies irregularly to correspondence in Spanish.

Radio Sicuani, Jirón 2 de Mayo 206, Sicuani, Canchis, Cusco, Peru; or P.O. Box 45, Sicuani, Peru. Contact: Mario Ochoa Vargas, Director.

Radio Soledad, Centro Minero de Retama, Distrito de Parcoy, Provincia de Pataz, La Libertad, Peru. Contact: Vicente Valdivieso, Locutor. Return postage necessary.

Radio Sudamérica, Jirón Ramón Castilla 704, 2º piso, Cutervo, Cajamarca, Peru. Contact: Jorge Paredes Guerra, Administrador; or Amadeo Mario Muñoz Guivar, Propietario.

Radio Tacna, Casilla de Correo 370, Tacna, Peru. Phone: +51 (54) 714-871.Fax: +51 (54) 723 745. E-mail: radiotac@principal.unjbg.edu.pe. URL: http://principal.unjbg.edu.pe/radio/radta.htm. Contact: (nontechnical and technical) Ing. Alfonso Cáceres Contreras, Sub-Gerente/Jefe Técnico; (administration) Yolanda Vda. de Cáceres C., Directora Gerente. Free stickers and samples of Correo local newspaper. $1 or return postage helpful. Audio cassettes of Peruvian and other music $2 plus postage. Replies irregularly to correspondence in English and Spanish.

Radio Tarma, Casilla de Correo 167, Tarma, Peru. Contact: Mario Monteverde Pumareda, Gerente General. Sometimes sends 100 Inti banknote in return when $1 enclosed. Free stickers. $1 or return postage required. Replies irregularly to correspondence in Spanish.

Radio Tayacaja, Correo Central, Distrito de Pampas,

Tayacaja, Huancavelica, Peru. Phone: +51 (64) 22-02-17, Anexo 238. Contact: (general) J. Jorge Flores Cárdenas; (technical) Ing. Larry Guido Flores Lezama. Free stickers and pennants. Replies to correspondence in Spanish. Hopes to replace transmitter.

Radio Tingo María, Jirón Callao 115 (or Av. Raimondi No. 592), Casilla de Correo 25, Tingo María, Leoncio Prado, Peru. Contact: Gina A. de la Cruz Ricalde, Administradora; or Ricardo Abad Vásquez, Gerente. Free brochures. $1 required. Replies slowly to correspondence in Spanish.

Radio Tropical, S.A., Casilla de Correo 31, Tarapoto, Peru. Fax: +51 (94) 522 155. Contact: Mery A. Rengifo Tenazoa; or Luis F. Mori Roatogui, Gerente. Free stickers, occasionally free pennants, and station history booklet. $1 or return postage required. Replies occasionally to correspondence in Spanish.

Radio Unión, Apartado 833, Lima 27, Peru. Phone: +51 (14) 408-657. Fax: +51 (14) 407 594. E-mail: runion@amauta.rcp.net.pe. Contact: Juan Zubiaga S., Gerente; or Juan Carlos Sologuren, Dpto. de Administración, who collects stamps. Free satin pennants and stickers. IRC required, and enclosing used or new stamps from various countries is especially appreciated. Replies irregularly to correspondence and tape recordings, especially from young women, with Spanish preferred.

Radio Victoria, Reynel 320, Mirones Bajo, Lima 1, Peru. Fax: +51 (14) 427 1195. Contact: Marta Flores Ushinahua. This station is owned by the Brazilian-run Pentecostal Church "Dios Es Amor." Their program "La Voz de la Liberación" is produced locally and aired over numerous Peruvian shortwave stations.

Radio Villa Rica

GENERAL CORRESPONDENCE: Jirón Virrey Toledo 544, Huancavelica, Peru. Contact: Srta. Maritza Pozo Manrique. Free informative pamphlets. Local storybooks and poems from Huancavelica $15; cassettes of Peruvian and Andean regional music $20; also sells cloth and wooden folk articles. Replies occasionally to correspondence in Spanish.

TECHNICAL CORRESPONDENCE: Apartado 92, Huancavelica, Peru. Contact: Fidel Hilario Huamani, Director. $3 required in return postage for a reply to a reception report from abroad.

Radio Visión 2000 (when active), Radiodifusora Comercial Visión 2000, Jirón Prolongación Mariscal Sucre s/n, Bambamarca, Hualgayoc, Cajamacra, Peru. Contact: Víctor Marino Tello Cruzado, Propietario. Return postage required. Replies slowly to correspondence in Spanish.

PHILIPPINES World Time +8

NOTE: Philippine stations sometimes send publications with lists of Philippine young ladies seeking "pen pal" courtships.

DZRM—Philippine Broadcasting Service (when operating), Bureau of Broadcasting Services, Media Center, Bohol Avenue, Quezon City, Philippines.

☞Far East Broadcasting Company—FEBC Radio International (External Service)

MAIN OFFICE: P.O. Box 1, Valenzuela, Metro Manila, Philippines 0560. Phone: +63 (2) 292-5603, or +63 (2) 292-9403. Fax: +63 (2) 292 9430, but lacks funds to provide faxed replies. E-mail: febcomphil@febc.jmf.org.ph; or ieoffice@febc.org.ph; (English Department) english@febc.jmf.org.ph; (Peter McIntyre, Host "DX Dial") dx@febc.jmf.org.ph or pm@febc.jfm.org.ph; (Jane Colley) jane@febc.jmf.org.ph; (Roger Foyle) foyle@febc.jmf.org.ph; (Mrs. Fay Olympia) alvarez@febc.jmf.org.ph; (Christine Johnson) cjohnson@febc.jmf.org.ph; (Larry Podmore) lpodmore@febc.jmf.org.ph. URL: www.febc.org/. (For some really exotic musical clips, visit the station's RealAudio page: www.febc.org/music.html.) Contact: (general) Peter McIntyre, Manager, International Operations Division & Producer, "DX Dial"; Jane Colley, Head, Audience Relations; Roger P. Foyle, Audience Relations Counsellor & Acting DX Secretary; Ella McIntyre, Pro-

FEBC

What appears to be the Paris of Ernest Hemingway is actually today's Majayjay in the Philippines' Laguna Province.

ducer, "Mailbag" and "Let's Hear from You"; Fay Olympia, English Programme Supervisor; Ms. Madini Tluanga, Producer, "Good Morning from Manila"; Christine D. Johnson, Head, Overseas English Service; or David Miller, Chief News Editor, FEB-News Bureau; (administration) Carlos Peña, Managing Director; (engineering) Ing. Renato Valentin, Frequency Manager; Larry Podmore, IBG Chief Engineer. Free stickers, calendar cards and DX Club Registration. Three IRCs appreciated for airmail reply. Plans to add a new 100 kW shortwave transmitter.

NEW DELHI BUREAU, NONTECHNICAL: c/o FEBA, Box 6, New Delhi-110 001, India.

Far East Broadcasting Company (Domestic Service), Bgy. Bayanan Baco Radyo DZB2, c/o ONF Calapan, Orr. Mindoro, Philippines 5200. Contact: (general) Dangio Onday, Program Supervisor/OIC; (technical) Danilo Flores, Broadcast Technician.

Radyo Pilipinas, the Voice of Democracy, Philippine Broadcasting Service, 4th Floor, PIA Building, Visayas Avenue, Quezon City 1100, Metro Manila, Philippines. Phone: (general) +63 (2) 924-2620; +63 (2) 920-3963; or +63 (2) 924-2548; (engineering) +63 (2) 924-2268. Fax: +63 (2) 924 2745. Contact: (nontechnical) Evelyn Salvador Agato, Officer-in-Charge; Mercy Lumba; Leo Romano, Producer, "Listeners and Friends"; or Richard Lorenzo, Production Coordinator; (technical) Danilo Alberto, Supervisor; or Mike Pangilinan, Engineer. Free postcards & stickers.

Radio Veritas Asia

STUDIOS AND ADMINISTRATIVE HEADQUARTERS: P.O. Box 2642, Quezon City, Philippines 1166. Phone: +63 (2) 939-0011/12/13/14, +63 (2) 939-4465, +63 (2) 939-4692, +63 (2) 939-7121 or +63 (2) 939-7476. Fax: (general) +63 (2) 907 436 or +63 (2) 938 1940; (Frequency and Monitoring) +63 (2) 939 7556.

E-mail: veritas@mnl.sequel.net. URL: www.catholic.org.tw/vntaiwan/veritas/. Contact: (administration) Ms. Erlinda G. So, Manager; or Alejandro Limoanco, Admin. Director; (general) Ms. Cleofe R. Labindao, Audience Relations Supervisor; or Msgr. Pietro Nguyen Van Tai, Program Director; (technical) Ing. Floremundo L. Kiguchi, Technical Director; Ing. Honorio Llavore, Assistant Technical Director; or Frequency and Monitoring Department. Free caps, T-shirts, stickers, pennants, rulers, pens, postcards and calendars.

TRANSMITTER SITE: Radio Veritas Asia, Palauig, Zambales, Philippines. Contact: Fr. Hugo Delbaere, CICM, Technical Consultant.

BRUSSELS BUREAUS AND MAIL DROPS: Catholic Radio and Television Network, 32-34 Rue de l' Association, B-1000 Brussels, Belgium; or UNDA, 12 Rue de l'Orme, B-1040 Brussels, Belgium.

Voice of America/VOA-IBB—Poro and Tinang Relay Stations. Phone: +63 (2) 813-0470/1/2. Fax: +63 (2) 813 0469. Contact: Frank Smith, Manager; or David Strawman, Deputy Manager. These numbers for urgent technical matters only. Otherwise, does not welcome direct correspondence; *see* USA for acceptable VOA Washington address and related information.

PIRATE

Pirate radio stations are usually one-person operations airing home-brew entertainment and/or iconoclastic viewpoints. In order to avoid detection by the authorities, they tend to appear irregularly, with little concern for the niceties of conventional program scheduling. Most are found in Europe chiefly on weekends, and mainly during evenings in North America, often just above 6200 kHz, just below 7000 kHz and just above 7375 kHz. These *sub rosa* stations and their addresses are subject to unusually abrupt change or termination, sometimes as a result of forays by radio authorities.

Two worthy sources of current addresses and other information on American pirate radio activity are: *The Pirate Radio Directory*, by Andrew Yoder and George Zeller [Tiare Publications, P.O. Box 493, Lake Geneva WI 53147 USA, U.S. toll-free phone 1-800-420-0579; or for specific inquiries, contact author Zeller directly: (fax) +1 (216) 696 0770; (e-mail) George.Zeller@acclink.com], an excellent annual reference; and A*C*E, P.O. Box 12112, Norfolk VA 23541 USA (e-mail: pradio@erols.com; URL: www.frn.net/ace/), a club which publishes a periodical ($20/year U.S., US$21 Canada, $27 elsewhere) for serious pirate radio enthusiasts.

A show on a specialized form of American pirate activity—low-powered local (usually FM) stations—is "Micro-Power Radio in the U.S.," aired over Radio for Peace International, Costa Rica, some Mondays at 2130 and some Thursdays at 2200 World Time on 6200 or 7385 kHz, plus 15050 kHz. For further information, send an e-mail message to: sues@ricochet.net; or paul_w_griffin@bmug.org.
For Europirate DX news, try:
SRSNEWS, Swedish Report Service, Ostra Porten 29, SE-442 54 Ytterby, Sweden. E-mail: srs@ice.warp.slink.se. URL: www-pp.kdt.net/jonny/index.html.
Pirate Connection, P.O. Box 4580, SE-203 20 Malmoe, Sweden; or P.O. Box 7085, Kansas City, Missouri 64113, USA. Phone: (home, Sweden) +46 (40) 611-1775; (mobile, Sweden) +46 (70) 581-5047. E-mail: etoxspz@eto.ericsson.se, xtdspz@lmd.ericsson.se or spz@exallon.se. URL: www-pp.hogia.net/jonny/pc. Six issues annually for about $23. Related to SRSNEWS, above.
Pirate Chat, 21 Green Park, Bath, Avon, BA1 1HZ, United Kingdom.
FRS Goes DX, P.O. Box 2727, NL-6049 ZG Herten, Holland. E-mail: FRSH@pi.net; or peter.verbruggen@tip.nl. URL: http://home.pi.net/~freak55/home.htm.
Free-DX, 3 Greenway, Harold Park, Romford, Essex, RM3 0HH, United Kingdom.
FRC-Finland, P.O. Box 82, FIN-40101 Jyvaskyla, Finland.
Pirate Express, Postfach 220342, Wuppertal, Germany.
A regularly updated list of addresses for European "Free Radio" stations can be found at the URL: www.club.innet.be/~ind1570/freerad.htm.
For up-to-date listener discussions and other pirate-radio information on the Internet, the usenet URLs are: alt.radio.pirate and rec.radio.pirate.

POLAND World Time +1 (+2 midyear)
Radio Maryja, ul. Żwirki i Wigury 80, PL-87-100 Toruń, Poland. Phone: +48 (56) 655-2361. Fax: +48 (56) 655 2362. URL: www.man.torun.pl/RadioMaryja/index.htm. Contact: Tadeusz Rydzk, Dyrektor. Replies to correspondence in Polish. Transmits via the facilities of the Voice of Russia.
📻Polish Radio Warsaw
STATION: External Service, P.O. Box 46, PL-00-977 Warsaw, Poland. Phone: (general) +48 (22) 645-9305 or +48 (22) 444-123; (English Section) +48 (22) 645-9262; (German Section) +48 (22) 645-9333; (placement liaison) +48 (2) 645-9002. Fax: (general and administration) +48 (22) 645 5917 or +48 (22) 645 5919; (placement liaison) +48 (2) 645 5906. E-mail (general): piatka@radio.com.pl; (English Section) rafalk@radio.com.pl; (Polskie Radio parent organization) polskie.radio@radio.com.pl. URLs: (RealAudio in English and Polish) www.wrn.org/stations/poland.html; (text in Polish) http://apollo.radio.com.pl/piatka/; (Polish Radio parent organization) http://apollo.com.pl/. Contact: (general) Rafał Kiepuszewski, Head, English Section & Producer, "Postbag"; or Ann Plapan, Corresponding Secretary; (administration) Jerzy M. Nowakowski, Managing Director; Bogumila Berdychowska, Deputy Director; or Maciej Lętowski, Executive Manager. Free stickers, pens, key rings and possibly T-shirts. DX Listeners' Club.

TRANSMISSION AUTHORITY: PAR (National Radiocommunication Agency), ul. Kasprzaka 18/20, PL-01-211 Warsaw, Poland. Phone: +48 (22) 658-5140. Fax: +48 (22) 658 5175. E-mail: (Grodzicka) z.wizimirski@par.gov.pl; (Trzos) ltrzos@ire.pw.edu.pl. Contact: Ms. Filomena Grodzicka, Head of BC Section; Lukasz Trzos; Ms. Urszula Rzepa or Jan Kondej.

PORTUGAL World Time exactly (+1 midyear); Azores World Time –1 (World Time midyear)
RDP Internacional—Rádio Portugal, Box 1011, P-1001 Lisbon, Portugal. Phone: (main office) +351 (1) 347-5065/8; (engineering) +351 (1) 387-1109. Fax: (main office) +351 (1) 347 4475; (engineering) +351 (1) 387 1381. URL: www.rdp.pt/. Contact: (general) "Listeners' Mailbag," English Service; or Arlindo de Carvalho; (administration) José Manuel Nunes, Chairman; (technical) Winnie Almeida, English Section; Eng. Francisco Mascarenhas; or Rui de Jesús, Frequency Manager. Free stickers, paper pennants and calendars. May send literature from the Portuguese National Tourist Office.
Rádio Renascença, Rua Ivens 14, P-1294 Lisbon Codex, Portugal. Phone: +351 (1) 347-5270. Fax: +351 (1) 342 2658. Contact: C. Pabil, Director-Manager.
Radio Trans Europe (transmission facilities), 6º esq., Rua Braamcamp 84, P-1200 Lisbon, Portugal. E-mail: boydw@rte.ie. Transmitter located at Sines.
Voice of Orthodoxy—see Belarus.

QATAR World Time +3
Qatar Broadcasting Service, P.O. Box 3939, Doha, Qatar. Phone: (director) +974 86-48-05; (under secretary) +974 86-48-23; (engineering) +974 86-45-18; (main Arabic service audio feed) +974 895-895. Fax: +974 82 28 88 or +974 83 14 47. Contact: Jassem Mohamed Al-Qattan, Head of Public Relations. May send booklet on Qatar Broadcasting Service. Rarely replies, but return postage helpful.

ROMANIA World Time +2 (+3 midyear)
📻Radio România International
STATION: P.O. Box 111, R-70756 Bucharest, Romania; or Romanian embassies worldwide. Phone: (general) +40 (1) 312-3645; (English Department) +40 (1) 617-2856; (engineering) +40 (1) 312-1057. Fax: (general) +40 (1) 223 2613 [if no connection, try via office of the Director General of Radio România, but mark fax "Pentru RRI"; that fax is +40 (1) 222 5641]; (Engineering Services) +40 (1) 312 1056/7 or +40 (1) 615 6992. E-mail: rri@radio.ror.ro; (Nisipeanu) emisie@radio.ror.ro. URL: (general) http://indis.ici.ro/romania/news/rri.html; (RealAudio in English) www.wrn.org/stations/romania/html. Contact: (communications in English, Romanian or German) Frederica Dochinoiu; or Dan Balamat, "Listeners' Letterbox"; (radio enthusiasts' issues, English only) "DX Mailbag," English Department; (communications in French or Romanian) Doru Vasile Ionescu, Director; (technical) Ms. Sorin Floricu, Radu Ianculescu or Marius Nisipeanu, Engineering Services. Free stickers, pennants, posters, pins and assorted other items. Can provide supplementary materials for "Romanian by Radio" course on audio cassettes. Listeners' Club. Annual contests. Replies slowly but regularly. Concerns about frequency management should be directed to the PTT (see below), with copies to the Romanian Autonomous Company (see farther below) and to a suitable official at RRI.
TRANSMISSION AND FREQUENCY MANAGEMENT, PTT: General Directorate of Regulations, Ministry of Communications, 14a Al. Libertatii, R-70060 Bucharest, Romania. Phone: +40 (1) 400-1060. Fax: +40 (1) 400 1230. Contact: Mrs. Elena Danila, Head of Frequency Management Department.
TRANSMISSION AND FREQUENCY MANAGEMENT, AUTONOMOUS COMPANY: Romanian Autonomous Company for Radio Communications, 14a Al. Libertatii, R-70060 Bucharest, Romania. Phone: +40 (1) 400-1072. Fax: +40 (1) 400 1228. Contact: Mr. Marian Ionita.

RUSSIA (Times given for republics, oblasts and krays):
- World Time +2 (+3 midyear) Kaliningradskaya;
- World Time +3 (+4 midyear) Arkhangel'skaya (incl. Nenetskiy), Astrakhanskaya, Belgorodskaya, Bryanskaya, Ivanovskaya, Kaluzhskaya, Karelia, Kirovskaya, Komi, Kostromskaya, Kurskaya, Lipetskaya, Moscovskaya, Murmanskaya, Nizhegorodskaya, Novgorodskaya, Orlovskaya, Penzenskaya, Pskovskaya, Riazanskaya, Samarskaya, Sankt-Peterburgskaya, Smolenskaya, Tambovskaya, Tulskaya, Tverskaya, Vladimirskaya, Vologodskaya, Volgogradskaya, Voronezhskaya, Yaroslavskaya;
- World Time +4 (+5 midyear) Checheno-Ingushia, Chuvashia, Dagestan, Kabardino-Balkaria, Kalmykia, Krasnodarskiy, Mari-Yel, Mordovia, Severnaya Osetia, Stavropolskiy, Tatarstan, Udmurtia;
- World Time +5 (+6 midyear) Bashkortostan, Chelyabinskaya, Kurganskaya, Orenburgskaya, Permskaya, Yekaterinburgskaya, Tyumenskaya;
- World Time +6 (+7 midyear) Altayskiy, Omskaya;
- World Time +7 (+8 midyear) Kemerovskaya, Krasnoyarskiy (incl. Evenkiyskiy), Novosibirskaya, Tomskaya, Tuva;
- World Time +8 (+9 midyear) Buryatia, Irkutskaya;
- World Time +9 (+10 midyear) Amurskaya, Chitinskaya, Sakha (West);
- World Time +10 (+11 midyear) Khabarovskiy, Primorskiy, Sakha (Center), Yevreyskaya;
- World Time +11 (+12 midyear) Magadanskaya (exc. Chukotskiy), Sakha (East), Sakhalinskaya;
- World Time +12 (+13 midyear) Chukotskiy, Kamchatskaya, Koryakskiy;
- World Time +13 (+14 midyear) all points east of longtitude 172.30 E.

WARNING—MAIL THEFT: Airmail correspondence containing funds or IRCs from North America and Japan may not arrive safely even if sent by registered air mail, as such mail enters via Moscow Airport. However, funds sent from Europe, North America and Japan via surface mail enter via St. Petersburg, and thus stand a better chance of arriving safely. Airmail service is otherwise now almost on a par with that of other advanced countries.

VERIFICATION OF STATIONS USING TRANSMITTERS IN ST. PETERSBURG AND KALININGRAD: Transmissions of certain world band stations—such as the Voice of Russia, Mayak and China Radio International—when emanating from transmitters located in St. Petersburg and Kaliningrad, may be verified directly from: World Band Verification QSL Service, The State Enterprise for Broadcasting and Radio Communications No. 2 (GPR-2), ul. Akademika Pavlova 13A, 197376 St. Petersburg, Russia. Fax: +7 (812) 234 2971 during working hours. Contact: Mikhail V. Sergeyev, Chief Engineer; or Mikhail Timofeyev, verifier. Free stickers. Two IRCs required for a reply, which upon request includes a copy of "Broadcast Schedule," which gives transmission details (excluding powers) for all transmissions emanating from three distinct transmitter locations: Kaliningrad-Bolshakovo, St. Petersburg and St. Petersburg-Popovka. This organization—which has 26 shortwave, three longwave, 15 mediumwave AM and nine FM transmitters—relays broadcasts for clients for the equivalent of about $0.70–1.00 per kW/hour.

Government Radio Agencies

C.I.S. FREQUENCY MANAGEMENT ENGINEERING OFFICE: The Main Centre for Control of Broadcasting Networks, ul. Nikolskaya 7, 103012 Moscow, Russia. Phone: +7 (095) 298-3302. Fax: +7 (095) 956 7546 or +7 (095) 921 1624. E-mail: (Titov) titov@mccbn.ru. Contact: (general) Mrs. Antonia Ostakhova or Ms. Margarita Ovetchkina; (administration) Anatoliy T. Titov, Chief Director. This office plans the frequency usage for transmitters throughout much of the C.I.S. Correspondence should be concerned only with significant technical observations or engineering suggestions concerning frequency management improvement—not regular requests for verifications. Correspondence in Russian preferred, but English accepted.

STATE ENTERPRISE FOR BROADCASTING AND RADIO COMMUNICATIONS NO. 2 (GPR-2)—see VERIFICATION OF STATIONS USING TRANSMITTERS IN ST. PETERSBURG AND KALININGRAD, above.

STATE RADIO COMPANY: AS "Radioagency Co., Pyatnitskaya 25, 113326 Moscow, Russia. Phone: (Khlebnikov and Petrunicheva) +7 (095) 233-6474; (Komissarova) +7 (095) 233-6660; (Staviskaia) +7 (095) 233-7003. Fax: (Khlebnikov, Petrunicheva and Komissarova) +7 (095) 233 1342; (Staviskaia) +7 (095) 230 2828 or +7 (095) 233 7648. Contact: Valentin Khlebnikov, Mrs. Maris Petrunicheva, Mrs. Lyudmila Komissarova or Mrs. Rachel Staviskaia.

STATE TRANSMISSION AUTHORITY: Russian Ministry of Telecommunication, ul. Tverskaya 7, 103375 Moscow, Russia. Phone: +7 (095) 201-6568. Fax: +7 (095) 292 7086 or +7 (095) 292 7128. Contact: Anatoly C. Batiouchkine.

STATE TV AND RADIO COMPANY: Russian State TV & Radio Company, ul. Yamskogo 5, Polya 19/21, 125124 Moscow, Russia. Phone: +7 (095) 213-1054, +7 (095) 213-1054 or +7 (095) 250-0511. Fax: +7 (095) 250 0105. Contact: Ivan Sitilenlov.

Adventist World Radio, the Voice of Hope, AWR-Russia, The Voice of Hope Media Center, P.O. Box 170, 300 000 Tula-Centre, Russia. Fax: +7 (087) 233 1218. E-mail: (Kulakov) 74532.2000@compuserve.com. URL: www.awr.org/awr-russia/. Contact: Peter Kulakov, Manager. Free home study Bible guides and other religious material, some small souvenirs. AWR terminated its external shortwave transmissions from Russia in October 1996, but still brodcasts via Russian domestic medium wave (AM), shortwave and FM channels. Often reception reports sent here are redirected to the AWR Europe office (*see* under Italy)—*see* also AWR listings under Costa Rica, Guam, Guatemala, Kenya and USA).

Adygey Radio (Radio Maykop), ul. Zhukovskogo 24, 352700 Maykop, Republic of Adygeya, Russia. Contact: A.T. Kerashev, Chairman. English accepted but Russian preferred. Return postage helpful.

Arkhangel'sk Radio, Dom Radio, ul. Popova 2, 163000 Arkhangel'sk, Arkhangel'skaya Oblast, Russia; or U1PR, Valentin G. Kalasnikov, ul. Suvorov 2, kv. 16, Arkhangel'sk, Arkhangel'skaya Oblast, Russia. Replies irregularly to correspondence in Russian.

Bashkir Radio, ul. Gafuri 9, 450076 Ufa, Bashkortostan, Russia.

Buryat Radio, Dom Radio, ul. Erbanova 7, 670000 Ulan-Ude, Republic of Buryatia, Russia. Contact: Z.A. Telin or L.S. Shikhanova.

Chita Radio, ul. Kostushko-Grigorovicha 27, 672090 Chita, Chitinskaya Oblast, Russia. Contact: (technical) V.A. Klimov, Chief Engineer; V.A. Moorzin, Head of Broadcasting; or A.A. Anufriyev.

Evenkiyskaya Radio, ul. 50 let Oktyabrya 28, 663370 Tura, Evenkiyskiy Avt. Okrug, Russia. Contact: B. Yuryev, Engineer. Replies to correspondence in Russian.

FEBC Russia, P.O. Box 2128, Khabarovsk 680020, Russia.

Islamskaya Volna (Islamic Wave), Islamic Center of Moscow Region, Moscow Jami Mosque, Vypolzov per. 7, 129090 Moscow, Russia. Phone: +7 (095) 233-6423/6, +7 (095) 233-6629 or +7 (095) 281-4904. Contact: Sheikh Ravil Gainutdin. Return postage necessary.

Kabardino-Balkar Radio (Radio Nalchik), ul. Nogmova 38, 360000 Nalchik, Republic of Kabardino-Balkariya, Russia. Contact: Kamal Makitov, Vice-Chairman. Replies to correspondence in Russian.

Kala Aturaya (Voice of Assyria), ul. Pyatnitskaya 25, 113326 Moscow. Contact: Marona Arsanis, Chief Editor. Return postage helpful. Replies irregularly.

Kamchatka Radio, RTV Center, Dom Radio, ul. Sovietskaya 62-G, 683000 Petropavlovsk-Kamchatskiy, Kamchatskaya Oblast, Russia. Contact: A. Borodin, Chief OTK; or V.I. Aibabin.

$1 required. Replies in Russian to correspondence in Russian or English.

Khabarovsk Radio, RTV Center, ul. Lenina 71, 680013 Khabarovsk, Khabarovskiy Kray, Russia; or Dom Radio, pl. Slavy, 682632 Khabarovsk, Khabarovskiy Kray, Russia. Contact: (technical) V.N. Kononov, Glavnyy Inzhener.

Khanty-Mansiysk Radio, Dom Radio, ul. Mira 7, 626200 Khanty-Mansiysk, Khanty-Mansiyskiy Avt. Okrug, Tyumenskaya Oblast, Russia. Contact: (technical) Vladimir Sokolov, Engineer.

Koryak Radio, ul. Obukhova 4, 684620 Palana, Koryakskiy Khrebet, Russia.

Krasnoyarsk Radio, RTV Center, Sovietskaya 128, 660017 Krasnoyarsk, Krasnoyarskiy Kray, Russia. Contact: Valeriy Korotchenko; or Anatoliy A. Potehin, RAØAKE. Free local information booklets in English/Russian. Replies in Russian to correspondence in English or Russian. Return postage helpful.

Magadan Radio, RTV Center, ul. Kommuny 8/12, 685013 Magadan, Magadanskaya Oblast, Russia. Contact: Viktor Loktionov or V.G. Kuznetsov. Return postage helpful. May reply to correspondence in Russian.

Mariy Radio, Mari Yel, ul. Osipenko 50, 424014 Yoshkar-Ola, Russia.

Mayak—see Radio Odin and Mayak, below.

Mukto Probaho—see Thailand.

Murmansk Radio, sopka Varnichnaya, 183042 Murmansk, Murmanskaya Oblast, Russia; or RTV Center, Sopka Varnichaya, 183042 Murmansk, Murmanskaya Oblast, Russia.

Northern European Radio Relay Service (NERRS) (when inaugurated), World Band Verification QSL Service, The State Enterprise for Broadcasting and Radio Communications No. 2 (GPR-2), ul. Akademika Pavlova 13A, 197376 St. Petersburg, Russia. Fax: +7 (812) 234 2971. This planned operation hopes to air non-controversial commercial world band programs to Europe.

Primorsk Radio, RTV Center, ul. Uborevieha 20A, 690000 Vladivostok, Primorskiy Kray, Russia. Contact: A.G. Giryuk. Return postage helpful.

Radio Alef (when active, a joint project of Voice of Russia and the Jewish Children's Association "Banim Banot"), P.O. Box 72, 123154 Moscow, Russia.

Radio Kudymkar, 617240 Kudymkar, Komi-Permytskiy Avt. Okrug, Permskaya Oblast, Russia.

Radio Lena, ul. Semena Dezhneva 75-4, Radiocenter, 677002 Yakutsk, Russia.

Radio Maykop—see Adygey Radio, above.

Radio Nalchik—see Radio Kabardino-Balkar, above.

Radio Novaya Volna (New Wave Radio, when operating; an independent program last traced over Radio Odin), ul. Akademika Koroleva 19, 127427 Moscow, Russia. Fax: +7 (095) 215 0847. Contact: Vladimir Razin, Editor-in-Chief.

Radio Odin and **Mayak**, ul. Akademika Koroleva 12, 127427 Moscow, Russia. Phone: (general) +7 (095) 217-9340; (English Service) +7 (095) 233-6578; (administration) +7 (095) 217-7888. Fax: +7 (095) 215 0847. Contact: (administration) Vladimir Povolyaev, Director. Correspondence in Russian preferred, but English increasingly accepted. For verification of reception from transmitters located in St. Petersburg and Kaliningrad, see NOTE, above, shortly after the country heading, "RUSSIA."

Radio Perm, ul. Teknicheskaya 7, 614600 Perm, Permskaya Oblast, Russia. Contact: M. Levin, Senior Editor; or A. Losev, Acting Chief Editor.

Radio Rossii (Russia's Radio), Room 121, ul. Yamskogo 5-R, Polya 19/21, 125124 Moscow, Russia. Phone: +7 (095) 213-1054 or +7 (095) 250-0511. Fax: +7 (095) 250 0105 or +7 (095) 233 6449. Contact: Sergei Yerofeyev, Director of International Operations [sic]; or Sergei Davidov, Director. Free English-language information sheet. For verification of reception from transmitters located in St. Petersburg and Kaliningrad, see NOTE, above, shortly after the country heading, "RUSSIA."

Radio Rossii-Nostalgie
MOSCOW OFFICE: Phone: +7 (095) 956-1245. French-managed leased-time program aired over a variety of Russian transmitters.
PARIS HEADQUARTERS: 9-11 Rue Franquet, F-75015 Paris, France. Phone: +33 (1) 53-68-80-00. Fax: +33 (1) 45 32 10 31. Contact: (technical) Hervé Pichat, Chef Technique.

Radio Samorodinka, P.O. Box 898, Center, 101000 Moscow, Russia. Contact: L.S. Shiskin, Editor. This station may be licensed as other than a regular broadcaster.

Radio Seven, ul. Gagarina 6-A, 443079 Samara, Samaraskaya Oblast, Russia. Contact: A.P. Nenashjev; or Mrs. A.S. Shamsutdinova, Editor.

Radio Slavyanka, kv. 160, ul. Marshala Shaposhnikova 14, 103168 Moscow, Russia.

Radio Yunost, ul. Pyatnitskaya 25, 113326 Moscow, Russia. Fax: +7 (095) 233 6244. Contact: Yevgeniy Vasilyevich Pavlov, Director General. Although this station's logo shows Radiostantsiya Yunost, it consistently identifies as Radio Yunost.

Radiostantsiya Atlantika (program of Murmansk Radio, aired via the Russian service of Voice of Russia), per. Rusanova 7-A, 183767 Murmansk, Russia.

Radiostansiya Tikhiy Okean (program of Primorsk Radio, also aired via Voice of Russia transmitters), RTV Center, ul. Uborevieha 20A, 690000 Vladivostok, Primorskiy Kray, Russia.

Radiostantsiya Yakutsk, ul. Semena Dezhneva 75/2, Radiocenter, 677000 Yakutsk, Russia.

Radiostantsiya Yunost—see Radio Yunost.

Sakha Radio, Dom Radio, ul. Ordzhonikidze 48, 677007 Yakutsk, Sakha (Yakutia) Republic, Russia. Fax: +7 (095) 230 2919. Contact: (general) Alexandra Borisova; Lia Sharoborina, Advertising Editor; or Albina Danilova, Producer, "Your Letters"; (technical) Sergei Bobnev, Technical Director. Russian books $15; audio cassettes $10. Free station stickers and original Yakutian souvenirs. Replies to correspondence in English.

Sakhalin Radio, Dom Radio, ul. Komsomolskaya 209, 693000 Yuzhno-Sakhalinsk, Sakhalin Is., Sakhalinskaya Oblast, Russia. Contact: V. Belyaev, Chairman of Sakhalinsk RTV Committee.

Tyumen' Radio, RTV Center, ul. Permyakova 6, 625013 Tyumen', Tyumenskaya Oblast, Russia. Contact: (technical) V.D. Kizerov, Engineer, Technical Center. Sometimes replies to correspondence in Russian. Return postage helpful.

Voice of Russia, ul. Pyatnitskaya 25, Moscow 113326, Russia. Phone: (World Service) +7 (095) 233-6980 or +7 (095) 233-6586; (International Directorate) +7 (095) 233-7801; (Programmes Directorate) +7 (095) 233-6793; (Commercial Dept.) +7 (095) 233-7934; (Audience Research) +7 (095) 233-6278; (Chairman's Secretariat) +7 (095) 233-6331; (News Directorate) +7 (095) 233-6513. Fax: (Chairman's Secretariat) +7 (095) 230 2828; (World Service) +7 (095) 233 7693; (International Relations) +7 (095) 233 7648; (News Directorate) +7 (095) 233 7567; (technical) +7 (095) 233 1342. E-mail: (general) letters@vor.ru; (administrative) chairman@vor.ru; (backup e-mail address) root@avrora.msk.ru. URL: www.vor.ru/. Contact: (English Service—listeners' questions to be answered over the air) Joe Adamov; (English Service—all other general correspondence) Ms. Olga Troshina, World Service Letters Department; (general correspondence, all languages) Victor Kopytin, Director of International Relations Department; Vladimir Zhamkin, Editor-in-Chief; Yevgeny Nilov, Deputy Editor-in-Chief; Anatoly Morozov, Deputy Editor-in-Chief; (Japanese) Yelena Sopova, Japanese Department; (verifications, all services) Mrs. Eugenia Stepanova, c/o English Service; (administration) Yuri Minayev, First Deputy Chairman, Voice of Russia; Armen Ogannesian, Chairman, World Service, Voice of Russia; (technical) Valentin Khleknikov, Frequency Coordinator; Leonid Maevski, Engineering Services; or Maria Petrunicheva, Engineering Services. For verification of reception from trans-

RNW

Veronica Wilson hails from Sierra Leone, and started her career with the BBC's African Service. Ms. Wilson now produces shows for Radio Netherlands' English service.

mitters located in St. Petersburg and Kaliningrad, *see NOTE*, above, shortly after the country heading, "RUSSIA." For verification from transmitters in Khabarovsk, you can also write directly to the Voice of Russia, Dom Radio, Lenina 4, Khabarovsk 680020, Russia. For engineering correspondence concerning frequency management problems, besides "technical," preceding, *see NOTE* on C.I.S. Frequency Management towards the beginning of this "Russia" listing. Free stickers, booklets and sundry other souvenirs occasionally available upon request. Sells audio cassettes of Russian folk and classical music, as well as a Russian language-learning course. Although not officially a part of the Voice of Russia, an organization selling Russian art and handcrafts that sprung from contacts made with the Voice of Russia is "Cheiypouka," Box 266, Main St., Stonington ME 04681 USA; phone +1 (207) 367-5021.

Voice of Assyria—*see* Kala Aturaya, above.

RWANDA   World Time +2

Deutsche Welle—Relay Station Kigali—Correspondence should be directed to the main offices in Cologne, Germany (*see*).

Radio Rwanda, B.P. 404, Kigali, Rwanda. Fax: +250 (7) 6185. Contact: Marcel Singirankabo. $1 required. Rarely replies, with correspondence in French preferred.

ST. HELENA   World Time exactly

Radio St. Helena (when operating once each year), Broadway House, Main Street, Jamestown, St. Helena, South Atlantic Ocean. Phone: +290 4669. Fax: +290 4542. E-mail: tony@sthelena.se; or (Radio St. Helena Day Coordinator, Sweden) sthelena.coordinator@sthelena.se. URL: www.sthelena.se. Contact: (general) Tony Leo, Station Manager; (listeners' questions) Ralph Peters, Presenter, "Evening Shuttle." $1, required. Replies regularly but slowly; verifications can take several months or even a year. Radio St. Helena Day T-shirts (small/medium/large/XL/XXL) available for $25 airmail from: South Atlantic Travel & Trade, Box 6014, SE-600 06 Norrköping, Sweden. Is on the air on world band only once each year—"Radio St Helena Day"—usually late October on 11092.5 kHz in the upper-sideband (USB) mode.

SAO TOME E PRINCIPE   World Time exactly

Voice of America/VOA-IBB—São Tomé Relay Station, P.O. Box 522, São Tomé, São Tomé e Príncipe. Phone: +23 912

22-800. Fax: +23 912 22 435. These numbers are for timely and significant technical matters only. Contact: Jack Fisher, Relay Manager; or Manuel Neves, Transmitter Plant Technician. Replies direct if $1 included with correspondence, otherwise all communications should be directed to the usual VOA address in Washington (*see* USA).

SAUDI ARABIA   World Time +3

Broadcasting Service of The Kingdom of Saudi Arabia, P.O. Box 61718, Riyadh-11575, Saudi Arabia. Phone: (general) +966 (1) 404-2795; (administration) +966 (1) 442-5493; (technical) +966 (1) 442-5170. Fax: (general) +966 (1) 402 8177; (Frequency Management) +966 (1) 404 1692. Contact: (general) Mutlaq A. Albegami, European Service Manager; (technical) Sulaiman Samnan, Director of Frequency Management; or A. Shah, Department of Frequency Management. Free travel information and book on Saudi history.

Radio Islam from Holy Mecca (Idha'at Islam min Mecca al-Mukarama)—program with the same contact details as Broadcasting Service of the Kingdom of Saudi Arabia, above.

SENEGAL   World Time exactly

Office de Radiodiffusion-Télévision du Sénégal, B.P. 1765, Dakar, Senegal. Phone: +221 23-63-49. Fax: + 221 22 34 90. Contact: (technical) Joseph Nesseim, Directeur des Services Techniques. Free stickers and Senegalese stamps. Return postage, $1 or 2 IRCs required; as Mr. Nesseim collects stamps, unusual stamps may be even more appreciated. Replies to correspondence in French.

SEYCHELLES   World Time +4

BBC World Service—Indian Ocean Relay Station, P.O. Box 448, Victoria, Mahé, Seychelles; or Grand Anse, Mahé, Seychelles. Phone: +248 78-269. Fax: +248 78 500. Contact: (administration) Peter J. Loveday, Station Manager; (technical) Peter Lee, Resident Engineer; Nigel Bird, Resident Engineer; or Steve Welch, Assistant Resident Engineer. Nontechnical correspondence should be sent to the BBC World Service in London (*see*).

Far East Broadcasting Association—FEBA Radio

MAIN OFFICE: P.O. Box 234, Mahé, Seychelles, Indian Ocean. Phone: (main office) +248 241-215; (engineering) +248 241-353. E-mail: spepper@febaradio.org.uk. URL: www.feba.org.uk. Contact: Station Director; or Richard Whittington, Schedule Engineer. Free stickers, pennants and station information sheet. $1 or one IRC helpful. Also, *see* FEBC Radio International—USA and United Kingdom.

CANADIAN OFFICE: 6850 Antrim Avenue, Burnaby BC, V5J 4M4 Canada. Fax: +1 (604) 430 5272. E-mail: dpatter@ axionet.com.

INDIA OFFICE: FEBA India, P.O. Box 2526, 7 Commissariat Road, Bangalore-560 025, India. Fax: +91 (80) 584 701. E-mail: 6186706@mcimail.com. Contact: Peter Muthl Raj.

SIERRA LEONE   World Time exactly

NOTE: Due to civil unrest mail to Sierra Leone has been temporarily suspended.

Sierra Leone Broadcasting Service, New England, Freetown, Sierra Leone. Phone: +232 (22) 240-123; +232 (22) 240-173; +232 (22) 240-497 or 232 (22) 241-919. Fax: +232 (22) 240 922. Contact: (general) Denis Smith, Acting Head of Programmes; (technical) B.D.H. Taylor, Acting Chief Engineer; or Steve Conteh, Project Engineer.

SINGAPORE   World Time +8

BBC World Service—Far Eastern Relay Station, 26 Olive Road, Singapore. Phone: + 65 260-1511. Fax: +65 253 8131. Contact: (technical) Far East Resident Engineer. Nontechnical correspondence should be sent to the BBC World Service in London (*see*).

📻**Radio Corporation of Singapore**, Farrer Road, P.O. Box 968, Singapore 912899; or (physical location) Caldecott Broadcast Centre, Caldecott Hill, Andrew Road, Singapore 299939. Phone: +65 251-8622 or +65 359-7340. Fax: +65 256

9533, +65 256 9556 or +65 256 9338. E-mail: radio@
mediacity.com.sg. URL: http://rcs.com.sg/. Contact: (general)
Lillian Tan, Public Relations Division; Lim Heng Tow, Manager, International & Community Relations; Tan Eng Lai,
Promotion Executive; Hui Wong, Producer/Presenter; or Lucy
Leong; (administration) Anthony Chia, Director General;
(technical) Asaad Sameer Bagharib, V.P. Engineering; or Lee
Wai Meng. Free regular and Post-It stickers, pens, umbrellas,
mugs, towels, wallets and lapel pins. Do not include currency
in envelope.

Radio Japan via Singapore—For verification direct from
the Singaporean transmitters, contact the BBC World Service—Far Eastern Relay Station (see above) Nontechnical
correspondence should be sent to Radio Japan in Tokyo
(see).

☞Radio Singapore International, Farrer Road, P.O. Box
5300, Singapore 912899, Singapore; or (physical address)
Caldecott Broadcast Centre, Annex Building Level 1, Andrew
Road, Singapore 299939. Phone: (general) + 65 359-7662;
(programme listings) +65 353-5300; (publicity) +65 350-
3708 or +65 256-0401. Fax: +65 259 1357 or +65 259 1380.
E-mail: rsieng@pacific.net.sg. URL: http://.rsi.com.sg/. Contact: (general) Anushia Kanagabasai, Producer, "You Asked
For It"; Belinda Yeo, Producer, "Dateline RSI"; or Mrs.
Sakuntala Gupta, Programme Manager, English Service;
(administration) S. Chandra Mohan, Station Director; (technical) Selena Kaw, Office of the Administrative Executive; or
Yong Wui Pin, Engineer. Free souvenir T-shirts and key chains
to selected listeners. Do not include currency in envelope.

SLOVAKIA   World Time +1 (+2 midyear)
Radio Slovakia International, Mýtna 1, P.O. Box 55, SK-810
05 Bratislava, Slovakia. Phone: (Chief Editor) +421 (7) 49-62-
81; (Deputy Chief Editor) +421 (7) 49-62-82; (English Service)
+421 (7) 49-80-75; (Russian Service) +421 (7) 49-82-76;
(Slovak Service) +421 (7) 49-82-47; (French Service) +421 (7)
49-82-67; (German Service) +421 (7) 49-62-83. Phone/fax:
(technical) +421 (7) 49-76-59. Fax: (French and English Services) +421 (7) 49 82 67; (English Service) +421 (7) 49 62 82;
(other language services) +421 (7) 49 82 47; (technical) +421
(7) 39 89 23. E-mail: slrozv@ba-cvt.sanet.sk. URLs:
www.slovakradio.sk/rsi.html. Contact: Helga Dingová, Director of English Broadcasting; Alan Jones, Producer "Listeners' Tribune"; (administration) PhDr. Karol Palkovič, Head of
External Broadcasting; (technical) Edita Chocholatá, Frequency Coordinator; Jozef Krátky, Ing. "Slovak Lesson"
course, but no accompanying printed materials. Free stickers, pennants, pocket calendars and other small souvenirs
and publications. Reader feedback suggests station may
not always receive mail addressed to it; so, if you get no
reply, keep trying.

SOLOMON ISLANDS   World Time +11
Solomon Islands Broadcasting Corporation, P.O. Box
654, Honiara, Solomon Islands. Phone: +677 20051. Fax:
+677 23159. Contact: (general) Julian Maka'a, Producer,
"Listeners From Far Away"; Cornelius Teasi; John Babera; or
Program Director; (administration) James T. Kilua, General
Manager; (technical) George Tora, Chief Engineer. IRC or $1
helpful. Problems with the domestic mail system may cause
delays.

SOMALIA   World Time +3
Radio Mogadishu—Currently, there are three stations operating under the rubric Radio Mogadishu. None is known to
reply to listener correspondence.

SOMALILAND   World Time +3
NOTE: "Somaliland," claimed as an independent nation, is
diplomatically recognized only as part of Somalia.
Radio Hargeisa, P.O. Box 14, Hargeisa, Somaliland, Somalia. Contact: Sulayman Abdel-Rahman, announcer. Most
likely to respond to correspondence in Somali or Arabic.

SOUTH AFRICA   World Time +2
BBC World Service via South Africa—For verification
direct from the South African transmitters, contact Sentech
(see below). Nontechnical correspondence should be sent to
the BBC World Service in London (see).
☞Channel Africa, P.O. Box 91313, Auckland Park 2006,
South Africa. Phone: + 27 (11) 714-2551 or +27 (11) 714-3942;
(technical) +27 (11) 714-3409. Fax: (general) +27 (11) 482
3506, + 27 (11) 714 2546, +27 (11) 714 4956 or +27 (11) 714 6377;
(technical) +27 (11) 714 5812. E-mail: (general) africancan@
sabc.co.za; (English News) vorstern@sabc.co.za. URL: (general, including news about South Africa) www.sabc.co.za/
units/chanafr/index.html; (RealAudio in English) www.wrn.org/
stations/africa/html; (technical) see Sentech, below. Contact: (general) Tony Machilika, Head of English Service;
Robert Michel, Head of Research and Strategic Planning; or
Noeleen Vorster, Corporate Communications Manager; (technical) Mrs. H. Meyer, Supervisor Operations; or Lucienne
Libotte, Technology Operations. T-shirts $11 and watches
$25. Prices do not include shipping and handling. Free Share
newsletter from the Department of Foreign Affairs, stickers
and calendars. Reception reports are best directed to Sentech
(see below), which operates the transmission facilities.
Radiosondergrense (Radio Without Boundaries), Posbus
91312, Auckland Park 2006, South Africa. Phone: (general)
+27 (89) 110-2525; (live studio on-air line) +27 (89) 110-4553;
(management) +27 (11) 714-2702; (administration) +27 (11)
714-4406. Fax: +27 (11) 714 6445. E-mail: (Shaikh) shaikhm@
sabc.co.za. Contact: (general) Mohamed Shaikh, Manager;
(administration) Sarel Myburgh. Reception reports are best
directed to Sentech (see below), which operates the shortwave transmission facilities. A domestic service of the South
African Broadcasting Corporation (see below), and formerly
known as Afrikaans Stereo.
Sentech (Pty) Ltd, Shortwave Services, Private Bag X06,
Honeydew 2040, South Africa. Phone: (shortwave) +27 (11)
475-1596 or (Otto) +27 (11) 471-4658; (general) +27 (11) 475-
5600. Fax: +27 (11) 475 5112 or (Otto) +27 (11) 471 4605. E-mail:
(Otto) ottok@sentech.co.za; (Smuts) smutsn@sentech.co.za.
URL: (shortwave) www.sentech.co.za/meyerton.html; (gen-
eral, homepage) www.sentech.co.za/. Contact: Mr. N. Smuts,
Managing Director; Rodgers Gamuti, Client Manager; or
Kathy Otto. Sentech is currently issuing its own verification
cards, and is the best place to direct reception reports for all
South African world band stations. Four additional 100 kW
Brown Boveri transmitters are expected to be on the air
shortly for use to such nearby targets as Mozambique,
Zambia and Zimbabwe.
South African Broadcasting Corporation
ADMINISTRATION AND GENERAL TECHNICAL MATTERS:
Private Bag X1, Auckland Park 2006, South Africa. Phone:
(Reddy) +27 (11) 714-2306; (technical) +27 (11) 714-3409.
Fax: (general) +27 (11) 714 5055; (Reddy) +27 (11) 726 2914;
(technical) +27 (11) 714 3106 or +27 (11) 714 5812. E-mail:
format is lastnameinitial@sabc.co.za, so to reach, say, Govin
Reddy, it would be reddyg@sabc.co.za. URL: www.sabc.co.za.
Contact: Govin Reddy, Chief Executive of Radio. Free stickers
and ballpoint pens. Reception reports are best directed to
Sentech (see above), which operates the transmission
facilities.
RADIO PROGRAMME SALES: Private Bag X1, Auckland Park
2006, South Africa. Phone: (general enquiries) +27 (11) 714-
5681, +27 (11) 714-6039 or +27 (11) 714-4044; (actuality
programs) +27 (11) 714-4709; (music) +27 (11) 714-4315. Fax:
+27 (11) 714 3671. E-mail: botham@sabc.co.za; snymane@
sabc.co.za; or corbinm@sabc.co.za. Offers a wide range of
music, book readings, radio drama, comedy and other types
of programs.
Trans World Radio Africa
NONTECHNICAL CORRESPONDENCE: Trans World Radio—
South Africa, Private Bag 987, Pretoria 0001, South Africa.

Phone: +27 (12) 807-0053. Fax: +27 (12) 807 1266. URL: www.icon.co.za/~ttatlow/Welcome.htm.
TECHNICAL CORRESPONDENCE: Reception reports and other technical correspondence are best directed to Sentech (see above) or to TWR's Swaziland office (see). Also, see USA.

SPAIN   World Time +1 (+2 midyear)
Radio Exterior de España (Spanish National Radio)
MAIN OFFICE: Apartado 156.202, E-28080 Madrid, Spain. Phone: +34 (1) 346-1081/1083/1149/1160. Fax: +34 (1) 346 1813/1815. E-mail: radioexterior.espana@rtve.es. URL: www.rtve.es/rtve/_rne/_radios/_ree/radioe00.htm. Contact: Pilar Salvador M., Relaciones con la Audiencia; Nuria Alonso Veiga, Head of Information Service; or Penelope Eades, Foreign Language Programmer. Free stickers, calendars, pennants and tourist information. Reception reports can be sent to: Radio Exterior de España, Relaciones con la Audiencia, Sección DX, Apartado de Correos 156.202, E-28080 Madrid, Spain.
NOBLEJAS TRANSMITTER SITE: Centro Emisor de RNE en Onda Corta, Ctra. Dos Barrios s/n, E-45350 Noblejas-Toledo, Spain.
RUSSIAN OFFICE: P.O Box 88, 109044 Moscow, Russia.
Costa Rican Relay Facility—see Costa Rica.
TRANSCRIPTION SERVICE: Radio Nacional de España, Servicio de Transcripciones, Apartado 156.200, Casa de la Radio (Prado del Rey), E-28223 Madrid, Spain.
WASHINGTON NEWS BUREAU: National Press Building, 529 14th Street NW, Suite 1288, Washington DC 20045 USA. Phone: +1 (202) 783-0768. Contact: Luz María Rodríguez.

SRI LANKA   World Time +6:00
Deutsche Welle—Relay Station Sri Lanka, 92/2 Rt. Hon. D.S. Senanayake Mwts, Colombo 8, Sri Lanka. Nontechnical correspondence should be sent to Deutsche Welle in Germany (see).
Radio Japan/NHK, c/o SLBC, P.O. Box 574, Torrington Square, Colombo 7, Sri Lanka. This address for technical correspondence only. General nontechnical listener correspondence should be sent to the usual Radio Japan address in Japan. News-oriented correspondence may also be sent to the NHK Bangkok Bureau (see Radio Japan, Japan).
Sri Lanka Broadcasting Corporation, P.O. Box 574, Independence Square, Colombo 7, Sri Lanka. Phone: (domestic service) +94 (1) 697-491; (external service) +94 (1) 695-661. Fax: +94 (1) 695 488. E-mail: slbc@sri.lanka.net; or slbcweb@srilanka.net. Contact: N. Jayhweera, Director of Audience Research; or Icumar Ratnayake, Controller, "Mailbag Program"; (SLBC administration) Newton Gunaratne, Deputy Director-General; (technical) H.M.N.R. Jayawardena, Frequency Engineer.
Voice of America/VOA-IBB—Sri Lanka Relay—A new shortwave relay facility is currently under construction in Sri Lanka. However, the project suffered a setback when a 500 kW transmitter was destroyed by fire. The damage is being assessed but VOA is still hoping for a September 1997 start-up date for the new relay station.

SUDAN   World Time +2
National Unity Radio—see Sudan National Radio Corporation, below, for details.
Sudan National Radio Corporation, P.O. Box 572, Omdurman, Sudan. Phone: +249 (11) 53-151 or +249 (11) 52-100. Contact: (general) Mohammed Elfatih El Sumoal; (technical) Abbas Sidig, Director General, Engineering and Technical Affairs; Mohammed Elmahdi Khalil, Administrator, Engineering and Technical Affairs; or Adil Didahammed, Engineering Department. Replies irregularly. Return postage necessary.

SURINAME   World Time –3
Radio Apintie, Postbus 595, Paramaribo, Suriname. Phone: +597 40-05-00. Fax: +597 40 06 84. Contact: Ch. E. Vervuurt, Director. Free pennant. Return postage or $1 required.

SWAZILAND   World Time +2
Swaziland Commercial Radio
NONTECHNICAL CORRESPONDENCE: P.O. Box 5569, Rivonia 2128, Transvaal, South Africa. Phone: +27 (11) 884-8400. Fax: +27 (11) 883 1982. Contact: Rob Vickers, Manager—Religion. IRC helpful. Replies irregularly.
TECHNICAL CORRESPONDENCE: P.O. Box 99,Amsterdam 2375, South Africa. Contact: Guy Doult, Chief Engineer.
SOUTH AFRICA BUREAU: P.O. Box 1586,Alberton 1450, Republic of South Africa. Phone: +27 (11) 434-4333. Fax: +27 (11) 434 4777.
Trans World Radio—Swaziland
MAIN OFFICE: P.O. Box 64, Manzini, Swaziland. Phone: +268 52-781/2/3. Fax: +268 55 333. E-mail: (James Burnett) jburnett.twr.org; (technical) sstavrop@twr.org. URL (transmission schedule): www.icon.co.za/~ttatlow/schedule.htm. Contact: (general) Dawn-Lynn Prediger, DX Secretary; Mrs. L. Stavropoulos; Greg Shaw, Follow-up Department; Peter A. Prediger, Station Director; or Program Manager; (technical) Chief Engineer; or James Burnett, Regional Engineer. Free stickers, postcards and calendars. May swap canceled stamps. $1, return postage or 3 IRCs required. Also, see USA.
AFRICA REGIONAL OFFICE: P.O. Box 4232,Kempton Park 1610, South Africa. Contact: Stephen Boakye-Yiadom, African Regional Director.
CÔTE D'IVOIRE OFFICE: B.P. 2131, Abidjan 06, Côte d'Ivoire.
KENYA OFFICE: P.O. Box 21514 Nairobi, Kenya.
MALAWI OFFICE: P. O. Box 52 Lilongwe, Malawi.
SOUTH AFRICA OFFICE: P.O. Box 36000, Menlo Park 0102, South Africa.
ZIMBABWE OFFICE: P.O. Box H-74, Hatfield, Harare, Zimbabwe.

SWEDEN   World Time +1 (+2 midyear)
IBRA Radio (program)
MAIN OFFICE: International Broadcasting Association, Box 396, SE-105 36 Stockholm, Sweden. Phone: +46 (8) 619-2540; Fax: +46 (8) 619 2539. E-mail: hq@ibra.se/; URLs: www.ibra.org/. Contact: Mikael Stjernberg, Public Relations Manager. Free pennants and stickers. IBRA Radio is heard as a program over various world band radio stations, including the Voice of Hope, Lebanon, Trans World Radio, Monaco, and the Voice of Russia.
CANADA OFFICE: P.O. Box 444, Niagara Falls ON, L2E 6T8 Canada.
CYPRUS OFFICE: P.O. Box 7420, 3315 Limassol, Cyprus. Contact: Rashad Saleem. Free schedules, calendars and stickers.
Radio Sweden
MAIN OFFICE: SE-105 10 Stockholm, Sweden. Phone: (general) +46 (8) 784-7281, +46 (8) 784-7288 or +46 (8) 784-5000; (listener voice mail) +46 (8) 784-7287; (Technical Department) +46 (8) 784-7286. Fax: (general) +46 (8) 667 6283; (audience contact and Technical Department) +46 (8) 660 2990; (polling to receive schedule) +46 8 667 3701. E-mail: info@rs.sr.se; (Beckman, Technical Manager) rolf-b@stab.sr.se. URL: (RealAudio in Swedish, and text): www.sr.se/rs/index.htm; (RealAudio in English) www.sr.se/rs; (MediaScan page) www.sr.se/rs/english/media/media.htm; (George Wood) www.abc.se/~m8914; (English Service page) www.sr.se/rs/english/. Contact: (general) Alan Pryke, Host, "In Touch with Stockholm" [include your telephone number]; Sarah Roxström, Head, English Service; Greta Grandin, Program Assistant, English Service; George Wood, Producer, MediaScan; Olimpia Seldon, Assistant to the Director; or Charlotte Adler, Public Relations & Information; (administration) Finn Norgren, Director; (technical) Rolf Erik Beckman, Head, Technical Department. T-shirts (two sizes) $12 or £8. Payment for T-shirts may be made by international money order, Swedish postal giro account No. 43 36 56-6 or internationally negotiable bank check.
TRANSMISSION AUTHORITY: TERACOM, Svensk Rundradio AB, P.O. Box 17666, SE-118 92 Stockholm, Sweden. Phone:

(general) +46 (8) 671-2000; (Nilsson) +46 (8) 671-2066. Fax: (Nilsson) +46 (8) 671 2060 or +46 (8) 671 2080. E-mail: mni@teracom.se. URL: www.teracom.se. Contact: (Frequency Planning Dept.—head office): Magnus Nilsson. Free stickers; sometimes free T-shirts to those monitoring during special test transmissions. Seeks monitoring feedback for new frequency usages.

NEW YORK NEWS BUREAU: Swedish Broadcasting, 825 Third Avenue, New York NY 10022 USA. Phone: +1 (212) 688-6872 or +1 (212) 643-8855. Fax: +1 (212) 594 6413. Contact: Elizabeth Johansson or Ann Hedengren.

WASHINGTON NEWS BUREAU: Swedish Broadcasting, 2030 M Street NW, Suite 700, Washington DC 20036 USA. Phone: +1 (202) 785-1727. Contact: Folke Rydén, Lisa Carlsson or Steffan Ekendahl.

SWITZERLAND World Time +1 (+2 midyear)

European Broadcasting Union, Case Postal 67, CH-1218 Grand-Saconnex, Geneva, Switzerland. Phone: +41 (22) 717-2111. Fax: +41 (22) 798 5897. URL: www.ebu.ch. Contact: Jean-Bernard Munch, Secretary-General.

International Telecommunication Union, Place des Nations, CH-1211 Geneva 20, Switzerland. Phone: +41 (22) 730-5111. Fax: +41 (22) 733 7256. URL: www.itu.ch/. The ITU is the world's official regulatory body for all telecommunication activities, including world band radio. Offers a wide range of official multilingual telecommunication publications in print and/or digital formats.

Swiss Radio International

MAIN OFFICE: Giacomettistrasse 1, CH-3000 Berne 15, Switzerland. Phone: (general) +41 (31) 350-9222; (English Department) +41 (31) 350-9790; (French Department) +41 (31) 350-9555; (German Department) +41 (31) 350-9535; (Italian Department) +41 (31) 350-9531). Fax: (general) +41 (31) 350 9569; (administration) +41 (31) 350 9744 or +41 (31) 350 9581; (Communication and Marketing) +41 (31) 350 9544; (Programme Department) +41 (31) 350 9569; (English Department) +41 (31) 350 9580; (French Department) +41 (31) 350 9664; (German Department) +41 (31) 350 9562; (Italian Department) +41 (31) 350 9678. E-mail: language@sri.srg-ssr.ch (e.g. english@sri.srg-ssr.ch). URLs: (general) www.srg-ssr.ch/SRI/; (RealAudio in English and Portuguese) http://srgtserver.tech-srg-ssr.ch/sri/index.html. Contact: (general) Nancy Thöny, Listeners' Letters, English Programmes; Marlies Schmutz, Listeners' Letters, German Programmes; Thérèse Schafter, Listeners' Letters, French Programmes; Esther Niedhammer, Listeners' Letters, Italian Programmes; Beatrice Lombard, Promotion; Giovanni D'Amico, Audience Officer; (administration) Ulrich Kündig, General Manager; Nicolas Lombard, Deputy General Manager; Walter Fankhauser, Head, Communication & Marketing Services; Rose-Marie Malinverni, Head, Editorial Co-ordination Unit; Ron Grünig, Head, English Programmes; James Jeanneret, Head, German Programmes; Philippe Zahne, Head, French Programmes; Fabio Mariani, Head, Italian Programmes; (technical) Paul Badertscher, Head, Engineering Services; Bob Zanotti. Free station flyers, posters, stickers and pennants. Sells CDs of Swiss music, plus audio and video (PAL/NTSC) cassettes; also, Swiss watches and clocks, microphone lighters, letter openers, books, T-shirts, sweatshirts and Swiss Army knives. VISA/EURO/AX or cash, but no personal checks. For catalog, write Nicolas D. Lombard, Head, SRI Enterprises, c/o the above address, fax +41 (31) 350 9581, or e-mail shopping@sri.srg-ssr.ch.

TRANSMISSION AUTHORITY: Swiss Telecom PTT, Direction Radiocom, HF Broadcasting / RC115, Speichergaße 6, CH-3030 Berne, Switzerland. Phone: +41 (31) 338-3490. Fax: +41 (31) 338 6554. E-mail: TRC83490@gdr.telco.swissptt.ch. Contact: Ulrich Wegmüller, Frequency Manager; (administration) Dr. Walter G. Tiedweg, Head Radio Division.

WASHINGTON NEWS BUREAU: 2030 M Street NW, Washington DC 20554 USA. Phone: (general) +1 (202) 775-0894 or +1

(202) 429-9668; (French-language radio) +1 (202) 296-0277; (German-language radio) +1 (202) 7477. Fax: +1 (202) 833 2777. Contact: Christophe Erbeck, reporter.

United Nations Radio, Room G209, Palais des Nations, CH-1211 Geneva 10, Switzerland. Phone: +41 (22) 917-4222. Fax: +41 (22) 917 0123. E-mail: audio-visual@un.org. URLs: (RealAudio) www.nexus.org/IRN/index.html; www.wrn.org/stations/un.html.

SYRIA World Time +2 (+3 midyear)

Radio Damascus, Syrian Radio & Television, Ommayad Square, Damascus, Syria. Phone: +963 (11) 720-700. Contact: Mr. Afaf, Director General; Lisa Arslanian; or Mrs. Wafa Ghawi. Free stickers, paper pennants and *The Syria Times* newspaper. Replies can be highly erratic, but as of late have been more regular, if sometimes slow.

TAHITI—*see* FRENCH POLYNESIA.

TAJIKISTAN World Time +5

Radio Tajikistan, ul Chapayeva 31, Dushanbe 734025, Tajikistan. Contact: Gulom Makhmudovich, Deputy Chairman; Raisamuhtan Dinova Vuncha, English Service; Gulnaz Abdullaeva, English Service Editor; or Mrs. Raisa Muhutdinova, Editor-in-Chief, English Department. Correspondence in Russian, Farsi, Dari, Tajik or Uzbek preferred, and correspondence in English is best directed to the English service. Mr Abdullaeva collects maps of different countries, so enclosing a map may help in getting a reply. Used Russian stamps appreciated, for whatever reason. Return postage (IRCs or 1$) appreciated, but enclosing currency notes is risky due to the high level of postal theft in the country.

Radio Pay-i 'Ajam—*see* Tajik Radio for details.

Tajik Radio, ul Chapayeva 31, Dushanbe 735025, Tajikistan. Contact: Mirbobo Mirrakhimov, Chairman of State Television and Radio Corporation. Correspondence in Russian, Tajik or Uzbek preferred.

TANZANIA World Time +3

Radio Tanzania, P.O. Box 9191, Dar es Salaam, Tanzania. Phone: +255 (51) 860-760. Fax: +255 (51) 865 577. Contact: (general) Abdul Ngarawa, Director of Broadcasting; Mrs. Edda Sanga, Controller of Programs; Abisay Steven, Head of English Service and International Relations Unit; or Ahmed Jongo, Producer, "Your Answer"; (technical) Taha Usi, Chief Engineer; or Emmanuel Mangula, Deputy Chief Engineer. Replies to correspondence in English.

Radio Tanzania Zanzibar, P.O. Box 1178, Zanzibar, Tanzania. Phone: +255 (54) 31-088. Fax: + 255 (54) 57 207. Contact: (general) Yusuf Omar Chunda, Director Department of Information and Broadcasting; Ali Bakari Muombwa; or Kassim S. Kassim; (technical) Nassor M. Suleiman, Maintenance Engineer. $1 return postage helpful.

THAILAND World Time +7

BBC World Service—Asia Relay Station, P.O. Box 20, Muang Nakhon, Sawan 60000, Thailand.

Mukto Probaho

MAIN ADDRESS: P.O. Box 9406, Calcutta 700016, India. Contact: Sk Abdullah. Correspondence in English and reception reports welcomed. Members' Club. This daily Bengali-language Christian religious program/listener-response show, produced by a studio associated with IBRA Radio (*see* Sweden), is aired via transmission facilities of the Voice of Russia. Sometimes verifies via IBRA Radio in Sweden.

BANGKOK ADDRESS: GPO Box 1605, Bangkok 10501, Thailand.

Radio Thailand World Service, 236 Vibhavadi Rangsit Highway, Din Daeng, Huaykhwang, Bangkok 10400, Thailand. Phone: +66 (2) 277-0122, +66 (2) 277-1814 or +66 (2) 277-1840. Fax: +66 (2) 277 7095 or +66 (2) 271 3514. Contact: Mrs. Amporn Samosorn, Chief of External Services; or Patra Lamjiack. Free pennants. Replies irregularly, especially to those who persist.

Voice of America/VOA-IBB—Relay Station Thailand, Udon Thani, Thailand. Phone: +66 (42) 271-490/1. Only matters of urgent importance should be directed to this site. All other correspondence should be directed to the regular VOA address in Washington (see USA).

TOGO World Time exactly
Radio Lomé, B.P. 434, Lomé, Togo. Phone: + 228 (21) 2492. Contact: (nontechnical) Batchoudi Malúlaba or Geraldo Isidine. Return postage, $1 or 2 IRCs helpful. French preferred but English accepted.

TONGA World Time +13
Tonga Broadcasting Commission (when operating), A3Z, P.O. Box 36, Nuku'alofa, Tonga, SW Pacific. Phone: +676 23295, +676 23555 or +676 23556. Fax: +676 24417. Contact: (general) Tavake Fusimalohi, General Manager; (technical) Sioeli Maka Tohi, Chief Engineer. Station is currently off the air due to cyclone damage. Plans to return to shortwave if a new transmitter can be obtained from UNESCO.

TUNISIA World Time +1
☞**Radiodiffusion Télévision Tunisienne**, 71 Avenue de la Liberté, TN-1070 Tunis, Tunisia; or try ONT, 13 Rue de Bizerte, TN-1006 Tunis, Tunisia. Phone: +216 (1) 287-300. Fax: +216 (1) 781 058. E-mail: info@radiotunis.com. URL: (includes RealAudio) www.radiotunis.com/news.html. Contact: Mongai Caffai, Director General; Mohamed Abdelkafi, Director; Masmoudi Mahmoud; or Smaoui Sadok, Le Sous-Directeur Technique. Replies irregularly and slowly to correspondence in French or Arabic. $1 helpful.

TURKEY World Time +2 (+3 midyear)
Radyo Çinarli, Çinarli Anadolu Teknik ve Endüstri Meslek Lisesi Deneme Radyosu, Çinarli, TR-35.110 İzmir, Turkey. Phone: +90 (232) 486-6434; (technical) +90 (232) 461-7442. Fax: +90 (232) 435 1032. Contact: (general) Ahmet Ayaydin, School Manager; (technical) Göksel Uysal, Technical Manager. Station is run by the local technical institute. Free studio photos and, occasionally, other small souvenirs. Correspondence in English accepted.
Turkish Radio-Television Corporation—Voice of Turkey
MAIN OFFICE, NONTECHNICAL: P.K. 333, TR-06.443 Yenisehir Ankara, Turkey. Phone: (general) +90 (312) 490-9800/9806/9808/9809; (English Department) +90 (312) 490-9842. Fax: +90 (312) 490 9845/6. Contact: (English) Osman Erkan, Host, "Letterbox" and Head of English Department; (other languages) Rafet Esit, Foreign Languages Section Chief; (administration) Savaş Kiratli, Head of the External Services Dept.; or A. Akad Gukuriva, Deputy Director General; (technical) Mete Coşkun. Free stickers, pennants, women's embroidery artwork swatches and tourist literature.
MAIN OFFICE, TECHNICAL (FOR EMIRLER AND ÇAKIRLAR TRANSMITTER SITES): Gene Mudurluk Teknik, TRT Sitesi, Kkat : 5/C, Or-An, TR-06.450 Ankara, Turkey. Phone: +90 (312) 490-1730/2. Fax: +90 (312) 490 1733. E-mail: (Boratav, Engineer) boratav@pallas.dialup.ankara.edu.tr. Contact: Turgay Cakimci, Frequency Manager; Vural Tekeli, Deputy Director General, Engineering; or Ms. F. Elvan Boratav, International Technical Relations Department.
OR-AN OFFICE: Diş Yayınlar Dairesi Başkanlığı, Turan Güneş Bulvarı, Or-An Çankaya, Ankara, Turkey.
SAN FRANCISCO OFFICE, SCHEDULES: 2654 17th Avenue, San Francisco CA 94116 USA. Phone: +1 (415) 564-9968. Contact: George Poppin. This address, a volunteer office, only provides TRT schedules to listeners. All other correspondence should be sent directly to Ankara.
Türkiye Polis Radyosu (Turkish Police Radio), T.C. Içişleri Bakanliği, Emniyet Genel Müdürlüğü, Ankara, Turkey. Contact: Fatih Umutlu. Tourist literature for return postage. Replies irregularly.
Meteoroloji Sesi Radyosu (Voice of Meteorology), T.C. Tarim Bakanliği, Devlet Meteoroloji İşleri, Genel Müdürlüğü, P.K. 401, Ankara, Turkey. Phone: +90 (312) 359-7545, X-281.

Fax: +90 (312) 314 1196. Contact: (nontechnical) Gühekin Takinalp; or Abdullah Gölpinar; (technical) Mehmet Örmeci, Director General. Free tourist literature. Return postage helpful.

TURKMENISTAN World Time +5
"Turkmen Milliyet"—see Turkmen Radio, below.
Turkmen Radio, Ulitsa Mollanepes 3, 744000 Ashgabat, Turkmenistan. Phone: +7 (3632) 251-515. Fax: +7 (3632) 251 421. Contact: K. Karayev; or Yu M. Pashaev, Deputy Chairman of State Television and Radio Company; (technical) A.A Armanklichev, Deputy Chief, Technical Department. This country is currently under strict censorship and media people are closely watched. A lot of foreign mail addressed to a particular person may attract the attention of the secret service. Best bet is not to address your mail to particular individual but to the station itself.

UGANDA World Time +3
Radio Uganda
GENERAL OFFICE: P.O. Box 7142, Kampala, Uganda. Phone: +256 (41) 257-256. Fax: +256 (41) 256 888. Contact: Charles Byekwaso, Controller of Programmes; or Mrs. Florence Sewanyana, Head of Public Relations. $1 or return postage required. Replies infrequently and slowly.
ENGINEERING DIVISION: P.O. Box 2038, Kampala, Uganda. Contact: Leopold B. Lubega, Principal Broadcasting Engineer; or Rachel Nakibuuka. Four IRCs or $2 required. Enclosing a self addressed envelope may also help to get a reply.

UKRAINE World Time +2 (+3 midyear)
WARNING-MAIL THEFT: For the time being, letters to Ukrainian stations, especially those containing funds or IRCs, are more likely to arrive safely if sent by registered mail.
For Those at Sea, (Dly Tech Kto v More), Krymskoye Radio, ul. Krymskaya d. 6, 333000 Simferopol, Ukraine. Contact: Konstantin Lepin, who collects stamps and is a fan of American jazz. Via the Russian service of Voice of Russia (Golos Rossii), Russia (see).
Government Transmission Authority: RRT/Concern of Broadcasting, Radiocommunication & Television, 10 Dorogajtshaya St., 254112 Kiev, Ukraine. Phone: +380 (44) 226-2262 or +380 (44) 440-8688. Fax: +380 (44) 440 8722. Contact: Alexey Karpenko; Nikolai P. Kiriliuk, Head of Operative Management Service; or Mrs. Liudmila Deretskaya, Interpreter.
Radio Ukraine International, Kreshchatik str., 26, 252001 Kiev, Ukraine. Phone: +380 (44) 228-7356, +380 (44) 228-2534 or +380 (44) 229-1757. Fax: +380 (44) 229 4585. Contact: (administration) Inna Chichinadze, Vice-Director of RUI; (technical) see Ukrainian Radio, below. Free stickers, calendars and Ukrainian stamps.
Radio Lugansk, ul. Dem'ochina 25, 348000 Lugansk, Ukraine. Contact: A.N. Mospanova.
Ukrainian Radio, Kreshchatik str., 26, 252001 Kiev, Ukraine. Phone: +380 (44) 226-2253. Fax: (administration) +380 (44) 229 4226 or +380 (44) 229 4585. (technical) +380 (44) 220 6733. Contact: (administration) Volodimyr Reznikov, President of National Radio Company of Ukraine; or Victor Nabrusko, First Vice-President of National Radio Company of Ukraine; (technical) Anatoly Ivanov, Frequency Coordination, Engineering Services.

UNITED ARAB EMIRATES World Time +4
UAE Radio from Abu Dhabi, Ministry of Information & Culture, P.O. Box 63, Abu Dhabi, United Arab Emirates. Phone: +971 (2) 451-000. Fax: (station) +971 (2) 451 155; (Ministry of Information & Culture) +971 (2) 452 504. Contact: (general) Aïda Hamza, Director, Foreign Language Services; or Abdul Hadi Mubarak, Producer, "Live Program"; (technical) Ibrahim Rashid, Director General, Technical Department; or Fauzi Saleh, Chief Engineer. Free stickers, postcards and stamps. Do not enclose money with correspondence.

UAE Radio in Dubai, P.O. Box 1695, Dubai, United Arab Emirates. Phone: +971 (4) 370-255. Fax: +971 (4) 374 111 +971 (4) 370 283 or +971 (4) 371 079. Contact: Ms. Khulud Halaby; or Sameer Aga, Producer, "Cassette Club Cinarabic"; (technical) K.F. Fenner, Chief Engineer—Radio; or Ahmed Al Muhaideb, Assistant Controller, Engineering. Free pennants. Replies irregularly.

UNITED KINGDOM World Time exactly (+1 midyear)

Adventist World Radio, the Voice of Hope, AWR Branch Administrative Office, Newbold College, Binfield, Bracknell, Berks. RG42 4AN, United Kingdom. Phone: +44 (1344) 401-401. Fax: +44 (1344) 401 409. E-mail: 74617.2230@compuserve.com. Contact: Andrea Steele, Director Public Relations & Development. Also, see AWR listings under Costa Rica, Guam, Guatemala, Italy, Kenya, Russia and USA.

BBC Monitoring, Caversham Park, Reading RG4 8TZ, United Kingdom. Phone: (general) +44 (118) 947-2742; (Customer Service) +44 (118) 946-9338; (Foreign Media Unit—Broadcast Schedules/monitoring) +44 (118) 946-9261; (Marketing Department) +44 (118) 946-9204. Fax: (Customer Service) +44 (118) 946 1020; (Foreign Media Unit) +44 (118) 946 1993; (Marketing Department) +44 (118) 946 3828. E-mail: (Customer Service) csu@mon.bbc.co.uk; (Marketing Department) stephen_innes@mon.bbc.co.uk; (Foreign Media Unit/World Media) fmu@mon.bbc.co.uk; (Kenny) dave_kenny@mon.bbc.co.uk; (publications and real time services) marketing@mon.bbc.co.uk. URL: www.monitor.bbc.co.uk/Welcome.html. Contact: (administration) Andrew Hills, Director of Monitoring; (World Media) Chris McWhinnie, Editor "World Media"; (World Media Schedules) Dave Kenny, Sub Editor, "World Media"; (Publication Sales) Stephen Innes, Marketing. BBC Monitoring produces the weekly publication *World Media*. Available on yearly subscription, costing £390.00. Price excludes postage overseas. *World Media* is also available online through the Internet or via a direct dial-in bulletin board at an annual cost of £425.00. Broadcasting Schedules, issued weekly by e-mail at an annual cost of £99.00. VISA/MC/AX. The Technical Operations Unit provides detailed observations of broadcasts on the long, medium and short wave bands. This unit provides tailored channel occupancy observations, reception reports, *Broadcast Schedules Database* (constantly updated on over 100 countries) and the *Broadcast Research Log* (a record of broadcasting developments compiled daily). BBC Monitoring works in conjunction with the Foreign Broadcast Information Service (see USA).

📻BBC World Service

MAIN OFFICE, NONTECHNICAL: Bush House, Strand, London WC2B 4PH, United Kingdom. Phone: (general) +44 (171) 240-3456; (Press Office) +44 (171) 557-2947/1; (Marketing) +44 (171) 557-1142; (administration) +44 (171) 557-2057. Fax: (Audience Relations) +44 (171) 557-1258; ("Write On" listeners' letters program) +44 (171) 497 0287; (International Broadcasting & Audience Research) +44 (171) 557-1254. E-mail: (general listener correspondence) worldservice.letters@bbc.co.uk; (general BBC inquiries concerning domestic and external services) correspondence@bbc.co.uk. URLs: (general, including snippets of RealAudio) www.bbc.co.uk/worldservice/; (World Service program information) www.bbc.co.uk/worldservice/schedules/; (frequency database by language/stream and country) www.bbc.co.uk/worldservice/freq.html. Contact: Penny Long, Presenter, or Nick Baker, Executive Producer of "Write On"; Graham L. Mytton, Controller, Marketing; Sam Younger, Managing Director. Offers *BBC On Air* magazine (see below). Also, see Antigua, Ascension, Oman, Seychelles, Singapore and Thailand, which are where technical correspondence concerning these BBC relay transmissions should be sent if you seek a reply with full verification data, as no such data are provided via the London address. The present facility at Masirah, Oman, is scheduled to be replaced in 2001 by a new site at

Al-Ashkharah, also in Oman, which is to include four 300 kW shortwave transmitters.

SAN FRANCISCO OFFICE, SCHEDULES: 2654 17th Avenue, San Francisco CA 94116 USA. Phone: +1 (415) 564-9968. Contact: George Poppin. This address, a volunteer office, only provides BBC World Service schedules to listeners. All other correspondence should be sent directly to the main office in London.

TECHNICAL: See Merlin Communications International, below.

BBC World Service—Publication and Product Sales

BBC ENGLISH magazine, Bush House, Strand, London WC2B 4PH, United Kingdom. Phone: (editorial office) +44 (171) 557-1110. Fax: +44 (171) 557 1316.

BBC WORLD SERVICE SHOP, Bush House Arcade, Strand, London WC2B 4PH, United Kingdom. Phone: +44 (171) 557-2576. Fax: +44 (171) 240 4811. Sells numerous audio/video (video PAL/VHS only) cassettes, publications (including PASSPORT TO WORLD BAND RADIO), portable world band radios, T-shirts, sweatshirts and other BBC souvenirs available from BBC World Service Shop.

BBC ON AIR monthly program guide, Room 227 NW, Bush House, Strand, London WC2B 4PH, United Kingdom. Phone: (editorial office) +44 (171) 557-2211; (Circulation Manager) +44 (171) 557-2855; (advertising) +44 (171) 557-2873; (subscription voice mail) +44 (171) 557-2211. Fax: +44 (171) 240 4899. E-mail: on.air.magazine@bbc.co.uk. Contact: (editorial) Vicky Payne, Editor; (subscriptions) Rosemarie Reid, Circulation Manager; (advertising) Paul Cosgrove. Subscription $30 or £18 per year. VISA/MC/AX/Barclay/EURO/Access, Postal Order, International Money Draft or cheque in pounds sterling.

GERMAN BUREAU: Am-Taubertsberg 4, D-55122 Mainz, Germany.

Commonwealth Broadcasting Association, CBA Secretariat, Room 312, Yalding House, 152-156 Great Portland Street, London W1N 6AJ, United Kingdom. Phone: +44 (171) 765-5144 or +44 (171) 765-5151. Fax: +44 (171) 765 5152. E-mail: (general) cba@bbc.co.uk; (Smith) elizabeth.smith@bbc.co.uk. URL: www.oneworld.org/cba/. Contact: Elizabeth Smith, Secretary-General; Colin Lloyd, Manager—Training & Development. Publishes the annual *Who's Who in Commonwealth Broadcasting* and the quarterly *Combroad*.

Merlin Communications International Limited, Room 724 NE Wing, Bush House, P.O. Box 76, Strand, London WC2B 4PH, United Kingdom. Phone: (general) +44 (171) 557-2748; (Control Room) +44 (171) 557-2672; (Reception Analysis) +44 (171) 557-2155. Fax: (general) +44 (171) 379 3205; (Sones) +44 (171) 240 8926. Contact: Caroline Sones, Business Development Executive. This company is responsible for, amongst other things, the operation and maintenance of the BBC World Service's UK and overseas transmitter sites.

Far East Broadcasting Association (FEBA), Ivy Arch Road, Worthing, West Sussex BN14 8BX, United Kingdom. Phone: +44 (1903) 237-281. Fax: +44 (1903) 205 294. E-mail: reception@febaradio.org.uk. URL: www.feba.org.uk. Contact: Tony Ford. This office is the headquarters for FEBA worldwide.

UCB Europe—see Ireland.

📻World Radio Network Ltd, Wyvil Court, 10 Wyvil Road, London SW8 2TY, United Kingdom. Phone: +44 (171) 896-9000. Fax: +44 (171) 896 9007. E-mail: (general) online@wrn.org or wrn@cityscape.co.uk; (Cohen) jeffc@wrn.org. URLs: (general and Web radio) www.wrn.org; (sound files) http://town.org/radio/wrn.html. Contact: Karl Miosga, Managing Director; Jeffrey Cohen, President; or Simon Spanswick. Provides Web RealAudio and StreamWorks, plus program placement via satellite in various countries for nearly two dozen international broadcasters.

UNITED NATIONS World Time –5 (–4 midyear)

📻United Nations Radio, R/S-850, United Nations, New York NY 10017 USA; or write the station over which UN Radio was heard (Radio Myanmar, Radio Cairo, China Radio International, Sierra Leone Broadcasting Service, Radio Zambia, Radio Tanzania, Polish Radio Warsaw, HCJB/Ecuador, /Italy, All India Radio, RFPI/Costa Rica). Fax: +1 (212) 963 1307. E-mail: audio-visual@un.org. URLs: (RealAudio) www.nexus.org/IRN/index.html; www.wrn.org/stations/un.html. Contact: (general) Sylvester E. Rowe, Chief, Radio and Video Service; or Ayman El-Amir, Chief, Radio Section, Department of Public Information; (technical and nontechnical) Sandra Guy, Secretary. Free stamps and *UN Frequency* publication.

GENEVA OFFICE: see Switzerland.

PARIS OFFICE: UNESCO Radio, 7 Pl.de Fontenoy, F-75018 Paris, France. Fax: +33 (1) 45 67 30 72. Contact: Erin Faherty, Executive Radio Producer.

URUGUAY World Time −3

Emisora Ciudad de Montevideo, Canelones 2061, 11200 Montevideo, Uruguay. Fax: +598 (2) 420 700. Contact: Aramazd Yizmeyian, Director General. Free stickers. Return postage helpful.

La Voz de Artigas (when active), Av. Lecueder 483, 55000 Artigas, Uruguay. Phone: +598 (642) 2447 or +598 (642) 3445. Fax: +598 (642) 4744. Contact: (general) Sra. Solange Murillo Ricciardi, Co-Propietario; or Luis Murillo; (technical) Roberto Murillo Ricciardi. Free stickers and pennants. Replies to correspondence in English, Spanish, French, Italian and Portuguese.

Radiodifusion Nacional—*see* SODRE, below.

📻Radio Monte Carlo, Av. 18 de Julio 1224 piso 1, 11100 Montevideo, Uruguay. Phone:+598 (2) 905-423, +598 (2) 905-612, +598 (2) 914-433 or +598 (2) 983-987. Fax: +598 (2) 917 762. E-mail: cx20@netgate.comintur.com.uy. URL: (includes RealAudio) http://netgate.comintur.com.uy/cx20/. Contact: Ana Ferreira de Errázquin, Secretaria, Departamento de Prensa de la Cooperativa de Radioemisoras; Déborah Ibarra, Secretaria; Emilia Sánchez Vega, Secretaria; or Ulises Graceras. Correspondence in Spanish preferred.

📻Radio Oriental—Same mailing address and phone/fax numbers as Radio Monte Carlo, above. E-mail: cx12@netgate.comintur.com.uy. URL: (includes RealAudio) http://netgate.comintur.com.uy/cx12/. Correspondence in Spanish preferred.

SODRE

PUBLICITY AND TECHNICAL: Radiodifusión Nacional, Casilla 1412, 11000 Montevideo, Uruguay. E-mail: radioact@chasque.apc.org. URL: (Radioactividades) www.chasque.apc.org/radioact. Contact: (general) Roberto Belo, Radioactividades Producer; (publicity) Daniel Ayala González, Publicidad; (technical) Francisco Escobar, Depto. Técnico. Reception reports may also be sent to: Casilla 7011, Montevideo, Uruguay.

OTHER: "Radioactividades," Casilla 801 (or Casilla 6541), 11000 Montevideo, Uruguay. Fax: +598 (2) 48 71 27. Contact: Daniel Muñoz Faccioli.

USA World Time −4 Atlantic, including Puerto Rico and Virgin Islands; −5 (−4 midyear) Eastern, excluding Indiana; −5 Indiana, except northwest and southwest portions; −6 (−5 midyear) Central, including northwest and southwest Indiana; −7 (−6 midyear) Mountain, except Arizona; −7 Arizona; −8 (−7 midyear) Pacific; −9 (−8 midyear) Alaska, except Aleutian Islands; −10 (−9 midyear) Aleutian Islands; −10 Hawaii; −11 Samoa

Note on Disestablishmentarian Programs: Contact and related information for many American politically oriented shows that are of an anti-establishment bent are listed separately earlier in this chapter, under Disestablishmentarian, following the entries for Denmark.

📻Adventist World Radio, the Voice of Hope

WORLD HEADQUARTERS: 12501 Old Columbia Pike, Silver Spring MD 20904-6600 USA. Phone: +1 (301) 680-6304. Fax: +1 (301) 680 6303. E-mail: 74617.1621@compuserve.com.

URL: (World Wide Website includes RealAudio in English and Japanese) www.awr.org/. Contact: (general) Don Jacobsen, President. Most correspondence and all reception reports are best sent to the station from which the transmission you heard actually emanated (*see* Costa Rica, Guam, Guatemala, Italy (Italy also for Armenia, Germany and Slovakia transmissions) and Russia, rather than to the World Headquarters. Free religious printed matter, stickers, program schedules and other small souvenirs. IRC or $1 appreciated.

INTERNATIONAL RELATIONS: 903 Tanninger Drive, Indianapolis IN 46239 USA. Phone/fax: +1 (317) 891-8540. Contact: Dr. Adrian M. Peterson, International Relations. Provides publications with regular news releases and technical information. Annual DX contest in association with "Wavescan" program, *see* below. Issues some special verification cards. QSL stamps and certificates also available from this address in return for reception reports.

DX PROGRAM: "Wavescan," prepared by Adrian Peterson (*see* preceding); aired on all AWR facilities and also available via RealAudio at www.awr.org/online_programs.html.

LISTENER NEWSLETTER: Current, published quarterly by AWR, is available through AWR stations: Costa Rica, Guam and Italy. Free, but IRCs appreciated.

PUBLIC RELATIONS & DEVELOPMENT—see United Kingdom.

FREQUENCY MANAGEMENT OFFICE: AWR-Europe, Postfach 100252, D-64202 Darmstadt, Germany. Phone: +49 (6151) 390-920. Fax: +49 (6151) 390-913. E-mail: 102555.257@compuserve.com. Contact: Claudius Dedio, Frequency Manager. Implied by various reports is that this office will shortly be merged into the Public Relations & Development Office in the United Kingdom (*see*) or AWR's Italian facility (*see*).

Also, *see* AWR listings under Costa Rica, Guam, Guatemala, Kenya and Russia.

BBC World Service via WYFR—Family Radio. For verification direct from WYFR's transmitters, contact WYFR—Family Radio (*see* below). Nontechnical correspondence should be sent to the BBC World Service in London (*see*).

Broadcasting Board of Governors (BBG), 330 Independence Avenue SW, Room 3360, Washington DC 20547 USA. Phone: +1 (202) 401-3736. Fax: +1 (202) 401 3376. Contact: (general) Kathleen Harrington, Public Relations; (administration) David Burke, Chairman. The BBG, created in 1994 and headed by nine members nominated by the President, is the overseeing agency for all official non-military United States international broadcasting operations, including the VOA, RFE-RL, Radio Martí and Radio Free Asia.

Central Intelligence Agency, Washington DC 20505 USA. Phone: (press liason) +1 (703) 482-7668; (general) +1 (703) 482-1100. URLs: (general) www.odci.gov/cia/; (Public Affairs) www.odci.gov/cia/public_affairs/pas.html. Contact: (general) Dennis Boxx, Director, Public Affairs; Kent Harrington, Press Liason; (administration) Nora Slatkin, Executive Director. Although the CIA is not believed to be operating any broadcasting stations at present, it is known to have done so in the past, usually in the form of "black" clandestine stations, and could do so again in the future. Additionally, the Agency is reliably reported to have funded a variety of organizations over the years, and may still be funding a relatively small number of organizations today, which operate, control or influence world band programs and stations. Also, *see* Foreign Broadcast Information Service, below.

C-SPAN, 400 N Capitol Street NW, Suite 650, Washington DC 20001 USA. Phone: +1 (202) 626-4863 or +1 (202) 737-3220. Fax: +1 (202) 737 3323. URL: www.c-span.org/. Contact: Thomas Patton, Audio Network; or Rayne Pollack, Manager, Press Relations. Relays selected international radio broadcasts over cable systems within the United States.

Disestablishmentarian Programs—see Disestablishmentarian listing earlier in this chapter, following the entries for "Denmark."

FEBC Radio International

INTERNATIONAL HEADQUARTERS: Far East Broadcasting

Company, Inc., P.O. Box 1, La Mirada CA 90637 USA. Phone: +1 (310) 947-4651. Fax: +1 (310) 943 0160. E-mail: 3350911@mcimail.com; febc-usa@xc.org. URL: http://febc.org. Operates world band stations in the Northern Mariana Islands, the Philippines and the Seychelles.

UNITED KINGDOM OFFICE: FEBA Radio, Ivy Arch Road, Worthing, West Sussex BN14 8BX, United Kingdom. Phone: +44 (903) 237-281. Fax: +44 (903) 205 294.

Federal Communications Commission
ORGANIZATION: 1919 M Street NW, Washington DC 20554 USA (a scheduled move to the Portals complex in southwest Washington appears to have been postponed, if not deferred indefinitely, because of a lack of funds). Phone: (toll-free for licensed or prospective private broadcasters within the United States) (888) 225-5322 or (888) 322-8255; (general) +1 (202) 418-0200; (public affairs) +1 (202) 418-0500; (public affairs, recorded listing of releases and texts) +1 (202) 418-2222; (international bureau, technical) + 1 (202) 739-0509; (international bureau, administration) +1 (202) 418-0420; (international bureau, legal) +1 (202) 739-0415; (international bureau, notifications and WARC) +1 (202) 418-2156. Fax: (general) +1 (202) 418 0232; (public affairs) +1 (202) 418 2809; (international bureau, technical) +1 (202) 887 6124 or +1 (202) 418 0398; (international bureau, administration) +1 (202) 418 2818; (international bureau, legal) +1 (202) 887 0175. E-mail: (general) fccinfo@fcc.gov; (specific individuals) format is initiallastname@fcc.gov, so to reach, say, Tom Polzin it would be tpolzin@fcc.gov. URLs: (shortwave broadcasting, direct) www.fcc.gov/ib/pnd/neg/hf_web/hf.html; (shortwave broadcasting via welcome page) www.fcc.Welcome.html, then follow the links to the International Bureau, Hot Topics and HF-Broadcasting; (general) http://fcc.gov/; (FTP) ftp://ftp.fcc.gov (shortwave broadcasting files can be downloaded from /pub/Bureaus/International/). Contact: (public affairs) Patricia Chew or Sharon Hurd; (public affairs, administration) Susan Lewis Sallet, Director; Maureen P. Peratino, Deputy Director; David H. Fiske, Deputy Director; Sharon Jenkins, Chief, Consumer Assistance Branch; (international bureau, technical) Thomas E. Polzin, James Ballis, Larry W. Olson, Acting Chief, Planning; or Charles Magnuson, Planning and Negotiations Division, International Bureau, Room 892; (international bureau, legal) Jonathan Stern, Esq., Senior Legal Advisor, Suite 800; (international bureau, notifications and WARC) Charles Breig, Chief; (international bureau, administration) Donald H. Gips, Chief; Ruth Milkman, Deputy Chief; Roderick K. Porter, Deputy Chief. The FCC, whose International Bureau has recently been functioning exceptionally well, regulates all private broadcasting within the United States, and is not affiliated with the Voice of America/IBB. However, the FCC as a whole is being drastically downsized to save funds, and in the process plans no longer to concern itself with complaints from the public about powerline and other illegal electrical interference to radio receivers.

POTENTIAL OF DOMESTIC SHORTWAVE BROADCASTING: In 1995, the International Bureau discovered, to its surprise, that there may not be a valid legal basis for the present FCC rule prohibiting domestic shortwave broadcasting. (Currently, private U.S. world band stations must be configured to broadcast internationally, a relatively costly proposition.) Although the Bureau has no plans to act on its own in this regard, it may do so should forces within the broadcasting industry—such as AM stations wishing to increase audience size via low-power regional shortwave simulcasting—demonstrate a strong interest in having the rule-making procedure opened on that issue.

Foreign Broadcast Information Service, P.O. Box 2604, Washington DC 20013 USA. Phone: +1 (202) 338-6735. Parented by the CIA (*see*, above) and working in concert with BBC Monitoring (*see* United Kingdom) and selected other organizations, the F.B.I.S., with listening posts in various countries outside the United States, monitors broadcasts worldwide for intelligence-gathering purposes. However, it never engages in broadcasting or jamming of any sort, directly or indirectly.

☞**Fundamental Broadcasting Network**, Grace Missionary Baptist Church, Newport NC 28570 USA. Phone: +1 (919) 223-6088. URL: (includes RealAudio) www.clis.com/fbn/. E-mail: fbn@bmd.clis.com. Alternative address: Morehead City NC 28557 USA. Phone: +1 (919) 240-1600. Fax: + (919) 726 2251. Contact: Pastor Clyde Eborn. Provides programming for WGTG, USA.

George Jacobs and Associates, Inc., 8701 Georgia Avenue, Suite 410, Silver Spring MD 20910 USA. Phone: +1 (301) 587-8800. Fax: +1 (301) 587 8801. E-mail: gja@gjainc.com; or gjacobs@clark.net. URL: www.gjainc.com/. Contact: (technical) Bob German or Mrs. Anne Case; (administration) George Jacobs, P.E. This firm provides frequency management and other engineering services for a variety of private U.S. and other world band stations, but does not correspond with the general public.

Government Broadcasting Regulatory Authority—For private international broadcasting, see Federal Communications Commission, above; also, see the non-governmental National Association of Shortwave Broadcasters, below. For non-military governmental international broadcasting, see Broadcasting Board of Governors (BBG).

Herald Broadcasting Syndicate—Shortwave Broadcasts (all locations), Shotwave Broadcasts, P.O. Box 1524, Boston MA 02117-1524 USA. Phone: (general, toll-free within U.S.) 1-800-288-7090 or (general elsewhere) +1 (617) 450-2929 [with either number, extension 2060 to hear recorded frequency information, or 2929 for Shortwave Helpline and request printed schedules and information]. Fax: +1 (617) 450 2283. E-mail: (letters and reception reports) letterbox@csps.com; or (religious questions) sentinel@csps.com. URL: (*The Christian Science Monitor* newspaper) www.csmonitor.com; or (information about The Christian Science Church in Boston) www.tfccs.com. Contact: Catherine Aitken-Smith, Director of International Broadcasting, Herald Broadcasting Syndicate (representative for station activity in Boston); or Tina Hammers, Frequency and Production Coordinator. Free schedules and information about Christian Science. *The Christian Science Monitor* newspaper and a full line of Christian Science books are available from: 1 Norway Street, Boston MA 02115 USA. *Science and Health with Key to the Scriptures* by Mary Baker Eddy is available in English $14.95 paperback ($16.95 in French, German, Portuguese or Spanish paperback; $24.95 in Czech or Russian hardcover) from Science and Health, P.O. Box 1875, Boston MA 02117 USA. Also, *see* Northern Mariana Islands.

Herald Broadcasting Syndicate—WSHB Cypress Creek, Rt. 2, Box 107A, Pineland SC 29934 USA. Phone: (general) +1 (803) 625-5555; (station manager) +1 (803) 625-5551; (engineer) +1 (803) 625-5554. Fax: +1 (803) 625 5559. E-mail: (station manager) cee@csms.com; (engineer) tony@csms.com; (QSL coordinator) judy@csms.com. URL: www.tfccs.com. Contact: (technical) Antonio L. (Tony") Kobatake, Chief Transmitter/Service Engineer; C. Ed Evans, Senior Station Manager; or Judy P. Cooke, QSL Coordinator. Visitors welcome from 9 to 4 Monday through Friday; for other times, contact transmitter site beforehand to make arrangements. This address for technical feedback on South Carolina transmissions only; other inquiries should be directed to the P.O. Box 1524, Boston address.

International Broadcasting Bureau (IBB)—*see* Voice of America/VOA. Also, RFE-RL (technical).

KAIJ
ADMINISTRATION OFFICE: Two-if-by-Sea Broadcasting Co., 22720 SE 410th St., Enumclaw WA 89022 USA. Phone/fax: (Mike Parker, California) +1 (818) 606-1254; (Washington State office, if and when operating) +1 (206) 825 4517. Contact: Mike Parker (mark envelope, "please forward"). Relays programs of Dr. Gene Scott. Replies occasionally.

STUDIO: Faith Center, 1615 S. Glendale Avenue, Glendale CA 91025 USA. Phone: +1 (818) 246-8121. Contact: Dr. Gene Scott, President.

TRANSMITTER: RR#3 Box 120, Frisco TX 75034 USA (physical location: Highway 380, 3.6 miles west of State Rt. 289, near Denton TX). Phone: +1 (214) 346-2758. Contact: Walt Green or Fred Bethel. Station encourages mail to be sent to administration office, which seldom replies, or the studio (*see above*).

KGEI—Voice of Friendship—The original owners discontinued transmission from Redwood City, California, during last half of 1994 because of the high cost of operation at that location. However, another organization, the Calvary Chapel of Costa Mesa, California, hopes to reactivate operation from near Twin Falls, Idaho, in the United States, although they have not as yet filed an application with the Federal Communications Commission. They plan to use the KGEI— Voice of Friendship call sign and the aging California 250 kW transmitter, donated by the former owners, for religious transmissions to Latin America, especially Mexico.

KJES—King Jesus Eternal Savior

STATION: The Lord's Ranch, 230 High Valley Road, Vado NM 88072 USA. Phone: +1 (505) 233-2090. Fax: +1 (505) 233 3019. E-mail: KJES@aol.com. Contact: Michael Reuter, Manager. $1 or return postage appreciated.

SPONSORING ORGANIZATION: Our Lady's Youth Center, P.O. Box 1422, El Paso TX 79948 USA. Phone: +1 (915) 533-9122.

KNLS—New Life Station

OPERATIONS CENTER: 605 Bradley Ct., Franklin TN 37067 USA (letters sent to the Alaska transmitter site are usually forwarded to Franklin). Phone: +1 (615) 371-8707 ext.107. Fax: +1 (615) 371 8791. E-mail: knls@aol.com. URLs: www.knls.org; www.montara.com/WCB/aaaindex.htm. Contact: (general) Wesley Jones, Director, Follow-Up Teaching; or Steven Towell, Senior Producer, English Language Service; (technical) Mike Osborne, Production Manager and Webeditor. Free *Alaska Calling!* newsletter, pennants, stickers, English-language and Russian-language religious tapes and literature, and English-language learning course materials for Russian speakers. Free information about Alaska. Radio-related publications and bibles available; 2 IRCs appreciated for each book. Special, individually numbered, limited edition, verification cards issued for each new transmission period to the first 200 listeners providing confirmed reception reports. Swaps canceled stamps from different countries to help listeners round out their stamp collections. Accepts faxed reports. Return postage appreciated.

TRANSMITTER SITE: P.O. Box 473, Anchor Point AK 99556 USA. Phone: +1 (907) 235-8262. Fax: +1 (907) 235 2326. Contact: (technical) Kevin Chambers, Engineer.

KTBN—Trinity Broadcasting Network:

GENERAL CORRESPONDENCE: P.O. Box A, Santa Ana CA 92711 USA. Phone: +1 (714) 832-2950. Fax: +1 (714) 731 4196 or +1 (714) 665 2101. E-mail: tbntalk@tbn.org. URLs: (Trinity Broadcasting Network, including RealAudio) www.tbn.org; (KTBN) www.tbn.org/ktbn.html. Contact: Dr. Paul F. Crouch, Managing Director; Jay Jones, Producer, "Music of Praise"; or Programming Department. Monthly TBN newsletter. Free booklets, stickers and small souvenirs sometimes available. Return postage (IRC or SASE) helpful.

TECHNICAL CORRESPONDENCE: Engineering/QSL Department, 2442 Michelle Drive, Tustin CA 92780-7015 USA. Phone: +1 (714) 665-2145. Fax: +1 (714) 730 0661. E-mail: bmiller@tbn.org. Contact: Chris Hiser, QSL Manager; or W. Ben Miller, Vice President of Engineering.

KVOH—High Adventure Radio

MAIN OFFICE: P.O. Box 100, Simi Valley CA 93062 USA. Phone: +1 (805) 520-9460; toll-free (within USA) 1-800-517-HOPE. Fax: +1 (805) 520 7823. E-mail: highadventure@guns.net; kvoh@themall.net. URL: www.highadventure.org. Contact: (listeners' correspondence) Pat Kowalick, "Listeners' Letterbox"; (administration, High Adventure Ministries)

George Otis, President and Chairman; (administration, KVOH) Paul Johnson, General Manager, KVOH; (technical) Paul Hunter, Network Chief Engineer. Free program schedules and *Voice of Hope* book. Sells books, audio and video cassettes, T-shirts and world band radios. Booklist available on request. VISA/MC. Plans to add further languages and increase broadcasting hours. Also, *see* Lebanon. Return postage (IRCs) required. Replies as time permits.

VICTORIA, AUSTRALIA OFFICE, NONTECHNICAL: P.O. Box 295, Vermont, Victoria 3133, Australia. Phone: +61 (3) 9801-4648. Fax: +61 (3) 9887 1145. Contact: Roger Pearce, Director; or Helen Pearce.

WESTERN AUSTRALIA OFFICE, NONTECHNICAL: 79 Sycamore Drive, Duncraig WA 6023, Australia. Phone: +61 (9) 9345-1777. Fax: +61 (9) 9345 5407. Contact: Caron or Peter Hedgeland.

CANADA OFFICE, NONTECHNICAL: Box 425, Station "E", Toronto, M6H 4E3 Canada. Phone/fax: +1 (416) 898-5447. Contact: Don McLaughlin, Director.

PALAU OFFICE, NONTECHNICAL: P.O. Box 66, Koror, Palau 96940, Pacific Islands. Phone: +680 488-2162. Fax: +680 488 2163. Contact: Regina Subris.

SINGAPORE OFFICE, NONTECHNICAL: 105 Cairhill Circle, Hilltops #13-107, Singapore 0922, Singapore. Phone/fax: + 65 737-1682. Contact: Cyril Seah.

U.K. OFFICE: P.O. Box 109, Hereford HR4 9XR, United Kingdom. Phone: +44 (1432) 359-099 or (mobile) +44 (0589) 078-444. Fax: +44 (1432) 263 408. E-mail: 101602.3273@compuserve.com. Contact: Peter Darg, Director; or Helen Darg. This office verifies reports of Voice of Hope ("European Beacon") broadcasts via Tbilisi, Georgia.

KWHR-World Harvest Radio:

ADMINISTRATION OFFICE: see WHRI, USA, below.

TRANSMITTER: Although located 6½ miles southwest of Naalehu, 8 miles north of South Cape, and 2000 feet west of South Point (Ka La) Road (the antennas are easily visible from this road) on otherwise friendly Big Island, Hawaii, the folks at this rural transmitter site maintain no post office box in or near Naalehu, and their telephone number is unlisted, reportedly because of hostile phone calls from a local individual. Best bet is to contact them via their administration office (*see* WHRI, below), or to drive in unannounced (it's just off South Point Road) the next time you vacation on Big Island. If you learn more, please let us know! A new transmitter serving the South Pacific is due to come online during August 1997.

Leinwoll (Stanley)—Telecommunication Consultant, 305 E. 86th Street, Suite 21S-W, New York NY 10028 USA. Phone: +1 (212) 987-0456. Fax: +1 (212) 987 3532. Contact: Stanley Leinwoll, President. This firm provides frequency management and other engineering services for a variety of private U.S. world band stations, but does not correspond with the general public.

National Association of Shortwave Broadcasters

HEADQUARTERS: 11185 Columbia Pike, Silver Spring MD 20901 USA. Phone: +1 (301) 593-5409. Fax: +1 (301) 681 0099. Contact: Tulio R. Haylock, Secretary-Treasurer. Association of most private U.S. world band stations, as well as a group of other international broadcasters, equipment manufacturers and organizations related to shortwave broadcasting. Includes committees on various subjects, such as digital shortwave radio. Interfaces with the Federal Communications Commission's International Bureau and other broadcasting-related organizations to advance the interests of its members. Publishes *NASB Newsletter* for members and associate members; free sample upon request on letterhead of an appropriate organization. Annual one-day convention held near Washington DC's National Airport early each spring; non-members wishing to attend should contact the Secretary-Treasurer in advance; convention fee typically $50 per person.

MEMBERSHIP OFFICE: 276 N. Bobwhite, Orange CA 92669 USA. Phone/fax: (membership information) +1 (714) 771-1843.

Contact: William E. "Ted" Haney, Membership Chairman, NASB. Full Membership (only for private U.S. shortwave broadcasters) $500 or more /year; Associate Membership (other organizations, subject to approval): $500/year.

Public Radio International, 100 North Sixth Street, Suite 900A, Minneapolis MN 55403 USA. Phone: (general) +1 (612) 338-5000, (New Business Development) +1 (612) 330-9238. Fax: +1 (612) 330 9222. URL: www.pri.org/. Contact: Beth Talisman, Senior Manager, New Business Development; or Stephen Salyer, President and CEO. Makes available selected international broadcasts for those PRI radio stations within the United States which choose to air them in whole or in part, often after having taped them for later replay. Interestingly, PRI's placement of international programs seems to have increased, rather than decreased, the interest in world band listening within the United States.

Radio Free Asia, Suite 300, 2025 M Street NW, Washington DC 20036 USA. Phone: (general) +1 (202) 530-4900 or +1 (202) 457-6975; (programming) +1 (202) 530-4907; (president) +1 (202) 457-6948; (technical) +1 (202) 822-6234. Fax: +1 (202) 457 6996 or +1 (202) 530 7794/95. E-mail: the format is lastnameinitial@rfa.org; so to reach, say, David Baden, it would be badend@rfa.org. URL: www.rfa.org. Contact: (administration) Richard Richter, President; Craig Perry, Vice President; Daniel Southerland, Executive Editor; (listener contact) Ms. Arin Basu, Secretary; (technical) David Baden, Director of Technical Operations. Free stickers. RFA, originally created in 1996 as the Asia Pacific Network, is funded as a private nonprofit U.S. corporation by a grant from the Broadcasting Board of Governors, a politically bi-partisan body appointed by the President (see).

Radio Martí, Office of Cuba Broadcasting, 400 6th Street SW, Washington DC 20547 USA. Phone: +1 (202) 401-7013. Fax: +1 (202) 401 3340. E-mail: (technical) rseifert@usia.gov. Contact: (general) Rolando Bonachea, Director of Radio; or Agustín Alles, Director of News; (technical) Rick Seifert, Engineering Supervisor; or Mike Pallone, Technical Director. This station, which reportedly is friendly to the Cuban American National Foundation (see "La Voz de la Fundación," under Disestablishmentarian), is in the process of moving to new facilities in Miami.

"Radio Newyork International," 97 High Street, Kennebunk ME 04043 USA. Phone: (Weiner) +1 (207) 985-7547; (Becker) +1 (316) 825-4209. E-mail: AnitaM1061@aol.com. Contact: Allan Weiner, Scott Becker or Anita McCormick. Two "RNI the Video" NTSC cassettes $24.95 each; two "Best of Voyages Broadcast Services" audio cassettes $14.95 each, or both $24.95. Also, Offshore Society sells T-shirts, tote bags and such. Last heard as an entertainment program, rather than the original disestablishmentarian offshore exercise. However, Weiner, along with partner Becker, plan to finish outfitting their new ship, the Electra, as a shortwave station under the name "Lightwave Mission Broadcasting," providing enough financial backing can be found, such as via contributions to their "Offshore Society."

📻RFE-RL

PRAGUE HEADQUARTERS: Vinohradská 1, 110 00 Prague 1, Czech Republic. Phone: (switchboard) +420 (2) 2112-1111 or +420 (2) 2422-752; (President) +420 (2) 2112-3000/3001; (Technical Operations) +420 (2) 2112-3700; (Broadcast Operations) +420 (2) 2112-3550. Fax: (President) +420 (2) 2112 3002; (Broadcast Operations) +420 (2) 2112 3586; (news & current affairs) +420 (2) 2112 3600; (information services) +420 (2) 2112 2006. E-mail: the format is lastnameinitial@rferl.org; so to reach, say, David Walcutt, it would be walcuttd@rferl.org. URL: (general, including RealAudio) www.rferl.org/; (broadcast services) www.rferl.org/bd/index.html. Contact: Tom Morgan, Director of Technical Operations; Luke Springer, Director of Broadcast Operations; Thomas A. Dine, President; or Robert McMahon, Director of News & Current Affairs.

WASHINGTON OFFICE: 1201 Connecticut Avenue NW, Wash-

Among the growing roster of world band stations also broadcasting on the Web is Washington's VOA. Web radio is explained and detailed in the annual Passport to Web Radio.

ington DC 20036 USA. Phone: (general) +1 (202) 457-6900; (news) +1 (202) 457-6950; (technical) +1 (202) 457-6963. Fax: +1 (202) 457 6992; (technical) +1 (202) 457 6995. E-mail and URL: *see above.* Contact: (general) Jane Lester, Secretary of the Corporation; (news) Oleh Zwadiuk, Washington Bureau Chief; (technical) David Walcutt, Broadcast Operations Liaison Officer. This organization has changed considerably from Cold War days, with its remaining transmission facilities now being a part of the International Broadcasting Bureau (IBB), *see.*

📻Rock-it Radio, P.O. Box 5617, Ventura CA 93005 USA. E-mail: Rockitrad@aol.com. URL: www.alpcom.it/hamradio/freewaves/rock_html; (RealAudio during weekends) www.nexus.org/IRN. Contact: Bennie Dingo. Independent radio program featuring rare and unreleased Rock and Roll of the 1950's. Reception reports requested. Program is aired via IRRS Milan and WRMI-Radio Miami International—*see* Italy and USA below.

Trans World Radio, International Headquarters, P.O. Box 8700, Cary NC 27512-8700 USA. Phone: +1 (919) 460-3700. Fax: +1 (919) 460 3702. E-mail: info2@twr.org. URL: www.gospelcom.net/twr/twr_index.htm. Contact: (general) Jon Vaught, Public Relations; Richard Greene, Director, Public Relations; Joe Fort, Director, Broadcaster Relations; or Bill Danick; (technical) Glenn W. Sink, Assistant Vice President, International Operations. Free "Towers to Eternity" publication for those living in the U.S. Technical correspondence should be sent to the office nearest the country where the transmitter is located—Guam, Monaco or Swaziland.

📻University Network, P.O. Box 1, Los Angeles CA 90053 USA. Phone: (toll-free within U.S.) 1-800-338-3030; (elsewhere, call collect) +1 (818) 240-8151. E-mail: drgenescott@drgenescott.org. URLs (including RealAudio): www.drgenescott.org/; http://207.155.78.66/. Contact: Dr. Gene Scott. Sells audio and video tapes and books relating to Dr. Scott's teaching. Free copies of *The Truth About* and *The University Cathedral Pulpit* publications. Transmits via its own facilities (KAIJ, USA and Caribbean Beacon, Anguilla) as well as those of WWCR (USA) and Voice of Russia.

USA Radio Network, 2290 Springlake #107, Dallas TX 75234 USA. E-mail: newsroom@usaradio.com. URL:

No miniskirts, please! WEWN's Sister M. Raphael, torn between St. Anthony and St. Francis. WEWN, a traditionalist Roman Catholic station led by the feisty Mother Angelica, is not associated with the Vatican. Nevertheless, it is much better heard throughout the Americas than the official Vatican Radio.

www.usaradio.com/. Does not broadcast on shortwave, but some of its news and other programs are heard via WHRI and WWCR, USA.

📻 Voice of America/VOA-IBB—All Transmitter Locations
MAIN OFFICE, NONTECHNICAL: United States Information Agency (USIA), International Broadcasting Bureau (IBB), 330 Independence Avenue SW, Washington DC 20547 USA. If contacting the VOA directly is impractical, write c/o the American Embassy or USIS Center in your country. Phone: (to hear VOA-English live) +1 (202) 619-1979; (Office of External Affairs) +1 (202) 619-2358 or +1 (202) 619-2039; (Audience Mail Division) +1 (202) 619-2770; (Africa Division) +1 (202) 619-1666 or +1 (202) 619-2879; ("Communications World") +1 (202) 619-3047; (Office of Research) +1 (202) 619-4965; (Computer Services) +1 (202) 619-2020; (administration) +1 (202) 619-1088. Fax: (general information for listeners outside the United States) +1 (202) 376 1066; (Public Liaison for listeners within the United States) +1 (202) 619 1241; (Office of External Affairs) +1 (202) 205 0634 or +1 (202) 205 2875; (Africa Division) +1 (202) 619 1664; ("Communications World," Audience Mail Division and Office of Research) +1 (202) 619 0211; (administration) +1 (202) 619 0085; ("Communications World") +1 (202) 619 2543. E-mail: (general inquires outside the United States) letters@voa.gov; (reception reports from outside the United States) qsl@voa.gov; (reception reports from within the United States) qsl-usa@voa.gov; ("Communications World") cw@voa.gov; (Office of Research) gmackenz@usia.gov. URLs: www.voa.gov/; (text only) www.voa.gov/text-only.html; (text, plus audio in .au and .wav) www.voa.gov; gopher://gopher.voa.gov; ftp://ftp.voa.gov; (RealAudio) www.voa.gov/programs/audio/realaudio or www.wrn.org/stations/voa.html. Contact: Mrs. Betty Lacy Thompson, Chief, Audience Mail Division, B/K. G759A Cohen; Leo Sarkisian; Rita Rochelle, Africa Division; Kim Andrew Elliott, Producer, "Communications World"; Kevin Klose, Director; Chris Kern, Chief of Computer Services; or George Mackenzie, Audience Research Officer. Free stickers and calendars. Free "Music Time in Africa" calendar, to non-U.S. addresses only, from Mrs. Rita Rochelle, Africa Division, Room 1622. If you're an American and miffed because you can't receive these goodies from the VOA, don't blame the station—they're only following the law. The VOA occasionally hosts international broadcasting conventions, and as of 1996 has been accepting limited supplemental funding from the U.S. Agency for International Development (AID).
MAIN OFFICE, TECHNICAL: United States Information Agency (USIA), International Broadcasting Bureau (IBB), 330 Independence Avenue SW, Washington DC 20547 USA. Contact: Mrs. Irene Greene, QSL Desk, Audience Mail Division, Room G-759-C; (administration) Robert Kamosa, Head, IBB-Engineering. E-mail: qsl@voa.gov. Also, see Ascension, Botswana, Greece, Morocco, Philippines, São Tomé e Príncipe, Sri Lanka and Thailand.
FREQUENCY AND MONITORING OFFICE, TECHNICAL: USIA/IBB/EOF: Frequency Management & Monitoring Division, United States Information Agency (USIA), International Broadcasting Bureau (IBB), 4611 Cohen Bldg., 330 Independence Avenue SW, Washington DC 20547 USA. Phone: +1 (202) 619-1669. Fax: +1 (202) 619 1680 or +1 (202) 619 1781. E-mail: dan_ferguson@beng.voa.gov or bw@his.com. URL: (general) http://voa.his.com/; (monitoring results database) http://fmds.ibb.his.com/. Contact: Daniel Ferguson or Bill Whitacre.
LABOR REPRESENTATION: AFGE Local 1812/USIA, 301 4th Street SW, Room 348, Washington DC 20547 USA. Phone: +1 (202) 619-4759. Contact: Stacey Rose-Blass. Local 1812 is active in trying to maintain the VOA as an active force in international broadcasting.

Voice of America/VOA-IBB—Delano Relay Station, Rt. 1, Box 1350, Delano CA 93215 USA. Phone: +1 (805) 725-0150 or +1 (805) 861-4136. Fax: +1 (805) 725 6511. Contact: (technical) Jim O'Neill, Engineer; or Perry G. Pitts, Manager. Nontechnical correspondence should be sent to the VOA address in Washington.

Voice of America/VOA-IBB—Greenville Relay Station, P.O. Box 1826, Greenville NC 27834 USA. Phone: +1 (919) 758-2171 or +1 (919) 752-7115. Fax: +1 (919) 752 5959. Contact: (technical) Bruce Hunter, Manager. Nontechnical correspondence should be sent to the VOA address in Washington.

📻 WEWN—EWTN Worldwide Catholic Radio
STATION OFFICE: Eternal Word Radio Network (EWTN), Catholic Radio Service, P.O. Box 100234, Birmingham AL 35210 USA; WEWN Catholic Shortwave Radio, 5817 Old Leeds Rd., Birmingham AL 35210 USA. Phone: (toll-free within U.S.) 1-800-585-9396; (elsewhere) +1 (205) 672-7200. Fax: +1 (205) 672 9988. E-mail: (general) 70413.40@compuserve.com; (information and listener feedback) viewer@ewtn.com; (Spanish) gbujanda@ewtn.com. URLs: (EWTN) www.ewtn.com/; (WEWN) www.ewtn.com/WEWN/radio1.htm; (RealAudio) www.AudioNet.com/lightsource/EWTN/canvas.html. Contact: (general) Mrs. Gwen Carr, Office Manager; W. Glen Tapley, Director of Network Radio Operations; or Father John Mary Klobacher, Chaplain, co-host of "Live Wire" call-in program; (marketing) Scott Hults, Director of Radio Marketing and Program Development; (administration) William Steltemeier, President; (technical) Frank Phillips, Vice President of Radio; Joseph A. Dentici, Frequency Manager; or Matt Cadak, Chief Engineer. Listener correspondence welcomed; responds to correspondence on-air and by mail. Free *Gabriel's Horn* newsletter and bumper stickers; also, free *At Mary's Knee* quarterly newsletter for children. Sells numerous religious publications ranging from $2 to $20, as well as T-shirts ($10-12), sweatshirts ($15 donation) and world band radios ($50 to $225); list available upon request (VISA/MC). IRC or return postage appreciated for correspondence. Volunteers needed for placing articles or ads in parish or Diocesan publications, as well as other parish activities. Although a Catholic entity, WEWN is not an official station of the Vatican, which operates its own Vatican Radio (see). Rather, WEWN reflects the activities of Mother M. Angelica and the Eternal Word Foundation, Inc. Donations and bequests accepted by the Eternal Word Foundation.

TRANSMISSION FACILITY: P.O. Box 176, Vandiver AL 35176 USA. Phone and fax: *see* Station Office, above. Contact: Bernard Lockhart, Marketing Manager; or Norman Williams, Manager, Planning & Installation.

RELIGIOUS ORDER and EWTN ORGANIZATIONAL HEAD-QUARTERS: Our Lady of The Angels Monastery, 5817 Old Leeds Road, Birmingham AL 35210 USA. Phone: +1 (205) 956-5987. Fax: +1 (205) 951 0142.

WGTG—With Glory To God, Box 1131, Copperhill TN 37317 USA; or 2710 Hawk Drive, Marietta GA 30066 USA. Phone/fax: +1 (706) 492-5944. Contact: (general) Roseanne Frantz, Program Director; or "Mail Bag"; (technical) Dave Frantz, Chief Engineer. $1 or 3 IRCs for verification response. WGTG is a family-run Christian station partly supported by listener donations. Comments on reception quality, and especially audio quality, are welcomed. SASE appreciated. Hopes to add four more AM/SSB transmitters, nominally of 50 kW apiece.

PROGRAM PROVIDER: Fundamental Broadcasting Network (*see*). A nonprofit organization, FBN feeds program material to WGTG via satellite.

WHRI—World Harvest Radio, WHRI/KWHR, LeSEA Broadcasting, P.O. Box 12, South Bend IN 46624 USA. Phone: +1 (219) 291-8200. Fax: (station) +1 (219) 291 9043. E-mail: whri@lesea.com; (Brashier) jbrashier@whri.com; (Hill) jhill@whri.com. URLs (including RealAudio): www.whri.com/; (LeSEA Broadcasting parent organization) www.lesea.com/. Contact: (listener contact) Loren Holycross; (general) Joe Brashier, Vice President; or Joe Hill, Operations Manager; (technical) Douglas Garlinger, Chief Engineer. Free stickers. WHRI T-shirts (one for $12, two for $20) from 61300 S. Ironwood Road, South Bend IN 46614 USA. Return postage appreciated. Carries programs from various political organizations; these may be contacted either directly (*see* Disestablishmentarian, earlier in this chapter) or via WHRI.

WINB—World International Broadcasters, World International Broadcast Network, P.O. Box 88, Red Lion PA 17356 USA. Phone: (general) +1 (717) 244-5360; (administration) +1 (717) 246-1681; (studio) +1 (717) 244-3145. Fax: +1 (717) 244 9316. Contact: (general) Mrs. Sally Spyker, Correspondence Secretary; John Stockdale, Manager; Clyde H. Campbell, C.F.O.; or John H. Norris, Owner; (technical) Fred W. Wise, Technical Director. Return postage helpful outside United States. No giveaways or items for sale.

WJCR—Jesus Christ Radio, P.O. Box 91, Upton KY 42784 USA. Phone: +1 (502) 369-8614. URL: www.mindspring.com/~brunner/wjcr.html. Contact: (general) Pastor Don Powell, President; Gerri Powell; Trish Powell; or A.L. Burile; (technical) Louis Tate, Chief Engineer. Free religious printed matter. Return postage or $1 appreciated. Actively solicits listener contributions.

WMLK—Assemblies of Yahweh, P.O. Box C, Bethel PA 19507 USA. Toll free telephone (U.S only) 1-800-523 3827; (elsewhere) +1 (717) 933-4518. URL: http://marvin.ecc.cc.mo.us/~rdimmett/snb1.html. Contact: (general) Elder Jacob O. Meyer, Manager & Producer of "The Open Door to the Living World"; (technical) Gary McAvin, Engineer. Free *Yahweh* magazine, stickers and religious material. Bibles, audio tapes and religious paperback books offered. Enclosing return postage ($1 or IRCs) helps speeds things up. Plans to increase transmitter power to 100 kW in the near future.

WRMI—Radio Miami Internacional

MAIN OFFICE: P.O. Box 526852, Miami FL 33152 USA. Phone: +1 (305) 267-1728. Fax: +1 (305) 267 9253. E-mail: 71163.1735@compuserve.com; or wrmi@compuserve.com. URL: http://home.nexus.org/WRMI/. Contact: (general) Jeff White, General Manager; (technical) Indalecio "Kiko" Espinosa, Chief Engineer. Free station stickers and tourist brochures. Sells PASSPORT TO WORLD BAND RADIO $23-33 (Depending where in the world it is sent), Grundig Yacht Boy 400 radios $205-220 (ditto), T-shirts $15 (worldwide), baseball-style hats $10 (worldwide)—all postpaid by air-

mail. No cards. Sells "public access" airtime to nearly anyone to say virtually anything for $1 or more per minute. Radio Miami Internacional also acts as a broker for Cuban exile programs aired via U.S. stations WHRI and WRNO. Technical correspondence may be sent to either WRMI or the station over which the program was heard. Hopes to add one or more new antennas and an additional 50 kW transmitter in the foreseeable future.

VENEZUELA OFFICE: Apartado 2122, Valencia 2001, Venezuela. Phone:/fax: + 58 (45) 810-362. Contact: Yoslen Silva.

WRNO, Box 100, New Orleans LA 70181 USA; or 4539 I-10 Service Road North, Metairie LA 70006 USA. Phone: +1 (504) 889-2424. Fax: +1 (504) 889 0602. URL: www.wrnoworldwide.com/. Contact: Paul Heingarten, Operations Manager. Single copy of program guide for 2 IRCs or an SASE. Stickers available for SASE. T-shirts available for $10. Sells World Band radios. Carries programs from various organizations; these may be contacted either directly (*see* Disestablishmentarian, earlier in this section) or via WRNO. Correct reception reports verified for 2 IRCs or an SASE.

WSHB—*see* Herald Broadcasting Syndicate, above.

WWBS, P.O. Box 18174, Macon GA 31209 USA. Phone: +1 (912) 745-1485. E-mail: charlesK4LNL@june.com. Contact: Charles C. Josey; or Joanne Josey. Granted authorization to operate a 50 kilowatt transmitter on 11910 kHz, and expected to start operation early 1998.

WWCR—World Wide Christian Radio, F.W. Robbert Broadcasting Co., 1300 WWCR Avenue, Nashville TN 37218 USA. Phone: (general) +1 (615) 255-1300. Fax: +1 (615) 255 1311. E-mail: (general) wwcr@aol.com; (head of operations) wwcrl@aol.com; ("Ask WWCR" program) askwwcr@aol.com. URL: www.wwcr.com. Contact: (general) Chuck Adair, Sales Representative; (administration) George McClintock, K4BTY, General Manager; or Adam W. Lock, Sr., WA2JAL, Head of Operations; (technical) Watt Hairston, Chief Engineer. Free program guide, updated monthly. Free stickers and small souvenirs sometimes available. Return postage helpful. For items sold on the air, contact the producers of the programs, and *not* WWCR. Replies as time permits. Carries programs from various political organizations; these may be contacted directly (*see* Disestablishmentarian, earlier in this chapter).

WWV/WWVB (official time and frequency stations), Frequency-Time Broadcast Services Section, Time and Frequency Division, NIST, Mail Station 847, 325 Broadway, Boulder CO 80303 USA. Phone: (tape recording of latest shortwave technical propagation data and forecast) +1 (303) 497-3235; (live WWV audio) +1 (303) 499-7111; (Broadcast Manager) +1 (303) 497-3281; (Public Affairs) +1 (303) 497-3246; (Institute for Telecommunications Sciences) +1 (303) 497-3484. Phone/fax: (technical, call first before trying to fax) +1 (303) 497-3914. Fax: (Public Affairs) +1 (303) 497 3371. Contact: (general) Fred P. McGehan, Public Affairs Officer; (administration) Roger Beehler, Broadcast Manager; (technical) John B. Milton, Engineer-in-Charge; or Matt Deutsch, Engineer. Along with branch sister station WWVH in Hawaii (*see* below), WWV and WWVB are the official time and frequency stations of the United States, operating over longwave (WWVB) on 60 kHz, and over shortwave (WWV) on 2500, 5000, 10000, 15000 and 20000 kHz. Free Special Publication 432 "NIST Time & Frequency Services" pamphlet. Don't enclose return postage, money or IRCs, as they will only have to be returned by station. Plans to increase power of WWVB, currently 13 kW, before end of decade.

WWVH (official time and frequency station), NIST—Hawaii, P.O. Box 417, Kekaha, Kauai HI 96752 USA. Phone: +1 (808) 335-4361; (live audio) +1 (808) 335-4363. Fax: +1 (808) 335 4747. Contact: (technical) Dean T. Okayama, Engineer-in-Charge. E-mail: None planned. Along with headquarters sister stations WWV and WWVB (*see* preceding), WWVH is the official time and frequency station of the United States, operating on 2500, 5000, 10000 and 15000 kHz. Free Special Publication 432 "NIST Time & Frequency Services" pamphlet.

Modesto Marchena, owner and manager of Venezuela's Radio Frontera. Frontera's transmitter tends to be used sporadically, mainly during the day.

WYFR—Family Radio
NONTECHNICAL: Family Stations, Inc., 290 Hegenberger Road, Oakland CA 94621 USA. Phone: (toll-free, U.S. only) 1-800-543-1495; (elsewhere) +1 (510) 568-6200. Fax: +1 (510) 562 1023. E-mail: famradio@lanminds.com; shortwave@familyradio.com; or if you have a question about a particular song, carlah@lanminds.com. URLs: (Family Radio Network) www.familyradio.com; (WYFR) www.familyradio.com/wyfr.htm; (RealAudio) http://familyradio.com/raguide.htm. Contact: Shortwave Department. Free gospel tracts (33 languages), books, booklets, quarterly *Family Radio News* magazine and frequency schedule. 2 IRCs helpful.
TECHNICAL: WYFR—Family Radio, 10400 NW 240th Street, Okeechobee FL 34972 USA. Phone: +1 (941) 763-0281. Fax: +1 (941) 763 8867. Contact: Dan Elyea, Engineering Manager.

UZBEKISTAN World Time +5
WARNING—MAIL THEFT: Due to increasing local mail theft, Radio Tashkent suggests that those wishing to correspond should try using one of the drop-mailing addresses listed below.
Radio Tashkent
STATION: 49 Khorezm Street, 740047 Tashkent, Uzbekistan. Phone: +7 (3712) 441-210 or +7 (3712) 440 021. Contact: V. Danchev, Correspondence Section; Lenora Hannanowa; Zulfiya Ibragimova; Mrs. G. Babadjanova, Chief Director of Programs; or Mrs. Florida Perevertailo, Producer, "At Listeners' Request." Free pennants, badges, wallet calendars and postcards. Books in English by Uzbek writers are apparently available for purchase. Station offers free membership to two clubs: The "Salum Aleikum Listeners' Club" is open to anyone who asks to join, whereas "Radio Tashkent DX Club" is open to listeners who send in ten reception reports that are verified by the station.
LONDON OFFICE: 72 Wigmore Street, London W18 9L, United Kingdom.
FRANKFURT OFFICE: Radio Taschkent, c/o Uzbekistan Airways, Merkurhaus, Raum 215, Hauptbahnhof 10, D-60329 Frankfurt, Germany.
BANGKOK OFFICE: 848-850 Ramapur Road, Bangkok 10050, Thailand.
Uzbek Radio—see Radio Tashkent for details.

VANUATU World Time +12 (+11 midyear)
Radio Vanuatu, Information & Public Relations, P.M.B. 049, Port Vila, Vanuatu. Phone: +678 22999 or +678 23026. Fax: +678 22026. Contact: Ambong Thompson, Head of Programmes; or Allan Kalfabun, Sales & Marketing Consultant, who is interested in exchanging letters and souvenirs from other countries; (technical) K.J. Page, Principal Engineer.

VATICAN CITY STATE World Time +1 (+2 midyear)
Vatican Radio
MAIN AND PROMOTION OFFICES: 00120 Città del Vaticano, Vatican City State. Phone: (general) +39 (6) 698-83551; (Promotion Office and schedules) +39 (6) 698-83045 or +39 (6) 698-83463; (technical) +39 (6) 698-85258 or +39 (6) 988-3995. Fax: (general) +39 (6) 698 84565 or +39 (6) 698 83237;

(technical) +39 (6) 698 85125 or +39 (6) 698 85062. E-mail: sedoc@vatiradio.va. URLs: (general, including RealAudio) www.vatican.va/news_services/radio/radio_en.htm; (RealAudio in English, German and French, plus text) www.wrn.org/vatican-radio/. Contact: (general) Elisabetta Vitalini Sacconi, Promotion Office and schedules; Eileen O'Neill, Head of Program Development, English Service; Fr. Lech Rynkiewicz; Fr. Federico Lombardi, S.J., Program Manager; P. Moreau, Ufficio Promozione; Solange de Maillardoz, International Relations; or Veronica Scarisbrick, Producer, "On the Air;" (administration) Fr. Pasquale Borgomeo, S.J., Direttore Generale; (technical) Umberto Tolaini, Frequency Manager, Direzione Tecnica; Sergio Salvatori, Assistant Frequency Manager, Direzione Tecnica; Eugenio Matis SJ, Technical Director; or Giovanni Serra, Frequency Management Department. Correspondence sought on religious and programming matters, rather than the technical minutiae of radio. Free station stickers and paper pennants. Music CDs $13; *Pope John Paul II: The Pope of the Rosary* double CD/cassette $19.98 plus shipping; "Sixty Years . . . a Single Day" PAL video on Vatican Radio for 15,000 lire, including postage, from the Promotion Office. Vatican Radio's annual budget is $10 million.
TOKYO OFFICE: 2-10-10 Shiomi, Koto-ku, Tokyo 135, Japan. Fax: +81 (3) 5632 4457.

VENEZUELA   World Time –4
Ecos del Torbes, Apartado 152, San Cristóbal 5001-A, Táchira, Venezuela. Phone: +58 (76) 438-244 or (studio): +58 (76) 421-949. Contact: (general) Daphne González Zerpa, Directora; (technical) Ing. Iván Escobar S., Jefe Técnico.
Observatorio Cagigal—YVTO, Apartado 6745, Armada 84-DHN, Caracas 103, Venezuela. Phone: +58 (2) 481—2761. E-mail: armdhn@ven.net. Contact: Jesús Alberto Escalona, Director Técnico; or Colonel José Fuentes Goitia, Director. $1 or return postage helpful.
Radio Amazonas, Av. Simón Bolívar 4, Puerto Ayacucho 7101, Amazonas, Venezuela; or if no reply try Francisco José Ocaña at: Urb. 23 de Enero, Calle Nicolás Briceño, No. 18-266, Barinas 5201, Venezuela. Contact: Luis Jairo, Director. Francisco José Ocano is a keen collector of U.S. radio station stickers. Sending a few stickers with your letter as well as enclosing $2 may help.
Radio Frontera (when active), Edificio Radio, San Antonio del Táchira, Táchira, Venezuela. Phone: +58 (76) 782-92. Fax: +58 (76) 785 08. Contact: Modesto Marchena, Gerente General. May reply to correspondence in Spanish. $1 or return postage suggested. If no reply, try sending your reports to Venezuelan DXer Antonio J. Contín, Calle Los Lirios #1219, Urbanización Miraflores 4013, Cabimas, Estado Zulia, Venezuela. In return for this service he requests you send $2-3 and would like any spare Latin American pennants and stickers you might have.
Radio Mundial Los Andes (Radio Los Andes 1040) (if reactivated), Calle 44 No. 3-57, Mérida, Venezuela. Phone: +58 (74) 639-286. Contact: Celso Pacheco, Director. May reply to correspondence in Spanish. $1 or return postage suggested.
Radio Nacional de Venezuela (when operating)
MAIN OFFICE: Apartado 3979, Caracas 1050, Venezuela (although transmitter site is at Campo Carabobo near Valencia, some three hours drive away from Caracas). Phone: +58 (2) 745-166. URL: (when operating) http://165.247.176.136/Radio-Nacional/. Contact: Martin G. Delfin, English News Director; Jaime Alsina, Director; Ing. Dionisio Atencio; or Sra. Haydee Briceno, Gerente. Free 50th anniversary stickers, while they last, and other small souvenirs. If no response, try Apartado 50700, Caracas 1050, Venezuela.
MIAMI POSTAL ADDRESS: Jet Cargo International, M-7, P.O. Box 020010, Miami FL 33102 USA. Contact: Martin G. Delfin, English News Director.
Radio Occidente, Carrera 4a. No. 6-46, Tovar 5143, Mérida, Venezuela.

Radio Rumbos (when operating)
MAIN ADDRESS: Apartado 2618, Caracas 1010A, Venezuela. Phone: +58 (2) 261-0666. Fax: +58 (2) 335 164. Contact: (general) Andrés Felipe Serrano, Vice-Presidente; (technical) Ing. José Corrales; or Jaime L. Ferguson, Departamento Técnico. Free pamphlets, keychains and stickers. $1 or IRC required. Replies occasionally to correspondence in Spanish.
MIAMI ADDRESS: P.O. Box 020010, Miami FL 33102 USA.
Radio Táchira, Apartado 152, San Cristóbal 5001-A, Táchira, Venezuela. Phone: +58 (76) 430-009. Contact: Desirée González Zerpa, Directora; Sra. Albertina, Secretaria; or Eleázar Silva Malavé, Gerente.
Radio Valera, Av. 10 No. 9-31, Valera 3102, Trujillo, Venezuela. Phone: +58 (71) 53-744. Replies to correspondence in Spanish. Return postage required. This station has been on the same world band frequency for almost 50 years, which is a record for Latin America. If no response try via Antonio J. Contín. (see Radio Frontera, above).

VIETNAM   World Time +7
Bac Thai Broadcasting Service—contact via Voice of Vietnam—Overseas Service, below.
Lai Chau Broadcasting Service—contact via Voice of Vietnam—Overseas Service, below.
Lam Dong Broadcasting Service, Da Lat, Vietnam. Contact: Hoang Van Trung. Replies slowly to correspondence in Vietnamese, but French may also suffice.
Son La Broadcasting Service, Son La, Vietnam. Contact: Nguyen Hang, Director. Replies slowly to correspondence in Vietnamese, but French may also suffice.
Voice of Vietnam—Domestic Service (Dài Tiêng Nói Viêt Nam, TNVN)—Addresses and contact numbers as for all sections of Voice of Vietnam—Overseas Service, below. Contact: Phan Quang, Director General.
Voice of Vietnam—Overseas Service
TRANSMISSION FACILITY (MAIN ADDRESS FOR NONTECHNICAL CORRESPONDENCE AND GENERAL VERIFICATIONS): 58 Quán Sú, Hànôi, Vietnam. Phone: +84 (4) 825-7870. Fax: +84 (4) 825 5765. Contact: Dao Dinh Tuan, Director of External Broadcasting. Free paper pennant and, occasionally upon request, Vietnamese stamps. $1 helpful, but IRCs apparently of no use. Replies slowly. Don't send stamps on letters to Vietnam. They're often cut off the letters and the station doesn't receive them. Frankings printed by machines stand a better chance of getting through.
STUDIOS (NONTECHNICAL CORRESPONDENCE AND GENERAL VERIFICATIONS): 45 Ba Trieu Street, Hànôi, Vietnam. Phone: +84 (4) 825-5669. Fax: +84 (4) 826 1122. Contact and other data: as in *Transmission Facility*, preceding.
TECHNICAL CORRESPONDENCE: Office of Radio Reception Quality, Central Department of Radio and Television Broadcast Engineering, Vietnam General Corporation of Posts and Telecommunications, Hànôi, Vietnam.
Yen Bai Broadcasting Station—contact via Voice of Vietnam, Overseas Service, above.

YEMEN   World Time +3
Republic of Yemen Radio, Ministry of Information, P.O. Box 2371, San'a, Yemen; or P.O. Box 2182, San'a, Yemen. Phone: +967 (1) 231-181. Fax: +967 (1) 230 761. Contact: (general) English Service; (technical) Abdullah Farhan, Technical Director.

YUGOSLAVIA   World Time +1 (+2 midyear)
Radiotelevizija Srbije, Hilendarska 2/IV, 11000 Belgrade, Serbia, Yugoslavia. Fax: +381 (11) 332 014. Contact: (technical) B. Miletic, Operations Manager of HF Broadcasting.
Radio Yugoslavia, Hilendarska 2, P.O. Box 200, 11000 Belgrade, Serbia, Yugoslavia. Phone: +381 (11) 346-884 or +381 (11) 346-801; (listener voice mail) +381 (11) 344-455. Fax: +381 (11) 332 014. Contact: (general) Nikola Ivanovic, Director; Aleksandar Georgiev; Aleksandar Popovic, Head of Public Relations; Pance Zafirovski, Head of Programs; or

Christian Voice

From Zambia's Christian Voice: administrator Julie Chinene (T-shirt), news producer and announcer Mwiza Lemba, engineer John Kawele and producer-announcer Mofya Phiri.

Slobodan Topović, Producer, "Post Office Box 200/Radio Hams' Corner"; (technical) B. Miletic, Operations Manager of HF Broadcasting; Technical Department; or Rodoljub Medan, Chief Engineer. Free pennants, stickers, pins and tourist information. $1 helpful.

ZAMBIA   World Time +2
Radio Christian Voice
STATION: Private Bag E606, Lusaka, Zambia. Phone: +260 (1) 274-251. Fax: +260 (1) 274 526. E-mail: cvoice@zamnet.zm. Contact: Andrew Flynn, Head of Transmission; Philip Haggar, Station Manager; B. Phiri; or Lenganji Nanyangwe, Assistant to Station Manager. Free calendars and stickers pens, as available. Free religious books and items under selected circumstances. Sells T-shirts and sundry other items. $1 or 2 IRCs appreciated for reply. This station broadcasts Christian teachings and music, as well as news and programs on farming, sport, education, health, business and children's affairs.
U. K. OFFICE: Christian Vision, Ryder Street, West Bromwich, West Midlands, B70 0EJ, United Kingdom.
Radio Zambia, ZNBC Broadcasting House, P.O. Box 50015, Lusaka, Zambia. Phone: (general) +260 (1) 254-989; (Public Relations) +260 (1) 254-989, X-216; (engineering) +260 (1) 250-380. Fax: +260 (1) 254 317 or +260 (1) 250 5424. Contact: (general) Keith Nalumango, Public Relations Manager; or Frank Mutubila, Director of Programmes and Producer of "Tell the Nation" listeners' letters program; (administration) Duncan H. Mbazima, Director-General; (technical) Edward H. Mwanza, Principal Engineer, Planning & Development; or Felix Katundu Chabala, Director of Engineering. Free *Zamwaves* newsletter. Sometimes gives away stickers and small publications. $1 required, and postal correspondence should be sent via registered mail. Tours given of the station Tuesdays to Fridays between 9:00 AM and noon local time; inquire in advance. Used to reply slowly and irregularly, but seems to be better now.

ZIMBABWE   World Time +2
Zimbabwe Broadcasting Corporation, P.O. Box HG444, Highlands, Harare, Zimbabwe. Phone: +263 (4) 498-610, or +263 (4) 498-630. Fax: (general) +263 (4) 498 613; (technical) +263 (4) 498 608. Contact: (general) Charles Warikandwa; (administration) Edward Moyo, Director General; or Thomas Mandigora, Director of Programmes; (technical) I. Magoryo, Engineer. $1 helpful.

CREDITS: Craig Tyson (Australia), Editor. Also, Tony Jones (Paraguay), Henrik Klemetz (Colombia), Marie Lamb (USA) and Lawrence Magne (USA). Special thanks to Ask-DX/Anatoly Klepov (Russia), Gabriel Iván Barrera (Argentina), Cumbre DX/Hans Johnson (USA), Graeme Dixon/ New Zealand, India Broadbase/Manosij Guha (India), Tetsuya Hirahara (Japan), Takayuki Inoue (Japan/Latin America), Kotanet Communications Ltd./Risto Kotalampi (Finland), Ian McFarland (Canada), Número Uno (USA), Toshimichi Ohtake (Japan), George Poppin (USA), Radio Nuevo Mundo (Japan) and Relámpago DX (Japan).

Weird Words

Glossary of Terms and Abbreviations Used in World Band Radio

All sorts of terms and abbreviations are used in world band radio. Some are specialized and benefit from explanation; several are foreign words that need translation; and yet others are simply adaptations of everyday usage.

Here, then, is PASSPORT'S guide to what's what in world band buzzwords—including what each one means. For a thorough writeup on nomenclature used in evaluating how well a world band radio performs, see the Radio Database International White Paper, How to Interpret Receiver Specifications and Lab Tests.

Active Antenna. An antenna that electronically amplifies signals. Active antennas are typically mounted indoors, but some models can also be mounted outdoors. Active antennas take up relatively little space, but their amplification circuits may introduce certain types of problems that can result in unwanted sounds being heard. See Passive Antenna.

Adjacent-Channel Rejection. See Selectivity.

AGC. See Automatic Gain Control.

Alt. Freq. Alternative frequency or channel. Frequency or channel that may be used unexpectedly in place of the regularly scheduled one.

Amateur Radio. See Hams.

AM Band. The local radio band, which currently runs from 520 to 1611 kHz (530–1705 kHz in the Western Hemisphere), within the Medium Frequency (MF) range of the radio spectrum. Outside North America, it is usually called the mediumwave (MW) band. However, in one or two Latin American countries it is sometimes called, by the general public and a few stations, onda larga—strictly speaking, a misnomer.

Amplified Antenna. See Active Antenna.

Analog Frequency Readout. Needle-and-dial or "slide-rule" tuning, greatly inferior to synthesized tuning for scanning the world band airwaves. See Synthesizer.

Audio Quality, Audio Fidelity. At PASSPORT, audio quality refers to what in computer testing is called "benchmark" quality. This means, primarily, the freedom from distortion of a signal fed through a receiver's entire circuitry—not just the audio stage—from the antenna input through to the speaker terminals. A lesser characteristic of audio quality is the audio bandwidth needed for pleasant world band reception of music. Also, see Enhanced Fidelity.

Automatic Gain Control (AGC). Smooths out fluctuations in signal strength brought about by fading, a regular occurrence with world band signals.

AV. A Voz—Portuguese for "The Voice." In PASSPORT, this term is also used to represent "The Voice of."

Bandwidth. A key variable that determines selectivity (see), bandwidth is the amount of radio signal at –6 dB a radio's circuitry will let pass through, and thus be heard. With world band channel spacing at 5 kHz, the best single bandwidths are usually in the vicinity of 3 to 6 kHz. Better radios offer two or more selectable bandwidths: one of 5 to 7 kHz or so for when a station is in the clear, and one or more others between 2 to 4 kHz for when a station is hemmed in by other stations next to it. Proper selectivity is a key determinant of the aural quality of what you hear.

Baud. Measurement of the speed by which radioteletype (see), radiofax (see) and other digital data are transmitted. Baud is properly written entirely in lower case, and thus is abbreviated as b (baud), kb (kilobaud) or Mb (Megabaud). Baud rate standards are usually set by the international CCITT regulatory body.

BC. Broadcasting, Broadcasting Company, Broadcasting Corporation.

Broadcast. A radio or television transmission meant for the general public. *Compare* Utility Stations, Hams.

BS. Broadcasting Station, Broadcasting Service.

Cd. Ciudad—Spanish for "City."

Channel. An everyday term to indicate where a station is supposed to be located on the dial. World band channels are spaced exactly 5 kHz apart. Stations operating outside this norm are "off-channel" (for these, PASSPORT provides resolution to better than 1 kHz to aid in station identification).

Chugging, Chuffing. The sound made by some synthesized tuning systems when the tuning knob is turned. Called "chugging" or "chuffing," as it is suggestive of the rhythmic "chug, chug" sound of a steam engine or "chugalug" gulping.

Cl. Club, Clube.

Cult. Cultura, Cultural.

Default. The setting at which a control of a digitally operated electronic device, including many world band radios, normally operates, and to which it will eventually return.

Dipole Antenna. *See* Passive Antenna.

Digital Frequency Display, Digital Tuning. *See* Synthesizer.

Digital Signal Processing. Technique in which computer-type circuitry is used to enhance the readability or other characteristics of an analog audio signal. Used on a very few world band supersets; also available as an add-on accessory.

Domestic Service. *See* DS.

DS. Domestic Service—Broadcasting intended primarily for audiences in the broadcaster's home country. However, some domestic programs are beamed on world band to expatriates and other kinfolk abroad, as well as interested foreigners. *Compare* ES.

DSP. *See* Digital Signal Processing.

DX, DXers, DXing. From an old telegraph term "to DX"; that is, to communicate over a great distance. Thus, DXers are those who specialize in finding distant or exotic stations that are considered to be rare catches. Few world band listeners are considered to be regular DXers, but many others seek out DX stations every now and then—usually by bandscanning, which is greatly facilitated by PASSPORT's Blue Pages.

Dynamic Range. The ability of a receiver to handle weak signals in the presence of strong competing signals within or near the same world band segment (see World Band Spectrum). Sets with inferior dynamic range sometimes "overload," especially with external antennas, causing a mishmash of false signals up and down—and even beyond—the segment being received.

Earliest Heard (or Latest Heard). See key at the bottom of each Blue Page. If the PASSPORT monitoring team cannot establish the definite sign-on (or sign-off) time of a station, the earliest (or latest) time that the station could be traced is indicated by a left-facing or right-facing "arrowhead flag." This means that the station almost certainly operates beyond the time shown by that "flag." It also means that, unless you live relatively close to the station, you're unlikely to be able to hear it beyond that "flagged" time.

EBS. Economic Broadcasting Station, a type of station found in China.

ECSS. Exalted-carrier selectable sideband, a term no longer in general use except to refer to manually and carefully tuning in a conventional AM-mode signal using the receiver's single-sideband circuitry. See Synchronous Detector.

Ed, Educ. Educational, Educação, Educadora.

Electrical Noise. *See* Noise.

Em. Emissora, Emisora, Emissor, Emetteur—in effect, "station" in various languages.

Enhanced Fidelity. Radios with good audio performance and certain types of high-tech circuitry can improve upon the fidelity of world band reception. Among the newer fidelity-enhancing techniques is synchronous detection (see). Another potential technological advance to enhance fidelity is digital world band transmission, which is actively being researched in the United States and elsewhere.

EP. Emissor Provincial—Portuguese for "Provincial Station."

ER. Emissor Regional—Portuguese for "Regional Station."

Ergonomics. How handy and comfortable—intuitive—a set is to operate, especially hour after hour.

ES. External Service—Broadcasting intended primarily for audiences abroad. *Compare* DS.

External Service. *See* ES.

F. Friday.

Fax. *See* Radiofax.

Feeder, Shortwave. A utility transmission from the broadcaster's home country to a relay site or placement facility some distance away. Although these specialized transmissions carry world band programming, they are not intended to be received by the general public. Many world band radios can process these quasi-broadcasts anyway. Feeders operate in lower sideband (LSB), upper sideband (USB) or independent sideband (termed ISL if heard on the lower side, ISU if heard on the upper side) modes. Most shortwave feeders have by now been replaced by satellite feeders. See Single Sideband, Utility Stations.

Frequency. The standard term to indicate where a station is located on the dial—regardless of whether it is "on-channel" or "off-channel" (see Channel). Measured in kilohertz (kHz) or Megahertz (MHz), which differ only in the placement of a decimal; e.g., 5975 kHz is the same as 5.975 MHz. Either measurement is equally valid, but to minimize confusion PASSPORT and most stations designate frequencies only in kHz.

Frequency Synthesizer. *See* Synthesizer, Frequency.

Front-End Selectivity. The ability of the initial stage of receiving circuitry to admit only limited frequency ranges into succeeding stages of circuitry. Good front-end selectivity keeps signals from other, powerful bands or segments from being superimposed upon the frequency range you're tuning. For example, a receiver with good front-end selectivity will receive only shortwave signals within the range 3200-3400 kHz. However, a receiver with mediocre front-end selectivity might allow powerful local mediumwave AM stations from 520-1700 kHz to be heard "ghosting in" between 3200 and 3400 kHz, along with the desired shortwave signals. Obviously, mediumwave AM signals don't belong on shortwave. Receivers with inadequate front-end selectivity can benefit by the addition of a preselector (see).

GMT. Greenwich Mean Time—See World Time.

Hams. Government-licensed amateur radio hobbyists who *transmit* to each other by radio, often by single sideband

Located in a weathered old building, La Voz del Rio Tarqui, 3285 kHz, is one of Ecuador's more dilapidated and irregular world band stations. The inside is even more rundown than the outside.

(see), for pleasure within special amateur bands. Many of these bands are within the shortwave spectrum (see). This is the same spectrum used by world band radio, but world band and ham radio, which laymen sometimes confuse with each other, are two very separate entities. The easiest way is to think of hams as making something like phone calls, whereas world band stations are like long-distance versions of ordinary FM or mediumwave AM stations.

Harmonic, Harmonic Radiation, Harmonic Signal. Weak spurious repeat of a signal in multiple(s) of the fundamental, or "real," frequency. Thus, the third harmonic of a mediumwave AM station on 1120 kHz might be heard faintly on 4480 kHz within the world band spectrum. Stations almost always try to avoid harmonic radiation, but in rare cases have been known to amplify a harmonic signal so they can operate inexpensively on a second frequency. Also, see Subharmonic.

Hash. Electrical noise. See Noise.

High Fidelity. See Enhanced Fidelity.

Image Rejection. A key type of spurious-signal rejection (see).

Independent Sideband. See Single Sideband.

Interference. Sounds from other signals, notably on adjacent channels or the same channel ("co-channel"), that are disturbing the one you are trying to hear. Worthy radios reduce interference by having good selectivity (see). Nearby television sets and cable television wiring may also generate a special type of radio interference called TVI, a "growl" usually heard every 15 kHz or so.

International Telecommunication Union (ITU). The regulatory body, headquartered in Geneva, for all international telecommunications, including world band radio. Sometimes incorrectly referred to as the "International Telecommunications Union." In recent years, the ITU has become increasingly ineffective as a regulatory body for world band, with much of its former role having been taken up by groups of affiliated international broadcasters voluntarily coordinating their schedules a number of times each year.

Inverted-L Antenna. See Passive Antenna.

Ionosphere. See Propagation.

Irr. Irregular operation or hours of operation; i.e., schedule tends to be unpredictable.

ISB. Independent sideband. See Single Sideband.

ISL. Independent sideband, lower. See Feeder.

ISU. Independent sideband, upper. See Feeder.

ITU. See International Telecommunication Union.

Jamming. Deliberate interference to a transmission with the intent of discouraging listening. Jamming is practiced much less now than it was during the Cold War.

Keypad. On a world band radio, like a computer, a keypad can be used to control many variables. However, unlike a computer, the keypad on most world band radios consists of ten numeric or multifunction keys, usually supplemented by two more keys, as on a telephone keypad. Keypads are used primarily so you can enter a station's frequency for reception, and the best keypads have real keys (not a membrane) in the standard telephone format of 3×4 with "zero" under the "8" key. Many keypads are also used for presets, but this means you have to remember code numbers for stations (e.g., BBC 5975 kHz is "07"); handier radios either have separate keys for presets, or use LCD-displayed "pages" to access presets.

kHz. Kilohertz, the most common unit for measuring where a station is on the world band dial. Formerly known as "kilocycles per second," or kc/s. 1,000 kilohertz equals one Megahertz.

Kilohertz. See kHz.

kW. Kilowatt(s), the most common unit of measurement for transmitter power (see).

LCD. Liquid-crystal display. LCDs, if properly designed, are fairly easily seen in bright light, but require side lighting (also called "backlighting") under darker conditions. LCDs, being gray on gray, also tend to have mediocre contrast, and sometimes can be read from only a certain angle or angles, but they consume nearly no battery power.

LED. Light-emitting diode. LEDs are very easily read in the dark or in normal room light, but consume battery power and are hard to read in bright light.

Loc. Local.

Location. The physical location of a station's transmitter, which may be different from the studio location. Transmitter location is useful as a guide to reception location. For example, if you're in eastern North America and wish to listen to the Voice of Russia, a transmitter located in St. Petersburg will almost certainly provide better reception than one located in Siberia.

Longwave Band. The 148.5–283.5 kHz portion of the low-frequency (LF) radio spectrum used in Europe, the Near East, North Africa, Russia and Mongolia for domestic broadcasting. As a practical matter, these longwave signals, which have nothing to do with world band or other shortwave signals, are not usually audible in other parts of the world.

Longwire Antenna. See Passive Antenna.

LSB. Lower Sideband. See Feeder, Single Sideband.

LV. La Voix, La Voz—French and Spanish for "The Voice." In PASSPORT, this term is also used to represent "The Voice of."

M. Monday.

Mediumwave Band, Mediumwave AM Band. See AM Band.

Megahertz. See MHz.

Memory, Memories. See Preset.

Meters. An outdated unit of measurement used for individual world band segments of the shortwave spectrum. The frequency range covered by a given meters designation—also known as "wavelength"—can be gleaned from the following formula: *frequency (kHz) = 299,792 ÷ meters*. Thus, 49 meters comes out to a frequency of 6118 kHz—well within the range of frequencies included in that segment (see World Band Spectrum). Inversely, meters can be derived from the following: *meters = 299,792 ÷ frequency (kHz)*.

MHz. Megahertz, a common unit to measure where a station is on the dial. Formerly known as "Megacycles per second," or Mc/s One Megahertz equals 1,000 kilohertz.

Mode. Method of transmission of radio signals. World band radio broadcasts are almost always in the analog AM mode, the same mode used in the mediumwave AM band (see). The AM mode consists of three components: two "sidebands" and one "carrier." Each sideband contains the same programming as the other, and the carrier carries no programming, so a few stations have experimented with the single-sideband (SSB) mode. SSB contains only one sideband, either the lower sideband (LSB) or upper sideband (USB), and a reduced carrier. It requires special radio circuitry to be demodulated, or made intelligible, which is the main reason SSB has not succeeded, and is not expected to succeed, as a world band mode. There are yet other modes used on shortwave, but not for world band. These include CW (Morse-type code), radiofax, RTTY (radioteletype) and narrow-band FM used by utility and ham stations. Narrow-band FM is not used for music, and is different from usual FM. See Single Sideband, ISB, ISL, ISU, LSB and USB.

N. New, Nueva, Nuevo, Nouvelle, Nacional, National, Nationale.

Nac. Nacional. Spanish and Portuguese for "National."

Nat, Natl, Nat'l. National, Nationale.

Noise. Static, buzzes, pops and the like caused by the earth's atmosphere (typically lightning), and to a lesser extent by galactic noise. Also, electrical noise emanates from such man-made sources as electric blankets, fish-tank heaters, heating pads, electrical and gasoline motors, light dimmers, flickering light bulbs, non-incandescent lights, computers and computer peripherals, office machines, electrical fences, and faulty electrical utility wiring and related components.

Other. Programs are in a language other than one of the world's primary languages.

Overloading. See Dynamic Range.

Passive Antenna. An antenna that is not electronically amplified. Typically, these are mounted outdoors, although the "tape-measure" type that comes as an accessory with some portables is usually strung indoors. For world band reception, virtually all outboard models for consumers are made from wire. The two most common designs are the inverted-L (so-called "longwire") and trapped dipole (either horizontal or sloper). These antennas are preferable to active antennas (see), and are reviewed in detail in the Radio Database International White Paper, PASSPORT *Evaluation of Popular Outdoor Antennas (Unamplified)*.

PBS. People's Broadcasting Station.

PLL (Phase-Locked Loop). With world band receivers, a PLL circuit means that the radio can be tuned digitally, often using a number of handy tuning techniques, such as a keypad and presets (see).

Power. Transmitter power *before* amplification by the antenna, expressed in kilowatts (kW). The present range of world band powers is 0.01 to 1,000 kW.

Power Lock. See Travel Power Lock.

PR. People's Republic.

Preselector. A device—typically outboard, but sometimes inboard—that effectively limits the range of frequencies which can enter a receiver's circuitry or the circuitry of an active antenna (see); that is, which improves front-end selectivity (see). For example, a preselector may let in the range 15000-16000 kHz, thus helping ensure that your receiver or active antenna will encounter no problems within that range caused by signals from, say, 5800-6200 kHz or local mediumwave AM signals (520-1705 kHz). This range usually can be varied, manually or automatically, according to the frequency to which the receiver is being tuned. A preselector may be passive (unamplified) or active (amplified).

Preset. Allows you to select a station pre-stored in a radio's memory. The handiest presets require only one push of a button, as on a car radio.

Propagation. World band signals travel, like a basketball, up and down from the station to your radio. The "floor" below is the earth's surface, whereas the "player's hand" on high is the *ionosphere*, a gaseous layer that envelops the planet. While the earth's surface remains pretty much the same from day to day, the ionosphere—nature's own passive "satellite"—varies in how it propagates radio signals, depending on how much sunlight hits the "bounce points."

Thus, some world band segments do well mainly by day, whereas others are best by night. During winter there's less sunlight, so the "night bands" become unusually active, whereas the "day bands" become correspondingly less useful (see World Band Spectrum). Day-to-day changes in the sun's weather also cause short-term changes in world band radio reception; this explains why some days you can hear rare signals.

Additionally, the 11-year sunspot cycle has a long-term effect on propagation. Currently, the sunspot cycle is exiting its trough. This means that while the upper world band segments have been less active than usual in recent years, there will be a significant and welcome improvement in world band reception towards the end of the decade and beyond.

PS. Provincial Station, Pangsong.

Pto. Puerto, Porto.

QSL. See Verification.

R. Radio, Radiodiffusion, Radiodifusora, Radiodifusão, Radiophonikos, Radiostantsiya, Radyo, Radyosu, and so forth.

Radiofax, Radio Facsimile. Like ordinary telefax (facsimile by telephone lines), but by radio.

Radioteletype (RTTY). Characters, but not illustrations, transmitted by radio. See Baud.

Receiver. Synonym for a radio, but sometimes—especially when called a "communications receiver"—implying a radio with superior tough-signal performance.

Reduced Carrier. See Single Sideband.

Reg. Regional.

Relay. A retransmission facility, often highlighted in "Worldwide Broadcasts in English" and "Voices from Home" in PASSPORT's WorldScan® section. Relay facilities are generally considered to be located outside the broadcaster's country. Being closer to the target audience, they usually provide superior reception. See Feeder.

Rep. Republic, République, República.

RN. See R and N.

RS. Radio Station, Radiostantsiya, Radiostudiya, Radiophonikos Stathmos.

RT, RTV. Radiodiffusion Télévision, Radio Télévision, and so forth.

RTTY. See Radioteletype.

S. As an icon **S**: aired summer (midyear) only. As an ordinary letter: San, Santa, Santo, São, Saint, Sainte. Also, South.

Sa. Saturday.

Scan, Scanning. Circuitry within a radio that allows it to bandscan or memory-scan automatically.

Segments. See Shortwave Spectrum.

Selectivity. The ability of a radio to reject interference (see) from signals on adjacent channels. Thus, also known as adjacent-channel rejection, a key variable in radio quality. Also, see "Bandwidth" and "Synchronous Detector".

Sensitivity. The ability of a radio to receive weak signals; thus, also known as weak-signal sensitivity. Of special importance if you're listening during the day, or if you're located in such parts of the world as Western North America, Hawaii and Australasia, where signals tend to be relatively weak.

Shortwave Spectrum. The shortwave spectrum—also known as the High Frequency (HF) spectrum—is, strictly speaking, that portion of the radio spectrum from 3-30 MHz (3,000-30,000 kHz). However, common usage places it from 2.3-30 MHz (2,000-30,000 kHz). World band operates on shortwave within 14 discrete segments between 2.3-26.1 MHz, with the rest of the shortwave spectrum being occupied by hams (see) and utility stations (see). Also, see World Band Spectrum, as well as the detailed "Best Times and Frequencies" piece elsewhere in this edition.

Sideband. See Mode.

Single Sideband, Independent Sideband. Spectrum- and power-conserving modes of transmission commonly used by utility stations and hams. Few broadcasters use, or are expected ever to use, these modes. Many world band radios are already capable of demodulating single-sideband transmissions, and some can even process independent-sideband signals. Certain single-sideband transmissions operate with a minimum of carrier reduction, which allows them to be listened to, albeit with some distortion, on ordinary radios not equipped to demodulate single sideband. Properly designed synchronous detectors (see) may prevent such distortion. See Feeder, Mode.

Site. See Location.

Slew Controls. Elevator-button-type up and down controls to tune a radio. On many radios with synthesized tuning, slewing is used in lieu of tuning by knob. Better is when slew controls are complemented by a tuning knob, which is more versatile.

Sloper Antenna. See Passive Antenna.

SPR. Spurious (false) extra signal from a transmitter actually operating on another frequency. One such type is harmonic (see).

Spurious-Signal Rejection. The ability of a radio receiver not to produce false, or "ghost," signals that might otherwise interfere with the clarity of the station you're trying to hear. See Image Rejection.

St, Sta, Sto. Abbreviations for words that mean "Saint."

Static. See Noise.

Su. Sunday.

Subharmonic. A harmonic heard at 1 times the operating frequency. Thus, the subharmonic of a station on 3360 kHz might be heard faintly on 5040 kHz. Also, see Harmonic.

Synchronous Detector. World band radios are increasingly coming equipped with this high-tech circuit that greatly reduces fading distortion. Better synchronous detectors also allow for selectable sideband; that is, the ability to select the clearer of the two sidebands of a world band or other AM-mode signal. See Mode.

Synchronous Selectable Sideband. See Synchronous Detector.

Synthesizer, Frequency. Simple radios often use archaic needle-and-dial tuning that makes it difficult to find a desired channel or to tell which station you are hearing, except by ear. Other models utilize a digital frequency synthesizer to tune in signals without your having to hunt and peck. Among other things, such synthesizers allow for push-button tuning and presets, and display the exact frequency digitally—pluses that make tuning in the world considerably easier. Virtually a "must" feature.

Target. Where a transmission is beamed.

Th. Thursday.

Travel Power Lock. Control to disable the on/off switch to prevent a radio from switching on accidentally.

Transmitter Power. See Power.

Trapped Dipole Antenna. See Passive Antenna.

Tu. Tuesday.

Universal Day. See World Time.

Universal Time. See World Time.

USB. Upper Sideband. See Feeder, Single Sideband.

UTC. See World Time.

Utility Stations. Most signals within the shortwave spectrum are not world band stations. Rather, they are utility stations—radio telephones, ships at sea, aircraft and the like—that transmit strange sounds (growls, gurgles, dih-dah sounds, etc.) point-to-point and are not intended to be heard by the general public. Compare Broadcast, Hams and Feeders.

v. Variable frequency; i.e., one that is unstable or drifting because of a transmitter malfunction or to avoid jamming.

Verification. A card or letter from a station verifying that a listener indeed heard that particular station. In order to stand a chance of qualifying for a verification card or letter, you need to provide the station heard with the following information in a three-number "SIO" code, in which "SIO 555" is best and "SIO 111" is worst:

- **S**ignal strength, with 5 being of excellent quality, comparable to that of a local mediumwave AM station, and 1 being inaudible or at least so weak as to be virtually unintelligible. 2 (faint, but somewhat intelligible), 3 (moderate strength) and 4 (good strength) represent the signal-strength levels usually encountered with world band stations.

- **I**nterference from other stations, with 5 indicating no interference whatsoever, and 1 indicating such extreme interference that the desired signal is virtually drowned out. 2 (heavy interference), 3 (moderate interference) and 4 (slight interference) represent the differing degrees of interference more typically encountered with world band signals. If possible, indicate the names of the interfering station(s) and the channel(s) they are on. Otherwise, at least describe what the interference sounds like.

- **O**verall quality of the signal, with 5 being best, 1 worst.
- In addition to providing SIO findings, you should indicate which programs you've heard, as well as comments on how you liked or disliked those programs. Refer to the "Addresses PLUS" section of this edition for information on where and to whom your report should be sent, and whether return postage should be included.
- Because of the time involved in listening, few stations wish to receive tape recordings of their transmissions.

Vo. Voice of.

W. As an icon 🎼: aired winter only. As a regular letter: Wednesday.

Wavelength. See Meters.

Weak-Signal Sensitivity. See Sensitivity.

World Band Radio. Similar to regular mediumwave AM band and FM band radio, except that world band stations can be heard over enormous distances and thus often carry news, music and entertainment programs created especially for audiences abroad. Some world band stations have audiences of up to 120 million each day. Some 600 million people worldwide are believed to listen to world band radio.

World Band Spectrum. See "Best Times and Frequencies" elsewhere in this edition.

World Day. See World Time.

World Time. Also known as Coordinated Universal Time (UTC), Greenwich Mean Time (GMT) and Zulu time (Z). With nearly 170 countries on world band radio, if each announced its own local time you would need a calculator to figure it all out. To get around this, a single international time—World Time—is used. The difference between World Time and local time is detailed in the "Addresses PLUS" section of this edition, the "Compleat Idiot's Guide to Getting Started" and especially in the last page of this edition. It is also determined simply by listening to World Time announcements given on the hour by world band stations—or minute by minute by WWV and WWVH in the United States on such frequencies as 5000, 10000 and 15000 kHz, or CHU in Canada on 3330, 7335 and 14670 kHz. A 24-hour clock format is used, so "1800 World Time" means 6:00 PM World Time. If you're in, say, North America, Eastern Time is five hours behind World Time winters and four hours behind World Time summers, so 1800 World Time would be 1:00 PM EST or 2:00 PM EDT. The easiest solution is to use a 24-hour clock set to World Time. Many radios already have these built in, and World Time clocks are also available as accessories. World Time also applies to the days of the week. So if it's 9:00 PM (21:00) Wednesday in New York during the winter, it's 0200 *Thursday* World Time.

WS. World Service.

1998 DIRECTORY OF ADVERTISERS

Advertising Manager: Mary Kroszner
IBS, Ltd.
Box 300, 825 Cherry Lane
Penn's Park, PA 18943, USA
Phone: 215/794-3410
Fax: 215/794-3396
E-Mail: mwk@passport.com

Channel-by-Channel Guide to World Band Schedules

If you scan the world band airwaves, you'll discover lots more stations than those aimed your way. That's because shortwave signals are capriciously scattered by the heavens, so you can often hear stations not targeted to your area.

Passport's Blue Pages Help Identify Stations

But just dialing around can be frustrating if you don't have a "map"—Passport's Blue Pages. Let's say that you've stumbled across something Asian-sounding on 7410 kHz at 2035 World Time. Passport's Blue Pages show All India Radio in a distinctive tongue beamed to Western Europe, with a hefty 250 kW of power. These clues suggest this is probably what you're hearing, even if you're not in Europe. The Blue Pages also show that

English from India will commence on that same channel in about ten minutes.

Schedules for Entire Year

Times and days of the week are in World Time; for local times, see Addresses PLUS. Some stations are shown as one hour earlier (◀) or later (▶) midyear—typically April through October. Stations may also extend their hours during holidays or for sports events.

To be as helpful as possible throughout the year, Passport's Blue Pages include not just observed activity and factual schedules, but also those which we have creatively opined will take place. This predictive information is original from us, and although it's of real value when tuning the airwaves, it is inherently not so exact as factual data.

Guide to Blue Pages Format

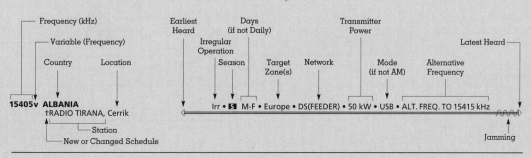

FREQUENCY　　COUNTRY, STATION, LOCATION　　　　　　　TARGET • NETWORK • POWER (kW)　　　　World Time

0 1 2 3 4 5 6 7 8 9 10 11 12 13 14 15 16 17 18 19 20 21 22 23 24

Freq	Country / Station, Location	Details
2310	**AUSTRALIA** ABC/CAAMA RADIO, Alice Springs	ENGLISH, ETC • Australasia • DS • 50 kW
2325	**AUSTRALIA** ABC/CAAMA RADIO, Tennant Creek	ENGLISH, ETC • Australasia • DS • 50 kW
2340	**CHINA** FUJIAN PEOPLE'S BS, Fuzhou	DS-1 • 10 kW / TAIWAN SVC • 10 kW
2360	**GUATEMALA** R MAYA DE BARILLAS, Huehuetenango	DS • 0.5 kW
2380	**BRAZIL** RADIO EDUCADORA, Limeira	DS • 0.25 kW • ➡ / Su • DS • 0.25 kW • ➡
2390	**GUATEMALA** LA VOZ DE ATITLAN, Santiago Atitlán	SPANISH, ETC • DS • 1 kW / Su • SPANISH, ETC • DS • 1 kW
	MEXICO †RADIO HUAYACOCOTLA, Huayacocotla	➡ • Tu-Su • DS • 0.5 kW / ➡ • M-Sa • DS • 0.5 kW
	USA WWCR, Nashville, Tennessee	E North Am • 100 kW
2410	**PAPUA NEW GUINEA** RADIO ENGA, Wabag	DS • 10 kW
2415	**CHINA** WENZHOU PEOPLE'S BS, Wenzhou	DS
2420	**BRAZIL** †RADIO SAO CARLOS, São Carlos	DS • 0.5 kW
2445	**CHINA** JIANGXI PEOPLE'S BS, Nanchang	DS-1 • 10 kW
2460	**CHINA** YUNNAN PEOPLE'S BS, Kunming	DS-1 • 15 kW
2460v	**BRAZIL** RADIO ALVORADA, Rio Branco	DS • 1 kW / Irr • DS • 1 kW
2475	**CHINA** ZHEJIANG PEOPLE'S BS, Hangzhou	DS-1 • 10 kW
2485	**AUSTRALIA** ABC/R RUM JUNGLE, Katherine	Australasia • DS • 50 kW
2490	**BRAZIL** RADIO 8 SETEMBRO, Descalvado	DS • 0.25 kW • ➡
2490v	**INDONESIA** †RRI, Ujung Pandang, Sulawesi	DS
2500	**AUSTRALIA** VNG, Llandilo	WORLD TIME • 1 kW
	USA WWV, Fort Collins, Colorado	WEATHER/WORLD TIME • 2.5 kW
	WWVH, Kekaha, Hawai'i	WEATHER/WORLD TIME • 5 kW
2560	**CHINA** †XINJIANG PEOPLE'S BC STN, Urümqi	DS-CHINESE • 15 kW
2580v	**INDONESIA** †RPD TENGAH SELATAN, Soë, Timur	DS
2625v	**KOREA (DPR)** †FRONTLINE SOLDIERS RADIO	DS
2695	**INDONESIA** RPD ENDE, Ende, Flores	DS
2754	**CHINA** †VO THE STRAIT-PLA, Fuzhou	SPR (2X1377 KHZ)
2850v	**KOREA (DPR)** KOREAN CENTRAL BS, Pyongyang	DS • 100 kW
2899v	**INDONESIA** †RPD NGADA, Bajawa, N Tenggara	DS • 0.5 kW
2960v	**INDONESIA** †RPD MANGGARAI, Ruteng, Flores	DS • 0.3 kW
3025v	**KOREA (DPR)** †FRONTLINE SOLDIERS RADIO	DS
3121v	**INDONESIA** †RSPD HALMAHERA, Soasiu, Maluku	DS
3200	**SWAZILAND** †TRANS WORLD RADIO, Manzini	S Africa • 25 kW / 🅂 • S Africa • 25 kW / S Africa • 50 kW / F-Su • S Africa • 25/50 kW / M-F • S Africa • 25/50 kW / S Africa • 25/50 kW
3200.4	**ARGENTINA** RADIO ARMONIA, Tres de Febrero	DS (2X1600.2 KHZ) • SPR / Irr • ARABIC & SPANISH • DS-RAMADAN • SPR
3205	**BRAZIL** R RIBEIRAO PRETO, Ribeirão Preto	DS • 1 kW • ➡
	PAPUA NEW GUINEA RADIO SANDAUN, Vanimo	DS • 10 kW
3205v	**INDONESIA** †RRI, Bandung, Jawa	DS-TEMP INACTIVE • 10 kW
3210 (con'd)	**MOZAMBIQUE** †RADIO MOCAMBIQUE, Maputo	DS • 100 kW

0 1 2 3 4 5 6 7 8 9 10 11 12 13 14 15 16 17 18 19 20 21 22 23 24

SEASONAL 🅂 OR 🅆　　　1-HR TIMESHIFT MIDYEAR ⬅ OR ➡　　　JAMMING / OR ∧　　　EARLIEST HEARD ◁　　　LATEST HEARD ▷　　　NEW FOR 1998 †

FREQUENCY   COUNTRY, STATION, LOCATION   TARGET • NETWORK • POWER (kW)   World Time

Freq	Country, Station, Location	Schedule
3210 (con'd)	SPAIN — R EXTERIOR ESPANA, Via Costa Rica	Tu-Sa • C America • 100 kW / M-F • C America • 100 kW
	USA — WWCR, Nashville, Tennessee	E North Am • 100 kW / S • E North Am • 100 kW
3215	SOUTH AFRICA — S AF AMATEUR R LEAGUE, Meyerton	M • ENGLISH & AFRIKAANS • S Africa • 100 kW
	USA — WWCR, Nashville, Tennessee	E North Am • 100 kW
3215v	INDONESIA — †RRI, Manado, Sulawesi	Irr • DS • 10 kW
3220	CHINA — †CENTRAL PEOPLE'S BS	W • DS-1
	ECUADOR — †HCJB-VO THE ANDES, Quito	8 kW
	KOREA (DPR) — †HAMGYONG PS, Hamhung	DS
	RADIO PYONGYANG, Hamhung	DS
	PAPUA NEW GUINEA — RADIO MOROBE, Lae	DS • 10 kW
3222	TOGO — RADIO KARA, Lama-Kara	FRENCH, ETC • DS • 10 kW
3223	INDIA — †ALL INDIA RADIO, Simla	DS • 50 kW / Sa/Su • DS • 50 kW / Sa/Su • ENGLISH, ETC • DS • 50 kW
	INDONESIA — †RRI, Mataram, Lombok	Irr • DS • 5 kW
3225v	INDONESIA — †RRI, Tanjungpinang, Riau	Irr • DS • 10 kW
3230v	NEPAL — RADIO NEPAL, Harriharpur	DS • 7.5/100 kW • ALT. FREQ. TO 7164v kHz / Sa • DS • 7.5/100 kW • ALT. FREQ. TO 7164v kHz
	PERU — R SOL DE LOS ANDES, Juliaca	SPANISH, QUECHUA & AYMARA • DS • 1 kW
3232v	INDONESIA — RRI, Bukittinggi, Sumatera	DS • 10 kW
3234.8	PERU — †R LUZ Y SONIDO, Huánuco	SPANISH & QUECHUA • DS • 1 kW
3235	PAPUA NEW GUINEA — RADIO WEST NEW BRITAIN, Kimbe	DS • 10 kW
3240	SWAZILAND — †TRANS WORLD RADIO, Manzini	S Africa • 25/50 kW / S Africa • 25 kW
3245	BRAZIL — †RADIO CLUBE, Varginha	DS • 1 kW
	INDIA — †ALL INDIA RADIO, Lucknow	Irr • DS-B • 50 kW / DS-B • 50 kW / ENGLISH, ETC • DS-B • 50 kW
	PAPUA NEW GUINEA — RADIO GULF, Kerema	DS • 10 kW
3249.5	HONDURAS — RADIO LUZ Y VIDA, San Luis	DS • 1 kW
3250	KOREA (DPR) — †RADIO PYONGYANG, Pyongyang	E Asia • 100 kW
3250v	INDONESIA — RRI, Banjarmasin, Kalimantan	DS • 10 kW
3255	BRAZIL — RADIO DIF 6 DE AGOSTO, Xapuri	DS • 2 kW / Irr • DS • 2 kW
	UNITED KINGDOM — BBC, Via Meyerton, South Africa	S Africa • 100 kW / S • S Africa • 50 kW / S Africa • 50 kW
3259	JAPAN — NHK, Fukuoka	Irr • DS-1(FEEDER) • 0.6 kW • USB
3260	CHINA — GUIZHOU PEOPLE'S BS, Guiyang	DS-1 • 10 kW
	ECUADOR — ESTEREO CARRIZAL, Calceta	DS-TEMP INACTIVE • 1 kW
	NIGER — LA VOIX DU SAHEL, Niamey	M-Sa • FRENCH, ETC • DS-TEMP INACTIVE • 4 kW / Sa • FRENCH, ETC • DS-TEMP INACTIVE • 4 kW / FRENCH, ETC • DS-TEMP INACTIVE • 4 kW
	PAPUA NEW GUINEA — RADIO MADANG, Madang	DS • 10 kW
	PERU — LA VOZ DE OXAPAMPA, Oxapampa	SPANISH, ETC • DS • 2.5 kW
3265	CONGO (REPUBLIC) — RTV CONGOLAISE, Brazzaville	FRENCH, ETC • DS • 50 kW • ALT. FREQ. TO 5985 kHz
3265v	INDONESIA — RRI, Bengkulu, Sumatera	DS • 10 kW
(con'd)	RRI, Gorontalo, Sulawesi	DS • 10 kW

ENGLISH ▬   ARABIC ⌇⌇⌇   CHINESE ▯▯▯   FRENCH ═   GERMAN ▬   RUSSIAN ═   SPANISH ▬   OTHER ▬

FREQUENCY	COUNTRY, STATION, LOCATION	TARGET • NETWORK • POWER (kW)	World Time

World Time scale: 0 1 2 3 4 5 6 7 8 9 10 11 12 13 14 15 16 17 18 19 20 21 22 23 24

Frequency	Country/Station	Details
3265v (con'd)	**INDONESIA** RRI, Gorontalo, Sulawesi	Sa • DS • 10 kW
3270	**NAMIBIA** NAMIBIAN BC CORP, Windhoek	ENGLISH, ETC • DS • 100 kW • ⬕
3272v	**MOZAMBIQUE** †DELEGACAO DE BEIRA, Beira	DS-A • 100 kW • ALT. FREQ. TO 3280v kHz
3275	**PAPUA NEW GUINEA** RADIO SOUTHERN HIGHLANDS, Mendi	DS • 10 kW
3277	**INDIA** †RADIO KASHMIR, Srinagar	DS • 50 kW • ALT. FREQ. TO 4950 kHz; ENGLISH, ETC • DS • 50 kW • ALT. FREQ. TO 4950 kHz
3280	**CHINA** VOICE OF PUJIANG, Shanghai	E Asia
	ECUADOR LA VOZ DEL NAPO, Tena	SPANISH, ETC • DS • 2.5 kW; M-Sa • DS • 2.5 kW; Su • SPANISH, ETC • DS • 2.5 kW
3280v	**MOZAMBIQUE** †DELEGACAO DE BEIRA, Beira	DS-A • 100 kW • ALT. FREQ. TO 3272v kHz
3283v	**PERU** †ESTACION WARI, Ayacucho	SPANISH & QUECHUA • DS
3285v	**ECUADOR** †LA VOZ DEL RIO TARQUI, Cuenca	DS-TEMP INACTIVE • 0.5 kW
3288v	**MADAGASCAR** RTV MALAGASY, Antananarivo	DS-1 • 10 kW
3289.8	**ECUADOR** RADIO CENTRO, Ambato	DS • 5 kW
3290	**GUYANA** †VOICE OF GUYANA, Georgetown	DS • 5 kW; DS • 5 kW • ALT. FREQ. TO 5950 kHz
	NAMIBIA NAMIBIAN BC CORP, Windhoek	ENGLISH, GERMAN & AFRIKAANS • DS • 100 kW • ⬕
	PAPUA NEW GUINEA RADIO CENTRAL, Port Moresby	ENGLISH, ETC • DS • 10 kW
3300	**GUATEMALA** †RADIO CULTURAL, Guatemala City	M • DS • 10 kW; Tu-Su • DS • 10 kW; M-Sa • DS • 10 kW; Su • DS • 10 kW; DS • 10 kW
3305	**INDIA** †ALL INDIA RADIO, Ranchi	DS • 10 kW; ENGLISH & HINDI • DS • 10 kW; ENGLISH, ETC • DS • 10 kW
	PAPUA NEW GUINEA RADIO WESTERN, Daru	ENGLISH, ETC • DS • 10 kW
3306	**ZIMBABWE** ZIMBABWE BC CORP, Gweru	DS-2 • 100 kW
3315	**INDIA** †ALL INDIA RADIO, Bhopal	ENGLISH, ETC • DS • 50 kW; DS • 50 kW
	PAPUA NEW GUINEA RADIO MANUS, Lorengau	ENGLISH, ETC • DS • 10 kW; Irr • Sa • ENGLISH, ETC • DS • 10 kW
3316	**SIERRA LEONE** †SIERRA LEONE BS, Goderich	Irr • DS • 10 kW; ENGLISH, ETC • DS • 10 kW
3320	**KOREA (DPR)** PYONGYANG BC STN, Pyongyang	E Asia
	SOUTH AFRICA †SOUTH AFRICAN BC, Meyerton	S Africa • DS-R SONDERGRENSE • 100 kW; W S Africa • DS-R SONDERGRENSE • 100 kW
3324.8	**GUATEMALA** R MAYA DE BARILLAS, Huehuetenango	DS • 1 kW
3325	**INDONESIA** RRI, Palangkaráya, Kalimantan	DS • 10 kW
	PAPUA NEW GUINEA †RADIO BOUGAINVILLE, Rabaul	ENGLISH, ETC • DS • 10 kW
3326	**NIGERIA** RADIO NIGERIA, Lagos	DS-1 • 50 kW
3329.5	**PERU** †ONDAS DEL HUALLAGA, Huánuco	SPANISH & QUECHUA • DS • 0.5 kW • ALT. FREQ. TO 3330.5 kHz; Su • SPANISH & QUECHUA • DS • 0.5 kW • ALT. FREQ. TO 3330.5 kHz
3330	**CANADA** CHU, Ottawa	WORLD TIME • 3 kW • USB
	ZAMBIA †CHRISTIAN VOICE, Lusaka	S Africa • 100 kW • ALT. FREQ. TO 6065 kHz; S Africa • 100 kW • ALT. FREQ. TO 4965 kHz
3330.5	**PERU** †ONDAS DEL HUALLAGA, Huánuco	SPANISH & QUECHUA • DS • 0.5 kW • ALT. FREQ. TO 3329.5 kHz; Su • SPANISH & QUECHUA • DS • 0.5 kW • ALT. FREQ. TO 3329.5 kHz
3331	**COMOROS** RADIO COMORO, Moroni	FRENCH, ARABIC, ETC • DS-TEMP INACTIVE • 4 kW

World Time scale: 0 1 2 3 4 5 6 7 8 9 10 11 12 13 14 15 16 17 18 19 20 21 22 23 24

FREQUENCY COUNTRY, STATION, LOCATION	TARGET • NETWORK • POWER (kW)	World Time

World Time scale: 0 1 2 3 4 5 6 7 8 9 10 11 12 13 14 15 16 17 18 19 20 21 22 23 24

3335 CHINA (TAIWAN)
  †CENTRAL BC SYSTEM, T'ai-pei — E Asia • NETWORK 1 • 10 kW
  PAPUA NEW GUINEA
  RADIO EAST SEPIK, Wewak — DS-TEMP INACTIVE • 10 kW
3340 PERU
  †RADIO ALTURA, Cerro de Pasco — DS • 1 kW
  Tu-Su • DS • 1 kW

  UGANDA
  RADIO UGANDA, Kampala — ENGLISH, ETC • DS • 50 kW • ALT. FREQ. TO 4976 kHz
3345 DENMARK
  †WORLD MUSIC RADIO, Via South Africa — Sa/Su • S Africa • 100 kW
  INDIA
  †ALL INDIA RADIO, Jaipur — DS • 50 kW
  Irr • DS • 50 kW
  ENGLISH, ETC • DS • 50 kW

  PAPUA NEW GUINEA
  RADIO NORTHERN, Popondetta — ENGLISH, ETC • DS • 10 kW
  SOUTH AFRICA
  †CHANNEL AFRICA, Meyerton — S Africa • 100 kW   S • S Africa • 100 kW
3345v INDONESIA
  RRI, Ternate, Maluku — DS • 10 kW
  PHILIPPINES
  †RADYO MINDORO, Baco, Mindoro — Su • DS • 1 kW   DS • 1 kW
3350 KOREA (DPR)
  SOUTH PYONGYANG PS, Pyŏngsong — DS
3354v ANGOLA
  RADIO NACIONAL, Luanda — DS-ANTENNA 2 • 10 kW
  S Africa • 10 kW

3355 PAPUA NEW GUINEA
  RADIO SIMBU, Kundiawa — DS • 10 kW
3355v INDONESIA
  †RRI, Jambi, Sumatera — DS • 7.5 kW
  Irr • DS • 0.6 kW
  RRI, Sumenep, Jawa
3356 BOTSWANA
  RADIO BOTSWANA, Gaborone — ENGLISH, ETC • DS • 50 kW
3358v MADAGASCAR
  RTV MALAGASY, Antananarivo — DS-1 • 30/100 kW
3360 ECUADOR
  †LA VOZ DEL UPANO, Macas — DS-VERY IRREGULAR • 10 kW
  GUATEMALA
  LA VOZ DE NAHUALA, Nahualá — SPANISH, ETC • DS • 0.5/1 kW
  Su • SPANISH, ETC • DS • 0.5/1 kW

3365 BRAZIL
  RADIO CULTURA, Araraquara — DS • 1 kW
  INDIA
  †ALL INDIA RADIO, Delhi — DS • 50 kW
  ENGLISH, ETC • DS • 50 kW

  PAPUA NEW GUINEA
  RADIO MILNE BAY, Alotau — ENGLISH, ETC • DS • 10 kW
3366 GHANA
  †GHANA BC CORP, Accra — Sa/Su//Holidays • DS-2 • 50 kW
  DS-2 • 50 kW

3370 GUATEMALA
  RADIO TEZULUTLAN, Cobán — DS • 1 kW
  Tu-Su • SPANISH, ETC • DS • 1 kW   SPANISH, ETC • DS • 1 kW
  M-Sa • SPANISH, ETC • DS • 1 kW   Su • SPANISH, ETC • DS • 1 kW
  M-Sa • DS • 1 kW

3370v MOZAMBIQUE
  DELEGACAO DE BEIRA, Beira — DS • 10 kW
3373.5 JAPAN
  NHK, Osaka — Irr • DS-2(FEEDER) • 0.3 kW • USB
3375 ANGOLA
  RADIO NACIONAL, Luanda — DS-NATIONAL • 10 kW
  BRAZIL
  †RADIO CLUBE, Dourados — DS • 3.5 kW •
  †RADIO EDUCADORA, Guajará Mirim — M-Sa • DS • 5 kW
  DS • 5 kW

  PAPUA NEW GUINEA
  R WESTERN HIGHLANDS, Mount Hagen — DS • 10 kW
3375v BRAZIL
  †RADIO NACIONAL, S Gab Cachoeira — DS • 2.5/10 kW
3380 GUATEMALA
  RADIO CHORTIS, Jocotán — DS-SPANISH, CHORTI • 1 kW
  Tu-Su • DS • 1 kW   M-Sa • DS-SPANISH, CHORTI • 1 kW

  MALAWI
  †MALAWI BC CORP, Limbe — ENGLISH, ETC • DS • 100 kW
3385 BRAZIL
  †R EDUCACAO RURAL, Tefé — DS • 1 kW
  Tu-Su • DS • 1 kW

(con'd)

World Time scale: 0 1 2 3 4 5 6 7 8 9 10 11 12 13 14 15 16 17 18 19 20 21 22 23 24

ENGLISH ▬ ARABIC ※ CHINESE ⬚⬚ FRENCH ═ GERMAN ▬ RUSSIAN ═ SPANISH ▬ OTHER ▬

FREQUENCY   COUNTRY, STATION, LOCATION   TARGET • NETWORK • POWER (kW)   World Time

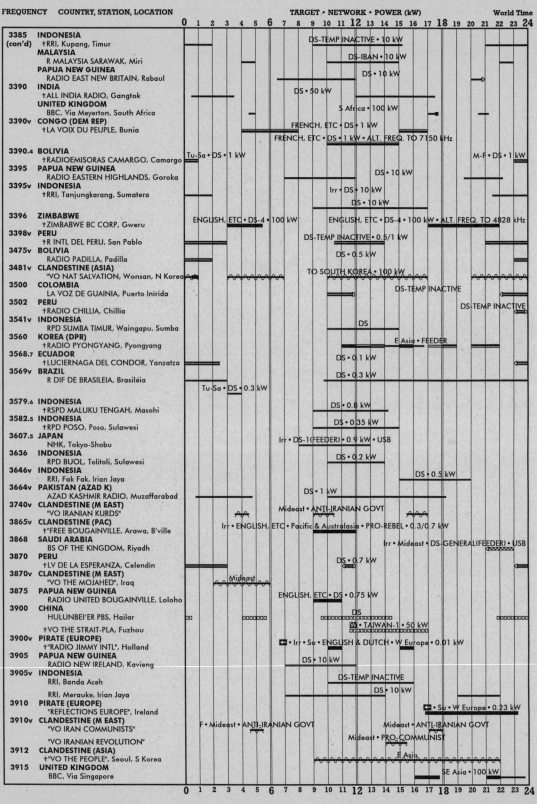

FREQUENCY	COUNTRY, STATION, LOCATION	TARGET • NETWORK • POWER (kW)
3385 (con'd)	INDONESIA †RRI, Kupang, Timur	DS-TEMP INACTIVE • 10 kW
	MALAYSIA R MALAYSIA SARAWAK, Miri	DS-IBAN • 10 kW
	PAPUA NEW GUINEA RADIO EAST NEW BRITAIN, Rabaul	DS • 10 kW
3390	INDIA †ALL INDIA RADIO, Gangtok	DS • 50 kW
	UNITED KINGDOM BBC, Via Meyerton, South Africa	S Africa • 100 kW
3390v	CONGO (DEM REP) †LA VOIX DU PEUPLE, Bunia	FRENCH, ETC • DS • 1 kW FRENCH, ETC • DS • 1 kW • ALT. FREQ. TO 7150 kHz
3390.4	BOLIVIA †RADIOEMISORAS CAMARGO, Camargo	Tu-Sa • DS • 1 kW M-F • DS • 1 kW
3395	PAPUA NEW GUINEA RADIO EASTERN HIGHLANDS, Goroka	DS • 10 kW
3395v	INDONESIA †RRI, Tanjungkarang, Sumatera	Irr • DS • 10 kW DS • 10 kW
3396	ZIMBABWE †ZIMBABWE BC CORP, Gweru	ENGLISH, ETC • DS-4 • 100 kW ENGLISH, ETC • DS-4 • 100 kW • ALT. FREQ. TO 4828 kHz
3398v	PERU †R INTL DEL PERU, San Pablo	DS-TEMP INACTIVE • 0.5/1 kW
3475v	BOLIVIA RADIO PADILLA, Padilla	DS • 0.5 kW
3481v	CLANDESTINE (ASIA) "VO NAT SALVATION, Wonsan, N Korea"	TO SOUTH KOREA • 100 kW
3500	COLOMBIA LA VOZ DE GUAINIA, Puerto Inirida	DS-TEMP INACTIVE
3502	PERU †RADIO CHILLIA, Chillia	DS-TEMP INACTIVE
3541v	INDONESIA RPD SUMBA TIMUR, Waingapu, Sumba	DS
3560	KOREA (DPR) †RADIO PYONGYANG, Pyongyang	E Asia • FEEDER
3568.7	ECUADOR †LUCIERNAGA DEL CONDOR, Yanzatza	DS • 0.1 kW
3569v	BRAZIL R DIF DE BRASILEIA, Brasiléia	DS • 0.3 kW Tu-Sa • DS • 0.3 kW
3579.6	INDONESIA †RSPD MALUKU TENGAH, Masohi	DS • 0.8 kW
3582.5	INDONESIA †RPD POSO, Poso, Sulawesi	DS • 0.35 kW
3607.5	JAPAN NHK, Tokyo-Shobu	Irr • DS-1(FEEDER) • 0.9 kW • USB
3636	INDONESIA RPD BUOL, Tolitoli, Sulawesi	DS • 0.2 kW
3646v	INDONESIA RRI, Fak Fak, Irian Jaya	DS • 0.5 kW
3664v	PAKISTAN (AZAD K) AZAD KASHMIR RADIO, Muzaffarabad	DS • 1 kW
3740v	CLANDESTINE (M EAST) "VO IRANIAN KURDS"	Mideast • ANTI-IRANIAN GOVT
3865v	CLANDESTINE (PAC) †"FREE BOUGAINVILLE, Arawa, B'ville	Irr • ENGLISH, ETC • Pacific & Australasia • PRO-REBEL • 0.3/0.7 kW
3868	SAUDI ARABIA BS OF THE KINGDOM, Riyadh	Irr • Mideast • DS-GENERAL(FEEDER) • USB
3870	PERU †LV DE LA ESPERANZA, Celendin	DS • 0.7 kW
3870v	CLANDESTINE (M EAST) "VO THE MOJAHED", Iraq	Mideast
3875	PAPUA NEW GUINEA RADIO UNITED BOUGAINVILLE, Loloho	ENGLISH, ETC • DS • 0.75 kW
3900	CHINA HULUNBEI'ER PBS, Hailar	DS
	†VO THE STRAIT-PLA, Fuzhou	W • TAIWAN-1 • 50 kW
3900v	PIRATE (EUROPE) †"RADIO JIMMY INTL", Holland	Irr • Su • ENGLISH & DUTCH • W Europe • 0.01 kW
3905	PAPUA NEW GUINEA RADIO NEW IRELAND, Kavieng	DS • 10 kW
3905v	INDONESIA RRI, Banda Aceh	DS-TEMP INACTIVE
	RRI, Merauke, Irian Jaya	DS • 10 kW
3910	PIRATE (EUROPE) "REFLECTIONS EUROPE", Ireland	Su • W Europe • 0.23 kW
3910v	CLANDESTINE (M EAST) "VO IRAN COMMUNISTS"	F • Mideast • ANTI-IRANIAN GOVT Mideast • ANTI-IRANIAN GOVT
	"VO IRANIAN REVOLUTION"	Mideast • PRO-COMMUNIST
3912	CLANDESTINE (ASIA) †"VO THE PEOPLE", Seoul, S Korea	E Asia
3915	UNITED KINGDOM BBC, Via Singapore	SE Asia • 100 kW

FREQUENCY   COUNTRY, STATION, LOCATION   TARGET • NETWORK • POWER (kW)   World Time

		0 1 2 3 4 5 6 7 8 9 10 11 12 13 14 15 16 17 18 19 20 21 22 23 24

3920 KOREA (DPR)
NORTH PYONGYANG PS, Sinuiju — DS

3920v PIRATE (EUROPE)
†"INTL MUSIC RADIO", Switzerland — Irr • Su • ENGLISH, ETC • Europe
— Irr • Sa • ENGLISH, ETC • Europe
— Irr • Sa • W Europe

"R RODE KONING", Holland — Irr • Su • W Europe
†"RADIO METEOOR", Holland — Irr • W/Sa • W Europe • 0.04 kW
— Irr • Su • W Europe • 0.04 kW

3922v PIRATE (EUROPE)
"LIVE WIRE RADIO", England — Irr • Su • W Europe • 0.15 kW • ALT. FREQ. TO 3945v kHz
— Irr • Sa • W Europe • 0.15 kW • ALT. FREQ. TO 3945v kHz

VARIOUS STATIONS — Irr • Su • GERMAN, FRENCH, ETC • W Europe • 0.01/0.75 kW
— Irr • Sa/Su • GERMAN, FRENCH, ETC • W Europe • 0.01/0.75 kW

3923v PIRATE (EUROPE)
†"RADIO GRENSJAGER", Belgium — Irr • Su • W Europe • 0.1 kW
— Irr • Sa • W Europe • 0.1 kW
RUSSIA
RADIO SAMORODINKA, Moscow — DS • 0.01 kW

3925 JAPAN
RADIO TAMPA, Multiple Locations — DS-1 • 10/50 kW
RADIO TAMPA, Tokyo-Nagara — DS-1 • 50 kW

3927v PIRATE (EUROPE)
†"RADIO SPACEMAN", Holland — Irr • Su • W Europe • 0.1 kW
— Irr • Sa • W Europe • 0.1 kW
"SUBTERRANEAN SOUNDS" — Irr • Su • W Europe • ALT. FREQ. TO 3945v kHz
— Irr • Sa • W Europe • ALT. FREQ. TO 3945v kHz

3930 KOREA (REPUBLIC)
KOREAN BC SYSTEM, Hwasung — DS-1 • 5 kW
M-Sa • DS-1 • 5 kW
Su • DS-1 • 5 kW

3934v INDONESIA
†RRI, Semarang, Jawa — DS-TEMP INACTIVE • 5/10 kW
3935 NEW ZEALAND
RADIO READING SVC, Levin — DS • 1 kW
3940 CHINA
HUBEI PEOPLE'S BS, Wuhan — DS-1
M-Sa • DS-1

3940v CLANDESTINE (M EAST)
†"VO IRAQI PEOPLE" — Mideast • PRO-COMMUNIST
3945 INDIA
†ALL INDIA RADIO, Gorakhpur — S Asia • 50 kW
DS • 50 kW
ENGLISH, ETC • DS • 50 kW

JAPAN
RADIO TAMPA, Tokyo-Nagara — DS-2 • 10 kW
VANUATU
†RADIO VANUATU, Vila, Efate Island — ENGLISH, FRENCH, ETC • DS • 10 kW
VATICAN STATE
VATICAN RADIO, Vatican City — Europe • 10 kW • ALT. FREQ. TO 4005 kHz
3945v PIRATE (EUROPE)
"LIVE WIRE RADIO", England — Irr • Su • W Europe • 0.15 kW • ALT. FREQ. TO 3922v kHz
— Irr • Sa • W Europe • 0.15 kW • ALT. FREQ. TO 3922v kHz
"SUBTERRANEAN SOUNDS" — Irr • Su • W Europe • ALT. FREQ. TO 3927v kHz
— Irr • Sa • W Europe • ALT. FREQ. TO 3927v kHz

3946 INDONESIA
†RRI, Tanjungkarang, Sumatera — DS • 2.5 kW
PIRATE (EUROPE)
†"RADIO KORAK", Holland — Irr • Su • W Europe
— Irr • Sa • W Europe
3946v PIRATE (EUROPE)
†"RADIO FREE LONDON", England — Irr • Su • W Europe • 0.02 kW
— Irr • Sa • W Europe • 0.02 kW
— Su • W Europe • 0.02 kW • ALT. FREQ. TO 5804.6 kHz

3950 CHINA
QINGHAI PEOPLE'S BS, Xining — DS-1 • 10 kW
Su • DS-1 • 10 kW

3955 SOUTH AFRICA
†CHANNEL AFRICA, Meyerton — S Africa • 250 kW
UNITED KINGDOM
BBC, Skelton, Cumbria — W • Europe • 250 kW
3959v INDONESIA
†RRI, Palu, Sulawesi — DS • 10 kW
3959.7 INDONESIA
†RRI, Padang, Sumatera — DS • 0.5 kW
3960 CHINA
†XINJIANG PEOPLE'S BC STN, Urümqi — W • DS-CHINESE • 50 kW
KOREA (DPR)
CHAGONG PROVINCIAL, Kanggye — DS
MONGOLIA
MONGOL RADIO, Dalandzadgad — DS-1 • 12 kW

	0 1 2 3 4 5 6 7 8 9 10 11 12 13 14 15 16 17 18 19 20 21 22 23 24

ENGLISH ▬   ARABIC ᙛᙛ   CHINESE ▫▫▫   FRENCH ═   GERMAN ▬   RUSSIAN ═   SPANISH ▬   OTHER ▬

FREQUENCY	COUNTRY, STATION, LOCATION	TARGET • NETWORK • POWER (kW)	World Time

World Time scale: 0 1 2 3 4 5 6 7 8 9 10 11 12 13 14 15 16 17 18 19 20 21 22 23 24

3965	FRANCE	
	†R FRANCE INTL, Issoudun-Allouis	W • N Africa • 250 kW • ALT. FREQ. TO 3970 kHz W • Europe • 250 kW
	RUSSIA	
	†MAYAK, Arkhangel'sk	S • DS • 20 kW
3970	CAMEROON	
	CAMEROON RTV, Buea	FRENCH, ENGLISH, ETC • DS • 4 kW
	CHINA	
	NEI MONGGOL PBS, Hohhot	DS
	FRANCE	
	†R FRANCE INTL, Issoudun-Allouis	W • N Africa • 250 kW • ALT. FREQ. TO 3965 kHz
	JAPAN	
	NHK, Nagoya	Irr • DS-1 (FEEDER) • 0.3 kW • USB
	NHK, Sapporo	Irr • DS-1 (FEEDER) • 0.6 kW
	KOREA (DPR)	
	KANGWONG PS, Wonsan	DS
	RADIO PYONGYANG, Wonsan	DS
	KOREA (REPUBLIC)	
	†RADIO KOREA INTL, Via Skelton, UK	W • Europe • 250 kW
		S • Europe • 250 kW
	NIGERIA	
	RADIO NIGERIA, Enugu	ENGLISH, ETC • DS-TEMP INACTIVE • 100 kW
3975	HUNGARY	
	RADIO BUDAPEST, Jászberény	⇄ • Europe • 250 kW
		W • Europe • 250 kW
		S • Su • Europe • 250 kW
		⇄ • M-Sa • Europe • 250 kW
3976v	INDONESIA	
	RRI, Pontianak, Kalimantan	DS • 1 kW
3985	CHINA	
	CHINA RADIO INTL, Via Switzerland	⇄ • Europe • 250 kW
	CLANDESTINE (ASIA)	
	†"ECHO OF HOPE", Seoul, South Korea	E Asia • 50 kW
	FRANCE	
	R FRANCE INTL, Issoudun-Allouis	W • Europe • 250 kW
	ITALY	
	†IRRS-SHORTWAVE, Milan	⇄ • M-F • Europe • 8.5 kW ⇄ • F-Su • ENGLISH, ETC • Europe • 8.5 kW
		⇄ • ENGLISH, ETC • Europe • 8.5 kW
	UNITED KINGDOM	
	BBC, Skelton, Cumbria	W M-F • Europe • 250 kW
3987v	INDONESIA	
	†RRI, Manokwari, Irian Jaya	DS-TEMP INACTIVE • 1 kW
3990	CHINA	
	XINJIANG PEOPLE'S BC STN, Urümqi	W • DS-UIGHUR • 50 kW
	UNITED KINGDOM	
	BBC, Via Zyyi, Cyprus	W M-F • E Europe & Mideast • 250 kW
		W • E Europe & Mideast • 250 kW
3995	GERMANY	
	†DEUTSCHE WELLE, Jülich	W • E Europe • 100 kW
	†DEUTSCHE WELLE, Wertachtal	Europe • 500 kW
		W • Europe • 500 kW
	RUSSIA	
	MAYAK, Khabarovsk	W • DS • 50 kW
3996	INDONESIA	
	†RRI, Kendari, Sulawesi	DS • 5 kW
4000	ERITREA	
	†VO BROAD MASSES, Asmera	E Africa • 10 kW
4000v	CAMEROON	
	CAMEROON RTV, Bafoussam	FRENCH, ENGLISH, ETC • DS • 20 kW
	INDONESIA	
	†RRI, Kendari, Sulawesi	DS • 5 kW
4000.4	PERU	
	†RADIO SAN JUAN, Trujillo	DS-TEMP INACTIVE
4002v	INDONESIA	
	†RRI, Padang, Sumatera	DS • 10 kW
4005	PERU	
	†RADIO LV DEL CAMPESINO, El Faique	DS-TEMP INACTIVE
	VATICAN STATE	
	VATICAN RADIO, Vatican City	⇄ • Europe • 10 kW • ALT. FREQ. TO 3945 kHz
		⇄ • Europe • 10 kW • ALT. FREQ. TO 4010 kHz
		⇄ • M-Sa • Europe • 10 kW • ALT. FREQ. TO 4010 kHz
4010	KYRGYZSTAN	
	KYRGYZ RADIO, Bishkek	⇄ • ENGLISH, ETC • DS-1 • 50 kW ⇄ • Sa • DS-1 • 50 kW
		⇄ • RUSSIAN, ETC • DS-1 • 50 kW
		⇄ • Su-F • RUSSIAN, ETC • DS-1 • 50 kW
	RUSSIA	
	VOICE OF RUSSIA, Vladivostok	W • E Asia • 100 kW
	VATICAN STATE	
	VATICAN RADIO, Vatican City	⇄ • Europe • 10 kW • ALT. FREQ. TO 4005 kHz
		⇄ • M-Sa • Europe • 10 kW • ALT. FREQ. TO 4005 kHz

World Time scale: 0 1 2 3 4 5 6 7 8 9 10 11 12 13 14 15 16 17 18 19 20 21 22 23 24

FREQUENCY   COUNTRY, STATION, LOCATION   TARGET • NETWORK • POWER (kW)   World Time

0 1 2 3 4 5 6 7 8 9 10 11 12 13 14 15 16 17 18 19 20 21 22 23 24

Frequency	Country, Station, Location	Target • Network • Power
4020	**CHINA** †CHINA RADIO INTL, Beijing	W • E Asia • FEEDER
4030	**RUSSIA** CHUKOT RADIO, Anadyr'	RUSSIAN, ETC • DS-TEMP INACTIVE • 15 kW
4035	**CHINA** XIZANG PEOPLE'S BC STN, Lhasa	DS-TIBETAN • 50 kW
4039.2	**PERU** †RADIO MARGINAL, Tocache	DS • 1 kW Irr • DS • 1 kW
4040	**ARMENIA** ARMENIAN RADIO, Kamo	DS-1 • 15 kW
	RUSSIA †EVENKIYSKAYA RADIO, Tura	RUSSIAN, ETC • DS-LOCAL, R ROSSII • 5 kW
4050	**KYRGYZSTAN** KYRGYZ RADIO, Bishkek	RUSSIAN, ETC • DS-2 • 100 kW Tu • DS-2 • 100 kW W-M • DS-2 • 100 kW
	RUSSIA †SAKHALIN RADIO, Yuzhno-Sakhalinsk	DS-TEMP INACTIVE • 20 kW
4050.6	**PERU** †RADIO CRISTAL, Arequipa	DS
4070v	**CLANDESTINE (M EAST)** †"VO IRAQI KURDS", Salāh al-Dīn	Mideast • PRO-KDP ARABIC, ETC • Europe • PRO-KDP
4081v	**MONGOLIA** MONGOL RADIO, Ulaanbaatar	DS-1 • 50 kW
4085v	**CLANDESTINE (M EAST)** "VO KURDISH PEOPLE", Sulaymānīyah	ARABIC, ETC • Mideast • ANTI-IRAQI GOVT • ALT. FREQ. TO 4120v kHz
4110v	**CLANDESTINE (M EAST)** "VOICE OF ISLAM"	Mideast
4115v	**CLANDESTINE (ASIA)** "VO KASHMIR FREEDOM", Pakistan	S Asia • ANTI-INDIAN GOVT
4120v	**CLANDESTINE (ASIA)** "VO NAT SALVATION, Pyongyang	TO SOUTH KOREA • 100 kW
	CLANDESTINE (M EAST) "VO KURDISH PEOPLE", Sulaymānīyah	ARABIC, ETC • Mideast • ANTI-IRAQI GOVT • ALT. FREQ. TO 4085v kHz
4131	**CHINA** †VO THE STRAIT-PLA, Fuzhou	SPR (3X1377 KHZ)
4183v	**PERU** LA VOZ DE SAYAPULLO, Sayapullo	DS
4190	**CHINA** CENTRAL PEOPLE'S BS, Beijing	W • DS-MINORITIES • 50 kW
4190v	**CLANDESTINE (M EAST)** "VOICE OF THE WORKER"	Mideast • ANTI-IRANIAN GOVT
	PERU RADIO SELVA, Moyobamba	DS
	†SUPER R SAN IGNACIO, San Ignacio	DS-TEMP INACTIVE
4190.7	**PERU** †RADIO SUPER, San Ignacio	DS
4215v	**VIETNAM** †UNIDENTIFIED	DS
4250v	**CLANDESTINE (M EAST)** "VO THE MOJAHED", Iraq	Mideast
4279.4	**PERU** RADIO CAJAMARCA, Baños del Inca	DS
4285v	**CLANDESTINE (M EAST)** "VO IRANIAN KURDS"	Mideast • ANTI-IRANIAN GOVT
4330	**CHINA** XINJIANG PEOPLE'S BC STN, Urümqi	DS-KAZAKH • 50 kW
4350v	**CLANDESTINE (M EAST)** "VO KURD STRUGGLE"	Mideast • ANTI-IRANIAN GOVT
4400v	**CLANDESTINE (ASIA)** "VO NAT SALVATION, North Korea	TO SOUTH KOREA • 100 kW
	CLANDESTINE (M EAST) "VOICE OF ISLAM"	Mideast
4405	**KOREA (DPR)** †RADIO PYONGYANG, Pyongyang	E Asia • FEEDER
4409v	**BOLIVIA** RADIO ECO, Reyes	DS • 1 kW
4419v	**PERU** RADIO BAMBAMARCA, Bambamarca	"FRECUENCIA LIDER" • 0.85 kW
4420v	**PERU** †RADIO SAN JUAN, Aramango	DS
4450	**BOLIVIA** RADIO ESTACION FRONTERA, Cobija	DS
4450v	**CLANDESTINE (ASIA)** "VO NAT SALVATION, Pyongyang	TO SOUTH KOREA • 100 kW
4460	**CHINA** †CENTRAL PEOPLE'S BS, Beijing	W • DS-1 • 10/15 kW DS-1 • 10/15 kW
4460v	**CLANDESTINE (M EAST)** "VO THE MOJAHED", Iraq	Mideast
4461	**PERU** †RADIO NORANDINA, Celendín	DS • 1 kW

0 1 2 3 4 5 6 7 8 9 10 11 12 13 14 15 16 17 18 19 20 21 22 23 24

ENGLISH ■■■   ARABIC ⧢⧢⧢   CHINESE ▭▭▭   FRENCH ═══   GERMAN ■■■   RUSSIAN ═══   SPANISH ■■■   OTHER ▬▬

FREQUENCY	COUNTRY, STATION, LOCATION	TARGET • NETWORK • POWER (kW)	World Time

World Time scale: 0 1 2 3 4 5 6 7 8 9 10 11 12 13 14 15 16 17 18 19 20 21 22 23 24

4472v	BOLIVIA	
	RADIO MOVIMA, Santa Ana	DS / Irr • DS / M-Sa • DS / Su • DS
4485	RUSSIA	
	†BASHKIR RADIO, Ufa	RUSSIAN, ETC • DS-LOCAL, R ROSSII • 15 kW
	KAMCHATKA RADIO, Petropavlovsk-K	DS-TEMP INACTIVE • 100 kW
4485.2	PERU	
	R FRECUENCIA VH, Celendin	DS-LV DE CELENDIN • 0.5 kW
4500	CHINA	
	†XINJIANG PEOPLE'S BC STN, Urümqi	DS-CHINESE • 50 kW
4505.2	PERU	
	RADIO HORIZONTE, Chiclayo	DS • 0.5 kW
4508.7	BOLIVIA	
	RADIO SAN JOAQUIN, San Joaquín	DS-TEMP INACTIVE
4510.2	PERU	
	R PAUCARTAMBO, Paucartambo (Pasco)	DS • 0.25 kW / Tu-Su • DS • 0.25 kW / M-Sa • DS • 0.25 kW / Sa/Su • DS • 0.25 kW
4520	RUSSIA	
	†KORYAK RADIO, Palana	RUSSIAN, ETC • DS-LOCAL, R ROSSII • 2 kW
4530.3	BOLIVIA	
	RADIO HITACHI, Guayaramerin	Irr • Tu-Su • DS / M-Sa • DS
4545	KAZAKHSTAN	
	KAZAKH RADIO, Almaty	RUSSIAN, GERMAN, ETC • DS-1 • 20 kW
4549.4	BOLIVIA	
	RADIODIFUSORAS TROPICO, Trinidad	Tu-Sa • DS • 0.75/3 kW • ALT. FREQ. TO 4552.3 kHz / DS • 0.75/3 kW • ALT. FREQ. TO 4552.3 kHz / M-Sa • DS • 0.75/3 kW • ALT. FREQ. TO 4552.3 kHz
4552.3	BOLIVIA	
	RADIODIFUSORAS TROPICO, Trinidad	Tu-Su • DS • 0.75/3 kW • ALT. FREQ. TO 4549.4 kHz / DS • 0.75/3 kW • ALT. FREQ. TO 4549.4 kHz / M-Sa • DS • 0.75/3 kW • ALT. FREQ. TO 4549.4 kHz
4557v	CLANDESTINE (ASIA)	
	"VO NAT SALVATION, Haeju, N Korea	TO SOUTH KOREA • 100 kW
4567v	PERU	
	†RADIO GOTAS DE ORO, Chiclayo	Irr • DS
4593.5	PERU	
	†ESTACION X, Yurimaguas	DS-TEMP INACTIVE
4599.3	BOLIVIA	
	RADIO VILLAMONTES, Villamontes	Irr • DS • 1 kW / DS • 1 kW
4600	BOLIVIA	
	†RADIO PERLA DEL ACRE, Cobija	Tu-Su • DS • 0.2 kW / M-Sa • DS • 0.2 kW
4606v	INDONESIA	
	†RRI, Serui, Irian Jaya	DS • 0.5 kW
4606.6	PERU	
	RADIO AYAVIRI, Ayaviri	SPANISH & QUECHUA • DS-"LV DE MELGAR" • 1 kW
4623v	PERU	
	†RADIO SOLEDAD, Parcoy	DS(4515-4680V KHZ) / Irr • DS(4515-4680V KHZ)
4627.3	PERU	
	†RADIO COSMOS, Celendin	DS-TEMP INACTIVE
4630.8	BOLIVIA	
	†RADIO 11 DE OCTUBRE, Cobija	DS
4635	TAJIKISTAN	
	†TAJIK RADIO, Dushanbe	RUSSIAN, ETC • DS-1 • 50 kW / Irr • DS-1 • 100 kW
4649	BOLIVIA	
	RADIO SANTA ANA, Santa Ana	DS • 1 kW / Irr • DS • 1 kW
4682v	BOLIVIA	
	RADIO PAITITI, Guayaramerín	DS • 0.75 kW / Tu-Su • DS • 0.75 kW / Irr • DS • 0.75 kW
4690v	LAOS	
	†LAO NATIONAL RADIO, Vientiane	DS
4697v	INDONESIA	
	RK INFORMASI PER'N, Surabaya, Jawa	DS • 2.5 kW
4702v	VIETNAM	
	VOICE OF VIETNAM	DS
4702.3	BOLIVIA	
	RADIO ECO, San Borja	DS • 1 kW
4719v	INDONESIA	
	RRI, Ujung Pandang, Sulawesi	DS • 50 kW • ALT. FREQ. TO 4753v kHz
4719.8	BOLIVIA	
	RADIO ABAROA, Riberalta	DS • 0.5 kW
4725	MYANMAR (BURMA)	
	RADIO MYANMAR, Yangon	DS • 50 kW
4732v	BOLIVIA	
	RADIO LA PALABRA, Sta Ana de Yacuma	DS • 0.1 kW / M-Sa • DS • 0.1 kW

World Time scale: 0 1 2 3 4 5 6 7 8 9 10 11 12 13 14 15 16 17 18 19 20 21 22 23 24

FREQUENCY   COUNTRY, STATION, LOCATION

TARGET • NETWORK • POWER (kW)

World Time

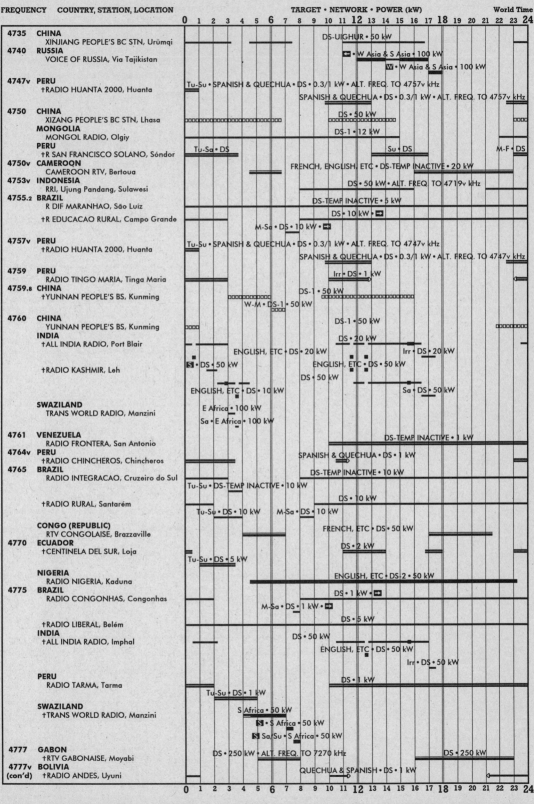

Freq	Country / Station / Location	Schedule details
4735	**CHINA** XINJIANG PEOPLE'S BC STN, Urümqi	DS-UIGHUR • 50 kW
4740	**RUSSIA** VOICE OF RUSSIA, Via Tajikistan	W Asia & S Asia • 100 kW / W • W Asia & S Asia • 100 kW
4747v	**PERU** †RADIO HUANTA 2000, Huanta	Tu-Su • SPANISH & QUECHUA • DS • 0.3/1 kW • ALT. FREQ. TO 4757v kHz / SPANISH & QUECHUA • DS • 0.3/1 kW • ALT. FREQ. TO 4757v kHz
4750	**CHINA** XIZANG PEOPLE'S BC STN, Lhasa	DS • 50 kW
	MONGOLIA MONGOL RADIO, Olgiy	DS-1 • 12 kW
	PERU †R SAN FRANCISCO SOLANO, Sóndor	Tu-Sa • DS / Su • DS / M-F • DS
4750v	**CAMEROON** CAMEROON RTV, Bertoua	FRENCH, ENGLISH, ETC • DS-TEMP INACTIVE • 20 kW
4753v	**INDONESIA** RRI, Ujung Pandang, Sulawesi	DS • 50 kW • ALT. FREQ. TO 4719v kHz
4755.2	**BRAZIL** R DIF MARANHAO, São Luiz	DS-TEMP INACTIVE • 5 kW
	†R EDUCACAO RURAL, Campo Grande	DS • 10 kW • / M-Sa • DS • 10 kW •
4757v	**PERU** †RADIO HUANTA 2000, Huanta	Tu-Su • SPANISH & QUECHUA • DS • 0.3/1 kW • ALT. FREQ. TO 4747v kHz / SPANISH & QUECHUA • DS • 0.3/1 kW • ALT. FREQ. TO 4747v kHz
4759	**PERU** RADIO TINGO MARIA, Tinga Maria	Irr • DS • 1 kW
4759.8	**CHINA** †YUNNAN PEOPLE'S BS, Kunming	DS-1 • 50 kW / W-M • DS-1 • 50 kW
4760	**CHINA** YUNNAN PEOPLE'S BS, Kunming	DS-1 • 50 kW
	INDIA †ALL INDIA RADIO, Port Blair	DS • 20 kW / ENGLISH, ETC • DS • 20 kW / Irr • DS • 20 kW
	†RADIO KASHMIR, Leh	S • DS • 50 kW / ENGLISH, ETC • DS • 50 kW / DS • 50 kW / ENGLISH, ETC • DS • 10 kW / Sa • DS • 50 kW
	SWAZILAND TRANS WORLD RADIO, Manzini	E Africa • 100 kW / Sa • E Africa • 100 kW
4761	**VENEZUELA** RADIO FRONTERA, San Antonio	DS-TEMP INACTIVE • 1 kW
4764v	**PERU** †RADIO CHINCHEROS, Chincheros	SPANISH & QUECHUA • DS • 1 kW
4765	**BRAZIL** RADIO INTEGRACAO, Cruzeiro do Sul	Tu-Su • DS-TEMP INACTIVE • 10 kW / DS-TEMP INACTIVE • 10 kW
	†RADIO RURAL, Santarém	DS • 10 kW / Tu-Su • DS • 10 kW / M-Sa • DS • 10 kW
	CONGO (REPUBLIC) RTV CONGOLAISE, Brazzaville	FRENCH, ETC • DS • 50 kW
4770	**ECUADOR** †CENTINELA DEL SUR, Loja	DS • 2 kW / Tu-Su • DS • 5 kW
	NIGERIA RADIO NIGERIA, Kaduna	ENGLISH, ETC • DS • 2 • 50 kW
4775	**BRAZIL** RADIO CONGONHAS, Congonhas	DS • 1 kW • / M-Sa • DS • 1 kW •
	†RADIO LIBERAL, Belém	DS • 5 kW
	INDIA †ALL INDIA RADIO, Imphal	DS • 50 kW / ENGLISH, ETC • DS • 50 kW / Irr • DS • 50 kW
	PERU RADIO TARMA, Tarma	DS • 1 kW / Tu-Su • DS • 1 kW
	SWAZILAND †TRANS WORLD RADIO, Manzini	S Africa • 50 kW / S • S Africa • 50 kW / Sa/Su • S Africa • 50 kW
4777	**GABON** †RTV GABONAISE, Moyabi	DS • 250 kW • ALT. FREQ. TO 7270 kHz / DS • 250 kW
4777v (con'd)	**BOLIVIA** †RADIO ANDES, Uyuni	QUECHUA & SPANISH • DS • 1 kW

ENGLISH ▬   ARABIC ⬚⬚⬚   CHINESE ▭▭▭   FRENCH ▬▬   GERMAN ▬▬   RUSSIAN ▬▬   SPANISH ▬   OTHER ▬

FREQUENCY	COUNTRY, STATION, LOCATION	TARGET • NETWORK • POWER (kW)	World Time

World Time scale: 0 1 2 3 4 5 6 7 8 9 10 11 12 13 14 15 16 17 18 19 20 21 22 23 24

Frequency	Country / Station / Location	Notes
4777v (con'd)	BOLIVIA — †RADIO ANDES, Uyuni	M-Sa • QUECHUA & SPANISH • DS • 1 kW
	INDONESIA — †RRI, Jakarta, Jawa	DS • 50 kW
4779.8	ECUADOR — RADIO ORIENTAL, Tena	DS • 1 kW
	GUATEMALA — RADIO COATAN, San Sebastián	SPANISH, ETC • DS • 1 kW
4780	PERU — RADIO BAHIA, Chimbote	DS
4780v	DOMINICAN REPUBLIC — ONDA MUSICAL, Santo Domingo	DS
4783v	MALI — RTV MALIENNE, Bamako	FRENCH, ETC • DS • 50 kW / M-Sa • FRENCH, ETC • DS • 50 kW / Su • DS • 50 kW
4785	AZERBAIJAN — AZERBAIJANI RADIO, Baku	DS-1/RUSSIAN, AZERI • 100 kW
	BRAZIL — RADIO BRASIL, Campinas	DS • 1 kW • ⮕
	RADIO CAIARI, Pôrto Velho	DS • 1 kW
		Tu-Su • DS • 1 kW
	CHINA — ZHEJIANG PEOPLE'S BS, Qu Xian	DS-1 • 10 kW
	PERU — RADIO COOPERATIVA, Satipo	DS • 1 kW
4785.6	ECUADOR — †RADIO FEDERACION, Sucúa	DS-TEMP INACTIVE
4789v	INDONESIA — RRI, Fak Fak, Irian Jaya	DS • 1 kW
4790	INDIA — †ALL INDIA RADIO, Chennai	SE Asia • 100 kW
	PAKISTAN (AZAD K) — †AZAD KASHMIR RADIO, Via Islamabad	DS • 100 kW
	PERU — RADIO ATLANTIDA, Iquitos	DS • 1/3 kW / Su • DS • 1/3 kW
	SAUDI ARABIA — BS OF THE KINGDOM, Jiddah	DS-2(0.5X9580 KHZ) • SPR
4795	BRAZIL — RADIO AQUIDAUANA, Aquidauana	DS • 1 kW • ⮕
	CAMEROON — CAMEROON RTV, Douala	FRENCH, ENGLISH, ETC • DS-TEMP INACTIVE • 100 kW / FRENCH, ENGLISH, ETC • DE-TEMP INACTIVE • 100 kW
	UKRAINE — RADIO UKRAINE, Khar'kov	ⓦ • Europe • 100 kW / ⓦ • W Asia • 100 kW
4795.4	ECUADOR — †LV DE LOS CARAS, Bahía de Caráquez	Irr • Su • DS • 5 kW
4796v	VIETNAM — SON LA BC STATION, Son La	DS
4799.8	DOMINICAN REPUBLIC — RADIO N-103, Santiago	Irr • DS • 1 kW
	GUATEMALA — R BUENAS NUEVAS, San Sebastián	SPANISH, ETC • DS • 1 kW
4800	CHINA — CENTRAL PEOPLE'S BS, Shijiazhuang	DS-2 • 10/50 kW / DS-MINORITIES • 10/50 kW
	ECUADOR — RADIO POPULAR DE CUENCA, Cuenca	DS-TEMP INACTIVE • 5 kW
	INDIA — †ALL INDIA RADIO, Hyderabad	DS • 50 kW / M-Sa • DS • 50 kW / ENGLISH, ETC • DS • 50 kW
	LESOTHO — RADIO LESOTHO, Maseru	DS-ENGLISH, SESOTHO • 100 kW
	RUSSIA — YAKUT RADIO, Yakutsk	DS-RUSSIAN, YAKUT • 50 kW
4800.6	ARGENTINA — RADIO ARMONIA, Tres de Febrero	DS (3X1600.2 KHZ) • SPR / Irr • ARABIC & SPANISH • DS-RAMADAN • SPR
4800.7	MEXICO — †RADIO XERTA, México City	⮕ • Irr • TESTS • 2.5/5 kW
4801v	PERU — RADIO ONDA AZUL, Puno	SPANISH, ETC • DS-TEMP INACTIVE • 1.5 kW / M-Sa • SPANISH, ETC • DS-TEMP INACTIVE • 1.5 kW
4805	BRAZIL — R DIF DO AMAZONAS, Manaus	DS • 5 kW
4805v	INDONESIA — RRI, Kupang, Timur	DS-TEMP INACTIVE • 0.3 kW

World Time scale: 0 1 2 3 4 5 6 7 8 9 10 11 12 13 14 15 16 17 18 19 20 21 22 23 24

FREQUENCY   COUNTRY, STATION, LOCATION   TARGET • NETWORK • POWER (kW)   World Time

0 1 2 3 4 5 6 7 8 9 10 11 12 13 14 15 16 17 18 19 20 21 22 23 24

Frequency	Country, Station, Location	Target • Network • Power
4810	**ARMENIA**	
	ARMENIAN RADIO, Kamo	DS-1 • 100 kW
	VOICE OF ARMENIA, Kamo	E Europe, Mideast & W Asia • 100 kW
		M-F • E Europe, Mideast & W Asia • 100 kW
		Sa/Su • E Europe, Mideast & W Asia • 1000 kW
	RUSSIA	
	R TIKHIY OKEAN, Vladivostok	E Asia • 100 kW
4810.2	**PERU**	DS-TEMP INACTIVE
	RADIO SAN MARTIN, Tarapoto	M-Sa • DS-TEMP INACTIVE
4815	**BRAZIL**	
	RADIO CABOCLA, Benjamim Constant	DS-TEMP INACTIVE • 10 kW
	†RADIO DIFUSORA, Londrina	DS • 10 kW
		Irr • M • DS • 10 kW
		Tu-Sa • DS • 10 kW
	BURKINA FASO	
	RADIO BURKINA, Ouagadougou	FRENCH, ETC • DS • 50 kW
	CHINA	
	†CHINA RADIO INTL, Togtoh	E Asia • 10 kW
		W • E Asia • 10 kW
	ECUADOR	
	†RADIO BUEN PASTOR, Saraguro	DS • 1 kW
		QUECHUA • DS • 1 kW
4815v	**PAKISTAN**	
	PAKISTAN BC CORP, Islamabad	W • DS • 10 kW
4819v	**HONDURAS**	
	†LA VOZ EVANGELICA, Tegucigalpa	DS • 5/10 kW
		M • DS • 5/10 kW
		Tu-Su • DS • 5/10 kW
4820	**BOTSWANA**	
	RADIO BOTSWANA, Gaborone	ENGLISH, ETC • DS • 50 kW • ALT. FREQ. TO 4830 kHz
	CHINA	
	XIZANG PEOPLE'S BC STN, Lhasa	DS-TIBETAN • 50 kW
	INDIA	
	ALL INDIA RADIO, Calcutta	DS • 50 kW
		ENGLISH, ETC • DS • 50 kW
	KAZAKHSTAN	
	KAZAKH RADIO, Almaty	DS-2 • 50 kW
	†R ALMATY/R KAZAKHSTAN, Almaty	C Asia • 50 kW
	RUSSIA	
	KHANTY-MANSIYSK R, Khanty-Mansiysk	DS-LOCAL, R ROSSII • 50 kW
	UKRAINE	
	RADIO UKRAINE, Khar'kov	W • Europe • 100 kW
4820.2	**ANGOLA**	
	EP DA HUILA, Lubango	DS • 25 kW
4824.4	**PERU**	
	†LA VOZ DE LA SELVA, Iquitos	Tu-Su • DS • 10 kW
		M-Sa • DS • 10 kW
		DS • 10 kW
4825	**BRAZIL**	
	R CANCAO NOVA, Cachoeira Paulista	DS • 10 kW
	RADIO EDUCADORA, Bragança	DS-TEMP INACTIVE • 10 kW
	GUATEMALA	
	†RADIO MAM, Cabricán	Su-F • SPANISH, ETC • DS • 0.5/1 kW
		M-F • SPANISH, ETC • DS • 0.5/1 kW
		M-Sa • SPANISH, ETC • DS • 0.5/1 kW
	RUSSIA	
	†YAKUT RADIO, Yakutsk	RUSSIAN, ETC • DS-LOCAL, R ROSSII • 50 kW
4826v	**MAURITANIA**	
	RADIO MAURITANIE, Nouakchott	ARABIC, FRENCH, ETC • DS • 100 kW • ALT. FREQ. TO 4845 kHz
		Irr • ARABIC & FRENCH • DS-RAMADAN • 100 kW • ALT. FREQ. TO 4845 kHz
4826.3	**PERU**	
	RADIO SICUANI, Sicuani	QUECHUA • DS • 0.35/1 kW
		DS • 0.35/1 kW
4828	**ZIMBABWE**	
	†ZIMBABWE BC CORP, Gweru	ENGLISH, ETC • DS-4 • 100 kW • ALT. FREQ. TO 3396 kHz
4828v	**MONGOLIA**	
	MONGOL RADIO, Altai	DS-1 • 12 kW
4830	**BOLIVIA**	
	†RADIO GRIGOTA, Santa Cruz	DS-TEMP INACTIVE • 1 kW
	BOTSWANA	
	RADIO BOTSWANA, Gaborone	ENGLISH, ETC • DS • 50 kW • ALT. FREQ. TO 4820 kHz
	CHINA	
	†CHINA HUAYI BC COMPANY, Fuzhou	E Asia • 15 kW
		Irr • E Asia • 15 kW
(con'd)	**THAILAND**	
	†RADIO THAILAND, Pathum Thani	DS • 10 kW

0 1 2 3 4 5 6 7 8 9 10 11 12 13 14 15 16 17 18 19 20 21 22 23 24

ENGLISH ■■   ARABIC ᔕᔕ   CHINESE □□□   FRENCH ══   GERMAN ▬▬   RUSSIAN ══   SPANISH ▬▬   OTHER ──

| FREQUENCY | COUNTRY, STATION, LOCATION | TARGET • NETWORK • POWER (kW) | World Time |

0 1 2 3 4 5 6 7 8 9 10 11 12 13 14 15 16 17 18 19 20 21 22 23 24

Frequency	Country / Station	Details
4830 (con'd)	**VENEZUELA** — RADIO TACHIRA, San Cristóbal	DS • 10 kW / Irr • DS • 10 kW
4830.7	**PERU** — †RADIO LIRCAY, Lircay	DS • 1 kW
4832v	**COSTA RICA** — †RADIO RELOJ, San José	Irr • DS • 3 kW • ALT. FREQ. TO 6006 kHz / Irr • DS • 3 kW
4834.8	**PERU** — RADIO MARANON, Jaen	DS-TEMP INACTIVE • 1 kW / Tu-Su • DS-TEMP INACTIVE • 1 kW / M-Sa • DS-TEMP INACTIVE • 1 kW
4835	**AUSTRALIA** — ABC/CAAMA RADIO, Alice Springs	ENGLISH, ETC • Australasia • DS • 50 kW
	GUATEMALA — †RADIO TEZULUTLAN, Cobán	DS • 5 kW / Tu-Su • DS • 5 kW / M-Sa • SPANISH, ETC • DS • 5 kW / Su • SPANISH, ETC • DS • 5 kW / SPANISH, ETC • DS • 5 kW
	MALI — RTV MALIENNE, Bamako	FRENCH, ETC • DS • 50 kW / M-Sa • FRENCH, ETC • DS • 50 kW / Su • DS • 50 kW
4840	**CHINA** — †HEILONGJIANG PBS, Harbin	DS-1 • 50 kW
	INDIA — †ALL INDIA RADIO, Mumbai	DS • 50 kW / ENGLISH, ETC • DS • 50 kW
	PERU — †RADIO ANDAHUAYLAS, Andahuaylas	SPANISH & QUECHUA • DS • 2 kW / Irr • DS • 2 kW
	VENEZUELA — †RADIO VALERA, Valera	Irr • DS • 1 kW / Irr • Tu-Su • DS • 1 kW
4845	**BOLIVIA** — †RADIO FIDES, La Paz	DS • 5 kW / Tu-Su • DS • 5 kW / Sa/Su • DS • 5 kW / Irr • DS • 5 kW
	BRAZIL — RADIO METEOROLOGIA, Ibitinga	DS • 1 kW
	GUATEMALA — RADIO K'EKCHI, San Cristóbal V	SPANISH, ETC • DS • 1.3 kW / Tu-Su • SPANISH, ETC • DS • 1.3 kW / Su • SPANISH, ETC • DS • 1.3 kW / M-Sa • SPANISH, ETC • DS • 1.3 kW
	MALAYSIA — †RADIO MALAYSIA, Kajang	DS-6 (TAMIL) • 50 kW
	MAURITANIA — RADIO MAURITANIE, Nouakchott	ARABIC, FRENCH, ETC • DS • 100 kW • ALT. FREQ. TO 4826v kHz / Irr • ARABIC & FRENCH • DS-RAMADAN • 100 kW • ALT. FREQ. TO 4826v kHz
	PERU — RADIO LIDER, Cusco	Tu-Su • DS • 1 kW / M-Sa • DS • 1 kW / DS • 1 kW
4845v	**INDONESIA** — RRI, Ambon, Maluku	DS • 10 kW
4845.2	**BRAZIL** — †R CULT ONDAS TROPICAIS, Manaus	DS
4850	**CAMEROON** — †CAMEROON RTV, Buea	FRENCH, ENGLISH, ETC • DS
	CHINA — †CENTRAL PEOPLE'S BS	DS-1 / W-M • DS-1
	INDIA — †ALL INDIA RADIO, Kohima	DS • 50 kW / ENGLISH, ETC • DS • 50 kW / Irr • DS • 50 kW
	MONGOLIA — MONGOL RADIO, Ulaanbaatar	DS-1 • 50 kW
	UZBEKISTAN — UZBEK RADIO, Tashkent	DS-2 • 50 kW
4850v	**ECUADOR** — †EMISORAS LUZ Y VIDA, Loja	Irr • DS • 5 kW
4855	**BOLIVIA** — RADIO CENTENARIO, Santa Cruz	M-Sa • DS • 1 kW / DS • 1 kW / Tu-Sa • DS • 1 kW / Su-F • DS • 1 kW / M-F • DS • 1 kW / Su • DS • 1 kW
(con'd)	**BRAZIL** — RADIO TROPICAL, Barra do Garças	DS-TEMP INACTIVE • 1 kW

0 1 2 3 4 5 6 7 8 9 10 11 12 13 14 15 16 17 18 19 20 21 22 23 24

FREQUENCY   COUNTRY, STATION, LOCATION

TARGET • NETWORK • POWER (kW)

World Time

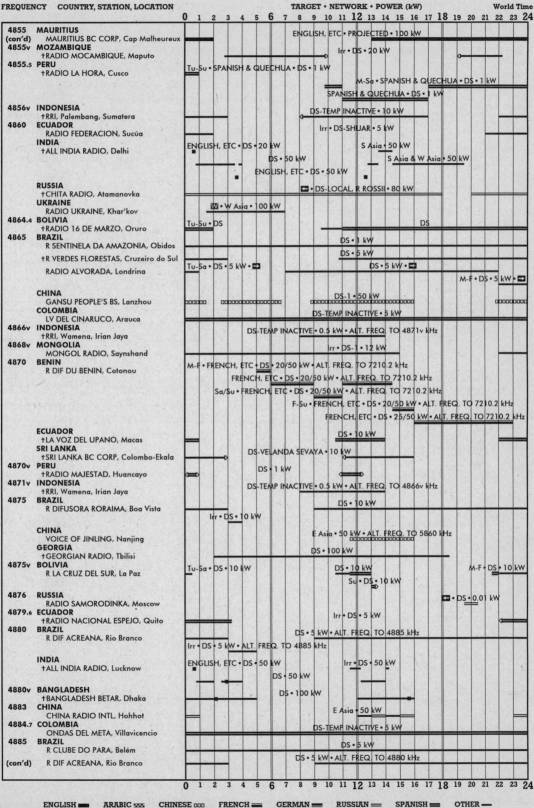

Frequency	Country, Station, Location	Target • Network • Power
4855 (con'd)	**MAURITIUS** MAURITIUS BC CORP, Cap Malheureux	ENGLISH, ETC • PROJECTED • 100 kW
4855v	**MOZAMBIQUE** †RADIO MOCAMBIQUE, Maputo	Irr • DS • 20 kW
4855.5	**PERU** †RADIO LA HORA, Cusco	Tu-Su • SPANISH & QUECHUA • DS • 1 kW / M-Sa • SPANISH & QUECHUA • DS • 1 kW / SPANISH & QUECHUA • DS • 1 kW
4856v	**INDONESIA** †RRI, Palembang, Sumatera	DS-TEMP INACTIVE • 10 kW
4860	**ECUADOR** RADIO FEDERACION, Sucúa	Irr • DS-SHUAR • 5 kW
	INDIA †ALL INDIA RADIO, Delhi	ENGLISH, ETC • DS • 20 kW / S Asia • 50 kW / DS • 50 kW / S Asia & W Asia • 50 kW / ENGLISH, ETC • DS • 50 kW
	RUSSIA †CHITA RADIO, Atamanovka	DS-LOCAL, R ROSSII • 80 kW
	UKRAINE RADIO UKRAINE, Khar'kov	W • W Asia • 100 kW
4864.4	**BOLIVIA** †RADIO 16 DE MARZO, Oruro	Tu-Su • DS / DS
4865	**BRAZIL** R SENTINELA DA AMAZONIA, Obidos	DS • 1 kW
	†R VERDES FLORESTAS, Cruzeiro do Sul	DS • 5 kW
	RADIO ALVORADA, Londrina	Tu-Sa • DS • 5 kW • ➡ / DS • 5 kW • ➡ / M-F • DS • 5 kW • ➡
	CHINA GANSU PEOPLE'S BS, Lanzhou	DS-1 • 50 kW
	COLOMBIA LV DEL CINARUCO, Arauca	DS-TEMP INACTIVE • 5 kW
4866v	**INDONESIA** †RRI, Wamena, Irian Jaya	DS-TEMP INACTIVE • 0.5 kW • ALT. FREQ. TO 4871v kHz
4868v	**MONGOLIA** MONGOL RADIO, Saynshand	Irr • DS-1 • 12 kW
4870	**BENIN** R DIF DU BENIN, Cotonou	M-F • FRENCH, ETC • DS • 20/50 kW • ALT. FREQ. TO 7210.2 kHz / FRENCH, ETC • DS • 20/50 kW • ALT. FREQ. TO 7210.2 kHz / Sa/Su • FRENCH, ETC • DS • 20/50 kW • ALT. FREQ. TO 7210.2 kHz / F-Su • FRENCH, ETC • DS • 20/50 kW • ALT. FREQ. TO 7210.2 kHz / FRENCH, ETC • DS • 25/50 kW • ALT. FREQ. TO 7210.2 kHz
	ECUADOR †LA VOZ DEL UPANO, Macas	DS • 10 kW
	SRI LANKA †SRI LANKA BC CORP, Colombo-Ekala	DS-VELANDA SEVAYA • 10 kW
4870v	**PERU** †RADIO MAJESTAD, Huancayo	DS • 1 kW
4871v	**INDONESIA** †RRI, Wamena, Irian Jaya	DS-TEMP INACTIVE • 0.5 kW • ALT. FREQ. TO 4866v kHz
4875	**BRAZIL** R DIFUSORA RORAIMA, Boa Vista	DS • 10 kW / Irr • DS • 10 kW
	CHINA VOICE OF JINLING, Nanjing	E Asia • 50 kW • ALT. FREQ. TO 5860 kHz
	GEORGIA †GEORGIAN RADIO, Tbilisi	DS • 100 kW
4875v	**BOLIVIA** R LA CRUZ DEL SUR, La Paz	Tu-Sa • DS • 10 kW / DS • 10 kW / M-F • DS • 10 kW / Su • DS • 10 kW
4876	**RUSSIA** RADIO SAMORODINKA, Moscow	DS • 0.01 kW
4879.6	**ECUADOR** †RADIO NACIONAL ESPEJO, Quito	Irr • DS • 5 kW
4880	**BRAZIL** R DIF ACREANA, Rio Branco	DS • 5 kW • ALT. FREQ. TO 4885 kHz / Irr • DS • 5 kW • ALT. FREQ. TO 4885 kHz
	INDIA †ALL INDIA RADIO, Lucknow	ENGLISH, ETC • DS • 50 kW / Irr • DS • 50 kW / DS • 50 kW
4880v	**BANGLADESH** †BANGLADESH BETAR, Dhaka	DS • 100 kW
4883	**CHINA** CHINA RADIO INTL, Hohhot	E Asia • 50 kW
4884.7	**COLOMBIA** ONDAS DEL META, Villavicencio	DS-TEMP INACTIVE • 5 kW
4885	**BRAZIL** R CLUBE DO PARA, Belém	DS • 5 kW
(con'd)	R DIF ACREANA, Rio Branco	DS • 5 kW • ALT. FREQ. TO 4880 kHz

ENGLISH ▬▬   ARABIC ⊠⊠⊠   CHINESE □□□   FRENCH ▭▭   GERMAN ▬▬   RUSSIAN ══   SPANISH ▬▬   OTHER ▬

| FREQUENCY | COUNTRY, STATION, LOCATION | TARGET • NETWORK • POWER (kW) | World Time |

0 1 2 3 4 5 6 7 8 9 10 11 12 13 14 15 16 17 18 19 20 21 22 23 24

4885 BRAZIL
(con'd) R DIF ACREANA, Rio Branco — Irr • DS • 5 kW • ALT. FREQ. TO 4880 kHz

RADIO CARAJA, Anápolis — DS-TEMP INACTIVE • 0.25/1 kW •

KENYA
†KENYA BC CORP, Nairobi — DS-GENERAL • 100 kW • ALT. FREQ. TO 4935 kHz

4885.6 BOLIVIA
†RADIO SARARENDA, Camiri — Irr • M-Sa • DS • 1 kW   M-F • DS • 1 kW
M-Sa • DS • 1 kW   Irr • M-F • DS • 1 kW

4886.6 PERU
RADIO VILLA RICA, Huancavelica — DS • 1 kW
Irr • DS • 1 kW   M-Sa • DS • 1 kW
Su • QUECHUA • DS • 1 kW

4888v PERU
RADIO HUANTA, Huanta — DS • 0.5 kW
Irr • Tu-Su • DS • 0.5 kW   M-Sa • DS • 0.5 kW

4890 FRANCE
R FRANCE INTL, Via Moyabi, Gabon — C Africa • 250 kW
PAPUA NEW GUINEA
†NBC, Port Moresby — DS • 100 kW • ALT. FREQ. TO 9675 kHz
ENGLISH, ETC • DS • 100 kW
M-Sa • ENGLISH, ETC • DS • 100 kW
M-Sa • ENGLISH, ETC • DS • 100 kW • ALT. FREQ. TO 9675 kHz

4890v PERU
†RADIO CHOTA, Chota — DS
Irr • DS

SENEGAL
RTV DU SENEGAL, Dakar — FRENCH, ETC • DS • 100 kW • ALT. FREQ. TO 7170v kHz
4895 BRAZIL
RADIO BARE, Manaus — DS • 1 kW
RADIO IPB AM, Campo Grande — DS • 5 kW
COLOMBIA
†LV DEL RIO ARAUCA, Arauca — Irr • DS-TEMP INACTIVE • 10 kW
INDIA
†ALL INDIA RADIO, Kurseong — DS • 20 kW
ENGLISH, ETC • DS • 20 kW
MALAYSIA
R MALAYSIA SARAWAK, Kuching — DS-IBAN • 10 kW
PERU
†RADIO CHANCHAMAYO, La Merced — Tu-Su • DS • 0.4 kW   M-Sa • DS • 0.4 kW
RUSSIA
†TYUMEN RADIO, Tyumen — DS-LOCAL, R ROSSII • 50 kW
4895v PAKISTAN
PAKISTAN BC CORP, Islamabad — DS
4897v MONGOLIA
MONGOL RADIO, Murun — DS-1 • 12 kW
4900 CHINA
VO THE STRAIT-PLA, Fuzhou — TAIWAN-2 • 50 kW
4901v BOLIVIA
R SAN IGNACIO, S Ignacio de Moxos — Irr • DS • 0.5 kW
4902 SRI LANKA
SRI LANKA BC CORP, Colombo-Ekala — DS-SINHALA 1 • 10 kW
4904.5 CHAD
RADIODIF NATIONALE, N'Djamena — FRENCH, ETC • DS • 100 kW   FRENCH, ETC • DS • 100 kW • ALT. FREQ. TO 6165 kHz
Sa/Su • FRENCH, ETC • DS • 100 kW • ALT. FREQ. TO 6165 kHz
Sa • FRENCH, ETC • DS • 100 kW • ALT. FREQ. TO 6165 kHz
4904.8 PERU
RADIO LA OROYA, La Oroya — DS • 0.45/1 kW
4905 BRAZIL
†RADIO ANHANGUERA, Araguaína — DS • 1 kW •
CHINA
CENTRAL PEOPLE'S BS — DS-2
4905.3 COLOMBIA
ECOS DEL ORINOCO, Puerto Carreño — DS-TEMP INACTIVE
4906v MOZAMBIQUE
†RADIO MOCAMBIQUE, Maputo — DS-INTERPROVINCIAL • 10 kW • ALT. FREQ. TO 4926v kHz
DS-INTERPROVINCIAL • 7.5 kW • ALT. FREQ. TO 4926v kHz

4910 AUSTRALIA
ABC/CAAMA RADIO, Tennant Creek — ENGLISH, ETC • Australasia • DS • 50 kW
INDIA
†ALL INDIA RADIO, Jaipur — DS • 50 kW
ZAMBIA
†RADIO ZAMBIA-ZNBC, Lusaka — ENGLISH, ETC • DS-1 • 100 kW • ALT. FREQ. TO 6265 kHz
4910v CAMBODIA
RADIO PHNOM PENH, Phnom Penh — DS-TEMP INACTIVE • 50 kW
4910.6 HONDURAS
LV DE LA MOSQUITIA, Puerto Lempira — Irr • DS • 0.1/0.5 kW
4914.4 PERU
†RADIO CORA, Lima-Puente Piedra — DS • 10 kW
Tu-Sa • DS • 10 kW

0 1 2 3 4 5 6 7 8 9 10 11 12 13 14 15 16 17 18 19 20 21 22 23 24

SEASONAL ⑤ OR Ⓦ   1-HR TIMESHIFT MIDYEAR ◆ OR ◆   JAMMING / OR ∧   EARLIEST HEARD ◁   LATEST HEARD ▷   NEW FOR 1998 †

FREQUENCY   COUNTRY, STATION, LOCATION   TARGET • NETWORK • POWER (kW)   World Time

	0 1 2 3 4 5 6 7 8 9 10 11 12 13 14 15 16 17 18 19 20 21 22 23 24

4915 **BRAZIL**
  †RADIO ANHANGUERA, Goiânia — DS • 10 kW • ▣
  RADIO NACIONAL, Macapá — Irr • DS • 10 kW
CHINA
  GUANGXI PEOPLE'S BS, Nanning — CHINESE, ETC • DS-1 • 10 kW
COLOMBIA
  †ARMONIAS DEL CAQUETA, Florencia — DS • 3 kW
GHANA
  †GHANA BC CORP, Accra — ENGLISH, ETC • DS-1 • 50 kW
  Sa/Su//Holidays • ENGLISH, ETC • DS-1 • 50 kW
  Irr • M-F • DS-EDUCATIONAL • 50 kW
KENYA
  KENYA BC CORP, Nairobi — M-F • DS-CENTRAL • 100 kW
PAKISTAN
  PAKISTAN BC CORP, Islamabad — DS • 10 kW
4919 **ECUADOR**
  RADIO QUITO, Quito — DS • 5 kW
4920 **INDIA**
  †ALL INDIA RADIO, Chennai — DS • 50 kW
  ENGLISH, ETC • DS • 50 kW
4925 **BRAZIL**
  †RADIO DIFUSORA, Taubaté — DS • 0.5/1 kW
4925v **INDONESIA**
  †RRI, Jambi, Sumatera — DS • 7.5 kW
4926v **BOLIVIA**
  †RADIO SAN MIGUEL, Riberalta — DS • 1 kW
  Tu-Su • DS • 1 kW
  Su • DS • 1 kW
CHINA
  HONGHE PEOPLE'S BS, Honghe — DS
EQUATORIAL GUINEA
  RADIO NACIONAL, Bata — DS-SPANISH, ETC • 50 kW • ALT. FREQ. TO 5004v kHz
MOZAMBIQUE
  †RADIO MOCAMBIQUE, Maputo — DS-INTERPROVINCIAL • 10 kW • ALT. FREQ. TO 4906v kHz
  DS-INTERPROVINCIAL • 7.5 kW • ALT. FREQ. TO 4906v kHz
4927v **INDONESIA**
  †RRI, Jambi, Sumatera — DS • 7.5 kW
4930 **DOMINICAN REPUBLIC**
  RADIO BARAHONA, Barahona — Irr • DS • 1 kW
NAMIBIA
  NAMIBIAN BC CORP, Windhoek — ENGLISH, ETC • DS • 100 kW • ▣
RUSSIA
  MAYAK — DS
TURKMENISTAN
  TURKMEN RADIO, Ashgabat — RUSSIAN, ETC • DS-2/MAYAK • 50 kW
4930.6 **HONDURAS**
  †R INTERNACIONAL, San Pedro Sula — DS • 1 kW
4931v **INDONESIA**
  †RRI, Surakarta, Jawa — Irr • DS • 10 kW
4935 **BRAZIL**
  RADIO CAPIXABA, Vitória — DS • 1 kW
  RADIO DIFUSORA, Jataí — DS • 2.5 kW • ▣
KENYA
  †KENYA BC CORP, Nairobi — DS-GENERAL • 100 kW • ALT. FREQ. TO 4885 kHz
PERU
  RADIO TROPICAL, Tarapoto — DS • 3 kW
  Tu-Su • DS • 3 kW   M-Sa • DS • 3 kW
4939.2 **BOLIVIA**
  RADIO NORTE, Montero — Tu-Sa • DS • 1 kW   M-Sa • DS • 1 kW
  DS • 1 kW
  Su • DS • 1 kW
4939.5 **VENEZUELA**
  †RADIO AMAZONAS, Puerto Ayacucho — DS • 1 kW
4940 **CHINA**
  VO THE STRAIT-PLA, Fuzhou — TAIWAN-1 • 50 kW
INDIA
  †ALL INDIA RADIO, Guwahati — DS • 50 kW
  DS-A • 50 kW
  Irr • DS • 50 kW
  Irr • ENGLISH & HINDI • DS • 50 kW
RUSSIA
  VOICE OF RUSSIA, Via Tajikistan — ▣ • W Asia & S Asia • 100 kW
SRI LANKA
  †SRI LANKA BC CORP, Colombo-Ekala — DS • 10 kW
4945 **BOLIVIA**
  †RADIO ILLIMANI, La Paz — DS • 10 kW
  Tu-Su • DS • 10 kW   Irr • M-Sa • DS • 10 kW
  M-Sa • DS • 10 kW

(con'd)

	0 1 2 3 4 5 6 7 8 9 10 11 12 13 14 15 16 17 18 19 20 21 22 23 24

ENGLISH ▬   ARABIC ▨▨   CHINESE □□□   FRENCH ▬   GERMAN ▬   RUSSIAN ═   SPANISH ▬   OTHER —

FREQUENCY	COUNTRY, STATION, LOCATION	TARGET • NETWORK • POWER (kW)	World Time

```
                                                    0  1  2  3  4  5  6  7  8  9  10 11 12 13 14 15 16 17 18 19 20 21 22 23 24
```

4945
(con'd) **BRAZIL**
　　　†A VOZ DO SAO FRANCISCO, Petrolina — DS • 2 kW
　　　RADIO DIFUSORA, Poços de Caldas — DS • 1 kW • ⇨
　　　　Tu-Su • DS • 1 kW • ⇨
　　　RADIO PROGRESSO, Pôrto Velho — DS-TEMP INACTIVE • 7.5 kW

4949.8 ECUADOR
　　　RADIO BAHA'I, Otavalo — QUECHUA • DS • 3 kW
　　　　DS • 3 kW

4950 ANGOLA
　　　RADIO NACIONAL, Luanda — DS-NATIONAL
　　　CHINA
　　　VOICE OF PUJIANG, Shanghai — E Asia
　　　XILINGOL PEOPLE'S BS, Abagnar Qi — DS-MONGOLIAN
　　　INDIA
　　　†RADIO KASHMIR, Srinagar — DS • 50 kW ... DS • 50 kW • ALT. FREQ. TO 3277 kHz
　　　　ENGLISH, ETC • DS • 50 kW • ALT. FREQ. TO 3277 kHz
　　　PERU
　　　R MADRE DE DIOS, Puerto Maldonado — DS • 5 kW • ALT. FREQ. TO 4953 kHz
　　　　M-Sa • DS • 5 kW • ALT. FREQ. TO 4953 kHz
　　　USA
　　　†VOA, Via São Tomé — Sa • W Africa & C Africa • 100 kW
　　　　W Africa & C Africa • 100 kW
　　　　M-F • W Africa & C Africa • 100 kW
　　　　Sa/Su • W Africa & C Africa • 100 kW

4953 PERU
　　　R MADRE DE DIOS, Puerto Maldonado — DS • 5 kW • ALT. FREQ. TO 4950 kHz
　　　　M-Sa • DS • 5 kW • ALT. FREQ. TO 4950 kHz

4955 BRAZIL
　　　†RADIO CLUBE, Rondonópolis — Irr • M • DS • 2.5 kW • ⇨ ... DS • 2.5 kW • ⇨
　　　　M-Sa • DS • 2.5 kW • ⇨ ... Irr • Su • DS • 2.5 kW • ⇨
　　　COLOMBIA
　　　RADIO NACIONAL, Santafé de Bogotá — DS • 20 kW
　　　PERU
　　　RADIO CULTURAL AMAUTA, Huanta — Tu-Su • DS • 1 kW
　　　　QUECHUA • DS • 1 kW
　　　　DS • 1 kW
　　　　M-Sa • DS • 1 kW

4955.2 BRAZIL
　　　RADIO CULTURA, Campos — DS • 2.5 kW • ⇨
　　　RADIO MARAJOARA, Belém — DS-TEMP INACTIVE • 10 kW

4957.5 AZERBAIJAN
　　　AZERBAIJANI RADIO, Baku — DS-2/RUSSIAN, AZERI • 50 kW

4959v MADAGASCAR
　　　†RTV MALAGASY, Antananarivo — DS-1 • 30/100 kW • ALT. FREQ. TO 5009v kHz
　　　VIETNAM
　　　VOICE OF VIETNAM, Hanoi — DS-2 • 50 kW

4959.8 DOMINICAN REPUBLIC
　　　RADIO CIMA, Santo Domingo — Irr • DS • 1 kW

4960 CHINA
　　　CHINA RADIO INTL, Beijing — E Asia • FEEDER
　　　ECUADOR
　　　RADIO FEDERACION, Sucúa — DS-SHUAR • 5 kW
　　　　Tu-Su • DS-SHUAR • 5 kW
　　　USA
　　　†VOA, Via São Tomé — Su-Th • W Africa & C Africa • 100 kW
　　　　W Africa & C Africa • 100 kW
　　　　M-F • W Africa & C Africa • 100 kW
　　　VANUATU
　　　RADIO VANUATU, Vila, Efate Island — ENGLISH, FRENCH, ETC • DS • 10 kW • ALT. FREQ. TO 7260 kHz • ⇨

4960.5 HONDURAS
　　　†RADIO HRET, Puerto Lempira — Tu-Su • DS-TEMP INACTIVE ... DS-TEMP INACTIVE

4964.5 PERU
　　　RADIO LA MERCED, La Merced — Tu-Su • DS • 1 kW ... M-Sa • DS • 1 kW
　　　　DS • 1 kW

4965 BRAZIL
　　　RADIO ALVORADA, Parintins — DS • 5 kW
　　　NAMIBIA
　　　NAMIBIAN BC CORP, Windhoek — ENGLISH, GERMAN & AFRIKAANS • DS • 100 kW • ⇨
　　　ZAMBIA
　　　CHRISTIAN VOICE, Lusaka — S Africa • 100 kW • ALT. FREQ. TO 3330 kHz

4965v BOLIVIA
　　　RADIO JUAN XXIII, San Ignacio Velasco — Tu-Su • DS • 3 kW ... Irr • M-Sa • DS • 3 kW
　　　　DS • 3 kW ... M-Sa • DS • 3 kW
　　　　Su • DS • 3 kW

4965.8 PERU
　　　R SAN MIGUEL, Cusco — SPANISH & QUECHUA • DS • 5 kW
　　　　M-Sa • SPANISH & QUECHUA • DS • 5 kW

```
                                                    0  1  2  3  4  5  6  7  8  9  10 11 12 13 14 15 16 17 18 19 20 21 22 23 24
```

FREQUENCY   COUNTRY, STATION, LOCATION

TARGET • NETWORK • POWER (kW)

World Time

0 1 2 3 4 5 6 7 8 9 10 11 12 13 14 15 16 17 18 19 20 21 22 23 24

Frequency	Country, Station, Location	Schedule
4969v	PERU †RADIO IMAGEN, Tarapoto	DS • 1 kW / Tu-Su • DS • 1 kW / M-Sa • DS • 1 kW
4970	CHINA XINJIANG PEOPLE'S BC STN, Urümqi	DS-KAZAKH • 50 kW
	INDIA †ALL INDIA RADIO, Shillong	Irr • DS • 50 kW / DS • 50 kW / ENGLISH, ETC • DS • 50 kW
	MALAYSIA R MALAYSIA KOTA KINABALU	DS • 10 kW
	VENEZUELA RADIO RUMBOS, Villa de Cura	DS-TEMP INACTIVE • 10 kW / Sa/Su • DS-TEMP INACTIVE • 10 kW
4974.8	PERU †RADIO DEL PACIFICO, Lima	DS • 5 kW
4975	BRAZIL †RADIO MUNDIAL, São Paulo	DS • 1 kW
	RADIO TIMBIRA, São Luís	DS-TEMP INACTIVE • 2.5 kW
	CHINA FUJIAN PEOPLE'S BS, Jianyang	DS-1 • 10 kW / TAIWAN SVC • 10 kW
	RUSSIA VOICE OF RUSSIA, Via Tajikistan	• W Asia & S Asia • 100 kW
	TAJIKISTAN †RADIO TAJIKISTAN, Dushanbe	W Asia & C Asia • 100 kW • ALT. FREQ. TO 7245 kHz
4975v	COLOMBIA †ONDAS DEL ORTEGUAZA, Florencia	DS-TODELAR • 1 kW
4976	UGANDA RADIO UGANDA, Kampala	ENGLISH, ETC • DS • 50 kW • ALT. FREQ. TO 3340 kHz
4980	CHINA †XINJIANG PEOPLE'S BC STN, Urümqi	DS-MONGOLIAN • 50 kW
	VENEZUELA ECOS DEL TORBES, San Cristóbal	DS • 10 kW
4985	BRAZIL †R BRASIL CENTRAL, Goiânia	DS • 10 kW •
4990	ARMENIA VOICE OF ARMENIA, Kamo	• Mideast & N Africa • 100 kW / • M-F • Mideast & N Africa • 100 kW / • Sa/Su • Mideast & N Africa • 100 kW
	CHINA HUNAN PEOPLE'S BS, Changsha	DS-1 • 10 kW
	INDIA †ALL INDIA RADIO, Itanagar	DS • 50 kW
	NIGERIA RADIO NIGERIA, Lagos	ENGLISH, ETC • DS-TEMP INACTIVE • 50 kW
4991	BOLIVIA RADIO ANIMAS, Animas	Tu-Su • SPANISH & QUECHUA • DS • 1 kW / M-Sa • SPANISH & QUECHUA • DS • 1 kW / SPANISH & QUECHUA • DS • 1 kW
	SURINAME †RADIO APINTIE, Paramaribo	DS • 0.05/0.35 kW • ALT. FREQ. TO 5005.7 kHz / Tu-Su • DS • 0.05/0.35 kW • ALT. FREQ. TO 5005.7 kHz
4991v	PERU RADIO ANCASH, Huaraz	SPANISH & QUECHUA • DS • 5 kW
4995	MONGOLIA MONGOL RADIO, Choybalsan	Irr • DS-1 • 12 kW
4995.6	PERU RADIO ANDINA, Huancayo	DS • 1 kW / Tu-Su • DS • 1 kW / M-Sa • DS • 1 kW / Irr • Tu-Su • DS • 1 kW
5000	AUSTRALIA VNG, Llandilo	WORLD TIME • 10 kW
	ERITREA †VO BROAD MASSES, Asmera	M-F • E Africa • 2 kW / E Africa • 2 kW / Sa/Su • E Africa • 2 kW
	USA WWV, Fort Collins, Colorado	WEATHER/WORLD TIME • 10 kW
	WWVH, Kekaha, Hawai'i	WEATHER/WORLD TIME • 10 kW
	VENEZUELA OBSERVATORIO CAGIGAL, Caracas	DS • 2 kW
5004v	EQUATORIAL GUINEA RADIO NACIONAL, Bata	DS-SPANISH, ETC • 50 kW • ALT. FREQ. TO 4926v kHz
5004.8	BOLIVIA †RADIO LIBERTAD, La Paz	Tu-Sa • DS-TEMP INACTIVE • 1/5 kW / DS-TEMP INACTIVE • 1/5 kW / Sa • DS-TEMP INACTIVE • 1/5 kW / Su-F • DS-TEMP INACTIVE • 1/5 kW / M-F • DS-TEMP INACTIVE • 1/5 kW / Sa/Su • DS-TEMP INACTIVE • 1/5 kW

0 1 2 3 4 5 6 7 8 9 10 11 12 13 14 15 16 17 18 19 20 21 22 23 24

ENGLISH ▬   ARABIC ⧓⧓⧓   CHINESE □□□   FRENCH ══   GERMAN ▬▬   RUSSIAN ══   SPANISH ══   OTHER ▬▬

FREQUENCY	COUNTRY, STATION, LOCATION	TARGET • NETWORK • POWER (kW)	World Time

0 1 2 3 4 5 6 7 8 9 10 11 12 13 14 15 16 17 18 19 20 21 22 23 24

5005	**MALAYSIA**	
	R MALAYSIA SARAWAK, Sibu	DS-IBAN • 10 kW
	NEPAL	
	RADIO NEPAL, Harriharpur	DS • 40/100 kW
		Sa • DS • 40/100 kW
5005.6	**PERU**	
	†RADIO JAEN, Jaén	DS • 0.25 kW
5005.7	**SURINAME**	
	†RADIO APINTIE, Paramaribo	DS • 0.05/0.35 kW • ALT. FREQ. TO 4991 kHz
		Tu-Su • DS • 0.05/0.35 kW • ALT. FREQ. TO 4991 kHz
5009v	**MADAGASCAR**	
	†RTV MALAGASY, Antananarivo	DS-1 • 30/100 kW • ALT. FREQ. TO 4959v kHz
5010	**CAMEROON**	
	CAMEROON RTV, Garoua	FRENCH, ETC • DS • 100 kW FRENCH, ETC • DS • 100 kW • ALT. FREQ. TO 7240 kHz
		M-F • DS • 100 kW DS • 100 kW • ALT. FREQ. TO 7240 kHz
		Sa/Su • FRENCH, ETC • DS • 100 kW
	CHINA	
	GUANGXI ECONOMIC BS, Nanning	CHINESE, ETC • 10 kW
	INDIA	
	†ALL INDIA RADIO, Thiruvananthapuram	DS • 50 kW Irr • Su • DS • 50 kW
		Irr • DS • 50 kW
5010.3	**ECUADOR**	
	†ESCUELAS RADIOFONICAS, Riobamba	Irr • SPANISH, ETC • DS-TEMP INACTIVE • 1 kW
		Irr • SPANISH & QUECHUA • DS-TEMP INACTIVE • 1 kW
5012v	**DOMINICAN REPUBLIC**	
	RADIO CRISTAL INTL, Santo Domingo	1 kW
5014v	**BRAZIL**	
	RADIO PIONEIRA, Teresina	DS • 1 kW
	PERU	
	ESTACION TARAPOTO, Tarapoto	DS-TEMP INACTIVE • 0.7 kW
5015	**BRAZIL**	
	R BRASIL TROPICAL, Cuiabá	DS • 0.25/0.5 kW
	RADIO COPACABANA, Rio de Janeiro	DS • 0.25 kW
	RUSSIA	
	R TIKHIY OKEAN, Vladivostok	◨ • E Asia • 50 kW
	†VLADIVOSTOK R, Vladivostok	◨ • DS • 50 kW
	TURKMENISTAN	
	†TURKMEN RADIO, Ashgabat	RUSSIAN, ETC • DS-1 • 100 kW
		Tu/Th-Sa • DS-1 • 100 kW
		W/Su/M • DS-1 • 100 kW
5016v	**PERU**	
	RADIO JULIACA, Juliaca	SPANISH, QUECHUA & AYMARA • DS • 0.5 kW
5019v	**COLOMBIA**	
	†ECOS DEL ATRATO, Quibdó	DS-CARACOL • 2 kW
5019.8	**PERU**	
	RADIO HORIZONTE, Chachapoyas	Tu-Su • DS • 5 kW M-Sa • DS • 5 kW
		DS • 5 kW
5020	**CHINA**	
	JIANGXI PEOPLE'S BS, Nanchang	DS-1 • 10 kW
		Su • DS-1 • 10 kW
	SOLOMON ISLANDS	
	SOLOMON ISLANDS BC, Honiara	Su • DS-ENGLISH, PIDGIN • 10 kW
		M-F • DS-ENGLISH, PIDGIN • 10 kW
		Sa • DS-ENGLISH, PIDGIN • 10 kW
	SRI LANKA	
	SRI LANKA BC CORP, Colombo-Ekala	DS-TAMIL • 10 kW
5020v	**CHINA**	
	XIZANG PEOPLE'S BC STN, Lhasa	DS-TIBETAN • 50 kW
	NIGER	
	LA VOIX DU SAHEL, Niamey	M-Sa • FRENCH, ETC • DS • 20/100 kW Sa • FRENCH, ETC • DS • 20/100 kW
		FRENCH, ETC • DS • 20/100 kW
5025	**AUSTRALIA**	
	ABC/R RUM JUNGLE, Katherine	Australasia • DS • 50 kW
	BENIN	
	†R DIF DU BENIN, Parakou	M-F • FRENCH, ETC • DS • 20 kW FRENCH, ETC • DS • 20 kW • ALT. FREQ. TO 7190 kHz
		FRENCH, ETC • DS • 20 kW
		Sa/Su • FRENCH, ETC • DS • 20 kW • ALT. FREQ. TO 7190 kHz
		F-Su • FRENCH, ETC • DS • 20 kW • ALT. FREQ. TO 7190 kHz
	CUBA	
	RADIO REBELDE, Havana	DS • 10 kW
	PAKISTAN	
	PAKISTAN BC CORP, Quetta	DS • 10 kW
	PERU	
	RADIO QUILLABAMBA, Quillabamba	SPANISH & QUECHUA • DS • 5 kW
		Su • DS • 5 kW Irr • SPANISH, ETC • DS • 5 kW
5025v	**BHUTAN**	
	†BHUTAN BC SERVICE, Thimbu	M-Sa • DS • 50 kW • ALT. FREQ. TO 5030 kHz • ◨

0 1 2 3 4 5 6 7 8 9 10 11 12 13 14 15 16 17 18 19 20 21 22 23 24

FREQUENCY   COUNTRY, STATION, LOCATION

TARGET • NETWORK • POWER (kW)   World Time

0 1 2 3 4 5 6 7 8 9 10 11 12 13 14 15 16 17 18 19 20 21 22 23 24

Frequency	Country, Station, Location	Schedule
5026	**UGANDA** — RADIO UGANDA, Kampala	ENGLISH, ETC • DS • 20 kW
5029v	**VIETNAM** — †VOICE OF VIETNAM, Hanoi	DS
5030	**BHUTAN** — †BHUTAN BC SERVICE, Thimbu	M-Sa • DS • 50 kW • ALT. FREQ. TO 5025v kHz
	CHINA — †CENTRAL PEOPLE'S BS	DS-1
	COSTA RICA — †ADVENTIST WORLD R, Cahuita	Su/M • C America • 20 kW; Tu-Sa • C America • 20 kW; C America • 20 kW; M-Sa • C America • 20 kW; Su • C America • 20 kW
	MALAYSIA — R MALAYSIA SARAWAK, Kuching	DS-BIDAYUH • 10 kW
5030.6	**PERU** — †RADIO LOS ANDES, Huamachuco	DS
5034v	**CENTRAL AFRICAN REP** — RADIO CENTRAFRIQUE, Bangui	FRENCH, ETC • DS • 100 kW; Irr • FRENCH, ETC • DS • 100 kW
5035	**BRAZIL** — R EDUCACAO RURAL, Coari	DS • 5 kW
	UZBEKISTAN — RADIO TASHKENT, Tashkent	Europe • 100 kW
5035v	**BRAZIL** — RADIO APARECIDA, Aparecida	DS • 10 kW
5039.2	**PERU** — RADIO LIBERTAD, Junin	DS • 1 kW; Tu-Su • DS • 1 kW; M-Sa • DS • 1 kW
5039.8	**CHINA** — FUJIAN PEOPLE'S BS, Fuzhou	DS-1 • 10 kW
5040	**COLOMBIA** — †LA VOZ DE YOPAL, Yopal	Irr • DS-TEMP INACTIVE • 1 kW
	ECUADOR — †LA VOZ DEL UPANO, Macas	Irr • DS • 10 kW
	GEORGIA — †GEORGIAN RADIO, Tbilisi	DS-1 • 100 kW
	GUATEMALA — LA VOZ DE NAHUALA, Nahualá	SPANISH, ETC • DS (1.5X3360 KHZ) • SPR; Su • SPANISH, ETC • DS (1.5X3360 KHZ) • SPR
	INDONESIA — †RRI, Pekanbaru, Sumatera	DS • 50 kW
	UZBEKISTAN — RADIO TASHKENT, Tashkent	W • E Asia • 100 kW
5043v	**ANGOLA** — EP DE BENGUELA, Benguela	DS-TEMP INACTIVE • 1 kW
5045	**BRAZIL** — †R CULTURA DO PARA, Belém	DS • 10 kW; Irr • DS • 10 kW
5046v	**INDONESIA** — †RRI, Yogyakarta, Jawa	DS-TEMP INACTIVE • 20 kW
5046.3	**PERU** — †RADIO INTEGRACION, Abancay	SPANISH & QUECHUA • DS
5047	**TOGO** — RADIO LOME, Lomé-Togblekope	FRENCH, ETC • DS • 100 kW; DS • 100 kW
5049.7	**PERU** — RADIO TAYACAJA, Pampas	DS
5050	**CHINA** — GUANGXI BC STATION, Nanning	SE Asia • 50 kW; TAIWAN-1 • 50 kW
	†VO THE STRAIT-PLA, Fuzhou	TAIWAN-1 • 50 kW
	INDIA — †ALL INDIA RADIO, Aizawl	ENGLISH, ETC • DS • 50 kW; DS • 50 kW; Irr • DS • 50 kW
	TANZANIA — RADIO TANZANIA, Dar es Salaam	E Africa • 10/100 kW; Sa/Su • E Africa • 10/100 kW; E Africa • DS-NATIONAL • 10/100 kW
5050.5	**ECUADOR** — †RADIO JESUS DEL GRAN PODER, Quito	DS • 5 kW
	PERU — RADIO MUNICIPAL, Cangallo	DS-TEMP INACTIVE
5053.6	**PERU** — RADIO ACOBAMBA, Acobamba	DS
5054.6	**COSTA RICA** — FARO DEL CARIBE, San José	DS • 5 kW
5055 (con'd)	**BRAZIL** — †R JORNAL "A CRITICA", Manaus	DS • 5 kW

0 1 2 3 4 5 6 7 8 9 10 11 12 13 14 15 16 17 18 19 20 21 22 23 24

ENGLISH ▬ ARABIC ▧ CHINESE ▭▭▭ FRENCH ▬▬ GERMAN ▬▬ RUSSIAN ═ SPANISH ▬▬ OTHER ──

FREQUENCY	COUNTRY, STATION, LOCATION	TARGET • NETWORK • POWER (kW)	World Time

World Time scale: 0 1 2 3 4 5 6 7 8 9 10 11 12 13 14 15 16 17 18 19 20 21 22 23 24

Frequency	Country / Station / Location	Details
5055 (con'd)	BRAZIL — †RADIO DIFUSORA, Cáceres	DS • 1 kW ⇨ ; M-Sa • DS • 1 kW ⇨
	FRENCH GUIANA — RFO-GUYANE, Cayenne	DS • 10 kW
	PAKISTAN — RADIO PAKISTAN, Islamabad	S Asia • 100 kW
5055v	INDONESIA — RRI, Nabire, Irian Jaya	DS
5056.2	PERU — RADIO ONDA IMPERIAL, Cusco	DS • 0.15 kW
5059v	INDONESIA — RRI, Yogyakarta, Jawa	DS
5060	CHINA — †XINJIANG PEOPLE'S BC STN, Changji	DS-MONGOLIAN • 10 kW
	UZBEKISTAN — RADIO TASHKENT, Tashkent	⬛ • E Asia • 50/100 kW ; ⑤ • E Asia • 50 kW ; Europe • 100 kW ; ⑩ • S Asia • 100 kW
5060v	ECUADOR — RADIO PROGRESO, Loja	Irr • DS • 5 kW
5065	USA — †WWCR, Nashville, Tennessee	E North Am & Europe • 100 kW • ALT. FREQ. TO 5070 kHz ; ⑩ M • E North Am & Europe • 100 kW • ALT. FREQ. TO 5070 kHz ; ⑤ M • E North Am & Europe • 100 kW • ALT. FREQ. TO 5070 kHz ; Tu-Su • E North Am & Europe • 100 kW • ALT. FREQ. TO 5070 kHz ; ⑩ • E North Am & Europe • 100 kW • ALT. FREQ. TO 5070 kHz
5066v	CONGO (DEM REP) — †LA VOIX DU PEUPLE, Bunia	FRENCH, ETC • DS • 1 kW
5068.7	PERU — ONDAS SUR ORIENTE, Quillabamba	DS • 1 kW
5070	USA — †WWCR, Nashville, Tennessee	E North Am & Europe • 100 kW • ALT. FREQ. TO 5065 kHz ; ⑩ M • E North Am & Europe • 100 kW • ALT. FREQ. TO 5065 kHz ; ⑤ M • E North Am & Europe • 100 kW • ALT. FREQ. TO 5065 kHz ; Tu-Su • E North Am & Europe • 100 kW • ALT. FREQ. TO 5065 kHz ; ⑩ • E North Am & Europe • 100 kW • ALT. FREQ. TO 5065 kHz
5076.8	COLOMBIA — CARACOL COLOMBIA, Santafé Bogotá	DS • 50 kW
5084v	PERU — RADIO MUNDO, Cusco	QUECHUA & SPANISH • DS • 1 kW
5085	USA — †WGTG, McCaysville, Georgia	W North Am & C America • 20/50 kW ; ⑩ • W North Am & C America • 20/50 kW
5090	CHINA — †CENTRAL PEOPLE'S BS, Beijing	⑩ W-M • NETWORK 6 • 50 kW ; ⑩ • CHINESE, ETC • NETWORK 6 • 50 kW
5097.4	PERU — RADIO ECO, Iquitos	DS-TEMP INACTIVE • 1 kW
5100	LIBERIA — †LIBERIAN COMM'S NETWORK, Totota	ENGLISH & FRENCH • DS-"RADIO LIBERIA" • 10 kW
5125	CHINA — †CENTRAL PEOPLE'S BS, Beijing	⑩ • CHINESE, ETC • TAIWAN SERVICE • 50 kW
5131	PERU — RADIO VISION 2000, Bambamarca	DS-TEMP INACTIVE
5139.8	PERU — RADIO AMAUTA, San Pablo	DS
5145	CHINA — CHINA RADIO INTL, Beijing	E Asia • 120 kW
5163	CHINA — †CENTRAL PEOPLE'S BS, Baoji	⑩ • DS-2 • 50 kW ; DS-2 • 50 kW
5170v	CLANDESTINE (M EAST) — "VO THE MOJAHED", Iraq	Mideast
5220	CHINA — †CHINA RADIO INTL, Beijing	E Asia • FEEDER • 10 kW
	FRANCE — R FRANCE INTL, Via Beijing, China	E Asia • FEEDER • 10 kW
	SPAIN — †R EXTERIOR ESPANA, Via Beijing, China	E Asia • FEEDER • 10 kW
5236v	PERU — †RADIO APURIMAC, Abancay	Irr • Tu-Su • DS • 0.5 kW ; Irr • M-Sa • DS • 0.5 kW ; Irr • DS • 0.5 kW
5250	CHINA — †CHINA RADIO INTL, Beijing	E Asia • FEEDER ; ⑤ • E Asia • FEEDER
5260	KAZAKHSTAN — KAZAKH RADIO, Almaty	⬛ • DS-1 • 20 kW
5264v	PERU — †RADIO 5264, Chiriaco	DS-TEMP INACTIVE

World Time scale: 0 1 2 3 4 5 6 7 8 9 10 11 12 13 14 15 16 17 18 19 20 21 22 23 24

FREQUENCY   COUNTRY, STATION, LOCATION   TARGET • NETWORK • POWER (kW)   World Time

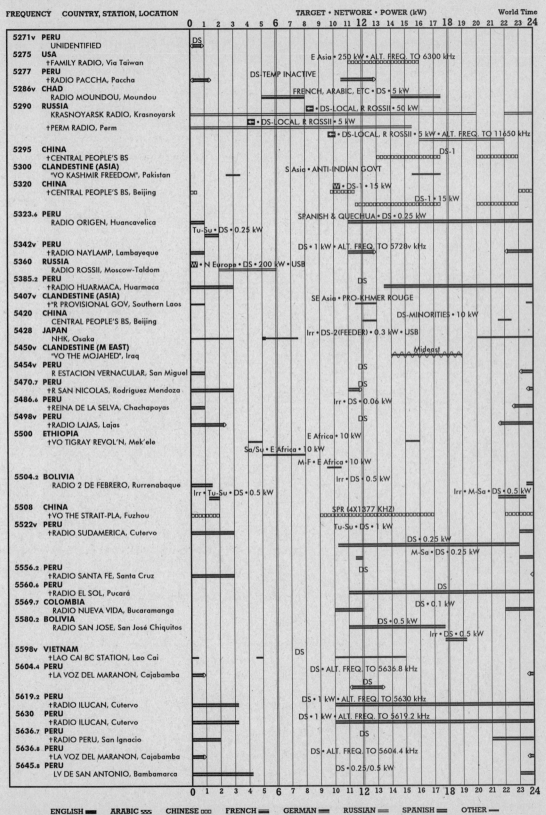

FREQUENCY	COUNTRY, STATION, LOCATION	TARGET • NETWORK • POWER
5271v	**PERU**	
	UNIDENTIFIED	DS
5275	**USA**	
	†FAMILY RADIO, Via Taiwan	E Asia • 250 kW • ALT. FREQ. TO 6300 kHz
5277	**PERU**	
	†RADIO PACCHA, Paccha	DS-TEMP INACTIVE
5286v	**CHAD**	
	RADIO MOUNDOU, Moundou	FRENCH, ARABIC, ETC • DS • 5 kW
5290	**RUSSIA**	
	KRASNOYARSK RADIO, Krasnoyarsk	DS-LOCAL, R ROSSII • 50 kW
	†PERM RADIO, Perm	DS-LOCAL, R ROSSII • 5 kW
		DS-LOCAL, R ROSSII • 5 kW • ALT. FREQ. TO 11650 kHz
5295	**CHINA**	
	†CENTRAL PEOPLE'S BS	DS-1
5300	**CLANDESTINE (ASIA)**	
	"VO KASHMIR FREEDOM", Pakistan	S Asia • ANTI-INDIAN GOVT
5320	**CHINA**	
	†CENTRAL PEOPLE'S BS, Beijing	W • DS-1 • 15 kW
		DS-1 • 15 kW
5323.6	**PERU**	
	RADIO ORIGEN, Huancavelica	SPANISH & QUECHUA • DS • 0.25 kW
		Tu-Su • DS • 0.25 kW
5342v	**PERU**	
	†RADIO NAYLAMP, Lambayeque	DS • 1 kW • ALT. FREQ. TO 5728v kHz
5360	**RUSSIA**	
	RADIO ROSSII, Moscow-Taldom	W • N Europe • DS • 200 kW • USB
5385.2	**PERU**	
	†RADIO HUARMACA, Huarmaca	DS
5407v	**CLANDESTINE (ASIA)**	
	†"R PROVISIONAL GOV", Southern Laos	SE Asia • PRO-KHMER ROUGE
5420	**CHINA**	
	CENTRAL PEOPLE'S BS, Beijing	DS-MINORITIES • 10 kW
5428	**JAPAN**	
	NHK, Osaka	Irr • DS-2(FEEDER) • 0.3 kW • USB
5450v	**CLANDESTINE (M EAST)**	
	"VO THE MOJAHED", Iraq	Mideast
5454v	**PERU**	
	R ESTACION VERNACULAR, San Miguel	DS
5470.7	**PERU**	
	†R SAN NICOLAS, Rodríguez Mendoza	DS
5486.6	**PERU**	
	†REINA DE LA SELVA, Chachapoyas	Irr • DS • 0.06 kW
5498v	**PERU**	
	†RADIO LAJAS, Lajas	DS
5500	**ETHIOPIA**	
	†VO TIGRAY REVOL'N, Mek'ele	E Africa • 10 kW
		Sa/Su • E Africa • 10 kW
		M-F • E Africa • 10 kW
5504.2	**BOLIVIA**	
	RADIO 2 DE FEBRERO, Rurrenabaque	Irr • DS • 0.5 kW
		Irr • Tu-Su • DS • 0.5 kW Irr • M-Sa • DS • 0.5 kW
5508	**CHINA**	
	†VO THE STRAIT-PLA, Fuzhou	SPR (4X1377 KHZ)
5522v	**PERU**	
	†RADIO SUDAMERICA, Cutervo	Tu-Su • DS • 1 kW
		DS • 0.25 kW
		M-Sa • DS • 0.25 kW
5556.2	**PERU**	
	†RADIO SANTA FE, Santa Cruz	DS
5560.6	**PERU**	
	†RADIO EL SOL, Pucará	DS
5569.7	**COLOMBIA**	
	RADIO NUEVA VIDA, Bucaramanga	DS • 0.1 kW
5580.2	**BOLIVIA**	
	RADIO SAN JOSE, San José Chiquitos	DS • 0.5 kW
		Irr • DS • 0.5 kW
5598v	**VIETNAM**	
	†LAO CAI BC STATION, Lao Cai	DS
5604.4	**PERU**	
	†LA VOZ DEL MARANON, Cajabamba	DS • ALT. FREQ. TO 5636.8 kHz
		DS
5619.2	**PERU**	
	†RADIO ILUCAN, Cutervo	DS • 1 kW • ALT. FREQ. TO 5630 kHz
5630	**PERU**	
	†RADIO ILUCAN, Cutervo	DS • 1 kW • ALT. FREQ. TO 5619.2 kHz
5636.7	**PERU**	
	†RADIO PERU, San Ignacio	DS
5636.8	**PERU**	
	†LA VOZ DEL MARANON, Cajabamba	DS • ALT. FREQ. TO 5604.4 kHz
5645.8	**PERU**	
	LV DE SAN ANTONIO, Bambamarca	DS • 0.25/0.5 kW

ENGLISH ▬   ARABIC ▨   CHINESE □□□   FRENCH ▬▬   GERMAN ▬▬   RUSSIAN ══   SPANISH ▭   OTHER ▬▬

FREQUENCY   COUNTRY, STATION, LOCATION

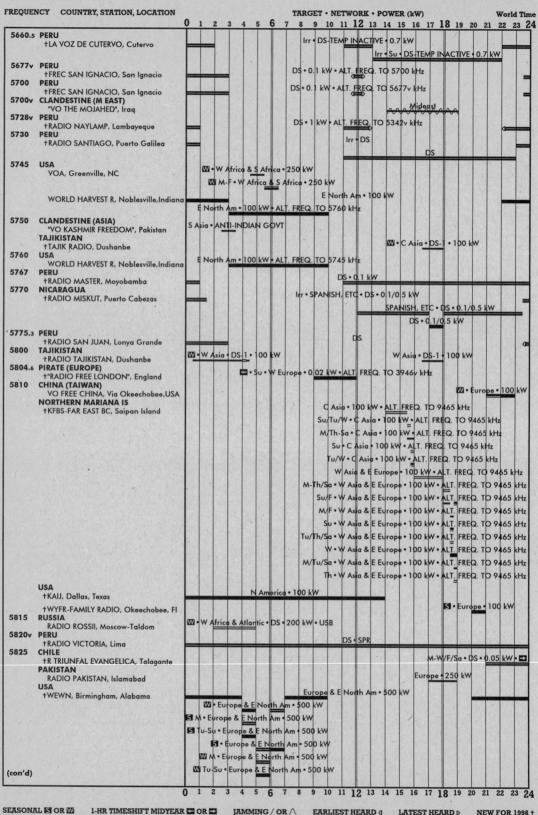

FREQUENCY	COUNTRY, STATION, LOCATION	TARGET • NETWORK • POWER (kW)
5660.5	PERU †LA VOZ DE CUTERVO, Cutervo	Irr • DS-TEMP INACTIVE • 0.7 kW / Irr • Su • DS-TEMP INACTIVE • 0.7 kW
5677v	PERU †FREC SAN IGNACIO, San Ignacio	DS • 0.1 kW • ALT. FREQ. TO 5700 kHz
5700	PERU †FREC SAN IGNACIO, San Ignacio	DS • 0.1 kW • ALT. FREQ. TO 5677v kHz
5700v	CLANDESTINE (M EAST) "VO THE MOJAHED", Iraq	Mideast
5728v	PERU †RADIO NAYLAMP, Lambayeque	DS • 1 kW • ALT. FREQ. TO 5342v kHz
5730	PERU †RADIO SANTIAGO, Puerto Galilea	Irr • DS / DS
5745	USA VOA, Greenville, NC	W • W Africa & S Africa • 250 kW / M-F • W Africa & S Africa • 250 kW
	WORLD HARVEST R, Noblesville, Indiana	E North Am • 100 kW / E North Am • 100 kW • ALT. FREQ. TO 5760 kHz
5750	CLANDESTINE (ASIA) "VO KASHMIR FREEDOM", Pakistan	S Asia • ANTI-INDIAN GOVT
	TAJIKISTAN †TAJIK RADIO, Dushanbe	W • C Asia • DS-1 • 100 kW
5760	USA WORLD HARVEST R, Noblesville, Indiana	E North Am • 100 kW • ALT. FREQ. TO 5745 kHz
5767	PERU †RADIO MASTER, Moyobamba	DS • 0.1 kW
5770	NICARAGUA †RADIO MISKUT, Puerto Cabezas	Irr • SPANISH, ETC • DS 0.1/0.5 kW / SPANISH, ETC • DS • 0.1/0.5 kW / DS • 0.1/0.5 kW
5775.3	PERU †RADIO SAN JUAN, Lonya Grande	DS
5800	TAJIKISTAN †RADIO TAJIKISTAN, Dushanbe	W • W Asia • DS-1 • 100 kW / W Asia • DS-1 • 100 kW
5804.6	PIRATE (EUROPE) †"RADIO FREE LONDON", England	• Su • W Europe • 0.02 kW • ALT. FREQ. TO 3946v kHz
5810	CHINA (TAIWAN) VO FREE CHINA, Via Okeechobee, USA	W • Europe • 100 kW
	NORTHERN MARIANA IS †KFBS-FAR EAST BC, Saipan Island	C Asia • 100 kW • ALT. FREQ. TO 9465 kHz / Su/Tu/W • C Asia • 100 kW • ALT. FREQ. TO 9465 kHz / M/Th-Sa • C Asia • 100 kW • ALT. FREQ. TO 9465 kHz / Su • C Asia • 100 kW • ALT. FREQ. TO 9465 kHz / Tu/W • C Asia • 100 kW • ALT. FREQ. TO 9465 kHz / W Asia & E Europe • 100 kW • ALT. FREQ. TO 9465 kHz / M-Th/Sa • W Asia & E Europe • 100 kW • ALT. FREQ. TO 9465 kHz / Su/F • W Asia & E Europe • 100 kW • ALT. FREQ. TO 9465 kHz / M/F • W Asia & E Europe • 100 kW • ALT. FREQ. TO 9465 kHz / Su • W Asia & E Europe • 100 kW • ALT. FREQ. TO 9465 kHz / Tu/Th/Sa • W Asia & E Europe • 100 kW • ALT. FREQ. TO 9465 kHz / W • W Asia & E Europe • 100 kW • ALT. FREQ. TO 9465 kHz / M/Tu/Sa • W Asia & E Europe • 100 kW • ALT. FREQ. TO 9465 kHz / Th • W Asia & E Europe • 100 kW • ALT. FREQ. TO 9465 kHz
	USA †KAIJ, Dallas, Texas	N America • 100 kW
	†WYFR-FAMILY RADIO, Okeechobee, Fl	S • Europe • 100 kW
5815	RUSSIA RADIO ROSSII, Moscow-Taldom	W • W Africa & Atlantic • DS • 200 kW • USB
5820v	PERU †RADIO VICTORIA, Lima	DS • SPR
5825	CHILE †R TRIUNFAL EVANGELICA, Talagante	M-W/F/Sa • DS • 0.05 kW •
	PAKISTAN RADIO PAKISTAN, Islamabad	Europe • 250 kW
	USA †WEWN, Birmingham, Alabama	Europe & E North Am • 500 kW / W • Europe & E North Am • 500 kW / S M • Europe & E North Am • 500 kW / S Tu-Su • Europe & E North Am • 500 kW / S • Europe & E North Am • 500 kW / W M • Europe & E North Am • 500 kW / W Tu-Su • Europe & E North Am • 500 kW

(con'd)

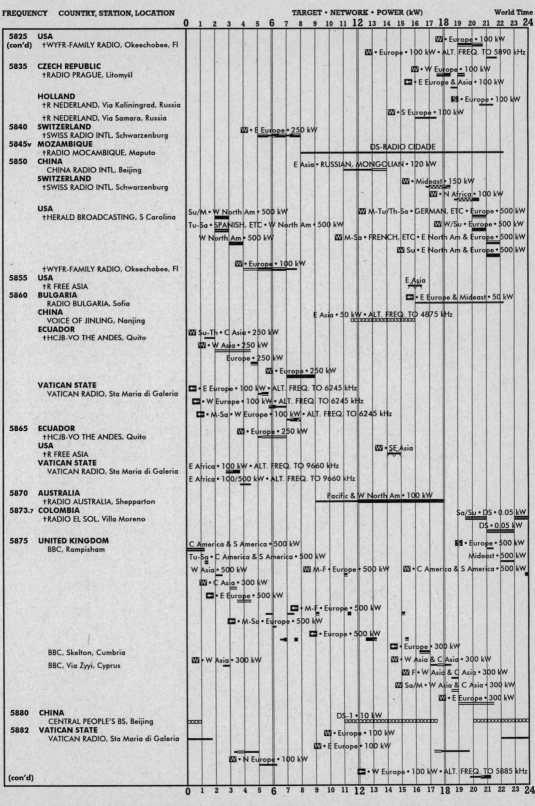

FREQUENCY	COUNTRY, STATION, LOCATION		Broadcast Schedule
5825 (con'd)	USA	†WYFR-FAMILY RADIO, Okeechobee, Fl	W • Europe • 100 kW; W • Europe • 100 kW • ALT. FREQ. TO 5890 kHz
5835	CZECH REPUBLIC	†RADIO PRAGUE, Litomyšl	W • W Europe • 100 kW; W • E Europe & Asia • 100 kW
	HOLLAND	†R NEDERLAND, Via Kaliningrad, Russia	S • Europe • 100 kW
		†R NEDERLAND, Via Samara, Russia	W • S Europe • 100 kW
5840	SWITZERLAND	†SWISS RADIO INTL, Schwarzenburg	W • E Europe • 250 kW
5845v	MOZAMBIQUE	†RADIO MOCAMBIQUE, Maputo	DS-RADIO CIDADE
5850	CHINA	CHINA RADIO INTL, Beijing	E Asia • RUSSIAN, MONGOLIAN • 120 kW
	SWITZERLAND	†SWISS RADIO INTL, Schwarzenburg	W • Mideast • 150 kW; W • N Africa • 100 kW
	USA	†HERALD BROADCASTING, S Carolina	Su/M • W North Am • 500 kW; W M-Tu/Th-Sa • GERMAN, ETC • Europe • 500 kW; Tu-Sa • SPANISH, ETC • W North Am • 500 kW; W W/Su • Europe • 500 kW; W North Am • 500 kW; W M-Sa • FRENCH, ETC • E North Am & Europe • 500 kW; W Su • E North Am & Europe • 500 kW
		†WYFR-FAMILY RADIO, Okeechobee, Fl	W • Europe • 100 kW
5855	USA	†R FREE ASIA	E Asia
5860	BULGARIA	RADIO BULGARIA, Sofia	E Europe & Mideast • 50 kW
	CHINA	VOICE OF JINLING, Nanjing	E Asia • 50 kW • ALT. FREQ. TO 4875 kHz
	ECUADOR	†HCJB-VO THE ANDES, Quito	W Su-Th • C Asia • 250 kW; W • W Asia • 250 kW; Europe • 250 kW; W • Europe • 250 kW
	VATICAN STATE	VATICAN RADIO, Sta Maria di Galeria	E Europe • 100 kW • ALT. FREQ. TO 6245 kHz; W Europe • 100 kW • ALT. FREQ. TO 6245 kHz; M-Sa • W Europe • 100 kW • ALT. FREQ. TO 6245 kHz
5865	ECUADOR	†HCJB-VO THE ANDES, Quito	W • Europe • 250 kW
	USA	†R FREE ASIA	W • SE Asia
	VATICAN STATE	VATICAN RADIO, Sta Maria di Galeria	E Africa • 100 kW • ALT. FREQ. TO 9660 kHz; E Africa • 100/500 kW • ALT. FREQ. TO 9660 kHz
5870	AUSTRALIA	†RADIO AUSTRALIA, Shepparton	Pacific & W North Am • 100 kW
5873.7	COLOMBIA	†RADIO EL SOL, Villa Moreno	Sa/Su • DS • 0.05 kW; DS • 0.05 kW
5875	UNITED KINGDOM	BBC, Rampisham	C America & S America • 500 kW; S • Europe • 500 kW; Tu-Sa • C America & S America • 500 kW; Mideast • 500 kW; W Asia • 500 kW; W M-F • Europe • 500 kW; W • C America & S America • 500 kW; W • C Asia • 300 kW; E Europe • 500 kW; M-F • Europe • 500 kW; M-Sa • Europe • 500 kW; Europe • 500 kW
		BBC, Skelton, Cumbria	Europe • 300 kW; W • W Asia • 300 kW
		BBC, Via Zyyi, Cyprus	F • W Asia & C Asia • 300 kW; W Sa/M • W Asia & C Asia • 300 kW; W • E Europe • 300 kW
5880	CHINA	CENTRAL PEOPLE'S BS, Beijing	DS-1 • 10 kW
5882	VATICAN STATE	VATICAN RADIO, Sta Maria di Galeria	W • Europe • 100 kW; W • E Europe • 100 kW; W • N Europe • 100 kW; W Europe • 100 kW • ALT. FREQ. TO 5885 kHz
(con'd)			

ENGLISH ▬   ARABIC ▨   CHINESE ▫▫▫   FRENCH ▬   GERMAN ▬   RUSSIAN ═   SPANISH ▬   OTHER ▬

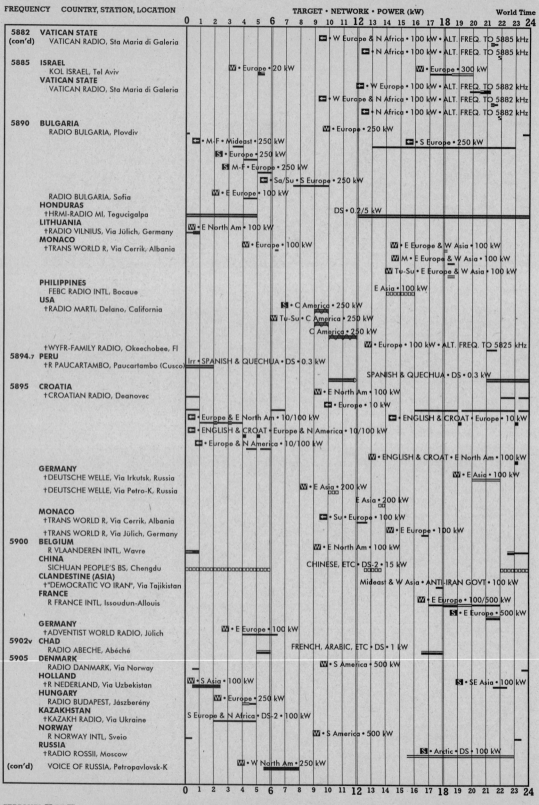

FREQUENCY	COUNTRY, STATION, LOCATION	TARGET • NETWORK • POWER (kW)	World Time

0 1 2 3 4 5 6 7 8 9 10 11 12 13 14 15 16 17 18 19 20 21 22 23 24

Frequency	Country / Station / Location	Schedule
5905 (con'd)	**SLOVAKIA** †ADVENTIST WORLD R, Rimavská Sobota	W • E Africa • 250 kW / W Europe • 250 kW
	UKRAINE RADIO UKRAINE, Kiev	S Europe & N Africa • 100/200 kW / W • S Europe & N Africa • 100 kW
	RADIO UKRAINE, Multiple Locations	W • W Europe, W Africa & S America • 100/1000 kW
	UNITED KINGDOM BBC, Via Irkutsk, Russia	W • E Asia • 200 kW
	BBC, Via Yekaterinburg, Russia	W • E Europe • 200 kW / W Sa/Su • E Europe • 200 kW
	VIETNAM †VOICE OF VIETNAM, Via Armavir, Russia	W • C America • 500 kW
5910	**BELGIUM** R VLAANDEREN INTL, Wavre	W • Europe • 200 kW / W • Europe • 200 kW
	HUNGARY RADIO BUDAPEST, Jászberény	S • Europe • 250 kW
	IRELAND †WEST COAST R IRELAND, Via Germany	W Th • E North Am • 100 kW
	RUSSIA †RADIO ROSSII, Moscow	Arctic • DS • 100 kW / W • Arctic • DS • 100 kW
	USA †VOA, Via Novosibirsk, Russia	W • E Asia • 200 kW
5915	**BELGIUM** R VLAANDEREN INTL, Wavre	W Su • Europe • 200 kW / W Sa/Su • Europe • 200 kW
	CHINA CENTRAL PEOPLE'S BS, Beijing	DS-1 • 50 kW
	FRANCE R FRANCE INTL, Issoudun-Allouis	E Europe • 100 kW / W • E Europe • 100 kW / S • E Europe • 100 kW
	HUNGARY RADIO BUDAPEST, Jászberény	S • Europe • 250 kW
	ISRAEL KOL ISRAEL, Tel Aviv	Mideast • DS-D • 50 kW
	POLAND †POLISH RADIO WARSAW, Warsaw	E Europe • 100 kW
	RUSSIA VOICE OF RUSSIA, Armavir	W • C America • 500 kW
	SLOVAKIA †R SLOVAKIA INTL, Rimavská Sobota	S • W Europe • 250 kW / W Europe • 250 kW / E Europe & W Asia • 250 kW
	UKRAINE RADIO UKRAINE, Kiev	S • S Europe & N Africa • 200 kW
	RADIO UKRAINE, Nikolayev	W • W Europe & E North Am • 1000 kW
5919.5	**CHINA** GUANGXI PEOPLE'S BS, Nanning	CHINESE, ETC • DS-3 • 10 kW
5920	**CROATIA** †CROATIAN RADIO, Deanovec	M-F • ENGLISH & CROAT • Europe • 10 kW / Sa/Su • Europe • 10 kW / Europe • 10 kW / M-F • Europe • 10 kW / Sa/Su • ENGLISH & CROAT • Europe • 10 kW / ENGLISH & CROAT • Europe • 10 kW
	FRANCE †R FRANCE INTL, Issoudun-Allouis	W • C America • 500 kW
	†R FRANCE INTL, Multiple Locations	C America & N America • 500 kW
	†R FRANCE INTL, Via French Guiana	C America & N America • 500 kW / C America • 500 kW
	HUNGARY RADIO BUDAPEST, Jászberény	W • Europe • 250 kW
	PAKISTAN RADIO PAKISTAN, Islamabad	S Asia • 100 kW
	RUSSIA †MAYAK, Arkhangel'sk	S • DS • 20 kW
	VOICE OF RUSSIA, Kaliningrad	W • Europe • 240 kW
	VOICE OF RUSSIA, Komsomol'sk 'Amure	W • W North Am • 240 kW
5924v	**VIETNAM** VOICE OF VIETNAM, Hanoi	DS / DS-1

0 1 2 3 4 5 6 7 8 9 10 11 12 13 14 15 16 17 18 19 20 21 22 23 24

ENGLISH ▬   ARABIC ⁘⁘⁘   CHINESE ▭▭▭   FRENCH ═══   GERMAN ▬▬   RUSSIAN ══   SPANISH ▬▬   OTHER ▬

FREQUENCY	COUNTRY, STATION, LOCATION	TARGET • NETWORK • POWER (kW)	World Time

World Time scale: 0 1 2 3 4 5 6 7 8 9 10 11 12 13 14 15 16 17 18 19 20 21 22 23 24

5925	**ESTONIA**	
	RADIO ESTONIA, Tallinn	⬅ • Su • N Europe • 100 kW / ⬅ • M-F • N Europe • 100 kW
		⬅ • M-F • GERMAN, ETC • N Europe • 100 kW
		⬅ • M/Th • N Europe • 100 kW
		⬅ • Tu/F • N Europe • 100 kW
	FRANCE	
	R FRANCE INTL, Issoudun-Allouis	N Africa • 500 kW / W • Mideast & W Asia • 500 kW
		W • N Africa • 500 kW
	GERMANY	
	DEUTSCHE WELLE, Via Irkutsk, Russia	W • E Asia • 250 kW
	DEUTSCHE WELLE, Via N'sibirsk, Russia	W • E Asia • 1000 kW
	DEUTSCHE WELLE, Via Samara, Russia	W Asia & C Asia • 200 kW
	HUNGARY	
	RADIO BUDAPEST, Jászberény	W M-Sa • Europe • 250 kW
	RADIO BUDAPEST, Szekésfehérvár	W Su • W Europe • 100 kW
	RUSSIA	
	†MAYAK, St Petersburg	S • N Europe • DS • 100 kW
	VOICE OF RUSSIA, Armavir	S • Mideast • 100 kW
	VOICE OF RUSSIA, Samara	W • N Africa • 250 kW
5927v	**BOLIVIA**	
	RADIO MINERIA, Oruro	Irr • DS
		SPANISH & QUECHUA • DS
		M-Sa • SPANISH & QUECHUA • DS
5930	**CZECH REPUBLIC**	
	†RADIO PRAGUE, Litomyšl	E North Am • 100 kW / S • W Europe • 100 kW
		C America • 100 kW / W Europe • 100 kW
		N America • 100 kW / W • W Africa • 100 kW
		⬅ • W Europe • 100 kW
		⬅ • Europe • 100 kW
		W • E North Am • 100 kW
		W • S America • 100 kW
		W • C America • 100 kW
	DENMARK	
	RADIO DANMARK, Via Norway	W • Australasia • 500 kW
	HOLLAND	
	†R NEDERLAND, Via Petro-K, Russia	W • E Asia • 240 kW
		S • E Asia • 240 kW
	HUNGARY	
	RADIO BUDAPEST, Jászberény	⬅ • Europe • 250 kW
	NORWAY	
	R NORWAY INTL, Kvitsøy	W M-Sa • Australasia • 500 kW
		W Su • Australasia • 500 kW
	RUSSIA	
	MURMANSK RADIO, Monchegorsk	⬅ • DS-LOCAL, R ROSSII • 50 kW
	VOICE OF RUSSIA, Petropavlovsk-K	W • W North Am • 100 kW
	SLOVAKIA	
	R SLOVAKIA INTL, Rimavská Sobota	E North Am & C America • 250 kW
	USA	
	†R FREE ASIA	S • SE Asia
5933v	**MOZAMBIQUE**	
	†RADIO MOCAMBIQUE, Maputo	DS-INTERPROVINCIAL • 10 kW
5935	**BULGARIA**	
	RADIO BULGARIA, Sofia	W • E Europe • 100 kW
	CHINA	
	XIZANG PEOPLE'S BC STN, Lhasa	DS • 50 kW
	GERMANY	
	†DEUTSCHE WELLE, Via Samara, Russia	⬅ • W Asia • 250 kW
	HUNGARY	
	RADIO BUDAPEST, Szekésfehérvár	⬅ • N Europe • 100 kW
	LATVIA	
	RADIO LATVIA, Riga	⬅ • Sa • N Europe • 100 kW
		⬅ • Sa • 100 kW
		⬅ • M-Sa • 100 kW
		⬅ • M-F • 100 kW
	RUSSIA	
	†MAYAK, St Petersburg	S • E Europe & Mideast • DS • 200 kW
		W • E Europe & Mideast • DS • 240 kW
	VOICE OF RUSSIA, Samara	W • Mideast & N Africa • 200 kW
		⬅ • Mideast • 200/250 kW
	SWEDEN	
	†IBRA RADIO, Via Samara Russia	Mideast • 250 kW
	USA	
(con'd)	WWCR, Nashville, Tennessee	E North Am & Europe • 100 kW

World Time scale: 0 1 2 3 4 5 6 7 8 9 10 11 12 13 14 15 16 17 18 19 20 21 22 23 24

SEASONAL S OR W   1-HR TIMESHIFT MIDYEAR ⬅ OR ⬅   JAMMING / OR ∧   EARLIEST HEARD ◁   LATEST HEARD ▷   NEW FOR 1998 †

FREQUENCY   COUNTRY, STATION, LOCATION   TARGET • NETWORK • POWER (kW)   World Time

0 1 2 3 4 5 6 7 8 9 10 11 12 13 14 15 16 17 18 19 20 21 22 23 24

Frequency	Country, Station, Location	Schedule
5935 (con'd)	**USA** WWCR, Nashville, Tennessee	W • E North Am & Europe • 100 kW
5940	**BULGARIA** RADIO BULGARIA, Plovdiv	W M-F • S Europe • 250 kW
	RADIO BULGARIA, Sofia	W Sa/Su • E Europe & Mideast • 50 kW
	RUSSIA †MAGADAN RADIO, Magadan	C • RUSSIAN, ETC • DS-LOCAL, R ROSSII • 100 kW
		C M-F • DS-RADIO ROSSII • 100 kW
	†R TIKHIY OKEAN, Magadan	C • Sa/Su • NP • 100 kW
	VOICE OF RUSSIA, Armavir	W • E North Am • 700/1000 kW
		W • N Europe • 700/1000 kW
	VOICE OF RUSSIA, Petropavlovsk-K	W • E Asia • 100 kW
	SLOVAKIA †ADVENTIST WORLD R, Rimavská Sobota	C • Europe • 250 kW
		C • Su • Europe • 250 kW
	†R SLOVAKIA INTL, Rimavská Sobota	W • W Europe • 250 kW
	UKRAINE RADIO UKRAINE, Kiev	W • S Europe & N Africa • 100 kW
	VIETNAM †VOICE OF VIETNAM, Via Armavir, Russia	W • E North Am • 700/1000 kW
5945	**AUSTRIA** †R AUSTRIA INTL, Vienna	Europe • 100 kW
		W • Europe • 100 kW
		S • Europe • 100 kW
	BULGARIA RADIO BULGARIA, Plovdiv	W • Mideast • 500 kW
		S M-F • E Europe & Mideast • 50 kW
	RADIO BULGARIA, Sofia	W • E Europe & Mideast • 50 kW
	FRANCE †R FRANCE INTL, Issoudun-Allouis	W • E Africa & Mideast • 500 kW
		W • E Africa & Mideast • 100/500 kW
		S • N Africa • 500 kW
		W • N Africa & E Africa • 100/500 kW
	†R FRANCE INTL, Via Novosibirsk, Russia	W • E Asia • 240 kW
	GERMANY †DEUTSCHE WELLE, Via Samara, Russia	W • W Asia & C Asia • 200 kW
	HUNGARY RADIO BUDAPEST, Jászberény	W Su • W Europe • 250 kW
	RADIO BUDAPEST, Székésfehérvár	W • E Europe • 100 kW
	RUSSIA †MAYAK, Volgograd	W • N Asia • DS • 100 kW
5950	**CHINA** HEILONGJIANG EBS, Harbin	DS • 50 kW
	HEILONGJIANG KOREAN BS, Harbin	Su • DS • 50 kW / Su-F • DS • 50 kW
		DS • 50 kW
	XIZANG PEOPLE'S BC STN, Lhasa	DS-TIBETAN • 50 kW
	CHINA (TAIWAN) †BC CORP CHINA, Via Okeechobee, USA	E North Am • 100 kW
	†VO FREE CHINA, Via Okeechobee, USA	E North Am • 100 kW
		E North Am & C America • 100 kW
		C America • 100 kW
	GUAM KSDA-ADVENTIST WORLD RADIO, Agat	E Asia • 100 kW
	GUYANA †VOICE OF GUYANA, Georgetown	DS • 5 kW • ALT. FREQ. TO 3290 kHz
	HUNGARY RADIO BUDAPEST, Jászberény	W • Europe • 250 kW
	RUSSIA †MAYAK, Arkhangel'sk	W • DS • 20 kW
		DS • 20 kW
	VOICE OF RUSSIA, Samara	W • Europe • 240 kW
	USA WYFR-FAMILY RADIO, Okeechobee, Fl	E North Am • 100 kW
	YEMEN †REP OF YEMEN RADIO, San'ā	DS • 300 kW
		Irr • DS-RAMADAN • 300 kW
5952.3	**BOLIVIA** †RADIO PIO DOCE, Llallagua-Siglo XX	Tu-Su • SPANISH, ETC • DS • 1 kW SPANISH, ETC • DS • 1 kW M-Sa • SPANISH, ETC • DS • 1 kW
		Su • SPANISH, ETC • DS • 1 kW
5954v	**COSTA RICA** †RADIO CASINO, Limón	DS • 0.7 kW
5955	**BRAZIL** RADIO GAZETA, São Paulo	DS • 10 kW
	CAMEROON	
(con'd)	CAMEROON RTV, Bafoussam	FRENCH, ENGLISH, ETC • DS • 20 kW

0 1 2 3 4 5 6 7 8 9 10 11 12 13 14 15 16 17 18 19 20 21 22 23 24

ENGLISH ▬   ARABIC ⣿   CHINESE ⣿   FRENCH ▬   GERMAN ▬   RUSSIAN ▬   SPANISH ▬   OTHER ▬

FREQUENCY	COUNTRY, STATION, LOCATION	TARGET • NETWORK • POWER (kW)	World Time

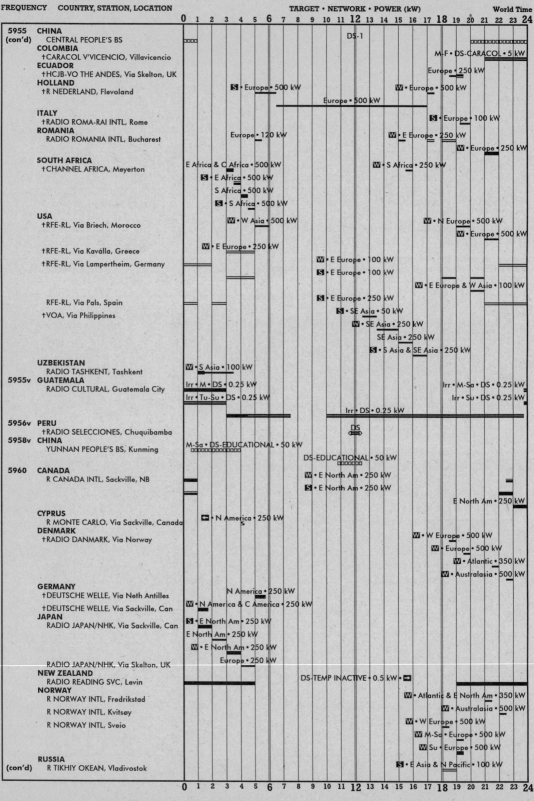

5955 (con'd)
- **CHINA** — CENTRAL PEOPLE'S BS — DS-1
- **COLOMBIA** — †CARACOL V'VICENCIO, Villavicencio — M-F • DS-CARACOL • 5 kW
- **ECUADOR** — †HCJB-VO THE ANDES, Via Skelton, UK — Europe • 250 kW
- **HOLLAND** — †R NEDERLAND, Flevoland — S • Europe • 500 kW — W • Europe • 500 kW — Europe • 500 kW
- **ITALY** — †RADIO ROMA-RAI INTL, Rome — S • Europe • 100 kW
- **ROMANIA** — RADIO ROMANIA INTL, Bucharest — Europe • 120 kW — W • E Europe • 250 kW — W • Europe • 250 kW
- **SOUTH AFRICA** — †CHANNEL AFRICA, Meyerton — E Africa & C Africa • 500 kW — W • S Africa • 250 kW — S • E Africa • 500 kW — S Africa • 500 kW — S • S Africa • 500 kW
- **USA** — †RFE-RL, Via Briech, Morocco — W • W Asia • 500 kW — W • N Europe • 500 kW — W • Europe • 500 kW
  - †RFE-RL, Via Kaválla, Greece — W • E Europe • 250 kW
  - †RFE-RL, Via Lampertheim, Germany — W • E Europe • 100 kW — S • E Europe • 100 kW — W • E Europe & W Asia • 100 kW
  - RFE-RL, Via Pals, Spain — S • E Europe • 250 kW
  - †VOA, Via Philippines — S • SE Asia • 50 kW — W • SE Asia • 250 kW — SE Asia • 250 kW — S • S Asia & SE Asia • 250 kW
- **UZBEKISTAN** — RADIO TASHKENT, Tashkent — W • S Asia • 100 kW

5955v
- **GUATEMALA** — RADIO CULTURAL, Guatemala City — Irr • M • DS • 0.25 kW — Irr • M-Sa • DS • 0.25 kW — Irr • Tu-Su • DS • 0.25 kW — Irr • Su • DS • 0.25 kW — Irr • DS • 0.25 kW

5956v
- **PERU** — †RADIO SELECCIONES, Chuquibamba — DS

5958v
- **CHINA** — YUNNAN PEOPLE'S BS, Kunming — M-Sa • DS-EDUCATIONAL • 50 kW — DS-EDUCATIONAL • 50 kW

5960
- **CANADA** — R CANADA INTL, Sackville, NB — W • E North Am • 250 kW — S • E North Am • 250 kW — E North Am • 250 kW
- **CYPRUS** — R MONTE CARLO, Via Sackville, Canada — N America • 250 kW
- **DENMARK** — †RADIO DANMARK, Via Norway — W • W Europe • 500 kW — W • Europe • 500 kW — W • Atlantic • 350 kW — W • Australasia • 500 kW
- **GERMANY** — †DEUTSCHE WELLE, Via Neth Antilles — N America • 250 kW — †DEUTSCHE WELLE, Via Sackville, Can — W • N America & C America • 250 kW
- **JAPAN** — RADIO JAPAN/NHK, Via Sackville, Can — S • E North Am • 250 kW — E North Am • 250 kW — W • E North Am • 250 kW — Europe • 250 kW
  - RADIO JAPAN/NHK, Via Skelton, UK
- **NEW ZEALAND** — RADIO READING SVC, Levin — DS-TEMP INACTIVE • 0.5 kW •
- **NORWAY** — R NORWAY INTL, Fredrikstad — W • Atlantic & E North Am • 350 kW — W • Australasia • 500 kW
  - R NORWAY INTL, Kvitsøy — W • W Europe • 500 kW
  - R NORWAY INTL, Sveio — W M-Sa • Europe • 500 kW — W Su • Europe • 500 kW

(con'd)
- **RUSSIA** — R TIKHIY OKEAN, Vladivostok — S • E Asia & N Pacific • 100 kW

FREQUENCY   COUNTRY, STATION, LOCATION   TARGET • NETWORK • POWER (kW)   World Time

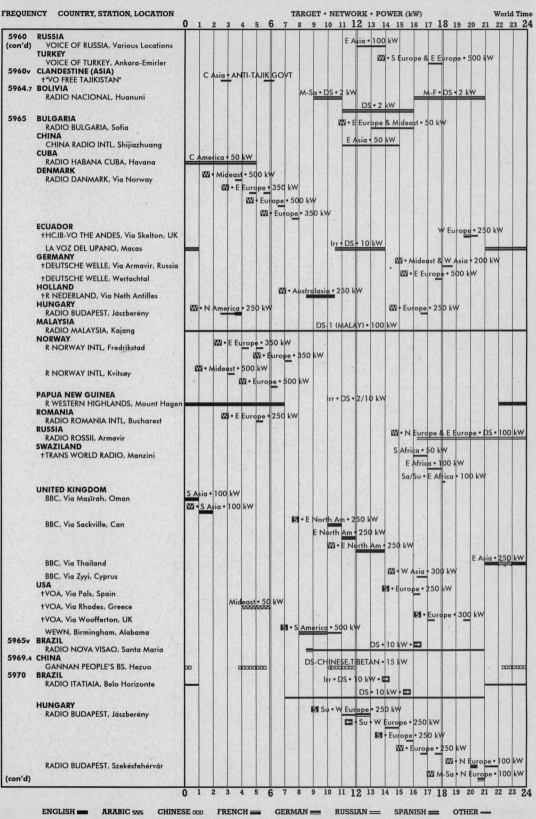

Frequency	Country, Station, Location	Details
5960 (con'd)	**RUSSIA** VOICE OF RUSSIA, Various Locations	E Asia • 100 kW
	TURKEY VOICE OF TURKEY, Ankara-Emirler	W • S Europe & E Europe • 500 kW
5960v	**CLANDESTINE (ASIA)** †"VO FREE TAJIKISTAN"	C Asia • ANTI-TAJIK GOVT
5964.7	**BOLIVIA** RADIO NACIONAL, Huanuni	M-Sa • DS • 2 kW M-F • DS • 2 kW DS • 2 kW
5965	**BULGARIA** RADIO BULGARIA, Sofia	W • E Europe & Mideast • 50 kW
	CHINA CHINA RADIO INTL, Shijiazhuang	E Asia • 50 kW
	CUBA RADIO HABANA CUBA, Havana	C America • 50 kW
	DENMARK RADIO DANMARK, Via Norway	W • Mideast • 500 kW W • E Europe • 350 kW W • Europe • 500 kW W • Europe • 350 kW
	ECUADOR †HCJB-VO THE ANDES, Via Skelton, UK	W Europe • 250 kW
	LA VOZ DEL UPANO, Macas	Irr • DS • 10 kW
	GERMANY †DEUTSCHE WELLE, Via Armavir, Russia	W • Mideast & W Asia • 200 kW
	†DEUTSCHE WELLE, Wertachtal	W • E Europe • 500 kW
	HOLLAND †R NEDERLAND, Via Neth Antilles	W • Australasia • 250 kW
	HUNGARY RADIO BUDAPEST, Jászberény	W • N America • 250 kW W • Europe • 250 kW
	MALAYSIA RADIO MALAYSIA, Kajang	DS-1 (MALAY) • 100 kW
	NORWAY R NORWAY INTL, Fredrikstad	W • E Europe • 350 kW W • Europe • 350 kW
	R NORWAY INTL, Kvitsøy	W • Mideast • 500 kW W • Europe • 500 kW
	PAPUA NEW GUINEA R WESTERN HIGHLANDS, Mount Hagen	Irr • DS • 2/10 kW
	ROMANIA RADIO ROMANIA INTL, Bucharest	W • E Europe • 250 kW
	RUSSIA RADIO ROSSII, Armavir	W • N Europe & E Europe • DS • 100 kW
	SWAZILAND †TRANS WORLD RADIO, Manzini	S Africa • 50 kW E Africa • 100 kW Sa/Su • E Africa • 100 kW
	UNITED KINGDOM BBC, Via Maşirah, Oman	S Asia • 100 kW W • S Asia • 100 kW
	BBC, Via Sackville, Can	S • E North Am • 250 kW E North Am • 250 kW W • E North Am • 250 kW
	BBC, Via Thailand	E Asia • 250 kW
	BBC, Via Zyyi, Cyprus	W • W Asia • 300 kW
	USA †VOA, Via Pals, Spain	S • Europe • 250 kW
	†VOA, Via Rhodes, Greece	Mideast • 50 kW
	†VOA, Via Woofferton, UK	S • Europe • 300 kW
	WEWN, Birmingham, Alabama	S • S America • 500 kW
5965v	**BRAZIL** RADIO NOVA VISAO, Santa Maria	DS • 10 kW • ▭
5969.4	**CHINA** GANNAN PEOPLE'S BS, Hezuo	DS-CHINESE,TIBETAN • 15 kW
5970	**BRAZIL** RADIO ITATIAIA, Belo Horizonte	Irr • DS • 10 kW • ▭ DS • 10 kW • ▭
	HUNGARY RADIO BUDAPEST, Jászberény	S • Su • W Europe • 250 kW ▭ • Su • W Europe • 250 kW S • Europe • 250 kW W • Europe • 250 kW
	RADIO BUDAPEST, Székésfehérvár	W • N Europe • 100 kW W M-Sa • N Europe • 100 kW
(con'd)		

ENGLISH ▬   ARABIC ✗✗✗   CHINESE ▫▫▫   FRENCH ▬▬   GERMAN ▬▬   RUSSIAN ══   SPANISH ▬▬   OTHER ▬

FREQUENCY   COUNTRY, STATION, LOCATION

TARGET • NETWORK • POWER (kW)   World Time

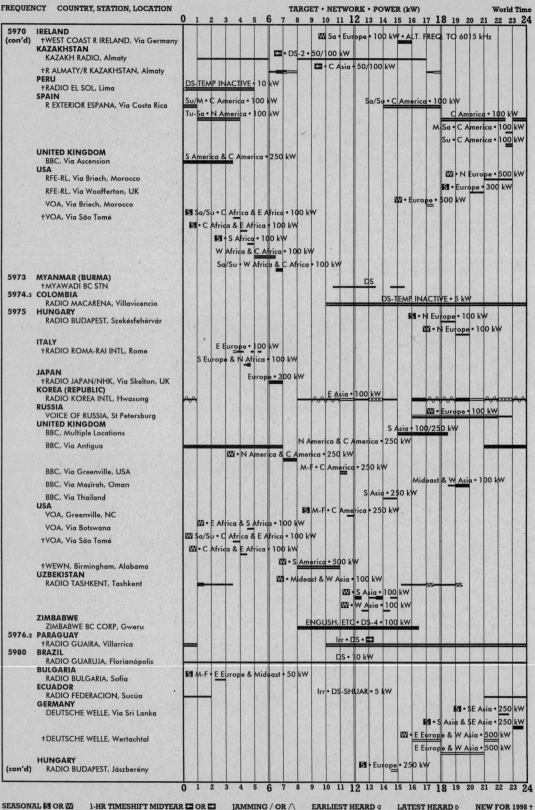

5970 IRELAND
(con'd) †WEST COAST R IRELAND, Via Germany
      KAZAKHSTAN
          KAZAKH RADIO, Almaty
      †R ALMATY/R KAZAKHSTAN, Almaty
      PERU
          †RADIO EL SOL, Lima
      SPAIN
          R EXTERIOR ESPANA, Via Costa Rica

      UNITED KINGDOM
          BBC, Via Ascension
      USA
          RFE-RL, Via Briech, Morocco
          RFE-RL, Via Woofferton, UK
          VOA, Via Briech, Morocco
      †VOA, Via São Tomé

5973 MYANMAR (BURMA)
          †MYAWADI BC STN
5974.3 COLOMBIA
          RADIO MACARENA, Villavicencio
5975 HUNGARY
          RADIO BUDAPEST, Szekésfehérvár

      ITALY
          †RADIO ROMA-RAI INTL, Rome

      JAPAN
          †RADIO JAPAN/NHK, Via Skelton, UK
      KOREA (REPUBLIC)
          RADIO KOREA INTL, Hwasung
      RUSSIA
          VOICE OF RUSSIA, St Petersburg
      UNITED KINGDOM
          BBC, Multiple Locations
          BBC, Via Antigua

          BBC, Via Greenville, USA
          BBC, Via Maşirah, Oman
          BBC, Via Thailand
      USA
          VOA, Greenville, NC
          VOA, Via Botswana
      †VOA, Via São Tomé

      †WEWN, Birmingham, Alabama
      UZBEKISTAN
          RADIO TASHKENT, Tashkent

      ZIMBABWE
          ZIMBABWE BC CORP, Gweru
5976.2 PARAGUAY
          †RADIO GUAIRA, Villarrica
5980 BRAZIL
          RADIO GUARUJA, Florianópolis
      BULGARIA
          RADIO BULGARIA, Sofia
      ECUADOR
          RADIO FEDERACION, Sucúa
      GERMANY
          DEUTSCHE WELLE, Via Sri Lanka

      †DEUTSCHE WELLE, Wertachtal

      HUNGARY
(con'd) RADIO BUDAPEST, Jászberény

FREQUENCY   COUNTRY, STATION, LOCATION   TARGET • NETWORK • POWER (kW)   World Time

0 1 2 3 4 5 6 7 8 9 10 11 12 13 14 15 16 17 18 19 20 21 22 23 24

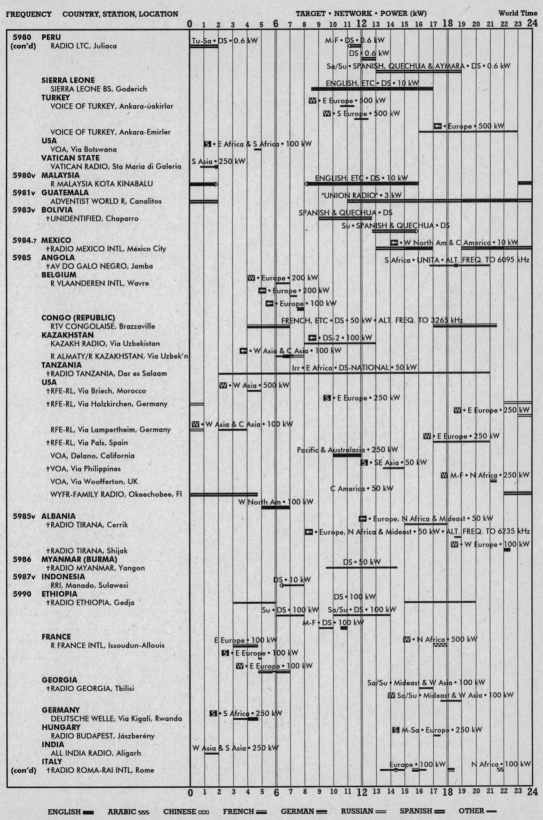

Frequency	Country, Station, Location	Schedule details
5980 (con'd)	**PERU** — RADIO LTC, Juliaca	Tu-Sa • DS • 0.6 kW; M-F • DS • 0.6 kW; DS • 0.6 kW; Sa/Su • SPANISH, QUECHUA & AYMARA • DS • 0.6 kW
	SIERRA LEONE — SIERRA LEONE BS, Goderich	ENGLISH, ETC • DS • 10 kW
	TURKEY — VOICE OF TURKEY, Ankara-úakirlar	W • E Europe • 500 kW; W • S Europe • 500 kW
	VOICE OF TURKEY, Ankara-Emirler	Europe • 500 kW
	USA — VOA, Via Botswana	S • E Africa & S Africa • 100 kW
	VATICAN STATE — VATICAN RADIO, Sta Maria di Galeria	S Asia • 250 kW
5980v	**MALAYSIA** — R MALAYSIA KOTA KINABALU	ENGLISH, ETC • DS • 10 kW
5981v	**GUATEMALA** — ADVENTIST WORLD R, Canalitos	"UNION RADIO" • 3 kW
5983v	**BOLIVIA** — †UNIDENTIFIED, Chaparro	SPANISH & QUECHUA • DS; Su • SPANISH & QUECHUA • DS
5984.7	**MEXICO** — †RADIO MEXICO INTL, México City	W North Am & C America • 10 kW
5985	**ANGOLA** — †AV DO GALO NEGRO, Jamba	S Africa • UNITA • ALT. FREQ. TO 6095 kHz
	BELGIUM — R VLAANDEREN INTL, Wavre	W • Europe • 200 kW; Europe • 200 kW; Europe • 100 kW
	CONGO (REPUBLIC) — RTV CONGOLAISE, Brazzaville	FRENCH, ETC • DS • 50 kW • ALT. FREQ. TO 3265 kHz
	KAZAKHSTAN — KAZAKH RADIO, Via Uzbekistan	DS-2 • 100 kW
	R ALMATY/R KAZAKHSTAN, Via Uzbek'n	W Asia & C Asia • 100 kW
	TANZANIA — †RADIO TANZANIA, Dar es Salaam	Irr • E Africa • DS-NATIONAL • 50 kW
	USA — †RFE-RL, Via Briech, Morocco	W • W Asia • 500 kW
	†RFE-RL, Via Holzkirchen, Germany	S • E Europe • 250 kW; W • E Europe • 250 kW
	RFE-RL, Via Lampertheim, Germany	W • W Asia & C Asia • 100 kW; W • E Europe • 250 kW
	†RFE-RL, Via Pals, Spain	Pacific & Australasia • 250 kW
	VOA, Delano, California	S • SE Asia • 50 kW
	†VOA, Via Philippines	W M-F • N Africa • 250 kW
	VOA, Via Woofferton, UK	C America • 50 kW
	WYFR-FAMILY RADIO, Okeechobee, Fl	W North Am • 100 kW
5985v	**ALBANIA** — †RADIO TIRANA, Cerrik	Europe, N Africa & Mideast • 50 kW; Europe, N Africa & Mideast • 50 kW • ALT. FREQ. TO 6235 kHz
	†RADIO TIRANA, Shijak	W • W Europe • 100 kW
5986	**MYANMAR (BURMA)** — †RADIO MYANMAR, Yangon	DS • 50 kW
5987v	**INDONESIA** — RRI, Manado, Sulawesi	DS • 10 kW
5990	**ETHIOPIA** — †RADIO ETHIOPIA, Gedja	DS • 100 kW; Su • DS • 100 kW; Sa/Su • DS • 100 kW; M-F • DS • 100 kW
	FRANCE — R FRANCE INTL, Issoudun-Allouis	E Europe • 100 kW; W • N Africa • 500 kW; S • E Europe • 100 kW; W • E Europe • 100 kW
	GEORGIA — †RADIO GEORGIA, Tbilisi	Sa/Su • Mideast & W Asia • 100 kW; W Sa/Su • Mideast & W Asia • 100 kW
	GERMANY — DEUTSCHE WELLE, Via Kigali, Rwanda	S • S Africa • 250 kW
	HUNGARY — RADIO BUDAPEST, Jászberény	S M-Sa • Europe • 250 kW
	INDIA — ALL INDIA RADIO, Aligarh	W Asia & S Asia • 250 kW
(con'd)	**ITALY** — †RADIO ROMA-RAI INTL, Rome	Europe • 100 kW; N Africa • 100 kW

0 1 2 3 4 5 6 7 8 9 10 11 12 13 14 15 16 17 18 19 20 21 22 23 24

ENGLISH ■   ARABIC ▨   CHINESE □□□   FRENCH ▬   GERMAN ▬   RUSSIAN ═   SPANISH ▬   OTHER ▬

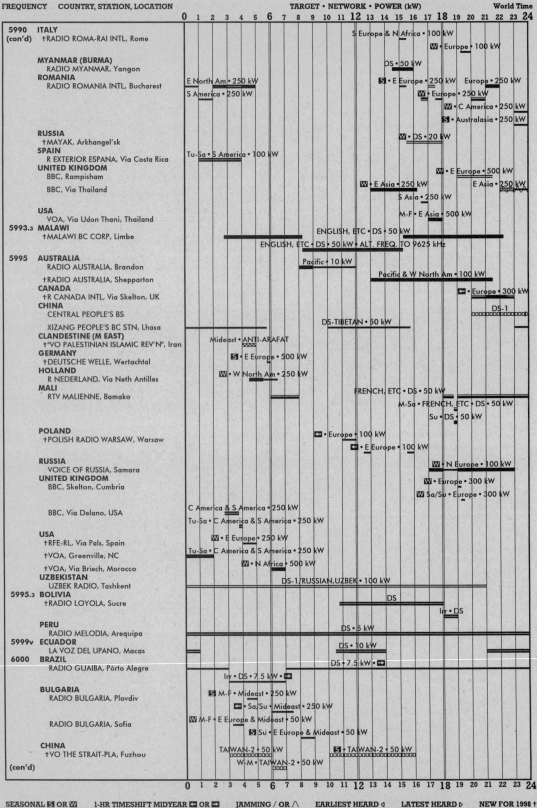

FREQUENCY   COUNTRY, STATION, LOCATION   TARGET • NETWORK • POWER (kW)   World Time

5990 ITALY
(con'd) †RADIO ROMA-RAI INTL, Rome — S Europe & N Africa • 100 kW / W • Europe • 100 kW

MYANMAR (BURMA)
RADIO MYANMAR, Yangon — DS • 50 kW

ROMANIA
RADIO ROMANIA INTL, Bucharest — E North Am • 250 kW / S America • 250 kW / S • E Europe • 250 kW / Europe • 250 kW / W • Europe • 250 kW / W • C America • 250 kW / S • Australasia • 250 kW

RUSSIA
†MAYAK, Arkhangel'sk — W • DS • 20 kW

SPAIN
R EXTERIOR ESPANA, Via Costa Rica — Tu-Sa • S America • 100 kW

UNITED KINGDOM
BBC, Rampisham — W • E Europe • 500 kW

BBC, Via Thailand — W • E Asia • 250 kW / E Asia • 250 kW / S Asia • 250 kW

USA
VOA, Via Udon Thani, Thailand — M-F • E Asia • 500 kW

5993.3 MALAWI
†MALAWI BC CORP, Limbe — ENGLISH, ETC • DS • 50 kW / ENGLISH, ETC • DS • 50 kW • ALT. FREQ. TO 9625 kHz

5995 AUSTRALIA
RADIO AUSTRALIA, Brandon — Pacific • 10 kW

†RADIO AUSTRALIA, Shepparton — Pacific & W North Am • 100 kW

CANADA
†R CANADA INTL, Via Skelton, UK — • Europe • 300 kW

CHINA
CENTRAL PEOPLE'S BS — DS-1

XIZANG PEOPLE'S BC STN, Lhasa — DS-TIBETAN • 50 kW

CLANDESTINE (M EAST)
†"VO PALESTINIAN ISLAMIC REV'N", Iran — Mideast • ANTI-ARAFAT

GERMANY
†DEUTSCHE WELLE, Wertachtal — S • E Europe • 500 kW

HOLLAND
R NEDERLAND, Via Neth Antilles — W • W North Am • 250 kW

MALI
RTV MALIENNE, Bamako — FRENCH, ETC • DS • 50 kW / M-Sa • FRENCH, ETC • DS • 50 kW / Su • DS • 50 kW

POLAND
†POLISH RADIO WARSAW, Warsaw — • Europe • 100 kW / • E Europe • 100 kW

RUSSIA
VOICE OF RUSSIA, Samara — W • N Europe • 100 kW

UNITED KINGDOM
BBC, Skelton, Cumbria — W • Europe • 300 kW / W Sa/Su • Europe • 300 kW

BBC, Via Delano, USA — C America & S America • 250 kW / Tu-Sa • C America & S America • 250 kW

USA
†RFE-RL, Via Pals, Spain — W • E Europe • 250 kW

†VOA, Greenville, NC — Tu-Sa • C America & S America • 250 kW

†VOA, Via Briech, Morocco — W • N Africa • 500 kW

UZBEKISTAN
UZBEK RADIO, Tashkent — DS-1/RUSSIAN,UZBEK • 100 kW

5995.3 BOLIVIA
†RADIO LOYOLA, Sucre — DS / Irr • DS

PERU
RADIO MELODIA, Arequipa — DS • 5 kW

5999v ECUADOR
LA VOZ DEL UPANO, Macas — DS • 10 kW

6000 BRAZIL
RADIO GUAIBA, Pôrto Alegre — DS • 7.5 kW • / Irr • DS • 7.5 kW •

BULGARIA
RADIO BULGARIA, Plovdiv — S M-F • Mideast • 250 kW / • Sa/Su • Mideast • 250 kW

RADIO BULGARIA, Sofia — W M-F • E Europe & Mideast • 50 kW / S Su • E Europe & Mideast • 50 kW

CHINA
†VO THE STRAIT-PLA, Fuzhou — TAIWAN-2 • 50 kW / S • TAIWAN-2 • 50 kW / W-M • TAIWAN-2 • 50 kW

(con'd)

FREQUENCY   COUNTRY, STATION, LOCATION

TARGET • NETWORK • POWER (kW)

World Time

0 1 2 3 4 5 6 7 8 9 10 11 12 13 14 15 16 17 18 19 20 21 22 23 24

Frequency	Country, Station, Location	Target • Network • Power
6000 (con'd)	**CUBA** †RADIO HABANA CUBA, Havana	E North Am • 250 kW
		W • W North Am • 100 kW
		W M • W North Am • 100 kW
	GERMANY †DEUTSCHE WELLE, Via Samara, Russia	W • E Europe • 200 kW
	DEUTSCHE WELLE, Wertachtal	W • SE Asia • 500 kW
	HUNGARY RADIO BUDAPEST, Szekésfehérvár	W Su • Europe • 20 kW
	INDIA †RADIO KASHMIR, Leh	DS • 50 kW
		ENGLISH & HINDI • DS • 50 kW
	POLAND †POLISH RADIO WARSAW, Warsaw	• N Europe & E Europe • 100 kW
		• M-Sa • W Europe • 100 kW
		• Su • Europe • 100 kW
		• W Europe • 100 kW
		• E Europe • 100 kW
	RUSSIA VOICE OF RUSSIA, Samara	W • S Europe • 240 kW
	SINGAPORE R SINGAPORE INTL, Kranji	SE Asia • 250 kW
	RADIO CORP OF SINGAPORE, Kranji	DS • 250 kW
	SOUTH AFRICA †CHANNEL AFRICA, Meyerton	E Africa & C Africa • 250 kW
	†SOUTH AFRICAN BC, Meyerton	W • S Africa • DS-R SONDERGRENSE • 100 kW
		S Africa • DS-R SONDERGRENSE • 100 kW
		S • S Africa • DS-R SONDERGRENSE • 100 kW
	SWEDEN RADIO SWEDEN, Hörby	W • E Europe • 500 kW
		• E Europe • 500 kW
	USA WEWN, Birmingham, Alabama	C America & S America • 500 kW
6005	**CAMEROON** CAMEROON RTV, Buea	FRENCH, ENGLISH ETC • DS • 4 kW
	CANADA CFCX, Montréal, Québec	Irr • E North Am • DS-RELAY CIQC • 0.5 kW
		Irr • E North Am • DS-RELAY CKOI • 0.5 kW
	CHINA GANSU PEOPLE'S BS, Lanzhou	DS-1 • 15 kW
	GERMANY DEUTSCHLANDRADIO, Berlin	Europe • 100 kW
	IRAN VO THE ISLAMIC REP, Tehrān	W • Europe • 500 kW
		W Asia & S Asia • 500 kW • ALT. FREQ. TO 6175 kHz
	VO THE ISLAMIC REP, Zāhedān	W Asia • DS • 500 kW • ALT. FREQ. TO 6175 kHz
	JAPAN NHK, Nagoya	Irr • DS-1(FEEDER) • 0.3 kW • USB
	NHK, Sapporo	Irr • DS-1(FEEDER) • 0.6 kW
	RUSSIA ADYGEY RADIO, Armavir	W M/F • Mideast & W Asia • 100 kW
	KABARDINO-BALKAR R, Armavir	W Su/W • Mideast & W Asia • 100 kW
	VOICE OF RUSSIA, Armavir	W • Mideast & W Asia • 100 kW
		W Su-F • Mideast & W Asia • 100 kW
	UNITED KINGDOM BBC, Via Ascension	W Africa & S Africa • 250 kW
		W Africa • 250 kW
	BBC, Via Seychelles	S • E Africa • 250 kW
		E Africa • 250 kW
6006	**COSTA RICA** †RADIO RELOJ, San José	Irr • DS • 3 kW • ALT. FREQ. TO 4832v kHz
6010	**BAHRAIN** RADIO BAHRAIN, Abu Hayan	DS-TEMP INACTIVE • 60 kW
	BRAZIL R INCONFIDENCIA, Belo Horizonte	DS
	CHINA †CHINA RADIO INTL, Kunming	W • SE Asia • 50 kW
		SE Asia • 50 kW
	GERMANY †DEUTSCHE WELLE, Wertachtal	W • E Europe • 500 kW
		W • Europe • 500 kW
		W • E Asia • 500 kW
	ITALY †RADIO ROMA-RAI INTL, Rome	E North Am • 100 kW
(con'd)		E Europe • 100 kW • ALT. FREQ. TO 6020 kHz

0 1 2 3 4 5 6 7 8 9 10 11 12 13 14 15 16 17 18 19 20 21 22 23 24

ENGLISH ▪▪   ARABIC ⬚⬚⬚   CHINESE □□□   FRENCH ▬▬   GERMAN ▬▬   RUSSIAN ══   SPANISH ══   OTHER ▬

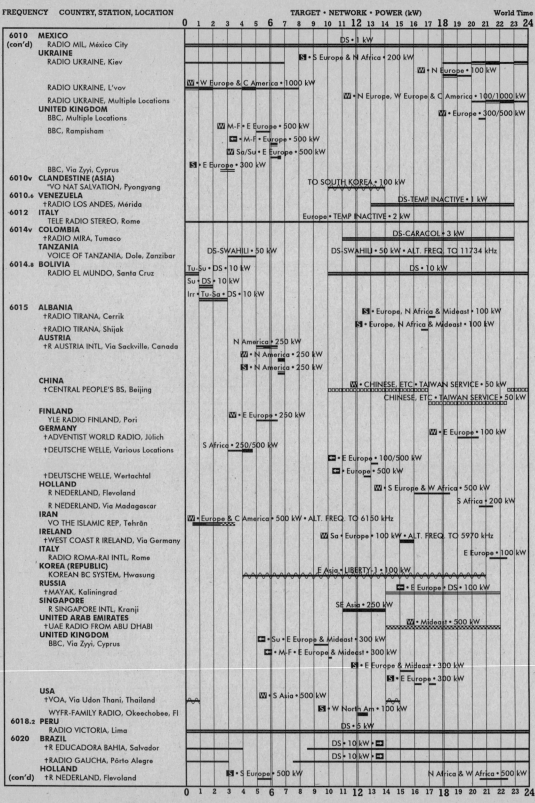

FREQUENCY	COUNTRY, STATION, LOCATION	TARGET • NETWORK • POWER (kW)

0 1 2 3 4 5 6 7 8 9 10 11 12 13 14 15 16 17 18 19 20 21 22 23 24   World Time

- **6010** **MEXICO**
  - (con'd)   RADIO MIL, México City — DS • 1 kW
  - **UKRAINE**
    - RADIO UKRAINE, Kiev — S • S Europe & N Africa • 200 kW
    - — W • N Europe • 100 kW
    - RADIO UKRAINE, L'vov — W • W Europe & C America • 1000 kW
    - RADIO UKRAINE, Multiple Locations — W • N Europe, W Europe & C America • 100/1000 kW
    - — W • Europe • 300/500 kW
  - **UNITED KINGDOM**
    - BBC, Multiple Locations — W • M-F • E Europe • 500 kW
    - BBC, Rampisham — M-F • Europe • 500 kW
    - — W • Sa/Su • E Europe • 500 kW
    - BBC, Via Zyyi, Cyprus — S • E Europe • 300 kW
- **6010v** **CLANDESTINE (ASIA)**
  - "VO NAT SALVATION, Pyongyang — TO SOUTH KOREA • 100 kW
- **6010.6** **VENEZUELA**
  - †RADIO LOS ANDES, Mérida — DS-TEMP INACTIVE • 1 kW
- **6012** **ITALY**
  - TELE RADIO STEREO, Rome — Europe • TEMP INACTIVE • 2 kW
- **6014v** **COLOMBIA**
  - †RADIO MIRA, Tumaco — DS-CARACOL • 3 kW
  - **TANZANIA**
    - VOICE OF TANZANIA, Dole, Zanzibar — DS-SWAHILI • 50 kW — DS-SWAHILI • 50 kW • ALT. FREQ. TO 11734 kHz
- **6014.8** **BOLIVIA**
  - RADIO EL MUNDO, Santa Cruz — Tu-Su • DS • 10 kW — DS • 10 kW
  - — Su • DS • 10 kW
  - — Irr • Tu-Sa • DS • 10 kW
- **6015** **ALBANIA**
  - †RADIO TIRANA, Cerrik — S • Europe, N Africa & Mideast • 100 kW
  - †RADIO TIRANA, Shijak — S • Europe, N Africa & Mideast • 100 kW
  - **AUSTRIA**
    - †R AUSTRIA INTL, Via Sackville, Canada — N America • 250 kW
    - — W • N America • 250 kW
    - — S • N America • 250 kW
  - **CHINA**
    - †CENTRAL PEOPLE'S BS, Beijing — W • CHINESE, ETC • TAIWAN SERVICE • 50 kW
    - — CHINESE, ETC • TAIWAN SERVICE • 50 kW
  - **FINLAND**
    - YLE RADIO FINLAND, Pori — W • E Europe • 250 kW
  - **GERMANY**
    - †ADVENTIST WORLD RADIO, Jülich — W • E Europe • 100 kW
    - †DEUTSCHE WELLE, Various Locations — S Africa • 250/500 kW — E Europe • 100/500 kW
    - †DEUTSCHE WELLE, Wertachtal — Europe • 500 kW
  - **HOLLAND**
    - R NEDERLAND, Flevoland — W • S Europe & W Africa • 500 kW
    - R NEDERLAND, Via Madagascar — S Africa • 200 kW
  - **IRAN**
    - VO THE ISLAMIC REP, Tehrān — W • Europe & C America • 500 kW • ALT. FREQ. TO 6150 kHz
  - **IRELAND**
    - †WEST COAST R IRELAND, Via Germany — W • Sa • Europe • 100 kW • ALT. FREQ. TO 5970 kHz
  - **ITALY**
    - RADIO ROMA-RAI INTL, Rome — E Europe • 100 kW
  - **KOREA (REPUBLIC)**
    - KOREAN BC SYSTEM, Hwasung — E Asia • LIBERTY-1 • 100 kW
  - **RUSSIA**
    - †MAYAK, Kaliningrad — E Europe • DS • 100 kW
  - **SINGAPORE**
    - R SINGAPORE INTL, Kranji — SE Asia • 250 kW
  - **UNITED ARAB EMIRATES**
    - †UAE RADIO FROM ABU DHABI — W • Mideast • 500 kW
  - **UNITED KINGDOM**
    - BBC, Via Zyyi, Cyprus — Su • E Europe & Mideast • 300 kW
    - — M-F • E Europe & Mideast • 300 kW
    - — S • E Europe & Mideast • 300 kW
    - — S • E Europe • 300 kW
  - **USA**
    - †VOA, Via Udon Thani, Thailand — W • S Asia • 500 kW
    - WYFR-FAMILY RADIO, Okeechobee, Fl — S • W North Am • 100 kW
- **6018.2** **PERU**
  - RADIO VICTORIA, Lima — DS • 5 kW
- **6020** **BRAZIL**
  - †R EDUCADORA BAHIA, Salvador — DS • 10 kW
  - †RADIO GAUCHA, Pôrto Alegre — DS • 10 kW
  - **HOLLAND**
  - (con'd) †R NEDERLAND, Flevoland — S • S Europe • 500 kW — N Africa & W Africa • 500 kW

0 1 2 3 4 5 6 7 8 9 10 11 12 13 14 15 16 17 18 19 20 21 22 23 24

SEASONAL **S** OR **W**   1-HR TIMESHIFT MIDYEAR ◪ OR ◪   JAMMING / OR ∧   EARLIEST HEARD ◁   LATEST HEARD ▷   NEW FOR 1998 †

FREQUENCY   COUNTRY, STATION, LOCATION   TARGET • NETWORK • POWER (kW)   World Time

FREQUENCY	COUNTRY, STATION, LOCATION	TARGET • NETWORK • POWER (kW)
6020 (con'd)	**HOLLAND** †R NEDERLAND, Flevoland	W • S Europe • 500 kW W • C America • 500 kW
	R NEDERLAND, Various Locations	E North Am • 250/500 kW C America • 250/500 kW
	†R NEDERLAND, Via Madagascar	S Africa • 200 kW
	†R NEDERLAND, Via Neth Antilles	W North Am & C America • 250 kW , ETC • C America • 250 kW C America • 250 kW
	INDIA †ALL INDIA RADIO, Simla	DS • 50 kW ENGLISH, ETC • DS • 50 kW Su • DS • 50 kW
	ITALY RADIO ROMA-RAI INTL, Rome	E Europe • 100 kW • ALT FREQ. TO 6010 kHz
	RUSSIA †MAYAK, Arkhangel'sk	W • DS • 20 kW
	†MAYAK, Komsomol'sk 'Amure	W • DS • 100 kW
	R TIKHIY OKEAN, Khabarovsk	W • E Asia & N Pacific • 100 kW
	UKRAINE RADIO UKRAINE, Kiev	S • E Europe • 100 kW
	RADIO UKRAINE, Nikolayev	W • W Europe & E North Am • 1000 kW W • N Europe & E North Am • 1000 kW
	UNITED KINGDOM BBC, Via Zyyi, Cyprus	W • E Europe & Mideast • 300 kW W • E Europe • 300 kW
	USA KWHR, Naalehu, Hawai'i	Australasia • 100 kW
	†RFE-RL, Via Kaválla, Greece	W • Mideast & W Asia • 250 kW
	†VOA, Via Woofferton, UK	W • Europe • 250 kW
6020v	**SAUDI ARABIA** BS OF THE KINGDOM, Jiddah	Mideast & E Africa • DS-2 • 50 kW
6025	**BOLIVIA** †RADIO ILLIMANI, La Paz	DS • 10 kW Tu-Su • DS • 10 kW Irr • M-Sa • DS • 10 kW M-Sa • DS • 10 kW
	CANADA R CANADA INTL, Via Germany	W • Mideast • 500 kW
	R CANADA INTL, Via Skelton, UK	W • Mideast • 300 kW
	DOMINICAN REPUBLIC †R AMANECER INTL, Sto Domingo	DS • 1/5 kW
	GERMANY †DEUTSCHE WELLE, Wertachtal	S • E Europe • 500 kW
	HUNGARY RADIO KOSSUTH, Szekésfehérvár	M-Sa • Europe • DS • 100 kW • Europe • DS • 100 kW
	IRAN VO THE ISLAMIC REP, Tehrän	Mideast & N Africa • 500 kW
	MALAYSIA RADIO MALAYSIA, Kajang	DS-5 • 100 kW
	NIGERIA RADIO NIGERIA, Enugu	ENGLISH, ETC • DS • 10 kW
	USA †VOA, Via Kaválla, Greece	W • W Asia & S Asia • 250 kW
	†VOA, Via Philippines	E Asia • 250 kW
	UZBEKISTAN RADIO TASHKENT, Tashkent	W • W Asia & S Asia • 100 kW
6029.6	**CHILE** RADIO SANTA MARIA, Coyhaique	DS • 10 kW • M-Sa • DS • 10 kW •
6030	**BHUTAN** †BHUTAN BC SERVICE, Thimbu	Su • DS • 50 kW •
	BRAZIL RADIO GLOBO, Rio de Janeiro	DS • 10 kW • Irr • DS • 10 kW •
	CANADA CFVP-CKMX, Calgary, Alberta	W North Am • DS • 0.1 kW
	R CANADA INTL, Via In-Kimjae, Korea	W • E Asia • 250 kW
	CHINA †CENTRAL PEOPLE'S BS	DS-1 W-M • DS-1
	FINLAND YLE RADIO FINLAND, Pori	W • E Europe • 250 kW
	GERMANY SUDDEUTSCHER R'FUNK, Mühlacker	• Europe • DS-1 • 20 kW
(con'd)	**HOLLAND** R NEDERLAND, Via Neth Antilles	, ETC • C America • 250 kW

World Time scale (top and bottom): 0 1 2 3 4 5 6 7 8 9 10 11 12 13 14 15 16 17 18 19 20 21 22 23 24

FREQUENCY	COUNTRY, STATION, LOCATION	TARGET • NETWORK • POWER (kW)	World Time

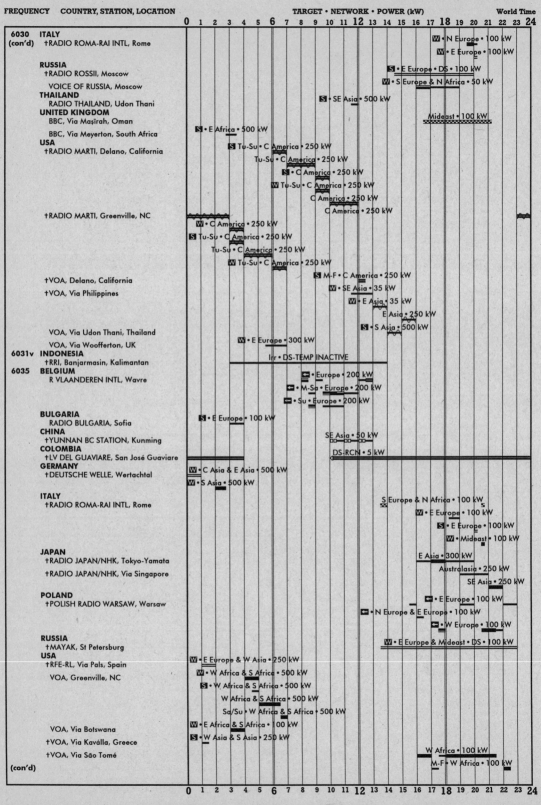

6030
(con'd) ITALY
†RADIO ROMA-RAI INTL, Rome — W • N Europe • 100 kW / W • E Europe • 100 kW

RUSSIA
†RADIO ROSSII, Moscow — S • E Europe • DS • 100 kW
VOICE OF RUSSIA, Moscow — W • S Europe & N Africa • 50 kW
THAILAND
RADIO THAILAND, Udon Thani — S • SE Asia • 500 kW
UNITED KINGDOM
BBC, Via Maşīrah, Oman — Mideast • 100 kW
BBC, Via Meyerton, South Africa — S • E Africa • 500 kW
USA
†RADIO MARTI, Delano, California — S Tu-Su • C America • 250 kW / Tu-Su • C America • 250 kW / S • C America • 250 kW / W Tu-Su • C America • 250 kW / C America • 250 kW / C America • 250 kW

†RADIO MARTI, Greenville, NC — W • C America • 250 kW / S Tu-Su • C America • 250 kW / Tu-Su • C America • 250 kW / W Tu-Su • C America • 250 kW

†VOA, Delano, California — S M-F • C America • 250 kW
†VOA, Via Philippines — W • SE Asia • 35 kW / W • E Asia • 35 kW / E Asia • 250 kW

VOA, Via Udon Thani, Thailand — S • S Asia • 500 kW
VOA, Via Woofferton, UK — W • E Europe • 300 kW
6031v INDONESIA
†RRI, Banjarmasin, Kalimantan — Irr • DS-TEMP INACTIVE
6035 BELGIUM
R VLAANDEREN INTL, Wavre — • Europe • 200 kW / • M-Sa • Europe • 200 kW / • Su • Europe • 200 kW

BULGARIA
RADIO BULGARIA, Sofia — S • E Europe • 100 kW
CHINA
†YUNNAN BC STATION, Kunming — SE Asia • 50 kW
COLOMBIA
†LV DEL GUAVIARE, San José Guaviare — DS-RCN • 5 kW
GERMANY
†DEUTSCHE WELLE, Wertachtal — W • C Asia & E Asia • 500 kW / W • S Asia • 500 kW

ITALY
†RADIO ROMA-RAI INTL, Rome — S Europe & N Africa • 100 kW / W • E Europe • 100 kW / S • E Europe • 100 kW / W • Mideast • 100 kW

JAPAN
†RADIO JAPAN/NHK, Tokyo-Yamata — E Asia • 300 kW
†RADIO JAPAN/NHK, Via Singapore — Australasia • 250 kW / SE Asia • 250 kW

POLAND
†POLISH RADIO WARSAW, Warsaw — • E Europe • 100 kW / • N Europe & E Europe • 100 kW / • W Europe • 100 kW

RUSSIA
†MAYAK, St Petersburg — W • E Europe & Mideast • DS • 100 kW
USA
†RFE-RL, Via Pals, Spain — W • E Europe & W Asia • 250 kW
VOA, Greenville, NC — W • W Africa & S Africa • 500 kW / S • W Africa & S Africa • 500 kW / W Africa & S Africa • 500 kW / Sa/Su • W Africa & S Africa • 500 kW

VOA, Via Botswana — W • E Africa & S Africa • 100 kW
†VOA, Via Kaválla, Greece — S • W Asia & S Asia • 250 kW
†VOA, Via São Tomé — W Africa • 100 kW / M-F • W Africa • 100 kW

(con'd)

| FREQUENCY | COUNTRY, STATION, LOCATION | | TARGET • NETWORK • POWER (kW) | World Time |

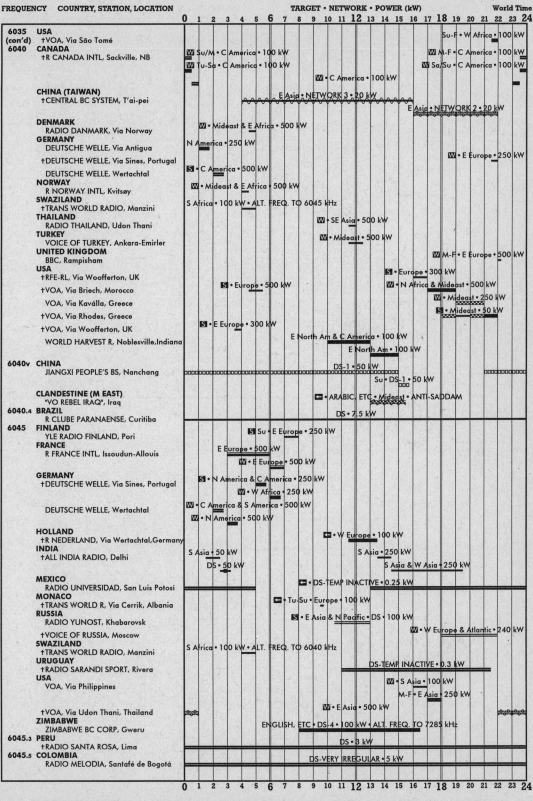

World Time scale: 0 1 2 3 4 5 6 7 8 9 10 11 12 13 14 15 16 17 18 19 20 21 22 23 24

6035 **USA**
(con'd) †VOA, Via São Tomé — Su-F • W Africa • 100 kW
6040 **CANADA**
†R CANADA INTL, Sackville, NB
- W Su/M • C America • 100 kW
- W Tu-Sa • C America • 100 kW
- W M-F • C America • 100 kW
- W Sa/Su • C America • 100 kW
- W • C America • 100 kW

CHINA (TAIWAN)
†CENTRAL BC SYSTEM, T'ai-pei — E Asia • NETWORK 3 • 20 kW / E Asia • NETWORK 2 • 20 kW

DENMARK
RADIO DANMARK, Via Norway — W • Mideast & E Africa • 500 kW
GERMANY
DEUTSCHE WELLE, Via Antigua — N America • 250 kW
†DEUTSCHE WELLE, Via Sines, Portugal — W • E Europe • 250 kW
DEUTSCHE WELLE, Wertachtal — S • C America • 500 kW
NORWAY
R NORWAY INTL, Kvitsøy — W • Mideast & E Africa • 500 kW
SWAZILAND
†TRANS WORLD RADIO, Manzini — S Africa • 100 kW • ALT. FREQ. TO 6045 kHz
THAILAND
RADIO THAILAND, Udon Thani — W • SE Asia • 500 kW
TURKEY
VOICE OF TURKEY, Ankara-Emirler — W • Mideast • 500 kW
UNITED KINGDOM
BBC, Rampisham — W M-F • E Europe • 500 kW
USA
†RFE-RL, Via Woofferton, UK — S • Europe • 300 kW
†VOA, Via Briech, Morocco — S • Europe • 500 kW / W • N Africa & Mideast • 500 kW
VOA, Via Kaválla, Greece — W • Mideast • 250 kW
†VOA, Via Rhodes, Greece — S • Mideast • 50 kW
†VOA, Via Woofferton, UK — S • E Europe • 300 kW
WORLD HARVEST R, Noblesville, Indiana — E North Am & C America • 100 kW / E North Am • 100 kW

6040v **CHINA**
JIANGXI PEOPLE'S BS, Nanchang — DS-1 • 50 kW / Su • DS-1 • 50 kW

CLANDESTINE (M EAST)
"VO REBEL IRAQ", Iraq — • ARABIC, ETC • Mideast • ANTI-SADDAM
6040.4 **BRAZIL**
R CLUBE PARANAENSE, Curitiba — DS • 7.5 kW
6045 **FINLAND**
YLE RADIO FINLAND, Pori — S Su • E Europe • 250 kW
FRANCE
R FRANCE INTL, Issoudun-Allouis — E Europe • 500 kW / W • E Europe • 500 kW
GERMANY
†DEUTSCHE WELLE, Via Sines, Portugal — S • N America & C America • 250 kW / W • W Africa • 250 kW
DEUTSCHE WELLE, Wertachtal — W • C America & S America • 500 kW / W • N America • 500 kW
HOLLAND
†R NEDERLAND, Via Wertachtal, Germany — • W Europe • 100 kW
INDIA
†ALL INDIA RADIO, Delhi — S Asia • 50 kW / S Asia • 250 kW / DS • 50 kW / S Asia & W Asia • 250 kW
MEXICO
RADIO UNIVERSIDAD, San Luis Potosí — • DS-TEMP INACTIVE • 0.25 kW
MONACO
†TRANS WORLD R, Via Cerrik, Albania — • Tu-Su • Europe • 100 kW
RUSSIA
RADIO YUNOST, Khabarovsk — S • E Asia & N Pacific • DS • 100 kW
†VOICE OF RUSSIA, Moscow — W • W Europe & Atlantic • 240 kW
SWAZILAND
†TRANS WORLD RADIO, Manzini — S Africa • 100 kW • ALT. FREQ. TO 6040 kHz
URUGUAY
†RADIO SARANDI SPORT, Rivera — DS-TEMP INACTIVE • 0.3 kW
USA
VOA, Via Philippines — W • S Asia • 100 kW / M-F • E Asia • 250 kW
†VOA, Via Udon Thani, Thailand — W • E Asia • 500 kW
ZIMBABWE
ZIMBABWE BC CORP, Gweru — ENGLISH, ETC • DS-4 • 100 kW • ALT. FREQ. TO 7285 kHz
6045.3 **PERU**
†RADIO SANTA ROSA, Lima — DS • 3 kW
6045.5 **COLOMBIA**
RADIO MELODIA, Santafé de Bogotá — DS-VERY IRREGULAR • 5 kW

World Time scale: 0 1 2 3 4 5 6 7 8 9 10 11 12 13 14 15 16 17 18 19 20 21 22 23 24

ENGLISH ▬ ARABIC ▨ CHINESE □□□ FRENCH ▬ GERMAN ▬ RUSSIAN ═ SPANISH ▬ OTHER ▬

FREQUENCY	COUNTRY, STATION, LOCATION	TARGET • NETWORK • POWER (kW)	World Time

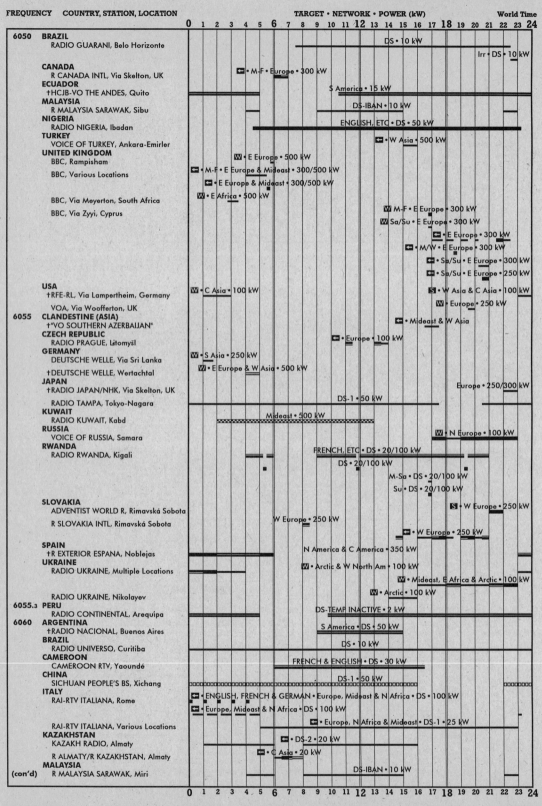

SEASONAL 🅂 OR 🆆   1-HR TIMESHIFT MIDYEAR 🔁 OR 🔄   JAMMING / OR /\   EARLIEST HEARD ◁   LATEST HEARD ▷   NEW FOR 1998 †

FREQUENCY   COUNTRY, STATION, LOCATION

TARGET • NETWORK • POWER (kW)

World Time

0 1 2 3 4 5 6 7 8 9 10 11 12 13 14 15 16 17 18 19 20 21 22 23 24

Frequency	Country, Station, Location	Target • Network • Power
6060 (con'd)	**NIGER** LA VOIX DU SAHEL, Niamey	FRENCH, ETC • DS-TEMP INACTIVE • 4/20 kW / Sa • FRENCH, ETC • DS-TEMP INACTIVE • 4/20 kW
	RUSSIA MAYAK, Blagoveshchensk	☐ • DS • 5 kW
	†RADIO ROSSII, Moscow	W • Europe • DS • 100 kW
	UNITED KINGDOM BBC, Via Singapore	W • S Asia • 250 kW
	USA RFE-RL, Via Woofferton, UK	W • E Europe • 250 kW
	VOA, Via Kaválla, Greece	W • W Asia • 250 kW
	†VOA, Via Lampertheim, Germany	W • E Europe • 100 kW
	†VOA, Via Philippines	SE Asia • 50 kW / W • SE Asia • 50 kW
	†VOA, Via Udon Thani, Thailand	W • S Asia • 500 kW / S • E Asia • 500 kW
	VOA, Via Woofferton, UK	W • Europe • 300 kW / W • W Asia • 250 kW
6063.8	**COLOMBIA** †COLMUNDO BOGOTA, Santafé Bogotá	DS • 5 kW
6065	**ARMENIA** ARMENIAN RADIO, Kamo	☐ • DS-1 • 100 kW
	GERMANY DEUTSCHE WELLE, Wertachtal	W • Africa • 500 kW
	INDIA †ALL INDIA RADIO, Kohima	DS • 50 kW
	RUSSIA R TIKHIY OKEAN, Khabarovsk	☐ • E Asia • 100 kW • USB
	SWEDEN RADIO SWEDEN, Hörby	S America • 500 kW / ☐ • M-F • Europe • 500 kW / ☐ • Sa • Europe • 500 kW / ☐ • Su • Europe • 500 kW / ☐ • Sa/Su • Europe • 500 kW / ☐ • Europe • 500 kW / ☐ • Europe & Mideast • 500 kW / ☐ • M-F • Europe & Mideast • 500 kW / ☐ • Sa/Su • Europe & Mideast • 500 kW
	UNITED KINGDOM BBC, Skelton, Cumbria	W • C Asia • 300 kW
	BBC, Via Maṣīrah, Oman	W Asia & S Asia • 100 kW
	BBC, Via Singapore	S • W Asia & S Asia • 100 kW
	BBC, Via Tokyo, Japan	W • E Asia • 300 kW
	USA †VOA, Via Kaválla, Greece	S • E Europe • 250 kW
	WYFR-FAMILY RADIO, Okeechobee, Fl	E North Am • 100 kW
	VATICAN STATE VATICAN RADIO, Sta Maria di Galeria	W • E Asia • 500 kW / W • SE Asia • 500 kW
	ZAMBIA †CHRISTIAN VOICE, Lusaka	S Africa • 100 kW • ALT. FREQ. TO 3330 kHz / S Africa • 100 kW
6070	**CANADA** CFRX-CFRB, Mississauga, Ontario	☐ • E North Am • DS • 1 kW
	CUBA †RADIO HABANA CUBA, Havana	C America & W North Am • 50 kW / C America & W North Am • 100 kW / Su • C America & W North Am • 100 kW
	JAPAN †RADIO JAPAN/NHK, Via French Guiana	S America • 500 kW
	KOREA (DPR) †RADIO PYONGYANG, Pyongyang	E Asia • 100 kW
	NEW ZEALAND †R NEW ZEALAND INTL, Rangitaiki	Irr • W • Pacific • SPORTS • 100 kW / W • M-F • ENGLISH, ETC • Pacific • 100 kW
	PAKISTAN PAKISTAN BC CORP, Islamabad	DS • 100 kW
	PERU †RADIO CHASKI, Cusco	SPANISH & QUECHUA • DS • ALT. FREQ. TO 6088 kHz
	SWAZILAND †TRANS WORLD RADIO, Manzini	S Africa • 25 kW • ALT. FREQ. TO 6100 kHz
	THAILAND †RADIO THAILAND, Pathum Thani	DS • 10 kW
	UNITED KINGDOM BBC, Via Meyerton, South Africa	S Africa • 500 kW
	USA VOA, Via Rhodes, Greece	W • Mideast • 50 kW
6070v	**INDONESIA** †RRI, Jayapura, Irian Jaya	DS • 20 kW

0 1 2 3 4 5 6 7 8 9 10 11 12 13 14 15 16 17 18 19 20 21 22 23 24

ENGLISH ▬ ARABIC ⠶⠶ CHINESE ▫▫▫ FRENCH ▬▬ GERMAN ▭▭ RUSSIAN ═ SPANISH ▬▬ OTHER —

FREQUENCY	COUNTRY, STATION, LOCATION	TARGET • NETWORK • POWER (kW)	World Time

World Time scale: 0 1 2 3 4 5 6 7 8 9 10 11 12 13 14 15 16 17 18 19 20 21 22 23 24

Frequency	Country / Station / Location	Target • Network • Power
6074.4	**URUGUAY** LA VOZ DE ARTIGAS, Artigas	DS-VERY IRREGULAR • 2.5 kW
6075	**COSTA RICA** †RADIO 88 ESTEREO, Pérez Zeledón	DS-PROJECTED • 1 kW / M-Sa • DS-PROJECTED • 1 kW
	GERMANY †DEUTSCHE WELLE, Multiple Locations	Europe • 250/500 kW / Europe & N America • 250/500 kW / Europe & Africa • 250/500 kW
	KAZAKHSTAN KAZAKH RADIO, Almaty	DS-2 • 20 kW
	R ALMATY/R KAZAKHSTAN, Almaty	C Asia • 20 kW
	MADAGASCAR †RADIO TSIOKA VAO, Tana	FRENCH, ETC • DS
	PHILIPPINES †RADIO VERITAS ASIA, Palauig	E Asia • 250 kW
	RUSSIA †MAYAK, Saransk	W • W Asia • DS • 150 kW
	SRI LANKA SRI LANKA BC CORP, Colombo-Ekala	S Asia • 10 kW
6080	**AUSTRALIA** †RADIO AUSTRALIA, Shepparton	Pacific & E Asia • 100 kW / Pacific • 100 kW / E Asia • 100 kW
	BELARUS BELARUSSIAN R, Brest	DS-1 • 10 kW
	BRAZIL †RADIO ANHANGUERA, Goiânia	DS • 10 kW
	RADIO NOVAS DE PAZ, Curitiba	DS • 10 kW / Sa/Su • DS • 10 kW
	CHILE †R PATAGONIA CHILENA, Coyhaique	DS • 1 kW / Su • DS • 1 kW / M-Sa • DS • 1 kW
	CHINA HULUNBEI'ER PBS, Hailar	DS-MONGOLIAN • 15 kW
	ECUADOR †HCJB-VO THE ANDES, Quito	8 kW
	GEORGIA †RADIO GEORGIA, Tbilisi	Tu/Th • Mideast & W Asia • 100 kW / S Sa/Su • Mideast & W Asia • 100 kW / W • Europe • 100 kW / N Europe • 100 kW
	RUSSIA †VOICE OF RUSSIA, Khabarovsk	W • E Asia • 100 kW
	†VOICE OF RUSSIA, Vladivostok	S • E Asia • 100 kW
	UKRAINE RADIO UKRAINE, Kiev	W • W Asia • 200 kW
	RADIO UKRAINE, Various Locations	W Asia • 100/200 kW
	UNITED KINGDOM BBC, Via Singapore	SE Asia • 250 kW
	USA VOA, Via São Tomé	S Africa • 100 kW / W Africa • 100 kW / Sa/Su • W Africa • 100 kW
6081v	**PAKISTAN** PAKISTAN BC CORP, Islamabad	DS • 10 kW
6085	**CHINA (TAIWAN)** †CENTRAL BC SYSTEM, T'ai-pei	E Asia • NETWORK 2 • 100 kW
	GERMANY BAYERISCHER RUNDFUNK, Ismaning	DS-1, ARD-NACHT • 100 kW
	†DEUTSCHE WELLE, Via Sackville, Can	N America • 250 kW
	HUNGARY RADIO BUDAPEST, Diósd	S • S America • 100 kW / S Su • S America • 100 kW
	INDIA †ALL INDIA RADIO, Gangtok	DS • 50 kW
	OMAN †RADIO OMAN, Sib	W • Mideast & W Asia • DS • 100 kW / Mideast & W Asia • DS • 100 kW • ALT. FREQ. TO 6120 kHz
	RADIO OMAN, Thamarīt	E Africa • DS • 100 kW / W • E Africa • DS • 100 kW
	USA †VOA, Via Philippines	W • SE Asia • 100 kW
	†WYFR-FAMILY RADIO, Okeechobee, Fl	E North Am • 100 kW / C America • 100 kW
6085.3	**BOLIVIA** RADIO SAN GABRIEL, La Paz	DS • 5 kW / Tu-Su • DS • 5 kW / M-Sa • DS • 5 kW / Tu-Sa • DS • 5 kW / M-F • DS • 5 kW

World Time scale: 0 1 2 3 4 5 6 7 8 9 10 11 12 13 14 15 16 17 18 19 20 21 22 23 24

SEASONAL S OR W   **1-HR TIMESHIFT MIDYEAR** ◄ OR ►   **JAMMING** / OR ∧   **EARLIEST HEARD** ◄   **LATEST HEARD** ►   **NEW FOR 1998** †

FREQUENCY   COUNTRY, STATION, LOCATION

TARGET • NETWORK • POWER (kW)

World Time

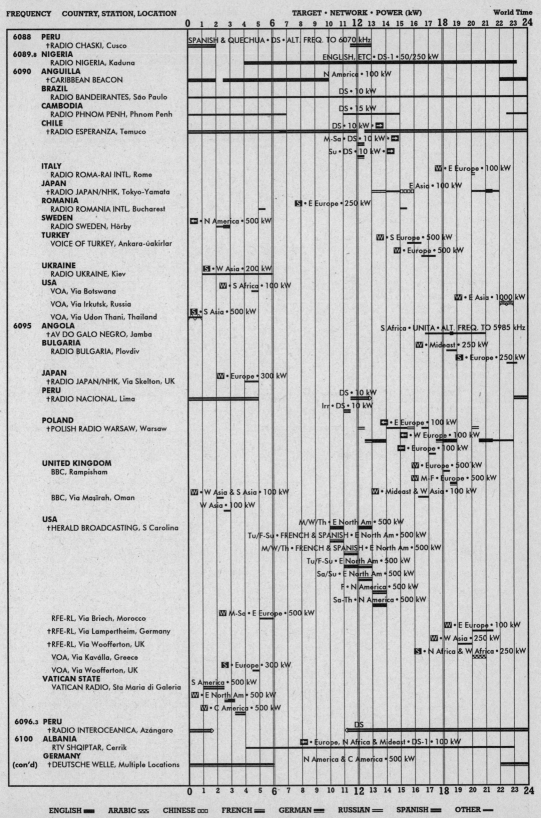

Frequency	Country, Station, Location	Target • Network • Power (kW)
6088	**PERU** †RADIO CHASKI, Cusco	SPANISH & QUECHUA • DS • ALT. FREQ. TO 6070 kHz
6089.8	**NIGERIA** RADIO NIGERIA, Kaduna	ENGLISH, ETC • DS-1 • 50/250 kW
6090	**ANGUILLA** †CARIBBEAN BEACON	N America • 100 kW
	BRAZIL RADIO BANDEIRANTES, São Paulo	DS • 10 kW
	CAMBODIA RADIO PHNOM PENH, Phnom Penh	DS • 15 kW
	CHILE †RADIO ESPERANZA, Temuco	DS • 10 kW • ➡ / M-Sa • DS • 10 kW • ➡ / Su • DS • 10 kW • ➡
	ITALY RADIO ROMA-RAI INTL, Rome	W • E Europe • 100 kW
	JAPAN †RADIO JAPAN/NHK, Tokyo-Yamata	E Asia • 100 kW
	ROMANIA RADIO ROMANIA INTL, Bucharest	S • E Europe • 250 kW
	SWEDEN RADIO SWEDEN, Hörby	⬅ • N America • 500 kW
	TURKEY VOICE OF TURKEY, Ankara-úakirlar	W • S Europe • 500 kW / W • Europe • 500 kW
	UKRAINE RADIO UKRAINE, Kiev	S • W Asia • 200 kW
	USA VOA, Via Botswana	W • S Africa • 100 kW
	VOA, Via Irkutsk, Russia	W • E Asia • 1000 kW
	VOA, Via Udon Thani, Thailand	S • S Asia • 500 kW
6095	**ANGOLA** †AV DO GALO NEGRO, Jamba	S Africa • UNITA • ALT. FREQ. TO 5985 kHz
	BULGARIA RADIO BULGARIA, Plovdiv	W • Mideast • 250 kW / S • Europe • 250 kW
	JAPAN †RADIO JAPAN/NHK, Via Skelton, UK	W • Europe • 300 kW
	PERU †RADIO NACIONAL, Lima	DS • 10 kW / Irr • DS • 10 kW
	POLAND †POLISH RADIO WARSAW, Warsaw	⬅ • E Europe • 100 kW / ⬅ • W Europe • 100 kW / ⬅ • Europe • 100 kW
	UNITED KINGDOM BBC, Rampisham	W • Europe • 500 kW / W M-F • Europe • 500 kW
	BBC, Via Maṣīrah, Oman	W • W Asia & S Asia • 100 kW / W • Mideast & W Asia • 100 kW / W Asia • 100 kW
	USA †HERALD BROADCASTING, S Carolina	M/W/Th • E North Am • 500 kW / Tu/F-Su • FRENCH & SPANISH • E North Am • 500 kW / M/W/Th • FRENCH & SPANISH • E North Am • 500 kW / Tu/F-Su • E North Am • 500 kW / Sa/Su • E North Am • 500 kW / F • N America • 500 kW / Sa-Th • N America • 500 kW
	RFE-RL, Via Briech, Morocco	W M-Sa • E Europe • 500 kW
	†RFE-RL, Via Lampertheim, Germany	W • E Europe • 100 kW
	†RFE-RL, Via Woofferton, UK	W • W Asia • 250 kW
	VOA, Via Kaválla, Greece	S • N Africa & W Africa • 250 kW
	VOA, Via Woofferton, UK	S • Europe • 300 kW
	VATICAN STATE VATICAN RADIO, Sta Maria di Galeria	S America • 500 kW / W • E North Am • 500 kW / W • C America • 500 kW
6096.3	**PERU** †RADIO INTEROCEANICA, Azángaro	DS
6100	**ALBANIA** RTV SHQIPTAR, Cerrik	⬅ • Europe, N Africa & Mideast • DS-1 • 100 kW
(con'd)	**GERMANY** †DEUTSCHE WELLE, Multiple Locations	N America & C America • 500 kW

ENGLISH ▬▬   ARABIC ⨯⨯⨯   CHINESE □□□   FRENCH ▬▬▬   GERMAN ▬▬   RUSSIAN ══   SPANISH ▬▬▬   OTHER ▬▬

FREQUENCY	COUNTRY, STATION, LOCATION	TARGET • NETWORK • POWER (kW)	World Time

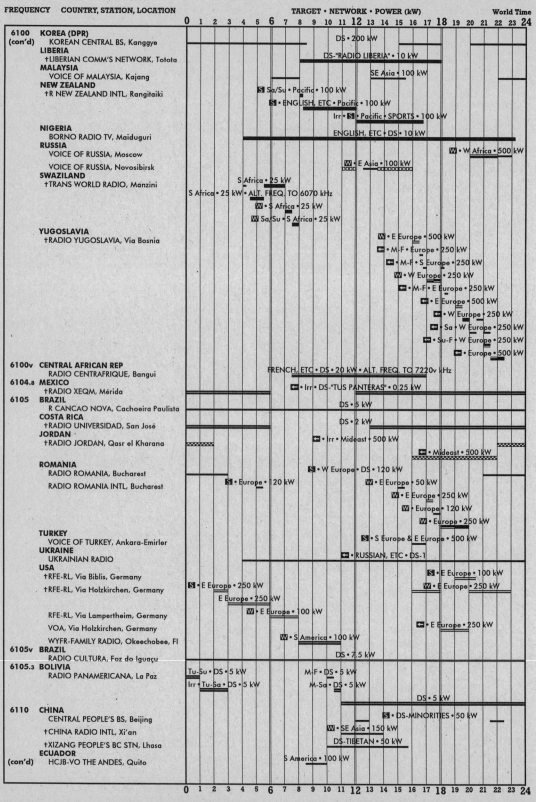

6100 (con'd) — KOREA (DPR) — KOREAN CENTRAL BS, Kanggye — DS • 200 kW
LIBERIA — †LIBERIAN COMM'S NETWORK, Totota — DS-"RADIO LIBERIA" • 10 kW
MALAYSIA — VOICE OF MALAYSIA, Kajang — SE Asia • 100 kW
NEW ZEALAND — †R NEW ZEALAND INTL, Rangitaiki — S Sa/Su • Pacific • 100 kW — S • ENGLISH, ETC • Pacific • 100 kW — Irr • S • Pacific • SPORTS • 100 kW
NIGERIA — BORNO RADIO TV, Maiduguri — ENGLISH, ETC • DS • 10 kW
RUSSIA — VOICE OF RUSSIA, Moscow — W • W Africa • 500 kW
VOICE OF RUSSIA, Novosibirsk — W • E Asia • 100 kW
SWAZILAND — †TRANS WORLD RADIO, Manzini — S Africa • 25 kW — S Africa • 25 kW • ALT. FREQ. TO 6070 kHz — W • S Africa • 25 kW — W Sa/Su • S Africa • 25 kW
YUGOSLAVIA — †RADIO YUGOSLAVIA, Via Bosnia — W • E Europe • 500 kW — M-F • Europe • 250 kW — M-F • S Europe • 250 kW — W • W Europe • 250 kW — M-F • E Europe • 250 kW — E Europe • 500 kW — W Europe • 250 kW — Sa • W Europe • 250 kW — Su-F • W Europe • 250 kW — Europe • 500 kW

6100v CENTRAL AFRICAN REP — RADIO CENTRAFRIQUE, Bangui — FRENCH, ETC • DS • 20 kW • ALT. FREQ. TO 7220v kHz
6104.8 MEXICO — †RADIO XEQM, Mérida — Irr • DS-"TUS PANTERAS" • 0.25 kW
6105 BRAZIL — R CANCAO NOVA, Cachoeira Paulista — DS • 5 kW
COSTA RICA — †RADIO UNIVERSIDAD, San José — DS • 2 kW
JORDAN — †RADIO JORDAN, Qasr el Kharana — Irr • Mideast • 500 kW — Mideast • 500 kW
ROMANIA — RADIO ROMANIA, Bucharest — S • W Europe • DS • 120 kW
RADIO ROMANIA INTL, Bucharest — S • Europe • 120 kW — W • E Europe • 50 kW — W • E Europe • 250 kW — W • Europe • 120 kW — W • Europe • 250 kW
TURKEY — VOICE OF TURKEY, Ankara-Emirler — S • S Europe & E Europe • 500 kW
UKRAINE — UKRAINIAN RADIO — RUSSIAN, ETC • DS-1
USA — †RFE-RL, Via Biblis, Germany — S • E Europe • 100 kW
†RFE-RL, Via Holzkirchen, Germany — S • E Europe • 250 kW — W • E Europe • 250 kW — E Europe • 250 kW
RFE-RL, Via Lampertheim, Germany — W • E Europe • 100 kW
VOA, Via Holzkirchen, Germany — E Europe • 250 kW
WYFR-FAMILY RADIO, Okeechobee, Fl — W • S America • 100 kW
6105v BRAZIL — RADIO CULTURA, Foz do Iguaçu — DS • 7.5 kW
6105.3 BOLIVIA — RADIO PANAMERICANA, La Paz — Tu-Su • DS • 5 kW — M-F • DS • 5 kW — Irr • Tu-Sa • DS • 5 kW — M-Sa • DS • 5 kW — DS • 5 kW
6110 CHINA — CENTRAL PEOPLE'S BS, Beijing — S • DS-MINORITIES • 50 kW
†CHINA RADIO INTL, Xi'an — W • SE Asia • 150 kW
†XIZANG PEOPLE'S BC STN, Lhasa — DS-TIBETAN • 50 kW
ECUADOR (con'd) — HCJB-VO THE ANDES, Quito — S America • 100 kW

FREQUENCY   COUNTRY, STATION, LOCATION

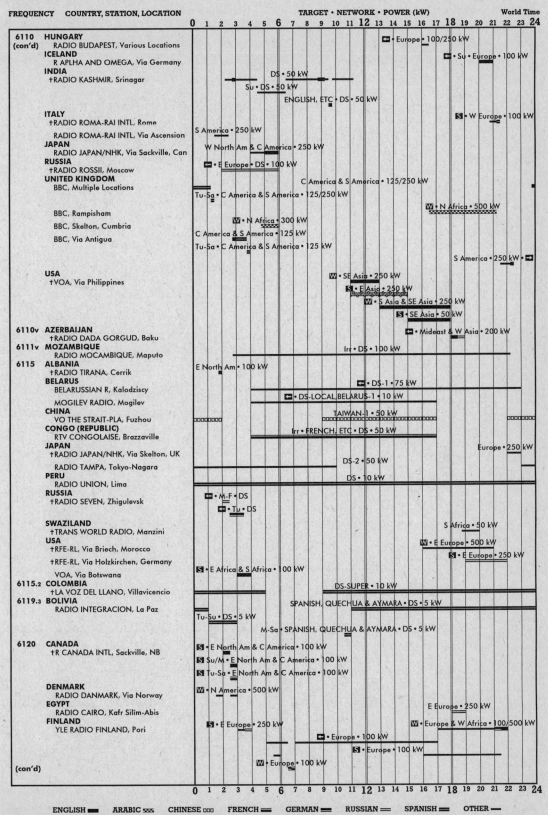

Frequency	Country, Station, Location	Notes
6110 (con'd)	**HUNGARY** RADIO BUDAPEST, Various Locations	Europe • 100/250 kW
	ICELAND R APLHA AND OMEGA, Via Germany	Su • Europe • 100 kW
	INDIA †RADIO KASHMIR, Srinagar	DS • 50 kW; Su • DS • 50 kW; ENGLISH, ETC • DS • 50 kW
	ITALY †RADIO ROMA-RAI INTL, Rome	W Europe • 100 kW
	RADIO ROMA-RAI INTL, Via Ascension	S America • 250 kW
	JAPAN RADIO JAPAN/NHK, Via Sackville, Can	W North Am & C America • 250 kW
	RUSSIA †RADIO ROSSII, Moscow	E Europe • DS • 100 kW
	UNITED KINGDOM BBC, Multiple Locations	C America & S America • 125/250 kW; Tu-Sa • C America & S America • 125/250 kW
		N Africa • 500 kW
	BBC, Rampisham	W • N Africa • 300 kW
	BBC, Skelton, Cumbria	C America & S America • 125 kW; Tu-Sa • C America & S America • 125 kW
	BBC, Via Antigua	S America • 250 kW
	USA †VOA, Via Philippines	W • SE Asia • 250 kW; S • E Asia • 250 kW; W • S Asia & SE Asia • 250 kW; S • SE Asia • 50 kW
6110v	**AZERBAIJAN** †RADIO DADA GORGUD, Baku	Mideast & W Asia • 200 kW
6111v	**MOZAMBIQUE** RADIO MOCAMBIQUE, Maputo	Irr • DS • 100 kW
6115	**ALBANIA** †RADIO TIRANA, Cerrik	E North Am • 100 kW
	BELARUS BELARUSSIAN R, Kalodziscy	DS-1 • 75 kW
	MOGILEV RADIO, Mogilev	DS-LOCAL, BELARUS-1 • 10 kW
	CHINA VO THE STRAIT-PLA, Fuzhou	TAIWAN-1 • 50 kW
	CONGO (REPUBLIC) RTV CONGOLAISE, Brazzaville	Irr • FRENCH, ETC • DS • 50 kW
	JAPAN †RADIO JAPAN/NHK, Via Skelton, UK	Europe • 250 kW
	RADIO TAMPA, Tokyo-Nagara	DS-2 • 50 kW
	PERU RADIO UNION, Lima	DS • 10 kW
	RUSSIA †RADIO SEVEN, Zhigulevsk	M-F • DS; Tu • DS
	SWAZILAND †TRANS WORLD RADIO, Manzini	S Africa • 50 kW
	USA †RFE-RL, Via Briech, Morocco	W • E Europe • 500 kW
	†RFE-RL, Via Holzkirchen, Germany	S • E Europe • 250 kW
	VOA, Via Botswana	S • E Africa & S Africa • 100 kW
6115.2	**COLOMBIA** †LA VOZ DEL LLANO, Villavicencio	DS-SUPER • 10 kW
6119.3	**BOLIVIA** RADIO INTEGRACION, La Paz	SPANISH, QUECHUA & AYMARA • DS • 5 kW; Tu-Su • DS • 5 kW; M-Sa • SPANISH, QUECHUA & AYMARA • DS • 5 kW
6120	**CANADA** †R CANADA INTL, Sackville, NB	S • E North Am & C America • 100 kW; S Su/M • E North Am & C America • 100 kW; S Tu-Sa • E North Am & C America • 100 kW
	DENMARK RADIO DANMARK, Via Norway	W • N America • 500 kW
	EGYPT RADIO CAIRO, Kafr Silim-Abis	E Europe • 250 kW
	FINLAND YLE RADIO FINLAND, Pori	W • Europe & W Africa • 100/500 kW; S • E Europe • 250 kW; Europe • 100 kW; S • Europe • 100 kW; W • Europe • 100 kW

(con'd)

ENGLISH ▬▬   ARABIC ⨯⨯⨯   CHINESE ▭▭▭   FRENCH ══   GERMAN ▬▬   RUSSIAN ══   SPANISH ▬▬   OTHER ──

FREQUENCY	COUNTRY, STATION, LOCATION	TARGET • NETWORK • POWER (kW)	World Time

0 1 2 3 4 5 6 7 8 9 10 11 12 13 14 15 16 17 18 19 20 21 22 23 24

6120
(con'd) **FRANCE**
R FRANCE INTL, Via Tokyo, Japan — SE Asia • 300 kW
GERMANY
DEUTSCHE WELLE, Via Sines, Portugal — W • N America • 250 kW
JAPAN
RADIO JAPAN/NHK, Via Sackville, Can — S • E North Am • 250 kW
E North Am • 250 kW
W • E North Am • 250 kW

NORWAY
R NORWAY INTL, Sveio — W • N America • 500 kW
OMAN
†RADIO OMAN, Sīb — Mideast & W Asia • DS • 100 kW / Mideast & W Asia • DS • 100 kW • ALT. FREQ. TO 6085 kHz
SINGAPORE
R SINGAPORE INTL, Kranji — SE Asia • 250 kW
SOUTH AFRICA
†CHANNEL AFRICA, Meyerton — S • S Africa • 250 kW
S Africa • 100 kW

UNITED KINGDOM
BBC, Via Tokyo, Japan — W • E Asia • 300 kW
Irr • W • E Asia • 300 kW

USA
KWHR, Naalehu, Hawai'i — Australasia • 100 kW
†VOA, Via Philippines — S • SE Asia • 35 kW
†VOA, Via São Tomé — W Africa & C Africa • 100 kW
M-F • W Africa & C Africa • 100 kW
†VOA, Via Woofferton, UK — W • E Europe • 300 kW

6120v ALBANIA
†RADIO TIRANA, Shijak — N America • 100 kW • ALT. FREQ. TO 6190v kHz
BRAZIL
RADIO GLOBO, São Paulo — Irr • DS • 7.5 kW • ⊡
DS • 7.5 kW • ⊡

6125 CHINA
CENTRAL PEOPLE'S BS, Shijiazhuang — DS-1 • 50 kW
ECUADOR
HCJB-VO THE ANDES, Quito — S America • 100 kW
KOREA (DPR)
†RADIO PYONGYANG, Pyongyang — E Asia • 200 kW
RUSSIA
†MARIY RADIO, Yoshkar Ola — ⊡ • RUSSIAN, ETC • DS-LOCAL, R ROSSII • 5 kW
†RADIO ROSSII, Samara — W • W Asia & C Asia • DS • 100 kW
SPAIN
†R EXTERIOR ESPANA, Noblejas — S America • 350 kW
Sa/Su • W Europe • 350 kW
M • Europe • 350 kW
M-F • Europe • 350 kW
Sa • W Europe • 350 kW
Sa/Su • Europe • 350 kW

UNITED KINGDOM
BBC, Rampisham — W • E Europe • 500 kW
BBC, Skelton, Cumbria — S • M-F • Europe • 250 kW
BBC, Via Zyyi, Cyprus — W • E Europe • 250 kW
W • Sa/Su • E Europe • 250 kW

URUGUAY
SODRE, Montevideo — DS-RELAY CX38 • 0.2 kW
USA
VOA, Via Woofferton, UK — S • Europe • 250 kW
Europe • 300 kW
W • Europe • 300 kW

6130 CANADA
CHNX-CHNS, Halifax, NS — E North Am • DS • 0.05/0.5 kW
GERMANY
†DEUTSCHE WELLE, Via Sri Lanka — W • SE Asia • 250 kW
W • S Asia & SE Asia • 250 kW
†DEUTSCHE WELLE, Wertachtal — W • E Europe • 500 kW / S • E Europe • 500 kW
W • E Europe & Mideast • 500 kW
GHANA
†GHANA BC CORP, Accra — M-F • DS-2 • 50 kW
JAPAN
NHK, Fukuoka — Irr • DS-1 (FEEDER) • 0.6 kW • USB
LAOS
†LAO NATIONAL RADIO, Vientiane — DS • 10 kW
PORTUGAL
RDP INTERNATIONAL, Lisbon — ⊡ • M-F • Europe • 100 kW • ALT. FREQ. TO 6155 kHz / ⊡ • M-F • Europe • 100 kW
⊡ • Europe • 100/250 kW

(con'd)

0 1 2 3 4 5 6 7 8 9 10 11 12 13 14 15 16 17 18 19 20 21 22 23 24

SEASONAL S OR W   1-HR TIMESHIFT MIDYEAR ⊡ OR ⊡   JAMMING / OR ∧   EARLIEST HEARD ◁   LATEST HEARD ▷   NEW FOR 1998 †

FREQUENCY   COUNTRY, STATION, LOCATION

TARGET • NETWORK • POWER (kW)

World Time

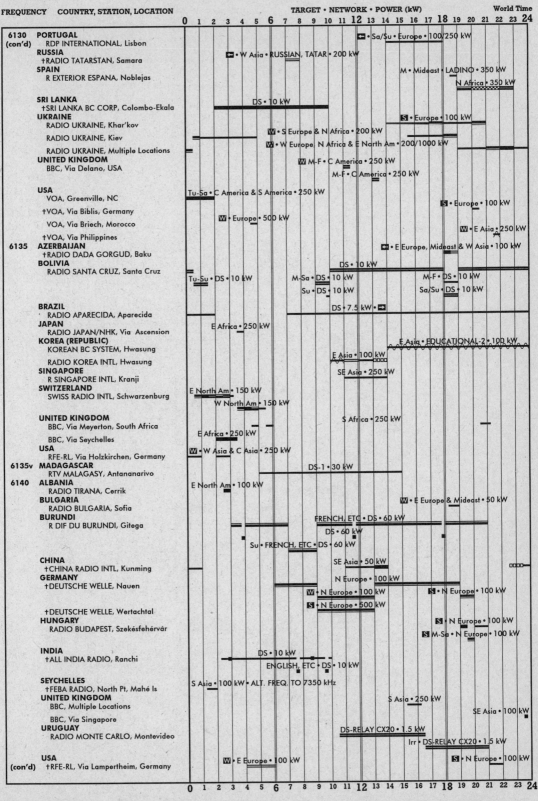

Frequency	Country, Station, Location	Target • Network • Power (kW)
6130 (con'd)	**PORTUGAL** RDP INTERNATIONAL, Lisbon	• Sa/Su • Europe • 100/250 kW
	RUSSIA †RADIO TATARSTAN, Samara	• W Asia • RUSSIAN, TATAR • 200 kW
	SPAIN R EXTERIOR ESPANA, Noblejas	M • Mideast • LADINO • 350 kW / N Africa • 350 kW
	SRI LANKA †SRI LANKA BC CORP, Colombo-Ekala	DS • 10 kW
	UKRAINE RADIO UKRAINE, Khar'kov	S • Europe • 100 kW
	RADIO UKRAINE, Kiev	W • S Europe & N Africa • 200 kW
	RADIO UKRAINE, Multiple Locations	W • W Europe, N Africa & E North Am • 200/1000 kW
	UNITED KINGDOM BBC, Via Delano, USA	W M-F • C America • 250 kW / M-F • C America • 250 kW
	USA VOA, Greenville, NC	Tu-Sa • C America & S America • 250 kW
	†VOA, Via Biblis, Germany	S • Europe • 100 kW
	VOA, Via Briech, Morocco	W • Europe • 500 kW
	†VOA, Via Philippines	W • E Asia • 250 kW
6135	**AZERBAIJAN** †RADIO DADA GORGUD, Baku	• E Europe, Mideast & W Asia • 100 kW
	BOLIVIA RADIO SANTA CRUZ, Santa Cruz	DS • 10 kW / Tu-Su • DS • 10 kW / M-Sa • DS • 10 kW / Su • DS • 10 kW / M-F • DS • 10 kW / Sa/Su • DS • 10 kW
	BRAZIL RADIO APARECIDA, Aparecida	DS • 7.5 kW •
	JAPAN RADIO JAPAN/NHK, Via Ascension	E Africa • 250 kW
	KOREA (REPUBLIC) KOREAN BC SYSTEM, Hwasung	E Asia • EDUCATIONAL-2 • 100 kW
	RADIO KOREA INTL, Hwasung	E Asia • 100 kW
	SINGAPORE R SINGAPORE INTL, Kranji	SE Asia • 250 kW
	SWITZERLAND SWISS RADIO INTL, Schwarzenburg	E North Am • 150 kW / W North Am • 150 kW
	UNITED KINGDOM BBC, Via Meyerton, South Africa	S Africa • 250 kW
	BBC, Via Seychelles	E Africa • 250 kW
	USA RFE-RL, Via Holzkirchen, Germany	W • W Asia & C Asia • 250 kW
6135v	**MADAGASCAR** RTV MALAGASY, Antananarivo	DS-1 • 30 kW
6140	**ALBANIA** RADIO TIRANA, Cerrik	E North Am • 100 kW
	BULGARIA RADIO BULGARIA, Sofia	W • E Europe & Mideast • 50 kW
	BURUNDI R DIF DU BURUNDI, Gitega	FRENCH, ETC • DS • 60 kW / DS • 60 kW / Su • FRENCH, ETC • DS • 60 kW
	CHINA †CHINA RADIO INTL, Kunming	SE Asia • 50 kW
	GERMANY †DEUTSCHE WELLE, Nauen	N Europe • 100 kW / W • N Europe • 100 kW / S • N Europe • 100 kW
	†DEUTSCHE WELLE, Wertachtal	S • N Europe • 500 kW
	HUNGARY RADIO BUDAPEST, Szekésfehérvár	S • N Europe • 100 kW / S M-Sa • N Europe • 100 kW
	INDIA †ALL INDIA RADIO, Ranchi	DS • 10 kW / ENGLISH, ETC • DS • 10 kW
	SEYCHELLES †FEBA RADIO, North Pt, Mahé Is	S Asia • 100 kW • ALT. FREQ. TO 7350 kHz
	UNITED KINGDOM BBC, Multiple Locations	S Asia • 250 kW
	BBC, Via Singapore	SE Asia • 100 kW
	URUGUAY RADIO MONTE CARLO, Montevideo	DS-RELAY CX20 • 1.5 kW / Irr • DS-RELAY CX20 • 1.5 kW
	USA (con'd) †RFE-RL, Via Lampertheim, Germany	W • E Europe • 100 kW / S • N Europe • 100 kW

ENGLISH ▬   ARABIC ▨   CHINESE ▢▢▢   FRENCH ▭   GERMAN ▭   RUSSIAN ═   SPANISH ▬   OTHER —

FREQUENCY	COUNTRY, STATION, LOCATION	TARGET • NETWORK • POWER (kW)	World Time

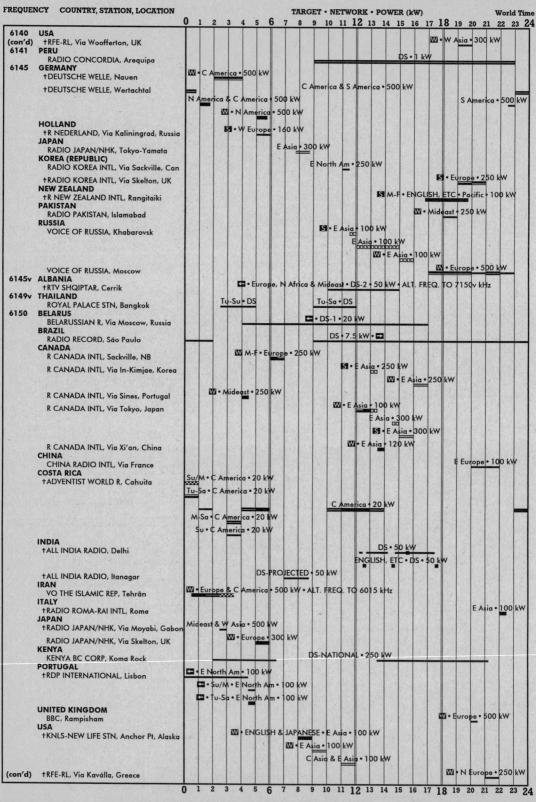

0 1 2 3 4 5 6 7 8 9 10 11 12 13 14 15 16 17 18 19 20 21 22 23 24

6140 **USA**
(con'd) †RFE-RL, Via Woofferton, UK — W • W Asia • 300 kW
6141 **PERU** — DS • 1 kW
RADIO CONCORDIA, Arequipa
6145 **GERMANY**
†DEUTSCHE WELLE, Nauen — W • C America • 500 kW
C America & S America • 500 kW
†DEUTSCHE WELLE, Wertachtal — N America & C America • 500 kW
S America • 500 kW
W • N America • 500 kW
HOLLAND
†R NEDERLAND, Via Kaliningrad, Russia — S • W Europe • 160 kW
JAPAN
RADIO JAPAN/NHK, Tokyo-Yamata — E Asia • 300 kW
KOREA (REPUBLIC)
RADIO KOREA INTL, Via Sackville, Can — E North Am • 250 kW
†RADIO KOREA INTL, Via Skelton, UK — S • Europe • 250 kW
NEW ZEALAND
†R NEW ZEALAND INTL, Rangitaiki — S • M-F • ENGLISH, ETC • Pacific • 100 kW
PAKISTAN
RADIO PAKISTAN, Islamabad — W • Mideast • 250 kW
RUSSIA
VOICE OF RUSSIA, Khabarovsk — S • E Asia • 100 kW
E Asia • 100 kW
W • E Asia • 100 kW
VOICE OF RUSSIA, Moscow — W • Europe • 500 kW
6145v **ALBANIA**
†RTV SHQIPTAR, Cerrik — • Europe, N Africa & Mideast • DS-2 • 50 kW • ALT. FREQ. TO 7150v kHz
6149v **THAILAND**
ROYAL PALACE STN, Bangkok — Tu-Su • DS   Tu-Sa • DS
6150 **BELARUS**
BELARUSSIAN R, Via Moscow, Russia — • DS-1 • 20 kW
BRAZIL
RADIO RECORD, São Paulo — DS • 7.5 kW • ▱
CANADA
R CANADA INTL, Sackville, NB — W • M-F • Europe • 250 kW
R CANADA INTL, Via In-Kimjae, Korea — S • E Asia • 250 kW
W • E Asia • 250 kW
R CANADA INTL, Via Sines, Portugal — W • Mideast • 250 kW
R CANADA INTL, Via Tokyo, Japan — W • E Asia • 100 kW
E Asia • 300 kW
S • E Asia • 300 kW
R CANADA INTL, Via Xi'an, China — W • E Asia • 120 kW
CHINA
CHINA RADIO INTL, Via France — E Europe • 100 kW
COSTA RICA
†ADVENTIST WORLD R, Cahuita — Su/M • C America • 20 kW
Tu-Sa • C America • 20 kW
C America • 20 kW
M-Sa • C America • 20 kW
Su • C America • 20 kW
INDIA
†ALL INDIA RADIO, Delhi — DS • 50 kW
ENGLISH, ETC • DS • 50 kW
†ALL INDIA RADIO, Itanagar — DS-PROJECTED • 50 kW
IRAN
VO THE ISLAMIC REP, Tehrān — W • Europe & C America • 500 kW • ALT. FREQ. TO 6015 kHz
ITALY
†RADIO ROMA-RAI INTL, Rome — E Asia • 100 kW
JAPAN
†RADIO JAPAN/NHK, Via Moyabi, Gabon — Mideast & W Asia • 500 kW
RADIO JAPAN/NHK, Via Skelton, UK — W • Europe • 300 kW
KENYA
KENYA BC CORP, Koma Rock — DS-NATIONAL • 250 kW
PORTUGAL
†RDP INTERNATIONAL, Lisbon — • E North Am • 100 kW
• Su/M • E North Am • 100 kW
• Tu-Sa • E North Am • 100 kW
UNITED KINGDOM
BBC, Rampisham — W • Europe • 500 kW
USA
†KNLS-NEW LIFE STN, Anchor Pt, Alaska — W • ENGLISH & JAPANESE • E Asia • 100 kW
W • E Asia • 100 kW
C Asia & E Asia • 100 kW
(con'd) †RFE-RL, Via Kaválla, Greece — W • N Europe • 250 kW

0 1 2 3 4 5 6 7 8 9 10 11 12 13 14 15 16 17 18 19 20 21 22 23 24

SEASONAL 🅂 OR 🅆   1-HR TIMESHIFT MIDYEAR ▱ OR ▱   JAMMING / OR ∧   EARLIEST HEARD ◁   LATEST HEARD ▷   NEW FOR 1998 †

FREQUENCY   COUNTRY, STATION, LOCATION

TARGET • NETWORK • POWER (kW)

World Time

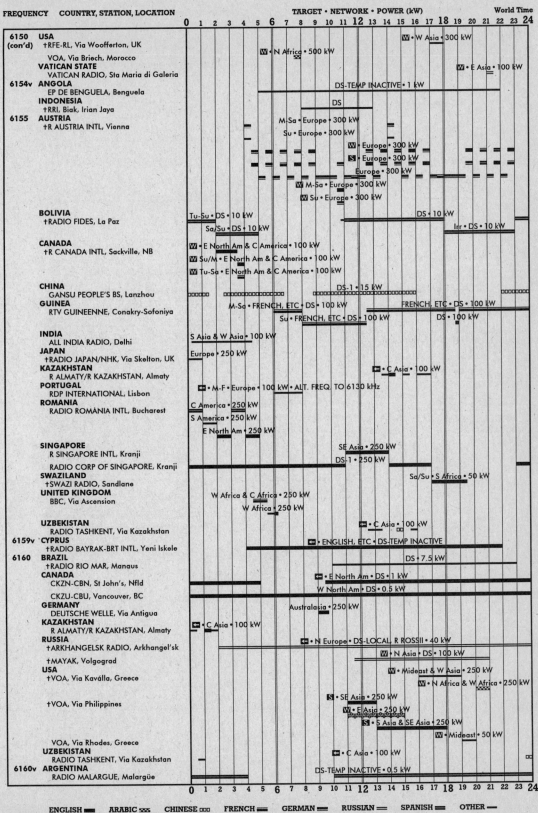

Frequency	Country, Station, Location
6150 (con'd)	**USA**
	†RFE-RL, Via Woofferton, UK
	VOA, Via Briech, Morocco
	VATICAN STATE
	VATICAN RADIO, Sta Maria di Galeria
6154v	**ANGOLA**
	EP DE BENGUELA, Benguela
	INDONESIA
	†RRI, Biak, Irian Jaya
6155	**AUSTRIA**
	†R AUSTRIA INTL, Vienna
	BOLIVIA
	†RADIO FIDES, La Paz
	CANADA
	†R CANADA INTL, Sackville, NB
	CHINA
	GANSU PEOPLE'S BS, Lanzhou
	GUINEA
	RTV GUINEENNE, Conakry-Sofoniya
	INDIA
	ALL INDIA RADIO, Delhi
	JAPAN
	†RADIO JAPAN/NHK, Via Skelton, UK
	KAZAKHSTAN
	R ALMATY/R KAZAKHSTAN, Almaty
	PORTUGAL
	RDP INTERNATIONAL, Lisbon
	ROMANIA
	RADIO ROMÂNIA INTL, Bucharest
	SINGAPORE
	R SINGAPORE INTL, Kranji
	RADIO CORP OF SINGAPORE, Kranji
	SWAZILAND
	†SWAZI RADIO, Sandlane
	UNITED KINGDOM
	BBC, Via Ascension
	UZBEKISTAN
	RADIO TASHKENT, Via Kazakhstan
6159v	**CYPRUS**
	†RADIO BAYRAK-BRT INTL, Yeni Iskele
6160	**BRAZIL**
	†RADIO RIO MAR, Manaus
	CANADA
	CKZN-CBN, St John's, Nfld
	CKZU-CBU, Vancouver, BC
	GERMANY
	DEUTSCHE WELLE, Via Antigua
	KAZAKHSTAN
	R ALMATY/R KAZAKHSTAN, Almaty
	RUSSIA
	†ARKHANGELSK RADIO, Arkhangel'sk
	†MAYAK, Volgograd
	USA
	†VOA, Via Kaválla, Greece
	†VOA, Via Philippines
	VOA, Via Rhodes, Greece
	UZBEKISTAN
	RADIO TASHKENT, Via Kazakhstan
6160v	**ARGENTINA**
	RADIO MALARGUE, Malargüe

ENGLISH ▬   ARABIC ▨   CHINESE ▫▫▫   FRENCH ▬   GERMAN ▬   RUSSIAN ═   SPANISH ▬   OTHER ▬

FREQUENCY   COUNTRY, STATION, LOCATION   TARGET • NETWORK • POWER (kW)   World Time

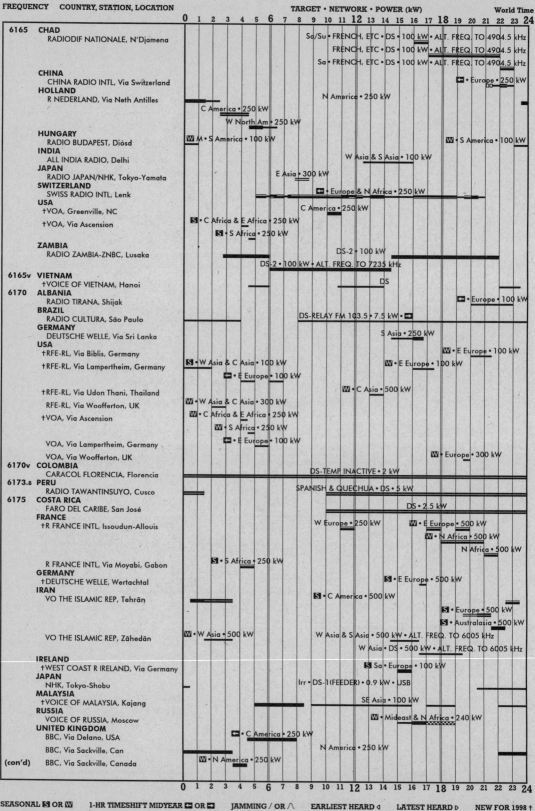

6165 CHAD
RADIODIF NATIONALE, N'Djamena
- Sa/Su • FRENCH, ETC • DS • 100 kW • ALT. FREQ. TO 4904.5 kHz
- FRENCH, ETC • DS • 100 kW • ALT. FREQ. TO 4904.5 kHz
- Sa • FRENCH, ETC • DS • 100 kW • ALT. FREQ. TO 4904.5 kHz

CHINA
CHINA RADIO INTL, Via Switzerland
- Europe • 250 kW

HOLLAND
R NEDERLAND, Via Neth Antilles
- N America • 250 kW
- C America • 250 kW
- W North Am • 250 kW

HUNGARY
RADIO BUDAPEST, Diósd
- W M • S America • 100 kW
- W • S America • 100 kW

INDIA
ALL INDIA RADIO, Delhi
- W Asia & S Asia • 100 kW

JAPAN
RADIO JAPAN/NHK, Tokyo-Yamata
- E Asia • 300 kW

SWITZERLAND
SWISS RADIO INTL, Lenk
- Europe & N Africa • 250 kW

USA
†VOA, Greenville, NC
- C America • 250 kW

†VOA, Via Ascension
- S • C Africa & E Africa • 250 kW
- S • S Africa • 250 kW

ZAMBIA
RADIO ZAMBIA-ZNBC, Lusaka
- DS-2 • 100 kW
- DS-2 • 100 kW • ALT. FREQ. TO 7235 kHz

6165v VIETNAM
†VOICE OF VIETNAM, Hanoi
- DS

6170 ALBANIA
RADIO TIRANA, Shijak
- Europe • 100 kW

BRAZIL
RADIO CULTURA, São Paulo
- DS-RELAY FM 103.5 • 7.5 kW •

GERMANY
DEUTSCHE WELLE, Via Sri Lanka
- S Asia • 250 kW

USA
†RFE-RL, Via Biblis, Germany
- W • E Europe • 100 kW

†RFE-RL, Via Lampertheim, Germany
- S • W Asia & C Asia • 100 kW
- W • E Europe • 100 kW
- E Europe • 100 kW

†RFE-RL, Via Udon Thani, Thailand
- W • C Asia • 500 kW

RFE-RL, Via Woofferton, UK
- W • W Asia & C Asia • 300 kW

†VOA, Via Ascension
- W • C Africa & E Africa • 250 kW
- W • S Africa • 250 kW
- E Europe • 100 kW

VOA, Via Lampertheim, Germany

VOA, Via Woofferton, UK
- W • Europe • 300 kW

6170v COLOMBIA
CARACOL FLORENCIA, Florencia
- DS-TEMP INACTIVE • 2 kW

6173.8 PERU
RADIO TAWANTINSUYO, Cusco
- SPANISH & QUECHUA • DS • 5 kW

6175 COSTA RICA
FARO DEL CARIBE, San José
- DS • 2.5 kW

FRANCE
†R FRANCE INTL, Issoudun-Allouis
- W Europe • 250 kW
- W • E Europe • 500 kW
- W • N Africa • 500 kW
- N Africa • 500 kW

R FRANCE INTL, Via Moyabi, Gabon
- S • S Africa • 250 kW

GERMANY
†DEUTSCHE WELLE, Wertachtal
- S • E Europe • 500 kW

IRAN
VO THE ISLAMIC REP, Tehrān
- S • C America • 500 kW
- S • Europe • 500 kW
- S • Australasia • 500 kW

VO THE ISLAMIC REP, Zāhedān
- W • W Asia • 500 kW
- W Asia & S Asia • 500 kW • ALT. FREQ. TO 6005 kHz
- W Asia • DS • 500 kW • ALT. FREQ. TO 6005 kHz

IRELAND
†WEST COAST R IRELAND, Via Germany
- S Sa • Europe • 100 kW

JAPAN
NHK, Tokyo-Shobu
- Irr • DS-1 (FEEDER) • 0.9 kW • USB

MALAYSIA
†VOICE OF MALAYSIA, Kajang
- SE Asia • 100 kW

RUSSIA
VOICE OF RUSSIA, Moscow
- W • Mideast & N Africa • 240 kW

UNITED KINGDOM
BBC, Via Delano, USA
- C America • 250 kW

BBC, Via Sackville, Can
- N America • 250 kW

(con'd) BBC, Via Sackville, Canada
- W • N America • 250 kW

FREQUENCY   COUNTRY, STATION, LOCATION

TARGET • NETWORK • POWER (kW)

World Time

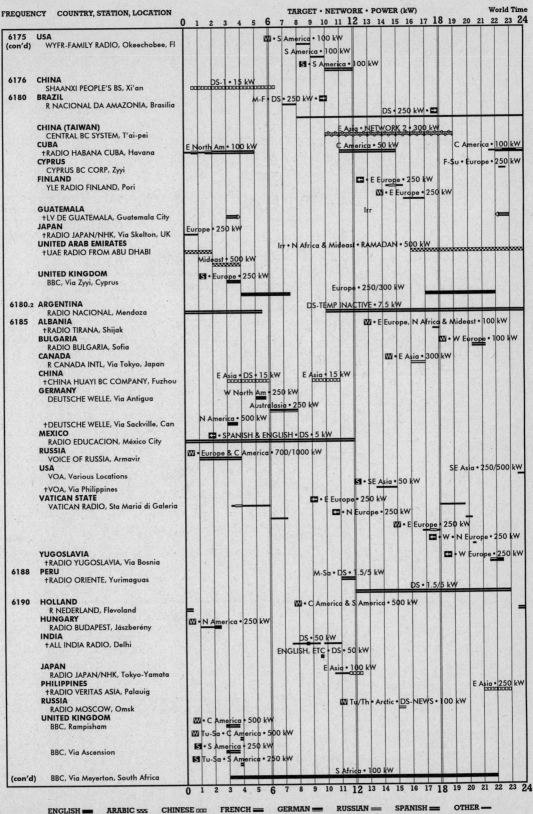

FREQUENCY	COUNTRY, STATION, LOCATION	TARGET • NETWORK • POWER (kW)
6175 (con'd)	**USA** WYFR-FAMILY RADIO, Okeechobee, Fl	W • S America • 100 kW / S America • 100 kW / S • S America • 100 kW
6176	**CHINA** SHAANXI PEOPLE'S BS, Xi'an	DS-1 • 15 kW
6180	**BRAZIL** R NACIONAL DA AMAZONIA, Brasilia	M-F • DS • 250 kW • / DS • 250 kW •
	CHINA (TAIWAN) CENTRAL BC SYSTEM, T'ai-pei	E Asia • NETWORK 2 • 300 kW
	CUBA †RADIO HABANA CUBA, Havana	E North Am • 100 kW / C America • 50 kW / C America • 100 kW
	CYPRUS CYPRUS BC CORP, Zyyi	F-Su • Europe • 250 kW
	FINLAND YLE RADIO FINLAND, Pori	• E Europe • 250 kW / W • E Europe • 250 kW
	GUATEMALA †LV DE GUATEMALA, Guatemala City	Irr
	JAPAN †RADIO JAPAN/NHK, Via Skelton, UK	Europe • 250 kW
	UNITED ARAB EMIRATES †UAE RADIO FROM ABU DHABI	Irr • N Africa & Mideast • RAMADAN • 500 kW / Mideast • 500 kW
	UNITED KINGDOM BBC, Via Zyyi, Cyprus	S • Europe • 250 kW / Europe • 250/300 kW
6180.2	**ARGENTINA** RADIO NACIONAL, Mendoza	DS-TEMP INACTIVE • 7.5 kW
6185	**ALBANIA** †RADIO TIRANA, Shijak	W • E Europe, N Africa & Mideast • 100 kW
	BULGARIA RADIO BULGARIA, Sofia	W • W Europe • 100 kW
	CANADA R CANADA INTL, Via Tokyo, Japan	W • E Asia • 300 kW
	CHINA †CHINA HUAYI BC COMPANY, Fuzhou	E Asia • DS • 15 kW / E Asia • 15 kW
	GERMANY DEUTSCHE WELLE, Via Antigua	W North Am • 250 kW / Australasia • 250 kW
	†DEUTSCHE WELLE, Via Sackville, Can	N America • 500 kW
	MEXICO RADIO EDUCACION, México City	• SPANISH & ENGLISH • DS • 5 kW
	RUSSIA VOICE OF RUSSIA, Armavir	W • Europe & C America • 700/1000 kW
	USA VOA, Various Locations	SE Asia • 250/500 kW
	†VOA, Via Philippines	S • SE Asia • 50 kW
	VATICAN STATE VATICAN RADIO, Sta Maria di Galeria	• E Europe • 250 kW / • N Europe • 250 kW / W • E Europe • 250 kW / • W • N Europe • 250 kW / • W Europe • 250 kW
	YUGOSLAVIA †RADIO YUGOSLAVIA, Via Bosnia	
6188	**PERU** †RADIO ORIENTE, Yurimaguas	M-Sa • DS • 1.5/5 kW / DS • 1.5/5 kW
6190	**HOLLAND** R NEDERLAND, Flevoland	W • C America & S America • 500 kW
	HUNGARY RADIO BUDAPEST, Jászberény	W • N America • 250 kW
	INDIA †ALL INDIA RADIO, Delhi	DS • 50 kW / ENGLISH, ETC • DS • 50 kW
	JAPAN RADIO JAPAN/NHK, Tokyo-Yamata	E Asia • 100 kW
	PHILIPPINES †RADIO VERITAS ASIA, Palauig	E Asia • 250 kW
	RUSSIA RADIO MOSCOW, Omsk	W Tu/Th • Arctic • DS-NEWS • 100 kW
	UNITED KINGDOM BBC, Rampisham	W • C America • 500 kW / W Tu-Sa • C America • 500 kW
	BBC, Via Ascension	S • S America • 250 kW / S Tu-Sa • S America • 250 kW
(con'd)	BBC, Via Meyerton, South Africa	S Africa • 100 kW

ENGLISH ▬   ARABIC ⠿   CHINESE ▫▫▫   FRENCH ▬▬   GERMAN ▬   RUSSIAN ═   SPANISH ▬▬   OTHER ──

FREQUENCY   COUNTRY, STATION, LOCATION

TARGET • NETWORK • POWER (kW)

World Time

0 1 2 3 4 5 6 7 8 9 10 11 12 13 14 15 16 17 18 19 20 21 22 23 24

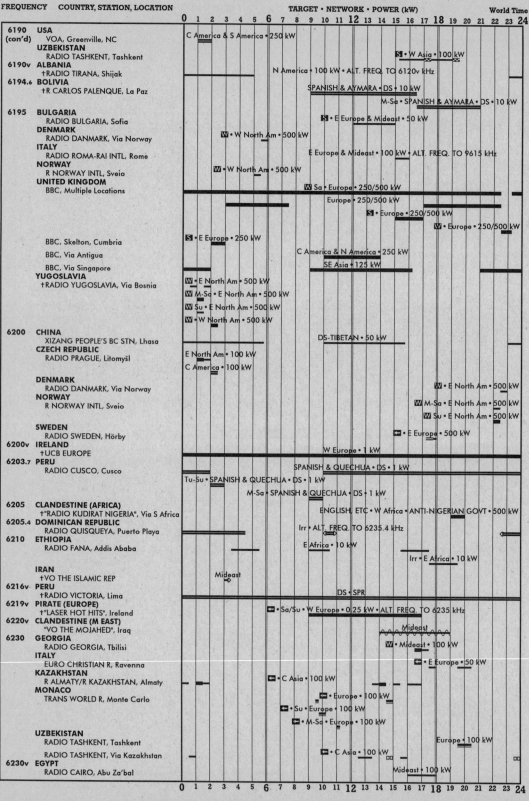

Frequency	Country, Station, Location	Target • Network • Power
6190 (con'd)	USA — VOA, Greenville, NC	C America & S America • 250 kW
	UZBEKISTAN — RADIO TASHKENT, Tashkent	S • W Asia • 100 kW
6190v	ALBANIA — †RADIO TIRANA, Shijak	N America • 100 kW • ALT. FREQ. TO 6120v kHz
6194.6	BOLIVIA — †R CARLOS PALENQUE, La Paz	SPANISH & AYMARA • DS • 10 kW / M-Sa • SPANISH & AYMARA • DS • 10 kW
6195	BULGARIA — RADIO BULGARIA, Sofia	S • E Europe & Mideast • 50 kW
	DENMARK — RADIO DANMARK, Via Norway	W • W North Am • 500 kW
	ITALY — RADIO ROMA-RAI INTL, Rome	E Europe & Mideast • 100 kW • ALT. FREQ. TO 9615 kHz
	NORWAY — R NORWAY INTL, Sveio	W • W North Am • 500 kW
	UNITED KINGDOM — BBC, Multiple Locations	W Sa • Europe • 250/500 kW / Europe • 250/500 kW / S • Europe • 250/500 kW / W • Europe • 250/500 kW
	BBC, Skelton, Cumbria	S • E Europe • 250 kW
	BBC, Via Antigua	C America & N America • 250 kW
	BBC, Via Singapore	SE Asia • 125 kW
	YUGOSLAVIA — †RADIO YUGOSLAVIA, Via Bosnia	W • E North Am • 500 kW / W M-Sa • E North Am • 500 kW / W Su • E North Am • 500 kW / W • W North Am • 500 kW
6200	CHINA — XIZANG PEOPLE'S BC STN, Lhasa	DS-TIBETAN • 50 kW
	CZECH REPUBLIC — RADIO PRAGUE, Litomyšl	E North Am • 100 kW / C America • 100 kW
	DENMARK — RADIO DANMARK, Via Norway	W • E North Am • 500 kW
	NORWAY — R NORWAY INTL, Sveio	W M-Sa • E North Am • 500 kW / W Su • E North Am • 500 kW
	SWEDEN — RADIO SWEDEN, Hörby	E Europe • 500 kW
6200v	IRELAND — †UCB EUROPE	W Europe • 1 kW
6203.7	PERU — RADIO CUSCO, Cusco	SPANISH & QUECHUA • DS • 1 kW / Tu-Su • SPANISH & QUECHUA • DS • 1 kW / M-Sa • SPANISH & QUECHUA • DS • 1 kW
6205	CLANDESTINE (AFRICA) — †"RADIO KUDIRAT NIGERIA", Via S Africa	ENGLISH, ETC • W Africa • ANTI-NIGERIAN GOVT • 500 kW
6205.4	DOMINICAN REPUBLIC — RADIO QUISQUEYA, Puerto Playa	Irr • ALT. FREQ. TO 6235.4 kHz
6210	ETHIOPIA — RADIO FANA, Addis Ababa	E Africa • 10 kW / Irr • E Africa • 10 kW
	IRAN — †VO THE ISLAMIC REP	Mideast
6216v	PERU — †RADIO VICTORIA, Lima	DS • SPR
6219v	PIRATE (EUROPE) — †"LASER HOT HITS", Ireland	Sa/Su • W Europe • 0.25 kW • ALT. FREQ. TO 6235 kHz
6220v	CLANDESTINE (M EAST) — "VO THE MOJAHED", Iraq	Mideast
6230	GEORGIA — RADIO GEORGIA, Tbilisi	W • Mideast • 100 kW
	ITALY — EURO CHRISTIAN R, Ravenna	E Europe • 50 kW
	KAZAKHSTAN — R ALMATY/R KAZAKHSTAN, Almaty	C Asia • 100 kW
	MONACO — TRANS WORLD R, Monte Carlo	Europe • 100 kW / Su • Europe • 100 kW / M-Sa • Europe • 100 kW
	UZBEKISTAN — RADIO TASHKENT, Tashkent	Europe • 100 kW
	RADIO TASHKENT, Via Kazakhstan	C Asia • 100 kW
6230v	EGYPT — RADIO CAIRO, Abu Za'bal	Mideast • 100 kW

0 1 2 3 4 5 6 7 8 9 10 11 12 13 14 15 16 17 18 19 20 21 22 23 24

FREQUENCY   COUNTRY, STATION, LOCATION

TARGET • NETWORK • POWER (kW)

World Time

0 1 2 3 4 5 6 7 8 9 10 11 12 13 14 15 16 17 18 19 20 21 22 23 24

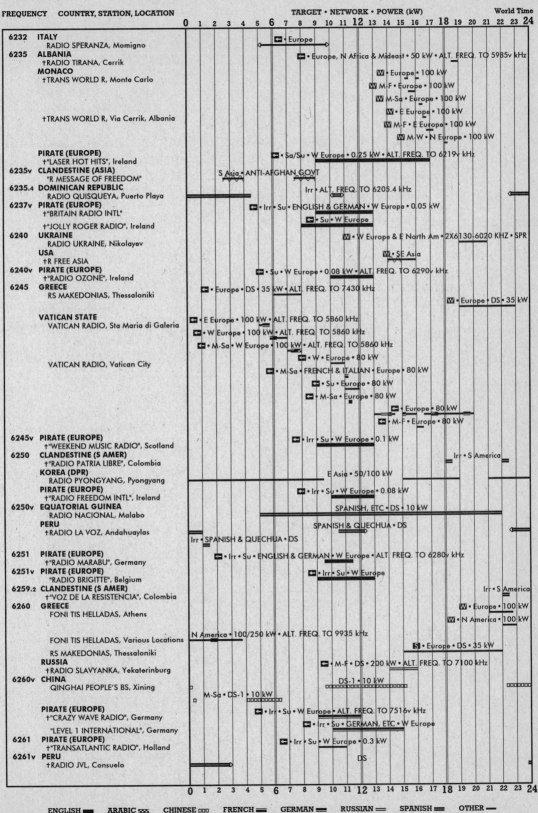

FREQUENCY	COUNTRY, STATION, LOCATION	TARGET • NETWORK • POWER (kW)
6232	**ITALY** RADIO SPERANZA, Momigno	• Europe
6235	**ALBANIA** †RADIO TIRANA, Cerrik	• Europe, N Africa & Mideast • 50 kW • ALT. FREQ. TO 5985v kHz
	MONACO †TRANS WORLD R, Monte Carlo	W • Europe • 100 kW
		W M-F • Europe • 100 kW
		W M-Sa • Europe • 100 kW
		W • E Europe • 100 kW
	†TRANS WORLD R, Via Cerrik, Albania	W M-F • E Europe • 100 kW
		W M-W • N Europe • 100 kW
	PIRATE (EUROPE) †"LASER HOT HITS", Ireland	• Sa/Su • W Europe • 0.25 kW • ALT. FREQ. TO 6219v kHz
6235v	**CLANDESTINE (ASIA)** "R MESSAGE OF FREEDOM"	S Asia • ANTI-AFGHAN GOVT
6235.4	**DOMINICAN REPUBLIC** RADIO QUISQUEYA, Puerto Playa	Irr • ALT. FREQ. TO 6205.4 kHz
6237v	**PIRATE (EUROPE)** †"BRITAIN RADIO INTL"	• Irr • Su • ENGLISH & GERMAN • W Europe • 0.05 kW
	†"JOLLY ROGER RADIO", Ireland	• Su • W Europe
6240	**UKRAINE** RADIO UKRAINE, Nikolayev	W • W Europe & E North Am • 2X6130-6020 KHZ • SPR
	USA †R FREE ASIA	W • SE Asia
6240v	**PIRATE (EUROPE)** †"RADIO OZONE", Ireland	• Su • W Europe • 0.08 kW • ALT. FREQ. TO 6290v kHz
6245	**GREECE** RS MAKEDONIAS, Thessaloniki	• Europe • DS • 35 kW • ALT. FREQ. TO 7430 kHz
		W • Europe • DS • 35 kW
	VATICAN STATE VATICAN RADIO, Sta Maria di Galeria	• E Europe • 100 kW • ALT. FREQ. TO 5860 kHz
		• W Europe • 100 kW • ALT. FREQ. TO 5860 kHz
		• M-Sa • W Europe • 100 kW • ALT. FREQ. TO 5860 kHz
	VATICAN RADIO, Vatican City	• W • Europe • 80 kW
		• M-Sa • FRENCH & ITALIAN • Europe • 80 kW
		• Su • Europe • 80 kW
		• M-Sa • Europe • 80 kW
		• Europe • 80 kW
		• M-F • Europe • 80 kW
6245v	**PIRATE (EUROPE)** †"WEEKEND MUSIC RADIO", Scotland	• Irr • Su • W Europe • 0.1 kW
6250	**CLANDESTINE (S AMER)** †"RADIO PATRIA LIBRE", Colombia	Irr • S America
	KOREA (DPR) RADIO PYONGYANG, Pyongyang	E Asia • 50/100 kW
	PIRATE (EUROPE) †"RADIO FREEDOM INTL", Ireland	• Irr • Su • W Europe • 0.08 kW
6250v	**EQUATORIAL GUINEA** RADIO NACIONAL, Malabo	SPANISH, ETC • DS • 10 kW
	PERU †RADIO LA VOZ, Andahuaylas	SPANISH & QUECHUA • DS
		Irr • SPANISH & QUECHUA • DS
6251	**PIRATE (EUROPE)** †"RADIO MARABU", Germany	• Irr • Su • ENGLISH & GERMAN • W Europe • ALT. FREQ. TO 6280v kHz
6251v	**PIRATE (EUROPE)** "RADIO BRIGITTE", Belgium	• Irr • Su • W Europe
6259.2	**CLANDESTINE (S AMER)** †"VOZ DE LA RESISTENCIA", Colombia	Irr • S America
6260	**GREECE** FONI TIS HELLADAS, Athens	W • Europe • 100 kW
		W • N America • 100 kW
	FONI TIS HELLADAS, Various Locations	N America • 100/250 kW • ALT. FREQ. TO 9935 kHz
	RS MAKEDONIAS, Thessaloniki	S • Europe • DS • 35 kW
	RUSSIA †RADIO SLAVYANKA, Yekaterinburg	• M-F • DS • 200 kW • ALT. FREQ. TO 7100 kHz
6260v	**CHINA** QINGHAI PEOPLE'S BS, Xining	DS-1 • 10 kW
		M-Sa • DS-1 • 10 kW
	PIRATE (EUROPE) †"CRAZY WAVE RADIO", Germany	• Irr • Su • W Europe • ALT. FREQ. TO 7516v kHz
	"LEVEL 1 INTERNATIONAL", Germany	• Irr • Su • GERMAN, ETC • W Europe
6261	**PIRATE (EUROPE)** †"TRANSATLANTIC RADIO", Holland	• Irr • Su • W Europe • 0.3 kW
6261v	**PERU** †RADIO JVL, Consuelo	DS

0 1 2 3 4 5 6 7 8 9 10 11 12 13 14 15 16 17 18 19 20 21 22 23 24

ENGLISH ▬   ARABIC ≋   CHINESE ▫▫▫   FRENCH ▬   GERMAN ▬   RUSSIAN ▬   SPANISH ▬   OTHER ▬

FREQUENCY   COUNTRY, STATION, LOCATION

TARGET • NETWORK • POWER (kW)

World Time

0 1 2 3 4 5 6 7 8 9 10 11 12 13 14 15 16 17 18 19 20 21 22 23 24

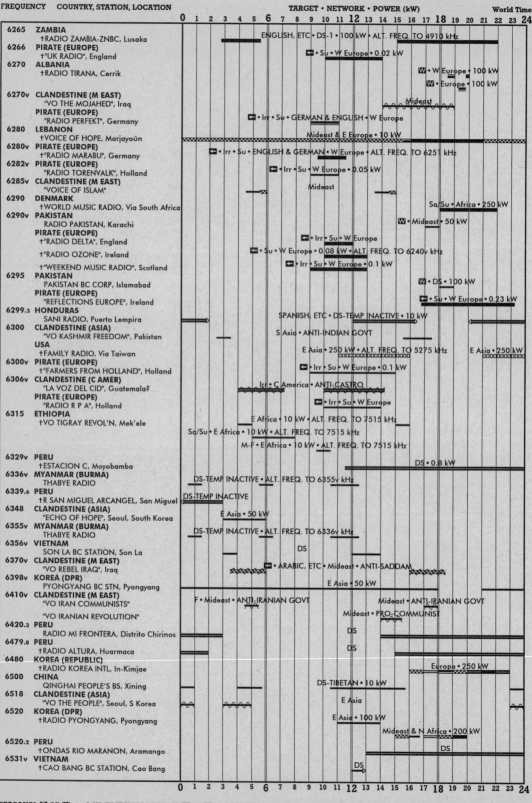

6265 ZAMBIA
†RADIO ZAMBIA-ZNBC, Lusaka — ENGLISH, ETC • DS-1 • 100 kW • ALT. FREQ. TO 4910 kHz

6266 PIRATE (EUROPE)
†"UK RADIO", England — Su • W Europe • 0.02 kW

6270 ALBANIA
†RADIO TIRANA, Cerrik — W • W Europe • 100 kW / W • Europe • 100 kW

6270v CLANDESTINE (M EAST)
"VO THE MOJAHED", Iraq — Mideast

PIRATE (EUROPE)
"RADIO PERFEKT", Germany — Irr • Su • GERMAN & ENGLISH • W Europe

6280 LEBANON
†VOICE OF HOPE, Marjayoûn — Mideast & E Europe • 10 kW

6280v PIRATE (EUROPE)
†"RADIO MARABU", Germany — Irr • Su • ENGLISH & GERMAN • W Europe • ALT. FREQ. TO 6251 kHz

6282v PIRATE (EUROPE)
"RADIO TORENVALK", Holland — Irr • Su • W Europe • 0.05 kW

6285v CLANDESTINE (M EAST)
"VOICE OF ISLAM" — Mideast

6290 DENMARK
†WORLD MUSIC RADIO, Via South Africa — Sa/Su • Africa • 250 kW

6290v PAKISTAN
RADIO PAKISTAN, Karachi — W • Mideast • 50 kW

PIRATE (EUROPE)
†"RADIO DELTA", England — Irr • Su • W Europe

†"RADIO OZONE", Ireland — Su • W Europe • 0.08 kW • ALT. FREQ. TO 6240v kHz

†"WEEKEND MUSIC RADIO", Scotland — Irr • Su • W Europe • 0.1 kW

6295 PAKISTAN
PAKISTAN BC CORP, Islamabad — W • DS • 100 kW

PIRATE (EUROPE)
"REFLECTIONS EUROPE", Ireland — Su • W Europe • 0.23 kW

6299.3 HONDURAS
SANI RADIO, Puerto Lempira — SPANISH, ETC • DS-TEMP INACTIVE • 10 kW

6300 CLANDESTINE (ASIA)
"VO KASHMIR FREEDOM", Pakistan — S Asia • ANTI-INDIAN GOVT

USA
†FAMILY RADIO, Via Taiwan — E Asia • 250 kW • ALT. FREQ. TO 5275 kHz / E Asia • 250 kW

6300v PIRATE (EUROPE)
†"FARMERS FROM HOLLAND", Holland — Irr • Su • W Europe • 0.1 kW

6306v CLANDESTINE (C AMER)
"LA VOZ DEL CID", Guatemala? — Irr • C America • ANTI-CASTRO

PIRATE (EUROPE)
"RADIO R P A", Holland — Irr • Su • W Europe

6315 ETHIOPIA
†VO TIGRAY REVOL'N, Mek'ele — E Africa • 10 kW • ALT. FREQ. TO 7515 kHz / Sa/Su • E Africa • 10 kW • ALT. FREQ. TO 7515 kHz / M-F • E Africa • 10 kW • ALT. FREQ. TO 7515 kHz

6329v PERU
†ESTACION C, Moyobamba — DS • 0.8 kW

6336v MYANMAR (BURMA)
THABYE RADIO — DS-TEMP INACTIVE • ALT. FREQ. TO 6355v kHz

6339.6 PERU
†R SAN MIGUEL ARCANGEL, San Miguel — DS-TEMP INACTIVE

6348 CLANDESTINE (ASIA)
"ECHO OF HOPE", Seoul, South Korea — E Asia • 50 kW

6355v MYANMAR (BURMA)
THABYE RADIO — DS-TEMP INACTIVE • ALT. FREQ. TO 6336v kHz

6356v VIETNAM
SON LA BC STATION, Son La — DS

6370v CLANDESTINE (M EAST)
"VO REBEL IRAQ", Iraq — ARABIC, ETC • Mideast • ANTI-SADDAM

6398v KOREA (DPR)
PYONGYANG BC STN, Pyongyang — E Asia • 50 kW

6410v CLANDESTINE (M EAST)
"VO IRAN COMMUNISTS" — F • Mideast • ANTI-IRANIAN GOVT / Mideast • ANTI-IRANIAN GOVT

"VO IRANIAN REVOLUTION" — Mideast • PRO-COMMUNIST

6420.3 PERU
RADIO MI FRONTERA, Distrito Chirinos — DS

6479.8 PERU
†RADIO ALTURA, Huarmaca — DS

6480 KOREA (REPUBLIC)
†RADIO KOREA INTL, In-Kimjae — Europe • 250 kW

6500 CHINA
QINGHAI PEOPLE'S BS, Xining — DS-TIBETAN • 10 kW

6518 CLANDESTINE (ASIA)
"VO THE PEOPLE", Seoul, S Korea — E Asia

6520 KOREA (DPR)
†RADIO PYONGYANG, Pyongyang — E Asia • 100 kW / Mideast & N Africa • 200 kW

6520.2 PERU
†ONDAS RIO MARANON, Aramango — DS

6531v VIETNAM
†CAO BANG BC STATION, Cao Bang — DS

0 1 2 3 4 5 6 7 8 9 10 11 12 13 14 15 16 17 18 19 20 21 22 23 24

SEASONAL 🅂 OR 🅆   1-HR TIMESHIFT MIDYEAR ⮂ OR ⮊   JAMMING / OR ∧   EARLIEST HEARD ◁   LATEST HEARD ▷   NEW FOR 1998 †

FREQUENCY   COUNTRY, STATION, LOCATION   TARGET • NETWORK • POWER (kW)   World Time

Frequency	Country, Station, Location	Target • Network • Power
6535.8	PERU	DS • 0.8 kW
	†R DIF HUANCABAMBA, Huancabamba	Irr • DS • 0.8 kW
6544v	SOMALIA	Su-Th • DS • USB
	†HOLY KORAN RADIO, Mogadishu	DS • USB
6545v	VIETNAM	DS
	†YEN BAI BC STATION, Yen Bai	
6549.5	LEBANON	DS-PHALANGE • 8 kW
	VOICE OF LEBANON, Beirūt-Ashrafiyah	
6550	CANADA	E Asia • FEEDER • 10/50 kW
	R CANADA INTL, Via Beijing, China	
	CHINA	W • E Asia • FEEDER • 10 kW
	†CHINA RADIO INTL, Beijing	
6557	BOLIVIA	Tu-Sa • DS M-F • DS
	†R ESTACION COLONIA, Yapacani	
6560v	IRAQ	DS
	REP OF IRAQ RADIO	
6570	MYANMAR (BURMA)	DS • 10 kW
	DEFENSE FORCES BC, Taunggyi	
6575	KOREA (DPR)	E Asia • 200 kW Europe • 200 kW
	†RADIO PYONGYANG, Pyongyang	
6580v	VIETNAM	DS
	CAO BANG BC STATION, Cao Bang	
6590	CHINA	E Asia • FEEDER • 10 kW
	†CHINA RADIO INTL, Beijing	
	RUSSIA	E Asia • FEEDER • 10 kW
	VOICE OF RUSSIA, Via Beijing, China	
6600	CLANDESTINE (ASIA)	E Asia
	"VO THE PEOPLE", Seoul, S Korea	
6670.2	PERU	DS-TEMP INACTIVE
	R SANTA MONICA, Santiago de Chuco	
6676.2	PERU	DS
	†RADIO HUAMACHUCO, Huamachuco	
6700v	VIETNAM	DS
	LAO CAI BC STATION, Lao Cai	
6726v	PERU	DS • 0.5 kW
	†RADIO SATELITE, Santa Cruz	
6732v	SOMALIA	DS-PRO UTHMAN ATO • USB
	†RADIO MOGADISHU, Mogadishu	ARABIC, ETC • DS-PRO UTHMAN ATO • USB
6750	CHINA	DS-1
	CENTRAL PEOPLE'S BS	
6754.7	PERU	Irr • DS
	RADIO LA MERCED, Tongod	
6790	CHINA	W • CHINESE, ETC • NETWORK 6 • 50 kW
	†CENTRAL PEOPLE'S BS, Beijing	S • CHINESE, ETC • NETWORK 6 • 50 kW • ALT. FREQ. TO 11000 kHz
6797v	PERU	DS • 1 kW
	†R ONDAS DEL RIO MAYO, N Cajamarca	
6805	RUSSIA	W • DS • 200 kW • USB
	RADIO ROSSII, Moscow-Taldom	
6822v	SOMALIA	PRO-ALI M MUHAMMAD • USB
	RADIO MOGADISHU, Mogadishu	
6840	CHINA	DS-1 • 50 kW
	CENTRAL PEOPLE'S BS	W-M • DS-1 • 50 kW
6870v	SOMALIA	PRO-AYDID • USB • ALT. FREQ. TO 6890v kHz
	†RADIO MOGADISHU, Mogadishu	Su-Th • PRO-AYDID • USB • ALT. FREQ. TO 6890v kHz
6890	CHINA	W • DS-2 • 10/50 kW
	CENTRAL PEOPLE'S BS, Beijing	W Th/Sa-Tu • DS-2 • 10/50 kW DS-2 • 10/50 kW
6890v	SOMALIA	PRO-AYDID • USB • ALT. FREQ. TO 6870v kHz
	†RADIO MOGADISHU, Mogadishu	Su-Th • PRO-AYDID • USB • ALT. FREQ. TO 6870v kHz
6895.3	PERU	DS • 0.25 kW
	†R SAN MIGUEL, El Faique	
6900	TURKEY	DS • 5 kW
	METEOROLOJI SESI RADYOSU, Ankara	
6920	CHINA	W • WAS/SAS
	†CHINA RADIO INTL	W
	†CHINA RADIO INTL, Xi'an	W • S Africa • 120 kW
6925.6	PIRATE (S AMERICA)	Irr • SPANISH & ENGLISH • S America
	†"RADIO COCHIGUAZ"	
6933	CHINA	Europe • 120 kW
	CHINA RADIO INTL, Beijing	
6937v	CHINA	DS-MINORITIES • 50 kW
	†YUNNAN PEOPLE'S BS, Kunming	

World Time scale: 0 1 2 3 4 5 6 7 8 9 10 11 12 13 14 15 16 17 18 19 20 21 22 23 24

ENGLISH ▄▄   ARABIC ≈≈≈   CHINESE □□□   FRENCH ▬▬   GERMAN ▬▬   RUSSIAN ══   SPANISH ▬▬   OTHER —

FREQUENCY   COUNTRY, STATION, LOCATION

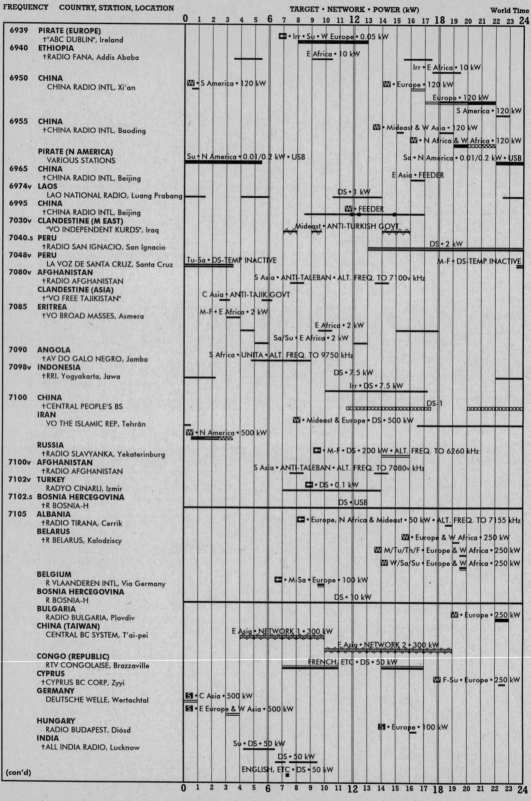

Frequency	Country, Station, Location	Details
6939	PIRATE (EUROPE) †"ABC DUBLIN", Ireland	Irr • Su • W Europe • 0.05 kW
6940	ETHIOPIA †RADIO FANA, Addis Ababa	E Africa • 10 kW / Irr • E Africa • 10 kW
6950	CHINA CHINA RADIO INTL, Xi'an	Ⓦ • S America • 120 kW / Ⓦ • Europe • 120 kW / Europe • 120 kW / S America • 120 kW
6955	CHINA †CHINA RADIO INTL, Baoding	Ⓦ • Mideast & W Asia • 120 kW / Ⓦ • N Africa & W Africa • 120 kW
	PIRATE (N AMERICA) VARIOUS STATIONS	Su • N America • 0.01/0.2 kW • USB / Sa • N America • 0.01/0.2 kW • USB
6965	CHINA †CHINA RADIO INTL, Beijing	E Asia • FEEDER
6974v	LAOS LAO NATIONAL RADIO, Luang Prabang	DS • 1 kW
6995	CHINA †CHINA RADIO INTL, Beijing	Ⓦ • FEEDER
7030v	CLANDESTINE (M EAST) "VO INDEPENDENT KURDS", Iraq	Mideast • ANTI-TURKISH GOVT
7040.5	PERU †RADIO SAN IGNACIO, San Ignacio	DS • 2 kW
7048v	PERU LA VOZ DE SANTA CRUZ, Santa Cruz	Tu-Sa • DS-TEMP INACTIVE / M-F • DS-TEMP INACTIVE
7080v	AFGHANISTAN †RADIO AFGHANISTAN	S Asia • ANTI-TALEBAN • ALT. FREQ. TO 7100v kHz
	CLANDESTINE (ASIA) †"VO FREE TAJIKISTAN"	C Asia • ANTI-TAJIK GOVT
7085	ERITREA †VO BROAD MASSES, Asmera	M-F • E Africa • 2 kW / E Africa • 2 kW / Sa/Su • E Africa • 2 kW
7090	ANGOLA †AV DO GALO NEGRO, Jamba	S Africa • UNITA • ALT. FREQ. TO 9750 kHz
7098v	INDONESIA †RRI, Yogyakarta, Jawa	DS • 7.5 kW / Irr • DS • 7.5 kW
7100	CHINA †CENTRAL PEOPLE'S BS	DS-1
	IRAN VO THE ISLAMIC REP, Tehrān	Ⓦ • Mideast & Europe • DS • 500 kW / Ⓦ • N America • 500 kW
	RUSSIA †RADIO SLAVYANKA, Yekaterinburg	⬅ • M-F • DS • 200 kW • ALT. FREQ. TO 6260 kHz
7100v	AFGHANISTAN †RADIO AFGHANISTAN	S Asia • ANTI-TALEBAN • ALT. FREQ. TO 7080v kHz
7102v	TURKEY RADYO CINARLI, Izmir	⬅ • DS • 0.1 kW
7102.5	BOSNIA HERCEGOVINA †R BOSNIA-H	DS • USB
7105	ALBANIA †RADIO TIRANA, Cerrik	⬅ • Europe, N Africa & Mideast • 50 kW • ALT. FREQ. TO 7155 kHz
	BELARUS †R BELARUS, Kalodziscy	Ⓦ • Europe & W Africa • 250 kW / Ⓦ M/Tu/Th/F • Europe & W Africa • 250 kW / Ⓦ W/Sa/Su • Europe & W Africa • 250 kW
	BELGIUM R VLAANDEREN INTL, Via Germany	⬅ • M-Sa • Europe • 100 kW
	BOSNIA HERCEGOVINA R BOSNIA-H	DS • 10 kW
	BULGARIA RADIO BULGARIA, Plovdiv	Ⓦ • Europe • 250 kW
	CHINA (TAIWAN) CENTRAL BC SYSTEM, T'ai-pei	E Asia • NETWORK 1 • 300 kW / E Asia • NETWORK 2 • 300 kW
	CONGO (REPUBLIC) RTV CONGOLAISE, Brazzaville	FRENCH, ETC • DS • 50 kW
	CYPRUS †CYPRUS BC CORP, Zyyi	Ⓦ F-Su • Europe • 250 kW
	GERMANY DEUTSCHE WELLE, Wertachtal	⑤ • C Asia • 500 kW / ⑤ • E Europe & W Asia • 500 kW
	HUNGARY RADIO BUDAPEST, Diósd	⑤ • Europe • 100 kW
	INDIA †ALL INDIA RADIO, Lucknow	Su • DS • 50 kW / DS • 50 kW / ENGLISH, ETC • DS • 50 kW

(con'd)

FREQUENCY   COUNTRY, STATION, LOCATION

TARGET • NETWORK • POWER (kW)

World Time

0 1 2 3 4 5 6 7 8 9 10 11 12 13 14 15 16 17 18 19 20 21 22 23 24

FREQUENCY	COUNTRY, STATION, LOCATION	TARGET • NETWORK • POWER (kW)
7105 (con'd)	ROMANIA RADIO ROMANIA INTL, Bucharest	W • Europe • 250 kW ; W • FRENCH & GERMAN • Europe • 250 kW ; W • Mideast • 250 kW ; Europe • 250 kW ; E Europe • 250 kW ; S • Europe • 120 kW ; Australasia • 250 kW
	RUSSIA RADIO ROSSII, Moscow	S • Arctic • DS • 100 kW
	VOICE OF RUSSIA, Via Belarus	W • W Europe & W Africa • 250 kW
	UNITED KINGDOM BBC, Rampisham	W • E Europe • 500 kW ; W • Mideast & W Asia • 500 kW ; W • Sa/Su • E Europe • 500 kW ; W • M-F • E Europe • 500 kW
	BBC, Via Ascension	W Africa & C Africa • 250 kW ; W Africa • 250 kW
	BBC, Via Maşīrah, Oman	W • S Asia • 100 kW ; W • W Asia • 100 kW
	BBC, Via Singapore	S Asia • 100 kW
	BBC, Via Zyyi, Cyprus	W • W Asia & S Asia • 250 kW ; W • E Europe • 250 kW
	USA †RFE-RL, Via Biblis, Germany	W • E Europe • 100 kW
	†RFE-RL, Via Kaválla, Greece	S • W Asia • 250 kW
	VOA, Via Ascension	S Africa • 250 kW
	†VOA, Via Rhodes, Greece	S • Mideast • 50 kW
	UZBEKISTAN RADIO TASHKENT, Tashkent	W • W Asia • 20 kW
	UZBEK RADIO, Tashkent	W • DS-2 • 20 kW
7108v	CHINA NEI MONGGOL PBS, Hohhot	DS • 15 kW
7110	ALBANIA †RADIO TIRANA, Cerrik	S • Europe, N Africa & Mideast • 100 kW
	†RADIO TIRANA, Shijak	S • W Europe • 100 kW
	CHINA CHINA RADIO INTL, Hohhot	E Asia • 50 kW ; W • Australasia • 120 kW
	†CHINA RADIO INTL, Kunming	
	†CHINA RADIO INTL	S
	CHINA RADIO INTL, Xi'an	Europe & N Africa • 120 kW
	ETHIOPIA †RADIO ETHIOPIA, Gedja	DS • 100 kW ; Su • DS • 100 kW ; Sa/Su • DS • 100 kW ; M-F • DS • 100 kW
	FRANCE R FRANCE INTL, Via Xi'an, China	S Asia • 150 kW
	GERMANY †ADVENTIST WORLD RADIO, Jülich	• E Europe • 100 kW
	INDIA †ALL INDIA RADIO, Delhi	ENGLISH, ETC • DS • 50 kW ; DS • 50 kW
	ITALY RADIO ROMA-RAI INTL, Rome	S • E Europe • 100 kW ; E Europe • 100 kW • ALT. FREQ. TO 7130 kHz ; Europe • 100 kW ; W • E Europe • 100 kW ; Mideast • 100 kW ; E Europe • 100 kW
	JAPAN †RADIO JAPAN/NHK, Tokyo-Yamata	Europe • 300 kW
	PAKISTAN PAKISTAN BC CORP, Peshawar	DS • 10 kW ; S • DS • 10 kW
	RUSSIA †RADIO ROSSII, Yekaterinburg	W • N Asia • DS • 240 kW
	TURKEY VOICE OF TURKEY, Ankara-úakirlar	S • E Europe • 500 kW ; S • S Europe • 500 kW ; S • Europe • 500 kW
	VOICE OF TURKEY, Ankara-Emirler	W • S Europe • 500 kW ; • E Europe • 500 kW

(con'd)

0 1 2 3 4 5 6 7 8 9 10 11 12 13 14 15 16 17 18 19 20 21 22 23 24

ENGLISH ▬   ARABIC ≋   CHINESE ▫▫▫   FRENCH ▬   GERMAN ▬   RUSSIAN ▬   SPANISH ▬   OTHER ▬

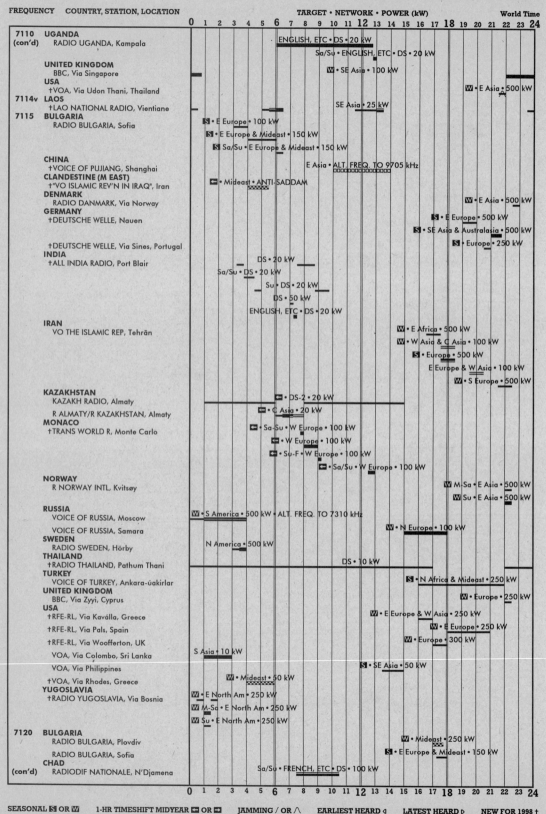

FREQUENCY   COUNTRY, STATION, LOCATION

TARGET • NETWORK • POWER (kW)

World Time

0 1 2 3 4 5 6 7 8 9 10 11 12 13 14 15 16 17 18 19 20 21 22 23 24

7110 UGANDA
(con'd) RADIO UGANDA, Kampala — ENGLISH, ETC • DS • 20 kW
Sa/Su • ENGLISH, ETC • DS • 20 kW

UNITED KINGDOM
  BBC, Via Singapore — W • SE Asia • 100 kW
USA
  †VOA, Via Udon Thani, Thailand — W • E Asia • 500 kW
7114v LAOS
  †LAO NATIONAL RADIO, Vientiane — SE Asia • 25 kW
7115 BULGARIA
  RADIO BULGARIA, Sofia — S • E Europe • 100 kW
S • E Europe & Mideast • 150 kW
S • Sa/Su • E Europe & Mideast • 150 kW

CHINA
  †VOICE OF PUJIANG, Shanghai — E Asia • ALT. FREQ. TO 9705 kHz
CLANDESTINE (M EAST)
  †"VO ISLAMIC REV'N IN IRAQ", Iran — • Mideast • ANTI-SADDAM
DENMARK
  RADIO DANMARK, Via Norway — W • E Asia • 500 kW
GERMANY
  †DEUTSCHE WELLE, Nauen — S • E Europe • 500 kW
S • SE Asia & Australasia • 500 kW
  †DEUTSCHE WELLE, Via Sines, Portugal — S • Europe • 250 kW
INDIA
  †ALL INDIA RADIO, Port Blair — DS • 20 kW
Sa/Su • DS • 20 kW
Su • DS • 20 kW
DS • 50 kW
ENGLISH, ETC • DS • 20 kW

IRAN
  VO THE ISLAMIC REP, Tehrãn — W • E Africa • 500 kW
W • W Asia & C Asia • 100 kW
S • Europe • 500 kW
E Europe & W Asia • 100 kW
W • S Europe • 500 kW

KAZAKHSTAN
  KAZAKH RADIO, Almaty — • DS-2 • 20 kW
  R ALMATY/R KAZAKHSTAN, Almaty — • C Asia • 20 kW
MONACO
  †TRANS WORLD R, Monte Carlo — • Sa-Su • W Europe • 100 kW
• W Europe • 100 kW
• Su-F • W Europe • 100 kW
• Sa/Su • W Europe • 100 kW

NORWAY
  R NORWAY INTL, Kvitsøy — W • M-Sa • E Asia • 500 kW
W • Su • E Asia • 500 kW

RUSSIA
  VOICE OF RUSSIA, Moscow — W • S America • 500 kW • ALT. FREQ. TO 7310 kHz
  VOICE OF RUSSIA, Samara — W • N Europe • 100 kW
SWEDEN
  RADIO SWEDEN, Hörby — N America • 500 kW
THAILAND
  †RADIO THAILAND, Pathum Thani — DS • 10 kW
TURKEY
  VOICE OF TURKEY, Ankara-úakirlar — S • N Africa & Mideast • 250 kW
UNITED KINGDOM
  BBC, Via Zyyi, Cyprus — W • Europe • 250 kW
USA
  †RFE-RL, Via Kaválla, Greece — W • E Europe & W Asia • 250 kW
  †RFE-RL, Via Pals, Spain — W • E Europe • 250 kW
  †RFE-RL, Via Woofferton, UK — W • Europe • 300 kW
  VOA, Via Colombo, Sri Lanka — S Asia • 10 kW
  VOA, Via Philippines — S • SE Asia • 50 kW
  †VOA, Via Rhodes, Greece — W • Mideast • 50 kW
YUGOSLAVIA
  †RADIO YUGOSLAVIA, Via Bosnia — W • E North Am • 250 kW
W • M-Sa • E North Am • 250 kW
W • Su • E North Am • 250 kW

7120 BULGARIA
  RADIO BULGARIA, Plovdiv — W • Mideast • 250 kW
  RADIO BULGARIA, Sofia — S • E Europe & Mideast • 150 kW
CHAD
(con'd) RADIODIF NATIONALE, N'Djamena — Sa/Su • FRENCH, ETC • DS • 100 kW

0 1 2 3 4 5 6 7 8 9 10 11 12 13 14 15 16 17 18 19 20 21 22 23 24

FREQUENCY   COUNTRY, STATION, LOCATION

TARGET • NETWORK • POWER (kW)

World Time

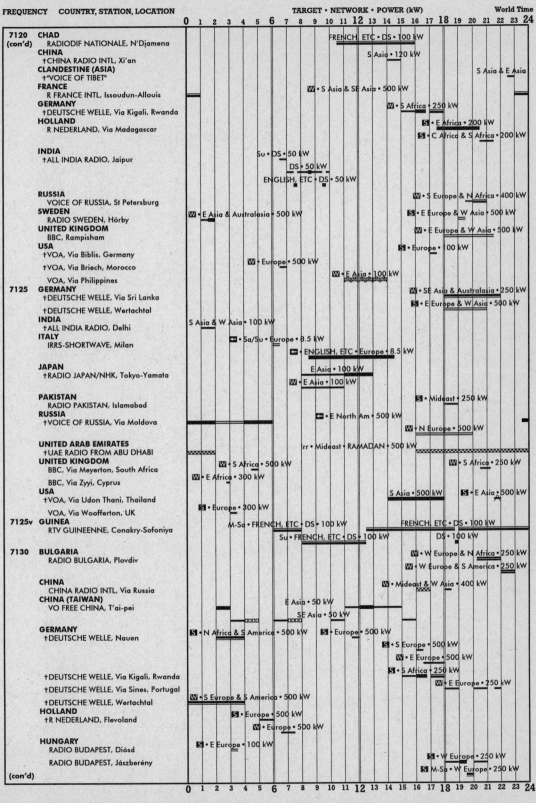

Frequency	Country, Station, Location	Details
7120 (con'd)	**CHAD** RADIODIF NATIONALE, N'Djamena	FRENCH, ETC • DS • 100 kW
	CHINA †CHINA RADIO INTL, Xi'an	S Asia • 120 kW
	CLANDESTINE (ASIA) †"VOICE OF TIBET"	S Asia & E Asia
	FRANCE R FRANCE INTL, Issoudun-Allouis	W • S Asia & SE Asia • 500 kW
	GERMANY †DEUTSCHE WELLE, Via Kigali, Rwanda	W • S Africa • 250 kW
	HOLLAND R NEDERLAND, Via Madagascar	S • E Africa • 200 kW / S • C Africa & S Africa • 200 kW
	INDIA †ALL INDIA RADIO, Jaipur	Su • DS • 50 kW / DS • 50 kW / ENGLISH, ETC • DS • 50 kW
	RUSSIA VOICE OF RUSSIA, St Petersburg	W • S Europe & N Africa • 400 kW
	SWEDEN RADIO SWEDEN, Hörby	W • E Asia & Australasia • 500 kW / S • E Europe & W Asia • 500 kW
	UNITED KINGDOM BBC, Rampisham	W • E Europe & W Asia • 500 kW
	USA †VOA, Via Biblis, Germany	S • Europe • 100 kW
	†VOA, Via Briech, Morocco	W • Europe • 500 kW
	VOA, Via Philippines	W • E Asia • 100 kW
7125	**GERMANY** †DEUTSCHE WELLE, Via Sri Lanka	W • SE Asia & Australasia • 250 kW
	†DEUTSCHE WELLE, Wertachtal	S • E Europe & W Asia • 500 kW
	INDIA †ALL INDIA RADIO, Delhi	S Asia & W Asia • 100 kW
	ITALY IRRS-SHORTWAVE, Milan	• Sa/Su • Europe • 8.5 kW / ENGLISH, ETC • Europe • 8.5 kW
	JAPAN †RADIO JAPAN/NHK, Tokyo-Yamata	E Asia • 100 kW / W • E Asia • 100 kW
	PAKISTAN RADIO PAKISTAN, Islamabad	S • Mideast • 250 kW
	RUSSIA †VOICE OF RUSSIA, Via Moldova	• E North Am • 500 kW / W • N Europe • 500 kW
	UNITED ARAB EMIRATES †UAE RADIO FROM ABU DHABI	Irr • Mideast • RAMADAN • 500 kW
	UNITED KINGDOM BBC, Via Meyerton, South Africa	W • S Africa • 500 kW / W • S Africa • 250 kW
	BBC, Via Zyyi, Cyprus	W • E Africa • 300 kW
	USA †VOA, Via Udon Thani, Thailand	S Asia • 500 kW / S • E Asia • 500 kW
	VOA, Via Woofferton, UK	S • Europe • 300 kW
7125v	**GUINEA** RTV GUINEENNE, Conakry-Sofoniya	M-Sa • FRENCH, ETC • DS • 100 kW / FRENCH, ETC • DS • 100 kW / Su • FRENCH, ETC • DS • 100 kW / DS • 100 kW
7130	**BULGARIA** RADIO BULGARIA, Plovdiv	W • W Europe & N Africa • 250 kW / W • W Europe & S America • 250 kW
	CHINA CHINA RADIO INTL, Via Russia	W • Mideast & W Asia • 400 kW
	CHINA (TAIWAN) VO FREE CHINA, T'ai-pei	E Asia • 50 kW / SE Asia • 50 kW
	GERMANY †DEUTSCHE WELLE, Nauen	S • N Africa & S America • 500 kW / S • Europe • 500 kW / S • S Europe • 500 kW / W • E Europe • 500 kW
	†DEUTSCHE WELLE, Via Kigali, Rwanda	S • S Africa • 250 kW
	†DEUTSCHE WELLE, Via Sines, Portugal	W • E Europe • 250 kW
	†DEUTSCHE WELLE, Wertachtal	W • S Europe & S America • 500 kW
	HOLLAND †R NEDERLAND, Flevoland	S • Europe • 500 kW / W • Europe • 500 kW
	HUNGARY RADIO BUDAPEST, Diósd	S • E Europe • 100 kW
	RADIO BUDAPEST, Jászberény	S • W Europe • 250 kW / S M-Sa • W Europe • 250 kW
(con'd)		

ENGLISH ▬   ARABIC ▨   CHINESE ▫▫▫   FRENCH ▭▭   GERMAN ▬▬   RUSSIAN ══   SPANISH ▭▭   OTHER ▬

FREQUENCY	COUNTRY, STATION, LOCATION	TARGET • NETWORK • POWER (kW)	World Time

World Time scale: 0 1 2 3 4 5 6 7 8 9 10 11 12 13 14 15 16 17 18 19 20 21 22 23 24

7130 INDIA
(con'd) †ALL INDIA RADIO, Shillong — DS • 50 kW
— ENGLISH, ETC • DS • 50 kW

IRAN
VO THE ISLAMIC REP, Tehrān — **S** • Mideast & Europe • DS • 500 kW
— **S** • Mideast • 500 kW

ITALY
RADIO ROMA-RAI INTL, Rome — E Europe • 100 kW • ALT. FREQ. TO 7110 kHz
KAZAKHSTAN
†KAZAKH RADIO, Via Ukraine — **W** • S Europe & N Africa • DS-2 • 100 kW
MALAWI
†MALAWI BC CORP, Limbe — ENGLISH, ETC • DS • 100 kW
RUSSIA
VOICE OF RUSSIA, St Petersburg — **W** • Mideast & W Asia • 400 kW
— **⇨** • Mideast & W Asia • 400 kW

UNITED KINGDOM
BBC, Via Zyyi, Cyprus — **W** • E Europe & W Asia • 300 kW
USA
†VOA, Via Briech, Morocco — **W** • Europe • 500 kW

VOA, Via Philippines — **S** • SE Asia • 50 kW

†VOA, Via Udon Thani, Thailand — **W** • SE Asia • 500 kW

VOA, Via Woofferton, UK — Europe • 300 kW
YUGOSLAVIA
†RADIO YUGOSLAVIA, Via Bosnia — **W** • W North Am • 250 kW
7135 BULGARIA
RADIO BULGARIA, Sofia — **S** Su • E Europe & Mideast • 150 kW
FRANCE
†R FRANCE INTL, Issoudun-Allouis — **W** • E Europe • 500 kW
— **S** • E Europe • 500 kW
— E Europe • 500 kW

R FRANCE INTL, Multiple Locations — Africa • 100/250/500 kW
GERMANY
†DEUTSCHE WELLE, Wertachtal — **S** • E Europe & W Asia • 500 kW
ROMANIA
RADIO ROMANIA INTL, Bucharest — **W** • E Europe • 250 kW
— Europe • 120 kW
RUSSIA
R TIKHIY OKEAN, Komsomol'sk 'Amure — **W** • SE Asia • 1000 kW

VOICE OF RUSSIA, Irkutsk — **W** • E Asia • 250 kW
UKRAINE
RADIO UKRAINE, Kiev — **W** • W Asia • 100 kW
UNITED KINGDOM
BBC, Via Singapore — SE Asia • 100 kW
— **W** • S Asia • 100 kW
— **W** • SE Asia • 100 kW

USA
†VOA, Via Briech, Morocco — **S** • S Asia • 500 kW

VOA, Via Philippines — **S** • SE Asia • 250 kW

†VOA, Via São Tomé — W Africa & C Africa • 100 kW
7140 BELARUS
GRODNO RADIO, Grodno — **⇨** • DS-LOCAL, BELARUS-1 • 10 kW
FRANCE
R FRANCE INTL, Via Tokyo, Japan — **W** • E Asia • 300 kW
— E Asia • 300 kW

GERMANY
DEUTSCHE WELLE, Via N'sibirsk, Russia — **S** • SE Asia • 1000 kW
INDIA
ALL INDIA RADIO, Delhi — S Asia • 100 kW
— DS • 100 kW
— ENGLISH, ETC • DS • 100 kW

ALL INDIA RADIO, Hyderabad — DS • 50 kW
— Su • DS • 50 kW — Su • DS-A • 50 kW
— Sa/Su • DS-A • 50 kW

JAPAN
†RADIO JAPAN/NHK, Tokyo-Yamata — Australasia • 100 kW
KENYA
KENYA BC CORP, Nairobi — DS-NATIONAL • 100 kW
RUSSIA
VOICE OF RUSSIA, Moscow — **W** • Europe • 500 kW

VOICE OF RUSSIA, St Petersburg — **W** • S Europe • 400 kW

†YAKUT RADIO, Yakutsk — **⇨** • RUSSIAN, ETC • DS-LOCAL, R ROSSII • 50 kW
UNITED KINGDOM
BBC, Via Zyyi, Cyprus — Mideast & E Africa • 300 kW
USA
†VOA, Via Udon Thani, Thailand — **W** • E Asia • 500 kW
7140v ITALY
RADIO MARIA, Spoleto — DS • 1 kW

World Time scale (bottom): 0 1 2 3 4 5 6 7 8 9 10 11 12 13 14 15 16 17 18 19 20 21 22 23 24

FREQUENCY　　COUNTRY, STATION, LOCATION　　　　　　　TARGET • NETWORK • POWER (kW)　　　　　World Time

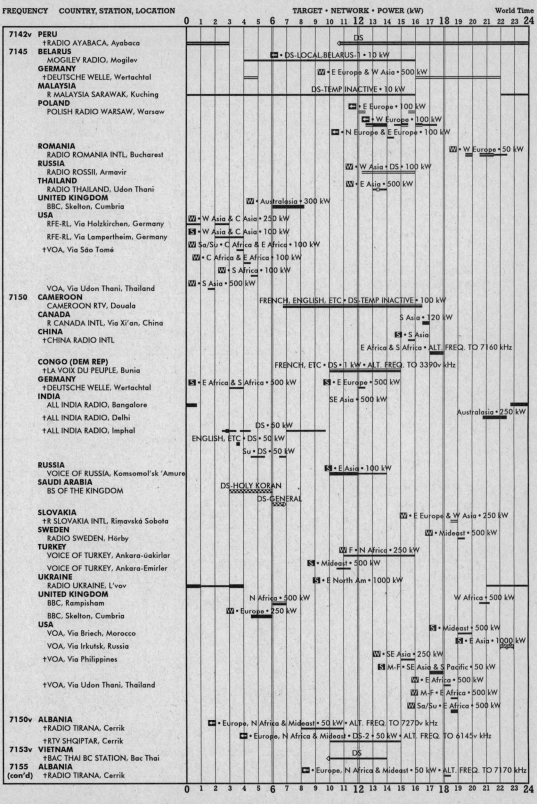

FREQUENCY	COUNTRY, STATION, LOCATION	TARGET • NETWORK • POWER (kW)
7142v	**PERU**	
	†RADIO AYABACA, Ayabaca	DS
7145	**BELARUS**	
	MOGILEV RADIO, Mogilev	🔲 • DS-LOCAL, BELARUS-1 • 10 kW
	GERMANY	
	†DEUTSCHE WELLE, Wertachtal	W • E Europe & W Asia • 500 kW
	MALAYSIA	
	R MALAYSIA SARAWAK, Kuching	DS-TEMP INACTIVE • 10 kW
	POLAND	
	POLISH RADIO WARSAW, Warsaw	🔲 • E Europe • 100 kW
		🔲 • W Europe • 100 kW
		🔲 • N Europe & E Europe • 100 kW
	ROMANIA	
	RADIO ROMANIA INTL, Bucharest	W • W Europe • 50 kW
	RUSSIA	
	RADIO ROSSII, Armavir	W • W Asia • DS • 100 kW
	THAILAND	
	RADIO THAILAND, Udon Thani	W • E Asia • 500 kW
	UNITED KINGDOM	
	BBC, Skelton, Cumbria	W • Australasia • 300 kW
	USA	
	RFE-RL, Via Holzkirchen, Germany	W • W Asia & C Asia • 250 kW
	RFE-RL, Via Lampertheim, Germany	S • W Asia & C Asia • 100 kW
	†VOA, Via São Tomé	W Sa/Su • C Africa & E Africa • 100 kW
		W • C Africa & E Africa • 100 kW
		W • S Africa • 100 kW
	VOA, Via Udon Thani, Thailand	W • S Asia • 500 kW
7150	**CAMEROON**	
	CAMEROON RTV, Douala	FRENCH, ENGLISH, ETC • DS-TEMP INACTIVE • 100 kW
	CANADA	
	R CANADA INTL, Via Xi'an, China	S Asia • 120 kW
	CHINA	
	†CHINA RADIO INTL	S • S Asia
		E Africa & S Africa • ALT. FREQ. TO 7160 kHz
	CONGO (DEM REP)	
	†LA VOIX DU PEUPLE, Bunia	FRENCH, ETC • DS • 1 kW • ALT. FREQ. TO 3390v kHz
	GERMANY	
	†DEUTSCHE WELLE, Wertachtal	S • E Africa & S Africa • 500 kW
		S • E Europe • 500 kW
	INDIA	
	ALL INDIA RADIO, Bangalore	SE Asia • 500 kW
	†ALL INDIA RADIO, Delhi	Australasia • 250 kW
	†ALL INDIA RADIO, Imphal	DS • 50 kW
		ENGLISH, ETC • DS • 50 kW
		Su • DS • 50 kW
	RUSSIA	
	VOICE OF RUSSIA, Komsomol'sk 'Amure	S • E Asia • 100 kW
	SAUDI ARABIA	
	BS OF THE KINGDOM	DS-HOLY KORAN
		DS-GENERAL
	SLOVAKIA	
	†R SLOVAKIA INTL, Rimavská Sobota	W • E Europe & W Asia • 250 kW
	SWEDEN	
	RADIO SWEDEN, Hörby	W • Mideast • 500 kW
	TURKEY	
	VOICE OF TURKEY, Ankara-úakirlar	W F • N Africa • 250 kW
	VOICE OF TURKEY, Ankara-Emirler	S • Mideast • 500 kW
	UKRAINE	
	RADIO UKRAINE, L'vov	S • E North Am • 1000 kW
	UNITED KINGDOM	
	BBC, Rampisham	N Africa • 500 kW
		W Africa • 500 kW
	BBC, Skelton, Cumbria	W • Europe • 250 kW
	USA	
	VOA, Via Briech, Morocco	S • Mideast • 500 kW
	VOA, Via Irkutsk, Russia	S • E Asia • 1000 kW
	†VOA, Via Philippines	W • SE Asia • 250 kW
		S M-F • SE Asia & S Pacific • 50 kW
	†VOA, Via Udon Thani, Thailand	W • E Africa • 500 kW
		W M-F • E Africa • 500 kW
		W Sa/Su • E Africa • 500 kW
7150v	**ALBANIA**	
	†RADIO TIRANA, Cerrik	🔲 • Europe, N Africa & Mideast • 50 kW • ALT. FREQ. TO 7270v kHz
	†RTV SHQIPTAR, Cerrik	🔲 • Europe, N Africa & Mideast • DS-2 • 50 kW • ALT. FREQ. TO 6145v kHz
7153v	**VIETNAM**	
	†BAC THAI BC STATION, Bac Thai	DS
7155 (con'd)	**ALBANIA**	
	†RADIO TIRANA, Cerrik	🔲 • Europe, N Africa & Mideast • 50 kW • ALT. FREQ. TO 7170 kHz

ENGLISH ▬　ARABIC ▨　CHINESE ▢▢▢　FRENCH ▬▬　GERMAN ▬▬　RUSSIAN ═══　SPANISH ▬▬　OTHER ▬

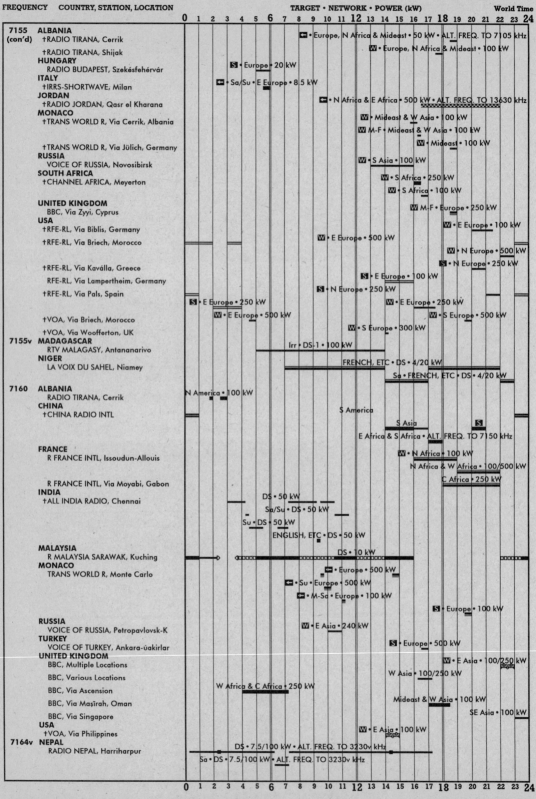

FREQUENCY	COUNTRY, STATION, LOCATION	TARGET • NETWORK • POWER (kW)	World Time

7155 ALBANIA (con'd)
†RADIO TIRANA, Cerrik — Europe, N Africa & Mideast • 50 kW • ALT. FREQ. TO 7105 kHz
†RADIO TIRANA, Shijak — W • Europe, N Africa & Mideast • 100 kW
HUNGARY
RADIO BUDAPEST, Székesfehérvár — S • Europe • 20 kW
ITALY
†IRRS-SHORTWAVE, Milan — Sa/Su • E Europe • 8.5 kW
JORDAN
†RADIO JORDAN, Qasr el Kharana — N Africa & E Africa • 500 kW • ALT. FREQ. TO 13630 kHz
MONACO
†TRANS WORLD R, Via Cerrik, Albania — W • Mideast & W Asia • 100 kW
— W • M-F • Mideast & W Asia • 100 kW
†TRANS WORLD R, Via Jülich, Germany — W • Mideast • 100 kW
RUSSIA
VOICE OF RUSSIA, Novosibirsk — W • S Asia • 100 kW
SOUTH AFRICA
†CHANNEL AFRICA, Meyerton — W • S Africa • 250 kW
— W • S Africa • 100 kW
UNITED KINGDOM
BBC, Via Zyyi, Cyprus — W M-F • Europe • 250 kW
USA
†RFE-RL, Via Biblis, Germany — W • E Europe • 100 kW
†RFE-RL, Via Briech, Morocco — W • E Europe • 500 kW
— W • N Europe • 500 kW
†RFE-RL, Via Kaválla, Greece — S • N Europe • 250 kW
RFE-RL, Via Lampertheim, Germany — S • E Europe • 100 kW
†RFE-RL, Via Pals, Spain — S • N Europe • 250 kW
— S • E Europe • 250 kW
— W • E Europe • 250 kW
†VOA, Via Briech, Morocco — W • E Europe • 500 kW
— W • S Europe • 500 kW
†VOA, Via Woofferton, UK — W • S Europe • 300 kW
7155v MADAGASCAR
RTV MALAGASY, Antananarivo — Irr • DS-1 • 100 kW
NIGER
LA VOIX DU SAHEL, Niamey — FRENCH, ETC • DS • 4/20 kW
— Sa • FRENCH, ETC • DS • 4/20 kW
7160 ALBANIA
RADIO TIRANA, Cerrik — N America • 100 kW
CHINA
†CHINA RADIO INTL — S America
— S Asia — S
— E Africa & S Africa • ALT. FREQ. TO 7150 kHz
FRANCE
R FRANCE INTL, Issoudun-Allouis — W • N Africa • 100 kW
— N Africa & W Africa • 100/500 kW
R FRANCE INTL, Via Moyabi, Gabon — C Africa • 250 kW
INDIA
†ALL INDIA RADIO, Chennai — DS • 50 kW
— Sa/Su • DS • 50 kW
— Su • DS • 50 kW
— ENGLISH, ETC • DS • 50 kW
MALAYSIA
R MALAYSIA SARAWAK, Kuching — DS • 10 kW
MONACO
TRANS WORLD R, Monte Carlo — Europe • 500 kW
— Su • Europe • 500 kW
— M-Sa • Europe • 100 kW
— S • Europe • 100 kW
RUSSIA
VOICE OF RUSSIA, Petropavlovsk-K — W • E Asia • 240 kW
TURKEY
VOICE OF TURKEY, Ankara-úakirlar — S • Europe • 500 kW
UNITED KINGDOM
BBC, Multiple Locations — W • E Asia • 100/250 kW
BBC, Various Locations — W Asia • 100/250 kW
BBC, Via Ascension — W Africa & C Africa • 250 kW
BBC, Via Maṣīrah, Oman — Mideast & W Asia • 100 kW
BBC, Via Singapore — SE Asia • 100 kW
USA
†VOA, Via Philippines — W • E Asia • 100 kW
7164v NEPAL
RADIO NEPAL, Harriharpur — DS • 7.5/100 kW • ALT. FREQ. TO 3230v kHz
— Sa • DS • 7.5/100 kW • ALT. FREQ. TO 3230v kHz

FREQUENCY   COUNTRY, STATION, LOCATION   TARGET • NETWORK • POWER (kW)   World Time

0 1 2 3 4 5 6 7 8 9 10 11 12 13 14 15 16 17 18 19 20 21 22 23 24

7165   **CROATIA**
  †CROATIAN RADIO, Deanovec

  • Europe & Australasia • 10/100 kW
  • M-F • ENGLISH & CROAT • Europe & Australasia • 10/100 kW
  • Sa/Su • Europe & Australasia • 10/100 kW
  • M-F • Europe & Australasia • 10/100 kW
  • Sa/Su • ENGLISH & CROAT • Europe & Australasia • 10/100 kW
  • Europe • 10 kW
  • ENGLISH & CROAT • Europe • 10 kW

  DENMARK
    RADIO DANMARK, Via Norway   Mideast • 500 kW
  ETHIOPIA
    RADIO ETHIOPIA, Gedja   E Africa • 100 kW
  GERMANY
    †DEUTSCHE WELLE, Wertachtal   W • Europe • 500 kW
                                          W • E Europe • 500 kW
  INDIA
    †ALL INDIA RADIO, Aligarh   W • SE Asia • 250 kW
  NORWAY
    R NORWAY INTL, Kvitsøy   Mideast • 500 kW
  RUSSIA
    VOICE OF RUSSIA, Novosibirsk   W • Mideast & W Asia • 1000 kW
  TURKEY
    VOICE OF TURKEY, Ankara-úakirlar   • S Europe • 500 kW
                                          S • Europe • 500 kW

  UNITED KINGDOM
    BBC, Rampisham   W • S Europe • 500 kW
  USA
    RFE-RL, Various Locations   • M-Sa • E Europe • 300/500 kW

    RFE-RL, Via Briech, Morocco   S • E Europe • 500 kW
                                          E Europe • 500 kW
                                          • S Europe • 500 kW

    RFE-RL, Via Pals, Spain   W • E Europe • 250 kW

    RFE-RL, Via Udon Thani, Thailand   W • E Europe • 500 kW

    †RFE-RL, Via Woofferton, UK   • E Europe • 300 kW
                                          • Su • E Europe • 300 kW

                                          W • E Europe • 300 kW
                                          S • E Europe • 250 kW
  YUGOSLAVIA
    †RADIO YUGOSLAVIA, Via Bosnia   • E Europe • 250 kW
7170   **ALBANIA**
    †RADIO TIRANA, Cerrik   • Europe, N Africa & Mideast • 50 kW • ALT. FREQ. TO 7155 kHz
                                          W • W Europe • 100 kW
  CHINA
    †CHINA RADIO INTL, Beijing   E Asia • 120 kW

    CHINA RADIO INTL, Via Russia   W • Europe • 240 kW

    XIZANG PEOPLE'S BC STN, Lhasa   DS • 50 kW
  GERMANY
    †DEUTSCHE WELLE, Nauen   S • W Europe • 500 kW
  OMAN
    †RADIO OMAN, Sīb   Mideast & W Asia • DS • 100 kW   W • Mideast & W Asia • DS • 100 kW
  PAKISTAN
    PAKISTAN BC CORP, Quetta   DS • 10 kW
  RUSSIA
    R TIKHIY OKEAN, Khabarovsk   S • E Asia & N Pacific • 240 kW
    R TIKHIY OKEAN, Komsomol'sk 'Amure   W • SE Asia • 1000 kW
    VOICE OF RUSSIA, Moscow   W • Europe • 240 kW
  SINGAPORE
    RADIO CORP OF SINGAPORE, Kranji   DS-TAMIL • 100 kW
  SWEDEN
    RADIO SWEDEN, Hörby   S • E Europe & W Asia • 500 kW
  USA
    †RFE-RL, Via Lampertheim, Germany   S • E Europe & W Asia • 250 kW
    †VOA, Via Kaválla, Greece   S • E Africa • 250 kW
                                          S M-F • E Africa • 250 kW
                                          S Sa/Su • E Africa • 250 kW
                                          S M-F • E Asia & Australasia • 250 kW
    †VOA, Via Philippines   N Africa • 300 kW
    †VOA, Via Woofferton, UK   W • N Africa • 300 kW

7170v **SENEGAL**
    RTV DU SENEGAL, Dakar   M-Sa • FRENCH, ETC • DS • 100 kW
                                          FRENCH, ETC • DS • 100 kW
                                          FRENCH, ETC • DS • 100 kW • ALT. FREQ. TO 4890v kHz

0 1 2 3 4 5 6 7 8 9 10 11 12 13 14 15 16 17 18 19 20 21 22 23 24

ENGLISH ▬   ARABIC ⌇⌇⌇   CHINESE ▢▢▢   FRENCH ▬▬   GERMAN ▬▬   RUSSIAN ══   SPANISH ▭▭   OTHER ▬▬

FREQUENCY	COUNTRY, STATION, LOCATION	TARGET • NETWORK • POWER (kW)	World Time

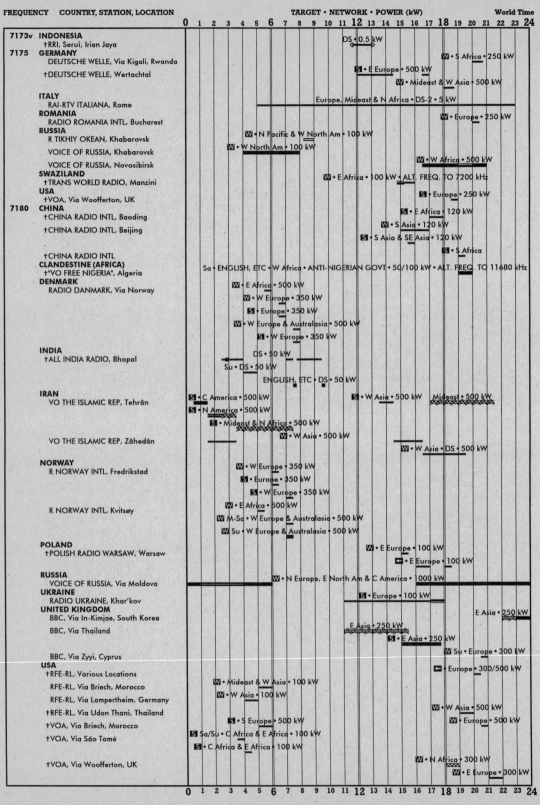

7173v INDONESIA
†RRI, Serui, Irian Jaya — DS • 0.5 kW

7175 GERMANY
DEUTSCHE WELLE, Via Kigali, Rwanda — W • S Africa • 250 kW
†DEUTSCHE WELLE, Wertachtal — S • E Europe • 500 kW; W • Mideast & W Asia • 500 kW

ITALY
RAI-RTV ITALIANA, Rome — Europe, Mideast & N Africa • DS-2 • 5 kW

ROMANIA
RADIO ROMANIA INTL, Bucharest — W • Europe • 250 kW

RUSSIA
R TIKHIY OKEAN, Khabarovsk — W • N Pacific & W North Am • 100 kW
VOICE OF RUSSIA, Khabarovsk — W • W North Am • 100 kW
VOICE OF RUSSIA, Novosibirsk — W • W Africa • 500 kW

SWAZILAND
†TRANS WORLD RADIO, Manzini — W • E Africa • 100 kW • ALT. FREQ. TO 7200 kHz

USA
†VOA, Via Woofferton, UK — S • Europe • 250 kW

7180 CHINA
†CHINA RADIO INTL, Baoding — S • E Africa • 120 kW
†CHINA RADIO INTL, Beijing — W • S Asia • 120 kW; S • S Asia & SE Asia • 120 kW
†CHINA RADIO INTL — S • S Africa

CLANDESTINE (AFRICA)
†"VO FREE NIGERIA", Algeria — Sa • ENGLISH, ETC • W Africa • ANTI-NIGERIAN GOVT • 50/100 kW • ALT. FREQ. TO 11680 kHz

DENMARK
RADIO DANMARK, Via Norway — W • E Africa • 500 kW; W • W Europe • 350 kW; S • Europe • 350 kW; W • W Europe & Australasia • 500 kW; S • W Europe • 350 kW

INDIA
†ALL INDIA RADIO, Bhopal — DS • 50 kW; Su • DS • 50 kW; ENGLISH, ETC • DS • 50 kW

IRAN
VO THE ISLAMIC REP, Tehrān — S • C America • 500 kW; S • N America • 500 kW; S • Mideast & N Africa • 500 kW; S • W Asia • 500 kW; Mideast • 500 kW
VO THE ISLAMIC REP, Zāhedān — W • W Asia • 500 kW; W • W Asia • DS • 500 kW

NORWAY
R NORWAY INTL, Fredrikstad — W • W Europe • 350 kW; S • Europe • 350 kW; S • W Europe • 350 kW
R NORWAY INTL, Kvitsøy — W • E Africa • 500 kW; W M-Sa • W Europe & Australasia • 500 kW; W Su • W Europe & Australasia • 500 kW

POLAND
†POLISH RADIO WARSAW, Warsaw — W • E Europe • 100 kW; E Europe • 100 kW

RUSSIA
VOICE OF RUSSIA, Via Moldova — W • N Europe, E North Am & C America • 1000 kW

UKRAINE
RADIO UKRAINE, Khar'kov — S • Europe • 100 kW

UNITED KINGDOM
BBC, Via In-Kimjae, South Korea — E Asia • 250 kW
BBC, Via Thailand — E Asia • 250 kW; S • E Asia • 250 kW
BBC, Via Zyyi, Cyprus — W Su • Europe • 300 kW

USA
†RFE-RL, Various Locations — Europe • 300/500 kW
RFE-RL, Via Briech, Morocco — W • Mideast & W Asia • 100 kW
RFE-RL, Via Lampertheim, Germany — W • W Asia • 100 kW
†RFE-RL, Via Udon Thani, Thailand — W • W Asia • 500 kW
†VOA, Via Briech, Morocco — S • S Europe • 500 kW; W • Europe • 500 kW
†VOA, Via São Tomé — S Sa/Su • C Africa & E Africa • 100 kW; S • C Africa & E Africa • 100 kW
†VOA, Via Woofferton, UK — W • N Africa • 300 kW; W • E Europe • 300 kW

SEASONAL S OR W   1-HR TIMESHIFT MIDYEAR ⊟ OR ⊡   JAMMING / OR ∧   EARLIEST HEARD ◁   LATEST HEARD ▷   NEW FOR 1998 †

FREQUENCY   COUNTRY, STATION, LOCATION   TARGET • NETWORK • POWER (kW)   World Time
0 1 2 3 4 5 6 7 8 9 10 11 12 13 14 15 16 17 18 19 20 21 22 23 24

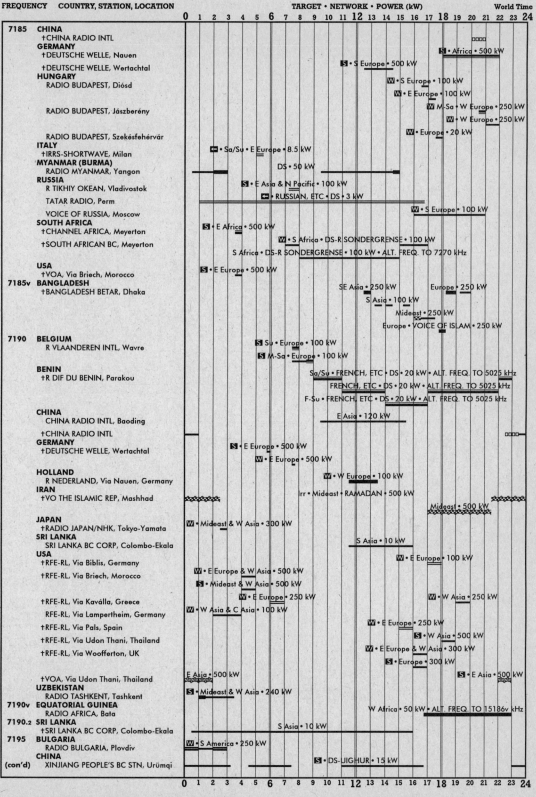

7185 **CHINA**
  †CHINA RADIO INTL
  GERMANY
  †DEUTSCHE WELLE, Nauen — S • Africa • 500 kW
  †DEUTSCHE WELLE, Wertachtal — S • S Europe • 500 kW
  HUNGARY
  RADIO BUDAPEST, Diósd — W • S Europe • 100 kW
  — W • E Europe • 100 kW
  RADIO BUDAPEST, Jászberény — W • M-Sa • W Europe • 250 kW
  — W • W Europe • 250 kW
  RADIO BUDAPEST, Szekésfehérvár — W • Europe • 20 kW
  ITALY
  †IRRS-SHORTWAVE, Milan — • Sa/Su • E Europe • 8.5 kW
  MYANMAR (BURMA)
  RADIO MYANMAR, Yangon — DS • 50 kW
  RUSSIA
  R TIKHIY OKEAN, Vladivostok — S • E Asia & N Pacific • 100 kW
  TATAR RADIO, Perm — • RUSSIAN, ETC • DS • 3 kW
  VOICE OF RUSSIA, Moscow — W • S Europe • 100 kW
  SOUTH AFRICA
  †CHANNEL AFRICA, Meyerton — S • E Africa • 500 kW
  †SOUTH AFRICAN BC, Meyerton — W • S Africa • DS-R SONDERGRENSE • 100 kW
  S Africa • DS-R SONDERGRENSE • 100 kW • ALT. FREQ. TO 7270 kHz
  USA
  †VOA, Via Briech, Morocco — • E Europe • 500 kW
7185v **BANGLADESH**
  †BANGLADESH BETAR, Dhaka — SE Asia • 250 kW   Europe • 250 kW
  S Asia • 100 kW
  Mideast • 250 kW
  Europe • VOICE OF ISLAM • 250 kW
7190 **BELGIUM**
  R VLAANDEREN INTL, Wavre — S • Su • Europe • 100 kW
  — S • M-Sa • Europe • 100 kW
  BENIN
  †R DIF DU BENIN, Parakou — Sa/Su • FRENCH, ETC • DS • 20 kW • ALT. FREQ. TO 5025 kHz
  FRENCH, ETC • DS • 20 kW • ALT. FREQ. TO 5025 kHz
  F-Su • FRENCH, ETC • DS • 20 kW • ALT. FREQ. TO 5025 kHz
  CHINA
  CHINA RADIO INTL, Baoding — E Asia • 120 kW
  †CHINA RADIO INTL
  GERMANY
  †DEUTSCHE WELLE, Wertachtal — S • E Europe • 500 kW
  — W • E Europe • 500 kW
  HOLLAND
  R NEDERLAND, Via Nauen, Germany — W • W Europe • 100 kW
  IRAN
  †VO THE ISLAMIC REP, Mashhad — Irr • Mideast • RAMADAN • 500 kW   Mideast • 500 kW
  JAPAN
  †RADIO JAPAN/NHK, Tokyo-Yamata — W • Mideast & W Asia • 300 kW
  SRI LANKA
  SRI LANKA BC CORP, Colombo-Ekala — S Asia • 10 kW
  USA
  †RFE-RL, Via Biblis, Germany — W • E Europe • 100 kW
  †RFE-RL, Via Briech, Morocco — W • E Europe & W Asia • 500 kW
  — S • Mideast & W Asia • 500 kW
  †RFE-RL, Via Kaválla, Greece — W • E Europe • 250 kW   W • W Asia • 250 kW
  RFE-RL, Via Lampertheim, Germany — W • W Asia & C Asia • 100 kW
  †RFE-RL, Via Pals, Spain — W • E Europe • 250 kW
  †RFE-RL, Via Udon Thani, Thailand — S • W Asia • 500 kW
  †RFE-RL, Via Woofferton, UK — W • E Europe & W Asia • 300 kW
  — S • Europe • 300 kW
  †VOA, Via Udon Thani, Thailand — E Asia • 500 kW   S • E Asia • 500 kW
  UZBEKISTAN
  RADIO TASHKENT, Tashkent — S • Mideast & W Asia • 240 kW
7190v **EQUATORIAL GUINEA**
  RADIO AFRICA, Bata — W Africa • 50 kW • ALT. FREQ. TO 15186v kHz
7190.2 **SRI LANKA**
  †SRI LANKA BC CORP, Colombo-Ekala — S Asia • 10 kW
7195 **BULGARIA**
  RADIO BULGARIA, Plovdiv — W • S America • 250 kW
  CHINA
(con'd) XINJIANG PEOPLE'S BC STN, Urümqi — S • DS-UIGHUR • 15 kW

0 1 2 3 4 5 6 7 8 9 10 11 12 13 14 15 16 17 18 19 20 21 22 23 24

ENGLISH ▬   ARABIC ⌇⌇⌇   CHINESE ▭▭▭   FRENCH ▬   GERMAN ▬   RUSSIAN ═══   SPANISH ▬   OTHER ▬

FREQUENCY	COUNTRY, STATION, LOCATION	TARGET • NETWORK • POWER (kW) — World Time

0 1 2 3 4 5 6 7 8 9 10 11 12 13 14 15 16 17 18 19 20 21 22 23 24

7195 (con'd)	**CHINA**	
	XIZANG PEOPLE'S BC STN, Lhasa	DS-TIBETAN • 50 kW
	GERMANY	
	DEUTSCHE WELLE, Via Kigali, Rwanda	W • S Africa • 250 kW
	ROMANIA	
	RADIO ROMANIA INTL, Bucharest	S • E Europe • 250 kW
		S • S Europe • 250 kW
		W • Europe • 250 kW
		Europe • 250 kW
	RUSSIA	
	R TIKHIY OKEAN, Chita	W • SE Asia • 240 kW
	VOICE OF RUSSIA, Komsomol'sk 'Amure	W • E Asia & SE Asia • 100 kW
	UNITED KINGDOM	
	BBC, Rampisham	W • M-F • N Africa • 500 kW
	USA	
	VOA, Via Briech, Morocco	S • W Africa • 500 kW
		S • Sa/Su • W Africa • 500 kW
		S • S Asia & E Asia • 250 kW
	VOA, Via Philippines	S • SE Asia • 250 kW
		W • N Africa • 300 kW
	†VOA, Via Woofferton, UK	W • S Europe • 300 kW
7195v	**UGANDA**	
	RADIO UGANDA, Kampala	ENGLISH, ETC • DS • 20 kW
		Sa/Su • ENGLISH, ETC • DS • 20 kW
7200	**AFGHANISTAN**	
	RADIO AFGHANISTAN, Kabul	TEMP INACTIVE • 100 kW
		F • TEMP INACTIVE • 100 kW
	CANADA	
	R CANADA INTL, Via Germany	W • Mideast • 500 kW
	R CANADA INTL, Via Skelton, UK	W • Europe • 300 kW
	JAPAN	
	†RADIO JAPAN/NHK, Tokyo-Yamata	SE Asia • 100 kW
		SE Asia • 300 kW
	KOREA (DPR)	
	†RADIO PYONGYANG, Pyongyang	E Asia • 200 kW
	RUSSIA	
	†MARIY RADIO, Yoshkar Ola	⬌ • RUSSIAN, ETC • DS-LOCAL, R ROSSII • 5 kW
	†RADIO ROSSII, St Petersburg	S • W Asia • DS • 400 kW
	VOICE OF RUSSIA, Moscow	W • E Africa & S Africa • 240 kW
	†YAKUT RADIO, Yakutsk	⬌ • RUSSIAN, ETC • DS-LOCAL, R ROSSII • 100 kW
	SUDAN	
	REP OF SUDAN RADIO, Sawba	DS • 100 kW
	SWAZILAND	
	†TRANS WORLD RADIO, Manzini	W • E Africa • 100 kW • ALT. FREQ. TO 7175 kHz
	USA	
	†VOA, Various Locations	W • S Asia & E Asia • 250/500 kW
	†VOA, Via Kaválla, Greece	W • Mideast & W Asia • 250 kW
	†VOA, Via Philippines	E Asia • 100 kW
		W • SE Asia • 250 kW
	YUGOSLAVIA	
	RTV SRBIJE, Belgrade	⬌ • Europe, N Africa & Mideast • DS-1 • 100 kW
7203v	**CONGO (DEM REP)**	
	R NAC CONGOLAISE, Lubumbashi	FRENCH, ETC • DS-TEMP INACTIVE • 10 kW
7205	**BELARUS**	
	†R BELARUS, Via Ukraine	W • Europe • 100 kW
		W • M/Tu/Th/F • Europe • 100 kW
		W • W/Sa/Su • Europe • 100 kW
	CYPRUS	
	CYPRUS BC CORP, Zyyi	S • F-Su • Europe • 250 kW
	DENMARK	
	RADIO DANMARK, Via Norway	S • Australasia • 500 kW
	NORWAY	
	R NORWAY INTL, Kvitsøy	S • Australasia • 500 kW
	POLAND	
	†POLISH RADIO WARSAW, Warsaw	⬌ • Su • Europe • 100 kW
	RUSSIA	
	†TRANS WORLD RADIO, Vladivostok	E Asia & SE Asia • 1000 kW
	VOICE OF RUSSIA, Moscow	W • C America • 240 kW
		W • N Europe & W Europe • 240 kW
	†VOICE OF RUSSIA, Vladivostok	E Asia & SE Asia • 1000 kW
		W • E Asia & SE Asia • 1000 kW
	SOUTH AFRICA	
	S AF AMATEUR R LEAGUE, Meyerton	Su • ENGLISH & AFRIKAANS • S Africa • 100 kW
	UKRAINE	
(con'd)	RADIO UKRAINE, Kiev	W • W Europe • 100 kW

0 1 2 3 4 5 6 7 8 9 10 11 12 13 14 15 16 17 18 19 20 21 22 23 24

SEASONAL S OR W   1-HR TIMESHIFT MIDYEAR ⬅ OR ➡   JAMMING / OR ∧   EARLIEST HEARD ◁   LATEST HEARD ▷   NEW FOR 1998 †

FREQUENCY   COUNTRY, STATION, LOCATION   TARGET • NETWORK • POWER (kW)   World Time

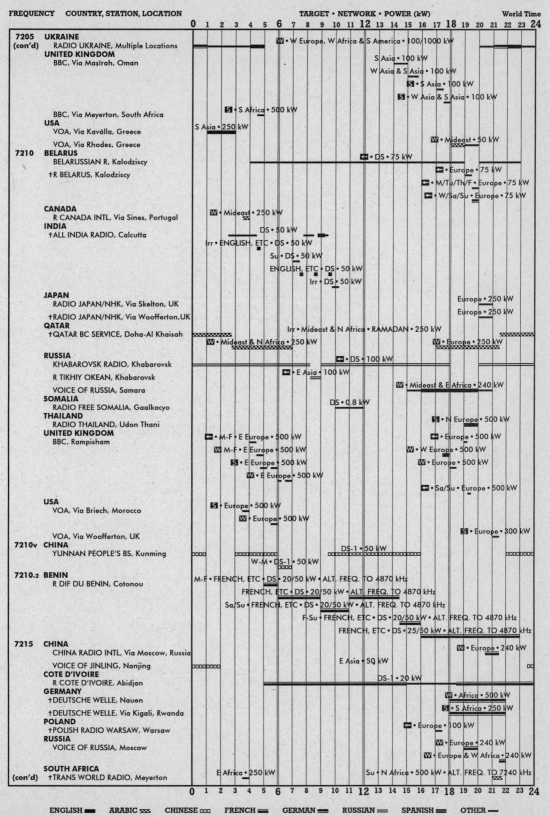

7205	**UKRAINE**	
(con'd)	RADIO UKRAINE, Multiple Locations	W • W Europe, W Africa & S America • 100/1000 kW
	UNITED KINGDOM	
	BBC, Via Maṣīrah, Oman	S Asia • 100 kW
		W Asia & S Asia • 100 kW
		S • S Asia • 100 kW
		S • W Asia & S Asia • 100 kW
	BBC, Via Meyerton, South Africa	S • S Africa • 500 kW
	USA	
	VOA, Via Kaválla, Greece	S Asia • 250 kW
	VOA, Via Rhodes, Greece	W • Mideast • 50 kW
7210	**BELARUS**	
	BELARUSSIAN R, Kalodziscy	DS • 75 kW
	†R BELARUS, Kalodziscy	• Europe • 75 kW
		• M/Tu/Th/F • Europe • 75 kW
		• W/Sa/Su • Europe • 75 kW
	CANADA	
	R CANADA INTL, Via Sines, Portugal	W • Mideast • 250 kW
	INDIA	
	†ALL INDIA RADIO, Calcutta	DS • 50 kW
		Irr • ENGLISH, ETC • DS • 50 kW
		Su • DS • 50 kW
		ENGLISH, ETC • DS • 50 kW
		Irr • DS • 50 kW
	JAPAN	
	RADIO JAPAN/NHK, Via Skelton, UK	Europe • 250 kW
	†RADIO JAPAN/NHK, Via Woofferton,UK	Europe • 250 kW
	QATAR	
	†QATAR BC SERVICE, Doha-Al Khaisah	Irr • Mideast & N Africa • RAMADAN • 250 kW
		W • Mideast & N Africa • 250 kW W • Europe • 250 kW
	RUSSIA	
	KHABAROVSK RADIO, Khabarovsk	DS • 100 kW
	R TIKHIY OKEAN, Khabarovsk	E Asia • 100 kW
	VOICE OF RUSSIA, Samara	W • Mideast & E Africa • 240 kW
	SOMALIA	
	RADIO FREE SOMALIA, Gaalkacyo	DS • 0.8 kW
	THAILAND	
	RADIO THAILAND, Udon Thani	S • N Europe • 500 kW
	UNITED KINGDOM	
	BBC, Rampisham	• M-F • E Europe • 500 kW • Europe • 500 kW
		W M-F E Europe • 500 kW W • W Europe • 500 kW
		S • E Europe • 500 kW W • Europe • 500 kW
		W • E Europe • 500 kW
		• Sa/Su • Europe • 500 kW
	USA	
	VOA, Via Briech, Morocco	S • Europe • 500 kW
		W • Europe • 500 kW
	VOA, Via Woofferton, UK	S • Europe • 300 kW
7210v	**CHINA**	
	YUNNAN PEOPLE'S BS, Kunming	DS-1 • 50 kW
		W-M • DS-1 • 50 kW
7210.2	**BENIN**	
	R DIF DU BENIN, Cotonou	M-F • FRENCH, ETC • DS • 20/50 kW • ALT. FREQ. TO 4870 kHz
		FRENCH, ETC • DS • 20/50 kW • ALT. FREQ. TO 4870 kHz
		Sa/Su • FRENCH, ETC • DS • 20/50 kW • ALT. FREQ. TO 4870 kHz
		F-Su • FRENCH, ETC • DS • 20/50 kW • ALT. FREQ. TO 4870 kHz
		FRENCH, ETC • DS • 25/50 kW • ALT. FREQ. TO 4870 kHz
7215	**CHINA**	
	CHINA RADIO INTL, Via Moscow, Russia	W • Europe • 240 kW
	VOICE OF JINLING, Nanjing	E Asia • 50 kW
	COTE D'IVOIRE	
	R COTE D'IVOIRE, Abidjan	DS-1 • 20 kW
	GERMANY	
	†DEUTSCHE WELLE, Nauen	W • Africa • 500 kW
	†DEUTSCHE WELLE, Via Kigali, Rwanda	S • S Africa • 250 kW
	POLAND	
	†POLISH RADIO WARSAW, Warsaw	• Europe • 100 kW
	RUSSIA	
	VOICE OF RUSSIA, Moscow	W • Europe • 240 kW
		W • Europe & W Africa • 240 kW
	SOUTH AFRICA	
(con'd)	†TRANS WORLD RADIO, Meyerton	E Africa • 250 kW Su • N Africa • 500 kW • ALT. FREQ. TO 7240 kHz

ENGLISH ▬ ARABIC ▨ CHINESE ▯▯▯ FRENCH ▬ GERMAN ▬ RUSSIAN ═ SPANISH ▬ OTHER ▬

FREQUENCY   COUNTRY, STATION, LOCATION   TARGET • NETWORK • POWER (kW)   World Time

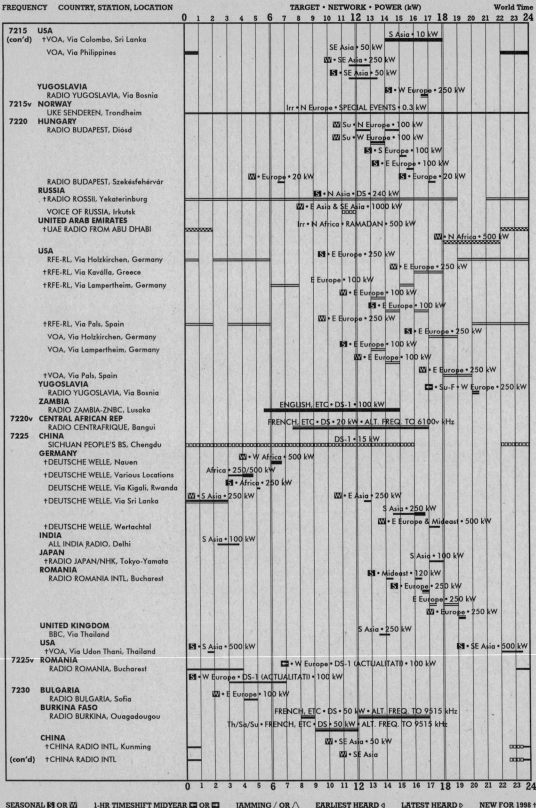

FREQUENCY	COUNTRY, STATION, LOCATION	TARGET • NETWORK • POWER (kW)
7215 (con'd)	USA †VOA, Via Colombo, Sri Lanka	S Asia • 10 kW
	VOA, Via Philippines	SE Asia • 50 kW; W • SE Asia • 250 kW; S • SE Asia • 50 kW
	YUGOSLAVIA RADIO YUGOSLAVIA, Via Bosnia	S • W Europe • 250 kW
7215v	NORWAY UKE SENDEREN, Trondheim	Irr • N Europe • SPECIAL EVENTS • 0.3 kW
7220	HUNGARY RADIO BUDAPEST, Diósd	W Su • N Europe • 100 kW; W Su • W Europe • 100 kW; S • S Europe • 100 kW; S • E Europe • 100 kW
	RADIO BUDAPEST, Székésfehérvár	W • Europe • 20 kW; S • Europe • 20 kW
	RUSSIA †RADIO ROSSII, Yekaterinburg	S • N Asia • DS • 240 kW
	VOICE OF RUSSIA, Irkutsk	W • E Asia & SE Asia • 1000 kW
	UNITED ARAB EMIRATES †UAE RADIO FROM ABU DHABI	Irr • N Africa • RAMADAN • 500 kW; W • N Africa • 500 kW
	USA RFE-RL, Via Holzkirchen, Germany	S • E Europe • 250 kW
	†RFE-RL, Via Kaválla, Greece	W • E Europe • 250 kW
	†RFE-RL, Via Lampertheim, Germany	E Europe • 100 kW; W • E Europe • 100 kW; S • E Europe • 100 kW
	†RFE-RL, Via Pals, Spain	W • E Europe • 250 kW; S • E Europe • 250 kW
	VOA, Via Holzkirchen, Germany	S • E Europe • 100 kW
	VOA, Via Lampertheim, Germany	W • E Europe • 100 kW
	†VOA, Via Pals, Spain	W • E Europe • 250 kW
	YUGOSLAVIA RADIO YUGOSLAVIA, Via Bosnia	Su-F • W Europe • 250 kW
	ZAMBIA RADIO ZAMBIA-ZNBC, Lusaka	ENGLISH, ETC • DS-1 • 100 kW
7220v	CENTRAL AFRICAN REP RADIO CENTRAFRIQUE, Bangui	FRENCH, ETC • DS • 20 kW • ALT. FREQ. TO 6100v kHz
7225	CHINA SICHUAN PEOPLE'S BS, Chengdu	DS-1 • 15 kW
	GERMANY †DEUTSCHE WELLE, Nauen	W • W Africa • 500 kW
	†DEUTSCHE WELLE, Various Locations	Africa • 250/500 kW
	DEUTSCHE WELLE, Via Kigali, Rwanda	S • Africa • 250 kW
	†DEUTSCHE WELLE, Via Sri Lanka	W • S Asia • 250 kW; W • E Asia • 250 kW
	†DEUTSCHE WELLE, Wertachtal	S Asia • 250 kW; W • E Europe & Mideast • 500 kW
	INDIA ALL INDIA RADIO, Delhi	S Asia • 100 kW
	JAPAN †RADIO JAPAN/NHK, Tokyo-Yamata	S Asia • 100 kW
	ROMANIA RADIO ROMANIA INTL, Bucharest	S • Mideast • 120 kW; S • Europe • 250 kW; E Europe • 250 kW; W • Europe • 250 kW
	UNITED KINGDOM BBC, Via Thailand	S Asia • 250 kW
	USA †VOA, Via Udon Thani, Thailand	S • S Asia • 500 kW; S • SE Asia • 500 kW
7225v	ROMANIA RADIO ROMANIA, Bucharest	• W Europe • DS-1 (ACTUALITATI) • 100 kW; S • W Europe • DS-1 (ACTUALITATI) • 100 kW
7230	BULGARIA RADIO BULGARIA, Sofia	W • E Europe • 100 kW
	BURKINA FASO RADIO BURKINA, Ouagadougou	FRENCH, ETC • DS • 50 kW • ALT. FREQ. TO 9515 kHz; Th/Sa/Su • FRENCH, ETC • DS • 50 kW • ALT. FREQ. TO 9515 kHz
	CHINA †CHINA RADIO INTL, Kunming	W • SE Asia • 50 kW
(con'd)	†CHINA RADIO INTL	W • SE Asia

FREQUENCY   COUNTRY, STATION, LOCATION   TARGET • NETWORK • POWER (kW)   World Time

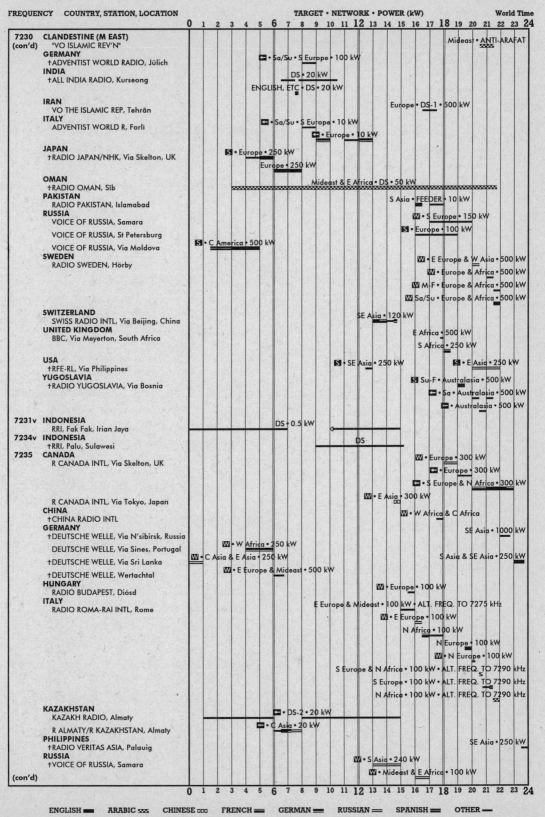

Frequency	Country, Station, Location	Target • Network • Power
7230 (con'd)	**CLANDESTINE (M EAST)** "VO ISLAMIC REV'N"	Mideast • ANTI-ARAFAT
	GERMANY †ADVENTIST WORLD RADIO, Jülich	• Sa/Su • S Europe • 100 kW
	INDIA †ALL INDIA RADIO, Kurseong	DS • 20 kW / ENGLISH, ETC • DS • 20 kW
	IRAN VO THE ISLAMIC REP, Tehrān	Europe • DS-1 • 500 kW
	ITALY ADVENTIST WORLD R, Forli	• Sa/Su • S Europe • 10 kW / • Europe • 10 kW
	JAPAN †RADIO JAPAN/NHK, Via Skelton, UK	S • Europe • 250 kW / Europe • 250 kW
	OMAN †RADIO OMAN, Sib	Mideast & E Africa • DS • 50 kW
	PAKISTAN RADIO PAKISTAN, Islamabad	S Asia • FEEDER • 10 kW
	RUSSIA VOICE OF RUSSIA, Samara	W • S Europe • 150 kW
	VOICE OF RUSSIA, St Petersburg	S • Europe • 100 kW
	VOICE OF RUSSIA, Via Moldova	S • C America • 500 kW
	SWEDEN RADIO SWEDEN, Hörby	W • E Europe & W Asia • 500 kW / W • Europe & Africa • 500 kW / W M-F • Europe & Africa • 500 kW / W Sa/Su • Europe & Africa • 500 kW
	SWITZERLAND SWISS RADIO INTL, Via Beijing, China	SE Asia • 120 kW
	UNITED KINGDOM BBC, Via Meyerton, South Africa	E Africa • 500 kW / S Africa • 250 kW
	USA †RFE-RL, Via Philippines	S • SE Asia • 250 kW / S • E Asia • 250 kW
	YUGOSLAVIA †RADIO YUGOSLAVIA, Via Bosnia	S Su-F • Australasia • 500 kW / • Sa • Australasia • 500 kW / • Australasia • 500 kW
7231v	**INDONESIA** RRI, Fak Fak, Irian Jaya	DS • 0.5 kW
7234v	**INDONESIA** †RRI, Palu, Sulawesi	DS
7235	**CANADA** R CANADA INTL, Via Skelton, UK	W • Europe • 300 kW / • Europe • 300 kW / • S Europe & N Africa • 300 kW
	R CANADA INTL, Via Tokyo, Japan	W • E Asia • 300 kW
	CHINA †CHINA RADIO INTL	W • W Africa & C Africa
	GERMANY †DEUTSCHE WELLE, Via N'sibirsk, Russia	SE Asia • 1000 kW
	DEUTSCHE WELLE, Via Sines, Portugal	W • W Africa • 250 kW
	†DEUTSCHE WELLE, Via Sri Lanka	W • C Asia & E Asia • 250 kW / S Asia & SE Asia • 250 kW
	†DEUTSCHE WELLE, Wertachtal	W • E Europe & Mideast • 500 kW
	HUNGARY RADIO BUDAPEST, Diósd	W • Europe • 100 kW
	ITALY RADIO ROMA-RAI INTL, Rome	E Europe & Mideast • 100 kW • ALT. FREQ. TO 7275 kHz / W • E Europe • 100 kW / N Africa • 100 kW / N Europe • 100 kW / W • N Europe • 100 kW / S Europe & N Africa • 100 kW • ALT. FREQ. TO 7290 kHz / S Europe • 100 kW • ALT. FREQ. TO 7290 kHz / N Africa • 100 kW • ALT. FREQ. TO 7290 kHz
	KAZAKHSTAN KAZAKH RADIO, Almaty	• DS-2 • 20 kW
	R ALMATY/R KAZAKHSTAN, Almaty	• C Asia • 20 kW
	PHILIPPINES †RADIO VERITAS ASIA, Palauig	SE Asia • 250 kW
	RUSSIA †VOICE OF RUSSIA, Samara	W • S Asia • 240 kW / W • Mideast & E Africa • 100 kW
(con'd)		

ENGLISH ▬   ARABIC ⧖   CHINESE ▫▫▫   FRENCH ▬▬   GERMAN ▬   RUSSIAN ═   SPANISH ▬   OTHER ▬

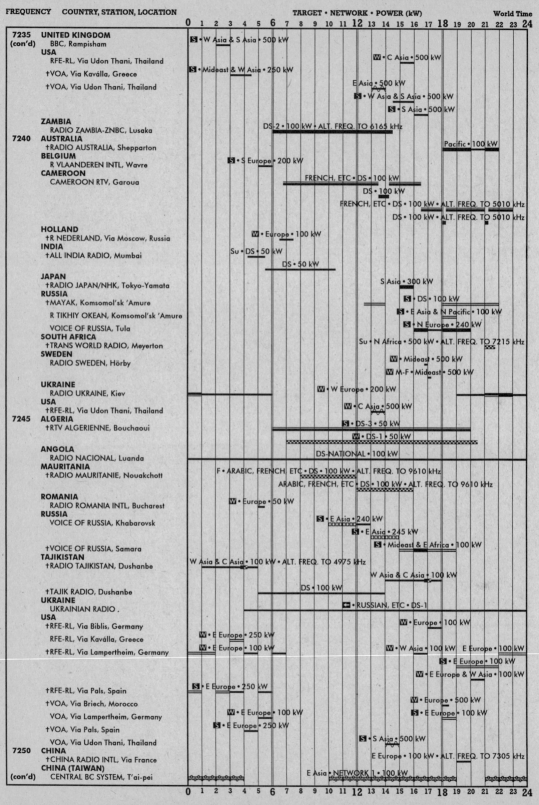

FREQUENCY   COUNTRY, STATION, LOCATION   TARGET • NETWORK • POWER (kW)   World Time

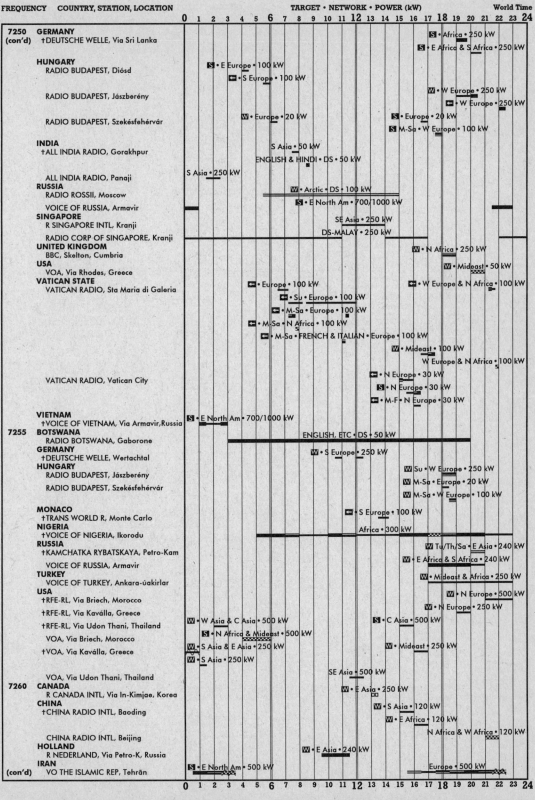

7250 **GERMANY**
(con'd) †DEUTSCHE WELLE, Via Sri Lanka
- S • Africa • 250 kW
- S • E Africa & S Africa • 250 kW

HUNGARY
RADIO BUDAPEST, Diósd
- S • E Europe • 100 kW
- S Europe • 100 kW

RADIO BUDAPEST, Jászberény
- W • W Europe • 250 kW
- W Europe • 250 kW

RADIO BUDAPEST, Szekésfehérvár
- W • Europe • 20 kW
- S • Europe • 20 kW
- M-Sa • W Europe • 100 kW

INDIA
†ALL INDIA RADIO, Gorakhpur
- S Asia • 50 kW
- ENGLISH & HINDI • DS • 50 kW

ALL INDIA RADIO, Panaji
- S Asia • 250 kW

RUSSIA
RADIO ROSSII, Moscow
- W • Arctic • DS • 100 kW

VOICE OF RUSSIA, Armavir
- S • E North Am • 700/1000 kW

SINGAPORE
R SINGAPORE INTL, Kranji
- SE Asia • 250 kW

RADIO CORP OF SINGAPORE, Kranji
- DS-MALAY • 250 kW

UNITED KINGDOM
BBC, Skelton, Cumbria
- W • N Africa • 250 kW

USA
VOA, Via Rhodes, Greece
- W • Mideast • 50 kW

VATICAN STATE
VATICAN RADIO, Sta Maria di Galeria
- Europe • 100 kW
- W • W Europe & N Africa • 100 kW
- Su • Europe • 100 kW
- M-Sa • Europe • 100 kW
- M-Sa • N Africa • 100 kW
- M-Sa • FRENCH & ITALIAN • Europe • 100 kW
- W • Mideast • 100 kW
- W Europe & N Africa • 100 kW

VATICAN RADIO, Vatican City
- N Europe • 30 kW
- S • N Europe • 30 kW
- M-F • N Europe • 30 kW

VIETNAM
†VOICE OF VIETNAM, Via Armavir, Russia
- S • E North Am • 700/1000 kW

7255 **BOTSWANA**
RADIO BOTSWANA, Gaborone
- ENGLISH, ETC • DS • 50 kW

GERMANY
†DEUTSCHE WELLE, Wertachtal
- W • S Europe • 250 kW

HUNGARY
RADIO BUDAPEST, Jászberény
- W Su • W Europe • 250 kW

RADIO BUDAPEST, Szekésfehérvár
- W M-Sa • Europe • 20 kW
- W M-Sa • W Europe • 100 kW

MONACO
†TRANS WORLD R, Monte Carlo
- S Europe • 100 kW

NIGERIA
†VOICE OF NIGERIA, Ikorodu
- Africa • 300 kW

RUSSIA
†KAMCHATKA RYBATSKAYA, Petro-Kam
- W Tu/Th/Sa • E Asia • 240 kW

VOICE OF RUSSIA, Armavir
- W • E Africa & S Africa • 240 kW

TURKEY
VOICE OF TURKEY, Ankara-úakirlar
- W • Mideast & Africa • 250 kW

USA
†RFE-RL, Via Briech, Morocco
- W • N Europe • 500 kW

†RFE-RL, Via Kaválla, Greece
- W • N Europe • 250 kW

†RFE-RL, Via Udon Thani, Thailand
- W • W Asia & C Asia • 500 kW
- S • C Asia • 500 kW

VOA, Via Briech, Morocco
- S • N Africa & Mideast • 500 kW

†VOA, Via Kaválla, Greece
- W • S Asia & E Asia • 250 kW
- W • Mideast • 250 kW

VOA, Via Udon Thani, Thailand
- W • S Asia • 250 kW
- SE Asia • 500 kW

7260 **CANADA**
R CANADA INTL, Via In-Kimjae, Korea
- W • E Asia • 250 kW

CHINA
†CHINA RADIO INTL, Baoding
- W • S Asia • 120 kW
- W • E Africa • 120 kW
- N Africa & W Africa • 120 kW

CHINA RADIO INTL, Beijing

HOLLAND
R NEDERLAND, Via Petro-K, Russia
- W • E Asia • 240 kW

IRAN
(con'd) VO THE ISLAMIC REP, Tehrān
- S • E North Am • 500 kW
- Europe • 500 kW

World Time: 0 1 2 3 4 5 6 7 8 9 10 11 12 13 14 15 16 17 18 19 20 21 22 23 24

ENGLISH ▬ ARABIC ▨ CHINESE ☐☐☐ FRENCH ▬▬ GERMAN ▬▬ RUSSIAN ═ SPANISH ▬▬ OTHER ▬

FREQUENCY   COUNTRY, STATION, LOCATION   TARGET • NETWORK • POWER (kW)   World Time

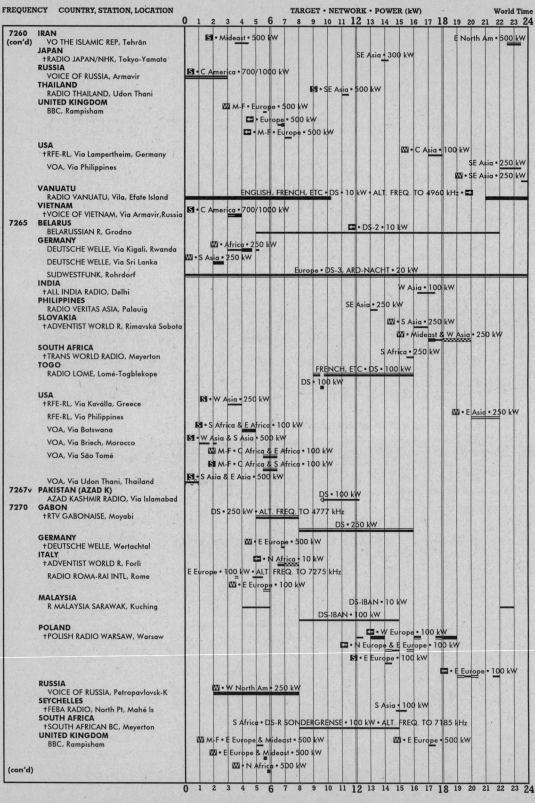

FREQUENCY	COUNTRY, STATION, LOCATION	TARGET • NETWORK • POWER (kW)
7260 (con'd)	**IRAN** VO THE ISLAMIC REP, Tehrān	S • Mideast • 500 kW ... E North Am • 500 kW
	JAPAN †RADIO JAPAN/NHK, Tokyo-Yamata	SE Asia • 300 kW
	RUSSIA VOICE OF RUSSIA, Armavir	S • C America • 700/1000 kW
	THAILAND RADIO THAILAND, Udon Thani	S • SE Asia • 500 kW
	UNITED KINGDOM BBC, Rampisham	W • M-F • Europe • 500 kW / Europe • 500 kW / M-F • Europe • 500 kW
	USA †RFE-RL, Via Lampertheim, Germany	W • C Asia • 100 kW
	VOA, Via Philippines	SE Asia • 250 kW / W • SE Asia • 250 kW
	VANUATU RADIO VANUATU, Vila, Efate Island	ENGLISH, FRENCH, ETC • DS • 10 kW • ALT. FREQ. TO 4960 kHz •
	VIETNAM †VOICE OF VIETNAM, Via Armavir, Russia	S • C America • 700/1000 kW
7265	**BELARUS** BELARUSSIAN R, Grodno	• DS-2 • 10 kW
	GERMANY DEUTSCHE WELLE, Via Kigali, Rwanda	W • Africa • 250 kW
	DEUTSCHE WELLE, Via Sri Lanka	W • S Asia • 250 kW
	SUDWESTFUNK, Rohrdorf	Europe • DS-3, ARD-NACHT • 20 kW
	INDIA †ALL INDIA RADIO, Delhi	W Asia • 100 kW
	PHILIPPINES RADIO VERITAS ASIA, Palauig	SE Asia • 250 kW
	SLOVAKIA †ADVENTIST WORLD R, Rimavská Sobota	W • S Asia • 250 kW / W • Mideast & W Asia • 250 kW
	SOUTH AFRICA †TRANS WORLD RADIO, Meyerton	S Africa • 250 kW
	TOGO RADIO LOME, Lomé-Togblekope	FRENCH, ETC • DS • 100 kW / DS • 100 kW
	USA †RFE-RL, Via Kaválla, Greece	S • W Asia • 250 kW
	RFE-RL, Via Philippines	W • E Asia • 250 kW
	VOA, Via Botswana	S • S Africa & E Africa • 100 kW
	VOA, Via Briech, Morocco	S • W Asia & S Asia • 500 kW
	VOA, Via São Tomé	W • M-F • C Africa & E Africa • 100 kW / S • M-F • C Africa & S Africa • 100 kW
	VOA, Via Udon Thani, Thailand	S • S Asia & E Asia • 500 kW
7267v	**PAKISTAN (AZAD K)** AZAD KASHMIR RADIO, Via Islamabad	DS • 100 kW
7270	**GABON** †RTV GABONAISE, Moyabi	DS • 250 kW • ALT. FREQ. TO 4777 kHz / DS • 250 kW
	GERMANY †DEUTSCHE WELLE, Wertachtal	W • E Europe • 500 kW
	ITALY †ADVENTIST WORLD R, Forli	• N Africa • 10 kW
	RADIO ROMA-RAI INTL, Rome	E Europe • 100 kW • ALT. FREQ. TO 7275 kHz / W • E Europe • 100 kW
	MALAYSIA R MALAYSIA SARAWAK, Kuching	DS-IBAN • 10 kW / DS-IBAN • 100 kW
	POLAND †POLISH RADIO WARSAW, Warsaw	• W Europe • 100 kW / • N Europe & E Europe • 100 kW / S • E Europe • 100 kW / • E Europe • 100 kW
	RUSSIA VOICE OF RUSSIA, Petropavlovsk-K	W • W North Am • 250 kW
	SEYCHELLES †FEBA RADIO, North Pt, Mahé Is	S Asia • 100 kW
	SOUTH AFRICA †SOUTH AFRICAN BC, Meyerton	S Africa • DS-R SONDERGRENSE • 100 kW • ALT. FREQ. TO 7185 kHz
	UNITED KINGDOM BBC, Rampisham	W • M-F • E Europe & Mideast • 500 kW / W • E Europe & Mideast • 500 kW / W • E Europe • 500 kW / W • N Africa • 500 kW

(con'd)

FREQUENCY   COUNTRY, STATION, LOCATION

TARGET • NETWORK • POWER (kW)

World Time

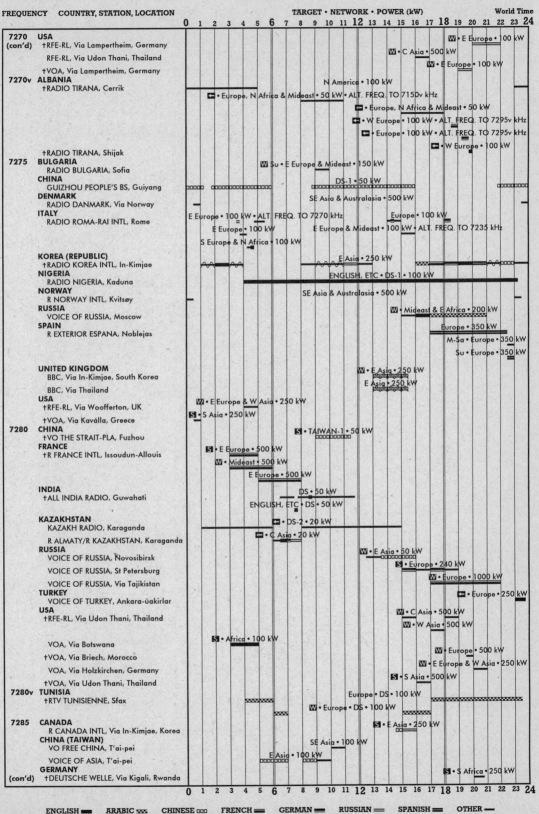

FREQUENCY	COUNTRY, STATION, LOCATION	TARGET • NETWORK • POWER (kW)
7270 (con'd)	USA	
	†RFE-RL, Via Lampertheim, Germany	W • E Europe • 100 kW
	RFE-RL, Via Udon Thani, Thailand	W • C Asia • 500 kW
	†VOA, Via Lampertheim, Germany	W • E Europe • 100 kW
7270v	ALBANIA	N America • 100 kW
	†RADIO TIRANA, Cerrik	← • Europe, N Africa & Mideast • 50 kW • ALT. FREQ. TO 7150v kHz
		■ • Europe, N Africa & Mideast • 50 kW
		← • W Europe • 100 kW • ALT. FREQ. TO 7295v kHz
		← • Europe • 100 kW • ALT. FREQ. TO 7295v kHz
		← • W Europe • 100 kW
	†RADIO TIRANA, Shijak	
7275	BULGARIA	
	RADIO BULGARIA, Sofia	W Su • E Europe & Mideast • 150 kW
	CHINA	
	GUIZHOU PEOPLE'S BS, Guiyang	DS-1 • 50 kW
	DENMARK	
	RADIO DANMARK, Via Norway	SE Asia & Australasia • 500 kW
	ITALY	E Europe • 100 kW • ALT. FREQ. TO 7270 kHz Europe • 100 kW
	RADIO ROMA-RAI INTL, Rome	E Europe • 100 kW E Europe & Mideast • 100 kW • ALT. FREQ. TO 7235 kHz
		S Europe & N Africa • 100 kW
	KOREA (REPUBLIC)	E Asia • 250 kW
	†RADIO KOREA INTL, In-Kimjae	
	NIGERIA	ENGLISH, ETC • DS-1 • 100 kW
	RADIO NIGERIA, Kaduna	
	NORWAY	SE Asia & Australasia • 500 kW
	R NORWAY INTL, Kvitsøy	
	RUSSIA	W • Mideast & E Africa • 200 kW
	VOICE OF RUSSIA, Moscow	
	SPAIN	Europe • 350 kW
	R EXTERIOR ESPANA, Noblejas	M-Sa • Europe • 350 kW
		Su • Europe • 350 kW
	UNITED KINGDOM	W • E Asia • 250 kW
	BBC, Via In-Kimjae, South Korea	E Asia • 250 kW
	BBC, Via Thailand	
	USA	W • E Europe & W Asia • 250 kW
	†RFE-RL, Via Woofferton, UK	
	†VOA, Via Kaválla, Greece	S • S Asia • 250 kW
7280	CHINA	S • TAIWAN-1 • 50 kW
	†VO THE STRAIT-PLA, Fuzhou	
	FRANCE	S • E Europe • 500 kW
	†R FRANCE INTL, Issoudun-Allouis	W • Mideast • 500 kW
		E Europe • 500 kW
	INDIA	DS • 50 kW
	†ALL INDIA RADIO, Guwahati	ENGLISH, ETC • DS • 50 kW
	KAZAKHSTAN	← • DS-2 • 20 kW
	KAZAKH RADIO, Karaganda	
	R ALMATY/R KAZAKHSTAN, Karaganda	← • C Asia • 20 kW
	RUSSIA	W • E Asia • 50 kW
	VOICE OF RUSSIA, Novosibirsk	
	VOICE OF RUSSIA, St Petersburg	S • Europe • 240 kW
	VOICE OF RUSSIA, Via Tajikistan	W • Europe • 1000 kW
	TURKEY	← • Europe • 250 kW
	VOICE OF TURKEY, Ankara-úakirlar	
	USA	W • C Asia • 500 kW
	†RFE-RL, Via Udon Thani, Thailand	W • W Asia • 500 kW
	VOA, Via Botswana	S • Africa • 100 kW
	†VOA, Via Briech, Morocco	W • Europe • 500 kW
	VOA, Via Holzkirchen, Germany	W • E Europe & W Asia • 250 kW
	†VOA, Via Udon Thani, Thailand	S • S Asia • 500 kW
7280v	TUNISIA	Europe • DS • 100 kW
	†RTV TUNISIENNE, Sfax	W • Europe • DS • 100 kW
7285	CANADA	S • E Asia • 250 kW
	R CANADA INTL, Via In-Kimjae, Korea	
	CHINA (TAIWAN)	SE Asia • 100 kW
	VO FREE CHINA, T'ai-pei	
	VOICE OF ASIA, T'ai-pei	E Asia • 100 kW
	GERMANY	S • S Africa • 250 kW
(con'd)	†DEUTSCHE WELLE, Via Kigali, Rwanda	

ENGLISH ▬▬   ARABIC ⧓⧓⧓   CHINESE □□□   FRENCH ▬▬   GERMAN ▬▬   RUSSIAN ══   SPANISH ▬▬   OTHER ▬▬

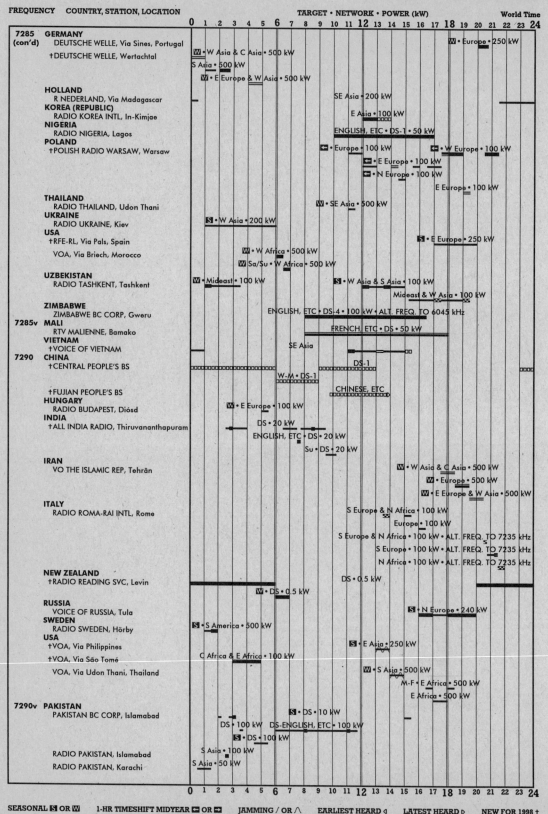

FREQUENCY   COUNTRY, STATION, LOCATION

TARGET • NETWORK • POWER (kW)

World Time

7285	GERMANY	
(con'd)	DEUTSCHE WELLE, Via Sines, Portugal	W • Europe • 250 kW
	†DEUTSCHE WELLE, Wertachtal	W • W Asia & C Asia • 500 kW / S Asia • 500 kW / W • E Europe & W Asia • 500 kW
	HOLLAND	
	R NEDERLAND, Via Madagascar	SE Asia • 200 kW
	KOREA (REPUBLIC)	
	RADIO KOREA INTL, In-Kimjae	E Asia • 100 kW
	NIGERIA	
	RADIO NIGERIA, Lagos	ENGLISH, ETC • DS-1 • 50 kW
	POLAND	
	†POLISH RADIO WARSAW, Warsaw	• Europe • 100 kW / • W Europe • 100 kW / • E Europe • 100 kW / • N Europe • 100 kW / E Europe • 100 kW
	THAILAND	
	RADIO THAILAND, Udon Thani	W • SE Asia • 500 kW
	UKRAINE	
	RADIO UKRAINE, Kiev	S • W Asia • 200 kW
	USA	
	†RFE-RL, Via Pals, Spain	S • E Europe • 250 kW
	VOA, Via Briech, Morocco	W • W Africa • 500 kW / W • Sa/Su • W Africa • 500 kW
	UZBEKISTAN	
	RADIO TASHKENT, Tashkent	W • Mideast • 100 kW / S • W Asia & S Asia • 100 kW / Mideast & W Asia • 100 kW
	ZIMBABWE	
	ZIMBABWE BC CORP, Gweru	ENGLISH, ETC • DS-4 • 100 kW • ALT. FREQ. TO 6045 kHz
7285v	MALI	
	RTV MALIENNE, Bamako	FRENCH, ETC • DS • 50 kW
	VIETNAM	
	†VOICE OF VIETNAM	SE Asia
7290	CHINA	
	†CENTRAL PEOPLE'S BS	DS-1 / W-M • DS-1
	†FUJIAN PEOPLE'S BS	CHINESE, ETC
	HUNGARY	
	RADIO BUDAPEST, Diósd	W • E Europe • 100 kW
	INDIA	
	†ALL INDIA RADIO, Thiruvananthapuram	DS • 20 kW / ENGLISH, ETC • DS • 20 kW / Su • DS • 20 kW
	IRAN	
	VO THE ISLAMIC REP, Tehrān	W • W Asia & C Asia • 500 kW / W • Europe • 500 kW / W • E Europe & W Asia • 500 kW
	ITALY	
	RADIO ROMA-RAI INTL, Rome	S Europe & N Africa • 100 kW / Europe • 100 kW / S Europe & N Africa • 100 kW • ALT. FREQ. TO 7235 kHz / S Europe • 100 kW • ALT. FREQ. TO 7235 kHz / N Africa • 100 kW • ALT. FREQ. TO 7235 kHz
	NEW ZEALAND	
	†RADIO READING SVC, Levin	DS • 0.5 kW / W • DS • 0.5 kW
	RUSSIA	
	VOICE OF RUSSIA, Tula	S • N Europe • 240 kW
	SWEDEN	
	RADIO SWEDEN, Hörby	S • S America • 500 kW
	USA	
	†VOA, Via Philippines	S • E Asia • 250 kW
	†VOA, Via São Tomé	C Africa & E Africa • 100 kW
	VOA, Via Udon Thani, Thailand	W • S Asia • 500 kW / M-F • E Africa • 500 kW / E Africa • 500 kW
7290v	PAKISTAN	
	PAKISTAN BC CORP, Islamabad	S • DS • 10 kW / DS • 100 kW / DS-ENGLISH, ETC • 100 kW / S • DS • 100 kW
	RADIO PAKISTAN, Islamabad	S Asia • 100 kW
	RADIO PAKISTAN, Karachi	S Asia • 50 kW

FREQUENCY   COUNTRY, STATION, LOCATION

TARGET • NETWORK • POWER (kW)   World Time

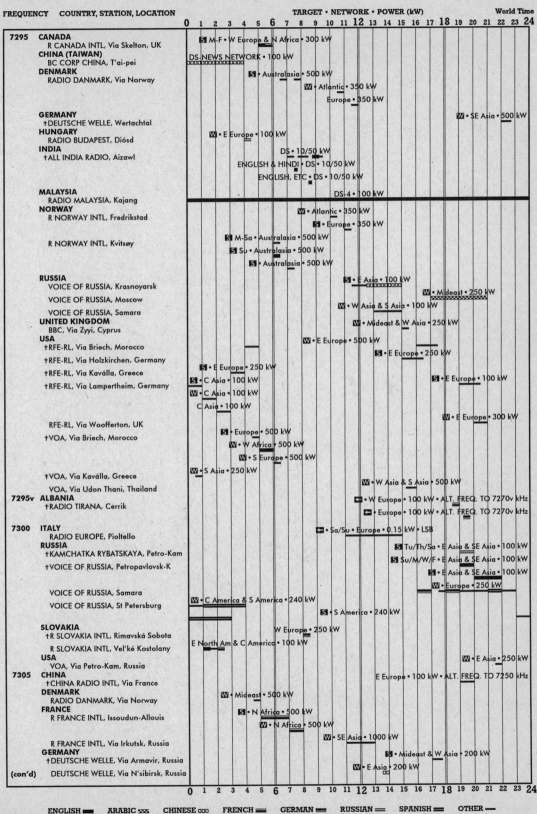

7295 **CANADA**	
R CANADA INTL, Via Skelton, UK	S · M-F · W Europe & N Africa · 300 kW
CHINA (TAIWAN)	
BC CORP CHINA, T'ai-pei	DS-NEWS NETWORK · 100 kW
DENMARK	
RADIO DANMARK, Via Norway	S · Australasia · 500 kW
	W · Atlantic · 350 kW
	Europe · 350 kW
GERMANY	
†DEUTSCHE WELLE, Wertachtal	W · SE Asia · 500 kW
HUNGARY	
RADIO BUDAPEST, Diósd	W · E Europe · 100 kW
INDIA	
†ALL INDIA RADIO, Aizawl	DS · 10/50 kW
	ENGLISH & HINDI · DS · 10/50 kW
	ENGLISH, ETC · DS · 10/50 kW
MALAYSIA	
RADIO MALAYSIA, Kajang	DS-4 · 100 kW
NORWAY	
R NORWAY INTL, Fredrikstad	W · Atlantic · 350 kW
	S · Europe · 350 kW
R NORWAY INTL, Kvitsøy	S · M-Sa · Australasia · 500 kW
	S · Su · Australasia · 500 kW
	S · Australasia · 500 kW
RUSSIA	
VOICE OF RUSSIA, Krasnoyarsk	S · E Asia · 100 kW
VOICE OF RUSSIA, Moscow	W · Mideast · 250 kW
VOICE OF RUSSIA, Samara	W · W Asia & S Asia · 100 kW
UNITED KINGDOM	
BBC, Via Zyyi, Cyprus	W · Mideast & W Asia · 250 kW
USA	
†RFE-RL, Via Briech, Morocco	W · E Europe · 500 kW
†RFE-RL, Via Holzkirchen, Germany	S · E Europe · 250 kW
†RFE-RL, Via Kaválla, Greece	S · E Europe · 250 kW
†RFE-RL, Via Lampertheim, Germany	S · C Asia · 100 kW S · E Europe · 100 kW
	W · C Asia · 100 kW
	C Asia · 100 kW
RFE-RL, Via Woofferton, UK	W · E Europe · 300 kW
†VOA, Via Briech, Morocco	S · Europe · 500 kW
	W · W Africa · 500 kW
	S · S Europe · 500 kW
†VOA, Via Kaválla, Greece	W · S Asia · 250 kW
VOA, Via Udon Thani, Thailand	W · W Asia & S Asia · 500 kW
7295v **ALBANIA**	
†RADIO TIRANA, Cerrik	⬅ · W Europe · 100 kW · ALT. FREQ. TO 7270v kHz
	⬅ · Europe · 100 kW · ALT. FREQ. TO 7270v kHz
7300 **ITALY**	
RADIO EUROPE, Pioltello	⬅ · Sa/Su · Europe · 0.15 kW · LSB
RUSSIA	
†KAMCHATKA RYBATSKAYA, Petro-Kam	S · Tu/Th/Sa · E Asia & SE Asia · 100 kW
†VOICE OF RUSSIA, Petropavlovsk-K	S · Su/M/W/F · E Asia & SE Asia · 100 kW
	S · E Asia & SE Asia · 100 kW
VOICE OF RUSSIA, Samara	W · Europe · 250 kW
VOICE OF RUSSIA, St Petersburg	W · C America & S America · 240 kW
	S · S America · 240 kW
SLOVAKIA	
†R SLOVAKIA INTL, Rimavská Sobota	W Europe · 250 kW
R SLOVAKIA INTL, Vel'ké Kostolany	E North Am & C America · 100 kW
USA	
VOA, Via Petro-Kam, Russia	W · E Asia · 250 kW
7305 **CHINA**	
†CHINA RADIO INTL, Via France	E Europe · 100 kW · ALT. FREQ. TO 7250 kHz
DENMARK	
RADIO DANMARK, Via Norway	W · Mideast · 500 kW
FRANCE	
R FRANCE INTL, Issoudun-Allouis	S · N Africa · 500 kW
	W · N Africa · 500 kW
R FRANCE INTL, Via Irkutsk, Russia	W · SE Asia · 1000 kW
GERMANY	
†DEUTSCHE WELLE, Via Armavir, Russia	S · Mideast & W Asia · 200 kW
(con'd) DEUTSCHE WELLE, Via N'sibirsk, Russia	W · E Asia · 200 kW

ENGLISH ▬   ARABIC ⧚   CHINESE ⬚⬚⬚   FRENCH ══   GERMAN ▬▬   RUSSIA ══   SPANISH ▬▬   OTHER ▬

FREQUENCY   COUNTRY, STATION, LOCATION

TARGET • NETWORK • POWER (kW)

World Time

0 1 2 3 4 5 6 7 8 9 10 11 12 13 14 15 16 17 18 19 20 21 22 23 24

Frequency	Country, Station, Location	Target • Network • Power
7305 (con'd)	**GERMANY** DEUTSCHE WELLE, Via N'sibirsk, Russia	W • S Asia • 500 kW
	HOLLAND R NEDERLAND, Via Kazakhstan	W • S Asia • 1000 kW
	NORWAY R NORWAY INTL, Kvitsøy	W • Mideast • 500 kW
	PAKISTAN RADIO PAKISTAN, Islamabad	W • Mideast • 100 kW • ALT. FREQ. TO 7395 kHz
	RUSSIA VOICE OF RUSSIA, Irkutsk	W • SE Asia • 1000 kW
	VATICAN STATE VATICAN RADIO, Sta Maria di Galeria	S America • 250 kW
		W • E Africa • 250 kW
		C America & S America • 250 kW
		W • Mideast • 100 kW
		E North Am • 250/500 kW
		W • E Asia • 500 kW
		E Asia • 500 kW
		SE Asia • 500 kW
7310	**HOLLAND** †R NEDERLAND, Via Kaliningrad, Russia	S • W Europe • 160 kW
	RUSSIA †MAYAK, Arkhangel'sk	W • DS • 20 kW
	†VOICE OF RUSSIA, Armavir	W • Europe • 700/1000 kW
	VOICE OF RUSSIA, Kaliningrad	S • Europe • 240 kW
	VOICE OF RUSSIA, Moscow	W • S America • 500 kW • ALT. FREQ. TO 7115 kHz
7315	**CHINA** †CENTRAL PEOPLE'S BS	DS-1
		W-M • DS-1
	DENMARK RADIO DANMARK, Via Norway	W • Australasia • 500 kW
	FRANCE †R FRANCE INTL, Issoudun-Allouis	Mideast • 500 kW
		W • E Europe • 500 kW
		W • Mideast • 500 kW
		W • E Africa • 500 kW
		E Africa • 500 kW
	†R FRANCE INTL, Via Vladivostok	W • E Asia • 1000 kW
	GERMANY †DEUTSCHE WELLE, Various Locations	S • S Asia & SE Asia • 500 kW
	†DEUTSCHE WELLE, Via N'sibirsk, Russia	W • E Asia • 200 kW
	DEUTSCHE WELLE, Via Samara, Russia	W • S Asia • 250 kW
	RUSSIA †VOICE OF RUSSIA, Chita	S • E Asia & SE Asia • 1000 kW
	VOICE OF RUSSIA, Petropavlovsk-K	S • E Asia • 100 kW
	SLOVAKIA †ADVENTIST WORLD R, Rimavská Sobota	W • S Asia • 250 kW
	SWAZILAND †TRANS WORLD RADIO, Manzini	S Africa • 50 kW
		M-Th • S Africa • 50 kW
	USA WORLD HARVEST R, Noblesville, Indiana	M • SPANISH & PORTUGUESE • C America • 100 kW
		Tu-Su • C America • 100 kW
		M • C America • 100 kW
		C America • 100 kW
		M-F • C America • 100 kW
		Sa/Su • C America • 100 kW
7320	**RUSSIA** MAGADAN RADIO, Magadan	RUSSIAN, ETC • DS-LOCAL, R ROSSII • 100 kW
	R TIKHIY OKEAN, Magadan	M-F • DS-RADIO ROSSII • 100 kW
		Sa/Su • N Pacific • 100 kW
	VOICE OF RUSSIA, Moscow	W • Europe • 500 kW
	UKRAINE RADIO UKRAINE, Khar'kov	S • W Asia • 100 kW
	UNITED KINGDOM BBC, Rampisham	E Europe • 500 kW
	BBC, Via Zyyi, Cyprus	S • S Asia • 300 kW
		W • C Asia • 250 kW
7325	**AUSTRIA** †R AUSTRIA INTL, Vienna	E North Am • 500 kW • ALT. FREQ. TO 9655 kHz
	FRANCE R FRANCE INTL, Issoudun-Allouis	W • N Africa • 500 kW
	RUSSIA RADIO ROSSII, Armavir	W • W Asia • DS • 100 kW
	†RADIO ROSSII, Samara	S • Mideast & W Asia • DS • 100 kW
	VOICE OF RUSSIA, Armavir	W • C Africa & S Africa • 700/1000 kW
	SWEDEN	
(con'd)	RADIO SWEDEN, Hörby	W • Europe & Africa • 500 kW

0 1 2 3 4 5 6 7 8 9 10 11 12 13 14 15 16 17 18 19 20 21 22 23 24

FREQUENCY   COUNTRY, STATION, LOCATION   TARGET • NETWORK • POWER (kW)   World Time

0 1 2 3 4 5 6 7 8 9 10 11 12 13 14 15 16 17 18 19 20 21 22 23 24

7325	**UNITED KINGDOM**		
(con'd)	BBC, Multiple Locations	N Africa • 300/500 kW
	BBC, Rampisham	⑤ M-F • E Europe • 500 kW W • E Europe • 500 kW
		⑤ M-F • Europe • 500 kW W • M/W • E Europe • 500 kW
		Europe • 500 kW
	BBC, Skelton, Cumbria	S America • 300 kW W • S Europe • 300 kW
		Europe • 300 kW
	BBC, Via Zyyi, Cyprus	W • S Asia • 250 kW W • Mideast • 250 kW
7330	**RUSSIA**	
	VOICE OF RUSSIA, Komsomol'sk 'Amure	W • W North Am • 200 kW
	VOICE OF RUSSIA, Moscow	W • S America • 240 kW W • W Europe • 240 kW
	VOICE OF RUSSIA, Yekaterinburg	W • Europe • 200 kW
		⑤ • S Europe • 200 kW
	UNITED KINGDOM	
	BBC, Via Chita, Russia	W • E Asia • 500 kW
	BBC, Via Vladivostok, Russia	W • E Asia • 500 kW
	USA	
	†VOA, Via Botswana	⑤ • E Africa • 100 kW
		⑤ • M-F • E Africa • 100 kW
		⑤ • Sa/Su • E Africa • 100 kW
7335	**BULGARIA**	
	RADIO BULGARIA, Plovdiv	W • C America • 250 kW
		W • Europe • 500 kW
	CANADA	
	CHU, Ottawa	WORLD TIME • 10 kW • USB
	CHINA	
	†CHINA RADIO INTL	
	CHINA RADIO INTL, Xi'an	S Asia
		E Africa & S Africa • 150 kW
		Europe & N Africa • 150 kW
		Africa • 150 kW
	RUSSIA	
	RADIO ROSSII, St Petersburg	W • E Europe & Mideast • DS • 500 kW
	VATICAN STATE	
	VATICAN RADIO, Sta Maria di Galeria	W • S Asia • 500 kW
7340	**GERMANY**	
	DEUTSCHE WELLE, Via N'sibirsk, Russia	W • E Asia • 1000 kW
	RUSSIA	
	RADIO ROSSII, St Petersburg	W • E Europe & Mideast • DS • 500 kW
	†VOICE OF RUSSIA, Moscow	W • Europe • 500 kW
		W • W Europe & Atlantic • 250 kW
	USA	
	†VOA, Via Botswana	C Africa & E Africa • 100 kW ⑤ • Africa • 100 kW
		Sa/Su • C Africa & E Africa • 100 kW ⑤ M-F • Africa • 100 kW
		⑤ Sa/Su • Africa • 100 kW
7345	**BULGARIA**	
	RADIO BULGARIA, Sofia	⑤ M-F • Europe • 50 kW
	CHINA	
	†CENTRAL PEOPLE'S BS	DS-1
		W • DS-1
	CZECH REPUBLIC	
	†RADIO PRAGUE, Litomyšl	E North Am • 100 kW
		S America • 100 kW
		➤ • W Europe • 100 kW
		W • W Europe • 100 kW W • W Africa • 100 kW
		➤ • N Europe • 100 kW
		W • C America • 100 kW
	RUSSIA	
	†MAYAK, Saransk	⑤ • W Asia • DS • 150 kW
	†RADIO ROSSII, Armavir	⑤ • W Asia • DS • 100 kW
	VOICE OF RUSSIA, Petropavlovsk-K	W • W North Am • 100 kW
	†YAKUT RADIO, Yakutsk	RUSSIAN, ETC • DS-LOCAL, R ROSSII • 50 kW
	SEYCHELLES	
	†FEBA RADIO, North Pt, Mahé Is	W • W Asia & S Asia • 100 kW
	SLOVAKIA	
	R SLOVAKIA INTL, Rimavská Sobota	➤ • W Europe • 250 kW
		⑤ • E Europe & W Asia • 250 kW
	†R SLOVAKIA INTL, Various Locations	➤ • S Europe • 100/250 kW
		➤ • W Europe • 100/250 kW
	†R SLOVAKIA INTL, Vel'ké Kostolany	⑤ • E Europe • 100 kW

0 1 2 3 4 5 6 7 8 9 10 11 12 13 14 15 16 17 18 19 20 21 22 23 24

ENGLISH ▬   ARABIC ⧓   CHINESE ▭▭▭   FRENCH ══   GERMAN ▬▬   RUSSIAN ══   SPANISH ▬▬   OTHER ▬

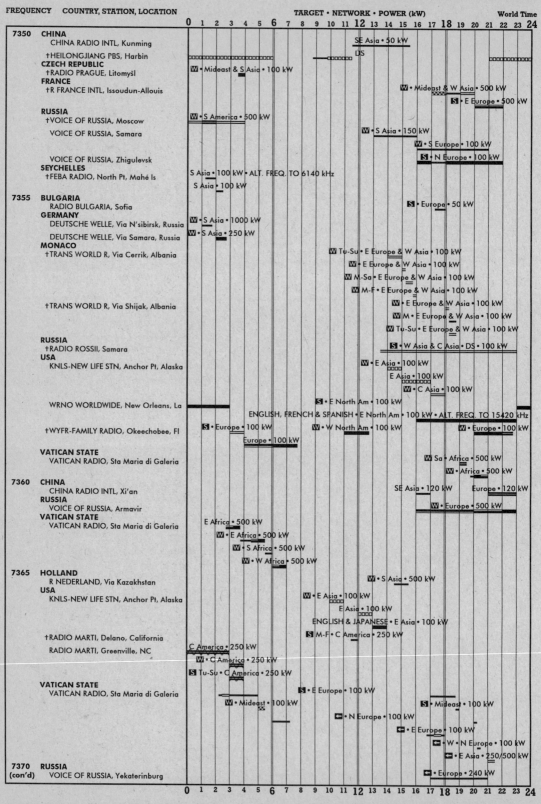

FREQUENCY   COUNTRY, STATION, LOCATION

TARGET • NETWORK • POWER (kW)

World Time

7350	**CHINA**
	CHINA RADIO INTL, Kunming — SE Asia • 50 kW
	†HEILONGJIANG PBS, Harbin — DS
	CZECH REPUBLIC
	†RADIO PRAGUE, Litomyšl — W • Mideast & S Asia • 100 kW
	FRANCE
	†R FRANCE INTL, Issoudun-Allouis — W • Mideast & W Asia • 500 kW / S • E Europe • 500 kW
	RUSSIA
	†VOICE OF RUSSIA, Moscow — W • S America • 500 kW
	VOICE OF RUSSIA, Samara — W • S Asia • 150 kW / W • S Europe • 100 kW
	VOICE OF RUSSIA, Zhigulevsk — S • N Europe • 100 kW
	SEYCHELLES
	†FEBA RADIO, North Pt, Mahé Is — S Asia • 100 kW • ALT. FREQ. TO 6140 kHz / S Asia • 100 kW
7355	**BULGARIA**
	RADIO BULGARIA, Sofia — S • Europe • 50 kW
	GERMANY
	DEUTSCHE WELLE, Via N'sibirsk, Russia — W • S Asia • 1000 kW
	DEUTSCHE WELLE, Via Samara, Russia — W • S Asia • 250 kW
	MONACO
	†TRANS WORLD R, Via Cerrik, Albania — W Tu-Su • E Europe & W Asia • 100 kW / W • E Europe & W Asia • 100 kW / W M-Sa • E Europe & W Asia • 100 kW / W M-F • E Europe & W Asia • 100 kW
	†TRANS WORLD R, Via Shijak, Albania — W • E Europe & W Asia • 100 kW / W M • E Europe & W Asia • 100 kW / W Tu-Su • E Europe & W Asia • 100 kW
	RUSSIA
	†RADIO ROSSII, Samara — S • W Asia & C Asia • DS • 100 kW
	USA
	KNLS-NEW LIFE STN, Anchor Pt, Alaska — W • E Asia • 100 kW / E Asia • 100 kW / W • C Asia • 100 kW
	WRNO WORLDWIDE, New Orleans, La — S • E North Am • 100 kW / ENGLISH, FRENCH & SPANISH • E North Am • 100 kW • ALT. FREQ. TO 15420 kHz
	†WYFR-FAMILY RADIO, Okeechobee, Fl — S • Europe • 100 kW / W • W North Am • 100 kW / W • Europe • 100 kW / Europe • 100 kW
	VATICAN STATE
	VATICAN RADIO, Sta Maria di Galeria — W Sa • Africa • 500 kW / W • Africa • 500 kW
7360	**CHINA**
	CHINA RADIO INTL, Xi'an — SE Asia • 120 kW / Europe • 120 kW
	RUSSIA
	VOICE OF RUSSIA, Armavir — W • Europe • 500 kW
	VATICAN STATE
	VATICAN RADIO, Sta Maria di Galeria — E Africa • 500 kW / W • E Africa • 500 kW / W • S Africa • 500 kW / W • W Africa • 500 kW
7365	**HOLLAND**
	R NEDERLAND, Via Kazakhstan — W • S Asia • 500 kW
	USA
	KNLS-NEW LIFE STN, Anchor Pt, Alaska — W • E Asia • 100 kW / E Asia • 100 kW / ENGLISH & JAPANESE • E Asia • 100 kW
	†RADIO MARTI, Delano, California — S M-F • C America • 250 kW
	RADIO MARTI, Greenville, NC — C America • 250 kW / W • C America • 250 kW / S Tu-Su • C America • 250 kW
	VATICAN STATE
	VATICAN RADIO, Sta Maria di Galeria — S • E Europe • 100 kW / W • Mideast • 100 kW / S • Mideast • 100 kW / ⇨ • N Europe • 100 kW / ⇨ • E Europe • 100 kW / ⇨ • W N Europe • 100 kW / ⇨ • E Asia • 250/500 kW
7370 (con'd)	**RUSSIA**
	VOICE OF RUSSIA, Yekaterinburg — ⇨ • Europe • 240 kW

FREQUENCY   COUNTRY, STATION, LOCATION   TARGET • NETWORK • POWER (kW)   World Time

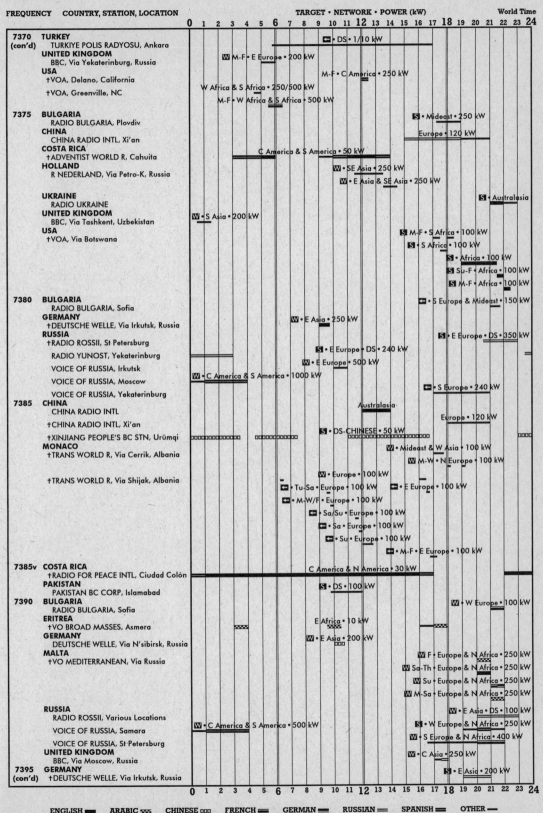

7370	**TURKEY**	
(con'd)	TURKIYE POLIS RADYOSU, Ankara	◻ • DS • 1/10 kW
	UNITED KINGDOM	
	BBC, Via Yekaterinburg, Russia	W M-F • E Europe • 200 kW
	USA	
	†VOA, Delano, California	M-F • C America • 250 kW
	†VOA, Greenville, NC	W Africa & S Africa • 250/500 kW M-F • W Africa & S Africa • 500 kW
7375	**BULGARIA**	
	RADIO BULGARIA, Plovdiv	S • Mideast • 250 kW
	CHINA	
	CHINA RADIO INTL, Xi'an	Europe • 120 kW
	COSTA RICA	
	†ADVENTIST WORLD R, Cahuita	C America & S America • 50 kW
	HOLLAND	
	R NEDERLAND, Via Petro-K, Russia	W • SE Asia • 250 kW W • E Asia & SE Asia • 250 kW
	UKRAINE	
	RADIO UKRAINE	S • Australasia
	UNITED KINGDOM	
	BBC, Via Tashkent, Uzbekistan	W • S Asia • 200 kW
	USA	
	†VOA, Via Botswana	S M-F • S Africa • 100 kW S • S Africa • 100 kW S • Africa • 100 kW S Su-F • Africa • 100 kW S M-F • Africa • 100 kW
7380	**BULGARIA**	
	RADIO BULGARIA, Sofia	◻ • S Europe & Mideast • 150 kW
	GERMANY	
	†DEUTSCHE WELLE, Via Irkutsk, Russia	W • E Asia • 250 kW
	RUSSIA	
	†RADIO ROSSII, St Petersburg	S • E Europe • DS • 350 kW
	RADIO YUNOST, Yekaterinburg	S • E Europe • DS • 240 kW
	VOICE OF RUSSIA, Irkutsk	W • E Europe • 500 kW
	VOICE OF RUSSIA, Moscow	W • C America & S America • 1000 kW
	VOICE OF RUSSIA, Yekaterinburg	◻ • S Europe • 240 kW
7385	**CHINA**	
	CHINA RADIO INTL	Australasia
	†CHINA RADIO INTL, Xi'an	Europe • 120 kW
	†XINJIANG PEOPLE'S BC STN, Urümqi	S • DS-CHINESE • 50 kW
	MONACO	
	†TRANS WORLD R, Via Cerrik, Albania	W • Mideast & W Asia • 100 kW W M-W • N Europe • 100 kW
	†TRANS WORLD R, Via Shijak, Albania	W • Europe • 100 kW ◻ • Tu-Sa • Europe • 100 kW ◻ • E Europe • 100 kW ◻ • M-W/F • Europe • 100 kW ◻ • Sa/Su • Europe • 100 kW ◻ • Sa • Europe • 100 kW ◻ • Su • Europe • 100 kW ◻ • M-F • E Europe • 100 kW
7385v	**COSTA RICA**	
	†RADIO FOR PEACE INTL, Ciudad Colón	C America & N America • 30 kW
	PAKISTAN	
	PAKISTAN BC CORP, Islamabad	S • DS • 100 kW
7390	**BULGARIA**	
	RADIO BULGARIA, Sofia	W • W Europe • 100 kW
	ERITREA	
	†VO BROAD MASSES, Asmera	E Africa • 10 kW
	GERMANY	
	DEUTSCHE WELLE, Via N'sibirsk, Russia	W • E Asia • 200 kW
	MALTA	
	†VO MEDITERRANEAN, Via Russia	W F • Europe & N Africa • 250 kW W Sa-Th • Europe & N Africa • 250 kW W Su • Europe & N Africa • 250 kW W M-Sa • Europe & N Africa • 250 kW
	RUSSIA	
	RADIO ROSSII, Various Locations	W • E Asia • DS • 100 kW W • C America & S America • 500 kW
	VOICE OF RUSSIA, Samara	S • W Europe & N Africa • 250 kW
	VOICE OF RUSSIA, St Petersburg	W • S Europe & N Africa • 400 kW
	UNITED KINGDOM	
	BBC, Via Moscow, Russia	W • C Asia • 250 kW
7395	**GERMANY**	
(con'd)	†DEUTSCHE WELLE, Via Irkutsk, Russia	S • E Asia • 200 kW

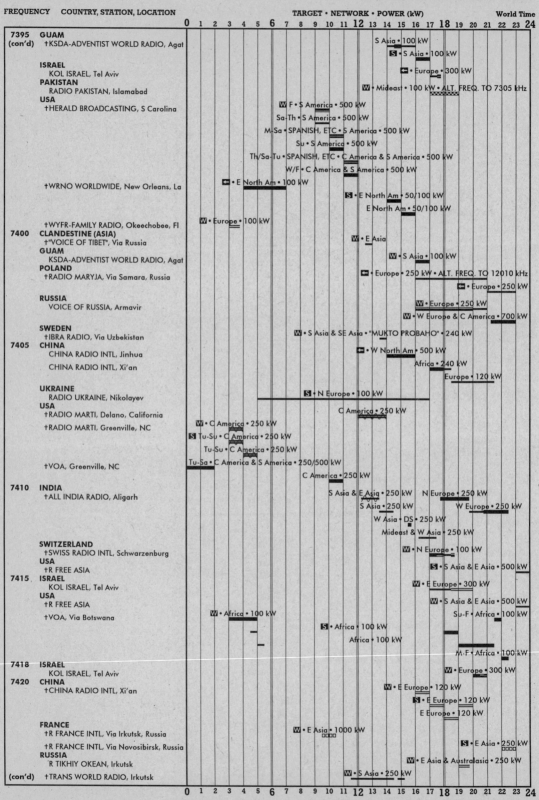

7395 GUAM
(con'd) †KSDA-ADVENTIST WORLD RADIO, Agat — S Asia • 100 kW — S Asia • 100 kW

ISRAEL
KOL ISRAEL, Tel Aviv — Europe • 300 kW
PAKISTAN
RADIO PAKISTAN, Islamabad — Mideast • 100 kW • ALT. FREQ. TO 7305 kHz
USA
†HERALD BROADCASTING, S Carolina — F • S America • 500 kW
Sa-Th • S America • 500 kW
M-Sa • SPANISH, ETC • S America • 500 kW
Su • S America • 500 kW
Th/Sa-Tu • SPANISH, ETC • C America & S America • 500 kW
W/F • C America & S America • 500 kW
†WRNO WORLDWIDE, New Orleans, La — E North Am • 100 kW
E North Am • 50/100 kW
E North Am • 50/100 kW
†WYFR-FAMILY RADIO, Okeechobee, Fl — Europe • 100 kW

7400 CLANDESTINE (ASIA)
†"VOICE OF TIBET", Via Russia — E Asia
GUAM
KSDA-ADVENTIST WORLD RADIO, Agat — S Asia • 100 kW
POLAND
†RADIO MARYJA, Via Samara, Russia — Europe • 250 kW • ALT. FREQ. TO 12010 kHz
Europe • 250 kW

RUSSIA
VOICE OF RUSSIA, Armavir — Europe • 250 kW
W Europe & C America • 700 kW

SWEDEN
†IBRA RADIO, Via Uzbekistan — S Asia & SE Asia • "MUKTO PROBAHO" • 240 kW
7405 CHINA
CHINA RADIO INTL, Jinhua — W North Am • 500 kW
CHINA RADIO INTL, Xi'an — Africa • 240 kW
Europe • 120 kW

UKRAINE
RADIO UKRAINE, Nikolayev — N Europe • 100 kW
USA
†RADIO MARTI, Delano, California — C America • 250 kW
†RADIO MARTI, Greenville, NC — C America • 250 kW
Tu-Su • C America • 250 kW
Tu-Su • C America • 250 kW
†VOA, Greenville, NC — Tu-Sa • C America & S America • 250/500 kW
C America • 250 kW

7410 INDIA
†ALL INDIA RADIO, Aligarh — S Asia & E Asia • 250 kW — N Europe • 250 kW
S Asia • 250 kW — W Europe • 250 kW
W Asia • DS • 250 kW
Mideast & W Asia • 250 kW

SWITZERLAND
†SWISS RADIO INTL, Schwarzenburg — N Europe • 100 kW
USA
†R FREE ASIA — S Asia & E Asia • 500 kW
7415 ISRAEL
KOL ISRAEL, Tel Aviv — E Europe • 300 kW
USA
†R FREE ASIA — S Asia & E Asia • 500 kW
†VOA, Via Botswana — Africa • 100 kW — Su-F • Africa • 100 kW
Africa • 100 kW
Africa • 100 kW
M-F • Africa • 100 kW

7418 ISRAEL
KOL ISRAEL, Tel Aviv — Europe • 300 kW
7420 CHINA
†CHINA RADIO INTL, Xi'an — E Europe • 120 kW
E Europe • 120 kW
E Europe • 120 kW

FRANCE
†R FRANCE INTL, Via Irkutsk, Russia — E Asia • 1000 kW
†R FRANCE INTL, Via Novosibirsk, Russia — E Asia • 250 kW
RUSSIA
R TIKHIY OKEAN, Irkutsk — E Asia & Australasia • 250 kW
(con'd) †TRANS WORLD RADIO, Irkutsk — S Asia • 250 kW

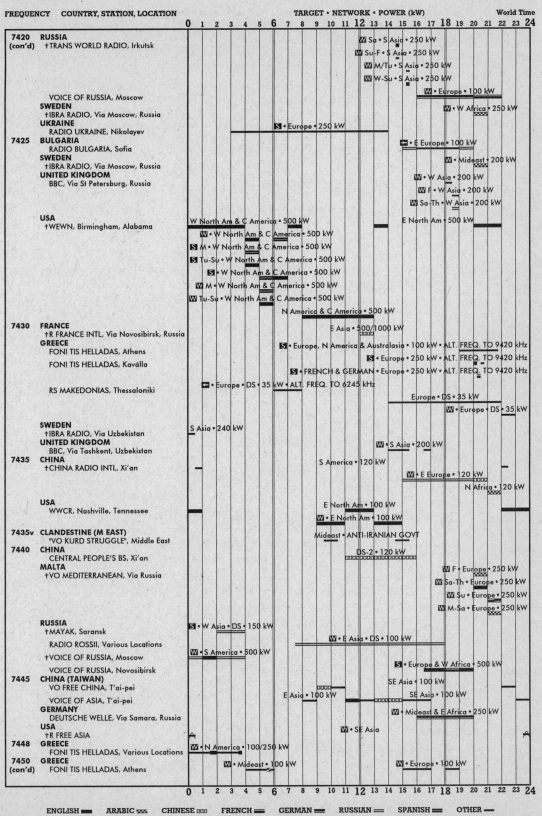

FREQUENCY   COUNTRY, STATION, LOCATION   TARGET • NETWORK • POWER (kW)   World Time

Freq	Country/Station	Details
7420 (con'd)	**RUSSIA** †TRANS WORLD RADIO, Irkutsk	W Sa • S Asia • 250 kW / W Su-F • S Asia • 250 kW / W M/Tu • S Asia • 250 kW / W W-Su • S Asia • 250 kW
	VOICE OF RUSSIA, Moscow	W • Europe • 100 kW
	SWEDEN †IBRA RADIO, Via Moscow, Russia	W • W Africa • 250 kW
	UKRAINE RADIO UKRAINE, Nikolayev	S • Europe • 250 kW
7425	**BULGARIA** RADIO BULGARIA, Sofia	• E Europe • 100 kW
	SWEDEN †IBRA RADIO, Via Moscow, Russia	W • Mideast • 200 kW
	UNITED KINGDOM BBC, Via St Petersburg, Russia	W • W Asia • 200 kW / W F • W Asia • 200 kW / W Sa-Th • W Asia • 200 kW
	USA †WEWN, Birmingham, Alabama	W North Am & C America • 500 kW ... E North Am • 500 kW / W • W North Am & C America • 500 kW / S M • W North Am & C America • 500 kW / S Tu-Su • W North Am & C America • 500 kW / S • W North Am & C America • 500 kW / W M • W North Am & C America • 500 kW / W Tu-Su • W North Am & C America • 500 kW / N America & C America • 500 kW
7430	**FRANCE** †R FRANCE INTL, Via Novosibirsk, Russia	E Asia • 500/1000 kW
	GREECE FONI TIS HELLADAS, Athens	S • Europe, N America & Australasia • 100 kW • ALT. FREQ. TO 9420 kHz
	FONI TIS HELLADAS, Kaválla	S • Europe • 250 kW • ALT. FREQ. TO 9420 kHz / S • FRENCH & GERMAN • Europe • 250 kW • ALT. FREQ. TO 9420 kHz
	RS MAKEDONIAS, Thessaloniki	• Europe • DS • 35 kW • ALT. FREQ. TO 6245 kHz / Europe • DS • 35 kW / W • Europe • DS • 35 kW
	SWEDEN †IBRA RADIO, Via Uzbekistan	S Asia • 240 kW
	UNITED KINGDOM BBC, Via Tashkent, Uzbekistan	W • S Asia • 200 kW
7435	**CHINA** †CHINA RADIO INTL, Xi'an	S America • 120 kW / W • E Europe • 120 kW / N Africa • 120 kW
	USA WWCR, Nashville, Tennessee	E North Am • 100 kW ... / W • E North Am • 100 kW
7435v	**CLANDESTINE (M EAST)** "VO KURD STRUGGLE", Middle East	Mideast • ANTI-IRANIAN GOVT
7440	**CHINA** CENTRAL PEOPLE'S BS, Xi'an	DS-2 • 120 kW
	MALTA †VO MEDITERRANEAN, Via Russia	W F • Europe • 250 kW / W Sa-Th • Europe • 250 kW / W Su • Europe • 250 kW / W M-Sa • Europe • 250 kW
	RUSSIA †MAYAK, Saransk	S • W Asia • DS • 150 kW
	RADIO ROSSII, Various Locations	W • E Asia • DS • 100 kW
	†VOICE OF RUSSIA, Moscow	W • S America • 500 kW
	VOICE OF RUSSIA, Novosibirsk	S • Europe & W Africa • 500 kW
7445	**CHINA (TAIWAN)** VO FREE CHINA, T'ai-pei	SE Asia • 100 kW
	VOICE OF ASIA, T'ai-pei	E Asia • 100 kW / SE Asia • 100 kW
	GERMANY DEUTSCHE WELLE, Via Samara, Russia	W • Mideast & E Africa • 250 kW
	USA †R FREE ASIA	W • SE Asia
7448	**GREECE** FONI TIS HELLADAS, Various Locations	W • N America • 100/250 kW
7450 (con'd)	**GREECE** FONI TIS HELLADAS, Athens	W • Mideast • 100 kW / W • Europe • 100 kW

0 1 2 3 4 5 6 7 8 9 10 11 12 13 14 15 16 17 18 19 20 21 22 23 24

ENGLISH ▬ ARABIC ⌇⌇ CHINESE ▫▫▫ FRENCH ═ GERMAN ▬ RUSSIAN ═ SPANISH ▬ OTHER ▬

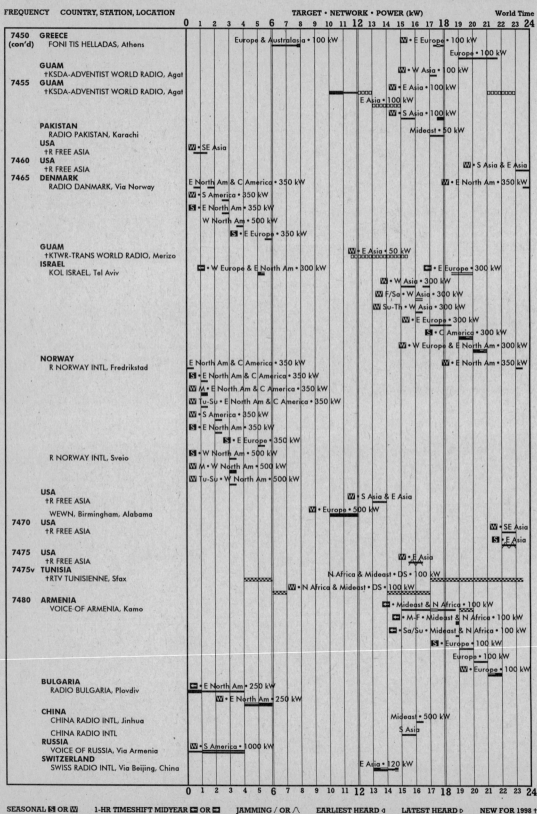

FREQUENCY   COUNTRY, STATION, LOCATION

TARGET • NETWORK • POWER (kW)

World Time

7450 (con'd)	**GREECE** FONI TIS HELLADAS, Athens
	GUAM †KSDA-ADVENTIST WORLD RADIO, Agat
7455	**GUAM** †KSDA-ADVENTIST WORLD RADIO, Agat
	PAKISTAN RADIO PAKISTAN, Karachi
	USA †R FREE ASIA
7460	**USA** †R FREE ASIA
7465	**DENMARK** RADIO DANMARK, Via Norway
	GUAM †KTWR-TRANS WORLD RADIO, Merizo
	ISRAEL KOL ISRAEL, Tel Aviv
	NORWAY R NORWAY INTL, Fredrikstad
	R NORWAY INTL, Sveio
	USA †R FREE ASIA
	WEWN, Birmingham, Alabama
7470	**USA** †R FREE ASIA
7475	**USA** †R FREE ASIA
7475v	**TUNISIA** †RTV TUNISIENNE, Sfax
7480	**ARMENIA** VOICE-OF ARMENIA, Kamo
	BULGARIA RADIO BULGARIA, Plovdiv
	CHINA CHINA RADIO INTL, Jinhua
	CHINA RADIO INTL
	RUSSIA VOICE OF RUSSIA, Via Armenia
	SWITZERLAND SWISS RADIO INTL, Via Beijing, China

Greece: Europe & Australasia • 100 kW / W • E Europe • 100 kW / Europe • 100 kW

Guam KSDA: W • W Asia • 100 kW

Guam KSDA 7455: W • E Asia • 100 kW / E Asia • 100 kW / W • S Asia • 100 kW / Mideast • 50 kW

USA R Free Asia: W • SE Asia

USA R Free Asia 7460: W • S Asia & E Asia

Denmark: E North Am & C America • 350 kW / W • E North Am • 350 kW / W • S America • 350 kW / S • E North Am • 350 kW / W North Am • 500 kW / S • E Europe • 350 kW

Guam KTWR: W • E Asia • 50 kW

Israel: ⊡ • W Europe & E North Am • 300 kW / ⊡ • E Europe • 300 kW / W • W Asia • 300 kW / W F/Sa • W Asia • 300 kW / W Su-Th • W Asia • 300 kW / W • E Europe • 300 kW / S • C America • 300 kW / W • W Europe & E North Am • 300 kW

Norway Fredrikstad: E North Am & C America • 350 kW / S • E North Am & C America • 350 kW / W M • E North Am & C America • 350 kW / W Tu-Su • E North Am & C America • 350 kW / W • S America • 350 kW / S • E North Am • 350 kW / S • E Europe • 350 kW / W • E North Am • 350 kW

Norway Sveio: S • W North Am • 500 kW / W M • W North Am • 500 kW / W Tu-Su • W North Am • 500 kW

USA R Free Asia: W • S Asia & E Asia / W • Europe • 500 kW

USA 7470: W • SE Asia / S • E Asia

USA 7475: W • E Asia

Tunisia 7475v: N Africa & Mideast • DS • 100 kW / W • N Africa & Mideast • DS • 100 kW

Armenia 7480: ⊡ • Mideast & N Africa • 100 kW / W • M-F • Mideast & N Africa • 100 kW / ⊡ • Sa/Su • Mideast & N Africa • 100 kW / S • Europe • 100 kW / Europe • 100 kW / W • Europe • 100 kW

Bulgaria: ⊡ • E North Am • 250 kW / W • E North Am • 250 kW

China Jinhua: Mideast • 500 kW

China Radio Intl: S Asia

Russia: W • S America • 1000 kW

Switzerland: E Asia • 120 kW

FREQUENCY   COUNTRY, STATION, LOCATION   TARGET • NETWORK • POWER (kW)   World Time

0 1 2 3 4 5 6 7 8 9 10 11 12 13 14 15 16 17 18 19 20 21 22 23 24

7485   **DENMARK**
     RADIO DANMARK, Via Norway
- E Europe • 350 kW
- S • E Europe • 350 kW
- W • W Africa • 350 kW
- S • Europe • 350 kW
- S • Europe & Mideast • 350 kW

     NORWAY
     R NORWAY INTL, Fredrikstad
- E Europe • 350 kW
- W • W Africa • 350 kW
- S • Europe • 350 kW
- W M-Sa • W Africa • 350 kW
- W Su • W Africa • 350 kW
- S • Europe & Mideast • 350 kW

     R NORWAY INTL, Sveio
- S M-Sa • Europe • 500 kW
- S Su • Europe • 500 kW

7490   **DENMARK**
     RADIO DANMARK, Via Norway — S • S America • 500 kW
     NORWAY
     R NORWAY INTL, Sveio — S • S America • 500 kW
     RUSSIA
     R TIKHIY OKEAN, Khabarovsk — • E Asia • 100 kW • USB
     VOICE OF RUSSIA, Khabarovsk — E Asia • 100 kW • USB
     USA
     WJCR, Upton, Kentucky — E North Am • 50 kW

7495   **USA**
     †R FREE ASIA — W • E Asia

7495v   **ISRAEL**
     RESHET BET, Tel Aviv — W • W Europe & E North Am • DS • 50 kW

7500   **ITALY**
     †RADIO INTERNAZIONALE, Padova — • Irr • Europe • 1 kW
     MOLDOVA
     †RADIO MOLDOVA INTL, Via Romania
- W • E North Am • 100 kW
- W • Europe • 100 kW
- W • E Europe & W Asia • 100 kW

7504   **CHINA**
     CENTRAL PEOPLE'S BS, Xi'an
- DS-1 • 120 kW
- Th/Sa-M • DS-1 • 120 kW

7510   **TAJIKISTAN**
     †RADIO TAJIKISTAN, Dushanbe — S • C Asia • DS-1 • 100 kW
     USA
     †HERALD BROADCASTING, S Carolina
- W • SPANISH, ETC • Europe • 500 kW
- W Tu/TH/F • GERMAN, ETC • Europe • 500 kW
- W W/Sa-M • Europe • 500 kW
- M-W/F/Sa • SPANISH & FRENCH • Europe • 500 kW
- Su/Th • Europe • 500 kW
- M/Tu/Th-Sa • SPANISH, FRENCH, ETC • Europe • 500 kW
- Su/W • S Europe & W Africa • 500 kW

     KTBN, Salt Lake City, Utah
- W • E North Am • 100 kW
- E North Am • 100 kW

7515   **ETHIOPIA**
     †VO TIGRAY REVOL'N, Mek'ele
- E Africa • 10 kW • ALT. FREQ. TO 6315 kHz
- Sa/Su • E Africa • 10 kW • ALT. FREQ. TO 6315 kHz
- M-F • E Africa • 10 kW • ALT. FREQ. TO 6315 kHz

     USA
     †R FREE ASIA — W • SE Asia

7516   **CHINA**
     CENTRAL PEOPLE'S BS, Beijing — DS-2 • 50 kW

7516v   **PIRATE (EUROPE)**
     †"CRAZY WAVE RADIO", Germany — • Irr • Su • W Europe • ALT. FREQ. TO 6260v kHz

7520   **CHINA (TAIWAN)**
     †VO FREE CHINA, Via Okeechobee, USA — Europe • 100 kW
     DENMARK
     RADIO DANMARK, Via Norway
- S • W North Am • 500 kW
- W • Europe • 350 kW
     MOLDOVA
     †RADIO MOLDOVA INTL, Via Romania
- S • E North Am • 100 kW
- S • Europe • 100 kW
- S • E Europe & W Asia • 100 kW

     NORWAY
     R NORWAY INTL, Fredrikstad — W • Europe • 350 kW
     R NORWAY INTL, Sveio
- S M • W North Am • 500 kW
- S Tu-Su • W North Am • 500 kW

     USA
     †R FREE ASIA
- W • SE Asia
- W • E Asia

(con'd)

0 1 2 3 4 5 6 7 8 9 10 11 12 13 14 15 16 17 18 19 20 21 22 23 24

ENGLISH ▬   ARABIC ⨉⨉   CHINESE ☐☐☐   FRENCH ▭▭   GERMAN ▬▬   RUSSIAN ══   SPANISH ▬▬   OTHER ▬

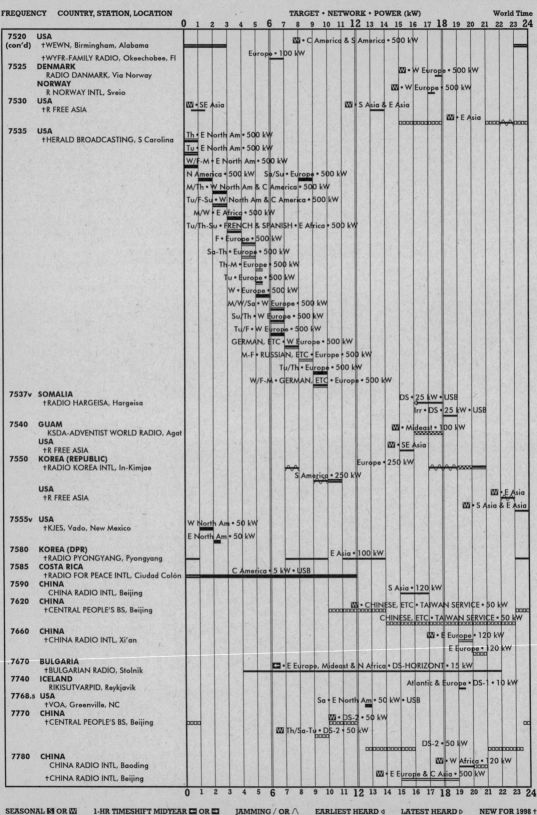

FREQUENCY   COUNTRY, STATION, LOCATION   TARGET • NETWORK • POWER (kW)   World Time

Frequency	Country, Station, Location	Details
7520 (con'd)	USA	
	†WEWN, Birmingham, Alabama	W • C America & S America • 500 kW
	†WYFR-FAMILY RADIO, Okeechobee, Fl	Europe • 100 kW
7525	DENMARK	
	RADIO DANMARK, Via Norway	W • W Europe • 500 kW
	NORWAY	
	R NORWAY INTL, Sveio	W • W Europe • 500 kW
7530	USA	
	†R FREE ASIA	W • SE Asia / W • S Asia & E Asia / W • E Asia
7535	USA	
	†HERALD BROADCASTING, S Carolina	Th • E North Am • 500 kW
		Tu • E North Am • 500 kW
		W/F-M • E North Am • 500 kW
		N America • 500 kW Sa/Su • Europe • 500 kW
		M/Th • W North Am & C America • 500 kW
		Tu/F-Su • W North Am & C America • 500 kW
		M/W • E Africa • 500 kW
		Tu/Th-Su • FRENCH & SPANISH • E Africa • 500 kW
		F • Europe • 500 kW
		Sa-Th • Europe • 500 kW
		Th-M • Europe • 500 kW
		Tu • Europe • 500 kW
		W • Europe • 500 kW
		M/W/Sa • W Europe • 500 kW
		Su/Th • W Europe • 500 kW
		Tu/F • W Europe • 500 kW
		GERMAN, ETC • W Europe • 500 kW
		M-F • RUSSIAN, ETC • Europe • 500 kW
		Tu/Th • Europe • 500 kW
		W/F-M • GERMAN, ETC • Europe • 500 kW
7537v	SOMALIA	
	†RADIO HARGEISA, Hargeisa	DS • 25 kW • USB / Irr • DS • 25 kW • USB
7540	GUAM	
	KSDA-ADVENTIST WORLD RADIO, Agat	W • Mideast • 100 kW
	USA	
	†R FREE ASIA	W • SE Asia
7550	KOREA (REPUBLIC)	
	†RADIO KOREA INTL, In-Kimjae	Europe • 250 kW / S America • 250 kW
	USA	
	†R FREE ASIA	W • E Asia / W • S Asia & E Asia
7555v	USA	
	†KJES, Vado, New Mexico	W North Am • 50 kW / E North Am • 50 kW
7580	KOREA (DPR)	
	†RADIO PYONGYANG, Pyongyang	E Asia • 100 kW
7585	COSTA RICA	
	†RADIO FOR PEACE INTL, Ciudad Colón	C America • 5 kW • USB
7590	CHINA	
	CHINA RADIO INTL, Beijing	S Asia • 120 kW
7620	CHINA	
	†CENTRAL PEOPLE'S BS, Beijing	W • CHINESE, ETC • TAIWAN SERVICE • 50 kW / CHINESE, ETC • TAIWAN SERVICE • 50 kW
7660	CHINA	
	†CHINA RADIO INTL, Xi'an	W • E Europe • 120 kW / E Europe • 120 kW
7670	BULGARIA	
	†BULGARIAN RADIO, Stolnik	⬅ • E Europe, Mideast & N Africa • DS-HORIZONT • 15 kW
7740	ICELAND	
	RIKISUTVARPID, Reykjavik	Atlantic & Europe • DS-1 • 10 kW
7768.s	USA	
	†VOA, Greenville, NC	Sa • E North Am • 50 kW • USB
7770	CHINA	
	†CENTRAL PEOPLE'S BS, Beijing	W • DS-2 • 50 kW / W Th/Sa-Tu • DS-2 • 50 kW / DS-2 • 50 kW
7780	CHINA	
	CHINA RADIO INTL, Baoding	W • W Africa • 120 kW
	†CHINA RADIO INTL, Beijing	W • E Europe & C Asia • 500 kW

FREQUENCY   COUNTRY, STATION, LOCATION

TARGET • NETWORK • POWER (kW)

World Time

0 1 2 3 4 5 6 7 8 9 10 11 12 13 14 15 16 17 18 19 20 21 22 23 24

Freq	Country / Station / Location	Schedule
7800	**CHINA** — CHINA RADIO INTL, Kunming	Europe & N Africa • 50 kW
7820	**CHINA** — CHINA RADIO INTL, Beijing	C Asia • 120 kW
7935	**CHINA** — †CENTRAL PEOPLE'S BS, Beijing	W • DS-1 • 15 kW — DS-1 • 15 kW
7970	**RUSSIA** — RADIO ROSSII, Moscow-Taldom	W • W Africa & Atlantic • DS • 200 kW • USB
8000v	**CLANDESTINE (AFRICA)** — †"VOICE OF SUDAN", Eritrea	N Africa & E Africa • PRO-NDA
8005	**RUSSIA** — †RADIO ROSSII, Moscow-Taldom	W • DS • 200 kW • USB — S • DS • 200 kW • USB
8260	**CHINA** — †CHINA RADIO INTL, Beijing	S • E Asia • FEEDER • 10 kW
8566	**CHINA** — CENTRAL PEOPLE'S BS, Beijing	W • DS-MINORITIES / DS-MINORITIES
8660	**CHINA** — †CHINA RADIO INTL, Beijing	S • SE Asia • FEEDER • 10 kW
9022	**IRAN** — VO THE ISLAMIC REP, Tehrān	N America • 500 kW / Europe • 500 kW / E North Am • 500 kW
9025.3	**CLANDESTINE (AFRICA)** — †"VOICE OF SUDAN", Eritrea	N Africa & E Africa • PRO-NDA
9064	**CHINA** — CENTRAL PEOPLE'S BS, Beijing	DS-2 • 15 kW / Th/Sa-Tu • DS-2 • 15 kW
9080	**CHINA** — †CENTRAL PEOPLE'S BS, Beijing	DS-1 • 50 kW / W • DS-1 • 50 kW
9170	**CHINA** — †CENTRAL PEOPLE'S BS, Beijing	CHINESE, ETC • NETWORK 6 • 50 kW / S • CHINESE, ETC • NETWORK 6 • 50 kW
9181	**JAPAN** — NHK, Osaka	Irr • DS-2(FEEDER) • 0.3 kW • USB
9200	**SUDAN** — †RADIO OMDURMAN, Omdurman	E Africa • 100 kW / Europe, Mideast & Africa • 100 kW
	†REP OF SUDAN RADIO, Omdurman	DS • 100 kW
9275	**ICELAND** — RIKISUTVARPID, Reykjavik	Atlantic & Europe • DS-1 • 10 kW / Atlantic & E North Am • DS-1 • 10 kW
9280	**CHINA (TAIWAN)** — BC CORP CHINA, T'ai-pei	E Asia • DS(FM-1) • 100 kW
	VOICE OF ASIA, T'ai-pei	E Asia • 100 kW
	USA — FAMILY RADIO, Via Taiwan	E Asia • 250 kW
9290	**CHINA** — CENTRAL PEOPLE'S BS, Beijing	DS-1 • 50 kW / W-M • DS-1 • 50 kW
9310	**USA** — †VOICE OF HOPE, Via Tbilisi, Georgia	Europe • 100 kW
9325	**KOREA (DPR)** — †RADIO PYONGYANG, Kujang-dong	Europe • 200 kW
9340	**CHINA** — †CENTRAL PEOPLE'S BS	DS-1 / W-M • DS-1
9345	**KOREA (DPR)** — †RADIO PYONGYANG, Pyongyang	Asia • 200 kW / Europe • 200 kW
9355	**USA** — †HERALD BROADCASTING, Via Saipan	W F • E Asia • 100 kW / W Su/M/W/F • Europe & Mideast • 100 kW / W Th/Sa-Tu • E Asia • 100 kW / S F-Tu • Australasia • 100 kW / W W • E Asia • 100 kW / W Tu/Th/Sa • Europe & Mideast • 100 kW / Su/M/W/F • E Asia • 100 kW / Tu/Th/Sa • E Asia • 100 kW / M/W/F • SE Asia • 100 kW / Su/Tu/Th/Sa • SE Asia • 100 kW / S Asia • 100 kW / E Asia • 100 kW / W M/W/F • FRENCH, GERMAN, ETC • Europe & Mideast • 100 kW / W Su/Tu/Th/Sa • Europe & Mideast • 100 kW / S W/Th • GERMAN, ETC • Australasia • 100 kW

(con'd)

0 1 2 3 4 5 6 7 8 9 10 11 12 13 14 15 16 17 18 19 20 21 22 23 24

ENGLISH ▬   ARABIC ≈≈   CHINESE □□□   FRENCH ▬   GERMAN ▬   RUSSIAN ══   SPANISH ▬   OTHER ▬

FREQUENCY	COUNTRY, STATION, LOCATION	TARGET • NETWORK • POWER (kW)	World Time

World Time scale: 0 1 2 3 4 5 6 7 8 9 10 11 12 13 14 15 16 17 18 19 20 21 22 23 24

9355 (con'd)	USA †WYFR-FAMILY RADIO, Okeechobee, Fl	Europe • 100 kW / S • Europe • 100 kW / W • W North Am • 100 kW
9365	CHINA †CHINA RADIO INTL, Kunming	Europe • 120 kW
	RUSSIA VOICE OF RUSSIA, Via Armenia	S • Mideast & E Africa • 100 kW / S • S America • 1000 kW
	USA †R FREE ASIA	S • SE Asia / S • S Asia & E Asia
9370	GUAM †KSDA-ADVENTIST WORLD RADIO, Agat	E Asia • 100 kW / S • W Asia • 100 kW / S Asia • 100 kW / S • E Asia • 100 kW / SE Asia • 100 kW / W • E Asia • 100 kW
	RUSSIA VOICE OF RUSSIA, Via Armenia	W • S America • 1000 kW
	USA †WEWN, Birmingham, Alabama	S America • 500 kW
9375	GREECE FONI TIS HELLADAS, Athens	S • E Europe • 100 kW
	FONI TIS HELLADAS, Kaválla	W • Europe • 250 kW • ALT. FREQ. TO 9380 kHz / W • FRENCH & GERMAN • Europe • 250 kW • ALT. FREQ. TO 9380 kHz / • E Europe • 250 kW
9380	CHINA †CENTRAL PEOPLE'S BS, Beijing	S • CHINESE, ETC • TAIWAN SERVICE • 50 kW
	CLANDESTINE (M EAST) "VO IRAQI PEOPLE"	• Mideast • ANTI-SADDAM
	GREECE FONI TIS HELLADAS, Kaválla	• Europe • 250 kW • ALT. FREQ. TO 9375 kHz / W • FRENCH & GERMAN • Europe • 250 kW • ALT. FREQ. TO 9375 kHz
9385	GUAM KSDA-ADVENTIST WORLD RADIO, Agat	S • S Asia • 100 kW
	USA †HERALD BROADCASTING, Via Saipan	S • Australasia • 100 kW / Th-Tu • S Africa • 100 kW / M-Sa • GERMAN, ETC • Australasia • 100 kW • ALT. FREQ. TO 9430 kHz / Su • Australasia • 100 kW • ALT. FREQ. TO 9430 kHz / W • S Africa • 100 kW / F-M • S Africa • 100 kW / Tu-Th • GERMAN, ETC • S Africa • 100 kW
9388	ISRAEL RESHET BET, Tel Aviv	S • W Europe & E North Am • DS • 50 kW
9390	CHINA CENTRAL PEOPLE'S BS	W • DS-MINORITIES
	ISRAEL KOL ISRAEL, Tel Aviv	W • W Europe & E North Am • 300 kW
	RESHET BET, Tel Aviv	W • W Europe & E North Am • DS • 50 kW
9395	GREECE FONI TIS HELLADAS, Athens	W • Europe • 100 kW / S • C America & S America • 100 kW
	USA †R FREE ASIA	S • E Asia
9400	MOLDOVA RADIO MOLDOVA INTL, Via Romania	S America • 100 kW / E North Am • 100 kW
	PAKISTAN RADIO PAKISTAN, Islamabad	Mideast • 100 kW / N Africa & W Africa • 100 kW
	PHILIPPINES †FEBC RADIO INTL, Bocaue	E Asia • 40/50 kW • ALT. FREQ. TO 9405 kHz
	USA †WGTG, McCaysville, Georgia	W North Am & C America • 20/50 kW / S • W North Am & C America • 20/50 kW
9405	PHILIPPINES †FEBC RADIO INTL, Bocaue	E Asia • 100 kW / E Asia • 40/50 kW • ALT. FREQ. TO 9400 kHz
9410	UNITED KINGDOM BBC, Multiple Locations	S • Europe • 250/500 kW / Europe • 250/300/500 kW
	BBC, Via Zyyi, Cyprus	W Asia & S Asia • 300 kW / W • W Asia & S Asia • 300 kW
9415	AUSTRALIA †RADIO AUSTRALIA, Shepparton	Pacific & W North Am • 100 kW
(con'd)	BULGARIA RADIO BULGARIA, Plovdiv	• S America • 500 kW

World Time scale: 0 1 2 3 4 5 6 7 8 9 10 11 12 13 14 15 16 17 18 19 20 21 22 23 24

SEASONAL S OR W   1-HR TIMESHIFT MIDYEAR ◘ OR ◘   JAMMING / OR ∧   EARLIEST HEARD ◁   LATEST HEARD ▷   NEW FOR 1998 †

FREQUENCY   COUNTRY, STATION, LOCATION   TARGET • NETWORK • POWER (kW)   World Time

0 1 2 3 4 5 6 7 8 9 10 11 12 13 14 15 16 17 18 19 20 21 22 23 24

9415 (con'd)	**ECUADOR** †HCJB-VO THE ANDES, Quito	W • E North Am • 100 kW W • Europe • 100 kW E Asia • 250 kW
	USA †R FREE ASIA	W • S Asia & E Asia W • SE Asia
9420	**ECUADOR** †HCJB-VO THE ANDES, Quito	Europe • 100 kW • ALT. FREQ. TO 9765 kHz
	GREECE FONI TIS HELLADAS, Athens	W • N America • 100 kW W • Mideast • 100 kW W • Europe • 100 kW W • ARABIC & ENGLISH • Mideast • 100 kW W • Europe & N America • 100 kW S • Mideast • 100 kW S • Europe, N America & Australasia • 100 kW • ALT. FREQ. TO 7430 kHz
	FONI TIS HELLADAS, Kaválla	Mideast • 250 kW • ALT. FREQ. TO 9425 kHz E Europe • 250 kW E Europe • 250 kW • ALT. FREQ. TO 9425 kHz S • Europe • 250 kW • ALT. FREQ. TO 7430 kHz S • FRENCH & GERMAN • Europe • 250 kW • ALT. FREQ. TO 7430 kHz
	SEYCHELLES †FEBA RADIO, North Pt, Mahé Is	S Africa • 75 kW F-W • S Africa • 75 kW
	USA †R FREE ASIA	S • E Asia
9425	**GREECE** FONI TIS HELLADAS, Athens	S • Europe & Australasia • 100 kW S • E Europe • 100 kW Mideast • 100 kW E Europe • 100 kW W • Europe • 100 kW S • C America & Australasia • 100 kW W • C America & S America • 100 kW W • C America • 100 kW
	FONI TIS HELLADAS, Kaválla	Mideast • 250 kW • ALT. FREQ. TO 9420 kHz E Europe • 250 kW • ALT. FREQ. TO 9420 kHz Australasia • 250 kW
9430	**BULGARIA** RADIO BULGARIA, Plovdiv	S • Mideast • 250 kW W • N Africa & W Africa • 500 kW W • W Africa & S America • 500 kW
	CZECH REPUBLIC †RADIO PRAGUE, Litomyšl	W • E Africa • 100 kW W • C Africa • 100 kW W • Australasia • 100 kW W • W Africa & S America • 100 kW W • S Asia & Australasia • 100 kW
	GUAM †KTWR-TRANS WORLD RADIO, Merizo	S Asia • 100 kW • ALT. FREQ. TO 11835 kHz SE Asia • 100 kW
	SWEDEN RADIO SWEDEN, Hörby	S • Europe & Africa • 500 kW S • M-F • Europe & Africa • 500 kW S • Sa/Su • Europe & Africa • 500 kW
	USA †HERALD BROADCASTING, S Carolina	M/W/F • C America & S America • 500 kW Su/Tu/Th/Sa • C America & S America • 500 kW M • C America & S America • 500 kW Tu-Su • SPANISH, ETC • C America & S America • 500 kW
	†HERALD BROADCASTING, Via Saipan	W Su/M/W/F • E Asia • 100 kW W Tu/Th/Sa • RUSSIAN, ETC • E Asia • 100 kW M-Sa • GERMAN, ETC • Australasia • 100 kW • ALT. FREQ. TO 9385 kHz Su • Australasia • 100 kW • ALT. FREQ. TO 9385 kHz
9435	**AUSTRALIA** †RADIO AUSTRALIA, Shepparton	E Asia & SE Asia • 100 kW
	ISRAEL KOL ISRAEL, Tel Aviv	S • Europe • 20 kW W • W Asia • 300 kW W F/Sa • W Asia • 300 kW W Su-Th • W Asia • 300 kW • Europe • 300 kW • W Europe & E North Am • 300 kW
(con'd)	**SWEDEN** RADIO SWEDEN, Hörby	S • E Asia & Australasia • 500 kW

0 1 2 3 4 5 6 7 8 9 10 11 12 13 14 15 16 17 18 19 20 21 22 23 24

ENGLISH ▬ ARABIC ⁑ CHINESE □□□ FRENCH ▬ GERMAN ▬ RUSSIAN ═ SPANISH ▬ OTHER ▬

FREQUENCY   COUNTRY, STATION, LOCATION

TARGET • NETWORK • POWER (kW)

World Time

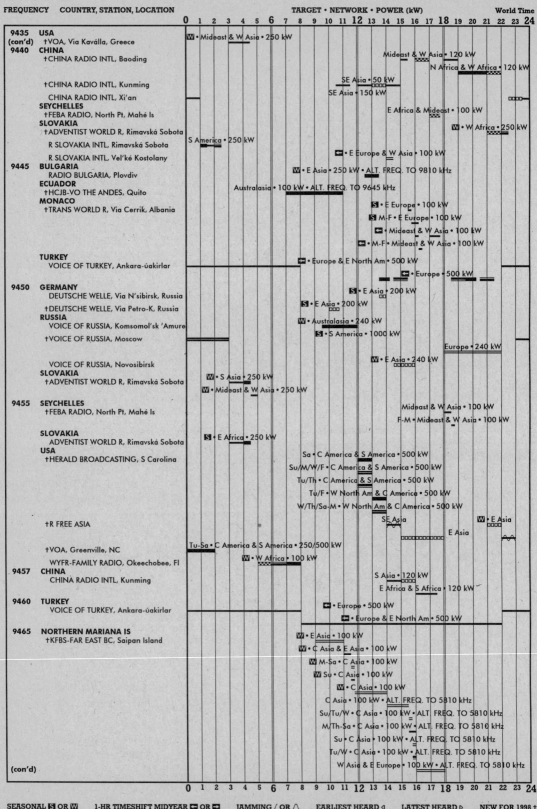

9435	USA	
(con'd)	†VOA, Via Kaválla, Greece	W • Mideast & W Asia • 250 kW
9440	CHINA	
	†CHINA RADIO INTL, Baoding	Mideast & W Asia • 120 kW / N Africa & W Africa • 120 kW
	†CHINA RADIO INTL, Kunming	SE Asia • 50 kW / SE Asia • 150 kW
	CHINA RADIO INTL, Xi'an	
	SEYCHELLES	
	†FEBA RADIO, North Pt, Mahé Is	E Africa & Mideast • 100 kW
	SLOVAKIA	
	†ADVENTIST WORLD R, Rimavská Sobota	W • W Africa • 250 kW
	R SLOVAKIA INTL, Rimavská Sobota	S America • 250 kW
	R SLOVAKIA INTL, Vel'ké Kostolany	• E Europe & W Asia • 100 kW
9445	BULGARIA	
	RADIO BULGARIA, Plovdiv	W • E Asia • 250 kW • ALT. FREQ. TO 9810 kHz
	ECUADOR	
	†HCJB-VO THE ANDES, Quito	Australasia • 100 kW • ALT. FREQ. TO 9645 kHz
	MONACO	
	†TRANS WORLD R, Via Cerrik, Albania	S • E Europe • 100 kW / S M-F • E Europe • 100 kW / • Mideast & W Asia • 100 kW / • M-F • Mideast & W Asia • 100 kW
	TURKEY	
	VOICE OF TURKEY, Ankara-úakirlar	• Europe & E North Am • 500 kW / • Europe • 500 kW
9450	GERMANY	
	DEUTSCHE WELLE, Via N'sibirsk, Russia	S • E Asia • 200 kW
	†DEUTSCHE WELLE, Via Petro-K, Russia	S • E Asia • 200 kW
	RUSSIA	
	VOICE OF RUSSIA, Komsomol'sk 'Amure	W • Australasia • 240 kW
	†VOICE OF RUSSIA, Moscow	S • S America • 1000 kW / Europe • 240 kW
	VOICE OF RUSSIA, Novosibirsk	W • E Asia • 240 kW
	SLOVAKIA	
	†ADVENTIST WORLD R, Rimavská Sobota	W • S Asia • 250 kW / W • Mideast & W Asia • 250 kW
9455	SEYCHELLES	
	†FEBA RADIO, North Pt, Mahé Is	Mideast & W Asia • 100 kW / F-M • Mideast & W Asia • 100 kW
	SLOVAKIA	
	ADVENTIST WORLD R, Rimavská Sobota	S • E Africa • 250 kW
	USA	
	†HERALD BROADCASTING, S Carolina	Sa • C America & S America • 500 kW / Su/M/W/F • C America & S America • 500 kW / Tu/Th • C America & S America • 500 kW / Tu/F • W North Am & C America • 500 kW / W/Th/Sa-M • W North Am & C America • 500 kW
	†R FREE ASIA	SE Asia / E Asia / W • E Asia
	†VOA, Greenville, NC	Tu-Sa • C America & S America • 250/500 kW
	WYFR-FAMILY RADIO, Okeechobee, Fl	W • W Africa • 100 kW
9457	CHINA	
	CHINA RADIO INTL, Kunming	S Asia • 120 kW / E Africa & S Africa • 120 kW
9460	TURKEY	
	VOICE OF TURKEY, Ankara-úakirlar	• Europe • 500 kW / • Europe & E North Am • 500 kW
9465	NORTHERN MARIANA IS	
	†KFBS-FAR EAST BC, Saipan Island	W • E Asia • 100 kW / W • C Asia & E Asia • 100 kW / W M-Sa • C Asia • 100 kW / W Su • C Asia • 100 kW / W • C Asia • 100 kW / C Asia • 100 kW • ALT. FREQ. TO 5810 kHz / Su/Tu/W • C Asia • 100 kW • ALT. FREQ. TO 5810 kHz / M/Th-Sa • C Asia • 100 kW • ALT. FREQ. TO 5810 kHz / Su • C Asia • 100 kW • ALT. FREQ. TO 5810 kHz / Tu/W • C Asia • 100 kW • ALT. FREQ. TO 5810 kHz / W Asia & E Europe • 100 kW • ALT. FREQ. TO 5810 kHz
(con'd)		

FREQUENCY   COUNTRY, STATION, LOCATION   TARGET • NETWORK • POWER (kW)   World Time

0 1 2 3 4 5 6 7 8 9 10 11 **12** 13 14 15 16 17 **18** 19 20 21 22 23 **24**

9465 **NORTHERN MARIANA IS**	
(con'd) †KFBS-FAR EAST BC, Saipan Island	M-Th/Sa • W Asia & E Europe • 100 kW • ALT. FREQ. TO 5810 kHz
	Su/F • W Asia & E Europe • 100 kW • ALT. FREQ. TO 5810 kHz
	M/F • W Asia & E Europe • 100 kW • ALT. FREQ. TO 5810 kHz
	Su • W Asia & E Europe • 100 kW • ALT. FREQ. TO 5810 kHz
	Tu/Th/Sa • W Asia & E Europe • 100 kW • ALT. FREQ. TO 5810 kHz
	W • W Asia & E Europe • 100 kW • ALT. FREQ. TO 5810 kHz
	M/Tu/Sa • W Asia & E Europe • 100 kW • ALT. FREQ. TO 5810 kHz
	Th • W Asia & E Europe • 100 kW • ALT. FREQ. TO 5810 kHz
SLOVAKIA	
†ADVENTIST WORLD R, Rimavská Sobota	W • E Africa • 250 kW W • S Asia • 250 kW W • N Africa • 250 kW
USA	
†FAMILY RADIO, Via Taiwan	E Asia • 250 kW • ALT. FREQ. TO 9630 kHz
WMLK, Bethel, Pennsylvania	Su-F • Europe, Mideast & N America • 50/100 kW
9470 CROATIA	
†CROATIAN RADIO, Via Jülich, Germany	ENGLISH & CROAT • Australasia • 100 kW
	Australasia • 100 kW
GERMANY	
†DEUTSCHE WELLE, Via Samara, Russia	S • E Europe • 200 kW
MONACO	
TRANS WORLD R, Via Cerrik, Albania	S • Europe • 100 kW
RUSSIA	
†MAYAK, Saransk	S • W Asia • DS • 150 kW
VOICE OF RUSSIA, Armavir	W • C Africa & S Africa • 100 kW
VOICE OF RUSSIA, Moscow	S • S America • 500 kW
	S • Europe • 500 kW
VOICE OF RUSSIA, Novosibirsk	W • E Asia • 100 kW
9475 EGYPT	
RADIO CAIRO, Kafr Silîm-Abis	N America • 250 kW
GUAM	
KTWR-TRANS WORLD RADIO, Merizo	E Asia • 100 kW
PHILIPPINES	
FEBC RADIO INTL, Bocaue	E Asia • 50 kW
SLOVAKIA	
†ADVENTIST WORLD R, Rimavská Sobota	W • E Africa • 250 kW
USA	
WWCR, Nashville, Tennessee	E North Am • 100 kW
	W • ENGLISH & SPANISH • E North Am • 100 kW
	S • E North Am • 100 kW
9480 BULGARIA	
RADIO BULGARIA, Sofia	S • Su • Europe • 50 kW
	S • Sa/Su • Europe • 50 kW
CHINA	
CHINA RADIO INTL, Baoding	E Asia • 120 kW Mideast • 120 kW
CZECH REPUBLIC	
RADIO PRAGUE, Litomyšl	S • Mideast • 100 kW
DENMARK	
RADIO DANMARK, Via Norway	S • Europe • 350 kW W • W North Am • 500 kW
	W • E Asia • 500 kW
GERMANY	
†DEUTSCHE WELLE, Via N'sibirsk, Russia	W • S Asia & SE Asia • 500 kW
MONACO	
TRANS WORLD R, Via Cerrik, Albania	S • Europe • 100 kW
NORWAY	
R NORWAY INTL, Fredrikstad	S • Europe • 350 kW
R NORWAY INTL, Kvitsøy	W • E Asia • 500 kW
R NORWAY INTL, Sveio	W • W North Am • 500 kW
RUSSIA	
VOICE OF RUSSIA, Novosibirsk	• E Asia • 100/240 kW
†VOICE OF RUSSIA, St Petersburg	S • S America • 500 kW
	S • N Europe • 500 kW
	W • S Europe & N Africa • 200 kW
USA	
†VOA, Greenville, NC	W • C America & S America • 250 kW
	W Africa & S Africa • 500 kW
	S • W Africa • 500 kW
	M-F • W Africa & S Africa • 500 kW
9485 CZECH REPUBLIC	
†RADIO PRAGUE, Litomyšl	S • S America • 100 kW
DENMARK	
RADIO DANMARK, Via Norway	W • W North Am • 500 kW
	S • Australasia • 500 kW
(con'd)	S • E North Am • 350 kW

0 1 2 3 4 5 6 7 8 9 10 11 **12** 13 14 15 16 17 **18** 19 20 21 22 23 **24**

ENGLISH ▬   ARABIC ⋙   CHINESE ▭▭▭   FRENCH ▬▬   GERMAN ▬   RUSSIAN ═   SPANISH ▬▬   OTHER ▬

FREQUENCY	COUNTRY, STATION, LOCATION	TARGET • NETWORK • POWER (kW)	World Time

0 1 2 3 4 5 6 7 8 9 10 11 12 13 14 15 16 17 18 19 20 21 22 23 24

9485 **FRANCE**
(con'd) †R FRANCE INTL, Issoudun-Allouis — W • N Africa, Mideast & E Africa • 100/500 kW
— W • Mideast & E Africa • 500 kW
— W • E Africa • 100 kW
— E Africa • 100 kW

MONACO
TRANS WORLD R, Monte Carlo — M-Sa • E Europe & W Asia • 100 kW • ALT. FREQ. TO 9490 kHz
NORWAY
R NORWAY INTL, Fredrikstad — S • E North Am • 350 kW
R NORWAY INTL, Kvitsøy — S • M-Sa • Australasia • 500 kW
— S • Su • Australasia • 500 kW

R NORWAY INTL, Sveio — W • W North Am • 500 kW
SLOVAKIA
R SLOVAKIA INTL, Vel'ké Kostolany — E Europe & W Asia • 100 kW
9485v **PAKISTAN**
RADIO PAKISTAN, Islamabad — Mideast • 100 kW
9490 **FRANCE**
R FRANCE INTL, Via French Guiana — S • S America • 500 kW
MONACO
TRANS WORLD R, Monte Carlo — E Europe & W Asia • 100 kW
— M-Sa • E Europe & W Asia • 100 kW • ALT. FREQ. TO 9485 kHz
— S • Mideast • 100 kW
— Su • Mideast & W Asia • 100 kW

TRANS WORLD R, Via Cerrik, Albania — Europe • 100 kW
— M-Sa • Europe • 100 kW
— Sa/Su • Europe • 100 kW
— Sa • Europe • 100 kW
— Su • Europe • 100 kW

RUSSIA
RADIO MOSCOW, Samara — S • Tu/Th • Arctic • DS-NEWS • 100 kW
VOICE OF RUSSIA, Samara — W • W Asia & S Asia • 100 kW
— S • S Europe & W Africa • 240 kW
— W • W Africa • 200 kW

9494.8 **GEORGIA**
†REP ABKHAZIA R — RUSSIAN, ETC • DS-LOCAL,MAYAK,ETC
9495 **AUSTRIA**
†R AUSTRIA INTL, Vienna — W • S America • 100 kW — W • S Africa • 500 kW
CROATIA
†CROATIAN RADIO, Via Jülich, Germany — S • ENGLISH & CROAT • E North Am • 100 kW
— S • E North Am • 100 kW

CZECH REPUBLIC
†RADIO PRAGUE, Litomyšl — S • S Asia & Australasia • 100 kW • ALT. FREQ. TO 11600 kHz
DENMARK
RADIO DANMARK, Via Norway — S • Australasia • 500 kW
FRANCE
†R FRANCE INTL, Issoudun-Allouis — W • E Europe • 500 kW
— Irr • E Europe • 500 kW
— S • E Europe • 500 kW

GUAM
†KSDA-ADVENTIST WORLD RADIO, Agat — E Asia • 100 kW
— W • E Asia • 100 kW
— W • SE Asia • 100 kW

NORTHERN MARIANA IS
†KFBS-FAR EAST BC, Saipan Island — E Asia • 100 kW
— W Asia & C Asia • 100 kW

NORWAY
R NORWAY INTL, Kvitsøy — S • Australasia • 500 kW
PHILIPPINES
FEBC RADIO INTL, Bocaue — SE Asia • 100 kW
USA
†VOA, Greenville, NC — S • C America & S America • 250 kW

WORLD HARVEST R, Noblesville, Indiana — ENGLISH & SPANISH • N America & C America • 100 kW
9500 **BULGARIA**
RADIO BULGARIA, Sofia — S • W Europe • 100 kW
RUSSIA
MAYAK, Blagoveshchensk — DS • 5 kW
SEYCHELLES
†FEBA RADIO, North Pt, Mahé Is — C Africa & S Africa • 75 kW
— Th-M • C Africa & S Africa • 75 kW

SWAZILAND
†TRANS WORLD RADIO, Manzini — C Africa • 100 kW
— Sa/Su • C Africa • 100 kW — Su/F • E Africa • 100 kW

VATICAN STATE
(con'd) VATICAN RADIO, Sta Maria di Galeria — W • Su • E Europe • 100 kW — W • SE Asia • 500 kW

0 1 2 3 4 5 6 7 8 9 10 11 12 13 14 15 16 17 18 19 20 21 22 23 24

FREQUENCY　　COUNTRY, STATION, LOCATION　　　　　TARGET • NETWORK • POWER (kW)　　　　World Time

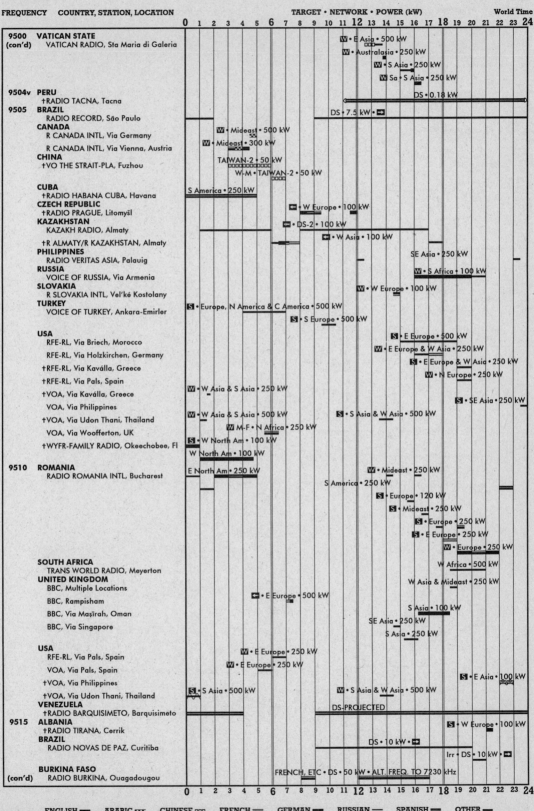

9500 (con'd)	**VATICAN STATE** VATICAN RADIO, Sta Maria di Galeria	W • E Asia • 500 kW; W • Australasia • 250 kW; W • S Asia • 250 kW; Sa • S Asia • 250 kW
9504v	**PERU** †RADIO TACNA, Tacna	DS • 0.18 kW
9505	**BRAZIL** RADIO RECORD, São Paulo	DS • 7.5 kW
	CANADA R CANADA INTL, Via Germany	W • Mideast • 500 kW
	R CANADA INTL, Via Vienna, Austria	W • Mideast • 300 kW
	CHINA †VO THE STRAIT-PLA, Fuzhou	TAIWAN-2 • 50 kW; W-M • TAIWAN-2 • 50 kW
	CUBA †RADIO HABANA CUBA, Havana	S America • 250 kW
	CZECH REPUBLIC †RADIO PRAGUE, Litomyšl	W Europe • 100 kW
	KAZAKHSTAN KAZAKH RADIO, Almaty	DS-2 • 100 kW
	†R ALMATY/R KAZAKHSTAN, Almaty	W • W Asia • 100 kW
	PHILIPPINES RADIO VERITAS ASIA, Palauig	SE Asia • 250 kW
	RUSSIA VOICE OF RUSSIA, Via Armenia	W • S Africa • 100 kW
	SLOVAKIA R SLOVAKIA INTL, Vel'ké Kostolany	W • W Europe • 100 kW
	TURKEY VOICE OF TURKEY, Ankara-Emirler	S • Europe, N America & C America • 500 kW; S • S Europe • 500 kW
	USA RFE-RL, Via Briech, Morocco	S • E Europe • 500 kW
	RFE-RL, Via Holzkirchen, Germany	W • E Europe & W Asia • 250 kW
	†RFE-RL, Via Kaválla, Greece	S • E Europe & W Asia • 250 kW
	†RFE-RL, Via Pals, Spain	W • N Europe • 250 kW
	†VOA, Via Kaválla, Greece	W • W Asia & S Asia • 250 kW; S • SE Asia • 250 kW
	VOA, Via Philippines	W • W Asia & S Asia • 500 kW; S • S Asia & W Asia • 500 kW
	†VOA, Via Udon Thani, Thailand	W M-F • N Africa • 250 kW
	VOA, Via Woofferton, UK	S • W North Am • 100 kW
	†WYFR-FAMILY RADIO, Okeechobee, Fl	W North Am • 100 kW
9510	**ROMANIA** RADIO ROMANIA INTL, Bucharest	E North Am • 250 kW; W • Mideast • 250 kW; S America • 250 kW; S • Europe • 120 kW; S • Mideast • 250 kW; S • Europe • 250 kW; S • E Europe • 250 kW; W • Europe • 250 kW
	SOUTH AFRICA TRANS WORLD RADIO, Meyerton	W Africa • 500 kW
	UNITED KINGDOM BBC, Multiple Locations	W Asia & Mideast • 250 kW
	BBC, Rampisham	S • E Europe • 500 kW
	BBC, Via Maşīrah, Oman	S Asia • 100 kW; SE Asia • 250 kW
	BBC, Via Singapore	S Asia • 250 kW
	USA RFE-RL, Via Pals, Spain	W • E Europe • 250 kW
	VOA, Via Pals, Spain	W • E Europe • 250 kW
	†VOA, Via Philippines	S • E Asia • 100 kW
	†VOA, Via Udon Thani, Thailand	S • S Asia • 500 kW; W • S Asia & W Asia • 500 kW
	VENEZUELA †RADIO BARQUISIMETO, Barquisimeto	DS-PROJECTED
9515	**ALBANIA** †RADIO TIRANA, Cerrik	S • W Europe • 100 kW
	BRAZIL RADIO NOVAS DE PAZ, Curitiba	DS • 10 kW; Irr • DS • 10 kW
(con'd)	**BURKINA FASO** RADIO BURKINA, Ouagadougou	FRENCH, ETC • DS • 50 kW • ALT. FREQ. TO 7230 kHz

ENGLISH ▬　ARABIC ⁵⁵⁵　CHINESE ▫▫▫　FRENCH ▭▭　GERMAN ▬▬　RUSSIAN ═　SPANISH ▭　OTHER ▬

FREQUENCY   COUNTRY, STATION, LOCATION   TARGET • NETWORK • POWER (kW)   World Time

0 1 2 3 4 5 6 7 8 9 10 11 12 13 14 15 16 17 18 19 20 21 22 23 24

Frequency	Country / Station / Location	Details
9515 (con'd)	**BURKINA FASO** RADIO BURKINA, Ouagadougou	Th/Sa/Su • FRENCH, ETC • DS • 50 kW • ALT. FREQ. TO 7230 kHz
	GERMANY DEUTSCHE WELLE, Wertachtal	W • S Asia • 500 kW
	HOLLAND †R NEDERLAND, Via Madagascar	S • SE Asia • 200 kW
	ITALY RAI-RTV ITALIANA, Caltanissetta	• Europe, N Africa & Mideast • DS-1 • 5 kW
	JAPAN RADIO JAPAN/NHK, Via Moyabi, Gabon	Mideast • 500 kW / W • Mideast • 500 kW
	KOREA (REPUBLIC) †RADIO KOREA INTL, In-Kimjae	Mideast & Africa • 250 kW
	UNITED KINGDOM BBC, Via Delano, USA	C America & S America • 250 kW / Tu-Sa • C America & S America • 250 kW
	BBC, Via Meyerton, South Africa	W • S Africa • 500 kW / S Africa • 500 kW
	BBC, Via Sackville, Can	S • E North Am • 250 kW / E North Am • 250 kW / Sa • E North Am • 250 kW
	USA †VOA, Via Philippines	W • SE Asia • 100 kW
9515v	**PAKISTAN** RADIO PAKISTAN, Karachi	S Asia • 50 kW / Mideast • 50 kW • ALT. FREQ. TO 9785 kHz
9520	**CROATIA** †CROATIAN RADIO, Via Jülich, Germany	S America • 100 kW
	DENMARK RADIO DANMARK, Via Norway	W • Mideast • 500 kW
	NORWAY R NORWAY INTL, Kvitsøy	W M-Sa • Mideast • 500 kW / W Su • Mideast • 500 kW
	PHILIPPINES †RADIO VERITAS ASIA, Palauig	E Asia • 250 kW / S Asia • 250 kW
	RUSSIA VOICE OF RUSSIA, Armavir	S • C America • 700/1000 kW
	SWAZILAND †TRANS WORLD RADIO, Manzini	S Africa • 100 kW • ALT. FREQ. TO 9525 kHz / W • S Africa • 100 kW • ALT. FREQ. TO 9525 kHz / W Sa/Su • S Africa • 100 kW • ALT. FREQ. TO 9525 kHz
	USA RFE-RL, Various Locations	• E Europe & W Asia • 100/250 kW
	VOA, Various Locations	• E Europe & W Asia • 100/250 kW
	†VOA, Via Philippines	W • E Asia • 100 kW
	†VOA, Via Woofferton, UK	S • E Europe & W Asia • 300 kW
9525	**DENMARK** RADIO DANMARK, Via Norway	S • S America • 500 kW
	INDONESIA RRI, Jakarta, Jawa	Irr • DS • 250 kW
	VOICE OF INDONESIA, Jakarta, Jawa	Asia & Pacific • 250 kW / Europe • 250 kW
	IRAN VO THE ISLAMIC REP, Tehrān	S • Mideast • 500 kW
	ITALY RADIO ROMA-RAI INTL, Rome	S • E Europe • 100 kW
	NORWAY R NORWAY INTL, Sveio	S • S America • 500 kW
	POLAND †POLISH RADIO WARSAW, Warsaw	• N Europe & E Europe • 100 kW / • W Europe • 100 kW
	SOUTH AFRICA †CHANNEL AFRICA, Meyerton	W • S Africa & W Africa • 500 kW
	SWAZILAND †TRANS WORLD RADIO, Manzini	S Africa • 100 kW • ALT. FREQ. TO 9520 kHz / W • S Africa • 100 kW • ALT. FREQ. TO 9520 kHz / W Sa/Su • S Africa • 100 kW • ALT. FREQ. TO 9520 kHz
	USA VOA, Greenville, NC	• M-F • C America • 250/500 kW
	VOA, Via Philippines	W M-F • E Asia, SE Asia & S Pacific • 50 kW / Australasia • 100 kW
9530	**CHINA** †CENTRAL PEOPLE'S BS	DS-1 • ALT. FREQ. TO 9610 kHz
	GUAM KSDA-ADVENTIST WORLD RADIO, Agat	E Asia • 100 kW
	ROMANIA RADIO ROMANIA INTL, Bucharest	S • Mideast • 250 kW / W • W Europe • 120 kW / W • Mideast • 250 kW
(con'd)		

0 1 2 3 4 5 6 7 8 9 10 11 12 13 14 15 16 17 18 19 20 21 22 23 24

FREQUENCY   COUNTRY, STATION, LOCATION

TARGET • NETWORK • POWER (kW)

World Time

0 1 2 3 4 5 6 7 8 9 10 11 12 13 14 15 16 17 18 19 20 21 22 23 24

Frequency	Country, Station, Location	Schedule details
9530 (con'd)	**RUSSIA**	▣ • RUSSIAN, ETC • DS-LOCAL, R ROSSII • 100 kW
	†MAGADAN RADIO, Magadan	▣ • M-F • DS-RADIO ROSSII • 100 kW
	†R TIKHIY OKEAN, Magadan	▣ • Irr • M-F • N Pacific • 100 kW
		▣ • Sa/Su • N Pacific • 100 kW
	R TIKHIY OKEAN, Vladivostok	W • E Asia • 100 kW
	SOUTH AFRICA	
	†TRANS WORLD RADIO, Meyerton	S • E Africa • 250 kW • ALT. FREQ. TO 9850 kHz
		Sa • E Africa • 250 kW • ALT. FREQ. TO 9850 kHz
	THAILAND	
	†RADIO THAILAND, Udon Thani	W • SE Asia & Australasia • 500 kW
	USA	
	†VOA, Via Philippines	W • E Asia • 250 kW
	VOA, Via Woofferton, UK	W • N Africa • 300 kW
	UZBEKISTAN	
	RADIO TASHKENT, Tashkent	S • Mideast • 100 kW
9530v	**CHINA**	
	XIZANG PEOPLE'S BC STN, Lhasa	DS • 50 kW
9534.8	**ANGOLA**	
	RADIO NACIONAL, Luanda	DS-ANTENNA 2 • 100 kW
		S Africa • 100 kW
9535	**CANADA**	
	R CANADA INTL, Sackville, NB	Su/M • C America & S America • 100/250 kW
		W M-F • C America & S America • 250 kW
		S Tu-Sa • C America & S America • 100 kW
		W Sa/Su • C America & S America • 250 kW
		C America & S America • 100/250 kW
		W • C America & S America • 250 kW
		S • C America & S America • 100 kW
		W Su/M • C America & S America • 250 kW
		S Su/M • C America & S America • 100 kW
		Tu-Sa • C America & S America • 100/250 kW
	R CANADA INTL, Via Xi'an, China	E Asia • 120 kW
	CHINA	
	†CHINA RADIO INTL, Kunming	S Africa • 50 kW • ALT. FREQ. TO 9670 kHz
	†CHINA RADIO INTL	S Asia E Europe
	†CHINA RADIO INTL, Xi'an	E Asia • 150 kW
	GERMANY	
	†DEUTSCHE WELLE, Via Sackville, Can	S • N America & C America • 250 kW
	DEUTSCHE WELLE, Via Sines, Portugal	N America & C America • 250 kW
	†DEUTSCHE WELLE, Via Sri Lanka	S • SE Asia • 250 kW
	ITALY	
	RADIO ROMA-RAI INTL, Rome	S • N Africa • 100 kW
	JAPAN	
	NHK, Fukuoka	Irr • DS-1(FEEDER) • 0.6 kW • USB
	NHK, Sapporo	Irr • DS-1(FEEDER) • 0.6 kW • USB
	†RADIO JAPAN/NHK, Tokyo-Yamata	W • W North Am • 300 kW
		W North Am • 300 kW
	PHILIPPINES	
	†RADIO VERITAS ASIA, Palauig	SE Asia • 250 kW • ALT. FREQ. TO 9615 kHz
	SWITZERLAND	
	SWISS RADIO INTL, Schwarzenburg	S • E Europe • 250 kW
		▣ • S Europe & W Europe • 250 kW
	THAILAND	
	†RADIO THAILAND, Udon Thani	W • N Europe • 500 kW
		W • Europe • 500 kW
	TURKEY	
	VOICE OF TURKEY, Ankara-Emirler	S • Europe • 500 kW
	USA	
	†RFE-RL, Via Biblis, Germany	S • E Europe • 100 kW
	VOA, Via Kaválla, Greece	S • N Africa & Mideast • 250 kW
	VOA, Via Philippines	S • SE Asia • 50 kW
	VOA, Via Udon Thani, Thailand	SE Asia • 500 kW
		S • S Asia & W Asia • 500 kW
9540	**BRAZIL**	
	†R EDUCADORA BAHIA, Salvador	DS • 10 kW • ▣
	IRAN	
	VO THE ISLAMIC REP, Tehrān	S • Europe & Mideast • 500 kW
	OMAN	
	RADIO OMAN, Thamarīt	S • E Africa • DS • 100 kW
		E Africa • DS • 100 kW
	POLAND	
	†POLISH RADIO WARSAW, Warsaw	▣ • W Europe • 100 kW
	SPAIN	
(con'd)	†R EXTERIOR ESPANA, Noblejas	N America & C America • 350 kW

0 1 2 3 4 5 6 7 8 9 10 11 12 13 14 15 16 17 18 19 20 21 22 23 24

ENGLISH ▬ ARABIC ⌇⌇⌇ CHINESE □□□ FRENCH ━ GERMAN ▬ RUSSIAN ═ SPANISH ▬ OTHER ▬

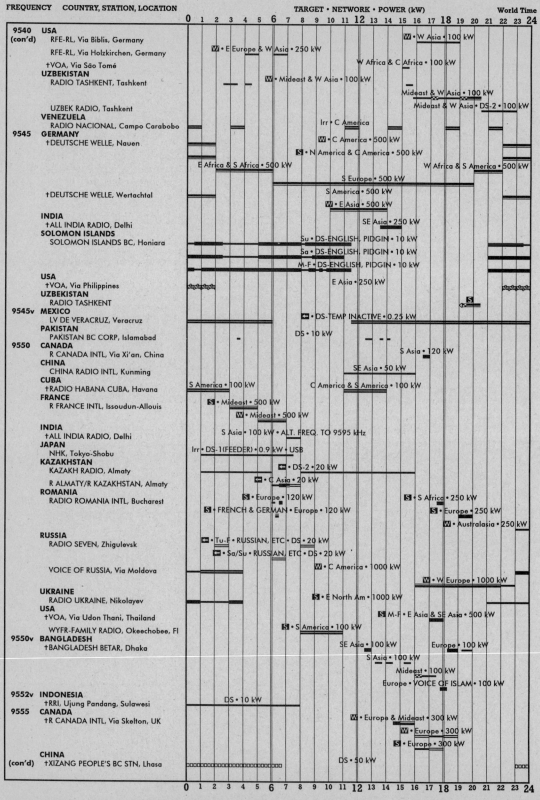

FREQUENCY   COUNTRY, STATION, LOCATION

TARGET • NETWORK • POWER (kW)

World Time

9540
(con'd) USA
         RFE-RL, Via Biblis, Germany
         RFE-RL, Via Holzkirchen, Germany
         †VOA, Via São Tomé
         UZBEKISTAN
         RADIO TASHKENT, Tashkent

         UZBEK RADIO, Tashkent
         VENEZUELA
         RADIO NACIONAL, Campo Carabobo
9545   GERMANY
         †DEUTSCHE WELLE, Nauen

         †DEUTSCHE WELLE, Wertachtal

         INDIA
         †ALL INDIA RADIO, Delhi
         SOLOMON ISLANDS
         SOLOMON ISLANDS BC, Honiara

         USA
         †VOA, Via Philippines
         UZBEKISTAN
         RADIO TASHKENT
9545v   MEXICO
         LV DE VERACRUZ, Veracruz
         PAKISTAN
         PAKISTAN BC CORP, Islamabad
9550   CANADA
         R CANADA INTL, Via Xi'an, China
         CHINA
         CHINA RADIO INTL, Kunming
         CUBA
         †RADIO HABANA CUBA, Havana
         FRANCE
         R FRANCE INTL, Issoudun-Allouis

         INDIA
         †ALL INDIA RADIO, Delhi
         JAPAN
         NHK, Tokyo-Shobu
         KAZAKHSTAN
         KAZAKH RADIO, Almaty

         R ALMATY/R KAZAKHSTAN, Almaty
         ROMANIA
         RADIO ROMANIA INTL, Bucharest

         RUSSIA
         RADIO SEVEN, Zhigulevsk

         VOICE OF RUSSIA, Via Moldova

         UKRAINE
         RADIO UKRAINE, Nikolayev
         USA
         †VOA, Via Udon Thani, Thailand
         WYFR-FAMILY RADIO, Okeechobee, Fl
9550v   BANGLADESH
         †BANGLADESH BETAR, Dhaka

9552v   INDONESIA
         †RRI, Ujung Pandang, Sulawesi
9555   CANADA
         †R CANADA INTL, Via Skelton, UK

         CHINA
(con'd) †XIZANG PEOPLE'S BC STN, Lhasa

SEASONAL ⑤ OR ⑩   1-HR TIMESHIFT MIDYEAR ⇦ OR ⇨   JAMMING / OR ∧   EARLIEST HEARD ◁   LATEST HEARD ▷   NEW FOR 1998 †

FREQUENCY   COUNTRY, STATION, LOCATION

TARGET • NETWORK • POWER (kW)

World Time

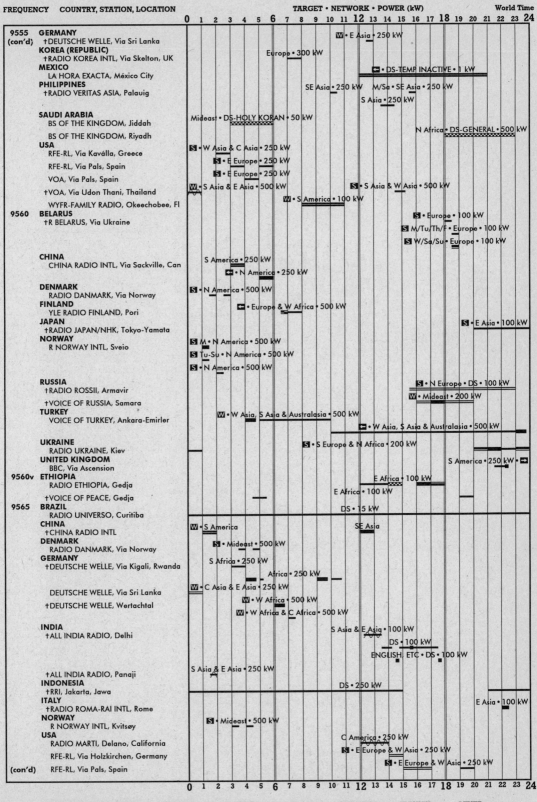

FREQUENCY	COUNTRY, STATION, LOCATION	TARGET • NETWORK • POWER (kW)
9555 (con'd)	GERMANY	
	†DEUTSCHE WELLE, Via Sri Lanka	W • E Asia • 250 kW
	KOREA (REPUBLIC)	
	†RADIO KOREA INTL, Via Skelton, UK	Europe • 300 kW
	MEXICO	
	LA HORA EXACTA, México City	DS-TEMP INACTIVE • 1 kW
	PHILIPPINES	
	†RADIO VERITAS ASIA, Palauig	SE Asia • 250 kW M/Sa • SE Asia • 250 kW
		S Asia • 250 kW
	SAUDI ARABIA	
	BS OF THE KINGDOM, Jiddah	Mideast • DS-HOLY KORAN • 50 kW
	BS OF THE KINGDOM, Riyadh	N Africa • DS-GENERAL • 500 kW
	USA	
	RFE-RL, Via Kaválla, Greece	S • W Asia & C Asia • 250 kW
	RFE-RL, Via Pals, Spain	S • E Europe • 250 kW
	VOA, Via Pals, Spain	S • E Europe • 250 kW
	VOA, Via Udon Thani, Thailand	W • S Asia & E Asia • 500 kW S • S Asia & W Asia • 500 kW
	WYFR-FAMILY RADIO, Okeechobee, Fl	W • S America • 100 kW
9560	BELARUS	
	†R BELARUS, Via Ukraine	S • Europe • 100 kW
		S M/Tu/Th/F • Europe • 100 kW
		S W/Sa/Su • Europe • 100 kW
	CHINA	
	CHINA RADIO INTL, Via Sackville, Can	S America • 250 kW
		N America • 250 kW
	DENMARK	
	RADIO DANMARK, Via Norway	S • N America • 500 kW
	FINLAND	
	YLE RADIO FINLAND, Pori	Europe & W Africa • 500 kW
	JAPAN	
	†RADIO JAPAN/NHK, Tokyo-Yamata	S • E Asia • 100 kW
	NORWAY	
	R NORWAY INTL, Sveio	S M • N America • 500 kW
		S Tu-Su • N America • 500 kW
		S • N America • 500 kW
	RUSSIA	
	†RADIO ROSSII, Armavir	S • N Europe • DS • 100 kW
	†VOICE OF RUSSIA, Samara	W • Mideast • 200 kW
	TURKEY	
	VOICE OF TURKEY, Ankara-Emirler	W • W Asia, S Asia & Australasia • 500 kW
		W Asia, S Asia & Australasia • 500 kW
	UKRAINE	
	RADIO UKRAINE, Kiev	S • S Europe & N Africa • 200 kW
	UNITED KINGDOM	
	BBC, Via Ascension	S America • 250 kW
9560v	ETHIOPIA	
	RADIO ETHIOPIA, Gedja	E Africa • 100 kW
	†VOICE OF PEACE, Gedja	E Africa • 100 kW
9565	BRAZIL	
	RADIO UNIVERSO, Curitiba	DS • 15 kW
	CHINA	
	†CHINA RADIO INTL	W • S America SE Asia
	DENMARK	
	RADIO DANMARK, Via Norway	S • Mideast • 500 kW
	GERMANY	
	†DEUTSCHE WELLE, Via Kigali, Rwanda	S Africa • 250 kW
		Africa • 250 kW
	DEUTSCHE WELLE, Via Sri Lanka	W • C Asia & E Asia • 250 kW
	†DEUTSCHE WELLE, Wertachtal	W • W Africa • 500 kW
		W • W Africa & C Africa • 500 kW
	INDIA	
	†ALL INDIA RADIO, Delhi	S Asia & E Asia • 100 kW
		DS • 100 kW
		ENGLISH ETC • DS • 100 kW
	†ALL INDIA RADIO, Panaji	S Asia & E Asia • 250 kW
	INDONESIA	
	†RRI, Jakarta, Jawa	DS • 250 kW
	ITALY	
	†RADIO ROMA-RAI INTL, Rome	E Asia • 100 kW
	NORWAY	
	R NORWAY INTL, Kvitsøy	S • Mideast • 500 kW
	USA	
	RADIO MARTI, Delano, California	C America • 250 kW
	RFE-RL, Via Holzkirchen, Germany	S • E Europe & W Asia • 250 kW
(con'd)	RFE-RL, Via Pals, Spain	S • E Europe & W Asia • 250 kW

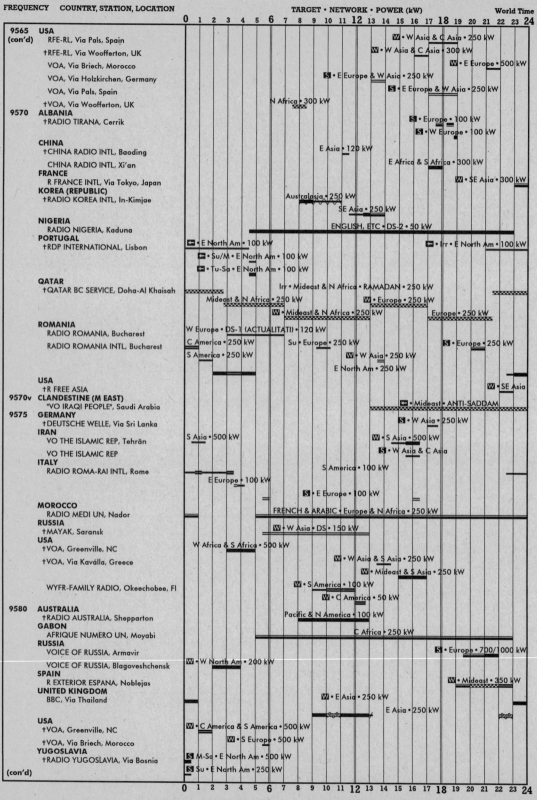

FREQUENCY	COUNTRY, STATION, LOCATION	TARGET • NETWORK • POWER (kW)

9565 USA (con'd)
- RFE-RL, Via Pals, Spain — W • W Asia & C Asia • 250 kW
- †RFE-RL, Via Woofferton, UK — W • W Asia & C Asia • 300 kW
- VOA, Via Briech, Morocco — W • E Europe • 500 kW
- VOA, Via Holzkirchen, Germany — S • E Europe & W Asia • 250 kW
- VOA, Via Pals, Spain — S • E Europe & W Asia • 250 kW
- †VOA, Via Woofferton, UK — N Africa • 300 kW

9570 ALBANIA
- †RADIO TIRANA, Cerrik — S • Europe • 100 kW / S • W Europe • 100 kW

CHINA
- †CHINA RADIO INTL, Baoding — E Asia • 120 kW
- CHINA RADIO INTL, Xi'an — E Africa & S Africa • 300 kW

FRANCE
- R FRANCE INTL, Via Tokyo, Japan — W • SE Asia • 300 kW

KOREA (REPUBLIC)
- †RADIO KOREA INTL, In-Kimjae — Australasia • 250 kW / SE Asia • 250 kW

NIGERIA
- RADIO NIGERIA, Kaduna — ENGLISH, ETC • DS-2 • 50 kW

PORTUGAL
- †RDP INTERNATIONAL, Lisbon — E North Am • 100 kW / Irr • E North Am • 100 kW / Su/M • E North Am • 100 kW / Tu-Sa • E North Am • 100 kW

QATAR
- †QATAR BC SERVICE, Doha-Al Khaisah — Irr • Mideast & N Africa • RAMADAN • 250 kW / Mideast & N Africa • 250 kW / Europe • 250 kW / W • Mideast & N Africa • 250 kW / Europe • 250 kW

ROMANIA
- RADIO ROMANIA, Bucharest — W Europe • DS-1 (ACTUALITATI) • 120 kW
- RADIO ROMANIA INTL, Bucharest — C America • 250 kW / Su • Europe • 250 kW / S • Europe • 250 kW / S America • 250 kW / E North Am • 250 kW

USA
- †R FREE ASIA — W • SE Asia

9570v CLANDESTINE (M EAST)
- "VO IRAQI PEOPLE", Saudi Arabia — Mideast • ANTI-SADDAM

9575 GERMANY
- †DEUTSCHE WELLE, Via Sri Lanka — S • W Asia • 250 kW

IRAN
- VO THE ISLAMIC REP, Tehrān — S Asia • 500 kW / W • S Asia • 500 kW
- VO THE ISLAMIC REP — S • W Asia & C Asia

ITALY
- RADIO ROMA-RAI INTL, Rome — S America • 100 kW / E Europe • 100 kW / S • E Europe • 100 kW

MOROCCO
- RADIO MEDI UN, Nador — FRENCH & ARABIC • Europe & N Africa • 250 kW

RUSSIA
- †MAYAK, Saransk — W • W Asia • DS • 150 kW

USA
- †VOA, Greenville, NC — W Africa & S Africa • 500 kW
- †VOA, Via Kaválla, Greece — W • W Asia & S Asia • 250 kW / W • Mideast & S Asia • 250 kW
- WYFR-FAMILY RADIO, Okeechobee, Fl — W • S America • 100 kW / W • C America • 50 kW

9580 AUSTRALIA
- †RADIO AUSTRALIA, Shepparton — Pacific & N America • 100 kW

GABON
- AFRIQUE NUMERO UN, Moyabi — C Africa • 250 kW

RUSSIA
- VOICE OF RUSSIA, Armavir — S • Europe • 700/1000 kW
- VOICE OF RUSSIA, Blagoveshchensk — W • W North Am • 200 kW

SPAIN
- R EXTERIOR ESPANA, Noblejas — W • Mideast • 350 kW

UNITED KINGDOM
- BBC, Via Thailand — W • E Asia • 250 kW / E Asia • 250 kW

USA
- †VOA, Greenville, NC — W • C America & S America • 500 kW
- †VOA, Via Briech, Morocco — W • S Europe • 500 kW

YUGOSLAVIA
- †RADIO YUGOSLAVIA, Via Bosnia — S • M-Sa • E North Am • 500 kW / S • Su • E North Am • 250 kW

(con'd)

FREQUENCY   COUNTRY, STATION, LOCATION   TARGET • NETWORK • POWER (kW)   World Time

0 1 2 3 4 5 6 7 8 9 10 11 12 13 14 15 16 17 18 19 20 21 22 23 24

Frequency	Country, Station, Location	Schedule
9580 (con'd)	**YUGOSLAVIA** †RADIO YUGOSLAVIA, Via Bosnia	S • E North Am • 250/500 kW; S • W North Am • 500 kW
9580v	**SAUDI ARABIA** BS OF THE KINGDOM, Jiddah	Mideast & E Africa • DS-2 • 50 kW
9585	**BRAZIL** RADIO GLOBO, São Paulo	Irr • DS • 10 kW •; DS • 10 kW •
	CUBA †RADIO HABANA CUBA, Havana	W • Europe & E North Am • 20 kW • USB
	GERMANY †DEUTSCHE WELLE, Via Sri Lanka	W • E Asia • 250 kW
	†DEUTSCHE WELLE, Wertachtal	W • S Asia • 500 kW
	PAKISTAN RADIO PAKISTAN, Islamabad	S Asia & SE Asia • 100 kW
	QATAR QATAR BC SERVICE, Doha-Al Khaisah	S • Mideast & N Africa • 250 kW
	RUSSIA VOICE OF RUSSIA, Via Moldova	W • Mideast & N Africa • 500 kW
	UNITED KINGDOM BBC, Rampisham	W • E Europe • 500 kW
	BBC, Various Locations	• W Asia • 300/500 kW
	USA †RFE-RL, Via Briech, Morocco	W • C Asia • 500 kW
	RFE-RL, Via Udon Thani, Thailand	S • Europe • 500 kW
	†VOA, Via Briech, Morocco	S • S Europe • 500 kW
	†VOA, Via Udon Thani, Thailand	S • S Asia & W Asia • 500 kW; S • E Asia • 500 kW
	VOA, Via Woofferton, UK	S • N Africa • 300 kW
9590	**DENMARK** RADIO DANMARK, Via Norway	W • W Africa • 500 kW; Europe • 350 kW; W • C Africa • 500 kW; S • W Africa & Australasia • 500 kW; W • E Europe • 500 kW; Europe • 500 kW; W • E Africa • 500 kW; W • Australasia • 500 kW; S • Mideast • 350 kW; S • Australasia • 500 kW; S • Atlantic • 350 kW
	GREECE †FONI TIS HELLADAS, Via G'ville, USA	E North Am • 250 kW
	GUAM KTWR-TRANS WORLD RADIO, Merizo	E Asia • 100 kW
	HOLLAND R NEDERLAND, Via Madagascar	SE Asia • 200 kW
	R NEDERLAND, Via Neth Antilles	S • C America & W North Am • 250 kW; S • W North Am • 250 kW
	NORWAY R NORWAY INTL, Fredrikstad	W • Europe • 350 kW; S Su • Mideast • 350 kW; S M-Sa • Europe • 350 kW; S • Atlantic • 350 kW; S Su • Europe • 350 kW; S • Europe • 350 kW; W M-Sa • Europe • 350 kW; W Su • Europe • 350 kW; S M-Sa • Mideast • 350 kW
	R NORWAY INTL, Kvitsøy	W • Australasia • 500 kW; W • E Europe • 500 kW; W • E Africa • 500 kW; W • C Africa • 500 kW; W M-Sa • C Africa • 500 kW; W Su • C Africa • 500 kW; S M-Sa • Australasia • 500 kW; S Su • Australasia • 500 kW
	R NORWAY INTL, Sveio	W • W Africa • 500 kW; S M-Sa • W Africa & Australasia • 500 kW; S Su • W Africa & Australasia • 500 kW; S • Europe • 500 kW
	ROMANIA RADIO ROMANIA INTL, Bucharest	W Su • W Europe • 250 kW
	TURKEY VOICE OF TURKEY, Ankara-Emirler	• N Africa • 500 kW
	UNITED KINGDOM BBC, Via Delano, USA	C America & S America • 250 kW; W • C America & S America • 250 kW
(con'd)		

0 1 2 3 4 5 6 7 8 9 10 11 12 13 14 15 16 17 18 19 20 21 22 23 24

ENGLISH ▬   ARABIC ▨   CHINESE ▢▢▢   FRENCH ═══   GERMAN ▬▬   RUSSIAN ══   SPANISH ▬▬   OTHER ▬

FREQUENCY   COUNTRY, STATION, LOCATION   TARGET • NETWORK • POWER (kW)   World Time

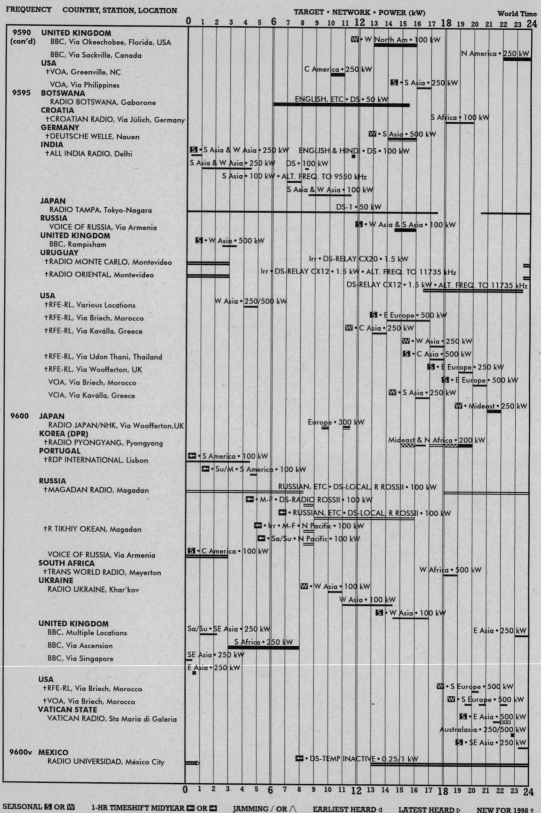

Frequency	Country, Station, Location	Target • Network • Power
9590 (con'd)	UNITED KINGDOM	
	BBC, Via Okeechobee, Florida, USA	W • W North Am • 100 kW
	BBC, Via Sackville, Canada	N America • 250 kW
	USA	
	†VOA, Greenville, NC	C America • 250 kW
	VOA, Via Philippines	S • S Asia • 250 kW
9595	BOTSWANA	
	RADIO BOTSWANA, Gaborone	ENGLISH, ETC • DS • 50 kW
	CROATIA	
	†CROATIAN RADIO, Via Jülich, Germany	S Africa • 100 kW
	GERMANY	
	†DEUTSCHE WELLE, Nauen	W • S Asia • 500 kW
	INDIA	
	†ALL INDIA RADIO, Delhi	S • S Asia & W Asia • 250 kW ENGLISH & HINDI • DS • 100 kW
		S Asia & W Asia • 250 kW DS • 100 kW
		S Asia • 100 kW • ALT. FREQ. TO 9550 kHz
		S Asia & W Asia • 100 kW
	JAPAN	
	RADIO TAMPA, Tokyo-Nagara	DS-1 • 50 kW
	RUSSIA	
	VOICE OF RUSSIA, Via Armenia	S • W Asia & S Asia • 100 kW
	UNITED KINGDOM	
	BBC, Rampisham	S • W Asia • 500 kW
	URUGUAY	
	†RADIO MONTE CARLO, Montevideo	Irr • DS-RELAY CX20 • 1.5 kW
	†RADIO ORIENTAL, Montevideo	Irr • DS-RELAY CX12 • 1.5 kW • ALT. FREQ. TO 11735 kHz
		DS-RELAY CX12 • 1.5 kW • ALT. FREQ. TO 11735 kHz
	USA	
	†RFE-RL, Various Locations	W Asia • 250/500 kW
	†RFE-RL, Via Briech, Morocco	S • E Europe • 500 kW
	†RFE-RL, Via Kaválla, Greece	W • C Asia • 250 kW
		W • W Asia • 250 kW
		S • C Asia • 500 kW
	†RFE-RL, Via Udon Thani, Thailand	S • E Europe • 250 kW
	†RFE-RL, Via Woofferton, UK	S • E Europe • 500 kW
	VOA, Via Briech, Morocco	W • S Asia • 250 kW
	VOA, Via Kaválla, Greece	W • Mideast • 250 kW
9600	JAPAN	
	RADIO JAPAN/NHK, Via Woofferton, UK	Europe • 300 kW
	KOREA (DPR)	
	†RADIO PYONGYANG, Pyongyang	Mideast & N Africa • 200 kW
	PORTUGAL	
	†RDP INTERNATIONAL, Lisbon	⇄ • S America • 100 kW
		⇄ • Su/M • S America • 100 kW
	RUSSIA	
	†MAGADAN RADIO, Magadan	RUSSIAN, ETC • DS-LOCAL, R ROSSII • 100 kW
		⇄ • M-F • DS-RADIO ROSSII • 100 kW
		⇄ • RUSSIAN, ETC • DS-LOCAL, R ROSSII • 100 kW
	†R TIKHIY OKEAN, Magadan	⇄ • Irr • M-F • N Pacific • 100 kW
		⇄ • Sa/Su • N Pacific • 100 kW
	VOICE OF RUSSIA, Via Armenia	S • C America • 100 kW
	SOUTH AFRICA	
	†TRANS WORLD RADIO, Meyerton	W Africa • 500 kW
	UKRAINE	
	RADIO UKRAINE, Khar'kov	W • W Asia • 100 kW
		W Asia • 100 kW
		S • W Asia • 100 kW
	UNITED KINGDOM	
	BBC, Multiple Locations	Sa/Su • SE Asia • 250 kW
		E Asia • 250 kW
	BBC, Via Ascension	S Africa • 250 kW
	BBC, Via Singapore	SE Asia • 250 kW
		E Asia • 250 kW
	USA	
	†RFE-RL, Via Briech, Morocco	W • S Europe • 500 kW
	†VOA, Via Briech, Morocco	W • S Europe • 500 kW
	VATICAN STATE	
	VATICAN RADIO, Sta Maria di Galeria	S • E Asia • 500 kW
		Australasia • 250/500 kW
		S • SE Asia • 250 kW
9600v	MEXICO	
	RADIO UNIVERSIDAD, México City	⇄ • DS-TEMP INACTIVE • 0.25/1 kW

World Time: 0 1 2 3 4 5 6 7 8 9 10 11 12 13 14 15 16 17 18 19 20 21 22 23 24

FREQUENCY   COUNTRY, STATION, LOCATION   TARGET • NETWORK • POWER (kW)   World Time

0 1 2 3 4 5 6 7 8 9 10 11 12 13 14 15 16 17 18 19 20 21 22 23 24

9605 FRANCE
†R FRANCE INTL, Issoudun-Allouis
W • E Europe • 100 kW
Irr • E Europe • 100 kW
S • E Europe • 100 kW

GERMANY
DEUTSCHE WELLE, Via Antigua
S • S America • 250 kW
HOLLAND
R NEDERLAND, Via Madagascar
W • E Africa • 200 kW
UNITED ARAB EMIRATES
†UAE RADIO FROM ABU DHABI
Irr • Mideast • RAMADAN • 500 kW
W • Australasia • 500 kW
W • Mideast • 500 kW
S • Mideast • 500 kW

UNITED KINGDOM
BBC, Via Maṣīrah, Oman
S • S Asia • 100 kW
S Asia • 100 kW

BBC, Via Singapore
SE Asia • 250 kW
S Asia • 250 kW

BBC, Via Zyyi, Cyprus
W • W Asia & S Asia • 250 kW
S • E Europe • 300 kW

USA
†RFE-RL, Via Briech, Morocco
W • E Europe • 500 kW
W Su • E Europe • 500 kW

VOA, Via Kaválla, Greece
S • Mideast • 250 kW
WYFR-FAMILY RADIO, Okeechobee, Fl
W • S America • 100 kW   S America • 100 kW
C America • 100 kW
W • C America • 100 kW

VATICAN STATE
VATICAN RADIO, Sta Maria di Galeria
S • S America • 500 kW
S America • 500 kW
S • E North Am & C America • 500 kW

9610 CHINA
†CENTRAL PEOPLE'S BS
DS-1 • ALT. FREQ. TO 9530 kHz
CHINA (TAIWAN)
BC CORP CHINA, T'ai-pei
DS-NEWS NETWORK • 250 kW
†VO FREE CHINA, T'ai-pei
Australasia • 250 kW   Europe • 250 kW
SE Asia • 250 kW

CLANDESTINE (M EAST)
†"VO ISLAMIC REV'N IN IRAQ", Iran
• Mideast • ANTI-SADDAM
CONGO (REPUBLIC)
†RTV CONGOLAISE, Brazzaville
FRENCH, ETC • DS • 50 kW
Irr • DS • 50 kW

MAURITANIA
†RADIO MAURITANIE, Nouakchott
F • ARABIC, FRENCH, ETC • DS • 100 kW • ALT. FREQ. TO 7245 kHz
ARABIC, FRENCH, ETC • DS • 100 kW • ALT. FREQ. TO 7245 kHz

RUSSIA
†MAYAK, Arkhangel'sk
S • DS • 20 kW
†VOICE OF RUSSIA, Yekaterinburg
S • W Europe • 240 kW
UKRAINE
RADIO UKRAINE, Nikolayev
W • Arctic • 100 kW
UNITED KINGDOM
BBC, Rampisham
W • E Europe • 500 kW
W Sa/Su • E Europe • 500 kW

BBC, Via Ascension
W Africa • 250 kW
BBC, Via Meyerton, South Africa
S • E Africa • 500 kW
BBC, Via Seychelles
E Africa • 250 kW
USA
†RFE-RL, Via Holzkirchen, Germany
S • E Europe • 250 kW
9612v INDONESIA
RRI, Jayapura, Irian Jaya
Irr • DS
9615 BRAZIL
RADIO CULTURA, São Paulo
DS • 7.5 kW •
CANADA
R CANADA INTL, Via Germany
W • Mideast • 500 kW
GERMANY
†DEUTSCHE WELLE, Via Kigali, Rwanda
W • W Africa • 250 kW
†DEUTSCHE WELLE, Via Sines, Portugal
W • S Europe • 250 kW
S • Europe • 250 kW

DEUTSCHE WELLE, Via Sri Lanka
S Asia • 250 kW
†DEUTSCHE WELLE, Wertachtal
S • N America & C America • 500 kW
S • N America • 500 kW

HOLLAND
(con'd)   R NEDERLAND, Via Neth Antilles
S • Australasia • 250 kW

0 1 2 3 4 5 6 7 8 9 10 11 12 13 14 15 16 17 18 19 20 21 22 23 24

ENGLISH ▬   ARABIC ⌗   CHINESE ▯▯▯   FRENCH ▭   GERMAN ▬   RUSSIAN ═   SPANISH ▭   OTHER ▬

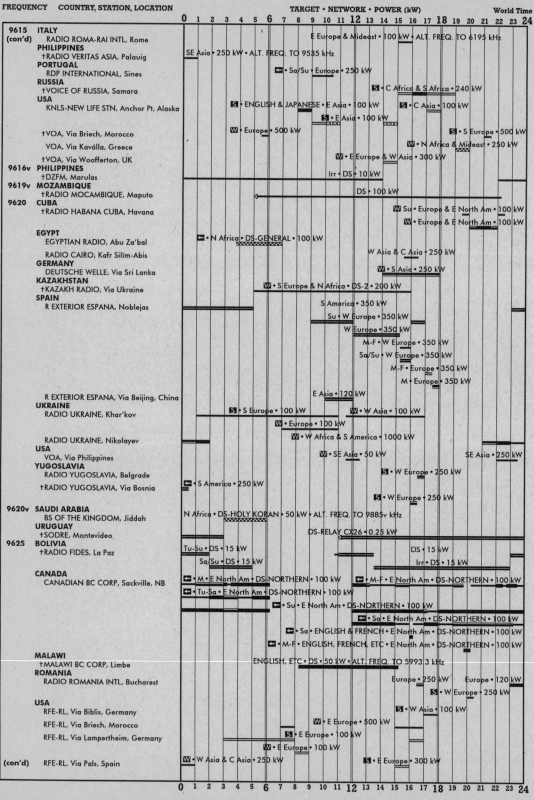

FREQUENCY   COUNTRY, STATION, LOCATION

TARGET • NETWORK • POWER (kW)

World Time

9615	ITALY
(con'd)	RADIO ROMA-RAI INTL, Rome
	PHILIPPINES
	†RADIO VERITAS ASIA, Palauig
	PORTUGAL
	RDP INTERNATIONAL, Sines
	RUSSIA
	†VOICE OF RUSSIA, Samara
	USA
	KNLS-NEW LIFE STN, Anchor Pt, Alaska
	†VOA, Via Briech, Morocco
	VOA, Via Kaválla, Greece
	†VOA, Via Woofferton, UK
9616v	PHILIPPINES
	†DZFM, Marulas
9619v	MOZAMBIQUE
	†RADIO MOCAMBIQUE, Maputo
9620	CUBA
	†RADIO HABANA CUBA, Havana
	EGYPT
	EGYPTIAN RADIO, Abu Za'bal
	RADIO CAIRO, Kafr Silim-Abis
	GERMANY
	DEUTSCHE WELLE, Via Sri Lanka
	KAZAKHSTAN
	†KAZAKH RADIO, Via Ukraine
	SPAIN
	R EXTERIOR ESPANA, Noblejas
	R EXTERIOR ESPANA, Via Beijing, China
	UKRAINE
	RADIO UKRAINE, Khar'kov
	RADIO UKRAINE, Nikolayev
	USA
	VOA, Via Philippines
	YUGOSLAVIA
	RADIO YUGOSLAVIA, Belgrade
	†RADIO YUGOSLAVIA, Via Bosnia
9620v	SAUDI ARABIA
	BS OF THE KINGDOM, Jiddah
	URUGUAY
	†SODRE, Montevideo
9625	BOLIVIA
	†RADIO FIDES, La Paz
	CANADA
	CANADIAN BC CORP, Sackville, NB
	MALAWI
	†MALAWI BC CORP, Limbe
	ROMANIA
	RADIO ROMANIA INTL, Bucharest
	USA
	RFE-RL, Via Biblis, Germany
	RFE-RL, Via Briech, Morocco
	RFE-RL, Via Lampertheim, Germany
(con'd)	RFE-RL, Via Pals, Spain

Target/network/power entries (by station):

- E Europe & Mideast • 100 kW • ALT. FREQ. TO 6195 kHz
- SE Asia • 250 kW • ALT. FREQ. TO 9535 kHz
- S • Sa/Su • Europe • 250 kW
- S • C Africa & S Africa • 240 kW
- S • ENGLISH & JAPANESE • E Asia • 100 kW
- S • C Asia • 100 kW
- S • E Asia • 100 kW
- W • Europe • 500 kW
- S • S Europe • 500 kW
- W • N Africa & Mideast • 250 kW
- W • E Europe & W Asia • 300 kW
- Irr • DS • 10 kW
- DS • 100 kW
- W • Su • Europe & E North Am • 100 kW
- W • Europe & E North Am • 100 kW
- N Africa • DS-GENERAL • 100 kW
- W Asia & C Asia • 250 kW
- W • S Asia • 250 kW
- W • S Europe & N Africa • DS-2 • 200 kW
- S America • 350 kW
- Su • W Europe • 350 kW
- W Europe • 350 kW
- M-F • W Europe • 350 kW
- Sa/Su • W Europe • 350 kW
- M-F • Europe • 350 kW
- M • Europe • 350 kW
- E Asia • 120 kW
- S • S Europe • 100 kW
- W • W Asia • 100 kW
- W • Europe • 100 kW
- W • W Africa & S America • 1000 kW
- W • SE Asia • 50 kW
- SE Asia • 250 kW
- S • W Europe • 250 kW
- S America • 250 kW
- S • W Europe • 250 kW
- N Africa • DS-HOLY KORAN • 50 kW • ALT. FREQ. TO 9885v kHz
- DS-RELAY CX26 • 0.25 kW
- Tu-Su • DS • 15 kW
- DS • 15 kW
- Sa/Su • DS • 15 kW
- Irr • DS • 15 kW
- M • E North Am • DS-NORTHERN • 100 kW
- M-F • E North Am • DS-NORTHERN • 100 kW
- Tu-Sa • E North Am • DS-NORTHERN • 100 kW
- Su • E North Am • DS-NORTHERN • 100 kW
- Sa • E North Am • DS-NORTHERN • 100 kW
- Sa • ENGLISH & FRENCH • E North Am • DS-NORTHERN • 100 kW
- M-F • ENGLISH, FRENCH, ETC • E North Am • DS-NORTHERN • 100 kW
- ENGLISH, ETC • DS • 50 kW • ALT. FREQ. TO 5993.3 kHz
- Europe • 250 kW
- Europe • 120 kW
- S • W Europe • 250 kW
- S • W Asia • 100 kW
- W • E Europe • 500 kW
- S • E Europe • 100 kW
- W • E Europe • 100 kW
- W • W Asia & C Asia • 250 kW
- S • E Europe • 300 kW

FREQUENCY   COUNTRY, STATION, LOCATION

TARGET • NETWORK • POWER (kW)

World Time

0 1 2 3 4 5 6 7 8 9 10 11 12 13 14 15 16 17 18 19 20 21 22 23 24

Frequency	Country, Station, Location	Target • Network • Power
9625 (con'd)	USA	
	RFE-RL, Via Pals, Spain	S • W Asia & C Asia • 250 kW
		W Asia & C Asia • 250 kW
		E Europe • 250 kW
		W • E Europe • 250 kW
		S • E Europe & W Asia • 250 kW
		W • E Europe • 300 kW
	RFE-RL, Via Woofferton, UK	W • E Europe • 500 kW
	†VOA, Via Briech, Morocco	W • E Europe • 100 kW
	VOA, Via Lampertheim, Germany	S • S Europe • 250 kW
	†VOA, Via Woofferton, UK	S • S America • 100 kW
	WYFR-FAMILY RADIO, Okeechobee, Fl	
9630	BRAZIL	
	RADIO APARECIDA, Aparecida	DS • 10 kW • ➡
	CHINA (TAIWAN)	E Asia • NETWORK 2 • 300 kW
	CENTRAL BC SYSTEM, T'ai-pei	Mideast & N Africa • 250 kW • ALT. FREQ. TO 9955 kHz
	†VO FREE CHINA, T'ai-pei	
	INDONESIA	DS • 250 kW
	†RRI, Jakarta, Jawa	
	JORDAN	
	RADIO JORDAN, Qasr el Kharana	← • N Africa & E Africa • 500 kW
	PORTUGAL	
	RDP INTERNATIONAL, Sines	← • M-F • Europe • 250 kW
	RUSSIA	
	VOICE OF RUSSIA, Via Moldova	W • W Africa • 500 kW
	SPAIN	
	R EXTERIOR ESPANA, Via Costa Rica	M-F • N America • 100 kW
	TURKEY	
	VOICE OF TURKEY, Ankara-Emirler	← • W Asia • 500 kW
		← • W Asia & S Asia • 500 kW
	UNITED KINGDOM	
	BBC, Via Seychelles	E Africa • 250 kW
	USA	E Asia • 250 kW • ALT. FREQ. TO 9465 kHz
	†FAMILY RADIO, Via Taiwan	S • Africa • 100 kW
	VOA, Via Botswana	S • Sa/Su • Africa • 100 kW
9635	FINLAND	
	YLE RADIO FINLAND, Pori	W • Mideast & E Africa • 500 kW
	GUAM	S • SE Asia • 100 kW
	KSDA-ADVENTIST WORLD RADIO, Agat	
	PORTUGAL	← • C America & S America • 100 kW
	†RDP INTERNATIONAL, Lisbon	← • Su/M • C America & S America • 100 kW
	RUSSIA	
	VOICE OF RUSSIA, Via Kazakhstan	W • Mideast • 240 kW
	TURKEY	
	VOICE OF TURKEY, Ankara-Emirler	S • S Europe • 500 kW
	UNITED KINGDOM	
	BBC, Multiple Locations	W • Europe • 250/500 kW
	BBC, Rampisham	W Su • Europe • 500 kW
	BBC, Via Zyyi, Cyprus	S • E Europe • 250 kW W • Europe • 250 kW
		E Europe • 250 kW
		W • E Europe • 250 kW
	USA	
	†RFE-RL, Via Briech, Morocco	S • Mideast & W Asia • 500 kW
	RFE-RL, Via Pals, Spain	S • E Europe & W Asia • 250 kW
	†VOA, Via Udon Thani, Thailand	S • S Asia • 500 kW W • S Asia • 500 kW
9635v	MALI	
	RTV MALIENNE, Bamako	FRENCH, ETC • DS • 50 kW
9637v	MOZAMBIQUE	
	DELEGACAO DE BEIRA, Beira	DS-B • 100 kW
9640	CANADA	
	†R CANADA INTL, Sackville, NB	← • E North Am • 100/250 kW
		← • M-F • E North Am • 100/250 kW
		W Su • E North Am • 100 kW
	GERMANY	
	†DEUTSCHE WELLE, Various Locations	W • N America & C America • 250/500 kW Africa • 250/500 kW
	DEUTSCHE WELLE, Via Antigua	S • N America • 250 kW W • S America • 250 kW
	†DEUTSCHE WELLE, Via Sines, Portugal	W • S America • 250 kW
		S America • 250 kW
	DEUTSCHE WELLE, Via Sri Lanka	S • C Asia & E Asia • 250 kW
	†DEUTSCHE WELLE, Wertachtal	S • E Europe & Mideast • 500 kW
		W • W Africa • 500 kW
	KOREA (DPR)	
(con'd)	†RADIO PYONGYANG, Pyongyang	Mideast • 200 kW

0 1 2 3 4 5 6 7 8 9 10 11 12 13 14 15 16 17 18 19 20 21 22 23 24

ENGLISH ▬   ARABIC ﹏   CHINESE ▫▫▫   FRENCH ▬   GERMAN ▬   RUSSIAN ═   SPANISH ▬   OTHER ▬

FREQUENCY   COUNTRY, STATION, LOCATION   TARGET • NETWORK • POWER (kW)   World Time

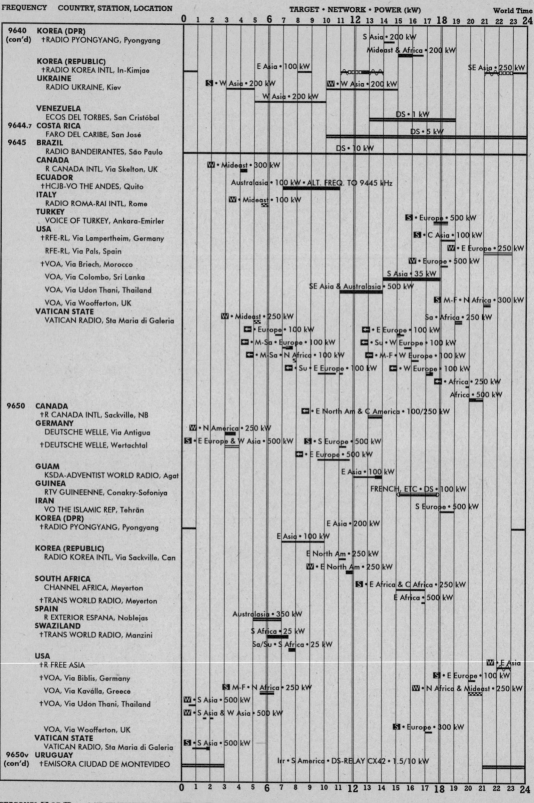

Frequency	Country, Station, Location	Target • Network • Power
9640 (con'd)	**KOREA (DPR)** †RADIO PYONGYANG, Pyongyang	S Asia • 200 kW; Mideast & Africa • 200 kW
	KOREA (REPUBLIC) †RADIO KOREA INTL, In-Kimjae	E Asia • 100 kW; SE Asia • 250 kW
	UKRAINE RADIO UKRAINE, Kiev	S • W Asia • 200 kW; W • W Asia • 200 kW; W Asia • 200 kW
	VENEZUELA ECOS DEL TORBES, San Cristóbal	DS • 1 kW
9644.7	**COSTA RICA** FARO DEL CARIBE, San José	DS • 5 kW
9645	**BRAZIL** RADIO BANDEIRANTES, São Paulo	DS • 10 kW
	CANADA R CANADA INTL, Via Skelton, UK	W • Mideast • 300 kW
	ECUADOR †HCJB-VO THE ANDES, Quito	Australasia • 100 kW • ALT. FREQ. TO 9445 kHz
	ITALY RADIO ROMA-RAI INTL, Rome	W • Mideast • 100 kW
	TURKEY VOICE OF TURKEY, Ankara-Emirler	S • Europe • 500 kW
	USA †RFE-RL, Via Lampertheim, Germany	S • C Asia • 100 kW
	RFE-RL, Via Pals, Spain	W • E Europe • 250 kW
	†VOA, Via Briech, Morocco	W • Europe • 500 kW
	VOA, Via Colombo, Sri Lanka	S Asia • 35 kW
	VOA, Via Udon Thani, Thailand	SE Asia & Australasia • 500 kW
	VOA, Via Woofferton, UK	S • M-F • N Africa • 300 kW
	VATICAN STATE VATICAN RADIO, Sta Maria di Galeria	W • Mideast • 250 kW; Sa • Africa • 250 kW; □ • Europe • 100 kW; □ • E Europe • 100 kW; □ • M-Sa • Europe • 100 kW; □ • Su • W Europe • 100 kW; □ • M Sa • N Africa • 100 kW; □ • M-F • W Europe • 100 kW; □ • Su • E Europe • 100 kW; □ • W Europe • 100 kW; □ • Africa • 250 kW; Africa • 500 kW
9650	**CANADA** †R CANADA INTL, Sackville, NB	□ • E North Am & C America • 100/250 kW
	GERMANY DEUTSCHE WELLE, Via Antigua	W • N America • 250 kW
	†DEUTSCHE WELLE, Wertachtal	S • E Europe & W Asia • 500 kW; S • S Europe • 500 kW; □ • E Europe • 500 kW
	GUAM KSDA-ADVENTIST WORLD RADIO, Agat	E Asia • 100 kW
	GUINEA RTV GUINEENNE, Conakry-Sofoniya	FRENCH, ETC • DS • 100 kW
	IRAN VO THE ISLAMIC REP, Tehrān	S Europe • 500 kW
	KOREA (DPR) †RADIO PYONGYANG, Pyongyang	E Asia • 200 kW; E Asia • 100 kW
	KOREA (REPUBLIC) RADIO KOREA INTL, Via Sackville, Can	E North Am • 250 kW; W • E North Am • 250 kW
	SOUTH AFRICA CHANNEL AFRICA, Meyerton	S • E Africa & C Africa • 250 kW; E Africa • 500 kW
	†TRANS WORLD RADIO, Meyerton	
	SPAIN R EXTERIOR ESPANA, Noblejas	Australasia • 350 kW
	SWAZILAND †TRANS WORLD RADIO, Manzini	S Africa • 25 kW; Sa/Su • S Africa • 25 kW
	USA †R FREE ASIA	W • E Asia
	†VOA, Via Biblis, Germany	S • E Europe • 100 kW
	VOA, Via Kaválla, Greece	S • M-F • N Africa • 250 kW; W • N Africa & Mideast • 250 kW
	†VOA, Via Udon Thani, Thailand	W • S Asia • 500 kW; W • S Asia & W Asia • 500 kW
	VOA, Via Woofferton, UK	S • Europe • 300 kW
	VATICAN STATE VATICAN RADIO, Sta Maria di Galeria	S • S Asia • 500 kW
9650v (con'd)	**URUGUAY** †EMISORA CIUDAD DE MONTEVIDEO	Irr • S America • DS-RELAY CX42 • 1.5/10 kW

FREQUENCY   COUNTRY, STATION, LOCATION

TARGET • NETWORK • POWER (kW)

World Time

0 1 2 3 4 5 6 7 8 9 10 11 12 13 14 15 16 17 18 19 20 21 22 23 24

Frequency	Country / Station / Location	Schedule
9650v (con'd)	URUGUAY †EMISORA CIUDAD DE MONTEVIDEO	S America • DS-RELAY CX42 • 1.5/10 kW
9655	AUSTRIA †R AUSTRIA INTL, Vienna	E North Am • 500 kW • ALT. FREQ. TO 7325 kHz; W • Mideast • 100 kW; W M-Sa • Mideast • 100 kW
	CHINA †CHINA RADIO INTL	W Asia & E Europe; S • W Asia & E Europe; W • E Europe
	FINLAND YLE RADIO FINLAND, Pori	S • E Europe • 250 kW
	FRANCE R FRANCE INTL, Issoudun-Allouis	N Africa • 500 kW; S • N Africa • 500 kW
	GERMANY †DEUTSCHE WELLE, Via Sri Lanka	S • S Asia • 250 kW; S • SE Asia & Australasia • 250 kW
	RUSSIA †RADIO ROSSII, Irkutsk	S • DS • 100 kW
	SOUTH AFRICA CHANNEL AFRICA, Meyerton	W • S Africa • 250 kW
	SWEDEN RADIO SWEDEN, Hörby	▭ • Mideast • 500 kW; S M-F • Europe & Africa • 500 kW; S Sa/Su • Europe & Africa • 500 kW; S • Europe & Africa • 500 kW
	TURKEY VOICE OF TURKEY, Ankara-úakirlar	S • Mideast & E Africa • 250 kW; W • Mideast & E Africa • 250 kW
	VOICE OF TURKEY, Ankara-Emirler	▭ • Europe & E North Am • 500 kW
9655v	THAILAND †RADIO THAILAND, Pathum Thani	Asia • 100 kW
9659v	VENEZUELA RADIO RUMBOS, Caracas	DS-TEMP INACTIVE • 10 kW; Sa/Su • DS-TEMP INACTIVE • 10 kW
9660	AUSTRALIA †RADIO AUSTRALIA, Brandon	Pacific • 10 kW
	CANADA R CANADA INTL, Via Tokyo, Japan	S • E Asia • 100 kW
	FRANCE †R FRANCE INTL, Via Tokyo, Japan	E Asia • 300 kW
	PERU RADIO NOR PERUANA, Chachapoyas	DS-TEMP INACTIVE • 1 kW
	PHILIPPINES †RADIO VERITAS ASIA, Palauig	S Asia • 250 kW; C Asia • 250 kW
	UNITED KINGDOM BBC, Via Brandon, Australia	Pacific • 10 kW
	USA †RFE-RL, Via Briech, Morocco	S M-Sa • E Europe • 500 kW; S • E Europe • 500 kW; S Su • E Europe • 500 kW
	†RFE-RL, Via Holzkirchen, Germany	S • W Asia & C Asia • 250 kW; W • W Asia & C Asia • 250 kW; S • C Asia • 250 kW
	RFE-RL, Via Kaválla, Greece	W • E Europe • 250 kW
	RFE-RL, Via Lampertheim, Germany	W • C Asia • 100 kW
	†VOA, Via Briech, Morocco	S • S Europe • 500 kW
	VOA, Via Kaválla, Greece	W • E Europe • 250 kW
	VOA, Via Lampertheim, Germany	W • E Europe • 100 kW
	†VOA, Via Woofferton, UK	S • N Africa • 300 kW
	VATICAN STATE VATICAN RADIO, Sta Maria di Galeria	E Africa • 100 kW • ALT. FREQ. TO 5865 kHz; W Sa • E Africa • 500 kW; E Africa • 100/500 kW • ALT. FREQ. TO 5865 kHz; W Su-F • E Africa • 500 kW; Africa • 100/250 kW; W • E Africa • 500 kW; E Africa • 100/250 kW; W • S Africa • 500 kW; W • Africa • 250 kW
9665	BRAZIL RADIO MARUMBY, Florianópolis	DS • 10 kW • ▭
	CHINA CHINA RADIO INTL, Via Brasília, Brazil	C America & S America • 250 kW
	GERMANY DEUTSCHE WELLE, Wertachtal	W • E Asia • 500 kW
(con'd)	IRAN VO THE ISLAMIC REP, Tehrän	S • N Africa • 500 kW

0 1 2 3 4 5 6 7 8 9 10 11 12 13 14 15 16 17 18 19 20 21 22 23 24

ENGLISH ▬   ARABIC ⌇⌇⌇   CHINESE ▭▭▭   FRENCH ▬▬   GERMAN ▬▬   RUSSIAN ═══   SPANISH ▬▬   OTHER ▬▬

FREQUENCY   COUNTRY, STATION, LOCATION

TARGET • NETWORK • POWER (kW)   World Time

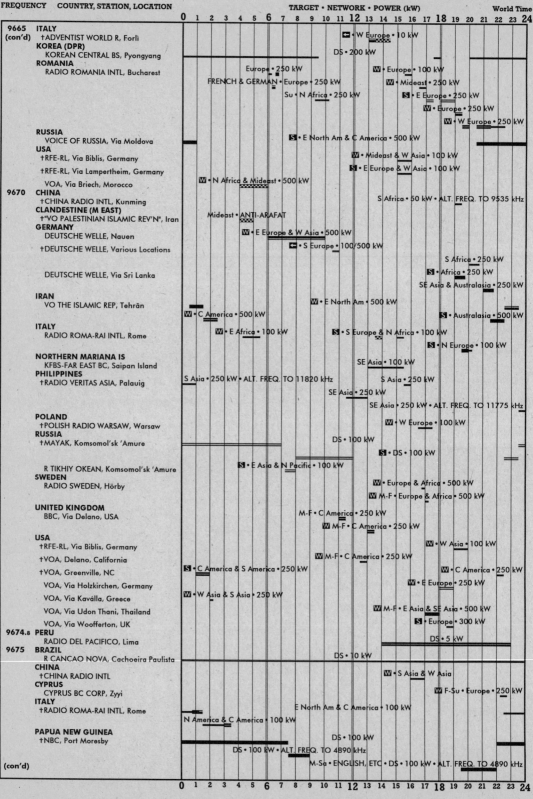

FREQUENCY	COUNTRY, STATION, LOCATION	TARGET • NETWORK • POWER (kW)
9665 (con'd)	ITALY †ADVENTIST WORLD R, Forli	W Europe • 10 kW
	KOREA (DPR) KOREAN CENTRAL BS, Pyongyang	DS • 200 kW
	ROMANIA RADIO ROMANIA INTL, Bucharest	Europe • 250 kW / W • Europe • 100 kW / FRENCH & GERMAN • Europe • 250 kW / W • Mideast • 250 kW / Su • N Africa • 250 kW / S • E Europe • 250 kW / W • Europe • 250 kW / W • W Europe • 250 kW
	RUSSIA VOICE OF RUSSIA, Via Moldova	S • E North Am & C America • 500 kW
	USA †RFE-RL, Via Biblis, Germany	W • Mideast & W Asia • 100 kW
	†RFE-RL, Via Lampertheim, Germany	S • E Europe & W Asia • 100 kW
	VOA, Via Briech, Morocco	W • N Africa & Mideast • 500 kW
9670	CHINA †CHINA RADIO INTL, Kunming	S Africa • 50 kW • ALT. FREQ. TO 9535 kHz
	CLANDESTINE (M EAST) †"VO PALESTINIAN ISLAMIC REV'N", Iran	Mideast • ANTI-ARAFAT
	GERMANY DEUTSCHE WELLE, Nauen	W • E Europe & W Asia • 500 kW
	†DEUTSCHE WELLE, Various Locations	S Europe • 100/500 kW
	DEUTSCHE WELLE, Via Sri Lanka	S Africa • 250 kW / S • Africa • 250 kW / SE Asia & Australasia • 250 kW
	IRAN VO THE ISLAMIC REP, Tehrän	W • E North Am • 500 kW / W • C America • 500 kW / S • Australasia • 500 kW
	ITALY RADIO ROMA-RAI INTL, Rome	W • E Africa • 100 kW / S • S Europe & N Africa • 100 kW / S • N Europe • 100 kW
	NORTHERN MARIANA IS KFBS-FAR EAST BC, Saipan Island	SE Asia • 100 kW
	PHILIPPINES †RADIO VERITAS ASIA, Palauig	S Asia • 250 kW • ALT. FREQ. TO 11820 kHz / S Asia • 250 kW / SE Asia • 250 kW / SE Asia • 250 kW • ALT. FREQ. TO 11775 kHz
	POLAND †POLISH RADIO WARSAW, Warsaw	W • W Europe • 100 kW
	RUSSIA †MAYAK, Komsomol'sk 'Amure	DS • 100 kW
		S • DS • 100 kW
	R TIKHIY OKEAN, Komsomol'sk 'Amure	S • E Asia & N Pacific • 100 kW
	SWEDEN RADIO SWEDEN, Hörby	W • Europe & Africa • 500 kW / W M-F • Europe & Africa • 500 kW
	UNITED KINGDOM BBC, Via Delano, USA	M-F • C America • 250 kW / W M-F • C America • 250 kW
	USA †RFE-RL, Via Biblis, Germany	W • W Asia • 100 kW
	†VOA, Delano, California	W M-F • C America • 250 kW
	†VOA, Greenville, NC	S • C America & S America • 250 kW / W • C America • 250 kW
	VOA, Via Holzkirchen, Germany	W • E Europe • 250 kW
	VOA, Via Kaválla, Greece	W • W Asia & S Asia • 250 kW
	VOA, Via Udon Thani, Thailand	W M-F • E Asia & SE Asia • 500 kW
	VOA, Via Woofferton, UK	S • Europe • 300 kW
9674.8	PERU RADIO DEL PACIFICO, Lima	DS • 5 kW
9675	BRAZIL R CANCAO NOVA, Cachoeira Paulista	DS • 10 kW
	CHINA †CHINA RADIO INTL	W • S Asia & W Asia
	CYPRUS CYPRUS BC CORP, Zyyi	W F-Su • Europe • 250 kW
	ITALY †RADIO ROMA-RAI INTL, Rome	E North Am & C America • 100 kW / N America & C America • 100 kW
	PAPUA NEW GUINEA †NBC, Port Moresby	DS • 100 kW / DS • 100 kW • ALT. FREQ. TO 4890 kHz
(con'd)		M-Sa • ENGLISH, ETC • DS • 100 kW • ALT. FREQ. TO 4890 kHz

FREQUENCY   COUNTRY, STATION, LOCATION   TARGET • NETWORK • POWER (kW)   World Time

Time scale: 0 1 2 3 4 5 6 7 8 9 10 11 12 13 14 15 16 17 18 19 20 21 22 23 24

Frequency	Country, Station, Location	Target • Network • Power (kW)
9675 (con'd)	**RUSSIA** VOICE OF RUSSIA, Tula	S • Mideast & S Africa • 100 kW
	SOUTH AFRICA †CHANNEL AFRICA, Meyerton	S • W Africa • 500 kW
		S • S Africa & W Africa • 500 kW
	TURKEY VOICE OF TURKEY, Ankara-úakirlar	S • Mideast • 250 kW
	VOICE OF TURKEY, Ankara-Emirler	• E Europe & W Asia • 500 kW
		S • Europe • 500 kW
	USA †RFE-RL, Via Holzkirchen, Germany	W • C Asia • 250 kW
	†VOA, Via São Tomé	E Africa • 100 kW
9680	**BULGARIA** RADIO BULGARIA, Sofia	S • Europe • 100 kW
	CANADA R CANADA INTL, Via Tokyo, Japan	S • E Asia • 300 kW
	CHINA (TAIWAN) VO FREE CHINA, Via Okeechobee, USA	W North Am • 100 kW
	FINLAND YLE RADIO FINLAND, Pori	W • Mideast • 500 kW
	GERMANY †DEUTSCHE WELLE, Via Kigali, Rwanda	S • S Asia & SE Asia • 250 kW
	INDONESIA RRI, Jakarta, Jawa	DS • 100 kW
	PHILIPPINES †RADIO VERITAS ASIA, Palauig	Mideast • 250 kW • ALT. FREQ. TO 11715 kHz
		W/F/Su • Mideast • 250 kW • ALT. FREQ. TO 11715 kHz
	PORTUGAL †RADIO RENASCENCA, Muge	• Europe • DS-TEMP INACTIVE • 100 kW
	RUSSIA VOICE OF RUSSIA, Kaliningrad	W • Europe • 100 kW
	THAILAND †RADIO THAILAND, Udon Thani	W • S Asia & E Africa • 500 kW
		S • Europe • 500 kW
	TURKEY VOICE OF TURKEY, Ankara-úakirlar	W • Mideast • 250 kW
	USA †RFE-RL, Via Biblis, Germany	S • W Asia & C Asia • 100 kW
		W • W Asia • 100 kW
		W • E Europe & W Asia • 100 kW
	†RFE-RL, Via Briech, Morocco	S • E Europe & W Asia • 500 kW
		S Europe • 500 kW
	†RFE-RL, Via Kaválla, Greece	S • W Asia • 250 kW
	†RFE-RL, Via Udon Thani, Thailand	W • C Asia • 500 kW
	†VOA, Via Briech, Morocco	S • N Africa • 500 kW
		W • S Europe • 500 kW
	VOA, Via Kaválla, Greece	Mideast & W Asia • 250 kW
	VOA, Via Philippines	W • E Asia • 250 kW
	WYFR-FAMILY RADIO, Okeechobee, Fl	W • S America • 100 kW
9685	**BRAZIL** RADIO GAZETA, São Paulo	DS • 7.5 kW
	IRAN VO THE ISLAMIC REP, Tehrãn	W • S America • 500 kW
		E Africa • 500 kW
		W • C America • 500 kW
		S • S America • 500 kW
	JAPAN †RADIO JAPAN/NHK, Tokyo-Yamata	S America • 300 kW
	†RADIO JAPAN/NHK, Via French Guiana	S America • 500 kW
	RUSSIA VOICE OF RUSSIA, Irkutsk	W • SE Asia • 1000 kW
	SOUTH AFRICA †CHANNEL AFRICA, Meyerton	E Africa & C Africa • 500 kW
		S Africa • 500 kW
	SPAIN R EXTERIOR ESPANA, Noblejas	Europe • 350 kW
	TANZANIA RADIO TANZANIA, Dar es Salaam	Irr • E Africa • 10/100 kW
	TURKEY VOICE OF TURKEY, Ankara-úakirlar	• Mideast & W Asia • 250 kW
	VOICE OF TURKEY, Ankara-Emirler	W • S Europe • 500 kW
	UKRAINE RADIO UKRAINE, L'vov	S • E North Am • 1000 kW
	UNITED KINGDOM BBC, Skelton, Cumbria	W • E Europe • 250 kW
		W M/W • E Europe • 250 kW
9690	**ARGENTINA** R ARGENTINA-RAE, Buenos Aires	Tu-Sa • S America • 100 kW
		M-F • S America • 100 kW
(con'd)	RADIO NACIONAL, Buenos Aires	Su/M • S America • 100 kW
		Sa/Su • S America • 100 kW

Time scale: 0 1 2 3 4 5 6 7 8 9 10 11 12 13 14 15 16 17 18 19 20 21 22 23 24

ENGLISH ▪▪   ARABIC ⟋⟋⟋   CHINESE ▫▫▫   FRENCH ▬▬   GERMAN ▬▬   RUSSIAN ══   SPANISH ▬▬▬   OTHER ▬

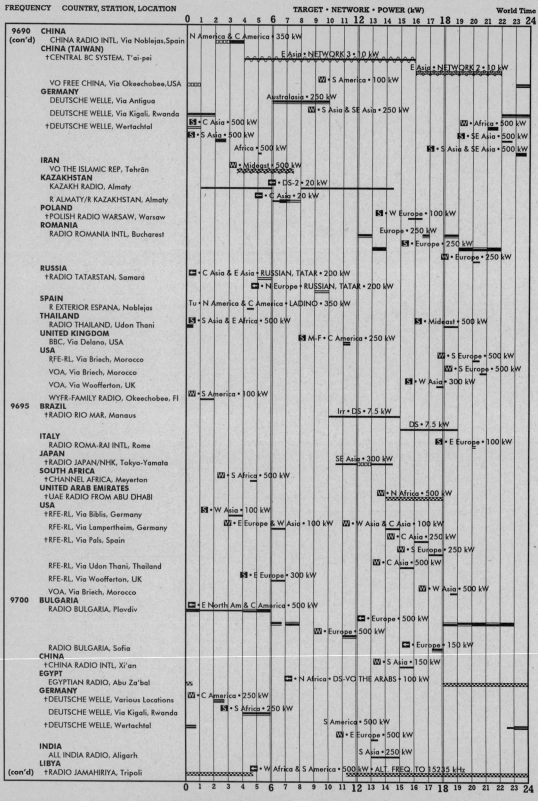

FREQUENCY   COUNTRY, STATION, LOCATION

TARGET • NETWORK • POWER (kW)

World Time

9690 (con'd)	CHINA
	CHINA RADIO INTL, Via Noblejas, Spain	N America & C America • 350 kW
	CHINA (TAIWAN)
	†CENTRAL BC SYSTEM, T'ai-pei	E Asia • NETWORK 3 • 10 kW / E Asia • NETWORK 2 • 10 kW
	VO FREE CHINA, Via Okeechobee, USA	W • S America • 100 kW
	GERMANY
	DEUTSCHE WELLE, Via Antigua	Australasia • 250 kW
	DEUTSCHE WELLE, Via Kigali, Rwanda	W • S Asia & SE Asia • 250 kW
	†DEUTSCHE WELLE, Wertachtal	S • C Asia • 500 kW / W • Africa • 500 kW
		S • S Asia • 500 kW / S • SE Asia • 500 kW
		Africa • 500 kW / S • S Asia & SE Asia • 500 kW
	IRAN
	VO THE ISLAMIC REP, Tehrān	W • Mideast • 500 kW
	KAZAKHSTAN
	KAZAKH RADIO, Almaty	DS-2 • 20 kW
	R ALMATY/R KAZAKHSTAN, Almaty	C Asia • 20 kW
	POLAND
	†POLISH RADIO WARSAW, Warsaw	S • W Europe • 100 kW
	ROMANIA
	RADIO ROMANIA INTL, Bucharest	Europe • 250 kW
		S • Europe • 250 kW
		W • Europe • 250 kW
	RUSSIA
	†RADIO TATARSTAN, Samara	C Asia & E Asia • RUSSIAN, TATAR • 200 kW
		N Europe • RUSSIAN, TATAR • 200 kW
	SPAIN
	R EXTERIOR ESPANA, Noblejas	Tu • N America & C America • LADINO • 350 kW
	THAILAND
	RADIO THAILAND, Udon Thani	S • S Asia & E Africa • 500 kW / S • Mideast • 500 kW
	UNITED KINGDOM
	BBC, Via Delano, USA	S • M-F • C America • 250 kW
	USA
	RFE-RL, Via Briech, Morocco	W • S Europe • 500 kW
	VOA, Via Briech, Morocco	W • S Europe • 500 kW
	VOA, Via Woofferton, UK	S • W Asia • 300 kW
	WYFR-FAMILY RADIO, Okeechobee, Fl	W • S America • 100 kW
9695	BRAZIL
	†RADIO RIO MAR, Manaus	Irr • DS • 7.5 kW
		DS • 7.5 kW
	ITALY
	RADIO ROMA-RAI INTL, Rome	S • E Europe • 100 kW
	JAPAN
	†RADIO JAPAN/NHK, Tokyo-Yamata	SE Asia • 300 kW
	SOUTH AFRICA
	†CHANNEL AFRICA, Meyerton	W • S Africa • 500 kW
	UNITED ARAB EMIRATES
	†UAE RADIO FROM ABU DHABI	W • N Africa • 500 kW
	USA
	†RFE-RL, Via Biblis, Germany	S • W Asia • 100 kW
	RFE-RL, Via Lampertheim, Germany	W • E Europe & W Asia • 100 kW / W • W Asia & C Asia • 100 kW
	†RFE-RL, Via Pals, Spain	W • C Asia • 250 kW
		W • S Europe • 250 kW
	RFE-RL, Via Udon Thani, Thailand	W • C Asia • 500 kW
	RFE-RL, Via Woofferton, UK	S • E Europe • 300 kW
	VOA, Via Briech, Morocco	W • W Asia • 500 kW
9700	BULGARIA
	RADIO BULGARIA, Plovdiv	E North Am & C America • 500 kW
		Europe • 500 kW
		W • Europe • 500 kW
		Europe • 150 kW
	RADIO BULGARIA, Sofia
	CHINA
	†CHINA RADIO INTL, Xi'an	W • S Asia • 150 kW
	EGYPT
	EGYPTIAN RADIO, Abu Za'bal	N Africa • DS-VO THE ARABS • 100 kW
	GERMANY
	†DEUTSCHE WELLE, Various Locations	W • C America • 250 kW
	DEUTSCHE WELLE, Via Kigali, Rwanda	S • S Africa • 250 kW
	†DEUTSCHE WELLE, Wertachtal	S America • 500 kW
		W • E Europe • 500 kW
	INDIA
	ALL INDIA RADIO, Aligarh	S Asia • 250 kW
	LIBYA
(con'd)	†RADIO JAMAHIRIYA, Tripoli	W • Africa & S America • 500 kW • ALT. FREQ. TO 15235 kHz

FREQUENCY   COUNTRY, STATION, LOCATION   TARGET • NETWORK • POWER (kW)   World Time

0 1 2 3 4 5 6 7 8 9 10 11 12 13 14 15 16 17 18 19 20 21 22 23 24

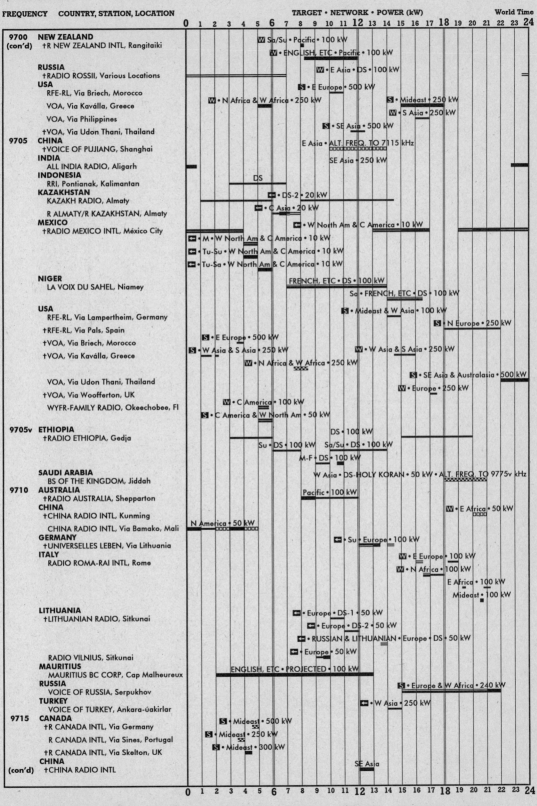

Freq	Country/Station/Location	Schedule
9700	**NEW ZEALAND**	
(con'd)	†R NEW ZEALAND INTL, Rangitaiki	W • Sa/Su • Pacific • 100 kW
		W • ENGLISH, ETC • Pacific • 100 kW
	RUSSIA	
	†RADIO ROSSII, Various Locations	W • E Asia • DS • 100 kW
	USA	
	RFE-RL, Via Briech, Morocco	S • E Europe • 500 kW
	VOA, Via Kaválla, Greece	W • N Africa & W Africa • 250 kW S • Mideast • 250 kW
	VOA, Via Philippines	W • S Asia • 250 kW
	†VOA, Via Udon Thani, Thailand	S • SE Asia • 500 kW
9705	**CHINA**	
	†VOICE OF PUJIANG, Shanghai	E Asia • ALT. FREQ. TO 7115 kHz
	INDIA	
	ALL INDIA RADIO, Aligarh	SE Asia • 250 kW
	INDONESIA	
	RRI, Pontianak, Kalimantan	DS
	KAZAKHSTAN	
	KAZAKH RADIO, Almaty	• DS-2 • 20 kW
	R ALMATY/R KAZAKHSTAN, Almaty	• C Asia • 20 kW
	MEXICO	
	†RADIO MEXICO INTL, México City	• W North Am & C America • 10 kW
		• M • W North Am & C America • 10 kW
		• Tu-Su • W North Am & C America • 10 kW
		• Tu-Sa • W North Am & C America • 10 kW
	NIGER	
	LA VOIX DU SAHEL, Niamey	FRENCH, ETC • DS • 100 kW
		Sa • FRENCH, ETC • DS • 100 kW
	USA	
	RFE-RL, Via Lampertheim, Germany	S • Mideast & W Asia • 100 kW
	†RFE-RL, Via Pals, Spain	S • N Europe • 250 kW
	†VOA, Via Briech, Morocco	S • E Europe • 500 kW
	†VOA, Via Kaválla, Greece	S • W Asia & S Asia • 250 kW W • W Asia & S Asia • 250 kW
		W • N Africa & W Africa • 250 kW
	VOA, Via Udon Thani, Thailand	S • SE Asia & Australasia • 500 kW
	†VOA, Via Woofferton, UK	W • Europe • 250 kW
	WYFR-FAMILY RADIO, Okeechobee, Fl	W • C America • 100 kW
		S • C America & W North Am • 50 kW
9705v	**ETHIOPIA**	
	†RADIO ETHIOPIA, Gedja	DS • 100 kW
		Su • DS • 100 kW Sa/Su • DS • 100 kW
		M-F • DS • 100 kW
	SAUDI ARABIA	
	BS OF THE KINGDOM, Jiddah	W Asia • DS-HOLY KORAN • 50 kW • ALT. FREQ. TO 9775v kHz
9710	**AUSTRALIA**	
	†RADIO AUSTRALIA, Shepparton	Pacific • 100 kW
	CHINA	
	†CHINA RADIO INTL, Kunming	W • E Africa • 50 kW
	CHINA RADIO INTL, Via Bamako, Mali	N America • 50 kW
	GERMANY	
	†UNIVERSELLES LEBEN, Via Lithuania	• Su • Europe • 100 kW
	ITALY	
	RADIO ROMA-RAI INTL, Rome	W • E Europe • 100 kW
		W • N Africa • 100 kW
		E Africa • 100 kW
		Mideast • 100 kW
	LITHUANIA	
	†LITHUANIAN RADIO, Sitkunai	• Europe • DS-1 • 50 kW
		• Europe • DS-2 • 50 kW
		• RUSSIAN & LITHUANIAN • Europe • DS • 50 kW
		• Europe • 50 kW
	RADIO VILNIUS, Sitkunai	
	MAURITIUS	
	MAURITIUS BC CORP, Cap Malheureux	ENGLISH, ETC • PROJECTED • 100 kW
	RUSSIA	
	VOICE OF RUSSIA, Serpukhov	S • Europe & W Africa • 240 kW
	TURKEY	
	VOICE OF TURKEY, Ankara-úakirlar	• W Asia • 250 kW
9715	**CANADA**	
	†R CANADA INTL, Via Germany	S • Mideast • 500 kW
	R CANADA INTL, Via Sines, Portugal	S • Mideast • 250 kW
	†R CANADA INTL, Via Skelton, UK	S • Mideast • 300 kW
	CHINA	
(con'd)	†CHINA RADIO INTL	SE Asia

0 1 2 3 4 5 6 7 8 9 10 11 12 13 14 15 16 17 18 19 20 21 22 23 24

ENGLISH ▬ ARABIC ▨▨ CHINESE □□□ FRENCH ═══ GERMAN ▭▭ RUSSIAN ══ SPANISH ▬▬ OTHER ──

FREQUENCY	COUNTRY, STATION, LOCATION	TARGET • NETWORK • POWER (kW)	World Time

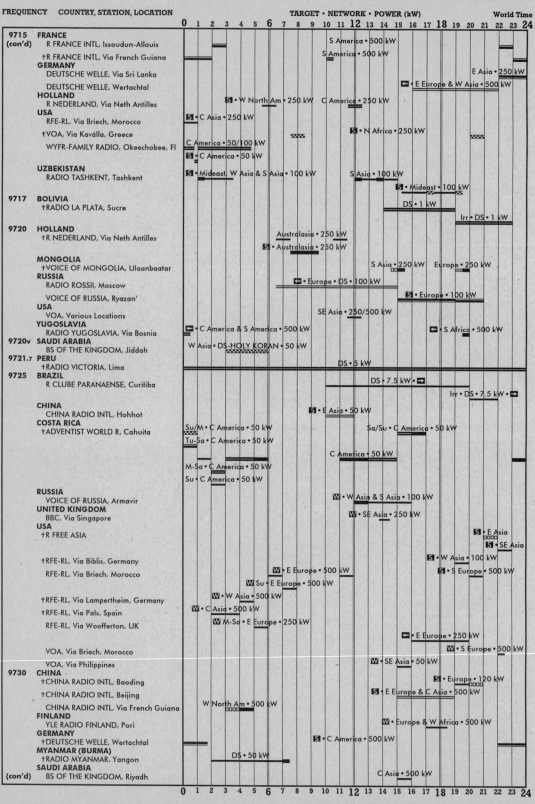

FREQUENCY	COUNTRY, STATION, LOCATION	Target • Network • Power
9715 (con'd)	**FRANCE**	
	R FRANCE INTL, Issoudun-Allouis	S America • 500 kW
	†R FRANCE INTL, Via French Guiana	S America • 500 kW
	GERMANY	
	DEUTSCHE WELLE, Via Sri Lanka	E Asia • 250 kW
	DEUTSCHE WELLE, Wertachtal	E Europe & W Asia • 500 kW
	HOLLAND	
	R NEDERLAND, Via Neth Antilles	S • W North Am • 250 kW C America • 250 kW
	USA	
	RFE-RL, Via Briech, Morocco	S • C Asia • 250 kW
	†VOA, Via Kaválla, Greece	S • N Africa • 250 kW
	WYFR-FAMILY RADIO, Okeechobee, Fl	C America • 50/100 kW S • C America • 50 kW
	UZBEKISTAN	
	RADIO TASHKENT, Tashkent	S • Mideast, W Asia & S Asia • 100 kW S Asia • 100 kW
		S • Mideast • 100 kW
9717	**BOLIVIA**	
	†RADIO LA PLATA, Sucre	DS • 1 kW
		Irr • DS • 1 kW
9720	**HOLLAND**	
	†R NEDERLAND, Via Neth Antilles	Australasia • 250 kW
		S • Australasia • 250 kW
	MONGOLIA	
	†VOICE OF MONGOLIA, Ulaanbaatar	S Asia • 250 kW Europe • 250 kW
	RUSSIA	
	RADIO ROSSII, Moscow	E Europe • DS • 100 kW
	VOICE OF RUSSIA, Ryazan'	S • Europe • 100 kW
	USA	
	VOA, Various Locations	SE Asia • 250/500 kW
	YUGOSLAVIA	
	RADIO YUGOSLAVIA, Via Bosnia	C America & S America • 500 kW S Africa • 500 kW
9720v	**SAUDI ARABIA**	
	BS OF THE KINGDOM, Jiddah	W Asia • DS-HOLY KORAN • 50 kW
9721.7	**PERU**	
	†RADIO VICTORIA, Lima	DS • 5 kW
9725	**BRAZIL**	
	R CLUBE PARANAENSE, Curitiba	DS • 7.5 kW • ◻▸
		Irr • DS • 7.5 kW • ◻▸
	CHINA	
	CHINA RADIO INTL, Hohhot	S • E Asia • 50 kW
	COSTA RICA	
	†ADVENTIST WORLD R, Cahuita	Su/M • C America • 50 kW Sa/Su • C America • 50 kW
		Tu-Sa • C America • 50 kW
		C America • 50 kW
		M-Sa • C America • 50 kW
		Su • C America • 50 kW
	RUSSIA	
	VOICE OF RUSSIA, Armavir	W • W Asia & S Asia • 100 kW
	UNITED KINGDOM	
	BBC, Via Singapore	W • SE Asia • 250 kW
	USA	
	†R FREE ASIA	S • E Asia
		S • SE Asia
	†RFE-RL, Via Biblis, Germany	S • W Asia • 100 kW
	RFE-RL, Via Briech, Morocco	W • E Europe • 500 kW S • S Europe • 500 kW
		W Su • E Europe • 500 kW
	†RFE-RL, Via Lampertheim, Germany	W • W Asia • 500 kW
	†RFE-RL, Via Pals, Spain	W • C Asia • 500 kW
	RFE-RL, Via Woofferton, UK	W M-Sa • E Europe • 250 kW
		◻▸ • E Europe • 250 kW
	VOA, Via Briech, Morocco	W • S Europe • 500 kW
	VOA, Via Philippines	W • SE Asia • 50 kW
9730	**CHINA**	
	†CHINA RADIO INTL, Baoding	S • Europe • 120 kW
	†CHINA RADIO INTL, Beijing	S • E Europe & C Asia • 500 kW
	CHINA RADIO INTL, Via French Guiana	W North Am • 500 kW
	FINLAND	
	YLE RADIO FINLAND, Pori	W • Europe & W Africa • 500 kW
	GERMANY	
	†DEUTSCHE WELLE, Wertachtal	S • C America • 500 kW
	MYANMAR (BURMA)	
	†RADIO MYANMAR, Yangon	DS • 50 kW
	SAUDI ARABIA	
(con'd)	BS OF THE KINGDOM, Riyadh	C Asia • 500 kW

FREQUENCY   COUNTRY, STATION, LOCATION   TARGET • NETWORK • POWER (kW)   World Time

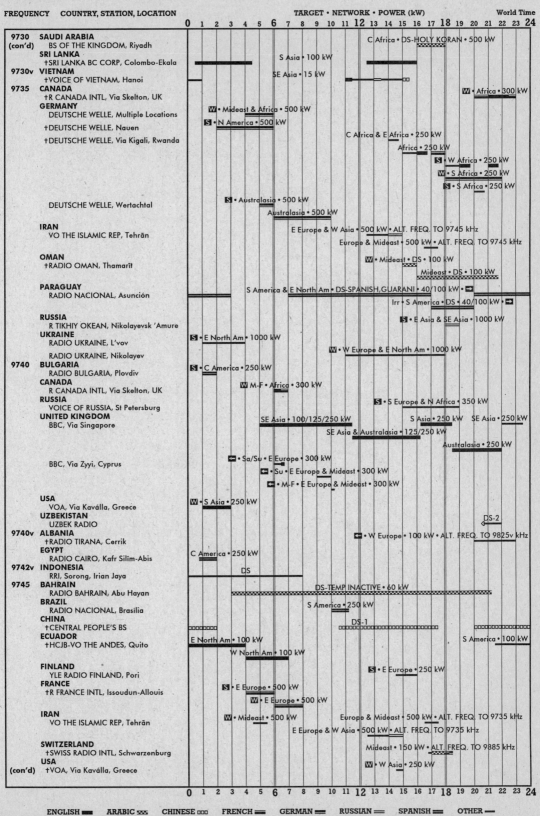

Frequency	Country, Station, Location	Schedule
9730 (con'd)	**SAUDI ARABIA** BS OF THE KINGDOM, Riyadh	C Africa • DS-HOLY KORAN • 500 kW
	SRI LANKA †SRI LANKA BC CORP, Colombo-Ekala	S Asia • 100 kW
9730v	**VIETNAM** †VOICE OF VIETNAM, Hanoi	SE Asia • 15 kW
9735	**CANADA** †R CANADA INTL, Via Skelton, UK	W • Africa • 300 kW
	GERMANY DEUTSCHE WELLE, Multiple Locations	W • Mideast & Africa • 500 kW
	†DEUTSCHE WELLE, Nauen	S • N America • 500 kW
	†DEUTSCHE WELLE, Via Kigali, Rwanda	C Africa & E Africa • 250 kW / Africa • 250 kW / S • W Africa • 250 kW / W • S Africa • 250 kW / S • S Africa • 250 kW
	DEUTSCHE WELLE, Wertachtal	S • Australasia • 500 kW / Australasia • 500 kW
	IRAN VO THE ISLAMIC REP, Tehrān	E Europe & W Asia • 500 kW • ALT. FREQ. TO 9745 kHz / Europe & Mideast • 500 kW • ALT. FREQ. TO 9745 kHz
	OMAN †RADIO OMAN, Thamarīt	W • Mideast • DS • 100 kW / Mideast • DS • 100 kW
	PARAGUAY RADIO NACIONAL, Asunción	S America & E North Am • DS-SPANISH, GUARANI • 40/100 kW • ▭➡ / Irr • S America • DS • 40/100 kW • ➡
	RUSSIA R TIKHIY OKEAN, Nikolayevsk 'Amure	S • E Asia & SE Asia • 1000 kW
	UKRAINE RADIO UKRAINE, L'vov	S • E North Am • 1000 kW
	RADIO UKRAINE, Nikolayev	W • W Europe & E North Am • 1000 kW
9740	**BULGARIA** RADIO BULGARIA, Plovdiv	S • C America • 250 kW
	CANADA R CANADA INTL, Via Skelton, UK	W • M-F • Africa • 300 kW
	RUSSIA VOICE OF RUSSIA, St Petersburg	S • S Europe & N Africa • 350 kW
	UNITED KINGDOM BBC, Via Singapore	SE Asia • 100/125/250 kW / S Asia • 250 kW / SE Asia • 250 kW / SE Asia & Australasia • 125/250 kW / Australasia • 250 kW
	BBC, Via Zyyi, Cyprus	▭ • Sa/Su • E Europe • 300 kW / ▭ • Su • E Europe & Mideast • 300 kW / ▭ • M-F • E Europe & Mideast • 300 kW
	USA VOA, Via Kaválla, Greece	W • S Asia • 250 kW
	UZBEKISTAN UZBEK RADIO	DS-2
9740v	**ALBANIA** †RADIO TIRANA, Cerrik	▭ • W Europe • 100 kW • ALT. FREQ. TO 9825v kHz
	EGYPT RADIO CAIRO, Kafr Silim-Abis	C America • 250 kW
9742v	**INDONESIA** RRI, Sorong, Irian Jaya	DS
9745	**BAHRAIN** RADIO BAHRAIN, Abu Hayan	DS-TEMP INACTIVE • 60 kW
	BRAZIL RADIO NACIONAL, Brasília	S America • 250 kW
	CHINA †CENTRAL PEOPLE'S BS	DS-1
	ECUADOR †HCJB-VO THE ANDES, Quito	E North Am • 100 kW / S America • 100 kW / W North Am • 100 kW
	FINLAND YLE RADIO FINLAND, Pori	S • E Europe • 250 kW
	FRANCE †R FRANCE INTL, Issoudun-Allouis	S • E Europe • 500 kW / W • E Europe • 500 kW
	IRAN VO THE ISLAMIC REP, Tehrān	W • Mideast • 500 kW / Europe & Mideast • 500 kW • ALT. FREQ. TO 9735 kHz / E Europe & W Asia • 500 kW • ALT. FREQ. TO 9735 kHz
	SWITZERLAND †SWISS RADIO INTL, Schwarzenburg	Mideast • 150 kW • ALT. FREQ. TO 9885 kHz
(con'd)	**USA** †VOA, Via Kaválla, Greece	W • W Asia • 250 kW

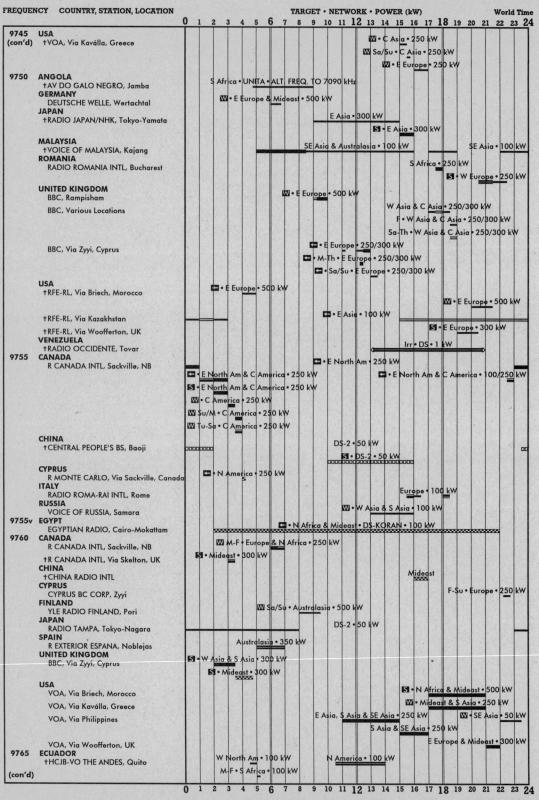

FREQUENCY   COUNTRY, STATION, LOCATION

Frequency	Country, Station, Location	Target • Network • Power (kW)

9745 (con'd) **USA**
  †VOA, Via Kaválla, Greece — W • C Asia • 250 kW; W Sa/Su • C Asia • 250 kW; W • E Europe • 250 kW

9750 **ANGOLA**
  †AV DO GALO NEGRO, Jamba — S Africa • UNITA • ALT. FREQ. TO 7090 kHz
  GERMANY
  DEUTSCHE WELLE, Wertachtal — W • E Europe & Mideast • 500 kW
  JAPAN
  †RADIO JAPAN/NHK, Tokyo-Yamata — E Asia • 300 kW; S • E Asia • 300 kW
  MALAYSIA
  †VOICE OF MALAYSIA, Kajang — SE Asia & Australasia • 100 kW; SE Asia • 100 kW
  ROMANIA
  RADIO ROMANIA INTL, Bucharest — S Africa • 250 kW; S • W Europe • 250 kW
  UNITED KINGDOM
  BBC, Rampisham — W • E Europe • 500 kW
  BBC, Various Locations — W Asia & C Asia • 250/300 kW; F • W Asia & C Asia • 250/300 kW; Sa-Th • W Asia & C Asia • 250/300 kW
  BBC, Via Zyyi, Cyprus — • E Europe • 250/300 kW; M-Th • E Europe • 250/300 kW; Sa/Su • E Europe • 250/300 kW
  USA
  †RFE-RL, Via Briech, Morocco — • E Europe • 500 kW; W • E Europe • 500 kW
  †RFE-RL, Via Kazakhstan — • E Asia • 100 kW
  †RFE-RL, Via Woofferton, UK — S • E Europe • 300 kW
  VENEZUELA
  †RADIO OCCIDENTE, Tovar — Irr • DS • 1 kW

9755 **CANADA**
  R CANADA INTL, Sackville, NB — • E North Am • 250 kW; • E North Am & C America • 250 kW; • E North Am & C America • 100/250 kW; S • E North Am & C America • 250 kW; W • C America • 250 kW; W Su/M • C America • 250 kW; W Tu-Sa • C America • 250 kW
  CHINA
  †CENTRAL PEOPLE'S BS, Baoji — DS-2 • 50 kW; S • DS-2 • 50 kW
  CYPRUS
  R MONTE CARLO, Via Sackville, Canada — • N America • 250 kW
  ITALY
  RADIO ROMA-RAI INTL, Rome — Europe • 100 kW
  RUSSIA
  VOICE OF RUSSIA, Samara — W • W Asia & S Asia • 100 kW

9755v **EGYPT**
  EGYPTIAN RADIO, Cairo-Mokattam — • N Africa & Mideast • DS-KORAN • 100 kW

9760 **CANADA**
  R CANADA INTL, Sackville, NB — W M-F • Europe & N Africa • 250 kW
  †R CANADA INTL, Via Skelton, UK — S • Mideast • 300 kW
  CHINA
  †CHINA RADIO INTL — Mideast
  CYPRUS
  CYPRUS BC CORP, Zyyi — F-Su • Europe • 250 kW
  FINLAND
  YLE RADIO FINLAND, Pori — W Sa/Su • Australasia • 500 kW
  JAPAN
  RADIO TAMPA, Tokyo-Nagara — DS-2 • 50 kW
  SPAIN
  R EXTERIOR ESPANA, Noblejas — Australasia • 350 kW
  UNITED KINGDOM
  BBC, Via Zyyi, Cyprus — S • W Asia & S Asia • 300 kW; S • Mideast • 300 kW
  USA
  VOA, Via Briech, Morocco — S • N Africa & Mideast • 500 kW
  VOA, Via Kaválla, Greece — W • Mideast & S Asia • 250 kW
  VOA, Via Philippines — E Asia, S Asia & SE Asia • 250 kW; W • SE Asia • 50 kW; S Asia & SE Asia • 250 kW
  VOA, Via Woofferton, UK — E Europe & Mideast • 300 kW

9765 **ECUADOR**
  †HCJB-VO THE ANDES, Quito — W North Am • 100 kW; N America • 100 kW; M-F • S Africa • 100 kW

(con'd)

FREQUENCY	COUNTRY, STATION, LOCATION	TARGET • NETWORK • POWER (kW)	World Time

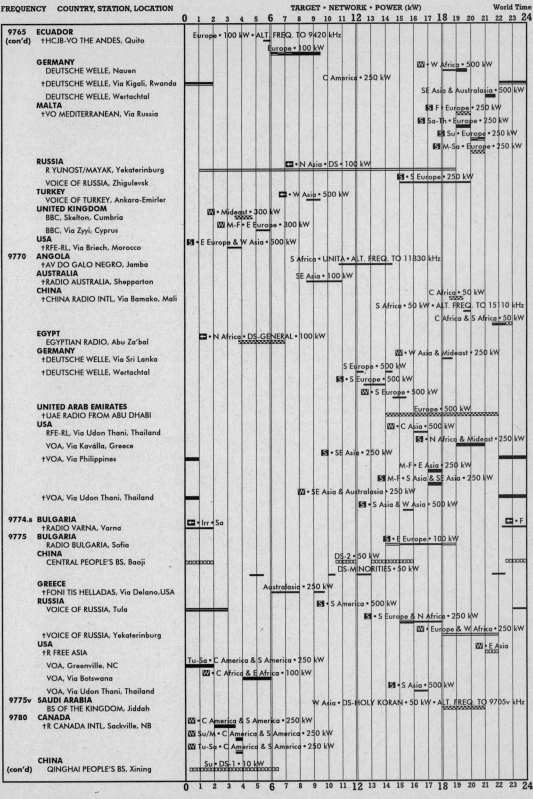

```
FREQUENCY   COUNTRY, STATION, LOCATION                          TARGET • NETWORK • POWER (kW)                    World Time
                                              0  1  2  3  4  5  6  7  8  9  10 11 12 13 14 15 16 17 18 19 20 21 22 23 24

9765        ECUADOR
(con'd)       †HCJB-VO THE ANDES, Quito          Europe • 100 kW • ALT. FREQ. TO 9420 kHz
                                                   Europe • 100 kW

            GERMANY
              DEUTSCHE WELLE, Nauen                                                              W • W Africa • 500 kW
              †DEUTSCHE WELLE, Via Kigali, Rwanda                        C America • 250 kW
              DEUTSCHE WELLE, Wertachtal                                                           SE Asia & Australasia • 500 kW
            MALTA
              †VO MEDITERRANEAN, Via Russia                                                       S  F • Europe • 250 kW
                                                                                                 S  Sa-Th • Europe • 250 kW
                                                                                                 S  Su • Europe • 250 kW
                                                                                                 S  M-Sa • Europe • 250 kW

            RUSSIA
              R YUNOST/MAYAK, Yekaterinburg                         ← • N Asia • DS • 100 kW
              VOICE OF RUSSIA, Zhigulevsk                                                         S • S Europe • 250 kW
            TURKEY
              VOICE OF TURKEY, Ankara-Emirler                    ← • W Asia • 500 kW
            UNITED KINGDOM
              BBC, Skelton, Cumbria                W • Mideast • 300 kW
              BBC, Via Zyyi, Cyprus                  W • M-F • E Europe • 300 kW
            USA
              †RFE-RL, Via Briech, Morocco         S • E Europe & W Asia • 500 kW
9770        ANGOLA
              †AV DO GALO NEGRO, Jamba                          S Africa • UNITA • ALT. FREQ. TO 11830 kHz
            AUSTRALIA
              †RADIO AUSTRALIA, Shepparton                      SE Asia • 100 kW
            CHINA
              †CHINA RADIO INTL, Via Bamako, Mali                                    C Africa • 50 kW
                                                                      S Africa • 50 kW • ALT. FREQ. TO 15110 kHz
                                                                                    C Africa & S Africa • 50 kW

            EGYPT
              EGYPTIAN RADIO, Abu Za'bal             ← • N Africa • DS-GENERAL • 100 kW
            GERMANY
              †DEUTSCHE WELLE, Via Sri Lanka                                          W • W Asia & Mideast • 250 kW
              †DEUTSCHE WELLE, Wertachtal                                 S Europe • 500 kW
                                                                    S • S Europe • 500 kW
                                                                    W • S Europe • 500 kW

            UNITED ARAB EMIRATES
              †UAE RADIO FROM ABU DHABI                                               Europe • 500 kW
            USA
              RFE-RL, Via Udon Thani, Thailand                                     W • C Asia • 500 kW
              VOA, Via Kaválla, Greece                                               S • N Africa & Mideast • 250 kW
              †VOA, Via Philippines                                   S • SE Asia • 250 kW
                                                                                    M-F • E Asia • 250 kW
                                                                                 S  M-F • S Asia & SE Asia • 250 kW
              †VOA, Via Udon Thani, Thailand        W • SE Asia & Australasia • 250 kW
                                                                    S • S Asia & W Asia • 500 kW
9774.8      BULGARIA
              †RADIO VARNA, Varna                   ← • Irr • Sa                                             ← • F
9775        BULGARIA
              RADIO BULGARIA, Sofia                                                  S • E Europe • 100 kW
            CHINA
              CENTRAL PEOPLE'S BS, Baoji                                    DS-2 • 50 kW
                                                                          DS-MINORITIES • 50 kW

            GREECE
              †FONI TIS HELLADAS, Via Delano, USA       Australasia • 250 kW
            RUSSIA
              VOICE OF RUSSIA, Tula                                  S • S America • 500 kW
                                                                    S • S Europe & N Africa • 250 kW
                                                                                 W • Europe & W Africa • 250 kW
              †VOICE OF RUSSIA, Yekaterinburg                                            W • E Asia
            USA
              †R FREE ASIA                          Tu-Sa • C America & S America • 250 kW
              VOA, Greenville, NC                    W • C Africa & E Africa • 100 kW
              VOA, Via Botswana                                                      S • S Asia • 500 kW
              VOA, Via Udon Thani, Thailand
9775v       SAUDI ARABIA
              BS OF THE KINGDOM, Jiddah              W Asia • DS-HOLY KORAN • 50 kW • ALT. FREQ. TO 9705v kHz
9780        CANADA
              †R CANADA INTL, Sackville, NB         W • C America & S America • 250 kW
                                                    W Su/M • C America & S America • 250 kW
                                                    W Tu-Sa • C America & S America • 250 kW

            CHINA
(con'd)       QINGHAI PEOPLE'S BS, Xining            Su • DS-1 • 10 kW

                                              0  1  2  3  4  5  6  7  8  9  10 11 12 13 14 15 16 17 18 19 20 21 22 23 24
```

ENGLISH ■■ ARABIC ▨▨ CHINESE □□□ FRENCH ▬▬ GERMAN ▬▬ RUSSIAN ══ SPANISH ▬▬ OTHER ▬

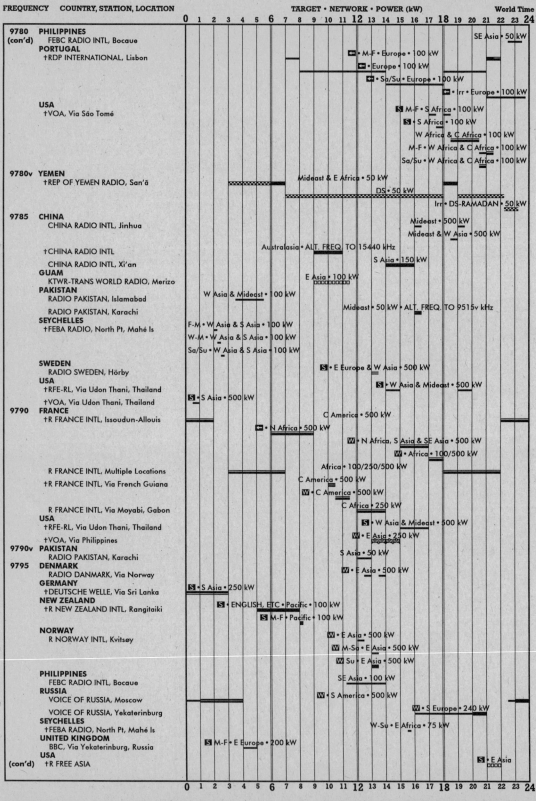

FREQUENCY   COUNTRY, STATION, LOCATION   TARGET • NETWORK • POWER (kW)   World Time

0 1 2 3 4 5 6 7 8 9 10 11 12 13 14 15 16 17 18 19 20 21 22 23 24

9780 **PHILIPPINES**
(con'd)   FEBC RADIO INTL, Bocaue   SE Asia • 50 kW
    PORTUGAL
      †RDP INTERNATIONAL, Lisbon   M-F • Europe • 100 kW
                         Europe • 100 kW
                         Sa/Su • Europe • 100 kW
                         Irr • Europe • 100 kW
    USA
      †VOA, Via São Tomé   M-F • S Africa • 100 kW
                         S Africa • 100 kW
                         W Africa & C Africa • 100 kW
                         M-F • W Africa & C Africa • 100 kW
                         Sa/Su • W Africa & C Africa • 100 kW

9780v **YEMEN**
      †REP OF YEMEN RADIO, San'ā   Mideast & E Africa • 50 kW
                         DS • 50 kW
                         Irr • DS-RAMADAN • 50 kW

9785 **CHINA**
    CHINA RADIO INTL, Jinhua   Mideast • 500 kW
                         Mideast & W Asia • 500 kW
      †CHINA RADIO INTL   Australasia • ALT. FREQ. TO 15440 kHz
      CHINA RADIO INTL, Xi'an   S Asia • 150 kW
    GUAM
      KTWR-TRANS WORLD RADIO, Merizo   E Asia • 100 kW
    PAKISTAN
      RADIO PAKISTAN, Islamabad   W Asia & Mideast • 100 kW
      RADIO PAKISTAN, Karachi   Mideast • 50 kW • ALT. FREQ. TO 9515v kHz
    SEYCHELLES
      †FEBA RADIO, North Pt, Mahé Is   F-M • W Asia & S Asia • 100 kW
                         W-M • W Asia & S Asia • 100 kW
                         Sa/Su • W Asia & S Asia • 100 kW
    SWEDEN
      RADIO SWEDEN, Hörby   E Europe & W Asia • 500 kW
    USA
      †RFE-RL, Via Udon Thani, Thailand   W Asia & Mideast • 500 kW
      †VOA, Via Udon Thani, Thailand   S Asia • 500 kW

9790 **FRANCE**
      †R FRANCE INTL, Issoudun-Allouis   C America • 500 kW
                         N Africa • 500 kW
                         W • N Africa, S Asia & SE Asia • 500 kW
                         W • Africa • 100/500 kW
      R FRANCE INTL, Multiple Locations   Africa • 100/250/500 kW
      †R FRANCE INTL, Via French Guiana   C America • 500 kW
                         W • C America • 500 kW
      R FRANCE INTL, Via Moyabi, Gabon   C Africa • 250 kW
    USA
      †RFE-RL, Via Udon Thani, Thailand   W Asia & Mideast • 500 kW
      †VOA, Via Philippines   W • E Asia • 250 kW

9790v **PAKISTAN**
      RADIO PAKISTAN, Karachi   S Asia • 50 kW

9795 **DENMARK**
      RADIO DANMARK, Via Norway   W • E Asia • 500 kW
    GERMANY
      †DEUTSCHE WELLE, Via Sri Lanka   S Asia • 250 kW
    NEW ZEALAND
      †R NEW ZEALAND INTL, Rangitaiki   ENGLISH, ETC • Pacific • 100 kW
                         M-F • Pacific • 100 kW
    NORWAY
      R NORWAY INTL, Kvitsøy   W • E Asia • 500 kW
                         W M-Sa • E Asia • 500 kW
                         W Su • E Asia • 500 kW
    PHILIPPINES
      FEBC RADIO INTL, Bocaue   SE Asia • 100 kW
    RUSSIA
      VOICE OF RUSSIA, Moscow   W • S America • 500 kW
      VOICE OF RUSSIA, Yekaterinburg   W • S Europe • 240 kW
    SEYCHELLES
      †FEBA RADIO, North Pt, Mahé Is   W-Su • E Africa • 75 kW
    UNITED KINGDOM
      BBC, Via Yekaterinburg, Russia   M-F • E Europe • 200 kW
    USA
(con'd)   †R FREE ASIA   S • E Asia

0 1 2 3 4 5 6 7 8 9 10 11 12 13 14 15 16 17 18 19 20 21 22 23 24

SEASONAL S OR W   1-HR TIMESHIFT MIDYEAR ◄ OR ►   JAMMING / OR /\   EARLIEST HEARD ◄   LATEST HEARD ►   NEW FOR 1998 †

FREQUENCY   COUNTRY, STATION, LOCATION   TARGET • NETWORK • POWER (kW)   World Time

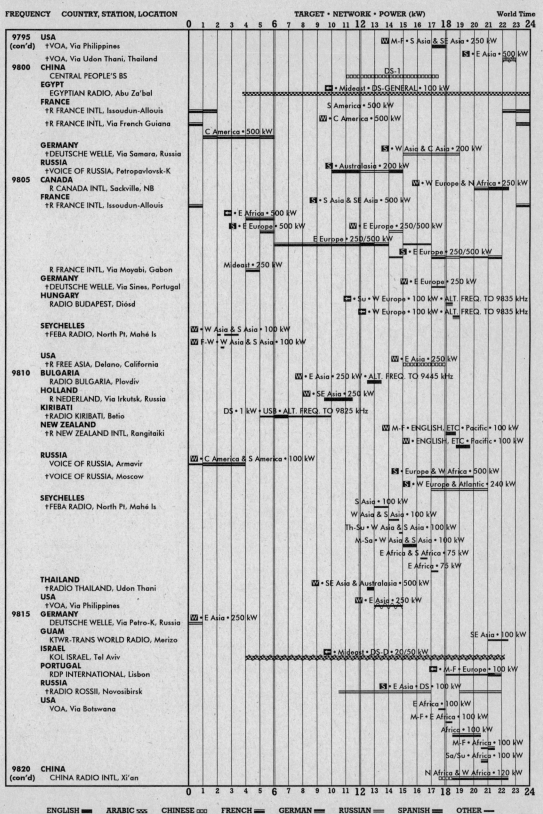

FREQUENCY	COUNTRY, STATION, LOCATION	TARGET • NETWORK • POWER (kW)
9795 (con'd)	USA	
	†VOA, Via Philippines	W • M-F • S Asia & SE Asia • 250 kW
	†VOA, Via Udon Thani, Thailand	S • E Asia • 500 kW
9800	CHINA	
	CENTRAL PEOPLE'S BS	DS-1
	EGYPT	
	EGYPTIAN RADIO, Abu Za'bal	• Mideast • DS-GENERAL • 100 kW
	FRANCE	
	†R FRANCE INTL, Issoudun-Allouis	S America • 500 kW
	†R FRANCE INTL, Via French Guiana	W • C America • 500 kW / C America • 500 kW
	GERMANY	
	†DEUTSCHE WELLE, Via Samara, Russia	S • W Asia & C Asia • 200 kW
	RUSSIA	
	†VOICE OF RUSSIA, Petropavlovsk-K	S • Australasia • 200 kW
9805	CANADA	
	R CANADA INTL, Sackville, NB	W • W Europe & N Africa • 250 kW
	FRANCE	
	†R FRANCE INTL, Issoudun-Allouis	S • S Asia & SE Asia • 500 kW
		• E Africa • 500 kW
		S • E Europe • 500 kW W • E Europe • 250/500 kW
		E Europe • 250/500 kW
		S • E Europe • 250/500 kW
	R FRANCE INTL, Via Moyabi, Gabon	Mideast • 250 kW
	GERMANY	
	†DEUTSCHE WELLE, Via Sines, Portugal	• W Europe • 250 kW
	HUNGARY	
	RADIO BUDAPEST, Diósd	• Su • W Europe • 100 kW • ALT. FREQ. TO 9835 kHz
		• W Europe • 100 kW • ALT. FREQ. TO 9835 kHz
	SEYCHELLES	
	†FEBA RADIO, North Pt, Mahé Is	W • W Asia & S Asia • 100 kW
		W F-W • W Asia & S Asia • 100 kW
	USA	
	†R FREE ASIA, Delano, California	W • E Asia • 250 kW
9810	BULGARIA	
	RADIO BULGARIA, Plovdiv	W • E Asia • 250 kW • ALT. FREQ. TO 9445 kHz
	HOLLAND	
	R NEDERLAND, Via Irkutsk, Russia	W • SE Asia • 250 kW
	KIRIBATI	
	†RADIO KIRIBATI, Betio	DS • 1 kW • USB • ALT. FREQ. TO 9825 kHz
	NEW ZEALAND	
	†R NEW ZEALAND INTL, Rangitaiki	W • M-F • ENGLISH, ETC • Pacific • 100 kW
		W • ENGLISH, ETC • Pacific • 100 kW
	RUSSIA	
	VOICE OF RUSSIA, Armavir	W • C America & S America • 100 kW
	†VOICE OF RUSSIA, Moscow	S • Europe & W Africa • 500 kW
		S • W Europe & Atlantic • 240 kW
	SEYCHELLES	
	†FEBA RADIO, North Pt, Mahé Is	S Asia • 100 kW
		W Asia & S Asia • 100 kW
		Th-Su • W Asia & S Asia • 100 kW
		M-Sa • W Asia & S Asia • 100 kW
		E Africa & S Africa • 75 kW
		E Africa • 75 kW
	THAILAND	
	†RADIO THAILAND, Udon Thani	W • SE Asia & Australasia • 500 kW
	USA	
	†VOA, Via Philippines	W • E Asia • 250 kW
9815	GERMANY	
	DEUTSCHE WELLE, Via Petro-K, Russia	W • E Asia • 250 kW
	GUAM	
	KTWR-TRANS WORLD RADIO, Merizo	SE Asia • 100 kW
	ISRAEL	
	KOL ISRAEL, Tel Aviv	• Mideast • DS-D • 20/50 kW
	PORTUGAL	
	RDP INTERNATIONAL, Lisbon	• M-F • Europe • 100 kW
	RUSSIA	
	†RADIO ROSSII, Novosibirsk	S • E Asia • DS • 100 kW
	USA	
	VOA, Via Botswana	E Africa • 100 kW
		M-F • E Africa • 100 kW
		Africa • 100 kW
		M-F • Africa • 100 kW
		Sa/Su • Africa • 100 kW
9820 (con'd)	CHINA	
	CHINA RADIO INTL, Xi'an	N Africa & W Africa • 120 kW

ENGLISH ▬   ARABIC ⧆⧆⧆   CHINESE □□□   FRENCH ═   GERMAN ▬▬   RUSSIAN ══   SPANISH ▬▬   OTHER ▬

FREQUENCY   COUNTRY, STATION, LOCATION   TARGET • NETWORK • POWER (kW)   World Time

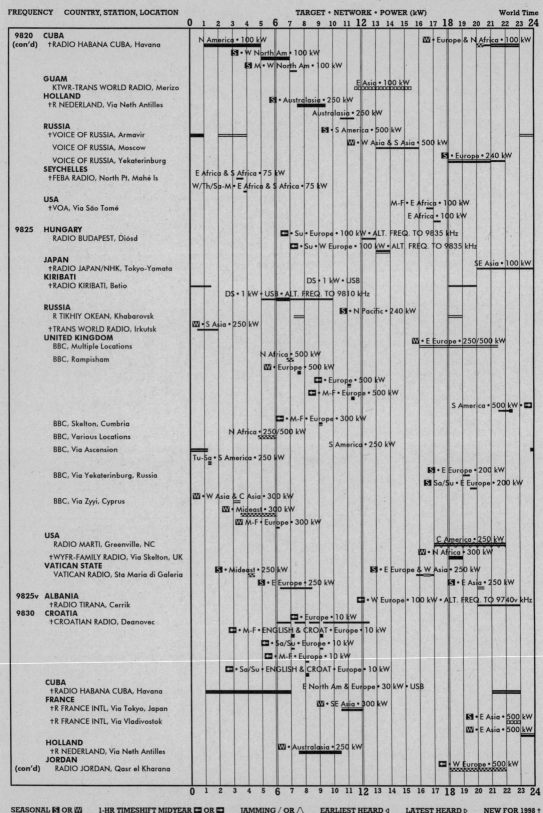

9820	CUBA	
(con'd)	†RADIO HABANA CUBA, Havana	N America • 100 kW ... W • Europe & N Africa • 100 kW
		S • W North Am • 100 kW
		S • M • W North Am • 100 kW
	GUAM	
	KTWR-TRANS WORLD RADIO, Merizo	E Asia • 100 kW
	HOLLAND	
	†R NEDERLAND, Via Neth Antilles	S • Australasia • 250 kW
		Australasia • 250 kW
	RUSSIA	
	†VOICE OF RUSSIA, Armavir	S • S America • 500 kW
	VOICE OF RUSSIA, Moscow	W • W Asia & S Asia • 500 kW
	VOICE OF RUSSIA, Yekaterinburg	S • Europe • 240 kW
	SEYCHELLES	
	†FEBA RADIO, North Pt, Mahé Is	E Africa & S Africa • 75 kW
		W/Th/Sa-M • E Africa & S Africa • 75 kW
	USA	
	†VOA, Via São Tomé	M-F • E Africa • 100 kW
		E Africa • 100 kW
9825	HUNGARY	
	RADIO BUDAPEST, Diósd	• Su • Europe • 100 kW • ALT. FREQ. TO 9835 kHz
		• Su • W Europe • 100 kW • ALT. FREQ. TO 9835 kHz
	JAPAN	
	†RADIO JAPAN/NHK, Tokyo-Yamata	SE Asia • 100 kW
	KIRIBATI	
	†RADIO KIRIBATI, Betio	DS • 1 kW • USB
		DS • 1 kW • USB • ALT. FREQ. TO 9810 kHz
	RUSSIA	
	R TIKHIY OKEAN, Khabarovsk	S • N Pacific • 240 kW
	†TRANS WORLD RADIO, Irkutsk	W • S Asia • 250 kW
	UNITED KINGDOM	
	BBC, Multiple Locations	W • E Europe • 250/500 kW
	BBC, Rampisham	N Africa • 500 kW
		W • Europe • 500 kW
		• Europe • 500 kW
		• M-F • Europe • 500 kW
		S America • 500 kW •
	BBC, Skelton, Cumbria	• M-F • Europe • 300 kW
	BBC, Various Locations	N Africa • 250/500 kW
		S America • 250 kW
	BBC, Via Ascension	Tu-Sa • S America • 250 kW
	BBC, Via Yekaterinburg, Russia	S • E Europe • 200 kW
		S • Sa/Su • E Europe • 200 kW
	BBC, Via Zyyi, Cyprus	W • W Asia & C Asia • 300 kW
		W • Mideast • 300 kW
		W • M-F • Europe • 300 kW
	USA	
	RADIO MARTI, Greenville, NC	C America • 250 kW
	†WYFR-FAMILY RADIO, Via Skelton, UK	W • N Africa • 300 kW
	VATICAN STATE	
	VATICAN RADIO, Sta Maria di Galeria	S • Mideast • 250 kW
		S • E Europe & W Asia • 250 kW
		S • E Europe • 250 kW
		S • E Asia • 250 kW
9825v	ALBANIA	
	†RADIO TIRANA, Cerrik	• W Europe • 100 kW • ALT. FREQ. TO 9740v kHz
9830	CROATIA	
	†CROATIAN RADIO, Deanovec	• Europe • 10 kW
		• M-F • ENGLISH & CROAT • Europe • 10 kW
		• Sa/Su • Europe • 10 kW
		• M-F • Europe • 10 kW
		• Sa/Su • ENGLISH & CROAT • Europe • 10 kW
	CUBA	
	†RADIO HABANA CUBA, Havana	E North Am & Europe • 30 kW • USB
	FRANCE	
	†R FRANCE INTL, Via Tokyo, Japan	W • SE Asia • 300 kW
	†R FRANCE INTL, Via Vladivostok	S • E Asia • 500 kW
		W • E Asia • 500 kW
	HOLLAND	
	†R NEDERLAND, Via Neth Antilles	W • Australasia • 250 kW
	JORDAN	
(con'd)	RADIO JORDAN, Qasr el Kharana	• W Europe • 500 kW

SEASONAL ⑤ OR Ⓦ   1-HR TIMESHIFT MIDYEAR ⊏ OR ⊐   JAMMING / OR ∧   EARLIEST HEARD ◁   LATEST HEARD ▷   NEW FOR 1998 †

FREQUENCY   COUNTRY, STATION, LOCATION   TARGET • NETWORK • POWER (kW)   World Time

0 1 2 3 4 5 6 7 8 9 10 11 12 13 14 15 16 17 18 19 20 21 22 23 24

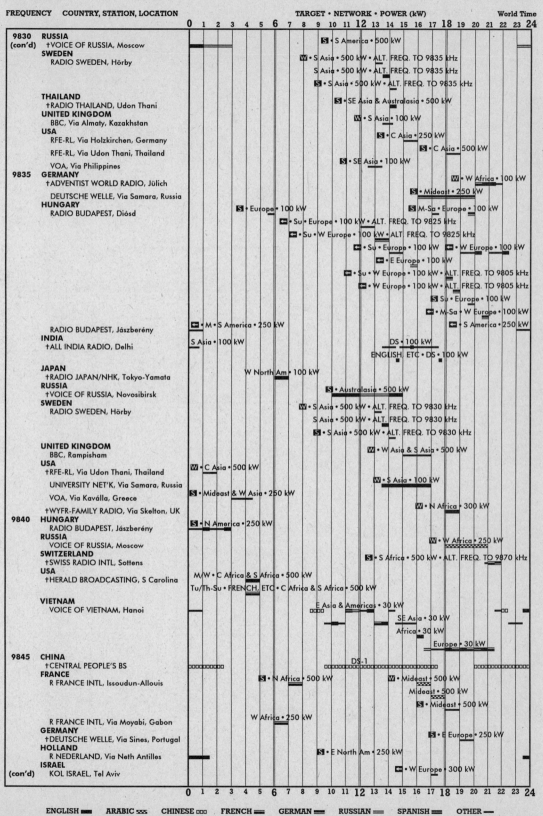

9830
(con'd)   RUSSIA
     †VOICE OF RUSSIA, Moscow — S • S America • 500 kW
   SWEDEN
     RADIO SWEDEN, Hörby — W • S Asia • 500 kW • ALT. FREQ. TO 9835 kHz
         S Asia • 500 kW • ALT. FREQ. TO 9835 kHz
         S • S Asia • 500 kW • ALT. FREQ. TO 9835 kHz

   THAILAND
     †RADIO THAILAND, Udon Thani — S • SE Asia & Australasia • 500 kW
   UNITED KINGDOM
     BBC, Via Almaty, Kazakhstan — W • S Asia • 100 kW
   USA
     RFE-RL, Via Holzkirchen, Germany — S • C Asia • 250 kW
     RFE-RL, Via Udon Thani, Thailand — S • C Asia • 500 kW
     VOA, Via Philippines — S • SE Asia • 100 kW

9835   GERMANY
     †ADVENTIST WORLD RADIO, Jülich — W • W Africa • 100 kW
     DEUTSCHE WELLE, Via Samara, Russia — S • Mideast • 250 kW
   HUNGARY
     RADIO BUDAPEST, Diósd — S • Europe • 100 kW
         S • M-Sa • Europe • 100 kW
         • Su • Europe • 100 kW • ALT. FREQ. TO 9825 kHz
         • Su • W Europe • 100 kW • ALT. FREQ. TO 9825 kHz
         • Su • Europe • 100 kW • W Europe • 100 kW
         • Su • E Europe • 100 kW
         • Su • W Europe • 100 kW • ALT. FREQ. TO 9805 kHz
         • W Europe • 100 kW • ALT. FREQ. TO 9805 kHz
         S • Su • Europe • 100 kW
         • M-Sa • W Europe • 100 kW

     RADIO BUDAPEST, Jászberény — • M • S America • 250 kW
         • S America • 250 kW
   INDIA
     †ALL INDIA RADIO, Delhi — S Asia • 100 kW
         DS • 100 kW
         ENGLISH, ETC • DS • 100 kW

   JAPAN
     †RADIO JAPAN/NHK, Tokyo-Yamata — W North Am • 100 kW
   RUSSIA
     †VOICE OF RUSSIA, Novosibirsk — S • Australasia • 500 kW
   SWEDEN
     RADIO SWEDEN, Hörby — W • S Asia • 500 kW • ALT. FREQ. TO 9830 kHz
         S Asia • 500 kW • ALT. FREQ. TO 9830 kHz
         S • S Asia • 500 kW • ALT. FREQ. TO 9830 kHz

   UNITED KINGDOM
     BBC, Rampisham — W • W Asia & S Asia • 500 kW
   USA
     †RFE-RL, Via Udon Thani, Thailand — W • C Asia • 500 kW
     UNIVERSITY NET'K, Via Samara, Russia — W • S Asia • 100 kW
     VOA, Via Kaválla, Greece — S • Mideast & W Asia • 250 kW
     †WYFR-FAMILY RADIO, Via Skelton, UK — W • N Africa • 300 kW

9840   HUNGARY
     RADIO BUDAPEST, Jászberény — S • N America • 250 kW
   RUSSIA
     VOICE OF RUSSIA, Moscow — W • W Africa • 250 kW
   SWITZERLAND
     †SWISS RADIO INTL, Sottens — S • S Africa • 500 kW • ALT. FREQ. TO 9870 kHz
   USA
     †HERALD BROADCASTING, S Carolina — M/W • C Africa & S Africa • 500 kW
         Tu/Th-Su • FRENCH, ETC • C Africa & S Africa • 500 kW

   VIETNAM
     VOICE OF VIETNAM, Hanoi — E Asia & Americas • 30 kW
         SE Asia • 30 kW
         Africa • 30 kW
         Europe • 30 kW

9845   CHINA
     †CENTRAL PEOPLE'S BS — DS-1
   FRANCE
     R FRANCE INTL, Issoudun-Allouis — S • N Africa • 500 kW
         W • Mideast • 500 kW
         Mideast • 500 kW
         S • Mideast • 500 kW

     R FRANCE INTL, Via Moyabi, Gabon — W Africa • 250 kW
   GERMANY
     †DEUTSCHE WELLE, Via Sines, Portugal — S • E Europe • 250 kW
   HOLLAND
     R NEDERLAND, Via Neth Antilles — S • E North Am • 250 kW
   ISRAEL
(con'd)   KOL ISRAEL, Tel Aviv — • W Europe • 300 kW

0 1 2 3 4 5 6 7 8 9 10 11 12 13 14 15 16 17 18 19 20 21 22 23 24

ENGLISH ▬▬   ARABIC ≋≋≋   CHINESE □□□   FRENCH ▬▬   GERMAN ▬▬   RUSSIAN ══   SPANISH ▬▬   OTHER ▬▬

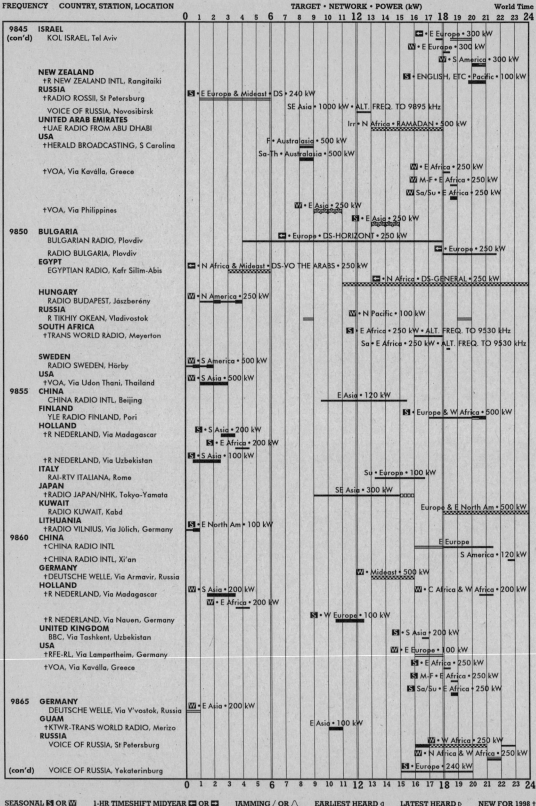

9845 ISRAEL
(con'd) KOL ISRAEL, Tel Aviv — E Europe • 300 kW / W • E Europe • 300 kW / W • S America • 300 kW

NEW ZEALAND
†R NEW ZEALAND INTL, Rangitaiki — S • ENGLISH, ETC • Pacific • 100 kW
RUSSIA
†RADIO ROSSII, St Petersburg — S • E Europe & Mideast • DS • 240 kW

VOICE OF RUSSIA, Novosibirsk — SE Asia • 1000 kW • ALT. FREQ. TO 9895 kHz
UNITED ARAB EMIRATES
†UAE RADIO FROM ABU DHABI — Irr • N Africa • RAMADAN • 500 kW
USA
†HERALD BROADCASTING, S Carolina — F • Australasia • 500 kW / Sa-Th • Australasia • 500 kW

†VOA, Via Kaválla, Greece — W • E Africa • 250 kW / W M-F • E Africa • 250 kW / W Sa/Su • E Africa • 250 kW

†VOA, Via Philippines — W • E Asia • 250 kW / S • E Asia • 250 kW

9850 BULGARIA
BULGARIAN RADIO, Plovdiv — Europe • DS-HORIZONT • 250 kW

RADIO BULGARIA, Plovdiv — Europe • 250 kW
EGYPT
EGYPTIAN RADIO, Kafr Silīm-Abis — N Africa & Mideast • DS-VO THE ARABS • 250 kW / N Africa • DS-GENERAL • 250 kW

HUNGARY
RADIO BUDAPEST, Jászberény — W • N America • 250 kW
RUSSIA
R TIKHIY OKEAN, Vladivostok — W • N Pacific • 100 kW
SOUTH AFRICA
†TRANS WORLD RADIO, Meyerton — S • E Africa • 250 kW • ALT. FREQ. TO 9530 kHz / Sa • E Africa • 250 kW • ALT. FREQ. TO 9530 kHz

SWEDEN
RADIO SWEDEN, Hörby — W • S America • 500 kW
USA
†VOA, Via Udon Thani, Thailand — W • S Asia • 500 kW
9855 CHINA
CHINA RADIO INTL, Beijing — E Asia • 120 kW
FINLAND
YLE RADIO FINLAND, Pori — S • Europe & W Africa • 500 kW
HOLLAND
†R NEDERLAND, Via Madagascar — S • S Asia • 200 kW / S • E Africa • 200 kW

†R NEDERLAND, Via Uzbekistan — S • S Asia • 100 kW
ITALY
RAI-RTV ITALIANA, Rome — Su • Europe • 100 kW
JAPAN
†RADIO JAPAN/NHK, Tokyo-Yamata — SE Asia • 300 kW
KUWAIT
RADIO KUWAIT, Kabd — Europe & E North Am • 500 kW
LITHUANIA
†RADIO VILNIUS, Via Jülich, Germany — S • E North Am • 100 kW
9860 CHINA
†CHINA RADIO INTL — E Europe

†CHINA RADIO INTL, Xi'an — S America • 120 kW
GERMANY
†DEUTSCHE WELLE, Via Armavir, Russia — W • Mideast • 500 kW
HOLLAND
†R NEDERLAND, Via Madagascar — W • S Asia • 200 kW / W • C Africa & W Africa • 200 kW / W • E Africa • 200 kW

†R NEDERLAND, Via Nauen, Germany — S • W Europe • 100 kW
UNITED KINGDOM
BBC, Via Tashkent, Uzbekistan — S • S Asia • 200 kW
USA
†RFE-RL, Via Lampertheim, Germany — W • E Europe • 100 kW

†VOA, Via Kaválla, Greece — S • E Africa • 250 kW / S M-F • E Africa • 250 kW / S Sa/Su • E Africa • 250 kW

9865 GERMANY
DEUTSCHE WELLE, Via V'vostok, Russia — W • E Asia • 200 kW
GUAM
†KTWR-TRANS WORLD RADIO, Merizo — E Asia • 100 kW
RUSSIA
VOICE OF RUSSIA, St Petersburg — W • W Africa • 250 kW / W • N Africa & W Africa • 250 kW

(con'd) VOICE OF RUSSIA, Yekaterinburg — S • Europe • 240 kW

SEASONAL S OR W   1-HR TIMESHIFT MIDYEAR ◪ OR ◪   JAMMING / OR ∧   EARLIEST HEARD ◁   LATEST HEARD ▷   NEW FOR 1998 †

FREQUENCY   COUNTRY, STATION, LOCATION   TARGET • NETWORK • POWER (kW)   World Time

0 1 2 3 4 5 6 7 8 9 10 11 12 13 14 15 16 17 18 19 20 21 22 23 24

Freq	Country, Station, Location	Notes
9865 (con'd)	SEYCHELLES †FEBA RADIO, North Pt, Mahé Is	F-M • E Africa • 100 kW; E Africa • 100 kW
	SWEDEN RADIO SWEDEN, Hörby	W • W Asia & C Asia • 500 kW
	USA VOA, Via Rhodes, Greece	S • Mideast • 50 kW
9870	AUSTRIA †R AUSTRIA INTL, Vienna	S America • 300 kW; C America • 300 kW; M-Sa • S America • 300 kW; Su • S America • 300 kW
	CHINA †CHINA RADIO INTL	SE Asia
	CLANDESTINE (AFRICA) †"VO OROMO LIBERATION", Via Ukraine	M/W/Sa • E Africa • 100 kW • ALT. FREQ. TO 9930 kHz
	GERMANY †DEUTSCHE WELLE, Via Sines, Portugal	W • E Europe • 250 kW
	GUAM †KTWR-TRANS WORLD RADIO, Merizo	SE Asia • 100 kW; E Asia • 100 kW
	KOREA (REPUBLIC) †RADIO KOREA INTL, In-Kimjae	Mideast & Africa • 250 kW
	RUSSIA †RADIO ROSSII, Novosibirsk	S • E Asia • DS • 100 kW
	SAUDI ARABIA BS OF THE KINGDOM, Riyadh	W Europe • DS-GENERAL • 500 kW
	SWITZERLAND †SWISS RADIO INTL, Sottens	S • S Africa • 500 kW • ALT. FREQ. TO 9840 kHz
	UKRAINE RADIO UKRAINE, Nikolayev	W • W Europe & E North Am • 1000 kW
	UNITED KINGDOM BBC, Skelton, Cumbria	N Africa • 300 kW
9875	GERMANY †DEUTSCHE WELLE, Via N'sibirsk, Russia	S • S Asia • 500 kW
	IRELAND †WEST COAST R IRELAND, Via Germany	S • Th • E North Am • 100 kW
	KOREA (REPUBLIC) †RADIO KOREA INTL, Via Skelton, UK	S • N Europe • 300 kW
	PHILIPPINES †FEBC RADIO INTL, Bocaue	SE Asia • 100 kW
	RUSSIA VOICE OF RUSSIA, Armavir	W • S Asia & SE Asia • 240 kW
	VOICE OF RUSSIA, Irkutsk	S • E Asia • 500 kW
	UKRAINE RADIO UKRAINE, L'vov	S • S Africa • 1000 kW
	USA RFE-RL, Via Udon Thani, Thailand	S • W Asia & Mideast • 500 kW
9880	CHINA †CHINA RADIO INTL, Beijing	SE Asia • 120 kW
	†CHINA RADIO INTL	S • S Asia & W Asia
	CHINA RADIO INTL, Via Moscow, Russia	S • Europe • 250 kW
	KUWAIT RADIO KUWAIT, Kabd	Mideast • 500 kW
	RUSSIA VOICE OF RUSSIA, Moscow	S • Europe • 250 kW
9885	RUSSIA †MAYAK, St Petersburg	S • E Europe & Mideast • DS • 200 kW
	SWITZERLAND †SWISS RADIO INTL, Schwarzenburg	W Africa • 150 kW; W • C Asia & S Asia • 150 kW; Mideast • 150 kW • ALT. FREQ. TO 9745 kHz; W • W Africa • 150 kW; S • N Africa • 250 kW; W • E Africa • 150 kW; S • W Africa • 150 kW; S America • 500 kW
	†SWISS RADIO INTL, Sottens	E North Am • 500 kW; N America • 500 kW; W • E Asia • 500 kW
	SWISS RADIO INTL, Via French Guiana	Australasia • 500 kW
	THAILAND †RADIO THAILAND, Udon Thani	S • SE Asia & Australasia • 500 kW
	USA †VOA, Via Botswana	Africa • 100 kW
	†VOA, Via Philippines	W • SE Asia • 50 kW
9885v	SAUDI ARABIA BS OF THE KINGDOM, Jiddah	N Africa • DS-HOLY KORAN • 50 kW • ALT. FREQ. TO 9620v kHz
9890	CHINA CHINA RADIO INTL, Via Samara, Russia	S • Europe • 250 kW
	HOLLAND (con'd) R NEDERLAND, Via Madagascar	S • S Asia • 200 kW

0 1 2 3 4 5 6 7 8 9 10 11 12 13 14 15 16 17 18 19 20 21 22 23 24

ENGLISH ▬▬   ARABIC ∽∽∽   CHINESE □□□   FRENCH ▬▬   GERMAN ▬▬   RUSSIAN ══   SPANISH ▬▬   OTHER ──

FREQUENCY   COUNTRY, STATION, LOCATION   TARGET • NETWORK • POWER (kW)   World Time

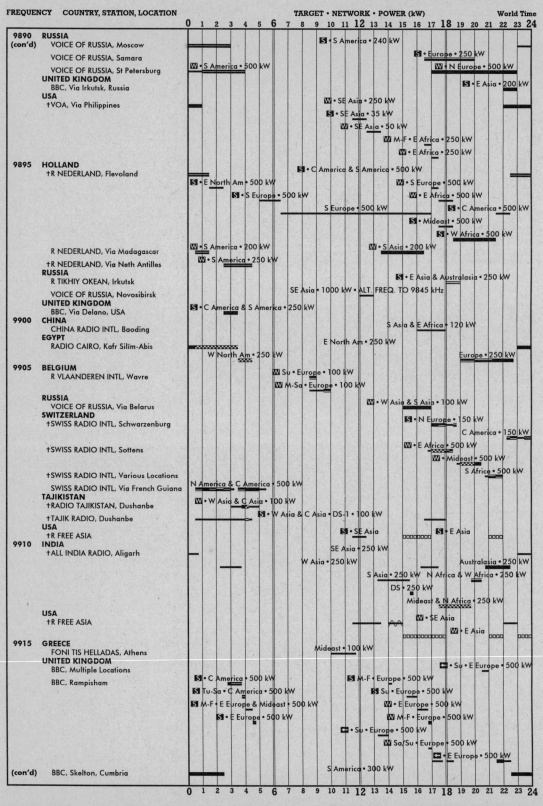

Frequency	Country, Station, Location	Target • Network • Power
9890 (con'd)	**RUSSIA** VOICE OF RUSSIA, Moscow	S • S America • 240 kW
	VOICE OF RUSSIA, Samara	S • Europe • 250 kW
	VOICE OF RUSSIA, St Petersburg	W • S America • 500 kW / W • N Europe • 500 kW
	UNITED KINGDOM BBC, Via Irkutsk, Russia	S • E Asia • 200 kW
	USA †VOA, Via Philippines	W • SE Asia • 250 kW / S • SE Asia • 35 kW / W • SE Asia • 50 kW / W • M-F • E Africa • 250 kW / W • E Africa • 250 kW
9895	**HOLLAND** †R NEDERLAND, Flevoland	S • C America & S America • 500 kW / S • E North Am • 500 kW / S • S Europe • 500 kW / W • S Europe • 500 kW / W • E Africa • 500 kW / S Europe • 500 kW / S • C America • 500 kW / S • Mideast • 500 kW / S • W Africa • 500 kW
	R NEDERLAND, Via Madagascar	W • S America • 200 kW / W • S Asia • 200 kW
	†R NEDERLAND, Via Neth Antilles	W • S America • 250 kW
	RUSSIA R TIKHIY OKEAN, Irkutsk	S • E Asia & Australasia • 250 kW
	VOICE OF RUSSIA, Novosibirsk	SE Asia • 1000 kW • ALT. FREQ. TO 9845 kHz
	UNITED KINGDOM BBC, Via Delano, USA	S • C America & S America • 250 kW
9900	**CHINA** CHINA RADIO INTL, Baoding	S Asia & E Africa • 120 kW
	EGYPT RADIO CAIRO, Kafr Silim-Abis	E North Am • 250 kW / W North Am • 250 kW / Europe • 250 kW
9905	**BELGIUM** R VLAANDEREN INTL, Wavre	W • Su • Europe • 100 kW / W • M-Sa • Europe • 100 kW
	RUSSIA VOICE OF RUSSIA, Via Belarus	W • W Asia & S Asia • 100 kW
	SWITZERLAND †SWISS RADIO INTL, Schwarzenburg	S • N Europe • 150 kW / C America • 150 kW
	†SWISS RADIO INTL, Sottens	W • E Africa • 500 kW / W • Mideast • 500 kW / S Africa • 500 kW
	†SWISS RADIO INTL, Various Locations	N America & C America • 500 kW
	SWISS RADIO INTL, Via French Guiana	
	TAJIKISTAN †RADIO TAJIKISTAN, Dushanbe	W • W Asia & C Asia • 100 kW
	†TAJIK RADIO, Dushanbe	S • W Asia & C Asia • DS-1 • 100 kW
	USA †R FREE ASIA	S • SE Asia / S • E Asia
9910	**INDIA** †ALL INDIA RADIO, Aligarh	SE Asia • 250 kW / W Asia • 250 kW / Australasia • 250 kW / S Asia • 250 kW N Africa & W Africa • 250 kW / DS • 250 kW / Mideast & N Africa • 250 kW
	USA †R FREE ASIA	W • SE Asia / W • E Asia
9915	**GREECE** FONI TIS HELLADAS, Athens	Mideast • 100 kW
	UNITED KINGDOM BBC, Multiple Locations	• Su • E Europe • 500 kW
	BBC, Rampisham	S • C America • 500 kW / S • M-F • Europe • 500 kW / S Tu-Sa • C America • 500 kW / S • Su • Europe • 500 kW / S • M-F • E Europe & Mideast • 500 kW / W • E Europe • 500 kW / W • M-F • Europe • 500 kW / S • E Europe • 500 kW / • Su • Europe • 500 kW / W • Sa/Su • Europe • 500 kW / • E Europe • 500 kW
(con'd)	BBC, Skelton, Cumbria	S America • 300 kW

FREQUENCY   COUNTRY, STATION, LOCATION   TARGET • NETWORK • POWER (kW)   World Time

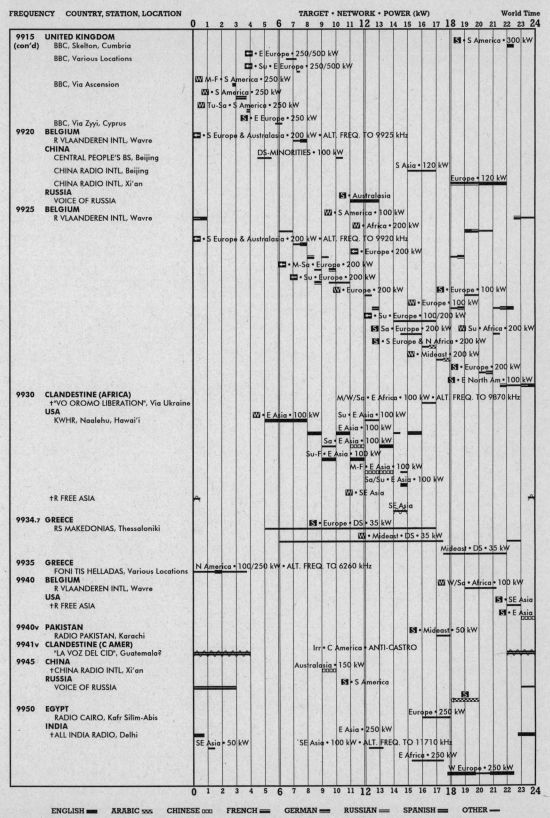

9915	**UNITED KINGDOM**
(con'd)	BBC, Skelton, Cumbria — S America • 300 kW
	BBC, Various Locations — E Europe • 250/500 kW
	Su • E Europe • 250/500 kW
	BBC, Via Ascension — M-F • S America • 250 kW
	S America • 250 kW
	Tu-Sa • S America • 250 kW
	BBC, Via Zyyi, Cyprus — E Europe • 250 kW
9920	**BELGIUM**
	R VLAANDEREN INTL, Wavre — S Europe & Australasia • 200 kW • ALT. FREQ. TO 9925 kHz
	CHINA
	CENTRAL PEOPLE'S BS, Beijing — DS-MINORITIES • 100 kW
	CHINA RADIO INTL, Beijing — S Asia • 120 kW
	CHINA RADIO INTL, Xi'an — Europe • 120 kW
	RUSSIA
	VOICE OF RUSSIA — Australasia
9925	**BELGIUM**
	R VLAANDEREN INTL, Wavre — W • S America • 100 kW
	W • Africa • 200 kW
	S Europe & Australasia • 200 kW • ALT. FREQ. TO 9920 kHz
	Europe • 200 kW
	M-Sa • Europe • 200 kW
	Su • Europe • 200 kW
	W • Europe • 200 kW
	Europe • 100 kW
	W • Europe • 100 kW
	Su • Europe • 100/200 kW
	Sa • Europe • 200 kW W Su • Africa • 200 kW
	S • S Europe & N Africa • 200 kW
	W • Mideast • 200 kW
	S • Europe • 200 kW
	S • E North Am • 100 kW
9930	**CLANDESTINE (AFRICA)**
	†"VO OROMO LIBERATION", Via Ukraine — M/W/Sa • E Africa • 100 kW • ALT. FREQ. TO 9870 kHz
	USA
	KWHR, Naalehu, Hawai'i — W • E Asia • 100 kW Su • E Asia • 100 kW
	E Asia • 100 kW
	Sa • E Asia • 100 kW
	Su-F • E Asia • 100 kW
	M-F • E Asia • 100 kW
	Sa/Su • E Asia • 100 kW
	†R FREE ASIA — W • SE Asia
	SE Asia
9934.7	**GREECE**
	RS MAKEDONIAS, Thessaloniki — S • Europe • DS • 35 kW
	W • Mideast • DS • 35 kW
	Mideast • DS • 35 kW
9935	**GREECE**
	FONI TIS HELLADAS, Various Locations — N America • 100/250 kW • ALT. FREQ. TO 6260 kHz
9940	**BELGIUM**
	R VLAANDEREN INTL, Wavre — W W/Sa • Africa • 100 kW
	USA
	†R FREE ASIA — S • SE Asia
	S • E Asia
9940v	**PAKISTAN**
	RADIO PAKISTAN, Karachi — S • Mideast • 50 kW
9941v	**CLANDESTINE (C AMER)**
	"LA VOZ DEL CID", Guatemala? — Irr • C America • ANTI-CASTRO
9945	**CHINA**
	†CHINA RADIO INTL, Xi'an — Australasia • 150 kW
	RUSSIA
	VOICE OF RUSSIA — S • S America
9950	**EGYPT**
	RADIO CAIRO, Kafr Silim-Abis — Europe • 250 kW
	INDIA
	†ALL INDIA RADIO, Delhi — E Asia • 250 kW
	SE Asia • 50 kW SE Asia • 100 kW • ALT. FREQ. TO 11710 kHz
	E Africa • 250 kW
	W Europe • 250 kW

ENGLISH ▬   ARABIC ⌇⌇⌇   CHINESE □□□   FRENCH ▬▬   GERMAN ▬▬   RUSSIAN ══   SPANISH ══   OTHER ▬

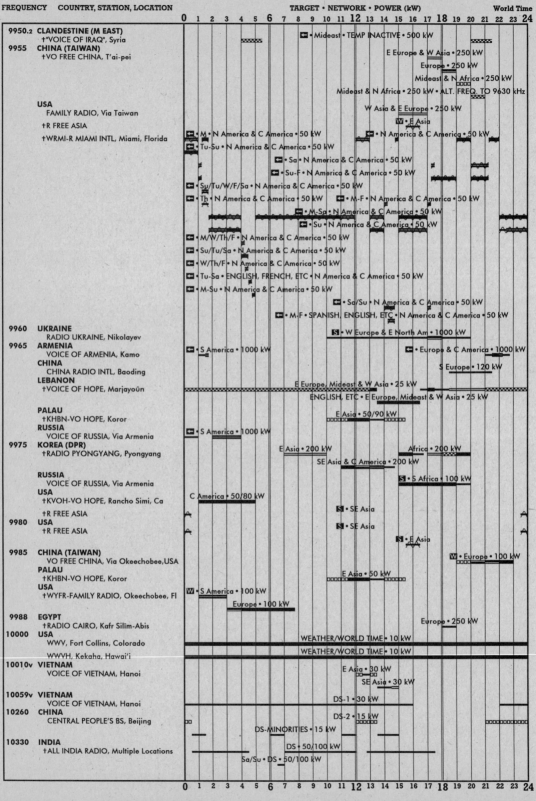

FREQUENCY   COUNTRY, STATION, LOCATION   TARGET • NETWORK • POWER (kW)   World Time

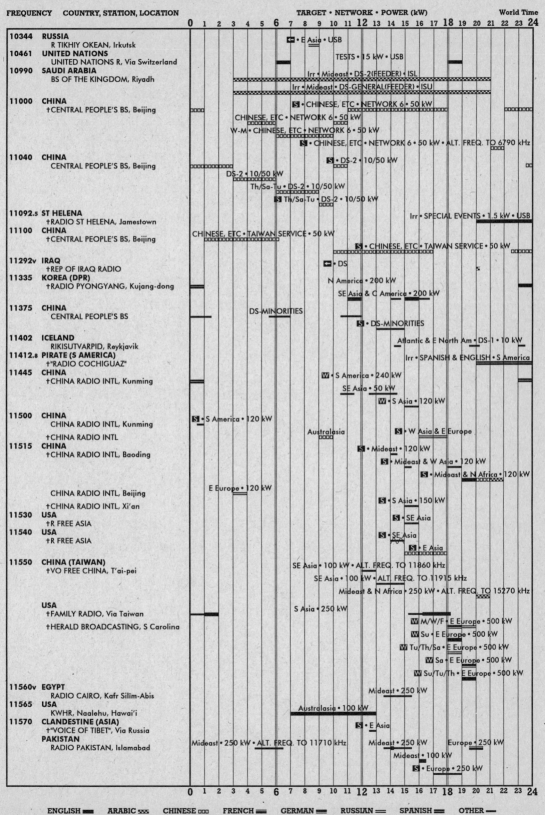

Frequency	Country, Station, Location	Schedule details
10344	**RUSSIA** — R TIKHIY OKEAN, Irkutsk	• E Asia • USB
10461	**UNITED NATIONS** — UNITED NATIONS R, Via Switzerland	TESTS • 15 kW • USB
10990	**SAUDI ARABIA** — BS OF THE KINGDOM, Riyadh	Irr • Mideast • DS-2(FEEDER) • ISL / Irr • Mideast • DS-GENERAL(FEEDER) • ISU
11000	**CHINA** — †CENTRAL PEOPLE'S BS, Beijing	• CHINESE, ETC • NETWORK 6 • 50 kW / CHINESE, ETC • NETWORK 6 • 50 kW / W-M • CHINESE, ETC • NETWORK 6 • 50 kW / • CHINESE, ETC • NETWORK 6 • 50 kW • ALT. FREQ. TO 6790 kHz
11040	**CHINA** — CENTRAL PEOPLE'S BS, Beijing	• DS-2 • 10/50 kW / DS-2 • 10/50 kW / Th/Sa-Tu • DS-2 • 10/50 kW / Th/Sa-Tu • DS-2 • 10/50 kW
11092.5	**ST HELENA** — †RADIO ST HELENA, Jamestown	Irr • SPECIAL EVENTS • 1.5 kW • USB
11100	**CHINA** — †CENTRAL PEOPLE'S BS, Beijing	CHINESE, ETC • TAIWAN SERVICE • 50 kW / • CHINESE, ETC • TAIWAN SERVICE • 50 kW
11292v	**IRAQ** — †REP OF IRAQ RADIO	• DS
11335	**KOREA (DPR)** — †RADIO PYONGYANG, Kujang-dong	N America • 200 kW / SE Asia & C America • 200 kW
11375	**CHINA** — CENTRAL PEOPLE'S BS	DS-MINORITIES / • DS-MINORITIES
11402	**ICELAND** — RIKISUTVARPID, Reykjavik	Atlantic & E North Am • DS-1 • 10 kW
11412.8	**PIRATE (S AMERICA)** — †"RADIO COCHIGUAZ"	Irr • SPANISH & ENGLISH • S America
11445	**CHINA** — †CHINA RADIO INTL, Kunming	• S America • 240 kW / SE Asia • 50 kW / • S Asia • 120 kW
11500	**CHINA** — CHINA RADIO INTL, Kunming / †CHINA RADIO INTL	• S America • 120 kW / Australasia / • W Asia & E Europe
11515	**CHINA** — †CHINA RADIO INTL, Baoding / CHINA RADIO INTL, Beijing / †CHINA RADIO INTL, Xi'an	• Mideast • 120 kW / • Mideast & W Asia • 120 kW / • Mideast & N Africa • 120 kW / E Europe • 120 kW / • S Asia • 150 kW
11530	**USA** — †R FREE ASIA	• SE Asia
11540	**USA** — †R FREE ASIA	• SE Asia / • E Asia
11550	**CHINA (TAIWAN)** — †VO FREE CHINA, T'ai-pei	SE Asia • 100 kW • ALT. FREQ. TO 11860 kHz / SE Asia • 100 kW • ALT. FREQ. TO 11915 kHz / Mideast & N Africa • 250 kW • ALT. FREQ. TO 15270 kHz
	USA — †FAMILY RADIO, Via Taiwan	S Asia • 250 kW
	†HERALD BROADCASTING, S Carolina	M/W/F • E Europe • 500 kW / Su • E Europe • 500 kW / Tu/Th/Sa • E Europe • 500 kW / Sa • E Europe • 500 kW / Su/Tu/Th • E Europe • 500 kW
11560v	**EGYPT** — RADIO CAIRO, Kafr Silim-Abis	Mideast • 250 kW
11565	**USA** — KWHR, Naalehu, Hawai'i	Australasia • 100 kW
11570	**CLANDESTINE (ASIA)** — †"VOICE OF TIBET", Via Russia	• E Asia
	PAKISTAN — RADIO PAKISTAN, Islamabad	Mideast • 250 kW • ALT. FREQ. TO 11710 kHz / Mideast • 250 kW / Europe • 250 kW / Mideast • 100 kW / • Europe • 250 kW

FREQUENCY   COUNTRY, STATION, LOCATION

TARGET • NETWORK • POWER (kW)

World Time

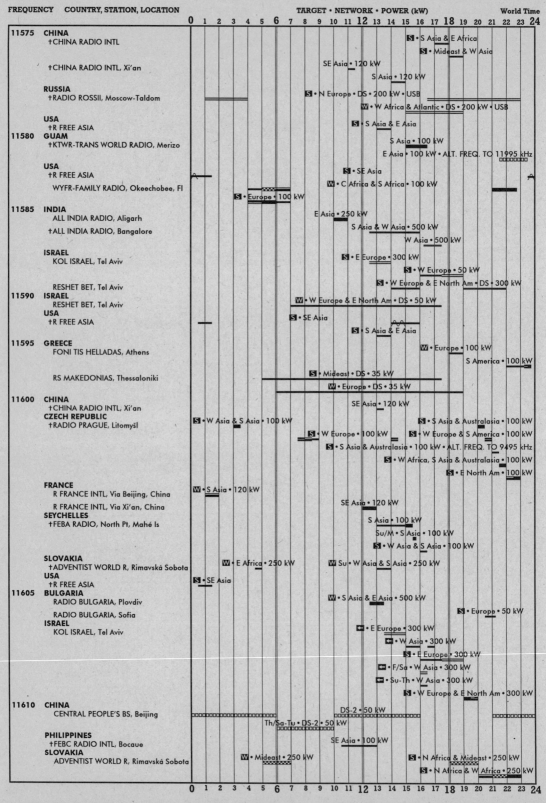

FREQUENCY	COUNTRY, STATION, LOCATION	TARGET • NETWORK • POWER (kW)
11575	CHINA	
	†CHINA RADIO INTL	S • S Asia & E Africa
		S • Mideast & W Asia
	†CHINA RADIO INTL, Xi'an	SE Asia • 120 kW
		S Asia • 120 kW
	RUSSIA	
	†RADIO ROSSII, Moscow-Taldom	S • N Europe • DS • 200 kW • USB
		W • W Africa & Atlantic • DS • 200 kW • USB
	USA	
	†R FREE ASIA	S • S Asia & E Asia
11580	GUAM	
	†KTWR-TRANS WORLD RADIO, Merizo	S Asia • 100 kW
		E Asia • 100 kW • ALT. FREQ. TO 11995 kHz
	USA	
	†R FREE ASIA	S • SE Asia
	WYFR-FAMILY RADIO, Okeechobee, Fl	W • C Africa & S Africa • 100 kW
		S • Europe • 100 kW
11585	INDIA	
	ALL INDIA RADIO, Aligarh	E Asia • 250 kW
	†ALL INDIA RADIO, Bangalore	S Asia & W Asia • 500 kW
		W Asia • 500 kW
	ISRAEL	
	KOL ISRAEL, Tel Aviv	S • E Europe • 300 kW
		S • W Europe • 50 kW
	RESHET BET, Tel Aviv	S • W Europe & E North Am • DS • 300 kW
11590	ISRAEL	
	RESHET BET, Tel Aviv	W • W Europe & E North Am • DS • 50 kW
	USA	
	†R FREE ASIA	S • SE Asia
		S • S Asia & E Asia
11595	GREECE	
	FONI TIS HELLADAS, Athens	W • Europe • 100 kW
		S America • 100 kW
	RS MAKEDONIAS, Thessaloniki	S • Mideast • DS • 35 kW
		W • Europe • DS • 35 kW
11600	CHINA	
	†CHINA RADIO INTL, Xi'an	SE Asia • 120 kW
	CZECH REPUBLIC	
	†RADIO PRAGUE, Litomyšl	S • W Asia & S Asia • 100 kW
		S • S Asia & Australasia • 100 kW
		S • W Europe • 100 kW
		S • W Europe & S America • 100 kW
		S • S Asia & Australasia • 100 kW • ALT. FREQ. TO 9495 kHz
		S • W Africa, S Asia & Australasia • 100 kW
		S • E North Am • 100 kW
	FRANCE	
	R FRANCE INTL, Via Beijing, China	W • S Asia • 120 kW
	R FRANCE INTL, Via Xi'an, China	SE Asia • 120 kW
	SEYCHELLES	
	†FEBA RADIO, North Pt, Mahé Is	S Asia • 100 kW
		Su/M • S Asia • 100 kW
		S • W Asia & S Asia • 100 kW
	SLOVAKIA	
	†ADVENTIST WORLD R, Rimavská Sobota	W • E Africa • 250 kW
		W Su • W Asia & S Asia • 250 kW
	USA	
	†R FREE ASIA	S • SE Asia
11605	BULGARIA	
	RADIO BULGARIA, Plovdiv	W • S Asia & E Asia • 500 kW
	RADIO BULGARIA, Sofia	S • Europe • 50 kW
	ISRAEL	
	KOL ISRAEL, Tel Aviv	• E Europe • 300 kW
		• W Asia • 300 kW
		S • E Europe • 300 kW
		• F/Sa • W Asia • 300 kW
		• Su-Th • W Asia • 300 kW
		S • W Europe & E North Am • 300 kW
11610	CHINA	
	CENTRAL PEOPLE'S BS, Beijing	DS-2 • 50 kW
		Th/Sa-Tu • DS-2 • 50 kW
	PHILIPPINES	
	†FEBC RADIO INTL, Bocaue	SE Asia • 100 kW
	SLOVAKIA	
	ADVENTIST WORLD R, Rimavská Sobota	W • Mideast • 250 kW
		S • N Africa & Mideast • 250 kW
		S • N Africa & W Africa • 250 kW

SEASONAL S OR W   1-HR TIMESHIFT MIDYEAR ◧ OR ◧   JAMMING / OR ∧   EARLIEST HEARD ◁   LATEST HEARD ▷   NEW FOR 1998 †

FREQUENCY   COUNTRY, STATION, LOCATION   TARGET • NETWORK • POWER (kW)   World Time

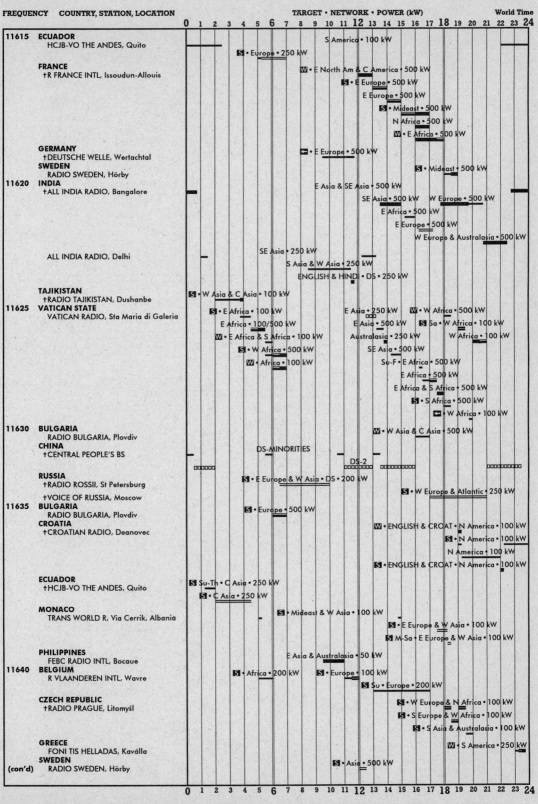

Frequency	Country / Station / Location	Target • Network • Power
11615	**ECUADOR** HCJB-VO THE ANDES, Quito	S America • 100 kW
		S • Europe • 250 kW
	FRANCE †R FRANCE INTL, Issoudun-Allouis	W • E North Am & C America • 500 kW
		S • E Europe • 500 kW
		E Europe • 500 kW
		S • Mideast • 500 kW
		N Africa • 500 kW
		W • E Africa • 500 kW
	GERMANY †DEUTSCHE WELLE, Wertachtal	← • E Europe • 500 kW
	SWEDEN RADIO SWEDEN, Hörby	S • Mideast • 500 kW
11620	**INDIA** †ALL INDIA RADIO, Bangalore	E Asia & SE Asia • 500 kW
		SE Asia • 500 kW W Europe • 500 kW
		E Africa • 500 kW
		E Europe • 500 kW
		W Europe & Australasia • 500 kW
	ALL INDIA RADIO, Delhi	SE Asia • 250 kW
		S Asia & W Asia • 250 kW
		ENGLISH & HINDI • DS • 250 kW
	TAJIKISTAN †RADIO TAJIKISTAN, Dushanbe	S • W Asia & C Asia • 100 kW
11625	**VATICAN STATE** VATICAN RADIO, Sta Maria di Galeria	S • E Africa • 100 kW E Asia • 250 kW W • W Africa • 500 kW
		E Africa • 100/500 kW E Asia • 500 kW S • Sa • W Africa • 100 kW
		W • E Africa & S Africa • 100 kW Australasia • 250 kW W Africa • 100 kW
		S • W Africa • 500 kW SE Asia • 500 kW
		W • Africa • 100 kW Su-F • E Africa • 500 kW
		E Africa • 500 kW
		E Africa & S Africa • 500 kW
		S • S Africa • 500 kW
		← • W Africa • 100 kW
11630	**BULGARIA** RADIO BULGARIA, Plovdiv	W • W Asia & C Asia • 500 kW
	CHINA †CENTRAL PEOPLE'S BS	DS-MINORITIES
		DS-2
	RUSSIA †RADIO ROSSII, St Petersburg	S • E Europe & W Asia • DS • 200 kW
	†VOICE OF RUSSIA, Moscow	S • W Europe & Atlantic • 250 kW
11635	**BULGARIA** RADIO BULGARIA, Plovdiv	S • Europe • 500 kW
	CROATIA †CROATIAN RADIO, Deanovec	W • ENGLISH & CROAT • N America • 100 kW
		S • N America • 100 kW
		N America • 100 kW
		S • ENGLISH & CROAT • N America • 100 kW
	ECUADOR †HCJB-VO THE ANDES, Quito	S Su-Th • C Asia • 250 kW
		S • C Asia • 250 kW
	MONACO TRANS WORLD R, Via Cerrik, Albania	S • Mideast & W Asia • 100 kW
		S • E Europe & W Asia • 100 kW
		S M-Sa • E Europe & W Asia • 100 kW
	PHILIPPINES FEBC RADIO INTL, Bocaue	E Asia & Australasia • 50 kW
11640	**BELGIUM** R VLAANDEREN INTL, Wavre	S • Africa • 200 kW S • Europe • 100 kW
		S • Su • Europe • 200 kW
	CZECH REPUBLIC †RADIO PRAGUE, Litomyšl	S • W Europe & N Africa • 100 kW
		S • S Europe & W Africa • 100 kW
		S • S Asia & Australasia • 100 kW
	GREECE FONI TIS HELLADAS, Kaválla	W • S America • 250 kW
	SWEDEN (con'd) RADIO SWEDEN, Hörby	S • Asia • 500 kW

ENGLISH ▬   ARABIC ≋   CHINESE ▫▫▫   FRENCH ═   GERMAN ▬▬   RUSSIAN ═   SPANISH ▭   OTHER ▬

FREQUENCY	COUNTRY, STATION, LOCATION	TARGET • NETWORK • POWER (kW)	World Time

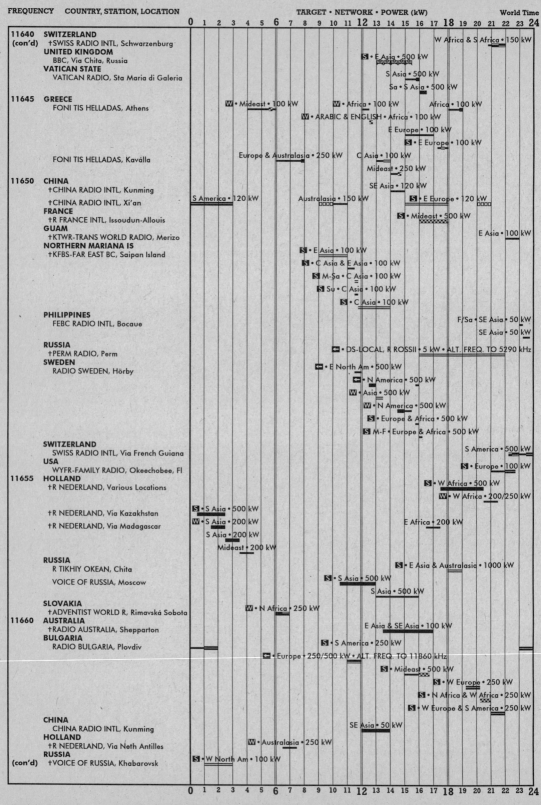

11640
(con'd)　†SWISS RADIO INTL, Schwarzenburg — W Africa & S Africa • 150 kW
SWITZERLAND

UNITED KINGDOM
　BBC, Via Chita, Russia — 🅂 • E Asia • 500 kW

VATICAN STATE
　VATICAN RADIO, Sta Maria di Galeria — S Asia • 500 kW
　Sa • S Asia • 500 kW

11645　**GREECE**
　FONI TIS HELLADAS, Athens — 🅆 • Mideast • 100 kW ／ 🅆 • Africa • 100 kW ／ Africa • 100 kW
　🅆 • ARABIC & ENGLISH • Africa • 100 kW
　E Europe • 100 kW
　🅂 • E Europe • 100 kW

　FONI TIS HELLADAS, Kaválla — Europe & Australasia • 250 kW ／ C Asia • 100 kW
　Mideast • 250 kW

11650　**CHINA**
　†CHINA RADIO INTL, Kunming — SE Asia • 120 kW
　†CHINA RADIO INTL, Xi'an — S America • 120 kW ／ Australasia • 150 kW ／ 🅂 • E Europe • 120 kW

FRANCE
　†R FRANCE INTL, Issoudun-Allouis — 🅂 • Mideast • 500 kW

GUAM
　†KTWR-TRANS WORLD RADIO, Merizo — E Asia • 100 kW

NORTHERN MARIANA IS
　†KFBS-FAR EAST BC, Saipan Island — 🅂 • E Asia • 100 kW
　🅂 • C Asia & E Asia • 100 kW
　🅂 • M-Sa • C Asia • 100 kW
　🅂 • Su • C Asia • 100 kW
　🅂 • C Asia • 100 kW

PHILIPPINES
　FEBC RADIO INTL, Bocaue — F/Sa • SE Asia • 50 kW
　SE Asia • 50 kW

RUSSIA
　†PERM RADIO, Perm — ⯈ • DS-LOCAL, R ROSSII • 5 kW • ALT. FREQ. TO 5290 kHz

SWEDEN
　RADIO SWEDEN, Hörby — ⯇ • E North Am • 500 kW
　⯇ • N America • 500 kW
　🅆 • Asia • 500 kW
　🅆 • N America • 500 kW
　🅂 • Europe & Africa • 500 kW
　🅂 • M-F • Europe & Africa • 500 kW

SWITZERLAND
　SWISS RADIO INTL, Via French Guiana — S America • 500 kW

USA
　WYFR-FAMILY RADIO, Okeechobee, Fl — 🅂 • Europe • 100 kW

11655　**HOLLAND**
　†R NEDERLAND, Various Locations — 🅂 • W Africa • 500 kW
　🅆 • W Africa • 200/250 kW

　†R NEDERLAND, Via Kazakhstan — 🅂 • S Asia • 500 kW
　†R NEDERLAND, Via Madagascar — 🅆 • S Asia • 200 kW ／ E Africa • 200 kW
　S Asia • 200 kW
　Mideast • 200 kW

RUSSIA
　R TIKHIY OKEAN, Chita — 🅂 • E Asia & Australasia • 1000 kW
　VOICE OF RUSSIA, Moscow — 🅂 • S Asia • 500 kW
　S Asia • 500 kW

SLOVAKIA
　†ADVENTIST WORLD R, Rimavská Sobota — 🅆 • N Africa • 250 kW

11660　**AUSTRALIA**
　†RADIO AUSTRALIA, Shepparton — E Asia & SE Asia • 100 kW

BULGARIA
　RADIO BULGARIA, Plovdiv — 🅂 • S America • 250 kW
　⯇ • Europe • 250/500 kW • ALT. FREQ. TO 11860 kHz
　🅂 • Mideast • 500 kW
　🅂 • W Europe • 250 kW
　🅂 • N Africa & W Africa • 250 kW
　🅂 • W Europe & S America • 250 kW

CHINA
　CHINA RADIO INTL, Kunming — SE Asia • 50 kW

HOLLAND
　†R NEDERLAND, Via Neth Antilles — 🅆 • Australasia • 250 kW

RUSSIA
(con'd)　†VOICE OF RUSSIA, Khabarovsk — 🅂 • W North Am • 100 kW

FREQUENCY	COUNTRY, STATION, LOCATION	TARGET • NETWORK • POWER (kW) — World Time

11660 (con'd) USA
†RFE-RL, Via Kaválla, Greece — S • C Asia • 250 kW
†VOA, Via Briech, Morocco — S • Europe • 500 kW

11665 GUAM
†KTWR-TRANS WORLD RADIO, Merizo — E Asia • 100 kW; S • E Asia • 100 kW

IRELAND
†WEST COAST R IRELAND, Via Germany — W • Th • Africa & Australasia • 100 kW

JAPAN
†RADIO JAPAN/NHK, Tokyo-Yamata — SE Asia • 300 kW

RUSSIA
†VOICE OF RUSSIA, Samara — S • SE Asia • 100 kW

USA
†RFE-RL, Via Lampertheim, Germany — S • C Asia • 100 kW
†WYFR-FAMILY RADIO, Okeechobee, Fl — W • Europe • 100 kW

11665v EGYPT
EGYPTIAN RADIO, Abu Za'bal — C Africa & E Africa • DS-VO THE ARABS • 100 kW; Mideast • DS-GENERAL • 100 kW

11670 FRANCE
†R FRANCE INTL, Issoudun-Allouis — E Europe • 500 kW; S • C America • 500 kW; W • E Europe • 500 kW; C America • 500 kW; S • E Europe • 500 kW
†R FRANCE INTL, Via French Guiana — S • C America • 500 kW; Irr • S America • 500 kW; S America • 500 kW; C America • 500 kW; S • S America • 500 kW; W • C America • 500 kW

USA
†VOA, Via Kaválla, Greece — W • Mideast • 250 kW; S • N Africa & Mideast • 250 kW

11675 CHINA
†CENTRAL PEOPLE'S BS — DS-1 • ALT. FREQ. TO 11825 kHz; W-M • DS-1 • ALT. FREQ. TO 11825 kHz; S • DS-1 • ALT. FREQ. TO 11825 kHz
†CHINA RADIO INTL, Xi'an — S • S Asia • 120 kW

KUWAIT
RADIO KUWAIT, Kabd — W North Am • 500 kW

RUSSIA
†VOICE OF RUSSIA, Via Moldova — S • N Europe • 1000 kW
†VOICE OF RUSSIA, Yekaterinburg — S • E Asia • 240 kW

SEYCHELLES
†FEBA RADIO, North Pt, Mahé Is — FRENCH, ETC • S Africa • 75 kW; F-M • E Africa • 75 kW • ALT. FREQ. TO 11705 kHz

11680 CLANDESTINE (AFRICA)
†"VO FREE NIGERIA", Algeria — So • ENGLISH, ETC • W Africa • ANTI-NIGERIAN GOVT • 50/100 kW • ALT. FREQ. TO 7180 kHz

HOLLAND
R NEDERLAND, Flevoland — S • S America • 500 kW

UNITED KINGDOM
BBC, Rampisham — Tu/F • Atlantic & S America • FALKLANDS SVC • 500 kW
BBC, Skelton, Cumbria — W • N Africa • 300 kW
BBC, Various Locations — E Europe • 250/500 kW; Su • Europe • 500 kW; Sa/Su • E Europe • 250/500 kW; W • E Europe & Mideast • 500 kW
BBC, Via Zyyi, Cyprus — W M-F • Europe • 300 kW

11680v KOREA (DPR)
KOREAN CENTRAL BS, Pyongyang — DS • 100/200 kW

11685 CHINA
†CHINA RADIO INTL, Kunming — S • SE Asia • 120 kW; SE Asia • 120 kW
†CHINA RADIO INTL, Xi'an — S • E Europe • 120 kW

FRANCE
†R FRANCE INTL, Issoudun-Allouis — S • Mideast • 500 kW; W • Mideast • 500 kW

ISRAEL
KOL ISRAEL, Tel Aviv — S • E Europe • 300 kW; W • W Europe & E North Am • 300 kW

RUSSIA
†MAYAK, St Petersburg — S • N Europe • DS • 100 kW

UNITED KINGDOM (con'd)
BBC, Via Maşīrah, Oman — S Asia • 100 kW

ENGLISH ▬ ARABIC ⊠ CHINESE □□□ FRENCH ═ GERMAN ▬ RUSSIAN ═ SPANISH ▬ OTHER —

FREQUENCY   COUNTRY, STATION, LOCATION

TARGET • NETWORK • POWER (kW)

World Time

0 1 2 3 4 5 6 7 8 9 10 11 12 13 14 15 16 17 18 19 20 21 22 23 24

FREQUENCY	COUNTRY, STATION, LOCATION	Schedule
11685 (con'd)	UNITED KINGDOM	
	BBC, Via Singapore	Sa/Su • SE Asia • 250 kW; SE Asia • 100 kW; W • S Asia • 100 kW; S Asia • 100 kW
	BBC, Via Thailand	S Asia • 250 kW
11690	BELARUS	
	BELARUSSIAN R, Mogilev	DS-1 • 10 kW
	BELGIUM	
	R VLAANDEREN INTL, Wavre	S • S America • 100 kW
	CANADA	
	R CANADA INTL, Sackville, NB	S • Europe • 250 kW
	JAPAN	
	†RADIO JAPAN/NHK, Tokyo-Yamata	SE Asia • 300 kW
	JORDAN	
	†RADIO JORDAN, Qasr el Kharana	W Europe & E North Am • 500 kW
	SEYCHELLES	
	†FEBA RADIO, North Pt, Mahé Is	S • W Asia & S Asia • 100 kW; S F-W • W Asia & S Asia • 100 kW; W Asia & S Asia • 100 kW • ALT. FREQ. TO 11695 kHz
	USA	
	RFE-RL, Via Lampertheim, Germany	S • C Asia • 100 kW
11695	AUSTRALIA	
	†RADIO AUSTRALIA, Shepparton	E Asia & SE Asia • 100 kW
	CLANDESTINE (M EAST)	
	"FREE IRAQ NEWS"	Irr • Mideast • ANTI-SADDAM
	INDIA	
	†ALL INDIA RADIO, Bangalore	S Asia & E Asia • 500 kW; S Asia • 500 kW
	ISRAEL	
	KOL ISRAEL, Tel Aviv	S • W Asia • 300 kW; S F/Sa • W Asia • 300 kW; S Su-Th • W Asia • 300 kW
	RUSSIA	
	VOICE OF RUSSIA, Armavir	W • W Asia & S Asia • 700/1000 kW
	VOICE OF RUSSIA, Irkutsk	S • E Asia • 240 kW
	VOICE OF RUSSIA, Serpukhov	S • Mideast • 250 kW
	SEYCHELLES	
	†FEBA RADIO, North Pt, Mahé Is	W Asia & S Asia • 100 kW • ALT. FREQ. TO 11690 kHz; Mideast & E Africa • 100 kW; Su/F • Mideast & E Africa • 100 kW
	USA	
	VOA, Greenville, NC	Tu-Sa • C America & S America • 250/500 kW
	†WYFR-FAMILY RADIO, Okeechobee, Fl	W • Europe • 100 kW
11695v	CHINA	
	CHINA RADIO INTL, Via Bamako, Mali	N America • 50 kW
11700	CANADA	
	R CANADA INTL, Sackville, NB	S • Europe • 250 kW
	CHINA	
	CHINA RADIO INTL, Beijing	SE Asia • 120 kW
	FRANCE	
	†R FRANCE INTL, Issoudun-Allouis	S • E Africa • 500 kW; W • E North Am • 500 kW; W • W Africa • 500 kW
	R FRANCE INTL, Multiple Locations	E Africa • 100/250/500 kW; Africa • 100/250/500 kW
	R FRANCE INTL, Via Beijing, China	Australasia • 120 kW
	R FRANCE INTL, Via Moyabi, Gabon	W Africa • 250 kW
	GUAM	
	KTWR-TRANS WORLD RADIO, Merizo	E Asia • 100 kW
	KOREA (DPR)	
	†RADIO PYONGYANG, Kujang-dong	N America • 200 kW
	RUSSIA	
	VOICE OF RUSSIA, Yekaterinburg	S • S Asia • 100 kW
11705	CANADA	
	R CANADA INTL, Via Tokyo, Japan	SE Asia • 300 kW
	FRANCE	
	†R FRANCE INTL, Issoudun-Allouis	S • N Africa • 500 kW; W • Africa • 500 kW; Africa • 250/500 kW; S • Africa • 250/500 kW
	GERMANY	
	DEUTSCHE WELLE, Via Sri Lanka	S • C Asia & E Asia • 250 kW
	†DEUTSCHE WELLE, Wertachtal	S • E Europe & Mideast • 500 kW; S • Mideast & W Asia • 500 kW
	GUAM	
(con'd)	†KTWR-TRANS WORLD RADIO, Merizo	S • E Asia • 100 kW

0 1 2 3 4 5 6 7 8 9 10 11 12 13 14 15 16 17 18 19 20 21 22 23 24

SEASONAL ⑤ OR Ⓦ   1-HR TIMESHIFT MIDYEAR ⇇ OR ⇉   JAMMING / OR ∧   EARLIEST HEARD ◁   LATEST HEARD ▷   NEW FOR 1998 †

FREQUENCY   COUNTRY, STATION, LOCATION

TARGET • NETWORK • POWER (kW)

World Time

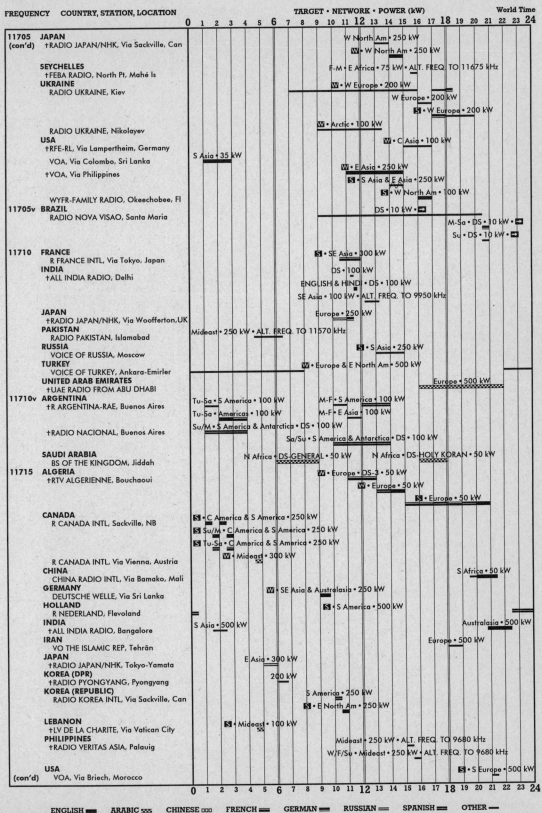

FREQUENCY	COUNTRY, STATION, LOCATION	TARGET • NETWORK • POWER (kW)
11705 (con'd)	JAPAN †RADIO JAPAN/NHK, Via Sackville, Can	W North Am • 250 kW / W • W North Am • 250 kW
	SEYCHELLES †FEBA RADIO, North Pt, Mahé Is	F-M • E Africa • 75 kW • ALT. FREQ. TO 11675 kHz
	UKRAINE RADIO UKRAINE, Kiev	W • W Europe • 200 kW / W Europe • 200 kW / S • W Europe • 200 kW
	RADIO UKRAINE, Nikolayev	W • Arctic • 100 kW
	USA †RFE-RL, Via Lampertheim, Germany	W • C Asia • 100 kW
	VOA, Via Colombo, Sri Lanka	S Asia • 35 kW
	†VOA, Via Philippines	W • E Asia • 250 kW / S • S Asia & E Asia • 250 kW
	WYFR-FAMILY RADIO, Okeechobee, Fl	S • W North Am • 100 kW
11705v	BRAZIL RADIO NOVA VISAO, Santa Maria	DS • 10 kW • ➡ / M-Sa • DS • 10 kW • ➡ / Su • DS • 10 kW • ➡
11710	FRANCE R FRANCE INTL, Via Tokyo, Japan	S • SE Asia • 300 kW
	INDIA †ALL INDIA RADIO, Delhi	DS • 100 kW / ENGLISH & HINDI • DS • 100 kW / SE Asia • 100 kW • ALT. FREQ. TO 9950 kHz
	JAPAN †RADIO JAPAN/NHK, Via Woofferton, UK	Europe • 250 kW
	PAKISTAN RADIO PAKISTAN, Islamabad	Mideast • 250 kW • ALT. FREQ. TO 11570 kHz
	RUSSIA VOICE OF RUSSIA, Moscow	S • S Asia • 250 kW
	TURKEY VOICE OF TURKEY, Ankara-Emirler	W • Europe & E North Am • 500 kW
	UNITED ARAB EMIRATES †UAE RADIO FROM ABU DHABI	Europe • 500 kW
11710v	ARGENTINA †R ARGENTINA-RAE, Buenos Aires	Tu-Sa • S America • 100 kW / M-F • S America • 100 kW / Tu-Sa • Americas • 100 kW / M-F • E Asia • 100 kW
	†RADIO NACIONAL, Buenos Aires	Su/M • S America & Antarctica • DS • 100 kW / Sa/Su • S America & Antarctica • DS • 100 kW
	SAUDI ARABIA BS OF THE KINGDOM, Jiddah	N Africa • DS-GENERAL • 50 kW / N Africa • DS-HOLY KORAN • 50 kW
11715	ALGERIA †RTV ALGERIENNE, Bouchaoui	W • Europe • DS-3 • 50 kW / W • Europe • 50 kW / S • Europe • 50 kW
	CANADA R CANADA INTL, Sackville, NB	S • C America & S America • 250 kW / S • Su/M • C America & S America • 250 kW / S • Tu-Sa • C America & S America • 250 kW
	R CANADA INTL, Via Vienna, Austria	W • Mideast • 300 kW
	CHINA CHINA RADIO INTL, Via Bamako, Mali	S Africa • 50 kW
	GERMANY DEUTSCHE WELLE, Via Sri Lanka	W • SE Asia & Australasia • 250 kW
	HOLLAND R NEDERLAND, Flevoland	S • S America • 500 kW
	INDIA †ALL INDIA RADIO, Bangalore	S Asia • 500 kW / Australasia • 500 kW
	IRAN VO THE ISLAMIC REP, Tehrān	Europe • 500 kW
	JAPAN †RADIO JAPAN/NHK, Tokyo-Yamata	E Asia • 300 kW
	KOREA (DPR) †RADIO PYONGYANG, Pyongyang	200 kW
	KOREA (REPUBLIC) RADIO KOREA INTL, Via Sackville, Can	S America • 250 kW / S • E North Am • 250 kW
	LEBANON †LV DE LA CHARITE, Via Vatican City	S • Mideast • 100 kW
	PHILIPPINES †RADIO VERITAS ASIA, Palauig	Mideast • 250 kW • ALT. FREQ. TO 9680 kHz / W/F/Su • Mideast • 250 kW • ALT. FREQ. TO 9680 kHz
(con'd)	USA VOA, Via Briech, Morocco	S • S Europe • 500 kW

ENGLISH ▬▬   ARABIC ⩘⩘⩘   CHINESE □□□   FRENCH ▬▬   GERMAN ▬▬   RUSSIAN ══   SPANISH ▬▬   OTHER ──

FREQUENCY	COUNTRY, STATION, LOCATION	TARGET • NETWORK • POWER (kW)

World Time: 0 1 2 3 4 5 6 7 8 9 10 11 12 13 14 15 16 17 18 19 20 21 22 23 24

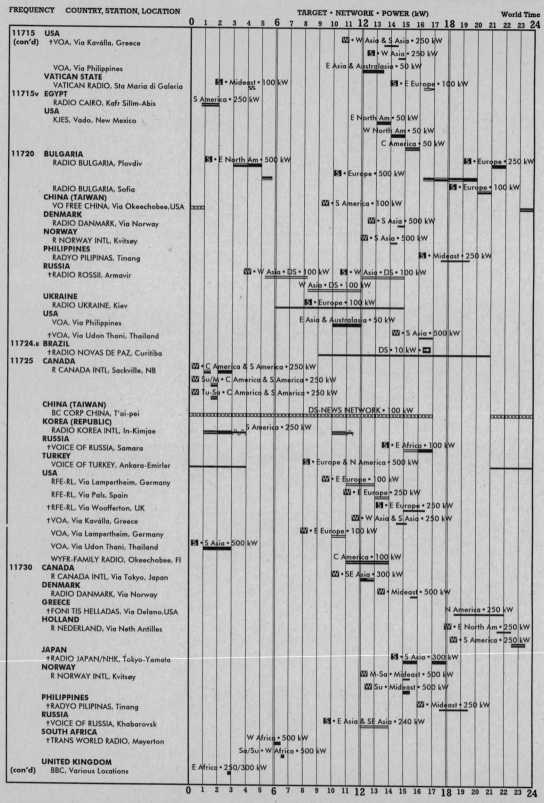

11715 USA
(con'd)   †VOA, Via Kavála, Greece — W • W Asia & S Asia • 250 kW / S • W Asia • 250 kW

   VOA, Via Philippines — E Asia & Australasia • 50 kW

VATICAN STATE
   VATICAN RADIO, Sta Maria di Galeria — S • Mideast • 100 kW / S • E Europe • 100 kW

11715v EGYPT
   RADIO CAIRO, Kafr Silim-Abis — S America • 250 kW

USA
   KJES, Vado, New Mexico — E North Am • 50 kW / W North Am • 50 kW / C America • 50 kW

11720 BULGARIA
   RADIO BULGARIA, Plovdiv — S • E North Am • 500 kW / S • Europe • 250 kW

   RADIO BULGARIA, Sofia — S • Europe • 500 kW / S • Europe • 100 kW

CHINA (TAIWAN)
   VO FREE CHINA, Via Okeechobee,USA — W • S America • 100 kW

DENMARK
   RADIO DANMARK, Via Norway — W • S Asia • 500 kW

NORWAY
   R NORWAY INTL, Kvitsøy — W • S Asia • 500 kW

PHILIPPINES
   RADYO PILIPINAS, Tinang — S • Mideast • 250 kW

RUSSIA
   †RADIO ROSSII, Armavir — W • W Asia • DS • 100 kW / S • W Asia • DS • 100 kW / W Asia • DS • 100 kW

UKRAINE
   RADIO UKRAINE, Kiev — S • Europe • 100 kW

USA
   VOA, Via Philippines — E Asia & Australasia • 50 kW

   †VOA, Via Udon Thani, Thailand — W • S Asia • 500 kW

11724.8 BRAZIL
   †RADIO NOVAS DE PAZ, Curitiba — DS • 10 kW •

11725 CANADA
   R CANADA INTL, Sackville, NB — W • C America & S America • 250 kW / W Su/M • C America & S America • 250 kW / W Tu-Sa • C America & S America • 250 kW

CHINA (TAIWAN)
   BC CORP CHINA, T'ai-pei — DS-NEWS NETWORK • 100 kW

KOREA (REPUBLIC)
   RADIO KOREA INTL, In-Kimjae — S America • 250 kW

RUSSIA
   †VOICE OF RUSSIA, Samara — S • E Africa • 100 kW

TURKEY
   VOICE OF TURKEY, Ankara-Emirler — S • Europe & N America • 500 kW

USA
   RFE-RL, Via Lampertheim, Germany — W • E Europe • 100 kW

   RFE-RL, Via Pals, Spain — W • E Europe • 250 kW

   †RFE-RL, Via Woofferton, UK — S • E Europe • 250 kW

   †VOA, Via Kavála, Greece — W • W Asia & S Asia • 250 kW

   VOA, Via Lampertheim, Germany — W • E Europe • 100 kW

   VOA, Via Udon Thani, Thailand — S • S Asia • 500 kW

   WYFR-FAMILY RADIO, Okeechobee, Fl — C America • 100 kW

11730 CANADA
   R CANADA INTL, Via Tokyo, Japan — W • SE Asia • 300 kW

DENMARK
   RADIO DANMARK, Via Norway — W • Mideast • 500 kW

GREECE
   †FONI TIS HELLADAS, Via Delano,USA — N America • 250 kW

HOLLAND
   R NEDERLAND, Via Neth Antilles — W • E North Am • 250 kW / W • S America • 250 kW

JAPAN
   †RADIO JAPAN/NHK, Tokyo-Yamata — S • S Asia • 300 kW

NORWAY
   R NORWAY INTL, Kvitsøy — W M-Sa • Mideast • 500 kW / W Su • Mideast • 500 kW

PHILIPPINES
   †RADYO PILIPINAS, Tinang — W • Mideast • 250 kW

RUSSIA
   †VOICE OF RUSSIA, Khabarovsk — S • E Asia & SE Asia • 240 kW

SOUTH AFRICA
   †TRANS WORLD RADIO, Meyerton — W Africa • 500 kW / Sa/Su • W Africa • 500 kW

UNITED KINGDOM
(con'd)   BBC, Various Locations — E Africa • 250/300 kW

World Time: 0 1 2 3 4 5 6 7 8 9 10 11 12 13 14 15 16 17 18 19 20 21 22 23 24

SEASONAL S OR W   1-HR TIMESHIFT MIDYEAR ◲ OR ◳   JAMMING / OR ∧   EARLIEST HEARD ◁   LATEST HEARD ▷   NEW FOR 1998 †

FREQUENCY   COUNTRY, STATION, LOCATION

TARGET • NETWORK • POWER (kW)

World Time

0 1 2 3 4 5 6 7 8 9 10 11 12 13 14 15 16 17 18 19 20 21 22 23 24

Frequency	Country, Station, Location	Target • Network • Power
11730 (con'd)	UNITED KINGDOM	
	BBC, Via Seychelles	E Africa • 250 kW
	BBC, Via Zyyi, Cyprus	N Africa & Mideast • 250/300 kW
	USA	
	†RFE-RL, Via Holzkirchen, Germany	W • Mideast & W Asia • 250 kW
	†RFE-RL, Via Pals, Spain	W • E Europe & W Asia • 250 kW
	†VOA, Via Philippines	S • S Asia & E Asia • 250 kW
	†VOA, Via Udon Thani, Thailand	W • E Asia • 500 kW
11730v	TUNISIA	
	†RTV TUNISIENNE, Sfax	S • Europe • DS • 100 kW / Europe • DS • 100 kW
11734	TANZANIA	
	†VOICE OF TANZANIA, Dole, Zanzibar	DS-SWAHILI • 50 kW • ALT. FREQ. TO 6014v kHz / Irr • DS-SWAHILI • 50 kW
11735	CANADA	
	R CANADA INTL, Via Skelton, UK	S • E Europe • 300 kW
	DENMARK	
	RADIO DANMARK, Via Norway	W • E Africa • 500 kW
	FINLAND	
	†YLE RADIO FINLAND, Pori	W • N America • 500 kW
	GERMANY	
	DEUTSCHE WELLE, Via Sri Lanka	SE Asia • 250 kW / W • SE Asia • 250 kW
	KOREA (DPR)	
	†RADIO PYONGYANG, Kujang-dong	Africa • 200 kW / SE Asia & C America • 200 kW
	NEW ZEALAND	
	†R NEW ZEALAND INTL, Rangitaiki	ENGLISH, ETC • Pacific • 100 kW • →
	NORWAY	
	R NORWAY INTL, Kvitsøy	W • E Africa • 500 kW
	URUGUAY	
	†RADIO ORIENTAL, Montevideo	Irr • DS-RELAY CX12 • 1.5 kW • ALT. FREQ. TO 9595 kHz / DS-RELAY CX12 • 1.5 kW • ALT. FREQ. TO 9595 kHz
	USA	
	†RFE-RL, Via Kaválla, Greece	S • C Asia • 250 kW
	†VOA, Via Pals, Spain	S • S Europe • 250 kW
11740	CHINA	
	†CENTRAL PEOPLE'S BS	DS-2 • 50 kW / W • DS-2 • 50 kW
	CHINA (TAIWAN)	
	†BC CORP CHINA, Via Okeechobee, USA	C America • 100 kW
	VO FREE CHINA, Via Okeechobee, USA	C America • 100 kW
	INDIA	
	†ALL INDIA RADIO, Bangalore	SE Asia • 500 kW / SE Asia • DS • 500 kW
	IRAN	
	VO THE ISLAMIC REP, Tehrān	E Africa • 500 kW
	ITALY	
	RADIO ROMA-RAI INTL, Rome	E Africa • 100 kW
	JAPAN	
	†RADIO JAPAN/NHK, Via Singapore	SE Asia • 250 kW
	KOREA (DPR)	
	†RADIO PYONGYANG, Pyongyang	Europe • 200 kW / EU • 200 kW / Asia • 200 kW
	QATAR	
	QATAR BC SERVICE, Doha-Al Khaisah	S • Europe • 250 kW
	ROMANIA	
	RADIO ROMANIA INTL, Bucharest	S • E Asia • 250 kW / S • Mideast • 250 kW / S • Su • W Asia • 250 kW / Mideast • 250 kW / W • S Asia • 250 kW / W • S Africa • 250 kW
	SAUDI ARABIA	
	BS OF THE KINGDOM, Riyadh	C Asia • DS-HOLY KORAN • 500 kW • ALT. FREQ. TO 11935 kHz
	UNITED KINGDOM	
	BBC, Via Zyyi, Cyprus	Mideast • 300 kW
	USA	
	†RFE-RL, Via Kaválla, Greece	S • Mideast & W Asia • 250 kW
	†WINB-WORLD INTL BC, Red Lion, Pa	Europe • 50 kW
	WYFR-FAMILY RADIO, Okeechobee, Fl	W • S America • 100 kW
	VATICAN STATE	
	VATICAN RADIO, Sta Maria di Galeria	⊡ • W Europe & N Africa • 100 kW / ⊡ • M-Sa • W Europe & N Africa • 100 kW / ⊡ • Su • E Europe • 100 kW / ⊡ • Su • W Europe • 100 kW / ⊡ • M-Sa • FRENCH & ITALIAN • W Europe • 100 kW

(con'd)

0 1 2 3 4 5 6 7 8 9 10 11 12 13 14 15 16 17 18 19 20 21 22 23 24

ENGLISH ▬   ARABIC ⌇⌇⌇   CHINESE □□□   FRENCH ═   GERMAN ▬   RUSSIAN ═   SPANISH ▬   OTHER ▬

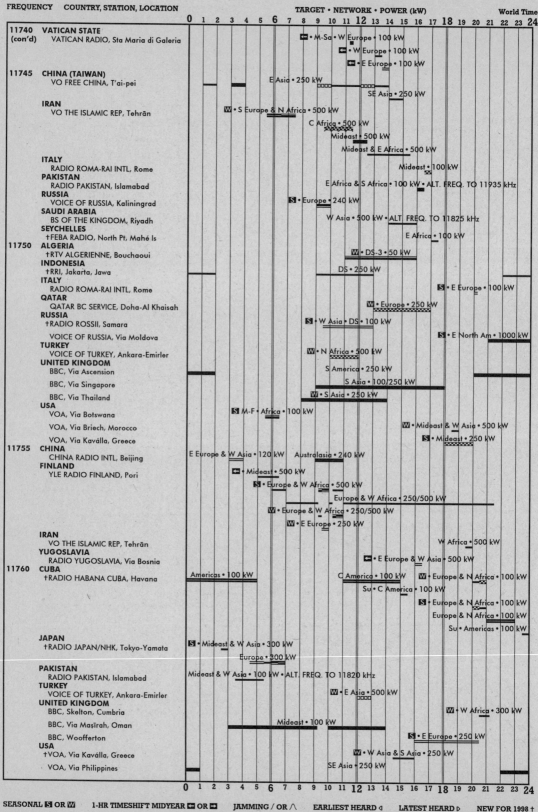

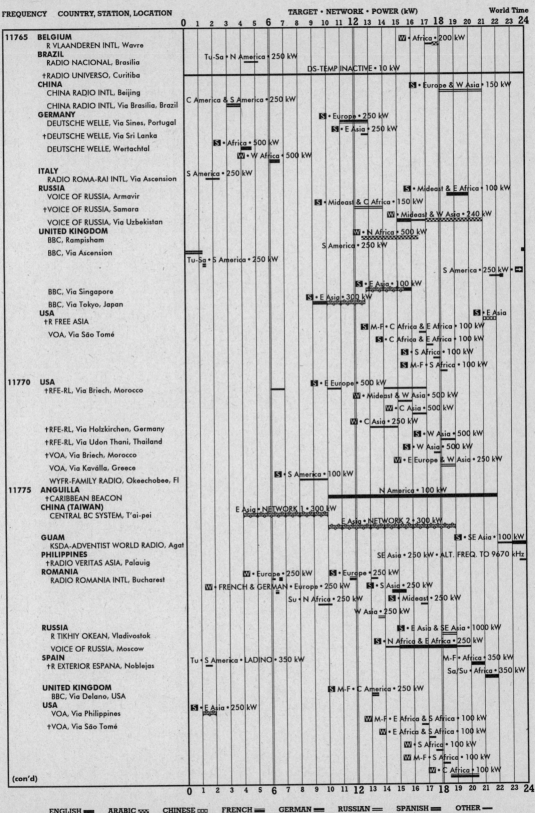

11765 BELGIUM
R VLAANDEREN INTL, Wavre — W • Africa • 200 kW
BRAZIL
RADIO NACIONAL, Brasília — Tu-Sa • N America • 250 kW
†RADIO UNIVERSO, Curitiba — DS-TEMP INACTIVE • 10 kW
CHINA
CHINA RADIO INTL, Beijing — S • Europe & W Asia • 150 kW
CHINA RADIO INTL, Via Brasília, Brazil — C America & S America • 250 kW
GERMANY
DEUTSCHE WELLE, Via Sines, Portugal — S • Europe • 250 kW
S • E Asia • 250 kW
†DEUTSCHE WELLE, Via Sri Lanka — S • Africa • 500 kW
DEUTSCHE WELLE, Wertachtal — W • W Africa • 500 kW
ITALY
RADIO ROMA-RAI INTL, Via Ascension — S America • 250 kW
RUSSIA
VOICE OF RUSSIA, Armavir — S • Mideast & E Africa • 100 kW
†VOICE OF RUSSIA, Samara — S • Mideast & C Africa • 150 kW
VOICE OF RUSSIA, Via Uzbekistan — W • Mideast & W Asia • 240 kW
UNITED KINGDOM
BBC, Rampisham — W • N Africa • 500 kW
S America • 250 kW
BBC, Via Ascension — Tu-Sa • S America • 250 kW
S America • 250 kW
BBC, Via Singapore — S • E Asia • 100 kW
BBC, Via Tokyo, Japan — S • E Asia • 300 kW
USA
†R FREE ASIA — S • E Asia
VOA, Via São Tomé — S • M-F • C Africa & E Africa • 100 kW
S • C Africa & E Africa • 100 kW
S • S Africa • 100 kW
S • M-F • S Africa • 100 kW

11770 USA
†RFE-RL, Via Briech, Morocco — S • E Europe • 500 kW
W • Mideast & W Asia • 500 kW
W • C Asia • 500 kW
†RFE-RL, Via Holzkirchen, Germany — W • C Asia • 250 kW
†RFE-RL, Via Udon Thani, Thailand — S • W Asia • 500 kW
†VOA, Via Briech, Morocco — S • W Asia • 500 kW
VOA, Via Kavála, Greece — W • E Europe & W Asia • 250 kW
WYFR-FAMILY RADIO, Okeechobee, Fl — S • S America • 100 kW

11775 ANGUILLA
†CARIBBEAN BEACON — N America • 100 kW
CHINA (TAIWAN)
CENTRAL BC SYSTEM, T'ai-pei — E Asia • NETWORK 1 • 300 kW
E Asia • NETWORK 2 • 300 kW
GUAM
KSDA-ADVENTIST WORLD RADIO, Agat — S • SE Asia • 100 kW
PHILIPPINES
†RADIO VERITAS ASIA, Palauig — SE Asia • 250 kW • ALT. FREQ. TO 9670 kHz
ROMANIA
RADIO ROMANIA INTL, Bucharest — W • Europe • 250 kW
S • Europe • 250 kW
W • FRENCH & GERMAN • Europe • 250 kW
S • S Asia • 250 kW
Su • N Africa • 250 kW
S • Mideast • 250 kW
W Asia • 250 kW
RUSSIA
R TIKHIY OKEAN, Vladivostok — S • E Asia & SE Asia • 1000 kW
VOICE OF RUSSIA, Moscow — S • N Africa & E Africa • 250 kW
SPAIN
†R EXTERIOR ESPANA, Noblejas — Tu • S America • LADINO • 350 kW
M-F • Africa • 350 kW
Sa/Su • Africa • 350 kW
UNITED KINGDOM
BBC, Via Delano, USA — S • M-F • C America • 250 kW
USA
VOA, Via Philippines — S • E Asia • 250 kW
†VOA, Via São Tomé — W M-F • E Africa & S Africa • 100 kW
W • E Africa & S Africa • 100 kW
W • S Africa • 100 kW
W M-F • S Africa • 100 kW
W • C Africa • 100 kW

(con'd)

ENGLISH ▬   ARABIC ▨   CHINESE ▥   FRENCH ═   GERMAN ▬   RUSSIAN ═   SPANISH ═   OTHER ─

FREQUENCY   COUNTRY, STATION, LOCATION   TARGET • NETWORK • POWER (kW)   World Time

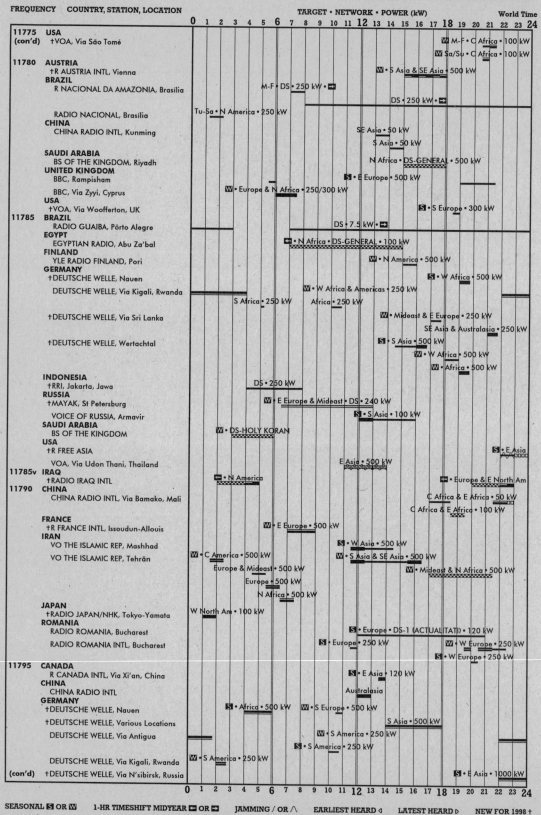

| | | 0 | 1 | 2 | 3 | 4 | 5 | 6 | 7 | 8 | 9 | 10 | 11 | 12 | 13 | 14 | 15 | 16 | 17 | 18 | 19 | 20 | 21 | 22 | 23 | 24 |

11775 USA
(con'd)   †VOA, Via São Tomé — W • M-F • C Africa • 100 kW ; W • Sa/Su • C Africa • 100 kW

11780 AUSTRIA
        †R AUSTRIA INTL, Vienna — W • S Asia & SE Asia • 500 kW
      BRAZIL
        R NACIONAL DA AMAZONIA, Brasília — M-F • DS • 250 kW • ; DS • 250 kW •

        RADIO NACIONAL, Brasília — Tu-Sa • N America • 250 kW
      CHINA
        CHINA RADIO INTL, Kunming — SE Asia • 50 kW ; S Asia • 50 kW

      SAUDI ARABIA
        BS OF THE KINGDOM, Riyadh — N Africa • DS-GENERAL • 500 kW
      UNITED KINGDOM
        BBC, Rampisham — S • E Europe • 500 kW

        BBC, Via Zyyi, Cyprus — W • Europe & N Africa • 250/300 kW
      USA
        †VOA, Via Woofferton, UK — S • S Europe • 300 kW
11785 BRAZIL
        RADIO GUAIBA, Pôrto Alegre — DS • 7.5 kW •
      EGYPT
        EGYPTIAN RADIO, Abu Za'bal — • N Africa • DS-GENERAL • 100 kW
      FINLAND
        YLE RADIO FINLAND, Pori — W • N America • 500 kW
      GERMANY
        †DEUTSCHE WELLE, Nauen — S • W Africa • 500 kW

        DEUTSCHE WELLE, Via Kigali, Rwanda — S Africa • 250 kW ; W • W Africa & Americas • 250 kW ; Africa • 250 kW

        †DEUTSCHE WELLE, Via Sri Lanka — W • Mideast & E Europe • 250 kW ; SE Asia & Australasia • 250 kW

        †DEUTSCHE WELLE, Wertachtal — S • S Asia • 500 kW ; W • W Africa • 500 kW ; W • Africa • 500 kW

      INDONESIA
        †RRI, Jakarta, Jawa — DS • 250 kW
      RUSSIA
        †MAYAK, St Petersburg — W • E Europe & Mideast • DS • 240 kW

        VOICE OF RUSSIA, Armavir — S • S Asia • 100 kW
      SAUDI ARABIA
        BS OF THE KINGDOM — W • DS-HOLY KORAN
      USA
        †R FREE ASIA — S • E Asia

        VOA, Via Udon Thani, Thailand — E Asia • 500 kW
11785v IRAQ
        †RADIO IRAQ INTL — • N America ; • Europe & E North Am
11790 CHINA
        CHINA RADIO INTL, Via Bamako, Mali — C Africa & E Africa • 50 kW ; C Africa & E Africa • 100 kW

      FRANCE
        †R FRANCE INTL, Issoudun-Allouis — W • E Europe • 500 kW
      IRAN
        VO THE ISLAMIC REP, Mashhad — S • W Asia • 500 kW
        VO THE ISLAMIC REP, Tehrãn — W • C America • 500 kW ; W • S Asia & SE Asia • 500 kW ; W • Mideast & N Africa • 500 kW ; Europe & Mideast • 500 kW ; Europe • 500 kW ; N Africa • 500 kW

      JAPAN
        †RADIO JAPAN/NHK, Tokyo-Yamata — W North Am • 100 kW
      ROMANIA
        RADIO ROMANIA, Bucharest — S • Europe • DS-1 (ACTUALITATI) • 120 kW
        RADIO ROMANIA INTL, Bucharest — S • Europe • 250 kW ; W • W Europe • 250 kW ; S • W Europe • 250 kW

11795 CANADA
        R CANADA INTL, Via Xi'an, China — S • E Asia • 120 kW
      CHINA
        CHINA RADIO INTL — Australasia
      GERMANY
        †DEUTSCHE WELLE, Nauen — S • Africa • 500 kW ; W • S Europe • 500 kW

        †DEUTSCHE WELLE, Various Locations — S Asia • 500 kW

        DEUTSCHE WELLE, Via Antigua — W • S America • 250 kW ; S • S America • 250 kW

        DEUTSCHE WELLE, Via Kigali, Rwanda — W • S America • 250 kW
(con'd)   †DEUTSCHE WELLE, Via N'sibirsk, Russia — S • E Asia • 1000 kW

| | 0 | 1 | 2 | 3 | 4 | 5 | 6 | 7 | 8 | 9 | 10 | 11 | 12 | 13 | 14 | 15 | 16 | 17 | 18 | 19 | 20 | 21 | 22 | 23 | 24 |

SEASONAL 𝗦 OR 𝗪   1-HR TIMESHIFT MIDYEAR ⮂ OR ⮀   JAMMING / OR ∧   EARLIEST HEARD ◁   LATEST HEARD ▷   NEW FOR 1998 †

FREQUENCY	COUNTRY, STATION, LOCATION	TARGET • NETWORK • POWER (kW)
11795 (con'd)	**GERMANY** †DEUTSCHE WELLE, Wertachtal	Australasia • 500 kW; W • E Asia • 500 kW; S • Africa • 500 kW; S • Mideast • 500 kW; W • W Africa & S America • 500 kW; W Africa & S America • 500 kW
	TURKEY VOICE OF TURKEY, Ankara-úakirlar	← • W Asia • 500 kW
	UNITED ARAB EMIRATES UAE RADIO IN DUBAI	Irr • Europe, E North Am & C America • RAMADAN • 300 kW; Europe • 300 kW
	USA †RFE-RL, Via Udon Thani, Thailand	S • C Asia • 500 kW
11800	**CHINA** †CENTRAL PEOPLE'S BS, Beijing	DS-1; W-M • DS-1; S • DS-1
	ITALY RADIO ROMA-RAI INTL, Rome	N America & C America • 100 kW; E North Am & C America • 100 kW; E Africa • 100 kW; W • E Africa • 100 kW; W • Mideast • 100 kW
	RUSSIA VOICE OF RUSSIA, Khabarovsk	S • S Pacific • 240 kW
	SRI LANKA †SRI LANKA BC CORP, Colombo-Ekala	S Asia • 100 kW • ALT. FREQ. TO 11905 kHz; Mideast • 100 kW; S Asia • 100 kW
	YUGOSLAVIA †RADIO YUGOSLAVIA, Via Bosnia	S • W North Am • 250 kW; W • N Africa & W Africa • 250 kW; ← • Mideast • 250 kW
11800v	**ETHIOPIA** RADIO ETHIOPIA, Gedja	E Africa • 100 kW
	†VOICE OF PEACE, Gedja	E Africa • 100 kW
11805	**ARMENIA** RADIO INTERCONTINENTAL, Kamo	W • Europe • 1000 kW
	FINLAND YLE RADIO FINLAND, Pori	S Sa/Su • W Africa & Australasia • 500 kW; W • E Asia • 500 kW; W • S Asia • 500 kW
	GEORGIA RADIO GEORGIA, Tbilisi	S • N Europe • 100 kW
	GERMANY †DEUTSCHE WELLE, Via Sines, Portugal	W • Europe • 250 kW
	PHILIPPINES †RADIO VERITAS ASIA, Palauig	E Europe & W Asia • 250 kW
	†RADYO PILIPINAS, Tinang	W • Mideast • 250 kW
	THAILAND RADIO THAILAND, Udon Thani	SE Asia • 500 kW
	UNITED KINGDOM BBC, Via Zyyi, Cyprus	← • Su • E Europe • 300 kW; ← • E Europe • 300 kW
	USA †RFE-RL, Via Lampertheim, Germany	S • C Asia • 100 kW
	RFE-RL, Via Pals, Spain	W • E Europe • 250 kW
	†VOA, Via Briech, Morocco	W • W Asia • 500 kW
	†VOA, Via Kaválla, Greece	N Africa & W Africa • 250 kW; S • N Africa • 250 kW
	†VOA, Via Pals, Spain	S • E Europe & W Asia • 250 kW
	†VOA, Via Philippines	S • S Asia • 250 kW; S • E Asia • 100 kW; SE Asia • 250 kW
11805v	**BRAZIL** RADIO GLOBO, Rio de Janeiro	DS • 10 kW • →; Irr • DS • 10 kW • →
11810	**GERMANY** †DEUTSCHE WELLE, Nauen	W • S America • 500 kW; S America • 500 kW
	DEUTSCHE WELLE, Via Antigua	S • C America • 250 kW; W • S America • 250 kW
	†DEUTSCHE WELLE, Via Kigali, Rwanda	C Africa & E Africa • 250 kW; S Africa • 250 kW; Africa • 250 kW; W Africa • 250 kW
	†DEUTSCHE WELLE, Via Sines, Portugal	S • N America & C America • 250 kW; W • W Africa • 250 kW
(con'd)	†DEUTSCHE WELLE, Via Sri Lanka	W • S Africa • 250 kW

World Time: 0 1 2 3 4 5 6 7 8 9 10 11 12 13 14 15 16 17 18 19 20 21 22 23 24

ENGLISH ▬ ARABIC ▦ CHINESE ▫▫▫ FRENCH ═ GERMAN ═ RUSSIAN ═ SPANISH ═ OTHER —

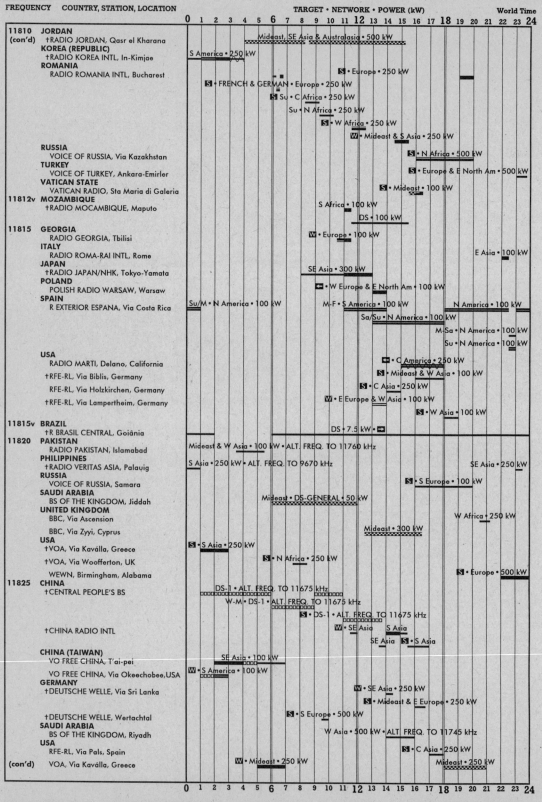

FREQUENCY	COUNTRY, STATION, LOCATION	TARGET • NETWORK • POWER (kW)
11810 (con'd)	JORDAN	
	†RADIO JORDAN, Qasr el Kharana	Mideast, SE Asia & Australasia • 500 kW
	KOREA (REPUBLIC)	
	†RADIO KOREA INTL, In-Kimjae	S America • 250 kW
	ROMANIA	
	RADIO ROMANIA INTL, Bucharest	S • Europe • 250 kW
		S • FRENCH & GERMAN • Europe • 250 kW
		S • Su • C Africa • 250 kW
		Su • N Africa • 250 kW
		S • W Africa • 250 kW
		W • Mideast & S Asia • 250 kW
	RUSSIA	
	VOICE OF RUSSIA, Via Kazakhstan	S • N Africa • 500 kW
	TURKEY	
	VOICE OF TURKEY, Ankara-Emirler	S • Europe & E North Am • 500 kW
	VATICAN STATE	
	VATICAN RADIO, Sta Maria di Galeria	S • Mideast • 100 kW
11812v	MOZAMBIQUE	
	†RADIO MOCAMBIQUE, Maputo	S Africa • 100 kW
		DS • 100 kW
11815	GEORGIA	
	RADIO GEORGIA, Tbilisi	W • Europe • 100 kW
	ITALY	
	RADIO ROMA-RAI INTL, Rome	E Asia • 100 kW
	JAPAN	
	†RADIO JAPAN/NHK, Tokyo-Yamata	SE Asia • 300 kW
	POLAND	
	POLISH RADIO WARSAW, Warsaw	• W Europe & E North Am • 100 kW
	SPAIN	
	R EXTERIOR ESPANA, Via Costa Rica	Su/M • N America • 100 kW M-F • S America • 100 kW N America • 100 kW
		Sa/Su • N America • 100 kW
		M-Sa • N America • 100 kW
		Su • N America • 100 kW
	USA	
	RADIO MARTI, Delano, California	• C America • 250 kW
	†RFE-RL, Via Biblis, Germany	S • Mideast & W Asia • 100 kW
	RFE-RL, Via Holzkirchen, Germany	S • C Asia • 250 kW
	†RFE-RL, Via Lampertheim, Germany	W • E Europe & W Asia • 100 kW
		S • W Asia • 100 kW
11815v	BRAZIL	
	†R BRASIL CENTRAL, Goiânia	DS • 7.5 kW •
11820	PAKISTAN	
	RADIO PAKISTAN, Islamabad	Mideast & W Asia • 100 kW • ALT. FREQ. TO 11760 kHz
	PHILIPPINES	
	†RADIO VERITAS ASIA, Palauig	S Asia • 250 kW • ALT. FREQ. TO 9670 kHz SE Asia • 250 kW
	RUSSIA	
	VOICE OF RUSSIA, Samara	S • S Europe • 100 kW
	SAUDI ARABIA	
	BS OF THE KINGDOM, Jiddah	Mideast • DS-GENERAL • 50 kW
	UNITED KINGDOM	
	BBC, Via Ascension	W Africa • 250 kW
	BBC, Via Zyyi, Cyprus	Mideast • 300 kW
	USA	
	†VOA, Via Kaválla, Greece	S • S Asia • 250 kW
	†VOA, Via Woofferton, UK	S • N Africa • 250 kW
	WEWN, Birmingham, Alabama	S • Europe • 500 kW
11825	CHINA	
	†CENTRAL PEOPLE'S BS	DS-1 • ALT. FREQ. TO 11675 kHz
		W-M • DS-1 • ALT. FREQ. TO 11675 kHz
		S • DS-1 • ALT. FREQ. TO 11675 kHz
	†CHINA RADIO INTL	W • SE Asia S Asia
		SE Asia S • S Asia
	CHINA (TAIWAN)	
	VO FREE CHINA, T'ai-pei	SE Asia • 100 kW
	VO FREE CHINA, Via Okeechobee, USA	W • S America • 100 kW
	GERMANY	
	†DEUTSCHE WELLE, Via Sri Lanka	W • SE Asia • 250 kW
		S • Mideast & E Europe • 250 kW
	†DEUTSCHE WELLE, Wertachtal	S • S Europe • 500 kW
	SAUDI ARABIA	
	BS OF THE KINGDOM, Riyadh	W Asia • 500 kW • ALT. FREQ. TO 11745 kHz
	USA	
	RFE-RL, Via Pals, Spain	S • C Asia • 250 kW
(con'd)	VOA, Via Kaválla, Greece	W • Mideast • 250 kW Mideast • 250 kW

FREQUENCY   COUNTRY, STATION, LOCATION

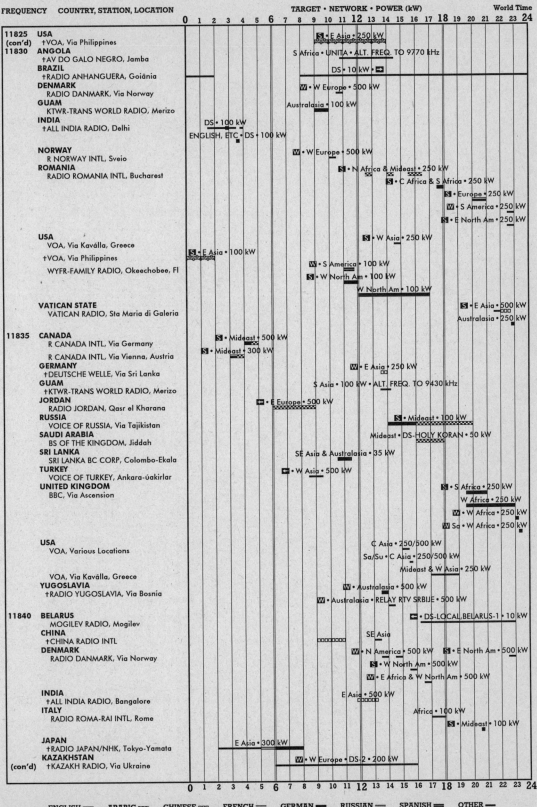

TARGET • NETWORK • POWER (kW)

World Time

Frequency	Country, Station, Location	Details
11825 (con'd)	USA · †VOA, Via Philippines	S • E Asia • 250 kW
11830	ANGOLA · †AV DO GALO NEGRO, Jamba	S Africa • UNITA • ALT. FREQ. TO 9770 kHz
	BRAZIL · †RADIO ANHANGUERA, Goiânia	DS • 10 kW
	DENMARK · RADIO DANMARK, Via Norway	W • W Europe • 500 kW
	GUAM · KTWR-TRANS WORLD RADIO, Merizo	Australasia • 100 kW
	INDIA · †ALL INDIA RADIO, Delhi	DS • 100 kW / ENGLISH, ETC • DS • 100 kW
	NORWAY · R NORWAY INTL, Sveio	W • W Europe • 500 kW
	ROMANIA · RADIO ROMANIA INTL, Bucharest	S • N Africa & Mideast • 250 kW / S • C Africa & S Africa • 250 kW / S • Europe • 250 kW / W • S America • 250 kW / S • E North Am • 250 kW
	USA · VOA, Via Kaválla, Greece	S • W Asia • 250 kW / S • E Asia • 100 kW
	†VOA, Via Philippines	W • S America • 100 kW
	WYFR-FAMILY RADIO, Okeechobee, Fl	S • W North Am • 100 kW / W North Am • 100 kW
	VATICAN STATE · VATICAN RADIO, Sta Maria di Galeria	S • E Asia • 500 kW / Australasia • 250 kW
11835	CANADA · R CANADA INTL, Via Germany	S • Mideast • 500 kW
	R CANADA INTL, Via Vienna, Austria	S • Mideast • 300 kW
	GERMANY · †DEUTSCHE WELLE, Via Sri Lanka	W • E Asia • 250 kW
	GUAM · †KTWR-TRANS WORLD RADIO, Merizo	S Asia • 100 kW • ALT. FREQ. TO 9430 kHz
	JORDAN · RADIO JORDAN, Qasr el Kharana	E Europe • 500 kW
	RUSSIA · VOICE OF RUSSIA, Via Tajikistan	S • Mideast • 100 kW
	SAUDI ARABIA · BS OF THE KINGDOM, Jiddah	Mideast • DS-HOLY KORAN • 50 kW
	SRI LANKA · SRI LANKA BC CORP, Colombo-Ekala	SE Asia & Australasia • 35 kW
	TURKEY · VOICE OF TURKEY, Ankara-úakirlar	W Asia • 500 kW
	UNITED KINGDOM · BBC, Via Ascension	S • S Africa • 250 kW / W Africa • 250 kW / W • W Africa • 250 kW / W • Sa • W Africa • 250 kW
	USA · VOA, Various Locations	C Asia • 250/500 kW / Sa/Su • C Asia • 250/500 kW / Mideast & W Asia • 250 kW
	VOA, Via Kaválla, Greece	
	YUGOSLAVIA · †RADIO YUGOSLAVIA, Via Bosnia	W • Australasia • 500 kW / W • Australasia • RELAY RTV SRBIJE • 500 kW
11840	BELARUS · MOGILEV RADIO, Mogilev	DS-LOCAL, BELARUS-1 • 10 kW
	CHINA · †CHINA RADIO INTL	SE Asia
	DENMARK · RADIO DANMARK, Via Norway	W • N America • 500 kW / S • E North Am • 500 kW / S • W North Am • 500 kW / W • E Africa & W North Am • 500 kW
	INDIA · †ALL INDIA RADIO, Bangalore	E Asia • 500 kW
	ITALY · RADIO ROMA-RAI INTL, Rome	Africa • 100 kW / S • Mideast • 100 kW
	JAPAN · †RADIO JAPAN/NHK, Tokyo-Yamata	E Asia • 300 kW
(con'd)	KAZAKHSTAN · †KAZAKH RADIO, Via Ukraine	W • W Europe • DS-2 • 200 kW

ENGLISH ▬ ARABIC ⊠ CHINESE ▦ FRENCH ═ GERMAN ▭ RUSSIAN ═ SPANISH ═ OTHER ─

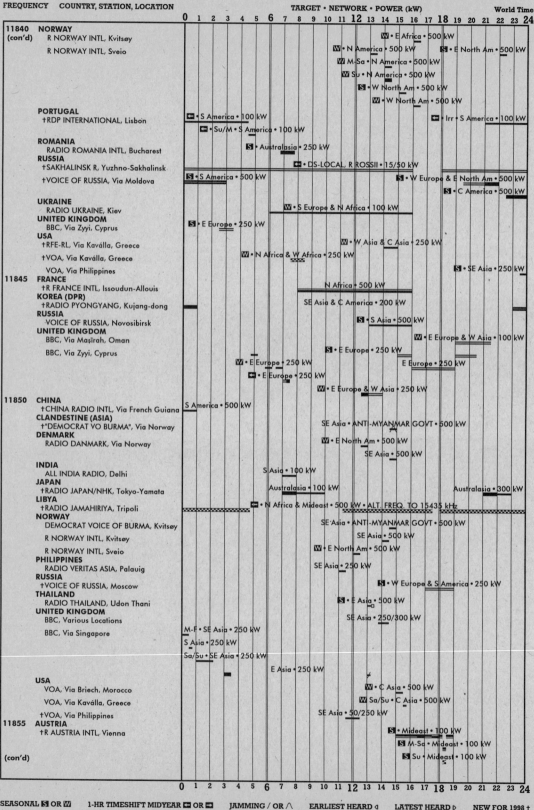

11840 NORWAY
(con'd)   R NORWAY INTL, Kvitsøy — W • E Africa • 500 kW

    R NORWAY INTL, Sveio — W • N America • 500 kW — S • E North Am • 500 kW
    W M-Sa • N America • 500 kW
    W Su • N America • 500 kW
    S • W North Am • 500 kW
    W • W North Am • 500 kW

PORTUGAL
    †RDP INTERNATIONAL, Lisbon — • S America • 100 kW — Irr • S America • 100 kW
    • Su/M • S America • 100 kW

ROMANIA
    RADIO ROMANIA INTL, Bucharest — S • Australasia • 250 kW
RUSSIA
    †SAKHALINSK R, Yuzhno-Sakhalinsk — • DS-LOCAL, R ROSSII • 15/50 kW
    †VOICE OF RUSSIA, Via Moldova — • S America • 500 kW — S • W Europe & E North Am • 500 kW
    S • C America • 500 kW

UKRAINE
    RADIO UKRAINE, Kiev — W • S Europe & N Africa • 100 kW
UNITED KINGDOM
    BBC, Via Zyyi, Cyprus — S • E Europe • 250 kW
USA
    †RFE-RL, Via Kaválla, Greece — W • W Asia & C Asia • 250 kW
    †VOA, Via Kaválla, Greece — W • N Africa & W Africa • 250 kW
    VOA, Via Philippines — S • SE Asia • 250 kW

11845 FRANCE
    †R FRANCE INTL, Issoudun-Allouis — N Africa • 500 kW
KOREA (DPR)
    †RADIO PYONGYANG, Kujang-dong — SE Asia & C America • 200 kW
RUSSIA
    VOICE OF RUSSIA, Novosibirsk — S • S Asia • 500 kW
UNITED KINGDOM
    BBC, Via Maṣīrah, Oman — W • E Europe & W Asia • 100 kW
    BBC, Via Zyyi, Cyprus — S • E Europe • 250 kW
    W • E Europe • 250 kW — E Europe • 250 kW
    • E Europe • 250 kW
    W • E Europe & W Asia • 250 kW

11850 CHINA
    †CHINA RADIO INTL, Via French Guiana — S America • 500 kW
CLANDESTINE (ASIA)
    †"DEMOCRAT VO BURMA", Via Norway — SE Asia • ANTI-MYANMAR GOVT • 500 kW
DENMARK
    RADIO DANMARK, Via Norway — W • E North Am • 500 kW
    SE Asia • 500 kW

INDIA
    ALL INDIA RADIO, Delhi — S Asia • 100 kW
JAPAN
    †RADIO JAPAN/NHK, Tokyo-Yamata — Australasia • 100 kW — Australasia • 300 kW
LIBYA
    †RADIO JAMAHIRIYA, Tripoli — • N Africa & Mideast • 500 kW • ALT. FREQ. TO 15435 kHz
NORWAY
    DEMOCRAT VOICE OF BURMA, Kvitsøy — SE Asia • ANTI-MYANMAR GOVT • 500 kW
    R NORWAY INTL, Kvitsøy — SE Asia • 500 kW
    R NORWAY INTL, Sveio — W • E North Am • 500 kW
PHILIPPINES
    RADIO VERITAS ASIA, Palauig — SE Asia • 250 kW
RUSSIA
    †VOICE OF RUSSIA, Moscow — S • W Europe & S America • 250 kW
THAILAND
    RADIO THAILAND, Udon Thani — S • E Asia • 500 kW
UNITED KINGDOM
    BBC, Various Locations — SE Asia • 250/300 kW
    BBC, Via Singapore — M-F • SE Asia • 250 kW
    S Asia • 250 kW
    Sa/Su • SE Asia • 250 kW
    E Asia • 250 kW

USA
    VOA, Via Briech, Morocco — W • C Asia • 500 kW
    VOA, Via Kaválla, Greece — W Sa/Su • C Asia • 500 kW
    †VOA, Via Philippines — SE Asia • 50/250 kW
11855 AUSTRIA
    †R AUSTRIA INTL, Vienna — S • Mideast • 100 kW
    S M-Sa • Mideast • 100 kW
    S Su • Mideast • 100 kW

(con'd)

FREQUENCY   COUNTRY, STATION, LOCATION   TARGET • NETWORK • POWER (kW)   World Time

0 1 2 3 4 5 6 7 8 9 10 11 12 13 14 15 16 17 18 19 20 21 22 23 24

Frequency	Country / Station / Location	Target • Network • Power
11855 (con'd)	**BULGARIA**	
	RADIO BULGARIA, Plovdiv	S • E Europe & W Asia • 250 kW
	CANADA	
	†R CANADA INTL, Sackville, NB	E North Am & C America • 100 kW
		Su-F • E North Am & C America • 100 kW
		Su • E North Am & C America • 100 kW
	CHINA (TAIWAN)	
	†BC CORP CHINA, Via Okeechobee,USA	W North Am • 100 kW
	INDIA	
	†ALL INDIA RADIO, Panaji	Mideast & W Asia • 250 kW
	ITALY	
	RADIO ROMA-RAI INTL, Rome	S • E Europe • 100 kW
	RUSSIA	
	VOICE OF RUSSIA, Petropavlovsk-K	S • E Asia • 250 kW
	THAILAND	
	RADIO THAILAND, Udon Thani	W • Mideast • 500 kW
	USA	
	RFE-RL, Via Briech, Morocco	W • E Europe • 500 kW
	†RFE-RL, Via Lampertheim, Germany	W • E Europe & W Asia • 100 kW
	RFE-RL, Via Pals, Spain	S • W Asia & C Asia • 250 kW
	RFE-RL, Via Woofferton, UK	S • N Europe • 250 kW
	VOA, Delano, California	S • C America • 250 kW
	†VOA, Various Locations	Mideast • 250/500 kW
	VOA, Via Ascension	W Africa • 250 kW
	VOA, Via Briech, Morocco	W • Mideast • 500 kW
	†VOA, Via Udon Thani, Thailand	W • E Asia • 500 kW
	†WYFR-FAMILY RADIO, Okeechobee, Fl	C America • 100 kW S • S America • 100 kW
11855v	**BRAZIL**	
	RADIO APARECIDA, Aparecida	DS • 0.5/1 kW •
11860	**BULGARIA**	
	RADIO BULGARIA, Plovdiv	Europe • 250/500 kW • ALT. FREQ. TO 11660 kHz
	CHINA (TAIWAN)	
	†VO FREE CHINA, T'ai-pei	SE Asia • 100 kW
		SE Asia • 100 kW • ALT. FREQ. TO 11550 kHz
	DENMARK	
	RADIO DANMARK, Via Norway	S • S Asia • 500 kW
		S • Australasia • 500 kW
	JAPAN	
	RADIO JAPAN/NHK, Via Singapore	SE Asia • 250 kW
	NORWAY	
	R NORWAY INTL, Kvitsøy	S • M-Sa • S Asia • 500 kW
		S • Su • S Asia • 500 kW
		S • S Asia • 500 kW
		S • Australasia • 500 kW
	SWITZERLAND	
	†SWISS RADIO INTL, Schwarzenburg	W Africa • 150 kW
	UNITED KINGDOM	
	BBC, Via Seychelles	E Africa • 250 kW
		M-F • E Africa • 250 kW
		Sa/Su • E Africa • 250 kW
	USA	
	RFE-RL, Via Philippines	S • E Asia • 250 kW
	VOA, Via Philippines	S • E Asia • 250 kW
11865	**GERMANY**	
	†DEUTSCHE WELLE, Nauen	S • E Europe & W Asia • 500 kW
		SE Asia • 250/500 kW W Africa • 500 kW
	†DEUTSCHE WELLE, Various Locations	S • S America • 250 kW
	†DEUTSCHE WELLE, Via Antigua	S • S America • 250 kW
	DEUTSCHE WELLE, Via Kigali, Rwanda	S • S America • 250 kW
	DEUTSCHE WELLE, Via Sines, Portugal	W • E Asia • 250 kW
	†DEUTSCHE WELLE, Via Sri Lanka	W • W Asia & Mideast • 250 kW
	†DEUTSCHE WELLE, Wertachtal	E Europe & Mideast • 500 kW
		W • E Asia • 500 kW W • S Asia • 500 kW S Africa • 500 kW
	RUSSIA	
	VOICE OF RUSSIA, Via Armenia	W • C Africa • 100 kW
	SWEDEN	
	RADIO SWEDEN, Hörby	Asia & Australasia • 500 kW • ALT. FREQ. TO 13740 kHz
	UNITED KINGDOM	
	BBC, Rampisham	S • E Europe • 500 kW
		S • Sa/Su • E Europe • 500 kW
(con'd)	BBC, Via Okeechobee, Florida, USA	S • W North Am • 100 kW

0 1 2 3 4 5 6 7 8 9 10 11 12 13 14 15 16 17 18 19 20 21 22 23 24

ENGLISH ▬   ARABIC ▧   CHINESE □□□   FRENCH ═   GERMAN ▬   RUSSIAN =   SPANISH ▬   OTHER ▬

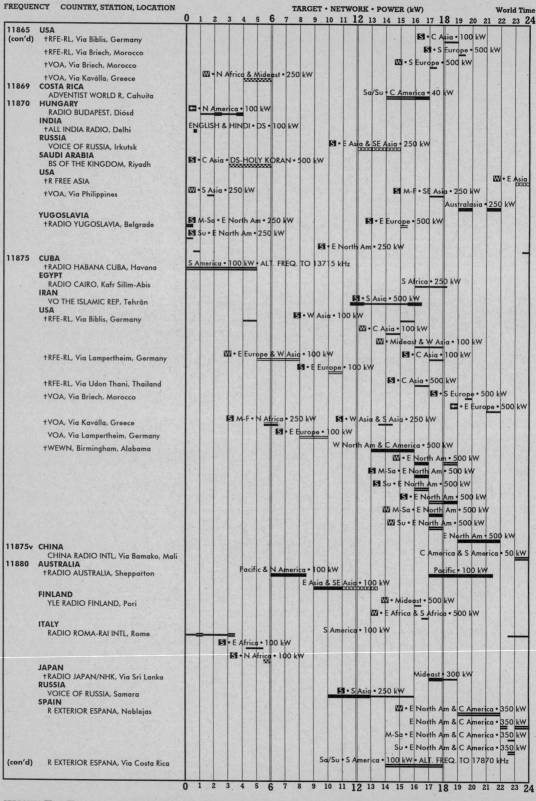

FREQUENCY   COUNTRY, STATION, LOCATION   TARGET • NETWORK • POWER (kW)   World Time

11865 USA
(con'd) †RFE-RL, Via Biblis, Germany — S • C Asia • 100 kW
         †RFE-RL, Via Briech, Morocco — S • S Europe • 500 kW
         †VOA, Via Briech, Morocco — W • S Europe • 500 kW
         †VOA, Via Kaválla, Greece — W • N Africa & Mideast • 250 kW
11869 COSTA RICA
         ADVENTIST WORLD R, Cahuita — Sa/Su • C America • 40 kW
11870 HUNGARY
         RADIO BUDAPEST, Diósd — N America • 100 kW
       INDIA
         †ALL INDIA RADIO, Delhi — ENGLISH & HINDI • DS • 100 kW
       RUSSIA
         VOICE OF RUSSIA, Irkutsk — S • E Asia & SE Asia • 250 kW
       SAUDI ARABIA
         BS OF THE KINGDOM, Riyadh — S • C Asia • DS-HOLY KORAN • 500 kW
       USA
         †R FREE ASIA — W • E Asia
         †VOA, Via Philippines — W • S Asia • 250 kW
                                    S M-F • SE Asia • 250 kW
                                    Australasia • 250 kW
         YUGOSLAVIA
         †RADIO YUGOSLAVIA, Belgrade — S M-Sa • E North Am • 250 kW
                                       S Su • E North Am • 250 kW
                                       S • E Europe • 500 kW
                                       S • E North Am • 250 kW
11875 CUBA
         †RADIO HABANA CUBA, Havana — S America • 100 kW • ALT. FREQ. TO 13715 kHz
       EGYPT
         RADIO CAIRO, Kafr Silim-Abis — S Africa • 250 kW
       IRAN
         VO THE ISLAMIC REP, Tehrān — S • S Asia • 500 kW
       USA
         †RFE-RL, Via Biblis, Germany — S • W Asia • 100 kW
                                        W • C Asia • 100 kW
                                        W • Mideast & W Asia • 100 kW
         †RFE-RL, Via Lampertheim, Germany — W • E Europe & W Asia • 100 kW
                                             S • C Asia • 100 kW
                                             S • E Europe • 100 kW
         †RFE-RL, Via Udon Thani, Thailand — S • C Asia • 500 kW
         †VOA, Via Briech, Morocco — S • S Europe • 500 kW
                                     E Europe • 500 kW
         †VOA, Via Kaválla, Greece — S M-F • N Africa • 250 kW
                                     S • W Asia & S Asia • 250 kW
         VOA, Via Lampertheim, Germany — S • E Europe • 100 kW
         †WEWN, Birmingham, Alabama — W North Am & C America • 500 kW
                                      W • E North Am • 500 kW
                                      S M-Sa • E North Am • 500 kW
                                      S Su • E North Am • 500 kW
                                      S • E North Am • 500 kW
                                      W M-Sa • E North Am • 500 kW
                                      W Su • E North Am • 500 kW
                                      E North Am • 500 kW
11875v CHINA
         CHINA RADIO INTL, Via Bamako, Mali — C America & S America • 50 kW
11880 AUSTRALIA
         †RADIO AUSTRALIA, Shepparton — Pacific & N America • 100 kW
                                        Pacific • 100 kW
                                        E Asia & SE Asia • 100 kW
         FINLAND
         YLE RADIO FINLAND, Pori — W • Mideast • 500 kW
                                   W • E Africa & S Africa • 500 kW
         ITALY
         RADIO ROMA-RAI INTL, Rome — S America • 100 kW
                                     S • E Africa • 100 kW
                                     S • N Africa • 100 kW
         JAPAN
         †RADIO JAPAN/NHK, Via Sri Lanka — Mideast • 300 kW
         RUSSIA
         VOICE OF RUSSIA, Samara — S • S Asia • 250 kW
         SPAIN
         R EXTERIOR ESPANA, Noblejas — W • E North Am & C America • 350 kW
                                       E North Am & C America • 350 kW
                                       M-Sa • E North Am & C America • 350 kW
                                       Su • E North Am & C America • 350 kW
(con'd) R EXTERIOR ESPANA, Via Costa Rica — Sa/Su • S America • 100 kW • ALT. FREQ. TO 17870 kHz

0 1 2 3 4 5 6 7 8 9 10 11 12 13 14 15 16 17 18 19 20 21 22 23 24

SEASONAL S OR W   1-HR TIMESHIFT MIDYEAR ◳ OR ◲   JAMMING / OR ∧   EARLIEST HEARD ◁   LATEST HEARD ▷   NEW FOR 1998 †

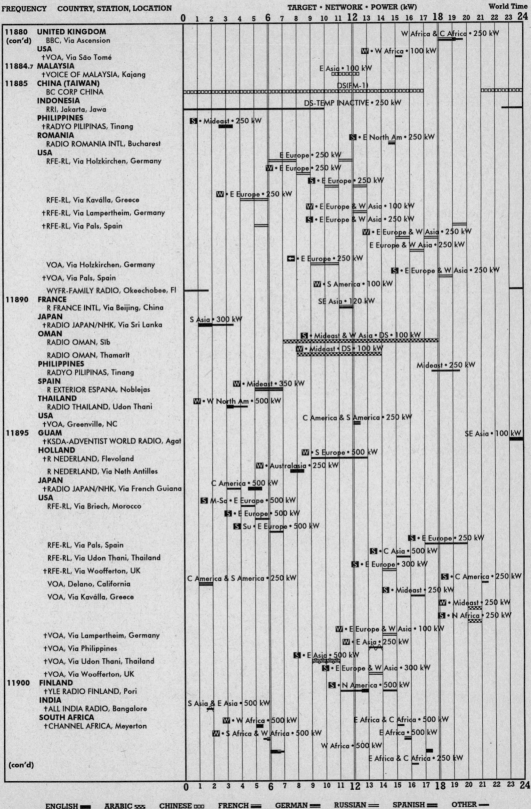

FREQUENCY   COUNTRY, STATION, LOCATION   TARGET • NETWORK • POWER (kW)   World Time

FREQUENCY	COUNTRY, STATION, LOCATION	TARGET • NETWORK • POWER (kW)
11880 (con'd)	UNITED KINGDOM — BBC, Via Ascension	W Africa & C Africa • 250 kW
	USA — †VOA, Via São Tomé	W • W Africa • 100 kW
11884.7	MALAYSIA — †VOICE OF MALAYSIA, Kajang	E Asia • 100 kW
11885	CHINA (TAIWAN) — BC CORP CHINA	DS (FM-1)
	INDONESIA — RRI, Jakarta, Jawa	DS-TEMP INACTIVE • 250 kW
	PHILIPPINES — †RADYO PILIPINAS, Tinang	S • Mideast • 250 kW
	ROMANIA — RADIO ROMANIA INTL, Bucharest	S • E North Am • 250 kW
	USA — RFE-RL, Via Holzkirchen, Germany	E Europe • 250 kW
		W • E Europe • 250 kW
		S • E Europe • 250 kW
	RFE-RL, Via Kaválla, Greece	W • E Europe • 250 kW
	†RFE-RL, Via Lampertheim, Germany	W • E Europe & W Asia • 100 kW
	†RFE-RL, Via Pals, Spain	S • E Europe & W Asia • 250 kW
		W • E Europe & W Asia • 250 kW
		E Europe & W Asia • 250 kW
	VOA, Via Holzkirchen, Germany	◘ • E Europe • 250 kW
	†VOA, Via Pals, Spain	S • E Europe & W Asia • 250 kW
	WYFR-FAMILY RADIO, Okeechobee, Fl	W • S America • 100 kW
11890	FRANCE — R FRANCE INTL, Via Beijing, China	SE Asia • 120 kW
	JAPAN — †RADIO JAPAN/NHK, Via Sri Lanka	S Asia • 300 kW
	OMAN — RADIO OMAN, Sīb	S • Mideast & W Asia • DS • 100 kW
	RADIO OMAN, Thamarīt	W • Mideast • DS • 100 kW
	PHILIPPINES — RADYO PILIPINAS, Tinang	Mideast • 250 kW
	SPAIN — R EXTERIOR ESPANA, Noblejas	W • Mideast • 350 kW
	THAILAND — RADIO THAILAND, Udon Thani	W • W North Am • 500 kW
	USA — †VOA, Greenville, NC	C America & S America • 250 kW
11895	GUAM — †KSDA-ADVENTIST WORLD RADIO, Agat	SE Asia • 100 kW
	HOLLAND — †R NEDERLAND, Flevoland	W • S Europe • 500 kW
	R NEDERLAND, Via Neth Antilles	W • Australasia • 250 kW
	JAPAN — †RADIO JAPAN/NHK, Via French Guiana	C America • 500 kW
	USA — RFE-RL, Via Briech, Morocco	S • M-Sa • E Europe • 500 kW
		S • E Europe • 500 kW
		S • Su • E Europe • 500 kW
	RFE-RL, Via Pals, Spain	S • E Europe • 250 kW
	RFE-RL, Via Udon Thani, Thailand	S • C Asia • 500 kW
	†RFE-RL, Via Woofferton, UK	S • E Europe • 300 kW
	VOA, Delano, California	C America & S America • 250 kW
		S • C America • 250 kW
	VOA, Via Kaválla, Greece	S • Mideast • 250 kW
		W • Mideast • 250 kW
		S • N Africa • 250 kW
	†VOA, Via Lampertheim, Germany	W • E Europe & W Asia • 100 kW
	†VOA, Via Philippines	W • E Asia • 250 kW
	†VOA, Via Udon Thani, Thailand	S • E Asia • 500 kW
	†VOA, Via Woofferton, UK	S • E Europe & W Asia • 300 kW
11900	FINLAND — †YLE RADIO FINLAND, Pori	S • N America • 500 kW
	INDIA — †ALL INDIA RADIO, Bangalore	S Asia & E Asia • 500 kW
	SOUTH AFRICA — †CHANNEL AFRICA, Meyerton	W • W Africa • 500 kW
		E Africa & C Africa • 500 kW
		W • S Africa & W Africa • 500 kW
		E Africa • 500 kW
		W Africa • 500 kW
		E Africa & C Africa • 250 kW

(con'd)

ENGLISH ▬ ARABIC ▨ CHINESE ▭▭ FRENCH ▬▬ GERMAN ▬▬ RUSSIAN ══ SPANISH ▬▬ OTHER ▬

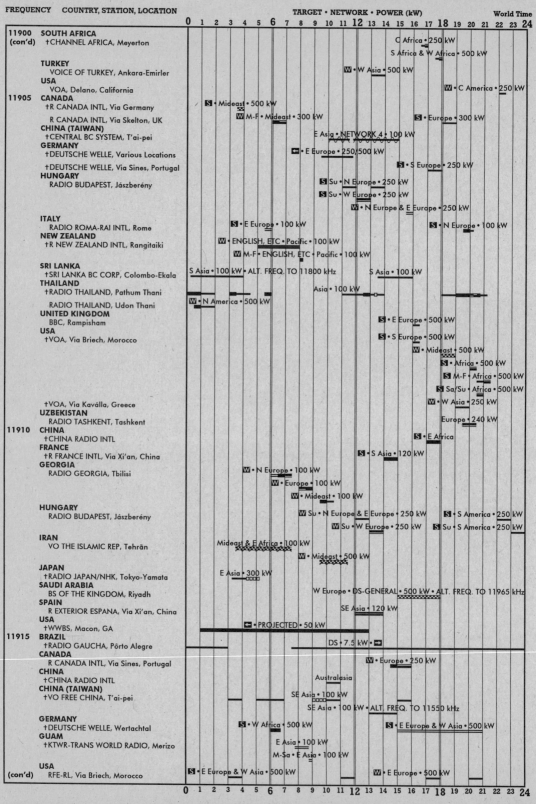

FREQUENCY   COUNTRY, STATION, LOCATION

TARGET • NETWORK • POWER (kW)   World Time

11900 **SOUTH AFRICA**	
(con'd) †CHANNEL AFRICA, Meyerton	C Africa • 250 kW / S Africa & W Africa • 500 kW
TURKEY	
VOICE OF TURKEY, Ankara-Emirler	W • W Asia • 500 kW
USA	
VOA, Delano, California	W • C America • 250 kW
11905 **CANADA**	
†R CANADA INTL, Via Germany	S • Mideast • 500 kW
R CANADA INTL, Via Skelton, UK	W • M-F • Mideast • 300 kW / S • Europe • 300 kW
CHINA (TAIWAN)	
†CENTRAL BC SYSTEM, T'ai-pei	E Asia • NETWORK 4 • 100 kW
GERMANY	
†DEUTSCHE WELLE, Various Locations	• E Europe • 250/500 kW
†DEUTSCHE WELLE, Via Sines, Portugal	S • S Europe • 250 kW
HUNGARY	
RADIO BUDAPEST, Jászberény	S Su • N Europe • 250 kW / S Su • W Europe • 250 kW / W • N Europe & E Europe • 250 kW
ITALY	
RADIO ROMA-RAI INTL, Rome	S • E Europe • 100 kW / S • N Europe • 100 kW
NEW ZEALAND	
†R NEW ZEALAND INTL, Rangitaiki	W • ENGLISH, ETC • Pacific • 100 kW / W M-F • ENGLISH, ETC • Pacific • 100 kW
SRI LANKA	
†SRI LANKA BC CORP, Colombo-Ekala	S Asia • 100 kW • ALT. FREQ. TO 11800 kHz / S Asia • 100 kW
THAILAND	
†RADIO THAILAND, Pathum Thani	Asia • 100 kW
RADIO THAILAND, Udon Thani	W • N America • 500 kW
UNITED KINGDOM	
BBC, Rampisham	S • E Europe • 500 kW
USA	
†VOA, Via Briech, Morocco	S • S Europe • 500 kW / W • Mideast • 500 kW / S • Africa • 500 kW / S M-F • Africa • 500 kW / S Sa/Su • Africa • 500 kW
†VOA, Via Kaválla, Greece	W • W Asia • 250 kW
UZBEKISTAN	
RADIO TASHKENT, Tashkent	Europe • 240 kW
11910 **CHINA**	
†CHINA RADIO INTL	S • E Africa
FRANCE	
†R FRANCE INTL, Via Xi'an, China	S • S Asia • 120 kW
GEORGIA	
RADIO GEORGIA, Tbilisi	W • N Europe • 100 kW / W • Europe • 100 kW / W • Mideast • 100 kW
HUNGARY	
RADIO BUDAPEST, Jászberény	S Su • N Europe & E Europe • 250 kW / S • S America • 250 kW / W Su • W Europe • 250 kW / S Su • S America • 250 kW
IRAN	
VO THE ISLAMIC REP, Tehrān	Mideast & E Africa • 100 kW / W • Mideast • 500 kW
JAPAN	
†RADIO JAPAN/NHK, Tokyo-Yamata	E Asia • 300 kW
SAUDI ARABIA	
BS OF THE KINGDOM, Riyadh	W Europe • DS-GENERAL • 500 kW • ALT. FREQ. TO 11965 kHz
SPAIN	
R EXTERIOR ESPANA, Via Xi'an, China	SE Asia • 120 kW
USA	
†WWBS, Macon, GA	• PROJECTED • 50 kW
11915 **BRAZIL**	
†RADIO GAUCHA, Pôrto Alegre	DS • 7.5 kW •
CANADA	
R CANADA INTL, Via Sines, Portugal	W • Europe • 250 kW
CHINA	
†CHINA RADIO INTL	Australasia
CHINA (TAIWAN)	
†VO FREE CHINA, T'ai-pei	SE Asia • 100 kW / SE Asia • 100 kW • ALT. FREQ. TO 11550 kHz
GERMANY	
†DEUTSCHE WELLE, Wertachtal	S • W Africa • 500 kW / S • E Europe & W Asia • 500 kW
GUAM	
†KTWR-TRANS WORLD RADIO, Merizo	E Asia • 100 kW / M-Sa • E Asia • 100 kW
USA	
(con'd) RFE-RL, Via Briech, Morocco	S • E Europe & W Asia • 500 kW / W • E Europe • 500 kW

0 1 2 3 4 5 6 7 8 9 10 11 12 13 14 15 16 17 18 19 20 21 22 23 24

SEASONAL S OR W   1-HR TIMESHIFT MIDYEAR � OR ▷   JAMMING / OR ∧   EARLIEST HEARD ◁   LATEST HEARD ▷   NEW FOR 1998 †

FREQUENCY	COUNTRY, STATION, LOCATION	TARGET • NETWORK • POWER (kW)	World Time

11915 USA
(con'd)
   RFE-RL, Via Kaválla, Greece — S • E Europe • 250 kW ; S • W Asia & C Asia • 250 kW
   RFE-RL, Via Udon Thani, Thailand — S • C Asia • 500 kW
   VOA, Via Kaválla, Greece — W • M-F • N Africa & W Africa • 250 kW

11920 BELARUS
   BELARUSSIAN R, Via Moscow, Russia — DS • 20 kW
JAPAN
   †RADIO JAPAN/NHK, Via Singapore — Australasia • 250 kW
MOROCCO
   RTV MAROCAINE, Briech — N Africa & Mideast • 500 kW
RUSSIA
   VOICE OF RUSSIA, Samara — S • Europe • 100 kW
SPAIN
   R EXTERIOR ESPANA, Noblejas — Europe • 350 kW
UNITED KINGDOM
   BBC, Via Singapore — SE Asia • 100 kW ; S Asia • 100 kW ; W Asia & S Asia • 300 kW
   BBC, Via Zyyi, Cyprus
USA
   VOA, Via Udon Thani, Thailand — W • E Africa • 500 kW

11925 BRAZIL
   RADIO BANDEIRANTES, São Paulo — DS • 10 kW
GERMANY
   †DEUTSCHE WELLE, Via Sri Lanka — S • E Asia • 250 kW
ITALY
   RADIO ROMA-RAI INTL, Via Singapore — Australasia • 250 kW
TURKEY
   VOICE OF TURKEY, Ankara-Emirler — W Asia • 500 kW
USA
   RFE-RL, Via Briech, Morocco — S • S Europe • 500 kW ; S • E Europe & W Asia • 500 kW
   RFE-RL, Via Pals, Spain — S • E Europe & W Asia • 250 kW
   †VOA, Via Philippines — E Asia • 250 kW

11930 IRAN
   RADIO ZAHEDAN, Zāhedān — Mideast • 500 kW
   †VO THE ISLAMIC REP, Zāhedān — Mideast • 500 kW
USA
   RADIO MARTI, Greenville, NC — C America • 250 kW
   †VOA, Via Philippines — E Asia • 250 kW ; W • SE Asia • 250 kW ; SE Asia • 250 kW ; W • SE Asia • 50 kW

11935 BRAZIL
   R CLUBE PARANAENSE, Curitiba — DS • 7.5 kW • ; Irr • DS • 7.5 kW •
CANADA
   †R CANADA INTL, Via Skelton, UK — • Europe & Mideast • 300 kW ; • Europe • 300 kW
CHINA
   †CENTRAL PEOPLE'S BS, Beijing — CHINESE, ETC • TAIWAN SERVICE • 50 kW ; S • CHINESE, ETC • TAIWAN SERVICE • 50 kW
CLANDESTINE (ASIA)
   †"VO SOUTHERN AZERBAIJAN" — • Mideast & W Asia
HOLLAND
   †R NEDERLAND, Flevoland — S • S Europe • 500 kW
INDIA
   ALL INDIA RADIO, Mumbai — E Africa • 100 kW
JORDAN
   RADIO JORDAN, Qasr el Kharana — • W Europe & E North Am • 500 kW
PAKISTAN
   RADIO PAKISTAN, Islamabad — S Asia & SE Asia • 100 kW ; E Africa & S Africa • 100 kW • ALT. FREQ. TO 11745 kHz
RUSSIA
   VOICE OF RUSSIA, Via Uzbekistan — S • Mideast • 100 kW
SAUDI ARABIA
   †BS OF THE KINGDOM, Riyadh — C Asia • DS-HOLY KORAN • 500 kW • ALT. FREQ. TO 11740 kHz ; N Africa • DS-HOLY KORAN • 500 kW
USA
   †RFE-RL, Via Pals, Spain — S • E Europe • 250 kW
   VOA, Greenville, NC — W • M-F • C America • 250 kW
VATICAN STATE
   VATICAN RADIO, Sta Maria di Galeria — S • S Asia • 250 kW

11939.4 PARAGUAY
   RADIO ENCARNACION, Encarnación — DS • 0.5 kW •

11940 CANADA
   R CANADA INTL, Sackville, NB — Su/M • C America & S America • 250 kW ; M-F • C America & S America • 250 kW ; W • Tu-Sa • C America & S America • 250 kW ; Sa/Su • C America & S America • 250 kW
(con'd)

ENGLISH ▬ ARABIC ✕✕✕ CHINESE ▫▫▫ FRENCH ▬ GERMAN ▬ RUSSIAN ═ SPANISH ▬ OTHER —

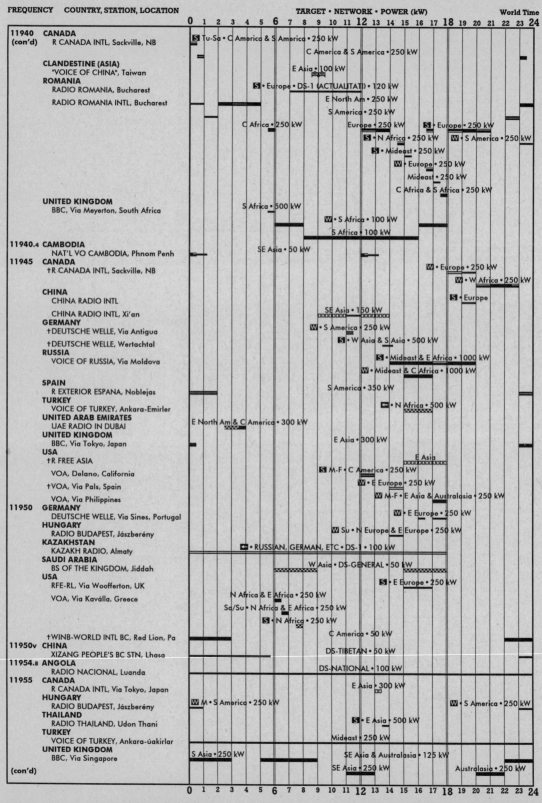

FREQUENCY   COUNTRY, STATION, LOCATION

TARGET • NETWORK • POWER (kW)   World Time

11940 **CANADA**	
(con'd) R CANADA INTL, Sackville, NB	**S** Tu-Sa • C America & S America • 250 kW
	C America & S America • 250 kW
CLANDESTINE (ASIA)	
"VOICE OF CHINA", Taiwan	E Asia • 100 kW
ROMANIA	
RADIO ROMANIA, Bucharest	**S** • Europe • DS-1 (ACTUALITATI) • 120 kW
RADIO ROMANIA INTL, Bucharest	E North Am • 250 kW
	S America • 250 kW
	C Africa • 250 kW
	Europe • 250 kW **S** • Europe • 250 kW
	S • N Africa • 250 kW **W** • S America • 250 kW
	S • Mideast • 250 kW
	W • Europe • 250 kW
	Mideast • 250 kW
	C Africa & S Africa • 250 kW
UNITED KINGDOM	
BBC, Via Meyerton, South Africa	S Africa • 500 kW
	W • S Africa • 100 kW
	S Africa • 100 kW
11940.4 **CAMBODIA**	
NAT'L VO CAMBODIA, Phnom Penh	SE Asia • 50 kW
11945 **CANADA**	
†R CANADA INTL, Sackville, NB	**W** • Europe • 250 kW
	W • W Africa • 250 kW
CHINA	
CHINA RADIO INTL	**S** • Europe
CHINA RADIO INTL, Xi'an	SE Asia • 150 kW
GERMANY	
†DEUTSCHE WELLE, Via Antigua	**W** • S America • 250 kW
†DEUTSCHE WELLE, Wertachtal	**S** • W Asia & S Asia • 500 kW
RUSSIA	
VOICE OF RUSSIA, Via Moldova	**S** • Mideast & E Africa • 1000 kW
	W • Mideast & C Africa • 1000 kW
SPAIN	
R EXTERIOR ESPANA, Noblejas	S America • 350 kW
TURKEY	
VOICE OF TURKEY, Ankara-Emirler	⬌ • N Africa • 500 kW
UNITED ARAB EMIRATES	
UAE RADIO IN DUBAI	E North Am & C America • 300 kW
UNITED KINGDOM	
BBC, Via Tokyo, Japan	E Asia • 300 kW
USA	
†R FREE ASIA	E Asia
VOA, Delano, California	**S** M-F • C America • 250 kW
†VOA, Via Pals, Spain	**W** • E Europe • 250 kW
VOA, Via Philippines	**W** M-F • E Asia & Australasia • 250 kW
11950 **GERMANY**	
DEUTSCHE WELLE, Via Sines, Portugal	**W** • E Europe • 250 kW
HUNGARY	
RADIO BUDAPEST, Jászberény	**W** Su • N Europe & E Europe • 250 kW
KAZAKHSTAN	
KAZAKH RADIO, Almaty	⬌ • RUSSIAN, GERMAN, ETC • DS-1 • 100 kW
SAUDI ARABIA	
BS OF THE KINGDOM, Jiddah	W Asia • DS-GENERAL • 50 kW
USA	
RFE-RL, Via Woofferton, UK	**S** • E Europe • 250 kW
VOA, Via Kaválla, Greece	N Africa & E Africa • 250 kW
	Sa/Su • N Africa & E Africa • 250 kW
	S • N Africa • 250 kW
†WINB-WORLD INTL BC, Red Lion, Pa	C America • 50 kW
11950v **CHINA**	
XIZANG PEOPLE'S BC STN, Lhasa	DS-TIBETAN • 50 kW
11954.8 **ANGOLA**	
RADIO NACIONAL, Luanda	DS-NATIONAL • 100 kW
11955 **CANADA**	
R CANADA INTL, Via Tokyo, Japan	E Asia • 300 kW
HUNGARY	
RADIO BUDAPEST, Jászberény	**W** M • S America • 250 kW **W** • S America • 250 kW
THAILAND	
RADIO THAILAND, Udon Thani	**S** • E Asia • 500 kW
TURKEY	
VOICE OF TURKEY, Ankara-úakirlar	Mideast • 250 kW
UNITED KINGDOM	
BBC, Via Singapore	S Asia • 250 kW SE Asia & Australasia • 125 kW
(con'd)	SE Asia • 250 kW Australasia • 250 kW

FREQUENCY   COUNTRY, STATION, LOCATION   TARGET • NETWORK • POWER (kW)   World Time

		0 1 2 3 4 5 6 7 8 9 10 11 12 13 14 15 16 17 18 19 20 21 22 23 24

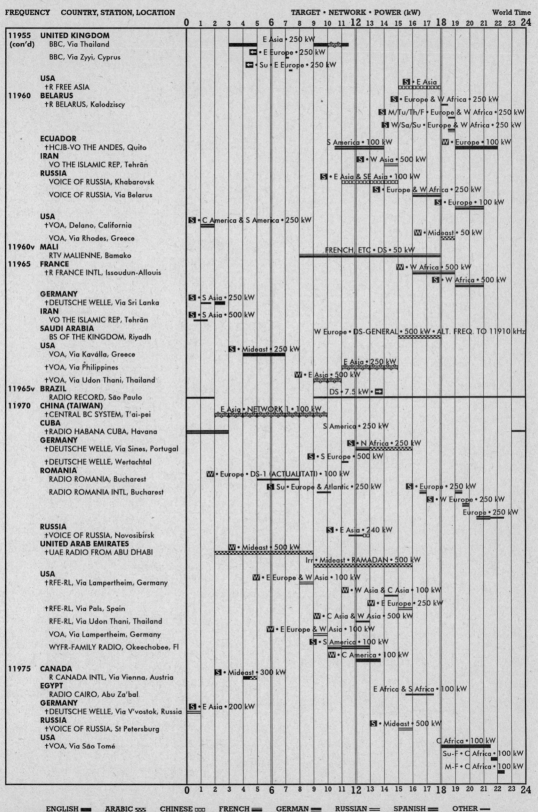

11955
(con'd) **UNITED KINGDOM**
  BBC, Via Thailand — E Asia • 250 kW
  BBC, Via Zyyi, Cyprus — E Europe • 250 kW
  — Su • E Europe • 250 kW

  USA
  †R FREE ASIA — S • E Asia
11960 **BELARUS**
  †R BELARUS, Kalodziscy — S • Europe & W Africa • 250 kW
  — S M/Tu/Th/F • Europe & W Africa • 250 kW
  — S W/Sa/Su • Europe & W Africa • 250 kW

  ECUADOR
  †HCJB-VO THE ANDES, Quito — S America • 100 kW — W • Europe • 100 kW
  IRAN
  VO THE ISLAMIC REP, Tehrān — S • W Asia • 500 kW
  RUSSIA
  VOICE OF RUSSIA, Khabarovsk — S • E Asia & SE Asia • 100 kW
  VOICE OF RUSSIA, Via Belarus — S • Europe & W Africa • 250 kW
  — S • Europe • 100 kW

  USA
  †VOA, Delano, California — S • C America & S America • 250 kW
  VOA, Via Rhodes, Greece — W • Mideast • 50 kW
11960v **MALI**
  RTV MALIENNE, Bamako — FRENCH, ETC • DS • 50 kW
11965 **FRANCE**
  †R FRANCE INTL, Issoudun-Allouis — W • W Africa • 500 kW
  — S • W Africa • 500 kW

  GERMANY
  †DEUTSCHE WELLE, Via Sri Lanka — S • S Asia • 250 kW
  IRAN
  VO THE ISLAMIC REP, Tehrān — S • S Asia • 500 kW
  SAUDI ARABIA
  BS OF THE KINGDOM, Riyadh — W Europe • DS-GENERAL • 500 kW • ALT. FREQ. TO 11910 kHz
  USA
  VOA, Via Kaválla, Greece — S • Mideast • 250 kW
  †VOA, Via Philippines — E Asia • 250 kW
  †VOA, Via Udon Thani, Thailand — W • E Asia • 500 kW
11965v **BRAZIL**
  RADIO RECORD, São Paulo — DS • 7.5 kW •
11970 **CHINA (TAIWAN)**
  †CENTRAL BC SYSTEM, T'ai-pei — E Asia • NETWORK 1 • 100 kW
  CUBA
  †RADIO HABANA CUBA, Havana — S America • 250 kW
  GERMANY
  †DEUTSCHE WELLE, Via Sines, Portugal — S • N Africa • 250 kW
  †DEUTSCHE WELLE, Wertachtal — S • S Europe • 500 kW
  ROMANIA
  RADIO ROMANIA, Bucharest — W • Europe • DS-1 (ACTUALITATI) • 100 kW
  RADIO ROMANIA INTL, Bucharest — S Su • Europe & Atlantic • 250 kW
  — S • Europe • 250 kW
  — S • W Europe • 250 kW
  — Europe • 250 kW

  RUSSIA
  †VOICE OF RUSSIA, Novosibirsk — S • E Asia • 240 kW
  UNITED ARAB EMIRATES
  †UAE RADIO FROM ABU DHABI — W • Mideast • 500 kW
  — Irr • Mideast • RAMADAN • 500 kW

  USA
  †RFE-RL, Via Lampertheim, Germany — W • E Europe & W Asia • 100 kW
  — W • W Asia & C Asia • 100 kW
  †RFE-RL, Via Pals, Spain — W • E Europe • 250 kW
  RFE-RL, Via Udon Thani, Thailand — W • C Asia & W Asia • 500 kW
  VOA, Via Lampertheim, Germany — W • E Europe & W Asia • 100 kW
  WYFR-FAMILY RADIO, Okeechobee, Fl — S • S America • 100 kW
  — W • C America • 100 kW

11975 **CANADA**
  R CANADA INTL, Via Vienna, Austria — S • Mideast • 300 kW
  EGYPT
  RADIO CAIRO, Abu Za'bal — E Africa & S Africa • 100 kW
  GERMANY
  †DEUTSCHE WELLE, Via V'vostok, Russia — S • E Asia • 200 kW
  RUSSIA
  †VOICE OF RUSSIA, St Petersburg — S • Mideast • 500 kW
  USA
  †VOA, Via São Tomé — C Africa • 100 kW
  — Su-F • C Africa • 100 kW
  — M-F • C Africa • 100 kW

	0 1 2 3 4 5 6 7 8 9 10 11 12 13 14 15 16 17 18 19 20 21 22 23 24

ENGLISH ▬ ARABIC ⌇⌇⌇ CHINESE ▫▫▫ FRENCH ▬ GERMAN ▬ RUSSIAN ═ SPANISH ▬ OTHER —

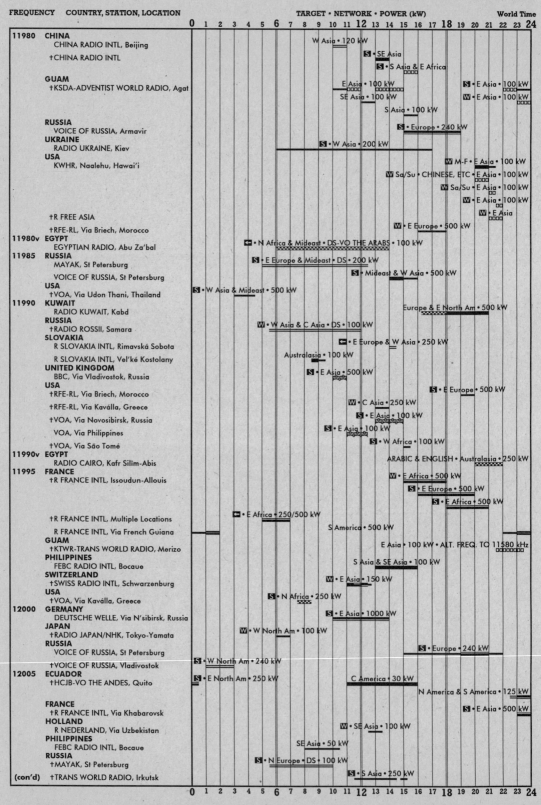

FREQUENCY	COUNTRY, STATION, LOCATION	TARGET • NETWORK • POWER (kW)	World Time

11980 CHINA
  CHINA RADIO INTL, Beijing — W Asia • 120 kW
  †CHINA RADIO INTL — S • SE Asia; S • S Asia & E Africa

  GUAM
  †KSDA-ADVENTIST WORLD RADIO, Agat — E Asia • 100 kW; SE Asia • 100 kW; S Asia • 100 kW; S • E Asia • 100 kW; W • E Asia • 100 kW

  RUSSIA
  VOICE OF RUSSIA, Armavir — S • Europe • 240 kW
  UKRAINE
  RADIO UKRAINE, Kiev — S • W Asia • 200 kW
  USA
  KWHR, Naalehu, Hawai'i — W M-F • E Asia • 100 kW; W Sa/Su • CHINESE, ETC • E Asia • 100 kW; W Sa/Su • E Asia • 100 kW; W • E Asia

  †R FREE ASIA

  †RFE-RL, Via Briech, Morocco — W • E Europe • 500 kW
11980v EGYPT
  EGYPTIAN RADIO, Abu Za'bal — ⬅ • N Africa & Mideast • DS-VO THE ARABS • 100 kW
11985 RUSSIA
  MAYAK, St Petersburg — S • E Europe & Mideast • DS • 200 kW
  VOICE OF RUSSIA, St Petersburg — S • Mideast & W Asia • 500 kW
  USA
  †VOA, Via Udon Thani, Thailand — S • W Asia & Mideast • 500 kW
11990 KUWAIT
  RADIO KUWAIT, Kabd — Europe & E North Am • 500 kW
  RUSSIA
  †RADIO ROSSII, Samara — W • W Asia & C Asia • DS • 100 kW
  SLOVAKIA
  R SLOVAKIA INTL, Rimavská Sobota — ⬅ • E Europe & W Asia • 250 kW
  R SLOVAKIA INTL, Vel'ké Kostolany — Australasia • 100 kW
  UNITED KINGDOM
  BBC, Via Vladivostok, Russia — S • E Asia • 500 kW
  USA
  †RFE-RL, Via Briech, Morocco — S • E Europe • 500 kW
  †RFE-RL, Via Kavála, Greece — W • C Asia • 250 kW
  †VOA, Via Novosibirsk, Russia — S • E Asia • 100 kW
  VOA, Via Philippines — S • E Asia • 100 kW
  †VOA, Via São Tomé — S • W Africa • 100 kW
11990v EGYPT
  RADIO CAIRO, Kafr Silim-Abis — ARABIC & ENGLISH • Australasia • 250 kW
11995 FRANCE
  †R FRANCE INTL, Issoudun-Allouis — W • E Africa • 500 kW; S • E Europe • 500 kW; S • E Africa • 500 kW

  †R FRANCE INTL, Multiple Locations — ⬅ • E Africa • 250/500 kW
  R FRANCE INTL, Via French Guiana — S America • 500 kW
  GUAM
  †KTWR-TRANS WORLD RADIO, Merizo — E Asia • 100 kW • ALT. FREQ. TO 11580 kHz
  PHILIPPINES
  FEBC RADIO INTL, Bocaue — S Asia & SE Asia • 100 kW
  SWITZERLAND
  †SWISS RADIO INTL, Schwarzenburg — W • E Asia • 150 kW
  USA
  †VOA, Via Kavála, Greece — S • N Africa • 250 kW
12000 GERMANY
  DEUTSCHE WELLE, Via N'sibirsk, Russia — S • E Asia • 1000 kW
  JAPAN
  †RADIO JAPAN/NHK, Tokyo-Yamata — W • W North Am • 100 kW
  RUSSIA
  VOICE OF RUSSIA, St Petersburg — S • Europe • 240 kW
  †VOICE OF RUSSIA, Vladivostok — S • W North Am • 240 kW
12005 ECUADOR
  †HCJB-VO THE ANDES, Quito — S • E North Am • 250 kW; C America • 30 kW; N America & S America • 125 kW

  FRANCE
  †R FRANCE INTL, Via Khabarovsk — S • E Asia • 500 kW
  HOLLAND
  R NEDERLAND, Via Uzbekistan — W • SE Asia • 100 kW
  PHILIPPINES
  FEBC RADIO INTL, Bocaue — SE Asia • 50 kW
  RUSSIA
  †MAYAK, St Petersburg — S • N Europe • DS • 100 kW
(con'd) †TRANS WORLD RADIO, Irkutsk — S • S Asia • 250 kW

FREQUENCY　　COUNTRY, STATION, LOCATION　　　　　　TARGET • NETWORK • POWER (kW)　　　　World Time

Freq	Country, Station, Location	Schedule
12005 (con'd)	**RUSSIA** †TRANS WORLD RADIO, Irkutsk	S Sa • S Asia • 250 kW / S Su-F • S Asia • 250 kW / S M/Tu • S Asia • 250 kW / S W-Su • S Asia • 250 kW
	VOICE OF RUSSIA, Khabarovsk	W • Australasia • 150 kW
	USA †VOA, Via Philippines	S M-F • SE Asia • 250 kW
12005v	**TUNISIA** †RTV TUNISIENNE, Sfax	N Africa & Mideast • DS • 100 kW / Irr • N Africa & Mideast • DS • 100 kW / W • N Africa & Mideast • DS • 100 kW
12008	**CLANDESTINE (AFRICA)** †"VOICE OF SUDAN", Eritrea	N Africa & E Africa • PRO-NDA
12010	**POLAND** †RADIO MARYJA, Via Samara, Russia	• Europe • 250 kW • ALT. FREQ. TO 7400 kHz
	RUSSIA VOICE OF RUSSIA, Petropavlovsk-K	S • W North Am • 100 kW
	VOICE OF RUSSIA, Samara	• Europe • 250 kW
	VOICE OF RUSSIA, Zhigulevsk	S • Europe • 240 kW
	USA †VOA, Via Philippines	S • E Asia • 250 kW / S • SE Asia • 250 kW
12015	**CHINA** CHINA RADIO INTL, Xi'an	SE Asia • 120 kW
	FRANCE R FRANCE INTL, Via Moyabi, Gabon	S Africa • 250 kW
	GERMANY †DEUTSCHE WELLE, Via Armavir, Russia	S • Mideast & E Africa • 500 kW
	†DEUTSCHE WELLE, Via Sines, Portugal	W • N Africa • 250 kW
	PAKISTAN RADIO PAKISTAN, Islamabad	S Asia & SE Asia • 100 kW
	RUSSIA R TIKHIY OKEAN, Chita	W • Australasia • 1000 kW
	†VOICE OF RUSSIA, Samara	W • S Asia & SE Asia • 240 kW
	SWEDEN †IBRA RADIO, Via Moscow, Russia	S • Mideast • 200 kW
	USA †RFE-RL, Via Holzkirchen, Germany	S • Mideast & W Asia • 250 kW
	†RFE-RL, Via Udon Thani, Thailand	S • C Asia • 500 kW
12015v	**MONGOLIA** †VOICE OF MONGOLIA, Ulaanbaatar	Europe • 100 kW
12020	**ECUADOR** †HCJB-VO THE ANDES, Quito	S • Europe • 100 kW • ALT. FREQ. TO 12025 kHz
	SWEDEN †IBRA RADIO, Via Moscow, Russia	S • W Africa • 250 kW
12020v	**VIETNAM** VOICE OF VIETNAM, Hanoi	W • Europe • 30 kW / W • DS • 30 kW / W • SE Asia • 30 kW / W • E Asia & Americas • 30 kW / W • Africa • 30 kW
12025	**ECUADOR** †HCJB-VO THE ANDES, Quito	S • Europe • 100 kW • ALT. FREQ. TO 12020 kHz / W • Europe • 250 kW / W • N Africa • 250 kW
	FRANCE †R FRANCE INTL, Issoudun-Allouis	S • N Africa & Mideast • 100/500 kW / S • Mideast & W Asia • 500 kW
	†R FRANCE INTL, Via Irkutsk, Russia	SE Asia • 1000 kW / S • E Asia • 500 kW / S • SE Asia • 500 kW
	GERMANY †DEUTSCHE WELLE, Via Sines, Portugal	W • N Africa • 250 kW
	RUSSIA †RADIO ROSSII, Armavir	S • W Asia • DS • 100 kW
	VOICE OF RUSSIA, Vladivostok	W • Australasia • 150 kW
	USA †VOA, Delano, California	W • C America & S America • 250 kW
	†VOA, Greenville, NC	W M-F • S America • 250 kW
	†VOA, Via Kamo, Armenia	S • S Asia & E Asia • 500 kW
	†VOA, Via Philippines	W • E Africa • 250 kW
12030	**CHINA** †CENTRAL PEOPLE'S BS	DS-1 / W-M • DS-1
(con'd)		

ENGLISH ■■　ARABIC ⧖⧖　CHINESE □□□　FRENCH ▬　GERMAN ▬▬　RUSSIAN ══　SPANISH ▬▬　OTHER —

FREQUENCY   COUNTRY, STATION, LOCATION

TARGET • NETWORK • POWER (kW)

World Time

0 1 2 3 4 5 6 7 8 9 10 11 12 13 14 15 16 17 18 19 20 21 22 23 24

FREQUENCY	COUNTRY, STATION, LOCATION	Schedule
12030 (con'd)	FRANCE †R FRANCE INTL, Issoudun-Allouis	W • S Asia & SE Asia • 500 kW Irr • S Asia & SE Asia • 500 kW S • S Asia & SE Asia • 500 kW
	JAPAN †RADIO JAPAN/NHK, Tokyo-Yamata	W North Am • 300 kW
	†RADIO JAPAN/NHK, Via Moyabi, Gabon	Europe • 500 kW
	RUSSIA VOICE OF RUSSIA, Moscow	S • Europe & N Africa • 150 kW
	VOICE OF RUSSIA, Petropavlovsk-K	W • W North Am • 250 kW
	UNITED KINGDOM BBC, Via Zyyi, Cyprus	F • W Asia • 250 kW Th/F • W Asia • 250 kW
	USA †VOA, Via Philippines	W • SE Asia • 50 kW
12035	CHINA CHINA RADIO INTL, Via Russia	S • Mideast • 250 kW
	RUSSIA †TRANS WORLD RADIO, Irkutsk	S • S Asia • 200 kW
	VOICE OF RUSSIA, Moscow	S • Mideast & E Africa • 250 kW
	†VOICE OF RUSSIA, Novosibirsk	S • E Asia • 100 kW
	SPAIN R EXTERIOR ESPANA, Noblejas	Europe • 350 kW Sa • Europe • 350 kW M-F • Europe • 350 kW Su-F • Europe • 350 kW Sa/Su • Europe • 350 kW
12035v	VIETNAM VOICE OF VIETNAM, Hanoi	DS-2
12040	RUSSIA R TIKHIY OKEAN, Vladivostok	S • W North Am • 120 kW
	†VOICE OF RUSSIA, Armavir	S • Europe & Atlantic • 700/1000 kW S • W Africa & S America • 700/1000 kW
	VOICE OF RUSSIA, Vladivostok	S • W North Am • 120 kW
	UKRAINE RADIO UKRAINE, Khar'kov	W • Europe • 100 kW
	UNITED KINGDOM BBC, Skelton, Cumbria	• E Europe • 250 kW • M-F • Europe • 300 kW • Su • Europe • 300 kW • Europe • 300 kW
	BBC, Via Zyyi, Cyprus	• M-F • E Europe • 250 kW • M-Th • E Europe • 250 kW
	BBC, Woofferton	W • E Europe • 250 kW
	USA †VOA, Via Philippines	W • E Asia • 250 kW W • E Africa • 250 kW E Asia • 250 kW W • S Asia & E Asia • 250 kW S • E Asia • 250 kW
	†VOA, Via Udon Thani, Thailand	S • E Asia • 500 kW
12045	GERMANY †DEUTSCHE WELLE, Via N'sibirsk, Russia	S • S Asia • 1000 kW S • S Asia & SE Asia • 250 kW
	DEUTSCHE WELLE, Via Petro-K, Russia	S • E Asia • 250 kW
	†DEUTSCHE WELLE, Via Samara, Russia	S • S Asia • 250 kW S • W Asia • 200 kW
	JAPAN †RADIO JAPAN/NHK, Via Sri Lanka	S Asia • 300 kW
	RUSSIA †RADIO ROSSII, St Petersburg	W • E Europe & W Asia • DS • 200 kW E Europe & W Asia • DS • 200 kW S • E Europe & W Asia • DS • 200 kW
12050	EGYPT EGYPTIAN RADIO, Mult Locations	• Europe & E North Am • DS-GENERAL • 250 kW • Europe, E North Am & E Africa • DS-GENERAL • 100/250 kW • Europe & N America • DS-GENERAL • 100/250 kW
	RUSSIA †KAMCHATKA RYBATSKAYA, Petro-Kam	S • Su/M/W/F • N Pacific & W North Am • 100 kW • Tu/Th/Sa • N Pacific & W North Am • 100 kW
	VOICE OF RUSSIA, Khabarovsk	S • W North Am • 100 kW
12055	GERMANY †DEUTSCHE WELLE, Via Irkutsk, Russia	S • E Asia • 250 kW
	DEUTSCHE WELLE, Via Samara, Russia	S • S Asia • 250 kW
	RUSSIA VOICE OF RUSSIA, Moscow	W • SE Asia • 250 kW

0 1 2 3 4 5 6 7 8 9 10 11 12 13 14 15 16 17 18 19 20 21 22 23 24

SEASONAL S OR W   1-HR TIMESHIFT MIDYEAR � OR ►   JAMMING / OR ∧   EARLIEST HEARD ◁   LATEST HEARD ▷   NEW FOR 1998 †

FREQUENCY   COUNTRY, STATION, LOCATION   TARGET • NETWORK • POWER (kW)   World Time

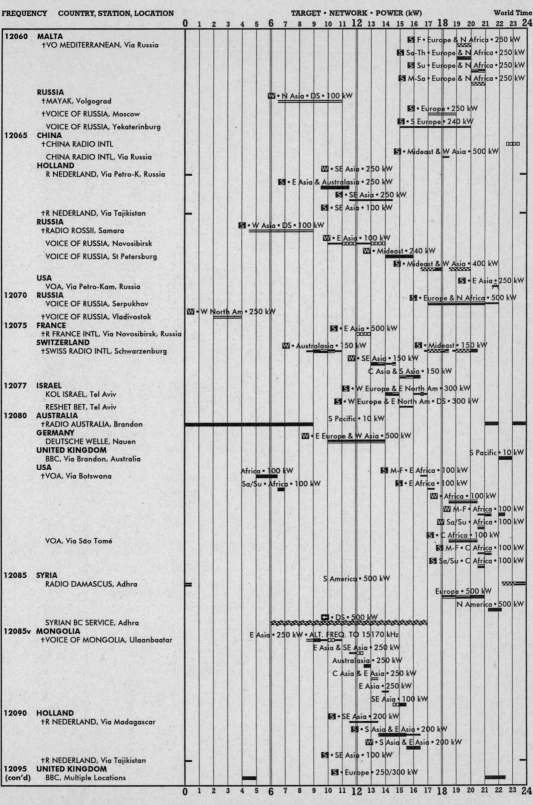

Frequency	Country, Station, Location	Target • Network • Power
12060	**MALTA**	
	†VO MEDITERRANEAN, Via Russia	F • Europe & N Africa • 250 kW
		Sa-Th • Europe & N Africa • 250 kW
		Su • Europe & N Africa • 250 kW
		M-Sa • Europe & N Africa • 250 kW
	RUSSIA	
	†MAYAK, Volgograd	W • N Asia • DS • 100 kW
	†VOICE OF RUSSIA, Moscow	Europe • 250 kW
	VOICE OF RUSSIA, Yekaterinburg	S Europe • 240 kW
12065	**CHINA**	
	†CHINA RADIO INTL	Mideast & W Asia • 500 kW
	CHINA RADIO INTL, Via Russia	
	HOLLAND	
	R NEDERLAND, Via Petro-K, Russia	W • SE Asia • 250 kW
		S • E Asia & Australasia • 250 kW
		SE Asia • 250 kW
	†R NEDERLAND, Via Tajikistan	SE Asia • 100 kW
	RUSSIA	
	†RADIO ROSSII, Samara	S • W Asia • DS • 100 kW
	VOICE OF RUSSIA, Novosibirsk	W • E Asia • 100 kW
	VOICE OF RUSSIA, St Petersburg	W • Mideast • 240 kW
		Mideast & W Asia • 400 kW
	USA	
	VOA, Via Petro-Kam, Russia	E Asia • 250 kW
12070	**RUSSIA**	
	VOICE OF RUSSIA, Serpukhov	Europe & N Africa • 500 kW
	†VOICE OF RUSSIA, Vladivostok	W • W North Am • 250 kW
12075	**FRANCE**	
	†R FRANCE INTL, Via Novosibirsk, Russia	E Asia • 500 kW
	SWITZERLAND	
	†SWISS RADIO INTL, Schwarzenburg	W • Australasia • 150 kW
		Mideast • 150 kW
		W • SE Asia • 150 kW
		C Asia & S Asia • 150 kW
12077	**ISRAEL**	
	KOL ISRAEL, Tel Aviv	W Europe & E North Am • 300 kW
	RESHET BET, Tel Aviv	W Europe & E North Am • DS • 300 kW
12080	**AUSTRALIA**	
	†RADIO AUSTRALIA, Brandon	S Pacific • 10 kW
	GERMANY	
	DEUTSCHE WELLE, Nauen	W • E Europe & W Asia • 500 kW
	UNITED KINGDOM	
	BBC, Via Brandon, Australia	S Pacific • 10 kW
	USA	
	†VOA, Via Botswana	Africa • 100 kW
		M-F • E Africa • 100 kW
		Sa/Su • Africa • 100 kW
		E Africa • 100 kW
		W • Africa • 100 kW
		W M-F • Africa • 100 kW
		W Sa/Su • Africa • 100 kW
		C Africa • 100 kW
	VOA, Via São Tomé	M-F • C Africa • 100 kW
		Sa/Su • C Africa • 100 kW
12085	**SYRIA**	
	RADIO DAMASCUS, Adhra	S America • 500 kW
		Europe • 500 kW
		N America • 500 kW
	SYRIAN BC SERVICE, Adhra	DS • 500 kW
12085v	**MONGOLIA**	
	†VOICE OF MONGOLIA, Ulaanbaatar	E Asia • 250 kW • ALT. FREQ. TO 15170 kHz
		E Asia & SE Asia • 250 kW
		Australasia • 250 kW
		C Asia & E Asia • 250 kW
		E Asia • 250 kW
		SE Asia • 100 kW
12090	**HOLLAND**	
	†R NEDERLAND, Via Madagascar	SE Asia • 200 kW
		S Asia & E Asia • 200 kW
		W • S Asia & E Asia • 200 kW
	†R NEDERLAND, Via Tajikistan	SE Asia • 100 kW
12095 (con'd)	**UNITED KINGDOM**	
	BBC, Multiple Locations	Europe • 250/300 kW

ENGLISH ▬   ARABIC ⧓   CHINESE ▫▫▫   FRENCH ▬   GERMAN ▬   RUSSIAN ═   SPANISH ▬   OTHER ▬

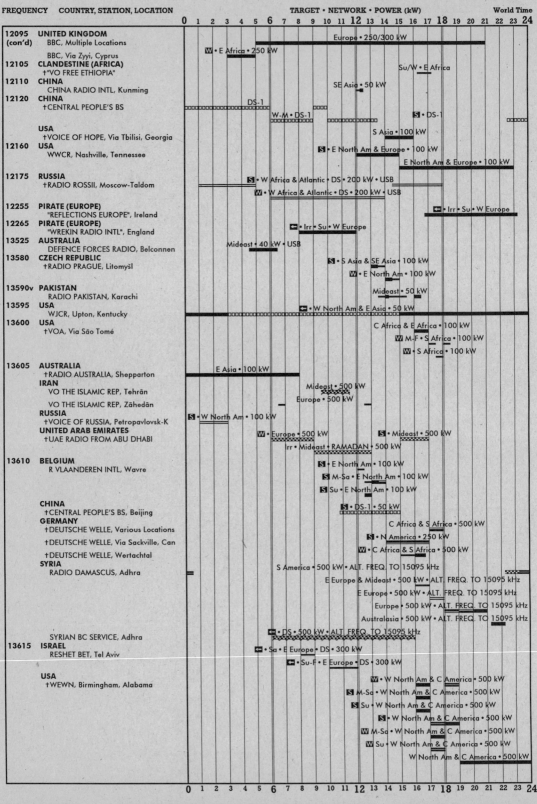

FREQUENCY   COUNTRY, STATION, LOCATION

TARGET • NETWORK • POWER (kW)

World Time

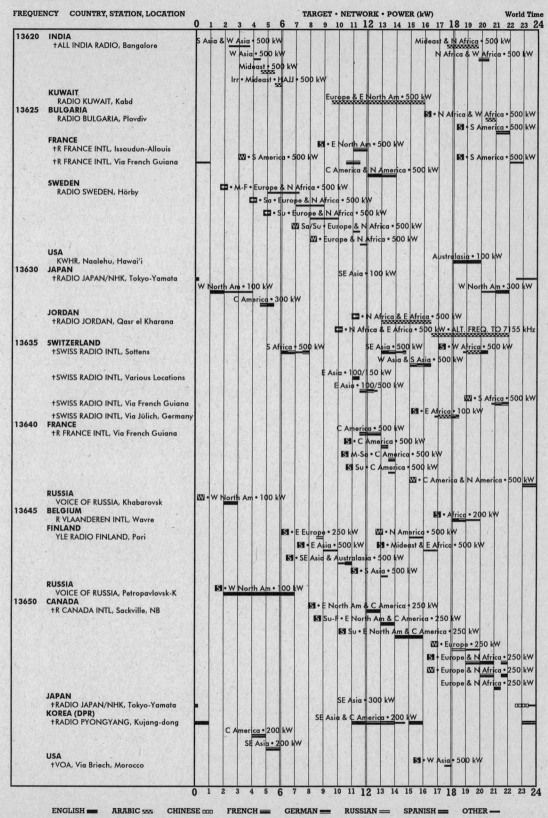

Frequency	Country, Station, Location	Target • Network • Power
13620	**INDIA** †ALL INDIA RADIO, Bangalore	S Asia & W Asia • 500 kW; Mideast & N Africa • 500 kW; W Asia • 500 kW; N Africa & W Africa • 500 kW; Mideast • 500 kW; Irr • Mideast • HAJJ • 500 kW
13625	**KUWAIT** RADIO KUWAIT, Kabd **BULGARIA** RADIO BULGARIA, Plovdiv	Europe & E North Am • 500 kW; S • N Africa & W Africa • 500 kW; S • S America • 500 kW
	FRANCE †R FRANCE INTL, Issoudun-Allouis †R FRANCE INTL, Via French Guiana	S • E North Am • 500 kW; W • S America • 500 kW; S • S America • 500 kW; C America & N America • 500 kW
	SWEDEN RADIO SWEDEN, Hörby	• M-F • Europe & N Africa • 500 kW; • Sa • Europe & N Africa • 500 kW; • Su • Europe & N Africa • 500 kW; W Sa/Su • Europe & N Africa • 500 kW; W • Europe & N Africa • 500 kW
13630	**USA** KWHR, Naalehu, Hawai'i **JAPAN** †RADIO JAPAN/NHK, Tokyo-Yamata	Australasia • 100 kW; SE Asia • 100 kW; W North Am • 100 kW; W North Am • 300 kW; C America • 300 kW
	JORDAN †RADIO JORDAN, Qasr el Kharana	• N Africa & E Africa • 500 kW; • N Africa & E Africa • 500 kW • ALT. FREQ. TO 7155 kHz
13635	**SWITZERLAND** †SWISS RADIO INTL, Sottens †SWISS RADIO INTL, Various Locations †SWISS RADIO INTL, Via French Guiana †SWISS RADIO INTL, Via Jülich, Germany	S Africa • 500 kW; SE Asia • 500 kW; W Africa • 500 kW; W Asia & S Asia • 500 kW; E Asia • 100/150 kW; E Asia • 100/500 kW; W • S Africa • 500 kW; S • E Africa • 100 kW
13640	**FRANCE** †R FRANCE INTL, Via French Guiana	C America • 500 kW; S • C America • 500 kW; S M-Sa • C America • 500 kW; S Su • C America • 500 kW; W • C America & N America • 500 kW
13645	**RUSSIA** VOICE OF RUSSIA, Khabarovsk **BELGIUM** R VLAANDEREN INTL, Wavre **FINLAND** YLE RADIO FINLAND, Pori	W • W North Am • 100 kW; S • Africa • 200 kW; S • E Europe • 250 kW; W • N America • 500 kW; S • E Asia • 500 kW; S • Mideast & E Africa • 500 kW; S • SE Asia & Australasia • 500 kW; S • S Asia • 500 kW
13650	**RUSSIA** VOICE OF RUSSIA, Petropavlovsk-K **CANADA** †R CANADA INTL, Sackville, NB	S • W North Am • 100 kW; S • E North Am & C America • 250 kW; S Su-F • E North Am & C America • 250 kW; S Su • E North Am & C America • 250 kW; W • Europe • 250 kW; S • Europe & N Africa • 250 kW; W • Europe & N Africa • 250 kW; Europe & N Africa • 250 kW
	JAPAN †RADIO JAPAN/NHK, Tokyo-Yamata **KOREA (DPR)** †RADIO PYONGYANG, Kujang-dong	SE Asia • 300 kW; SE Asia & C America • 200 kW; C America • 200 kW; SE Asia • 200 kW
	USA †VOA, Via Briech, Morocco	S • W Asia • 500 kW

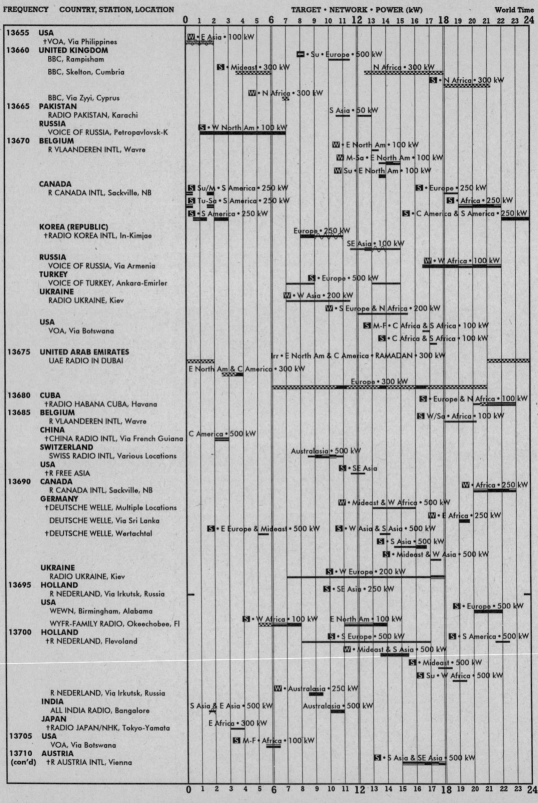

FREQUENCY　　COUNTRY, STATION, LOCATION　　　　　　　TARGET • NETWORK • POWER (kW)　　　　World Time

Frequency	Country, Station, Location	Target • Network • Power
13710 (con'd)	HOLLAND †R NEDERLAND, Via Irkutsk, Russia	S • E Asia & Australasia • 250 kW
	INDIA †ALL INDIA RADIO, Bangalore	SE Asia • 500 kW
	USA †R FREE ASIA	SE Asia
	†VOA, Via Botswana	W • M-F • Africa • 100 kW / Africa • 100 kW / W • Africa • 100 kW / W • Su-F • Africa • 100 kW
13715	CUBA †RADIO HABANA CUBA, Havana	S America • 100 kW • ALT. FREQ. TO 11875 kHz / S • Su • Europe & E North Am • 100 kW / S • Europe & E North Am • 100 kW
	SLOVAKIA †ADVENTIST WORLD R, Rimavská Sobota	W Africa • 250 kW
	R SLOVAKIA INTL, Rimavská Sobota	E Europe & W Asia • 250 kW
13720	GUAM †KSDA-ADVENTIST WORLD RADIO, Agat	Sa/Su • E Asia • 100 kW / SE Asia • 100 kW / W • SE Asia • 100 kW
	UKRAINE RADIO UKRAINE, Kiev	W • W Europe • 100 kW
	USA †VOA, Via Briech, Morocco	S • S Europe • 500 kW
13725	CUBA †RADIO HABANA CUBA, Havana	S • Europe & E North Am • 20 kW • USB
13730	AUSTRIA †R AUSTRIA INTL, Vienna	S • S America • 100 kW / N Europe • 100 kW / S Europe & W Africa • 100 kW
		M-Sa • E Europe • 100 kW / W Europe & E North Am • 300 kW / S • S Africa • 500 kW
		Su • E Europe • 100 kW / W • Su • N Europe • 100 kW / S • Mideast • 100 kW
		W • E Europe • 100 kW / M-Sa • S Europe & W Africa • 100 kW
		S • E Europe • 100 kW / Su • S Europe & W Africa • 100 kW
		E Europe • 100 kW / W • S Europe & W Africa • 100 kW
		W • N Europe • 100 kW / S • M-Sa • Mideast • 100 kW
		S • N Europe • 100 kW / S • Su • Mideast • 100 kW
		W • M-Sa • N Europe • 100 kW
		W • W Europe & E North Am • 300 kW
		S • W Europe & E North Am • 300 kW
		S • S Europe & W Africa • 100 kW
13740	CANADA †R CANADA INTL, Sackville, NB	S • C America • 250 kW
	SWEDEN RADIO SWEDEN, Hörby	S • Europe & Africa • 500 kW
		W • Sa/Su • E Asia & Australasia • 500 kW
		S • Asia & Australasia • 500 kW
		W • Asia & Australasia • 500 kW
		Asia & Australasia • 500 kW • ALT. FREQ. TO 11865 kHz
		S • N America • 500 kW
	USA †VOA, Delano, California	Tu-Sa • C America & S America • 250 kW
	VOA, Greenville, NC	C America • 250 kW
13745	UNITED KINGDOM BBC, Rampisham	E Europe • 500 kW / Su • E Europe • 500 kW / S • E Europe • 500 kW
13749.8	COSTA RICA †ADVENTIST WORLD R, Cahuita	Su/M • C America • 20 kW / Sa/Su • C America • 20 kW
		Tu-Sa • C America • 20 kW
		C America • 20 kW
		M-Sa • C America • 20 kW
		Su • C America • 20 kW
13750	ISRAEL KOL ISRAEL, Tel Aviv	W • S America • 300 kW
	RESHET BET, Tel Aviv	S • Europe • DS • 20/50 kW
13755	AUSTRALIA †RADIO AUSTRALIA, Shepparton	Pacific & W North Am • 100 kW
	HOLLAND †R NEDERLAND, Via Khabarovsk, Russia	S • SE Asia • 100 kW
	ISRAEL RESHET BET, Tel Aviv	W • Europe • DS • 20 kW
13760	KOREA (DPR) †RADIO PYONGYANG, Kujang-dong	N America • 200 kW
(con'd)	USA †VOA, Via Udon Thani, Thailand	E Asia • 500 kW

ENGLISH ▬　ARABIC ▩　CHINESE ☐☐☐　FRENCH ▬　GERMAN ▬　RUSSIAN ▭▭　SPANISH ▬　OTHER ▬

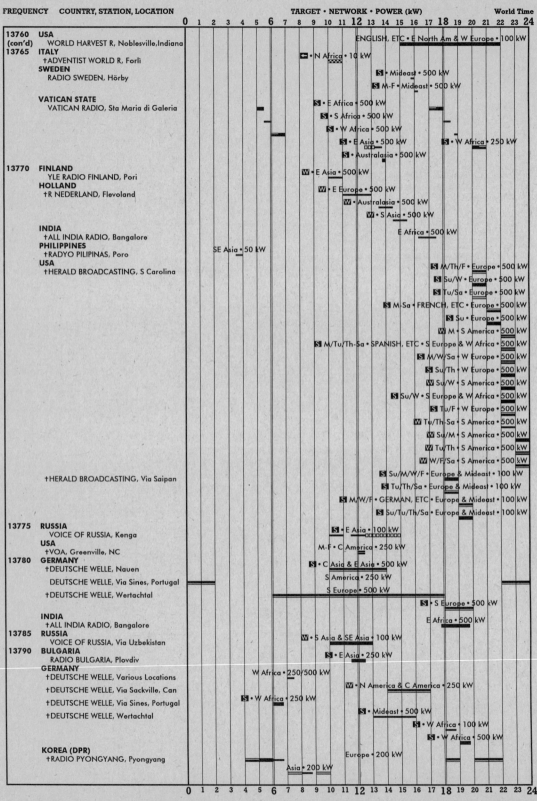

FREQUENCY   COUNTRY, STATION, LOCATION   TARGET • NETWORK • POWER (kW)   World Time

Frequency	Country, Station, Location	Target • Network • Power
13760 (con'd)	USA — WORLD HARVEST R, Noblesville, Indiana	ENGLISH, ETC • E North Am & W Europe • 100 kW
13765	ITALY — †ADVENTIST WORLD R, Forlì	N Africa • 10 kW
	SWEDEN — RADIO SWEDEN, Hörby	S • Mideast • 500 kW / S • M-F • Mideast • 500 kW
	VATICAN STATE — VATICAN RADIO, Sta Maria di Galeria	S • E Africa • 500 kW / S • S Africa • 500 kW / S • W Africa • 500 kW / S • E Asia • 500 kW / S • W Africa • 250 kW / S • Australasia • 500 kW
13770	FINLAND — YLE RADIO FINLAND, Pori	W • E Asia • 500 kW
	HOLLAND — †R NEDERLAND, Flevoland	W • E Europe • 500 kW / W • Australasia • 500 kW / W • S Asia • 500 kW
	INDIA — †ALL INDIA RADIO, Bangalore	E Africa • 500 kW
	PHILIPPINES — †RADYO PILIPINAS, Poro	SE Asia • 50 kW
	USA — †HERALD BROADCASTING, S Carolina	S • M/Th/F • Europe • 500 kW / S • Su/W • Europe • 500 kW / S • Tu/Sa • Europe • 500 kW / S • M-Sa • FRENCH, ETC • Europe • 500 kW / S • Su • Europe • 500 kW / W • M • S America • 500 kW / S • M/Tu/Th-Sa • SPANISH, ETC • S Europe & W Africa • 500 kW / S • M/W/Sa • W Europe • 500 kW / S • Su/Th • W Europe • 500 kW / W • Su/W • S America • 500 kW / S • Su/W • S Europe & W Africa • 500 kW / S • Tu/F • W Europe • 500 kW / W • Tu/Th-Sa • S America • 500 kW / W • Su/M • S America • 500 kW / W • Tu/Th • S America • 500 kW / W • W/F/Sa • S America • 500 kW
	†HERALD BROADCASTING, Via Saipan	S • Su/M/W/F • Europe & Mideast • 100 kW / S • Tu/Th/Sa • Europe & Mideast • 100 kW / S • M/W/F • GERMAN, ETC • Europe & Mideast • 100 kW / S • Su/Tu/Th/Sa • Europe & Mideast • 100 kW
13775	RUSSIA — VOICE OF RUSSIA, Kenga	S • E Asia • 100 kW
	USA — †VOA, Greenville, NC	M-F • C America • 250 kW
13780	GERMANY — †DEUTSCHE WELLE, Nauen	S • C Asia & E Asia • 500 kW
	DEUTSCHE WELLE, Via Sines, Portugal	S America • 250 kW
	†DEUTSCHE WELLE, Wertachtal	S Europe • 500 kW
	INDIA — †ALL INDIA RADIO, Bangalore	S • S Europe • 500 kW / E Africa • 500 kW
13785	RUSSIA — VOICE OF RUSSIA, Via Uzbekistan	W • S Asia & SE Asia • 100 kW
13790	BULGARIA — RADIO BULGARIA, Plovdiv	S • E Asia • 250 kW
	GERMANY — †DEUTSCHE WELLE, Various Locations	W Africa • 250/500 kW / W • N America & C America • 250 kW
	†DEUTSCHE WELLE, Via Sackville, Can	
	†DEUTSCHE WELLE, Via Sines, Portugal	S • W Africa • 250 kW
	†DEUTSCHE WELLE, Wertachtal	S • Mideast • 500 kW / S • W Africa • 100 kW / S • W Africa • 500 kW
	KOREA (DPR) — †RADIO PYONGYANG, Pyongyang	Europe • 200 kW / Asia • 200 kW

FREQUENCY   COUNTRY, STATION, LOCATION

TARGET • NETWORK • POWER (kW)   World Time

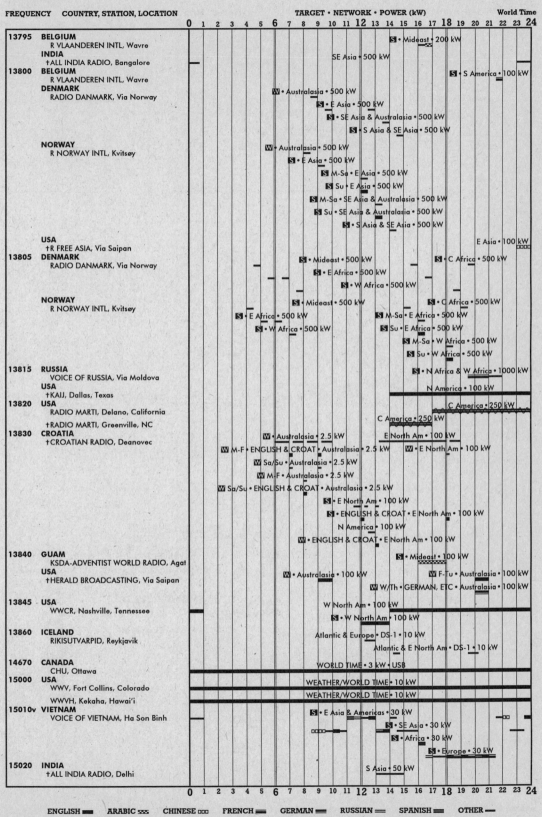

Frequency	Country, Station, Location	Target • Network • Power
13795	**BELGIUM** R VLAANDEREN INTL, Wavre	S • Mideast • 200 kW
	INDIA †ALL INDIA RADIO, Bangalore	SE Asia • 500 kW
13800	**BELGIUM** R VLAANDEREN INTL, Wavre	S • S America • 100 kW
	DENMARK RADIO DANMARK, Via Norway	W • Australasia • 500 kW; S • E Asia • 500 kW; S • SE Asia & Australasia • 500 kW; S • S Asia & SE Asia • 500 kW
	NORWAY R NORWAY INTL, Kvitsøy	W • Australasia • 500 kW; S • E Asia • 500 kW; S • M-Sa • E Asia • 500 kW; S • Su • E Asia • 500 kW; S • M-Sa • SE Asia & Australasia • 500 kW; S • Su • SE Asia & Australasia • 500 kW; S • S Asia & SE Asia • 500 kW
	USA †R FREE ASIA, Via Saipan	E Asia • 100 kW
13805	**DENMARK** RADIO DANMARK, Via Norway	S • Mideast • 500 kW; S • E Africa • 500 kW; S • W Africa • 500 kW; S • C Africa • 500 kW
	NORWAY R NORWAY INTL, Kvitsøy	S • E Africa • 500 kW; S • W Africa • 500 kW; S • Mideast • 500 kW; S • M-Sa • E Africa • 500 kW; S • Su • E Africa • 500 kW; S • C Africa • 500 kW; S • M-Sa • W Africa • 500 kW; S • Su • W Africa • 500 kW
13815	**RUSSIA** VOICE OF RUSSIA, Via Moldova	S • N Africa & W Africa • 1000 kW
	USA †KAIJ, Dallas, Texas	N America • 100 kW
13820	**USA** RADIO MARTI, Delano, California	C America • 250 kW; C America • 250 kW
	†RADIO MARTI, Greenville, NC	E North Am • 100 kW
13830	**CROATIA** †CROATIAN RADIO, Deanovec	W • Australasia • 2.5 kW; W M-F • ENGLISH & CROAT • Australasia • 2.5 kW; W • E North Am • 100 kW; W Sa/Su • Australasia • 2.5 kW; W M-F • Australasia • 2.5 kW; W Sa/Su • ENGLISH & CROAT • Australasia • 2.5 kW; S • E North Am • 100 kW; S • ENGLISH & CROAT • E North Am • 100 kW; N America • 100 kW; W • ENGLISH & CROAT • E North Am • 100 kW
13840	**GUAM** KSDA-ADVENTIST WORLD RADIO, Agat	S • Mideast • 100 kW
	USA †HERALD BROADCASTING, Via Saipan	W • Australasia • 100 kW; W F-Tu • Australasia • 100 kW; W W/Th • GERMAN, ETC • Australasia • 100 kW
13845	**USA** WWCR, Nashville, Tennessee	W North Am • 100 kW; S • W North Am • 100 kW
13860	**ICELAND** RIKISUTVARPID, Reykjavik	Atlantic & Europe • DS-1 • 10 kW; Atlantic & E North Am • DS-1 • 10 kW
14670	**CANADA** CHU, Ottawa	WORLD TIME • 3 kW • USB
15000	**USA** WWV, Fort Collins, Colorado	WEATHER/WORLD TIME • 10 kW
	WWVH, Kekaha, Hawai'i	WEATHER/WORLD TIME • 10 kW
15010v	**VIETNAM** VOICE OF VIETNAM, Ha Son Binh	S • E Asia & Americas • 30 kW; S • SE Asia • 30 kW; S • Africa • 30 kW; S • Europe • 30 kW
15020	**INDIA** †ALL INDIA RADIO, Delhi	S Asia • 50 kW

ENGLISH ▬   ARABIC ⧖   CHINESE ▭▭▭   FRENCH ▬▬   GERMAN ▬▬   RUSSIAN ═══   SPANISH ▬▬   OTHER ▬

FREQUENCY	COUNTRY, STATION, LOCATION	TARGET • NETWORK • POWER (kW)	World Time

World Time scale: 0 1 2 3 4 5 6 7 8 9 10 11 12 13 14 15 16 17 18 19 20 21 22 23 24

15050 INDIA
 †ALL INDIA RADIO, Aligarh
  - W Asia • 250 kW
  - SE Asia • 250 kW
  - Mideast • 250 kW
  - Australasia • 250 kW
  - Irr • Mideast • HAJJ • 250 kW

 ALL INDIA RADIO, Delhi
  - E Asia • 250 kW

15050v COSTA RICA
 †RADIO FOR PEACE INTL, Ciudad Colón
  - S • N America • 10 kW
  - N America • 10 kW

15060 SAUDI ARABIA
 BS OF THE KINGDOM, Riyadh
  - Mideast • 500 kW
  - N Africa • DS-GENERAL • 500 kW

15075 INDIA
 †ALL INDIA RADIO, Bangalore
  - W Asia, Mideast & E Africa • 500 kW
  - E Africa • 500 kW
  - S Asia • 50 kW

 †ALL INDIA RADIO, Delhi
  - E Africa • 250 kW

15084 IRAN
 VO THE ISLAMIC REP, Tehrān
  - DS • 500 kW

15095 PHILIPPINES
 †FEBC RADIO INTL, Bocaue
  - Europe • 500 kW
  - SE Asia • 50 kW

 SYRIA
 RADIO DAMASCUS, Adhra
  - S America • 500 kW • ALT. FREQ. TO 13610 kHz
  - E Europe & Mideast • 500 kW • ALT. FREQ. TO 13610 kHz
  - E Europe • 500 kW • ALT. FREQ. TO 13610 kHz
  - Europe • 500 kW • ALT. FREQ. TO 13610 kHz
  - Australasia • 500 kW • ALT. FREQ. TO 13610 kHz

 SYRIAN BC SERVICE, Adhra
  - DS • 500 kW • ALT. FREQ. TO 13610 kHz

15105 GERMANY
 †DEUTSCHE WELLE, Nauen
  - S • SE Asia • 500 kW
 DEUTSCHE WELLE, Via Antigua
  - S America • 250 kW
 DEUTSCHE WELLE, Via Sri Lanka
  - W • S Africa • 250 kW
 †DEUTSCHE WELLE, Wertachtal
  - S • Mideast & W Asia • 500 kW
  - S • E Asia • 500 kW

 ROMANIA
 RADIO ROMANIA, Bucharest
  - W • Europe, N Africa & Mideast • DS-1 (ACTUALITATI) • 100 kW
  - Europe, N Africa & Mideast • DS-1 (ACTUALITATI) • 100 kW
  - S • Europe, N Africa & Mideast • DS-1 (ACTUALITATI) • 100 kW

 UNITED KINGDOM
 BBC, Various Locations
  - N Africa • 250/500 kW
 BBC, Via Ascension
  - W Africa • 250 kW
  - W Africa & C Africa • 250 kW

 USA
 †RFE-RL, Via Briech, Morocco
  - S • E Europe • 500 kW
 WORLD HARVEST R, Noblesville, Indiana
  - C America • 100 kW

15110 CHINA
 †CHINA RADIO INTL, Via Bamako, Mali
  - C Africa & S Africa • 50 kW
  - S Africa • 50 kW • ALT. FREQ. TO 9770 kHz

 KUWAIT
 RADIO KUWAIT, Kabd
  - S Asia & SE Asia • 500 kW
 RUSSIA
 VOICE OF RUSSIA, Samara
  - S • S Asia • 240 kW
 SPAIN
 R EXTERIOR ESPANA, Noblejas
  - W • Mideast • 350 kW
  - S • Mideast • 350 kW
  - Mideast • 350 kW

15115 ECUADOR
 †HCJB-VO THE ANDES, Quito
  - N America & S America • 100 kW
 EGYPT
 EGYPTIAN RADIO, Abu Za'bal
  - W Africa • DS-GENERAL • 100 kW
 NEW ZEALAND
 †R NEW ZEALAND INTL, Rangitaiki
  - ENGLISH, ETC • Pacific • 100 kW
  - W • M-Th • Pacific • 100 kW
  - W • ENGLISH, ETC • Pacific • 100 kW

 THAILAND
 RADIO THAILAND, Udon Thani
  - Europe • 500 kW
 USA
 †RFE-RL, Via Briech, Morocco
  - S • E Europe • 500 kW
  - W • Mideast & W Asia • 500 kW

 RFE-RL, Via Pals, Spain
  - S • E Europe • 250 kW
 VOA, Via Pals, Spain
  - S • E Europe • 250 kW

15120 FINLAND
 YLE RADIO FINLAND, Pori
  - S • Sa/Su • E Asia & Australasia • 500 kW
 JAPAN
(con'd) RADIO JAPAN/NHK, Tokyo-Yamata
  - SE Asia • 100 kW

World Time scale: 0 1 2 3 4 5 6 7 8 9 10 11 12 13 14 15 16 17 18 19 20 21 22 23 24

FREQUENCY   COUNTRY, STATION, LOCATION   TARGET • NETWORK • POWER (kW)   World Time

	0 1 2 3 4 5 6 7 8 9 10 11 12 13 14 15 16 17 18 19 20 21 22 23 24

15120   **JAPAN**
(con'd)   RADIO JAPAN/NHK, Via Ascension — W Africa • 250 kW

PHILIPPINES
†RADYO PILIPINAS, Tinang — Mideast • 250 kW • ALT. FREQ. TO 15210 kHz

RUSSIA
VOICE OF RUSSIA, Via Armenia — W • S Asia • 1000 kW

SWEDEN
RADIO SWEDEN, Hörby — S Sa/Su • E Asia & Australasia • 500 kW
S • C America & S America • 500 kW

SWITZERLAND
†SWISS RADIO INTL, Schwarzenburg — S • SE Asia • 150 kW

UNITED KINGDOM
BBC, Rampisham — W M-F • E Europe • 500 kW

USA
VOA, Delano, California — ▣ • C America • 250 kW

†VOA, Greenville, NC — W • Europe • 500 kW

15120v   **CHINA**
CHINA RADIO INTL, Via Bamako, Mali — C America & S America • 50 kW

PAKISTAN
RADIO PAKISTAN, Karachi — S Asia & SE Asia • 50 kW • ALT. FREQ. TO 15190v kHz

15125   **CHINA (TAIWAN)**
BC CORP CHINA — S • DS(FM-1)

INDONESIA
†RRI, Jakarta, Jawa — DS(FM-1) ... Irr • DS • 100 kW

SPAIN
R EXTERIOR ESPANA, Noblejas — S • Mideast • 350 kW
S Sa/Su • C America & S America • 350 kW • ALT. FREQ. TO 17845 kHz
S Sa • C America & S America • 350 kW • ALT. FREQ. TO 17845 kHz

USA
†VOA, Via Briech, Morocco — W • S Europe • 500 kW
W • W Asia • 500 kW

15130   **CHINA (TAIWAN)**
VO FREE CHINA, Via Okeechobee, USA — S • S America • 100 kW

KOREA (DPR)
†RADIO PYONGYANG, Kujang-dong — N America • 200 kW

USA
†RFE-RL, Via Briech, Morocco — S • E Europe & W Asia • 500 kW

†RFE-RL, Via Lampertheim, Germany — S • E Europe & W Asia • 100 kW
S • C Asia • 100 kW

VOA, Via Lampertheim, Germany — S • E Europe & W Asia • 100 kW

WYFR-FAMILY RADIO, Okeechobee, Fl — S • S America • 100 kW
S • C America • 50 kW   S America • 100 kW
C America • 50 kW

15130v   **CHINA**
CHINA RADIO INTL, Via Bamako, Mali — S Africa • 50 kW

15135   **BRAZIL**
RADIO RECORD, São Paulo — Irr • DS • 7.5 kW • ▣

CHINA
CHINA RADIO INTL, Kunming — SE Asia • 120 kW

FRANCE
†R FRANCE INTL, Issoudun-Allouis — S • E Africa • 500 kW
E Africa • 500 kW
W • E Africa • 500 kW

GERMANY
†DEUTSCHE WELLE, Via Kigali, Rwanda — Africa • 250 kW   W • W Africa • 250 kW
W • Mideast & Africa • 250 kW
W Africa • 250 kW

INDIA
†ALL INDIA RADIO, Delhi — DS • 100 kW
ENGLISH, ETC • DS • 100 kW

USA
†VOA, Greenville, NC — S • Europe • 500 kW

15140   **ECUADOR**
†HCJB-VO THE ANDES, Quito — N America & S America • 50 kW

INDIA
ALL INDIA RADIO, Bangalore — E Europe • 500 kW

PALAU
KHBN-VO HOPE, Koror — E Asia & SE Asia • TEMP INACTIVE • 100 kW

USA
†VOA, Via Briech, Morocco — S • S Europe • 500 kW

15145   **FINLAND**
YLE RADIO FINLAND, Pori — S • E Africa • 500 kW

GERMANY
†DEUTSCHE WELLE, Via Madagascar — W • E Africa • 200 kW

†DEUTSCHE WELLE, Wertachtal — W • Mideast & W Asia • 500 kW
W • E Africa & S Africa • 500 kW

(con'd)

	0 1 2 3 4 5 6 7 8 9 10 11 12 13 14 15 16 17 18 19 20 21 22 23 24

ENGLISH ▬   ARABIC ⨯⨯⨯   CHINESE □□□   FRENCH ▬   GERMAN ▬   RUSSIAN ═   SPANISH ▬   OTHER ▬

FREQUENCY	COUNTRY, STATION, LOCATION	TARGET • NETWORK • POWER (kW)	World Time

Time scale: 0 1 2 3 4 5 6 7 8 9 10 11 12 13 14 15 16 17 18 19 20 21 22 23 24

Frequency	Country / Station / Location	Schedule
15145 (con'd)	**TURKEY** — VOICE OF TURKEY, Ankara	⮂ • W Asia • 250 kW
	USA — †RFE-RL, Via Kaválla, Greece	S • W Asia & C Asia • 250 kW
	RFE-RL, Via Lampertheim, Germany	S • E Europe & W Asia • 100 kW
	RFE-RL, Via Woofferton, UK	S • E Europe • 300 kW
	VOA, Via Kaválla, Greece	S • Mideast & W Asia • 250 kW
	†VOA, Via Philippines	W • SE Asia • 50 kW
	WYFR-FAMILY RADIO, Okeechobee, Fl	S • C America • 100 kW
15150	**CANADA** — R CANADA INTL, Sackville, NB	⮂ • Africa • 100 kW
	GREECE — FONI TIS HELLADAS, Various Locations	Africa • 100/250 kW
	INDONESIA — RRI, Jakarta, Jawa	DS • 100 kW
	USA — †VOA, Via Udon Thani, Thailand	S • E Asia • 500 kW
15155	**EGYPT** — RADIO CAIRO, Abu Za'bal	E Africa • 100 kW
	FRANCE — †R FRANCE INTL, Issoudun-Allouis	S • E Africa • 500 kW W • E Europe • 500 kW
		E Africa • 500 kW S • E Europe • 500 kW
		E Europe • 500 kW
	HOLLAND — R NEDERLAND, Via Neth Antilles	S • E North Am • 250 kW
15160	**EGYPT** — RADIO CAIRO	Mideast & W Asia
	HUNGARY — RADIO BUDAPEST, Jászberény	S • Australasia • 250 kW
		S • Su • Australasia • 250 kW
	USA — VOA, Delano, California	S • C America • 250 kW
	VOA, Via Kaválla, Greece	Mideast • 250 kW
	†VOA, Via Philippines	S • E Asia • 250 kW
15160v	**ALGERIA** — †RTV ALGERIENNE, Bouchaoui	W • Europe • 100 kW
		S • Europe • 100 kW
15165	**RUSSIA** — †MARIY RADIO, Yoshkar Ola	⮂ • RUSSIAN, ETC • DS-LOCAL, R ROSSII • 5 kW
	SAUDI ARABIA — BS OF THE KINGDOM, Jiddah	N Africa • DS-HOLY KORAN • 50 kW
	BS OF THE KINGDOM, Riyadh	E Africa • 500 kW • ALT. FREQ. TO 15335 kHz
	UZBEKISTAN — UZBEK RADIO, Tashkent	E Europe & W Asia • DS-2 • 50/100 kW
15167v	**FRENCH POLYNESIA** — †RFO POLYNESIE FRANCAISE, Papeete	Pacific • DS-FRENCH, TAHITIAN • 5 kW
15170	**MONGOLIA** — †VOICE OF MONGOLIA, Ulaanbaatar	E Asia • 250 kW • ALT. FREQ. TO 12085v kHz
	RUSSIA — VOICE OF RUSSIA, Via Armenia	S • S Asia & SE Asia • 100 kW
	USA — †R FREE ASIA	S • SE Asia
	†VOA, Via Briech, Morocco	S • S Europe • 500 kW
	WYFR-FAMILY RADIO, Okeechobee, Fl	W • S America • 100 kW
		S • C Africa & S Africa • 100 kW
15175	**BELARUS** — BELARUSSIAN R	⮂ • DS
	DENMARK — RADIO DANMARK, Via Norway	W • Australasia • 500 kW
	GREECE — FONI TIS HELLADAS, Kaválla	S • Europe & N America • 250 kW
	INDIA — †ALL INDIA RADIO, Bangalore	E Africa • 500 kW
	NORWAY — R NORWAY INTL, Kvitsøy	W • Australasia • 500 kW
	PAKISTAN — RADIO PAKISTAN, Islamabad	Mideast • 100 kW
	YUGOSLAVIA — †RADIO YUGOSLAVIA, Via Bosnia	⮂ • N Africa & W Africa • 250 kW
15175v	**SAUDI ARABIA** — BS OF THE KINGDOM, Riyadh	W Europe • DS-GENERAL • 500 kW • ALT. FREQ. TO 15230v kHz
15180	**CHINA** — CHINA RADIO INTL, Xi'an	E Asia • 150 kW
	INDIA — ALL INDIA RADIO, Delhi	E Africa • 250 kW
	KOREA (DPR) — †RADIO PYONGYANG, Kujang-dong	C America • 200 kW
		SE Asia • 200 kW
(con'd)		

FREQUENCY   COUNTRY, STATION, LOCATION

TARGET • NETWORK • POWER (kW)

World Time

0 1 2 3 4 5 6 7 8 9 10 11 12 13 14 15 16 17 18 19 20 21 22 23 24

Frequency	Country, Station, Location	Target • Network • Power
15180 (con'd)	ROMANIA RADIO ROMANIA INTL, Bucharest	S • E North Am • 250 kW
	RUSSIA VOICE OF RUSSIA, Komsomol'sk 'Amure	S • W North Am • 100 kW
	UNITED KINGDOM BBC, Skelton, Cumbria	N Africa • 300 kW
	USA VOA, Via Philippines	Pacific • 50 kW
15185	BULGARIA RADIO BULGARIA, Plovdiv	S • Europe • 250 kW
	FINLAND YLE RADIO FINLAND, Pori	S • S Asia • 500 kW
	GERMANY DEUTSCHE WELLE, Via Sri Lanka	E Asia • 250 kW
	DEUTSCHE WELLE, Wertachtal	S • W Africa • 500 kW
		W Africa • 500 kW
	INDIA †ALL INDIA RADIO, Delhi	ENGLISH & HINDI • DS • 100 kW
		DS • 100 kW
	TURKEY VOICE OF TURKEY, Ankara-Emirler	S • E Asia • 500 kW
	UNITED KINGDOM BBC, Via Zyyi, Cyprus	S • W Asia & C Asia • 250 kW
	USA VOA, Via Kaválla, Greece	S • W Asia & S Asia • 250 kW
	†VOA, Via Philippines	SE Asia & S Pacific • 50 kW
	VOA, Via Woofferton, UK	S • C Asia • 300 kW
		S • Sa/Su • C Asia • 300 kW
15186v	EQUATORIAL GUINEA RADIO AFRICA, Bata	M-F • S Africa • 50 kW W Africa • 50 kW • ALT. FREQ. TO 7190v kHz
	RADIO EAST AFRICA, Bata	Sa/Su • ENGLISH & FRENCH • E Africa • 50 kW
15189.8	BRAZIL R INCONFIDENCIA, Belo Horizonte	DS • 5 kW
15190	CHINA †CENTRAL PEOPLE'S BS	DS-1
		W-M • DS-1
	PHILIPPINES RADYO PILIPINAS, Tinang	Mideast • 250 kW
	UNITED KINGDOM BBC, Via Ascension	S America • 250 kW
		Sa/Su • S America • 250 kW
		M-F • S America • 250 kW
15190v	PAKISTAN RADIO PAKISTAN, Karachi	S Asia & SE Asia • 50 kW • ALT. FREQ. TO 15120v kHz
15195	CANADA R CANADA INTL, Via Tokyo, Japan	S • SE Asia • 300 kW
	FRANCE †R FRANCE INTL, Issoudun-Allouis	E Europe • 500 kW
		S • E Europe • 500 kW
	SWAZILAND TRANS WORLD RADIO, Manzini	W Asia & S Asia • 100 kW
	USA VOA, Via Kaválla, Greece	S • S Asia • 250 kW
	†VOA, Via Philippines	S • E Asia • 250 kW
15200	FRANCE R FRANCE INTL, Via French Guiana	W • S America • 500 kW S America • 500 kW
		S • C America • 500 kW
	GUAM †KTWR-TRANS WORLD RADIO, Merizo	SE Asia • 100 kW
	IRAN VO THE ISLAMIC REP, Tehrān	W Africa & C Africa • 500 kW
	PORTUGAL †RDP INTERNATIONAL, Lisbon	Sa/Su//Holidays • E North Am • 100 kW
	UZBEKISTAN †UZBEK RADIO, Tashkent	S • Mideast & W Asia • DS-2 • 100 kW
15205	GERMANY DEUTSCHE WELLE, Via Antigua	S America • 250 kW
	†DEUTSCHE WELLE, Via Madagascar	S • E Africa • 200 kW
	USA RFE-RL, Via Kaválla, Greece	S • C Asia • 250 kW
	RFE-RL, Via Pals, Spain	W • E Europe & W Asia • 250 kW
	†VOA, Via Briech, Morocco	S • S Europe • 500 kW
	VOA, Via Kaválla, Greece	S • Mideast & S Asia • 250 kW W • Mideast & S Asia • 250 kW
		Mideast & S Asia • 250 kW
	VOA, Via Pals, Spain	W • E Europe & W Asia • 250 kW
(con'd)	†VOA, Via Philippines	W • SE Asia • 50 kW SE Asia • 50 kW

0 1 2 3 4 5 6 7 8 9 10 11 12 13 14 15 16 17 18 19 20 21 22 23 24

ENGLISH ▬▬   ARABIC ⧓⧓⧓   CHINESE □□□   FRENCH ══   GERMAN ▬▬   RUSSIAN ══   SPANISH ══   OTHER ▬

FREQUENCY   COUNTRY, STATION, LOCATION   TARGET • NETWORK • POWER (kW)   World Time

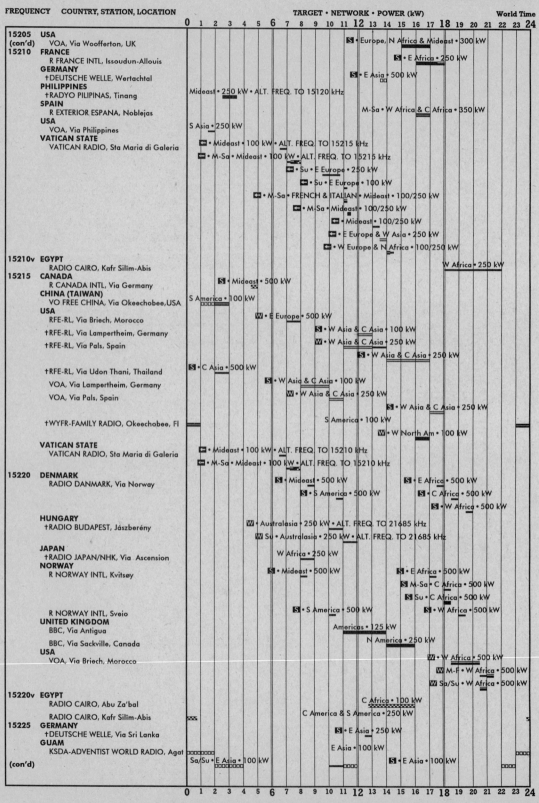

15205 **USA**
(con'd)   VOA, Via Woofferton, UK — Ⓢ • Europe, N Africa & Mideast • 300 kW
15210 **FRANCE**
   R FRANCE INTL, Issoudun-Allouis — Ⓢ • E Africa • 250 kW
   GERMANY
   †DEUTSCHE WELLE, Wertachtal — Ⓢ • E Asia • 500 kW
   PHILIPPINES
   †RADYO PILIPINAS, Tinang — Mideast • 250 kW • ALT. FREQ. TO 15120 kHz
   SPAIN
   R EXTERIOR ESPANA, Noblejas — M-Sa • W Africa & C Africa • 350 kW
   USA
   VOA, Via Philippines — S Asia • 250 kW
   VATICAN STATE
   VATICAN RADIO, Sta Maria di Galeria — ◨ • Mideast • 100 kW • ALT. FREQ. TO 15215 kHz
    ◨ • M-Sa • Mideast • 100 kW • ALT. FREQ. TO 15215 kHz
    ◨ • Su • E Europe • 250 kW
    ◨ • Su • E Europe • 100 kW
    ◨ • M-Sa • FRENCH & ITALIAN • Mideast • 100/250 kW
    ◨ • M-Sa • Mideast • 100/250 kW
    ◨ • Mideast • 100/250 kW
    ◨ • E Europe & W Asia • 250 kW
    ◨ • W Europe & N Africa • 100/250 kW

15210v **EGYPT**
   RADIO CAIRO, Kafr Silim-Abis — W Africa • 250 kW
15215 **CANADA**
   R CANADA INTL, Via Germany — Ⓢ • Mideast • 500 kW
   CHINA (TAIWAN)
   VO FREE CHINA, Via Okeechobee, USA — S America • 100 kW
   USA
   RFE-RL, Via Briech, Morocco — Ⓦ • E Europe • 500 kW
   †RFE-RL, Via Lampertheim, Germany — Ⓢ • W Asia & C Asia • 100 kW
   †RFE-RL, Via Pals, Spain — Ⓦ • W Asia & C Asia • 250 kW
    Ⓢ • W Asia & C Asia • 250 kW
   †RFE-RL, Via Udon Thani, Thailand — Ⓢ • C Asia • 500 kW
   VOA, Via Lampertheim, Germany — Ⓢ • W Asia & C Asia • 100 kW
   VOA, Via Pals, Spain — Ⓦ • W Asia & C Asia • 250 kW
    Ⓢ • W Asia & C Asia • 250 kW
   †WYFR-FAMILY RADIO, Okeechobee, Fl — S America • 100 kW
    Ⓦ • W North Am • 100 kW
   VATICAN STATE
   VATICAN RADIO, Sta Maria di Galeria — ◨ • Mideast • 100 kW • ALT. FREQ. TO 15210 kHz
    ◨ • M-Sa • Mideast • 100 kW • ALT. FREQ. TO 15210 kHz
15220 **DENMARK**
   RADIO DANMARK, Via Norway — Ⓢ • Mideast • 500 kW
    Ⓢ • E Africa • 500 kW
    Ⓢ • S America • 500 kW
    Ⓢ • C Africa • 500 kW
    Ⓢ • W Africa • 500 kW
   HUNGARY
   †RADIO BUDAPEST, Jászberény — Ⓦ • Australasia • 250 kW • ALT. FREQ. TO 21685 kHz
    Ⓦ Su • Australasia • 250 kW • ALT. FREQ. TO 21685 kHz
   JAPAN
   †RADIO JAPAN/NHK, Via Ascension — W Africa • 250 kW
   NORWAY
   R NORWAY INTL, Kvitsøy — Ⓢ • Mideast • 500 kW
    Ⓢ • E Africa • 500 kW
    Ⓢ M-Sa • C Africa • 500 kW
    Ⓢ Su • C Africa • 500 kW
   R NORWAY INTL, Sveio — Ⓢ • S America • 500 kW
    Ⓢ • W Africa • 500 kW
   UNITED KINGDOM
   BBC, Via Antigua — Americas • 125 kW
   BBC, Via Sackville, Canada — N America • 250 kW
   USA
   VOA, Via Briech, Morocco — Ⓦ • W Africa • 500 kW
    Ⓦ M-F • W Africa • 500 kW
    Ⓦ Sa/Su • W Africa • 500 kW

15220v **EGYPT**
   RADIO CAIRO, Abu Za'bal — C Africa • 100 kW
   RADIO CAIRO, Kafr Silim-Abis — C America & S America • 250 kW
15225 **GERMANY**
   †DEUTSCHE WELLE, Via Sri Lanka — Ⓢ • E Asia • 250 kW
   GUAM
   KSDA-ADVENTIST WORLD RADIO, Agat — E Asia • 100 kW
    Sa/Su • E Asia • 100 kW
(con'd)   Ⓢ • E Asia • 100 kW

0 1 2 3 4 5 6 7 8 9 10 11 12 13 14 15 16 17 18 19 20 21 22 23 24

SEASONAL Ⓢ OR Ⓦ   1-HR TIMESHIFT MIDYEAR ◨ OR ◨   JAMMING / OR ∧   EARLIEST HEARD ◁   LATEST HEARD ▷   NEW FOR 1998 †

FREQUENCY   COUNTRY, STATION, LOCATION   TARGET • NETWORK • POWER (kW)   World Time

0 1 2 3 4 5 6 7 8 9 10 11 12 13 14 15 16 17 18 19 20 21 22 23 24

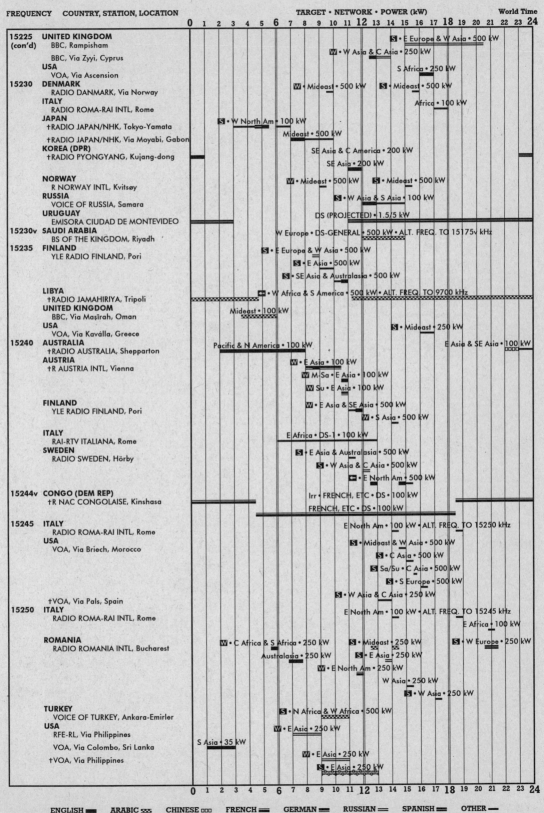

15225 **UNITED KINGDOM**
(con'd)   BBC, Rampisham — S • E Europe & W Asia • 500 kW

          BBC, Via Zyyi, Cyprus — W • W Asia & C Asia • 250 kW
          USA
          VOA, Via Ascension — S Africa • 250 kW
15230 **DENMARK**
          RADIO DANMARK, Via Norway — W • Mideast • 500 kW   S • Mideast • 500 kW
          ITALY
          RADIO ROMA-RAI INTL, Rome — Africa • 100 kW
          JAPAN
          †RADIO JAPAN/NHK, Tokyo-Yamata — S • W North Am • 100 kW

          †RADIO JAPAN/NHK, Via Moyabi, Gabon — Mideast • 500 kW
          KOREA (DPR)
          †RADIO PYONGYANG, Kujang-dong — SE Asia & C America • 200 kW
                                          SE Asia • 200 kW

          NORWAY
          R NORWAY INTL, Kvitsøy — W • Mideast • 500 kW   S • Mideast • 500 kW
          RUSSIA
          VOICE OF RUSSIA, Samara — S • W Asia & S Asia • 100 kW
          URUGUAY
          EMISORA CIUDAD DE MONTEVIDEO — DS (PROJECTED) • 1.5/5 kW
15230v **SAUDI ARABIA**
          BS OF THE KINGDOM, Riyadh — W Europe • DS-GENERAL • 500 kW • ALT. FREQ. TO 15175v kHz
15235 **FINLAND**
          YLE RADIO FINLAND, Pori — S • E Europe & W Asia • 500 kW
                                    S • E Asia • 500 kW
                                    S • SE Asia & Australasia • 500 kW

          LIBYA
          †RADIO JAMAHIRIYA, Tripoli — W Africa & S America • 500 kW • ALT. FREQ. TO 9700 kHz
          UNITED KINGDOM
          BBC, Via Maşirah, Oman — Mideast • 100 kW
          USA
          VOA, Via Kaválla, Greece — S • Mideast • 250 kW
15240 **AUSTRALIA**
          †RADIO AUSTRALIA, Shepparton — Pacific & N America • 100 kW   E Asia & SE Asia • 100 kW
          AUSTRIA
          †R AUSTRIA INTL, Vienna — W • E Asia • 100 kW
                                    W • M-Sa • E Asia • 100 kW
                                    W • Su • E Asia • 100 kW

          FINLAND
          YLE RADIO FINLAND, Pori — W • E Asia & SE Asia • 500 kW
                                    W • S Asia • 500 kW

          ITALY
          RAI-RTV ITALIANA, Rome — E Africa • DS-1 • 100 kW
          SWEDEN
          RADIO SWEDEN, Hörby — S • E Asia & Australasia • 500 kW
                                S • W Asia & C Asia • 500 kW
                                E North Am • 500 kW

15244v **CONGO (DEM REP)**
          †R NAC CONGOLAISE, Kinshasa — Irr • FRENCH, ETC • DS • 100 kW
                                        FRENCH, ETC • DS • 100 kW

15245 **ITALY**
          RADIO ROMA-RAI INTL, Rome — E North Am • 100 kW • ALT. FREQ. TO 15250 kHz
          USA
          VOA, Via Briech, Morocco — S • Mideast & W Asia • 500 kW
                                     S • C Asia • 500 kW
                                     S • Sa/Su • C Asia • 500 kW
                                     S • S Europe • 500 kW
                                     S • W Asia & C Asia • 250 kW
          †VOA, Via Pals, Spain
15250 **ITALY**
          RADIO ROMA-RAI INTL, Rome — E North Am • 100 kW • ALT. FREQ. TO 15245 kHz
                                      E Africa • 100 kW

          ROMANIA
          RADIO ROMANIA INTL, Bucharest — W • C Africa & S Africa • 250 kW   S • Mideast • 250 kW   S • W Europe • 250 kW
                                          Australasia • 250 kW   S • E Asia • 250 kW
                                          W • E North Am • 250 kW
                                          W Asia • 250 kW
                                          S • W Asia • 250 kW

          TURKEY
          VOICE OF TURKEY, Ankara-Emirler — S • N Africa & W Africa • 500 kW
          USA
          RFE-RL, Via Philippines — W • E Asia • 250 kW
          VOA, Via Colombo, Sri Lanka — S Asia • 35 kW
          †VOA, Via Philippines — W • E Asia • 250 kW
                                  S • E Asia • 250 kW

0 1 2 3 4 5 6 7 8 9 10 11 12 13 14 15 16 17 18 19 20 21 22 23 24

FREQUENCY	COUNTRY, STATION, LOCATION	TARGET • NETWORK • POWER (kW)	World Time

0 1 2 3 4 5 6 7 8 9 10 11 12 13 14 15 16 17 18 19 20 21 22 23 24

15255	**USA**	
	RFE-RL, Via Udon Thani, Thailand	S • C Asia & W Asia • 500 kW
	VOA, Via Briech, Morocco	S • E Europe • 500 kW
	VOA, Via Kaválla, Greece	S • Mideast • 250 kW
	VOA, Via Philippines	W • M-F • E Asia & Australasia • 50 kW
	WYFR-FAMILY RADIO, Okeechobee, Fl	S • S America • 100 kW
15255v	**EGYPT**	
	RADIO CAIRO, Abu Za'bal	C Africa & S Africa • 100 kW
15260	**CHINA**	
	CHINA RADIO INTL, Xi'an	SE Asia • 150 kW
	INDIA	
	ALL INDIA RADIO, Delhi	DS • 100 kW
		ENGLISH & HINDI • DS • 100 kW
	IRAN	
	†VO THE ISLAMIC REP, Tehrān	S • S Europe & N Africa • 500 kW S Asia & SE Asia • 500 kW
		S Europe & N Africa • 500 kW
		S • Mideast & N Africa • 500 kW
15265	**BRAZIL**	
	RADIO NACIONAL, Brasilia	Europe & Mideast • 250 kW
	QATAR	
	†QATAR BC SERVICE, Doha-Al Khaisah	Mideast & N Africa • 250 kW • ALT. FREQ. TO 15395 kHz
	UNITED ARAB EMIRATES	
	UAE RADIO FROM ABU DHABI	S • Europe • 500 kW S • N Africa • 500 kW
	USA	
	†VOA, Greenville, NC	M-F • S America • 250 kW
15270	**ARMENIA**	
	RADIO INTERCONTINENTAL, Kamo	⟷ • Europe • 1000 kW
		S • Europe • 1000 kW
	VOICE OF ARMENIA, Kamo	⟷ • Su • Europe • 1000 kW • ALT. FREQ. TO 15370 kHz
		⟷ • Su • Europe • 1000 kW
	CHINA (TAIWAN)	
	BC CORP CHINA, T'ai-pei	DS-NEWS NETWORK • 100 kW
	†VO FREE CHINA, T'ai-pei	SE Asia • 100 kW
		Mideast & N Africa • 250 kW • ALT. FREQ. TO 11550 kHz
	DENMARK	
	RADIO DANMARK, Via Norway	W • S America • 500 kW
	NORWAY	
	R NORWAY INTL, Sveio	W • S America • 500 kW
	PHILIPPINES	
	†RADYO PILIPINAS, Tinang	Mideast • 250 kW
	ROMANIA	
	RADIO ROMANIA INTL, Bucharest	S • E Asia • 250 kW
15275	**GERMANY**	
	†DEUTSCHE WELLE, Nauen	Africa • 500 kW S • S Asia • 500 kW
		S • Mideast • 100 kW
		W • S Europe • 500 kW
	†DEUTSCHE WELLE, Via Kigali, Rwanda	C America • 250 kW W • W Africa & Americas • 250 kW
		S • S Asia & SE Asia • 250 kW
		W • C America • 250 kW
	†DEUTSCHE WELLE, Wertachtal	S • W Africa & S America • 500 kW
15280	**CLANDESTINE (ASIA)**	
	"VOICE OF CHINA", Taiwan	E Asia • 100 kW
	UNITED ARAB EMIRATES	
	†UAE RADIO FROM ABU DHABI	W • Mideast • 500 kW
	UNITED KINGDOM	
	†BBC, Various Locations	E Asia & SE Asia • 100/250 kW
	†BBC, Via Maṣīrah, Oman	SE Asia • 100 kW
		W • S Asia • 100 kW
	BBC, Via Thailand	E Asia • 250 kW
	USA	
	†HERALD BROADCASTING, S Carolina	S • M • S America • 500 kW
		S • Tu/Th/F • S America • 500 kW
		S • W/Su • S America • 500 kW
		S • Su/M • S America • 500 kW
		S • Tu/Th • S America • 500 kW
		S • W/F/Sa • S America • 500 kW
		S • S Europe • 500 kW
	†VOA, Via Briech, Morocco	
15280v	**SAUDI ARABIA**	
	BS OF THE KINGDOM, Jiddah	Mideast • DS-HOLY KORAN • 50 kW
15285	**EGYPT**	
	EGYPTIAN RADIO, Abu Za'bal	⟷ • Mideast • DS-VO THE ARABS • 100 kW
	GERMANY	
(con'd)	†DEUTSCHE WELLE, Via Antigua	S • S America • 250 kW

0 1 2 3 4 5 6 7 8 9 10 11 12 13 14 15 16 17 18 19 20 21 22 23 24

SEASONAL S OR W   1-HR TIMESHIFT MIDYEAR ⟷ OR ⟶   JAMMING / OR /\   EARLIEST HEARD ◁   LATEST HEARD ▷   NEW FOR 1998 †

FREQUENCY COUNTRY, STATION, LOCATION

TARGET • NETWORK • POWER (kW)

World Time

0 1 2 3 4 5 6 7 8 9 10 11 12 13 14 15 16 17 18 19 20 21 22 23 24

Freq	Country, Station, Location	Target • Network • Power
15285 (con'd)	**GERMANY** †DEUTSCHE WELLE, Via Antigua	N America & C America • 250 kW
15290	**USA** †RFE-RL, Via Kazakhstan	E Asia • 100 kW
	VOA, Via Philippines	E Asia • 250 kW
15295	**ECUADOR** HCJB-VO THE ANDES, Quito	S America • 100 kW
	MALAYSIA †VOICE OF MALAYSIA, Kajang	Australasia • 100 kW / Mideast • 100 kW
	UZBEKISTAN RADIO TASHKENT, Tashkent	S Asia • 100 kW
15295v	**MOZAMBIQUE** RADIO MOCAMBIQUE, Maputo	Irr • DS • 100 kW
15300	**FRANCE** †R FRANCE INTL, Issoudun-Allouis	Africa • 500 kW
	†R FRANCE INTL, Multiple Locations	Africa • 500 kW
	USA †VOA, Via Philippines	E Asia • 250 kW
	†VOA, Via Udon Thani, Thailand	S Asia • 500 kW
15305	**CANADA** †R CANADA INTL, Sackville, NB	E North Am & C America • 250 kW
		Su • E North Am & C America • 100 kW
		M-Sa • Europe • 250 kW
		C America & S America • 100 kW
		M-F • C America & S America • 100 kW
		Sa/Su • C America & S America • 100 kW
	DENMARK RADIO DANMARK, Via Norway	E Asia • 500 kW
	NORWAY R NORWAY INTL, Kvitsøy	M-Sa • E Asia • 500 kW
		Su • E Asia • 500 kW
		E Asia • 500 kW
	USA VOA, Various Locations	Mideast • 250/500 kW
	†VOA, Via Briech, Morocco	Mideast • 500 kW
	VOA, Via Philippines	E Asia & Australasia • 35 kW
15310	**GUAM** KSDA-ADVENTIST WORLD RADIO, Agat	E Asia • 100 kW
	ITALY RADIO ROMA-RAI INTL, Rome	N Africa • 100 kW
	UNITED KINGDOM BBC, Via Maṣīrah, Oman	W Asia & S Asia • 100 kW
		S Asia • 100 kW
15315	**FRANCE** †R FRANCE INTL, Issoudun-Allouis	N Africa & W Africa • 500 kW
	HOLLAND R NEDERLAND, Via Neth Antilles	S America • 250 kW
		W Africa • 250 kW
	IRAN VO THE ISLAMIC REP, Tehrān	W Africa • 500 kW
	MOLDOVA RADIO MOLDOVA INTL, Via Romania	C America • 100 kW
	UNITED ARAB EMIRATES †UAE RADIO FROM ABU DHABI	E Asia • 500 kW / E Asia • 500 kW
	UNITED KINGDOM BBC, Via Delano, USA	M-F • C America & S America • 250 kW
15320	**CHINA (TAIWAN)** †CENTRAL BC SYSTEM, T'ai-pei	E Asia • NETWORK 1 • 100 kW
	ITALY RADIO ROMA-RAI INTL, Via Ascension	S Africa • 250 kW
	RUSSIA VOICE OF RUSSIA, Via Belarus	Mideast & W Asia • 100 kW
15325	**BRAZIL** RADIO GAZETA, São Paulo	DS • 1/10 kW
	CANADA †R CANADA INTL, Sackville, NB	Su • C America • 250 kW
		M-Sa • Europe • 100 kW
		Europe • 100/250 kW
		Europe • 250 kW
	R CANADA INTL, Via Sines, Portugal	Europe • 250 kW
		Europe • 250 kW
	R CANADA INTL, Via Skelton, UK	Europe • 300 kW
	UNITED KINGDOM BBC, Rampisham	E Europe • 500 kW
		Su • E Europe • 500 kW
	BBC, Via Zyyi, Cyprus	E Europe • 250 kW

0 1 2 3 4 5 6 7 8 9 10 11 12 13 14 15 16 17 18 19 20 21 22 23 24

ENGLISH ▬ ARABIC ⧉ CHINESE ▭ FRENCH ▬ GERMAN ▬ RUSSIAN ═ SPANISH ▬ OTHER —

FREQUENCY	COUNTRY, STATION, LOCATION	TARGET • NETWORK • POWER (kW)	World Time

0 1 2 3 4 5 6 7 8 9 10 11 12 13 14 15 16 17 18 19 20 21 22 23 24

15330	**CLANDESTINE (ASIA)**	
	†"DEMOCRAT VO BURMA", Via Germany	SE Asia • ANTI-MYANMAR GOVT • 100 kW
	FINLAND	
	YLE RADIO FINLAND, Pori	W Sa/Su • SE Asia & Australasia • 500 kW
	PHILIPPINES	
	†RADYO PILIPINAS, Poro	E Asia • 100 kW
	USA	
	RADIO MARTI, Delano, California	C America • 250 kW
	UZBEKISTAN	
	UZBEK RADIO, Tashkent	W • Mideast • DS-2 • 100 kW
15335	**EGYPT**	
	RADIO CAIRO, Kafr Silim-Abis	W Africa • 250 kW
	MOROCCO	
	RTV MAROCAINE, Briech	Europe • DS • 500 kW
	PHILIPPINES	
	RADIO VERITAS ASIA, Palauig	S Asia • 250 kW
	ROMANIA	
	RADIO ROMANIA INTL, Bucharest	Su • W Asia • 250 kW / S Asia • 250 kW
		Su • S Africa • 250 kW
	SAUDI ARABIA	
	BS OF THE KINGDOM, Riyadh	E Africa • 500 kW • ALT. FREQ. TO 15165 kHz
	USA	
	VOA, Greenville, NC	S • C America • 250 kW
15340	**CUBA**	
	†RADIO HABANA CUBA, Havana	S America • 50 kW
		S America • 100 kW
	DENMARK	
	RADIO DANMARK, Via Norway	S • N America • 500 kW
		S • W North Am • 350 kW
	INDIA	
	ALL INDIA RADIO, Bangalore	SE Asia • 500 kW
	ITALY	
	RADIO ROMA-RAI INTL, Rome	E Africa • 100 kW
	KOREA (DPR)	
	†RADIO PYONGYANG, Kujang-dong	C America • 200 kW
		C America & SE Asia • 200 kW
	NORWAY	
	R NORWAY INTL, Fredrikstad	S • W North Am • 350 kW
	R NORWAY INTL, Sveio	S • M-Sa • N America • 500 kW
		S • Su • N America • 500 kW
		S • N America • 500 kW
	ROMANIA	
	RADIO ROMANIA INTL, Bucharest	S • C Africa & S Africa • 250 kW / S • N Africa & Mideast • 250 kW
	RUSSIA	
	VOICE OF RUSSIA, Via Moldova	S • W Africa & S America • 500 kW
	UNITED KINGDOM	
	BBC, Rampisham	S • E Europe • 500 kW
	BBC, Via Singapore	E Asia • 100 kW / W • E Asia • 100 kW
	BBC, Via Zyyi, Cyprus	• Su • E Europe • 250 kW
		• E Europe • 250 kW
	USA	
	†RFE-RL, Via Kaválla, Greece	S • C Asia • 250 kW
	RFE-RL, Via Lampertheim, Germany	W • W Asia & C Asia • 100 kW
15345	**CHINA (TAIWAN)**	
	VO FREE CHINA, T'ai-pei	E Asia • 100 kW
		SE Asia • 100 kW
	MOROCCO	
	RTV MAROCAINE	DS • 100 kW
	SAUDI ARABIA	
	BS OF THE KINGDOM, Riyadh	S Asia • 500 kW
15345v	**ARGENTINA**	
	†R ARGENTINA-RAE, Buenos Aires	Tu-Sa • Americas • 50/100 kW / M-F • Europe & N Africa • 50/100 kW
		M-F • Americas • 50/100 kW
	†RADIO NACIONAL, Buenos Aires	Su/M • Americas • 50/100 kW
		M-F • ENA • 50/100 kW / Sa/Su • Europe & N Africa • 50/100 kW
		M-F • S America • 50/100 kW
15350	**IRAN**	
	†VO THE ISLAMIC REP	Mideast
	RUSSIA	
	VOICE OF RUSSIA, Armavir	S • Mideast & E Africa • 100 kW
	TURKEY	
	VOICE OF TURKEY, Ankara-Emirler	• Europe • 500 kW
15355	**JAPAN**	
	RADIO JAPAN/NHK, Via Moyabi, Gabon	S Africa • 500 kW
	JORDAN	
	RADIO JORDAN, Qasr el Kharana	• N Africa & C America • 500 kW
	USA	
(con'd)	RFE-RL, Via Briech, Morocco	S • C Asia • 500 kW

0 1 2 3 4 5 6 7 8 9 10 11 12 13 14 15 16 17 18 19 20 21 22 23 24

SEASONAL S OR W   1-HR TIMESHIFT MIDYEAR ◰ OR ◳   JAMMING / OR ∧   EARLIEST HEARD ◁   LATEST HEARD ▷   NEW FOR 1998 †

FREQUENCY	COUNTRY, STATION, LOCATION	TARGET • NETWORK • POWER (kW)	World Time

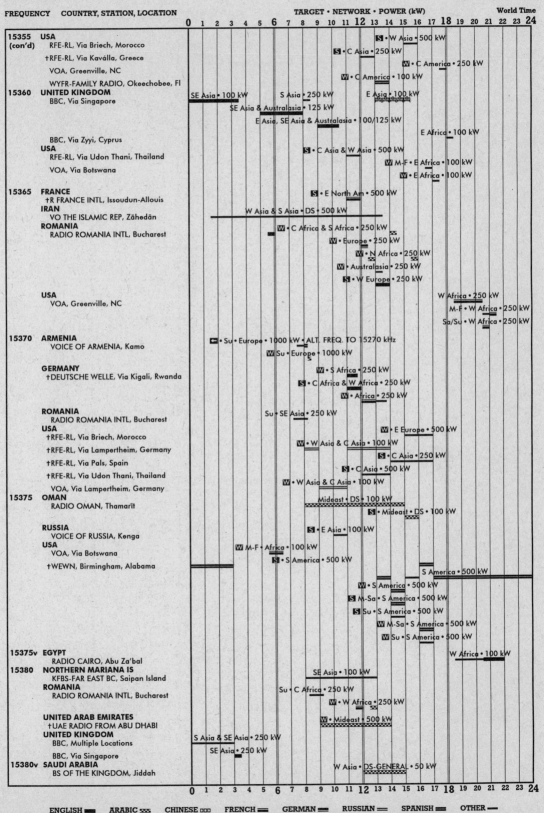

Frequency	Country, Station, Location	Target • Network • Power
15355 (con'd)	**USA**	S • W Asia • 500 kW
	RFE-RL, Via Briech, Morocco	S • C Asia • 250 kW
	†RFE-RL, Via Kaválla, Greece	W • C America • 250 kW
	VOA, Greenville, NC	W • C America • 100 kW
	WYFR-FAMILY RADIO, Okeechobee, Fl	
15360	**UNITED KINGDOM**	SE Asia • 100 kW S Asia • 250 kW E Asia • 100 kW
	BBC, Via Singapore	SE Asia & Australasia • 125 kW
		E Asia, SE Asia & Australasia • 100/125 kW
		E Africa • 100 kW
	BBC, Via Zyyi, Cyprus	
	USA	S • C Asia & W Asia • 500 kW
	RFE-RL, Via Udon Thani, Thailand	W • M-F • E Africa • 100 kW
	VOA, Via Botswana	W • E Africa • 100 kW
15365	**FRANCE**	S • E North Am • 500 kW
	†R FRANCE INTL, Issoudun-Allouis	
	IRAN	W Asia & S Asia • DS • 500 kW
	VO THE ISLAMIC REP, Zāhedān	
	ROMANIA	W • C Africa & S Africa • 250 kW
	RADIO ROMANIA INTL, Bucharest	W • Europe • 250 kW
		W • N Africa • 250 kW
		W • Australasia • 250 kW
		S • W Europe • 250 kW
	USA	W Africa • 250 kW
	VOA, Greenville, NC	M-F • W Africa • 250 kW
		Sa/Su • W Africa • 250 kW
15370	**ARMENIA**	• Su • Europe • 1000 kW • ALT. FREQ. TO 15270 kHz
	VOICE OF ARMENIA, Kamo	W Su • Europe • 1000 kW
	GERMANY	W • S Africa • 250 kW
	†DEUTSCHE WELLE, Via Kigali, Rwanda	S • C Africa & W Africa • 250 kW
		W • Africa • 250 kW
	ROMANIA	Su • SE Asia • 250 kW
	RADIO ROMANIA INTL, Bucharest	
	USA	W • E Europe • 500 kW
	†RFE-RL, Via Briech, Morocco	W • W Asia & C Asia • 100 kW
	†RFE-RL, Via Lampertheim, Germany	S • C Asia • 250 kW
	†RFE-RL, Via Pals, Spain	S • C Asia • 500 kW
	†RFE-RL, Via Udon Thani, Thailand	W • W Asia & C Asia • 100 kW
	VOA, Via Lampertheim, Germany	
15375	**OMAN**	Mideast • DS • 100 kW
	RADIO OMAN, Thamarīt	S • Mideast • DS • 100 kW
	RUSSIA	S • E Asia • 100 kW
	VOICE OF RUSSIA, Kenga	
	USA	W • M-F • Africa • 100 kW
	VOA, Via Botswana	S • S America • 500 kW
	†WEWN, Birmingham, Alabama	S America • 500 kW
		W • S America • 500 kW
		S M-Sa • S America • 500 kW
		S Su • S America • 500 kW
		W M-Sa • S America • 500 kW
		W Su • S America • 500 kW
15375v	**EGYPT**	W Africa • 100 kW
	RADIO CAIRO, Abu Za'bal	
15380	**NORTHERN MARIANA IS**	SE Asia • 100 kW
	KFBS-FAR EAST BC, Saipan Island	
	ROMANIA	Su • C Africa • 250 kW
	RADIO ROMANIA INTL, Bucharest	W • W Africa • 250 kW
	UNITED ARAB EMIRATES	W • Mideast • 500 kW
	†UAE RADIO FROM ABU DHABI	
	UNITED KINGDOM	S Asia & SE Asia • 250 kW
	BBC, Multiple Locations	SE Asia • 250 kW
	BBC, Via Singapore	
15380v	**SAUDI ARABIA**	W Asia • DS-GENERAL • 50 kW
	BS OF THE KINGDOM, Jiddah	

ENGLISH ▬   ARABIC ⧖   CHINESE ▫▫▫   FRENCH ══   GERMAN ▬▬   RUSSIAN ══   SPANISH ══   OTHER ▬

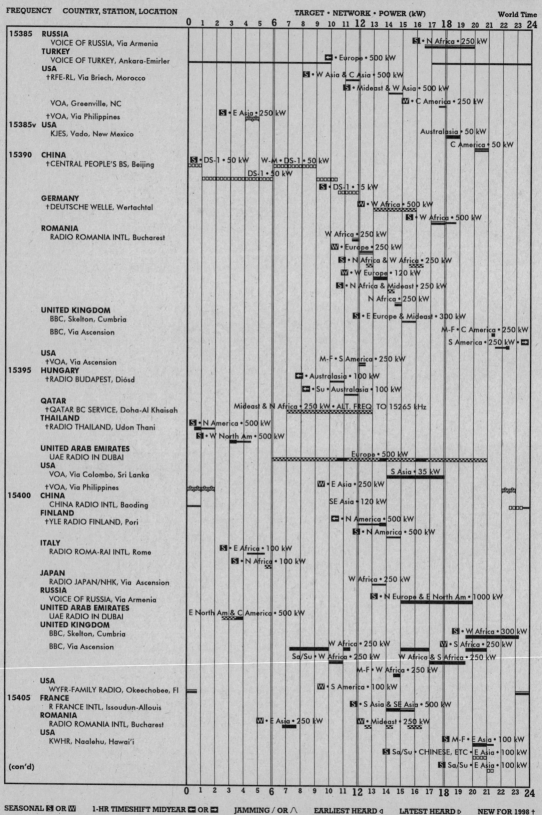

FREQUENCY   COUNTRY, STATION, LOCATION   TARGET • NETWORK • POWER (kW)   World Time

Frequency	Country, Station, Location	Target • Network • Power
15385	**RUSSIA** VOICE OF RUSSIA, Via Armenia	S • N Africa • 250 kW
	TURKEY VOICE OF TURKEY, Ankara-Emirler	Europe • 500 kW
	USA †RFE-RL, Via Briech, Morocco	S • W Asia & C Asia • 500 kW
		S • Mideast & W Asia • 500 kW
	VOA, Greenville, NC	W • C America • 250 kW
	†VOA, Via Philippines	S • E Asia • 250 kW
15385v	**USA** KJES, Vado, New Mexico	Australasia • 50 kW / C America • 50 kW
15390	**CHINA** †CENTRAL PEOPLE'S BS, Beijing	S • DS-1 • 50 kW / W-M • DS-1 • 50 kW / DS-1 • 50 kW / S • DS-1 • 15 kW
	GERMANY †DEUTSCHE WELLE, Wertachtal	W • W Africa • 500 kW / S • W Africa • 500 kW
	ROMANIA RADIO ROMANIA INTL, Bucharest	W Africa • 250 kW / W • Europe • 250 kW / S • N Africa & W Africa • 250 kW / W • W Europe • 120 kW / S • N Africa & Mideast • 250 kW / N Africa • 250 kW
	UNITED KINGDOM BBC, Skelton, Cumbria	S • E Europe & Mideast • 300 kW
	BBC, Via Ascension	M-F • C America • 250 kW / S America • 250 kW •
	USA †VOA, Via Ascension	M-F • S America • 250 kW
15395	**HUNGARY** †RADIO BUDAPEST, Diósd	Australasia • 100 kW / Su • Australasia • 100 kW
	QATAR †QATAR BC SERVICE, Doha-Al Khaisah	Mideast & N Africa • 250 kW • ALT. FREQ. TO 15265 kHz
	THAILAND †RADIO THAILAND, Udon Thani	S • N America • 500 kW / S • W North Am • 500 kW
	UNITED ARAB EMIRATES UAE RADIO IN DUBAI	Europe • 500 kW
	USA VOA, Via Colombo, Sri Lanka	S Asia • 35 kW
	†VOA, Via Philippines	W • E Asia • 250 kW
15400	**CHINA** CHINA RADIO INTL, Baoding	SE Asia • 120 kW
	FINLAND †YLE RADIO FINLAND, Pori	N America • 500 kW / S • N America • 500 kW
	ITALY RADIO ROMA-RAI INTL, Rome	S • E Africa • 100 kW / S • N Africa • 100 kW
	JAPAN RADIO JAPAN/NHK, Via Ascension	W Africa • 250 kW
	RUSSIA VOICE OF RUSSIA, Via Armenia	S • N Europe & E North Am • 1000 kW
	UNITED ARAB EMIRATES UAE RADIO IN DUBAI	E North Am & C America • 500 kW
	UNITED KINGDOM BBC, Skelton, Cumbria	S • W Africa • 300 kW
	BBC, Via Ascension	W Africa • 250 kW / W • S Africa • 250 kW / Sa/Su • W Africa • 250 kW / W Africa & S Africa • 250 kW / M-F • W Africa • 250 kW
	USA WYFR-FAMILY RADIO, Okeechobee, Fl	W • S America • 100 kW
15405	**FRANCE** R FRANCE INTL, Issoudun-Allouis	S • S Asia & SE Asia • 500 kW
	ROMANIA RADIO ROMANIA INTL, Bucharest	W • E Asia • 250 kW / W • Mideast • 250 kW
	USA KWHR, Naalehu, Hawai'i	S M-F • E Asia • 100 kW / S Sa/Su • CHINESE, ETC • E Asia • 100 kW / S Sa/Su • E Asia • 100 kW
(con'd)		

FREQUENCY	COUNTRY, STATION, LOCATION	TARGET • NETWORK • POWER (kW)	World Time

World Time scale: 0 1 2 3 4 5 6 7 8 9 10 11 12 13 14 15 16 17 18 19 20 21 22 23 24

Frequency	Country / Station / Location	Target • Network • Power
15405 (con'd)	**USA** — KWHR, Naalehu, Hawai'i	S • E Asia • 100 kW
15410	**AUSTRIA** — †R AUSTRIA INTL, Vienna	Mideast • 300 kW / W • Mideast • 300 kW / S • Mideast • 300 kW / M-Sa • Mideast • 300 kW / Su • Mideast • 300 kW
	GERMANY — DEUTSCHE WELLE, Via Antigua	S • S America • 250 kW
	†DEUTSCHE WELLE, Via Kigali, Rwanda	S Africa • 250 kW / W • W Africa • 250 kW / S • S Africa • 250 kW / Africa • 250 kW / C Africa & E Africa • 250 kW
	USA — VOA, Via Briech, Morocco	Africa • 500 kW / Su-F • Africa • 500 kW
	VOA, Via Philippines	• E Asia • 250 kW
15415	**AUSTRALIA** — †RADIO AUSTRALIA, Shepparton	E Asia & SE Asia • 100 kW
	GERMANY — DEUTSCHE WELLE, Via Sri Lanka	W • SE Asia • 250 kW
	GREECE — FONI TIS HELLADAS, Athens	E Asia • 100 kW • ALT. FREQ. TO 15630 kHz
	LIBYA — †RADIO JAMAHIRIYA, Tripoli	• Europe • 500 kW / • RUSSIAN, ETC • Europe • 500 kW
	SWITZERLAND — SWISS RADIO INTL, Schwarzenburg	S • E Asia • 150 kW
	TURKEY — VOICE OF TURKEY, Ankara-Emirler	S • W Asia • 500 kW
15420	**UNITED KINGDOM** — BBC, Various Locations	E Africa • 250 kW
	BBC, Via Meyerton, South Africa	E Africa • 250 kW
	BBC, Via Seychelles	E Africa • 250 kW / M-F • E Africa • 250 kW / Sa/Su • E Africa • 250 kW
	USA — WRNO WORLDWIDE, New Orleans, La	ENGLISH, FRENCH & SPANISH • E North Am • 100 kW • ALT. FREQ. TO 7355 kHz
15420v	**EGYPT** — RADIO CAIRO, Abu Za'bal	S America • 100 kW
15425	**CANADA** — R CANADA INTL, Sackville, NB	W • C America • 250 kW
	GERMANY — DEUTSCHE WELLE, Via Sri Lanka	W • W Africa • 250 kW
	†DEUTSCHE WELLE, Wertachtal	S • E Europe & W Asia • 500 kW
	SRI LANKA — †SRI LANKA BC CORP, Colombo-Ekala	S Asia • 35 kW
	USA — VOA, Via Philippines	SE Asia & Pacific • 50 kW
15430	**CANADA** — R CANADA INTL, Via Skelton, UK	S • M-F • Africa • 300 kW
	RUSSIA — †VOICE OF RUSSIA, Via Moldova	S • W Europe & E North Am • 500 kW / W Europe & E North Am • 500 kW / W • W Europe & E North Am • 500 kW
	SEYCHELLES — FEBA RADIO, North Pt, Mahé Is	S Africa • 75 kW / Sa/Su • S Africa • 75 kW
15435	**CHINA** — CHINA RADIO INTL, Beijing	S America • 120 kW / E Europe & W Asia • 120 kW
	FRANCE — †R FRANCE INTL, Via French Guiana	Irr • S America • 500 kW / S America • 500 kW
	JORDAN — †RADIO JORDAN, Qasr el Kharana	S America • 500 kW / • W Europe • 500 kW / • Sa-Th • W Europe • 500 kW
	LIBYA — †RADIO JAMAHIRIYA, Tripoli	• N Africa & Mideast • 500 kW • ALT. FREQ. TO 11850 kHz
	RUSSIA — R TIKHIY OKEAN, Irkutsk	S • Australasia • 1000 kW
(con'd)		

0 1 2 3 4 5 6 7 8 9 10 11 12 13 14 15 16 17 18 19 20 21 22 23 24

ENGLISH ▬ ARABIC ⊠⊠ CHINESE ▫▫▫ FRENCH ══ GERMAN ▬▬ RUSSIAN ═ SPANISH ══ OTHER ──

FREQUENCY   COUNTRY, STATION, LOCATION   TARGET • NETWORK • POWER (kW)   World Time

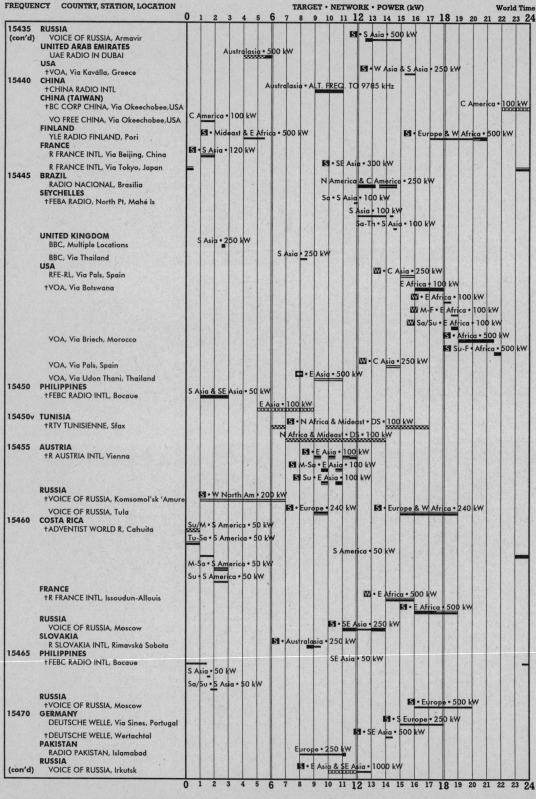

FREQUENCY	COUNTRY, STATION, LOCATION	TARGET • NETWORK • POWER (kW)
15435 (con'd)	**RUSSIA** VOICE OF RUSSIA, Armavir	S • S Asia • 500 kW
	UNITED ARAB EMIRATES UAE RADIO IN DUBAI	Australasia • 500 kW
	USA †VOA, Via Kaválla, Greece	S • W Asia & S Asia • 250 kW
15440	**CHINA** †CHINA RADIO INTL	Australasia • ALT. FREQ. TO 9785 kHz
	CHINA (TAIWAN) †BC CORP CHINA, Via Okeechobee, USA	C America • 100 kW
	VO FREE CHINA, Via Okeechobee, USA	C America • 100 kW
	FINLAND YLE RADIO FINLAND, Pori	S • Mideast & E Africa • 500 kW S • Europe & W Africa • 500 kW
	FRANCE R FRANCE INTL, Via Beijing, China	S • S Asia • 120 kW
	R FRANCE INTL, Via Tokyo, Japan	S • SE Asia • 300 kW
15445	**BRAZIL** RADIO NACIONAL, Brasilia	N America & C America • 250 kW
	SEYCHELLES †FEBA RADIO, North Pt, Mahé Is	Sa • S Asia • 100 kW
		S Asia • 100 kW
		Sa-Th • S Asia • 100 kW
	UNITED KINGDOM BBC, Multiple Locations	S Asia • 250 kW
	BBC, Via Thailand	S Asia • 250 kW
	USA RFE-RL, Via Pals, Spain	W • C Asia • 250 kW
	†VOA, Via Botswana	E Africa • 100 kW
		W • E Africa • 100 kW
		W • M-F • E Africa • 100 kW
		W • Sa/Su • E Africa • 100 kW
	VOA, Via Briech, Morocco	S • Africa • 500 kW
		S • Su-F • Africa • 500 kW
	VOA, Via Pals, Spain	W • C Asia • 250 kW
	VOA, Via Udon Thani, Thailand	• E Asia • 500 kW
15450	**PHILIPPINES** †FEBC RADIO INTL, Bocaue	S Asia & SE Asia • 50 kW
		E Asia • 100 kW
15450v	**TUNISIA** †RTV TUNISIENNE, Sfax	S • N Africa & Mideast • DS • 100 kW
		N Africa & Mideast • DS • 100 kW
15455	**AUSTRIA** †R AUSTRIA INTL, Vienna	S • E Asia • 100 kW
		S • M-Sa • E Asia • 100 kW
		S • Su • E Asia • 100 kW
	RUSSIA †VOICE OF RUSSIA, Komsomol'sk 'Amure	S • W North Am • 200 kW
	VOICE OF RUSSIA, Tula	S • Europe • 240 kW S • Europe & W Africa • 240 kW
15460	**COSTA RICA** †ADVENTIST WORLD R, Cahuita	Su/M • S America • 50 kW
		Tu-Sa • S America • 50 kW
		S America • 50 kW
		M-Sa • S America • 50 kW
		Su • S America • 50 kW
	FRANCE †R FRANCE INTL, Issoudun-Allouis	W • E Africa • 500 kW
		S • E Africa • 500 kW
	RUSSIA VOICE OF RUSSIA, Moscow	S • SE Asia • 250 kW
	SLOVAKIA R SLOVAKIA INTL, Rimavská Sobota	S • Australasia • 250 kW
15465	**PHILIPPINES** †FEBC RADIO INTL, Bocaue	SE Asia • 50 kW
		S Asia • 50 kW
		Sa/Su • S Asia • 50 kW
	RUSSIA †VOICE OF RUSSIA, Moscow	S • Europe • 500 kW
15470	**GERMANY** DEUTSCHE WELLE, Via Sines, Portugal	S • S Europe • 250 kW
	†DEUTSCHE WELLE, Wertachtal	S • SE Asia • 500 kW
	PAKISTAN RADIO PAKISTAN, Islamabad	Europe • 250 kW
	RUSSIA VOICE OF RUSSIA, Irkutsk	S • E Asia & SE Asia • 1000 kW

FREQUENCY   COUNTRY, STATION, LOCATION   TARGET • NETWORK • POWER (kW)   World Time

0 1 2 3 4 5 6 7 8 9 10 11 12 13 14 15 16 17 18 19 20 21 22 23 24

FREQUENCY	COUNTRY, STATION, LOCATION	TARGET • NETWORK • POWER (kW)
15470 (con'd)	RUSSIA	
	VOICE OF RUSSIA, Khabarovsk	W • Australasia • 240 kW
	VOICE OF RUSSIA, Moscow	S • SE Asia • 500 kW
	VOICE OF RUSSIA, Vladivostok	S • E Asia & Australasia • 1000 kW
	SWEDEN	
	†IBRA RADIO, Via Uzbekistan	S • S Asia & SE Asia • "MUKTO PROBAHO" • 240 kW
15475	GABON	
	AFRIQUE NUMERO UN, Moyabi	W Africa & E North Am • 250 kW
	JAPAN	
	†RADIO JAPAN/NHK, Tokyo-Yamata	E Asia • 300 kW • ALT. FREQ. TO 15500 kHz
		E Asia • 100 kW
	RUSSIA	
	†RADIO ROSSII, Irkutsk	S • DS • 100 kW
15475v	ANTARCTICA	
	†R NACIONAL-LRA36, Base Esperanza	SPANISH, ENGLISH & FRENCH • 1/3 kW
15480	CHINA	
	CENTRAL PEOPLE'S BS	DS-1
		W-M • DS-1
	DENMARK	
	RADIO DANMARK, Via Norway	S • S America • 500 kW
	EGYPT	
	EGYPTIAN RADIO	• DS-GENERAL
	ISRAEL	
	KOL ISRAEL, Tel Aviv	• Mideast • DS-D • 10/50 kW
	NORWAY	
	R NORWAY INTL, Sveio	S • S America • 500 kW
15485	PAKISTAN	
	RADIO PAKISTAN, Islamabad	S Asia & SE Asia • 100 kW • ALT. FREQ. TO 21730 kHz
	UNITED KINGDOM	
	BBC, Multiple Locations	W Europe & N Africa • 250/300 kW
	USA	
	†VOA, Via Udon Thani, Thailand	S • E Asia • 500 kW
15490	GERMANY	
	†DEUTSCHE WELLE, Via N'sibirsk, Russia	S • SE Asia & Australasia • 500 kW
	RUSSIA	
	R TIKHIY OKEAN, Vladivostok	S • E Asia & N Pacific • 200 kW
	VOICE OF RUSSIA, Armavir	W • S Asia & SE Asia • 400 kW
	VOICE OF RUSSIA, Irkutsk	S • SE Asia & Australasia • 1000 kW
	VOICE OF RUSSIA	S • S Asia
15495	KUWAIT	
	RADIO KUWAIT, Kabd	Mideast • 500 kW W Africa & C Africa • 500 kW
15500	CHINA	
	†CENTRAL PEOPLE'S BS, Beijing	S • DS-2 • 50 kW
		DS-2 • 50 kW
		Th/Sa-Tu • DS-2 • 50 kW
		S Th/Sa-Tu • DS-2 • 50 kW
	HOLLAND	
	†R NEDERLAND, Via Madagascar	W • SE Asia • 200 kW
	JAPAN	
	†RADIO JAPAN/NHK, Tokyo-Yamata	E Asia • 300 kW • ALT. FREQ. TO 15475 kHz
	USA	
	UNIVERSITY NET'K, Via Samara, Russia	S • S Asia • 100 kW
15505	KUWAIT	
	RADIO KUWAIT, Kabd	E Europe • 500 kW Europe & E North Am • 500 kW
		W Africa & C Africa • 500 kW
	USA	
	†VOA, Via Botswana	W M-F • Africa • 100 kW
		W • Africa • 100 kW
15510	AUSTRALIA	
	†RADIO AUSTRALIA, Shepparton	Pacific & C America • 100 kW
	BELGIUM	
	R VLAANDEREN INTL, Wavre	W M-Sa • Africa • 100 kW
		W • Africa • 100 kW
	RUSSIA	
	VOICE OF RUSSIA, Armavir	S • S Asia & SE Asia • 1000 kW
15515	FRANCE	
	†R FRANCE INTL, Via French Guiana	S • C America & N America • 500 kW
		C America & N America • 500 kW
		M-Sa • C America & N America • 500 kW
		Su • C America & N America • 500 kW
	PORTUGAL	
	RDP INTERNATIONAL, Lisbon	• Sa/Su • E Africa & S Africa • 300 kW • ALT. FREQ. TO 17680 kHz
		• E Africa & S Africa • 300 kW • ALT. FREQ. TO 17680 kHz
		• E Africa & S Africa • 300 kW
		• Irr • E Africa & S Africa • 300 kW
	USA	
(con'd)	†R FREE ASIA, Delano, California	S • E Asia • 250 kW

0 1 2 3 4 5 6 7 8 9 10 11 12 13 14 15 16 17 18 19 20 21 22 23 24

ENGLISH ▬▬   ARABIC ▨▨▨   CHINESE □□□   FRENCH ▭▭   GERMAN ▬▬   RUSSIAN ══   SPANISH ▬▬   OTHER ▬

FREQUENCY	COUNTRY, STATION, LOCATION	TARGET • NETWORK • POWER (kW)	World Time

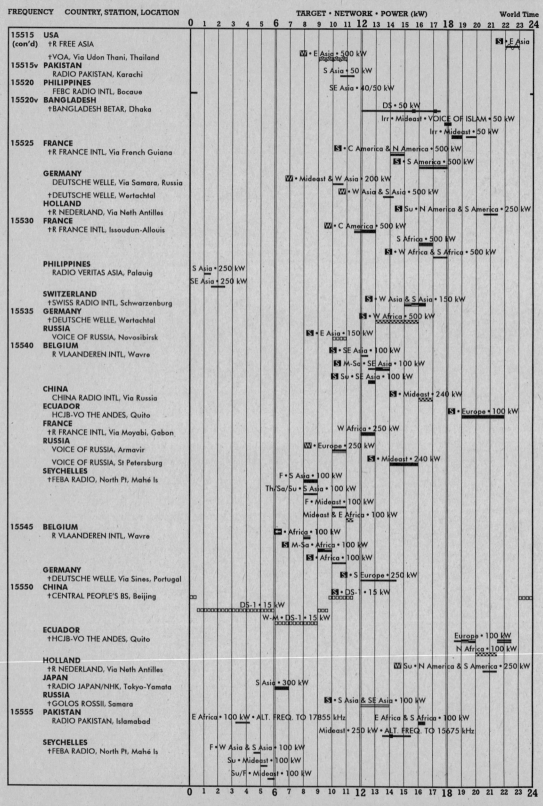

Frequency	Station	Schedule
15515 (con'd)	**USA** †R FREE ASIA	S • E Asia
	†VOA, Via Udon Thani, Thailand	W • E Asia • 500 kW
15515v	**PAKISTAN** RADIO PAKISTAN, Karachi	S Asia • 50 kW
15520	**PHILIPPINES** FEBC RADIO INTL, Bocaue	SE Asia • 40/50 kW
15520v	**BANGLADESH** †BANGLADESH BETAR, Dhaka	DS • 50 kW; Irr • Mideast • VOICE OF ISLAM • 50 kW; Irr • Mideast • 50 kW
15525	**FRANCE** †R FRANCE INTL, Via French Guiana	S • C America & N America • 500 kW; S • S America • 500 kW
	GERMANY DEUTSCHE WELLE, Via Samara, Russia	W • Mideast & W Asia • 200 kW
	†DEUTSCHE WELLE, Wertachtal	W • W Asia & S Asia • 500 kW
	HOLLAND †R NEDERLAND, Via Neth Antilles	Su • N America & S America • 250 kW
15530	**FRANCE** †R FRANCE INTL, Issoudun-Allouis	W • C America • 500 kW; S Africa • 500 kW; S • W Africa & S Africa • 500 kW
	PHILIPPINES RADIO VERITAS ASIA, Palauig	S Asia • 250 kW; SE Asia • 250 kW
	SWITZERLAND †SWISS RADIO INTL, Schwarzenburg	S • W Asia & S Asia • 150 kW
15535	**GERMANY** †DEUTSCHE WELLE, Wertachtal	S • W Africa • 500 kW
	RUSSIA VOICE OF RUSSIA, Novosibirsk	S • E Asia • 150 kW
15540	**BELGIUM** R VLAANDEREN INTL, Wavre	S • SE Asia • 100 kW; S M-Sa • SE Asia • 100 kW; S Su • SE Asia • 100 kW
	CHINA CHINA RADIO INTL, Via Russia	S • Mideast • 240 kW
	ECUADOR HCJB-VO THE ANDES, Quito	S • Europe • 100 kW
	FRANCE †R FRANCE INTL, Via Moyabi, Gabon	W Africa • 250 kW
	RUSSIA VOICE OF RUSSIA, Armavir	W • Europe • 250 kW
	VOICE OF RUSSIA, St Petersburg	S • Mideast • 240 kW
	SEYCHELLES †FEBA RADIO, North Pt, Mahé Is	F • S Asia • 100 kW; Th/Sa/Su • S Asia • 100 kW; F • Mideast • 100 kW; Mideast & E Africa • 100 kW
15545	**BELGIUM** R VLAANDEREN INTL, Wavre	◻ • Africa • 100 kW; S M-Sa • Africa • 100 kW; S • Africa • 100 kW
	GERMANY †DEUTSCHE WELLE, Via Sines, Portugal	S • S Europe • 250 kW
15550	**CHINA** †CENTRAL PEOPLE'S BS, Beijing	S • DS-1 • 15 kW; DS-1 • 15 kW; DS-1 • 15 kW; W-M • DS-1 • 15 kW
	ECUADOR †HCJB-VO THE ANDES, Quito	Europe • 100 kW; N Africa • 100 kW
	HOLLAND †R NEDERLAND, Via Neth Antilles	Su • N America & S America • 250 kW
	JAPAN †RADIO JAPAN/NHK, Tokyo-Yamata	S Asia • 300 kW
	RUSSIA †GOLOS ROSSII, Samara	S • S Asia & SE Asia • 100 kW
15555	**PAKISTAN** RADIO PAKISTAN, Islamabad	E Africa • 100 kW • ALT. FREQ. TO 17855 kHz; E Africa & S Africa • 100 kW; Mideast • 250 kW • ALT. FREQ. TO 15675 kHz
	SEYCHELLES †FEBA RADIO, North Pt, Mahé Is	F • W Asia & S Asia • 100 kW; Su • Mideast • 100 kW; Su/F • Mideast • 100 kW

FREQUENCY   COUNTRY, STATION, LOCATION

TARGET • NETWORK • POWER (kW)

World Time

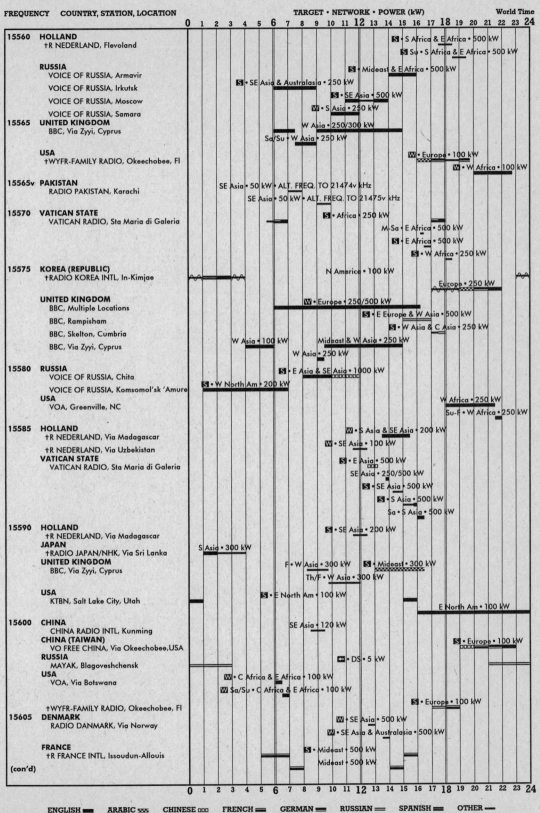

FREQUENCY	COUNTRY, STATION, LOCATION	Details
15560	**HOLLAND** †R NEDERLAND, Flevoland	S • S Africa & E Africa • 500 kW / Su • S Africa & E Africa • 500 kW
	RUSSIA VOICE OF RUSSIA, Armavir	S • Mideast & E Africa • 500 kW
	VOICE OF RUSSIA, Irkutsk	S • SE Asia & Australasia • 250 kW
	VOICE OF RUSSIA, Moscow	S • SE Asia • 500 kW
	VOICE OF RUSSIA, Samara	W • S Asia • 250 kW
15565	**UNITED KINGDOM** BBC, Via Zyyi, Cyprus	W Asia • 250/300 kW / Sa/Su • W Asia • 250 kW
	USA †WYFR-FAMILY RADIO, Okeechobee, Fl	W • Europe • 100 kW / W • W Africa • 100 kW
15565v	**PAKISTAN** RADIO PAKISTAN, Karachi	SE Asia • 50 kW • ALT. FREQ. TO 21474v kHz / SE Asia • 50 kW • ALT. FREQ. TO 21475v kHz
15570	**VATICAN STATE** VATICAN RADIO, Sta Maria di Galeria	S • Africa • 250 kW / M-Sa • E Africa • 500 kW / S • E Africa • 500 kW / S • W Africa • 250 kW
15575	**KOREA (REPUBLIC)** †RADIO KOREA INTL, In-Kimjae	N America • 100 kW / Europe • 250 kW
	UNITED KINGDOM BBC, Multiple Locations	W • Europe • 250/500 kW
	BBC, Rampisham	S • E Europe & W Asia • 500 kW
	BBC, Skelton, Cumbria	S • W Asia & C Asia • 250 kW
	BBC, Via Zyyi, Cyprus	W Asia • 100 kW / Mideast & W Asia • 250 kW / W Asia • 250 kW
15580	**RUSSIA** VOICE OF RUSSIA, Chita	S • E Asia & SE Asia • 1000 kW
	VOICE OF RUSSIA, Komsomol'sk 'Amure	S • W North Am • 200 kW
	USA VOA, Greenville, NC	W Africa • 250 kW / Su-F • W Africa • 250 kW
15585	**HOLLAND** †R NEDERLAND, Via Madagascar	W • S Asia & SE Asia • 200 kW
	†R NEDERLAND, Via Uzbekistan	W • SE Asia • 100 kW
	VATICAN STATE VATICAN RADIO, Sta Maria di Galeria	S • E Asia • 500 kW / SE Asia • 250/500 kW / S • SE Asia • 500 kW / S • S Asia • 500 kW / Sa • S Asia • 500 kW
15590	**HOLLAND** †R NEDERLAND, Via Madagascar	S • SE Asia • 200 kW
	JAPAN †RADIO JAPAN/NHK, Via Sri Lanka	S Asia • 300 kW
	UNITED KINGDOM BBC, Via Zyyi, Cyprus	F • W Asia • 300 kW / S • Mideast • 300 kW / Th/F • W Asia • 300 kW
	USA KTBN, Salt Lake City, Utah	S • E North Am • 100 kW / E North Am • 100 kW
15600	**CHINA** CHINA RADIO INTL, Kunming	SE Asia • 120 kW
	CHINA (TAIWAN) VO FREE CHINA, Via Okeechobee,USA	S • Europe • 100 kW
	RUSSIA MAYAK, Blagoveshchensk	• DS • 5 kW
	USA VOA, Via Botswana	W • C Africa & E Africa • 100 kW / W Sa/Su • C Africa & E Africa • 100 kW
	†WYFR-FAMILY RADIO, Okeechobee, Fl	S • Europe • 100 kW
15605	**DENMARK** RADIO DANMARK, Via Norway	W • SE Asia • 500 kW / W • SE Asia & Australasia • 500 kW
	FRANCE †R FRANCE INTL, Issoudun-Allouis	S • Mideast • 500 kW / Mideast • 500 kW
(con'd)		

FREQUENCY   COUNTRY, STATION, LOCATION   TARGET • NETWORK • POWER (kW)   World Time

Frequency	Country, Station, Location	Schedule
15605 (con'd)	**FRANCE** †R FRANCE INTL, Issoudun-Allouis	Mideast & S Asia • 500 kW
		W • Mideast & S Asia • 500 kW
		S • E Europe • 500 kW
	NORWAY R NORWAY INTL, Kvitsøy	W • SE Asia • 500 kW
		W M-Sa • SE Asia & Australasia • 500 kW
		W Su • SE Asia & Australasia • 500 kW
15610	**GERMANY** †DEUTSCHE WELLE, Via N'sibirsk, Russia	S • E Asia • 200 kW
15615	**ISRAEL** KOL ISRAEL, Tel Aviv	S • W Europe & E North Am • 300 kW
		S • W Africa & S America • 300 kW
	RESHET BET, Tel Aviv	S • W Europe & E North Am • DS • 300 kW
		W • E Europe • DS • 100 kW
15620	**BULGARIA** RADIO BULGARIA, Plovdiv	S • S Asia & E Asia • 500 kW
15625	**IRELAND** †WEST COAST R IRELAND, Via Germany	S Th • Africa & Australasia • 100 kW
	PAKISTAN RADIO PAKISTAN, Islamabad	S Asia & SE Asia • 100 kW
	TURKEY VOICE OF TURKEY, Ankara-úakirlar	S F • N Africa & E Africa • 250 kW
15630	**GREECE** FONI TIS HELLADAS, Athens	E Asia • 100 kW • ALT. FREQ. TO 15415 kHz
		S • Mideast • 100 kW
15635	**BULGARIA** RADIO BULGARIA, Plovdiv	S • W Asia & C Asia • 500 kW
15640	**CZECH REPUBLIC** †RADIO PRAGUE, Litomyšl	S • W Africa • 100 kW S • C Africa • 100 kW
	GERMANY †DEUTSCHE WELLE, Wertachtal	S • E Asia • 500 kW
	ISRAEL KOL ISRAEL, Tel Aviv	S Su-Th • W Europe & E North Am • 300 kW
		S • C America & S America • 300 kW
15650	**GREECE** FONI TIS HELLADAS, Athens	Mideast • 100 kW W • Africa • 100 kW
		Australasia • 100 kW
		W • ARABIC & ENGLISH • Africa • 100 kW
	FONI TIS HELLADAS, Various Locations	⇄ • Europe & N America • 100/250 kW
	ISRAEL KOL ISRAEL, Tel Aviv	S • W Europe & E North Am • 300 kW
		⇄ Tu • Mideast • 300 kW
15660	**USA** †R FREE ASIA	S • E Asia
15665	**USA** †HERALD BROADCASTING, S Carolina	S M/W/F • E Europe • 500 kW
		S Su • E Europe • 500 kW
		S Tu/Th/Sa • E Europe • 500 kW
		S Sa • E Europe • 500 kW
		S Su/Tu/Th • E Europe • 500 kW
		S • SPANISH, FRENCH, ETC • W Europe • 500 kW
		S Tu/Th/F • GERMAN, ETC • W Europe • 500 kW
		S W/Sa-M • W Europe • 500 kW
	†HERALD BROADCASTING, Via Saipan	E Asia • 100 kW
		Su • E Europe • 100 kW
		M-Sa • RUSSIAN, ETC • E Europe • 100 kW
		S Su/M/W/F • E Asia • 100 kW
		S Tu/Th/Sa • RUSSIAN, ETC • E Asia • 100 kW
		S F • E Asia • 100 kW
		S Th/Sa-Tu • E Asia • 100 kW
		S W • E Asia • 100 kW
	†WEWN, Birmingham, Alabama	Europe • 500 kW
		W • Europe • 500 kW
		S M-Sa • Europe • 500 kW
		S Su • Europe • 500 kW
		S • Europe • 500 kW
		W M-Sa • Europe • 500 kW
		W Su • Europe • 500 kW
15670 (con'd)	**CHINA** CENTRAL PEOPLE'S BS, Kunming	S • DS-MINORITIES • 50 kW

SEASONAL Ⓢ OR Ⓦ   1-HR TIMESHIFT MIDYEAR ⇄ OR ⇄   JAMMING / OR ⋀   EARLIEST HEARD ◁   LATEST HEARD ▷   NEW FOR 1998 †

FREQUENCY　　COUNTRY, STATION, LOCATION　　　　　　　TARGET • NETWORK • POWER (kW)　　　　　World Time

0　1　2　3　4　5　6　7　8　9　10　11　12　13　14　15　16　17　18　19　20　21　22　23　24

Frequency	Country / Station / Location	Schedule details
15670 (con'd)	CHINA — CENTRAL PEOPLE'S BS, Kunming	DS-MINORITIES • 50 kW
15675	PAKISTAN — RADIO PAKISTAN, Islamabad	Mideast • 250 kW • ALT. FREQ. TO 15555 kHz
15685	USA — WWCR, Nashville, Tennessee	S • ENGLISH, ETC • E North Am & Europe • 100 kW; ENGLISH, ETC • E North Am & Europe • 100 kW; F-Tu • E North Am & Europe • 100 kW; W/Th • E North Am & Europe • 100 kW; M-F • E North Am & Europe • 100 kW; Sa/Su • E North Am & Europe • 100 kW
15695	USA — †WYFR-FAMILY RADIO, Okeechobee, Fl	Europe • 100 kW; S • Europe • 100 kW
15710	CHINA — †CENTRAL PEOPLE'S BS, Beijing	CHINESE, ETC • TAIWAN SERVICE • 50 kW
15715	USA — †WINB-WORLD INTL BC, Red Lion, Pa	Europe • 50 kW
15725	USA — †HERALD BROADCASTING, Via Saipan	F • SE Asia • 100 kW; Th/Sa-Tu • SE Asia • 100 kW; W • SE Asia • 100 kW; N America • TEMP INACTIVE • 100 kW
	KAIJ, Dallas, Texas	
15745	USA — WEWN, Birmingham, Alabama	S • Europe • 500 kW
15770	INDIA — ALL INDIA RADIO, Aligarh	SE Asia • 250 kW
15880	CHINA — †CENTRAL PEOPLE'S BS, Beijing	CHINESE, ETC • NETWORK 6 • 50 kW; W-M • CHINESE, ETC • NETWORK 6 • 50 kW; S • W-M • NETWORK 6 • 50 kW; S • CHINESE, ETC • NETWORK 6 • 50 kW
16000	AUSTRALIA — VNG, Llandilo	WORLD TIME • 5 kW
16300	RUSSIA — †RADIO ROSSII, Moscow-Taldom	S • W Africa & Atlantic • DS • 200 kW • USB
16330	RUSSIA — †RADIO ROSSII, Moscow-Taldom	S • N Europe • DS • 200 kW • USB
17387	INDIA — ALL INDIA RADIO, Aligarh	E Africa • 250 kW; SE Asia • 250 kW; Australasia • 250 kW
	†ALL INDIA RADIO, Delhi	
17485	CZECH REPUBLIC — †RADIO PRAGUE, Litomyšl	S • Mideast & S Asia • 100 kW; W • Mideast & E Africa • 100 kW; E Africa • 100 kW; S • E Africa • 100 kW
	SLOVAKIA — †R SLOVAKIA INTL, Rimavská Sobota	W • Australasia • 250 kW
17500v	TUNISIA — †RTV TUNISIENNE, Sfax	N Africa & Mideast • DS • 100 kW • ALT. FREQ. TO 17735v kHz; S • N Africa & Mideast • DS • 100 kW • ALT. FREQ. TO 17735v kHz
17510	USA — †HERALD BROADCASTING, S Carolina	W Africa • 500 kW
	KWHR, Naalehu, Hawai'i	M • E Asia • 100 kW; Tu-Su • E Asia • 100 kW; E Asia • 100 kW; W • E Asia • 100 kW; Su-F • E Asia • 100 kW; Sa • E Asia • 100 kW; M-F • E Asia • 100 kW; Su • E Asia • 100 kW
17515	SWITZERLAND — SWISS RADIO INTL, Schwarzenburg	S • Australasia • 150 kW; S • E Asia • 150 kW
17520	UNITED NATIONS — UNITED NATIONS R, Via Switzerland	TESTS • 15 kW • USB
17525	RUSSIA — VOICE OF RUSSIA	S
17540v	PAKISTAN — RADIO PAKISTAN, Karachi	SE Asia • 50 kW
17545	ISRAEL — KOL ISRAEL, Tel Aviv	W • Australasia • 300 kW
	RESHET BET, Tel Aviv	S • Europe • DS • 20/50 kW; W • W Europe & E North Am • DS • 300 kW
	RESHET GIMEL, Tel Aviv	W • Th • SE Asia • DS • 300 kW
17550 (con'd)	CHINA — †CENTRAL PEOPLE'S BS	DS-1

0　1　2　3　4　5　6　7　8　9　10　11　12　13　14　15　16　17　18　19　20　21　22　23　24

ENGLISH ▬　ARABIC ≋　CHINESE □□□　FRENCH ▬　GERMAN ▬　RUSSIAN ＝　SPANISH ▬　OTHER ▬

FREQUENCY   COUNTRY, STATION, LOCATION

TARGET • NETWORK • POWER (kW)

World Time

0 1 2 3 4 5 6 7 8 9 10 11 12 13 14 15 16 17 18 19 20 21 22 23 24

17550	**CHINA**	
(con'd)	†CENTRAL PEOPLE'S BS	W-M • DS-1
	VATICAN STATE	
	VATICAN RADIO, Sta Maria di Galeria	S Su • E Africa & S Africa • 500 kW
		S M-Sa • FRENCH, ETC • Africa • 100 kW
		M-Sa • Africa • 100 kW
		S • Africa • 100 kW
17555	**USA**	
	KWHR, Naalehu, Hawai'i	Australasia • 100 kW
	WYFR-FAMILY RADIO, Okeechobee, Fl	W • Europe • 100 kW
		Europe • 100 kW
		S • Europe • 100 kW
17558v	**PAKISTAN**	
	RADIO PAKISTAN, Islamabad	Mideast & N Africa • 100 kW
17560	**FRANCE**	
	†R FRANCE INTL, Via French Guiana	S • S America • 500 kW
		S America • 500 kW
	R FRANCE INTL, Via Moyabi, Gabon	Mideast • 250 kW
	GERMANY	
	†DEUTSCHE WELLE, Wertachtal	S • W Africa • 500 kW
	RUSSIA	
	VOICE OF RUSSIA, Irkutsk	W • SE Asia • 100 kW
	VOICE OF RUSSIA, Vladivostok	S • Australasia • 200 kW
17570	**RUSSIA**	
	R TIKHIY OKEAN, Irkutsk	W • Australasia • 1000 kW
	VOICE OF RUSSIA, Various Locations	Australasia • 240/1000 kW
	SLOVAKIA	
	†R SLOVAKIA INTL, Rimavská Sobota	S • Australasia • 250 kW
17575	**FRANCE**	
	†R FRANCE INTL, Via French Guiana	Irr • S • C America & N America • 500 kW
		W • C America • 500 kW
17580	**HOLLAND**	
	R NEDERLAND, Via Madagascar	SE Asia • 200 kW
		W • SE Asia • 200 kW
	RUSSIA	
	VOICE OF RUSSIA, Novosibirsk	S • SE Asia • 500 kW
17585	**VATICAN STATE**	
	VATICAN RADIO, Sta Maria di Galeria	W • FRENCH & ITALIAN • Africa • 500 kW
		W • Africa • 500 kW
		W • Africa • 100 kW
17595	**BELGIUM**	
	R VLAANDEREN INTL, Wavre	⇨ • Su • Africa • 200 kW • ALT. FREQ. TO 17610 kHz
		⇨ • M-Sa • Africa • 200 kW • ALT. FREQ. TO 17610 kHz
		S • Africa • 200 kW • ALT. FREQ. TO 17690 kHz
		⇨ • Africa • 100 kW • ALT. FREQ. TO 17610 kHz
		W • Africa • 200 kW • ALT. FREQ. TO 17610 kHz
	EGYPT	
	RADIO CAIRO, Kafr Silim-Abis	S Asia • 250 kW
	PORTUGAL	
	RDP INTERNATIONAL, Lisbon	⇨ • Sa/Su • SE Asia • 100 kW
		⇨ • M-F • SE Asia • 300 kW
17600	**USA**	
	UNIVERSITY NET'K, Via Samara, Russia	W • S Asia • 100 kW
17605	**CHINA**	
	†CENTRAL PEOPLE'S BS, Beijing	S • DS-1 • 15 kW
		DS-1 • 15 kW
		W-M • DS-1 • 15 kW
	HOLLAND	
	R NEDERLAND, Via Neth Antilles	W Africa • 250 kW
		S • W Africa • 250 kW
17610	**BELGIUM**	
	R VLAANDEREN INTL, Wavre	⇨ • Su • Africa • 200 kW • ALT. FREQ. TO 17595 kHz
		⇨ • M-Sa • Africa • 200 kW • ALT. FREQ. TO 17595 kHz
		⇨ • Africa • 100 kW • ALT. FREQ. TO 17595 kHz
		W • Africa • 200 kW • ALT. FREQ. TO 17595 kHz
	RUSSIA	
	VOICE OF RUSSIA, Moscow	S • S Asia & SE Asia • 250 kW
	USA	
	†R FREE ASIA	W • SE Asia
17620	**FRANCE**	
	†R FRANCE INTL, Issoudun-Allouis	S • E Africa • 500 kW
		W Africa • 500 kW
		Africa • 500 kW
(con'd)	R FRANCE INTL, Via French Guiana	W • S America • 500 kW

0 1 2 3 4 5 6 7 8 9 10 11 12 13 14 15 16 17 18 19 20 21 22 23 24

SEASONAL S OR W   1-HR TIMESHIFT MIDYEAR ⇨ OR ⇦   JAMMING / OR ∧   EARLIEST HEARD ◁   LATEST HEARD ▷   NEW FOR 1998 †

FREQUENCY   COUNTRY, STATION, LOCATION

TARGET • NETWORK • POWER (kW)

World Time

0 1 2 3 4 5 6 7 8 9 10 11 12 13 14 15 16 17 18 19 20 21 22 23 24

Frequency	Country, Station, Location	Target • Network • Power
17620 (con'd)	FRANCE — R FRANCE INTL, Via French Guiana	S • C America • 500 kW
17630	FRANCE — †R FRANCE INTL, Via French Guiana	W • S America • 500 kW / S America • 500 kW / S • S America • 500 kW
	GABON — AFRIQUE NUMERO UN, Moyabi	W Africa • 250 kW
	JAPAN — †RADIO JAPAN/NHK, Via Moyabi, Gabon	Europe • 500 kW • ALT. FREQ. TO 17780 kHz
	UNITED ARAB EMIRATES — UAE RADIO IN DUBAI	N Africa • 300 kW
17640	BELGIUM — R VLAANDEREN INTL, Wavre	S • Africa • 200 kW
	UNITED KINGDOM — BBC, Multiple Locations	E Europe & Mideast • 250/300/500 kW
	BBC, Rampisham	S • E Europe • 500 kW
	BBC, Skelton, Cumbria	W • Europe • 300 kW
	BBC, Via Zyyi, Cyprus	W • E Africa • 250 kW
	USA — VOA, Greenville, NC	W Africa • 250 kW / M-F • W Africa • 250 kW / Sa/Su • W Africa • 250 kW
17645	GUAM — KSDA-ADVENTIST WORLD RADIO, Agat	S Asia & SE Asia • 100 kW
17650	FRANCE — †R FRANCE INTL, Issoudun-Allouis	W • S Asia • 500 kW / Mideast • 500 kW / S • Mideast • 500 kW
17655	HOLLAND — †R NEDERLAND, Via Khabarovsk, Russia	S • SE Asia • 100 kW
	UNITED KINGDOM — BBC, Via Tashkent, Uzbekistan	S Asia • 200 kW
	USA — UNIVERSITY NET'K, Via Armavir, Russia	S • S Asia • 200 kW
17665	UNITED KINGDOM — BBC, Skelton, Cumbria	W M-F • E Europe • 300 kW
17670	EGYPT — EGYPTIAN RADIO, Abu Za'bal	N Africa • DS-GENERAL • 100 kW
17680	CHINA — CHINA RADIO INTL, Kunming	SE Asia • 120 kW
	PORTUGAL — RDP INTERNATIONAL, Lisbon	Sa/Su • E Africa & S Africa • 300 kW • ALT. FREQ. TO 15515 kHz / E Africa & S Africa • 300 kW • ALT. FREQ. TO 15515 kHz
17685	JAPAN — †RADIO JAPAN/NHK, Tokyo-Yamata	Australasia • 300 kW / SE Asia • 300 kW
17690	BELGIUM — R VLAANDEREN INTL, Wavre	S • Africa • 200 kW • ALT. FREQ. TO 17595 kHz / Su • Africa • 200 kW
17690v	EGYPT — RADIO CAIRO, Kafr Silim-Abis	S Asia • 250 kW
17695	ISRAEL — †RESHET GIMEL, Tel Aviv	S Th • SE Asia • DS • 300 kW
	UNITED KINGDOM — BBC, Rampisham	S • E Europe & Mideast • 500 kW
	BBC, Various Locations	E Europe • 300/500 kW / Su • E Europe • 300/500 kW
	BBC, Via Zyyi, Cyprus	W • S Asia • 250 kW
	USA — †WEWN, Birmingham, Alabama	W • Europe • 500 kW
17700	CHINA — †CENTRAL PEOPLE'S BS	DS-2 • 50 kW / DS-2 • 50 kW / Th/Sa-Tu • DS-2 • 50 kW
	VATICAN STATE — VATICAN RADIO, Sta Maria di Galeria	S America • 500 kW
17705	INDIA — †ALL INDIA RADIO, Bangalore	E Asia • 500 kW
	PAKISTAN — RADIO PAKISTAN, Islamabad	SE Asia • 100 kW
	TURKEY — VOICE OF TURKEY, Ankara-Emirler	S • S Asia, SE Asia & Australasia • 500 kW
	UNITED KINGDOM — BBC, Various Locations	N Africa • 250/500 kW
	USA — VOA, Various Locations	M-F • C Africa & E Africa • 100/500 kW / C Africa & E Africa • 100/500 kW

0 1 2 3 4 5 6 7 8 9 10 11 12 13 14 15 16 17 18 19 20 21 22 23 24

ENGLISH ▬   ARABIC ⬚⬚⬚   CHINESE ⬚⬚⬚   FRENCH ▬   GERMAN ▬   RUSSIAN ═══   SPANISH ▬   OTHER ▬

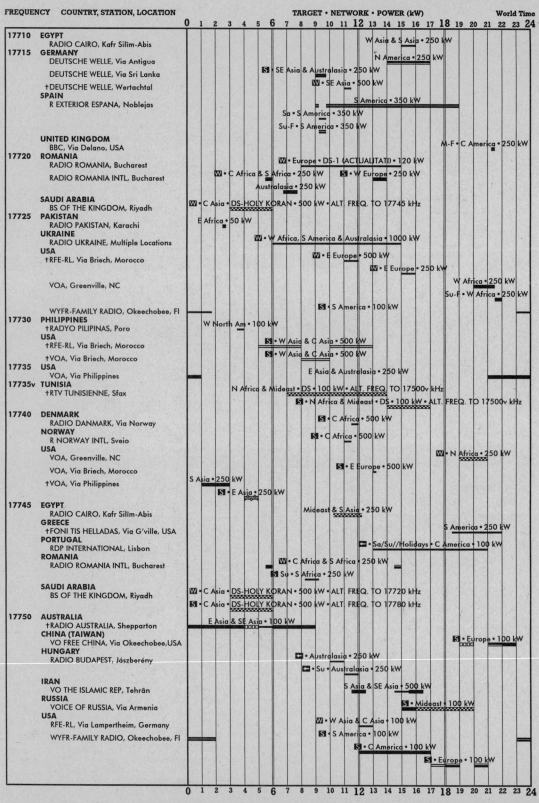

FREQUENCY   COUNTRY, STATION, LOCATION   TARGET • NETWORK • POWER (kW)   World Time

FREQUENCY	COUNTRY, STATION, LOCATION	TARGET • NETWORK • POWER (kW)
17710	EGYPT	
	RADIO CAIRO, Kafr Silim-Abis	W Asia & S Asia • 250 kW
17715	GERMANY	
	DEUTSCHE WELLE, Via Antigua	N America • 250 kW
	DEUTSCHE WELLE, Via Sri Lanka	S • SE Asia & Australasia • 250 kW
	†DEUTSCHE WELLE, Wertachtal	W • SE Asia • 500 kW
	SPAIN	
	R EXTERIOR ESPANA, Noblejas	S America • 350 kW
		Sa • S America • 350 kW
		Su-F • S America • 350 kW
	UNITED KINGDOM	
	BBC, Via Delano, USA	M-F • C America • 250 kW
17720	ROMANIA	
	RADIO ROMANIA, Bucharest	W • Europe • DS-1 (ACTUALITATI) • 120 kW
	RADIO ROMANIA INTL, Bucharest	W • C Africa & S Africa • 250 kW S • W Europe • 250 kW
		Australasia • 250 kW
	SAUDI ARABIA	
	BS OF THE KINGDOM, Riyadh	W • C Asia • DS-HOLY KORAN • 500 kW • ALT. FREQ. TO 17745 kHz
17725	PAKISTAN	
	RADIO PAKISTAN, Karachi	E Africa • 50 kW
	UKRAINE	
	RADIO UKRAINE, Multiple Locations	W • W Africa, S America & Australasia • 1000 kW
	USA	
	†RFE-RL, Via Briech, Morocco	W • E Europe • 500 kW
		W • E Europe • 250 kW
	VOA, Greenville, NC	W Africa • 250 kW
		Su-F • W Africa • 250 kW
	WYFR-FAMILY RADIO, Okeechobee, Fl	S • S America • 100 kW
17730	PHILIPPINES	
	†RADYO PILIPINAS, Poro	W North Am • 100 kW
	USA	
	†RFE-RL, Via Briech, Morocco	S • W Asia & C Asia • 500 kW
	†VOA, Via Briech, Morocco	S • W Asia & C Asia • 500 kW
17735	USA	
	VOA, Via Philippines	E Asia & Australasia • 250 kW
17735v	TUNISIA	
	†RTV TUNISIENNE, Sfax	N Africa & Mideast • DS • 100 kW • ALT. FREQ. TO 17500v kHz
		S • N Africa & Mideast • DS • 100 kW • ALT. FREQ. TO 17500v kHz
17740	DENMARK	
	RADIO DANMARK, Via Norway	S • C Africa • 500 kW
	NORWAY	
	R NORWAY INTL, Sveio	S • C Africa • 500 kW
	USA	
	VOA, Greenville, NC	W • N Africa • 250 kW
	VOA, Via Briech, Morocco	S • E Europe • 500 kW
	†VOA, Via Philippines	S Asia • 250 kW
		S • E Asia • 250 kW
17745	EGYPT	
	RADIO CAIRO, Kafr Silim-Abis	Mideast & S Asia • 250 kW
	GREECE	
	†FONI TIS HELLADAS, Via G'ville, USA	S America • 250 kW
	PORTUGAL	
	RDP INTERNATIONAL, Lisbon	• Sa/Su//Holidays • C America • 100 kW
	ROMANIA	
	RADIO ROMANIA INTL, Bucharest	W • C Africa & S Africa • 250 kW
		S • Su • S Africa • 250 kW
	SAUDI ARABIA	
	BS OF THE KINGDOM, Riyadh	W • C Asia • DS-HOLY KORAN • 500 kW • ALT. FREQ. TO 17720 kHz
		S • C Asia • DS-HOLY KORAN • 500 kW • ALT. FREQ. TO 17780 kHz
17750	AUSTRALIA	
	†RADIO AUSTRALIA, Shepparton	E Asia & SE Asia • 100 kW
	CHINA (TAIWAN)	
	VO FREE CHINA, Via Okeechobee,USA	S • Europe • 100 kW
	HUNGARY	
	RADIO BUDAPEST, Jászberény	• Australasia • 250 kW
		• Su • Australasia • 250 kW
	IRAN	
	VO THE ISLAMIC REP, Tehrān	S Asia & SE Asia • 500 kW
	RUSSIA	
	VOICE OF RUSSIA, Via Armenia	S • Mideast • 100 kW
	USA	
	RFE-RL, Via Lampertheim, Germany	W • W Asia & C Asia • 100 kW
		S • S America • 100 kW
	WYFR-FAMILY RADIO, Okeechobee, Fl	S • C America • 100 kW
		S • Europe • 100 kW

FREQUENCY   COUNTRY, STATION, LOCATION   TARGET • NETWORK • POWER (kW)   World Time

0 1 2 3 4 5 6 7 8 9 10 11 12 13 14 15 16 17 18 19 20 21 22 23 24

17755   **RUSSIA**
VOICE OF RUSSIA, Via Uzbekistan — W • S Asia & SE Asia • 240 kW
    S Asia & SE Asia • 240 kW
    S • S Asia & SE Asia • 240 kW

  SPAIN
R EXTERIOR ESPANA, Noblejas — W Africa & S Africa • 350 kW
  USA
VOA, Via Ascension — W Africa & C Africa • 250 kW
    M-F • W Africa • 250 kW

17760   **CHINA (TAIWAN)**
VO FREE CHINA, Via Okeechobee, USA — W • Europe • 100 kW
  SAUDI ARABIA
BS OF THE KINGDOM, Riyadh — E Africa & S Africa • 500 kW • ALT. FREQ. TO 17795 kHz
  UNITED ARAB EMIRATES
†UAE RADIO FROM ABU DHABI — S • N Africa • 500 kW
    W • Australasia • 500 kW

  UNITED KINGDOM
BBC, Via Singapore — E Asia & SE Asia • 250 kW
  USA
†WYFR-FAMILY RADIO, Okeechobee, Fl — W • C America • 100 kW
    W • Europe • 100 kW

17765   **GERMANY**
†DEUTSCHE WELLE, Nauen — S • Africa • 500 kW
  DEUTSCHE WELLE, Via Antigua — W • S America • 250 kW
    S America • 250 kW

  DEUTSCHE WELLE, Wertachtal — S • W Africa • 500 kW
  KOREA (DPR)
†RADIO PYONGYANG, Kujang-dong — C America • 200 kW
    SE Asia • 200 kW

  USA
†VOA, Via Philippines — E Asia • 250 kW
17770   **EGYPT**
RADIO CAIRO, Kafr Silim-Abis — SE Asia • 250 kW
  JAPAN
†RADIO JAPAN/NHK, Via Sri Lanka — Mideast & N Africa • 300 kW
  UNITED KINGDOM
BBC, Via Zyyi, Cyprus — E Africa • 250 kW
17770v   **EGYPT**
RADIO CAIRO, Kafr Silim-Abis — S America • 250 kW
17775   **RUSSIA**
VOICE OF RUSSIA, Via Uzbekistan — S • S Asia & SE Asia • 240 kW
  SAUDI ARABIA
BS OF THE KINGDOM, Riyadh — C Africa & W Africa • 500 kW
  USA
†KVOH-VO HOPE, Rancho Simi, Ca — C America • 50/80 kW
17780   **GERMANY**
†DEUTSCHE WELLE, Wertachtal — W • Mideast & W Asia • 500 kW
    W • Africa • 500 kW

  IRAN
VO THE ISLAMIC REP — Europe • 500 kW
  ITALY
RADIO ROMA-RAI INTL, Rome — E North Am • 100 kW
  RAI-RTV ITALIANA, Rome — Su • E North Am • 100 kW
  JAPAN
†RADIO JAPAN/NHK, Via Moyabi, Gabon — S Africa • 500 kW
    Europe • 500 kW • ALT. FREQ. TO 17630 kHz

  SAUDI ARABIA
BS OF THE KINGDOM, Riyadh — S • C Asia • DS-HOLY KORAN • 500 kW • ALT. FREQ. TO 17745 kHz
  USA
VOA, Via Philippines — W • S Asia • 250 kW
17785   **GERMANY**
†DEUTSCHE WELLE, Nauen — S • Mideast & E Africa • 500 kW
  INDIA
ALL INDIA RADIO, Bangalore — Mideast • 500 kW
    Irr • Mideast • HAJJ • 500 kW

  USA
†VOA, Via Ascension — S • M-F • E Africa & S Africa • 250 kW
    S • E Africa & S Africa • 250 kW

  †VOA, Via Briech, Morocco — W • Europe • 500 kW
    W • M-F • S Africa • 500 kW
    W • S Africa • 500 kW
    S Africa • 500 kW
    M-F • S Africa • 500 kW
    S • W Africa & S Africa • 500 kW

17790   **ROMANIA**
(con'd)   RADIO ROMANIA INTL, Bucharest — S Africa • 250 kW
    W • W Africa • 250 kW

0 1 2 3 4 5 6 7 8 9 10 11 12 13 14 15 16 17 18 19 20 21 22 23 24

ENGLISH ▬   ARABIC ⟩⟩⟩   CHINESE □□□   FRENCH ▬   GERMAN ▬   RUSSIAN =   SPANISH ▬   OTHER ▬

FREQUENCY	COUNTRY, STATION, LOCATION	TARGET • NETWORK • POWER (kW)	World Time

0 1 2 3 4 5 6 7 8 9 10 11 12 13 14 15 16 17 18 19 20 21 22 23 24

FREQUENCY	COUNTRY, STATION, LOCATION	TARGET • NETWORK • POWER (kW)
17790 (con'd)	ROMANIA — RADIO ROMANIA INTL, Bucharest	Su • SE Asia • 250 kW
		W Su • W Africa • 250 kW
		W • Australasia • 250 kW
	UKRAINE — RADIO UKRAINE, Nikolayev	S • S America • 1000 kW
	UNITED KINGDOM — BBC, Via Ascension	S America • 250 kW
	BBC, Via Maşīrah, Oman	S Asia • 100 kW
	BBC, Via Singapore	W • E Asia • 100 kW
17795	AUSTRALIA — †RADIO AUSTRALIA, Shepparton	Pacific & W North Am • 100 kW
	FRANCE — †R FRANCE INTL, Issoudun-Allouis	S • E Africa • 500 kW
		E Africa • 500 kW
	R FRANCE INTL, Via Moyabi, Gabon	S Africa • 250 kW
	RUSSIA — VOICE OF RUSSIA, Via Armenia	S • S Asia & SE Asia • 250/500 kW
	SAUDI ARABIA — BS OF THE KINGDOM, Riyadh	E Africa & S Africa • 500 kW • ALT. FREQ. TO 17760 kHz
17800	EGYPT — RADIO CAIRO, Kafr Silim-Abis	C Africa & S Africa • 250 kW
	FRANCE — †R FRANCE INTL, Issoudun-Allouis	S • E Africa • 500 kW
		E Africa • 500 kW
	GERMANY — †DEUTSCHE WELLE, Nauen	S • E Africa & S Africa • 100 kW
		W Africa • 250 kW
	†DEUTSCHE WELLE, Via Kigali, Rwanda	W • E Africa & S Africa • 500 kW
	†DEUTSCHE WELLE, Wertachtal	E Africa • 500 kW
		S • Africa • 500 kW
	USA — VOA, Greenville, NC	Africa • 250 kW
17805	BELARUS — BELARUSSIAN R, Grodno	DS • 10 kW
	CHINA (TAIWAN) — VO FREE CHINA, Via Okeechobee, USA	S • S America • 100 kW
	ROMANIA — RADIO ROMANIA INTL, Bucharest	W • Australasia • 250 kW
	USA — †R FREE ASIA	S • SE Asia
	RFE-RL, Via Pals, Spain	W • W Asia & C Asia • 250 kW
	VOA, Via Ascension	W M-F • E Africa & S Africa • 250 kW
		W • E Africa & S Africa • 250 kW
	VOA, Via Pals, Spain	W • W Asia & C Asia • 250 kW
17810	GERMANY — †DEUTSCHE WELLE, Via Antigua	N America & S America • 250 kW
	JAPAN — †RADIO JAPAN/NHK, Tokyo-Yamata	SE Asia • 300 kW
	UNITED KINGDOM — BBC, Via Ascension	W Africa & C Africa • 250 kW
	BBC, Via Zyyi, Cyprus	E Africa • 300 kW
17815	BRAZIL — RADIO CULTURA, São Paulo	DS • 1 kW
	JAPAN — RADIO JAPAN/NHK, Via Ascension	C Africa • 250 kW
	ROMANIA — RADIO ROMANIA INTL, Bucharest	S • W Europe • 250 kW
17820	CANADA — †R CANADA INTL, Sackville, NB	S M-Sa • Europe • 100 kW S • Africa • 100 kW
		W • W Europe & Africa • 250 kW
		M-Sa • Europe • 100 kW
		Europe • 100/250 kW
		W • Africa • 100 kW
		Africa • 100 kW
	GERMANY — †DEUTSCHE WELLE, Via Sri Lanka	E Asia • 250 kW S • E Asia • 250 kW
		S • SE Asia & Australasia • 250 kW
	†DEUTSCHE WELLE, Wertachtal	S • Mideast & W Asia • 500 kW
		E Asia • 500 kW
	JAPAN — RADIO JAPAN/NHK, Via Sri Lanka	Mideast & N Africa • 300 kW
	UNITED KINGDOM — BBC, Via Ascension	M-F • S America • 250 kW
(con'd)		

0 1 2 3 4 5 6 7 8 9 10 11 12 13 14 15 16 17 18 19 20 21 22 23 24

SEASONAL **S** OR **W**   1-HR TIMESHIFT MIDYEAR ⧄ OR ⧅   JAMMING / OR ∧   EARLIEST HEARD ◁   LATEST HEARD ▷   NEW FOR 1998 †

FREQUENCY   COUNTRY, STATION, LOCATION   TARGET • NETWORK • POWER (kW)   World Time

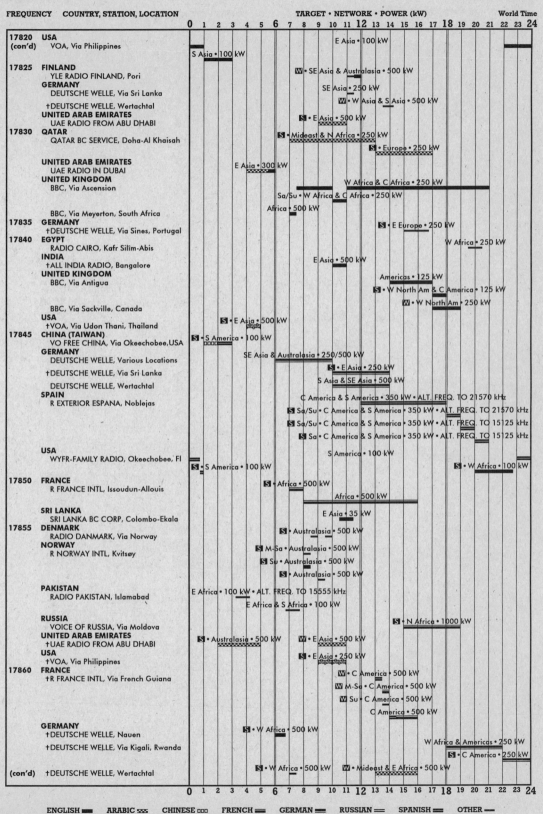

Frequency	Country, Station, Location	Target • Network • Power
17820 (con'd)	USA — VOA, Via Philippines	E Asia • 100 kW / S Asia • 100 kW
17825	FINLAND — YLE RADIO FINLAND, Pori	W • SE Asia & Australasia • 500 kW
	GERMANY — DEUTSCHE WELLE, Via Sri Lanka	SE Asia • 250 kW
	†DEUTSCHE WELLE, Wertachtal	W • W Asia & S Asia • 500 kW
	UNITED ARAB EMIRATES — UAE RADIO FROM ABU DHABI	S • E Asia • 500 kW
17830	QATAR — QATAR BC SERVICE, Doha-Al Khaisah	S • Mideast & N Africa • 250 kW / S • Europe • 250 kW
	UNITED ARAB EMIRATES — UAE RADIO IN DUBAI	E Asia • 300 kW
	UNITED KINGDOM — BBC, Via Ascension	W Africa & C Africa • 250 kW / Sa/Su • W Africa & C Africa • 250 kW
	BBC, Via Meyerton, South Africa	Africa • 500 kW
17835	GERMANY — †DEUTSCHE WELLE, Via Sines, Portugal	S • E Europe • 250 kW
17840	EGYPT — RADIO CAIRO, Kafr Silim-Abis	W Africa • 250 kW
	INDIA — †ALL INDIA RADIO, Bangalore	E Asia • 500 kW
	UNITED KINGDOM — BBC, Via Antigua	Americas • 125 kW / S • W North Am & C America • 125 kW / W • W North Am • 250 kW
	BBC, Via Sackville, Canada	S • E Asia • 500 kW
	USA — †VOA, Via Udon Thani, Thailand	
17845	CHINA (TAIWAN) — VO FREE CHINA, Via Okeechobee, USA	S • S America • 100 kW
	GERMANY — DEUTSCHE WELLE, Various Locations	SE Asia & Australasia • 250/500 kW
	†DEUTSCHE WELLE, Via Sri Lanka	S • E Asia • 250 kW
	DEUTSCHE WELLE, Wertachtal	S Asia & SE Asia • 500 kW
	SPAIN — R EXTERIOR ESPANA, Noblejas	C America & S America • 350 kW • ALT. FREQ. TO 21570 kHz / S Sa/Su • C America & S America • 350 kW • ALT. FREQ. TO 21570 kHz / S Sa/Su • C America & S America • 350 kW • ALT. FREQ. TO 15125 kHz / S Sa • C America & S America • 350 kW • ALT. FREQ. TO 15125 kHz
	USA — WYFR-FAMILY RADIO, Okeechobee, Fl	S America • 100 kW / S • S America • 100 kW / S • W Africa • 100 kW
17850	FRANCE — R FRANCE INTL, Issoudun-Allouis	S • Africa • 500 kW / Africa • 500 kW
	SRI LANKA — SRI LANKA BC CORP, Colombo-Ekala	E Asia • 35 kW
17855	DENMARK — RADIO DANMARK, Via Norway	S • Australasia • 500 kW
	NORWAY — R NORWAY INTL, Kvitsøy	S • M-Sa • Australasia • 500 kW / S Su • Australasia • 500 kW / S • Australasia • 500 kW
	PAKISTAN — RADIO PAKISTAN, Islamabad	E Africa • 100 kW • ALT. FREQ. TO 15555 kHz / E Africa & S Africa • 100 kW
	RUSSIA — VOICE OF RUSSIA, Via Moldova	S • N Africa • 1000 kW
	UNITED ARAB EMIRATES — †UAE RADIO FROM ABU DHABI	S • Australasia • 500 kW / W • E Asia • 500 kW
	USA — †VOA, Via Philippines	S • E Asia • 250 kW
17860	FRANCE — †R FRANCE INTL, Via French Guiana	W • C America • 500 kW / W M-Sa • C America • 500 kW / W Su • C America • 500 kW / C America • 500 kW
	GERMANY — †DEUTSCHE WELLE, Nauen	S • W Africa • 500 kW
	†DEUTSCHE WELLE, Via Kigali, Rwanda	W Africa & Americas • 250 kW / S • C America • 250 kW
(con'd)	†DEUTSCHE WELLE, Wertachtal	S • W Africa • 500 kW / W • Mideast & E Africa • 500 kW

ENGLISH ▬ ARABIC ▨ CHINESE ▭▭ FRENCH ▬ GERMAN ▬ RUSSIAN ═ SPANISH ▬ OTHER ▬

FREQUENCY   COUNTRY, STATION, LOCATION   TARGET • NETWORK • POWER (kW)   World Time

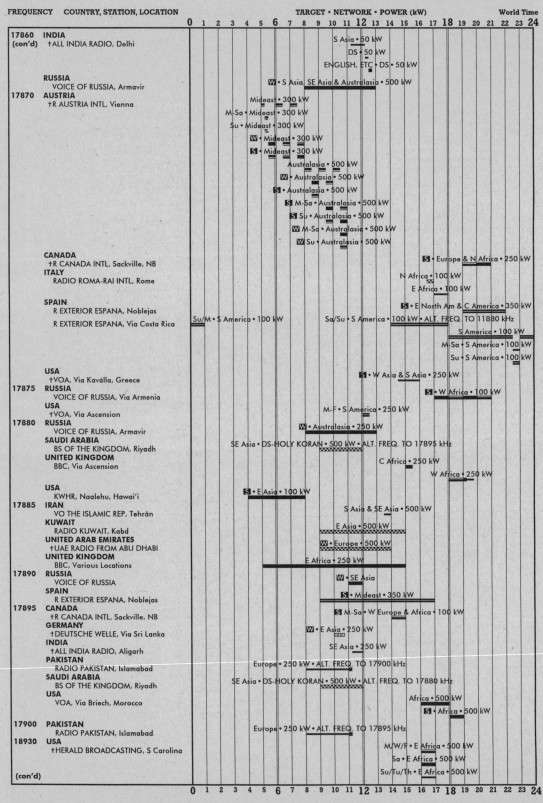

FREQUENCY	COUNTRY, STATION, LOCATION	TARGET • NETWORK • POWER (kW)
17860 (con'd)	INDIA †ALL INDIA RADIO, Delhi	S Asia • 50 kW / DS • 50 kW / ENGLISH, ETC • DS • 50 kW
	RUSSIA VOICE OF RUSSIA, Armavir	W • S Asia, SE Asia & Australasia • 500 kW
17870	AUSTRIA †R AUSTRIA INTL, Vienna	Mideast • 300 kW / M-Sa • Mideast • 300 kW / Su • Mideast • 300 kW / W • Mideast • 300 kW / S • Mideast • 300 kW / Australasia • 500 kW / W • Australasia • 500 kW / S • Australasia • 500 kW / S M-Sa • Australasia • 500 kW / S Su • Australasia • 500 kW / W M-Sa • Australasia • 500 kW / W Su • Australasia • 500 kW
	CANADA †R CANADA INTL, Sackville, NB	S • Europe & N Africa • 250 kW
	ITALY RADIO ROMA-RAI INTL, Rome	N Africa • 100 kW / E Africa • 100 kW
	SPAIN R EXTERIOR ESPANA, Noblejas	S • E North Am & C America • 350 kW
	R EXTERIOR ESPANA, Via Costa Rica	Su/M • S America • 100 kW / Sa/Su • S America • 100 kW • ALT. FREQ. TO 11880 kHz / S America • 100 kW / M-Sa • S America • 100 kW / Su • S America • 100 kW
	USA †VOA, Via Kaválla, Greece	S • W Asia & S Asia • 250 kW
17875	RUSSIA VOICE OF RUSSIA, Via Armenia	S • W Africa • 100 kW
	USA †VOA, Via Ascension	M-F • S America • 250 kW
17880	RUSSIA VOICE OF RUSSIA, Armavir	W • Australasia • 250 kW
	SAUDI ARABIA BS OF THE KINGDOM, Riyadh	SE Asia • DS-HOLY KORAN • 500 kW • ALT. FREQ. TO 17895 kHz
	UNITED KINGDOM BBC, Via Ascension	C Africa • 250 kW / W Africa • 250 kW
	USA KWHR, Naalehu, Hawai'i	S • E Asia • 100 kW
17885	IRAN VO THE ISLAMIC REP, Tehrān	S Asia & SE Asia • 500 kW
	KUWAIT RADIO KUWAIT, Kabd	E Asia • 500 kW
	UNITED ARAB EMIRATES †UAE RADIO FROM ABU DHABI	W • Europe • 500 kW
	UNITED KINGDOM BBC, Various Locations	E Africa • 250 kW
17890	RUSSIA VOICE OF RUSSIA	W • SE Asia
	SPAIN R EXTERIOR ESPANA, Noblejas	S • Mideast • 350 kW
17895	CANADA †R CANADA INTL, Sackville, NB	S M-Sa • W Europe & Africa • 100 kW
	GERMANY †DEUTSCHE WELLE, Via Sri Lanka	W • E Asia • 250 kW
	INDIA †ALL INDIA RADIO, Aligarh	SE Asia • 250 kW
	PAKISTAN RADIO PAKISTAN, Islamabad	Europe • 250 kW • ALT. FREQ. TO 17900 kHz
	SAUDI ARABIA BS OF THE KINGDOM, Riyadh	SE Asia • DS-HOLY KORAN • 500 kW • ALT. FREQ. TO 17880 kHz
	USA VOA, Via Briech, Morocco	Africa • 500 kW / S • Africa • 500 kW
17900	PAKISTAN RADIO PAKISTAN, Islamabad	Europe • 250 kW • ALT. FREQ. TO 17895 kHz
18930	USA †HERALD BROADCASTING, S Carolina	M/W/F • E Africa • 500 kW / Sa • E Africa • 500 kW / Su/Tu/Th • E Africa • 500 kW

(con'd)

FREQUENCY	COUNTRY, STATION, LOCATION	TARGET • NETWORK • POWER (kW) / World Time

Time scale across top: 0 1 2 3 4 5 6 7 8 9 10 11 12 13 14 15 16 17 18 19 20 21 22 23 24

Frequency	Country / Station / Location	Schedule details
18930 (con'd)	**USA** †HERALD BROADCASTING, S Carolina	M • C Africa • 500 kW Su/W/F • C Africa • 500 kW Tu/Th/Sa • C Africa • 500 kW M/Tu/Th/Sa • S Africa • 500 kW Su/W • S Africa • 500 kW
20000	**USA** WWV, Fort Collins, Colorado	WEATHER/WORLD TIME • 2.5 kW
21455	**ECUADOR** †HCJB-VO THE ANDES, Quito	Europe & Australasia • 0.25 kW • USB
21470	**UNITED KINGDOM** BBC, Via Zyyi, Cyprus	E Africa • 250 kW
21474v	**PAKISTAN** RADIO PAKISTAN, Karachi	SE Asia • 50 kW • ALT. FREQ. TO 15565v kHz
21475v	**PAKISTAN** RADIO PAKISTAN, Karachi	SE Asia • 50 kW • ALT. FREQ. TO 15565v kHz
21480	**HOLLAND** R NEDERLAND, Via Madagascar	E Asia • 200 kW
	UKRAINE RADIO UKRAINE, L'vov	W • W Africa & S America • 1000 kW
21485	**UNITED ARAB EMIRATES** UAE RADIO IN DUBAI	E North Am & C America • 500 kW
	USA VOA, Greenville, NC	W Africa & S Africa • 250 kW
21490	**JAPAN** RADIO JAPAN/NHK, Via Ascension	C Africa • 250 kW
	UNITED KINGDOM BBC, Various Locations	E Africa • 250 kW M-F • E Africa • 250 kW Sa/Su • E Africa • 250 kW
21495	**SAUDI ARABIA** BS OF THE KINGDOM, Riyadh	E Asia & SE Asia • DS-HOLY KORAN • 500 kW • ALT. FREQ. TO 21530 kHz
21515	**PORTUGAL** †RDP INTERNATIONAL, Lisbon	M-F • Mideast & S Asia • 100 kW Sa/Su • Mideast & S Asia • 100 kW Irr • Sa/Su • Mideast & S Asia • 100 kW
21520	**ITALY** RAI-RTV ITALIANA, Rome	Su • E Africa • 100 kW
21525	**USA** WYFR-FAMILY RADIO, Okeechobee, Fl	C Africa & S Africa • 100 kW S • C Africa & S Africa • 100 kW
21530	**SAUDI ARABIA** BS OF THE KINGDOM, Riyadh	E Asia & SE Asia • DS-HOLY KORAN • 500 kW • ALT. FREQ. TO 21495 kHz
21535	**ITALY** RADIO ROMA-RAI INTL, Rome	Su • S America • 100 kW
21560	**GERMANY** DEUTSCHE WELLE, Via Kigali, Rwanda	S • Mideast • 100 kW
21570	**SPAIN** R EXTERIOR ESPANA, Noblejas	C America & S America • 350 kW • ALT. FREQ. TO 17845 kHz S Sa/Su • C America & S America • 350 kW • ALT. FREQ. TO 17845 kHz
21580	**FRANCE** R FRANCE INTL, Issoudun-Allouis	W • C Africa & S Africa • 500 kW C Africa & S Africa • 500 kW S • C Africa & S Africa • 500 kW
21590	**HOLLAND** R NEDERLAND, Via Neth Antilles	W Africa • 250 kW
	UNITED KINGDOM BBC, Rampisham	Mideast • 500 kW
21600	**GERMANY** †DEUTSCHE WELLE, Wertachtal	Africa • 500 kW
21605	**UNITED ARAB EMIRATES** †UAE RADIO IN DUBAI	Europe • 300 kW
21610	**JAPAN** †RADIO JAPAN/NHK, Tokyo-Yamata	Australasia • 300 kW
21620	**FRANCE** †R FRANCE INTL, Issoudun-Allouis	W • E Africa • 500 kW / S • E Africa • 500 kW E Africa • 500 kW
21640	**GERMANY** †DEUTSCHE WELLE, Via Sri Lanka	S • SE Asia & Australasia • 250 kW S • E Asia • 250 kW
	UNITED KINGDOM BBC, Rampisham	W Africa • 500 kW
	BBC, Via Ascension	C Africa • 250 kW
21645	**FRANCE** R FRANCE INTL, Via French Guiana	W • C America • 500 kW
21655	**PORTUGAL** RDP INTERNATIONAL, Lisbon	Sa/Su • W Africa & S America • 100 kW W Africa & S America • 100 kW
(con'd)		

Time scale across bottom: 0 1 2 3 4 5 6 7 8 9 10 11 12 13 14 15 16 17 18 19 20 21 22 23 24

ENGLISH ▬ ARABIC ∼∼ CHINESE □□□ FRENCH ▬▬ GERMAN ▬ RUSSIAN ═ SPANISH ▬ OTHER ▬

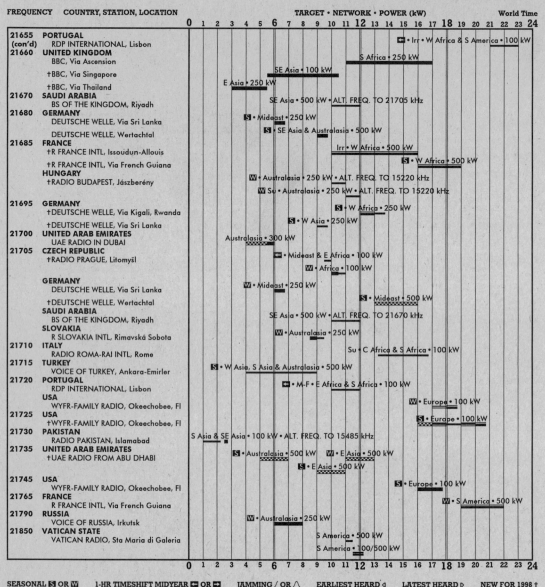

FREQUENCY	COUNTRY, STATION, LOCATION	TARGET • NETWORK • POWER (kW)	World Time

21655 (con'd) — **PORTUGAL** — RDP INTERNATIONAL, Lisbon — ◧ • Irr • W Africa & S America • 100 kW

21660 — **UNITED KINGDOM**
- BBC, Via Ascension — S Africa • 250 kW
- †BBC, Via Singapore — SE Asia • 100 kW
- †BBC, Via Thailand — E Asia • 250 kW

21670 — **SAUDI ARABIA** — BS OF THE KINGDOM, Riyadh — SE Asia • 500 kW • ALT. FREQ. TO 21705 kHz

21680 — **GERMANY**
- DEUTSCHE WELLE, Via Sri Lanka — Ⓢ • Mideast • 250 kW
- DEUTSCHE WELLE, Wertachtal — Ⓢ • SE Asia & Australasia • 500 kW

21685 — **FRANCE**
- †R FRANCE INTL, Issoudun-Allouis — Irr • W Africa • 500 kW
- †R FRANCE INTL, Via French Guiana — Ⓢ • W Africa • 500 kW

HUNGARY
- †RADIO BUDAPEST, Jászberény — Ⓦ • Australasia • 250 kW • ALT. FREQ. TO 15220 kHz — Ⓦ Su • Australasia • 250 kW • ALT. FREQ. TO 15220 kHz

21695 — **GERMANY**
- †DEUTSCHE WELLE, Via Kigali, Rwanda — Ⓢ • W Africa • 250 kW
- †DEUTSCHE WELLE, Via Sri Lanka — Ⓢ • W Asia • 250 kW

21700 — **UNITED ARAB EMIRATES** — UAE RADIO IN DUBAI — Australasia • 300 kW

21705 — **CZECH REPUBLIC** — †RADIO PRAGUE, Litomyšl — ◧ • Mideast & E Africa • 100 kW — Ⓦ • Africa • 100 kW

GERMANY
- DEUTSCHE WELLE, Via Sri Lanka — Ⓦ • Mideast • 250 kW
- †DEUTSCHE WELLE, Wertachtal — Ⓢ • Mideast • 500 kW

SAUDI ARABIA — BS OF THE KINGDOM, Riyadh — SE Asia • 500 kW • ALT. FREQ. TO 21670 kHz

SLOVAKIA — R SLOVAKIA INTL, Rimavská Sobota — Ⓦ • Australasia • 250 kW

21710 — **ITALY** — RADIO ROMA-RAI INTL, Rome — Su • C Africa & S Africa • 100 kW

21715 — **TURKEY** — VOICE OF TURKEY, Ankara-Emirler — Ⓢ • W Asia, S Asia & Australasia • 500 kW

21720 — **PORTUGAL** — RDP INTERNATIONAL, Lisbon — ◧ • M-F • E Africa & S Africa • 100 kW

USA — WYFR-FAMILY RADIO, Okeechobee, Fl — Ⓦ • Europe • 100 kW

21725 — **USA** — †WYFR-FAMILY RADIO, Okeechobee, Fl — Ⓢ • Europe • 100 kW

21730 — **PAKISTAN** — RADIO PAKISTAN, Islamabad — S Asia & SE Asia • 100 kW • ALT. FREQ. TO 15485 kHz

21735 — **UNITED ARAB EMIRATES** — †UAE RADIO FROM ABU DHABI — Ⓢ • Australasia • 500 kW — Ⓦ • E Asia • 500 kW — Ⓢ • E Asia • 500 kW

21745 — **USA** — WYFR-FAMILY RADIO, Okeechobee, Fl — Ⓢ • Europe • 100 kW

21765 — **FRANCE** — R FRANCE INTL, Via French Guiana — Ⓦ • S America • 500 kW

21790 — **RUSSIA** — VOICE OF RUSSIA, Irkutsk — Ⓦ • Australasia • 250 kW

21850 — **VATICAN STATE** — VATICAN RADIO, Sta Maria di Galeria — S America • 500 kW — S America • 100/500 kW

SEASONAL Ⓢ OR Ⓦ   1-HR TIMESHIFT MIDYEAR ◧ OR ◨   JAMMING / OR /\   EARLIEST HEARD ◁   LATEST HEARD ▷   NEW FOR 1998 †